HANDBOOK OF PERSONALITY

Theory and Research

Edited by

Lawrence A. Pervin

Rutgers University

THE GUILFORD PRESS
New York / London

© 1990 The Guilford Press
A Division of Guilford Publications, Inc.
72 Spring Street, New York, NY 10012

Printed in the United States of America

This book is printed on acid-free paper.

Last digit is print number: 9 8 7 6 5 4 3

Library of Congress Cataloging-in-Publication Data

Handbook of personality : theory and research / edited by Lawrence
  A. Pervin.
        p.   cm.
    Includes bibliographical references and index.
    ISBN 0-89862-430-4   ISBN 0-89862-593-9 (pbk)
    1. Personality.
BF698.H335   1990
155.2—dc20   90-37936
                                                  CIP

Preface

The initial idea for this book dates back to the spring of 1987 when Ken Craik invited me to participate in a colloquium series at Berkeley celebrating the 1937 textbooks of Allport and Stagner. I was particularly intrigued with this idea since Allport was a professor of mine, as was Murray, whose monumental *Explorations in Personality* was published the following year. In preparing for the colloquium I went back and read most of the major works of Allport and Stagner, which itself turned out to be an enlightening endeavor. Having completed graduate school in 1962, I had been involved in the field of personality for exactly half the period of the golden anniversary of the Allport and Stagner texts. Yet, I had never really reflected on where the field had been and was heading. At the same time, I reviewed the 1968 Borgatta and Lambert *Handbook of Personality: Theory and Research* and reflected on the changes that had occurred in the field. The 1977 *Handbook of Modern Personality Theory* edited by Cattell and Dreger was a noteworthy contribution but its coverage tended to represent a particular point of view. Thus, a new handbook, documenting the changes that had occurred, clearly seemed in order.

For some time the fields of social psychology and developmental psychology have been served by comprehensive handbooks, yet none has served a similar function in personality. Editing a handbook is an enormous responsibility. A handbook represents a definition of the field and therefore must be comprehensive and balanced, representative and definitive. Beyond this, however, a handbook should include guidelines for the future. Thus, in my letter to the contributors I expressed my hope that the chapters individually and collectively would set forth significant paths for future theory and research as well as serve a review function. To achieve these desired ends requires the participation and commitment of leading scholars in the field, and I am gratified that this handbook includes such a distinguished group of contributors. In particular, I am pleased that included here are not only traditional contributors to the personality literature but individuals from related fields whose views help so much to broaden and deepen our understanding of this complex area we define as personality.

Not only is editing a handbook an enormous responsibility but it also requires an enormous amount of coordination. Reading the prefaces to the *Handbook of Social Psychology* and *Handbook of Developmental Psychology* I was surprised to learn how long it took for the chapters to be handed in, how many chapters were by replacements for contributors who had originally agreed to write them, and how many areas were not ultimately represented because certain contributions were not forthcoming. Clearly this was a warning of what to expect. But on the whole, I must say that the contributors to this volume have been a very responsive and cooperative group. Thus, the manuscript was completed just eight months after the original target date, and about a year and a half after the time contributors were first contacted. This was important to ensure that chapters delivered on time were not out of date by the time the full manuscript was turned in. In a few cases, replacements had to be found for individuals who could not complete their contribution, most notably the chapter on the history of the field, which I had not originally planned to write. And, in a few cases the chapters never did arrive, most notably a chapter on research methods and strategies in the study of personality and one on industrial-organizational psychology and personality. I note these because it is important to understand that despite the effort to be comprehensive certain gaps are due to errors in editorial judgment while others are due to the vagaries of working with close to thirty distinguished individuals. Hopefully there are not too many of the former, fortunately there were very few of the latter.

As I have indicated, my appreciation goes to the contributors who have worked so conscientiously and been so cooperative. And, my appreciation goes to the Editor-in-Chief of Guilford Press, Seymour Weingarten, who was an early supporter of the project, and to the members of the Guilford staff, in particular Rowena Howells, who were so diligent in seeing the book through the various phases of the publication process.

LAWRENCE A. PERVIN
Princeton, NJ

Contributors

Richard D. Ashmore, PhD, Department of Psychology, Rutgers University, New Brunswick, New Jersey

Daryl J. Bem, PhD, Department of Psychology, Cornell University, Ithaca, New York

George A. Bonanno, MS, Department of Psychology, Yale University, New Haven, Connecticut

Nancy Cantor, PhD, Institute for Social Research, The University of Michigan, Ann Arbor, Michigan

Avshalom Caspi, PhD, Department of Psychology, University of Wisconsin, Madison, Wisconsin

Raymond B. Cattell, PhD, DSc, Forest Institute of Professional Psychology, Honolulu, Hawaii

Heather M. Chipuer, M.S., Center for Developmental and Health Genetics, College of Health and Human Development, Pennsylvania State University, University Park, Pennsylvania

Richard J. Contrada, PhD, Department of Psychology, Rutgers University, New Brunswick, New Jersey

Susan Cross, PhD, Department of Education, University of Texas at Austin, Austin, Texas

Seymour Epstein, PhD, Department of Psychology, University of Massachusetts at Amherst, Amherst, Massachusetts

Hans J. Eysenck, PhD, DSc, Institute of Psychiatry, De Crespigny Park, London, England

E. Tory Higgins, PhD, Department of Psychology, Columbia University, New York, New York

Oliver P. John, PhD, Institute of Personality Assessment and Research, University of California, Berkeley, California

John F. Kihlstrom, PhD, Amnesia and Cognition Unit, Department of Psychology, University of Arizona, Tucson, Arizona

Richard Koestner, PhD, Department of Psychology, McGill University, Montréal, Québec, Canada

Richard S. Lazarus, PhD, Department of Psychology, University of California, Berkeley, California

Howard Leventhal, PhD, Institute for Health, Healthcare Policy, and Aging Research, Rutgers University, New Brunswick, New Jersey

Michael Lewis, PhD, Institute for the Study of Child Development, Robert Wood Johnson Medical School, New Brunswick, New Jersey

John C. Loehlin, PhD, Department of Psychology, University of Texas at Austin, Austin, Texas

David Magnusson, PhD, Department of Psychology, University of Stockholm, Stockholm, Sweden

Hazel Markus, PhD, Department of Psychology, The University of Michigan, Ann Arbor, Michigan

David C. McClelland, PhD, The Center for Applied Social Science, Boston University, Boston, Massachusetts

Stanley B. Messer, PhD, Graduate School of Applied and Professional Psychology, Rutgers University, New Brunswick, New Jersey

Theodore Millon, PhD, Department of Psychiatry, Harvard Medical School, Cambridge, Massachusetts and Department of Psychiatry, University of Miami, Miami, Florida

Walter Mischel, PhD, Department of Psychology, Columbia University, New York, New York

Ann O'Leary, PhD, Department of Psychology, Rutgers University, New Brunswick, New Jersey

Lawrence A. Pervin, PhD, Department of Psychology, Rutgers University, New Brunswick, New Jersey

Robert Plomin, PhD, Center for Developmental and Health Genetics, College of Health and Human Development, Pennsylvania State University, University Park, Pennsylvania

Leonard G. Rorer, PhD, Department of Psychology, Miami University, Oxford, Ohio

Richard A. Shweder, PhD, Committee on Human Development, The University of Chicago, Chicago, Illinois

Dean Keith Simonton, PhD, Department of Psychology, University of California, Davis, California

Jerome L. Singer, PhD, Department of Psychology, Yale University, New Haven, Connecticut

Craig A. Smith, PhD, Department of Psychology and Human Development, Vanderbilt University, Nashville, Tennessee

Maria A. Sullivan, PhD, MD, Committee on Human Development, The University of Chicago, Chicago, Illinois

Seth Warren, PhD, private practice, Hoboken, New Jersey

Bernard Weiner, PhD, Department of Psychology, University of California, Los Angeles, California

Drew Westen, PhD, Department of Psychology, The University of Michigan, Ann Arbor, Michigan

Sabrina Zirkel, PhD, Department of Psychology, The University of Michigan, Ann Arbor, Michigan

Contents

PART THREE. INTERFACE WITH OTHER FIELDS

PART FOUR. RESEARCH TOPICS: INTRAPERSONAL AND INTERPERSONAL, PRIVATE AND PUBLIC ASPECTS OF PERSONALITY

PART ONE
INTRODUCTION

Chapter 1

A Brief History of Modern Personality Theory

Lawrence A. Pervin

Rutgers University

> The creator of theories is to some extent a product of his times and a full understanding of what has happened in the field of personality during the past thirty years requires that this period be viewed in a much longer time perspective.
>
> SANFORD (1963, p. 490)

Recently I read a review of the field of personality. In it, the authors touched upon a variety of themes and made a number of points, among which the following are particularly noteworthy:

1. Interest in the field has reached astonishing proportions.
2. There appear to be as many definitions of personality as there are authors.
3. Clarification of the concept of types would be an invaluable service to the field.
4. The tide has turned toward greater faith in the innate determination of traits.
5. There is increasing dissatisfaction with the more artificial pencil-and-paper or laboratory methods.
6. The principal source of disagreement is the issue of specificity versus generality, with common sense postulating the latter and experimental studies giving results that are interpreted in either direction, often according to the inclination of the author.
7. Although there is value in studying the same phenomenon in many subjects, there is particular value in seeing relations among the parts in the individual organism.
8. Though the formulation of adequate theories of personality lag behind research, this research is so flourishing that the outlook for a future systematic psychology of personality is bright indeed.

My point in citing this review is not to argue for or against any of the points made by the authors, but rather to argue in support of Sanford's emphasis on the value of a longer time perspective and an awareness of the history of the field. The review was written by Allport and Vernon in 1930!

In this brief overview of the history of modern personality theory, I attempt to capture some of the main themes and trends that have been present in the field. The early roots of the field are not detailed, since a number of resources are available to the interested reader (Allport, 1937; Burnham, 1968; Roback,

3

1927). It has been suggested that the study of personality as such was not formalized until the mid-1930s (Burnham, 1968; Murphy, 1949). This review covers roughly a 50-year period; thus, perhaps, it commemorates (a bit belatedly) the golden anniversary of modern personality theory.

In their landmark contribution to the field, *Theories of Personality*, Hall and Lindzey (1957) suggest four sources of influence upon personality theory: clinical observation, Gestalt psychology, experimental psychology, and the psychometric tradition. The clinical, experimental, and psychometric traditions have continued to flourish and exert profound influences on the field—each with its own conceptualization of the appropriate content to be emphasized and best method of investigation. My effort here is to keep in mind the simultaneous developments occurring in these approaches while tracing the overall development of the field. To a certain extent, developments in these approaches have been independent of one another. At the same time, occasionally a development in one has had an impact on the others, and inevitably developments in the field of psychology as a whole influence all three approaches. Thus, although for better or for worse the three traditions have remained independent of one another, some common themes emerge. The focus in this chapter is on these common themes—on what has remained stable and on what has changed, much as the field itself has struggled with the task of conceptualizing the interplay between the stable and dynamic properties of personality systems (Pervin, 1984).

THE BEGINNINGS OF MODERN PERSONALITY THEORY: ALLPORT AND MURRAY

> Out of their labors and other contemporaneous work developed the present field of study.
>   BURNHAM (1968, p. 73)

Allport's 1937 book, *Personality: A Psychological Interpretation*, represented an effort to define a new field of study—the psychology of personality. Although others had earlier written on personality (e.g., Lewin, *A Dynamic Theory of Personality*, 1935), Allport felt the need to articulate the objectives of a new movement. For him, psychology too often treated the individual "as something to be brushed aside so

the main business of accounting for the uniformity of events can get under way" (p. vii), and thus he embarked upon a lifelong effort to structure a field that would do justice to the richness and dignity of the individual.

Allport's book represents a remarkable effort. In it, he traced the history of interest in the field and the many meanings associated with the term "personality," concluding with his own frequently cited definition: "Personality is the dynamic organization within the individual of those psychophysical systems that determine his unique adjustments to his environment" (p. 48). It was this definition that emphasized many of the points so important to Allport: the organization of personality as a system, seen as the central problem of the field; the integration of the physical and the mental (body and mind); and the person as active and unique in efforts to grow and adapt to his or her surroundings.

Scanning the topics covered in this book gives one some sense of the enormity of the contribution—the development of personality; the self and its constraints; the transformation of motives; the structure of personality; the theory of traits; a survey of methods for the analysis of personality; the ability to judge people; and the unity of personality. In this book, Allport was critical of differential psychology as a method for the study of personality. He felt that it was elementaristic rather than organismic, focusing on the parts rather than on organization and patterning. The conception of the elements favored by psychometricians (i.e., factors) was rejected: "Factors fall short of our demand for a doctrine of elements that will offer as close an approximation as possible to the natural cleavages and individualized structural arrangements of each single life. The search must go on" (p. 248).

Similarly, Allport rejected the reduction of all motives to a single few, most or all of which are innate. Instead, he emphasized the goal-directedness of behavior. He described Murray's concept of needs as promising ("It leads to flexible and penetrating depictions of personality," p. 240), and propounded the concept of "functional autonomy" to suggest that adult motives are varied, self-sustaining, and functionally independent of their antecedents.

In his discussion of the search for the elements of personality, Allport gave careful consideration to the question of situational specificity, and rejected the view that behavior is composed entirely of countless specific habits. Instead, he emphasized the concept of "trait" as "a generalized and focalized neuropsychic system (peculiar to the individual), with the capacity to render many stimuli functionally equivalent, and to initiate and guide consistent (equivalent) forms of adaptive and expressive behavior" (p. 295). This conception of a trait is interesting in a number of ways. First, it emphasizes the capacity to render many stimuli functionally equivalent:

> Successful adaptation and mastery require a trait to remain loose-knit, so that its determinative influence may be modified or checked according to special demands of the moment. To serve as a successful *modus vivendi* a trait must remain plastic or lose its usefulness. (p. 332)

Second, it suggests that traits initiate and guide—characteristics generally associated with motivational concepts. Indeed, this was an issue with which Allport struggled. On the one hand, Allport suggested that traits had a motivational effect on behavior and possessed a teleonomic quality. Yet, not all motives were traits, nor were all traits motives; some were expressive or stylistic rather than driving.

Finally, there was Allport's concern for the individual and the place of such concern in the field of psychology as a whole. Here he contrasted his own effort to expand the traditional structure of psychology with "personalistic thought," where the goal was to demolish and reconstruct the entire edifice of general psychology from the ground up. "In this respect personalistic psychology is more extreme than the psychology of personality which is content to play its role within the many-sided science of psychology" (p. 550).

Of equally monumental proportions, though a very different effort, was Murray's *Explorations in Personality* (1938), with its emphasis on the emotional and motivational—an emphasis Murray viewed as setting it apart from academic psychology, where the tradition was to concentrate upon the perceptive and cognitive functions of the human mind or the behavior of animals. Murray criticized traditional academic psychology for its methods as well. Following Lewin, and in accord with Allport, he rejected statistical analyses that masked the different motives people had for the same behavior and that treated the uncommon as unhappy exceptions to the rule: "Averages obliterate the individual characters of individual organisms and so fail to reveal the complex interaction of forces which determines each concrete event" (p. viii).

In the course of $2\frac{1}{2}$ years of research, Murray and his associates (Erik Erikson, Jerome Frank, Christiana Morgan, Nevitt Sanford, and Robert White, among others) studied almost 100 subjects for periods from 2 weeks to 6 months:

> I take this opportunity to express the opinion that the reason why the results of so many researches in personality have been misleading or trivial is that experimenters have failed to obtain enough pertinent information about their subjects. Lacking these facts accurate generalizations are impossible. (p. ix)

If one was to understand adequately a single human event, a large number of determining variables as well as their relations had to be recognized. Thus evolved the strategy of a group of experimenters studying the same subjects—a strategy that has since been endorsed but rarely followed by others.

The result of this body of research was a proposal for a theory of personality, which Murray presented in part in the form of propositions. Like Allport's, many of these are noteworthy:

1. The objects of study are individual organisms, not aggregates of organisms.

2. The organism is from the beginning a whole; the whole and its parts are mutually related.

3. The organism is characterized from the beginning by rhythms of activity and rest.

4. Since at every moment an organism is within an environment, the organism and its milieu must be considered together.

5. In the organism the passage of time is marked by rhythms of assimilation, differentiation, and integration, making biography imperative.

6. Uniformities, if not identities, can be found in the episodes of an organism's life: "For an individual displays a tendency to react in a similar way to similar situations, and increasingly so with age. Thus there is sameness (consistency) as well as change (variability)" (p. 43).

7. Events must be interpreted in terms of many interacting forces and their relations, not ascribed to single causes.

8. To explain an event the psychologist must take account of both conscious and unconscious variables. Subjective reports are unreliable: "Children perceive inaccurately, are very little conscious of their inner states, and retain fallacious recollections of occurrences. Many adults are hardly better" (p. 15).

Of particular importance was Murray's elaboration of a theory of "needs" and corresponding environmental "press." Murray saw "need" as a hypothetical concept expressing an organism's potentiality or readiness to respond in a certain way under given conditions. Needs can be fused in action, can be subsidiated to one another, can be in conflict with one another, and can be conscious or unconscious. Needs were seen as having a complex relation to behavior, and it is here that Murray was careful to distinguish between needs and traits. Whereas traits are derived from observed consistencies or recurrent patterns in behavior, needs are internal processes that may or may not become manifest in behavior. In addition, the same action can be employed in the service of one need and an opposing need: "According to my prejudice, trait psychology is overconcerned with recurrence, with consistency, with what is clearly manifest (the surface of personality), with what is conscious, ordered, and rational" (p. 715).

It is interesting that Allport and Murray could share major points of emphasis (e.g., the importance of studying the individual and personality as a system), while at the same time differing on other fundamental issues (e.g., needs vs. traits, the value of psychoanalytic conceptualizations, and the relation of the abnormal to the normal).

Before I conclude this section, it is worth commenting on Stagner's (1937) *Psychology of Personality*, which appeared in the same year as did Allport's book. Stagner, too, defined personality in terms of individuality and emphasized the trait as the appropriate unit of study. He saw traits, however, as descriptions of behavior rather than as explanations. For Stagner, traits represented tendencies to respond, mental sets, or higher-order habits that are organized in terms of the meanings of situations for the person. They do not, however, indicate consistency of behavior across domains of situations. Thus a person can be consistent at home and at school, but not across the two: "It is said that a man who is a mouse in his office roars like a lion when he gets home" (p. 139). It may be interesting to note that in the later editions of his book Stagner (1948, 1961) continued to emphasize traits as descriptive rather than explanatory and added the concepts of "self" and "motives–goals" to capture the organization and persistence of personality.

TRACING DEVELOPMENTS THROUGH THE PRESENT

The preceding section on Allport and Murray has emphasized two organismic approaches to personality. Both personality theorists focused their attention on the individual and the unity of the individual. At the same time, important developments were occurring in learning theory, factor analysis, and structured personality inventories. Regional differences already were beginning to appear between clinical approaches based on the East Coast and those emerging in the Midwestern "dust bowl of empiricism."

During the 1930s and 1940s, major gains were being made in the area of learning theory, and the scientific logic of operationalism was being widely espoused (Hilgard, 1948; Hilgard & Marquis, 1940). Hull's stimulus–response (S-R) approach in particular, climaxed by his *Principles of Behavior* (1943), was having a marked influence on thinking in the areas of personality and social psychology, as witnessed in publications such as *Frustration and Aggression* (Dollard, Doob, Miller, Mowrer, & Sears, 1939), *Social Learning and Imitation* (Miller & Dollard, 1941), *Learning Theory and Personality Dynamics* (Mowrer, 1950), and *Personality and Psychotherapy* (Dollard & Miller, 1950). The last-mentioned book represented a brilliant effort to translate psychoanalysis into S-R learning terms—an effort that unfortunately has been lost to most current students of personality.

At the same time, the taxonomic, factor-analytic approach to personality was taking hold in the works of Cattell (*The Description and Measurement of Personality*, 1946) and Eysenck (*Dimensions of Personality*, 1947). Though not developed as a personality test, the Minnesota Multiphasic Personality Inventory (MMPI; Hathaway & McKinley, 1945) was gaining prominence, and its items would become the basis for many tests of personality concepts (e.g., ego strength, manifest anxiety). In addition, the MMPI would become the basis for major controversies concerning approaches to personality assessment and prediction (Holt, 1958; Meehl, 1954, 1956, 1957). In the clinical realm, psychoanalytic theory was continuing to exert a major influence on thinkers in the field, and the approach of Carl Rogers was beginning to take shape (Rogers, 1942, 1947).

Major wars inevitably have an impact upon society, including the pursuit of science in general and psychology in particular. World War I, for example, was associated with the development of the standardized test item (Woodworth, 1920), considered by some to be one of the most important innovations in modern psychology (Jackson & Paunonen, 1980, p. 505). World War II had a major impact on the field of personality in at least three ways. First, it led to the development of major graduate programs in clinical psychology, further tying developments in parts of personality to those in clinical psychology. To this day it is striking how many major personality theorists, of varying orientations, have been trained as clinicians. Second, the assessment effort of Murray and others in the Office of Strategic Services (Office of Strategic Services Assessment Staff, 1948) led to the development of the Institute of Personality Assessment and Research (IPAR) under the direction of MacKinnon. Third, concern with some of the social issues raised in the war led to studies published in *The Authoritarian Personality* (Adorno, Frenkel-Brunswik, Levinson, & Sanford, 1950), which, as we shall see, had a significant impact on personality research during the next decade.

With these developments, the future of personality theory and research would have appeared to be bright. And, indeed, the 1950s represented a period of many exciting developments. With the introduction of the *Annual Review of Psychology* series, the first personality review chapter appeared in which Sears (1950) divided the field into three categories: structure, dynamics, and development of motives and traits. Although this division was maintained for a period of time, it was eventually discontinued as the distinction between structure and dynamics became increasingly difficult to maintain. Bronfenbrenner (1953), in his review, sounded an optimistic note in terms of both the content considered and efforts to organize the field:

> Personality theory and research have indeed moved into areas which, like dreams, are at once both familiar and elusive. . . .
>
> Having concluded an appraisal of the year's accomplishments in personality theory and research, one naturally asks: how far have we come and where are we going? Somewhat to his own surprise, this reviewer finds himself heartened and impressed . . . the psychology of personality has moved far from what it once was—a jungle of disconnected, often irrelevant facts and fragmentary, footless speculations. (Bronfenbrenner, 1953, pp. 157, 176)

During this time Rogers (1951, 1954) continued with the development of his influential theory and approach to therapy; Rotter (1954) developed his social learning approach in an effort to integrate Hull, Tolman, and Adler; and Kelly (1955) developed his theory of personality, which Bruner (1956) considered to be the single greatest contribution to personality theory during the decade between 1945 and 1955. Cattell (1950, 1957) and Eysenck (1952b, 1953) continued with their important factor-analytic approach to personality. Finally, seeking to do for the field of personality what Hilgard (1948) had done for the field of learning, Hall and Lindzey (1957) proved to be remarkably successful with their *Theories of Personality*—a book that in its various editions went on to sell over 700,000 copies!

To a certain extent, there has always been a tension in the field between the more clinical approaches to personality and the more experimental approaches; I return to this topic later in the chapter. At the same time, there have historically been efforts to bridge the two. Early testimony to such efforts is given in Sears's (1944) review of experimental tests of psychoanalytic theory and in Hunt's (1944) influential *Personality and the Behavior Disorders*. In reviewing the literature on dynamics of personality, MacKinnon (1951) was led to conclude that a rapprochement was evolving between the laboratory/experimental and clinical streams of research.

During the 1950s, there were many noteworthy attempts at experimental study of phenomena traditionally of interest to clinicians. Illustrative here would be Klein's (1951) work on the relation of needs to perception and

McClelland, Atkinson, Clarke, and Lowell's (1953) work on achievement motivation. And, in marked contrast with later tensions between personality and social psychology, an interdisciplinary group in the newly formed Department of Social Relations at Harvard undertook investigation of the relations between *Opinions and Personality* (Smith, Bruner, & White, 1956).

The 1950s were also a time of development of the important concept of construct validity (Cronbach & Meehl, 1955) and the important emphasis on the multitrait–multimethod approach to convergent and discriminant validity (Campbell & Fiske, 1959). Personality psychologists clearly were becoming more sophisticated in their approaches to theory, assessment, and research. And this was a time of lively controversy in the field: the debate between Rogers and Skinner (1956) concerning the control of human behavior; the idiographic–nomothetic controversy (Allport, 1942; Beck, 1953; Eysenck, 1954; Holt, 1962); the controversy over clinical versus statistical approaches to prediction (Holt, 1958; Meehl, 1954, 1956, 1957); and the controversy surrounding factor analysis as a useful device for discovering the units of personality (Atkinson, 1960; Jensen, 1958). Finally, the 1950s were a time during which the drive concept was found to be inadequate as an explanatory motivational concept and the value of a broader conceptualization of motives, as expressed in White's (1959) "competence motivation," was recognized.

What has been presented so far represents a fairly bright picture of developments in the field during this time. However, it also was clear that storm clouds were on the horizon. First, some major efforts at assessment and prediction—what Wiggins (1973) refers to as "milestone" assessment studies—were not meeting with notable success. Second, questionnaire instruments were found to be plagued with the problems of response set, response bias, and response style (Jackson & Messick, 1958). Third, it was beginning to become clear that different investigators were using different methods to measure constructs identified with the same name, and that these different measures generally did not yield comparable results, leading to enormous confusion. Fourth, new minitheories, topics of research, and personality measures would explode on the scene and virtually dominate the field, only to disappear

and be replaced by other minitheories, topics of research, and personality measures. Thus, Eriksen (1957), in his chapter in the *Annual Review of Psychology*, was led to conclude that "Research in personality, as well as in psychology as a whole, shows many of the characteristics of a fad . . . with some notable exceptions, research tends to be characterized by one-shot experiments rather than programmatic attacks on a problem" (p. 185). Similarly Jensen (1958) suggested that

> Each year brings forth new findings which more often than not embarrass last year's theories. But theories in psychology are seldom disproved; they just fade away. . . .
>
> The formula for creating a research craze of proliferation and longevity consists of making available an easy-to-use measuring device with a significant label and fascinating content. Factorially it should be as multidimensional as possible, so that it will yield significant correlations with a host of other psychological measures. (pp. 295, 306)

Closing out the decade, Blake and Mouton (1959) concluded, "Gad, what a mess! constitutes one appraisal of the personality literature, which emphasizes its brittleness and the fact that results from one study frequently break and disappear under replication" (p. 226). These authors described the literature as consisting almost entirely of work on "AAA"—achievement, authoritarianism, and anxiety. In a further note, they suggested that interest in these topics was due to issues of social concern in the broader society, rather than merely to the availability of easy-to-use measures.

Carlson (1975) has suggested that personology virtually disappeared during the 1960s. Although this may be true for personology, it was not true for personality research. Whereas Sears's 1950 review included 39 references, the 1967 review contained 469 references (Klein, Barr, & Wolitzky, 1967). But the problems noted earlier continued to plague researchers in the field: questions concerning the construct validity of the measures used (Christie & Lindauer, 1963; Vannoy, 1965); questions concerning the accumulation of knowledge on such important and heavily researched areas as the self (Wylie, 1968); and questions concerning the amount of theoretical progress that had actually been made. Although London and Rosenhan (1964) could report the "slow but sure development of theoretical and methodological sophistication" (p. 447) and more good research than they could discuss, in the final review of the decade Adelson (1969) described the field of personality research as marked by "abundance, diffuseness, and diversity" with inexcusably low payoff, and suggested that "the sprawl and diversity can be seen as both a cause and a consequence of the virtual abandonment of large theoretical ambitions" (p. 217).

In addition to these problems internal to the field, and perhaps in some way related to them, there were three developments outside of personality that had important implications for its future. First, developments in the application of Skinner's work were having an impact on clinical psychology (Bandura, 1969; Ullmann & Krasner, 1965). On the one hand, this approach focused attention on the conditions in the environment that elicited and maintained overt behavior. On the other hand, it captured much of a field—clinical psychology—that previously had served as a breeding ground for personologists.

Second, the cognitive revolution (Miller, Galanter, & Pribram, 1960; Neisser, 1967; Newell, Shaw, & Simon, 1958) turned attention away from what had been traditional concerns of personality researchers. For example, as has been noted elsewhere (Pervin, 1984), during the 1960s interest in the concept of motivation declined so sharply as a topic of central concern that its utility as a scientific construct was seriously brought into question.

The third noteworthy development was that of experimental·social psychology. For reasons that have never been totally clear to me, programs in social psychology gradually emerged as stronger than programs in personality. Thus, on the one hand, personality was being pulled toward clinical programs that were behavioral in their focus; on the other hand, it was being pulled toward social programs that similarly questioned the basic assumptions of traditional personality theory—whether those of the individual-differences/psychometric school or those of the clinical/organismic school. No wonder that by 1971 Carlson could ask in an article title, "Where Is the Person in Personality Research?"

Given these developments, it is not surprising that research did not focus on the organization of personality variables in the individual. And, given these developments in personality and elsewhere in psychology, it is not surprising that a critique of traditional personality theory,

such as that formulated by Mischel (1968), would appear. The seeds of Mischel's critique were brewing in the concerns of personality psychologists with the generality versus specificity of traits and other personality variables (Holtzman, 1965; Klein et al., 1967); in the disappointment of personality psychologists with most personality questionnaires (Watson, 1959); and in the development of a social learning model (Bandura, 1973; Bandura & Walters, 1959, 1963; Peterson, 1968; Rotter, 1954).

Whether one agrees or disagrees with Mischel's critique, and whether or not one views the person–situation debate as having served a useful function in the development of personality as a field (Kenrick & Funder, 1988), it is clear that Mischel's critique served to focus research for much of the 1970s and beyond. Of particular importance was the development of an interaction focus (Endler & Magnusson, 1976; Magnusson & Endler, 1977). The history of the debate has been reviewed elsewhere (Pervin, 1984, 1985), so it may suffice here to note that the person–situation or internal–external issue is one that has been persistent throughout the history of the field—a point to which I return later in the chapter. And it may be noted that at the same time as considerable research has been devoted to demonstrating the longitudinal and cross-situational consistency of behavior, trait researchers have continued with their efforts to define the basic building blocks of personality and the hereditary components of these basic elements (Buss & Plomin, 1984; Digman & Inouye, 1986; McCrae & Costa, 1987).

A second issue that has dominated much of the research over the 1970s and 1980s involves conceptualization of the relations among cognition, affect, motivation, and behavior (Pervin, 1984, 1985). Writing in 1933, a psychologist suggested that "the 'will' has virtually passed out of our scientific psychology today; the 'emotion' is bound to do the same. In 1950 American psychologists will smile at both these terms as curiosities of the past" (Meyer, 1933, p. 300). At one point it seemed that this might indeed turn out to be the case, at first because of the onslaught of behaviorism and then because of the cognitive revolution. For a while, the work of Tomkins (1962) stood as a relatively lone voice emphasizing the importance of affect for motivation and personality. As noted above, the demise of the drive concept and emphasis on cognition threatened to remove the topic of motivation as a major source of concern to personality psychologists. Fortunately, the 1980s in particular have witnessed an enormous resurgence of interest in affect and motivation, strengthened in part by the efforts of psychologists working within a more cognitive framework. What started off as behavior therapy became cognitive-behavior therapy, and today cognitive-behavior therapists are paying increased attention to affect-related phenomena (Greenberg & Safran, 1989). Affect and cognition are now seen as having important implications for each other; we may hope that this will again point the way toward an emphasis on the organismic aspects of personality functioning. A final noteworthy aspect of this research has been an emphasis on biological variables on the one hand and cultural variables on the other, calling to mind Murphy's (1947) earlier emphasis on a biosocial approach to personality.

A third area of research during the 1980s that is worthy of particular note is that on the self. In writing *Current Controversies and Issues in Personality* in 1978, I debated whether to include a chapter on the self and finally decided to do so (Pervin, 1978). The title of the chapter ("Is the Concept of the Self Useful and Necessary?") was taken from a chapter by Allport (1955), in which he found it necessary to address this question. Hilgard (1949), in his presidential address to the American Psychological Association, also directed attention to the importance of the concept of the self, but Wylie's (1961) review of the literature hardly offered much promise for the future. Her later reviews of the literature similarly deplored the state of theory and measurement in relation to the construct of the self, and even went so far as to suggest that if the construct could not be formulated more precisely, it should be abandoned altogether (Wylie, 1968, 1974). Shortly thereafter, research on the self began to return to favor, in part following from ties to the cognitive revolution (Markus, 1977). Today, of course, it is a major topic within personality and in psychoanalytic theory, as well as showing signs of emerging or re-emerging as a major source of interest in cross-cultural research (Triandis, 1989).

Much of the current literature on the self is associated with a social-cognitive perspective, and there is little question that over the 1980s this perspective has had a major impact upon the field. Both the experimental and clinical traditions have been heavily influenced by the social-cognitive perspective. Of particular importance has been Bandura's (1986) effort to formulate a systematic social-cognitive theory of personality. Reviewing *Social Foundations of Thought and Action,* Baron (1987) described its breadth and sophistication as containing the outline of a grand theory of human behavior. Emphasizing the social origins of behavior and the importance of cognitive processes, this perspective has evolved both in terms of the kinds of phenomena considered and the settings in which research is conducted (Cantor & Kihlstrom, 1987).

Finally, I must note important developments in relating personality to health. Dating back to the early work of Glass and Singer (1972) on the effects of stress, and continuing with the research on learned helplessness (Peterson & Seligman, 1984), the Type A pattern (Booth-Keeley & Friedman, 1987), and other personality variables, the contribution of personality processes to health has grown to be an important area of research and theory. Although elements of this research follow from the behavioral tradition, at this point it is clear that personality factors play a major role in health-related functioning. And, although the roots of this area of research lie in the psychosomatic tradition, less specific ties are being drawn between areas of conflict and somatic difficulties. In addition, advances in research permit a greater specification of the exact processes contributing to the linkage between mind and body.

TOPICS THAT COME AND GO; ISSUES THAT REMAIN

> The dilemmas confronting the personality theorist today seem in a number of basic ways the same as they were in 1937.
>
> SANFORD (1963, p. 518)

> We share with Block the view that these earlier authors (Allport, Lewin, Murphy, Murray) frequently expressed central issues in personality theory more cogently than do the writings of some contemporary authors who seem to have rediscovered these same issues.
>
> JACKSON AND PAUNONEN
> (1980, pp. 504–505)

Throughout at least the past 30 years, various reviewers of the field have bemoaned the lack of cumulative knowledge. What we see over a 50-year span is a group of topics that are popular for a time and then fade away; a group of topics in which interest waxes and wanes; and some underlying issues that appear to remain throughout. Consider, for example, the popularity of research on rigidity during the 1950s; Eriksen (1957) referred to rigidity as the second biggest fad of that era, the trait of empathy being described as the first. Or consider the research on manifest anxiety, authoriarianism, dogmatism, the F Scale, and locus of control. The comments of Blake and Mouton (1959) on some of these were cynical but nevertheless instructive. They described research on anxiety as multiplying but not adding up—enough to make one anxious over the topic—and the concept of rigidity as continuing to be treated in a flexible manner. Interestingly enough, they called for more research that related persons to situations. Wiggins (1968) noted over 20 years ago that a quarter of the articles he reviewed had to do with response sets and styles. More recently, Carson (1989) noted that 20% of the material he assembled for review had to do with depression. What will be the dominant topic 20 years from now?

In addition to the topics that rise in interest and then permanently fade away, there are those that, like the phoenix, die and then reappear. Several examples of such topics have already been mentioned—emotions, motivation, and the self. Thus, Meyer (1933) could predict that the study of emotions would pass out of scientific psychology; yet 46 years later there was a complete chapter devoted to the topic in the *Annual Review* (Ekman & Oster, 1979). MacKinnon (1951) described the "notion" that all behavior is motivated as the most generally accepted notion of the time, and Eriksen (1957) described motivation as the most central and pervasive problem in psychology. A year later Jensen (1958) described motivation as the "liveliest and most vigorous, if not the most mature, area of psychological research" (p. 310). Yet by 1963 Sanford could note a decreased emphasis on motives, and, as noted, during the 1960s its utility as a scientific construct was seriously brought into question (Benjamin & Jones, 1978). Today, it is once more a concept of central importance to personality psychologists.

As for the third topic, in 1967 there was insufficient material on the self to warrant coverage in the *Annual Review* (Klein et al., 1967); however, by 1983 it was suggested that "interest in the self, far from being taboo, is now chic" (Loevinger & Knoll, 1983, p. 197). I could similarly note periods of increasing and declining interest in unconscious processes and in cultural differences. As someone trained in an interdisciplinary program, I have often been struck with the culture-bound nature of many of our conceptualizations. Thus, we may find ourselves caught up short when it is suggested that people in some cultures do not make attributions, at least in the form and content studied by attribution theorists, and that our conception of the self is a highly Westernized, individualistic conception.

One question we may ask concerns why there seem to be such trends and fashions in our research. Here the suggestion that the topics studied relate to those of importance in the broader society warrants careful consideration, regardless of whether one is skeptical of the view that a science of personality that is transhistorical is impossible (Blake & Mouton, 1959; Gergen & Gergen, 1988; Sampson, 1989). Another question that may be asked concerns whether there are issues that underlie all of these shifts in trends and fashions. Kluckhohn (1953) suggested that there are problems common to people of all cultures and that the number of solutions to them is finite. Perhaps something comparable to this exists in the field of personality as well. Sanford (1963) suggested that such fundamental issues as the nature–nurture issue, the internal–external issue, unconscious processes, the time dimension, and persistence and change are basic to differing views of the structure of personality. Here I would like to extend his list and suggest the topics discussed below as basic issues that historically have divided personality psychologists. These issues are not completely independent of one another, and a factor analysis or multidimensional scaling analysis undoubtedly would reduce them to a few factors or dimensions; however, there appears to be merit in considering them individually.

Definition of Personality

Historically, personality psychologists have varied in how concerned they are with definitions of personality and then with the definitions given. In the words of one psychologist, "What personality is, everybody knows; but nobody can tell" (Burnham, quoted in Allport & Vernon, 1930). MacKinnon (1951) noted that a concern with definitions of personality had almost disappeared from the literature. The following year, Eysenck (1952a) characterized personality as the most general and least well-defined term in psychology. Fifteen years later, Klein et al. (1967) concluded that there was no agreed-upon definition of personality or conception of its subject matter. Attention was drawn to the individual-differences and organismic views, which appear to have been the two main bases for distinguishing personality from other parts of psychology. Illustrative of the former would be the following:

> The concept of personality is a result of our observation of individual differences in human behavior. . . .
> All individual differences in the behavioral realm may be regarded as the subject matter of personality research. (Jensen, 1958, pp. 295, 302)

> It is in individual differences that we find the logical key to personality. . . . An individual's personality is his unique pattern of traits. (Guilford, 1959, p. 5)

> In our view, the science of personality revolves around the study of individual difference variables and behavioral predispositions which underlie trans-situational consistencies in behavior. (Sarason & Smith, 1971, p. 433)

Others have been critical of the individual-differences approach as unlikely to lead to an understanding of dynamic processes or the person as a whole. Illustrative of associated organismic definitions would be these quotations:

> As Wertheimer liked to put it, the essence of personality is cast not in a single tone or in a single melodic line, but in the wholeness of the musical conception. (Murphy, 1949, p. 646)

> I have assumed—in company, I believe, with most theorists in this field—that personality exists as an organized whole (system), that is constituted of parts or elements (subsystems), and separated somehow from an environment with which it interacts. (Sanford, 1963, p. 489)

> It is the interlocking, the structural or architectural totality rather than the sheer generality, of one or more traits that seems to call for the use of the term personality. Personality as a distinctive subject matter is concerned with the nature and scope of intra-individual integration. (Klein et al., 1967, p. 469)

In my own struggles to write a definition for my personality text, I have handled the issue by focusing both on individual differences and on the organization of component parts. However, it is my sense that the latter is what is truly distinctive about the field, and that recognizing this would lead to a greater emphasis in research on the system aspects of personality functioning. It may be of interest in this regard to note that Watson (1919) viewed personality as involving how the organism as a whole works. He noted that the parts of a gas engine may individually work well, but that there may be problems in terms of the interconnecting elements: "When we speak of the action of the individual as a whole, we mean something of this nature" (p. 423).

Relation of Personality Theory to Psychology and to Other Subdisciplines

In their classic text, Hall and Lindzey (1957) suggested that "personality theory has occupied a dissident role in the development of psychology. . . . The fact that personality theory has never been deeply embedded in the mainstream of academic psychology has had several important implications" (p. 4). As observed earlier in this chapter, Allport and Murray were both concerned about the lack of attention given to the individual in psychology generally. Their efforts may partly be viewed as a corrective emphasis in this regard. During the 1950s, personality was increasingly seen as indistinct from, or overlapping with, general psychology: "As general psychology becomes more adequate to deal with the whole range of human behavior, there is even less occasion to recognize personality study in the traditional sense as a discipline in any way distinct" (Child, 1954, p. 149). And warning was given that if personality was treated as a distinct area of theory and research, it was on its way to oblivion (Blake & Mouton, 1959, p. 203). However, others have suggested that personality is a distinctive subject matter (Klein et al., 1967), and one can even find the view that "whether we like it or not, personality psychology is the fundamental discipline" (Helson & Mitchell, 1978, p. 580).

The relation of personality to clinical and social psychology has also been an issue of concern. Whereas Sechrest (1976) suggested that the field faced an identity crisis and was too much identified with clinical and social psychology, others have been less concerned about the problem or actually supportive of closer ties to these other disciplines (Phares & Lamiell, 1977; Rorer & Widiger, 1983). Most recently, the issue has again risen with Carlson's (1984) suggestion that personality and social psychology "appear to be linked mainly by their deficiencies and appear to have little content worth sharing" (p. 1304), and Kenrick's (1986) response suggesting that we should walk across the lines separating us from the neighboring social and biological sciences while seeking to find our identity.

My own sense is that personality psychology cannot and should not proceed in isolation from psychology in general or from subdisciplines such as social, clinical, and developmental psychology in particular. Kenrick (1986) correctly points out that Allport was a social psychologist and Murray a physician. He might also have pointed out that they were supporters of the interdisciplinary Department of Social Relations, which, though it did split personality and social psychology from experimental psychology, joined personality with social psychology, clinical psychology, sociology, and anthropology. The price of keeping our focus on what is distinctive about personality need not be that we lose touch with the contributions made in other areas. And ultimately our identity will be defined by what we do and the contributions we make, rather than by what we stand in opposition to or whom we seek to keep out of our ranks.

View of Science within Psychology and Personality

Historically, there have been divisions within psychology concerning appropriate scientific methodology. Dashiell (1939) distinguished between the experimental and clinical attitudes, and Cronbach (1957) between the experimental and correlational disciplines of scientific psychology. Other efforts to characterize the disciplines within psychology

and personality have been made (Coan, 1968; Hogan, 1982; Thorndike, 1954), the most recent one being Kimble's (1984) distinction between the scientific and humanistic cultures. Two areas would appear to be of particular importance; Kimble refers to these as the "setting for discovery" and the "level of analysis." The former involves a preference for the laboratory as opposed to field research or case studies, the latter an emphasis on parts or wholes.

At times these divisions have taken on political characterizations and overtones. Thus, Hebb (1951) distinguished between a left wing and a right wing in psychology:

> The Right favors parsimony of explanatory ideas, a simple or mechanical account of behavior, and definiteness even at the cost of being narrow. The Left is prepared to postulate more freely and can better tolerate vagueness and lack of system in its account of behavior. (p. 40)

And we are well aware of the periodic splits within the American Psychological Association's Division of Personality and Social Psychology concerning program and journal emphasis.

The fact that these divisions have been the focus of attention now for at least 50 years should give us cause to ponder just what the basis for them is and to examine why they are so persistent. Beyond this, we should think about whether they have any utility to the field. As with a number of other issues covered in this section, there appears to be an ideological bent to the various positions—one that hardly does justice to the contributions and limitations of each, as well as to the potential profit from proceeding on the basis of more than one course of scientific discovery.

Personality Theories' Views of the Person

Kluckhohn (1953) suggested that all cultures have a view of basic human nature—evil, good, or neither. Similarly, a philosophical view of the person seems to underlie personality theories, particularly those that represent grand theories. At times it is a model that is most apparent (e.g., hydraulic equipment, telephone switchboard, computer), while at other times it is a more philosophical view: "Views about human nature influence which aspects of psychological functioning are studied most thoroughly and which remain unexamined. Theoretical conceptions similarly determine the paradigms used to collect evidence which, in turn, shape the particular theory" (Bandura, 1977, p. vi). Beyond these differing views of the person, differing views of reality have been suggested as making a rapprochement between therapeutic approaches difficult if not impossible (Messer, 1986; Woolfolk & Richardson, 1984).

The Idiographic–Nomothetic Issue

Periodically, the idiographic–nomothetic issue comes up in the field of personality (Allport, 1962; Hermans, 1988; Lamiell, 1987; Pervin, 1984). Though related to the earlier discussion of differing views of science, it is worthy of separate attention in that it often comes up as a separate issue. Although the issue is often associated with Allport, it is noteworthy that Lewin (1935) was critical of the view of lawfulness and individuality as antithetical, as well as critical of psychologists who viewed the individual event as fortuitous, unimportant, or scientifically uninteresting. We may also consider the contrast between Kohler's emphasis on the value of seeing relations in the individual organism among heart, lungs, and other systems (cited in Allport & Vernon, 1930, p. 715) and Sechrest's (1976) comment:

> [I]f anatomists had proceeded in the same way as personality psychologists we would know a great deal about minor variations in the location of the heart without ever realizing that for just about everyone everywhere it is located in the chest just slightly to the left of center. (p. 4)

It is unfortunate that various meanings of the term "idiographic" have become confused—a situation to which Allport himself contributed. Thus, the term has been used to describe a research method (i.e., intensive study of the individual), an approach to prediction (i.e., clinical vs. statistical prediction), a conception of personality (i.e., a holistic, dynamic view), and a view of science (i.e., history and art vs. physics and biology). It is the first meaning, the intensive study of the individual, that would appear to have the greatest to offer the field. In this sense, Allport, Freud, Pavlov, Piaget, and Skinner were all in favor of idiographic re-

search, and there is no need to view it as being in conflict with other approaches. It is merely another approach to research—one that offers the potential for observations perhaps not made as readily with alternative approaches.

The Internal–External Issue

> Is it governed from without, or governed from within? Is it merely reactive or is it active, mechanically determined or in some degree spontaneous? It is on this issue, above all others, that we find psychologists dividing.
>
> ALLPORT (1955, p. 6)

At its root, the internal–external issue underlies the person–situation controversy. It is, of course, related to differing views of the person, but once more it has been raised so often in its own context that it warrants separate mention. Considerable attention has been given to the person–situation controversy, so there is no need to elaborate upon it here. Suffice it to say that almost every reviewer in the *Annual Review of Psychology* has addressed the issue to some extent, and that although we are all pretty much interactionists at this point, there remains considerable disagreement about *what* in the person interacts *how* with *what* in the situation.

The Nature–Nurture Issue

As with the person–situation issue, it is unfortunate that heredity and environment have historically been viewed in polarized terms:

> The traditional questions of heredity and environment may be intrinsically unanswerable. Psychologists began by asking *which* type of factor, heredity or environmental, is responsible for individual differences in a given trait. Later, they tried to answer *how much* of the variance was attributable to heredity and how much to environment. It is the primary contention of this paper that a more fruitful approach is to be found in the question "How?" (Anastasi, 1958, p. 197)

It is clear that generally there has been a bias in psychology and in personality theory toward an emphasis on environment. Almost 40 years ago, Eysenck (1952a) noted such a bias and called for greater attention to hereditary determinants. At times the pendulum has started to swing in the direction of nature, only to return to an environmental emphasis. At this point, we are once more starting to see a strong emphasis on nature, with calls for caution in this regard (Plomin & Daniels, 1987). At the same time, we are also seeing greater attention paid to the complexity of the issue and a greater emphasis on reciprocal relations between nature and nurture.

The Time Dimension

According to Kluckhohn (1953), all cultures face the question of the significant time dimension—past, present, future. Once more we see a comparable issue among personality psychologists. All would agree that behavior can be influenced only by factors operating in the present. However, personality theorists differ in their concern with and conceptualization of the past and the future as determinants of behavior in the present. At one extreme, we have the psychoanalytic emphasis on the past, and at the other extreme Kelly's emphasis on the person as always looking toward the future. Generally, cognitive views are associated with an emphasis on the future (e.g., expectancies); drive, instinct, and mechanistic views tend to emphasize the past.

Persistence and Change in Personality

In her discussion of cultural differences in views of basic human nature, Kluckhohn (1953) also considers whether this basic nature is seen as mutable or immutable. Within personality theory, we find very basic differences in emphasis on persistence and change—whether in terms of the effects of early experience or in terms of the potential for change at any one point in time. Often there is a tie to an emphasis on heredity or biological factors. However, such a tie is neither logically necessary nor in fact inevitable. Thus, for example, we have someone such as Eysenck placing considerable emphasis on heredity and biological factors, but also placing relatively little emphasis on the fixity of the effects of early experience or personality functioning generally. Or, to take another example, we have Kagan emphasizing the biological/hereditary bases of temperament, while at the same time minimizing the permanent effects of early experience. All schools

of psychotherapy believe in the potential for change, but there are major differences in optimism concerning change—a well-emphasized difference between Rogers and Freud, as well as between behavior therapists and psychoanalysts. It is tempting to draw a connection between an emphasis on structure and one on persistence. However, it is clear that trait theorists tend to hold in common an emphasis on structure, but can vary considerably in the extent to which they see change (particularly change in trait structure) as possible.

Emphasis on Conscious versus Unconscious Processes

Concern with mental processes has varied from time to time. Personality psychologists have varied not only in their emphasis on such processes generally, but in their emphasis on the importance of unconscious processes in particular. The psychoanalytic emphasis on unconscious processes was rejected by many personality theorists, and for a time the subject almost dropped out of the empirical literature entirely. However, it has returned as a legitimate area of inquiry for cognitive psychologists, personality psychologists, and behavior therapists (Bowers & Meichenbaum, 1985; Brody, 1987; Hilgard, 1980. 1987).

This list of issues is not exhaustive. One could consider other issues as well, such as the importance of biological variables and relations among cognition, affect, and overt behavior. And some readers may consider some of the issues outlined above as unimportant or redundant with one another. The important point to be made is that certain issues have been recurrent in the field. At least half of the ones described above were described by Hall and Lindzey in 1957 and by Sanford in 1963. Will they still be present in an analysis of the field in 2020?

CONCLUSION

Writing in 1981, Tyler viewed psychology as extending its boundaries with the inclusion of new kinds of content, recognition of the complexity of the phenomena being studied, and the use of more varied research strategies. Recent research in personality shows evidence of these characteristics—interest in more varied phenomena, use of a greater diversity of methods, and awareness of the complexity of interactive forces responsible for any one event. There is hope for the future of the field in these developments; however, to return to the quotation by Sanford (1963) with which I have begun this chapter, this hope must be tempered by an awareness of the history of topics, issues, and developments over the past 50 years.

REFERENCES

Adelson, J. (1969). Personality. *Annual Review of Psychology, 20,* 217–252.

Adorno, T. W., Frenkel-Brunswik, E., Levinson, D. J., & Sanford, R. N. (1950). *The authoritarian personality.* New York: Harper.

Allport, G. W. (1937). *Personality: A psychological interpretation.* New York: Holt, Rinehart & Winston.

Allport, G. W. (1942). *The use of personal documents in psychological science* (Social Science Research Bulletin No. 49).

Allport, G. W. (1955). *Becoming: Basic considerations for a psychology of personality.* New Haven, CT: Yale University Press.

Allport, G. W. (1962). The general and the unique in psychological science. *Journal of Personality, 30,* 405–422.

Allport, G. W., & Vernon, P. E. (1930). The field of personality. *Psychological Bulletin, 27,* 677–730.

Anastasi, A. (1958). Heredity, environment, and the question "How?". *Psychological Review, 65,* 197–208.

Atkinson, J. W. (1960). Personality dynamics. *Annual Review of Psychology, 11,* 255–290.

Bandura, A. (1969). *Principles of behavior modification.* New York: Holt, Rinehart & Winston.

Bandura, A. (1973). *Aggression: A social learning analysis.* Englewood Cliffs, NJ: Prentice-Hall.

Bandura, A. (1977). *Social learning theory.* Englewood Cliffs, NJ: Prentice-Hall.

Bandura, A. (1986). *Social foundations of thought and action: A social cognitive theory.* Englewood Cliffs, NJ: Prentice-Hall.

Bandura, A., & Walters, R. H. (1959). *Adolescent aggression.* New York: Ronald Press.

Bandura, A., & Walters, R. H. (1963). *Social learning and personality development.* New York: Holt, Rinehart & Winston.

Baron, R. A. (1987). Outline of a grand theory. *Contemporary Psychology, 32,* 413–415.

Beck, S. J. (1953). The science of personality: Nomothetic or idiographic. *Psychological Review, 60,* 353–359.

Benjamin, L. T., & Jones, M. R. (1978). From motivational theory to social cognitive development: Twenty-five years of the Nebraska Symposium. In *Nebraska Symposium on Motivation* (Vol. 26, pp. ix–xix). Lincoln: University of Nebraska Press.

Blake, R. R., & Mouton, J. S. (1959). Personality. *Annual Review of Psychology, 10,* 203–232.

Booth-Keeley, S., & Friedman, H. S. (1987). Psychological predictors of heart disease: A quantitative review. *Psychological Bulletin, 101,* 343–362.

Bowers, K., & Meichenbaum, D. (Eds.). (1985). *The unconscious reconsidered.* New York: Wiley.

Brody, N. (Ed.). (1987). The unconscious [Special issue]. *Personality and Social Psychology Bulletin, 13*(3).

Bronfenbrenner, E. (1953). Personality. *Annual Review of Psychology, 4,* 157–182.

Bruner, J. S. (1956). You are your constructs. *Contemporary Psychology, 1,* 355–356.

Burnham, J. C. (1968). Historical background for the study of personality. In E. F. Borgatta & W. W. Lambert (Eds.), *Handbook of personality: Theory and research* (pp. 3–81). Chicago: McNally.

Buss, A. H., & Plomin, R. (1984). *Temperament: Early developing traits.* Hillsdale, NJ: Erlbaum.

Campbell, D. T., & Fiske, D. W. (1959). Convergent and discriminant validation by the multitrait–multimethod matrix. *Psychological Bulletin, 56,* 81–105.

Cantor, N., & Kihlstrom, J. F. (1987). *Personality and social intelligence.* Englewood Cliffs, NJ: Prentice-Hall.

Carlson, R. (1971). Where is the person in personality research? *Psychological Bulletin, 75,* 203–219.

Carlson, R. (1975). Personality. *Annual Review of Psychology, 26,* 393–414.

Carlson, R. (1984). What's social about social psychology? Where's the person in personality research? *Journal of Personality and Social Psychology, 47,* 1304–1309.

Carson, R. C. (1989). Personality. *Annual Review of Psychology, 40,* 227–248.

Cattell, R. B. (1946). *The description and measurement of personality.* Yonkers-on-Hudson, NY: World.

Cattell, R. B. (1950). *Personality.* New York: McGraw-Hill.

Cattell, R. B. (1957). *Personality and motivation structure and measurement.* Yonkers-on-Hudson, NY: World.

Child, I. L. (1954). Personality. *Annual Review of Psychology, 5,* 149–170.

Christie, R., & Lindauer, F. (1963). Personality structure. *Annual Review of Psychology, 14,* 201–230.

Coan, R. W. (1968). Dimensions of psychological theory. *American Psychologist, 23,* 715–722.

Cronbach, L. J. (1957). The two disciplines of scientific psychology. *American Psychologist, 12,* 671–684.

Cronbach, L. J., & Meehl, P. E. (1955). Construct validity in psychological tests. *Psychological Bulletin, 52,* 281–302.

Dashiell, J. F. (1939). Some rapprochements in contemporary psychology. *Psychological Bulletin, 36,* 1–24.

Digman, J. M., & Inouye, J. (1986). Further specification of the five robust factors of personality. *Journal of Personality and Social Psychology, 50,* 116–123.

Dollard, J., Doob, L. W., Miller, N. E., Mowrer, O. H., & Sears, R. R. (1939). *Frustration and aggression.* New Haven, CT: Yale University Press.

Dollard, J., & Miller, N. E. (1950). *Personality and psychotherapy.* New York: McGraw-Hill.

Ekman, P., & Oster, H. (1979). Facial expressions of emotion. *Annual Review of Psychology, 30,* 527–554.

Endler, N. S., & Magnusson, D. (Eds.). (1976). *Interactional psychology and personality.* Washington, DC: Hemisphere.

Eriksen, C. W. (1957). Personality. *Annual Review of Psychology, 8,* 185–210.

Eysenck, H. J. (1947). *Dimensions of personality.* London: Routledge & Kegan Paul.

Eysenck, H. J. (1952a). Personality. *Annual Review of Psychology, 3,* 151–174.

Eysenck, H. J. (1952b). *The scientific study of personality.* London: Routledge & Kegan Paul.

Eysenck, H. J. (1953). *The structure of human personality.* London: Methuen.

Eysenck, H. J. (1954). The science of personality: Nomothetic. *Psychological Review, 61,* 339–342.

Gergen, K. J., & Gergen, M. M. (1988). Narrative and the self as relationship. In L. Berkowitz (Eds.), *Advances in experimental social psychology* (Vol. 21, pp. 17–56). New York: Academic Press.

Glass, D. C., & Singer, J. E. (1972). *Urban stress.* New York: Academic Press.

Greenberg, L. S., & Safran, J. D. (1989). Emotion in psychotherapy. *American Psychologist, 44,* 19–29.

Guilford, J. P. (1959). *Personality.* New York: McGraw-Hill.

Hall, C. S., & Lindzey, G. (1957). *Theories of personality.* New York: Wiley.

Hathaway, S. R., & McKinley, J. C. (1945). *Manual for the Minnesota Multiphasic Personality Inventory.* New York: Psychological Corporation.

Hebb, D. O. (1951). The role of neurological ideas in psychology. *Journal of Personality, 20,* 39–55.

Helson, R., & Mitchell, V. (1978). Personality. *Annual Review of Psychology, 29,* 555–586.

Hermans, H. J. M. (1988). On the integration of nomothetic and idiographic research methods in the study of personal meaning. *Journal of Personality, 56,* 785–812.

Hilgard, E. R. (1948). *Theories of learning.* New York: Appleton-Century-Crofts.

Hilgard, E. R. (1949). Human motives and the concept of the self. *American Psychologist, 4,* 374–382.

Hilgard, E. R. (1980). Consciousness in contemporary psychology. *Annual Review of Psychology, 31,* 1–26.

Hilgard, E. R., & Marquis, D. G. (1940). *Conditioning and learning.* New York: Appleton-Century-Crofts.

Hogan, R. (1982). On adding apples and oranges in personality psychology. *Contemporary Psychology, 27,* 851–852.

Holt, R. R. (1958). Clinical and statistical prediction: A reformulation and some new data. *Journal of Abnormal Psychology, 56,* 1–12.

Holt, R. R. (1962). Individuality and generalization in the psychology of personality. *Journal of Personality, 30,* 377–404.

Holtzman, W. H. (1965). Personality structure. *Annual Review of Psychology, 16,* 119–156.

Hull, C. L. (1943). *Principles of behavior.* New York: Appleton-Century-Crofts.

Hunt, J. M. (Ed.). (1944). *Personality and the behavior disorders.* New York: Ronald Press.

Jackson, D. N., & Messick, S. (1958). Content and style in personality assessment. *Psychological Bulletin, 55,* 243–252.

Jackson, D. N., & Paunonen, S. V. (1980). Personality structure and assessment. *Annual Review of Psychology, 31,* 503–551.

Jensen, A. R. (1958). Personality. *Annual Review of Psychology, 9,* 295–322.

Kelly, G. A. (1955). *The psychology of personal constructs.* New York: Norton.

Kenrick, D. T. (1986). How strong is the case against contemporary social and personality psychology? A response to Carlson. *Journal of Personality and Social Psychology, 50,* 839–844.

Kenrick, D. T., & Funder, D. C. (1988). Profiting from controversy: Lessons from the person–situation debate. *American Psychologist, 43,* 23–34.

Kimble, G. A. (1984). Psychology's two cultures. *American Psychologist, 39,* 833–839.

Klein, G. S. (1951). The personal world through perception. In R. R. Blake & G. V. Ramsey (Eds.), *Perception: An approach to personality* (pp. 328–355). New York: Ronald Press.

Klein, G. S., Barr, H. L., & Wolitzky, D. L. (1967). Personality. *Annual Review of Psychology, 18,* 467–560.

Kluckhohn, F. R. (1953). Dominant and variant value orientations. In C. Kluckhohn, H. A. Murray, & D. M. Schneider (Eds.), *Personality in nature, society, and culture* (pp. 342–357). New York: Knopf.

Lamiell, J. T. (1987). *The psychology of personality: An epistemological inquiry.* New York: Columbia University Press.

Lewin, K. (1935). *A dynamic theory of personality.* New York: McGraw-Hill.

Loevinger, J., & Knoll, E. (1983). Personality: Stages, traits, and the self. *Annual Review of Psychology, 34,* 195–222.

London, P., & Rosenhan, D. (1964). Personality dynamics. *Annual Review of Psychology, 15,* 447–492.

MacKinnon, D. W. (1951). Personality. *Annual Review of Psychology, 2,* 113–136.

Magnusson, D., & Endler, N. S. (Eds.). (1977). *Personality at the crossroads: Current issues in interactional psychology.* Hillsdale, NJ: Erlbaum.

Markus, H. (1977). Self-schemata and processing information about the self. *Journal of Personality and Social Psychology, 35,* 63–78.

McClelland, D. C., Atkinson, J. W., Clarke, R. A., & Lowell, E. J. (1953). *The achievement motive.* New York: Appleton-Century-Crofts.

McCrae, R. R., & Costa, P. T. (1987). Validation of the five-factor model of personality across instruments and observers. *Journal of Personality and Social Psychology, 52,* 81–90.

Meehl, P. E. (1954). *Clinical versus statistical prediction: A theoretical analysis and a review of the evidence.* Minneapolis: University of Minnesota Press.

Meehl, P. E. (1956). Wanted—a good cookbook. *American Psychologist, 11,* 263–272.

Meehl, P. E. (1957). When shall we use our heads instead of the formula? *Journal of Counseling Psychology, 4,* 268–273.

Messer, S. B. (1986). Behavioral and psychoanalytic perspectives at therapeutic choice points. *American Psychologist, 41,* 1261–1272.

Meyer, M. F. (1933). That whale among the fishes—the theory of emotion. *Psychological Review, 40,* 292–300.

Miller, G. A., Galanter, E., & Pribram, K. H. (1960). *Plans and the structure of behavior.* New York: Holt.

Miller, N. E., & Dollard, J. H. (1941). *Social learning and imitation.* New Haven, CT: Yale University Press.

Mischel, W. (1968). *Personality assessment.* New York: Wiley.

Mowrer, O. H. (1950). *Learning theory and personality dynamics.* New York: Ronald Press.

Murphy, G. (1949). *Historical introduction to modern psychology* (2nd ed.). New York: Harcourt, Brace.

Murray, H. A. (1938). *Explorations in personality.* New York: Oxford University Press.

Neisser, U. (1967). *Cognitive psychology.* New York: Appleton-Century-Crofts.

Newell, A., Shaw, J. C., & Simon, H. A. (1958). Elements of a theory of human problem solving. *Psychological Review, 65,* 151–166.

Office of Strategic Services Assessment Staff. (1948). *Assessment of men.* New York: Rinehart.

Pervin, L. A. (1978). *Current controversies and issues in personality.* New York: Wiley.

Pervin, L. A. (1984). The stasis and flow of behavior: Toward a theory of goals. In M. M. Page (Ed.), *Personality: Current theory and research* (pp. 1–53). Lincoln: University of Nebraska Press.

Pervin, L. A. (1985). Personality. *Annual Review of Psychology, 36,* 83–114.

Peterson, C., & Seligman, M. E. P. (1984). Causal explanations as a risk factor for depression. *Psychological Review, 91,* 347–374.

Peterson, D. R. (1968). *The clinical study of social behavior.* New York: Appleton-Century-Crofts.

Phares, E. J., & Lamiell, J. T. (1977). Personality. *Annual Review of Psychology, 28,* 113–140.

Plomin, R., & Daniels, D. (1987). Why are children in the same family so different from one another? *Behavioral and Brain Sciences, 10,* 1–16.

Roback, A. A. (1927). *The psychology of character.* New York: Harcourt, Brace.

Rogers, C. R. (1942). *Counseling and psychotherapy.* Boston: Houghton Mifflin.

Rogers, C. R. (1947). Some observations on the organization of personality. *American Psychologist, 2,* 358–368.

Rogers, C. R. (1951). *Client-centered therapy.* Boston: Houghton Mifflin.

Rogers, C. R. (1954). The case of Mrs. Oak: A research analysis. In C. R. Rogers & R. F. Dymond (Eds.), *Psychotherapy and personality change* (pp. 259–348). Chicago: University of Chicago Press.

Rogers, C. R. (1956). Some issues concerning the control of human behavior. *Science, 124,* 1057–1066.

Rogers, C. R., & Skinner, B. F. (1956). Some issues concerning the control of human behavior: A symposium. *Science, 124,* 1057–1066.

Rorer, L. G., & Widiger, T. A. (1983). Personality structure and assessment. *Annual Review of Psychology, 34,* 431–463.

Rotter, J. B. (1954). *Social learning and clinical psychology.* Englewood Cliffs, NJ: Prentice-Hall.

Sampson, E. E. (1989). The challenge of social change for psychology. *American Psychologist, 44,* 914–921.

Sanford, N. (1963). Personality: Its place in psychology. In S. Koch (Ed.), *Psychology: A study of a science* (Vol. 5, pp. 488–592). New York: McGraw-Hill.

Sarason, I. G., & Smith, R. E. (1971). Personality. *Annual Review of Psychology, 22,* 393–446.

Sears, R. R. (1944). Experimental analysis of psychoanalytic phenomena. In J. McV. Hunt (Ed.), *Personality and the behavior disorders* (pp. 306–332). New York: Ronald Press.

Sears, R. R. (1950). Personality. *Annual Review of Psychology, 1,* 105–118.

Sechrest, L. (1976). Personality. *Annual Review of Psychology, 27,* 1–27.

Smith, M. B., Bruner, J., & White, R. W. (1956). *Opinions and personality.* New York: Wiley.

Stagner, R. (1937). *Psychology of personality* (2nd ed., 1948; 3rd ed., 1961). New York: McGraw-Hill.

Thorndike, R. L. (1954). The psychological value systems of psychologists. *American Psychologist, 9,* 787–790.

Tomkins, S. S. (1962). *Affect, imagery, and consciousness.* New York: Springer Verlag.

Triandis, H. C. (1989). The self and social behavior in differing cultural contexts. *Psychological Review, 96,* 506–520.

Tyler, L. E. (1981). More stately mansions: Psychology extends its boundaries. *Annual Review of Psychology, 32,* 1–20.

Ullmann, L. P., & Krasner, L. (Eds.). (1965). *Case studies in behavior modification.* New York: Holt, Rinehart & Winston.

Vannoy, J. S. (1965). Generality of cognitive complexity–simplicity as a personality construct. *Journal of Personality and Social Psychology, 2,* 385–396.

Watson, J. B. (1919). *Psychology from the standpoint of a behaviorist.* Philadelphia: J. B. Lippincott.

Watson, R. I. (1959). Historical review of objective personality testing: The search for objectivity. In B. M. Bass & I. A. Berg (Eds.), *Objective approaches to personality assessment* (pp. 1–23). Princeton, NJ: Van Nostrand.

White, R. W. (1959). Motivation reconsidered: The concept of competence. *Psychological Review, 66,* 297–332.

Wiggins, J. S. (1968). Personality structure. *Annual Review of Psychology, 19,* 293–350.

Wiggins, J. S. (1973). *Personality and prediction: Principles of personality assessment.* Reading, MA: Addison-Wesley.

Woodworth, R. S. (1920). *Personal data sheet.* Chicago: Stoelting.

Woolfolk, R. L., & Richardson, F. C. (1984). Behavior therapy and the ideology of modernity. *American Psychologist, 39,* 777–786.

Wylie, R. C. (1961). *The self concept.* Lincoln: University of Nebraska Press.

Wylie, R. C. (1968). The present status of self theory. In E. F. Borgatta & W. W. Lambert (Eds.), *Handbook of personality theory and research* (pp. 728–787). Chicago: Rand McNally.

Wylie, R. C. (1974). *The self concept* (rev. ed.). Lincoln: University of Nebraska Press.

PART TWO
THEORETICAL PERSPECTIVES

Chapter 2

Psychoanalytic Approaches to Personality

Drew Westen
University of Michigan

Perhaps the greatest challenge in trying to summarize the state of psychoanalysis as a theory of personality roughly a century after its inception is to delineate precisely what one means by "psychoanalysis." Fifty years ago, such a definition would have been relatively clear. Psychoanalysis was a well-guarded fortress, and most psychologists had little interest in scaling its walls. The password to enter was relatively unambiguous: Those who considered themselves psychoanalytic believed in the importance of unconscious processes, conflicts and defenses, the Oedipus complex, and the centrality of the sexual drive in the development of personality and neurosis; those who did not believed in none of these things. Psychologists who were caught in the moat—that is, those who accepted some of Freud's premises but rejected aspects of theory important to him, such as the centrality and sexuality or the Oedipus complex—would by and large leave the fold or be cast off as heretics, and their work would never be cited again in psychoanalytic literature (except for an occasional brief refutation). This ragtag army of the not-quite-analytic-enough came to be identified under the broader rubric of "psychodynamic"—that is, those who

believe in the importance of unconscious processes and conflicting forces within the mind but do not necessarily hold to the theory of libido and the pre-eminence of the Oedipus complex.

By the time of Freud's death, however, schisms had already emerged within psychoanalysis, particularly in London, between orthodox or classical psychoanalysis and what came to be known as "object relations" approaches. Today many of the major psychoanalytic journals publish papers from radically differing theoretical perspectives, including "self psychology," which at times seems to accept none of the basic psychoanalytic premises. Hence the use of the plural in the title of this chapter, "Psychoanalytic Approaches to Personality," reflecting the "pluralism" that characterizes contemporary psychoanalysis (Wallerstein, 1988).

Psychoanalysis has thus become less easy to define because its boundaries are more permeable. Perspectives that would at one time have been relegated to the wider ranks of the psychodynamic, such as more interpersonal approaches, are now part of mainstream psychoanalytic literature. Another factor rendering psychoanalytic approaches less distinct is that contemporary psychology has come to accept, at least to a degree, some of the postulates that once clearly demarcated psychoanalysis from other points of view. The cognitive revolution ushered in an interest in mental events, which had been largely extinguished by the behaviorists (with occasional spontaneous recoveries), and in the past decade a literature on unconscious processes has been flourishing (see, e.g., the volume edited by Bowers & Meichenbaum, 1984; see also Kihlstrom, 1987 and Chapter 17, this volume). Recently E. Tory Higgins, a leading exponent of the social-cognitive approach to personality, criticized exclusive reliance on the "faulty computer" metaphor for explaining errors in social cognition, calling instead for a conception of mental processes that would have been familiar to Freud and that echoes contemporary psychoanalytic emphasis on psychic conflict and compromise:

> It may be that people are not motivated solely to be accurate or correct. Indeed, people are likely to have multiple and conflicting motivations when processing information such that not all of them can be fully satisfied. . . . If one abandons this assumption [that people are motivated to be accurate], then an alternative perspective of people as "creatures of compromise" may be considered, a perspective suggesting that people's judgments and inferences must be understood in terms of the competing motivations that they are trying to satisfy. (Higgins & Bargh, 1987, p. 414)

Although there remain substantial differences between the views of academic psychologists and psychoanalytic theorists, the differences are now more subtle, so that mutual dismissal and slinging of epithets require considerably more finesse than was once the case.

What, then, is a psychoanalytic approach? Freud (1923/1961) defined psychoanalysis as a theory of the mind or personality, a method of investigation of unconscious processes, and a method of treatment. In the present discussion I focus on psychoanalysis as a theory of personality, although discussions of method invariably arise, since the evidence for psychoanalytic theory stems primarily from application of its method. At present, the psychoanalytic perspective on personality is probably best categorized prototypically rather than through any particular set of defining features. Psychoanalytic approaches are those that take as axiomatic the importance of conflicting mental processes; unconscious processes; compromises among competing psychological tendencies that may be negotiated unconsciously; defense and self-deception; the influence of the past on current functioning; the enduring effects of interpersonal patterns laid down in childhood; and the role of sexual and aggressive wishes in consciously and unconsciously influencing thought, feeling, and behavior. The degree to which an approach matches the prototype is the degree to which it can be considered psychoanalytic.

The chapter proceeds as follows: It begins with a brief discussion of the evolution of psychoanalytic theory. It then examines current issues and controversies in psychoanalysis. The next section describes empirical research on psychoanalytic theories and convergences of psychoanalytic approaches with other research traditions. The final section tries to place psychoanalytic theory in context as a theory of personality, enunciating its enduring contributions and suggesting possible directions for the future.

THE EVOLUTION OF PSYCHOANALYTIC THEORY

Freud's models of the mind, and the early revisionist theories of Adler, Jung, and the neo-Freudians, should be well known to readers of this volume and hence are described only briefly here. Freud developed a series of models and theories that he never attempted to integrate fully. Freud's psychological theorizing was, however, from the start guided by his interest and his data base: He was interested first and foremost in understanding psychopathology, and his primary data were the things that patients wittingly and unwittingly told about themselves in clinical hours. Of the greatest importance methodologically were free associations (which held the promise of revealing associational networks and mental transformations of ideas and feelings) and transference phenomena (in which patients revealed interpersonal cognitive–affective–behavioral patterns that the analyst could observe directly).

Freud's Models of the Mind

Fundamental to Freud's thinking about the mind was a simple assumption: that if there is a discontinuity in consciousness—something the person is doing but cannot report or explain—then the relevant mental processes necessary to "fill in the gaps" must be unconscious (see Rapaport, 1944/1967). This deceptively simple assumption was at once both brilliant and controversial. Freud was led to this assumption by patients, first described in the *Studies on Hysteria* (Breuer & Freud, 1893–1895/1955), who had symptoms with no organic origin; the patients were making every conscious effort to stop these symptoms, but could not. Freud's logic was simple: If the "force" behind the symptom is psychological but not conscious, that only leaves one possible explanation—namely, that the source of the symptom must be unconscious. Opposing the conscious will, Freud reasoned, must be an unconscious counterwill of equal or greater magnitude; the interplay of these forces was what he described as "psychodynamics." (See Erdelyi, 1985, for a vivid and readable account of Freud's discovery of psychodynamics.)

The Topographic Model

Freud's first model[1] of the mind, his topographic model, divided mental processes into "conscious," "preconscious," and "unconscious." Conscious thoughts are those of which the person is immediately aware; preconscious thoughts are those of which the person is not currently aware but can readily bring to consciousness; unconscious mental processes are those that are actively kept unconscious by repression because of their content. This model was first fully elaborated in *The Interpretation of Dreams* (1900/1953), in which Freud also distinguished the manifest content of a dream (the consciously recalled, often seemingly bizarre plot line) from the latent content (the underlying unconscious meaning, which Freud argued is an unconscious wish). The concept of latent wishes being transformed through various mental mechanisms to produce seemingly unintelligible but psychologically meaningful mental products became Freud's paradigm for symptom formation as well.

The Drive-Instinct and Energy Models

From his early publications onward, Freud was concerned with the nature of human motivation, and he attempted to bring together a psychological theory of adaptive and maladaptive mental processes with mechanistic and materialist conceptions of psychic energy, instinct, and drive rooted in the scientific thinking of his age (see Sulloway, 1979). His drive-instinct and energy models, which for present purposes I largely describe as a single model (though see Compton, 1981a, 1981b; Rapaport & Gill, 1959), evolved throughout his career, but always preserved their emphasis, first, on the conservation of psychic energy, and second, on the biological and animal origins of human motivation. Freud assumed that mental processes must be powered by energy, and that this energy must follow the same laws as other forms of energy in nature. A psychological motive to which energy has been attached can be consciously or unconsciously suppressed, but it cannot be destroyed. The act of suppression will itself require expenditure of energy, and the motive, if fueled by enough force, will likely be expressed by conversion to another form no longer under conscious control, such as a symptom, a dream, a joke, a slip of the tongue, behavior, ideology—the possible outlets are boundless.[2]

Freud also argued that basic human motivations are little different from those of other animals. The major differences between humans and animals in this respect stem from social requirements for inhibition of impulses in humans; the capacity of humans to express their motives in symbolic and derivative forms; and the greater capacity of humans either to obtain or to inhibit their desires, based on their capacity to adapt to their environment. Freud was dualistic in his instinct theory throughout much of his career, at first juxtaposing self-preservation and preservation of the species (through sex) as the two basic motives (e.g., Freud, 1914/1957), and and later asserting that sex and aggression are the basic human instincts from which all other motives ultimately flow. Freud's notion of the sexual drive, or "libido," is broader than common usage of the term, and is similar to its Platonic prototype: For Plato, Eros is a rich and malleable kind of desire, which has both relatively physical and sublime expressions. Libido, for Freud, refers as much to pleasure seeking, sensuality, and love as it does to sexual desire.

Ultimately Freud came to view life as a struggle between life and death instincts, although this was Freud at his most metaphysical, and "classical" analysts today tend to equate drive theory with Freud's dual-instinct theory of sex and aggression (e.g., Brenner, 1982). Perhaps what is most compelling about Freud's instinct theory is the notion that certain motives are simply rooted in the organism, and that there is nothing a person can do but to try to adapt to them, enjoy them or inhibit them when appropriate, and extrude them from one's experience of self when they are too threatening to acknowledge as one's own.

The Developmental Model

Although Freud's drive theory was dualistic, his primary focus was on the sexual drive, which he at times equated more generally with psychic energy. In his *Three Essays on the Theory of Sexuality* (1905/1953), in which he articulated his genetic or developmental model, he argued that the development of personality could be understood in terms of the vicissitudes of the sexual drive (broadly understood). From this springs his argument that stages in the development of libido are "psychosexual" stages—that is, stages in the development of both sexuality and personality.

Freud's psychosexual stages represent the child's evolving quest for pleasure and realization of the limitations of pleasure seeking. According to Freud, a drive has a source (a body zone), an aim (discharge), and an object (something with which to satisfy it). The sources or body zones on which libido is centered at different periods follow a timetable that is biologically determined, although the various modes of pleasure seeking associated with these zones have profound social implications as well. Freud's stages should be understood both concretely and metaphorically: They relate to specific bodily experiences, but these experiences are viewed as exemplars of larger psychological and psychosocial conflicts and concerns (see Erikson's [1963] elaborations of Freud's developmental theory).

In the "oral" stage, the child explores the world with its mouth, experiences considerable gratification and connection with people through its mouth, and exists in a state of dependency. The "anal" stage is characterized by the child's discovery that the anus can be a source of pleasurable excitation; by conflicts with socialization agents over compliance and defiance (the "terrible twos"), which Freud described in terms of conflicts over toilet training; and by the formation of attitudes toward order and disorder, giving and withholding, and messiness and cleanliness. The "phallic" stage is characterized by the child's discovery of the genitals and masturbation, an expanding social network, identification (particularly with same-sex parents), Oedipal conflicts, and the castration complex in boys and penis envy in girls. In the "latency" stage, sexual impulses undergo repression, and the child continues to identify with significant others and to learn culturally acceptable sublimations of sex and aggression. Finally, in the "genital" stage, conscious sexuality resurfaces, genital sex becomes the primary end of sexual activity, and the person becomes capable of mature relatedness to others.

These are among Freud's most controversial formulations, some of which are no longer central to contemporary psychoanalytic thinking; the extent to which one finds them credible depends in part upon whether one has observed such phenomena in a clinical (or child care) setting and how literally or metaphorically one chooses to take them. That little children masturbate or can be coy or competitive with their parents is manifestly obvious to anyone who has spent time with young children. (A friend's 3-year-old announced at the dinner table quite recently, "Daddy, I'm going to eat you up so I can have Mommy all to myself!") That penis envy is the key to understanding all women's personalities is another matter. Nevertheless, while Freud had a tendency to generalize from small and unrepresentative samples, he was not simply inventing concepts off the top of his head with no basis in clinical data when he postulated phenomena such as penis envy. At its most metaphorical, penis envy can refer to the envy developed by a little girl in a society in which men's activities seem more interesting and valued (see Horney, 1967). Given the concreteness of childhood cognition, it would not be surprising if a 5-year-old symbolized this in terms of having or not having a penis. At a less metaphorical level, as someone who was initially hostile to the concept of penis envy, I was astonished to hear more than one patient unacquainted with Freudian theory talk about her fantasies as a child that her vagina was a wound or physical defect. If the reader will forgive an anecdote (I cannot help it; I am psychoanalytic, and we break into anecdotes at the slightest provocation), prior to my entering psychology a coworker told me that her 6-year-old daughter had cried the night before in the bathtub because her younger brother, with whom she was bathing, had "one of those things" and she did not. I have always wondered about the impact of the mother's tongue-in-cheek reply to her daughter, "Don't worry, you'll get one someday." My coworker, incidentally, had never heard of penis envy.

The Structural Model

Whereas Freud's first model, the topographic model, categorized mental processes by their quality (vis-à-vis consciousness), his last basic model, the structural model (see Freud, 1923/1961, 1933/1964), categorized mental processes by their functions or purposes (Jahoda, 1977). With the introduction of the tripartite model of "id," "ego," and "superego," Freud's understanding of conflict shifted from conflict between consciousness and the unconscious to conflict between one's desires and the dictates of conscience or reality.

The id is the reservoir of sexual and aggressive energy and, like the topographic unconscious, operates on the basis of primary process thought (i.e., associative, wishful, illogical, nonvoluntary thought). The superego is the conscience, and is established through identification. The ego is the structure that must somehow balance the demands of desire, reality, and morality. To do this, the ego marshals mechanisms of defense as well as creative compromises among competing forces. Like the conscious and preconscious of the topographic model, the ego is characterized by the use of secondary-process thought (controlled, rational, voluntary, planful thinking). As Bettelheim (1983) observes, in the original German Freud's structural model was phrased in much more colloquial terms—the "I," the "it," and the "above-I"—so that Freud could actually speak to his patients about feeling that some moralistic part standing above the self was judging the self, or that an impulse felt like an impersonal, uncontrolled force, as in "It just came over me."

Developments in Psychoanalysis

Both during and since Freud's time, psychoanalysis has changed in significant ways. The first challenges to psychoanalysis from within were posed by the early revisionists, Adler and Jung, and by later neo-Freudians, who ultimately became challengers from without. The major developments since Freud's time within psychoanalysis are ego psychology, object relations theory, and evolving concepts of conflict and compromise in classical psychoanalysis.

Early Revisionists and Neo-Freudians

Since Adler, Jung, and later neo-Freudians are not, strictly speaking, psychoanalytic, I touch upon their work only briefly here. Adler (1929, 1939) and Jung (1971) were among the first prominent analysts to split with Freud, largely because they felt, to use Jung's phrasing, that Freud viewed the brain "as an appendage to the genital glands." Adler, for example, placed a greater focus on more conscious, everyday motives and experiences such as needs for achievement, as well on social motivation and the striving for superiority.

Since Adler and Jung's time, the ranks of the "psychodynamic" have become swollen with fallen analysts. Psychodynamic theorists such as Horney (1950), Fromm (1947, 1962), and Sullivan (1953) maintained aspects of the psychoanalytic approach, but placed much greater emphasis on the role of social forces in the genesis of personality. These later theorists also rejected Freud's view of libido as the primary motivational force in huma life. For example, Fromm criticized Freud's theory primarily on four interrelated grounds, all of which have considerable merit. First, he argued, Freud underestimated the extent to which humans are historically and culturally conditioned, so that basic motivations cannot be seen as entirely biologically determined. Second, humans are innately social creatures, and Freud's psychosexual stages are as much reflections of psychosocial dilemmas (giving or receiving, complying or defying) as they are of an unfolding ontogenetic blueprint (see also Erikson, 1963). Third, Freud treated acts of benevolence, altruism, and pursuit of ideals largely as reaction formations against their opposites, whereas Fromm proposed that humans have innately prosocial tendencies as well. Finally, Freud's psychology is a psychology of want—that is, of the need to reduce tensions; Fromm proposed that humans have other kinds of motivation as well, such as a need for relatedness to others, a need to be active and creative, and a need for a coherent sense of identity and meaning in life. Fromm, like Erikson, stressed conflicts specific to particular historical time periods and modes of production. He argued, foreshadowing Mahler (Mahler, Pine, & Bergman, 1975), that particularly in the present age a central conflict is between autonomy and individuation on the one hand, and the fear of aloneness and loss of connectedness on the other.

Ego Psychology

Although psychoanalytic theory evolved considerably during Freud's lifetime, in many ways it remained an "id psychology," focusing on the vicissitudes of the libidinal drive and the person's attempts to deal with impulses. A significant shift in psychoanalytic theory began to occur at about the time of Freud's death, with the development of ego psychology, which focuses on the functions and development of the ego (see Blanck & Blanck, 1974, 1979). During the same period in which Anna Freud (1936) was delineating various mechanisms of defense postulated to be used by the ego to cope with internal and external forces, Heinz Hartmann (1939/1958) and his colleagues were beginning to describe the interaction of motivational processes with ego functions that could not be reduced to derivatives of conflict. Perhaps the central point of their work was that motivational forces must be harnessed and employed by structures of thought and adaptation to the environment with a developmental history of their own, which interacts with but is not reducible to drive development.

Hartmann argued that the infant has inborn primary ego apparatuses, such as perceptual abilities, that are present from the start and are not derivative of conflict. Alongside drive development as adumbrated by Freud is the development of a conflict-free ego sphere that may become entangled in conflicts but is primarily an evolutionary endowment for purposes of adaptation. Hartmann and his colleagues (see Hartmann, Kris, & Loewenstein, 1946) were, to a significant extent, cognitive psychologists, and they actively read and attempted to integrate into psychoanalytic theory the work of Piaget and Werner. Hartmann (1939/1958) discussed means–end problem solving and the impact of automaticity of thought processes on cognitive development and adaptation, in ways that would be familiar to contemporary cognitive psychologists (e.g., Anderson, 1985).

Many other psychoanalysts have contributed to ego psychology as well. Rapaport (1951) and his colleagues systematically observed and described the organization and pathology of thinking in ways that have yet to be integrated into contemporary information-processing models. Menninger, Mayman, and Pruyser (1963) made a seminal (and relatively underappreciated) contribution to the understanding of adaptive functions and coping processes from a psychoanalytic point of view, elaborating the concept of levels of ego functioning and dyscontrol. In a work that has probably been equally unappreciated for its contributions to ego psychology, Redl and Wineman (1951) distinguished a vast number of quasi-independent ego functions in their study of delinquent adolescents, who manifested deficits in many domains of ego control. Bellak, Hurvich, and Gediman (1973) developed a taxonomy of ego functions that they operationalized for systematic empirical investigation. Erikson's (1963, 1968) contributions have been critical as well: his elaboration of stages of psychosocial/ego development parallel to Freud's psychosexual stages; his explication of processes of identity crisis and formation; and his elucidation of interactions of personality development with historical and cultural forces.

Object Relations Theory

Undoubtedly the major development in psychoanalysis since Freud has been the emergence of object relations theories of personality (for reviews, see Greenberg & Mitchell, 1983; see also Blatt & Lerner, 1983a; Eagle, 1984, 1987; Guntrip, 1971; Mitchell, 1988). Like most psychoanalytic terms, "object relations" carries many meanings, although, most broadly, the term denotes enduring patterns of interpersonal functioning in intimate relationships and the cognitive and affective processes mediating those patterns.

Although classical psychoanalytic theory focused on the vicissitudes of libido and aggression, from the start clinical practice has been oriented toward the "objects" of drives, and toward the individual's thoughts and feelings about those objects. Interest in object relations grew as clinicians began confronting patients with personality disorders who were unable to maintain satisfying relationships, and who seemed to be haunted by their fears and fantasies about the dangers of intimate relations with others and by unrealistic, often malevolent representations of significant others (Fairbairn, 1952; Guntrip, 1971; Klein, 1948). In contrast to classical psychoanalytic theory, object relations theory stresses the impact of actual deprivation in infancy and early childhood, the importance of self-representations and representations of others (called "object representations") in mediating interpersonal functioning, and the primary need for human relatedness that begins in infancy.

Psychoanalytic theory has seen a gradual shift from viewing objects as the repositories of drives (Freud, 1905/1953), to objects as fantasy figures (Klein, 1948; Fairbairn, 1952), to objects as psychic representations of real people (Sandler & Rosenblatt, 1962). Alongside this shift has been a continuing debate about whether human social motivation is best conceived of as motivated by the desire for sexual/ sensual pleasure or the desire for human contact and relatedness. Fairbairn (1952) and Sullivan (1953) clearly specified interpersonal alternatives to Freud's theories of motivation and psychic structure, with Fairbairn asserting that libido is object-seeking and not pleasure-seeking, and Sullivan developing a comprehensive model of the structure and development of personality that emphasized the distortions in personality and self-concept necessitated by the avoidance of interpersonally generated anxiety.

Two major developments in object relations theory in the 1960s were Sandler and Rosenblatt's (1962) paper on the representational world and Bowlby's (1969) enunciation of his theory of attachment.[3] Following Jacobson (1954) and others, Sandler and Rosenblatt described the cognitive–affective structure of the "representational world"—that is, of people's representations of the self and others—in ways that could profitably be assimilated by researchers studying social cognition. In the 1962 paper, for example, they described the self-concept as a self-schema, and elaborated the importance of distinguishing momentary from prototypic self-representations. Bowlby (1969, 1973, 1982) elaborated on Sandler and Rosenblatt's concept of "internal working models" of people and relationships, but added a powerful reformulation of motivational constructs such as "instinct" by integrating psychoanalytic thinking with control theory and ethology. He argued that attachment is a primary motivational system in humans as in other species, and that its evolutionary significance is the provision of security to immature members of the species. He suggested, further, that the expectations of relationships and the patterns of affective experience and regulation shaped in the first relationships are central determinants of later interpersonal functioning. As will be seen later, his theory has led to an enormous body of empirical research and a confirmation of many of these ideas. Also of considerable importance in the 1960s and 1970s was Mahler's research (Mahler et al., 1975), based on observation of infants and young children, in which she and her colleagues traced the development of separation–individuation—that is, of the child's struggle to develop a sense of autonomy and independent selfhood while maintaining an attachment to (or, in Mahler's theory, libidinal investment in) the primary caretaker.

Although numerous theorists have proposed models of object relations (e.g., Jacobson, 1964; Masterson, 1976), the two major contemporary object relations theories are Kernberg's (1975, 1976, 1984) attempt to wed drive theory, ego psychology, and object relations theory, and Kohut's (1968, 1971, 1977, 1984) self psychology. From the perspective of personality theory, one of Kernberg's central contributions (Kernberg, 1975) has been his development of a model of levels of personality organization, from extremely disturbed (psychotic) through relatively reality-oriented and adaptive (high-level neurotic or normal). His discussion of the clinical assessment of levels of personality organization in the first chapter of his book on severe personality disorders (Kernberg, 1984) would be of tremendous value to personality psychologists more generally.

Kernberg proposes a model of normal and pathological development that attempts to account for different levels of personality organization as assessed in adolescents and adults. The basic logic of Kernberg's developmental model is that development proceeds from a lack of awareness in infancy of the distinction between self and other, to a differentiation of representations based on affective valence (i.e., "good" vs. "bad" people and experiences), to an eventual construction of mature representations that integrate ambivalent feelings. Kernberg formulated his theory to account for phenomena observed in the treatment of severe personality disorders—notably, the tendency of these patients toward "splitting" (the separation of good and bad representations, so that the person cannot see the self or others at a particular time with any richness or complexity). The preschooler scolded by his or her mother who yells, "Mommy, I hate you! You don't love me!" is evidencing this normal developmental incapacity to retrieve memories of interactions with the mother associated with a different affective tone; later, according to Kernberg, splitting can be used defensively, to maintain idealizations of the self or significant others, or to protect the object from the person's own aggressive impulses.

Whereas Kernberg retains many elements of the classical theory of drive, conflict, and defense, Kohut's theory represents a much more radical departure. Kohut originally developed his theory as an attempt to explain the phenomenology and symptomatology of patients with narcissistic personality disorders (Kohut, 1966). Whereas in his early work Kohut defined the "self" as other analysts had since Hartmann (1950) as a collection of self-representations (and hence an ego structure, since cognition is an ego function), later Kohut (1971, 1977) came to view a psychology of the self as complementary to the classical theory of drive and defense. By the end of his life, Kohut (1984; Kohut & Wolf, 1978) argued that defects in the self, not conflicts, are critical in psychopathology, and that classical psychoanalysis has been superseded by self psychology. "Self" in this later work refers to a psychic structure on a par with, or superordinate to, id, ego, and superego. Kohut describes this structure as bipolar, with ambitions on one side, ideals on the other, and talents and skills driven by these two poles "arched" between them. Although Kohut's terminology can be confusing, the thrust of his argument is that having a core of ambitions and ideals, talents and skills with which to try to actualize them, and a cohesive and positive sense of self is what mental health is all about. The extent to which children develop these is determined, according to Kohut, by the extent to which their caretakers in the first years of life themselves are healthy along these dimensions, and can thus respond empathically when their children need them and can impart their own sense of security and self-esteem to their children. For Kohut, ambitions, ideals, and the need for self-esteem are three primary motivational systems in humans.[4]

Kohut's developmental theory, like that of most psychoanalytic theorists, proposes that the infant begins in a state of relatively poor differentiation of self and other, characterized by fragmented, unintegrated representations; he calls this the "stage of the fragmented self." At some time in the second year a "nuclear self," or core sense of self, emerges, with the bipolar structure described above. What he means by this is that the child is driven, on the one hand, by a fantasied sense of the self as omnipotent and omniscient, which Kohut calls the "grandiose self"; on the other hand, the child endows the parents with a similar greatness, creating what Kohut calls the "idealized parent imago." If primary caretakers are unempathic, chronically responding to their own needs rather than those of the infant, the child will develop defects in one or both poles of the self. This may lead to symptoms such as grandiosity, poor self-esteem, a desperate need to be attended to and admired, and severe problems in establishing a cohesive sense of identity.

Developments in Classical Psychoanalysis

Alongside these various developments in ego psychology and object relations theory have come changes in the classical model since Freud's time. Although these have been many, some of the major changes have come about through the systematizing and revisionist efforts of Charles Brenner. Freud developed many models of the mind and never made a concerted attempt to reconcile them, with the result that some psychoanalysts continued to speak in the language of the topographic model, whereas others spoke more in the language of Freud's later structural model. Arlow and Brenner (1964) made an important contribution by translating accounts of phenomena explained by the topographic model, such as dreams, into structural terms, and by demonstrating the superiority and comprehensiveness of the structural model. Since that time, Brenner in particular has been reformulating many basic Freudian constructs while attempting to preserve what is most important in the classical theory. His attempts at reformulation are set forth most succinctly in *The Mind in Conflict* (1982), which expresses the classical theory, as revised by decades of psychoanalytic practice, probably as clearly and persuasively as it could be expressed. (For a review of the development of Brenner's work, see also Richards, 1986).

Brenner's major contribution has been his elaboration of the concept of "compromise formation." Freud proposed that neurotic symptoms represent compromises among competing forces in the mind, particularly impulses, superego prohibitions, and the constraints of reality. In *The Interpretation of Dreams* (1900/1953), Freud proposed that compromise is critical in dream formation as well. Brenner's extension of Freud's theory was to suggest that *all* psychological events are compromise formations that include various elements of wishes, anxiety, depressive affect, defense, and superego prohibitions. For example, the academic who derives pleasure from his or her work may be simultaneously gratifying wishes to be superior to competitors, shaped in the Oedipal years, which are satisfied by feelings of intellectual superiority; gratifying wishes to be admired, which are achieved by being surrounded by a cadre of graduate students (probably an illusory gratification); allaying anxiety by mastering intellectual domains of uncertainty and solving small problems in the discipline; warding off depressive affect by bolstering self-esteem through publishing papers, making presentations, and winning the esteem of colleagues; and satisfying superego mandates by being disciplined in scientific method and seeking truth. One might quibble with Brenner's list of ingredients in a compromise formation: Notably absent are the need to see things as they really are, as well as cognitive processes leading to relatively veridical perception and cognition, which surely get expressed in beliefs along with more dynamic processes. Nevertheless, the basic point is that people are always synthesizing momentary compromises among multiple and competing mental processes. Some of these compromises are relatively stable and enduring, whereas others exist only briefly, since the "balance of forces" within the person is constantly changing in response to thoughts, feelings, fantasies, and environmental events.

CURRENT CONTROVERSIES IN PSYCHOANALYSIS

Currently psychoanalysis is in a state of flux, which some would probably describe as creative ferment, others as misguided foment, and still others simply as disarray. A number of interrelated issues critical to psychoanalytic theory are the subjects of debate and controversy. Many of these issues are critical to any comprehensive theory of personality, because they deal with such central questions as the roles of affect and cognition in motivation, the role of social experience in shaping personality, and the uses and limits of various forms of data for psychological theory.

Drive or Wish?

From the beginnings of psychoanalysis, Freud's theory of motivation has been both the heart and the Achilles heel of psychoanalytic theory. Psychoanalysis is, above all else, a theory of the complexities of human motivation and the ways in which motives interact, conflict, and attain surreptitious expression. Despite multiple changes in his motivational theories throughout his career, Freud was unflagging in his view of sexuality as the primary instinct in humans that draws them to each other and motivates much of their behavior, and in his corresponding implication of sexuality in the etiology of neurosis. As an inveterate biologist who never entirely relinquished his wish to ground his theory in physiology (Sulloway, 1979), Freud maintained a theory of psychic energy in his latest models of the mind that was a clear descendent of a purely physiological theory he developed in 1895 but abandoned and chose never to publish (Freud, 1950/1966; see Pribram & Gill, 1976).

The libido theory was, as noted earlier, the point of contention that drove many of Freud's adherents from the fold in the early part of this century and has been the target of considerable attack in recent years from both within and without psychoanalysis. Freud's model of a displaceable, transformable psychic energy, and the related drive-discharge model of motivation, is the "sick man of psychoanalytic theory" (Shevrin, 1984, p. 53), for which many have prescribed euthanasia (Gill, 1976; Rubenstein, 1976).[5] Holt (1976, 1985) has been particularly persuasive in this regard, arguing that Freud's mechanistic drive-discharge model is empirically and theoretically unsound and should be abandoned. The theory of a primary aggressive drive has similarly come under fire (Holt, 1976; Singer, 1988), and Freud's notion of the death instinct is an evolutionary impossibility that has never been accepted even by most orthodox analysts.

Interestingly, analysts with very different perspectives on classical psychoanalysis and drive theory have converged on the same motivational construct, the wish (Brenner, 1982; Dahl, 1983; Holt, 1976; Sandler & Sandler, 1978). "Wish" is an experience-near construct that does not rely on 19th-century energy concepts and is intuitively much more compelling. Brenner (1982) has argued for the continued utility of drive theory by suggesting that wishes are empirically observable derivatives of drives. Drives, in his view, are abstractions drawn from clinical observation of wishes; when one analyzes motives in psychoanalytic hours, he suggests, one consistently finds that these fall into two classes, sexual and aggressive.

From a clinical standpoint, Brenner is probably right that the two motivational systems that are most problematic and conflictual for people (at least in Western cultures) are those relating to sex and aggression, and clinical experience suggests that these infiltrate many areas of functioning in remarkably complex ways. At the same time, one has reason to question his account on several grounds. The clinical enterprise of analyzing neurotic symptoms may not provide an adequate observational base for motivations such as competence (White, 1959), which are only examined clinically to the extent that they are disrupted by conflicts involving other motive systems (see Pine, 1985). Brenner has confused the fact that sexual and aggressive impulses can be detected in a vast array of seemingly non-drive-determined psychic events, with the idea that these two motives are the *primary motivational determinants* of these events. Further, as several within the psychoanalytic tradition have argued (Holt, 1976; Sandler, 1987), the concept of sex in Freudian theory confounds love, sensuality, sexuality, pleasure seeking, affiliative needs, interests, and attachment motivation in ways that inhibit the development of a more widely acceptable psychoanalytically informed theory of motivation.

Interpreted more broadly, the concept of wish can be used to denote motivations for seeking many kinds of objects and experiences. Wishes are simultaneously cognitive and affective. The structure of a wish includes cognitive representations of wished-for states and representations of the person's current status vis-à-vis desired states; it also includes affects connected with anticipated attainment of the wish or arising from discrepancies between wished-for and attained states (Westen, 1985). Wishes and fears are in many respects opposites, since a person is motivated to narrow a discrepancy between possible and actual states in a wish, whereas maximization of a discrepancy of this sort is characteristic of a fear (Holt, 1976).[6]

Wishes may arise through interaction of biological and environmental events, as affects become associated in preprogrammed and learned ways with various cognitive representations and structures. For example, in the second half of the first year, separation from the mother may be an innate releasing mechanism for distress. When the return of the mother repeatedly quells this distress, the association of her representation with regulation of an aversive affective state and/or experience of a pleasurable state sets in motion a wish for proximity. This motive may be relatively autonomous from motives for oral gratification or other kinds of sensual contact with her.

From a psychoanalytic standpoint, what is critical to any reconceptualization of the concept of drive is that the denotation of passion be maintained. Psychoanalysts who have attempted to revise drive theory in the context of cognitive psychology have often proposed models of motivation that lose the emphasis on desire, impulse, fantasy, and emotional conflict (as opposed to cognitive conflict) that is the essence of the psychoanalytic account of motivation.[7] What the classical drive model provides, and what any reformulation must provide as well, is an account of motives that can be peremptory, can feel "it-like" or like nonself, and cannot be simply shut off. Furthermore, such a reformulation must account for motives that can be active consciously or unconsciously, can combine and interact in complex ways, can conflict with equally compelling fears or internal standards in which a person has invested emtionally, and can be seen as rooted to some significant extent in the biology of the organism.

The Classical Model, Object Relations, and the Self

One of the major sources of the contemporary pluralism in psychoanalysis relates to ambiguities about the relation between the classical theory of drive and conflict on the one hand, and approaches to object relations and the "self" on the other (see Eagle, 1987; Pine, 1988; Spruiell, 1988). The controversy centers around three issues. The first is the relation between object relations and drives. As noted earlier, object relations theorists have taken issue with the classical theory of drives. What Greenberg and Mitchell (1983) refer to as the "classical drive-structural model" asserts that the human organism is essentially pleasure-seeking, and that objects become important only insofar as they serve to release instinctual tension or satisfy drives. The relational model, in contrast, proposes that humans are essentially object-seeking, and that satisfaction of sensual or sexual pleasure is secondary to or derivative of basic needs for relatedness.

The second issue is the relation between object relations constructs and the structural model—that is, the id–ego–superego model. Are representations of self and others ego components, superego components, id components, or all three? Cognition is an ego function, so representations must be ego structures. At the same time, however, superego functions are seen as in part derived from internalization of parental objects and functions, and some theorists, such as Kernberg (1975), argue that object representations are components of drive structures (hence of id processes) as well.[8] To make matters more complicated, Kohut (1971, 1977) has argued for a special place for the "self" as a psychic structure (paralleling similar arguments in cognitive social psychology; see Markus, 1977, and Markus & Cross, Chapter 22, this volume; see also Kihlstrom & Cantor, 1983).[9]

Many psychoanalysts have been concerned that the shift in emphasis to a focus on representations, and particularly to such constructs as a unified or cohesive "self," has led psychoanalysis away from its most fundamental concepts: the notions of conflict and compromise. This concern is clearly not without foundation. From the perspective of current classical thinking (Brenner, 1982), representations of self and others are themselves compromise formations that reflect psychic conflict

as much as processes of person perception; hence, in this view, any attempt to divorce object relations from conflict psychology is likely to be misguided. Furthermore, many variants of self psychology, including Kohut's final statements of his approach, seem to regard conflicts between wishes on the one hand, and reality and internalized standards on the other, as relatively trivial, and to view the source of all psychological distress as unempathic parenting that leads to defective self-structure (see Kohut, 1984, p. 207).

A third and related issue confronting the integration of object relations concepts into psychoanalytic theory is the relation between psychosexual and object-relational development. Classical analysts view all psychological structures and processes in terms of conflict and compromise involving sexual or aggressive impulses; since object-relational difficulties are reducible to conflicts and pathological compromise formations at particular psychosexual stages, diagnoses based on level or degree of ego or object-relational disturbance, such as "borderline," are fundamentally mistaken. Although there is considerable merit to this perspective, the classical view tends to misinterpret phenomena that are clearly object-relational in terms of conflicts between wishes and prohibitions. Basic issues of relatedness described by character-disordered (and other, less disturbed) patients are filled with conflict—conflict between wishes to be intimate but fears that one cannot be vulnerable to another person without being hurt, humiliated, taken over, abused, or destroyed. However, these are not primarily conflicts between impulses and superego prohibitions, as in the classical model. They are laced with such conflicts, because any time a child feels abused, alone, or not attended to, he or she is likely to experience rage as well; however, the superego or Oedipal conflict may be secondary to the object-relational one.

Furthermore, the classical views tend to overestimate the role of motivation and to underestimate the importance of expectations derived in part from social learning. The pervasive expectations of malevolence in borderline patients, which have been documented in several studies (e.g., Lerner & St. Peter, 1984; Westen, Lohr, et al., in press; Westen, Ludolph, Lerner, Ruffins, & Wiss, in press) are typically interpreted from within the classical framework as projections of aggression. Although this is clearly part of the picture, recent research has begun to document extremely high frequencies of physical and especially sexual abuse in the developmental histories of borderline patients (Herman et al., 1989; Ogata, Silk, Goodrich, Lohr, & Westen, 1988; Westen, Ludolph, Misle, Ruffins, & Block, 1990; Zanarini, Gunderson, Marino, Schwartz, & Frankenburg, 1989). The malevolent object world of the borderline is thus likely to reflect in part real experiences of abuse, which are, in turn, perpetuated by behavioral expression of cognitive–dynamic interpersonal "scripts" that lead to further and confirmatory experiences of abuse (see Wachtel, 1977, on "cyclical psychodynamics"). The classical viewpoint also tends to deny that people can simply have deficits that are not currently maintained by conflict.[10]

In contrast to classical psychoanalytic theorists, some object relations theorists, such as Fairbairn (1952), have entirely abandoned the psychosexual model, instead embracing object-relational models of development. These models view "internationalizations" of object representations as the building blocks of psychic structure (Greenberg & Mitchell, 1983). In other words, our basic desires, competences, views of ourselves, and relationship patterns are shaped in our interactions with significant others and are formed by integrating aspects of those others and relationships into our personalities. A person's concept of self, for example, is shaped by both identification with and reflected appraisals of significant others, as well as by the need to disavow aspects of self that lead to anxiety about loss of love and other "danger situations" of childhood (see Sullivan, 1953). Because such models often abandon the Freudian focus on conflict and biologically based impulses, however, most object relations theorists have instead uneasily blended their models of development with Freud's psychosexual model. Freud initiated this hybridization in 1917 (Freud, 1917/1957) when he described the oral stage as "still narcissistic," aligning a psychosexual with an object-relational stage (see Compton, 1981b, p. 364).

The problem with this subtle blending of models is that the two views of development do not describe entirely the same developmental processes, and they need not covary. The psychosexual model suggests a continuum of fixation points that allegedly underlie different forms of neurotic pathology and different character structures. A personality constellation marked by obstinacy, parsimoniousness, and orderliness, in this view, reflects the way a child resolved feelings about the body and impulses during the anal stage.[11] Chronologically, the anal stage corresponds to Mahler's separation–individuation stage, particularly the rapprochement subphase. This hypothesized period has been associated theoretically with borderline personality disorders (Kernberg, 1975; Masterson, 1976). The problem is that there is no empirical relationship between borderline disorders and either "anal" character traits or related neurotic disorders in the obsessive–compulsive spectrum. What, then, is the relation between psychosexual fixation or regression and developmental disturbance in object relations during the same period? Are all list makers, misers, cantankerous souls, obsessive cleaners, or people whose sexual fantasies frequently center on touching or looking at a "good ass" borderline?

These are clearly "messy" issues, and though they admit to no easy solutions, a brief commentary is in order. With respect to the relation between motivations for object relations and Freud's libidinal drive, the antinomy between pleasure seeking and object seeking is only an antinomy in the context of Freud's specific meaning of libido, which confounds pleasure seeking with sexual pleasure seeking. People have a number of desires for connectedness with others, from wishes for physical proximity and security to desires for affiliation, intimacy, and a sense of belongingness. These are clearly mediated by affective systems—that is, characterized by "pleasure seeking" (and pain avoidance)—just as surely as are sexual desires. As Bowlby elucidated (1969, 1973), the child's attachment behavior is mediated by feelings such as separation distress, pleasure at being held in the mother's arms, or relief at reunion. There is no a priori reason why a child cannot be simultaneously motivated by several motive systems, each mediated by pleasurable and unpleasurable feelings, including both attachment and sensual/sexual gratification (Westen, 1985).

With respect to the place of object relations concepts in the structural model, one may question the utility of the structural model as anything more than a clinical heuristic for helping sort out the elements of a conflict, or wonder whether the concept of compromise formation may be able to account for most phenomena typically understood in more abstract structural terms. One may also fault the sloppiness of psychoanalytic terminology for creating a substantial part of the confusion and controversy. As noted earlier, the concept of "self" is a quagmire in psychoanalysis; equally problematic is the concept of "internalization," which is critical to object-relational accounts. When theorists speak of "internalized object relations" or "internalization of the mother," it is often difficult to know precisely what they mean. Frequently notions of internalization rely upon Freud's antiquated copy theory of perception (Schimek, 1975), as if somehow children store veridical percepts of important objects alongside their fantasy constructions. Equally problematic are classical analytic models of internalization that view the "taking in" of objects as some kind of act of oral incorporation.

One can distinguish several legitimate but distinct ways in which one can speak of internalization:

1. Formation of a person schema or object representation.
2. Formation of a relationship schema—that is, a representation of a relationship or set of relationships.
3. Formation of dynamic relationship paradigms and object-related fantasies—that is, cognitive–affective structures linking interpersonal wishes and fears with representations and action tendencies, and motivating interpersonal behavior.
4. Modeling, in which the person develops the competence to imitate some aspect of another's behavior.
5. Internalization of function, in which functions previously carried out by an external object become self-regulating functions, such as self-soothing in the face of pain or threat, and do not necessarily entail representation of specific people.
6. Moral internalization, in which moral injunctions are "cathected" as moral ideals.
7. Identification narrowly defined, which combines formation of an object representation, modeling and behavioral imitation, establishment of a motivational structure of "ideal object" to emulate, and adjustment of the self-concept or specific self-representations to reflect the altered ideal and behavior.

As can be seen, these various processes are not isomorphic. Any theorist who wishes to speak coherently of internalization of objects or "internalized object relations" must be able to specify precisely which processes he or she means in a particular instance, and to describe explicitly the ways in which cognitive and affective processes related to these representations could account for motivation if he or she abandons a drive model.

Finally, with respect to the difficulties of integrating psychosexual and object-relational developmental models, the concept of "developmental lines" (A. Freud, 1973) seems especially pertinent. There is little reason to believe that all of personality development can be captured in a single developmental process. Researchers studying cognitive development have similarly criticized Piaget on these grounds (e.g., Brainerd, 1978; Flavell, 1982; Cairns & Valsiner, 1984).[12] A more comprehensive psychoanalytic account of personality, and a correspondingly more thorough description of a single personality from a psychoanalytic perspective, will need to examine styles and developmental lines (various ego functions, object-relational processes, psychosexual phenomena); to explore subprocesses *within* each of these developmental lines; and to examine their complex interactions.

Metapsychology versus Clinical Theory

The last two decades have seen a growing disenchantment in some psychoanalytic circles with drive theory, energy concepts, aspects of the structural model, the distance of concepts such as "libidinal cathexis" and "drive fusion" from observable psychological events, and the persistent tendency in psychoanalytic literature for Freud's structures to be reified (as if "the ego" feels or chooses something). This has led many psychoanalytic theorists to suggest abandonment of much of Freud's theoretical superstructure, denoted his "metapsychology," in favor of the more experience-near concepts (e.g., repression, defense, conflict) that constitute what has been called the "clinical theory" of psychoanalysis (Klein, 1976; Schafer, 1976).[13] Schafer (1976) has advocated a move to "action language"—speaking of processes and actions instead of personified structures—as a way of preserving the sophisticated understanding of psychological processes embodied in psychoanalysis, while jettisoning what he believes to be an anachronistic and misleading language. Indeed, the consensus among many in the psychoanalytic community is that clinical thinking is far ahead of theoretical thinking at this point, and that attention to abstract theoretical nuance is at best a nuisance.

It seems to me that the diagnosis is probably correct, but the prescription is inadequate. One of the major problems with the prescription is that it is difficult to distinguish malignant from healthy cells: Delineation of precisely those elements that constitute metapsychology or clinical theory is problematic (Holt, 1985). Furthermore, the most basic clinical concepts are largely without foundation if one eliminates many of the more abstract theoretical or metapsychological principles that underlie them. For example, transference is probably the most important of all of Freud's clinical observations. Without developmental principles, however, why would one assume its roots in childhood? Without theoretical premises about conflicting mental forces or dynamics, why would one assume that the patient's thoughts and feelings about the analyst have any relation to important motivational forces, conflicts, or defenses?

From the perspective of personality psychology, a more pressing problem with attempts to retreat to clinical theory as a way of avoiding the problems of metapsychology is that doing this is both cognitively and philosophically untenable (see Holt, 1985; Peterfreund, 1975; Rubinstein, 1976). Abandonment of explicit principles of psychological functioning simply relegates them to the status of implicit and less systematic principles; to put the matter another way, it simply banishes them to our "scientific unconscious".[14]

Given the current renaissance of interest in the study of personality, it would truly be a pity if the subtle and sophisticated *working knowledge* of personality possessed by psychoanalytic clinicians were not assimilated by personality psychologists. Currently, it is too often not assimilated, in part because the theoretical superstructure of psychoanalysis is wanting. Through experience, supervision, and wrestling with existing theory, psychoanalytically informed practitioners tend to construct a largely unconscious "grammar" of personality. Although at the present time this intuitive grammar is probably in certain respects more sophisticated than the models used to account for it, a more refined "transformational grammar" would probably increase clinical

sophistication as well as our understanding of personality, just as the learning of grammatical rules by schoolchildren refines their speech.

The Epistemological Status of Psychoanalytic Data and Theory

Alongside these theoretical issues, a growing controversy has emerged over the epistemological status of psychoanalytic data and theory—that is, the kind of knowledge (if any) that psychoanalysis as a theory and a method affords. Current controversies center on three interrelated questions: Does psychoanalysis uncover actual memories and experiences, or is the reality that the patient constructs, and reconstructs, with the analyst the only reality that matters? Is psychoanalysis a science, or is it a hermeneutic enterprise like literary criticism? Finally, if psychoanalysis is a science, is it a good one, or are its data so contaminated by observer bias as to render them unscientific and useless?

Psychoanalytic Constructions: Narrative or Historical Truth?

One major point of contention, which is as much a point of theory as of epistemology, is the extent to which real events influence psychic events, and the correlative question of the extent to which actual historical events in the life of a patient are psychoanalytically knowable or useful. Freud initially believed hysteria to result from the effects of sexual abuse, but the extremely high prevalence of reports of actual seductions by his patients eventually led him to believe that many of these reports must represent childhood fantasies. It is now clear that Freud, in so shifting directions, vastly underestimated the prevalence of actual abuse; however, this shift was tremendously important theoretically, because with it Freud inaugurated a focus on "psychic reality" as opposed to "actual reality." This focus is a cornerstone of psychoanalytic thinking, and is most systematically adhered to theoretically in more classical circles (Arlow, 1985). The point is that the way a person reacts to an event is determined by the way he or she experiences it, which in turn is critically influenced by motives, fantasies, and affect-laden ideas.[15] In many ways, the shift in Freud's thinking parallels the similar shift in cognitive–behavioral thinking from viewing stimuli as causes to focusing on the influence on behavior of the way environmental events are construed and expected by the organism.[16]

The concept of psychic reality raises some challenging questions about the extent to which what matters psychologically is what actually happens or how the person construes what happens. Complicating things considerably is the fact that it is often exceedingly difficult to know where to place a patient's accounts of present and past relationships on the continuum from relatively accurate to relatively inaccurate and distorted—or, for that matter, where to place the patient's accounts of his or her past pscychic reality (i.e., wishes, fantasies, and ideas from the past). Spence (1982) has advanced an elegant argument that what happens in psychoanalytic treatment is not an act of archaeology, or recovering the past, but an act of mutual storymaking, in which patient and analyst construct a compelling narrative that provides the patient with an integrated view of his or her history and helps explain seemingly inexplicable aspects of the patient's life. Juxtaposed with historical truth is what Spence calls "narrative truth," which "depends on continuity and closure and the extent to which the fit of the pieces takes on an aesthetic finality. Narrative truth is what we have in mind when we say that such and such is a good story" (p. 31).

Although Spence makes an important distinction between therapeutic gains that may accrue from coming to understand oneself better, and gains that may accrue from coming to believe that one has done so, his argument is philosophically problematic. He seems to suppose that because reconstructions of the past are constructions and as such include elements of fiction, they are therefore *nothing but* fiction. The intermingling of reality with the observer's own cognitive structures is, however, true of all science and all cognition. As Morris Eagle (personal communication) has observed, the problem may not be so much Spence's argument, but his appellation of narrative truth as "truth": One could surely make an aesthetically pleasing story in which the Holocaust never happened, but most of us are outraged by neo-Nazi revisionists who claim truth status for this narrative. Coherence of structure and veridicality are two essential elements of a good theory, not criteria for competing brands of truth.

Science or Hermeneutics?

The question of the nature of truth in psychoanalysis—veridical reconstruction versus narrative coherence—dovetails with a question about precisely what kind of discipline psychoanalysis is or should be. Freud was quite clear in his view that psychoanalysis is a science, just like any other natural science (Freud, 1940/1964). Many analysts and psychoanalytic psychologists remain committed to the view that psychoanalysis, like other sciences, seeks general laws and attempts to establish causal connections among events—in this case, psychological events, such as thoughts, feelings, and behaviors (Brenner, 1980; Holt, 1985; Holzman, 1985).

On the other hand, several have suggested that psychoanalysis is not a science, but is instead a hermeneutic discipline, aimed at the *interpretive understanding* of human actions (Habermas, 1971; Ricoeur, 1971; Spence, 1982). In this view, the critical difference between humans and the objects of natural science such as planets or molecules is that humans confer meanings on their experiences, and that these meanings in turn influence what they do. Thus, as a social scientist (or, in this case, a psychoanalyst), what one endeavors to do is not to attribute causes but to *interpret* behavior and understand people's *reasons* for doing what they are doing—that is, their intentions. In psychoanalysis, these reasons are presumed often to be unconscious.

Many psychoanalysts have argued against this approach (see Edelson, 1985), contending that it trivializes psychoanalysis and ignores many of its factual assertions about stages of development, psychological mechanisms, and the like, which can be tested just as the hypotheses of any approach to human mental life and behavior can be tested. As Holzman (1985) observes, psychoanalysis is replete with causal theories (symptoms are caused by problematic compromise formations; repression of sexual wishes and fantasies is involved in the etiology of hysteria; etc.). Furthermore, reasons themselves have their causes (a person has sexual fantasies because sexual motivation is rooted in human biology; a particular sociopathic man has severe deficits in his moral development because he had no father, his mother was abusive, and he had a biological vulnerability to impulsivity).[17] Grunbaum (1984) has offered a trenchant critique of the hermeneutic account of psychoanalysis, arguing, among other things, that reasons are simultaneously causes. Whether an event is physical or psychological makes no difference to an account of causality: To be causal, an event X must simply *make a difference* to the occurrence of another event Y, and intentions can do this as well as material causes (see also Edelson, 1984, 1985; Holt, 1981).

There is little doubt that the "critique of the hermeneuts" by Grunbaum and others has, at least for now, put to rest the notion that psychoanalysis is and should be *nothing but* a hermeneutic affair. Whether that disposes of the hermeneutic approach to psychoanalysis in general is another matter (see the collection of essays on issues relevant to this in Messer, Sass, & Woolfolk, 1988). "Meaning" does not only mean "intention"; "meaning" has a number of "meanings," and carefully distinguishing them may suggest important ways in which psychoanalysis, and psychology in general, must be *in part* a hermeneutic discipline. Rogers (1959) was clear on one kind of meaning in his discussion of the way a particular kind of empathy allows one to understand another person by entering into his or her phenomenal experience—that is, to understand his or her subjectivity. There is very little in this kind of understanding that is causal, yet surely a good psychological theory must facilitate this, just as a good anthropological theory must facilitate understanding "from the native's point of view" (see Geertz, 1973).

A second meaning of "meaning" is derived from the psychoanalytic assertion that people use symbols in ways of which they are unaware. When one interprets the meaning of a hostile joke as a reflection of underlying anger, one is not only making a causal statement ("This comment was caused in part by his or her anger"), but is relying upon a set of rules of transformation, based on theory, that explains the way an underlying meaning has been expressed in a particular form. The relations between the latent content and the manifest content of a dream, a joke, an action, or a statement is analogous to the relation between deep structure and surface structure in linguistics: In each, an underlying meaning is converted through rules of transformation into a manifest form, which is typically only one way of expressing the underlying meaning. No one would suggest that Chomsky's transformational grammar is a causal theory—it is a system for

understanding the relation between what is latent and what is manifest—and it seems unlikely that anyone would challenge Chomsky to do large-n studies to demonstrate that there are indeed rules by which "He threw the ball" can be transformed into "The ball was thrown by him."

Though philosophers are of many opinions about the nature of social-scientific explanation and its relation to modes of explanation and proof in the natural sciences (see Benton, 1977; Boden, 1978; Ryan, 1970), it may be that a major difference between the social and natural sciences is that an adequate theory in the natural sciences must lead to accurate prediction, whereas an adequate theory in the social sciences must lead both to prediction *and* to interpretive understanding. An approach to personality that does not help the psychologist decode what is happening in an interpersonal situation in ways that a perspicacious layperson could not is no more adequate than a theory that does not generate testable hypotheses. When a female patient who frequently feels guilty about self-assertion and aggression chuckles while telling me that she is considering leaving her depressed, dependent boyfriend, I—as a clinician armed with psychoanalytic theory and hours of observation of this person—can readily explain why she is chuckling: She is feeling guilty about the possibility of hurting him, and her chuckling is a defense against the dysphoric affect (and perhaps against her anger and aggressive wishes as well, which she cannot allow herself to experience). There is not other theory in psychology that can as efficiently explain her laughter. (Perhaps amusement is a schema-triggered affect in the face of hurting someone? Or she has modeled laughter and is applying it in an inappropriate situation?)

A good personality theory is both nomothetic and idiographic, and idiographic explanation in humans often means interpretive understanding. Max Weber (1949) argued several decades ago that a social-scientific explanation must achieve both "adequacy at the level of meaning"—that is, interpretive understanding —and causal explanation. A psychological explanation of why abused children frequently enter into abusive marital relations as adults, for example, would need to explain how material and interpersonal causes in part produce meanings ("I am a bad person, and I deserve this in a relationship"), which in turn act as causes.

The Scientific Status of Psychoanalysis

If psychoanalysis is at least in part a causal–mechanical theory like those in the natural sciences, the question then arises as to whether it is a good theory, and whether its evidentiary basis is valid. The philosopher of science Sir Karl Popper (1957) argued that psychoanalysis, like Marxism, is a pseudoscience, not a true science, because it is inherently untestable. Psychoanalysis, he argued, is unfalsifiable because the logic of the theory is such that any negative finding can be explained away. How can one test hypotheses about aggressive impulses if such impulses can lead to either aggressive actions or reaction formations against them?

In his philosophical critique of psychoanalysis, Grunbaum (1984) argues that Popper's premise (that psychoanalysis is untestable) is wrong, but that his conclusion (psychoanalytic theory and data are problematic) is right. Grunbaum demonstrates that the hypotheses for which Freud claimed scientific status are causal hypotheses that can, in fact, be falsified. The major question, Grunbaum notes, is whether clinical data are scientifically valid as evidence that can be used to corroborate or falsify the theory. Freud's major argument for the truth of his claims was what Grunbaum calls the "tally argument": In the course of a treatment, those interpretations that tally with what is real in the patient will remain, those that do not will be weeded out, and the proof of the veracity of the interpretations is the fact that the patient improves. The problem with this, Grunbaum argues, is that there is no evidence that psychoanalysis is superior to any other form of treatment in eliminating neurotic symptoms. Furthermore, clinical data are so contaminated by suggestion—that is, by "demand characteristics" and by expectations of the analyst—that they cannot be used to support psychoanalytic concepts. Thus, there is minimal evidence in support of psychoanalytic theory, which is therefore at best of unknown validity.

Grunbaum's thesis is meticulously argued (see Grunbaum, 1986, for a précis), and most psychoanalytic commentators have been remarkably appreciative of his conclusions (see the series of commentaries in the *Behavioral and Brain Sciences*, 1986). Before the reader skips to the next chapter of this volume, satisfied that psychoanalysis has finally been done in, a few comments about Grunbaum's argument and conclusions are in order. First, as several authors have noted (e.g., Kline, 1986; Luborsky, 1986), Grunbaum considerably underestimates the amount of experimental evidence that exists in support of various psychoanalytic propositions, some of which are briefly reviewed in the next section of this chapter. Furthermore, psychotherapy research (see Messer & Warren, Chapter 14, this volume) has begun documenting many psychodynamic processes, such as transference and defense, by making systematic and quantitative use of precisely the kinds of data that Freud believed were crucial to formulating a theory of personality.

Second, as several commentators have pointed out as well (e.g., Holt, 1986; Shevrin, 1986), Grunbaum underestimates the extent to which patients tell clinicians things that the clinician neither expected nor suggested. The problems of perceiving only what one expects and unwittingly convincing one's patients to share one's preconceptions, to which both Grunbaum and Spence (along with a long line of others over the past century) repeatedly point, are indeed real, and are an especially problematic aspect of the psychoanalytic method of investigation of which Freud himself was well aware. Nevertheless, psychoanalysts had been describing unconscious processes for nearly a century before their experimental colleagues began even acknowledging the existence of such processes, and it was precisely the difference in method that led to the differences in observation and theory.[18]

As Marie Jahoda argues in an important book, *Freud and the Dilemmas of Psychology* (1977), the way to deal with impurities in one's method is to supplement that method with data from methods with different impurities (p. 157). She notes that the clinical method has several strengths that experimental methods do not. For example, because the observer knows the subject well, he or she is more likely to understand both the meanings and the context of the subject's communications and behavior. The clinical observer also sees the subject over many hours, in contrast to the typical 45-minute experiment.

An additional problem with Grunbaum's argument, as Cioffi (1986) points out, is that what Freud relied upon to demonstrate the validity of his inferences in a particular case was less the tally argument than the ability of those inferences to confer intelligibility upon data that would otherwise make little sense. For example, Kernberg's (1975) or Masterson's (1976) theory of borderline pathology allows one to understand why wrist cutting, severe separation distress, and manipulative behavior typically co-occur; this is certainly not intuitively obvious and is not well explained by other theories of personality. From a psychoanalytic perspective, when one sees these together, one has reason to infer an underlying personality organization, which then permits one to predict and understand why the patient keeps losing jobs.[19]

Some psychoanalysts do continue to view psychoanalytic data as the only valid data for a theory of mental processes (e.g., Arlow & Brenner, 1988; Brenner, 1982), much as many experimentalists view experimental data as the single path to psychological knowledge. There is, however, a growing consensus in the psychoanalytic community, shared by many leading analysts, that if psychoanalysis is to survive as a theory and a therapy, it must both generate and have contact with systematic experimental research (Cooper, 1984; Fisher & Greenberg, 1977; Holt, 1985; Holzman, 1985; Michels, 1988; Reiser, 1985; Wallerstein, 1988).

Implications for Personality Theory

As noted earlier, the points of controversy currently enlivening the psychoanalytic scene are not, strictly speaking, only psychoanalytic concerns; many of them point to fundamental issues for personality theory more generally. The debate about drive theory is a debate about the nature of human motivation, which branches into questions about the role of affect and cognition in motivation, the extent to which motives endure over time, and the interaction of nature and nurture in generating the motives that underlie human behavior. Trait approaches to personality tend to remain silent on motivational issues, whereas social learning and social-cognitive approaches tend to emphasize conscious, cognitive, rational, and environmentally induced motivations, and to study them without references to their developmental vicissitudes.

Although the relations among the drive model, object relations, and self psychology are distinctly psychoanalytic concerns, the issues raised are far more general. These include the extent to which people are to be understood as self-interested or as inherently social; the role of social processes, and particularly interactions with significant others in childhood, in forming aspects of personality; the relation between motivation and personality; the motivational status of cognitive representations, particularly representations of the self and others; and the nature of dimensions of "self." The issue of metapsychology versus clinical theory also raises a central question for personality psychology—namely, the extent to which research should be dominated by microtheories and studies of particular traits that are not part of a broader view of personality, or whether attempts at integrated frameworks for understanding personality (such as psychoanalysis and cognitive–social learning theory), should become the core of personality theory and research.

Perhaps of most importance to the field is a consideration of the epistemological questions that psychoanalysis has been confronting for the past decade. The relation between objective reality and psychic reality has been addressed in the personality literature largely in methodological terms, pertaining to the veridicality of self-reports.[20] Individual differences in capacity for veridical reporting are themselves a domain worthy of considerable study. The issue of hermeneutics is critical as well, particularly since life history research is once again beginning to receive attention (see, e.g., Rosenwald, 1988; Runyan, 1984), and since one could argue that a good personality theory must lead both to prediction and to interpretive understanding.

Finally, debates about the scientific status and validity of psychoanalytic data raise fundamental questions about necessary and sufficient data for personality theory and research. Clinical observation casts a broad net for observing psychologically meaningful phenomena. Scientists rarely test isolated hypotheses that are not part of a broader theoretical or paradigmatic network (see Kuhn, 1970), and the hypotheses they form stem from that framework, which relies upon data from many sources other than the laboratory (or the personality psychologist's laboratory, the introductory psychology subject pool). The specific "facts" corroborated in the psychologist's laboratory will always be so spotty in contrast to the wealth of observable human experience that these well-documented data must be woven together with knowledge and ideas with less documentation if our theories are to make any sense.

Indeed, one could make a strong case that the demand for certainty at the level of hypothesis testing in psychology leads to the certainty of falsehood at the level of theory. If psychologists base their theoretical frameworks exclusively on relatively "proven" experiments, they create a collective "availability heuristic" which leads them to understate the importance of processes and variables that, for technological, practical, or ethical reasons, are relatively inaccessible to the scientific community. One may have a choice between relatively rich theories containing numerous specific falsehoods, or relatively impoverished theories containing numerous likely truths that, when aggregated, produce a narrow and distorted view. We would probably do well to think of an evidentiary hierarchy, in which experimental demonstrations are especially convincing forms of evidence, and nonreplicable clinical observations are less compelling but important sources of data for theory building. This is particularly important for the field of personality, since it deals with phenomena of considerable complexity, many of which cannot be easily brought into a laboratory for systematic investigation.[21]

Between the context of discovery and the context of justification lies a context of scientific *committed belief*, and in this context, those who are wedded to a single method may be disadvantaged relative to those who are methodologically less monogamous. With this in mind, let us turn to empirical investigations of psychoanalytic hypotheses and points of contact with other domains of research.[22]

EMPIRICAL RESEARCH AND POINTS OF CONTACT WITH OTHER RESEARCH

When one considers not only research generated by psychoanalytic researchers but also the experimental evidence in other research traditions that corroborates, dovetails with, or refines basic psychoanalytic hypotheses, one finds that the empirical basis of psychoanalytic concepts is far better documented, and that psychoanalytic thinking is far more widely applicable, than is typically assumed. Limitations of space prevent anything more than a brief delineation here of areas of current research and salient issues. Experimental investigations of more classical Freudian hypotheses, such as those regarding dreams and psychosexual stages, have been thoroughly and competently reviewed elsewhere (Fisher & Greenberg, 1977; Kline, 1972, 1981), and are thus not described in any detail. Although psychoanalytic research has often been far from rigorous scientifically, most readers would be surprised to find that the construct validity of the anal character (and, to a lesser extent, the oral character) has been tested and supported in many studies, and that several psychoanalytic hypotheses about the Oedipus complex, the castration complex, and even penis envy have been subjected to empirical test. Fisher and Greenberg (1977) have impressively demonstrated the way in which empirical disconfirmations of the hypothesized relation between a boy's fear of his father and the strength of his superego can lead to refinements in the psychoanalytic theory of moral development (see also Westen, 1986). The discussions that follow focus on five domains in which psychoanalytic thinking has been empirically tested or could usefully be integrated with other empirical research traditions: the examination of unconscious processes; cognition and affect; object relations; developmental psychology; and neuropsychology.

Experimental Investigations of Unconscious Processes

Perhaps the major area of sophisticated experimental work from a psychoanalytic perspective has been the study of unconscious processes. During the 1940s and 1950s, and into the 1960s, researchers associated with the "New Look" in perception (see Bruner, 1973; Erdelyi, 1974, 1985) studied the way in which the selection and organization of perception are influenced by motives, expectations, and defenses. As early as 1917, Poetzl (1917/1960) had demonstrated, using tachistoscopic presentation of stimuli, that subliminal stimuli could influence subsequent dream content. A basic idea behind New Look research was that considerable cognitive processing goes on before a stimulus is ever consciously perceived. These investigators argued, further, that the emotional content of subliminally perceived stimuli can have an important impact on subsequent thought and behavior. The evidence is now clear that both of these suppositions are correct (Dixon, 1971, 1981).

The Return of the Unconscious in Psychology

The research of the New Look was, oddly, dismissed by most psychologists in the late 1950s just as the information-processing perspective, which could have assimilated its findings, began to emerge (see Erdelyi, 1974). For two decades this work has rarely been cited. In 1977, Nisbett and Wilson (1977a) demonstrated that people have minimal access to their cognitive processes; that they often "tell more than they can know" about these psychological events; and that the explanations people typically offer about why they did or thought as they did involve application of general attributional knowledge rather than access to their own cognitive processes. One study reported by Nisbett and Wilson documented that subjects are unaware of "spreading activation" (Collins & Loftus, 1975), whereby activation of one node of a network of association spreads activation to others, so that related nodes are primed and more likely to become conscious. After learning the word pair "ocean–moon," for example, subjects were more likely to respond with "Tide" to a question about laundry detergents, even though they had no conscious idea that a network was active and had influenced their response.

In 1980, Shevrin and Dickman marshaled evidence from several fields of research—notably, work on selective attention, subliminal perception, and cortical evoked potentials—to argue that a concept of unconscious psychological processes is both necessary for and implicit in much psychological research and theory. Within 4 years, two prominent psychologists not identified with psychoanalysis (Bowers & Meichenbaum, 1984) edited a volume entitled *The Unconscious Reconsidered* and stated unequivocally that unconscious processes pervasively influence thought, feeling, and behavior. Unconscious processes have now become a respectable area for research, mostly by nonanalytic psychologists (see Bargh, 1984; Kihlstrom, 1987 and Chapter 17, this volume). The issue of consciousness is rapidly becoming central to models of memory (see, e.g., Schacter, 1986; Squire, 1987), particularly since the discovery that amnesics may continue to learn certain skills and are subject to normal priming effects, even though they have no conscious

recollection of learning the skills or verbal material. This suggests that consciously retrievable memory is only one form of memory. Priming effects can similarly occur in normal subjects even when the initial verbal material (such as word pairs) is presented subliminally; in other words, networks of associations can be activated without any conscious processing at all.

Other research on selective and divided attention (see Hirst, 1986) and on automaticity of cognitive processes (see Bargh, 1984; Shiffrin & Schneider, 1977) demonstrates that even complex psychological processes can be carried out unconsciously (see also Lewicki, 1986; Marcel, 1983). Particularly striking is research using hypnosis, which demonstrates that actions carried out unconsciously can consume attentional capacity and thus cannot be conceived as simply routinized or automatic (Kihlstrom, 1987 and Chapter 17, this volume), as was previously the case in cognitive psychology. These studies not only document the existence of complex unconscious thought processes, but may also begin to provide experimental evidence for unconscious intentionality.

Research from a number of quarters even documents the existence of unconscious affective processes (see Greenberg & Safran, 1987; Westen, 1985). For example, Broadbent (1977) found that neutral words were more easily perceived than unpleasant words, which suggests preconscious processing of the affective significance of stimuli. Moray found that words paired with electric shocks in a classical conditioning procedure altered galvanic skin response (suggesting an emotional reaction) when presented to the unattended ear in a dichotic listening task; although the subject never consciously perceived the word that had been "tagged" with fear, presentation of the stimulus produced an emotional response that could be measured physiologically (see Moray, 1969). Heinemann and Emrich (1971), studying cortical evoked potentials, found that emotion-laden words presented subliminally elicited significantly greater alpha rhythms than neutral words even before subjects reported seeing anything, suggesting differential processing of emotional and neutral material outside of awareness. Morokoff (1985) assessed sexual arousal both by self-report and by vaginal photoplethysmography while female subjects viewed an erotic videotape. Women high in self-reported sex guilt reported less arousal but demonstrated significantly greater physiological arousal than women low in sex guilt, suggesting that their arousal was rendered unconscious by the need to defend against guilt. A recent study by Niedenthal and Cantor (1986) demonstrated, as had several New Look studies (e.g., Eagle, 1959), that unconscious affective processing can influence social categorization. Other research clearly documenting unconscious affective processes is described below.

From the perspective of psychoanalysis as a personality theory, this surge of interest in and acceptance of the pervasive role of unconscious processes is both remarkable and welcome, since this is one of the core assumptions that has distinguished psychoanalytic approaches from other perspectives in personality. Nevertheless, before the reader concludes that we are all Freudians now, it should be noted that the "cognitive unconscious" of theorists such as Kihlstrom remains vastly different from the dynamic unconscious of Freud. In fact, many researchers who study unconscious processes use the term "nonconscious" to underscore that they are not psychoanalytic, and Kihlstrom (1987) is careful to avoid any statement that people can be motivated to keep certain aspects of "declarative knowledge" unconscious. My guess is that this, too, will change. As psychology comes to focus more on the motivational role of affect, it should become clear that if affective processing can occur unconsciously, and if purposeful, nonautomatic, and complex thought can also occur unconsciously, then there is little reason to suppose that affectively motivated purposeful activity cannot occur without awareness. Surely an organism that required consciousness of every motive, as in a serial-processing model of goals coming in and out of consciousness, would be at a tremendous adaptive disadvantage. The idea that various cognitive, affective, and motivational processes could occur simultaneously and interact without conscious awareness is in fact more compatible with parallel distributed processing (PDP) models in cognitive science (Rumelhart, McClelland, and the PDP Research Group, 1986) than are contemporary social-cognitive motivational models that presume conscious processing of goals. McClelland and colleagues (McClelland, Koestner, & Weinberger, 1989) have recently gathered considerable evidence supporting the distinction between unconscious motives and the serial motives that guide

conscious action. Their evidence suggests that the two kinds of motives have different correlates and antecedents.

Furthermore, if one views defensive processes as ways of regulating affects (particularly aversive affects), then one could consider strategies for affect regulation as "procedures" or "skills"—that is, as aspects of "procedural knowledge," which is typically understood as unconscious—or one could view regulation of affect as involving a series of "production systems," to use the language of Anderson's (1983) ACT* model of cognition, that can be cued by various stimuli and internal events. As I discuss shortly, there is a body of experimental evidence that documents defensive processes more directly. Similarly, wishes have cognitive components that should presumably be located along networks of association, so that activation of a network should in certain cases prime wishes (as well as conflicting affective and behavioral tendencies) that remain below the threshold of consciousness.

Current Psychoanalytic Investigations Using Subliminal Stimulation

Two extensive programs of research using subliminal stimulation to test psychodynamic hypotheses are those of Silverman (1983; Silverman & Weinberger, 1985; Weinberger & Silverman, 1988) and Shevrin (1988; Shevrin & Dickman, 1980). Silverman's research involves presentation of verbal and pictorial stimuli "designed to stimulate the unconscious wishes, anxieties, and fantasies that psychoanalysis views as motivators of behavior" (Silverman, 1983, p. 70). Dozens of studies have now been carried out by Silverman and others, using stimuli such as the verbal messages, "I am losing Mommy," "Beating Dad is wrong," and "Mommy and I are one," to test for effects on thought or behavior. Two studies, for example, have used Blatt and colleagues' Depressive Experiences Questionnaire (DEQ) (Blatt, Quinlan, Chevron, McDonald, & Zuroff, 1982) to distinguish subjects whose depression is "anaclitic" (i.e., focused on issues of loss, separation, and emptiness) from those whose depression is "introjective" (i.e., based on a sense of guilt and failure to meet standards). Subjects distinguished by the DEQ responded differently to subliminal stimulation in theoretically expected ways (Dauber, 1984; Weinberger & Silverman, 1988). Another series of studies attempted to prime Oedipal competition in male college students, and then tested subjects' accuracy in a dart-throwing task. Though not all attempts at replication have been successful, several of these studies have found that presentation of the subliminal stimulus "Beating Dad is ok" leads to significantly better performance on the dart-throwing task than the stimulus "Beating Dad is wrong."

Silverman and others have also found that subliminal presentation of the stimulus "Mommy and I are one" to various clinical populations, particularly schizophrenics, reduces symptoms. Although one may raise theoretical questions about why a stimulus such as this would have an effect in contrast to various control stimuli, research using this paradigm (both from Silverman's laboratory and elsewhere) has largely been scientifically rigorous. A recent meta-analysis found small but significant effect sizes, leading its author to conclude that further replications of the basic design are at this point superfluous (Hardaway, in press). Interestingly, most of these studies have found effects only for subliminal stimulation, not for supraliminal presentation of stimuli.

Shevrin (1988; Shevrin & Dickman, 1980) has been exploring psychoanalytic hyptheses about unconscious processes by measuring the effects of subliminal exposure on a neurophysiological dependent variable, cortical evoked potential. His earlier reserach attempted to isolate brain wave correlates of repression. His current program of research follows implicitly if not explicitly from a critique of experimental methods that fail to consider the specific meanings of a stimulus for individual subjects (see Balay & Shevrin, 1988). Outpatient subjects with discrete symptoms—phobias and pathological grief reactions—are given an extensive battery of psychiatric interviews and projective tests, which are audiotaped. This material is then reviewed by a team of clinicians who choose from the transcribed protocol a series of words the patient has used, which fall into two classes: words the patient consciously relates to the symptom, and words related to the inferred dynamic conflict underlying the symptom. Although results at this point are preliminary, Shevrin has begun to find significant differences in patterns of cortical activity in response to these conscious and unconscious associates of the symptom and control words, and has found significant effects of subliminal versus supraliminal presentation.

Repressive Personality Styles and Processes

Several investigators have studied personality styles that entail a tendency toward rigid use of repressive defenses. The weight of the evidence from these studies is beginning to suggest not only that such individuals respond differently (both behaviorally and physiologically) from other subjects, but that their style of defending may have serious consequences for their health (Weinberger, in press; see also Bonanno & Singer, in press). To identify repressors, Weinberger et al. (1979) isolated individuals who simultaneously reported a low level of distress on the Taylor Manifest Anxiety Scale and a high level of social desirability, defensiveness, or over-control as measured by the Marlowe–Crowne Scale (Crowne & Marlow, 1964). The investigators found that the repressors (low anxiety, high social desirability) were distinguished from other subjects by greater reaction times when confronted with sexual and aggressive verbal stimuli; they also exhibited a combination of lower self-reported anxiety with higher anxiety as measured by multiple physiological indices during an emotionally stressful experimental procedure. Asendorpf and Scherer (1983) obtained similar results using a slightly different methodology. Subsequent studies (Davis, 1987; Davis & Schwartz, 1987) have found that repressors report fewer and later negative memories from childhood, and that this inhibition is restricted to memories of negative experiences that happened to themselves rather than to others. The link to health outcomes is now beginning to be documented (see Weinberger, in press). Studies have repeatedly found repressors to be more reactive physiologically on a plethora of measures related to heart disease and poor response to stress.

Weinberger's "repressive style" may actually be misnamed, since it is intended to refer to subjects who isolate their affects and report minimal reactivity, and hence applies best to rigidly defended obsessives, not hysterics, who are typically associated with repression as a preferred defensive mode (see Shapiro, 1965). Shedler (Shedler, Mayman, & Manis, 1988) is tapping a similar dimension, though perhaps casting a somewhat wider net, in isolating something like degree of defensiveness about oneself and one's inner experience that cuts across cognitive style, which he calls "defensive self-esteem." Shedler isolated subjects who reported minimal emotional disturbance on

Eysenck's Neuroticism scale (see Eysenck, Chapter 10, this volume) but who were simultaneously blindly judged on the basis of their early memories to be relatively disturbed; early memories were assessed by a clinician who is a leading researcher on the diagnostic uses of early memories. Subjects participated in a mildly stressful laboratory procedure, involving reading aloud, responding to Thematic Apperception Test (TAT) cards, and completing a phrase association task. In comparison to subjects in the genuine self-esteem group (rated healthy by both self-report and clinician judgment), subjects with defensive self-esteem were significantly more reactive ($p < .005$) on a combined index of heart rate and blood pressure used by cardiologists and empirically related to heart disease. Furthermore, although the defensive self-esteem subjects reported less subjective anxiety, their verbal productions were recorded and coded for manifestations of anxiety (laughing, sighing, stuttering, blocking, avoiding the content of the stimulus, etc.), and they were found to manifest significantly more behavioral indices of anxiety.[23]

Empirical Investigations of Defense Mechanisms

Another area of active research in psychoanalysis is the empirical study of defense mechanisms (for a comprehensive review, see Perry & Cooper, 1987). In the 1950s and 1960s, Blum and his students (see Blum, 1968) used hypnotic procedures, typically in combination with a projective task in which subjects responded to pictures of a cartoon dog ("Blacky") in various psychoanalytically relevant situations, to test hypotheses about defensive processes. For example, in a fascinating unpublished doctoral dissertation, Hedegard (1969) induced anxiety in subjects hypnotically, and asked subjects before and after anxiety induction to choose captions to the Blacky pictures. Supporting the notion that defenses form a hierarchy of relative adaptiveness, Hedegard found that higher levels of anxiety elicited less mature defenses.

The concept of hierarchical levels of defenses, originally developed by Anna Freud (1936), has been refined and studied empirically by Vaillant (1977). Theoretically, defenses involving rigidly held and gross distortions of reality are viewed as more pathological, and hence are expected to be used primarily by individuals with severe character pathology who do not have more adaptive defenses at their disposal (e.g., narcissistic personalities who find even minor inadequacies so intolerable that they must externalize the causes of any failure or project any impulse that threatens their tenuous self-esteem) or by relatively healthy people in times of severe stress (e.g., bereaved individuals who imagine the presence of recently deceased love ones). In several studies, Vaillant and others (see Vaillant, 1977, 1986) have begun testing this view. For example, Vaillant and Drake (1985) found a striking relationship between level of defense maturity on the one hand, and independently and reliably rated level of psychiatric health–sickness and presence–absence of a diagnosable personality disorder on the other. One notable aspect of this study is that it corroborated Vaillant's (1977) study of Harvard graduates with a sample of 306 subjects with an inner-city background. Perry and Cooper (1986, 1989) have been studying the defenses of a personality-disordered sample and have begun corroborating the notion of a hierarchy of defenses in research with this group.

Cognition, Affect, and Psychoanalysis

Freud's "cognitive psychology" was extensive (see Erdelyi, 1985), and although psychoanalysis is first and foremost a psychology of motivation, it has made many contributions to the understanding of cognition that have yet to be assimilated by cognitive psychologists. Freud's distinction between "primary-process" thought, which is organized by associations rather than by logic, and "secondary-process" thought, which is more rational and directed by conscious concerns, is similar in many respects to contemporary distinctions between automatic and controlled information processing. A critical difference between psychoanalytic approaches to cognition and information-processing approaches is that the former were tied from the start to considerations of affect, cognitive–affective interaction, and consciousness. For psychoanalysis, it is axiomatic that cognition is largely if not entirely in the service of affective and motivational processes, and that needs, wishes, and conflicts are involved in categorizing and selecting information to be consciously perceived and processed. In this section I touch only briefly on some of the major directions of psychoanalytic thinking about cognition, particularly as they bear on contemporary information-processing approaches.

Thought Disorder and the Menninger Group

A major impetus for psychoanalytic investigations of thinking in the middle of this century was the attempt to understand disordered thought in schizophrenics. Rapaport and his colleagues (see Allison, Blatt, & Zimet, 1968; Rapaport, 1951; Rapaport, Gill, & Schafer, 1945–1946) painstakingly analyzed the verbatim psychological testing protocols of hundreds of institutionalized patients, in an attempt to categorize the pathologic processes characterizing schizophrenic thought. For example, they found, from examination of Rorschach responses, that psychotic patients frequently contaminated one percept with another; that is, they superimposed one percept on another without recognizing the impossibility of the superimposition. Such patients were also found to make logical errors and category errors of various sorts, and to suffer from associative intrusions. These varieties of thought disorder were seen as manifestations of primary-process thinking (see Holt, 1967). Research on thought disorder in patients with borderline personality disorder (summarized in Gartner, Hurt, & Gartner, 1987) has found more attenuated forms of thought disturbance, such as egocentric or fanciful elaborations and intrusions of aggressive content into perceptions. To my knowledge, no one to date has integrated these various observations with contemporary information-processing theory and research, even though such phenomena must be explained by any theory of thinking.

Information Processing and Psychoanalysis

Many psychoanalytically oriented researchers and clinicians have attempted to bring psychoanalytic theory together with systems theory and information-processing approaches. In a rarely cited but important book, Blum (1961) developed a model of cognitive–dynamic interactions, based on systematic experimental research using hypnosis. Relying upon a computer model, Blum described networks of association, which he related to neural circuits; elaborated a theory of spreading activation (which he described as "reverberation" from an activated node in a network to related representations); described networks linking cognitive and affective representations; discussed cognitively controlled inhibitory mechanisms responsible for repression; and used an experimental paradigm for exploring cognitive–affective interactions that predated similar work in cognitive psychology by 20 years.

At the same time, Tomkins (1962) published the first of his massive volumes on affect, in which he argued that affect is a primary motivational system in humans that "amplifies" drives and stimulation (see also Plutchik, 1980). Tomkins' concept of "nuclear scenes" (see Singer & Bonanno, Chapter 16 this volume; Tomkins, 1986) was informed by psychoanalytic thinking and has been applied clinically by Carlson (1981, 1986). Menninger et al. (1963) reinterpreted Freud's concept of signal anxiety in terms of feedback activating defensive functions. Bowlby (1969, 1973), as noted earlier, relied on systems theory to develop a model of affect and motivation that has yet to be fully exploited by psychoanalytic thinkers. Peterfreund (1971) and Erdelyi (1985) have also explored links between information processing and psychoanalysis. Horowitz (1987, 1988) has developed a sophisticated "configurational analysis" of recurring "states of mind" that is meant to codify and systematize clinical assessment of personality processes; the theoretical underpinning of this approach is an integration of information-processing theory with psychoanalytic conceptions of motivation and defense (see Messer & Warren, Chapter 14, this volume).

Several psychoanalytic theorists have attempted to wed Freudian with Piagetian concepts of development, particularly in infancy, as well as with other approaches to learning and cognition. They have examined the interaction of the child's developing understanding of the self, others, and the world with evolving wishes and fears (e.g., Basch, 1977; Fast, 1985; Greenspan, 1979; Wolff, 1960). Klein (1976) and Singer (1985; Singer & Bonanno, Chapter 16, this volume) have reformulated many psychoanalytic observations in terms of cognitive–affective schemas. Following in the tradition of Dollard and Miller (1950), Wachtel (1977, 1987) has written extensively and with tremendous sophistication about links between psychoanalysis and learning theory, and I (Westen, 1985) have proposed a model of affect and cognitive–affective interaction that integrates aspects of psychoanalytic, cognitive, behavioral, systems, and attribution theories. Foulkes (1978) has attempted to integrate aspects of the psychoanalytic theory of dream interpretation with cognitive theory and research.

Another convergence with cognitive psychology is in the area of cognitive style (see Messer & Schacht, 1986). Shapiro (1965) has offered a description of various personality styles, which includes an analysis of preferred modes of defense as well as cognitive style. As he argues persuasively, cognitive and defensive style are intertwined: An obsessively oriented person who focuses on minor details, has difficulty choosing among various courses of action until all possible variables are considered, and takes pride in his or her rationality, has developed both a style of thinking (analytic, field-independent, left-hemisphere, etc.) and a characteristic mode of regulating affect to avoid aversive feelings (isolation of affect, intellectualization, etc.).

Empirical Investigations of Object Relations

A major area of contemporary research in psychoanalysis is the study of object relations (for a comprehensive review, see Blatt & Lerner, 1983a; see also Urist, 1980). Like research on repressive personality styles and processes, this research may have potential implications for physical as well as psychological health: Longitudinal, experimental, and quasi-experimental studies with both humans and animals suggest that quality and quantity of social relationships have a causal impact on health and mortality (see House, Landis, & Umberson, 1988). Although research on relationships and health has been carried out independently of the object relations literature (it typically relies instead on concepts of social support), if research can demonstrate a link between the cognitive and affective processes mediating interpersonal functioning described by object relations theorists and the capacity to sustain relationships, then there is good reason to believe that object-relational processes may influence morbidity and mortality.

Research on object relations over the last two decades has been extensive, though highly variable in degree of experimental rigor. Much of this research has involved coding of projective data. Although in previous eras this would have disqualified such research from serious consideration in the minds of many personality psychologists, recent social-cognitive research (Bargh, 1984; Higgins, King, & Mavin, 1982) suggests that chronically activated or accessible categories developed through experience are readily employed in the processing of social stimuli; in turn, this suggests that the characters subjects see in the Rorschach or the TAT are likely to bear the imprint of enduring cognitive–affective processes and structures. Mayman (1967, 1968) argued that the affective quality and cognitive structure of representations of self and others may be examined through projective tests. He hypothesized that the extent to which subjects describe characters who are psychologically rich, differentiated, and interacting in benign ways should predict relative psychological health and capacity for intimacy. Research since Mayman's initial studies, primarily by Mayman and his students and by Blatt at Yale, has consistently confirmed this hypothesis. For example, using an outpatient sample, Krohn and Mayman (1974) found that modal object relations scores from several different sources of projective data correlated highly, providing construct validity for the notion of levels of object relations, from relatively disturbed to relatively healthy. They also found that these scores could predict independently assessed therapist–supervisor ratings of the patient's level of object relations, based on extensive knowledge of the patient's actual interpersonal functioning with significant others as well as with the therapist.

Blatt (Blatt et al., 1976b; Blatt & Lerner, 1983a) has carried out an extensive program of research measuring several dimensions of object relations from Rorschach responses. In a series of studies, Blatt and colleagues have found predicted differences among various clinical and normal populations, as well as predicted developmental changes through adolescence. Blatt has also developed a parental representations scale for use with free-response parental descriptions (Blatt et al., 1979), which assesses dimensions such as the cognitive or conceptual level of the object and the degrees of ambivalence and malevolence expressed toward the object.

Bell (Bell, Billington, & Becker, 1986; Bell, Billington, Cicchetti, & Gibbons, 1988) adapted items from the object relations section of Bellak et al.'s (1973) method of assessing ego functions to form a self-report measure of object-relational functioning. The 45-item self-report inventory has been validated on several samples and yields four factors by factor analysis: Alienation, Egocentrism, Insecure Attachment, and Social Incompetence. Orlofsky and his colleagues have expanded upon Erikson's concept of intimacy and developed ways of assessing intimacy status that have been used in a number of studies (see Orlofsky, in press). Raskin has developed a self-report measure of narcissism that has now been validated in a series of studies (Emmons, 1987; Raskin, 1988). In one ingenious study, Raskin (in press) found that this narcissism scale could predict the number of times subjects used the first-person singular pronoun (as compared with the first-person plural) in a free-response situation. Millon's extensively validated and widely used self-report measure of personality disorders (see Millon, Chapter 13, this volume) also assesses several dimensions related to object relations, since personality disorders in the revised third edition of the *Diagnostic and Statistical Manual of Mental Disorders* (DSM-III-R) are in large measure disorders of interpersonal functioning.

Object Relations and Social Cognition

Since object relations theory and research examine the nature of representations of self and others and the mental processes that operate on those representations, this body of theory and research should be relevant to the study of social cognition. Each approach could stand to gain considerably from contact with the other (see Horowitz, 1988; Westen, in press-a). Object relations approaches pose important challenges to social-cognitive perspectives, largely because of the psychoanalytic understanding of affective and motivational processes. Object relations theories, and psychoanalytic theories more generally, point to the importance of unconscious schemas that are qualitatively different from those that are consciously accessible. Researchers in social cognition tend to assume that activated or "on-line" representations are accessible representations capable of becoming conscious, given the right level of activation. Clinical observation, by contrast, suggests that representations in phenomenal awareness may be defensively transformed versions of active but inaccessible representations, as when a narcissistic patient who has just been emotionally

devastated by being passed over for a promotion grandiosely announces that this simply confirms that the inferior cannot judge the superior, and denies that he or she has been upset at all. Psychoanalytic theory suggests that representations are far richer, far more affectively imbued, and far more complex and contradictory in their structure than social-cognitive research has implied. Most studies of social cognition have focused upon highly stereotyped, culturally patterned representations (such as "introverts" or "librarians"), and have thus methodologically excluded a focus on the idiosyncratic structure of individuals' representations.

Object relations approaches also point to motivational processes that have largely been overlooked by researchers in social cognition, although some movement in this direction has begun to occur (see the volume edited by Sorrentino & Higgins, 1986; see also Markus & Cross, Chapter 22, this volume, and Markus & Wurf, 1987). A critical object-relational dimension is the capacity for emotional investment in people. Emotional investment in another person means that one endows certain goals with respect to that person (protection of the person, concern for the person's welfare, proximity to the person, etc.) with personal significance, such that one's emotional state becomes a partial function of the relative attainment or nonattainment of those goals. Cognitive processes cannot account for individual differences in the capacity for mature emotional investment. Sociopaths know social rules; what they lack is not a knowledge of rules (what person could be unaware that a social rule exists that one should not steal or kill?) but an investment in them and an affective investment in the rights, feelings, and interests of others.[24]

Conversely, social-cognitive approaches pose important challenges to object relations theory. Object relations theory and research could benefit from reliance on controlled studies and methodologies of comparable rigor to current social-cognitive research. Furthermore, research in developmental social cognition (see Donaldson & Westerman, 1986; Harter, 1986; Shantz, 1983) challenges many object-relational accounts of development (Westen, 1989, in press-b,c). For example, explanations of pathological object relations in terms of developmental disturbances will require revision in light of evidence that many of the attributes ascribed to the Oedipal-age child in contrast to the pre-Oedipal child—cohesiveness of self-representations, capacity for amibivalent representations, transcendence of a need-gratifying interpersonal orientation—are in fact gradual attainments, solidified substantially during the latency and adolescent years.

Considerable obstacles to integration of work in object relations and social cognition do exist, such as vastly different philosophies of science, mutual denigration of the other's methods, incompatible metaphors, and the like. Nevertheless, some integrations have begun to occur.[26] My colleagues and I have been attempting to validate and test hypotheses comparing various clinical populations, using measures of several dimensions of object relations and social cognition derived from clinical observation, object relations theory and research, and research in developmental social cognition. Rather than treating level of object relations as a unitary dimension on which a person is likely to be globally fixated, we are beginning with the assumptions that individuals differ on many cognitive–affective–motivational dimensions relevant to their interpersonal functioning; that some of these covary and others do not; that some of these are chronically activated and others arc less so; that specific processes are activated under certain conditions; and that different sets of processes operate at different levels of consciousness. We also presume that the degree to which a specific process becomes activated (such as a tendency to make malevolent attributions) depends on several factors, including environmental events and cognitive structure (such as the extent to which the person expects malevolence in specific types of relationships, in specific situations, and from specific categories of people). Activation also depends upon motivational factors such as wishes and conflicts (such as the need to see another person as malevolent to protect the self from responsibility for an aggressive action), and level and type of affective arousal.

In this research we are attempting to study working representations—that is, momentarily active representations that shape thought and behavior, rather than the conscious, prototypical representations elicited by questions such as "Describe yourself " or "Do you think people can usually be trusted?" The method involves coding various structural dimensions from interpersonal interactions subjects describe in interviews, in projective tests such as the TAT, and in psychotherapy sessions. The dimensions we have been studying are the complexity of representations of people; the affective quality of relationship paradigms (the extent to which the person expects malevolence and pain or benevolence and pleasure in relationships); the capacity for emotional investment in relationships and in the ideals and standards that regulate relationships; and the logic, accuracy, and psychological mindedness of attributions (see Barends, Westen, Leigh, Silbert, & Byers, in press; Westen, in press-d; Westen, Lohr, Silk, Gold, & Kerber, in press). An assumption behind this method is that cognitive–affective structures may be inaccessible to introspection, both because of a lack of cognitive access to schematic structures and procedural knowledge, and because of motivational factors. Studies comparing reliably diagnosed borderline patients to psychiatric and normal comparison subjects have produced very consistent findings using adolescent (Westen, Ludolph, et al., in press) and adult (Westen, Lohr, et al., in press) samples; developmental studies have also documented developmental differences on all dimensions except affective quality of relationship paradigms between 2nd and 5th graders and between 9th and 12th graders, as predicted (Westen, Klepser, et al., 1989).

Transference and Information Processing

One of Freud's most important discoveries was "transference"—the displacement of thoughts, feelings, wishes, and interactional patterns from childhood figures onto people in adulthood (Freud, 1912/1958). Recent research (see Messer & Warren, Chapter 14, this volume) has begun to document transferential processes empirically, using psychotherapy transcripts. For example, Luborsky's painstaking analysis of Core Conflictual Relationship Themes (Luborsky, Crits-Christoph, & Mellon, 1986) demonstrates, as Freud proposed, that core relationship themes expressed toward the therapist are related to similar themes that occur outside of the treatment relationship.

Several authors (Hoffman, 1986; Singer, 1985; Wachtel, 1981; Westen, 1988) have explored the relationship between transference and social information processing; some have proposed that the concept of transference may be better differentiated by examining specific cognitive and affective components. For example, "transference" in psychotherapy refers to formation of a representation of the therapist or analyst that shares features with previous object representations and can become assimilated to older schemas. It also refers to various affective processes, such as attachment to, emotional investment in, and sexual, aggressive, and other feelings toward the therapist. Various schematic processes occur with transference, such as activation of schema-triggered affects (Fiske, 1982), in which features of the therapy situation evoke feelings associated with various person and situation schemas, many of which are triggered without the patient's awareness. Another aspect of transference is the activation of interpersonal "scripts" (Schank & Abelson, 1977; Tomkins, 1986)— that is, schemas that specify patterns of interpersonal interaction. Transference also refers to wishes and defenses, which are less easily understood from an information-processing perspective. It is probably more accurate to speak of "transferential processes" than "the transference," just as one would more accurately speak of specific "unconscious processes" than of "the unconscious."

Developmental Psychology and Psychoanalysis

Linkages between psychoanalysis and developmental psychology are so numerous that they can only be touched upon here. Freud's psychosexual model is not the only psychoanalytic theory of development; psychoanalytic theorists have discussed such phenomena as the relation between early relationships and later capacity for relatedness, and the development of ego functions such as self-observation and delay of gratification.

A Revised Theory of Infancy

One of Freud's least felicitous theories was his theory of infancy, which was based on analogies with schizophrenia and mania, as well as on conceptions of phylogeny and ontogeny inherited from German idealist philosophy (T. Horner, personal communication, 1987; Sulloway, 1979). Various psychoanalytic theorists from Freud onward have proposed that infants are oblivious to their social surroundings, hallucinate experiences of gratification, believe that

they are omnipotent and omniscient, confuse self and other, experience a symbiotic fusion with their mothers, and only begin to engage with the social world because hallucinatory wish-fulfillment is not successful and drive gratification is thus not available any other way. Few of these generalizations are probably true, and certainly not in their more sweeping forms. For the past decade, several in the psychoanalytic community have taken issue with this account of infancy from the perspective of developmental infant research (Basch, 1977; Horner, 1985; Lichtenberg, 1981; Peterfreund, 1978; Stern, 1985). In a major work, Stern (1985) proposed a critique and reformulation of psychoanalytic theories of the self and self–other differentiation in infancy, arguing that infants do not confuse self and other, and proposing that several senses of self develop throughout the first few years and continue to be a part of adult psychology. Beebe and Lachmann (1988) have begun to examine early interaction structures and expectations in the formation of self-representations and object representations.

Attachment Research and Internal Working Models

Bowlby's (1969, 1973, 1982) integration of psychoanalysis, ethology, and systems theory, which was based in part on psychoanalytic studies of children who had been separated from their mothers or had been reared without adequate caretaking, led to the development of an immense and important literature on attachment. Ainsworth (1979; Ainsworth, Blehar, Waters, & Wall, 1978) developed a procedure for measuring different styles of secure and insecure attachment in infancy, and subsequent research has found these to be predictive of later adjustment and interpersonal styles in the school years (see Bretherton, 1985; Sroufe & Fleeson, 1986), and to be influenced substantially by the quality of the primary caretaker's relatedness to the child (see Ricks, 1985; Zeanah and Zeanah, 1989).

Recent attachment research has moved to "the level of representation" (Main, Kaplan, & Cassidy, 1985). As noted earlier, Bowlby argued for the importance of a person's "internal working models" of significant others and of the attachment relationship for attachment-related behavior. The extent to which the child expects caretakers to be effective, consistent, and benign has been stressed by psychoanalytic theorists such as Erikson (1963). Main and her colleagues at Berkeley have developed procedures for assessing various qualities of these internal working models of attachment in children and adults. Research by Main and others (e.g., Cassidy & Kobak, 1987; Ricks, 1985) has begun to find striking associations between attachment status, nature of working models, and modes of regulating interpersonal affects in mothers and their children.

Not all attachment research has found predicted relationships among maternal attachment style, maternal behavior toward the infant, infant attachment category, and later social behavior (see Lamb, 1987); current research is focusing on conditions that lead to both continuity and change in the child's attachment status (see the volumes edited by Bretherton & Waters, 1985, and Belsky & Nezworski, 1987). Nevertheless, the overwhelming weight of evidence supports the basic psychoanalytic notion that interpersonal patterns of cognition, affect, and behavior laid down in the first few years are critical to later interpersonal functioning and psychological adjustment. Combined with research on adult transferential processes and on adult attachment (Kobak & Sceery, 1988; Main et al., 1985), these findings are particularly powerful.

Ego Development

Several researchers have developed measures of various ego functions or ego development. In some of the most methodologically sound research ever undertaken by a psychoanalytically informed personality researcher, Loevinger (1966, 1976) has developed a model and method for assessing ego development broadly conceived, which includes modes of interpersonal relatedness. Hundreds of studies have been conducted using her measure, which has demonstrated considerable predictive power (see a review by Hauser, 1976; see also Hauser et al., 1984).

As noted earlier, Bellak et al. (1973) have painstakingly assessed several dimensions of ego functioning in clinical and normal populations, although I am not aware of any developmental studies using their measures (though see relevant work by Santostefano, 1986). Haan (1977, 1982) has also conducted empirical research on ego functioning, which she has integrated with more mainstream research on stress and coping. Haan distinguishes between "defense" and "coping," the latter being more conscious, adaptive, and oriented toward problem solving.

Of particular importance for the psychoanalytic study of personality development is longitudinal research by Block and Block (1980) on dimensions they call "ego control" and "ego resiliency." "Ego control" refers to the characteristic ways in which a person experiences and regulates impulses and feelings. Individuals range from "overcontrolled," such as relatively rigid obsessives, to "undercontrolled," such as patients with severe personality disorders who are unable to delay gratification or pursue goals in a disciplined manner (on the clinical assessment of a related dimension, see Getsinger, 1980). "Ego resiliency" refers to the flexibility of the person's psychological resources for coping with the environment. Whereas at the "resilient" end of the continuum the person can respond appropriately to situational demands with appropriate problem solving and flexibility, at the "brittle" end the person may becomes disorganized under stress or when circumstances change. The Blocks and their colleagues have demonstrated remarkable stability in these personality dimensions over time, and have found significant relationships between these attributes and parental behavior.

An important attribute of the Blocks' conception of ego control and ego resiliency is similar to an attribute of the attachment construct to which Sroufe and Waters (1977; see also Sroufe & Fleeson, 1986) have called attention, and is critical for research in personality. These various constructs are not viewed as isolated traits that receive expression in every situation or take identical forms at various points in the lifespan. Rather, basic patterns established in the first few years of life solidify into an organization of cognitive–affective–behavioral processes, and this organization can be expressed in many ways at different points in time. Adults who were insecurely attached as infants are not likely to exhibit the same behaviors they did in infancy, but they are likely to behave in predictable ways—for example, feeling insecure in close relationships, clinging to friends, developing anxiety symptoms when moving to a new city, and the like. These manifestations are likely to be idiosyncratic but explicable from an understanding of the construct.

The Development of Self-Regulation and Metacognition

The literature on self-regulation (see the volume by Karoly & Kanfer, 1982, especially the chapter by Karoly; see also Brown & De-Loache, 1978; Harter, 1983; Rothbart & Posner, 1985) addresses several phenomena that psychoanalytic psychologists typically describe in terms of ego development. Research on the capacity to delay gratification and resistance to temptation (see Masters & Santrock, 1976; Mischel, Ebbeson, & Zeiss, 1972; Mischel & Moore, 1980) has elucidated ways in which children learn to regulate their own cognitive and affective processes. Studies on the development of the capacity to plan (Brown et al., 1983; Brown & DeLoache, 1978; Carter, Patterson, & Quasebarth, 1979) are also relevant to ego development.

Research on the ontogenesis of "metacognition" (see Flavell, 1979; Reeve & Brown, 1985; Wellman, 1985)—that is, cognition about cognition—is empirically examining a domain familiar to psychoanalytic psychologists as the "observing ego." This research focuses on children's knowledge about their own thought processes, and related research (see Masters & Carlson, 1984; Harris, in press) has examined children's knowledge of affective processes. A fundamental assumption of psychoanalytic forms of treatment is that greater knowledge of the way in which one's mental processes operate allows one to exercise greater control over one's own behavior; most researchers studying metacognition take this assumption as axiomatic as well. Research on perspective taking (Flavell, 1985; Selman, 1980) is also relevant to an understanding of the development of a person's capacity to self-observe—that is, to take the self as an object of thought and consider one's actions from the perspectives of significant others.

Neuropsychology and Psychoanalysis

A final domain with which psychoanalytic approaches may interface is neuropsychology. Work in this area is just beginning (Cooper, 1984; Hadley, 1983; Miller, 1986; Schwartz, 1987; Winson, 1985). Reiser's (1984) consideration of the interaction of learning mechanisms, meanings, neural processes, defenses, and physiological responses is probably the most successful to date. Cooper (1984) has described possible interactions of biological vulnerabilities and psychodynamic processes involved in anxiety symptoms.

Freud was himself a neurologist, and his theories were developed in the context of his understanding of the nervous system. His structural model of the mind is in many ways compatible with contemporary conceptualizations of the structure and evolution of the nervous system. Freud viewed the ego and superego as regulatory structures superimposed on the more phylogenetically and ontogenetically primitive id, and argued that our fundamental motivational structures are little different from those of other animals. From a neuropsychological perspective, the primitive brain stem of humans is indeed difficult to distinguish from the brain stem of many other animals; the critical differences between humans and other animals are found less in basic motivational centers than in the evolution of the neocortex. Consonant with psychoanalytic theory, the nervous system does appear to be organized hierarchically, with progressive regulation and inhibition of primitive motivational and behavioral tendencies exercised through development of higher cortical centers (see Kolb & Wishaw, 1985; Luria, 1962).

Increasing understanding of the relations among hypothalamic, limbic, and cortical structures in motivation (see LeDoux, 1986) is likely to lead to a better understanding of the relation between drive, affect, and conditioning on the one hand, and motivational states mediated by more complex cognitive processes on the other. Modular conceptions of neural functioning (see Gazzinaga, 1985), which view processing as occurring simultaneously in multiple specialized neural "circuits," are compatible not only with parallel distributed processing models in cognitive psychology; they are also compatible with the psychoanalytic supposition that a person can carry out several independent and often conflicting mental operations simultaneously, and that these may be combined and compromised with or without conscious attention.

Research in developmental neuropsychology may contribute to an understanding of the ontogeny of ego functions and object relations. The development of the prefrontal cortex and intercortical connections may be implicated in the attainment of the capacity for abstract thinking that is characteristic of Piagetian formal operations in adolescence (see Dean, 1985), and is thus likely to be relevant to the growing capacity for self-observation and self-regulation of thought and mood. An understanding of maturation of neural structures may also be critical to developing sophisticated, dynamically informed models of various forms of psychopathology, such as attention deficit disorders (see Mattes, 1981). Dynamic–neurological models may also be important for understanding a subgroup of patients with severe personality disorders (see Andronulis et al., 1980) in which neurological abnormalities (such as difficulties in verbally mediating behavior or regulating affect) may interact with social variables (such as inappropriate or abusive reponses to poor self-regulation) to produce dysfunctional interpersonal patterns, pathological representations of self and others, conflicts centered around success or vulnerability, or incapacity for emotional investment in others. These psychological processes or tendencies may in turn attain functional autonomy (or perhaps "dysfunctional autonomy" would be a better term) and lead to behavior characteristic of severe personality disorders or to defensive styles that prevent the person from developing compensatory strategies. This frequently appears to be the case in conduct-disordered adolescents with learning disabilities, whose repeated failures often lead to defensive strategies to preserve saelf-esteem, such as development of a negative identity as someone who is "bad" and "tough," or refusal to make any effort as a way of feeling in control of failure.

PSYCHOANALYSIS AND PERSONALITY THEORY

If there is a conclusion to be drawn from the preceding section, it is probably that the pervasive assumption that psychoanalysis is entirely without empirical grounding is simply wrong. If one means that no one has compared the responses of a sample of 4-year-old boys and a sample of 7-year-old boys (who have presumably entered the latency stage) to the question "Where would you most like to place your little penis?", then psychoanalysis has not been put to the test. But if one begins to treat aspects of psychoanalytic theory as components of a paradigmatic perspective, then it is clear that critical aspects of contemporary psychoanalytic thinking—the notion that much of mental life is unconscious, and that this extends to affec-

tive and motivational processes; the assertion that patterns of relatedness developed early in life may be expressed in later relationships and form the basis for patterns of thought, feeling, and behavior in intimate relationships; the notion that multiple simultaneous mental processes may converge, without conscious synthesis, to produce behavior; the conceptualization of mental representations of the self and others as critical mediators of interpersonal functioning; and the assertion that individuals differ in the extent to which they are able to regulate their impulses, feelings, and thoughts in adaptive, pleasurable, and socially acceptable ways—have not only been examined empirically, but appear accurate in the light of the best available evidence.

It should be clear by now, as well, that psychoanalytic approaches to personality have developed considerably since 1900. Rejecting "psychoanalysis" because one dislikes Freud's drive theory or psychosexual stage theory is like rejecting social-cognitive or cognitive social learning theory because one disagrees with its anti-mentalist behaviorist roots.

Directions for the Future

True to my stripes as a psychoanalytically oriented clinician and personality psychologist, I am probably better at interpreting the past than at predicting future behavior, so I describe only briefly here what I believe to be four directions that psychoanalysis, and psychoanalytic approaches to personality in particular, will (and, I think, must) take in the future.

1. *An expanded empiricism and the end of splendid isolation.* As noted earlier, many prominent analysts are now calling for psychoanalysis to upgrade its credentials as an empirical science. As suggested above, this process is in some respects already underway, though it is considerably obstructed by many institutional processes both within psychoanalysis (such as disdain for experimental work, and an institutional structure that Kernberg [1986] has likened to a religious order) and within academic psychology departments (such as disrespect for clinical data; the pressure for multiple quick publications, which leads almost inevitably to the use of measures of relatively simple phenomena that require no coding of data; and a general suspicion or dismissal of psychoanalytic ideas).[27]

2. *Examination of microstructures and pro-*

cesses. Perhaps the most important contribution of a mind like Freud's or Piaget's is to pose big questions and big solutions. The historian H. R. Trevor-Roper once said something to the effect that the function of genius is not to provide answers, but to pose questions that time and mediocrity will resolve. Freud, like Piaget, drew the big picture, and proposed broad stages and structures that could account for an astonishing array of observable phenomena. Scientific progress seems to require a dialectic not only between abstract theory and detailed observation, but also between the holistic purview of thinkers like Freud and Piaget and the more atomistic view characteristics of most academic psychology, at least in North America. The time has come in psychoanalysis for a move toward exploration of microprocesses, just as researchers in cognitive development have begun both mapping the specific processes involved in cognitive development that produce some of the phenomena Piaget observed and carrying out the painstaking work of refining and eliminating inadequate aspects of his theoretical superstructure (see the volume edited by Sternberg, 1984; see also Flavell, 1982). Whereas the psychoanalytic assessment of personality today largely involves assessment of level of object relations, level of ego functioning, and dynamic conflicts, assessment in the future will require a much more differentiated understanding of each of those domains.

3. *Attention to activating conditions.* Psychoanalysis is above all a dynamic theory, which in its sophisticated forms rarely posits trait-like phenomena that express themselves across all situations. Psychoanalytic research and theories of object relations and the self, however, must be careful to avoid static conceptions of processes, stages, and levels of functioning that are viewed as always operative. Future psychoanalytic research must pay careful attention to the activating conditions of various processes. We do not know, for example, whether borderline patients are uniformly unable to form relatively rich, differentiated representations of people, or whether they regress to the use of less mature split representations and illogical attributional processes under certain conditions, such as poorly modulated affect or conflicts centered around separation or aggression. These are precisely the kinds of questions that have the potential to be addressed empirically. Horowitz's (1987, 1988) analysis of states of mind represents an impor-

tant move in that direction, as do other approaches to analyzing the flux and flow of therapy hours (see Messer & Warren. Chapter 14, this volume). In many respects, a renewed emphasis on dynamics leads both to more classically psychoanalytic conceptions of conflict and compromise, and to contemporary currents in personality psychology focusing on conditions under which personality dispositions can be expected to be expressed.

4. *A cognitive–affective theory.* Finally, I suspect that the basic theoretical concepts used by psychoanalysis in the future will be denoted by terms such as "thoughts," "feelings," "wishes," "actions," and "compromise formations," rather than by more obscure terms lacking clear empirical[28] referents, such as "countercathexis," "symbiotic fusion," "drive derivative," and the like. Psychoanalytic approaches will also need to take cognition more seriously in the years ahead, avoiding the reduction of cognition to motivation that was pervasive in Freud's thinking (see Wachtel, 1987). For example, dreams in the classical theory are viewed as always expressing unconscious wishes, whereas one could just as easily propose that any salient concern, preoccupation, or way of looking at things can be expressed in a dream. Similarly, splitting is typically viewed as a defense, but it is just as likely at times to reflect a deficit in capacity to regulate the effects of mood on memory or a very unfortunate social learning history (as when a patient with a severely borderline mother developed the *accurate* expectation that people on whom one depends can be totally loving one moment and totally rejecting and vicious the next, which she then inappropriate generalized and could not transcend in an age-appropriately developmental manner).

The Enduring Contributions of Psychoanalysis to the Understanding of Personality

Psychoanalysis has contributed to personality psychology a number of fundamental insights and concepts:

1. *Unconscious processes.* Contemporary approaches based on experimental findings are likely to broaden our understanding of unconscious processes, but a reluctance to accept what Freud called "dynamic" unconscious processes is likely to lead to sterile, overly cognitive conceptualizations.

2. *Overdetermination, conflict, and compro-*

mise. Notions of conflict and compromise are crucial to an understanding of personality. Theexperimental data base is largely inadequate in exploring these issues, because such phenomena are idiosyncratic and not easily induced with the same stimulus across subjects. If serial processing models are inadequate for describing cognitive processes, there is little reason to presume their adequacy for describing affective and motivational processes.

3. *The bodily, the animal, and the uncomfortable.* Psychoanalysis repeatedly leads one to think about what one does not wish to think about. It is an approach to personality that one does not care to discuss with one's mother. Motivation and fantasy are rich and sometimes perverse, and any theory that is entirely comfortable to discuss is missing something very important about what it means to be human. Social learning research on the influence of television aggression on children's behavior is important and suggestive, but the social learning approach fails to ask a critical question: Why is it that aggressive television shows appeal to people so much? Would Freud be surprised to learn that the two variables that censors keep an eye on in television shows and movies are sex and aggression? One can read a thousand pages of social-cognitive theory and never know that people have genitals—or, for that matter, that they have bodies—let alone fantasies. I once evaluated a patient who had been treated for his "poor social skills" and difficulties in his marriage for a year by a nonanalytic therapist, who sent a glowing report of his progress in that treatment. Within the first session, however, he disclosed to me that he had had active fantasies of raping and murdering her, which were clearly tied to a core sexual fantasy that was troubling him in his relationship with his wife, and about which he never told his therapist because "she never asked." Psychoanalysis is the only theory of personality that suggests why one might want to ask.

4. *Defensive processes.* Studies described here provide relatively incontrovertible evidence of the existence of defensive processes. Given that children in our culture know about such processes by the time they are 9 or 10 (see Chandler, Paget, & Koch, 1978), it seems perplexing that defenses are not an integral component of most contemporary alternatives to psychoanalytic theory, and are ignored entirely as a potential confound in most personality research that relies on questionnaires.

5. *The concept of personality structure.* Central to contemporary psychoanlaysis is the concept of personality organization or structure. As noted previously, a search for simple behavioral regularities is likely to miss much about human beings that is important, because qualitatively different behaviors can stem from the same structure. A study from Jack Block's longitudinal project is especially illustrative. Shedler and Block (in press) found a systematic relationship between patterns of drug use at age 18, personality as assessed by Q-sort at age 18, personality as assessed in childhood, and quality of parenting as assessed at age 5. Subjects who had experimented with marijuana were the *most* well-adjusted in the sample, compared with those who had never tried the drug (who were described as relatively anxious, emotionally constricted, and lacking in social skills) and those who abused marijuana (who were observed to be alienated and impulsive). Mothers of both the abstainers and the abusers had been previously rated as relatively cold and unresponsive. As the authors point out, in the context of a relatively intact, flexible personality structure that permits experimentation and individuation in adolescence, drug use may be relatively healthy. Educational or social learning approaches that focus on "peer pressure" as a primary cause of adolescent drug abuse and encourage adolescents to "just say no" are missing the point because of their focus on discrete behaviors divorced from the personality structure in which they are embedded. The learning of behaviors occurs within the context of an organization of personality—that is, characteristic ways of coping with and defending against impulses and affects; of perceiving the self and others; of obtaining satisfaction of one's wishes and desires; of responding to environmental demands; and of finding meaning in one's activities, values, and relationships. Educational and social learning approaches also seriously underestimate the extent to which underlying personality dispositions influence what are often treated as "independent variables," such as the peers with whom people choose to associate and by whom they are pressured, which in turn influence subsequent responses (see Wachtel, 1987). Because of its basis in theory and its focus on personality organization, the psychoanalytic assessment of personality is comprehensive in a way that other approaches to assessment are not. In evaluating a patient, the psychoanalytically oriented clinician attempts to assess a number of interacting

personality processes. These include the person's affective experience, including emotions frequently experienced, intensity of affective experience, capacity to regulate aversive affects, and styles of regulating affects and impulses; dominant motivational tendencies, and conflicts among different motive systems (on empirical instruments for assessing conflicts, see Perry, Luborsky, Silberschatz, & Popp, 1989; Horowitz et al., 1989); object relations, including the cognitive structure and affective quality of representations of self and others, the capacity for relatedness to others, conflicts and fears impinging on that capacity, and patterns of interpersonal behavior; and cognitive patterns, including cognitive style, repetitive thoughts, content and structure of associative networks, ability to perceive reality in accurate and consensual ways, and capacity for planning and problem solving in ways that permit competent adaptive functioning. Whether or not researchers have developed valid and reliable methods for assessing all of these dimensions to date (which they have not), the theory provides a map of the domain of personality that permits systematic assessment.

6. *Viewing the present in the context of the past.* Axiomatic for a psychoanalytic account of any mental or behavioral event is that it must be viewed in the context of its development. Psychological experience is assumed to be so rich, and current thoughts, feelings, and actions are presumed to be so densely interconnected with networks of association at various levels of consciousness developed over time, that studying an adult form without its developmental antecedents is like trying to make sense of current political events without any knowledge of their history.

7. *The interpretation of meaning.* Perhaps above all, psychoanalytic approaches offer a way of interpreting what people mean by their communications and actions that allows the psychologist to understand human behavior in ways that may not seem intuitive to a layperson. Few approaches to personality even aspire to this, and it is not surprising that in contrast to experimentalists, whose stock in trade is the interpretation of statistical findings, the vast majority of clinicians, whose work requires that they understand personal meanings, rely exclusively or in part on psychodynamic conceptualizations (Pope, Tabachnick, & Keith-Spiegel, 1987). Learning to listen psychoanalytically and to interpret meanings in

this manner requires years of experience and supervision, just as does learning to design and conduct valid experiments.

8. *The clinical data base and the limitations of experimental research into personality.* Whereas the limitations of clinical data and inference are well known, the limitations of the experimental data base for personality research are less well established. One could make a strong case that several factors other than personality have been critical in shaping contemporary experimental research in personality. Two of these are the need for quickness (nQuick) and the need for large numbers of subjects for statistical analysis (nN). These two needs, driven by the higher-order factor, need for tenure (nTen), lead to an overreliance on questionnaire data. There is nothing intuitively sensible about the idea that the richness of human existence can be easily captured by 30–50 questions of the form "I am the kind of person who . . ." or the like. The correlation between nQuick, nN, and nTen on the one hand, and the use of questionnaires on the other, is probably far higher than the .30 that is typical in personality research.

Conclusion

A story is told of a student who asked his mentor, "Professor, what is science?" The professor paused and finally answered, "Science is looking for a black cat in a dark room." Momentarily satisfied, the student began to turn away, but then another question came to him. "Professor," he asked, "what is philosophy?" The academic furrowed his brow and after some thought replied, "Philosophy is looking for a black cat in a dark room where there is no black cat." Once again the student, satisfied that his question was answered, took leave of his mentor, only to return to ask one further question: "Professor, what is psychoanalysis?" "Psychoanalysis," the professor responded after a moment of deep contemplation, "is looking for a black cat in a dark room where there is no black cat—and finding one anyway."

Although (as this chapter has attempted to show) the cat has actually been there lurking in the dark more often than has been supposed, one can have little doubt that in the history of psychoanalysis, clinicians and theorists have mistaken more than one shadow for substance, and more than one of their own eyelashes for a feline whisker. The alternative, which personality psychologists who rely exclusively on more conservative empiricist methods have chosen, is to turn on the light, see what can be seen, and assume that what goes on in the dark is unknowable or unimportant. If psychoanalysis has, and will continue to have, anything to offer psychology of personality, it is the insight that we need not be in the dark about processes that are not manifestly observable, and that in the shadows sometimes lies the substance.

ACKNOWLEDGMENTS

I would like to thank the following people for their comments on an outline and/or a draft of this chapter: Robert Holt, Marie Jahoda, Stanley Messer, Christopher Peterson, Lawrence Pervin, George Rosenwald, Howard Shevrin, Jerome Singer, and Paul Wachtel.

NOTES

1. For the sake of simplicity, I use the terms "theory" and "model" interchangeably, since in the case of psychoanalysis one typically implies the other.
2. Although, as will be seen, Freud's theory of psychic energy is in many respects problematic (Holt, 1976), certain aspects of it are intuitively appealing. One is the notion that actively keeping knowledge from oneself may require expenditure of considerable psychic energy, particularly if the knowledge is of something significant or pressing, and that this may have a cost; this assertion has begun to be supported by research linking repressive personality styles to vulnerability to disease. A second aspect of the energy theory that seems sensible is the notion that motives differ in strength or intensity, and that more pressing motives are likely to find behavioral expression.
3. Sandler and Rosenblatt's paper, in my estimation, is one of the clearest-thinking papers in psychoanalysis since Freud, probably in part because the authors had a specific set of data they were trying to categorize, codify, and explain.
4. The reader well versed in personality theory will of course recognize here vintage Rogers (see Rogers, 1959), with the focus on the self, empathy, and the need for self-esteem, and the replacement of Freud's need-centered motiva-

tional theory with suggestions of an "actualizing tendency."
5. Freud actually developed several drive and energy theories, with multiple and incompatible notions of "drive discharge," "cathexis," and forms of "energy" (see Compton, 1981b; Klein, 1976). For example, Freud used the concepts of "cathexis" and "energy" in the sense of a general mental energy that can be attached to mental contents and bring them to consciousness ("attention cathexis"); his views in this respect are similar to contemporary cognitive conceptions of spreading activation and limits in conscious processing capacity. The relation between this form of cathexis (or "hypercathexis") and the taking of a sexual object ("object cathexis") is unclear. Equally unclear is how this diffuse mental energy can be synonymous with "libido," when libido is only one of the two basic drives; do these drives each have their own form of energy?
6. The reader acquainted with the history of psychological theories of motivation and personality will undoubtedly recognize that this concept of wish has been approached in various ways (see Pervin, 1982, for the history of similar constructs), both within psychoanalysis and without, by theorists drawing on systems theory and the notion of feedback (Bowlby, 1969; Klein, 1967; Menninger et al., 1963; Miller, Galanter, & Pribram, 1960; Peterfreund, 1971; Powers, 1973; Scheier & Carver, 1982).
7. As my colleague Carol Holden has put it (personal communication, 1985), such models provide "the id without the umph."
8. The problem is compounded still further if one recognizes that representations are themselves compromise formations containing id, ego, and superego elements (Boesky, 1988). This leads to an infinite regress: If each structure is comprised of elements of other structures, then what are the basic units or structures?
9. Unfortunately, Kohut, like most self theorists, has used the term in multiple and incompatible ways, conflating an organization of mental representations one has of oneself with a particular metapsychological structure. Freud similarly used the word "self" at times interchangeably with "ego," and was not always entirely clear whether he meant self-representations, the experiencing "I," or a hypothetical psychic structure. If one is to speak coherently about the self, one must carefully distinguish among several meanings, such as the system of conscious representations (William James's "me"), the system

of unconscious representations, the consciously experiencing person (James's "I"), the unconsciously experiencing person, the whole person (as when one refers to "myself" or "herself"—i.e., the "noumenal" object), and any other metapsychological meanings such as Kohut's.

10. This can have grave clinical implications, as when a leading analyst failed to notify Protective Services that his patient was abusing her child. In trying to avoid gratifying neurotic superego aims (the patient asked directly whether the analyst was going to "turn her in"), he failed to hear her plea for him to help her regulate her behavior in the light of a manifest defect in her capacities for self-regulation and relatedness to her child.

11. Although this theory may seem at face value preposterous to some, and probably overstates the influence of stage-specific factors rather than experience and social learning throughout childhood, it does seem likely that the child's attitudes toward yea-saying versus nay-saying, complying versus witholding and denying, and order and cleanliness versus disorder and messiness are significantly influenced by early experiences of conflict with parents over basic socialization demands, anal and otherwise.

12. Theorists of different persuasions may, of course, disagree on the relative importance of psychosexual development, object relations, and ego development, just as theorists of cognitive development debate the extent to which factors such as use of metacognitive strategies, limitations of space in working memory, and degree of automaticity distinguish children at different levels of cognitive development.

13. For discussions of usages of the concept of "metapsychology" in psychoanalysis, see Rapaport and Gill (1959) and Brenner (1980).

14. From a cognitive point of view, for better or for worse there is no replacement for schemas, and one has the choice of automatically applying procedural knowledge or subjecting it to conscious "declarative" scrutiny.

15. Stated in this way, the focus on psychic reality is undeniably important, and is an enduring contribution of psychoanalysis. Taken to its extreme, however, it can be misleading and clinically and socially destructive, as when a female patient's appropriate rage at sexual molestation by her father is interpreted as a reaction formation against Oedipal wishes. Furthermore, this view carried to its extreme and applied to the psychic reality of the analyst as well would vitiate any possible therapeutic connection between clinician and patient: The analyst would have to inform his or her patient, "It really does not matter what I say to you, because what I have heard you say is just my psychic reality, which has no necessary relation to what you have said, and what you in turn will hear has no necessary relation to what I have said." In reality (so to speak), the impact of what clinicians do say to their patients is mediated by the cognitive–affective structures of the patient, but it is no more a matter of indifference what the therapist says than it is what the mother or father did or did not do.

16. Actually, Freud's belief in the importance of psychic reality was present even in the days of the seduction hypothesis; as Schimek (1987) has demonstrated, Freud never believed in entirely unmediated environmental causes, and was to that extent a "Freudian" even before the advent of psychoanalysis.

17. Several have suggested that the "flight into hermeneutics" (Blight, 1981) is simply a way of avoiding falsification (see Holzman, 1985). Holt (1985) wryly describes the hermeneutic enterprise as something that "has been rediscovered periodically by those who hope to find some way to be intellectually respectable without having to exert themselves as strenuously as scientific method demands" (p. 303).

18. Clinical observation is always influenced, like all observation, by pre-existing schemas, but I, for one, am forever enlightened and amazed when a man who has no idea what it means that his therapist is psychoanalytic begins to talk about how he has two contradictory images of the therapist that seem to take him over at different times, one good and one bad; or when a woman remembers as a child looking at her genitals and thinking that they looked like a physical defect. What one makes of these statements is another matter, but they represent data that are unlikely to have been observed using other methods.

19. Although subject to typical schematic biases such as false confirmation (see Turk & Salovey, 1985), in making inferences about particular patients, clinicians are constantly making intuitive assessments of "convergent validity." As Jahoda notes, "No skilled analyst would ever venture a construction unless it was suggested in different contexts with different material from different sessions which were on the surface unrelated to each other but converged on the same underlying meaning" (1977, p. 115).

20. My colleagues and I have begun studying empirically the relation between aspects of object relations (such as the affective quality of relationship expectations or the "object world") and documented childhood experiences, such as history of neglect or sexual abuse. Our preliminary findings are intriguing.

21. The methodology adopted by many personality psychologists may often be inappropriate precisely because of one of the major aims of personality research, the understanding of individual differences: If things mean different things to different people, then one almost by definition does injustice to a phenomenon under study by aggregating across individuals and using the same objective stimulus conditions for every subject. Experimental stimuli may have vastly different subjective meanings or "subjective stimulus conditions."

22. For the remainder of this chapter, I use the term "empirical" as a shorthand, in the positivist–empiricist sense, to refer to data based on controlled observation best exemplified by the experimental situation, though I believe that this use of the term understates the extent to which clinical data are data (i.e., observable phenomena of utility for theory building).

23. It should be noted that a convergent finding in an entirely different area of research comes from studies of adult attachment. A similar style of verbal response by mothers has been associated with defensive denial of feelings in relationships, and has been shown to predict avoidant attachment in their children (Cassidy & Kobak, 1987; Main, Kaplan, & Cassidy, 1985; see also Hazen & Shaver, 1987). It is also important to note that repression and related defenses are not always pathological. The tendency to distort information in order to see oneself in a good light (see Greenwald & Pratkanis, 1984; Kunda, 1987) is a clear example of a normal defensive process that has been experimentally documented. Rather, the inflexible use of defenses that shut off access to negative feelings seems to be what is implicated in the research described above.

24. The social-cognitive literature is now beginning to assimilate the emphasis on the influence of affect, need, and defense that characterized research on person perception in the 1950s (Bruner & Tagiuri, 1954), which was in fact psychoanalytically informed, although motivational principles described in the contemporary literature still remain relatively rationalistic.

26. For attempted integrations, see Horowitz, 1987, 1988; Singer, 1985; Singer & Bonanno, Chapter 16, this volume; Singer & Salovey, in press, and Westen, 1985, 1988, 1989, in press-a).

27. The confluence of these factors, along with financial considerations, has led many of the most talented psychoanalytically trained PhDs to flee academia for more lucrative provated practice, and to create the illusion in academic psychology departments that psychoanalysis has all but gone the way of the Model T.

28. I am once again returning to the broader meaning of "empirical," including clinical as well as experimental observation.

REFERENCES

Adler, A. (1929). *The science of living.* Garden City, NY: Doubleday/Anchor.

Adler, A. (1939). *Social interest.* New York: G. P. Putnam.

Ainsworth, M. D. S. (1979). Infant–mother attachment. *American Psychologist, 34,* 932–937.

Ainsworth, M. D. S., Blehar, M. C., Waters, E., & Wall, S. (1978). *Patterns of attachment: A psychological study of the strange situation.* Hillsdale, NJ: Erlbaum.

Allison, J., Blatt, S. J., & Zimet, C. N. (1968). *The interpretation of psychological tests.* New York: Harper & Row.

Anderson, J. R. (1983). *The architecture of cognition.* Cambridge, MA: Harvard University Press.

Anderson, J. R. (1985). *Cognitive psychology and its implications,* 2nd edition. San Francisco: Freeman.

Andronulis, P. A., Glueck, B. C., Stroebel, C. F., Vogel, N. C., Shapiro, A., & Aldridge, D. M. (1980). Organic brain dysfunction and the borderline syndrome. *Psychiatric Clinics of North America, 4,* 47–66.

Arlow, J. (1985). The concept of psychic reality and related problems. *Journal of the American Psychoanalytic Association, 33,* 521–535.

Arlow, J., & Brenner, C. (1964). Psychoanalytic concepts and the structure model. *Journal of the American Psychoanalytic Association,* (Monograph No. 3).

Arlow, J., & Brenner, C. (1988). The future of psychoanalysis. *Psychoanalytic Quarterly, 62,* 1–14.

Asendorpf, J. B., & Scherer, K. R. (1983). The discrepant repressor: Differentiation between low anxiety, high anxiety, and repression of anxiety by autonomic-facial-verbal patterns of behavior. *Journal of Personality and Social Psychology, 45,* 1334–1346.

Balay, J., & Shevrin, H. (1988). The subliminal psychodynamic activation method: A critical review. *American Psychologist, 43,* 161–174.

Barends, A. Westen, D., Leigh, J. Silbert, D., & Byers, S. (in press). Assessing affect-tone of relationship paradigms from TAT and interview data. *Psychological Assessment: A Journal of Consulting and Clinical Psychology.*

Bargh, J. (1984). Automatic and conscious processing of

social information. In R. S. Wyer & T. K. Srull (Eds.), *Handbook of social cognition* (Vol. 3, pp. 1–43). Hillsdale, NJ: Erlbaum.

Basch, F. M. (1977). Developmental psychology and explanatory theory in psychoanalysis. *Annual of Psychoanalysis, 5,* 229–263.

Beebe, B., & Lachmann, F. M. (1988). The contribution of mother–infant mutual influence to the origins of self- and object-representations. *Psychoanalytic Psychology, 5,* 305–337.

Bell, M. B., Billington, R., & Becker, B. (1986). A scale for the assessment of object relations: Reliability, validity, and factorial invariance. *Journal of Clinical Psychology, 42,* 733–741.

Bell, M. B., Billington, R., Cicchetti, D., & Gibbons, J. (1988). Do object relations deficits distinguish BPD from other diagnostic groups? *Journal of Clinical Psychology, 44,* 511–516.

Bell, P. A., & Byrne, D. (1978). Repression-sensitization. In H. London & J. E. Exner (Eds.), *Dimensions of personality* (pp. 449–485). New York: Wiley.

Bellack, L., Hurvich, M., & Gediman, H. K. (1973). *Ego functions in schizophrenics, neurotics, and normals.* New York: Wiley.

Belsky, J., & Nezworski, T. (Eds.). (1987). *Clinical implications of attachment theory.* Hillsdale, NJ: Erlbaum.

Benton, T. (1977). *Philosophical foundations of the three sociologies.* London: Routledge & Kegan Paul.

Bettelheim, B. (1983). *Freud and man's soul.* New York: Knopf.

Blanck, G., & Blanck, R. (1974). *Ego psychology: Theory and practice.* New York: Columbia University Press.

Blanck, G., & Blanck, R. (1979). *Ego psychology II: Psychoanalytic developmental psychology.* New York: Columbia University Press.

Blatt, S. J., & Lerner, H. (1983a). Investigations in the psychoanalytic theory of object relations and object representations. In J. Masling (Ed.), *Empirical studies of psychoanalytic theories* (Vol. 1, pp. 189–249). Hillsdale, NJ: Erlbaum.

Blatt, S. J., & Lerner, H. (1983b). Psychodynamic perspectives on personality theory. In M. Hersen, et al. (Eds.), *The clinical psychology handbook* (pp. 87–106). New York: Pergamon Press.

Blatt, S. J., Brenneis, C. B., & Schimek, J. G. (1976). Normal development and psychopathological impairment of the concept of the object on the Rorschach. *Journal of Abnormal Psychology, 85,* 364–373.

Blatt, S. J., Wein, S., Chevron, E. S., & Quinlan, D. M. (1979). Parental representations and depression in normal young adults. *Journal of Abnormal Psychology, 78,* 388–397.

Blatt, S. J., Quinlan, D. M., Chevron, E. S., McDonald, C., & Zuroff, D. C. (1982). Dependency and self-criticism: Psychological dimensions of depression. *Journal of Consulting and Clinical Psychology, 50,* 113–124.

Blight, J. (1981). Must psychoanalysis retreat to hermeneutics? Psychoanalytic theory in the light of Popper's evolutionary epistemology. *Psychoanalysis and Contemporary Thought, 4,* 146–206.

Block, J., & Block, J. (1980). The role of ego-control and ego-resiliency in the organization of behavior. In W. A. Collins (Ed.), *Minnesota Symposium on Child Development* (Vol. 13). Hillsdale, NJ: Erlbaum

Blum, G. S. (1961). *A model of the mind.* New York: Wiley.

Blum, G. S. (1968). Assessment of psychodynamic variables by the Blacky pictures. In P. McReynolds (Ed.), *Advances in psychological assessment* (Vol. 1). Palo Alto, CA: Science and Behavior Press.

Boden, M. A. (1978). *Purposive explanation in psychology.* Sussex, England: Harvester.

Boesky, D. (1988). Comments on the structural theory of technique. *International Journal of Psycho-Analysis, 69,* 303–316.

Bonanno, G. A., & Singer, J. L. (in press). Repressive personality style: Theoretical and methodological implications for health and pathology. In J. L. Singer (Ed.), *Repression and dissociation.* Chicago: University of Chicago Press.

Bowers, K., & Meichenbaum, D. (Eds.). (1984). *The unconscious reconsidered.* New York: Wiley.

Bowlby, J. (1969). *Attachment and loss: Vol. 1. Attachment.* New York: Basic Books.

Bowlby, J. (1973). *Attachment and loss: Vol. 2. Separation.* New York: Basic Books.

Bowlby, J. (1982). Attachment and loss: Retrospect and prospect. *American Journal of Orthopsychiatry, 52,* 664–678.

Brainerd, C. J. (1978). The stage question in cognitive-developmental theory. *Behavioral and Brain Sciences, 2,* 173–213.

Brenner, C. (1980). Metapsychology and psychoanalytic theory. *Psychoanalytic Quarterly, 49,* 189–214.

Brenner, C. (1982). *The mind in conflict.* New York: International Universities Press.

Bretherton, I. (1985). Attachment theory: Retrospect and prospect. In I. Bretherton & E. Waters (Eds.), *Growing points of attachment theory and research. Monographs of the Society for Research in Child Development, 50*(1–2, Serial No. 209), 3–35.

Bretherton, I., & Waters, E. (Eds.). (1985). *Growing points of attachment theory and research. Monographs of the Society for Research in Child Development, 50*(1–2, Serial No. 209).

Broadbent, D. E. (1977). The hidden preattentive processes. *American Psychologist, 32,* 109–118.

Breuer, J., & Freud, S. (1955). Studies on hysteria. In J. Strachey (Ed. and Trans.), *The standard edition of the complete psychological works of Sigmund Freud* (Vol. 2, pp. 1–305). London: Hogarth Press. (Original work published 1893–1895)

Brown, A., & DeLoache, J. S. (1978). Skills, plans, and self-regulation. In R. S. Seigler (Ed.), *Children's thinking: What develops?* Hillsdale, New Jersey: Erlbaum.

Brown, A. L., Bransford, J. D. Ferrara, R. A., & Campione, J. C. (1983). Learning, remembering, and understanding. In J. H. Flavell & E. M. Markman (Eds.), *Handbook of child psychology* (4th ed.): *Vol. 3. Cognitive development.* New York: Wiley.

Bruner, J. S. (1973). *Beyond the information given: Studies in the psychology of knowing.* New York: Norton.

Bruner, J. S., & Tagiuri, R. (1954). The perception of people. In G. Lindzey (Ed.), *Handbook of social psychology* (pp. 634–654). Reading, MA: Addison-Wesley.

Cairns, R. B., & Valsiner, J. (1984). Child psychology. *Annual Review of Psychology, 35,* 553–577.

Carlson, R. (1981). Studies in script theory: I. Adult analogs of a childhood nuclear scene. *Journal of Personality and Social Psychology, 40,* 501–510.

Carlson, R. (1986). After analysis: A study of transference dreams following treatment. *Journal of Consulting and Clinical Psychology, 54,* 246–252.

Carter, D. B., Patterson, C. J., & Quasebarth, S. J. (1979). Development of children's plans for self-control. *Cognitive Therapy and Research, 3,* 407–413.

Cassidy, J., & Kobak, R. (1987). Avoidance and its relation to other defensive processes. In J. Belsky & T. Nezworsky (Eds.), *Clinical implication of attachment.* Hillsdale, NJ: Erlbaum.

Chandler, M. J., Paget, K. F., & Koch, D. A. (1978). The child's demystification of psychological defense mechanisms: A structural and developmental analysis. *Developmental Psychology, 41,* 197–205.

Cioffi, F. (1986). Did Freud rely on the tally argument to meet the argument from suggestibility? *Behavioral and Brain Sciences, 9,* 230–231.

Collins, A. M., & Loftus, E. S. (1975). A spreading-activation theory of semantic processing. *Psychological Review, 82,* 407–428.

Compton, A. (1981a). On the psychoanalytic theory of instinctual drives: III. The implications of libido and narcissism. *Psychoanalytic Quarterly, 50,* 345–362.

Compton, A. (1981b). On the psychoanalytic theory of instinctual drives. IV. Instinctual drives and the ego–id–superego model. *Psychoanalytic Quarterly, 50,* 363–392.

Cooper, A. (1984). Psychoanalysis at one hundred years: Beginnings of maturity. *Journal of the American Psychoanalytic Association, 32,* 245–267.

Cooper, A. (1985). Will neurobiology influence psychoanalysis? *American Journal of Psychiatry, 142,* 1395–1402.

Crowne, D. P., & Marlowe, D. (1964). *The approval motive: Studies in evaluative dependence.* New York: Wiley.

Dahl, H. (1983). On the definition and measurement of wishes. In J. Masling (Ed.), *Empirical studies of psychoanalytic theories* (Vol. 1). Hillsdale, NJ: Erlbaum.

Dauber, R. B. (1984). Subliminal psychodynamic activation in depression: On the role of autonomy in depressed college women. *Journal of Abnormal Psychology, 93,* 9–18.

Davis, P. (1987). Repression and the inaccessibility of affective memories. *Journal of Personality and Social Psychology, 53,* 585–593.

Davis, P., & Schwartz, G. (1987). Repression and the inaccessibility of affective memories. *Journal of Personality and Social Psychology, 52,* 155–162.

Dean, R. S. (1985). Foundation and rationale for neuropsychological bases of individual differences. In L. C. Hartlage & C. F. Telzrow (Eds.), *The neuropsychology of individual differences: A developmental perspective* (pp. 7–40). New York: Plenum.

Dixon, N. F. (1971). *Subliminal perception: The nature of a controversy.* New York: McGraw-Hill.

Dixon, N. F. (1981). *Preconscious processing.* New York: Wiley.

Dollard, J., & Miller, N. (1950). *Personality and psychotherapy: An analysis in terms of learning, thinking, and culture.* New York: McGraw-Hill.

Donaldson, S. K., & Westerman, M. A. (1986). Development of children's understanding of ambivalence and causal theories of emotion. *Developmental Psychology, 22,* 655–662.

Eagle, M. (1959). The effects of subliminal stimuli of aggressive content upon conscious cognition. *Journal of Personality, 27,* 678–68.

Eagle, M. (1984). *Recent developments in psychoanalysis.* New York: McGraw-Hill.

Eagle, M. (1987). Theoretical and clinical shifts in psychoanalysis. *American Journal of Orthopsychiatry, 57,* 175–185.

Edelson, M. (1984). *Hypothesis amd evidence in psychoanalysis.* Chicago: University of Chicago Press.

Edelson, M. (1985). The hermeneutic turn and the single case study in psychoanalysis. In D. N. Berg & K. K. Smith (Eds.), *Exploring clinical methods for social research.* Beverly Hills, CA: Sage.

Emmons, R. A. (1987). Narcissism: Theory and measurement. *Journal of Personality and Social Psychology, 52,* 11–17.

Erdelyi, M. (1974). A "new look" at the New Look in perception. *Psychological Review, 81,* 1–25.

Erdelyi, M. (1985). *Psychoanalysis: Freud's cognitive psychology.* San Francisco: W. H. Freeman.

Erikson, E. (1963). *Childhood and society* (rev. ed.). New York: Norton.

Erikson, E. (1968). *Identity: Youth and crisis.* New York: Norton.

Fairbairn, W. R. D. (1952). *Psychoanalytic studies of the personality.* London: Routledge & Kegan Paul.

Fast, I. (1985). *Event theory.* Hillsdale, NJ: Erlbaum.

Fisher, S., & Greenberg, R. P. (1977). *The scientific credibility of Freud's theories and therapy.* New York: Columbia University Press.

Fiske, S. (1982). Schema-triggered affect: Application to social perception. In M. S. Clarke & S. T. Fiske (Eds.), *Affect and cognition: The 17th annual Carnegie Symposium on Cognition.* Hillsdale, NJ: Erlbaum.

Flavell, J. H. (1979). Metacognition and cognitive monitoring: A new area of cognitive-developmental inquiry. *American Psychologist, 34,* 906–911

Flavell, J. H. (1982). Structures, stages, and sequences in cognitive development. In W. A. Collins (Ed.), *Minnesota Symposium on Child Development* (Vol. 15). Hillsdale, NJ: Erlbaum.

Flavell, J. (1985). *Cognitive development* (2nd ed.). Englewood Cliffs, NJ: Prentice-Hall.

Foulkes, D. (1978). *A grammar of dreams.* New York: Basic Books.

Freud, A. (1936). *The ego and the mechanisms of defense.* New York: International Universities Press.

Freud, A. (1973). The concept of developmental lines. In S. Sapir & A. Nitzburg (Eds.), *Children with learning problems: Readings in a developmental-interaction approach.* New York: Brunner/Mazel.

Freud, S. (1953). The interpretation of dreams. In J. Strachey (Ed. and Trans.), *The standard edition of the complete psychological works of Sigmund Freud* (Vol. 4, pp. 1–338; Vol. 5, pp. 339–621). London: Hogarth Press. (Original work published 1900)

Freud, S. (1953). Three essays on the theory of sexuality. In J. Strachey (Ed. and Trans.), *The standard edition of the complete psychological works of Sigmund Freud* (Vol. 7, pp. 123–245). London: Hogarth Press. (Original work published 1905)

Freud, S. (1957). On narcissism. In J. Strachey (Ed. and Trans.), *The standard edition of the complete psychological works of Sigmund Freud* (Vol. 14, pp. 67–102). London: Hogarth Press. (Original work published 1914)

Freud, S. (1957). The unconscious. In J. Strachey (Ed. and Trans.), *The standard edition of the complete psychological works of Sigmund Freud* (Vol. 14, pp. 159–215). London: Hogarth Press. (Original work published 1915)

Freud, S. (1957). Mourning and melancholia. In J. Strachey (Ed. and Trans.), *The standard edition of the complete psychological works of Sigmund Freud* (Vol. 14, pp. 237–260). London: Hogarth Press. (Original work published 1917)

Freud, S. (1958). The dynamics of transference. In J. Strachey (Ed. and Trans.), *The standard edition of the complete psychological works of Sigmund Freud* (Vol. 12, pp. 97–108). London: Hogarth Press. (Original work published 1912)

Freud, S. (1961). The ego and the id. In J. Strachey (Ed. and Trans.), *The standard edition of the complete psychological works of Sigmund Freud* (Vol. 19, pp. 1–66). London: Hogarth Press. (Original work published 1923)

Freud, S. (1964). New introductory lectures on psychoanalysis. In J. Strachey (Ed. and Trans.), *The standard edition of the complete psychological works of Sigmund Freud* (Vol. 22, pp. 1–182). London: Hogarth Press. (Original work published 1933)

Freud, S. (1964). An outline of psycho-analysis. In J. Strachey (Ed. and Trans.), *The standard edition of the complete psychological works of Sigmund Freud* (Vol. 23, pp. 139–207). London: Hogarth Press. (Original work published 1940)

Freud, S. (1966). Project for a scientific psychology. In J. Strachey (Ed. and Trans.), *The standard edition of the complete psychological works of Sigmund Freud* (Vol. 1, pp. 281–397). London: Hogarth Press. (Original work written 1895, published 1950)

Fromm, E. (1947). *Man for himself: An inquiry into the psychology of ethics.* New York: Holt, Rinehart & Winston.

Fromm, E. (1962). *The sane society.* Greenwich, CT: Fawcett Books.

Gartner, J., Hurt, S. W., & Gartner, A. (1987, September). *Psychological test signs of borderline personality disorder: A review of the empirical literature.* Paper presented at the annual convention of the American Psychological Association, New York.

Gazzaniga, M. S. (1985) *The social brain: Discovering the networks of the mind.* New York: Basic Books.

Geertz, C. (1973). *The interpretation of cultures.* New York: Basic Books.

Getsinger, S. H. (1980). Ego delay. In R. H. Woody (Ed.), *Encyclopedia of clinical assessment* (Vol. 1). San Francisco: Jossey-Bass.

Gill, M. M. (1976). Metapsychology is not psychology. In M. M. Gill & P. S. Holzman (Eds.), Psychology versus metapsychology: Psychoanalytic essays in memory of George S. Klein. *Psychological Issues, 9*(4, Monograph No. 36).

Greenberg, L. S., & Safran, J. D. (1987). *Emotion in psychotherapy.* New York: Guilford Press.

Greenberg, J. R., & Mitchell, S. A. (1983). *Object relations in psychoanalytic theory.* Cambridge, MA: Harvard University Press.

Greenspan, S. (1979). *Intelligence and adaptation.* New York: International Universities Press.

Greenwald, A. G., & Pratkanis, A. R. (1984). The self. In R. S. Wyer & T. K. Srull (Eds.), *Handbook of social cognition* (Vol. 3, pp. 129–178). Hillsdale, NJ: Erlbaum.

Grunbaum, A. (1984). *The foundations of psychoanalysis: A philosophical critique.* Berkeley: University of California Press.

Grunbaum, A. (1986). Précis of *The foundations of psychoanalysis: A philosophical critique. Behavioral and Brain Sciences, 9,* 217–284.

Guntrip, H. (1971). *Psychoanalytic theory, therapy, and the self.* New York: Basic Books.

Haan, N. (1977). *Coping and defending.* New York: Academic Press.

Haan, N. (1982). The assessment of coping, defense, and stress. In L. Goldberger and S. Breznits (Eds.), *Handbook of stress: Theoretical and clinical aspects.* New York: Free Press.

Habermas, J. (1971). *Knowledge and human interests* (J. J. Shapiro, Trans.). London: Heinemann.

Hadley, J. L. (1983). The representational system: A bridging concept for psychoanalysis and neurophysiology. *International Journal of Psycho-Analysis, 10,* 13–30.

Hardaway, R. (in press). Facts and fantasies in subliminal psychodynamic activation: A quantitative analysis. *Psychological Bulletin.*

Harris, D. (in press). *The child's concept of emotion.* Oxford, Blackwell.

Harter, S. (1983). The development of the self-system. In E. M. Hetherington (Vol. Ed.), *Handbook of child psychology Vol. 4. Social and personality development.* (pp. 275–386). New York: Wiley.

Harter, S. (1986). Cognitive-developmental processes in the integration of concepts about emotions and the self. *Social Cognition, 4,* 119–151.

Hartmann, H. (1950). Comments on the psychoanalytic theory of the ego. *Psychoanalytic Study of the Child, 5,* 74–96.

Hartmann, H. (1958). *Ego psychology and the problem of adaptation.* New York: International Universities Press. (Original work published 1939)

Hartmann, H., Kris, E., & Loewenstein, R. (1946). Comments on the formation of psychic structure. *Psychoanalytic Study of the Child, 2,* 11–38.

Hauser, S. (1976). Loevingers's model and measure of ego development: A critical review. *Psychological Bulletin, 83,* 928–955.

Hauser, S. T., Powers, S. I., Noam, G. G., Jacobson, A. M., Weiss, B., & Follansbee, D. J. (1984). Familial contexts of adolescent ego development. *Child Development, 55,* 195–213.

Hazen, C., & Shaver, P. (1987). Romantic love conceptualized as an attachment process. *Journal of Personality and Social Psychology, 52,* 511–524.

Hedegard, S. (1969). *A molecular analysis of psychological defenses.* Unpublished doctoral dissertation, University of Michigan.

Heinemann, L., & Emrich, H. (1971). Alpha activity during inhibitory brain processes. *Psychophysiology, 7,* 442–450.

Herman, J., Perry, J. C., & van der Kolk, B. A. (1989). Childhood trauma in borderline personality disorder. *American Journal of Psychiatry, 146,* 490–495.

Higgins, E. T., & Bargh, J. A. (1987). Social cognition and social perception. *Annual Review of Psychology, 38,* 369–425.

Higgins, E. T., King, G. A., & Mavin, G. H. (1982). Individual construct accessibility and subjective impressions and recall. *Journal of Personality and Social Psychology, 43,* 35–47.

Hirst, W. (1986). The psychology of attention. In J. E. LeDoux & W. Hirst (Eds.), *Mind and brain: Dialogues in cognitive neuroscience.* New York: Cambridge University Press.

Hoffman, M. (1986). Affect, cognition, and motivation.

In R. M. Sorrentino & E. T. Higgins (Eds.), *Handbook of motivation and cognition: Foundations of social behavior* (pp. 244–280). New York: Guilford Press.

Holt, R. R. (1967). The development of the primary process: A structural view. In R. R. Holt (Ed.), Motives and thought: Psychoanalytic essays in memory of David Rapaport. *Psychological Issues, 5*(2–3; Monograph 18/19).

Holt, R. R. (1976). Drive or wish? In M. M. Gill & P. S. Holzman (Eds.), Psychology versus metapsychology: Psychoanalytic essays in memory of George S. Klein. *Psychological Issues, 9*(4, Monograph No. 36).

Holt, R. R. (1981). The death and transfiguration of metapsychology. *International Review of Psycho-Analysis, 8,* 129–143.

Holt, R. R. (1985). The current status of psychoanalytic theory. *Psychoanalytic Psychology, 2,* 289–315.

Holt, R. R. (1986). Some reflections on testing psychoanalytic hypotheses. *Behavioral and Brain Sciences, 9,* 242–244.

Holzman, P. (1985). Psychoanalysis: Is the therapy destroying the science? *Journal of the American Psychoanalytic Association, 33,* 725–770.

Horner, T. (1985). The psychic life of the young infant: Review and critique of the psychoanalytic concepts of symbiosis and infantile omnipotence. *American Journal of Orthopsychiatry, 55,* 324–343.

Horney, K. (1950). *Neurosis and human growth.* New York: Norton.

Horney, K. (1967). *Feminine psychology.* New York: Norton.

Horowitz, M. J. (1987). *States of mind: Configurational analysis of individual psychology* (2nd ed). New York: Plenum Press.

Horowitz, M. J. (1988). *Introduction to psychodynamics: A Synthesis.* New York: Basic Books.

Horowitz, L. M., Rosenberg, S. E., Ureño, G., Kalehzan, B. M., & O'Halloran, P. (1989). Psychodynamic formulation, consensual response method, and interpersonal problems. *Journal of Consulting and Clinical Psychology, 57,* 599–606.

House, J. S., Landis, K. R., & Umberson, D. (1988). Social relationships and health. *Science, 241,* 540–545.

Jahoda, M. (1977). *Freud and the dilemmas of psychology.* London: Hogarth Press.

Jacobson, E. (1954). The self and the object world. *Psychoanalytic Study of the Child, 9,* 75–127.

Jacobson, E. (1964). *The self and the object world.* New York: International Universities Press.

Jung, C. G. (1971). *The portable Jung* (J. Campbell, Ed.). New York: Viking.

Karoly, P., & Kanfer, F. H., Eds. (1982). *Self-management and behavior change: From theory to practice.* New York: Pergamon Press.

Kernberg, O. (1975). *Borderline conditions and pathological narcissism.* New York: Jason Aronson.

Kernberg, O. (1976). *Object relations theory and clinical psychoanalysis.* New York: Jason Aronson.

Kernberg, O. (1984). *Severe personality disorders: Psychotherapeutic strategies.* New Haven, CT: Yale University Press.

Kernberg, O. F. (1986). Institutional problems of psychoanalytic education. *Journal of the American Psychoanalytic Association, 34,* 799–834.

Kihlstrom, J. F. (1987). The cognitive unconscious. *Science, 237,* 1445–1452.

Kihlstrom, J. F., & Cantor, N. (1983). Mental representations of the self. In L. Berkowitz (Ed.), *Advances in experimental social psychology* (Vol. 15). New York: Academic Press.

Klein, G. S. (1967). Peremptory ideation: Structure and force in motivated ideas. In R. R. Holt (Ed), Motives and thought: Psychoanalytic essays in honor of David Rapaport. *Psychological Issues, 5*(2–3 Monograph No. 18/19).

Klein, G. S. (1976). Freud's two theories of sexuality. In M. M. Gill & P. S. Holzman (Eds.), Psychology versus metapsychology: Psychoanalytic essays in memory of George S. Klein. *Psychological Issues, 9*(4, Monograph No. 36).

Klein, M. (1948). *Contributions to psycho-analysis, 1921–1945.* London: Hogarth Press.

Kline, P. (1972). *Fact and fantasy in Freudian theory (1st ed.).* London: Methuen.

Kline, P. (1981). *Fact and fantasy in Freudian theory (2nd ed.).* London: Methuen.

Kline, P. (1986). Grünbaum's philosophical critique of psychoanalysis: Or what I don't know isn't knowledge. *Behavioral and Brain Sciences, 9,* 245–246.

Kobak, R. R., & Sceery, A. (1988). Attachment in late adolescence: Working models, affect regulation, and representations of self and others. *Child Development, 59,* 135–146.

Kohut, H. (1966). Forms and transformations of narcissism. *Journal of the American Psychoanalytic Association, 14,* 243–272.

Kohut, H. (1968). The psychoanalytic treatment of narcissistic personality disorder. *Psychoanalytic Study of the Child, 23,* 86–113.

Kohut, H. (1971). *The analysis of the self: A systematic psychoanalytic approach to the treatment of narcissistic personality disorders.* New York: International Universities Press.

Kohut, H. (1977). *The restoration of the self.* New York: International Universities Press.

Kohut, H. (1984). *How does analysis cure?* (A. Goldberg, Ed., with collaboration of P. E. Stepansky). Chicago: University of Chicago Press.

Kohut, H., & Wolf, E. (1978). The disorders of the self and their treatment: An outline. *International Journal of Psycho-Analysis, 59,* 413–425.

Kolb, B., & Wishaw, I. Q. (1985). *Fundamentals of human neuropsychology (2nd ed.).* San Francisco: Freeman.

Krohn, A., & Mayman, M. (1974). Object representations in dreams and projective tests. *Bulletin of the Menninger Clinic, 38,* 445–466.

Kuhn, T. (1970). *The structure of scientific revolutions* (rev. ed.). Chicago: University of Chicago Press.

Kunda, Z. (1987). Motivated inference: Self-serving generation and evaluation of causal theories. *Journal of Personality and Social Psychology, 53,* 636–647.

Lamb, M. E. (1987). Predictive implications of individual differences in attachment. *Journal of Consulting and Clinical Psychology, 55,* 817–824.

Le Doux, J. E. (1986). The neuropsychology of emotion. In J. E. LeDoux & W. Hirst (Eds.), *Mind and brain: Dialogues in cognitive neuroscience* (pp. 301–354). New York: Cambridge University Press.

Lerner, H. D., & St. Peter, S. (1984). Patterns of object relations in neurotic, borderline, and schizophrenic patients. *Psychiatry, 47,* 77–92.

Lewicki, P. (1986). *Nonconscious social information processing.* New York: Academic Press.

Lichtenberg, J. D. (1981). Implications for psychoanalytic theory of research on the neonate. *International Review of Psycho-Analysis, 8,* 35–52.

Loevinger, J. (1966). The meaning and measurement of ego development. *American Psychologist, 21,* 195–206.

Loevinger, J. (1976). *Ego development.* San Francisco: Jossey-Bass.

Luborsky, L. (1986). Evidence to lessen Professor Grunbaum's concern about Freud's clinical inference method. *Behavioral and Brain Sciences, 9,* 247–249.

Luborsky, L., Crits-Christoph, P., & Mellon, J. (1986). Advent of direct measures of the transference concept. *Journal of Consulting and Clinical Psychology, 54,* 39–47.

Luria, A. (1962). *The role of speech in the regulation of normal and abnormal behaviors.* New York: Liveright Books.

McClelland, D. C., Koestner, R., & Weinberger, J. (1989). How do self-attributed and implicit motives differ? *Psychological Review, 96,* 690–702.

Mahler, M., Pine, F., & Bergman, A. (1975). *The psychological birth of the human infant: Symbiosis and individuation.* New York: Basic Books.

Main, M., Kaplan, N., & Cassidy, J. (1985). Security in infancy, childhood, and adulthood: A move to the level of representation. In I. Bretherton & E. Waters (Eds.), Growing points of attachment theory and research. *Monographs of the Society for Research in Child Development, 50*(1–2, Serial No. 209), 67–104.

Marcel, A. J. (1983). Conscious and unconscious perception: Experiments on visual masking and word recognition. *Cognitive Psychology, 15,* 197–237.

Markus, H. (1977). Self-schemata and processing information about the self. *Journal of Personality and Social Psychology, 35,* 63–78.

Markus, H., & Wurf, E. (1987). The dynamic self-concept: A social psychological perspective. *Annual Review of Psychology, 38,* 299–337.

Masters, J. C., & Carlson, C. R. (1984). Children's and adults' understanding of the causes and consequences of emotional states. In C. E. Izard, J. Kagan, & R. B. Zajonc (Eds.), *Emotions, cognitions, and behavior* (pp. 438–463). Cambridge, England: Cambridge University Press.

Masters, J. C., & Santrock, J. W. (1976). Studies on the self-regulation of behavior: Effects of contingent cognitive and affective events. *Developmental Psychology, 12,* 334–348.

Masterson, J. F. (1976). *Psychotherapy of the borderline adult: A developmental approach.* New York: Brunner/Mazel.

Mattes, J. A. (1981). The role of frontal lobe dysfunction in childhood hyperkinesis. *Comprehensive Psychiatry, 21,* 358–369.

Mayman, M. (1967). Object-representation and object relationships in Rorschach responses. *Journal of Projective Techniques and Personality Assessment, 31,* 17–24.

Mayman, M. (1968). Early memories and character structure. *Journal of Projective Techniques and Personality Assessment, 32,* 303–316.

Menninger, K., Mayman, M., & Pruyser, P. (1963). *The vital balance: The life process in mental health and illness.* New York: Viking.

Messer, S. B., & Schacht, T. E. (1986). A cognitive-dynamic theory of reflection-impulsivity. In J. Masling (Ed.), *Empirical studies of psychoanalytic theories* (Vol. 3, pp. 151–195). Hillsdale, New Jersey: Erlbaum.

Messer, S. B., Sass, L. A., & Woolfolk, R. L. (Eds.). (1988). *Hermeneutics and psychological theory: Interpretive perspectives on personality, psychotherapy, and psychopathology.* New Brunswick, NJ: Rutgers University Press.

Michels, R. (1988). The future of psychoanalysis. *Psychoanalytic Quarterly, 57,* 167–184.

Miller, G. A., Galanter, E., & Pribram, K. H. (1960). *Plans and the structure of behavior.* New York: Holt, Rinehart & Winston.

Miller, L. (1986, December). In search of the unconscious. *Psychology Today, 20*(12), 60–64.

Mitchell, S. A. (1988). *Relational concepts in psychoanalysis: An integration.* Cambridge: Harvard University Press.

Mischel, W., Ebbeson, E., & Zeiss, A. R. (1972). Cognitive and attentional mechanisms in delay of gratification. *Journal of Personality and Social Psychology, 21,* 204–218.

Mischel, W., & Moore, B. (1980). The role of ideation in voluntary delay for symbolically-presented rewards. *Cognitive Therapy and Research, 4,* 211–221.

Moray, N. (1969). *Attention: Selective processes in vision and hearing.* London: Hutchinson.

Morokoff, P. J. (1985). Effects of sex guilt, repression, sexual "arousibility," and sexual experience on female sexual arousal during erotica and fantasy. *Journal of Personality and Social Psychology, 49,* 177–187.

Niedenthal, P., & Cantor, N. (1986). Affective responses as guides to category-based inferences. *Motivation and Emotion, 10,* 217–221.

Nisbett, R., & Wilson, T. (1977a). Telling more than we can know: Verbal reports on mental processes. *Psychological Review, 84,* 231–259.

Nisbett, R. E., & Wilson, T. D. (1977b). The halo effect: Evidence for unconscious alteration of judgments. *Journal of Personality and Social Psychology, 35,* 250–256.

Ogata, S. N., Silk, K. R., Goodrich, S., Lohr, N. E., Westen, D., Hill, E. (1988). *Childhood abuse and clinical symptoms in borderline patients.* Unpublished manuscript, University of Michigan.

Orlofsky, J. L. (in press). Intimacy status: Theory and research. In J. E. Marcia, A. S. Waterman, D. R. Matteson, S. L. Archer, & J. L. Orlofsky (Eds.), *Ego identity: A handbook for psychosocial research.*

Perry, J. C., & Cooper, S. H. (1986). A preliminary report on defenses and conflicts associated with borderline personality disorder. *Journal of the American Psychoanalytic Association, 34,* 863–893.

Perry, J. C., & Cooper, S. H. (1987). Empirical studies of psychological defense mechanisms. In R. Michels & J. O. Cavenar, Jr. (Eds.), *Psychiatry.* Philadelphia: J. B. Lippincott.

Perry, J. C., & Cooper, S. H. (1989). An empirical study of defense mechanisms: I. Clinical interview and life vignette ratings. *Archives of General Psychiatry, 46,* 444–460.

Perry, J. C., Luborsky, L., Silberschatz, A, & Popp, C. (1989). An examination of three methods of psychodynamic formulation based on the same videotaped interview. *Psychiatry, 52,* 302–323.

Pervin, L. A. (1982). The stasis and flow of behavior: Toward a theory of goals. *Nebraska Symposium on Motivation.* Lincoln: University of Nebraska Press.

Peterfreund, E. (1971). Information, systems, and psychoanalysis: An evolutionary biological approach to psychoanalytic theory. *Psychological Issues, 7*(1/2, Monograph No. 25/26).

Peterfreund, E. (1975). The need for a new general theoretical frame of reference for psychoanalysis. *Psychoanalytic Quarterly*, 44, 534–549.

Peterfreund, E. (1978). Some critical comments on psychoanalytic conceptualizations of infancy. *International Journal of Psycho-Analysis*, 59, 427–441.

Pine, F. (1985). *Developmental theory and clinical process*. New Haven, CT: Yale University Press.

Pine, F. (1988). The four psychologies and their place in clinical work. *Journal of the American Psychoanalytic Association*, 571–596.

Plutchik, R. (1980). A general psychoevolutionary theory of emotion. In R. Plutchik & H. Kellerman (Eds.), *Emotion: Vol. 1. Theories of emotion*. New York: Academic Press.

Poetzl, O. (1960). The relationship between experimentally induced dream images and indirect vision. *Psychological Issues*, 2(Monograph No. 7), 41–120. (Original work published 1917)

Pope, K. S., Tabachnick, B. A., & Keith-Spiegel, P. (1987). Ethics of practice: The beliefs and behaviors of psychologists as therapists. *American Psychologist*, 42, 993–1006.

Popper, K. (1957). *The poverty of historicism*. London: Routledge & Kegan Paul.

Powers, W. T. (1973). *Behavior: The control of perception*. Chicago: Aldine.

Pribram, K. H., & Gill, M. M. (1976). *Freud's "Project" re-assessed: Preface to contemporary cognitive theory and neuropsychology*. New York: Basic Books.

Rapaport, D. (1951). *Organization and pathology of thought: Selected sources*. New York: Columbia University Press.

Rapaport, D. (1967). The scientific methodology of psychoanalysis. In M. Gill (Ed.), *The collected papers of David Rapaport*. New York: Basic Books. (Original work published 1944)

Rapaport, D., & Gill, M. M. (1959). The points of view and assumptions of metapsychology. *International Journal of Psycho-Analysis*, 40, 153–162.

Rapaport, D., Schafer, R., & Gill, M. (1945–1946). *Diagnostic psychological testing* (2 vols.). Chicago: Year Book Medical.

Raskin, R., & Terry, H. (1988). Principal-components analysis of the Narcissistic Personality Inventory and further evidence of its construct validity. *Journal of Personality and Social Psychology*, 54, 890–902.

Raskin, R. (in press). Narcissism and the use of personal pronouns. *Journal of Personality*.

Redl, R. A., & Wineman, D. (1951). *Children who hate*. New York: Collier.

Reeve, R. A., & Brown, A. (1985). Metacognition reconsidered: Implications for intervention research. *Journal of Abnormal Child Psychology*, 13, 343–356.

Reiser, M. F. (1984). *Mind, brain, body*. New York: Basic Books.

Reiser, M. (1985). Converging sectors of psychoanalysis and neurobiology: Mutual challenge and opportunity. *Journal of the American Psychoanalytic Association*, 33, 11–34.

Richards, A. (1986). Introduction. In A. Richards & M. S. Willick (Eds.), *Psychoanalysis, the science of mental conflict: Essays in honor of Charles Brenner* (pp. 1–27). Hillsdale, NJ: Erlbaum.

Ricks, M. H. (1985). The social transmission of parental behavior: Attachment across generations. In I. Bretherton & E. Waters (Eds.), Growing points of attachment theory and research. *Monographs of the Society for Research in Child Development*, 50, (1–2, Serial No. 209), 211–227.

Ricoeur, P. (1971). *Freud and philosophy: An essay on interpretation* (D. Savage, Trans.). New Haven, CT: Yale University Press.

Rogers, C. (1959). A theory of therapy, personality, and interpersonal relationships, as developed in the client-centered framework. In S. Koch (Ed.), *Psychology: A study of a science* (Vol. 3). New York: McGraw-Hill.

Rosenwald, G. (1988). A theory of multiple case research. *Journal of Personality*, 56, 239–264.

Rothbart, M. K., & Posner, M. I. (1985). Temperament and the development of self-regulation. In L. C. Hartlage & C. F. Telzrow (Eds.), *The neuropsychology of individual differences: A developmental perspective* (pp. 93–124). New York: Plenum.

Rubenstein, B. (1976). On the possibility of a strictly clinical theory: An essay on the philosophy of psychoanalysis. In M. M. Gill & P. S. Holzman (Eds.), Psychology versus metapsychology: Psychoanalytic essays in memory of George S. Klein. *Psychological Issues*, 9(4, Monograph No. 36).

Rumelhart, D. E., McClelland, J. L., & the PDP Research Group. (1986). *Parallel distributed processing: Explorations in the microstructures of cognition* (2 vols.). Cambridge, MA: MIT Press.

Runyan, W. M. (1984). *Life histories and psychobiography: Explorations in theory and method*. New York: Oxford University Press.

Ryan, A. (1970). *The philosophy of the social sciences*. London: Macmillan.

Sandler, J. (1987) *From safety to superego: Selected papers of Joseph Sandler*. New York: Guilford Press.

Sandler, J., & Rosenblatt, B. (1962). The concept of the representational world. *Psychoanalytic Study of the Child*, 17, 128–145.

Sandler, J., & Sandler, A. (1978). On the development of object relationships and affects. *International Journal of Psycho-Analysis*, 59, 285–296.

Santostefano, S. (1986). Cognitive controls, metaphors, and contexts: An approach to cognition and emotion. In D. J. Bearison & H. Zimiles (Eds.), *Thought and emotion: Developmental perspectives*. Hillsdale, NJ: Erlbaum.

Schacter, D. L. (1986). The psychology of memory. In J. E. LeDoux & W. Hirst (Eds.), *Mind and brain: Dialogues in cognitive neuroscience*. New York: Cambridge University Press.

Schafer, R. (1976). *A new language for psychoanalysis*. New Haven, CT: Yale University Press.

Schank, R. C., & Abelson, R. P. (1977). *Scripts, plans, goals, and understanding*. Hillsdale, NJ: Erlbaum.

Scheier, M. F., & Carver, C. S. (1982). Cognition, affect, and self-regulation. In M. S. Clark & S. T. Fiske (Eds.), *Affect and cognition: The 17th annual Carnegie Symposium on Cognition*. Hillsdale, NJ: Erlbaum.

Schimek, J. (1975). A critical re-examination of Freud's concept of unconscious mental representation. *International Review of Psycho-Analysis*, 2, 171–187.

Schimek, J. (1987). Fact and fantasy in the seduction theory: A historical review. *International Journal of Psycho-Analysis*, 35, 937–965.

Schwartz, A. (1987). Drives, affects, behavior—and learning: Approaches to a psychobiology of emotion and to an integration of psychoanalytic and neurobiologic thought. *Journal of the American Psychoanalytic Association*, 35, 467–506.

Selman, R. L. (1980). The child as a friendship philosopher. In S. R. Asher & J. M. Gottman (Eds.), *The development of friendships*. New York: Cambridge University Press.

Shantz, C. U. (1983). Social cognition. In J. H. Flavell & E. M. Markman (Vol. Eds.), *Handbook of child psychology* (4th ed.): Vol. 3. *Cognitive development*. New York: Wiley.

Shapiro, D. (1965). *Neurotic styles*. New York: Basic Books.

Shedler, J., & Block, J. (in press). Adolescent drug use and emotional health: A longitudinal perspective. *American Psychologist*.

Shedler, J., Mayman, M., & Manis, M. (1988). *Defensive self-esteem: Overview of research to date*. Unpublished manuscript, University of California–Berkeley.

Shevrin, H. (1984). The fate of the five metapsychological principles. *Psychoanalytic Inquiry*, 4, 33–58.

Shevrin, H. (1986). An argument for the evidential standing of psychoanalytic data. *Behavioral and Brain Sciences*, 9, 257–259.

Shevrin, H. (1988). Unconscious conflict: A convergent psychodynamic and electrophysiological approach. In M. J. Horowitz (Ed.), *Psychodynamics and cognition*. Chicago: University of Chicago Press.

Shevrin, H., & Dickman, S. (1980). The psychological unconscious: A necessary assumption for all psychological theory? *American Psychologist*, 35, 421–434.

Shiffrin, R. M., & Schneider, W. (1977). Controlled and automatic information processing: II. Perceptual learning, automatic attending, and a general theory. *Psychological Review*, 84, 127–190.

Silverman, L. H. (1983). The subliminal psychodynamic activation method: Overview and comprehensive listing of studies. In J. Masling (Ed.), *Empirical studies of psychoanalytic theories* (Vol. 1). New York: Analytic Press.

Silverman, L. H., & Weinberger, J. (1985). Mommy and I are one: Implications for psychotherapy. *American Psychologist*, 12, 1296–1308.

Singer, J. L. (1985). Transference and the human condition: A cognitive–affective perspective. *Psychoanalytic Psychology*, 2, 189–219.

Singer, J. L. (1988). Psychoanalytic theory in the context of contemporary psychology: The Helen Block Lewis Memorial Address. *Psychoanalytic Psychology*, 5, 95–125.

Singer, J. L., & Salovey, P. (in press). Organized knowledge structures in personality: Schemas, prototypes, and scripts. A review and research agenda. In M. Horowitz (Ed.), *Person schemas*. Chicago: University of Chicago Press.

Sorrentino, R. M., & Higgins, E. T. (Eds.). (1986). *Handbook of motivation and cognition: Foundations of social behavior*. New York: Guilford Press.

Spence, D. P. (1982). *Narrative truth and historical truth: Meaning and interpretation in psychoanalysis*. New York: Norton.

Spruiell, V. (1988). The indivisibility of Freudian object relations and drive theories. *Psychoanalytic Quarterly*, 57, 597–625.

Squire, L. R. (1987). *Memory and brain*. New York: Oxford University Press.

Sroufe, L. A., & Fleeson, J. (1986). Attachment and the construction of relationships. In W. W. Hartup & Z. Rubin (Eds.), *Relationships and development*. Hillsdale, New Jersey: Erlbaum.

Sroufe, L. A., & Waters, E. (1977). Attachment as an organizational construct. *Child Development*, 48, 1184–1199.

Stern, D. N. (1985). *The interpersonal world of the infant: A view from psychoanalysis and developmental psychology*. New York: Basic Books.

Sternberg, R., Ed. (1984). *Mechanisms of cognitive development*. San Francisco: Freeman.

Sullivan, H. S. (1953). *The interpersonal theory of psychiatry*. New York: Norton.

Sulloway, F. J. (1979). *Freud: Biologist of the mind*. New York: Basic Books.

Tomkins, S. (1962). *Affect, imagery, consciousness* (Vol. 1). New York: Springer.

Tomkins, S. (1986). Script theory. In J. Aronoff, A. I. Rabin, & R. Zucker (Eds.), *The emergence of personality* (pp. 147–216). New York: Springer.

Turk, D., & Salovey, P. (1985). Cognitive structures, cognitive processes, and cognitive-behavior modification: II. Judgments and inferences of the clinician. *Cognitive Therapy and Research*, 9, 19–33.

Urist, J. (1980). Object relations. In R. W. Woody (Ed.), *Encyclopedia of clinical assessment* (Vol. 2, pp. 821–833). San Francisco: Jossey-Bass.

Vaillant, G. E. (1977). *Adaptation to life*. Boston: Little, Brown.

Vaillant, G. E. (Ed.). (1986). *Empirical studies of ego mechanisms of defense*. Washington, DC: American Psychiatric Press.

Vaillant, G. E., & Drake, R. E. (1985). Maturity of defenses in relation to DSM-III Axis II personality disorder. *Archives of General Psychiatry*, 42, 597–601.

Wachtel, P. (1977). *Psychoanalysis and behavior therapy: Toward an integration*. New York: Basic Books.

Wachtel, P. (1981). Transference, schema, and assimilation: The relationship of Piaget to the psychoanalytic theory of transference. *Annual of Psychoanalysis*, 8, 59–76.

Wachtel, P. (1987). *Action and insight*. New York: Guilford Press.

Wallerstein, R. S. (1985). How does self psychology differ in practice? *International Journal of Psycho-Analysis*, 66, 391–404.

Wallerstein, R. S. (1988). One psychoanalysis or many? *International Journal of Psycho-Analysis* 69, 5–22.

Weber, M. (1949). *The methodology of the social sciences* (E. A. Shils & H. A. Finch, Eds. and Trans.). New York: Free Press.

Weinberger, D. A. (in press). The construct validity of the repressive coping style. In J. L. Singer (Ed.), *Repression and dissociation*. Chicago: University of Chicago Press.

Weinberger, D. A., Schwartz, G. E., & Davidson, R. J. (1979). Low-anxious, high-anxious, and repressive coping styles: Psychometric patterns and behavioral and psychological responses to stress. *Journal of Abnormal Psychology*, 88, 369–380.

Weinberger, J., & Silverman, J. (1988). *Testability and empirical verification of psychoanalytic dynamic propositions through subliminal psychodynamic activation*. Unpublished manuscript, H. A. Murray Center, Harvard University.

Weiss, R. S. (1986). Continuities and transformations in social relationships from childhood to adulthood. In W. W. Hartup & Z. Rubin (Eds.), *Relationships and development* (pp. 95–110). Hillsdale, NJ: Erlbaum.

Wellman, H. M. (1985). The origins of metacognition. In D. Forrest-Pressley, G. MacKinnon, & T. Waller

(Eds.), *Metacognition, cognition, and human performance* (pp. 1–31). New York: Academic Press.

Westen, D. (1985). *Self and society: Narcissism, collectivism, and the development of morals.* New York: Cambridge University Press.

Westen, D. (1986). The superego: A revised developmental model. *Journal of the American Academy of Psychoanalysis, 14,* 181–202.

Westen, D. (1988). Transference and information processing. *Clinical Psychology Review, 8,* 161–179.

Westen, D. (in press-a). Social cognition and object relations. *Psychological Bulletin.*

Westen, D. (in press-b). The relations among narcissism, egocentrism, self-concept, and self-esteem. *Psychoanalysis and Contemporary Thought.*

Westen, D. (in press-c). Toward a revised theory of borderline object relations: Implications of empirical research. *International Review of Psycho-Analysis.*

Westen, D. (in press-d). The clinical assessment of object relations using the TAT. *Journal of Personality Assessment.*

Westen, D., Lohr, N., Silk, K., Gold, L., & Kerber, K. (in press). Object relations and social cognition in borderlines, major depressives, and normals: A TAT analysis. *Psychological Assessment: A Journal of Consulting and Clinical Psychology.*

Westen, D., Klepser, J., Ruffins, S., Silverman, M., Boekamp, J., & Lifton, N. (1989). Object relations in childhood and adolescence: The development of working representations. Unpublished manuscript, University of Michigan.

Westen, D., Ludolph, P., Lerner, H., Ruffins, S., & Wiss, C. (in press). Object relations in borderline adolescents. *Journal of the American Academy of Child and Adolescent Psychiatry.*

Westen, D., Ludolph, P., Silk, K., Kellam, A., Gold, L., & Lohr, N. (in press). Object relations in borderline adolescents and adults: Developmental differences. *Adolescent Psychiatry.*

Westen, D., Ludolph, P., Misle, B., Ruffins, S., & Block, J. (1990). Physical and sexual abuse in female adolescents with borderline personality disorder. *American Journal of Orthopsychiatry, 60,* 55–66.

White, R. W. (1959). Motivation reconsidered: The concept of competence. *Psychological Review, 66,* 297–333.

Winson, J. (1985). *Brain and psyche: The biology of the unconscious.* New York: Anchor/Doubleday.

Wolff, P. H. (1960). The developmental psychologies of Jean Piaget and psychoanalysis. *Psychological Issues, 2* (Monograph 5).

Zanarini, M. C., Gunderson, J. G., Marino, M. F., Schwart, E. D., & Frankenburg, F. R. (1989). Childhood experiences of borderline patients. *Comprehensive Psychiatry, 30,* 18–25.

Zeanah, C. H., & Zeanah, P. D. (1989). Intergenerational transmission of maltreatment: Insights from attachment theory and research. *Psychiatry, 52,* 177–196.

Chapter 3

The "Big Five" Factor Taxonomy: Dimensions of Personality in the Natural Language and in Questionnaires

Oliver P. John

University of California at Berkeley

> Taxonomy is always a contentious issue because the world does not come to us in neat little packages.
>
> GOULD (1981, p. 158)

Like any field of scientific study, personality psychology needs a descriptive model or taxonomy of its subject matter. One of the central goals of scientific taxonomies is the definition of overarching domains within which large numbers of specific instances can be understood in a simplified way. In personality psychology, a taxonomy would permit researchers to study specified domains of personality characteristics, instead of examining separately the thousands of particular attributes that make human beings individual and unique. Moreover, a generally accepted taxonomy would greatly facilitate the accumulation and communication of empirical findings by offering a standard vocabulary or nomenclature (John, Angleitner, & Ostendorf, 1988).

Personality can be conceptualized from a variety of theoretical perspectives, and at various levels of abstraction or breadth (Hampson, John, & Goldberg, 1986), each of which can make unique contributions to our understanding of the complexities in human behavior and experience. However, the number of personality concepts, and of scales designed to measure them, has escalated without an end in sight (Goldberg, 1971). Researchers, as well as practitioners in the field of personality assessment, are faced with a bewildering array of personality scales from which to choose, with little guidance and no overall rationale at hand. Even worse, scales with the same name often measure concepts that are not the same, and scales with quite different names overlap considerably in their item content. Although diversity and scientific pluralism can be useful, the systematic accumulation of findings and the communication among researchers continues to be difficult in the present-day Babel of concepts and scales.

In spite of the tenacious need for diversity and individuality that seems to characterize personality psychologists as a group, there is also a deeply felt and widely acknowledged need for integration. Most every researcher in the field hopes, at one level or another, to be the one who devises the structure that will transform the present Babel into a community that speaks a common language. However, such an integration is unlikely to be achieved by any one researcher or by any one theoretical perspective. As Allport once put it, "each assessor has his own pet units and uses a pet battery of diagnostic devices" (1958, p. 258).

More likely to succeed than any one researcher or theory is a taxonomic structure that can represent in a common framework the various and diverse systems of personality description currently in use. Rather than replacing all these other systems, such a structure would primarily have a descriptive, integrative function. The descriptive taxonomy could also serve as the starting place for vigorous research and theorizing that would lead to an explication and revision of the preliminary taxonomy in causal and dynamic terms.

This chapter describes such a descriptive model, the "Big Five" dimensions of personality description, derived from analyses of the natural-language terms people use to describe themselves and others. The first part of the chapter describes the history of the lexical approach and the discovery of the five dimensions. The second part presents more recent research replicating and extending this model, both in English and in several other languages. In the third part, I present a consensual definition of the five dimensions, which I then use in the fourth part of the chapter to discuss numerous other dimensions of personality, temperament, mood, and interpersonal behavior proposed by researchers outside the lexical tradition. In the final sections, I address some criticisms of the Big Five structure, and discuss problems and issues that still await resolution.

THE LEXICAL APPROACH AND THE DISCOVERY OF THE BIG FIVE

One starting place for a shared descriptive taxonomy is the natural language of personality description. Beginning with Klages (1926/1932), Baumgarten (1933), and Allport and Odbert (1936), various psychologists have turned to natural-language dictionaries as a source of attributes for a scientific taxonomy. This work, beginning with the extraction of all personality-relevant terms included in unabridged dictionaries, has generally been guided by the "lexical" approach (see John et al., 1988), which posits that most of the socially relevant and salient personality characteristics have become encoded in the natural language (e.g., Allport, 1937). The personality vocabulary contained in the dictionaries of a natural language could thus provide an extensive yet finite set of attributes, including those that the people in the language community have found particularly important and useful in their daily interactions with each other.

Historical Background: The Allport–Odbert List of Personality Descriptors

The history of the lexical approach has recently been reviewed (John et al., 1988); a summary of this review is given in Figure 3.1. Following Baumgarten's (1933) work in German, Allport and Odbert (1936) provided the basis for later taxonomic work by listing the personality-relevant terms found in an unabridged dictionary. Allport and Odbert examined the 1925 edition of *Webster's New International Dictionary*, which contained about 550,000 separate terms. Terms were included in the list if they were judged to possess "the capacity . . . to distinguish the behavior of one human being from that of another" (Allport & Odbert, 1936, p. 24); thus terms referring to common, nondistinctive behaviors were eliminated. With the addition of a few common slang terms not (yet) included in *Webster's*, the final list amounted to almost 18,000 words. These are often, but misleadingly, referred to as 18,000 "trait" descriptors; actually, only about a fourth of these terms describe personality traits.

Allport and Odbert classified the attributes, on conceptual grounds, into four categories or "columns." Only the first column contained terms that designate possible personal traits and are relatively neutral in their evaluation (p. 38). Allport and Odbert defined traits as "generalized and personalized determining tendencies—consistent and stable modes of an individual's adjustment to his environment," such as aggressive, introverted, and sociable (p. 26). This definition of traits as relatively stable, internal, causal tendencies has influenced much subsequent research on personality structure.

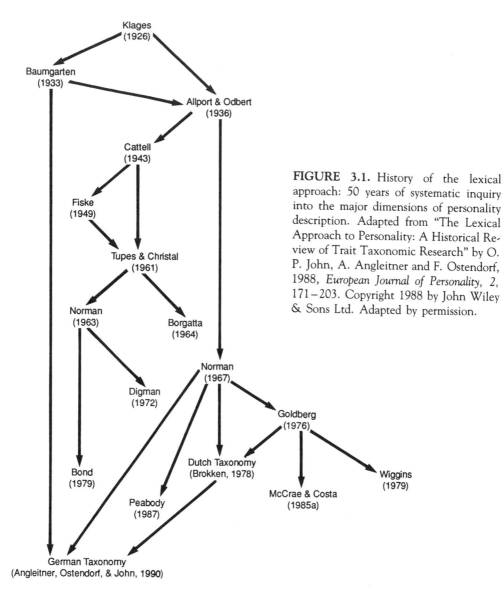

FIGURE 3.1. History of the lexical approach: 50 years of systematic inquiry into the major dimensions of personality description. Adapted from "The Lexical Approach to Personality: A Historical Review of Trait Taxonomic Research" by O. P. John, A. Angleitner and F. Ostendorf, 1988, *European Journal of Personality, 2,* 171–203. Copyright 1988 by John Wiley & Sons Ltd. Adapted by permission.

The terms included in the second category describe temporary states, moods, and activities. The majority of these words are verb forms, such as abashed, gibbering, and rejoicing. The third category consisted of evaluative terms "conveying social and characterial judgments of personal conduct, or designated influence on others," such as insignificant and worthy (p. 38). Most of these terms refer primarily to social evaluations, rather than to dispositions that are part of the structure of personality. A few of the terms included in this category describe differences in the "social stimulus value" an individual has for others, such as dazzling or irritating. Although these terms presuppose some traits in that individual, they do not indicate the psychological dispositions that give rise to the individual's dazzling or irritating effect on others. The fourth, a ragbag category, consisted of metaphorical and of doubtful terms, including physical qualities (e.g., lean, redhead), capacities and talents (e.g., gifted, prolific), and terms of lesser relevance for personality. These four categories obviously overlap and have fuzzy boundaries. Indeed, Allport and Odbert noted that some of the words could have been classified into more than one category, especially those assigned to the "trait" and the "state and activity" categories.

This observation has led some researchers (Allen & Potkay, 1981, 1983) to argue that the distinction between traits and states is altogether arbitrary and should be abolished. In response, we (Chaplin, John, & Goldberg, 1988) showed that although the discrete classification of some personality concepts (e.g., energetic, suspicious, antagonistic) is difficult, the classification of most instances is quite clear. Moreover, the prototypical cores of the categories can be differentiated from each other by a set of attributes. Prototypical *states* are temporary, brief, and externally caused; in contrast, prototypical *traits* are stable, long-lasting, and internally caused, and need to be observed more frequently and across a wider range of situations than states before they are attributed. These findings demonstrate that the conceptual distinctions made by Allport and Odbert (1936) are rooted in a common understanding of personality and can be made with considerable interjudge agreement.

Cattell's Reduction of the Allport–Odbert List to 35 Trait Variables

To be of practical value, however, a taxonomy must provide more than an alphabetical listing organized into four categories. A useful taxonomy must provide a systematic framework for distinguishing, ordering, and naming individual differences in people's behavior and experience (John, 1989a). Aiming for such a taxonomy, Cattell (1943) used the Allport and Odbert list as a starting point for his multidimensional model of personality structure. Because the size of the Allport–Odbert list was too overwhelming for research purposes, and because more than half of the terms included were uncommon and derivative forms unfamiliar even to most Americans, Cattell reduced the number of terms and then applied cluster- and factor-analytic techniques to the reduced set. This early work provided the foundation of Cattell's system of personality description, and, as shown in Figure 3.1, it served as the initial item selection pool for several other investigators.

Interested primarily in stable traits, Cattell began with Allport and Odbert's first category, the personal trait terms, to which he added approximately 100 of the state terms (Cattell, 1943). Semantically similar terms on the expanded list were grouped into rather loose "synonym" clusters, which were further grouped into antonym pairs. Together, these two semantic sorting steps yielded 160 mostly bipolar clusters intended to represent approximately 4,500 terms. Cattell (1943) then selected about 13 terms from each cluster and summarized them with a key term. Thus, at this stage Cattell had eliminated about half of the Allport and Odbert terms—mostly those that were archaic, uncommon, redundant, or derivative forms.

To examine the exhaustiveness of this collection of variables, Cattell reviewed the personological literature of the time, and concluded that his selection of variables was fairly complete. Nevertheless, Cattell added 11 new clusters and supplemented some of his initial clusters with terms derived from the psychological literature, particularly with ability traits (such as general intelligence and various special abilities) and with a number of specific-interest traits.[*] Unfortunately, the resulting set of 171 clusters (Cattell, 1946) was still much too large to be amenable to the factor-analytic techniques of the 1940s. In his empirical analyses, Cattell thus proceeded in two steps. First, he used a clustering approach to condense the 171 clusters to 35 "trait variables." Then he submitted the intercorrelations among this reduced set of variables to factor analysis.

In the clustering study, 100 adults were rated by one or two acquaintances on the 171 variables (Cattell, 1943; 1945b).[1] Cattell then used the correlations among the 171 variables, a matrix of 14,535 coefficients laid out on paper in its own room, to identify a smaller set of variables that would contain as many of the initial 171 clusters as possible. Although the exact procedures used at this point are difficult to reconstruct, Cattell (1943, pp. 500–503) eventually published provisional cluster labels, the traits forming the cluster core, and overlapping traits and clusters for 60 new "empirical" clusters. Although these clusters overlapped substantially, only 135 of the 171 original clusters were accounted for. Cattell claimed that "the analysis into clusters was made entirely blind, on mathematical criteria only" (1943, p. 504). However, given the number of undocumented and subjective decisions, the

---

[*]At some point Cattell must have changed these 171 clusters, because later he referred to a trait list of 181 or 182 clusters resulting from his semantic reduction steps (Cattell, 1957, 1979).

replicability and generalizability of this cluster solution must be considered doubtful at best.

Lack of funding for a factor analysis of all clusters hampered Cattell's further empirical efforts. Thus he (Cattell, 1945a) resorted to his own reviews of the literature for another drastic revision of the cluster solution he had so painstakingly derived. He retained only those of the "empirical" clusters that he judged to be confirmed by other studies, and combined and eliminated further clusters he deemed of lesser importance. According to Cattell (1945a), only 35 variables remained, although in later years he added "a few terms considered indispensable" (1957, p. 813). In the original publication, the 35 variables each subsumed 6–12 trait elements (Cattell, 1945a, pp. 71–74). In subsequent publications, these variables were further edited, augmented by short descriptions, and given bipolar adjective pairs as headings (Cattell, 1947, 1948, 1957). These changes were probably motivated by the realization that the initial variables were multifaceted and lacked coherence. Indeed, most subsequent investigators have not used the original variables, but instead have selected particular adjectives from the heterogeneous cluster descriptions provided by Cattell.

Cattell's 12 Primary Personality Factors

Having trimmed the 4,500 traits from Allport and Odbert's list to 35 variables, Cattell (1945a) was finally ready to proceed with factor analysis to identify, as he hoped, the major dimensions of personality. Thirteen small groups of adult male subjects participated. Two judges rank-ordered all the individuals in each group on each of the 35 variables; their judgments were pooled to yield mean rankings. The 35 variables were first intercorrelated within each group of subjects and then averaged across the 13 groups. The resulting averaged correlation matrix was factor-analyzed. Although Cattell interpreted 12 obliquely rotated factors, by today's standards he retained too many factors. The last three factors did not have a single loading exceeding .30; factors 6 through 12 had only secondary loadings, whereas the first five factors had rather substantial loadings.

However, even the largest five factors are difficult to interpret. The first factor (labeled by Cattell as "Cyclothyme vs. Paranoid Schi-

zothyme") is a Warm versus Cold (or Friendliness) dimension. The second factor, which Cattell noted was difficult to rotate, seems to reflect primarily intellectual characteristics but also Will and Conscientiousness: It includes "intellectual/analytical," "strong-willed/conscientious," "intellectual/wide interests," and "wise/mature/polished" as contrasted with "changeable/unreflective" and "changeable/unrealistic." Cattell (1945a, p. 89), however, interpreted this factor as "General Mental Capacity (Spearman's G in personality expression)." The third and the fourth factor overlap considerably and seem to reflect different aspects of Neuroticism, the third referring to more extremely pathological characteristics than the fourth. Finally, marker variables for the fifth factor were "assertive/boastful," "willful versus self-effacing," and "tough/talkative versus introspective." This factor seems to reflect, as Cattell suggests, "Dominance versus Submissiveness" (1945a, p. 89).

In interpreting the findings from his subsequent studies, Cattell (1947, 1948) concluded that he had replicated 9 of the 12 original factors, which he then used as the foundation of his system of personality measurement and theory (e.g., Cattell, 1957). For example, to assess these factors in self-reports, he constructed the Sixteen Personality Factors Questionnaire (16 PF; Cattell, Eber, & Tatsuoka, 1970); 12 of its 16 scales are said to match those found in the trait-rating studies, whereas the remaining 4 are said to be specific to the questionnaire domain. However, the high degree of correspondence Cattell claimed for his factors across self-reports, ratings by others, and objective test data has been questioned (e.g., Becker, 1960; Nowakowska, 1973). Moreover, reanalyses of Cattell's correlation matrices by others have not confirmed the number and nature of the factors he proposed (e.g., Tupes & Christal, 1961). Most recently, Digman and Takemoto-Chock (1981) concluded that Cattell's "original model, based on the unfortunate clerical errors noted here, cannot have been correct" (p. 168), although they suggested that the second-order factors of the 16 PF might show some correspondence between Cattell's system and subsequently derived dimensions, which are described below.

For his part, Cattell (e.g., 1974, 1979) continued to argue that his primary factors represent the most important dimensions of personality. However, although he claimed that his set of 35 trait variables was indeed "a truly representative list . . . derived from language" (1945a, p. 70), representativeness vis-à-vis the personality contents of the dictionary was never his sole, or even major, objective (Peabody, 1987; Peabody & Goldberg, 1989). Cattell was at least as concerned with ensuring the representation of those dimensions of personality, temperament, and intellect that had emerged from psychological research in the 1930s and 1940s. Indeed, as described above, Cattell twice used his literature reviews to evaluate and revise lists initially designed to represent the trait content in the dictionary.

In addition to the uncertainties raised by these drastic and subjective revisions, Cattell's semantic and empirical reduction steps were greatly hampered by the technical and computational limitations of his times. Cattell (1945a) realized that "naturally a factor analysis of these [35 variables] cannot be guaranteed to contain all the factors present among the original 171 traits of the personality sphere" (p. 71), and his concern with representativeness (or the lack thereof) is reflected in his later additions to the variable list. Everything considered, it is difficult to avoid the conclusion that Cattell's lists of variables and factors primarily represent those traits that he himself considered the most important. The evaluation of his 35-variable list thus depends on one's trust in Cattell's theoretical savvy and innovative genius, but cannot rest on the replicability of his empirical procedures. Nonetheless, it is possible that Cattell's trait selection, while probably not representative of the dictionary, may have contained traces of most of the major dimensions of personality description. This possibility is suggested by subsequent findings that, though initially based on selections from Cattell's list, have generalized to other, independently derived, and more extensive sets of personality attributes.

Discovery of Five Factors in Cattell's Variable Set

Cattell's innovative work, and the availability of a relatively short list of variables, stimulated other researchers to examine the dimensional structure of trait ratings. Fiske (1949) constructed much-simplified descriptions from 22 of Cattell's variables and used them to obtain trait ratings of 128 clinical psychology trainees. The factor structures derived from self-ratings, ratings by other trainees, and ratings by the psychological staff were similar, suggesting five factors. Tupes and Christal (1961) reanalyzed correlation matrices from eight different samples (including two of Cattell's), ranging from airmen with no more than high-school education to first-year graduate students, and included ratings by peers, supervisors, teachers, or experienced clinicians in settings as diverse as military training courses and sorority houses. In all the analyses, Tupes and Christal found "five relatively strong and recurrent factors and nothing more of any consequence" (1961, p. 14). They labeled these factors (I) Surgency (talkative, assertive, energetic), (II) Agreeableness (good-natured, cooperative, trustful), (III) Dependability (conscientious, responsible, orderly), (IV) Emotional Stability (calm, not neurotic, not easily upset), and (V) Culture (intellectual, cultured, polished, independent-minded).

THE BIG FIVE FACTORS IN PERSONALITY TRAIT RATINGS

The factors found by Tupes and Christal (1961) were later called the "Big Five" (Goldberg, 1981), to emphasize that each of these domains is extremely broad and summarizes a large number of distinct, more specific personality characteristics. The numbering convention from I to V, retained throughout this chapter, reflects the relative size of the factors. Factors I and II, which primarily summarize traits of interpersonal nature, tend to account for the largest percentage of variance in personality ratings; the next largest is Factor III, which primarily describes task behavior and socially prescribed impulse control. The two last factors are by far the smallest: Factor IV contrasts calm and relaxed confidence with nervous tension, temper, and proneness to anxiety and sadness, and Factor V describes the depth, complexity, and quality of a person's mental and experiential life. These five factors bear some resemblance to the first five in Cattell's (1945a) study, although that solution contained two separate Emotional Stability factors and combined Factors III and V into a single one (see John, 1990). Tupes and Christal's five-factor structure has been replicated by Norman (1963), Borgatta (1964), and Digman and Takemoto-Chock (1981). Because the scales included in these studies were derived from Cattell's 35 variables, these studies provide evidence that the relations among the variables *in this set* can be summarized by the five broad factors.

Subsequently, five-factor structures have been identified in sets of variables not derived directly from Cattell's list (e.g., Botwin & Buss, 1989; Conley, 1985a; De Raad, Mulder, Kloosterman, & Hofstee, 1988; Digman, 1963, 1972; Digman & Inouye, 1986; Field & Millsap, 1989; Goldberg, 1981, 1989; McCrae & Costa, 1985a, 1987; Peabody & Goldberg, 1989). Table 3.1 summarizes the factors emerging from both the earlier and the later studies. This table includes the labels the investigators assigned to the five dimensions as they interpreted them; Norman's (1963) labels, used most commonly in the literature, are given in boldface.

Several of the studies summarized in Table 3.1 involved considerable overlap among the variables rated by the subjects. For example, Digman included some scales that had been used by Tupes and Christal (1961) and by Norman (1963) (see Digman & Takemoto-Chock, 1981, p. 158). Similarly, McCrae and Costa, interested primarily in a reliable assessment of the five established factors, used 40 bipolar adjective scales selected by Goldberg (1989) to assess the Big Five, and added another 40 to represent each of the five dimensions as they interpreted them (i.e., including variables related to "Openness to Experience," their label for Factor V). From the same set of Goldberg's 40 bipolar scales, Botwin and Buss (1989) selected 20 single adjectives, four for each factor, to examine the generalizability of the Big Five structure in the assessment of act frequencies reported by subjects and their spouses.

TABLE 3.1. The Big Five Dimensions in Studies of Natural-Language Personality Descriptions from 1949 to 1989

Investigator(s)	I	II	III	IV	V
Fiske (1949)	Confident Self-Expression	Social Adaptability	Conformity	Emotional Control	Inquiring Intellect
Tupes & Christal (1961)	Surgency	Agreeableness	Dependability	Emotional Stability	Culture
Norman (1963)	**Surgency**	**Agreeableness**	**Conscientiousness**	**Emotional Stability**	**Culture**
Borgatta (1964)	Assertiveness	Likeability	Task Interest	Emotionality	Intelligence
Digman & Takemoto-Chock (1981)	Extraversion	Friendly Compliance	Will to Achieve	Ego Strength (Anxiety)	Intellect
Goldberg (1981, 1989)	Surgency	Agreeableness	Conscientiousness	Emotional Stability	Intellect
McCrae & Costa (1985a)	Extraversion	Agreeableness	Conscientiousness	Neuroticism	Openness to Experience
Conley (1985a)	Social Extraversion	Agreeableness	Impulse Control	Neuroticism	(Intellectual Interests)[a]
De Raad et al. (1988)	Extraversion	Agreeableness vs. Cold-Heartedness	Conscientiousness	Emotional Instability	Culture
Botwin & Buss (1989)	Extraverted	Agreeable-stable	Conscientious	Dominant–Assured	Intellectance–Culture
Field & Millsap (1989)	Extraversion	Agreeableness		Satisfaction	Intellect
Peabody & Goldberg (1989)	Power	Love	Work	Affect	Intellect

[a]This factor emerged only in Conley's male sample.

Thus, although these studies cover a wide range of different types of subjects, raters, and data sources, the number of studies employing variable sets truly independent of Cattell's selection is more limited than Table 3.1 might seem to suggest. Indeed, Waller and Ben-Porath (1987) have argued that "much of the evidence . . . stems from an assemblage of cognate studies better thought of as demonstrating the reliability rather than the validity (or comprehensiveness) of the five-factor paradigm" (p. 887). In the following section, several studies bearing on Waller and Ben-Porath's conclusion are considered in more detail.

Replication and Confirmation of the Five-Factor Structure

To demonstrate its comprehensiveness and validity as a model of the major dimensions in personality ratings, the Big Five structure has to be confirmed in variable selections independent of Cattell's work. One set of studies fulfilling this requirement consists of those *predating* Cattell's work. In one such study, Conley (1985a) used variables selected by Lowell Kelly prior to 1935, predating not only the publication of Cattell's 35 variables but even the Allport–Odbert listing. Conley analyzed trait ratings obtained in the 1930s, and again some 40 years laters, from a large sample of dating couples. Factor analyses of these ratings converged, as Conley (1985a, pp. 1278–1279) noted, on a version of the Big Five. Whereas the correspondences were apparent for the first four factors, the fifth emerged clearly only in the male sample, as Intellect or Intellectual Interests.

Field and Millsap (1989) also analyzed data collected several decades earlier. The variables included in their study were a set of "personal–social characteristics" selected 50 years ago by Caroline Tryon to assess the parents of the participants in the Berkeley Guidance Study. The raters interviewed the subjects (who were in their 60s at the initial assessment and in their 80s at the follow-up) and rated about 35 characteristics, including several indicators of the physical health of the aging participants (freshness, personal appearance, energy). Analyses of the interviewer ratings yielded five dimensions, four of which directly matched the Big Five. The health variables formed their own factor (interpreted as "Energy" by Field and Millsap), whereas Conscientiousness did

not emerge—a not very surprising finding, given the absence of any variables related to work, task behavior, or impulse control.

A more compelling, though cumbersome, way to test the comprehensiveness and generality of the Big Five is to construct variable sets according to criteria different from, and more explicit than, Cattell's. One such series of studies, still unpublished at the time of this writing, is based on the initial work of Norman and subsequent research by Goldberg (1989). To update the Allport and Odbert list and to rectify the imperfections of Cattell's reduction steps, Norman (1967) compiled an exhaustive list of personality-descriptive terms, organized into various categories. As I describe below, this updated and refined set was later used by Goldberg (1989; see also 1981, 1982) to identify the structure of personality trait ratings in a comprehensive pool of descriptors and to test the stability and generalizability of the resulting structure across methodological variations and data sources.

Retracing Cattell's Procedures: Norman's Updated List and Category System

Norman used the unabridged 1961 *Webster's Third New International Dictionary* to identify personality terms, but found that he needed to add only 171 new terms to the Allport–Odbert List resulting in a total set of 18,125. In a second step, Norman eliminated unsuitable terms from this exhaustive set, excluding (1) evaluative terms and mere quantifiers (e.g., awful, nice, gifted), (2) ambiguous, vague, and metaphorical terms (e.g., aesthetic, mannered), (3) very difficult, obscure, and little-known terms (e.g., eldritch, scait), and (4) terms referring to anatomical and physical dispositions and conditions, including physical and mental health (e.g., ill, senile, insane), physical dispositions (athletic, short) and conditions (jogging, obese), and physical attractiveness (handsome, pretty). In all, these exclusion criteria reduced the set by more than 50%. Norman's (1967) listing has provided the foundation for most contemporary taxonomies, because the exclusion and inclusion of terms were based on explicit criteria and on the consensus of a team of four judges.

The remaining 8,081 terms were then sorted into three major classes of personality descriptors: (1) stable traits; (2) temporary states and activities; and (3) social roles, relationships, and effects. The basic assumption underlying Norman's category system is that in the natural language an individual's personality may be described at different levels and with different conceptual units. In particular, individuals can be described by their enduring *traits* (e.g., irascible), by the internal *states* they typically experience (furious), by the *activities* they frequently engage in (yelling), by the *effects* they have on others (frightening), and by general *evaluations* of their conduct by society (unacceptable, bad).

The easiest way to illustrate these distinctions is to consider one particular personality characteristic across the categories. Norman classified "irascible" as a stable trait. At any given moment in time, this disposition may or may not be manifested in the individual's temporary conditions. Norman differentiated two kinds of such conditions, states and activities. "Furious," for example, would be a state descriptor, "yelling" an activity descriptor. Although the same trait may give raise to both kinds of temporary conditions, the concepts of state and activity are distinct from the concept of trait (Chaplin et al., 1988).

A fourth class of descriptors defined by Norman includes the effects that the expression of a trait in behavior and emotion has on others. Terms such as "frightening" and "intimidating" do not refer to traits, but to the effects "irascible" individuals have on others; these terms signify an individual's "social stimulus value" or reputation (Allport & Odbert, 1936). The mediating links between a trait and a social stimulus value are the individual's behaviors and emotional experiences; they are manifestations of the trait and constitute the stimulus that influences others in the individual's social environment. Finally, the natural language also includes descriptors even more evaluative than these social-effect terms—for example, "horrid," "terrible," and "bad." Norman argued, as had Allport and Odbert, that these terms contain too much evaluation and too little descriptive meaning to be useful for descriptive purposes, and thus assigned them to an exclusion category.

Although the conception of personality he abstracted from the natural language was broad and complex, Norman saw traits as central to the notion of personality. It appears that he viewed traits as enduring characteristics internal to the individual and causally effective—a view quite similar to that of Allport (1937).

In the trait category, Norman included individual differences in behavioral, emotional, and cognitive functioning; only dispositions related to physique and health were excluded.

A Hierarchical Structure: Norman's Preliminary Semantic Classification

Norman subsequently focused on the class of stable traits and accumulated rating data on 2,800 trait terms. Analyses of these data showed that the set of 2,800 still included many terms that were unfamiliar and unclear even to well-educated undergraduates, and Norman constructed a final list of almost 1,600 terms by omitting terms that were judged as too difficult or slangy, or elicited overly extreme self-ratings. In his earlier replication of the five-factor structure, Norman (1963) had selected only 20 variables from Cattell's set, using four variables to represent each factor. However, Norman realized that the Big Five needed a more extensive and precise definition than was possible in the 1963 report. The replacement of Cattell's list of 35 complex and multifaceted variables with a much more representative and comprehensive list of single-word descriptors finally made it possible to examine the meaning and composition of each of the broad factors. For that purpose, Norman constructed an initial semantic classification of all the descriptors included in his final list.

As a first step, Norman (see Goldberg, 1981, 1989) rationally sorted the almost 1,600 terms into 10 broad classes, one for each of the two poles of each of the Big Five dimensions. Using the findings from the previous factor analyses as a guide, he assigned almost all of the terms to a factor pole. However, whereas Norman (1963) had selected an equal number of markers for each of the Big Five in his factor analyses, his sorting showed that the Big Five do not represent equally "big" domains of English trait descriptors. The number of terms per factor and pole varied considerably, ranging from a low of 64 for IV (Neuroticism pole) to 274 for II (Disagreeableness pole), with an average of 155 terms. These findings are consistent with Peabody and Goldberg's (1989) later (and independent) finding that, when a representative selection is factored, IV and V tend to be the smallest factors.

Norman then sorted the terms within each of the 10 factor poles into more narrow semantic categories. For example, the sorting of the terms at the Neuroticism pole of Factor IV led to only three distinct categories, labeled Anxiety, Insecurity, and Self-Pity, whereas 12 categories emerged at the Disagreeableness pole of Factor II (Vindictiveness, Ill-Humor, Criticism, Disdain, Aggressiveness, Antagonism, Dogmatism, Temper, Distrust, Greed, Callousness, and Uncooperation). In all, there were 75 such middle-level categories, each containing a sizable number of terms. For example, the Dogmatism category consisted of almost 50 terms (e.g., biased, opinionated, stubborn, inflexible). Norman therefore examined the semantic relations among the terms within each of the 75 categories, and combined highly synonymous terms into sets—a procedure that led to a total of 571 synonym sets. This three-tiered hierarchical structuring allowed Norman to classify a total of 1,431 adjectives and 175 nouns, leaving only 25 words unclassified.

The 75 categories at the middle level of abstraction in Norman's taxonomy provide a compromise between the parsimonious but relatively undifferentiated superordinate level (10 factor poles) and the highly differentiated but unwieldy number of synonym sets at the most specific level. Moreover, the hierarchical nature of this classification provides the user with a quick and efficient elaboration of each middle-level category (by examining the synonym clusters included), as well as with a more general appraisal of its gist (by referring to the Big Five pole under which it is subsumed). However, despite its heuristic potential, Norman's hierarchical classification remained preliminary; the sorting was intuitive, was based on the judgments of only one person, and remained to be validated in studies of personality ratings.

Testing the Big Five in a Comprehensive Sample of English Trait Terms

Goldberg (1980, 1989) used the trait list assembled by Norman to examine whether the Big Five, "and nothing more of any consequence" (Tupes & Christal, 1961, p. 14), would emerge in this comprehensive pool of trait terms. Goldberg's second concern centered on the exact nature and composition of these broad factors. For these purposes, Goldberg constructed from Norman's listing an inventory of 1,710 trait adjectives that could be used in studies of

self- and peer descriptions. Among these adjectives were 1,431 that Norman had classified semantically into 75 content categories. Based on the self-ratings of 187 college students using these terms, Goldberg (1989; see also 1981, pp. 159–161) analyzed the correlations among 75 category-scale scores formed by summing the terms included in each of Norman's 75 categories. The first five factors replicated the Big Five across a variety of different methods of factor extraction and rotation. Moreover, Goldberg (1989) demonstrated that the first five factors remained virtually invariant when more than five were rotated. In the six-factor solution, Factor III separated into a more homogeneous variant of the Conscientiousness factor and a second factor, contrasting Norman's categories Grace, Formality, Vanity, Sophistication, Order, Evangelism, and Religiosity with Provinciality, Irreverence, and Rebelliousness. In the seven-factor solution, the three categories involving religiosity formed a small factor of their own. None of the further factors included more than one or two variables, and only the first seven showed factor invariance when up to 13 factors were rotated.

Norman's initial reliance on his 1963 factor analyses probably influenced the way in which he sorted terms into the 75 categories. To ensure complete independence from any *a priori* classification, and to reduce the strain on subjects who had to rate hundreds of terms, Goldberg (1989) used various abbreviated sets of more common terms, excluding terms on the basis of various criteria, such as difficulty, ambiguity, slanginess, and sex linkage. In a study of one such list, Goldberg obtained ratings of 475 very common trait adjectives, which he sorted into 131 sets of "tight synonym" clusters. In two samples of peer ratings and of self-ratings, the five-factor structures were very similar to each other and to the structure obtained from Norman's categorization of the adjectives included in the more comprehensive list of 1,710. The five-factor structures in the self-rating data were virtually indistinguishable from those in the peer rating data. Most important, however, were the results from the search for additional factors: No factor beyond the fifth was invariant across the four samples included in this study, providing little support for the small Culture and Religiosity factors that had emerged in the analyses of the 75 Norman categories.

Finally, the composition of the fifth factor in

Goldberg's analyses suggests an interpretation closer to Intellectual Interests and Openness to Experience than to the original Culture (Norman, 1963). In Goldberg's factor analysis of Norman's 75 categories, Factor V was defined by Originality, Wisdom, Objectivity, Knowledge, Reflection, and Art. When the 133 synonym clusters were factored, the highest positive loadings were consistently found for the two clusters labeled Intellectuality (intellectual, contemplative, meditative, philosophical, and introspective) and Creativity (creative, imaginative, inventive, ingenious, innovative), followed by Intelligence, Versatility, Wisdom, Perceptiveness, Art, Logic, Curiosity, and Nonconformity. Sophistication (cultured, refined, sophisticated, worldly, cosmopolitan, urbane) had a substantial positive loading, and Provinciality (provincial, unsophisticated) had a substantial negative loading, on Factor V in the peer ratings but not in the self-ratings, and Dignity (mannerly, dignified, formal) loaded more highly on Factor III than on Factor V. The finding that Nonconformity (nonconforming, unconventional, rebellious) loaded positively, and Conventionality (traditional, conventional, unprogressive) loaded negatively, on Factor V in all four samples is also inconsistent with the Culture interpretation and instead favors McCrae and Costa's (1985b) Openness to Experience interpretation. In all, these findings suggest that the fifth factor measures a broad domain of personality, rather than social class, education, or intelligence.

Indeed, even in Norman's (1963) studies, only one of the four variables included as a marker of Factor V is, strictly speaking, a measure of Cultural Sophistication: "polished, refined versus crude, boorish." The other three variables—"artistically sensitive versus insensitive"; "intellectual versus unreflective, narrow"; "imaginative versus simple, direct"— have more to do with creativity, cognitive complexity, and broad interests than with being cultured, well-educated, and from an upper-class background. Both in 1963 and today, Factor V seems to encompass a broad range of intellectual, creative, and artistic inclinations, preferences, and skills found foremost in highly original and creative individuals (Barron, 1968; Gough, 1979; Helson, 1967; MacKinnon, 1965).

In conclusion, the fifth factor is best considered a blend of several components of mental

and experiential functioning, and seems to have only small (though significant) correlations with measures of IQ and scholastic aptitude (e.g., Helson, 1985; McCrae & Costa, 1985a). In Peabody and Goldberg's (1989) studies, Factor V was interpreted as Intellect, including both *controlled* aspects (perceptive, reflective, intelligent) and *expressive* aspects (imaginative, curious, broad-minded). This interpretation of Factor V is more narrow than is Openness to Experience; it emphasizes the intellectual aspects but omits others, such as artistic interests, nonconformity, and progressive values, all of which reflect personal orientations and attitudes rather than skills or abilities. The data reviewed so far suggest that all these aspects together form one broad personality factor that closely resembles McCrae and Costa's (1985b, 1987) description of Openness to Experience, of which Intellect is but one part.

Cattell's 35 Variables versus Peabody's Representative Selection

Whereas Norman and Goldberg tried to ensure the comprehensiveness of their analyses by avoiding any *a priori* classification and retaining a large number of commonly understood descriptors from the dictionary, Peabody (1987) followed a different rationale. His goal was to select variables so as to achieve an adequate but limited representation of common English trait adjectives. For this purpose, he first classified a large number of descriptors used by previous investigators on the basis of their findings and identified 57 distinguishable groups of terms. On the basis of this classification, Peabody (1987) selected a pair of adjectives to represent the core of each group. The resulting set of 57 bipolar adjective scales has been used in numerous studies, with multiple samples of subjects, and with different kinds of rating instructions. In general, the findings from these studies (e.g., Peabody & Goldberg, 1989) have confirmed and further clarified the conclusions reached from the analyses of the more comprehensive variable sets.

Moreover, when Peabody and Goldberg (1989) compared their variable selection with that of Cattell, they found that Cattell's 35 variables included markers for all the domains among the 57 scales, but did so in an unrepresentative manner. Compared to Peabody's

(1987) selection, Cattell's variables seem to underrepresent traits related to Conscientiousness and Impulse Control (Factor III) as well as Intellect (a facet of Factor V), and to overrepresent traits related to Emotional Stability versus Neuroticism ([a pole of] Factor IV) and Culture (apparently only a minor facet related to Factors V and III). The overrepresentation of Emotional Stability is probably due to Cattell's addition of clusters from the extensive literature on psychopathology, whereas the underrepresentation of variables related to Intellect can be traced to Cattell's use of an actual intelligence test in his later studies. Peabody and Goldberg therefore concluded that the initial interpretation of Tupes and Christal's (1961) fifth factor as Culture was a historical accident.

In conclusion, studies using extensive variable sets, whether they are comprehensive or selected representatively, offer independent and compelling replications of the earlier findings based on more limited variable sets. Moreover, these newer studies suggest that the number of *replicable* factors in the domain of English trait adjectives is limited to five, and place the fifth factor—interpreted as a broad Openness to Experience factor, including mental, intellectual, and experiential components—firmly within the domain of personality, not ability.

Cross-Language and Cross-Cultural Studies

The findings reviewed so far suggest that the Big Five structure provides a replicable representation of the major dimensions of trait description in English. When representative (or at least large) sets of variables are factored, the five-factor structure seems to emerge reliably, across different types of samples, raters, and methodological variations. Generalizability across languages and cultures is another important criterion for evaluating personality taxonomies (John, Goldberg, & Angleitner, 1984). Taxonomic research in other languages and cultures can determine the usefulness of a given taxonomy in other cultural contexts and can test the hypothesis that there are universals in the encoding of individual differences across languages and cultures (Goldberg, 1981). The existence of cultural universals would be consistent with an evolutionary interpretation of the way individual differences have become en-

coded as personality categories into the natural language: If the tasks most central to human survival are universal, the most important individual differences, and the terms people use to label these individual differences, should be universal as well (Hogan, 1983).

Although central from the vantage point of the lexical approach, cross-language research is difficult and expensive to conduct, and consequently rare. In most comprehensive taxonomic studies, English has been the language of choice, primarily because the taxonomers were American (see John et al., 1984, 1988). The only non-English taxonomy projects that began with the dictionary involved Dutch and German, languages closely related to English. The Dutch project has been carried out by Hofstee and his colleagues at the University of Groningen in The Netherlands (Brokken, 1978; De Raad et al., 1988; see also John et al., 1988, for a review). The conclusions deriving from the Dutch project are remarkably consistent with those from the English research: Only five factors were replicable across different selections of trait adjectives and across different subject samples, and those five factors were easily identified by the Dutch team as the Big Five.

With respect to German, an inital study of German-American bilinguals provided support for cross-language generalizability (John et al., 1984). The unique advantage of the bilingual design (in which the same subject provides descriptions in both languages) is that sample differences can be controlled and that translation checks can be made at the level of individual items. Indeed, we found that a few of the carefully made translations were inadequate, with item–translation correlations approaching zero (John et al., 1984). This finding suggests that poor translation quality, undetected in monolingual investigations, can result in severe underestimations of cross-language generality. Nonetheless, when a 16-adjective scale was used for each of the Big Five in English and German, the cross-language correlations ranged from .84 for Factor III to .72 for Factor V. The dictionary-based German taxonomy project is well underway (Angleitner, Ostendorf, & John, 1990), and initial analyses of a representative set of about 450 trait adjectives have yielded the clearest replication of the Big Five so far (Angleitner & Ostendorf, 1989).

Because past research has focused almost exclusively on trait adjectives, the Dutch team has now begun to extend its taxonomic analyses to other types of personality descriptors, including personality verbs, such as "swindle," "love," "provoke," and "hesitate" (De Raad et al., 1988), and personality nouns, such as "nerd," "creep," and "joker." These analyses may provide a further test of the generality of the Big Five, examining whether the structures derived from trait adjectives generalize to other types of descriptors and whether there are additional dimensions unique to each type.

Extensions to non-Germanic languages and to cultures different from the industrialized West are just beginning to appear. In studies of interpersonal traits, White (1980) found overall similarities to Factors I and II for the A'ara (Solomon Islands) and Orissa (India) languages. Bond and his collaborators (Bond, 1979, 1983; Bond & Forgas, 1984; Bond, Nakazato, & Shiraishi, 1975; Nakazato, Bond, & Shiraishi, 1976) used translations of Norman's (1963) 20 variables and compared the factor structures of Hong Kong and Japanese samples with previous analyses of U.S. and Filipino (Guthrie & Bennett, 1971) data. Whereas the Japanese, Chinese, and U.S. data showed a notable degree of congruence, the Filipino data did not.

The latter finding is inconsistent with a recent and extensive study of Filipino samples, which provided support for the hypothesis of lexical universality (Church & Katigbak, 1989). These findings are more compelling than those based on the Guthrie and Bennett (1971) data, because Church and Katigbak (1989) used an "emic" (culture-specific) strategy in sampling descriptors in both languages, rather than simply translating descriptors from the Western language to the non-Western language under study. Given that Church and Katigbak (1989) had subjects generate behavioral exemplars, rather than providing established Big Five marker scales, their study provides the best evidence so far for the comprehensiveness and relevance of the Big Five in a non-Western culture. As the authors caution, however, "this does not mean that there are no unique concepts in either language. However, at a higher level of generality, similar structural dimensions emerge" (Church & Katigbak, 1989, p. 868).

In summary, the cross-language research suggests that the Big Five can be replicated very clearly in Germanic languages. The evidence for non-Western languages and cultures is more sparse, although it is encouraging; Factor V generally shows the weakest replicability. Nonetheless, conclusions about the linguistic, or even cultural, universality of the Big Five (Goldberg, 1981) would be premature.

TOWARD A CONSENSUAL DESCRIPTION OF THE BIG FIVE

After a period of dormancy during the 1970s, interest in the Big Five (and in issues of personality structure more generally) has been on the rise again. Nonetheless, the Big Five structure has not been generally accepted as a taxonomic superstructure in the field of personality (e.g., Briggs, 1989; Waller & Ben-Porath, 1987). One problem, it seems, is the perception that there is no *single* Big Five; this perception is evident in questions such as "*which* Big Five?" or "*whose* Big Five?" A quick perusal of Table 3.1 shows the variation in factor names chosen by different investigators. Indeed, to some psychologists, the columns in Table 3.1 may look like bedlam. The third factor, for example, has variously been interpreted as Conscientiousness, Dependability, Conformity, Prudence, Task Interest, and Will to Achieve. Factor V has been labeled Culture, Intellect, and Openness to Experience. It may appear as if each group of investigators has its own Big Five.

Some variation from study to study is, of course, to be expected with dimensions as broad and inclusive as the Big Five. Differences in factor solutions are likely to arise when researchers differ in the variables they include, thus representing different parts of a factor's total range of meaning. Moreover, researchers differ in their preferences for factor labels even when the factor patterns are quite similar. Consequently, there may be more commonality here than meets the eye. The fact that the labels differ does not necessarily mean that the factors are different, too.

In a research project currently underway, I have used a rather simple procedure to demonstrate that the five factors actually share a common set of features across studies (John, 1989a). Fuzzy and partially overlapping definitions, such as those implied by the labels in Table 3.1, are typical of natural categories (Rosch, 1978). However, such fuzzy categories can still be useful if they can be defined by their prototypical exemplars. Similarly, the Big Five may be defined with prototypical exemplars that occur consistently across studies. One way to integrate the various interpretations of the factors is to conceptually map the five dimensions into a common language.

In my application of such a prototype approach, I used the attributes included in the Adjective Check List (ACL; Gough & Heilbrun, 1965, 1983), an instrument developed prior to the discovery of the Big Five. In principle, the procedures I have used are similar to the approach taken by Jack Block in the studies that formed the basis for his book *Lives through Time* (Block, 1971). In that study, documents available about each child differed dramatically across both subjects and time. To integrate the vast amount of diverse information, Block used human judges as transducers, providing them with a standard descriptive language—in that case, the California Q-Sort. In the present case, I had available the findings from a large and varied set of factor-analytic investigations, each using somewhat different sets of variables, analytic procedures, and factor interpretations. To abstract what is common to this set of findings, human judges served as transducers, employing as the standard language the 300 terms included in the ACL.[2]

Conceptually Derived Prototype Descriptions of the Big Five

As the first step in my analysis of the Big Five, 10 judges reviewed the factor solutions and interpretations of the most important articles listed in Table 3.1, in order to form an understanding of the five dimensions. The judges then independently sorted each of the 300 items in the ACL into one of the Big Five domains or, if that was not possible, into a sixth category. Interjudge agreement was substantial; the coefficient alpha reliability of the judgments aggregated across the 10 raters ranged from .90 for Factor IV to .94 for Factor V, suggesting that the raters had formed a consensually shared understanding of the five dimensions.

Of the 300 ACL terms, 76 were assigned to one of the Big Five with perfect agreement, and another 36 were so classified by at least 90% of the judges. These 112 terms, presented in Table 3.2, form a relatively narrow, or "core," definition of the five factors, because agree-

ment should be lower for traits that are more peripheral to the meaning of the factors and are found less consistently in studies of the Big Five. The initial prototypes given in Table 3.2 are not based on a factor analysis of empirical data, but on judgments informed by a large set of factor-analytic findings. The terms in Table 3.2 should thus capture the definers of the Big Five dimensions appearing most consistently across numerous and diverse studies, and should provide a description of the Big Five independent of the vagaries of the particular (and usually small) sets of variables included in any one of the past studies.

Nonetheless, as with any rationally constructed measure, the validity of these categorizations must be demonstrated empirically. Therefore, the results from a preliminary analysis of the 112 terms are included in Table 3.2. If the initial prototypes adequately capture the composition of the Big Five, the 112 terms should clearly define five factors and should load on their respective factors. Because most of the past research on the Big Five has relied on personality ratings made by peers and by subjects themselves, it was decided to explore the degree to which the Big Five can also capture the personality formulations achieved by psychologists on the basis of intensive observations and interviews.

Initial Validation of the Prototypes in Observer Data

The ACL had been initially developed at the Institute of Personality Assessment and Research (IPAR) in Berkeley as a procedure for recording the personality evaluations by staff members of individuals examined in assessment programs (Gough & Heilbrun, 1983, p. 1). For the present analyses, I used a sample of 140 men and 140 women who had participated in groups of 10–15 in one of the IPAR assessment weekends (John, 1989b). Because each subject had been described on the ACL by 10 staff members, a factor analysis using these aggregated observer judgments could be performed. The varimax rotated factor loadings, shown in Table 3.2 for each adjective for its hypothesized factor, provide a compelling confirmation of the initial prototypes. With only one exception, each item loaded on its hypothesized factor in the expected direction; in addition, for 98 of the 112 items the highest loading was also

TABLE 3.2. Initial and Validated Big Five Prototypes: Consensually Selected ACL Marker Items and Their Factor Loadings in Personality Descriptions Obtained from 10 Psychologists Serving as Observers

Factor I		Factor II		Factor III	
Low	High	Low	High	Low	High
−.83 Quiet	.85 Talkative	−.52 Fault-finding	.87 Sympathetic	−.58 Careless	.80 Organized
−.80 Reserved	.83 Assertive	−.48 Cold	.85 Kind	−.53 Disorderly	.80 Thorough
−.75 Shy	.82 Active	−.45 Unfriendly	.85 Appreciative	−.50 Frivolous	.78 Planful
−.71 Silent	.82 Energetic	−.45 Quarrelsome	.84 Affectionate	−.49 Irresponsible	.78 Efficient
−.67 Withdrawn	.82 Outgoing	−.45 Hard-hearted	.84 Soft-hearted	−.40 Slipshod	.73 Responsible
−.66 Retiring	.80 Outspoken	−.38 Unkind	.82 Warm	−.39 Undependable	.72 Reliable
	.79 Dominant	−.33 Cruel	.81 Generous	−.37 Forgetful	.70 Dependable
	.73 Forceful	−.31 Stern[a]	.78 Trusting		.68 Conscientious
	.73 Enthusiastic	−.28 Thankless	.77 Helpful		.66 Precise
	.68 Show-off	−.24 Stingy[a]	.77 Forgiving		.66 Practical
	.68 Sociable		.74 Pleasant		.65 Deliberate
	.64 Spunky		.73 Good-natured		.46 Painstaking
	.64 Adventurous		.73 Friendly		.26 Cautious[a]
	.62 Noisy		.72 Cooperative		
	.58 Bossy		.67 Gentle		
			.66 Unselfish		
			.56 Praising		
			.51 Sensitive		

Factor IV		Factor V	
Low	High	Low	High
.73 Tense	.39 Stable[a]	−.74 Commonplace	.76 Wide interests
.72 Anxious	.35 Calm[a]	−.73 Narrow interests	.76 Imaginative
.72 Nervous	.21 Contented[a]	−.67 Simple	.72 Intelligent
.71 Moody	−.14 Unemotional[a]	−.55 Shallow	.73 Original
.71 Worrying		−.47 Unintelligent	.68 Insightful
.68 Touchy			.64 Curious
.64 Fearful			.59 Sophisticated
.63 High-strung			.59 Artistic
.63 Self-pitying			.59 Clever
.60 Temperamental			.58 Inventive
.59 Unstable			.56 Sharp-witted
.58 Self-punishing			.55 Ingenious
.54 Despondent			.45 Witty[a]
.51 Emotional			.45 Resourceful[a]
			.37 Wise
			.33 Logical[a]
			.29 Civilized[a]
			.22 Foresighted[a]
			.21 Polished[a]
			.20 Dignified[a]

Note. These 112 items were selected as initial prototypes for the Big Five because they were assigned to one factor by at least 90% of the judges (John, 1989a). The factor loadings, shown for the hypothesized factor, were based on a sample of 140 males and 140 females, each of whom had been described by 10 psychologists serving as observers during an assessment weekend at the Institute of Personality Assessment and Research at the University of California at Berkeley (see John, 1989b).
[a]Potentially misclassified items (i.e., loading more highly on a factor different from the one hypothesized in the original prototype definition).

on that factor, and most of the loadings were substantial.

Nonetheless, there were a few noteworthy deviations from the hypothesized structure (these are footnoted in Table 3.2), particularly for Factor V. First, most of the items referring to Culture (i.e., civilized, polished, dignified, foresighted, and logical) loaded more highly on Factor III (Conscientiousness) than on Factor V. These findings add to the growing body of evidence that characteristics related to Culture form only a minor part of Factor V (Peabody & Goldberg, 1989) and are often aligned more closely with Conscientiousness (McCrae & Costa, 1987; Goldberg, 1989). Moreover, two items (witty and resourceful) had slightly higher loadings on Factor I than on Factor V, suggesting that psychologists view these characteristics as involving both surgent and intellective aspects. In general, however, the items defining the fifth factor include both the "open" characteristics (e.g., imaginative, curious, artistic) highlighted by McCrae and Costa (1985a, 1985b) and the "intellectual" characteristics (intelligent, insightful, sophisticated) emphasized by Digman and Inouye (1981) and Peabody and Goldberg (1989); these findings suggest that this factor should no longer be interpreted as Culture, but instead as a broader concept defined jointly by Openness to Experience and Intellect. The other factors closely resemble those found in several of the earlier major studies, with the possible exception that in these data the Emotional Stability pole of Factor IV is represented only weakly.

The items defining each of the factors cover a broad range of content. For example, Factor I includes traits such as "active," "adventurous," "assertive," "dominant," "energetic," "enthusiastic," "outgoing," "sociable," and "show-off." In light of the enormous breadth of the five factors, the heterogeneity of the labels in Table 3.1 is more easily understood. Different investigators have focused on different components or facets of the total range of meaning subsumed by each factor. For example, the first factor seems to consist of at least five distinguishable components: Activity level (active, energetic), Dominance (assertive, bossy, forceful), Sociability (outgoing, sociable, talkative), Expressive Undercontrol (adventurous, outspoken, noisy, show-off), and Positive Emotionality (enthusiastic, spunky).

These five components are similar to five of the six facets Costa and McCrae (1985, 1989)

have included in their NEO Personality Inventory definition of the Extraversion domain—Activity, Assertiveness, Gregariousness, Excitement-Seeking, and Positive Emotions. Their sixth facet, Warmth, is here considered a component of Factor II; all 10 judges interpreted the past research to imply that Warmth is part of Agreeableness, and the loading of .82 confirms this interpretation of the literature. In addition to Warmth (affectionate, appreciative, gentle, warm), Factor II covers themes such as Sympathy (kind, sensitive, soft-hearted, sympathetic), Giving and Helping (cooperative, forgiving, helping, praising), and Trust, as contrasted with Hostility, Criticality, and Coldness.

More finely grained analyses, both rational and empirical, of the prototypes are needed to clarify and refine these initial groupings. Ultimately, the resulting components or facets may serve as a framework for establishing the similarities and differences among the alternative conceptions of the Big Five dimensions assembled in Table 3.1. Comparative analyses of this sort may also help uncover conceptual similarities between the Big Five and structural models of personality that have originated in different theoretical contexts and through different empirical procedures. In the following section, the prototypes presented in Table 3.2 are used to compare the Big Five to some of the major dimensions postulated within other models of personality structure. The results of these comparisons are summarized in Table 3.4, later in the chapter.

THE BIG FIVE AND OTHER STRUCTURAL MODELS

Item Pools Generated by Clinical Experts

The lexical approach is not the only route to obtaining a comprehensive and systematic set of personality descriptors. There seem to be two major alternatives. One frequently used alternative has been to accumulate large numbers of personality questionnaire items and to construct scales from these item pools—for example, by factor analysis or criterion-group comparisons. The other alternative is to capitalize on clinical expertise and ask experts to supply statements and descriptive phrases they have found particularly useful for personality description (e.g., Block, 1961). The resulting preliminary sample of descriptors can then be tried out in descriptions of large samples of individuals. Analyses of these descriptions may help identify redundant concepts that can be eliminated, as well as point to concepts that are still missing and need to be added.

Some Interesting Beginnings

One such list, the Minnesota–Ford Pool of Phenotypic Personality Items, was constructed in a project at the University of Minnesota under the direction of Paul Meehl (1962). This list of personality traits was compiled "as a pool of items to be used by diagnosticians and psychotherapists in describing their patients" and was intended as "practically exhaustive of personality traits in the phenotypic domain" (Meehl, 1962, p. 1). The items, initially culled from existing item pools, books, and other sources, were subjected to several rounds of screening, editing, and eliminating redundant elements. The exclusion criteria for eliminating items were quite similar to the procedures used by Norman (1967), including ambiguity and unfamiliarity of the descriptors, infrequency in the population, state descriptors, purely evaluative and excessively broad descriptors, and so on. The resulting pool of 1,808 items was further reduced to the final set of 329 descriptors rated by a group of psychotherapists as judicable "with an actual patient in mind." This pool was sorted into 13 major categories, such as Avocational Interests, Attitudes, Mood and Temperament, Manifest Interpersonal Patterns, Ethical Behavior, Self-Concept, and Ego Organization and Character Structure. Among the manifest interpersonal patterns, numerous traits were delineated into subcategories, including Dominance, Aggression, Affiliation, Giving and Taking, Conformity, Social Fear, and Spontaneity and Control.

Both in the procedures used and in the content categories postulated, this clinically oriented project is remarkably similar to the lexical taxonomies reviewed earlier. Unfortunately, however, the Minnesota–Ford project never advanced much closer than this to completion. Nonetheless, the unpublished catalog listing the category system and the descriptors included in them could prove to be of considerable value by permitting a replication of the lexical work in a set of descriptors assembled from a uniquely different set of sources.

An even earlier project, also largely uncompleted, has resulted in a list of 84 content categories representing a total of almost 2,000 self-report items. After a brief description of this project, Gough (in press) concluded:

> From the observational side, considerable evidence now exists that something on the order of five or six major variables may be specified . . . but additional study is still warranted to see if the list of major self-report dimensions can be extended. Large, diversified, and heterogeneous item pools such as that created for the PAR (Participation, Awareness, and Responsibility) project provide a good basis for carrying out such inquiry.

Block's California Q-Sort

Whereas the Minnesota–Ford and the PAR lists were never published, Block's (1961) 100-item California Q-Sort, developed according to clinical principles and in an iterative fashion, has been widely used. Block (1961) sought to devise a generally applicable, clinically based language for describing all important aspects of personality. The California Q-Sort was constructed primarily for use by psychologists to record observations and clinical impressions of participants in assessments and longitudinal studies (e.g., Block, 1971; Gough, 1987; Helson, 1967). Given its rather different origin, Block's set of variables would seem ideal for testing the generalizability of the Big Five. A factor analysis of self-reports obtained with the California Q-Sort suggested that the Big Five can be recaptured from this item set (McCrae, Costa, & Busch, 1986). However, analyses of the factor structure of the Q-Sort when employed by psychologists, clinicians, or other observers still remain to be done.

Moreover, no attempts have been made to relate the Big Five to Block's two major dimensions of ego functioning, Ego Resiliency and Ego Control (e.g., Block & Block, 1980), concepts central to the Development of the Q-Sort item set. However, Q-Sort-based criterion definitions of the prototypical ego-resilient and the prototypical ego-undercontrolling individual are now available and have been used, for example, by Funder and Block (1989) to study the nature and meaning of individual differences in delay of gratification.

According to these prototype definitions, ego-resilient individuals are calm and relaxed, are socially at ease, are able to see to the heart of important problems, and have insight into their own motives, whereas brittle individuals are self-defeating, are basically anxious, are uncomfortable with uncertainty, and feel a lack of personal meaning in life. In other words, ego-resilient individuals have the emotional and intellectual resources to engage the world effectively and to control anxiety; this suggests that Ego Resiliency should be associated most closely with Factor IV (e.g., as defined in Table 3.2, not anxious, not self-punishing, not despondent) and Factor V (e.g., wide interests, insightful, resourceful). On the other hand, Ego Control has been defined as the tendency to contain rather than express emotional and motivational impulses (Block & Block, 1980), as evident when *Q*-Sort descriptions such as "genuinely dependable," "fastidious," "uncomfortable with complexity," "prides self on being objective and rational," and "emotionally bland" are contrasted with "unable to delay gratification," "rapid personal tempo," "facial and gestural expressiveness," "rebellious and nonconforming," "unpredictable," and "direct expression of hostile feelings." In terms of the Big Five, high (vs. low) Ego Control should be positively related to Factor III (e.g., dependable, thorough, practical) and negatively to Factor I (e.g., active, adventurous, noisy, not reserved). That is, according to the *Q*-Sort items that characterize the prototypes, observers would probably see overcontrolling individuals as conscientious and introverted, and undercontrolling individuals as surgent (or extraverted) and lacking in conscientiousness.

The predicted relations between Ego Control and two of the Big Five dimensions suggests that dynamic person variables (such as Ego Control) may be manifested in rather distinct surface characteristics, depending on the behavioral domain and context. More specifically, undercontrol should be seen as expressive, energetic, and outgoing (i.e., high Surgency) in informal, social contexts, but as careless, frivolous, and undependable (low Conscientiousness) in more formal, task-oriented settings. Conversely, Block and Block (1980) have pointed out that a generalized tendency toward overcontrol can lead both to needless foregoing of pleasure in leisure settings *and* to adaptive self-control in work settings. The Big Five and the constructs of Ego Control and Ego Resiliency thus seem to operate at different levels of description: Whereas the Blocks have postulated regulatory processes within the individual that may lead to characteristic behavioral results in different contexts, the Big Five dimensions seem to describe individual differences in these behavioral "results" without directly specifying the nature of the underlying regulatory processes. These connections between theoretically postulated constructs and the empirically derived Big Five dimensions may eventually lead the way to a theoretical explication of the five dimensions resulting from the lexical approach.

Personality Dimensions Measured by Questionnaire

The work of many personality researchers, particularly those using factor analysis, has been aligned closely with the construction of self-report questionnaire instruments. The approach used to construct these questionnaire scales appears similar to the lexical approach, in that some sort of structural analysis (e.g., factor analysis, internal consistency, comparison groups) is applied to selected verbal stimuli to construct scales by grouping items from the pool administered to the subjects. In this kind of procedure, one crucial determinant of the results is the selection of the stimulus items (Peabody, 1987; Peabody & Goldberg, 1989). Therein lies the difference from the lexical approach: The stimuli being factored are questionnaire items, usually in sentence form, rather than trait-descriptive adjectives. The need for sentences, rather than single-word descriptors, raises further questions about the origin and nature of the items included in the analyses.

In practice, little attention is paid to the actual items (Angleitner, John, & Loehr, 1986). The number of personality-descriptive sentences is infinite, and it is hard if not impossible to define or describe them abstractly. Indeed, the specification of a comprehensive universe of personality-descriptive sentences has been much more complicated and much less systematic than the lexical procedures described earlier in this chapter (Angleitner et al., 1986). As a result, every questionnaire measures a somewhat different subset of dimensions (see Goldberg, 1971), and the field has separated into camps, with each camp adhering to a set of dimensions different in number, nature, and name.

Joint factor analyses of questionnaire scales from different inventories tended to yield two major dimensions, Extraversion and Neuroticism; however, despite the general and widely ranging correlates of these two dimensions, it is hard to believe that anyone would seriously believe that a two-factor model is sufficient. Besides the agreement on the two "secondary" factors of Extraversion and Neuroticism, questionnaire-based research has not made much progress toward a unified taxonomy of personality constructs. Given this continued state of confusion, convergences between questionnaire-based dimensions and the Big Five would be particularly useful but cannot be taken for granted.

Extraversion, Neuroticism, and Psychoticism

Several models of personality structure view traits as biologically based and temperamental dimensions of individual differences. H. J. Eysenck (e.g., 1967, 1986; see also Chapter 10,

this volume) has proposed three broad factors—Extraversion, Neuroticism, and Psychoticism—which he views as a sufficient model (or "paradigm") of personality. These factors were initially derived from exploratory factor analyses of responses to questionnaire items (e.g., Eysenck, 1944). Subsequently, Eysenck (see, e.g., 1986 for a review) has postulated various psychophysiological processes assumed to give rise to these individual differences and has examined the associations between his personality factors and a multitude of laboratory test measures.

The facets of the factors have been explicated most recently by Eysenck (1986, pp. 214–215; see also Eysenck & Eysenck, 1985, pp. 14–15). As shown in Table 3.3, each factor is defined in terms of nine subordinate traits.[3] For example, Extraversion is defined by descriptors such as active, assertive, venturesome, lively, and sociable. The subordinate

TABLE 3.3. Adjective Definers for the Personality Factors in Eysenck's and Tellegen's Three-Dimensional Systems

Eysenck (1986)

Extraversion	Neuroticism	Psychoticism
Active	Anxious	Aggressive
Assertive	Depressed	Antisocial
Carefree	Emotional	Cold
Dominant	Guilt feelings	Egocentric
Lively	Irrational	Impersonal
Sensation-seeking	Low self-esteem	Tough-minded
Sociable	Moody	Unempathic
Surgent	Shy	Creative
Venturesome	Tense	Impulsive

Tellegen (1982)

Positive Affect[a]	Negative Affect[a]	Constraint[b]
Alert	Afraid	Careful
Active	Ashamed	Cautious
Attentive	Distressed	Plodding
Determined	Guilty	Rational
Enthusiastic	Hostile	Reflective
Excited	Irritable	Sensible
Inspired	Jittery	Not careless
Interested	Nervous	Not impulsive
Proud	Scared	Not spontaneous
Strong	Upset	Not reckless

[a]From Watson, Clark, and Tellegen's (1988) scales for Positive and Negative Mood.
[b]Adjective definers were not available for Tellegen's (1982) Constraint factor; the adjectives listed here were taken from Tellegen's (1982, Table 2) description of the one scale with the highest loading on the Constraint factor, Control.

traits listed for Neuroticism include: anxious, depressed, emotional, tense, and moody. These definitions could hardly be more similar to the prototype definitions of Factors I+ and IV− given in Table 3.2. Eysenck's definers of Psychoticism are somewhat less consistent with any one of the Big Five dimensions, but share the greatest overlap with the low pole of Factor II. Seven of the nine definers (cold, antisocial, egocentric, unempathic, impersonal, tough-minded, and aggressive) are related to the antagonistic pole of Agreeableness. The remaining two definers, however, belong to other factors in the Big Five structure. Specifically, "creative" is central to the expressive-intellect component of Factor V, whereas the multi-faceted trait "impulsive" points to insufficient self-control, a characteristic typically associated with the low pole of Factor III (Conscientiousness).

In sum, this analysis suggests that Eysenck's Extraversion corresponds to Factor I and that Eysenck's Neuroticism is the polar opposite of Factor IV (Emotional Stability). Psychoticism should be related strongly and negatively to Agreeableness, moderately negatively to Conscientiousness, and (given the inclusion of creativity) moderately positively to measures of Openness to Experience. These predictions are borne out by the available data only in part (e.g., Borkenau & Ostendorf, 1989; McCrae & Costa, 1985c; Zuckerman, Kuhlman, & Camac, 1988). As anticipated, the correlations between measures of Extraversion and Factor I, and between measures of Neuroticism and Factor IV, tend to be so high that for all practical purposes, these concepts may be considered equivalent. For Psychoticism, however, the picture is more complex: Eysenck's Psychoticism scale correlated negatively and significantly with both Agreeableness and Conscientiousness, but not with Openness to Experience (McCrae & Costa, 1985c). Moreover, the correlations were moderate in size, suggesting that Agreeableness and Conscientiousness are not "primary" factors that combine into a broader, superordinate factor of Psychoticism. Moreover, the lack of correlation between Psychoticism and Openness to Experience (which has been shown to predict various measures of creativity, including objective tests and peer ratings) calls into question the inclusion of creativity within the conceptual definition of Psychoticism. These findings indicate the need to examine more closely the coherence and

meaning of the Psychoticism factor, which, as Eysenck (e.g., 1986, p. 106) readily admits, is not as replicable and well understood as are Extraversion and Neuroticism.

Four Constitutionally Based Dimensions of Temperament

Although Eysenck (e.g., 1967) assumes his dimensions to have a genetic and biological basis, the distinction between personality and temperament traits is not central to his work. Buss and Plomin (1975), by contrast, have developed a taxonomy designed to account exclusively for traits denoting individual differences in temperament. Temperament traits, according to their view, are constitutionally based—those traits that show a high degree of heritability, appear early in development (e.g., can be detected in parent ratings of very young children), and continue to be important throughout the individual's life span. Using these criteria, Buss and Plomin (1975) identified four dimensions—Emotionality, Activity, Sociability, and Impulsivity—which they considered the clearest examples of constitutionally based traits.[4]

For each of these four dimensions, Buss and Plomin (1975) developed questionnaire scales, each consisting of several subscales. For example, Activity was defined by subscales measuring tempo and vigor, Emotionality by scales for fear, anger, and general emotionality. Although Buss and Plomin's temperament scales measure dimensions that are defined less broadly than are the Big Five and Eysenck's personality factors, Activity and Emotionality can easily be matched to Factors I and IV of the Big Five, and to Eysenck's Extraversion and Neuroticism factors, respectively. Finding a direct match is more difficult for Impulsivity because of its multifaceted nature. Depending on its definition, Impulsivity may be related to Extraversion (expressive spontaneity), low Conscientiousness (distractibility), or low Emotional Stability (inability to delay gratification).

This analysis is generally consistent with the findings reported by McCrae and Costa (1985b), who conducted a joint factor analysis of Buss and Plomin's (1975) temperament scales with various other personality scales. As predicted, the Activity and Emotionality scales were related to other measures of Extraversion and low Emotional Stability, respectively. The four Impulsivity subscales, however, did not form a homogeneous set. The Persistence scale loaded positively, and the Quick Decision Time scale loaded negatively, on the Conscientiousness factor. The Poor Impulse Inhibition scale also had a negative loading on the Conscientiousness factor but a larger, positive loading on a Neuroticism factor, suggesting that the inability to resist cravings is a part of low Emotional Stability. The fourth Impulsivity scale, Sensation Seeking, was a definer of the Extraversion factor. Finally, the Sociability scale, which seems to combine the activity feature of Surgency with the warmth feature of Agreeableness, correlated most strongly with Extraversion (Factor I) in McCrae and Costa's (1985b) study. Zuckerman et al. (1988) found that Buss and Plomin's Sociability scale was more strongly associated with measures of affiliation than was the Activity scale, but that both were strongly related to Eysenck's broad Extraversion scale on the Eysenck Personality Questionnaire (EPQ).

In conclusion, then, Buss and Plomin's relatively pure temperamental traits map into three broader personality factors: The active and sociable temperaments are part of Factor I (Extraversion); the highly emotional temperament is part of Factor IV (low Emotional Stability); and several components of the impulsive temperament (low Persistence, quick Decision Time, and to some extent poor Impulse Inhibition) relate to lack of Conscientiousness (Factor III). That leaves two personality factors without a direct analogue among the temperament traits. One interpretation of this finding is that the Agreeableness and Openness to Experience factors summarize less heritable, and later-appearing, individual differences than do the other three factors. However, evidence for the differential heritability of personality characteristics is not well established (e.g., Tellegen et al., 1988), and dimensions related to Agreeableness and Openness to Experience have seldom been studied in behavior–genetic investigations. Thus, future studies may still establish a strong constitutional basis for Factors II and V.

Personality and Individual Differences in Mood

Another limited-domain taxonomy of individual differences has emerged from studies of mood and emotion. Tellegen (e.g., 1985) in particular has emphasized the link between personality and mood, and two of the second-order personality factors he postulates—independent dimensions of Positive Emotionality and Negative Emotionality—have been confirmed in extensive analyses of mood reports. Relatively short and internally consistent measures of these two factors in the domain of moods (referred to as Positive and Negative *Affect*) have recently been constructed (Watson, Clark, & Tellegen, 1988). Because each of these two self-report scales consists of 10 adjectives, the dimensions resulting from the analysis of moods can be compared directly to the personality dimensions represented by the Big Five adjective lists. For this purpose, the adjectives included in the Positive and Negative Mood scales are listed in the bottom half of Table 3.3. Also listed in Table 3.3 are some adjectives related to Tellegen's third personality factor, Constraint. Because the *Brief manual* for Tellegen's (1982) inventory did not include a separate description of the Constraint factor, Table 3.3 lists the 10 adjectives included in the description of the primary scale most closely related to the Constraint factor, namely Control.

Positive and Negative Affect and the Big Five Prototypes. Not surprisingly, only a few terms were identical across the adjective definers of the two Affect dimensions (Table 3.3) and the Big Five personality dimensions (Table 3.2). The affect terms are, with few exceptions, descriptors of temporary states (e.g., determined, afraid), whereas the Big Five terms from the ACL are descriptors of stable traits (e.g., assertive, fearful). However, if the state–trait distinction (see Chaplin et al., 1988) is set aside for a moment, the 10 Positive Affect descriptors in the Watson et al. list (e.g., enthusiastic, strong, determined, active, proud) would be indistinguishable from the terms marking the high pole of Surgency (e.g., enthusiastic, forceful, assertive, active, showoff). Similarly, the 10 Negative Affect descriptors (e.g., afraid, distressed, irritable, nervous, upset) would be indistinguishable from the traits representing low Emotional Stability (e.g., anxious, despondent, temperamental, nervous, worrying). Thus, the different factor labels notwithstanding, the degree of congruence between the affect factors and two of the Big Five factors is striking.

However, in addition to Surgency/ Extraversion and low Emotional Stability, Agreeableness is a third factor in the Big Five representation closely related to mood and affect, as suggested by adjective definers such as "affectionate," "gentle," "sympathetic," "warm," and "loving." As shown in Table 3.3, such *interpersonal* affects do not appear on Watson et al.'s (1988) list of affective states. Although these affects are clearly *positive* in nature, none of them apparently survived the item selection process employed in constructing the Positive Affect scale. Instead, the Positive Affect scale includes several relatively neutral states, such as "active," "alert," "interested," and "strong."[5]

Tellegen's Multidimensional Personality Questionnaire Compared to the Big Five. Over the past 15 years, Tellegen (e.g., 1982) has developed and refined a questionnaire, now called the Multidimensional Personality Questionnaire (MPQ). This inventory measures three higher-order traits as well as 11 more specific, "primary" personality dimensions. Positive Emotionality is defined by the primary scales Well-Being, Social Potency, Achievement, and Social Closeness; as Tellegen et al. (1988, p. 1033) noted, these "clear 'extraverted' features" resemble Factor I in the Big Five. Negative Emotionality, defined primarily by the Stress Reaction, Alienation, and Aggression scales, closely resembles the low Emotional Stability pole of Factor IV.

The third broad MPQ factor, Constraint, is marked by the Control, Harm Avoidance, and Traditionalism scales. The adjectives listed in Table 3.3, taken from the description of the Control scale, show that the Constraint factor shares central features with Factor III (Conscientiousness), including caution, deliberation, attention to detail, and appropriate impulse control, as contrasted with impulsiveness and distractibility. Fourth, Tellegen's MPQ includes a measure of Absorption, a concept originally developed by Tellegen and Atkinson (1974) via factor analyses of several homogeneous subscales. In its initial conception, Absorption was considered a broad personality factor combining attributes such as Reality Absorption, Fantasy Absorption, Dissociation, Devotion–Trust, Autonomy–Criticality, and Openness to Experience. This factor obviously overlaps with McCrae and Costa's (1985b) measure of Factor V, Openness to Experience, especially with its facets Openness to Fantasy, Openness to Ideas, and Openness to Aesthetics. Indeed, McCrae and Costa

(1985b) found that in both self-reports and spouse ratings, the correlation between NEO Personality Inventory Openness and the MPQ Absorption scale exceeded .50.

The alignment of the MPQ Positive Emotionality scale with Factor I in the Big Five would leave Factor II, Agreeableness, without a direct counterpart in Tellegen's system. However, the Social Closeness scale on the MPQ is described by characteristics such as "is warm and affectionate," "takes pleasure in, and values, close interpersonal ties," and "turns to others for comfort and help" (Tellegen, 1982, Table 2). These characteristics are central features of Agreeableness as shown by the definers listed in Table 3.2. Moreover, whereas Well-Being, Social Potency, and Achievement each correlate above .65 with the Positive Emotionality score, the correlation for Social Closeness hovers around .30. Apparently, the Social Closeness scale includes positive emotions of interpersonal origin and direction similar to Agreeableness and is distinguishable from the other markers of Positive Emotionality. Indeed, Tellegen et al. (1988) recently noted that, when four MPQ factors are retained, "Positive Emotionality essentially is split into *Agentic* Positive Emotionality and *Communal* Positive Emotionality, with Achievement being the salient marker of the former and Social Closeness of the latter" (p. 1037; emphasis added).

These considerations would seem to suggest that in the personality domain, Positive Emotionality consists of two distinct domains of individual differences, Surgency (agentic or instrumental positive emotionality) and Agreeableness (communal positive emotionality). Does this "bifurcation" of Positive Emotionality occur in the mood domain as well? That is, would positive interpersonal affects, such as love, sympathy, and affection, if included in the initial item pool, form a separate factor? Or would they be subsumed under the Positive Affect factor as defined by Watson et al. (1988)? Gotlib and Meyer (1986) identified two factors in an affect list including items related to the "communal" component of Positive Emotionality (e.g., loving, sympathetic, cooperative); however, because they did not compare this two-dimensional structure with a three-dimensional one, their findings—while consistent with the two-dimensional view—do not resolve the issue conclusively. Nonetheless, the available evidence suggests a substantive divergence between the mood and personality domains, with the latter appearing more complex than the former.

In conclusion, a four-dimensional representation of Tellegen's MPQ scales (with Absorption as a potential fifth factor) would be in close correspondence with the traditional Big Five structure. However, that representation implies a two-dimensional conception of Positive Emotionality and thus three dimensions related to Emotionality, thus sacrificing the theoretical elegance and integrative power achieved by the two-dimensional conception of Emotionality as positive and negative.

Dimensions in Broad-Band Personality Inventories

A seemingly infinite supply of personality dimensions comes from the ever-increasing number of commercially available questionnaires and inventories. Some of these inventories were constructed from a particular theoretical perspective, such as Murray's "needs" (e.g., the Personality Research Form; Jackson, 1984) or Jungian typology (e.g., the Myers–Briggs Type Indicator; Myers & McCaulley, 1985), whereas others were constructed from a more eclectic or pragmatic perspective, such as the recently revised California Psychological Inventory (CPI; Gough, 1987), Guilford's various questionnaires (Guilford, 1974, 1975), and the 16 PF (Cattell et al., 1970).

For the present review, I examined the test items and the primary scales included in the superordinate dimensions measured by each instrument. For example, Cattell et al. (1970) reported eight "secondary" factors, derived from factoring the intercorrelations among the 16 primary factors measured on the 16 PF. If we consider the loadings replicated across the sexes, three of these eight presumably broad factors had loadings from only one scale each; one represents the objective measure of intelligence included on the 16 PF (scale B), whereas the other two represent scale N (astute, polished) and scale I (tender-minded), respectively. The other five factors are similar to the familiar Big Five: (I) The factor labeled Exvia versus Invia by Cattell consists of the scales measuring "happy-go-lucky," "venturesome," "resourceful," "outgoing–warmhearted," and "assertive"; (II) Pathemia versus Cortertia measures "tender-minded" and "outgoing–warmhearted"; (III) Superego

Strength measures "conscientious," "controlled," and "not happy-go-lucky"; (IV) Adjustment versus Anxiety measures "emotionally stable," "not frustrated," "not insecure," "not suspicious," and "controlled"; and finally (V) Independence versus Subduedness measures "radical," "imaginative–Bohemian," "assertive," and "resourceful." Interestingly, the cluster of scales representing the Independence factor served as the starting point for the development of McCrae and Costa's (1985b) concept of Openness to Experience, and foreshadowed the importance of independence of judgment, progressive attitudes, and mental experiences such as imagination in that construct.

Whereas these conceptual analyses provide grounds for initial hypotheses, a series of recent studies (e.g., Borkenau & Ostendorf, 1989; Costa & McCrae, 1988; McCrae, 1989; McCrae & Costa, 1989a; Noller, Law, & Comrey, 1987) have provided empirical evidence for the congruence of questionnaire-based measures of personality and the Big Five. For example, Noller et al.'s (1987) joint factor analysis of the 16 PF, the Eysenck Personality Inventory (EPI), and Comrey's (1970) Personality Scales confirmed only the five Cattell secondaries described above and placed the Eysenck and Comrey scales on the appropriate factors. The congruences resulting from my conceptual analyses and from these empirical studies are summarized for all the questionnaires in Table 3.4. In the following section, only one of the broad-band questionnaires, and its relation to the Big Five, can be discussed.

The CPI, designed to study effectiveness in interpersonal functioning (Gough, 1987), is one of the most frequently used personality questionnaires. The 1987 revision of the CPI has 20 scales designed to reflect universal folk concepts of personality, covering three major themes: (1) externality, assessed by such scales as Dominance, Capacity for Status, Sociability, and Independence; (2) normative regulation of impulse, assessed by scales such as Responsibility, Socialization, Self-Control, Good Impression, and Achievement via Conformance; and (3) effective intellectual and social functioning, assessed by scales such as Intellectual Efficiency, Achievement via Independence, Tolerance, and Flexibility. Broadly conceived "structural" scales, referred to as "vectors," have been constructed to assess each of these three themes independently.

TABLE 3.4. The Big Five and Dimensions of Similar Breadth in Questionnaires and in Models of Personality and Interpersonal Behavior

Theorist(s)	Surgency (I)	Agreeableness (II)	Conscientiousness (III)	Emotional Stability (IV)	Intellect/ Openness to Experience (V)
Bales	Dominant–Initiative	Social–Emotional Orientation	Task Orientation[a]		
Block	Low Ego Control		High Ego Control	Ego Resiliency[b]	
Buss & Plomin	Activity		Impulsivity$_R$	Emotionality$_R$	
Cattell	Exvia (vs. Invia)	Pathemia (vs. Cortertia)	Superego Strength	Adjustment (vs. Anxiety)	Independence (vs. Subduedness)
Comrey scales (Noller et al.)	Extraversion and Activity	Femininity (vs. Masculinity)	Orderliness and Social Conformity	Emotional Stability	Rebelliousness
Eysenck	Extraversion	Psychoticism$_R$[c]		Neuroticism$_R$	
Gough					
CPI Vectors	Externality (vs. Internality)		Norm-Favoring (vs. Norm-Doubting)	Self-Realization[d]	
CPI Factors	Extraversion	Consensuality	Control		Flexibility
Guilford	Social Activity	Paranoid Disposition$_R$	Thinking Introversion	Emotional Stability	
Hogan	Ambition and Sociability	Likeability	Prudence (vs. Impulsivity)	Adjustment	Intellectance
Jackson	Outgoing, Social Leadership	Self-Protective Orientation$_R$	Work Orientation	Dependence$_R$	Aesthetic–Intellectual
Myers-Briggs	Extraversion (vs. Introversion)	Feeling (vs. Thinking)	Judging (vs. Perception)		Intuition (vs. Sensing)
Tellegen	Positive Emotionality Agentive	Communal	Constraint	Negative Emotionality$_R$	Absorption
Wiggins	Dominance	Love			

Note The subscript $_R$ means that a dimension is reverse-scored in the direction *opposite* that of the Big Five label listed in the column head.

[a]This dimension contrasts a work-directed, emotionally neutral orientation with an erratic, emotionally expressive orientation (Bales & Cohen, 1979), and thus seems to combine elements of both Factors III and IV.

[b]Resiliency seems to subsume aspects of both Factors IV and V, because an ego-resilient individual is considered both intellectually resourceful and effective in controlling anxiety (Block & Block, 1980).

[c]High scores on the EPQ Psychoticism scale are associated with low scores on Agreeableness and Conscientiousness (McCrae & Costa, 1985c).

[d]The third vector scale on the new CPI (Gough, 1987) measures levels of psychological integration and realization, and should reflect aspects of both Factor IV (e.g., Well-Being) and Factor V (e.g., Intellectual Efficiency).

The correlations between these vector scales and the primary, folk concept scales (see Gough, 1987) show that the vectors v.1 (Externality vs. Internality) and v.2 (Norm-Favoring vs. Norm-Doubting) share many conceptual features with Factors I and III in the Big Five representation. The third vector scale, Self-Realization, designed to assess the individual's level of effective functioning, is somewhat more difficult to place uniquely within the Big Five space. According to the

manual for the recent revision of the CPI (Gough, 1987), high scorers feel capable, are able to cope with the stresses of life, and are reasonably fulfilled. Low scorers feel they lack resolve, are vulnerable to life's traumas, and are not at all fulfilled (Gough, 1987, p. 20). This description would suggest the high scorer on v.3 to be emotionally stable and secure, the low scorer unstable and neurotic. This interpretation, linking v.3 to Factor IV, is supported by the high correlation between v.3 and the CPI

Well-Being scale; this scale assesses one's sense of good mental and physical health and of optimism about the future, as contrasted with concern about personal and health problems, worry about the future, and wariness of the intentions of others (Gough, 1987).

However, Gough's (1987) conception of v.3 goes far beyond Emotional Stability, as the high correlations between v.3 and scales such as Achievement via Independence. Intellectual efficiency, Psychological-Mindedness, and Tolerance show. Indeed, personality descriptions by observers suggest that high scorers are not only free of neurotic trends and conflicts (as suggested by Factor IV); they also are insightful, are comfortable with complexity, and have a wide range of interests (Gough, 1987)—mental and experiential attributes similar to those found on the fifth factor of the Big Five. An alternative, though generally convergent, summary of the major themes underlying the CPI is afforded by factor analysis of the 20 folk concept scales. The four factors and their interpretation by Gough (1987, pp. 33–34) seem to correspond to four of the Big Five dimensions, as shown in Table 3.4. In summary, notable similarities seem to exist between the Big Five and the CPI at the level of *broad* dimensions, or "themes," whether these themes are assessed by orthogonal factors or by specifically constructed vector scales. These conceptually derived associations now need to be examined empirically.

Personality Dimensions in Interpersonal Behavior

As the preceding sections have shown, components of Agreeableness, such as warmth, love, sympathy, hostility, distrust, and other interpersonal effects, have received little attention in temperament-based accounts of personality stucture. However, this dimension plays a central role in research on interpersonal behavior (e.g., White, 1980). Analyses of interpersonal behavior originated in the theoretical writings of Sullivan (1947), who viewed personality as a hypothetical construct that is inferred from interpersonal situations and that cannot be said to exist independently of such situations.

Dating back to Leary's (1957) interpersonal circle, research on interpersonal characteristics has emphasized two recurrent factors, variously labeled Power, Status, or Dominance, and Love, Affiliation, or Warmth. An excellent review of this research, and of the interpersonal model on which this research is based, can be found in Wiggins (1973), who emphasized the

> *empirical generalizability* of assessment variables conceived within an interpersonal framework. Despite substantial differences in universes of content, populations studied, media of observation, and strategies of test construction, the variables from different interpersonal assessment models have shown remarkable "convergences" of both substance and structure. (p. 475)

Probably the best known, and most refined, of the current taxonomic structures in the domain of interpersonal traits is that developed by Wiggins (1979). As a theoretical framework, Wiggins adopted a circumplex model—a circular arrangement of variables in a two-dimensional space defined by Power (or Dominance) and Love (or Warmth), which seem to be universally applicable to human interactions (White, 1980). Having selected the circumplex as an *a priori* theoretical structure, Wiggins then identified terms whose properties fit the constraints imposed by that structure.

Wiggins (1979) began with those 817 of Goldberg's 1,710 trait adjectives that seemed to refer to interpersonal behaviors ("what people do to each other"). Based on correlational analyses of self-ratings on these traits, the terms were assigned to 16 categories, arranged in the form of a circumplex. Successive refinements of these categories eventually led to 16 scales, each consisting of eight single adjectives. These scales quite closely approximate the postulated circular structure and provide a comprehensive framework that has brought some order and integration to the vast array of models and measures in the domain of interpersonal behavior (Wiggins & Broughton, 1985). The revised Interpersonal Adjective Scales (IAS-R), recently published by Wiggins, Phillips, and Trapnell (1989), measure eight facets of interpersonal behavior. Together, they define two dimensions that show considerable convergence with the Factor I and Factor II prototypes. In particular, traits measuring the Assured–Dominant and Unassured–Submissive facets overlap with those for Factor I, and the Warm–Agreeable and Cold-Hearted facets overlap with Factor II. These correspondences, noted by Wiggins et al. (1989), have also been demonstrated empirically (McCrae & Costa, 1989b).

Whereas most interpersonal theorists have examined only two dimensions, three independent dimensions have been studied by Bales and his colleagues (Bales, 1970; Bales & Cohen, 1979). Bales conducted research on small groups and was therefore interested in broad dimensions useful for the classification of interpersonal behavior and perception. He developed several different assessment instruments, including an on-line behavior-coding scheme, a set of adjective scales to permit the retrospective measurement of interpersonal events, and a questionnaire measuring interpersonal value orientations.

For the present purposes, the adjectival descriptors of his dimensions are most informative. The first dimension, called Dominant–Initiative, contrasts "active," "extraverted," "dominant," "self-confident," and "initiative" with "passive," "introverted," "submissive," and "inhibited," and thus closely matches Factor I in the Big Five framework. The second dimension, Social–Emotional Orientation, contrasts "friendly," "equalitarian," and "informal" with "unfriendly," "negativistic," and "individualistic," suggesting a close association with Factor II, Agreeableness. The third dimension, labeled Task Orientation, contrasts a work-directed, emotionally neutral orientation (task-oriented, problem-solving, analytical) with an erratic, emotionally expressive orientation (emotional, expressive, changeable, erratic), and thus seems to combine elements of both Factors III and IV: The task-oriented person, according to the descriptors used by Bales, is both conscientious and emotionally stable. Thus, the third dimension Bales added to the familiar two of the interpersonal circumplex seems to combine personality characteristics related to the successful completion of work assignments and tasks in groups—namely, high Conscientiousness and low Neuroticism.

Natural Language versus Questionnaires: Summary and Conclusions

The personality dimensions included in Table 3.4, although by no means a complete tabulation, emphasize the diversity of current conceptions of personality. However, they also point to some important convergences. First, almost every one of the theorists includes a dimension akin to Surgency or Extraversion. Although the labels and the exact definitions vary, nobody seems to doubt the fundamental importance of this dimension. The second dimension that is almost universally accepted is Emotional Stability, as contrasted with Neuroticism, Negative Emotionality, and Proneness to Anxiety. Interestingly, however, not all the researchers listed in Table 3.4 include a separate measure for this dimension. This is particularly true of the interpersonal approaches, such as those of Wiggins and Bales as well as the questionnaires primarily aimed at the assessment of basically healthy, well-functioning adults, such as Gough's CPI, the Myers–Briggs Type Indicator, and even Jackson's Personality Research Form. In contrast, all of the temperament-based models include Emotional Stability, usually labeled in the maladjusted, neurotic direction. There is less agreement on a third dimension, which appears in various guises, such as Control, Constraint, Superego Strength, and Work Orientation, as contrasted with Impulsivity, Psychoticism, and Play Orientation. The theme underlying most of these constructs involves the control or moderation of impulses in a normatively and socially appropriate way.

Whereas three broad dimensions have been emphasized by Buss and Plomin, Eysenck, Zuckerman, and other temperament-oriented theorists, the present review summarized in Table 3.4 points to two other broad dimensions of personality that are emphasized by other approaches (i.e., Agreeableness and Openness to Experience). In a comprehensive taxonomy, even at the broadest level, we need a "place" for scales measuring Communal and Feeling Orientation, Altruism, Nurturance, Love Styles, and Social Closeness, as contrasted with Narcissism, Hostility, and Anger Proneness. The existence of these scales, and the cross-cultural work on the interpersonal origin and consequences of personality, stress the need for a broad domain akin to Agreeableness, Warmth, or Love.

Similar arguments apply to the fifth and last factor included in the Big Five. For one, there are the concepts of Creativity, Originality, and Cognitive Complexity, which are measured by numerous questionnaire scales (Barron, 1968; Gough, 1979; Helson, 1967, 1985). Although these concepts are cognitive, or, more appropriately, *mental* in nature, they are clearly different from IQ. Second, limited-domain scales measuring concepts such as Absorption, Fantasy Proneness, Need for Cognition, Private

Self-Consciousness, Independence, and Autonomy would be difficult to subsume under Extraversion, Neuroticism, or Impulse Control. Indeed, the fifth factor is necessary because individual differences in intellectual and ceative functioning underlie artistic interests and performances, inventions and innovations, and even humor. Individual differences in these domains of human behavior and experience cannot be, and fortunately have not been, neglected by personality psychologists.

Finally, the correspondences sketched out in Table 3.4 should be considered with a healthy dose of skepticism. Some of these correspondences may be too broad, ignoring some important, implicative, and useful differences among the concepts proposed by different investigators. Other correspondences, although plausible, are entirely hypothetical and await empirical confirmation. Nonetheless, at this stage of development in the field, I am more impressed by the newly apparent similarities than by the continuing differences among the various models. Indeed, the Big Five are useful primarily because of their integrative and heuristic value, a value that becomes apparent in Tables 3.1 and 3.4. The availability of a taxonomy, even one as broad and incomplete as the Big Five, permits the comparison and potential integration of dimensions that, by their names alone, would seem entirely disparate.

SOME CRITICAL ISSUES

In the preceding sections, I have explored the criticism that the Big Five suffer from an imprecise specification (Briggs, 1989)—that everyone has his or her own version of the Big Five. As a step toward a more precise specification, I have presented prototype descriptions of the five factors, and have used them heuristically to uncover conceptual similarities between the Big Five and other systems of personality description. However, the opposite kind of criticism has also been voiced— namely, that the Big-Five structure is an artifact of a *particular* initial selection of variables. As I have shown in this review, much of the early factor-analytic work relied on relatively small sets of descriptors. In particular, several of these analyses have employed a common set of variables (namely, Cattell's), and the selection of variables in other studies may have been

prestructured so as to yield the Big Five. However, concerns about the generalizability of the Big Five (e.g., Waller & Ben-Porath, 1987) should now be alleviated; in the more recent studies reviewed here, the variable sets were either truly independent of Cattell's selection, or were much more extensive and selected more systematically.

Sampling Terms from Free Descriptions

A third concern is that the reliance on experimenter-imposed variable sets to define the universe of descriptors may have unduly excluded important characteristics from consideration. To assess the importance of this limitation, studies are needed that select characteristics on the basis of new criteria. Findings that item sets assembled according to clinical expertise, such as the California Q-Sort (Block, 1961) or the Myers–Briggs Type Indicator (Myers & McCaulley, 1985), yield dimensions similar to the Big Five are definitely encouraging. However, given that the Big Five were intended to represent the major dimensions of natural-language personality descriptions, another option is to investigate the characteristics people use in free descriptions of themselves and others. Would the Big Five be replicated if the set of descriptors factored was based on the content of subjects' free descriptions, rather than on those sets of terms selected by the taxonomers themselves?

Such a set of descriptors is available from a series of studies designed to elicit a large set of personality terms commonly used by college students (W. Chaplin and O. P. John, unpublished data, 1989). In one of these studies, more than 300 college students described their own personalities, generating terms for both their desirable *and* their undesirable characteristics. The 10 most frequently generated terms, with the percentage of subjects generating them in parentheses, were: "friendly" (34%), "caring" (25%), "intelligent" (22%), "happy" (20%) "lazy" (18%), "moody" (18%), "shy" (18%), "outgoing" (17%), "selfish" (16%), and "kind" (15%). Among these 10 terms were at least one for each of the Big Five domains: "outgoing" versus "shy" (Factor I), "kind" and "caring" versus "selfish" (II), "lazy" (low pole of III), happy versus moody (IV), and "intelligent" (V).

To further examine the content of these free

descriptions, self-ratings available for 60 of the most frequently used descriptors were factor-analyzed in a separate sample of subjects. These analyses yielded five factors closely resembling the Big Five prototypes presented here in Table 3.2. The largest factor was marked by "sincere," "kind," and "warm," obviously corresponding to Agreeableness. "Talkative" and "energetic" versus "quiet" and "shy" had the highest loadings on the second largest factor, thus closely resembling Surgency (Factor I). The next factor resembled Emotional Stability (Factor IV), with high loadings from descriptors such as "temperamental," "possessive," "moody," and "high-strung." Finally, the two remaining factors, substantially smaller that the other three, could nonetheless be identified by their highest-loading variables: "organized" and "responsible" for Conscientiousness (Factor III), and "intelligent" and "smart" versus "naive" for Factor V.

Similarly, Church and Katigbak (1989) used unstructured personality descriptions to obtain the Tagalog variables they used in their Filipino sample, and concluded that their approach, "in which informants provide their everyday language of personality, is a viable and cogent alternative to dictionary approaches" (p. 867). In conclusion, these findings provide little evidence for the conjecture that the Big Five structure is a result of any particular sampling of descriptors. Rather, they indicate that individuals of college age find all five dimensions sufficiently important to include at least some reference to them in free descriptions. Moreover, the findings suggest that college students in the United States were most concerned with the two interpersonal dimensions of Agreeableness and Surgency, thus replicating the dictionary-based finding that Factors II and I are "bigger" than Factors IV and V (Goldberg, 1989; Peabody, 1987; Peabody & Goldberg, 1989).

Hierarchy, Levels of Abstraction, and the Big Five

Another objection to the Big Five is that five dimensions cannot possibly capture all of the variance in human personality (Briggs, 1989; Mershon & Gorsuch, 1988) and that they are much too broad. However, the objection that five dimensions is too few overlooks the fact that personality can be conceptualized at different levels of abstraction or breadth. Indeed, many trait domains are hierarchically structured (Hampson et al., 1986).

The advantage of categories as broad as the Big Five is their enormous bandwidth. Their disadvantage, of course, is their low fidelity. In any hierarchical representation, one always loses information as one moves up the hierarchical levels. For example, categorizing something as a "guppy" is more informative than categorizing it as a "fish," which in turn is more informative than categorizing it as an "animal." Or, in psychometric terms, one necessarily loses item information as one aggregates items into scales, and one loses scale information as one aggregates scales into factors (John, Hampson, & Goldberg, 1989).

The Big Five dimensions represent a rather broad level in the hierarchy of personality descriptors. In that sense, they are to personality what the categories "plant" and "animal" are to the world of biological objects—extremely useful for some initial rough distinctions, but of less value for predicting specific behaviors of a particular object. The hierarchical level a researcher selects depends on the descriptive and predictive tasks to be addressed (Hampson et al., 1986). In principle, however, the number of attributes available for the description of an individual is infinite, limited only by one's objectives.

Norman, Goldberg, McCrae and Costa, and Hogan all recognized that there was a need in personality, just as in biology, "to have a system in which different levels of generality or inclusion are recognized" (Simpson, 1961, p. 12). A complete trait taxonomy must include middle-level categories, such as Dominance, Orderliness, and Creativity, and maybe even narrower descriptors, such as "talkative," "punctual," and "musical" (John et al., 1989). Therefore Norman and, more extensively, Goldberg (1982, 1989) have developed between 40 and 75 middle-level categories subordinate to the Big Five dimensions (for a review, see John et al., 1988). However, as Briggs (1989) noted, Norman's and Goldberg's middle-level categories have not been investigated systematically or included in any assessment instrument. Costa and McCrae's (1985, 1989) "facets," and Hogan's (1986) "homogeneous item composites," represent a step in the right direction. However, the two instruments differ notably at the level of Big Five subscales, indicating the need for further conceptual and empirical work to achieve a more explicit and consensual specification of the five factors at this lower level of abstraction.

CONCLUSIONS AND IMPLICATIONS

I have argued previously that a personality taxonomy should provide a systematic framework for distinguishing, ordering, and naming characteristics and types of individuals (John, 1989a, 1990). Ideally, that taxonomy would be built around principles that are causal and dynamic, that exist at multiple levels of abstraction or hierarchy, and that offer a standard nomenclature for scientists working in the field of personality. However, the Big Five structure, as presently developed, is far from that ideal. In contrast to the biological taxonomies, the five dimensions provide only a list of descriptive concepts specified at the highest level in the hierarchy, and a nomenclature that by no means has reached the status of a "standard." Still rooted in the "vernacular" English, the theoretical context of the Big Five is the accumulated knowledge about personality as it has been laid down over the ages in the natural language.

Natural Language, Description, and Explanation

The natural language from which the Big Five originated has numerous limitations and disadvantages. For one, the factors that influence the evolution of the personality lexicon in a language are not well understood, and may include criteria other than the sociocultural importance of the characteristics. Moreover, some psychologists feel that the individual differences *they* believe to be of foremost importance for the understanding of personality are simply too subtle or complex for laypeople to notice. In the context of psychodynamic explanation, this argument has logical merit. However, when asked not *why* but *what* a person did and *how* he or she did it, the astuteness of the lay observer is more difficult to challenge (Funder, 1987). Indeed, people are keenly interested in improving their understanding of personality and will readily acquire constructs created by psychologists (e.g., Extraversion, Defensiveness, Self-Monitoring).

More importantly, the comprehensiveness of the language-based taxonomy can be evaluated by comparing it to sets of attributes compiled from the personality literature. Although such a study has not been undertaken systematically, the present review of the questionnaire literature provides little evidence that *at the level of broad dimensions* psychologists have many more independent dimensions to offer than the natural language.[6] This literature also does not suggest that measures based on single adjectives are necessarily inferior to measures based on questionnaire items. There is no evidence that adjective scales show less convergence with questionnaire scales of equal length than do questionnaire scales with each other. This is not particularly surprising, for two reasons. First, items in sentence or short-phrase format may be far more abstract, ambiguous, and difficult to understand than is often assumed (Angleitner et al., 1986). Second, almost all commonly used assessment instruments include trait adjectives in a good percentage of their items, often in thinly disguised form. Questionnaire items such as "I'm an even-tempered person," "I rarely feel anxious or fearful," and "I'm known as a warm and friendly person" are not uncommon on the NEO Personality Inventory (Costa & McCrae, 1985, 1989). How different are subjects' responses to these items from subjects' self-ratings on the adjectives "even-tempered," "anxious," "fearful," "warm," and "friendly"? The inclusion in the California Q-Sort (Block, 1961) of items such as "Is a genuinely dependable and responsible person," "Tends to be self-defensive," and "Is productive; gets things done" illustrates either that the boundary between "single adjectives" and "phrases and sentences" is less clear than one would assume, or that clinicians and observers have long recognized the concise beauty and descriptive utility of trait adjectives.

The Big Five structure has the advantage that everybody can understand the words defining the factors, and that disagreements about their meanings can be reconciled by establishing their most common usage. Moreover, the natural language is not biased in favor of any existing scientific conceptions; although the atheoretical nature of the Big Five dimensions makes them less appealing to some psychologists, it also makes them more palatable to researchers who reject dimensions cast in a theoretical mold different from their own. Whatever the inadequacies of the natural language for scientific systematics, broad dimensions inferred from folk usage are *not* a bad place to start a taxonomy. Even in animal tax-onomy, as G. G. Simpson has pointed out, "the technical system evolved from the ver-nacular" (1961, pp. 12–13).

Obviously, a system that initially derives from the natural language does not need to reify such terms indefinitely. Indeed, several of the dimensions included among the Big Five, most notably Factors I (Surgency) and IV (Emotion-al Stability), have been the target of various physiological and mechanistic explanations (see Rothbart, in press, for a review). Sim-ilarly, Block and Block's (1980) notion of Ego Control may shed some light on the mech-anisms underlying Factors III and I. Likewise, Tellegen's (1985) interpretation of Factors I+ and IV– as persistent dispositions toward thinking and behaving in ways that foster, re-spectively, positive and negative affective ex-periences promises to connect the Big Five with individual differences in affective functioning, which in turn may be studied in more tightly controlled laboratory settings. In a sense, the Big Five differentiate domains of individual dif-ferences that from the perspective of the lay observer have similar surface manifestations. However, the structures and processes underly-ing them remain to be explicated. Explication in explanatory and mechanistic terms will cer-tainly have ramifications for the definition and assessment of the initial descriptive di-mensions.

Factor Names, Numbers, and Initials: Which Shall We Use?

Although the definitions and interpretations of the constructs that will eventually replace the Big Five may be different from what we know now, a more contemporary problem centers on the names or verbal labels used to refer to these factors. In this chapter, I have used two kinds of labeling conventions. I have referred to the factors both by Roman numerals (akin to, but less satisfactory than, the Latin-based nomen-clature in the biological taxonomies) and by the verbal labels used most commonly in the literature. However, Norman (1963) offered little in the way of a rationale for the selection of these particular labels. For example, the labels used by Norman (1963) differ vastly in their breadth or inclusiveness, as shown by their category-breadth values (Hampson, Gold-

berg, & John, 1987), given here in standard score form: Extraverted (2.35), Agreeable (1.54), Conscientious (.64), Stable (1.69), and Cultured (.44). According to these data, Conscientiousness and Culture are much too narrow to capture the enormous breadth of these two dimensions. The accumulation of new findings has already led to the abandon-ment of Culture as a label for Factor V, in favor of Intellect (Digman & Inouye, 1986; Peabody & Goldberg, 1989) or Openness to Experience (McCrae & Costa, 1985b). Neither label is truly satisfactory, however, because Intellect is too narrow and Openness to Experience, while broad enough, is somewhat vague.

Agreeableness is another problematic label. For one, it is ambiguous, referring either to "pleasing," in the sense of the person's social stimulus value, or to the behavioral tendency to "agree with others," thus incorrectly imply-ing submissiveness, which is more closely re-lated to Factor I. Agreeableness is also too detached, too neutral a label for a factor sup-posed to capture intensely affective com-ponents, such as love, compassion, and sym-pathy. Freud viewed love and work as central; following this lead, we could call Factor II sim-ply Love. However, Work is too narrow a label for Factor III. Even Conscientiousness is too narrow, because it omits a central component that Peabody and Goldberg (1989) call "favor-able impulse control." Thus, Responsibility, or even Degree of Socialization (see Gough, 1987), might be labels for Factor III at a level of breadth more appropriate than Conscien-tiousness.

More could be said about the many short-comings of the traditional labels, but better labels are hard to come by. The unsurpassed advantage of the traditional labels is that they are commonly known and used, thus prevent-ing Babel from taking over the literature on the Big Five. Moreover, the definition of the fac-tors in terms of facets or components should be elaborated and sharpened considerably before new names are devised. At this point, it seems premature to settle the scope and theoretical interpretation of the factors by devising new names. Rather, I believe that we should use the Roman numerals and go through the effort of memorizing what they stand for. Alternatively, we could use a mnemonic convention suggested by Robert McCrae (personal communication, July 28, 1989). The initials given below evoke multiple associations that represent more fully than a single word the broad range of meaning captured by each of the factors:

E: Extraversion, Energy, Enthusiasm (I)
A: Agreeableness, Altruism, Affection (II)
C: Conscientiousness, Control, Constraint (III)
N: Neuroticism, Negative Affectivity, Nervousness (IV)
O: Openness, Originality, Open-Mindedness (V)

The reader intrigued by anagrams may have noticed that these letters form the OCEAN of personality dimensions.

Summary and Future Directions

Now that the Big Five structure has been replicated in extensive analyses of English, the lexical approach still faces several major tasks. One is to spell out, with much more precision, the particular characteristics that comprise each of the factors, as well as those characteristics that fall in the fuzzy regions *between* factors. The second task involves further research on the Big Five in languages other than English and in cultures different from the industrialized West. Third, external validity and predictive utility are topics that have received conspicuously little attention in the present chapter and from researchers working in the taxonomic tradition. However, one of the criteria for the usefulness of a taxonomy is its success in predicting important outcomes in people's lives. Some promising work on divorce, alcoholism, and aging (e.g., Conley, 1985b; Field & Millsap, 1989) is already underway, but much remains to be done.

Finally, so far the Big Five dimensions have been employed in variable-centered, but not in person-centered, research. In his seminal paper on the units of personality description, Allport (1958) distinguished between, on the one hand, a dimensional model of personality characteristics and, on the other hand, the structure of personality within a particular individual:

Factors are simply a summary principle of classification of many measures. . . .[they] offer scalable dimensions; that is to say, they are common units in respect to which all personalities can be compared. None of them corresponds to the cleavages that exist in any single personality unless the single personal structure happens to be like that of the empirically derived average man. (pp. 251–252)

In other words, nomothetic dimensions such as the Big Five are derived from correlations among personality characteristics across, not within, individuals. They therefore represent the overall structure of the attributes as applied to a sample of individuals. However, nomothetic dimensions do not constitute a model of "personality structure" if by "structure" we mean the particular configuration, patterning, and dynamic organization of the individual's total set of characteristics. Idiographic analyses are necessary to elucidate the ways in which the attributes measured by each dimension combine in particular individuals, and typological analyses may identify groups or categories of individuals who have similar configurations of characteristics. We have yet to investigate the ways in which the Big Five dimensions combine into a coherent personality within individuals, and whether there exist groups or categories of individuals with similar configurations of these five personality characteristics.

Nonetheless, as Allport argued in 1958, "scalable dimensions are useful dimensions, and we hope that work will continue until we reach firmer agreement concerning their number and nature" (p. 252). As Allport had hoped, the work on scalable dimensions has continued since, and researchers have now reached a firmer agreement about them: Their number is five, and their nature can be summarized by the broad concepts of Surgency, Agreeableness, Conscientiousness, Emotional Stability versus Neuroticism, and Openness to Experience. In my view, the Big Five structure is a major step ahead—a long-due extension and improvement over earlier factor systems that tended to compete with each other, rather than to establish communalities and convergences. The Big Five structure captures, at a broad level of abstraction, the commonalities among most of the existing systems of personality description, and provides an integrative descriptive model for personality research.

ACKNOWLEDGMENTS

This chapter summarizes and updates previous reviews by John (1989a, 1990) and John et al. (1988).

The preparation of this chapter was supported in part by Biomedical Research Grant Nos. 87-20 and 88-24 from the University of California at Berkeley, and by Grant No. MH-39077 from the National Institute of Mental Health. The support and resources provided by the Institute of Personality Assessment and Research are also gratefully acknowledged. Alois Angleitner, Peter Borkenau, Jack Block, Paul DeBoeck, John M. Digman, Lewis R. Goldberg, Harrison Gough, Douglas, T. Kenrick, Robert Hogan, Robert R. McCrae, Warren Norman, Paul McReynolds, Dean Peabody, Leonard Rorer, and Auke Tellegen have variously offered comments and suggestions that greatly clarified the ideas presented here.

NOTES

1. The participants must have found it difficult to use this list, given the inclusion of psychological jargon for abilities, interests, and various components of neuroticism and psychoticism.

2. The choice of a standard language is always a compromise between, on the one hand, a set of descriptors as extensive and diverse as possible, and, on the other hand, a set not too large to prove impractical. The ACL seemed best suited for the present purposes because its 300 adjectives cover a broad range of individual differences but are limited to a number more manageable than even more extensive sets, such as Goldberg's set of 1,710.

3. Eysenck's definitions of his broad factors have evolved over time. For example, Impulsiveness, viewed initially as a component of Extraversion (Eysenck, 1967), was recently reassigned to Psychoticism (Eysenck, 1986). Excitability, formerly included among the five definers of Extraversion, no longer appears in the 1986 definitions. Apparently, the assignment of traits to factors has proceeded on conceptual and theoretical grounds; therefore, these assignments are not necessarily empirically valid. For example, Zuckerman, Kuhlman, and Camac (1988, pp. 103–104) found that "the primary locus of sensation seeking [is] in the P factor rather than in E," as suggested by Eysenck (1986).

4. In the 1984 revision of Buss and Plomin's book, Impulsivity has been dropped.

5. Indeed, one could argue that these terms are better examples of Potency or Vitality than of Positive Affect. On the other hand, these terms are clearly related to *interest*, which is typically regarded as a positive emotion.

6. Buss and Finn (1987) have urged that dimensions derived from recent research be given central status in the taxonomy. Many of their examples involve constructs that are relatively narrow and specific (e.g., Private Self-Consciousness), and thus likely to be part of broader factors (e.g., Openness) also represented in the natural language.

REFERENCES

Allen, B. P., & Potkay, C. R. (1981). On the arbitrary distinction between states and traits. *Journal of Personality and Social Psychology, 41,* 916–928.

Allen, B. P., & Potkay, C. R. (1983). Just as arbitrary as ever: Comments on Zuckerman's rejoinder. *Journal of Personality and Social Psychology, 44,* 1087–1089.

Allport, G. W. (1937). *Personality: A psychological interpretation.* New York: Holt.

Allport, G. W. (1958). What units shall we employ? In G. Lindzey (Ed.), *Assessment of human motives* (pp. 238–260). New York: Rinehart.

Allport, G. W., & Odbert, H. S. (1936). Trait-names: A psycho-lexical study. *Psychological Monographs, 47,* (No. 211).

Angleitner, A., John, O. P., & Loehr, F.-J. (1986). It's *what* you ask and *how* you ask it: An itemmetric analysis of personality questionnaires. In A. Angleitner & J. S. Wiggins (Eds.), *Personality assessment via questionnaires: Current issues in theory and measurement* (pp. 61–108). Berlin: Springer-Verlag.

Angleitner, A., & Ostendorf, F. (1989, July). *Personality factors via self and peer-ratings based on a representative sample of German trait-descriptive terms.* Paper presented at the First European Congress of Psychology, Amsterdam.

Angleitner, A., Ostendorf, F., & John, O. P. Towards a taxonomy of personality descriptors in German: A psycho-lexical study. *European Journal of Personality Psychology, 4.*

Bales, R. F. (1970). *Personality and interpersonal behavior.* New York: Holt, Rinehart, & Winston.

Bales, R. F., & Cohen, S. P. (1979). *SYMLOG: A system for the multiple level observation of groups.* New York: Free Press.

Barron, F. (1968). *Creativity and personal freedom.* Princeton, NJ: Van Nostrand.

Baumgarten, F. (1933). Die Charaktereigenschaften. [The character traits]. In *Beitraege zur Charakter- und Persoenlichkeitsforschung* (Whole No. 1). Bern: A. Francke.

Becker, W. C. (1960). The matching of behavior rating and questionnaire personality factors. *Psychological Bulletin, 57,* 201–212.

Block, J. (1961). *The Q-sort method in personality assessment and psychiatric research.* (Reprint Edition 1978). Palo Alto, CA: Consulting Psychologists Press.

Block, J. (1971). *Lives through time.* Berkeley, CA: Bancroft Books.

Block, J. H., & Block, J. (1980). The role of ego-control and ego-resiliency in the organization of behavior. In W. A. Collins (Ed.), *Minnesota Symposium on Child Psychology* (Vol. 13, pp. 39–101). Hillsdale, NJ: Erlbaum.

Bond, M. H. (1979). Dimensions used in perceiving peers: Cross-cultural comparisons of Hong Kong, Japanese, American and Filipino university students. *International Journal of Psychology, 14*, 47–56.

Bond, M. H. (1983). Linking person perception dimensions to behavioral intention dimensions: The Chinese connection. *Journal of Cross-Cultural Psychology, 14*, 41–63.

Bond, M. H., & Forgas, J. P. (1984). Linking person perception to behavior intention across cultures: The role of cultural collectivism. *Journal of Cross-Cultural Psychology, 15*, 337–352.

Bond, M. H., Nakazato, H., & Shiraishi, D. (1975). Universality and distinctiveness in dimensions of Japanese person perception. *Journal of Cross-Cultural Psychology, 6*, 346–357.

Borgatta, E. F. (1964). The structure of personality characteristics. *Behavioral Science, 9*, 8–17.

Borkenau, P., & Ostendorf, F. (1989). Descriptive consistency and social desirability in self- and peer reports. *European Journal of Personality, 3*, 31–45.

Botwin, M. D., & Buss, D. M. (1989). Structure of act-report data: Is the five-factor model of personality recaptured? *Journal of Personality and Social Psychology, 56*, 988–1001.

Briggs, S. R. (1989). The optimal level of measurement for personality constructs. In D. M. Buss & N. Cantor (Eds.), *Personality psychology: Recent trends and emerging directions* (pp. 246–260). New York: Springer.

Brokken, F. B. (1978). *The language of personality*. Meppel, The Netherlands: Krips.

Buss, A. H., & Finn, S. E. (1987). Classification of personality traits. *Journal of Personality and Social Psychology, 52*, 432–444.

Buss, A. H., & Plomin, R. (1975). *A temperament theory of personality development*. New York: Wiley.

Buss, A. H., & Plomin, R. (1984). *A temperament theory of personality development* (rev. ed.). New York: Wiley.

Cattell, R. B. (1943). The description of personality: Basic traits resolved into clusters. *Journal of Abnormal and Social Psychology, 38*, 476–506.

Cattell, R. B. (1945a). The description of personality: Principles and findings in a factor analysis. *American Journal of Psychology, 58*, 69–90.

Cattell, R. B. (1945b). The principal trait clusters for describing personality. *Psychological Bulletin, 42*, 129–161.

Cattell, R. B. (1946). *Description and measurement of personality*. Yonkers-on-Hudson, NY: World.

Cattell, R. B. (1947). Confirmation and clarification of primary personality factors. *Psychometrika, 12*, 197–220.

Cattell, R. B. (1948). The primary personality factors in women compared with those in men. *British Journal of Psychology, 1*, 114–130.

Cattell, R. B. (1957). *Personality and motivation structure and measurement*. Yonkers-on-Hudson, NY: World.

Cattell, R. B. (1974, Fall). A large sample cross-check on 16PF primary structure by parcelled factoring. *Journal of Multivariate Experimental Personality and Clinical Psychology*, pp. 79–95.

Cattell, R. B. (1979), *Personality and learning theory: Vol. 1. The structure of personality in its environment*. New York: Springer Publ.

Cattell, R. B., Eber, H. W., & Tatsuoka, M. M. (1970). *Handbook for the Sixteen Personality Factor Questionnaire (16PF)*. Champaign, IL: Institute for Personality and Ability Testing.

Chaplin, W. F., John, O. P., & Goldberg, L. R. (1988). Conceptions of states and traits: Dimensional attributes with ideals as prototypes. *Journal of Personality and Social Psychology, 54*, 541–557.

Church, T. A., & Katigbak, M. S. (1989). Internal, external, and self-report structure of personality in a non-Western culture. An investigation of cross-language and cross-cultural generalizability. *Journal of Personality and Social Psychology, 57*, 857–872.

Comrey, A. L. (1970). *Manual for the Comrey Personality Scales*. San Diego, CA: Educational and Industrial Testing Service.

Conley, J. J. (1985a). Longitudinal stability of personality traits: A multitrait–multimethod–multioccasion analysis. *Journal of Personality and Social Psychology, 49*, 1266–1282.

Conley, J. J. (1985b). A personality theory of adulthood and aging. In R. Hogan & W. H. Jones (Eds.), *Perspectives in personality* (Vol. 1, pp. 81–115). Greenwich, CT: JAI Press.

Costa, P. T., Jr., & McCrae, R. R. (1985). *The NEO Personality Inventory manual*. Odessa, FL: Psychological Assessment Resources.

Costa, P. T., Jr. & McCrae, R. R. (1988). From catalog to classification: Murray's needs and the five-factor model. *Journal of Personality and Social Psychology, 55*, 258–265.

Costa, P. T., Jr., & McCrae, R. R. (1989). *NEO PI/FFI Manual Supplement*. Odessa, FL: Psychological Assessment Resources.

De Raad, B., Mulder, E., Kloosterman, K., & Hofstee, W. K. (1988). Personality-descriptive verbs. *European Journal of Personality, 2*, 81–96.

Digman, J. M. (1963). Principal dimensions of child personality as seen in teachers' judgments. *Child Development, 34*, 43–60.

Digman, J. M. (1972). The structure of child personality as seen in behavior ratings. In R. M. Dreger (Ed.), *Multivariate personality research* (pp. 587–611). Baton Rouge, LA: Claitor's.

Digman, J. M., & Inouye, J. (1986). Further specification of the five robust factors of personality. *Journal of Personality and Social Psychology, 50*, 116–123.

Digman, J. M., & Takemoto-Chock, N. K. (1981). Factors in the natural language of personality: Re-analysis and comparison of six major studies. *Multivariate Behavioral Research, 16*, 149–170.

Eysenck, H. J. (1944). Types of personality: A factorial study of seven-hundred neurotics. *Journal of Mental Science, 90*, 851–861.

Eysenck, H. J. (1967). *The biological basis of personality*. Springfield, IL: Charles C Thomas.

Eysenck, H. J. (1986). Models and paradigms in personality research. In A. Angleitner, A. Furnham, & G. Van Heck (Eds.), *Personality psychology in Europe: Vol. 2. Current trends and controversies* (pp. 213–223). Lisse, The Netherlands: Swets & Zeitlinger.

Eysenck, H. J., & Eysenck, M. W. (1985). *Personality and individual differences: A natural science approach*. New York: Plenum.

Field, D., & Millsap, R. E. (1989). *Personality in advanced old age: Continuity or change?* Unpublished manuscript. Institute of Human Development, University of California at Berkeley, Berkeley.

Fiske, D. W. (1949). Consistency of the factorial structures of personality ratings from different sources. *Journal of Abnormal and Social Psychology, 44*, 329–344.

Funder, D. C. (1987). Errors and mistakes: Evaluating the accuracy of social judgment. *Psychological Bulletin, 101*, 75–90.

Funder, D. C., & Block, J. (1989). The role of ego-control, ego-resiliency, and IQ in delay of gratification in adolescents. *Journal of Personality and Social Psychology, 57*, 1041–1050.

Goldberg, L. R. (1971). A historical survey of personality scales and inventories. In P. McReynolds (Ed.), *Advances in psychological assessment* (Vol. 2, pp. 293–336). Palo Alto, CA: Science and Behavior Books.

Goldberg, L. R. (1976). Language and personality: Toward a taxonomy of trait-descriptive terms. *Istanbul Studies in Experimental Psychology, 12*, 1–23.

Goldberg, L. R. (1980, May). *Some ruminations about the structure of individual differences: Developing a common lexicon for the major characteristics of human personality.* Paper presented at the annual convention of the Western Psychological Association, Honolulu.

Goldberg, L. R. (1981). Language and individual differences: The search for universals in personality lexicons. In L. Wheeler (Ed.), *Review of personality and social psychology* (Vol. 2, pp. 141–165). Beverly Hills, CA: Sage.

Goldberg, L. R. (1982). From Ace to Zombie: Some explorations in the language of personality. In C. D. Spielberg & J. N. Butcher (Eds.), *Advances in personality assessment* (Vol. 1, pp. 203–234). Hillsdale, NJ: Erlbaum.

Goldberg, L. R. (1989). *An alternative "description of personality": The Big-Five factor structure.* Manuscript submitted for publication.

Gotlib, I. H., & Meyer, J. P. (1986). Factor analysis of the Multiple Affect Adjective Check List: A separation of positive and negative affect. *Journal of Personality and Social Psychology, 50*, 1161–1165.

Gough, H. G. (1979). A creative personality scale for the Adjective Check List. *Journal of Personality and Social Psychology, 37*, 1938–1405.

Gough, H. G. (1987). *The California Psychological Inventory administrator's guide.* Palo Alto, CA: Consulting Psychologists Press.

Gough, H. G. (in press). Some unfinished business. In D. Cicchetti & W. Grove (Eds.), *Thinking clearly about psychology: Essays in honor of Paul E. Meehl.* Minneapolis: University of Minnesota Press.

Gough, H. G., & Heilbrun, A. B., Jr. (1965). *The adjective check list manual.* Palo Alto, CA: Consulting Psychologists Press.

Gough, H. G., & Heilbrun, A. B., Jr. (1983). *The adjective check list manual* (rev. ed.). Palo Alto, CA: Consulting Psychologists Press.

Gould, S. J. (1981). *The mismeasure of man.* New York. Norton.

Guilford, J. P. (1974). Rotation problems in factor analysis. *Psychological Bulletin, 81*, 498–501.

Guilford, J. P. (1975). Factors and factors of personality. *Psychological Bulletin, 82*, 802–814.

Guthrie, G. M., & Bennett, A. B., Jr. (1971). Cultural differences in implicit personality theory. *International Journal of Psychology, 6*, 305–312.

Hampson, S. E., Goldberg, L. R., & John, O. P. (1987). Category-breadth and social-desirability values for 573 personality terms. *European Journal of Personality, 1*, 241–258.

Hampson, S. E., John, O. P., & Goldberg, L. R. (1986). Category breadth and hierarchical structure in personality: Studies of asymmetries in judgments of trait implications. *Journal of Personality and Social Psychology, 51*, 37–54.

Helson, R. (1967). Personality characteristics and developmental history of creative college women. *Genetic Psychology Monographs, 76*, 205–256.

Helson, R. (1985). Which of those young women with creative potential became productive? Personality in college and characteristics of parents. In R. Hogan & W. H. Jones (Eds.), *Perspectives in personality theory, measurement, and interpersonal dynamics* (Vol. 1, pp. 49–80). Greenwich, CT: JAI Press.

Hogan, R. (1983). A socioanalytic theory of personality. In M. M. Page (Ed.), *Nebraska Symposium on Motivation, 1982: Personality—Current theory and research.* Lincoln, NE: University of Nebraska Press.

Hogan, R. (1986). *Hogan Personality Inventory manual.* Minneapolis: National Computer Systems.

Jackson, D. N. (1984). *Personality Research Form manual* (3rd ed.). Port Huron, MI: Research Psychologists Press.

John, O. P. (1989a). Towards a taxonomy of personality descriptors. In D. M. Buss & N. Cantor (Eds.), *Personality psychology: Recent trends and emerging directions* (pp. 261–271). New York: Springer-Verlag.

John, O. P. (1989b, November). Big Five prototypes for the Adjective Check List using observer data. In O. P. John (Chair), *The Big Five: Historical perspective and current research.* Symposium presented at the annual meeting of the Society for Multivariate Experimental Psychology, Makaha, HI.

John, O. P. (1990). The search for basic dimensions of personality: A review and critique. In P. McReynolds, J. C. Rosen, & G. L. Chelune (Eds.), *Advances in psychological assessment* (Vol. 7, pp. 1–37). New York: Plenum Press.

John, O. P., Angleitner, A., & Ostendorf, F. (1988). The lexical approach to personality: A historical review of trait taxonomic research. *European Journal of Personality, 2*, 171–203.

John, O. P., Goldberg, L. R., & Angleitner, A. (1984). Better than the alphabet: Taxonomies of personality-descriptive terms in English, Dutch, and German. In H. Bonarius, G. van Heck, & N. Smid (Eds.), *Personality psychology in Europe: Theoretical and empirical developments* (pp. 83–100). Berwyn, PA: Swets North America.

John, O. P., Hampson, S. E., & Goldberg, L. R. (1989). *Is there a basic level of personality description?* Manuscript submitted for publication.

Klages, L. (1932). *The science of character* (Translated 1932). London: George Allen & Unwin. (Original work published 1926)

Leary, T. (1957). *Interpersonal diagnosis of personality.* New York: Ronald Press.

MacKinnon, D. W. (1965). Personality and the realization of creative potential. *American Psychologist, 20*, 273–281.

McCrae, R. R. (1989). Why I advocate the five-factor model: Joint factor analyses of the NEO-PI with other instruments. In D. M. Buss & N. Cantor (Eds.), *Personality psychology: Recent trends and emerging directions* (pp. 237–245). New York: Springer-Verlag.

McCrae, R. R., & Costa, P. T. (1985a). Updating Norman's adequate taxonomy: Intelligence and personality dimensions in natural language and in questionnaires. *Journal of Personality and Social Psychology, 49*, 710–721.

McCrae, R. R., & Costa, P. T. (1985b). Openness to experience. In R. Hogan & W. H. Jones (Eds.), *Perspectives in personality* (Vol. 1, pp. 145–172). Greenwich, CT: JAI Press.

McCrae, R. R., & Costa, P. T. (1985c). Comparison of EPI and psychoticism scales with measures of the five-factor model of personality. *Personality and Individual Differences, 6,* 587–597.

McCrae, R. R., & Costa, P. T. (1987). Validation of the five-factor model of personality across instruments and observers. *Journal of Personality and Social Psychology, 52,* 81–90.

McCrae, R. R., & Costa, P. T. (1989a). Reinterpreting the Myers–Briggs Type Indicator from the perspective of the five-factor model of personality. *Journal of Personality, 57,* 17–40.

McCrae, R. R., & Costa, P. T. (1989b). The structure of interpersonal traits: Wiggins's circumplex and the five-factor model. *Journal of Personality and Social Psychology, 56,* 586–595.

McCrae, R. R., Costa, P. T., & Busch, C. M. (1986). Evaluating comprehensiveness in personality systems: The California Q-Set and the five-factor model. *Journal of Personality, 54,* 430–446.

Meehl, P. E. (1962, August). *Minnesota–Ford pool of phenotypic personality items.* Minneapolis: Departments of Psychiatry and Psychology, University of Minnesota.

Mershon, B., & Gorsuch, R. L. (1988). Number of factors in the personality sphere: Does increase in factors increase predictability of real-life criteria? *Journal of Personality and Social Psychology, 55,* 675–680.

Myers, I. B., & McCaulley, M. H. (1985). *Manual: A guide to the development and use of the Myers–Briggs Type Indicator.* Palo Alto, CA: Consulting Psychologists Press.

Nakazato, H., Bond, M. H., & Shiraishi, D. (1976). Dimensions of personality perception: An examination of Norman's hypothesis. *Japanese Journal of Psychology, 47,* 139–148.

Noller, P., Law, H., & Comrey, A. L. (1987). Cattell, Comrey, and Eysenck personality factors compared: More evidence for the five robust factors? *Journal of Personality and Social Psychology, 53,* 775–782.

Norman, W. T. (1963). Toward an adequate taxonomy of personality attributes: Replicated factor structure in peer nomination personality ratings. *Journal of Abnormal and Social Psychology, 66,* 574–583.

Norman, W. T. (1967). *2,800 personality trait descriptors: Normative operating characteristics for a university population.* Ann Arbor: Department of Psychology, University of Michigan.

Nowakowska, M. (1973). The limitations of the factor-analytic approach to psychology with special application to Cattell's research strategy. *Theory and Decision, 4,* 109–139.

Peabody, D. (1987). Selecting representative trait adjectives. *Journal of Personality and Social Psychology, 52,* 59–71.

Peabody, D., & Goldberg, L. R. (1989). Some determinants of factor structures from personality-trait descriptors. *Journal of Personality and Social Psychology, 57,* 552–567.

Rosch, E. (1978). Principles of categorization. In E. Rosch & B. B. Lloyd (Eds.), *Cognition and categorization* (pp. 27–48). Hillsdale, NJ: Erlbaum.

Rothbart, M. (in press). Temperament and development. In G. A. Kohnstamm, L. Bates, and M. K. Rothbart (Eds.), *Handbook of temperament in childhood.* Chichester, England: Wiley.

Simpson, G. G. (1961). *Principles of animal taxonomy.* New York: Columbia University Press.

Sullivan, H. S. (1947). *Conceptions of modern psychiatry.* Washington, D.C.: William Alanson White Foundation.

Tellegen, A. (1982). *Brief manual for the Differential Personality Questionnaire.* Unpublished manuscript, University of Minnesota.

Tellegen, A. (1985). Structures of mood and personality and their relevance to assessing anxiety, with an emphasis on self-report. In A. H. Tuma & J. D. Maser (Eds.), *Anxiety and the anxiety disorders* (pp. 681–716). Hillsdale, NJ: Erlbaum.

Tellegen, A., & Atkinson, G. (1974). Openness to absorbing and self-altering experiences ("absorption"), a trait related to hypnotic susceptibility. *Journal of Abnormal Psychology, 83,* 268–277.

Tellegen, A., Lykken, D. T., Bouchard, T. J., Wilcox, K. J., Segal, N. L., & Rich, S. (1988). Personality similarity in twins reared part and together. *Journal of Personality and Social Psychology, 54,* 1031–1039.

Tupes, E. C., & Christal, R. C. (1961). *Recurrent personality factors based on trait ratings* (Tech. Rep. No. ASD-TR-61-97). Lackland Air Force Base, TX: U.S Air Force.

Waller, N. G., & Ben-Porath, Y. S. (1987). Is it time for clinical psychologists to embrace the five-factor model of personality? *American Psychologist, 42,* 887–889.

Watson, D., Clark, L. A., & Tellegen, A. (1988). Development and validation of brief measures of positive and negative affect: The PANAS scales. *Journal of Personality and Social Psychology, 54,* 1063–1070.

White, G. M. (1980). Conceptual universals in interpersonal language. *American Anthropologist, 82,* 759–781.

Wiggins, J. S. (1973). *Personality and prediction: Principles of personality assessment.* Reading, MA: Addison-Wesley.

Wiggins, J. S. (1979). A psychological taxonomy of trait-descriptive terms: The interpersonal domain. *Journal of Personality and Social Psychology, 37,* 395–412.

Wiggins, J. S., & Broughton, R. (1985). The interpersonal circle: A structural model for the integration of personality research. In R. Hogan & W. H. Jones (Eds.), *Perspectives in personality* (Vol. 1, pp. 1–47), Greenwich, CT: JAI Press.

Wiggins, J. S., Phillips, N., & Trapnell, P. (1989). Circular reasoning about interpersonal behavior: Evidence concerning some untested assumptions underlying diagnostic classification. *Journal of Personality and Social Psychology, 56,* 296–305.

Zuckerman, M., Kuhlman, D. M., & Camac, C. (1988). What lies beyond E and N? Factor analyses of scales believed to measure basic dimensions of personality. *Journal of Personality and Social Psychology, 54,* 96–107.

Chapter 4

Advances in Cattellian Personality Theory

Raymond B. Cattell
Forest Institute of Clinical Psychology

Science demands measurement! Measurement began in personality at the end of the Freudian, Jungian, and Adlerian phase of clinically derived theories. In its best usage it had a dynamic, not merely a static purpose. That is to say, it made measurements in order to discover laws of change. But for a long period—notably, from 1925 to 1955—it had first to define personality as it is at a given time.

When I began my career, I forsook the "mainstream" of existing concepts about personality types and traits, and started by factoring afresh the "personality sphere" of total human behavior. By 1925 Spearman had developed and proven the efficacy of factor analysis as an instrument to give foundation to his idea of a single general intelligence structure. It required little originality to see that this analytical method should apply also to isolating personality structures. But it required 50 years of refinement of the factor-analytic method to meet the new demands. And, from the beginning, psychologists stood back from learning the complexities of factor analysis, as the hosts of the barbarians stood back before the Great Wall of China. The story of the advances of multivariate experimental personality theory is therefore an extraordinary tale of isolation from the random mainstream of personality speculation. Time and again, salient discoveries have remained unknown and unincorporated in prevalent discussions of "unsolved" problems.

FACTORING OF THE PERSONALITY SPHERE

The first stage of the new approach was the factoring of a personality sphere of variables in ratings and questionnaire behavior items. This yielded at first 16 factors, embodied in the Sixteen Personality Factors Questionnaire (16 PF), and a further 12 in abnormal behavior in the Clinical Analysis Questionnaire (CAQ). Meanwhile, outside this systematic, difficult, and therefore slow progress, hundreds of questionnaires were spawned on subjective clinical and occupational hunches and were snatched up and standardized outside the Great Wall.

When the 16 PF and CAQ appeared, it was not realized that they constituted a new approach. In this approach one *first* found the personality structure and *then* constructed scales for each verified factor. The scales were in fact hostages for a personality theory, and that theory concerned the nature of 16 primary source traits and 7 second-order factors among them.

It was the next task of the programmatic research to determine the nature of these factors—as regards their persistence over the developmental age range, their life change plots, the degree of their inheritance, their physiological associations, and their predictive relevances ("validities") against all kinds of life behavior "criteria." The positive findings on persistence of pattern led to construction of the age-graded series of the High School Personality Questionnaire (HSPQ) (12–18 years), the Child Personality Questionnaire (CPQ) (8–12 years), the Early School Personality Questionnaire (ESPQ) (6–8 years), and the Pre-School Personality Questionnaire (PSPQ) (4–8 years), so valuable as a basis for developmental psychology.

It was also demonstrated that the primary and secondary factors were essentially the same in number and nature in other cultures—notably France, Germany, Italy, India, and Japan. This provided an international basis for personality research, so necessary to the international claims of science.

Meanwhile, outside the Great Wall of multivariate experimental research, many questionnaires proliferated and became established in respectable practice. These included the California scales, the Minnesota Multiphasic Personality Inventory (MMPI), the Edwards Personal Preference Schedule, the Eysenck Personality Inventory (EPI), and so forth. A period of troubles now began in that sponsors began to use factor analysis on such instruments, mostly "postmortem" (i.e., after the scales were constructed). Thus, Eysenck (Eysenck & Eysenck, 1964) concluded that his three scales were the same as three of the seven 16 PF secondaries, which he called "superfactors," though actually the broad secondaries have less predictive power than the primaries. Comrey (1970) reached similar conclusions regarding the Comrey Personality Scales. Digman and Inouye (1986) concluded that there were only five "robust factors," and so on in many other investigators' divergent conclusions about various instruments (Cattell & Gibbons, 1968; Howarth & Brown, 1971; etc.). These divergencies (notably those of Guilford) arose from degrees of obsoleteness in the factor-analytic method used—in the basic factors,

poor sample, poor structural rotation, absence of a test for number of factors, and so on.

In one of the "progressive rectification" studies practiced on the 16 PF, we (Cattell & Krug, 1989) used the last confirmatory factor-analytic design of Jöreskog and Sorbom (1967). This showed definitely that the 16 PF had at least 16 factors. This finding was crucial, since one of the constant objections by the designers of the 3-, 5-, 12-, and 13-factor questionnaires is that 16 is too many. The fact behind this criticism is that psychologists find 16 factors too many to learn about. As Meehl (1954) showed long ago, 6 factors are about the most a clinician can keep in mind; however, the computer can do far better. For example, the following behavioral equation gives a good estimate of a salesperson's annual earnings:

$$\begin{aligned} \text{Earnings} = {} & .21A + .10B + .10C \\ & + .10E + .21F + .10G \quad (1) \\ & - .10L - .31M + .21N \\ & - .31Q_2 + .21Q_3 \\ & - .21Q_4 + 3.8O \end{aligned}$$

And this behavioral equation gives an estimate of creativity:

$$\begin{aligned} \text{Creativity} = {} & .99 - .33A + .33B \quad (2) \\ & + .17E - .33F + .16A \\ & + .33I + .16M - .16N \\ & + .16Q_1 + .33Q_3 \end{aligned}$$

These equations leave no doubt of the complexity of human behavior. They also foreshadow the coming of "solid-state" computer practice by practicing psychologists. It will be noted, however, that there is more than Meehl's "actuarial" aspect to this use. One gets further prediction from knowing the nature of each factor—its life course, its genetic element, its interaction with the environment. Such knowledge is now becoming available. For example, we know that the hereditary influence is small on G (superego), but large on B (intelligence), F (surgency), and I (premsia) (Cattell, 1981, 1987). One of the first tasks in a course on personality should be to learn the names and natures of these 16 PF source traits. If psychology students balk at this, one might remind them that medical students learn hundreds of new names, that chemists know over 100 elements, and that astronomers have discovered a nameless number of galaxies.

Where do psychology students come from who find three or four factors all they can use to describe personality?

STRUCTURED LEARNING THEORY AND THE DYNAMIC CALCULUS

After tolerable clarity on *general* personality factors had been achieved (about 1960), it was natural that research turned to the last new modality of data—dynamic traits and interests. It was first necessary to turn from the pollsters' definition of attitude as "for or against" to a stimulus–response definition: "In *this* situation I want *so much* to do *this* with *that.*"

A survey of most of 50 alleged strength measurements—memory, perception, physiological—led by factoring to seven primary "components" (as they are called to distinguish them from substantive factors). These were novel, but contained the same devices across different attitudes, and are basic entities still requiring adequate interpretation today. They yield two secondaries: integrated (*I*) and unintegrated (*U*) interest strength in the given course of action (Cattell, Lawlis, McGill, & McGraw, 1979).

Factoring these objective device measures for a typical array of life interest attitudes surprisingly yielded the instinctive drives (sex, fear, assertion, protective impulses) now called "ergs" (sources of energy) and about the same number of clearly learned structures called "sems" or sentiments (e.g., attachments to home, job, sport, spouse). From these findings on structure (repeated on the child level), a Motivation Analysis Test (MAT), measuring five important ergs and five common sems, was constructed and validated. The bulk of multivariate experimental research in dynamics has rested on the use of this test (Cattell, Sealy, & Sweney, 1966).

It has been found, for instance, that the *U–I* difference indicates the strength of conflict in that area. It has also been shown by stimulation and deprivation (manipulative) research that *U* interest strength responds most to circumstances in the case of sex, hunger, and fear. It has also been shown that the superego sem in the MAT correlates with G in the 16 PF, thus offering two independent-instrument factor measures to proide a better instrument-free measure. Occupational profiles show characteristic adjustment patterns. For example, fear is high in the chronically unemployed, and the *U–I* conflict score is high on the career sem. But the main use of the MAT has been by psychiatrists and psychotherapists, who find it a valuable diagnostic tool and a suitable measure of gain in the therapeutic process (Cattell & Child, 1975).

Out of the use of the MAT has sprung a theoretical development called "structured learning theory." This differs from Pavlov–Skinner reflexology in (1) requiring explanation of the use of the known dynamic structures, and (2) taking account of the role of dynamic and general structures in explaining *new* learning. It presupposes five principles in learning:

1. Association
2. Means–end learning (Skinner's "conditioned response II")
3. Integration learning
4. Ergic goal modification (sublimation)
5. Energy saving

These are justified better than in the brief space here, in my book *Human Motivation and the Dynamic Calculus* (Cattell, 1985).

Structured learning propositions are embodied in a series of equations called the "dynamic calculus." In the first place, a given piece of learning is represented (a) as a result of the ergic and semic strengths involved, and (b) as a vector change rather than a scalar change as in reflexology. The former is represented in Figure 4.1 by a change in a particular attitude from (a) to (b). As an effect of learning on attitude (a), it changes its projection on Ergs I and II, showing that it now subsidiates more to (i.e., gets more satisfaction from) Erg II, and slightly less to Erg I. The change in total strength, of course, represents the scalar change in strength induced in the learning experience. This is a precision of learning law unknown in reflexology (Cattell, Horn, & Butcher, 1962).

The central equation for either the strength of an attitude or a learning change is as follows:

$$A_{hijk} = \Sigma b_{hjkx} E_{xi} + \Sigma b_{hjky} M_{yi} \\ + \Sigma b_{hjkme} M_{mi} E_{ei} + \Sigma b_{hjkem} E_{ei} M_{mi} \quad (3)$$

where *i* is the individual concerned, *j* is the particular course of action implicit in the given attitude, *h* is the recent stimulus to action, and *k* is the ambient situation. The series of *EM*'s

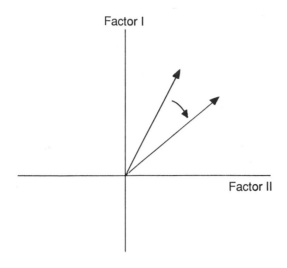

FIGURE 4.1. Change in the vector quantity of an attitude.

represents the strength of the ergic tensions. It will be seen that this supposes that the cognitive strength (which is the measure of an M) decides the amount of stimulus to an erg, E, according to past associations with satisfaction of the erg. Conversely, the strength of an ergic tension at the moment evokes cognitive associations in the sems involved.

This equation has only approximately been reached by factor analysis, which by its model analyzes to ΣM and ΣE, so further work with structural equations is necessary to determine the product terms. The next step in the dynamic calculus is the use of matrix representation in what is called "path learning analysis." This supposes that any commonly pursued life path (e.g., going to college, getting married) has, in a unit time (say, a year), a characteristic effect in changing traits. We (Cattell & Barton, 1975) showed this in a New Zealand study of

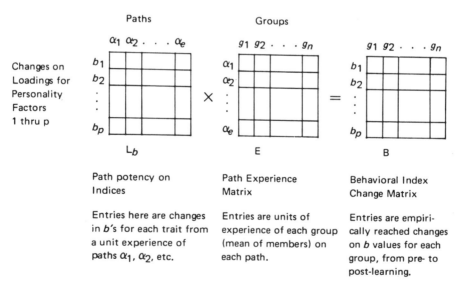

The solution for learning relation law matrix, L_b, is:

$$L_b = B\, E'\, (E\, E')^{-1}$$

Since obtaining behavioral indices requires a factor analysis we have either to compare R-technique results on groups, or P-technique results at different intervals of learning process progress in an individual. (These stages would replace g_1, g_2, etc., in E above.)

FIGURE 4.2. Path learning analysis method of calculating learning changes in the behavioral indices—b's. From *Personality and Learning Theory*, Vol. 2. (p. 299) by R. B. Cattell, 1980, New York: Springer Publishing Company. Copyright 1980 by Springer Publishing Company. Reprinted by permission.

18- to 23-year-olds, where marriage was found to raise G (the superego factor) and various other factors, and success in an occupation raised E (dominance), C (ego strength), and others. In short, life learning typically changes several factors to varying amounts. Since an individual is normally simultaneously following several paths to dealing with these effects, analyzing these paths one by one is thick with error. But a matrix multiplication, assuming that the changes are fractions of the original endowments, can be set out as shown in Figure 4.2 for a whole group of subjects at once (five persons).

The first matrix gives the discovered potencies of the various paths in altering the various traits, and the second the individuals' amounts of experience of those paths. In basic research, we would normally be seeking to obtain the first matrix from experimental records on the second and third; thus:

$$L = BE'(EE')^{-1} \qquad (4)$$

Further developments seek the relation of change to specific elements in path experience and are proposed elsewhere (Cattell, 1980, 1985).

To take the process of reward learning (e.g., in a maze), structural learning accepts the analysis as in Figure 4.3. Here it is supposed that the cognitive experience created at any decision point in the matrix, as at S and S_1, suffers a declining reverberation. The amount of engramming of this response will be a function of the amount of cognitive excitation, m_{23} and m_{13}, remaining when the rewarding goal of the maze is reached, and will be the product of M_1 or M_2 with the amount of satisfaction (tension reduction, or E_{ft}) on reaching the goal reward. This may be translated into an equation for engramming S_1,

$$N_{S_1} = \Sigma v_a s_a A_i + \Sigma v_p s_p P_i + \Sigma v_d s_d D_i \qquad (5)$$
$$+ KE_r m/t$$

where the v's include the structural learning from the individual's possession of abilities, A's;

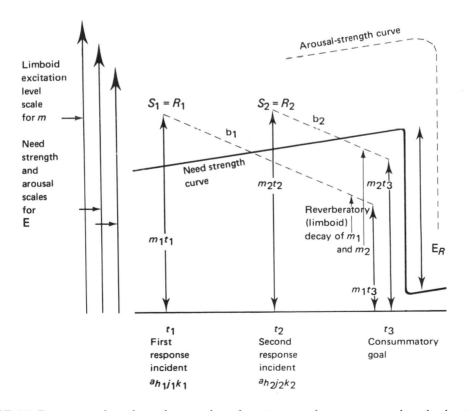

FIGURE 4.3 Engramming hypothesized as a product of cognitive reverberatory trace and need reduction as a goal. From *Personality and Learning Theory*, Vol. 2 (p. 267) by R. B. Cattell, 1980, New York: Springer Publishing Company. Copyright 1980 by Springer Publishing Company. Reprinted by permission.

personality traits, P's; and dynamic traits, D's. The m/t assumes the simplest linear reverberatory decay of the cognitive excitation; K is a standardizing constant; and E_r is the magnitude of reward.

Since a negative loading in a dynamic trait in the learning equation signifies that that trait is opposed to the final action, we can get an "index of conflict" in an equation such as the following:

$$A_{hijk} = b_{hjk1}P_{1i} + b_{hjk2}P_{2i} - b_{hjk3}\,P_{3i} - b_{hjk4}\,P_{4i} \qquad (6)$$

$$\text{as } C = \frac{(b_{hjk3} + b_{hjk4})}{(b_{hjk1} + b_{hjk2})} \qquad (7)$$

This C is best considered as an index of *indurated* conflict, which the individual has come to accept in the course of his or her life experience. Williams (1959) has shown by P-technique determination of the b's that the C index is lower in normals than in mental hospital patients.

The dynamic calculus covers some 38 equations systematizing concepts in integration, anxiety level, decision, control of impulse, relation to cultural elements, and most issues with which personality psychology is concerned. It has yielded for the treatment of edu-

cational progress the following formula:

$$\begin{aligned} \text{Achievement} = \qquad\qquad\qquad (8) \\ .44 \text{ superego} - .23 \text{ self-assertion} \\ + .35 \text{ self-sentiment} - .15 \text{ sex} \\ - .24 \text{ fear} + .21 \text{ pugnacity} \\ - .33 \text{ narcism} + .36 \text{ constructive erg} \end{aligned}$$

In clinical psychology, it has analyzed the process of varied expression of a sem according to situations. Incidentally, the model fully refutes the casual allegation that the situation is neglected by "trait theorists." Actually, each situation is represented by the profile of b's in every behavioral equation and permits objective classification of types of situations.

Finally, in that personality is seen as a process as well as a fixed profile, terms for states, S's, are added to the behavioral equation, recognizing that what a person does depends as much on the state he or she is in as on the person's traits. States have first been located on P-technique and dR-technique—the factoring of change scores. It has been shown (Boyle & Cattell, 1984) that state levels can be manipulated (e.g., by movies). The difficulty in practice of finding a person's state level *before* an actual use of the behavioral equation has been met by the "modulation theory." This supposes a specific state proneness or liability, L_{xi}, for

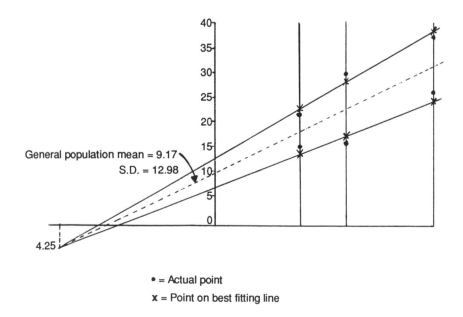

• = Actual point

x = Point on best fitting line

FIGURE 4.4 Illustrating by anxiety the essence of modulation theory.

each individual and a specific provocation force for each life situation, s_{jkx}. Then the formula has been shown (Cattell & Brennan, 1988) to hold that:

$$S_{xik} = s_{xk}L_{xi} \qquad (9)$$

This has the hitherto unattained quality in psychometrics of providing a *real* zero on any state scale—when s_{xk}, the stimulation of the given state, is absent. The derivation of the absolute zero in a given case, anxiety, is shown by taking two populations with different L values in Figure 4.4.

The dynamic calculus also opens a broad doorway into social psychology—first, by averaging the attitude vectors of members of a group to get the group's total synergy; and second, by using three matrices (the cultural syntality, C; the personal relevance matrix, P; and the impact matrix, I) in conjunction thus:

$$P \times C = I \qquad (10)$$

These are $N \times u$, $u \times u$, and $N \times u$, where N is the number of people and u is the number of cultural activities considered.

The dynamic calculus theory has been criticized (Eysenck & Eysenck, 1964) as having too many equations not yet tried on data. It is true that several are (clear, testable) hypotheses not yet tested out, however, in relation to the field generally, Madsen (1974) presents a quantitative analysis of 24 dynamic theories—including those of McDougall, Maslow, Pribram, Berlyne, Hebb, and Tolman—in which he places the dynamic calculus at the head of all in its ratio of experimental support to speculation. Certainly the expression of relations in formulas commands a precise possibility of testing each assertion.

THE DYNAMIC CALCULUS IN SYSTEMS THEORY AND CLINICAL WORK

In the further work on the dynamic calculus one encounters its statement in systems theory, as shown in the *vidas* systems model in Figure 4.5. This is an open system in which communications and feedback follow the internal arrows. The ergs, sems, and so on are not presented in separation, but as "classes" of reservoirs.

If we have to explain personality as it works in everyday life, we have to deal with a "flow" of stimuli and responses. What the individual literally does from hour to hour of the day is decided partly by stimuli occurring in relation to his or her sem structures and partly by the physiological states of the ergs, controlled by the ego structure (if all goes well). The phenomenon of persistence toward a goal with varied behavior—which is poorly accounted for by reflexology—arises from the main courses of response encountering different and immediate stimuli at different choice points in the dynamic lattice. The one primary assumption in the dynamic lattice is that behaviors continue only so long as they contribute ultimately to ergic goals, as shown by the paths from attitudes to sentiments to ergs in Figure 4.6.

It is this lattice that the clinician needs to unravel in diagnosis and therapy, and the complete way of doing so is by P-technique, as a successor to Freud's "free association." P-technique gives a cut across the lattice with the b values for the ergs and sems to which each attitude subsidiates. B curves can be obtained for each erg and sentiment, as shown in Figure 4.7 for the study of a clinical case (Cattell & Cross, 1952).

We (Birkett & Cattell, 1980) examined by P-technique the roots of the symptom in an episodic alcoholic and obtained the following behavioral equation:

$$
\begin{aligned}
\text{Symptom} = \quad & \qquad\qquad (11)\\
& .29 \text{ fear} + .23 \text{ self-sentiment}\\
& - .46 \text{ wife sem} - .61 \text{ narcism}\\
& - .23 \text{ superego}
\end{aligned}
$$

From this, one deduces that his drinking was motivated by fear and by affronts to the self-sentiment, and that it was opposed by the sentiment to his wife, by his narcissism and by his superego. When treatment proceeded on this basis, recovery was reached, though three previous psychiatric treatments had failed. After the factor analysis the result could be expressed as a structural equation summary, with the adjustment of the correlations to partials (see Cattell & Johnson, 1986, p. 368, Diagram 17.4).

DIRECTIONS FOR THE FUTURE

The main development in recent years in Cattellian theory has thus been the development of

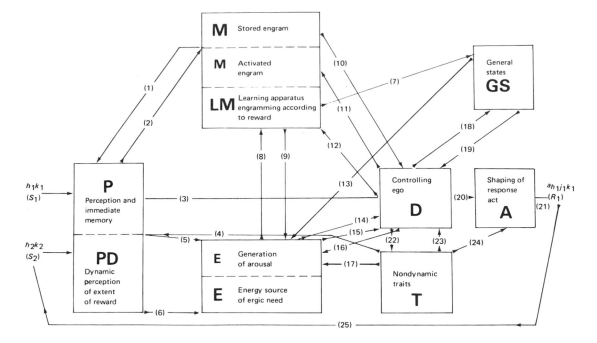

FIGURE 4.5. The full *vidas* systems model of personality. Channels and reservoirs: (1) Apperception information contributed; (2) referral to memory bank; (3) direct information on result of simple motor action; (4) trait effects on perception; (5) direct innate stimulation of ergs; (6) information on reward; (7) information on reward; (8) reciprocal action of ergic tension on M activation; (9) stimulation of ergs by sentiment; (10) cognitive feedback on final responses and results of earlier experience; (11) referral to sentiment "committee"; (12) invocation of controlling cues; (13) tempering effects of general states on ergs; (14) action urged by ergic demands; (15) information on degree of ergic gratification occurring; (16) invocation of controlling cues; (17) temperament limitations to arousal; (18) effect of ego decisions on general states, (19) effect of general states on ego decisions; (20) dynamic goal decisions sent for executive action; (21) emergence of response to stimulus S_1; (22) sensing fitness of action to ability and temperament traits; (23) call on abilities to help decision; (24) temperament–ability endowments shaping effectiveness of response; (25) response success or failure as new stimulus (S_2) input. From *Personality and Learning Theory*, Vol. 2 (p. 434) by R. B. Cattell, 1980, New York: Springer Publishing Company. Copyright 1980 by Springer Publishing Company. Reprinted by permission.

structured learning theory. It has already paid off well in the understanding of motivation and learning, taking the known structures into the behavioral equation. But the first new principle of structural learning—namely, that learning theory has to account for the rise of unitary traits—is not so well worked out yet in practice. We have the theory that the pre-existence of a social institution (e.g., family, occupation) simultaneously rewards all behaviors involved to produce correlation and a factor. But neither this nor the "budding" theory has yet received experimental attention. There is also need for experimental verification of the *ME* term in the motivational equation (Equation 3 above)— that is, that the cognitively unified channels of a sentiment are responsible for calling on the

energies of the ergs. Meanwhile, we write the equation with both pure ergic (*E*'s) and semic (*M*'s) terms, as well as the product terms, thus for response r_{ijhk}:

$$r_{ihjk} = b_{hjke}E_i + b_{hjkm}M_i + b_{hjkm}M_iE_i \\ + b_{hjke}E_iM_i \qquad (12)$$

Here the last term covers an as-yet-undiscovered tendency of the rise of an ergic tension (e.g., from physiological causes) to evoke the cognitive structure of a sem.

The trail thus ends in a systems theory of mutual internal reactions, which has been schematized in the proposed *vidas* systems theory model shown in Figure 4.5 above. Although all scientific researchers are com-

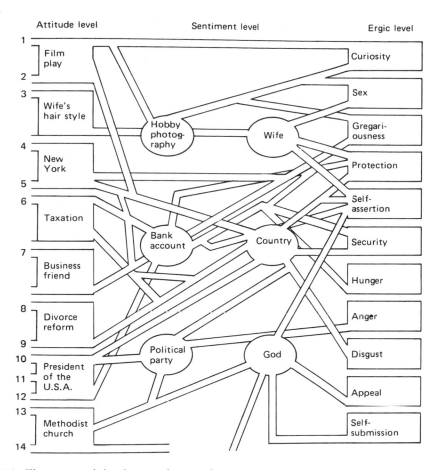

FIGURE 4.6. Illustration of the dynamic lattice, showing attitude subsidiation, sentiment structure, and ergic goals. From Cattell (1965). Copyright 1965 by Academic Press Inc. Reprinted by permission.

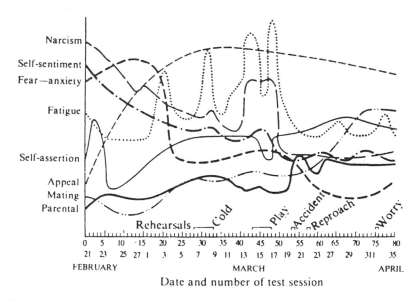

FIGURE 4.7 Ergs and sems in a P-technique experiment: Ergic tension (and sentiment) response to stimulus (S), internal state (P), and goal satisfaction (G). "Narcism" is narcissism. From "Comparison of the Ergic and Self-Sentiment Structures Found in Dynamic Traits by R- and P-Techniques" by R. B. Cattell and K. P. Cross, 1952, *Journal of Personality, 21*, pp. 250–271. Copyright 1952 by American Psychological Association. Reprinted by permission.

pelled today to recognize the ultimate truth that personality has to be represented as a system, the methods for investigating the structure of a system from observed behavior are still crude. Figure 4.5, therefore, is presented as a shrewd speculation to be investigated in time by improved equation methods.

REFERENCES

Boyle, G. G., & Cattell, R. B. (1984). Proof of the situational sensitivity of mood states and dynmaic traits—ergs and sentiments—to disturbing stimuli. *Personality and Individual Differences, 5,* 541–548.

Birkett, H., & Cattell, R. B. (1980). Can P-technique be practicably shortened? Some proposals and test of a 50-day abridgment. *Multivariate Experimental Clinical Research, 5,* 1–16.

Cattell, R. B. (1965). Methodological and conceptual advances in evaluating hereditary and environmental influences and their interaction. In S. G. Vandenberg (Ed.), *Methods and goals in human behavior genetics* (pp. 95–140). New York: Academic Press.

Cattell, R. B. (1973). *Personality and mood by questionnaire.* San Francisco: Jossey-Bass.

Cattell, R. B. (1980). *Personality and learning theory.* New York: Springer Publishing Company.

Cattell, R. B. (1985). *Human motivation and the dynamic calculus.* New York: Praeger.

Cattell, R. B. (1987). *Psychotherapy by structured learning theory.* New York: Springer Publishing Company.

Cattell, R. B., & Barton, K. (1975). Changes in personality over a five-year period and relationship to change in life events. *JSAS: Catalogue of Selected Documents in Psychology, 5,* 283.

Cattell, R. B., & Brennan, J. (1988). A check on modulcation theory calculations on anxiety and depression. Manuscript submitted for publication.

Cattell, R. B., & Child, D. (1975). *Motivation and dynamic structure.* New York: Holt, Rinehart & Winston.

Cattell, R. B., & Cross, K. P. (1952). Comparison of the ergic and self-sentiment structures found in dynamic traits by R- and P-techniques. *Journal of Personality, 21,* 250–271.

Cattell, R. B., & Gibbons, B. D. (1968). Personality factor structure of the combined Guilford and Cattell personality questionnaires. *Journal of Personality and Social Psychology, 9,* 107–120.

Cattell, R. B., Horn, J. L., & Butcher, J. (1962). The dynamic structure of attitudes in adults and description of some established factors and their measurement on the Motivational Analysis Test (MAT). *British Journal of Psychology, 67,* 89–149.

Cattell, R. B., & Johnson, R. (1986). *Functional psychological testing.* New York: Brunner/Mazel.

Cattell, R. B., & Krug, S. E. (1986). The number of factors in the 16 PF: Overview of the evidence with special emphasis on methodological problems. *Educational and Psychological Measurement, 46,* 509–526.

Cattell, R. B., Lawlis, F., McGill, J. C., & McGraw, A. (1979). Experimental check on the theory of motivational components, duplicated in two interest areas. *Multivariate Experimental Clinical Research, 4,* 33–52.

Cattell, R. B., Sealy, A. P., & Sweney, A. B. (1966). What can personality and motivation source trait measurements add to the prediction of school achievement? *British Journal of Educational Psychology, 36,* 280–295.

Comrey, A. L. (1970). *Manual for the Comrey Personality Scales.* San Diego: EYJS.

Digman, J. M., & Inouye, J. (1986). Further specification of the five robust factors of personality. *Journal of Personality and Social Psychology, 50,* 116–123.

Eysenck, H. J., & Eysenck, S. B. G. (1964). *Manual of the Eysenck Personality Inventory.* London: University of London Press.

Howarth, E., & Brown, J. A. (1971). An item–factor analysis of the 16 PF. *Personality, 2,* 117–139.

Jöreskog, K. G., & Sorbom, (1967). Some contributions to maximum likelihood factor analysis. *Psychometrika, 32,* 443–482.

Madsen, K. B. (1974). *Modern theories of motivation.* New York: Halsted Press.

Meehl, P. E. (1954). *Clinical versus statistical prediction.* Minneapolis: University of Minnesota Press.

Sweney, A. B., & Cartwright, D. S. (1966). Relations between conscious and unconscious manifestations of motivation in children. *Multivariate Behaviorial Research, 1,* 447–459.

Williams, J. R. (1959). A test of the validity of P-technique in the measurement of internal conflict. *Journal of Personality, 27,* 418–437

Chapter 5

Personality Dispositions Revisited and Revised: A View after Three Decades

Walter Mischel
Columbia University

The most enduring and crucial choices faced by personality psychologists concern the meaning and function of the field's basic units: How should one conceptualize traits or dispositions? What are they? How should they be assessed? For more than 40 years, the field has struggled with the nature and proper evaluation of personality dispositions; each decade devoted to a different facet of the same theme, in a progression that seems as clear now in retrospect as it was fuzzy then. This chapter considers some of these developments selectively, focusing on the nature of human dispositions relevant to social behavior and to the construct of personality.

A BRIEF HISTORY: THE PARADIGM CHALLENGE

Early Exuberance

To understand the present state of the psychology of personal dispositions, and to consider its future seriously, first requires a glimpse of the past in which much of the current agenda is still rooted. In the 1950s, the field of personality had a great growth spurt, both as a profession and as a science, stimulated on one side by demands for clinical psychologists in new health care facilities for millions of World War II veterans, and on the other by the opening of the Sputnik-launched space race, which fueled federal support for science in the United States. With this impetus, a new generation of clinically schooled "personologists" was trained to dedicate themselves to two-pronged careers as "scientist/practitioners." Most tried to straddle both roles; researchers devoted to testing their favorite hypotheses, and clinicians eager to apply the findings of their new psychological science to ameliorate the human condition.

In this ambitious decade, they created a huge research literature, intending to demonstrate the reliability and validity of an array of promising techniques—from Rorschachs and Thematic Apperception Tests to Minnesota Multiphasic Personality Inventories and interviews— inherited from an earlier generation of practitioners and pioneers. They assumed that these methods, if they did not provide X-rays of the human personality or directly pave Freud's royal road to the unconscious as originally hoped, at least would yield psychometrically sophisticated, reliable summary profiles to capture the gist of what the individual "is really like," stably over time and across situations. In this quest they were guided by the widely accepted "classic" view of dispositions. Shared by both trait and psychodynamic approaches, the traditional or classic assumptions about personality arose from a self-evidently true observation. On virtually every dimension of human behavior, there are substantial, distinctive differences in the response of different persons within the same social situation: Clearly, *within* the same objective stimulus situation, there often are also large differences *between* individuals. The second assumption is that individuals are characterized by *stable* and *broadly generalized* dispositions that endure over long periods of time and that generate consistencies in their social behavior across a wide range of situations. With this belief, assessors tried to predict behavior in many domains and contexts from a variety of personality indicators or "signs" from which they inferred these dispositions.

To illustrate, let us consider one effort, representative of the expectations and assessment strategies of its time (Mischel, 1965). The goal was to predict the probable success of Peace Corps teachers in Nigeria on the basis of a battery of measures while they were still in training. The results from this research highlight both the typical findings and the concerns that grew from them. Briefly, global ratings of the trainees made by the faculty, by the assessment board for the project, and by an interviewer were significantly intercorrelated. For example, the assessment board and the interview ratings correlated .72, showing that the assessors had similar impressions of the candidates' personalities in training. Independently, field performance of the Peace Corps teachers when they were on their assignments in Nigeria was assessed on six criterion subscales (which also were highly intercorrelated), and these were aggregated into a multiple-scale criterion. To illustrate the major findings, simple self-reports and self-ratings, as on anxiety-relevant items and attitudes to authority, yielded modest but often statistically significant correlations with outcome criteria, accounting for small but significant amounts of variance. On the other hand, more global and indirect measures failed

even to reach significance. For example, behavior in the interviews, one of the favorite global methods, predicted total criterion performance in Nigeria with a correlation of .13, accounting for a trivial percentage of the variance.

A three-person subcommittee of the assessment board based its pooled recommendations of each candidate on their discussion and review of all data from all observer sources during training. They thus integrated information from faculty evaluations, academic records, peer ratings, and interviews. A larger final assessment review board discussed these recommendations, considering each candidate individually. None of the separate predictions made by the training staff correlated significantly with criterion performance, to the dismay of those who were so confident in the power of their procedures. Especially notable is that even when the data were aggregated to enhance reliability, the resulting combined evaluations of each candidate by the total assessment board predicted aggregated performance outcomes in the field with a nonsignificant correlation of .20.

1968 Challenges to Classic Dispositional Assumptions

Findings like these were startling at a time when even small samples of behavior had seemed to promise a diagnostic X-ray to illuminate the core of personality—to allow rapid inferences from a few subtle signs observed by experts to broad generalizations about what the individual was like "on the whole," and then from these inferences about generalized global dispositions to predict specific outcomes. Were such predictive failures anomalies?

By the late 1960s, the yield from the many investigations of the preceding years was scrutinized to sift the conclusions. A thorough reexamination of the traditional global trait and psychodynamic approaches to the study of personality resulted, and to virtually everyone's surprise, challenged the dominant establishment views and indeed the core assumptions of personality and clinical psychologists.

On the one hand, a good deal of evidence was found that cognitive constructions about oneself and the world, including other people, are often extremely stable and highly resistant to change. Self-concepts, and the impressions of other people (including clinical judgments)—the theories that we have about ourselves and each other—these phenomena and many more of the same type were found to have consistency and even tenacious continuity (Mischel, 1968). Indeed, our constructions about other people are often built quickly and on the basis of little information (e.g., Bruner, Olver, & Greenfield, 1966), and soon become difficult to disconfirm. An impressive degree of continuity and consistency also was found for another aspect of cognition: namely, cognitive or information-processing styles (e.g., Kagan, 1969; Witkin, Goodenough, & Karp, 1967). These styles are often closely related to measures of intelligence and cognitive competence, and like "intelligence" itself, they tend to have higher consistency relative to more social dimensions of behavior (e.g., "conscientiousness," "honesty," "friendliness").

Apart from cognitive and intellective dimensions, the domain of social dispositions and interpersonal behavioral consistency proved much harder to document. In fact, a surprisingly reliable degree of behavioral specificity or "discriminativeness" (Mischel, 1973) was found regularly in the behavioral referents for such character traits as rigidity, social conformity, dependency, and aggression; for attitudes to authority; and for virtually any other nonintellective personality dimension (Mischel, 1968; Peterson, 1968; Vernon, 1964). In some readings of the literature, noncognitive personality dispositions began to seem much less global than traditional psychodynamic and trait positions had assumed them to be, with response patterns even in highly similar situations typically failing to be strongly related.

> Individuals show far less cross-situational consistency in their behavior than has been assumed by trait–state theories. The more dissimilar the evoking situations, the less likely they are to produce similar or consistent responses from the same individual. Even seemingly trivial situational differences may reduce correlations to zero. Response consistency tends to be greatest within the same response medium, within self-reports to paper-and-pencil tests, for example, or within directly observed non-verbal behavior. Intraindividual consistency is reduced drastically when dissimilar response modes are employed. Activities that are substantially associated with aspects of intelligence and with problem solving behavior—like achievement behaviors, cognitive styles, response speed—tend to be most consistent. (Mischel, 1968, p. 177)

Evidence of this sort, in smaller amounts, had been cited for many years (e.g., Dudycha, 1936; Hartshorne & May, 1928; Newcomb, 1929), indicating instability and lack of consistency across situations in domains of behavior expected to reflect generalized and stable traits. In the past, however, such data were interpreted to reflect the imperfections of tests and tools and the resulting unreliability and errors of measurements; the fallibility of clinical judges; and other similar methodological problems. Now the new criticisms also noted that these methodological sources constituted serious constraints, but took another step, suggesting that the observed inconsistency so often found in studies of noncognitive personality dimensions may reflect the state of nature and not just the noise of measurement. Of course, this need not imply a capriciously haphazard world, but it did suggest a world in which personality consistencies seem greater than they are and in which the organization of behavior seems simpler than it is (Mischel, 1969, pp. 1014–1015).

The Psychodynamic–Clinical Alternative

At the same time that global traits were challenged in their core assumptions, the dispositional paradigm of psychodynamic approaches also was questioned, but on different grounds. In contrast to the neglect of situational variables for which classic trait approaches were being criticized, psychodynamic approaches to personality dispositions had long recognized both the specificity and complexity of behavior, rejecting the idea of broad, overt behavioral consistencies across situations at the "surface" level. They believed that the observed inconsistencies in the individual's overt behavior could be understood as merely superficial diversities that masked the fundamentally consistent, underlying dispositions and dynamics (Mischel, 1971, p. 153). Thus, psychodynamic theories at an abstract level could readily deal with the facts of inconsistencies in the person's behavior. But they were subject to another problem. The embarrassment for them was in the failure to provide compelling empirical evidence that the inferences they generated about the underlying or genotypic dispositions were useful either for the prediction of behavior or for its therapeutic modification, especially when compared to simpler, less inferential, and less costly alternatives.

Perhaps the most serious challenges to classic dispositional approaches, both of the trait and of the psychodynamic type, arose primarily from the clinical experiences of the 1950s and early 1960s with clients seeking help. It was in that clinical context, not in the laboratory, that many clinicians came to doubt the value both of the psychodynamic and of the trait-dispositional portraits to which they were devoting most of their effort (e.g., Peterson, 1968; Vernon, 1964). Skepticism about the utility of such global assessments arose not from any lack of interest in the client's dispositions nor from a neglect of individual differences. Instead, it arose from a growing anxiety that psychodynamic and trait "personality diagnostics," too often generated without close attention to the clients' own views of their lives and specific behaviors, might be exercises in stereotyping that missed the uniqueness of individuals and pinned the persons instead on a continuum of clinician-supplied labels, as George Kelly (1955) had charged years earlier.

Many empirical studies had investigated the utility of clinicians' efforts to infer broad dispositions indirectly from specific symptomatic signs and to unravel disguises in order to uncover the hypothetical dispositions that might be their roots. The results on the whole threw doubt on the utility of clinical judgments even when the judges were well-trained, expert psychodynamicists, working with clients in clinical contexts and using their own preferred techniques (Bandura, 1969; Mischel, 1968; Peterson, 1968). Clinicians guided by concepts about underlying genotypic dispositions did not seem better able to predict behavior than the persons' own direct and simple self-reports, demographic variables, or in some cases the clinicians' secretaries (e.g., Mischel, 1968). The disappointments of expert clinical judgment were especially disconcerting when contrasted with evidence for the predictions possible from indices of directly relevant past behavior, such as an individual's past record of maladjustment and hospitalization (Lasky et al., 1959). A correlation of .61 was found, for example, between the weight of a patient's file folder and the incidence of rehospitalization. As results like these illustrate, even a simple measure of a person's past can sometimes powerfully predict relevant aspects of the future, in sharp contrast to more complex, indirect, costly efforts. It

should be equally evident that the simple fact that one cannot predict well from some previously favored measures and strategies denies neither the importance of individual differences nor the potential value of all sorts of assessments for all sorts of purposes (e.g., Mischel, 1983). It does not mean that individual differences are unpredictable, but it does indicate that the nature and locus of that predictability may be quite different from what had been assumed.

When concerns with clinical practice were combined with the evidence from empirical studies of global traits, the challenge in 1968 both to trait and to psychodynamic approaches to personality became considerable. A review of the utility of psychometrically measured traits, as well as of psychodynamic inferences about states and traits led to the following conclusion:

> [R]esponses have not served very userfully as indirect signs of internal predispositions. Actuarial methods of data combination are generally better than clinical–theoretical inferences. Base rates, direct self-reports, self-predictions, and especially indices of relevant past behavior typically provide the best as well as the cheapest predictions. Moreover, these predictions hold their own against, and usually exceed, those generated either clinically or statistically from complex inferences about underlying traits and states. In general, the predictive efficiency of simple, straightforward self-ratings and measures of directly relevant past performance has not been exceeded by more psychometrically sophisticated personality tests, by combining tests into batteries, by assigning differential weights to them, or by employing more complex statistical analyses involving multiple-regression equations. The conclusions for personality measures apply, on the whole, to diverse content areas including the prediction of college achievement, job and professional success, treatment outcomes, rehospitalization for psychiatric patients, parole violations for deliquent children, and so on. In light of these findings it is not surprising that large-scale applied efforts to predict behavior from personality inferences have been strikingly and consistently unsuccessful. . . . (Mischel, 1968, pp. 145–146)

Finally, beyond the empirical challenge questioning the utility of global traits was the practice of endowing such dispositions with causal powers in theoretical explanations of behavior. Allport (1937) had most articulately argued that behind the confusion of trait terms, the disagreement of judges, and the errors of empirical observation, trait terms ultimately refer to "bona fide mental structures" (p. 289) that generate (i.e., produce) consistencies in behavior not only over time, but also across situations. To the degree that traits also were commonly used as causal entities in explanation of the determinants of behavior, they became vulnerable to criticisms of circularity (Mischel, 1968; Peterson, 1968; Vernon, 1964). If descriptions of behavior are used to invoke traits, which in turn are offered as explanations of the same behavior from which they were inferred in the first place, the circularity of the reasoning becomes embarassing, as archly noted, for example, by Bandura (1969).

The critiques of traditional dispositional approaches that emerged at this juncture were first read by many as "situationist" attacks on personality itself and as unjustified denials of the importance of individual differences (e.g., Bowers, 1973). Reactions of this type were understandable, given a long tradition of dichotomizing the person and the situation and contrasting the relative importance of the two sources of variance, rather than clarifying how they interact psychologically. But while the challenge to traditional dispositional paradigms called attention to the significance of situations or contexts in the study of persons, its basic message was not a negation either of personality as a field or of individual differences as a phenomenon. On the contrary, the focus was on the idiographic nature of each person interacting with the specific contexts of his or her life and on the need to revise some favorite assumptions of traditional personality theories to take those unique interactions into account seriously. Far from denying individual differences in personality, the criticisms (e.g., Mischel, 1968; Peterson, 1968) were largely motivated to defend individuality and the uniqueness of each person against the tendency, prevalent in 1960s clinical and diagnostic efforts, to use a few ratings or few behavioral signs to categorize people into categories on an assessor's favorite nomothetic trait dimensions. It was common practice to assume in the 1960s that such assessments were useful to predict not just "average" levels of individual differences, but a person's specific behavior on specific criteria as well as "in general." It was not uncommon to undertake decision making about a

person's life and future on the basis of a relatively limited sampling of personological "signs" or "trait indicators." It was this type of practice that was challenged:

> Global traits and states are excessively crude, gross units to encompass adequately the extraordinary complexity and subtlety of the discriminations that people constantly make. Traditional trait–state conceptions of man have depicted him as victimized by his infantile history, as possessed by unchanging rigid trait attributes, and as driven inexorably by unconscious irrational forces. This conceptualization of man, besides being philosophically unappetizing, is contradicted by massive experimental data. The traditional trait–state conceptualizations of personality, while often paying lip service to man's complexity and to the uniqueness of each person, in fact lead to a grossly oversimplified view that misses both the richness and the uniqueness of individual lives. A more adequate conceptualization must take full account of man's extraordinary adaptiveness and capacities for discrimination, awareness, and self-regulation; it must also recognize that men can and do reconceptualize themselves and change, and that an understanding of how humans can constructively modify their behavior in systematic ways is the core of a truly dynamic personality psychology. (Mischel, 1968, p. 301)

In sum, the dissatisfactions that crystallized two decades ago were wide in range, reflecting many concerns. Global dispositional approaches were faulted as not useful for the planning of specific individual treatment programs, for the design of social change programs, or for the prediction of the specific behavior of individuals in specific contexts. Perhaps most troubling theoretically, they also were criticized for not yielding evidence of cross-situational consistency and for failing to provide a theoretically compelling analysis of the basic psychological processes that underlie the individual's cognition, affect, and actions (e.g., Mischel, 1973).

Aftermath of the Challenge

These challenges fueled a period of prolonged and heated controversy about personality dispositions and the construct of personality itself that consumed much attention throughout the 1970s and early 1980s (e.g., reviewed in Magnusson & Endler, 1977). The debate was multifaceted—engaging many segments of the field, spilling into adjacent areas, and spanning from one extreme that exaggerated the dilemma to another that trivialized it. The claims ranged from contentions that personality was a largely fictitious construction in the mind of the perceiver (e.g., Shweder, 1973), to counterarguments intended to prove that global dispositions as traditionally conceptualized were "alive and well" if one simply employed a more reliable measurement strategy to find them (e.g., Epstein, 1979). In the same period, social psychologists amassed evidence for the power of situational variables, and proposed that humans have a persistent tendency to invoke dispositions as favorite (albeit erroneous) explanations of social behavior (e.g., Nisbett & Ross, 1980; Ross, 1977; see also West, 1983). Indeed, the tendency to focus on dispositions in causal explanations soon was seen as a symptom of a "fundamental attribution error" committed by laypersons in everyday life, as well as by the psychologists who study them (Ross, 1977). Evidence of systematic judgmental errors in personality assessment and inferences, of course, had been noted often in the past. Typically, however, it was dismissed as mere "noise" of unreliable, imperfect methods, open to correction by improving the quality of measurement. Now such data began instead to be read as valid indicators of human nature, revealing the operation of "cognitive economics" or heuristics through which complex information tends to be reduced, simplified, and potentially distorted (e.g., Kahneman & Tversky, 1973; Mischel, 1973, 1979; Nisbett & Ross, 1980).

While these voices were insistent, so were those that, in response to these provocations, continued to seek methodological reforms through which the utility of generalized dispositions could be revealed and the status quo resumed. (They therefore focused on the methodological weakness of earlier efforts to demonstrate the utility of global dispositions and the need to obtain adequate reliability in the search for consistency by aggregating multiple observations and measures; e.g., Epstein, 1979). And in the same turbulent period it also began to be recognized, at least abstractly, that the person *and* the situation *and* the interaction among them had to be considered seriously in personality psychology (e.g., Magnusson & Endler, 1977).

In the abstract and as a general framework, "person–situation interactionism" was easily and widely embraced and even prematurely hailed as yielding a solution to the long-standing controversy and the growing confusion. The continuing challenge, however, still awaited answers: how to reconceptualize dispositions to take such interactions into account incisively, *a priori* in the form of specific predictions, and not just in post hoc attempts to deal with unpredicted and perhaps basically unpredictable higher-order interactions after they are found in the data (see Mischel, 1973, for discussion). Going beyond lip service about the importance of person–situation interaction to generate and test theory-based predictions of those interactions became and remains high on the agenda for personality psychology. In this direction, one senses a trend toward the collective building of a more cumulative theory of personality, a set of principles and constructs open to progressive revision and refinement on the basis of research findings—each version presented with different foci, specifics, and goals, but sharing a common general theoretical orientation. This body of theorizing is cumulative and frankly revisable, not "owned" by any single theorist or even "school." It is based instead on the most promising relevant findings from the diverse fields on which a comprehensive scientific attempt to understand personality can build. What seems to be evolving is not a single-owner, single-view theory of "what people are like," but a general shared perspective—a framework for the analysis and clarification of more specific issues and concerns basic for personality psychology about the processes and consequences of social-cognitive development in the person.

SOCIAL-COGNITIVE UNITS FOR PERSONALITY PSYCHOLOGY

In this vein, a set of person variables was proposed in the early 1970s (Mischel, 1973), based on theoretical developments in the fields of social learning and cognition that had been bypassed or ignored by personality theory at that juncture. In light of the complexity of the interactions between the individual and the situation that was emphasized by the critics of global trait assumptions, the focus in the search for person variables shifted. This shift called attention away from inferences about what broad traits a person *has*, to focus instead on what the person *does* in particular conditions in the coping process. Of course, what people do encompasses not just motor acts, but what they do cognitively and affectively, including the constructs they generate, the projects they plan and pursue, and the self-regulatory efforts they attempt in light of long-term goals (to illustrate from the vast array). Moreover, it was argued that these descriptions of what persons *do* need to include the specific psychological conditions in which they do it, thus providing more condition-qualified, "local," contingent, and specific characterizations of persons in contexts, in contrast to context-free traits.

Briefly, the cognitive–social learning approach to personality shifted the unit of study from global traits inferred from behavioral signs to the person's cognitions, affect, and action assessed in relation to the particular psychological conditions in which they occur. The focus thus changed from describing situation-free people with broad trait adjectives to analyzing the interactions between conditions and the cognitions and behaviors of interest.

In the 1960s, much personality research on social behavior was undertaken to study the processes of cognition and social learning through which potential behaviors are acquired, evoked, maintained, and modified (e.g., as reviewed in Bandura, 1969; Mischel, 1968). Less attention had been devoted to the psychological products within the person of these processes in the course of development. The cognitive–social learning reconceptualization of personality was intended to identify a set of interrelated person variables that capture these "products" of the individual's psychological history and that in turn mediate the manner in which new situations are interpreted. The goal was to identify person variables that are a synthesis of promising constructs in the areas of cognition and social learning. These variables were not expected to provide ways of accurately predicting broadly cross-situational behavioral differences between persons: The discriminativeness and idiosyncratic organization of behavior seem to be facts of nature, to be taken seriously in the study of dispositions. These variables should help to specify constructive ways of conceptualizing and studying specifically how persons mediate the impact of stimuli, generating their distinctive behavior in particular contexts. They also should help to conceptualize person–situation interactions in an evolving theoretical framework based as much on contributions from cognitive, social, developmental, and behav-

ioral psychology as from personality psychology itself.

Although the person variables that were proposed overlap and interact, each yields distinctive information about the probable specific interaction between the individual and any given psychological situation. Each may be assessed objectively. Most important theoretically, each is also amenable to study in two distinct but complementary ways. Each may be conceptualized as a person variable that is the *product* of the individual's social-cognitive development and on which individuals differ. Each also may be conceptualized in terms of the psychological *processes* relevant to understanding the operations of that variable and its psychological meaning. Thus, each variable has both a structural and a functional aspect in an emerging theory of personality. The following discussion briefly considers each of these person variables.

Competencies

Although a great deal of psychological research has clarified how people acquire knowledge and competencies, it is less clear how to conceptualize just what is acquired by the person. The concept of "cognitive and behavioral construction competencies" was intended to be broad enough to include the vast array of organized information that individuals acquire. The term "constructions" was used to emphasize the *constructive* manner in which information seems to be retrieved (e.g., Neisser, 1967) and the active organization through which it is categorized and transformed (Bower, 1970; Mandler, 1967, 1968). If cognitive psychology has a single message for personality students, it may be that rather than mimicking observed responses or returning memory traces from undisturbed storage vaults, observers selectively *construct* (generate) their renditions of the world of "reality." The concept of "construction competencies" also was intended to call attention to the person's *cognitive activities*—the operations and transformations that people perform on information, in contrast to some store of cognitions and responses that a person "has."

Although the particular cognitive processes remain far from clear, it is self-evident that persons can construct an enormous range of potential behaviors, and that they differ greatly in their construction capabilities. (Compare, e.g., the "construction potentials" of an acrobat, a writer, an actor, and a mathematician.) To assess competencies, one tries to specify the quality and range of the cognitive constructions and behavioral enactments of which the individual is capable. In this effort, rather than assessing "typical" behavior, one assesses *potential* behaviors or achievements, testing what the person *can* do rather than what he or she "typically" does. Increasing attention to cognitive competencies seemed warranted, given that "mental abilities" seem to have much better temporal and cross-situational stability and influence on social behavior and development than most of the social traits and motivations traditionally favored in personality research (e.g., Mischel, 1968, 1969).

The relevance of competencies for personality seemed plain because of the important, persistent contributions of indices of intelligence to networks of personality correlations found in assessment (Campbell & Fiske, 1959; Mischel, 1968). The relative temporal stability of competencies was also found to contribute substantially to the impression of consistency in personality more generally (Mischel, 1968). Historically, personality psychologists tried to "partial out" the role of intelligence, adhering to the traditional dichotomy between "abilities" and "personality." In spite of these efforts, cognitive competencies (e.g., as tested by "mental age" and IQ tests) proved to be among the best predictors of social development and interpersonal adjustment (e.g., Anderson, 1960). Enduring competencies relevant both to intelligence and to adaptive social coping also appear correlated with the ability to voluntarily delay gratification in the pursuit of goals early in life (e.g., Mischel, Shoda, & Peake, 1988; Mischel, Shoda, & Rodriguez, 1989).

An exciting theoretical trend in the field is to incorporate competencies as central constructs for personality psychology. Thus rather than trying to control for and partial out "IQ" or other ability indices, a contemporary movement is to reanalyze and deepen the notion of intelligence itself, in order to generate a more comprehensive conception of intelligent social behavior encompassing the range of social knowledge and coping skills on which people differ as they try to deal with real-life problems (e.g., Cantor & Kihlstrom, 1987; Cantor & Zirkel, Chapter 6, this volume; Mischel et al., 1989). Such a conception of mental ability focuses more on the individual's potential for flexibility, constructive alternativism, and problem solving in the coping process, in George Kelly's (1955) sense, than on a fixed static "IQ" in the psychometric sense.

Personal Constructs and Encoding Strategies

A second variable of special importance for personality psychology is another crucial component of information processing: the perceiver's ways of encoding or categorizing information from stimulus inputs to form social and personal constructs, including theories about the self, other people, and the world. Different individuals encode and categorize the same events in different ways, as seen in the differences among people in the personal constructs they generate (e.g., Argyle & Little, 1972; Kelly, 1955), and in the kinds of information to which they attend (Mischel, Ebbesen, & Zeiss, 1973), and it is the "stimulus as coded" (not necessarily the stimulus the psychologist has in mind) that informs them and to which they react. Because people can and do cognitively transform stimuli focusing on selected aspects, their selective attention, interpretation, and categorization of events substantially alter the meaning and impact of those stimuli (see Higgins, Chapter 12, this volume).

Skepticism about the usefulness of traditional trait constructs about broad dispositions, of course, in no way suggests that one should ignore the constructs that people have about themselves, about others, and about the world of situations they encounter. Personal construct systems, implicit personality theories (e.g., Hamilton, 1971; Schneider, 1973), and self-concepts (e.g., Gergen, 1968) have long constituted important ingredients for a basic variable of personality. The last decade has witnessed exploding research interest in the extensions, the applications, and the revisions of ideas about personal constructs and "self-schemas" to the areas of personality psychology. Although broad self-theories always were of interest to personality psychologists, in the 1970s they began to be articulated much more concretely and in researchable terms. The relevant work is too voluminous even to cite comprehesively here (e.g., Kihlstrom & Cantor, 1984). It encompasses studies of schemas, standards, scripts, templates, plans, prototypes, and other cognitive frameworks and knowledge packages hypothesized as mental structures that mediate the impact of social experience and guide information processing selectively (e.g., Cantor & Mischel, 1977, 1979; Markus, 1977; Nisbett & Ross, 1980; Rogers, Kuiper, & Kirker, 1977). It is not yet clear which routes will prove ultimately to be most useful, but there is little doubt that personal and social constructs, encoding strategies, and implicit theories will have an enduring place in the assessment of persons. The chapters by Cantor and Zirkel (Chapter 6) and by Higgins (Chapter 12) in this volume provide outstanding examples of work aimed in those directions.

The potential yield is exemplified in studies of knowledge accessibility and activation ("priming"), as discussed by Higgins (Chapter 12, this volume). His concept of "chronic accessibility" (Higgins, King, & Mavin, 1982) refers to the finding that certain categories or constructs are primed so frequently by some individuals that they may endure within the individuals in a state of potential activation, ready to be primed by minimal cues in the situation. This type of research opens a route for the analysis of dispositional preferences or "readiness" in ways specifically and incisively linked to the operation of social-cognitive processes. It thus facilitates the analysis and predictions of specific person–situation interactions, and further enables the study of personality in terms of both individual differences and the relevant psychological processes, within the same basic conceptual framework.

Expectancies

So far, the person variables considered deal with what individuals are capable of doing and how they categorize people, events, and themselves. To go from construction capacity and constructs to the construction of behavior in particular situations requires attention to the determinants of performance. The individual's "expectancies" are the person variables especially relevant here. It is often informative to know what a person *can* do and construes; however, to try to predict the person's behavior in particular situations, one needs to consider the specific expectancies about the perceived probable consequences of different behavioral possibilities in that situation (e.g., Mischel,

1966; Rotter, 1954). These "if _____, then _____" outcome expectations guide the selection (choice) of behaviors from among the enormous number that potentially could be constructed and enacted within any situation. In the absence of distinctive new information about the behavior–outcome relations likely in any situation, what the person enacts is likely to depend on relevant previous expectancies developed in situations encoded as similar (e.g., Mischel & Staub, 1965).

When the expected consequences for performance change, so does behavior. This simple fact of social learning makes predictable the lack of cross-situational consistency that was so unexpected and troubling for classic trait theory. When the consequences the person expects are not highly correlated across situations or response modes it is not surprising that responses will not covary strongly (Mischel, 1968). Thus, expectancies mediate the extent to which a person's behavior is cross-situationally consistent or discriminative. Because most social behaviors lead to positive consequences in some situations but not in others, highly discriminative specific expectancies tend to evolve, and the relatively low correlations typically found among a person's response patterns across situations become theoretically understandable rather than embarrassing. For example, the child who has been rewarded regularly in preschool for "dependency" (e.g., touching, holding, and being near) with the teacher but not with peers is unlikely to provide evidence for a high correlation between "dependency" assessed in these two situations (Mischel, 1969).

This type of analysis suggests that discriminative facility is highly functional, whereas "consistency" in the form of insufficient sensitivity to changing consequences may be an indicator of maladaptive functioning. Supporting such an interpretation is the finding that indiscriminate responding (i.e., "consistent" behavior across situations) often characterizes maladaptive, severely disturbed, or less mature persons more than it does well-functioning ones (Moos, 1968; Raush, Dittman, & Taylor, 1959). Moreover, the discriminativeness of human behavior, rather than constituting a "dilemma" for personality psychology, is predictable to the degree that most social behaviors generate positive consequences in some situations but negative ones in others. Thus even if those situations seem similar to the personality assessor, the individual's behavior will not be consistent across them.

The expectancy construct has several facets. One of these, "self-efficacy," defined as the individual's conviction that he or she can execute the behavior required by a particular situation, has come into focus in the last decade (Bandura, 1978, 1986). To assess self-efficacy, one asks persons to indicate their degree of confidence that they can do a particular task, which is described in detail. Perceptions of one's own efficacy may importantly guide and direct behavior. The close connection between high self-efficacy expectations and effective performance is illustrated in studies on people who received various treatments to help reduce their fear of snakes. Consistently high associations occurred between the degree to which such persons improved as a result of treatment (becoming able to handle snakes fearlessly) and their perceived self-efficacy (e.g., Bandura & Adams, 1977). Many studies of this type suggest strong links between self-perceptions of one's competence and the ability to actually behave competently. They also demonstrate again that when appropriate questions are asked, people can be excellent predictors of their own behaviors.

Expectancies, both about outcomes and about one's own efficacy, clearly seem to be central person variables. It may be tempting to transform them into widely generalized trait-like dispositions, to assume that they will have broad cross-situational consistency, and to forget their links to particular psychological conditions. Certainly expectancies are generalized to some degree (e.g., Mischel & Staub, 1965), but the level of generality must be determined empirically. For example, "locus of control" (internal vs. external) was found to have some generality, although the degree was less than originally anticipated, with distinct and unrelated expectancies for positive and negative outcomes and with highly specific behavioral correlates for each type even in young children (Mischel, Zeiss, & Zeiss, 1973). If expectancies are converted into global dispositions in assessment, they may well prove to be no more useful for a precise psychological analysis than other broad social dispositions have proved to be in the past. But when they are construed as condition-bound subjective hypotheses about behavior—outcome contingencies and personal competencies, expectancies may be readily and specifically assessed and may serve as useful predictors of performance (e.g., Bandura, 1986).

Subjective Values, Preferences, and Goals

The behaviors people choose to enact from among those they are capable of generating also depend on the "subjective values" of the outcomes that they expect them to yield. Different individuals value different outcomes and also share particular values and goals in different degrees, as they engage in "purposive" (goal-directed) behavior (see Cantor & Zirkel, Chapter 6, this volume). Therefore it is necessary to consider still another set of person variables: the subjective (perceived) values, both positive and negative, of particular classes of events, and the outcomes and goals that the person pursues or avoids. Included here are the stimuli that have acquired the power to induce positive or negative emotional states in the person, that function as powerful incentives or reinforcers for behavior, and that are the goals to which the behavior seems directed.

Illustrative assessments include measuring the individuals' actual choices in life-like situations, as well as verbal preferences and ratings for different choices and activities (Bullock & Merrill, 1980; Mischel & Grusec, 1966). Verbal reports (e.g., on questionnaires) about values, interests, and goals may often supply relevant information that is highly stable over time. Preferences also may be assessed more directly—for instance, by providing individuals opportunities to select the outcomes they want from a large array of alternatives. As an example, when hospitalized psychiatric patients earn tokens that they may exchange for objects or activities, the "prices" they are willing to pay for different options yield an index of their subjective value (e.g., Ayllon & Azrin, 1965). The fact that personal values, goals, and interests tend to have relatively high stability even over long periods of time (e.g., Mischel, 1968) makes them especially promising units for personality psychology.

Self-Regulatory System

The individual's "self-regulatory system" includes a number of components, all relevant to how complex, relatively long-term patterns of goal-directed behavior are planned, generated, and maintained even when the environment offers weak supports, impediments, and conflicting elements. To a considerable degree, individuals direct and control their own behavior toward delayed (i.e., future) outcomes and goals. They affect the quality of their performance by self-imposed goals and standards—by self-monitoring, self-evaluation, and self-produced consequences as they generate and pursue their plans and projects (e.g., Bandura, 1986; Cantor & Kihlstrom, 1987; Higgins, Chapter 12, this volume). Even in the absence of external constraints, people set performance goals for themselves, criticize or praise their own behavior (depending on how well it matches their expectations and standards), and encourage or demoralize their own efforts through their own ideation as they progress toward subgoals. Some of the main components in this process may be assessed relatively independently even if they are parts of an integral self-regulatory system, as briefly illustrated in the following examples dealing with various facets of self-regulation as a person variable.

For more than two decades, studies of goal setting and self-reinforcement (e.g., Bandura & Perloff, 1967; Bandura & Whalen, 1966; Mischel & Liebert, 1966) have made it plain that even young children will not indulge themselves with freely available immediate gratifications; instead, they set goals, follow rules, and impose standards and contingencies on their own behavior. Self-regulatory systems include the person's goals and "contingency rules" that guide behavior. Such rules specify the kinds of behavior appropriate (expected) under particular conditions, the performance levels (standards, goals) that the behavior must achieve, and the consequences (positive and negative) of attaining or failing to reach those standards. Like expectancies and subjective values, individual differences in how people self-regulate in their pursuit of goals have had a significant place in personality theorizing and research for many years (e.g., Mischel, 1966; Rotter, 1954; Rotter, Chance, & Phares, 1972), with increasingly precise specification of the mechanisms (e.g., Mischel et al., 1989).

The often long and difficult route to self-reinforcement as well as to external reinforcement in the pursuit of one's goals is mediated extensively by covert symbolic activities, including a variety of self-reactions, self-evaluation against standards, self-instructions, and cognitive-attentional strategies. These covert events can exert powerful effects. For example, if potentially reinforcing or noxious stimuli are imagined, they seem to influence behavior in the same way as when such stimuli are externally presented (e.g., Cautela, 1971). The self-statements one makes affect goal-directed behavior in a predictable manner (e.g., Bandura, 1977).

Just as adaptive cognitive patterns may help to sustain performance, ineffective strategies may accelerate anxiety and guarantee failure. For instance, when the person engages in anxious, self-preoccupying thoughts (e.g., "I'm no good at this—I'll never be able to do it"), performance may be seriously impaired. Such thoughts compete and interfere with task-relevant thoughts (e.g., "Now I have to recheck my answers"), and both the performance and the person consequently suffer (Sarason, 1979). People continuously judge and evaluate their own behavior, congratulating and condemning themselves for their own attributes and achievements. We assess our own characteristics and actions; we praise or abuse what we perceive to be our own achievements; and we self-administer social and material rewards and punishments for self-evaluated failures from the enormous array freely available to us. These self-regulatory processes are not limited to the individual's self-administration of such outcomes as the tokens, "prizes," or verbal approval and disapproval that have been favored in most early studies of self-reinforcement (e.g., Bandura, 1969; Kanfer & Marston, 1963; Kanfer & Phillips, 1970; Mahoney, 1974; Masters & Mokros, 1974; Mischel, Coates, & Raskoff, 1968). A pervasive but subtle feature of self-regulation is the person's selective attention to and processing of positive and negative information about the self (Mischel, Ebbesen, & Zeiss, 1973, 1976).

Everyone can access a wide range of "good" and "bad" information about the self (e.g., in the form of memories), and can focus on information and thoughts relevant to positive or negative attributes, to successes or failures, to strengths or weaknesses, selectively. Through selective attentional processes, individuals can expose themselves in different degrees to different types of information from the wide range that is potentially available—making themselves feel good or bad, calling themselves effective or inept, congratulating or condemning themselves. Research into this process helps specify the interactions between situational and dispositional variables that guide the process of selective attention to, and memory for, positive and negative information about the self (e.g., Mischel, Ebbesen, & Zeiss, 1973, 1976). Studies by other investigators have extended this type of paradigm to clarify how success–failure and positive–negative affect influence a wide variety of responses, including generosity to self and others as well as delay of gratification, in consistent, predictable ways (e.g., Rosenhan, Underwood, & Moore, 1974; Schwartz & Pollack, 1977; Seeman & Schwartz, 1974; Underwood, Froming, & Moore, 1977).

Research on self-regulation provides a number of illustrations showing how it is possible to combine the study of person variables (i.e., of the individual differences in the *products* of social-cognitive development) with the analysis of the social-cognitive processes through which persons interact with, and cope with, relevant psychological situations and conditions. It is the analysis of the type of interaction, attentive to both persons and conditions, that is becoming a distinctive feature of contemporary personality research. The examples below also illustrate the close interplay among different types of person variables that becomes apparent when one analyzes how the qualities of individuals mediate the impact of stimuli, and interact with situations, in the genesis of social behavior.

ILLUSTRATIVE SELF-REGULATORY RESEARCH: CONCURRENT STUDIES OF PROCESS AND PRODUCT

Many investigators have helped clarify how progress along the route to difficult or delayed goals is mediated by self-instructions, selective attention, and cognitive operations through which people can make purposeful self-control for the sake of achieving desired outcomes either relatively easy or difficult, and can enhance or undermine their own chances for success. Beginning with work on the role of self-instructions in self-control and specific reinforcement considerations (e.g., Bem, 1967; Luria, 1961; O'Leary, 1968), increasing attention has been devoted more recently to the planning and organization of complex behavioral sequences essential for sustained goal-directed behavior. For example, exciting developments have been occurring in the study of metacognition and heuristics for such complex

cognitive activities as reading and story comprehension (e.g., Brown, 1978), showing the important role of such processes as self-monitoring and rehearsal in self-directed behavior. At the same time, more is becoming known about the role of plans and cognitive rehearsal in self-control (Meichenbaum, 1977)—for example, in resistance to temptation (Mischel & Patterson, 1978) and in delay of gratification (Mischel, 1979, 1980; Mischel et al., 1989).

The Process

Some of the major strategies for transforming an aversive "self-control" situation into one that can be mastered effectively have been documented in detail (e.g., Mischel, 1974; Mischel, Ebbesen, & Zeiss, 1972; Mischel et al., 1989; Rodriguez, Mischel, & Shoda, 1989). In the self-imposed delay paradigm used in these studies, young children are free to continue to wait for a preferred outcome (e.g., a snack treat) that is more valuable but delayed, or to settle for an immediately available but less valued gratification. The findings suggest that persons can sustain delay most effectively for the sake of preferred but delayed gratifications if during the delay period they shift attention away from these gratifications, occupying themselves with cognitive distractions. Situational or self-induced conditions that shift attention from the tempting outcomes make voluntary delay of gratification much easier and increase waiting times appreciably. To bridge the delay necessary to obtain the desired goal and resist more immediate temptations, it is as if children must make internal notations of what they are waiting or working for, reminding themselves of it periodically and symbolically (e.g., Mischel & Moore, 1980), but spend the remaining time attending to other less frustrating internal and external stimuli. With increasing cognitive maturity, most individuals also become able to cognitively transform and abstract the desired but delayed gratifications by focusing on their nonarousing or symbolic features (rather than their consummatory, "hot" qualities), thereby making self-control easier for themselves.

It was shown that the effects of actual rewards physically present or absent in the situation could be completely overcome and even reversed by changing how children represented those rewards mentally during the delay period

(Mischel, 1974, 1981). For example, when, through pre-experimental instructions, preschoolers ideate about the rewards for which they are waiting in consummatory or "hot" ways (e.g., by focusing on their taste), they can hardly delay at all. In contrast, if they focus on the nonconsummatory or "cool" qualities of the rewards (i.e., on their abstract qualities), they can wait for them easily and even longer than if they can distract themselves from the rewards altogether. Thus, what is in the children's heads—not what is physically in front of them—crucially affects their ability to purposefully sustain delay in order to achieve their preferred but delayed goals. In these studies, regardless of the stimulus in their visual field, if the children imagine the real objects as present they cannot wait long for them. In constrast, if they imagine pictures (abstract representations) of the objects, they can wait for long time periods (indeed, even longer than when they are distracting themselves with abstract representations of objects that are comparable but not relevant to the rewards for which they are waiting). Understanding this process allows one to make fairly powerful predictions about specific behavior in specific delay-of-gratification situations.

The findings from this research also have implications for understanding person—situation interaction, and make the distinction between the power of the situation and of the person fuzzy. For example, does the fact that attention is focused away from the rewards in the delay situation (e.g., by covering the rewards or avoiding them cognitively) demonstrate the power of situational variables in self-control? It does in the sense that these findings show how specific changes in the situation can make delay either very difficult or very easy. But the same results also show that even young children can and do increase their own mastery and personal ability to control the effects of stimuli on them by modifying how they think about those stimuli, by "reframing" them cognitively, or by distracting themselves and focusing on other aspects of the situation while continuing in their goal-directed behavior. This process becomes possible in the course of development as children acquire increasing knowledge and understanding about a broad range of psychological principles, including those necessary for effective self-control. For example, children's spontaneous delay-of-gratification strategies show a clear developmental progression in knowledge of effec-tive delay rules to make self-imposed delay of gratification more manageable (Mischel & Mischel, 1983; Yates & Mischel, 1979). They progress from a systematic preference for seeing and thinking about the real blocked rewards, and hence using the worst delay strategy, to purposefully avoiding attention to the rewards and particularly refraining from "hot" (consummatory, arousing) ideation about the rewards. Systematically they come to prefer distraction from the temptation, self-instructions about the task contingency, and more abstract, nonconsummatory ideation about the rewards themselves.

These developmental shifts seem to reflect a growing recognition by the children of the principle that the more cognitively available and "hot" a temptation is, the more one will want it and the more difficult it will be to resist. With this insight, children can generate a diverse array of strategies for effectively managing otherwise formidable tasks, and for overcoming "stimulus control" with self-control. They are able to make themselves relatively immune to the physical situation and temptation, and are able to rearrange it psychologically to achieve mastery and attain their goals, guided by their comprehension of basic self-control rules. Knowledge of situational variables can become a key component of one's power over situations, enhancing the ability to control stimuli purposefully rather than being controlled or victimized by them.

Analyses of the situational and cognitive determinants affecting delay of gratification and self-control as a process have been accompanied by studies of the meaning of delay behavior as a quality of the person. They yielded a network of correlations showing that children who choose delayed, more valuable outcomes, as opposed to immediate, less valuable outcomes (e.g., Mischel, 1966, 1974) also tend to be more oriented toward the future, to have higher achievement motivation, to be more trusting and socially responsible, to be brighter and more mature, to have a higher level of aspiration, and to resist temptation and show less uncontrolled impulsivity.

The Product: Individual Differences

In contrast to this broad network of correlates found for delay choice preferences, little was known until the 1980s about the possible corre-lates of actual waiting time in the self-imposed delay paradigm. Studies now show that these seconds of waiting time seem to be remarkably robust indicators of a temporally stable and important human quality (e.g., Mischel & Peake, 1982; Mischel et al., 1988, 1989; Rodriguez, Mischel, & Shoda 1989). Most interesting are the long-term significant associations between the preschool child's delay behavior and indices of cognitive and social coping and competence obtained not only concurrently, but years later in adolescence and young adulthood. Such links spanning a decade were revealed in follow-up studies of children who participated in these delay-of-gratification experiments when they were preschoolers in the years from 1967 to 1974 at Stanford University's Bing School (e.g., Mischel et al., 1988; Shoda, Mischel, & Peake, 1990). The overall results suggest that this aspect of self-regulatory competence in early life is also linked to a broader construct of cognitive and social ability and achievement, related to intelligence but going beyond its narrow traditional definition (e.g., Mischel et al., 1989).

The links among children's knowledge of effective strategies, their spontaneous use of such strategies when attempting to control themselves in the pursuit of delayed goals, and their success in sustaining delay have also begun to be examined (Rodriguez et al., 1989). The delay paradigm was extended to a population of older children described as having a variety of social adjustment difficulties, such as aggressiveness and withdrawal; these children, aged 6–12 years, were assessed in a summer residential treatment facility. The children's knowledge of self-control processes was significantly related to the duration of their self-imposed delay. The children's spontaneous attention deployment during the delay period also was significantly correlated with their actual delay time: As the delay increased, those who were able to sustain self-control spent a higher proportion of the time distracting themselves from the frustrative situation than did those who terminated earlier. The relations among knowledge of self-control, spontaneous use of effective delay strategies, and duration of delay remained significant even when the effects of verbal intelligence were statistically controlled. Of greatest interest, the cognitive-attentional strategies that were identified in the experiments as allowing effective delay of gratification thus also seemed to be used spontaneously to a greater degree by individuals who delayed longer.

The cumulative findings from this research program give evidence both for the discriminativeness of delay behavior (across even seemingly similar contexts) and for its temporal stability and theoretical significance as a personal quality over many years. Preschool children who delay effectively in some contexts may not do so in other, even slightly different situations. For example, the correlation was .22 between preschool delay time when the experimenter was present versus absent during the delay, but the situation was otherwise identical (Mischel & Peake, 1982). Yet there are also important continuities linking preschoolers' delay time in certain conditions to indices of their cognitive and social competence, coping skills, and school performance years later. The same type of behavior thus may be discriminative and context-dependent, and nevertheless still indicative of a meaningful and stable set of human qualities. As this research illustrates, identifying both the situational parameters and the relevant individual differences within the same research paradigm should make it possible to draw on variance from both the person and the situation to predict their specific interaction with increasing precision, illuminating the same phenomena both as reflections of psychological processes and as variables on which individuals differ.

Person Variables in Delay

Theoretically, in terms of the operation of the person variables discussed previously, the choice of whether or not to delay gratification depends in part on an individual's relevant expectancies with regard to the alternative choices (e.g., Mischel, 1966, 1974). The choice also depends on the subjective values of the alternatives (e.g., Mischel, 1974; Mischel & Metzner, 1962; Mischel & Staub, 1965), as well as on how the particular delay situation is construed. After the initial choice to delay has been made, however, the ability to persist effectively in the face of the actual delay experience depends not only on those person variables affecting the original choice, but also on the availability of the necessary competencies for mastering and overcoming the aversiveness of the frustration and thus continuing to self-regulate in the pursuit of the chosen goal as the delay period continues. These competencies, essential for sustaining self-regulation, include such components as the individual's meta-cognitive understanding of the cognitions and strategies required for effective delay, and the cognitive skills (e.g., selective attention) needed to overcome the aversiveness of continuing with the self-imposed delay.

A Second Example

Another illustration of research on the interface of personality and cognition, guided by a different conception within a broadly social-cognitive framework and yielding complementary findings, comes from a research program by Carol Dweck and colleagues. Dweck and associates noted that when faced with failure, "helpless" children (those who believed that their failure was due to lack of ability) seemed to have self-defeating thoughts that virtually guaranteed failure. Moreover, after failure they performed more poorly than "mastery-oriented" children (those who saw their failure as due to lack of effort), who often actually performed better after failure. Both types of children were instructed "to think out loud" while solving problems (Diener & Dweck, 1978). As they began to experience failure, the children in the two groups soon said very different things to themselves. The helpless children made statements reflecting their lack of ability ("I'm getting confused" or "I never did have a good memory" or "I give up"), whereas the mastery-oriented children never talked about their lack of ability but seemed to search for a remedy, giving themselves instructions to encourage themselves and improve their performance (e.g., "I should slow down and try to figure this out") (Diener & Dweck, 1978, p. 450).

In subsequent studies and theorizing, Dweck and associates identified some of the specific psychological processes through which these adaptive and maladaptive patterns of positive and negative self-cognitions, affect, and performance may be generated and maintained as individuals pursue their goals (e.g., Dweck & Leggett, 1988). In their analysis, people's implicit theories (e.g., about the nature of their own abilities and dispositions) are linked to the types of goals they choose and the adaptive or maladaptive behaviors they display in the coping process. In other words, the motivational analysis offered by Dweck and Leggett specifies how individuals' implicit theories about their dispositions may orient them to particular types of goals, which in turn stimulate or set up different types of coping patterns.[1] Although the results still leave many questions unanswered, and much further empirical documentation of the theorizing is needed, their approach provides another interesting demonstration of the analysis of person–situation interactions within a social-cognitive framework.

TOWARD A CONDITIONAL VIEW OF DISPOSITIONS

The preceding section has outlined the types of person variables that seem to be promising units for the study of personality, both in terms of process and in terms of individual differences from a social-cognitive perspective. Many questions persist. The remainder of this chapter gives a selective overview of some of my own recent attempts to address those questions. They share one common aim: to refine the conception and understanding of dispositional constructs for personality psychology. Personality dispositions require attention not only to the units of personality (e.g., expectancies and values) of interest in psychological research and theory. It is also relevant to consider the types of categories or constructs used in more natural or "lay" analyses of social behavior. A social-cognitive analysis of dispositions considers, first, when and how dispositional constructs are used in social perception and judgment by the layperson. Second, it considers how dispositional constructs can be used by the personality psychologist to take appropriate account of psychological conditions and the discriminativeness of behavior, while also identifying the coherences that exist in personality. Investigations to address both of these concerns are beginning to build a basis for a conditional theory of personal dispositions (e.g., Mischel, 1984; Mischel & Peake, 1982; Wright & Mischel, 1987, 1988).

When and How Laypersons Use Dispositions

To try to study natural person categorization in laypersons' use of dispositions, my colleagues and I began by borrowing the cognitive-prototype perspective, and applied it to the categorization both of persons (Cantor & Mischel, 1979) and of situations (e.g., Cantor, Mischel, & Schwartz, 1982). At first, this cognitive-prototype approach to defining and studying dispositions focused on dispositions as natural categories about people, analyzable just as other natural object categories are (e.g., Rosch, Simpson, & Miller, 1976). As in the object domain, empirically people seem to have systematic, widely shared rules for assessing prototypicality in the person domain. There seem to be highly accessible, well-structured person and situation taxonomies with predictable formal properties analogous to those found for everyday objects (e.g., Cantor, 1978; Cantor & Kihlstrom, 1987; Cantor & Mischel, 1979). Especially provocative is the observation that social situations often seem to be characterized by the typical person–action combinations that people expect in them (Cantor et al., 1982). For example, people appear to have detailed, shared expectations about the kinds of behaviors and persons that are "best suited" and "worst suited" for different classes of situations. Social life thus appears to be described in terms of the interactions between different types of prototypic persons and different types of contexts, suggesting that lay perceivers may actually be guided spontaneously by a sort of implicit interactionism of person and situation. Work in other relevant directions has extended the cognitive-prototype approach pioneered by Rosch and associates to the analysis of dispositions based on a variety of semantic ratings (e.g., Hampson, John, & Goldberg, 1986; Higgins, Chapter 12, this volume).

We also asked whether lay observers of behavior tend habitually to employ major organizational dimensions other than traits (Hoffman, Mischel, & Mazze, 1981). Despite the traditional focus on traits as the pre-eminent units both of personality and of its perception, observers actually may categorize targets' behaviors in quite different terms, as suggested by a cognitive–social learning analysis (e.g., Mischel, 1973) that calls attention to such non-trait units. Some evidence suggests, in fact, that goal-based categories are a commonly invoked—and sometimes preferable—alternative to trait constructs in organizing social information.

First, let us consider the distinction between trait and goal concepts. They are similar in that they involve inferring a disposition on the part of the target (unlike concepts based on features of the environment). A trait, however, suggests a broader disposition (e.g., to behave in a particular style or manner, such as honestly),

whereas in the case of goals one infers a disposition to act toward a more specific outcome (e.g., admission to law school). One of the many questions here is whether trait and goal concepts might be differentially suited—and, therefore, perhaps employed differentially—for certain information-processing objectives. Addressing this question, we (Hoffman et al., 1981) reasoned that while the hallmark of trait categories seems to be their value for summarizing and generalizing diverse samples of behavior, goal categories may serve to link otherwise isolated actions into coherent, rule-guided patterns. We hypothesized that this special integrative function of goal concepts may allow them to serve as good recall cues for their category members—that is, for the behaviors conjoined by the goal category they share.

Specifically, we hypothesized that trait-based categories will be preferred by observers whose purpose is to form and communicate an impression of the target's personality or to make predictions of the target's behavior. In contrast, goal-based categories should be preferred by observers whose purpose is either to recall the target's behavior as accurately as possible or to empathize with the target. We found that observational purpose substantially influenced both the objective structure of subjects' categorizations and the constructs used as category labels. As expected, when both trait-based and goal-based structures were available in a set of behavioral data about people, subjects whose purpose was either to remember the behaviors or to understand them from a character's point of view (empathize) organized the data in terms of the character's *goals*. When the subjects' purpose was either to form a personality impression of the character or to predict his or her future behavior, the same data, in contrast, were organized in terms of the character's *traits*. A subsequent experiment (Hoffman et al., 1981) demonstrated that the categorizations produced by recall-oriented subjects actually facilitated the ability of a new sample of subjects to remember the episodes, relative to the categorizations produced by impression-oriented or control subjects. In a later series of studies, we (Hoffman, Mischel, & Baer, 1984) went on to show that individuals are especially likely to construe a person's behavior in global trait terms when they expect that they will have to communicate verbally about that person.

When people spontaneously use dispositional terms, they also may intuitively "hedge" those terms to qualify when or how they apply, although the hedges may be implicit and not immediately evident. The type of hedging seems to change in the course of development. For example, whereas younger children were found to use probabilistic qualifiers ("He sometimes is friendly"), at older ages conditional qualifiers emerge that indicate, at least implicitly, the psychological conditions in which the dispositionally relevant behaviors occur (Wright & Mischel, 1988). Clearly, it would be a gross oversimplification to view the layperson as a global trait theorist who relies exclusively on uncontextualized global traits in social perception.

In the Wright and Mischel (1988) study, younger (8-year-old) and older (12-year-old) children, as well as adults, were interviewed to obtain their verbal descriptions of 8-year-old and 12-year-old target children selected as either highly aggressive or highly withdrawn. The targets were selected from the interviewees' own living groups in a summer residential camp setting. Interview probes were directed systematically at eliciting everything they knew about [target] subjects. The verbatim interview transcripts were coded later, both to address the content of the behavior categories employed and to identify the occurrence of conditional statements (that qualified or hedged the contexts for the expected behavior) and probability modifiers (that hedged the certainty or uncertainty) in the assertions. Differences in verbal fluency as a function of age were, of course, taken into account in coding to avoid confounding.

Although this study was frankly exploratory, the results provide some evidence of sensitivity in natural discourse to the variability of people's behavior. Such sensitivity appears to be manifested both by children and adults, albeit in seemingly distinctive ways:

Children and adults both showed sensitivity to the variability of behavior in their descriptions of other people, but they did so in different ways. Children showed sensitivity to the variability of behavior in their use of probabilistic hedges (e.g., he sometimes B). In contrast, adults showed greater confidence in their dispositional attributions as reflected in their increased use of certainty statements (e.g., he always B). However, adults also used higher proportions of explicit conditionals that indicated more precisely the situations in which behaviors would occur. Thus, their certainty about their attributions was coupled with greater specification of the conditions in

which behaviors occur. (Wright & Mischel, 1988, p. 465)

Especially provocative was the finding pointing to the implicit forms of natural hedging or conditionalizing that adults seem to use when characterizing people under conversational (rather than laboratory) conditions. The adults in the study tended to place their conditional hedges near their high-certainty assertions, so that even when the qualifier was not attached directly to an utterance, it could function to hedge it situationally within normal conversational rules shared by speakers with similar world knowledge. Of course, the circumstances in which such implicit (as well as explicit) conditionalizing does and does not occur warrant much further research before final conclusions can be reached about human sensitivity to the conditional nature of dispositions.

To pursue this direction of work systematically, experimental methods were also used in which data about real individuals from the field study were presented in various situation–behavior combinations to perceivers (e.g., Shoda, Mischel, & Wright, 1989). With the goal of assessing how the relationship between behavior and the situation in which it occurs affects dispositional judgments, this relationship was manipulated experimentally. Adult subjects were exposed to sets of behaviors and situations based on the extensive observations of children's social interactions. In one condition, the relations between situations and behaviors reflected those observed in the children's actual social interactions (e.g., the child "hits when provoked"). In four other conditions, the behaviors (e.g., "hits") were presented either with situations unspecified (situation-free condition) or with their relations to situations systematically altered, while the total frequencies of each type of behavior and situation were held constant. Global personality impressions formed in the intact condition, in which situations were explicit, and those in the situation-free condition were found to be similar. It is notable, however, that judgments of the children's aggressiveness in the intact condition predicted individual differences in the targets' actual levels of aggressive behavior better than did judgments in the situation-free condition. As predicted, when the situation–behavior relations were increasingly altered, the targets were perceived as less plausible and increasingly maladjusted and odd. As this alteration increased, it also decreased correlations between the perceived level of the children's aggressiveness and behavioral criteria of their actual aggressive behavior. The results serve to demonstrate the important role of situational information in social perception and the prediction of behavior.

The studies cited illustrate one direction of research aimed at specifying the conditions affecting how and when perceivers use different types of categories in social perception. The growing literature on social cognition generally, and on the role of standards and knowledge activation in particular, is clarifying the relevant processes with increasing precision in a trend that promises to narrow some historically deep but scientifically artificial boundaries between the study of social psychology and of personality (e.g., see Higgins, Chapter 12, this volume).

Links between Perceived Dispositions and Social Behavior: The "Consistency Paradox"

How are the perceiver's dispositional judgments linked to coherences or regularities in the actions of the perceived? Interest and research in this question were stimulated by recognition of the so-called "consistency paradox" (e.g., Bem & Allen, 1974). This term refers to the notion that while intuition seems to support the belief that people are characterized by broad dispositions resulting in extensive cross-situational consistency, the research in the area has persistently failed to support this intuition. In studies of the consistency paradox, as a first step (Mischel & Peake, 1982, 1983) we replicated Bem and Allen's well-known 1974 study, greatly extending the behavioral referents and battery of measures employed. Specifically, a sample of Carleton College undergraduates volunteered to participate in extensive self-assessments relevant to their conscientiousness and friendliness. (The results for the two dimensions generally paralleled each other, but the review here is confined to conscientiousness.)

Each student was rated by his or her parents and a close friend, and was observed systematically in various situations relevant to the traits of interest in the college setting. The behavior measures included, for example, class attendance, study session attendance, assignment neatness, assignment punctuality, reserve reading punctuality for course sessions, room neat-

ness, and personal appearance neatness. To obtain referents for the trait constructs as perceived by the subjects, the specific behaviors selected as relevant to each trait were supplied by the subjects themselves as part of the pretesting at Carleton College. Behavior observations were aggregated over repeated occasions to enhance reliability. In addition, self-ratings of perceived consistency (vs. variability) for each trait were also obtained from the subjects, following the Bem and Allen procedures (as described in Mischel & Peake, 1982).

Congruent with earlier findings in the literature (Bem & Allen, 1974), raters agreed well with each other about the overall conscientiousness of people who view themselves as highly variable on that dimension. In our efforts to understand the consistency paradox, we found it more surprising and challenging that the students' perceptions of their own overall consistency or variability on conscientiousness were not related closely to the observed cross-situational consistency of their behavior (as assessed by mean pairwise correlation coefficients across the 19 behavioral measures). Although interjudge agreement was greater for those students who saw themselves overall as consistent in conscientiousness, their average behavioral consistency across the measures was not significantly greater than that of students who saw themselves as variable. In short, in this study, people who saw themselves as consistent on a dimension were seen with greater interjudge agreement by others, but their overall behavior was not necessarily more consistent cross-situationally. This finding directly contradicts the expectation that behavioral cross-situational consistency would be demonstrable at the level of specific situations, but only for that subset of people who view themselves as consistent on the particular dimension (Bem & Allen, 1974).

If, as the Carleton data suggest, the self-perception of consistency is unrelated to the level of cross-situational consistency in the referent behaviors, in what is it rooted? To try to answer this question, we turned again to the cognitive-prototype approach. Applied to the consistency paradox, the cognitive-prototype approach suggests that people judge their consistency not by seeking the average of all the observable features of a category, but by noting the reliable occurrence of some features that are central to the category, or more prototypic. Peake and I (Mischel & Peake, 1982) therefore proposed that consistency judgments rely heavily on the observation of central (prototypic) features, so that the impression of consistency will derive not from average levels of consistency across all the possible features of the category, but rather from the observation that some central features are reliably (stably) present. This perspective suggests that extensive cross-situational consistency may not be a basic ingredient for either the organization or the perception of personal consistency in a domain.

We hypothesized that the impression that a person is consistent with regard to a trait is not based mostly on the observation of average cross-situational consistency in all the potentially relevant behaviors (punctuality for classes, punctuality for appointments, desk neatness, etc.). Instead, we proposed that when people try to assess their variability (vs. consistency) with regard to a category of behavior, they scan the temporal stability of a limited number of behaviors that for them are most relevant (prototypic) to that category. That is, it was hypothesized that the impression of consistency is based extensively on the observation of *temporal* stability in those behaviors that are most relevant to the prototype. No relationship was expected between the impression of high consistency versus variability and overall cross-situational consistency. The results supported these expectations (Mischel & Peake, 1982). Those students who saw themselves as highly consistent in conscientiousness were significantly more temporally stable on these prototypic behaviors than were those who viewed themselves as more variable from situation to situation—an effect that was replicated in the domain of friendliness by Peake within the same sample of students (Peake, 1982). In contrast to the clear and consistent differences in temporal stability for the prototypic behaviors, the self-perceived low- and high-variability groups did not differ in mean temporal stability for the less prototypic behaviors. Finally, also as expected, self-perceived consistency and behavioral cross-situational consistency were unrelated in Mischel and Peake's (1982) study.

If these findings prove to be robust, they have intriguing implications. They suggest that people's intuitions of their consistency in personality are based on data, but that these data may not be highly generalized cross-situational consistencies in their behaviors on the whole. Intuitions about one's consistency may arise, instead, from the observation of temporal stability in prototypical behaviors. This would certainly not be an illusory or fictitious construction of consistency. It would simply locate perceived consistency in features of temporal stability rather than in the cross-situational consistency that has been pursued for so many years. It must be emphasized, however, that although the correlational results were suggestive and seem provocative, a more conclusive analysis of the process underlying self-perceptions of consistency awaits an experimental attack on the problem, as well as further correlational support.

Condition—Behavior Stabilities: In Search of Local Predictability

The classic trait strategy essentially treats situations as if they were error, and seeks to cancel their effects by aggregating across them to eliminate their role and to demonstrate stable individual differences. Both the strengths and limitations of this classic aggregation strategy are substantial, were appreciated as early as the 1920s (Hartshorne & May, 1928), and have more recently been restated and discussed in detail (e.g., Epstein, 1979, 1983; Mischel, 1983; Mischel & Peake, 1982; Shoda et al., 1989; Wright & Mischel, 1987, 1988). The approach that my associates and I favor, in contrast to the classic route, seeks consistencies by linking the behavior of interest to a circumscribed set of contexts, thus pursuing consistency on a more local, condition-bound, contingent, and specific (rather than global) level. Both approaches seem to accept the fact that average levels of consistency in behavior from situation to situation tend to be modest, even after aggregation over multiple occasions (e.g., Dudycha, 1936; Hartshorne & May, 1928; Mischel & Peake, 1982, 1983; Newcomb, 1929). Advocates of the traditional trait strategy propose circumventing this constraint by abandoning attempts to predict behavior from situation to situation altogether. Instead, they confine their predictive efforts to aggregates over multiple situations (e.g. Epstein, 1979). Such a strategy can enhance the resulting coefficients dramatically (as the Spearman–Brown formula has long recognized). But it bypasses rather than resolves the classic problems found in the search for coherences from situation to situation by "averaging out" the situation rather than predicting behavior in it (as discussed in Mischel & Peake, 1982, 1983).

And, of course, it places a low ceiling on the accuracy possible for predicting behavior in specific situations.

We have continued to explore the view that personality coherences involve prototypic features of behavior that are cross-situationally discriminative but meaningful, temporally stable dispositional indicators when they occur in certain diagnostic contexts. Instead of pursuing high levels of overall consistency from situation to situation for many aggregated behaviors in a wide range of aggregated contexts, the goal is to identify the distinctive "bundles" or sets of temporally stable prototypic condition–behavior relations that characterize the individual under predictable circumstances (e.g., Mischel, 1973; Wright & Mischel, 1987). Although these "if–then" condition–behavior relations may occur only some of the time, they may figure crucially both in the perception of personality and in its organization (e.g., Mischel & Peake, 1982; Wright & Mischel, 1987, 1988).

In this vein, we have been developing a conditional approach to dispositions in which dispositional constructs are viewed as clusters of if–then propositions. Rather than construing dispositions as generalized response tendencies aggregated over diverse situations, we view them as propositions summarizing contingencies between categories of conditions and categories of behavior. A basic unit in the analysis of dispositions, then, becomes the conditional frequency of acts that are central to a particular behavior category in circumscribed, "diagnostic" conditions (Wright & Mischel, 1987, 1988). This type of if–then proposition contrasts with the traditional focus on the overall frequency of dispositionally relevant behaviors aggregated across a wide range of situations. It calls explicit attention to inextricable specific links between conditions and actions in determining the implications of people's behavior for dispositional judgments about them (e.g., Shoda, 1990; Shoda, Mischel, & Wright, 1989). It equally highlights the interactive nature of the person–situation relations that characterize social behavior.

To summarize, although context sensitivity and discriminativeness across situations may be the rule rather than the exception for most social behavior, it is also possible to find specific coherences that differentiate individuals and that can be identified under predictable contingencies for at least some people and behaviors, suggesting "local areas" of relative predictability without resorting to aggregation across situations. Such local coherences seem to occur at least in situations requiring cognitive and self-regulatory competencies that make high demands and strain people's available competence, at least with regard to some categories of disadvantageous behavior (aggression, withdrawal). Moreover, we have found significant links between ratings on these dimensions and individuals' actual behavior in difficult situations at relatively molecular episodic levels of observation, even without benefit of aggregating across different behavioral features.

In the search for relatively specific or "local" levels (e.g., Wright, 1983; Wright & Mischel, 1987, 1988), we have been trying to specify the contingencies when individual differences will and will not make a predictable difference. To illustrate, one hypothesis we have been developing is that psychologically demanding, difficult situations will be especially diagnostic of important individual differences in characteristic modes of coping with stress. Psychologically difficult situations are defined as those calling for or demanding basic competencies that strain or tax the individual's own perceived level of such competencies. Supporting this hypothesis, we found that children judged to be good exemplars of two dispositional categories—aggressive and withdrawn—diverged into relatively stable aggressive versus withdrawn coping strategies in those situations characterized by sufficiently difficult cognitive, self-regulatory, and social competency requirements (Wright & Mischel, 1987). The same study also indicated that the demand level of situations was directly related to how closely dispositional judgments by observers predicted the children's behavior. For example, judgments of children's aggressiveness were only moderately correlated with their aggressive behavior in low-demand situations, but were more predictive of their aggressive behavior in situations in which competency requirements were high. Moreover, the same research indicated significant links between ratings on these dimensions and the individuals' actual behavior in difficult situations at relatively molecular episodic levels of observation, even without benefit of aggregating across different behavioral features.

Thus, if they are highly prototypic, even single features of behavior in diagnostic contexts may be sufficient to activate in the observer the larger dispositional category of which they are a part and that they represent. The analysis of how those behavioral features are organized and connected to the perception of personality dispositions and to the contexts in which they occur seems a necessary step in the search for a conception of personality structure that takes account of both the discriminativeness of social behavior and its coherences.

Constructive Alternativism: Multiple Perspectives for Multiple Goals

This chapter has begun by reviewing the critique of the global dispositional approach. It should be clear that the basic challenge was not and is not to the *existence* of dispositions, but to the assumptions about their nature. The challenge, then, has been focused on the limited utility of inferring broad context-free dispositions from behavioral signs as *the* basis for trying to explain the phenomena of personality and for predicting an individual's specific behavior in specific situations (Hunt, 1965; Mischel, 1968, 1973; Peterson, 1968; Vernon, 1964). The data available in 1968, like the data over two decades later, do not suggest that useful predictions cannot be made. They also do not imply that different people will not act differently with some consistency in different types of situations. Rather, the data both then and now do suggest that if predictive precision is the goal, the particular classes of conditions or equivalence units have to be taken into account much more carefully and seem to be considerably narrower and more local than traditional trait theories assumed. It should be self-evident that, instead of debating the existence of dispositions, the continuing need is to specify their nature with increasing precision, to determine their organization and structure, and to identify types of if–then, condition–behavior relations that constitute them in particular contexts and populations.

The discussion of dispositions presented in this chapter is deliberately selective and is intended to be neither exhaustive nor preemptive. I have focused on some basic psychological processes and underlying dispositionally relevant social behavior, and on such psychological person variables as the individual's competencies, constructs, expectancies, subjective values, rules, and self-regulatory system that mediate the effects of conditions on behavior. From the viewpoint of the experiencing person, however, it may be more useful to consider the same transactions in phenomenological terms, as personal projects, thoughts, feelings, intentions, goals, orientations, and other subjective (but communicable) internal states. From the perspective of the social perceiver (whether psychologist or layperson) who uses dispositional constructs in discourse and for various types of communication and prediction, it may be more useful to specify the if–then propositions (both explicit and implicit) that are the condition–behavior referents for such constructs, as also illustrated in this chapter. Each alternative perspective can point to goals worth pursuing in the search for useful dispositional constructs. Each allows glimpses into the diverse phenomena that constitute personality, and can facilitate progressive revision of the personality construct itself.

ACKNOWLEDGMENTS

Portions of this chapter draw extensively on my earlier publications cited in the references, especially from Mischel (1968, 1973, 1983, 1984) and from Mischel and Peake (1982). Preparation of this chapter was supported in part by Grant No. RO1 MH39349 from the National Institute of Mental Health.

NOTE

1. Interestingly, this analysis independently emerges with conclusions on the role of "cross-situational consistency" to be expected for personality dispositions that are entirely congruent with those underlying the critique of global trait theories (Mischel, 1968, 1973), summarized earlier in this chapter. As Dweck and Leggett (1988) point out, when different goals are available in different situations, it becomes unreasonable for investigators to expect—and unlikely that they will find—behavioral consistency across such situations. Equally congruent, their analysis "does not view such consistency as the hallmark of personality or as the focal phenomenon that personality constructs should strive to capture" (1988, p. 270).

REFERENCES

Allport, G. (1937). *Personality: A psychological interpretation*. New York: Holt.

Anderson, J. (1960). The prediction of adjustment over time. In I. Iscoe & H. Stevenson (Eds.), *Personality development in children*. Austin: University of Texas Press.

Argyle, M., & Little, B. R. (1972). Do personality traits apply to social behavior? *Journal of Theory of Social Behavior, 2*, 1–35.

Ayllon, T., & Azrin, N. H. (1965). The measurement and reinforcement of behavior of psychotics. *Journal of the Experimental Analysis of Behavior, 8*, 357–383.

Bandura, A. (1969). *Principles of behavior modification*. New York: Holt, Rinehart & Winston.

Bandura, A. (1977). *Social learning theory*. Englewood Cliffs, NJ: Prentice-Hall.

Bandura, A. (1978). The self system in reciprocal determinism. *American Psychologist, 33*, 344–358.

Bandura, A. (1986). *Social foundations of thought and action: A social cognitive theory*. Englewood Cliffs, NJ: Prentice-Hall.

Bandura, A., & Adams, N. E. (1977). Analysis of self-efficacy theory of behavioral change. *Cognitive Therapy and Research, 1*, 287–310.

Bandura, A., & Perloff, B. (1967). Relative efficacy of self-monitored and externally imposed reinforcement systems. *Journal of Personality and Social Psychology, 7*, 111–116.

Bandura, A., & Whalen, C. K. (1966). The influence of antecedent reinforcement and divergent modeling cues on patterns of self-reward. *Journal of Personality and Social Psychology, 3*, 373–382.

Bem, D. J. (1967). Self-perception: An alternative interpretation of cognitive dissonance phenomena. *Psychological Review, 74*, 183–200.

Bem, D. J., & Allen, A. (1974). On predicting some of the people some of the time: The search for cross-situational consistencies in behavior. *Psychological Review, 81*, 506–520.

Bower, G. H. (1970). Organizational factors in memory. *Cognitive Psychology, 1*, 18–46.

Bowers, K. S. (1973). Situationalism in psychology: An analysis and a critique. *Psychological Review, 80*, 307–336.

Brown, A. (1978). Development, schooling and the acquisition of knowledge about knowledge. In R. Anderson, R. Spiro, & W. Montague (Eds.), *Schooling and the acquisition of knowledge*. Hillsdale, NJ: Erlbaum.

Bruner, J. S., Olver, R. P., & Greenfield, P. M. (1966). *Studies in cognitive growth*. New York: Wiley.

Bullock, D., & Merrill, L. (1980). The impact of personal preference on consistency through time: The case of childhood aggression. *Child Development, 51*, 808–814.

Campbell, D., & Fiske, D. W. (1959). Convergent and discriminant validation. *Psychological Bulletin, 56*, 81–105.

Cantor, N. (1978). *Prototypicality and personality judgments*. Unpublished doctoral dissertation, Stanford University.

Cantor, N., & Kihlstrom, J. F. (1987). *Personality and Social Intelligence*. Englewood Cliffs, NJ: Prentice-Hall.

Cantor, N., & Mischel, W. (1977). Traits as prototypes: Effects on recognition memory. *Journal of Personality and Social Psychology, 35*, 38–48.

Cantor, N., & Mischel, W. (1979) Prototypes in person perception. In L. Berkowitz (Ed.), *Advances in experimental social psychology* (Vol. 12, pp. 3–52). New York: Academic Press.

Cantor, N., Mischel, W., & Schwartz, J. (1982). A prototype analysis of psychological situations. *Cognitive Psychology, 14*, 45–77.

Cautela, J. R. (1971). Covert conditioning. In A. Jacobs & L. B. Sachs (Eds.), *The psychology of private events*. New York: Academic Press.

Diener, C. O., & Dweck, C. S. (1978). An analysis of learned helplessness: Continuous changes in performance, strategy, and achievement cognitions following failure. *Journal of Personality and Social Psychology, 36*, 451–462.

Dudycha, G. J. (1936). An objective study of punctuality in relation to personality and achievement. *Archives of Psychology, 29* 1–53.

Dweck, C. S., & Leggett, E. L. (1988). A social-cognitive approach to motivation and personality. *Psychological Review, 95*, 256–273.

Epstein, S. (1979). The stability of behavior: On predicting most of the people much of the time. *Journal of Personality and Social Psychology, 37*, 1097–1126.

Epstein, S. (1983). The stability of confusion: A reply to Mischel and Peake. *Psychological Review, 90*, 179–184.

Gergen, K. J. (1968). Personal consistency and the presentation of self. In C. Gordon & K. J. Gergen (Eds.), *The self in social interaction*. New York: Wiley.

Hamilton, D. L. (1971). Implicit personality theories: Dimensions of interpersonal cognition. Paper presented at the meeting of the American Psychological Association, Washington, D.C.

Hampson, S. D., John, O. P., & Goldberg, L. R. (1986). Category breadth and hierarchical structure in personality: Studies of asymmetries in judgments of trait implications. *Journal of Personality and Social Psychology, 51*, 37–54.

Hartshorne, H., & May, M. A. (1928). *Studies in the nature of character, Studies in deceit* (Vol. 1). New York: Macmillan.

Higgins, E. T., Bargh, J. A., & Lombardi, W. (1989). Nature of priming effects on categorization. *Journal of Experimental Psychology: Learning, Memory, and Cognition, 11*, 59–69.

Higgins, E. T., King, G. A., & Mavin, G. H. (1982). Individual construct accessibility and subjective impressions and recall. *Journal of Personality and Social Psychology, 43*, 35–47.

Hoffman, C., Mischel, W., & Baer, J. S. (1984). Language and person cognition: Effects of communicative set on trait attribution. *Journal of Personality and Social Psychology, 46*, 1029–1043.

Hoffman, C. Mischel, W., & Mazze, K. (1981). The role of purpose in the organization of information about behavior: Trait-based versus goal-based categories in person cognition. *Journal of Personality and Social Psychology, 40*, 211–225.

Hunt, J. McV. (1965). Traditional personality theory in the light of recent evidence. *American Scientist, 53*, 80–96.

Kagan, J. (1969). Continuity in development. Paper presented at the meeting of the Society for Research in Child Development, Santa Monica, California.

Kahneman, D., & Tversky, A. (1973). On the psychology of prediction. *Psychological Review, 80,* 237–251.

Kanfer, F. H., & Marston, A. R. (1963). Determinants of self-reinforcement in human learning. *Journal of Experimental Psychology, 66,* 245–254.

Kanfer, F. H., & Phillips, J. S. (1970). *Learning foundations of behavior therapy.* New York: Wiley.

Kelly, G. (1955). *The psychology of personal constructs.* New York: Basic Books.

Kihlstrom, J. F., & Cantor, N. (1984). Mental representations of the self. In L. Berkowitz (Ed.), *Advances in experimental social psychology, Vol. 17. Theorizing in social psychology: Special topics.* New York: Academic Press.

Lasky, J. J., Hover, G. L., Smith, P. A., Bostian, D. W., Duffendack, S. C., & Nord, C. L. (1959). Posthospital adjustment as predicted by psychiatric patients and by their staff. *Journal of Consulting Psychology, 23,* 213–218.

Luria, A. R. (1961). *The role of speech in the regulation of normal and abnormal behavior.* New York: Pergamon Press.

Magnusson, D., & Endler, N. S. (1977). Interactional psychology: Present status and future prospects. In D. Magnusson & N. S. Endler (Eds.), *Personality at the crossroads: Current issues in interactional psychology.* Hillsdale, NJ: Erlbaum.

Mahoney, M. J. (1974). *Cognition and behavior modification.* Cambridge, MA: Ballinger.

Mandler, G. (1967). Organization and memory. In K. W. Spence & J. T. Spence (Eds.), *The psychology of learning and motivation: Advances in research and theory.* New York: Academic Press.

Mandler, G. (1968). Association and organization: Facts, fancies and theories. In T. R. Dixon & D. L. Horton (Eds.), *Verbal behavior and general behavior theory.* Englewood Cliffs, NJ: Prentice-Hall.

Markus, H. (1977). Self-schemata and processing information about the self. *Journal of Personality and Social Psychology, 35,* 63–78.

Masters, J. C., & Mokros, J. R. (1974). Self-reinforcement processes in children. In H. Reese (Ed.), *Advances in child development and behavior* (Vol. 9). New York: Academic Press.

Meichenbaum, D. (1977). *Cognitive-behavior modification.* New York: Plenum Press.

Mischel, W. (1965). Predicting the success of Peace Corps volunteers in Nigeria. *Journal of Personality and Social Psychology, 1,* 510–517.

Mischel, W. (1966). Theory and research on the antecedents of self-imposed delay of reward. In B. A. Maher (Ed.), *Progress in experimental personality research* (Vol. 3). New York: Academic Press.

Mischel, W. (1968). *Personality and assessment.* New York: Wiley.

Mischel, W. (1969). Continuity and change in personality. *American Psychologist, 24,* 1012–1018.

Mischel, W. (1971). *Introduction to personality.* New York: Holt, Rinehart & Winston.

Mischel, W. (1973). Toward a cognitive social-learning reconceptualization of personality. *Psychological Review, 80,* 252–283.

Mischel, W. (1974). Processes in delay of gratification. In L. Berkowitz (Ed.), *Advances in experimental social psychology* (Vol. 7). New York: Academic Press.

Mischel, W. (1979). On the interface of cognition and personality: Beyond the person-situation debate. *American Psychologist, 34,* 740–54.

Mischel, W. (1980). Personality and cognition: Something borrowed, something new? In N. Cantor & J. Kihlstrom (Eds.), *Personality, cognition, and social interaction.* Hillsdale, NJ: Erlbaum.

Mischel, W. (1981). Objective and subjective rules for delay of gratification. In W. Lens (Ed.), *Cognitions in human motivation and learning.* Hillsdale, NJ: Erlbaum.

Mischel, W., (1983). On the predictability of behavior and the structure of personality. In R. A. Zucker, J. Arnoff, & A. I. Rabin (Eds.), *Personality and the prediction of behavior* (pp. 269–305). New York: Academic Press.

Mischel, W. (1984). Convergences and challenges in the search for consistency. *American Psychologist, 39*(4), 351–364.

Mischel, W., Coates, B., & Raskoff, A. (1968). Effects of success and failure, on self-gratification. *Journal of Personality and Social Psychology, 10,* 381–390.

Mischel, W., Ebbesen, E. B., & Zeiss, A. R. (1973). Selective attention to the self: Situational and dispositional determinants. *Journal of Personality and Social Psychology, 27,* 129–142.

Mischel, W., Ebbesen, E. B., & Zeiss, A. M. (1976). Determinants of selective memory about the self. *Journal of Consulting and Clinical Psychology, 44,* 92–103.

Mischel, W., & Grusec, J. (1966). Determinants of the rehearsal and transmission of neutral and aversive behaviors. *Journal of Personality and Social Psychology, 11,* 363–373.

Mischel, W., & Liebert, R. M. (1966). Effects of discrepancies between observed and imposed criteria on their acquisition and transmission. *Journal of Personality and Social Psychology, 3,* 45–53.

Mischel, W., & Metzner, R. (1962). Preference for delayed reward as a function of age, intelligence, and length of delay interval. *Journal of Abnormal and Social Psychology, 64,* 425–31.

Mischel, W., & Mischel, H. N. (1983). The development of children's knowledge of self-control strategies. *Child Development, 54,* 603–619.

Mischel, W., & Moore, B. (1980). The role of ideation in voluntary delay for symbolically presented rewards. *Cognitive Therapy and Research, 4,* 211–221.

Mischel, W., & Patterson, C. J. (1978). Effective plans for self-control in children. In A. Collins (Eds.), *Minnesota symposia on child psychology* (Vol. XX). Minneapolis: University of Minnesota Press.

Mischel, W., & Peake, P. K. (1982). Beyond deja vu in the search for cross-situational consistency. *Psychological Review, 89,* 730–755.

Mischel, W., & Peake, P. K. (1983). Some facets of consistency: Replies to Epstein, Funder and Bem. *Psychological Review, 90,* 394–402.

Mischel, W., Shoda, Y., & Peake, P. K. (1988). The nature of adolescent competencies predicted by preschool delay of gratification. *Journal of Personality and Social Psychology, 54,* 687–696.

Mischel, W., Shoda, Y., & Rodriguez, M. L., (1989). Delay of gratification in children. *Science, 244,* 933–938.

Mischel, W., & Staub, E. (1965). Effects of expectancy on working and waiting for larger rewards. *Journal of Personality and Social Psychology, 2,* 625–633.

Mischel, W., Zeiss, R., & Zeiss, A. (1973). Internal-external control and persistence. Validation and implications of the Stanford Preschool Internal-External Scale. *Journal of Personality and Social Psychology, 29,* 265–278.

Moos, R. H. (1968). Situational analysis of a therapeutic community milieu. *Journal of Abnormal Psychology, 73,* 49–61.

Neisser, U. (1967). *Cognitive psychology.* New York: Appleton-Century-Crofts.

Newcomb, T. M. (1929). *Consistency of certain extrovert–introvert behavior patterns in 51 problem boys.* New York: Columbia University, Teachers College, Bureau of Publications.

Nisbett, R. E., & Ross, L. D. (1980). *Human inference: Strategies and shortcomings of social judgment. Century Psychology Series.* Englewood Cliffs, NJ: Prentice-Hall.

O'Leary, K. D. (1968). The effects of self-instruction on immoral behavior. *Journal of Experimental Child Psychology, 6,* 297–301.

Peak, P. K. (1982). Search for consistency: The Carleton Student Behavior Study (Doctoral dissertation, Stanford University, 1982). *Dissertation Abstracts, 43,* Section 8, Part B, 2746.

Peterson, D. R. (1968). *The clinical study of social behavior.* New York: Appleton-Century-Crofts.

Raush, H. L., Dittman, A. L., & Taylor, T. J. (1959). The interpersonal behavior of children in residential treatment. *Journal of Abnormal and Social Psychology, 58,* 9–26.

Rodriguez, M., Mischel, W., & Shoda, Y. (1989). Cognitive person variables in the delay of gratification of older children at-risk, *Journal of Personality and Social Psychology, 57,* 358–367.

Rogers, T. B., Kuiper, N. A., & Kirker, W. S. (1977). Self-reference and the encoding of personal information. *Journal of Personality and Social Psychology, 35,* 677–688.

Rosenhan, D. L., Underwood, B., & Moore, B. (1974). Affect moderates self-gratification and altruism. *Journal of Personality and Social Psychology, 30,* 546–552.

Rosch, E. H., Simpson, C., & Miller, R. S. (1976). Structural bases of typicality effects. *Journal of Experimental Psychology: Human Perception and Performance, 2,* 491–502.

Ross, L. (1977). The intuitive psychologists and his shortcomings: Distortions in the attribution process. In L. Berkowitz (Ed.), *Advances in experimental social psychology* (Vol. 10). New York: Academic Press.

Rotter, J. B. (1954). *Social learning and clinical psychology.* Englewood Cliffs, NJ: Prentice-Hall.

Rotter, J. B., Chance, J. D., & Phares, E. J. (Eds.). (1972). *Applications of a social learning theory of personality.* New York: Holt, Rinehart & Winston.

Sarason, I. G. (1979). Three lacunae of cognitive therapy. *Cognitive Therapy and Research, 3,* 223–235.

Sarason, I. G., Smith R. E., & Diener, E. (1975). Personality research: Components of variance attributable to the person and the situation. *Journal of Personality and Social Psychology, 32,* 199–204.

Schneider, D. J. (1973). Implicit personality theory: A review. *Psychological Bulletin, 79,* 294–309.

Schwartz, J. C., & Pollack, P. R. (1977). Affect and delay of gratification. *Journal of Research in Personality, 11,* 147–164.

Seeman, G., & Schwartz, J. C. (1974). Affective state and preference for immediate versus delayed reward. *Journal of Research in Personality, 7,* 384–394.

Shoda, Y. (1990). *Conditional analyses of personality coherence and dispositions.* Unpublished doctoral dissertation, Columbia University, New York.

Shoda, Y., Mischel, W., & Peake, P. K. (in press). Predicting adolescent cognitive and social competence from preschool delay of gratification: Identifying diagnostic conditions, *Developmental Psychology,*

Shoda, Y., Mischel, W., & Wright, J. C. (1989). Intuitive interactionism in person perception: Effects of situation-behavior relations on dispositional judgments. *Journal of Personality and Social Psychology, 56,* 41–53.

Shweder, R. A. (1973). How relevant is an individual difference theory of personality? *Journal of Personality, 43,* 455–485.

Underwood, B., Froming, W. J., & Moore, B. S. (1977). Mood, attention, and altruism: A search for mediating variables. *Developmental Psychology, 13,* 541–542.

Vernon, P. E. (1964). *Personality assessment: A critical survey.* New York: Wiley.

West, S. G. (1983). Personality and prediction: An introduction. *Journal of Personality, 51,* 275–285.

Witkin, H. A., Goodenough, D. R., & Karp, S. A. (1967). Stability of cognitive style from childhood to young adulthood. *Journal of Personality and Social Psychology, 7,* 291–300.

Wright, J. C. (1983). *The structure and perception of behavioral consistency.* Unpublished doctoral dissertation, Stanford University, Stanford, CA.

Wright, J. C., & Mischel. W. (1987). A conditional analysis of dispositional constructs: The local predictability of social behavior. *Journal of personality and Social Psychology, 53,* 1159–1177.

Wright, J. C., & Mischel. W. (1988). Conditional hedges and the intuitive psychology of traits. *Journal of Personality and Social Psychology, 3,* 454–469.

Yates, B. T., & Mischel, W. (1979). Young children's preferred attentional strategies for delaying gratification. *Journal of Personality and Social Psychology, 37,* 286–300.

Chapter 6

Personality, Cognition, and Purposive Behavior

Nancy Cantor and Sabrina Zirkel
University of Michigan

There are many ways to study personality and cognition, as there have been many traditions in this area (e.g., the "New Look" and cognitive styles; Freud and ego mechanisms of defense; trait theory and relations to cognitive processing). In this chapter, we examine personality and cognition via *purposive behavior,* focusing on cognitive–motivational units of individual difference as active elements in self-regulation and action control (Bandura, 1986; Kuhl, 1985; Mischel, 1973). We look at various units of analysis concerned with individuals' attempts to get what they want in their current life contexts.

Although it is always treacherous to try to argue for originality, the current cognitive personology does, in our opinion, have much that is timely to offer to the study of individuals' adaptive efforts. Certainly this is an effort built in large part on the insights of the New Look era and the empirical contributions of the cognitive-style theorists (e.g., see Baron, 1982; Witkin, Dyk, Faterson, Goodenough, & Karp, 1962). Nonetheless, some features of this enterprise are relatively novel. For example, the cognitive units of

analysis popular today, such as autobiographical selves, personal projects, and identity stories, are richly embedded in the everyday fabric of individuals' lives and experiences, desires and fears, in the past and in the present. At the same time, there is recognition of the imaginative nature of human thought, and units such as possible selves, self-ideals, personal strivings, and life tasks reveal the forward-looking, creative cognitive side of personality (Pervin, 1989a). The past and the future are also brought together in cognitive strategies of planning, simulation, monitoring, and retrospection, which are tailored to meet the individual's specific needs and experiences in particular life domains or social–cultural contexts (Showers & Cantor, 1985). In explicating these personality processes, there often is an explicit desire to understand the contextual influences on human action as mediated through a cognitive system. These cognitive processes of action control can be general, but are often quite specific, and they can be used persistently and too loyally; however, they can also be reworked, delimited in use, and sidestepped, with conscious effort, and thus allow for some personality change (Nasby & Kihlstrom, 1986). Therefore, a process approach can simultaneously address questions of specificity and of generality, of continuity and of change, in personality. Individuals keep knowledge of their personal pasts, think creatively about their personal futures, and work in their thoughts and in their actions to gain control in their everyday lives. A current cognitive personology can provide a window on some of their experiences. As Brian Little says: there is an attempt to "deal with the serious business of how people muddle through complex lives" (1989, p. 15).

In emphasizing the slice of work on personality and cognition that revolves around purposive social behavior, it is perhaps natural to blur the lines of division between motivational and cognitive approaches to personality; indeed, we step across that dividing line often in this chapter. However, it is worth noting from the outset that this cognitive–motivational integration is neither new to personality (e.g., McClelland's work on central social motives always involves the analysis of imaginative narratives), nor do we think that it is avoidable in taking account of likely cognitive contributions to individual differences *in vivo*. As noted elsewhere (Cantor & Kihlstrom, 1987, 1989), an important attraction of human social intelligence as a centerpiece for personality is that it serves as a source of autobiographical continuity for the individual, at the very same time as it facilitates a break with the past and provides a thrust to the future via imaginative self-reflection and goal setting. Cognition becomes then a tool for articulating, representing, and solidifying personal motivation in particular life settings and life periods. Many of the "cognitive" units of personality popular today, such as possible selves, self-identifications, and personal projects, represent the individual's goals, while simultaneously giving force and life to those goals via the impact of imaginative thought on affect and on action (Klinger, 1989). Whereas individual investigators still may differ as to the sources and form of personal motivation, there is at least some consensus that self-reflections, however nonconscious they may be, play a critical role in giving shape in everyday life to that motivation.

Our main objective in the present chapter, therefore, is to review some of the emerging trends in the study of personality, cognition, and purposive behavior. Toward this aim, we concentrate mainly on new units of analysis that emphasize the creative, forward-looking thoughts about self, others, and tasks that individuals have, and on the ways in which those intentions are constructed and negotiated in a broad sociocultural context. Individuals' proclivity to adopt a temporal perspective on themselves, thinking backwards and also anticipating alternative futures, greatly facilitates goal striving, opening the way for a strong cognitive contribution to purposive behavior (Bruner, 1986; Nuttin & Lens, 1986). Yet this power to break from the bonds of present life can be a recipe for disappointment and ineffective action control, if the intentional system is geared solely or even primarily to satisfy need-based motives, with little offsetting attention paid to the tasks and projects that need to be accomplished by a person in a particular age and social group. Similarly, there is little personal gain to be had when an individual strives to construct a self-image or a self-story that simply will not be tolerated in his or her current life context. Interpersonal scripts, once established, are difficult to change or even to avoid enacting, and thus social competence clearly revolves around negotiation skills. The various cognitive–motivational units of analysis under scrutiny today reflect these diverse components of social intelligence—the creativity, discriminativeness, and flexibility of intentional thoughts—in many ways. Nonetheless, it is our view that together they provide a sound basis for effective and intelligent action control, and we spend some time toward the end of the chapter in consideration of self-regulatory processes that complement these intentional structures. First, however, we briefly review the diverse perspectives that stand as the antecedents and the impetus for the "newer" generation of middle-level units of analysis in the study of personality and cognition.

HISTORICAL ROOTS AND CURRENT CONNECTIONS

The blending of cognitive, affective, and motivational units in the study of personality and cognition today comes from a long history of theorizing about personality development and functioning. Thus, our intention in providing a brief review of some of these traditions is to emphasize how such diverse perspectives are jointly informing current personality research. We believe that what is exciting and important about research in personality today is the breaking down of barriers, both within the discipline of personality and between different areas of psychology (e.g., clinical, cognitive, developmental, social). We begin by reviewing cognitive theorists, and follow this with an overview of those emphasizing the importance of goals and motives; we conclude the section with a discussion of how these perspectives are coming together in more contextualized units that bridge these different traditions.

The Cognitive Tradition

Some of the theorists to be described below would have considered themselves to be cognitive theorists, and others would almost certainly have not, but there is an element of the cognitive in all of them. Some (e.g., Kelly and Rotter) have concerned themselves with how people conceptualize the situations and events that they encounter, whereas others (e.g., Rogers and Sullivan) have concerned themselves more specifically with how people think about themselves and their relationships with the people around them. Though certainly a diverse group, these theorists are all "cognitive" in that each is centrally concerned in some way with self-reflection. Within this broad framework, however, they all have very different orientations, and whether or not they are actually cognitive in nature is less important than that these ideas are having enormous influence in personality and cognition as it exists today.

Early cognitive theorists realized that there are a myriad of ways for people to conceptualize the environment, and that these conceptualizations play a crucial role in understanding behavior. They remind us that it is not the events in a person's life that are important; more important for understanding personality are his or her interpretations of events. Kelly (1955) was among the first to insist that our conceptions of people emphasize the active, creative being, placing prime importance on the development and use of personal constructs. As each of us attempts to understand and predict the events of our lives, we abstract out patterns of events we anticipate will recur; these abstractions become the personal constructs or "schemas" through which we perceive the world. Kelly proposed a number of ways to assess personal constructs, noting that we can understand little about the general processes of people's cognitive representations of the world if we do not know the "alphabet" that they are using to build those representations. Rotter (1954) took a somewhat different approach; his social learning theory "cognitivized" behaviorism, focusing on cognitive representations of the contingencies of reinforcement as a means to understanding behavior. Rotter noted that in the real world of real people (as opposed to the laboratory world of rats), there is a great deal of ambiguity and flexibility in the interpretations and expectations that people can have concerning the specific opportunities situations offer. He proposed that, given the wide range of behaviors that could be reinforced in a given situation, it is critical to know more about people's representation of the situation's significance and potential reinforcement value if one is to make any meaningful predictions about their behavior.

Emphasis on the perceived opportunities in situations led to Rotter's (1966, 1975) work on locus of control. One way that people's interpretations of situations differ is in the extent to which they believe that they have control over the outcome of events, and these perceptions of the source of control will have important implications for the kinds of behavioral opportunities that they will perceive. Bandura's (1977) work with self-efficacy follows from this tradition, illustrating how one's sense of one's competence in a particular domain (independent of one's actual competence) predicts persistence and continued positive affect in the face of negative feedback. A perception of oneself as competent in a domain alters one's very perception of all feedback; unsuccessful outcomes are more likely to be assumed to result simply from low effort than from low ability. Self-efficacy naturally produces those kinds of self-serving attributional biases that social psychologists have found to be helpful in buffering stressful experiences (e.g., Taylor & Brown, 1988).

Kelly and Rotter have influenced almost all of what has come to be known as "cognitive personality theory," but this influence is most clearly seen among those researchers that emphasize the role played by perceptions and mental transformations of experiences. Mischel's work (Mischel, 1981; Mischel, Shoda, & Rodriguez, 1989) demonstrating enhanced delay of gratification through cognitive transformations of a desirable stimulus clearly stems from this tradition, as does Cantor and Kihlstrom's (1987) social intelligence viewpoint and many current cognitive–clinical viewpoints as well (Ingram, 1986).

A second cognitive tradition focuses more on the development and content of cognitive representations of the self than of the environment. Drawing from both psychoanalytic and sociological traditions, Sullivan (1953, 1964) argued for an interpersonal conception of personality, defining "personality" as the pattern of a person's relationships over time. Although not entirely relinquishing Freud's conceptions of basic drives, Sullivan posited that people are also motivated to develop a sense of security from their relationships with others, and that the motivation for security is probably more important for personality than are basic physiological drives. Personality development is seen as a process of working toward a greater sense of security in relationships, and this sense of security is considered to form the core of self-concepts. The self is seen not just as influenced by, but as actually *consisting of,* one's relationships with others. This theme has been picked up by Thorne (1987, 1989) in her study of interpersonal interactions. She focuses on how personality comes through in the ways that people recreate relationships over and over again. Building on Freud's (1912/1976) notion of transference, she looks at relationship patterns for clues to the ways individuals try to get security from others, finding that many seemingly maladaptive behaviors can be understood as attempts to gain security in relationships by replicating family patterns.

Within this tradition, others have focused more specifically on how a sense of oneself develops from others' reflected reactions. Rogers' (1951) emphasis on the importance of unconditional positive regard for the development of positive conceptions of the self illustrates one of the ways that relationships with others become encoded in the cognitive self. Similarly, Mead (1934) argued, with the concept of the "looking-glass self," that what we know about ourselves does not develop outside of our interactions with others, and object relations theorists point to the importance of the development of the dividing line between self and other for personality functioning (see Greenberg & Mitchell, 1983). More recently, Markus (Kitayama, Markus, & Tummala, 1989; Markus & Oyserman, 1989) has developed the concept of the "interpersonal self," parsimoniously allowing an understanding of a wide variety of cultural and gender differences by examining individual differences in the extent to which others are included in the self. Finally, in pointing to people's dialogues with "private audiences," Baldwin and Holmes (1987) bridge the self–other dividing line, with internalized "others" serving a pivotal role in self-regulation.

These theories recognize the importance of understanding how people think about themselves and their environment for making sense of human behavior. However, they offer us a somewhat incomplete view of people, in that we also need a way of thinking about the goal-directed nature of human beings. Next, we review those traditions that have emphasized the purposive dimension of personality, allowing a more complete understanding of how these cognitions move people from point A to point B.

Personality and Purpose

Many theorists over the years have stressed that personality might best be understood if we paid less attention to what people are *actually* doing and more attention to what they are *trying to do.* Behavior is interesting and important, but often it is ambiguous and misleading. One way to understand people and their actions better is to consider what is motivating them, what goals they are working toward. Within this broad framework, however, there have been large differences in how different theorists think about the relationship between personality and goal-directed behavior. The nomothetic–idiographic debate cuts through this work, with some theorists thinking about personality in terms of the extent to which particular nomothetic goals can be said to characterize a given individual's behavior (e.g., Murray, 1938), some focusing on individual differences in idiographic goals to illustrate underlying dispositional differences (e.g., F. Allport, 1937), and still others emphasizing the importance of age-graded normative goals or tasks (e.g., Erikson, 1950).

Among the more idiographic theorists,

Adler (1927) focused on the goals that people develop in order to overcome what he considered to be universal feelings of inferiority in highly specific and idiosyncratic domains. Having come from a psychoanalytic tradition, Adler felt that many if not most goals are unconscious, and that they are the results of the unique history of each individual. He believed that psychological health could be measured by the "appropriateness" of a person's goals. Also attending to idiosyncratic goals, F. Allport (1937) coined the term "teleonomic trend" to refer to the characteristic orientation of a person's behavior to a particular goal or set of goals, and assumed that these goals would help to provide a way of understanding the stability of people's personalities over time. Unlike Adler, however, F. Allport was less interested in goal *attainment;* rather, he felt that *enduring* goals were what provided the organizing force of personality. His ideas have had their clearest influence on Emmons' (1986, 1989) work with personal strivings, described as representations of "what an individual is typically trying to do" (Emmons, 1989, p. 92).

Murray (1938) provided a different approach to understanding the orientation toward the future in people's behavior. He internalized goals, calling them "needs," and although he assumed that a finite set of needs could characterize all people, he felt that the important individual differences would lie in the extent to which each person could be described as being motivated by one or another need. One person may be motivated to find intimacy (McAdams, 1980); another may be motivated to exert power over others (Winter, 1973); and still another may be motivated by achievement concerns (Veroff, 1982). Naturally, this perspective locates the source of individual differences mainly within the individual: It emphasizes people as the source of their own behavior, and in so doing initially gives less weight to contextual determinants. Yet, as Veroff (1983) recently argued, the very meaning of a motive changes with historical and cultural context, thus requiring close attention to what a motive actually is in the larger framework of a person's life settings.

Erikson's (1950) stages of development can also be conceived of as a series of goals, with people working toward achieving one kind of end state (e.g., trust) over another (e.g., mistrust). Inherently contextualized, Erikson's goals or stages are described as a normative series, with each individual expected to have to deal with each in one way or another at a relatively specific life stage. They are embedded in a particular cultural framework, focusing on the normative expectations that a given culture prescribes. For Erikson, the particular sociocultural context has important implications for the kinds of goals that people work on at any given point in time, and these struggles are not necessarily the same in different cultures. For example, "the task" of developing an identity would presumably differ for someone in the Third World as compared with a Western adolescent (Stewart & Healy, 1989).

In the Eriksonian model, personality comes from the personal history of negotiating the task(s) presented by these different life stages. Goals are not presumed to endure, and even those general concerns that do endure through several life stages will take on a new and different meaning as the particular features of life change over time. In this tradition, many current theorists assume that one cannot divorce the goals people are working toward from the complex fabric of their personal and sociological histories. Cantor and Kihlstrom (1987), for example, argue that one needs to study each individual's goals with his or her particular life stage closely in mind. They have developed the concept of a "life task" to capture precisely this kind of "normative" goal. Because life tasks are often initiated in this context of age and culture, they provide a common ground on which to compare people as to the unique meanings they give to these normative tasks.

We have seen a variety of ways of conceptualizing the purposive nature of human behavior, from the highly idiosyncratic, unstable goals of Adler to the enduring motives of Murray and to Erikson's normative series of goals. These goals can be conceived of at different levels of abstraction, with perhaps two broad classes of motives (e.g., Bakan's "agency" and "communion"; see Bakan, 1966) capturing most of them. However, many researchers are now turning to more "middle-level" units of analysis in order to incorporate a contextualized picture of goals. These middle-level units can accommodate the specific life situation of the individual and yet show enough regularity that individual-difference comparisons can easily be made. Researchers in many areas are finding that this richer, more completely contextualized understanding of a person offers opportunities to see new kinds of consistency, which are obscured when people are separated from the contexts in which they live. Seeing the world through the individual's eyes as the cognitivists do helps this enterprise, as does understanding the overarching goals that make a variety of behaviors cohere, but neither of these perspectives seems to suffice. Instead, individuals' goals also need to be assessed with an eye toward the interweaving of personality and culture—a topic to which we turn briefly now.

Personality and Culture

In recent years, there has been a resurgence of interest in studying the relationship between personality and culture. Interest in the field waned as the more process-oriented psychology developing in the 1960s became impatient with largely descriptive studies that consisted primarily of correlating personality styles with child-rearing practices. Recently, however, researchers have begun to re-examine the relationship of personality and culture with new constructs and methods, taking a more process-oriented approach and trying to understand how individuals, social structures, and cultural beliefs influence one another (House, 1981). In this resurgence, bidirectional models of influence are beginning to emerge, in which individuals' goals, preferences, and behaviors may be seen to emanate from the social roles that they are encouraged to enact in a given social structure; conversely, those same social structures are actually given form as a function of individuals and their cultural values and beliefs about appropriate roles. For example, Eagly (1987) shows how gender preferences come in part from repeatedly enacting certain prescribed social roles; yet the women's movement of the 1960s and 1970s also changed the very nature of those socially mandated roles, and the new roles may in turn change the goals and preferences of young girls and boys who enact them.

Culture also provides more than an understanding of personality development, however. Perhaps even more importantly for our purposes, culture provides the context in which personality is observed. Without a cultural framework, behavior has no meaning, and without meaning, behavior has no purpose (Shweder, in press). An understanding of pur-

posive behavior, then, requires an understanding of the cultural "language" in which it occurs. A culture provides people with a set of values and assumptive beliefs, and implicit inferences about how the world operates, which enable them to find meaning in and make sense of the events of their lives (Janoff-Bulman, 1989; Lakoff & Johnson, 1980). In Kellyan terms, a culture helps orient the kinds of personal constructs that are likely to develop; it prescribes the dimensions along which self-schemas are likely to develop; and it provides a set of culturally prescribed goals and tasks from which to choose. As Markus and Cross describe elsewhere in this volume (see Chapter 22), culture determines the very way in which we choose to draw the boundary between what is ourselves and what is "everything else out there." In other words, culture provides the cognitive tools through which we understand and regulate behavior.

Cultural context also provides important information for making judgments about, for example, such slippery constructs as "social competence" and "social adjustment." Sroufe (1979, in press) has pointed out that measures of adjustment in children need to consider age-graded differences in how a construct such as "dependency" is likely to be expressed. Insecurely attached babies may cling to their mothers, but it is obviously unreasonable to expect this same behavior from an "insecure" adolescent. One needs to consider the developmental, social, and cultural context when determining appropriate measures of a construct at different points in developmental time. For example, Caspi (1989) has found that dependent women tend to leave their parents' homes at an earlier age than do nondependent women. This is a surprising finding, unless one considers that perhaps these women are primarily leaving home to start their own families, thus expressing their dependency by creating new families with which to establish those all-important dependency relationships. It is only against a cultural background in which this is not the norm that the behavioral fact of "leaving home (early)" can be seen as a dependent act, and "starting a family (at a young age)" can be construed as evidence of a problem.

In order to achieve a contextualized understanding of personality, however, we need an adequate conceptualization of the lifespan. Lives can be construed as alternating between periods of relative stability and periods of change or transition (Levinson, 1978, 1986), with transitional periods characterized by demands such as adjusting to new roles and developing new social bonds, and periods of stability offering little change in these areas. Others have focused more on the specific life course trajectory that a culture prescribes. Erikson (1950) describes a normative series of life stages, and Elder (1975, 1985) has conceptualized the life course in terms of the age-graded series of roles that the culture prescribes (e.g., student, worker, spouse, parent). These two aspects of change over time (the cyclical nature of transitions and the culturally prescribed series of role changes) together provide a powerful tool for understanding personality change and stability over long periods of time. Stewart (1982) has focused on the transition versus stability dimension and has outlined a series of emotional stances that characterize adaptation to important life changes (e.g., moving away from home or getting a divorce), whereas Caspi (1987) has focused on the age stratification of roles and has demonstrated that personality is predictably reflected in the timing and nature of the assumption of these new roles. Cantor and her colleagues (Cantor, Norem, Niedenthal, Langston, & Brower, 1987) have looked closely at the cognitive strategies people use to achieve the normative goals presented by particular life transitions. These studies demonstrate that the general processes creating relationships between personality and goal-directed behavior, adjustment, and adaptation to important life changes can best be studied with detailed knowledge of the specific contexts in which these relationships unfold over the lifespan.

Thus, when we pay heed to these traditions, the "newer" units under consideration today are more completely contextualized. Behavior is thought to be created by a person in a particular context, and it is not necessarily expected to hold for other times or other contexts. For example, people are seen to negotiate an identity that is consistent both with desired images of the self and with situational goals and demands (Schlenker & Weigold, 1989). Individuals work toward achieving possible selves that account both for self-schemas and for particular situational demands likely to be encountered (Markus & Nurius, 1986). Decisions involving risk are based both on the likelihood of a payoff and on the need to use a number of strategies for protecting self-esteem (Josephs,

Steele, Larrick, & Nisbett, 1990). Cognitive development is seen as a product of maturational changes and of the situational pressures and opportunities afforded children at different ages; personal adjustment is seen as rooted in mastering these age-appropriate tasks (Higgins & Parsons, 1983). There is a strong movement to study questions of accuracy in more personally meaningful contexts (Miller & Cantor, 1982). Thus, rather than studying depressives' accuracy in perceptions of their ability to control a green light in a laboratory setting (Alloy & Abramson, 1979), researchers are finding ways to study the accuracy of depressives' perceptions of their romantic relationships (Fiske & Peterson, 1990). We also see a move to define accuracy itself more broadly—for example, as it is socially constructed (Hampson, 1989), as it is based on an understanding of normative act–context relationships (Wright, 1989; Wright & Mischel, 1987), as it reflects the perceivers' goals (Kruglanski, 1989), and under the constraints of limited experience with the stimulus material (Funder, 1989; Swann, 1984). In all of these areas, we see a move toward more detailed, contextualized understandings of personality.

These newer conceptualizations of personality and cognition, and their relationship to development and adjustment, are providing us with a substantial (albeit complicated) understanding of personality functioning. In our view, as researchers have developed better methods for assessing the complexity of life as people themselves experience it, they have also been able to develop more compelling, meaningful units to capture personality. We now turn to a review of a sampling of these new units.

MIDDLE-LEVEL UNITS OF ANALYSIS

Although parsimony of constructs may well be a virtue, one sign of health and growth among cognitive personality perspectives is the richness and diversity of middle-level units of analysis currently being pursued (Buss & Cantor, 1989). These units, related by family resemblance, are cognitive in that they are organized around individuals' beliefs about themselves and their worlds; their autobiographies and identities; and their projects, tasks, and concerns that give meaning to life. They are also infused with motivational content, and function as goals to energize and to organize purposive behavior. They are typically of a middle level in structural abstractness, as they can readily be concretized with reference to everyday activities and life settings, and generalized with reference to higher-order themes or meanings in life (Vallacher & Wegner, 1987). These are highly personalized structures, in the tradition of George Kelly's personal construct theory, though individuals living and working within shared sociocultural settings often develop this expertise in similar domains and use it for similar purposes. Moreover, although it is embedded in ongoing life experience, the content of these structures does not always remain faithful to a shared reality. For example, most of our most feared possible selves would be dismissed as ridiculous by our friends; similarly, we rarely reveal our imaginative musings about ideal selves, except perhaps to a "private audience" (Baldwin & Holmes, 1987). In what follows, we selectively illustrate these middle-level units that are personalized in content and yet serve some common cultural functions; contextually embedded and yet representative of higher-order meanings; reflective of a real past and yet looking toward an imagined future. These examples are chosen not to represent the full spectrum of such units under discussion in the literature, but rather to provide several illustrations of the ways in which forward-looking and contextually responsive cognitive–motivational units have been conceived and investigated.

Possible Selves and Self-Stories

A rich and traditionally important source of cognitive–motivational middle-level units is provided by individuals' personal stories about themselves, and by their remembrances of selves of the past and dreams of future selves (see Cantor & Kihlstrom, 1987, Ch. 5; Markus & Wurf, 1987). Most of these perspectives assume a complex view of self-concept, identity, and self-esteem—one that allows for multiple selves and self-identities (e.g., Linville, 1982; Rosenberg & Gara, 1985) and for domain specificity in self-esteem (e.g., Harter, 1983; Paulhus & Martin, 1987). They frequently stress the developmental and the temporal perspective on the self that individuals adopt, and the continual constructions and reconstructions of self-stories and autobiographical mem-

ories that simultaneously provide continuity of self and also document shifts over time in the self-narrative (Cohler, 1982; Kihlstrom & Cantor, 1984). There is an emphasis on multiple perspectives on the self, with individuals thinking about themselves as personal and as social objects (e.g., Cheek, 1989; Sampson, 1978), and it is not assumed that individuals are always conscious of their biases toward seeing the self or the world in certain lights (e.g., Lewicki, 1986). Most critically for the present exposition, these perspectives often stress the imaginative aspects of self-stories: Individuals construct self-ideals, future selves, imagoes, and possible selves, even as they compare and contrast these potential selves to the sometimes depressing reality of current self-concepts, feasible identities, and performance-based self-esteem. Moreover, sometimes these units of self are quite contextually defined and negotiated, at least with regard to their fluidity across current social interaction settings.

Markus' Possible Selves

In Markus' (e.g., Markus & Ruvolo, 1989) construct of "possible selves"—the set of hoped-for and feared selves, those that one could have been and may yet be—we see clearly the recruitment of imaginative capacity and temporal self-reflection in the service of creating, channeling, and preserving motivation and of guiding action. These are multiple selves, freed somewhat from the constraints of the here-and-now and of the current self-concept, but informed in detail and valence by those "now selves." Possible selves are specific in content (e.g., a lonely and old self of the future), diverse in terms of the domains of life typically represented (e.g., work, play, home life, intimacy, health, athletics, appearance), and, importantly, malleable as individuals negotiate different life periods and contexts (Cross & Markus, 1990).

Individuals can use their possible selves to effect self-change: For example, Oyserman and Markus (1988) found that some delinquent youths *balance* their feared negative possibilities with some positive possible selves, thereby embracing both the carrot and the stick of motivation. Individuals in crisis sometimes *recruit and elaborate* positive possible selves, perhaps to overwhelm their current negative selves and create perceived control for the recovery process (Porter, Markus, & Nurius, 1984).

Possible selves present a different picture of the self (to the self) than is captured by knowing where one stands *now,* and they often independently influence adjustment and well-being (Markus & Nurius, 1986). Possible selves can be highly "social" in content, representing the individual's version of desired or feared selves as reflected from peers, family, or culture, though they are assumed to be anchored for each person in very special recollections of self-in-context over the years. They present a picture—actually, many pictures, both good and bad—of where one has been and where one might go in particular life domains in the future, serving thus as "blueprints for change and growth across the lifespan" (Cross & Markus, 1990). They are a reminder of one's own potential role in one's (self-)development (Bandura, 1986).

McAdams' Self-Narratives

Working from a social motive tradition. McAdams (1985, 1989) suggests that individuals' "self-narratives," or personal narratives about their lives—the stories that they tell to "define who they are, who they have been, and who they may be in the future" (McAdams, 1988, p. 47)—provide both a coherence and a unity to the self. Narratives also serve as an expression of personal motive dispositions of intimacy, affiliation, and power. These stories follow a narrative structure, with plot themes, scenes, heroic figures (imagoes), and endings, and it is possible to see consistency in the relfection of personal motive dispositions in their content.

The deliberateness with which people "work on" their stories is assumed to vary with life period. For example, adolescence, as a time of heightened perspective taking and self-reflection, involves some fairly direct and explicit attempts at story building and identity consolidation, whereas later in the lifespan individuals may work either less deliberately or in a more focused way by thinking most about certain aspects of their story. The developmental–temporal perspective in self-narratives is a very central element, revealing the degree of temporal integrity the individual has attained in reviewing his or her past, present, and future self. Self-stories not only reflect motive dispositions; they also provide a forward-looking perspective on the self that encourages and shapes the continued expression of self in a story-consistent manner. Stories do

contain "turning points" as well as representing core themes and repeated scenes, but as the individual matures in adulthood there is increased emphasis placed on integrating imagoes in the service of a coherent (and perhaps more enactable) story line. In a sense, the core of the narrative is set early by personal motive dispositions, developed perhaps in tone and imagery in infancy and early childhood (see McAdams, 1989, Fig. 1), and then the expression is adapted over the lifespan to fit the particulars of the individual's life context.

Schlenker's Self-Identifications

In contrast to an emphasis on unity in the identity story, Schlenker and his colleagues (e.g., Schlenker & Weigold, 1989) have developed the notion of negotiated identity units called "self-identifications," which are fine-tuned to meet the demands and realities of different social audiences: "Identity can be regarded as a theory of self (or a schema) that is formed and maintained through actual or imagined interpersonal agreement about what the self is like" (p. 245). Not surprisingly (given their respective backgrounds as personality and social psychologists), whereas McAdams shows us how the self-story represents the core motive dispositions of the individual, Schlenker and Weigold explicate the process of social hypothesis testing about the self. In this process, individuals construct and (re)negotiate many sets of "desired identity images"—those images of self-in-context that mix desirability and feasibility—that guide their behavioral responses in particular interactions.

These desired identity images (and the entire process of self-identification) are not only contextually responsive but also contextually defined; that is, the desired identity is not necessarily consistent with the person's actual self-concept, but rather takes into account the current situation and the beliefs and goals of the social "audience" (see also Hampson, 1982). Desired identities are finely carved images that reflect what the person thinks he or she can do, should do, and is expected to do in that interaction. They reflect what the person is actually like—his or her values, preferences, and goals—but are explicitly *not* attempts to enact stable, enduring self-aspects in any exact or unedited form. In this regard, these desired identity images, and the process of identifying them and translating them *in vivo,* exemplify both the forward-looking potential afforded by self-reflection and the sensitivity of that process to an intricate social (as well as personal) agenda. Individuals are "multimotivated" in this scheme, working hard to be self-consistent but also sometimes to present the self in a new or more positive light, as well as to avoid overwhelming anxieties and self-threats (cf. Baumeister, 1982; Greenberg, Pyszczynski, & Solomon, 1986; Swann, 1985). Yet the self–other negotiation process also presents very real limits on self-identification and self-presentation: It is very hard for a person to get another person or a social group or culture to change its mind about him or her. The ultimate adaptation often comes from the individual as he or she actively and continuously (albeit rather automatically) weighs the costs and benefits of fulfilling various self-imperatives and social imperatives in an interaction (e.g., Snyder, 1979). These cognitive–motivational units represent not only what the person wants and can do, but also what the social world wants and will allow and/or reward at that time and in that place.

Higgins' Self-Guides

In his theory of self-concept discrepancy, Higgins (1987; see also Chapter 12, this volume) also takes a multiple-selves perspective. Individuals represent to themselves their "actual," "ideal," "ought," "can," and "future" selves, adopting different standpoints of self and other in construing the content of these "self-guides," and ultimately feeling the effects of a gap between the current self and a self-guide. Whereas individuals are assumed to be motivated to reduce these discrepancies (Carver & Scheier, 1981), sizable gaps can put the person at emotional risk for debilitating dejection (from ideal self-guide discrepancies) and agitation (from ought self-guide discrepancies). These different self-guides can be made alternatively salient by priming in a specific context; nonetheless, like motive dispositions, they are holistic/unitary structures, and experimental work shows that nondirective priming of one self-discrepant adjective in a self-guide is sufficient to elicit a full-blown emotional reaction of dejection or agitation (Strauman & Higgins, 1987).

Thus, the self-guide is not a fluid, negotiable structure—created "on-line," so to speak—yet its activation and the consequent elicitation of associated emotional states are affected by cues in the current context. Individuals are flexible thinkers in that they can adopt these different perspectives on the self and pull out these different slices of the self in response to very indirect environmental cues, but there is less control in the subsequent self-regulation of emotion and action once a self-guide is activated. Moreover, characteristic preferences for adopting certain self-guides, such as those that address desired selves or those that elucidate prescribed behavior, are established at quite a young age through exposure to different modes of socialization (e.g., those that stress ideal outcomes to strive for or instead focus attention on duties and obligations; see Higgins, Tykocinski, & Vookles, 1990). These self-guides—for example, a particular person's ideal self as seen from the perspective of important social figures—are relatively abstract knowledge structures, presumably carried through time fairly much intact, and certainly representing an abstracted and consolidated vision of self-across-contexts. Again, there is discriminative responding because the person can be induced to adopt different standpoints and to draw forth different domains of self: however, the context of those self-guides is not itself likely to shift perceptively from interaction to interaction, and the relatively strong emotional vulnerabilities are then consistently expressed as these abstract self-discrepancies are activated anew.

Finally, there is an important separation here between self- and other-standpoints on the self: The structures are distinct, and there may even be different motivational and emotional vulnerabilities that accrue from thinking of a discrepancy as viewed by ownself or by a social object. In any case, the individual is not portrayed as needing to balance and reconcile these different standpoints or these different self-domains in the context of an interaction (cf. Schlenker & Weigold, 1989).

Together, these units of the self present a variety of ways to look at the forward-looking motivation gained by taking a creative perspective on oneself over time and in one's imagination. In each case the function served or the process instigated by such self-reflection is slightly different, but the general thrust is to "work on the self" in some form or other. For example, McAdams' "successful" self-stories bring diverse selves in coordination in an integrated plot, whereas Markus' possible selves stand as figure against those past and present selves, holding forth the potential for new emergent properties to be realized. In Higgins' theory the motivation is to bring the actual self more in line with an ideal or ought vision of self, whereas Schlenker's model in some respects leads in the opposite direction, bringing the desired ideals back down to reality a bit. All of these views are dynamic self-models with multiple selves, multiple significant contexts defining "the" self, and multiple viewpoints from which to reflect on oneself. Moreover, they all suggest a role for self-reflection in the translation of personal intentions into behavior.

There are, of course, also differences among these perspectives—differences that may turn out to be significant as we come to understand more about the translation process. As self-regulatory guides, for example, McAdams' stories and imagoes may play a critical role in fostering the experience of self-continuity and in ensuring the consistent expression of personal motive dispositions over time and across life contexts. To be sure, in his model, imagoes represent caricatures of the self, and different parts of one's story are constructed (and reconstructed) in different life stages, but such self-reflection is still very much in the service of more enduring needs and themes of the individual. By contrast, in Markus' possible-selves model the individual takes a temporal perspective on the self mostly in the service of constructing alternative futures, in the service of hoped-for change rather than of self-continuity. As self-regulatory guides, possible selves represent ways of negotiating new selves in specific contexts, and especially in new life environments, cultural settings, and stages of life.

Similarly, whereas both Higgins' and Schlenker's models go a long way toward involving significant others in the self-regulatory process, in Higgins' case the self-guides encompass an abstracted image of the other, taken from many contexts and integrated into a powerful, holistic standard for behavior, and in Schlenker's self-identification process the focus is on the changing repertoire of desired identities constructed to incorporate quite specific audiences in a time-delimited fashion. In Higgins' model the impact of early childhood rearing patterns on styles of self-reflection—on ways of calling up an ideal or an ought standard, for example—suggest a basis for stability

in forms of action control; this stability is quite different from the negotiated self-perspective at the heart of Schlenker's theory. In one case the world is brought in as an internalized standard, and in the other case the self (or one of many selves) is brought out and fine-tuned in the process. These are, therefore, different ways of framing the self that potentially have different implications for how processes of enacting the self are conceptualized and studied. Most critically, these alternative models will probably lead to the asking of different empirical questions—questions of stability or of change, of determinism or of negotiation—as the implications of self-reflection are examined further.

Interpersonal Scripts and Private Audiences

Individuals have self-accounts that reflect how they characteristically relate to significant people in their environments, both now and in the past. These include "mental models" of how those relationships typically unfold or how they might be in the best of all possible worlds, and reflections on private dialogues with private audiences in the midst of interactions (Read & Miller, 1989; Singer & Kolligian, 1987). Importantly, these are "private" accounts, often requiring considerable self-reflection to put together as full accounts, and are rarely shared with or made directly "accountable" to the other social actors in an interaction, either now or in the past. Nonetheless, these interpersonal yet private units reflect traditional perspectives on the social nature of personality, and thus address our second theme of the "conditional" definition of personality units (Gergen & Gergen, 1988). Analysis of these interpersonal cognitive units, descriptive of individuals' repetitive forms of social dialogue and social interaction, provide a window both on the context-embedded, conditional features of personality, and on the higher-order meanings characterizing personal styles of social behavior that are posited to endure over time and place. Hence, these units provide a way to see the intricate texture of people's lives and also to characterize consistencies.

Whereas some of these interpersonal units are explicitly presented as forward-looking tools of motivation and self-regulation, there tends to be more emphasis here on consistencies emerging from the past, embellished, and carried forward repetitively into current social relationships (Pervin, 1989b). Furthermore, there is a thematic emphasis in content on the repetition of unsatisfactory or unsatisfying relationships of the past in the present, or rather the working through of those disappointments in the present (a legacy, often, of the Freudian analyses of transference; see Thorne, 1989). At the heart of these interpersonal units is the core affective reaction to events of the past that frequently involved some frustrating social relationship or pivotal interpersonal scene.

Thorne's Conditional Patterns

Inspired initially by her observations of the emergence of personality in interpersonal interaction settings—the "interpersonal press" (Thorne, 1987; see Murray, 1938)—Thorne (1989) has recently turned to look at individuals' internal representations of the key social conditions surrounding the expression of central dispositions. As she notes, these conditions are critical features of the dispositions themselves, such that a dominant person cannot express his or her dominance without a compliant social partner, and once the patterns of conditional behavior are established the individual can do much to create and recreate the necessary conditions. In this regard, the individual's self-account of that "conditional pattern," however fragmentary and nonconscious it is, may indeed be more instrumental in the perseverance of the dispositional expression than is the "actual" occurrence of the key social conditions. This is particularly likely to be true if, as she suspects, self-accounts of frustrating interaction episodes have more staying power than those conditional patterns based on more satisfying interactions. Starting with highly condensed accounts—for example, those emerging in complaints such as "I can't stand being dependent on others," or in autobiographical memories of "good times" and "bad times"—people can sometimes extend their narratives of these events in ways that reveal some pivotal interaction scenes from earlier years, which remain salient as recurrent conditions for their current behavior.

The key elements, then, of these conditional self-accounts are the frustrated wish that recurs and the typical reaction of both the person and his or her social partners; in addition, there is the generality of the pattern, as it occurs repeatedly with different partners. Whereas Thorne assumes that people have many such conditional patterns (and self-accounts thereof), the emphasis here is on demonstrating that personality coherence resides in the recurrence of these key elements. Moreover, though people may be motivated to change these frustrating patterns, the likelihood of significant change is clouded by the posited connection of current conditional patterns to core dispositions and to early childhood relationships (e.g., Shaver & Rubenstein, 1980). In that regard, this conditional account is similar to McAdams' narrative theory, wherein the creativity of personality comes in the embellishing and recreating of the conditions for dispositional expression, and is different from a negotiated self-perspective of the sort articulated by Schlenker and his colleagues.

Carlson's Nuclear Scenes

Building on Tomkins' (1979) script theory, Carlson (1981) demonstrates through cases history analysis the constructive process whereby individuals develop scripts—that is, rules for interpreting and responding to familiar (especially painful) scenes. These "nuclear scenes" from childhood that become the basis (via analogue processes) for adult scripts are highly particular, affectively laden, individualized events, not the universal scenes of Freud's Oedipal triangle or the cultural rituals that exemplify Erikson's age-graded tasks. Nor, in fact, are they linked necessarily in content to a core set of generalized dispositions (as in Thorne's model) or motives (as with McAdams' narrative accounts). Instead, the adult scripts—the guides for cognition, affect, and action in adulthood—are quite diverse in content and in number, and are particularized in the specific effect of these early events.

This is not a model in which early and significant social scenes become stretched and generalized over time to provide a pervasive set of conditions for dispositional displays; instead, it is one in which there is much inconsistency and variety in behavior precisely because the scripts are highly particular in content, even if only remotely connected to the earlier scenes (see Carlson, 1981, footnote 5, p. 509). Also, whereas Carlson emphasizes (as does Thorne) the power of early negative scenes to "recruit" material in later life, the process of script building is portrayed as a constant negotiation between current and past scenes, rather than a direct analogue or assimilation process. To be sure, that residue of negative affect from an early scene persists with power as a guiding framework for subsequent behavior; in fact, Carlson suggests that one clue to the presence of a nuclear script in case history material is a seeming gap between the power of current affect and the "realities" of a recent event as told by the individual. Nonetheless, the case history material also reveals a constant growth process, in which the connective tissue between the past and present stimuli are as "remote analogues of a nuclear scene in an *ever-growing* nuclear script" (p. 508; our italics). Therefore, this conditional account has somewhat more of the flavor of Schlenker's constructive process; however, the impetus for negotiation comes more from the negative affect of unresolved personal history than from the pressures of accountability to a social partnership.

Baldwin and Holmes' Private Audience

In contrast, Baldwin and Holmes (1987) have recently suggested another conditionalized unit of analysis—the "private audience"—that is centered on the notion of social accountability and the sensitivity of individuals to social appraisal. Individuals, according to this view, recruit and frame private social audiences. Sometimes these reflect actual standpoints on the self and sometimes they do not; sometimes they represent long-term, recurrent perspectives, and other times they draw on newly created sources of reflected appraisal. The interaction with a private audience is construed as a dialogue that, while sometimes quite deliberate and other times outside of awareness, is instrumental both in the course of individuals' task performance as a regulatory guide and after the fact as a source of self-evaluation. For example, individuals who are induced (through indirect instructions) to think about and visualize a particular private audience that, in their experience, holds exacting standards of evaluation and bestows performance-contingent praise or criticism demonstrate clear signs of working to please that audience and of taking a harsh evaluative stance to the self, even in unrelated task settings. Dialogues with a private audience can be powerful forms of self-regulation, serving to motivate performance and persistence, and to keep a person "on track" in his or her goal strivings; they tend to

be most effective when a person is in a state of private self-awareness, either brought on experimentally or reflecting a characteristic self-focus of attention (Scheier & Carver, 1980). These dialogues operate with different levels of awareness on the part of the individual. They range from distinct memories of private discussions with significant others to staunch disclaimers of any "social" influence on behavior or attitude statements, and people are very rarely aware that some subtle aspect of a context can induce a particular internal dialogue or train of thought (Bargh, 1982).

As a unit of personality, these private audiences have the potential either to represent internalized social objects with recurrent "control" over self-reflection and behavior (in the tradition of object relations theory; Eagle, 1984), or, alternatively, to symbolize the social sensitivity of the "private self" in its ongoing public interactions (in the tradition of the self-presentation literature; Goffman, 1959). Baldwin and Holmes refer both to the power of private audiences to "entrap" individuals in cycles of self-devaluation, and to the possibility that forceful new audiences can be used as tools of self-change. In either case, whether the audiences are recurrent or negotiated anew, this particular unit of analysis makes self-reflection and self-knowledge directly conditional upon (real or imagined) "social" messages. Furthermore, it might be reasonable to expect individual differences in the proclivity of people either to reinforce their "historical selves" by drawing repeatedly on certain private audiences, or to turn for some perhaps fresh self-perspective to ever-new private audiences. At the least, it is probably the case that any individual will turn first to history and familiarity in a new life setting, and then perhaps will gradually allow the opportunities afforded by a life transition or life change to induce some variation in the standard set of audiences.

Increasing attention is being accorded in recent literature to the importance of interpersonal cognitive units of analysis; to the goals and memories that partners share in relationships; to the scripts that certain social interactions repeatedly elicit; to the "accounts" that individuals give, jointly or alone, of the problems in a relationship; and so forth (e.g., Harvey, Agostineli, & Weber, 1989; Wegner, Guiliano, & Hertel, 1985). One obvious characteristic of all of these units is that they represent the socially situated or contextualized side of individuals' personalities, and we view this as a very important reason to pursue such approaches. As always, interpersonal units can also serve different purposes in the self-regulation process. For example, Baldwin and Holmes' private audiences are directly involved in action control, providing standards for behavioral decisions, even when the dialogues are nonconscious. In contrast, Thorne's conditional interaction patterns play a role more similar to McAdams' self-stories, serving as expressions of the individual's underlying social dispositions—ways of marking the kinds of relationships and interactions that a person tends to seek and enact on a regular basis.

Carlson's nuclear scenes and scripts stand somewhere in the middle of this comparison, with their form resembling the story accounts provided by Thorne's subjects; yet they serve perhaps more as active guides to behavior in particular social situations, along the line of Baldwin and Holmes' private audiences. Nonetheless, in both the Carlson and the Baldwin and Holmes approaches, it is assumed that some individuals will construct stable and highly generalized or overused audiences and scripts, thereby turning away from the potential for flexible responses to the particulars of a situation, and in fact leaving these persons vulnerable to rigid and self-defeating habits. And both Thorne and Carlson focus special attention on the interpersonal patterns and scripts that mark for a person those discouraging life events and scenes that he or she tries to avoid and instead repeats with some disappointing regularity. Though there is clearly good reason, as Thorne has articulated, for believing that individuals' memories of negative interactions, scolding private audiences, and demeaning relationships play special roles in ongoing self-regulation, future work on interpersonal units may build upon these promising contributions with attention to the positive scripts and "possible relationships" that people try to re-enact or to create anew (Read & Miller, 1989, p. 433).

Tasks, Strivings, and Projects

Cognitive–motivational units organized around individuals' current, self-articulated goals and tasks draw explicit attention to the future-oriented, forward-looking aspects of personality—those end states toward which individuals feel they are striving, the tasks and projects that they endorse in the process, and the thematic concerns that currently energize their purposive activities (see Pervin, 1983). These approaches rely often on individuals' own views of their current concerns and goals, as expressed in responses to questions such as "What are you trying to do?" "What gives meaning to your life?" "What are your current personal projects?" or "What are your life tasks in this transition?" Nonetheless, these consciously accessible goals and tasks are also assumed to derive from or at least to relate to (higher-order) motives and needs, and age-graded or culturally mandated tasks (Veroff, 1983). Nor do even the consciously accessible goals need to be readily in the forefront of consciousness as individuals behave, though when challenged in their strivings or tasks people may well think rather explicitly about their thwarted desires. Individuals can articulate their goals at many levels of abstraction, from the higher-order themes that energize their activity, to the concrete projects in which those themes are reflected and that organize and give special meaning to ongoing daily life activity (Baumeister, 1989). Moreover, there are many ways in which the conditional nature of individuals' goals can be conceptualized—from those that emerge consistently in a variety of interchangeable ways, to those that are defined by their constituent acts in context or those that change in predictable ways with life transitions.

Emmons' Personal Strivings

In defining the construct of "personal striving," Emmons (1989a) draws on Gordon Allport's (1953) description of motives as representing what a person is trying to do, to avoid, and to be in his or her life. Whereas personal strivings differ from traditional nomothetic social motives in that they are individually defined and typically more specific than those broad motives, they are similar in the intent to capture recurrent, stable, consistently expressed, characteristic forms of goal striving. Personal strivings are what the person is trying to do, often and in a variety of ways, in many different life settings and for relatively long periods of time. As such, they share much in common with the constructs of motive and trait dispositions, and in fact can be viewed as idiographic instantiations of those dispositions. Emmons (1989a,b) has demonstrated these links in both motive (e.g., intimacy and power mapping onto strivings) and trait (e.g., narcissism) domains. The construct, therefore, is organized around the individual's needs (and reflects his or her own versions of basic human needs and biological demands) and the creative ways in which those needs are fulfilled *in situ*. These are enduring personal goals, not, for example, ones that are likely to be abandoned in the face of obstacles or even of success.

In light of the interest in finding idiographic goals that nonetheless are dispositionally consistent—that is, ones that "rise above context," so to speak—the personal-striving approach places somewhat less emphasis on the conditional relations between strivings and particular actions in context (cf. Little, 1983) and on the reflection of cultural or age-graded mandates in individuals' strivings (cf. Cantor, in press). Emmons' assessments of strivings provide rich details on individuals' personal-striving systems, their appraisals of their current striving, and conflicts that they may have about their diverse goals, as well as reflecting on the choices that they make that are striving-consistent and their everyday experiences of success and failure. The assessment data provide the means for analyses that relate strivings to motives, and that relate striving appraisals to a variety of subjective well-being outcomes and to indices of emotional adjustment (e.g., Emmons & King, 1988, 1989). As with McAdams' work on motives and identity stories, the objective here is to show how people find ways to enact their strivings and the contexts in which to do so, and to demonstrate the roadblocks to well-being afforded by striving ambivalence or interference. As with motives, the particular enactment of a striving, and even at times the striving itself, will vary with setting and age period; however, the precipitant for change is more likely to reside in the pragmatics of the new life situation that require a different means to the desired end than in an attempt to solve a task or project emerging from that new setting. In this model, the individual's creativity is addressed more toward what he or she particularly wants to achieve than toward an analysis of what is out there for him or her to do or what "they" would like done. As a pragmatist, the individual adapts his or her striving-consistent behavior to fit the setting, group, or culture; nevertheless, this pragmatic adaptation

is not really a two-way negotiation, as the individual has basic personal needs (related to stable dispositions) to fulfill, and he or she will usually find ways to do that and settings that reward those special strivings (Emmons, Diener, & Larsen, 1986).

Little's Personal Projects

A slightly different way to capture individuals' self-defined goals is illustrated by Brian Little's (1983, 1989) model of "personal projects." This unit is built on Murray's (1938) notion of a "serial program" or extended series of acts, and the objective here is to capture "what individuals are doing" that gives meaning both to their daily activities and to their sense of purpose in life. The personal project is a highly contextualized unit in which the goal itself is not only expressed in but also defined by the set of interrelated acts-in-context that comprise the "project." Personal projects range in magnitude from very specific, contained efforts such as "finishing a term paper" to more extended, monumental efforts to "find a satisfying relationship." Nonetheless, they are defined with particular life contexts in mind; they serve to organize everyday activities; and the forward-looking agenda is constrained by the realities of negotiating in a particular environment. In fact, much of Little's empirical work on personal projects involves consideration of the strategies that people use to further their projects while negotiating the complex terrain of everyday life. For example, Palys and Little (1983) find that personal projects that extend too far in time rarely provide for satisfaction and subjective well-being. Little suggests a tradeoff between "meaning" and "manageability" in projects, with individuals striving to find the right balance, and with the point of balance changing even for one person with shifts in context and familiarity. Personal projects have to be constantly negotiated in an interpersonal context as well, and Little emphasizes the need for people to be competent at communicating their projects, at resolving interpersonal conflicts about projects, and at (re)shaping both the projects and the "environment" so that some progress can be made. As such, he sees the articulation of projects and of project conflicts in a social setting as a necessary first step to self-change, and he has developed therapeutic techniques to encourage such processes of project communication (see Little, 1989).

Cantor's Life Tasks

Cantor and Kihlstrom (1985, 1987) have suggested the current "life task," defined as the problem(s) that individuals see themselves as working on in a particular life period or life transition, as a way to characterize each individual's unique efforts to negotiate the demands of his or her age- and social/cultural-group in a personally viable manner. Life tasks are self-articulated problems that individuals are motivated to try to solve, to which they devote energy and time, and that they see as organizing their current daily life activity. Like personal projects, these tasks are given shape in the specific set of actions and subtasks that an individual sees as critical to master in that social environment in order to make progress on the task; as we (Zirkel & Cantor, 1990) have demonstrated for college students working on independence, even the most "mandated" of age-appropriate tasks can be alternatively construed by different participants. Although individuals give this form to their tasks by thinking about them as including certain projects or subtasks and excluding others, life tasks are always importantly embedded in and responsive to the "agenda" set by cultures and social groups for particular ages or life periods (e.g., Higgins & Parsons, 1983; Cantor & Langston, 1989). These are tasks—for example, "being on my own away from my family" or "setting career goals" for new college students—that individuals see as part of their mandate in mastering their new environment (Stewart & Healy, 1985). Whereas we assume that individuals are motivated to solve these tasks all of the time, our assessments often concentrate on individuals in life transitions, when the need to navigate the environment is perhaps greatest and the resources for doing so are somewhat taxed (Cantor et al., 1987).

The construct of life tasks is thus patterned on traditional lifespan developmental notions of tasks, though there is less presumption that all individuals must negotiate each age-appropriate task, or that they do it in some standard order (Erikson, 1950; Havighurst, 1953). In fact, Cantor and Fleeson (1990) have shown how part of the adjustment process for individuals in a new life period or life environment involves "trying on" and experimenting with those typical consensually validated life tasks in the service of comitment over time to a few personally meaningful ones. Life tasks are defined by an interaction between what is "out there" to be solved in any life period or setting, and what the person decides (in one way or another) to "take on" and make his or her own for the time being. In addition, individuals put their own mark on their life tasks by constructing strategies that "work" for them in pursuing a particular task in a particular context and at a particular time in life (Langston & Cantor, 1989; Norem, 1989). Whereas personal strivings are idiographically defined versions of social motives, life tasks can be viewed as individually defined versions of socially and culturally prescribed age-graded agendas; whereas Emmons shows us how individuals are motivated to find ways to fulfill their strivings, Cantor also views individuals as motivated to master their sociocultural contexts in personally comfortable ways. Moreover, whereas the emphasis in the analysis of strivings as idiographic motives is rightly on their persistence and generality, the focus for life tasks is on the dynamics of change and negotiation, and on the ways in which even familiar tasks such as "finding intimacy" or "being independent" really come to mean something entirely different in a new life period or setting. The dynamics of task negotiation sometimes include variations in the very core situations and actions of which the task is comprised, as when a college student "works on independence" in achievement arenas, and then goes off to start a new career and faces familiar issues of independence and self-assertion, but now in his or her newly emerging social life (Zirkel & Cantor, 1990). Of course, depending on one's perspective (as an analyst of consistency or of change), this form of life task redefinition can be taken as evidence either for the motive rising above the context or for people's goals taking their shape *in situ*; most likely, it is really a bit of both.

Klinger's Current Concerns

Eric Klinger's (1975, 1977, 1987) analyses of "current concerns" provide direct insights into the ongoing and ever-shifting process of goal commitment and disengagement, as revealed in the flow of thought, fantasy, and action, toward and away from specific goals. Current concerns are underlying goal states that direct thought and action largely through the emotional arousal that accompanies "on-line" commitment to a specific goal, and that in turn directs attention to goal-relevant stimuli in that context (Klinger, 1989). Whereas current concerns, such as "getting that person to like me" or "finishing a day's work," may well relate to higher-order life themes or motives (e.g., of affiliation and achievement), the emphasis in this approach is much more on the unfolding process of goal striving in context, and on the ebb and flow of commitment as individuals go about their daily lives.

Individuals have numerous current concerns that give meaning to and fill voids in their daily lives; Klinger, Barta, and Maxeiner (1980) have utilized thought sampling, retrospective self-reports, and experimental manipulations of divided attention to get a handle on the process by which some of these concerns become salient, and thus consume and direct thought and action until some point of disengagement occurs. Several principles of engagement or commitment (at this microprocess level) have emerged from their work: For example, people think more about goals to which they are imminently committed than about longer-term incentives, and they allocate processing time and energy to problematic goals that may well be thwarted in the current context. People think and fantasize not only about highly valued goals, but also about currently accessible ones (Higgins, King, & Mavin, 1982). Thus, the moment-to-moment texture of individuals' goal strivings is one shaped in context, with many bumps and ridges as some concerns surface and others recede in current importance. Also, this is an ever-changing cycle, so that "old" concerns may pop up again to direct thought and action at some later moment.

There are many ways to approach the question of individuals' self-articulated goals and tasks, and these four perspectives illustrate this diversity. Emmons focuses on the dispositional characteristics of his idiographic goal unit—on the creative ways in which people consistently and persistently strive for a desired end state. In so doing, he stresses the substitutability of diverse plans and actions in serving to fulfill any given higher-order striving, and the choice of appropriate life contexts in which to enact those strivings. The creativity of individuals is seen, then, in the ways in which underlying needs and traits can be enduringly expressed in personal strivings over contexts, over time, and across life periods.

In contrast, both the life tasks approach and the personal-projects approach represent personal goals more indirectly or interactively in the context of the tasks or projects that need to be, should be, or can be accomplished in a particular life period (for tasks) or life situation (for projects). Tasks and projects acquire their very meaning in context: They are often suggested by the culture or context, even sometimes imposed by those social structures or environments, and certainly always negotiated with the "agendas" of that broader social world in mind. In that sense, tasks and projects represent the needs and desires of the individual as inextricably bound with the opportunities and demands of the social environment. Whereas the personal-strivings model (and related motive approaches) importantly remind us of the biological and intrapsychic mandates that become expressed within individuals' goals and activities, the project and task approaches emphasize the impact of interpersonal and sociocultural or age-graded mandates, respectively. As a result, individuals' tasks and projects are less likely to be enduring, and more likely to change in regular, predictable ways with changes in those life environments from which they in part derive meaning and definition. The focus shifts thus more toward the unique ways in which individuals experiment with and ultimately negotiate personal versions of age-graded tasks or socially valued projects, in ways that follow as much from life changes as from enduring intrapsychic needs. Nonetheless, there is still a strongly idiographic flavor because individuals do experiment with these social agendas, and frequently find their own tasks and projects from within the broader array of "choices." Moreover, people's construals of consensual tasks or shared projects are often remarkably diverse, even when they live in ostensibly similar environments, and those alternative construals will in turn determine the nature of their plans and strategies in relevant domains.

Of course, despite these differences, there are many commonalties across all of these approaches, such as the emphasis on idiographic construal, on choices of life activities and of preoccupations (as revealed in experience- and thought-sampling procedures), and on the expression of intentions in action. And even the differences are not irreconcilable, as we all work toward answering questions of consistency and of change in more truly integrated person—situation models. In fact, at a more molecular level still, Klinger's work on charting the stream of concern-related thoughts, affects, and actions unites all such goal-based perspectives in a common cause—that is, in looking at the cognitive–intentional basis of action control. Klinger's process analyses combine these various emphases, with a focus both on what the person is currently *working on* in a particular life context and on what he or she is habitually *striving for* across many such endeavors. Klinger adds to this a sensitivity to the minute-by-minute ebb and flow of goal and task and of project engagement and disengagement—a perspective on purposive behavior to which we now turn more directly.

CREATIVE, DISCRIMINATIVE, AND FLEXIBLE ACTION CONTROL

In our view, one of the most important implications of pursuing these intentional middle-level units that are contextually responsive is the increasing emphasis on what G. W. Allport (1937) called the "doing" side of personality—attention to the diverse ways in which individuals navigate their social worlds while also maintaining self-esteem, constructing meaningful self-stories, and fulfilling at least some personal goals in the process (Cantor, 1989; Larsen, 1989). Whereas personality psychologists of diverse traditions have always paid heed to the importance of self-regulatory processes, the current emphasis on cognition and self-agency, as exemplified in Bandura's (1986) recent monograph or in Carver and Scheier's (1981) control theory exposition, seems to fit especially well with the many middle-level units of analysis described above. In fact, many of these approaches concentrate in empirical work on the enactment of selves and interpersonal scenes and goals in daily living, through the self-regulation of thought and action and the choice of situations and activities to pursue. Envisioning positive possible selves provides a motivational stimulus to persistence at hard tasks (Markus & Ruvolo, 1989); imagining a private audience that typically bestows unconditional approval buffers an individual against self-blame after a subpar performance (Baldwin & Holmes, 1987); playing through or simulating "worst-case scenarios" can serve as protection and can energize performance at risky life task ventures for some "defensive pessimists" (Norem & Cantor, 1986a, 1986b). The "doing" approaches that build upon these middle-level units are diverse in their particulars

but share a common perspective, in which the explication of the processes of social behavior involves the integration of motivation, affect, and cognition, and in which careful attention is accorded to behavioral measures (such as persistence, self-evaluation, or choice) that reveal this complex side of personality in action. In this section, we briefly and selectively review some aspects or principles of self-regulation that are receiving special scrutiny in these approaches, with an eye toward seeing how they follow from these middle-level constructs and how they shed light on sources of competence and on sources of problems in living.

In discussions of self-regulation, there is often reference, either explicit or implicit, to the *cognitive–behavioral strategy* as the basic unit of analysis. This is true, for example, in the problem-solving expert systems literature (e.g., Miller, Galanter, & Pribram, 1960; Newell & Simon, 1972); in the study of plans and self-control (e.g., Mischel, 1981); in models of motivated social cognition (e.g., Schank & Abelson, 1977; Showers & Cantor, 1985); and in the domain of cognitive therapy (e.g., Ingram, 1986). There are, of course, also many ways to define this unit of self-regulation, but for the present purposes a few key aspects seem most pertinent. Strategies are units organized around the flow of purposive behavior; therefore, they are centered in an individual's goal or intention, however subtle or unarticulated that impetus for action may be. The strategy unfolds over time and place, and comprises (1) the cognitive–affective work that an individual does to anticipate and prepare for action, to monitor behavior as it unfolds, and to look back on the outcomes and initiate corrective responses if need be; and (2) the more observable acts that make up the individual's "responses" (e.g., Cantor & Kihlstrom, 1987). Strategies chart the individual's efforts—cognitive, affective, and behavioral—to "take control" by simulating the future, keeping track of the present, and reaching back to examine or undo the past (Norem, 1989). As many have noted, individuals' proclivity to think about themselves and the future with alternative scenarios in mind constitutes a major cognitive contribution of self-reflection to human agency and coping (Bandura, 1986; Kahneman & Miller, 1986; Taylor & Schneider, 1989).

There are many models of self-regulation that can provide a context for looking at these processes of anticipation and mental simulation, of monitoring and evaluation, and of retrospection and self-correction (e.g., Carver & Scheier, 1981; Kuhl, 1985). In the following discussion, we focus on the action identification perspective articulated by Vallacher and Wegner (1987) as one vehicle for consideration of the processes that translate goals, selves, and interpersonal scripts into streams of intentional behavior. We choose this particular perspective as the defining context for discussion because it seems to make vivid the creative and discriminative capacities of individuals as they think of alternative ways to frame their pursuits, and as they tailor action to negotiate an effective path between personal needs and contextual requirements.

Action Identification and Action Control

In their work on action identification, Vallacher and Wegner (1987) have underlined the importance of conscious mental control over self-regulation, as represented by individuals' beliefs about what they think they are doing in any particular situation or delimited period of time. These authors argue that there is always some conscious cognitive control over action, but that what varies is the (hierarchical) level of identification at which a person is consciously operating. That is, individuals may "automatically" construct sentences to express an opinion in an argument, whereas they may be quite conscious of their (higher-level) desire to negotiate a desirable path between dogmatism and conformity. This theory establishes a highly elucidating context within which to view the process of translation of selves, scripts, and goals into concrete sequences of intended action in context. Vallacher and Wegner (1987) operate from the premise that people prefer an identification of action that proves effective in maintaining the action—a premise of intelligent self-regulation (Cantor & Kihlstrom, 1987). Individuals will gravitate toward the higher-level, more "meaningful" act identifications, but only insofar as they can continue to carry forth the necessary action as part of those higher-order intentions. Thus individuals are presumed to be sensitive to the difficulty of the required action in a given context, to their own expertise, and to cues in the surrounding context that signal alternative (perhaps more manageable) identifications or impending disruptions and difficulties likely with the present course of action (e.g., Klinger et al., 1980).

Actions identified at a high level are more stable (in reflecting intentions to which there is some high-level commitment) and yet also can be carried forth with a range of interchangeable lower-level acts, just as we have noted earlier that a personal striving can be enacted in a variety of substitutable forms, whereas most personal projects and life tasks have more clearly specified preferred forms of enactment in particular contexts. In contrast, when an individual's conscious action control (or attentive control) is maintained at a lower level (as in a new context), then he or she is both more sensitive to and more susceptible to contextual pressures that can sometimes change the intended course of action quite radically, raising competing intentions that must be dismissed or taken on instead. Both levels of action identification have their drawbacks, of course, as when an individual gets lost in the high-level intention and fails to adequately monitor the lower-level scripted behaviors, or becomes inflexible and unresponsive to the realities of the "actual" situation (e.g., Langer, 1989); conversely, a person may be "seduced" by contextual pressures to attempt infeasible higher-level actions or to be drawn away from his or her priorities in a way that may be regrettable later (e.g., Kuhl, 1985). Vallacher and Wegner acknowledge a variety of tradeoffs and breakdowns in the action identification process; nevertheless, they underline the creativity with which people do identify their actions in everyday life, and emphasize the dynamics of this process as people adjust their identifications and their actions in accord with performance feedback (Carver & Scheier, 1981).

Trading Off Meaning and Manageability

One of the most compelling aspects of this approach is its emphasis on individuals' attempts to find manageable or feasible ways to do things that promote their intentions—that is, the emphasis on intelligent action control. As Brian Little (1989) notes in his discussion of personal projects, people are constantly faced with a tradeoff between trying to do something "really meaningful" (i.e., high-level action identification) in their projects, and actually being able to make some progress on their current projects (i.e., a slightly lower, more concrete, and more time-delimited level of action identification). Often it is simply too hard to carry out projects and tasks at the highly meaningful, multidomain level that fits with the initial framing of personal goals, and some loss of "meaning" must be sacrificed to the practicalities of the current reality and of one's expertise.

The need for "modesty" in goal setting may be particularly acute in new environments, and at times of life transition generally (Stewart, 1982). For example, we (Zirkel & Cantor, 1990) found that new college students intent on "solving" their independence life task did better in this transition if they framed the task in a very specific, delimited way (e.g., "doing my laundry") than if they took on the broader possibilities of this age-graded task (e.g., "satisfying myself and my parents in my academic choices"). In times of life transition, individuals need to spend some time and effort in simply learning the terrain and discovering the new tasks of this environment or subculture from observation and experimentation (Cantor & Fleeson, 1990; Stewart, 1989). Thus, according to the action identification model, there are times when it is advantageous to sacrifice meaning at a high level for manageability at a slightly more modest level.

Showers' (1988, 1989a) work with socially anxious individuals suggests that the disruptive effects of personal anxiety on performance in important tasks can be somewhat reduced by techniques that keep individuals thinking about the concrete, "how-to" aspects of the interaction, perhaps because that strategy precludes a more debilitating self-focus of attention on personal deficits and past disappointments (Carver, 1979; Meichenbaum, 1977). Similarly, Harackiewicz's (1989) process analysis of factors that promote and detract from intrinsic motivation suggests that for some individuals the best plan is to remain at a low level of focus on the task-intrinsic aspects of the activity at hand, avoiding the disruptions of the competence valuation process induced by too high-level a focus of attention (Nicholls, 1984). As with mot self-regulatory strategies, there are probably alternative routes to successful action identification and action control in most contexts, and part of an individual-difference psychology is to understand why some strategies work well for some people in some contexts and not for others (Carver & Scheier, 1989; Norem & Cantor, in press).

Self-Efficacy and Monitoring Expertise

Another principle in the Vallacher and Wegner model is that individuals are sensitive to the limits of their own experise (or "action experience") in taking on tasks and in moving between levels of action identification. This fits very well with the traditional and current emphasis in the self-regulation literature on the decisive impact of expectancy orientations on action control (Rotter, 1966; Lazarus & Folkman, 1984; Scheier & Carver, 1985). Individuals not only evaluate their performance after the fact in light of their prior expectations for success and for failure, but also choose tasks, allocate effort, and monitor progress in light of those expectations. Bandura's (1977, 1986) self-efficacy model, for example, places special emphasis on "cognitively generated" motivation, derived from anticipating outcomes and planning action in accord with personal assessments of expertise and competence at the task at hand. In turn, those assessments of self-efficacy at a task are based upon a complicated internal metric, taking into account aspects of past performance history; current desires; the favorability of the circumstances; and personal mood state, optimism, and beliefs in the controllability of the situation (see Bandura, 1989). Self-efficacy judgments are specific to the current context and task, and they are importantly dynamic, varying from task to task and open to the kinds of updating at the heart of effective action regulation. As Bandura suggests, individuals will "take on" a challenge to the extent that they basically feel competent to try it; in action identification terms, optimistic self-efficacy evaluations provide an extra push to move to higher levels of action intentions.

Scheier and Carver (1985) have provided ample and compelling evidence that an optimistic expectancy orientation is a critical component of the self-regulatory process, keeping people on track in the pursuit of self-goals. At the core of their cybernetic model of action control are the implicit calculations that individuals repeatedly carry out (especially under conditions of heightened self-focus) to determine the likelihood of success at the task at hand. In so doing, sometimes individuals show the kinds of fine-tuned self-scrutiny that Vallacher and Wegner (1987), among others (e.g., Schlenker, 1980; Trope, 1986), basically imply. At other times it seems as if much of the impetus for these self-confident intentions and high-level identifications is based on illusory thinking (e.g., Alloy & Abramson, 1979; Gollwitzer & Kinney, in press; Langer, 1975) and on somewhat self-deceptive introspection (e.g., Wilson, 1985). In fact, the optimism that leads to high-level action identification is generally believed to be a major factor both in motivational persistence and in healthy adjustment, especially as contrasted with various states of pessimistic self-thought (e.g., Peterson & Seligman, 1987; Scheier & Carver, 1985).

Of course, as Vallacher & Wegner (1987) and others (e.g., Lazarus, 1983) have warned, there is also a cost to optimism (and high-level intentionality) if it somehow impedes the dynamic responsiveness and flexibility of the action identification process, and blinds the actor to impending disruptions or obstacles. On occasion, it is even the case that some highly competent individuals do better when they focus on those potential forthcoming obstacles, and presumably remain at a level of action identification slightly below what might seem warranted with their expertise (Cantor & Norem, 1989; Norem, 1987). Furthermore, as Oyserman and Markus (1988) have suggested, when personal history portends some trouble ahead in action control, there is good reason to believe that a "balanced" perspective on the future possibilities serves as an asset in self-regulation. Certainly, as Langer's (1989) work documents, it is not advisable to rely "mindlessly" on presumed expertise to such an extent that low-level action is not monitored much at all, thus violating the basic premise of intelligent and vigilant action control.

Self-Verification, Flexibility, and Malleability

One of the consequences for action control of individuals' firm commitments to their self-identities, personal strivings, and possible selves is that when given the opportunity they will operate at quite a high level of action identification, with great persistence and ingenuity, in preserving those beliefs and intentions (e.g., Markus, 1977; Swann, 1985). As Vallacher and Wegner note, individuals protect their high-level intentions by embracing a variety of interchangeable low-level paths to the same desired end, and by resisting alternative interpretations or purposes to pursue; "a person with a high level understanding

already knows what he or she is doing" (1987, p. 8). This kind of intense purposiveness is encouraged by the self-stories, personal strivings, and self-schemas in which individuals have invested much time and thought. As such, we see a variety of creative ways in which individuals create and maintain these high-level identifications in the course of everyday life. Swann and Hill (1982), for example, show how facile people are at behaviorally rejecting self-discrepant feedback, whereas Gollwitzer and Wicklund (1985) document the "substitutability" of alternative paths to self-completion in the face of some threat, and Steele (1988) explicates the various self-affirmations that people engage in without awareness when they have somehow been "forced" to behave in a self-discordant manner. As several personality psychologists have pointed out (Buss, 1987; Snyder, 1981), one of the common ways to persist in "being oneself" and "doing what one wants to do" is to be selective about the situations, tasks, and interactions that one enters (e.g., Niedenthal, Cantor, & Kihlstrom, 1985). In a related vein, it may be easier to protect a cherished identity or goal commitment, or to build a buffer against the demoralizing influence of negative feedback about the self, if one keeps one's various identities and strivings relatively compartmentalized (Linville, 1987; Showers, 1989b; cf. Emmons & King, 1989).

Of course, as there are always two sides to these action control strategies, there are times when it helps to be open to distraction from a high-level intention, or at least responsive to negative feedback. Wurf (1988), for example, showed how individuals with negative self-schemas that they desired very much to change sometimes sought out feedback about alternative ways of behaving, presumably in order to aid their self-change goals; and Norem (1989) found that "defensive pessimists" performed better when they believed that their negative self-characteristics were, in principle at least, changeable ones. In an elegant series of papers, Dweck and her colleagues (Dweck, 1986; Dweck & Leggett, 1988; Elliott & Dweck, 1988) have demonstrated a clear relationship between "learning goals" (and challenge-seeking behavior) and ingenuity in the face of difficulty, whereas "performance goals" that derive from a fixed view of individuals' talents and capacities are detrimental to motivation and to persistence precisely when these obstacles to performance arise. Schlenker and Weigold (1989) suggest that people are sometimes open to trying alternative desired identities when negative social feedback makes it clear that their ideal scenarios for self-enhancement are not feasible. In its broadest sense, these diverse perspectives all underline the need for social negotiation as individuals pursue their own intentions and (re)affirm their identities through action. Of course, there are special times that make this negotiable stance particularly critical: Stewart (1989), for example. suggests that newcomers in an environment have to be receptive to the social agendas of that environment in order to adjust, and ultimately to pursue more self-initiated intentions. Although the need to be accepting of the high-level identifications presented in a social context may be especially powerful in times of life transition, this kind of flexibility is probably important at all times (Norem, 1989).

Ruminations, Self-Defeating Strategies, and Dejection

There is—perhaps inevitably, when one is operating from a model of intelligent self-regulation—a tendency to emphasize the discriminativeness and creativity of purposive behavior, at the expense of capturing the pervasiveness of breakdowns in action control (cf. Cantor & Kihlstrom, 1989, and Pervin, 1989b). In actuality, there are numerous ways in which the action control system does typically break down, and it seems important to note a few of those cases here. Kuhl (1985), in distinguishing between a state orientation and an action orientation, vividly describes the negative consequences of persistent rumination. Individuals can get stuck in their perseverative ruminations, in their indecision about alternatives to pursue, in the commitment to "inexecutable or degenerated intentions," and in a cycle of regret and self-recrimination over mistaken choices and actions already taken. This state of self-regulatory breakdown often accompanies a depression when an individual feels captive to negative ruminations and self-blaming cognitions (e.g., Pyszczynski & Greenberg, 1987; Showers & Ruben, 1989). As Herrmann and Wortman (1985) point out, debilitating state orientation may also accompany a major life crisis or victimization experience, when basic assump-

tive beliefs cab be shattered in such a way as to preclude the mobilization of an action-oriented intention (see also Janoff-Bulman, 1989). Times of crisis illustrate the pervasive debilitating impact of negative affect and arousal upon action control, though Healy (1989) has also shown that the emotional disruption accompanying life changes also disrupts basic cognitive processes, such as perspective taking and information integration, that are critical to this action control process.

In a less dramatic way, the action control process can be said to break down when individuals persistently embrace self-defeating strategies of social behavior (Baumeister & Scher, 1988). Strategies can be self-defeating in a number of ways and at a number of points in the self-regulatory cycle, any one of which is not good for effective self-regulation. For example, Smith and Rhodewalt (1986) argue that Type A individuals create stressful interactions in part because they are constantly anticipating hostility and competition from others, and become committed sometimes without reason to a hostile stance that elicits its own hostile feedback (Snyder & Swann, 1978). Suzanne Miller (1987), in analyzing styles of information monitoring, raises the possibility that some people will monitor events too closely, thus learning things (e.g., the risks in a medical procedure) that make it more rather than less difficult to proceed with a task or intention. And frequently the self-defeating aspect of a strategy comes almost as a side effect after the "main event" has unfolded: For example, Langston and Cantor (1989) found that socially anxious individuals maintained active social lives at least in part by following the lead of others in an interaction, yet that same "other-directedness" then became fodder for their retrospective self-recriminations, thus exacerbating already low social self-esteem.

Whether in anticipation, monitoring, or retrospections, individuals can go astray in the self-regulatory process—by inaccurately "sizing up" the situation or, conversely, by monitoring too vigilantly, or in the relentlessness of their self-blame after the fact. Even a functional self-regulatory strategy can be used too rigidly or in too many situations, as when a defensive pessimist insists on simulating in exhausting detail the possible worst-case outcomes of relatively nonthreatening life events, and in the process saps his or her intrinsic motivation to pursue more important life tasks (Cantor & Norem,

1989). Moreover, these are only a few of the many ways that effective action can be impeded by the dysfunctional thoughts of normally competent individuals. As Vallacher and Wegner note, "People choke under pressure, suffer from evaluation apprehension, get distracted, lose concentration, revert to old habits, worry about failure, get overconfident, and in other ways manage to approach action with a dysfunctional mental set" (1987, p. 9).

In particular, many of these occasions of breakdown in effective action control seem to center in some way around failures in creativity, discriminativeness, or flexibility. For example, cognitive theories of depression often emphasize the rigidity of negative thinking about the self, and the failure even to imagine a different possible future, to simulate a non-worst-case outcome (e.g., Beck, 1967). Similarly, in their studies of aggressive children, Wright and Mischel (1987) emphasize a conditional definition of social competence that involves fine-tuning behavior to fit the demands of the situation, even when patience is taxed, as it often is for these children. The literature on close relationships is replete with examples of couples' failing to adopt a negotiable stance about their respective needs and desires, to make corrective changes in habitual behavior, or, if need be, to give up on intentions that simply will not work (Kelley, 1979). Failures of action control are not limited to any one population, nor are they hard to find in evidence in everyday life. However, people do occasionally engage in intelligent, effective action control. And the evidence for at least some measure of cognitive control of behavior is encouraging as a basis from which to consider interventions in these discouraging instances of self-regulation gone awry (e.g., Ingram, 1986; Nasby & Kihlstrom, 1986))

SUMMARY AND CONCLUSIONS: MODELS OF COMPETENCE

As we have noted at the outset of this chapter, several quite different traditions in personality psychology provide precedents for characterizing purposive behavior (in principle if not always in fact) as creative, discriminative, and negotiable. Social learning and cognitive theorists have always emphasized the power bestowed by cognition and self-reflection as individuals work to overcome stimulus control of behavior. Kelly (1955) assumed constructive alternativism in the construal and anticipation of social life events; Rotter (1954) radically departed from his behavioral colleagues in emphasizing the pivotal role played in self-regulation by expectancies, values, and generalized cognitive dispositions about control. Somewhat more recently, their intellectual heirs, Walter Mischel and Albert Bandura, have continued this tradition with theories of self-control and purposive behavior that regard creative construal and discriminative responding as the basis for social competence (e.g., Bandura, 1986; Mischel, 1973). Similarly, though from a different tradition, motive theorists—from Murray to McClelland and Atkinson and their heirs—have hailed the creative, constructive powers of individuals to think beyond the present, to desire an alternative future, and to fulfill personal needs in diverse ways (e.g., Atkinson, 1981; McClelland, 1975; Murray, 1938). Further precedents for thinking about personality as discriminative and negotiable can be found in the lifespan theory of Erik Erikson and in the interpersonal psychology of Harry Stack Sullivan. Each theory stresses the formative role of family, culture, and social organizations in setting up the tasks to be solved by the developing individual, and in emphasizing the rituals of everyday life that demonstrate "correct solutions" within which the individual negotiates his or her path. Of course, there are many other roots to the current interest in the creativity, discriminativeness, and flexibility of purposive behavior, but these stand out as salient influences on the particular middle-level units of analysis we have emphasized in this discussion.

There is the suggestion in all of these perspectives that it is difficult to be a fully functioning, competent individual, constructing (and pursuing) personal goals in a complex social and cultural context. In fact, many of the most famous treatises in these traditions vividly recount the failures and rigidities of individuals, and their proclivity for self-defeating behavior. Nonetheless, the perspectives that we have summarized here seem also to turn attention to people's competence—in framing goals that take account of what is out there as well as what is personally desired, and in the creative efforts undertaken to try to make those goals happen. Many of these middle-level units of analysis underline the broad temporal perspective that individuals take in thinking about themselves and their lives: Although individuals strive for continuity in their life stories, there is recognition of "turning points" that also pay heed to the possibilities for change (McAdams, 1988); similarly, though people know a great deal about what they are currently like, and even form self-theories about how they got that way (Epstein, 1973), they also look to the future as holding possible selves that diverge from the past, thus expanding the self in creative directions (Markus & Nurius, 1986). Discrepancies between what we are and what we would like to be or feel we should be can be overwhelmingly discouraging, as Higgins (1987) has shown, though sometimes people manage to negotiate desired identities in the course of social interactions that do not fall so far short of their intentions (Schlenker & Weigold, 1989). There is always a tension between what the person wants and the interpersonal conditions that seem almost magically to elicit well-worn and discouraging scripts (Carlson, 1981; Thorne, 1989); yet recognition of those eliciting conditions, and of the need to negotiate personal projects in a social setting, can form the basis of social communication that is a critical ingredient of social competence (Little, 1989).

There are many ways to see and to acknowledge the agendas of the social and cultural environment within which we live, and several of the units of analysis reviewed here suggest a direct representation of those "demands" within the goals and self-reflection of the individual. Baldwin and Holmes (1987) import the private audience right into the center of self-regulatory processes, whereas Cantor and Kihlstrom (1987) present the life task as a goal unit that reflects not just what the individual wants to accomplish, but also the tasks to be done in that age group and social environment. Social competence involves both the creativity and resiliency to find environments within which to express one's personal strivings and persist in one's current concerns (Emmons, 1989a; Klinger, 1989), and also the willingness to negotiate those goals and plans to fit the possibilities afforded by the existing social environment (e.g., Cantor, Mischel, & Schwartz, 1982b; Frese & Sabini, 1985). "Constructive thinking" or "social intelligence" involves a delicate balance of optimism and creativity (to get what one wants done in the service of building a future that differs in good ways from the present and past), and of realism

and flexibility (to negotiate socially responsible and feasible ways to do both what one wants and what is needed in the current context) (Cantor & Kihlstrom, 1987; Epstein, 1989).

Thus, our intention here is to suggest that the currently popular units of analysis of personality and cognition provide the basis for intelligent self-regulation of the sort that is described by Vallacher and Wegner, and that is also deeply rooted in the constructive alternativism of Kelly and the other early cognitivists. At the least, they provide a basis for thinking of standards of social competence, such as creativity, discriminativeness, and flexibility in thought and in action, that (as Baron, 1989, suggests) individuals may adopt upon reflection. All of these units rely in some form or other on individuals' self-articulated beliefs about what they think they are doing and what they think they want to be doing, thus making use of the creative powers of human social intelligence to anticipate, to retrospect, to simulate—that is, to build a different reality in the mind. Moreover, current self-regulatory models suggest that such thinking does then inform behavior as individuals find ways to carry forth plans and to persevere in intensions (e. g., Kuhl & Beckmann, 1985). In other words, what we think we are doing does influence what we actually do, even when our thoughts have become routinized or "mindless" (Cantor, Mischel, & Schwartz, 1982a), when cognitive control is shaped substantially by affect and arousal (Isen, 1984), or when personal intentions get disrupted and become fodder for ruminations rather than actions (Kuhl, 1985).

In fact, there are several exciting lines of work on cognition and action control that build upon the frequent occurrence of automatic or scripted social problem-solving strategies, which are often driven by affective reactions. For example, Linville and Clark (1989) have demonstrated the applicability of production systems—proceduralized knowledge based on "if–then" rules for automatically executing mental or physical actions—to well-practiced social coping strategies (e.g., self-protective attributions; goal setting in important but taxing tasks; self-handicapping or defensive pessimism under self-image pressure conditions). They note that production systems provide a representational system for the cognitive contribution to coping that encompasses automatic processing for highly learned tasks, as well as principles of learning and change that allow large repertoires of domain-specific strategies (productions) to be constructed and reconstructed in the face of new social experience. Moreover, productions are self-regulatory units that initiate and engage a variety of thoughts, affects, and actions in the coping response. Though more work needs to be done to fill in the operating details of such a system, it seems promising to us as one way to represent openness and variety in the action identification process, and also to pay heed to the overlearning of coping strategies, which can become so problematic in social problem-solving arenas.

Similarly, Klinger's (1989) recent program of research on the impact of affect and arousal on the pursuit of current concerns represents yet another example of the integration within self-regulatory models of thought, emotion, and action. In his experimental and thought-sampling studies, Klinger finds that states of current concern (i.e., intentional states) get translated into thought and action that persist when the individual becomes affectively aroused and is then more likely to notice goal-relevant cues in the environment. Affect and arousal often mediate the impact of intentional states on cognition and action control. Therefore, cognitive models of purposive behavior, such as those presented here, can now make contact more directly with the growing literature in personality on affect-based dispositions (e.g., Buss & Plomin, 1984; Larsen & Diener, 1987), in much the same way that others have explored the relationship between traits and memory processing (e.g, Humphreys & Revelle, 1984), or between styles of information processing and health behavior (e.g., Miller, 1987).

These kinds of integrated models of personality, cognition, and purposive behavior represent an exciting future development in this line of pursuit. Nonetheless, they also raise the specter of further ways in which an individual can lose control of the intention–action cycle. That is, competent action control involves not just creativity, discriminativeness, and flexibility, but also the integration in a smooth-running system of affect, cognition, and action in the service of personal motivation. Indeed, this is not a simple task by any means, even with the optimistic mind-set that we, as researchers and as social actors, may characteristically bring to the endeavor.

ACKNOWLEDGMENTS

We are pleased to acknowledge the technical assistance of Nancy G. Exelby, and the comments on this line of work of Christopher A. Langston, Julie K. Norem, William Fleeson, Hazel Markus, and Larry Pervin. This research was supported in part by Grant No. BNS 87-18467 from the National Science Foundation to Nancy Cantor and Julie K. Norem.

REFERENCES

Adler, A. (1927). *The practice and theory of individual psychology.* New York: Harcourt, Brace.

Alloy, L. B., & Abramson, L. Y. (1979). Judgement of contingency in depressed and nondepressed college students: Sadder but wiser? *Journal of Experimental Psychology: General, 108,* 441–487.

Allport, F. (1937). Teleonomic description in the study of personality. *Character and Personality, 5,* 202–214.

Allport, G. W. (1937). *Personality: A psychological interpretation.* New York: Holt.

Allport, G. W. (1953). The trend in motivational theory. *American Journal of Orthopsychiatry, 23,* 107–119.

Atkinson, J. W. (1981). Studying personality in the context of an advanced motivational psychology. *American Psychologist, 32*(2), 117–129.

Bakan, D., (1966). *The duality of human existence.* Boston: Beacon Press.

Baldwin, M. W., & Holmes, J. G. (1987). Salient private audiences and awareness of the self. *Journal of Personality and Social Psychology, 52,* 1087–1098.

Bandura, A. (1977). Self-efficacy: Toward a unifying theory of behavioral change. *Psychological Review, 84,* 191–215.

Bandura, A. (1986). *Social foundations of thought and action: A social cognitive theory.* Englewood Cliffs, NJ: Prentice-Hall.

Bandura, A. (1989). Self-regulation of motivation and action through internal standards and goal systems. In L. A. Pervin (Ed.), *Goal concepts in personality and social psychology* (pp. 19–86). Hillsdale, NJ: Erlbaum.

Bargh, J. A. (1982). Attentional automaticity in the processing of self-relevant information. *Journal of Personality and Social Psychology, 43,* 425–436.

Baron, J. (1982). Personality and intelligence. In R. Sternberg (Ed.), *Handbook of human intelligence* (pp. 308–352). Cambridge, England: Cambridge University Press.

Baron, J. (1989). Why a theory of social intelligence needs a theory of character. In R. Wyer & T. Srull (Eds.), *Advances in social cognition* (Vol. 2, pp. 61–70). Hillsdale, NJ: Erlbaum.

Baumeister, R. F. (1982). The self and mechanisms of agency. In J. Suls (Ed.), *Psychological perspectives on the self* (Vol. 1, pp. 3–39). Hillsdale, NJ: Erlbaum.

Baumeister, R. F. (1989). The problem of life's meaning. In D. M. Buss & N. Cantor (Eds.), *Personality psychology: Recent trends and emerging directions* (pp. 138–148). New York: Springer-Verlag.

Baumeister, R. F., & Scher, S. J. (1988). Self-defeating behavior patterns among normal individuals: Review and analysis of common self-destructive tendencies. *Psychological Bulletin, 104,* 3–22.

Beck, A. T. (1967). *Depression: Causes and treatment.* Philadelphia: University of Pennsylvania Press.

Bruner, J. (1986). *Actual minds, possible worlds.* Cambridge, MA: Harvard University Press.

Buss, A. H., & Plomin, R. (1984). *Temperament: Early developing personality traits.* Hillsdale, NJ: Erlbaum.

Buss, D. M. (1987). Selection, evocation, and manipulation. *Journal of Personality and Social Psychology, 53*(6), 1214–1221.

Buss, D. M., & Cantor, N. (Eds.). (1989). *Personality psychology: Recent trends and emerging directions.* New York: Springer-Verlag.

Cantor, N. (in press). *American Psychologist.*

Cantor, N., & Fleeson, W. (1990). Life tasks and self-regulatory processes. In M. Maehr & P. Pintrich (Eds.), *Advances in motivation and achievement* (Vol. 7). Greenwich, CT: JAI Press.

Cantor, N., & Kihlstrom, J. F. (1985). Social intelligence: The cognitive basis of personality. In P. Shaver (Ed.), *Review of personality and social psychology* (Vol. 6, pp. 15–33). Beverly Hills, CA: Sage.

Cantor, N., & Kihlstrom, J. F. (1987). *Personality and social intelligence.* Englewood Cliffs, NJ: Prentice-Hall.

Cantor, N., & Kihlstrom, J. F. (1989). Social intelligence and cognitive assessments of personality. In R. S. Wyer & T. K. Srull (Eds.), *Advances in social cognition* (Vol. 2, pp. 1–59). Hillsdale, NJ: Erlbaum.

Cantor, N., & Langston, C. A. (1989). Ups and downs of life tasks in a life transition. In L. A. Pervin (Ed.), *Goal concepts in personality and social psychology* (pp. 127–167). Hillsdale, NJ: Erlbaum.

Cantor, N., Mischel, W., & Schwartz, J. (1982a). Social knowledge: Structure, content, use and abuse. In A. Hastorf & A. Isen (Eds.), *Cognitive social psychology* (pp. 33–72). New York: Elsevier/North-Holland.

Cantor, N., Mischel, W., & Schwartz, J. (1982b). A prototype analysis of psychological situations. *Cognitive Psychology, 14,* 45–77.

Cantor, N., & Norem, J. K. (1989). Defensive pessimism and stress and coping. *Social Cognition, 7,* 92–112.

Cantor, N., Norem, J. K., Niedenthal, P. M., Langston, C. A., & Brower, A. M. (1987). Life tasks, self-concept ideals, and cognitive strategies in a life transition. *Journal of Personality and Social Psychology, 53*(6), 1178–1191.

Carlson, R. (1981). Studies in script theory: Adult analogs of a childhood nuclear scene. *Journal of Personality and Social Psychology, 40*(3), 501–510.

Carver, C. S. (1979). A cybernetic model of self-attention processes. *Journal of Personality and Social Psychology, 37,* 1251–1281.

Carver, C. S., & Scheier, M. F. (1981). *Attention and self-regulation: A control-theory approach to human behavior.* New York: Springer-Verlag.

Carver, C. S., & Scheier, M. F. (1989). Social intelligence and personality: Some unanswered questions and unresolved issues. In R. S. Wyer & T. K. Srull (Eds.), *Advances in social cognition* (Vol. 2, pp. 93–109). Hillsdale, NJ: Erlbaum.

Caspi, A. (1987). Personality and the life course. *Journal of Personality and Social Psychology, 53,* 1203–1213.

Caspi, A. (1989). On the continuities and consequences of personality: A life-course perspective. In D. M. Buss & N. Cantor (Eds.), *Personality psychology: Recent*

trends and emerging directions (pp. 85–98). New York: Springer-Verlag.

Cheek, J. M. (1989). Identity orientations and self-interpretation. In D. M. Buss & N. Cantor (Eds.), *Personality psychology: Recent trends and emerging directions* (pp.275–285). New York: Springer-Verlag.

Cohler, B. (1982). Personal narrative and life course. In P. Baltes & O. Brim, Jr. (Eds.), *Life-span development and behavior* (Vol. 4, pp. 205–241). New York: Academic Press.

Cross, S., & Markus, H. (in press 1990). Possible selves across the life span. *Human Development.*

Dweck, C. S. (1986). Motivational processes affecting learning. *American Psychologist, 41*(10), 1040–1048.

Dweck, C. S., & Leggett, E. L. (1988). A social-cognitive approach to motivation and personality. *Psychological Review, 95*(2), 256–373.

Eagle, M. N. (1984). *Recent developments in psychoanalysis: A critical evaluation.* New York: McGraw-Hill.

Eagly, A. (1987). *Sex differences in social behavior: A social role interpretation.* Hillsdale, NJ: Erlbaum.

Elder, G. H., Jr. (1975). Age differentiation and the life course. *Annual Review of Sociology, 1,* 165–190.

Elder, G. H., Jr. (1985). Perspectives on the life course. In G. H. Elder, Jr. (Ed.), *Life course dynamics: Trajectories and transitions, 1968–1980* (pp. 23–49). Ithaca, NY: Cornell University Press.

Elliott, E. S., & Dweck, C. S. (1988). Goals: An approach to motivation and achievement. *Journal of Personality and Social Psychology, 54*(1), 5–12.

Emmons, R. A. (1986). Personal strivings: An approach to personality and subjective well-being. *Journal of Personality and Social Psychology, 51*(5), 1058–1068.

Emmons, R. A. (1989a). The personal striving approach to personality. In L. A. Pervin (Ed.), *Goal concepts in personality and social psychology* (pp. 87–126). Hillsdale, NJ: Erlbaum.

Emmons, R. A. (1989b). Exploring the relations between motives and traits: The case of narcissism. In D. M. Buss & N. Cantor (Eds.), *Personality psychology: Recent trends and emerging directions* (pp. 32–44). New York: Springer-Verlag.

Emmons, R. A., Diener, E., & Larsen, R. J. (1986). Choice and avoidance of everyday situations and affect congruence: Two models of reciprocal interactionism. *Journal of Personality and Social Psychology, 51,* 815–826.

Emmons, R. A., & King, L. A. (1988). Conflict among personal strivings: Immediate and long-term implications for psychological and physical well-being. *Journal of Personality and Social Psychology. 54,* 1040–1048.

Emmons, R. A., & King, L. A. (1989). Personal striving differentiation and affective reactivity. *Journal of Personality and Social Psychology, 56*(3), 478–484.

Epstein, S. (1973). The self-concept revisited, or a theory of a theory. *American Psychologist, 28,* 404–416.

Epstein, S. (1989). *Constructive thinking: The intelligence of the experiential conceptual system.* Unpublished manuscript, University of Massachusetts–Amherst.

Erikson, E. H. (1950). *Childhood and society.* New York: Norton.

Fiske, V., & Peterson, C. (1990). *Love and depression: The nature of depressive romantic relationships.* Unpublished manuscript, University of Michigan.

Frese, M., and Sabini, J. (1985). *Goal directed behavior: The concept of action in psychology.* Hillsdale, NJ: Erlbaum.

Freud, S. (1976). *Therapy and technique.* New York: Macmillan. (Original work published 1912)

Funder, D. C. (1989). Accuracy in personality judgment and the dancing bear. In D. M. Buss & N. Cantor (Eds.), *Personality psychology: Recent trends and emerging directions* (pp. 210–223). New York: Springer-Verlag.

Gergen, K. J., & Gergen, M. (1988). Narrative and the self as relationship. In L. Berkowitz (Ed.), *Advances in experimental social psychology* (Vol. 21, pp. 17–56). New York: Academic Press.

Goffman, E. (1959). *The presentation of self in everyday life.* New York: Doubleday.

Gollwitzer, P. M., & Kinney, R. F. (1989). Effects of deliberative and implemental mindsets on illusion of control. *Journal of Personality and Social Psychology. 56* (4), 531–542.

Gollwitzer, P. M., & Wicklund, R. A. (1985). The pursuit of self-defining goals. In J. Kuhl & J. Beckmann (Eds.), *Action control: From cognition to behavior* (pp. 61–85). New York: Springer-Verlag.

Greenberg, J. R., & Mitchell, S. A. (1983). *Object relations in psychoanalytic theory.* Cambridge, MA: Harvard University Press.

Greenberg, J. R., Pyszczynski, T., & Solomon, S. (1986). The courses and consequences of a need for self-esteem: A terror management theory. In R. F. Baumeister (Ed.), *Public self and private self* (pp. 182–212). New York: Springer-Verlag.

Hampson, S. E. (1982). *The construction of personality: An introduction.* London: Routledge & Kegan Paul.

Hampson, S. E. (1989). Using traits to construct personality. In D. M. Buss & N. Cantor (Eds.), *Personality psychology: Recent trends and emerging directions* (pp. 286–293). New York: Springer-Verlag.

Harackiewicz, J. M. (1989). Performance evaluation and intrinsic motivation processes: The effects of achievement orientation and rewards. In D. M. Buss & N. Cantor (Eds.), *Personality psychology: Recent trends and emerging directions* (pp.. 128–137). New York: Springer-Verlag.

Harter, S. (1983). Developmental perspectives on the self-system. In E. M. Hetherington (Ed.), *Handbook of child psychology* (4th ed.): *Socialization, personality, and social development* (pp. 275–385) New York: Wiley.

Harvey, J., Agostineli, G., & Weber, A. (1989). Account-making and the formation of expectations about close relationships. In C. Hendrich (Ed.), *Review of personality and social psychology* (Vol. 10, pp. 39–62). Newbury Park, CA: Sage.

Havighurst, R. J. (1953). *Human development and education.* New York: Longmans, Green.

Healy, J. M., Jr. (1989). Emotional adaptation to life transitions: Early impact on integrative cognitive processes. In D. M. Buss & N. Cantor (Eds.), *Personality psychology: Recent trends and emerging directions* (pp. 115–127). New York: Springer-Verlag.

Herrmann, C., & Wortman, C. B. (1985). Action control and the coping process. In J. Kuhl & J. Beckmann (Eds.), *Action control: From cognition to behavior* (pp. 151–182). New York: Springer-Verlag.

Higgins, E. T. (1987). Self-discrepancy: A theory relating self and affect. *Psychological Review, 94,* 319–340.

Higgins, G., King, G., & Mavin, G. (1982). Individual construct accessibility and subjective impressions and recall. *Journal of Personality and Social Psychology, 43*(1), 35–47.

Higgins, E. T., & Parsons, J. E. (1983). Social cognition and the social life of the child: Stages as subcultures. In E. T. Higgins, D. N. Ruble, & W. W. Hartup (Eds.), *Social cognition and social development: A sociocultural perspective* (pp. 15–62). New York: Cambridge University Press.

Higgins, E. T., Tykocinski, O., & Vookles, J. (in press). Patterns of self-beliefs: The psychological significance of relations among the actual, ideal, ought, can, and future selves. In J. M. Olson & M. P. Zanna (Eds.), *The Ontario Symposium: Vol. 6. Self-inference processes.* Hillsdale, NJ: Erlbaum.

House, J. S. (1981). Social structure and personality. In M. Rosenberg & R. H. Turner (Eds.), *Social psychology: Sociological perspectives* (pp. 525–561). New York: Basic Books.

Humphreys, M. S., & Revelle, W. (1984). Personality, motivation, and performance: A theory of the relationship between individual differences and information processing. *Psychological Review, 91,* 153–184.

Ingram, R. E. (Ed.). (1986). *Information-processing approaches to clinical psychology.* New York: Academic Press.

Isen, A. (1984). Toward understanding the role of affect in cognition. In R. S. Wyer & T. K. Srull (Eds.), *Handbook of social cognition* (Vol. 3). Hillsdale, NJ: Erlbaum.

Janoff-Bulman, R. (1989). Assumptive worlds and the stress of traumatic events: Applications of the schema construct. *Social Cognition, 7,* 113–136.

Josephs, R. A., Steele, C. M., Larrick, R. P., & Nisbett, R. E. (1990). *The functioning of self-esteem in decision-making under risk.* Unpublished manuscript, University of Michigan.

Kahneman, D., & Miller, D. T. (1986). Norm theory: Comparing reality to its alternatives. *Psychological Review, 93,* 136–153.

Kelley, H. H. (1979). *Personal relationships: Their structures and processes.* Hillsdale, NJ: Erlbaum.

Kelly, G. A. (1955). *A theory of personality: The psychology of personal constructs.* New York: Norton.

Kihlstrom, J. F., & Cantor, N. (1984). Mental representations of the self. In L. Berkowitz (Ed.), *Advances in experimental social psychology* (Vol. 17, pp. 1–47). New York: Academic Press.

Kitayama, S., Markus, H., Tummula, P., Kurokawa, M., & Kato, K. *Culture and Self-cognition.* Unpublished manuscript, University of Oregon.

Klinger, E. (1975). Consequences of commitment to and disengagement from incentives. *Psychological Review, 82*(1), 1–25.

Klinger, E. (1977). *Meaning and void: Inner experience and the incentives in people's lives.* Minneapolis: University of Minnesota Press.

Klinger, E. (1987). Current concerns and disengagement from incentives. In F. Halisch & J. Kuhl (Eds.), *Motivation, intention and volition* (pp. 337–347). New York: Springer-Verlag.

Klinger, E. (1989). Goal-orientation as psychological linchpin: A commentary on Cantor and Kihlstrom's "Social intelligence and cognitive assessments of personality." In R. S. Wyer & T. K. Srull (Eds.), *Advances in social cognition* (Vol. 2, pp. 123–130). Hillsdale, NJ: Erlbaum.

Klinger, E., Barta, S. G., & Maxeiner, M. E. (1980). Motivational correlates of thought content frequency and commitment. *Journal of Personality and Social Psychology, 39*(6), 1222–1237.

Kruglanski, A. W. (1989). The psychology of being "right": On the problem of accuracy in social perception and cognition. *Psychological Bulletin, 106*(3), 395–409.

Kuhl, J. (1985). From cognition to behavior: Perspectives for future research on action control. In J. Kuhl & J. Beckmann (Eds.), *Action control: From cognition to behavior* (pp. 267–275). New York: Springer-Verlag.

Kuhl, J., & Beckmann, J. (Eds.). (1985). *Action control: From cognition to behavior.* New York: Springer-Verlag.

Lakoff, G., & Johnson, M. (1980). *Metaphors we live by.* Chicago: Chicago Press.

Langer, E. J. (1975). The illusion of control. *Journal of Personality and Social Psychology, 32*, 311–328.

Langer, E. J. (1989). *Mindlessness/mindfulness.* Reading, MA: Addison-Wesley.

Langston, C., & Cantor, N. (1989). Social anxiety and social constraint: When "making friends" is hard. *Journal of Personality and Social Psychology, 56*(4), 649–661.

Larsen, R. J. (1989). A process approach to personality psychology: Utilizing time as a facet of data. In D. M. Buss & N. Cantor (Eds.), *Personality psychology: Recent trends and emerging directions* (pp. 177–193). New York: Springer-Verlag.

Larsen, R., & Diener, E. (1987). Affect intensity as an individual difference characteristic. *Journal of Research in Personality, 21*, 1–39.

Lazarus, R. S. (1983). The costs and benefits of denial. In S. Breznitz (Ed.), *Denial of stress* (pp. 1–31). New York: International Universities Press.

Lazarus, R. S., & Folkman, S. (1984). *Stress, appraisal, and coping.* New York: Springer Publishing Company.

Levinson, D. (1978). *Seasons of a man's life.* New York: Knopf.

Levinson, D. (1986). A conception of adult development. *American Psychologist, 41*, 3–13.

Lewicki, P. (1986). *Nonconscious social information processing.* New York: Academic Press.

Linville, P. W. (1982). Affective consequences of complexity regarding the self and others. In M. Clark & S. Fiske (Eds.), *Affect and cognition: The 17th annual Carnegie Symposium on Cognition* (pp. 79–109). Hillsdale, NJ: Erlbaum.

Linville, P. W. (1987). Self-complexity as a cognitive buffer against stress-related illness and depression. *Journal of Personality and Social Psychology, 52*, 663–676.

Linville, P. W., & Clark, L. F. (1989). Production systems and social problem solving: Specificity, flexibility, and expertise. In R. S. Wyer & T. K. Srull (Eds.), *Advances in social cognition* (Vol. 2, pp. 131–152). Hillsdale, NJ: Erlbaum.

Little, B. (1983). Personal projects: A rationale and methods for investigation. *Environment and Behavior, 15*, 273–309.

Little, B. R. (1989). Personal projects analysis: Trivial pursuits, magnificient obsessions, and the search for coherence. In D. M. Buss & N. Cantor (Eds.), *Personality psychology: Recent trends and emerging directions* (pp. 15–31). New York: Springer-Verlag.

Markus, H. (1977). Self-schemata and processing information about the self. *Journal of Personality and Social Psychology, 35*, 63–78.

Markus, H., & Nurius, P. (1986). Possible selves. *American Psychologist, 41*(9), 954–969.

Markus, H., & Oyserman, D. (1989). Gender and thought: The role of the self-concept. In M. Crawford & M. Hamilton (Eds.), *Gender and thought* (pp. 100–127). New York: Springer-Verlag.

Markus, H., & Ruvolo, A. (1989). Possible selves: Personalized representations of goals. In L. A. Pervin (Ed.), *Goal concepts in personality and social psychology* (pp. 211–242). Hillsdale, NJ: Erlbaum.

Markus, H., & Wurf, E. (1987). The dynamic self-concept: A social psychological perspective. *Annual Review of Psychology, 38*, 299–337.

McAdams, D. P. (1980). A thematic coding system for the intimacy motive. *Journal of Research in Personality, 14*, 413–432.

McAdams, D P. (1985). *Power, intimacy, and the life story: Personological inquiries into identity.* New York: Guilford Press.

McAdams, D. P. (1988). Unity and purpose in human lives: The emergence of identity as a life story. In A. I. Rabin (Ed.), *Studying persons and lives.* New York: Springer Publishing Company.

McAdams, D. P. (1989). The development of a narrative identity. In D. M. Buss & N. Cantor (Eds.), *Personality psychology: Recent trends and emerging directions* (pp. 160–174). New York: Springer-Verlag.

McClelland, D. C. (1975). *Power: The inner experience.* New York: Irvington.

Mead, G. H. (1934). *Mind, self, and society.* Chicago: University of Chicago Press.

Meichebaum, D. (1977). *Cognitive behavior modification: An integrated approach.* New York: Plenum Press.

Miller, G. A., & Cantor, N. (1982) [Review of R. Nisbett & L. Ross, *Human inference: Strategies and shortcomings of social judgment*]. *Social Cognition, 1*(1), 83–93.

Miller, G. A., Galanter, E., & Pribram, K. H. (1960). *Plans and the structure of behavior.* New York: Holt, Rinehart, & Winston.

Miller, S. M. (1987). Monitoring and blunting: Validation of a questionnaire to assess styles of information seeking under threat. *Journal of Personality and Social Psychology, 52*(2), 345–353.

Mischel, W. (1973). Toward a cognitive social learning reconceptualization of personality. *Psychological Review, 80*, 252–283.

Mischel, W. (1981). Metacognition and the rules of delay. In J. Flavell & L. D. Ross (Eds.), *Social cognitive development: Frontiers and possible futures* (pp. 240–271). New York: Cambridge University Press.

Mischel W., Shoda, Y., & Rodriguez, M. I. (1989). Delay of gratification in children. *Science, 244*, 933–938.

Murray, H. A. (1938). *Exploration in personality.* New York: Oxford University Press.

Nasby, W., & Kihlstrom, J. F. (1986). Cognitive assessment of personality and psychopathology. In R. E. Ingram (Ed.), *Information-processing approaches to clinical psychology* (pp. 217–239) New York: Academic Press.

Newell, A., & Simon, H. A. (1972). *Human problem solving.* Englewood Cliffs, NJ: Prentice-Hall.

Nicholls, J. (1984). Achievement motivation: Conceptions of ability, subjective experiences, task choice, and performance. *Psychological Review, 92*(3), 328–346.

Niedenthal, P., Cantor, N., & Kihlstrom, J. (1985). Prototype-matching: A strategy for social decision-making. *Journal of Personality and Social Psychology, 48*(3), 575–584.

Norem, J. K. (1987). *Strategic realities: Optimism and defensive pessimism.* Unpublished doctoral dissertation, University of Michigan.

Norem, J. K. (1989). Cognitive strategies as personality: Effectiveness, specificity, flexibility, and change. In D. M. Buss & N. Cantor (Eds.), *Personality psychology: Recent trends and emerging directions* (pp. 45–60). New York: Springer-Verlag.

Norem, J. K., & Cantor, N. (1986a). Anticipatory and post hoc cushioning strategies: Optimism and defensive pessimism in "risky" situations. *Cognitive Therapy and Research, 10*(3), 347–362.

Norem, J. K., & Cantor, N. (1986b). Defensive pessimism: "Harnessing" anxiety as motivation. *Journal of Personality and Social Psychology, 51*(6), 1208–1217.

Norem, J. K., & Cantor, N. (in press). Cognitive strategies, coping and perceptions of competence. In R. J. Sternberg & J. Kolligian, Jr. (Eds.) *Perceptions of competence and incompetence across the lifespan.* New Haven, CT: Yale University Press.

Nuttin, J., & Lens, W. (1986). *Future time perspective and motivation.* Hillsdale, NJ: Erlbaum.

Oyserman, D., & Markus, H. (1988). *Possible selves and delinquency.* Unpublished manuscript, University of Michigan.

Palys, T. S., & Little, B. R. (1983). Perceived life satisfaction and the organization of personal project systems. *Journal of Personality and Social Psychology, 44,* 1221–1230.

Paulhus, D. L., & Martin, C. L. (1987). The structure of personality capabilities. *Journal of Personality and Social Psychology, 52*(2), 354–365.

Pervin, L. A. (1983). The stasis and flow of behavior: Toward a theory of goals. In M. M. Page (Ed.), *Nebraska Symposium on Motivation* (pp. 1–53). Lincoln: University of Nebraska Press.

Pervin, L. A. (Ed.). (1989a). *Goal concepts in personality and social psychology.* Hillsdale, NJ: Erlbaum.

Pervin, L. A. (1989b). Psychodynamic-systems reflections on a social intelligence model of personality. In R. S. Wyer & T. K. Srull (Eds.), *Advances in social cognition* (Vol. 2, pp. 153–161). Hillsdale, NJ: Erlbaum.

Peterson, C., & Seligman, M. (1987). Explanatory style and illness. *Journal of Personality, 55*(2), 237–265.

Porter, C., Markus, H., & Nurius, P. S. (1984). *Conceptions of possibility among people in crisis.* Unpublished manuscript, University of Michigan.

Pyszczynski, T., & Greenberg, J. (1987). Self-regulatory perseveration and the depressive self-focusing style: A self-awareness theory of reactive depression. *Psychological Bulletin, 102*(1), 122–138.

Read, S. J., & Miller, L. C. (1989). Interpersonalism: Toward a goal-based theory of persons and relationships. In L. Pervin (Ed.), *Goal concepts in personality and social psychology* (pp. 413–472). Hillsdale, NJ: Erlbaum.

Rogers, C. R. (1951). *Client-centered therapy.* Boston: Houghton Mifflin.

Rosenberg, S., & Gara, M. A. (1985). The multiplicity of personal identity. In P. Shaver (Ed.), *Review of personality and social psychology* (Vol. 6, pp. 87–114). Beverly Hills, CA: Sage.

Rotter, J. B. (1954). *Social learning and clinical psychology.* Englewood Cliffs, NJ: Prentice-Hall.

Rotter, J. B. (1966). Generalized expectancies for internal versus external control of reinforcement. *Psychological Monographs, 81* (1, Whole No. 609).

Rotter, J. B. (1975). Some problems and misconceptions related to the construct of internal versus external reinforcement. *Journal of Consulting and Clinical Psychology, 43,* 56–67.

Sampson, E. E. (1978). Personality and the location of identity. *Journal of Personality, 46,* 552–568.

Schank, R. C., & Abelson, R. P. (1977). *Scripts, plans, goals, and understanding: An inquiry into human knowledge structures.* Hillsdale, NJ: Erlbaum.

Scheier, M. F., & Carver, C. S. (1980). Private and public self-attention, resistance to change, and dissonance reduction. *Journal of Personality and Social Psychology, 39,* 390–405.

Scheier, M. F., & Carver, C. S. (1985). Optimism, coping, and health: Assessment and implications of generalized outcome expectancies. *Health Psychology, 4,* 219–247.

Schlenker, B. R. (1980). *Impression management: The self concept, social identity, and interpersonal relations.* Monterey, CA: Brooks/Cole.

Schlenker, B. R., & Weigold, M. F. (1989). Goals and the self-identification process: Constructing desired identities. In L. A. Pervin (Ed.), *Goal concepts in personality and social psychology* (pp. 243–290). Hillsdale, NJ: Erlbaum.

Shaver, P., & Rubenstein, C. (1980). Childhood attachment experience and adult loneliness. In L. Wheeler (Ed.), *Review of personality and social psychology* (Vol. 1, pp. 42–73). Beverly Hills, CA: Sage.

Showers, C. (1988). The effects of how and why thinking on perceptions of future negative events. *Cognitive Therapy and Research, 12,* 225–240.

Showers, C. (1989a). *Low level thinking as an anxiety-management strategy: Do socially anxious persons use an optimal approach?* Unpublished manuscript, Barnard College.

Showers, C. (1989b). *The organization of positive and negative components of the self.* Unpublished manuscript, Barnard College. New York.

Showers, C., & Cantor, N. (1985). Social cognition: A look at motivated strategies. *Annual Review of Psychology, 36,* 275–305.

Showers, C., & Ruben, C. (1989). *Distinguishing defensive pessimism from depression: Negative expectations and positive coping mechanisms.* Unpublished manuscript, Barnard College.

Shweder, R. (in press). Cultural psychology: What is it? In J. Stigler, R. Shweder, & G. Herdt (Eds.), *Cultural psychology: The Chicago Symposia on culture and human development.*

Singer, J. L., & Kolligian, J., Jr. (1987). Personality: Developments in the study of private experience. *Annual Review of Psychology, 38,* 533–574.

Smith, T. W., & Rhodewalt, F. (1986). On states, traits, and processes: A transactional alternative to the individual difference assumptions in Type A behavior and physiological reactivity. *Journal of Research in Personality, 20*(3), 229–251.

Snyder, M. (1979). Self-monitoring processes. In L. Berkowitz (Ed.), *Advances in experimental social psychology* (Vol. 12, pp. 85–128). New York: Academic Press.

Snyder, M. (1981). On the influence of individuals on situations. In N. Cantor & J. Kihlstrom (Eds.), *Personality, cognition, and social interaction* (pp. 309–329). Hillsdale, NJ: Erlbaum.

Snyder, M., & Swann, W. B. (1978). Behavioral confirmation in social interaction: From social perception to social reality. *Journal of Personality, 50,* 149–157.

Sroufe, L. A. (1979). The coherence of individual development. *American Psychologist, 34,* 834–841.

Sroufe, L. A. (in press). Pathways to adaptation and maladaptation: Psychopathology as developmental deviation. In D. Cicchetti (Ed.), *First Rochester Symposium on Developmental Psychopathology.* Hillsdale, NJ: Erlbaum.

Steele, C. (1988). The psychology of self-affirmation: Sustaining the integrity of the self. In L. Berkowitz (Ed.), *Advances in experimental social psychology* (Vol. 21, pp. 261–302). New York: Academic Press.

Stewart, A. J. (1982). The course of individual adaptation to life changes. *Journal of Personality and Social Psychology, 42,* 1100–1113.

Stewart, A. J. (1989). Social intelligence and adaptation to life changes. In R. S. Wyer & T. K. Srull (Eds.), *Advances in social cognition* (Vol. 2, pp. 187–196). Hillsdale, NJ: Erlbaum.

Stewart, A. J. & Healy, J. (1985). Personality and adaptation to change. In R. Hogan & W. Jones (Eds.), *Perspectives on personality: Theory, measurement, and interpersonal dynamics* (pp. 117–144). Greenwich, CT: JAI Press.

Stewart, A. J., & Healy, J. (1989). Linking individual development and social change. *American Psychologist, 44,* 30–42.

Strauman, T. J., & Higgins, E. T. (1987). Automatic activation of self-discrepancies and emotional syndromes: When cognitive structures influence affect. *Journal of Personality and Social Psychology, 53,* 1004–1014.

Sullivan, H. S. (1953). *The interpersonal theory of psychiatry.* New York: Norton.

Sullivan, H. S. (1964). *The fusion of psychiatry and social science.* New York: Norton.

Swann, W. B., Jr. (1984). Quest for accuracy in person perception: A matter of pragmatics. *Psychological Review, 91,* 457–477.

Swann, W. B., Jr. (1985). The self as architect of social reality. In B. R. Schlenker (Ed.), *The self and social life* (pp. 100–126). New York: McGraw-Hill.

Swann, W. B., Jr., & Hill, C. A. (1982). When our identities are mistaken: Reaffirming self-conceptions through social interaction. *Journal of Personality and Social Psychology, 43,* 59–66.

Taylor, S. E., & Brown, J. (1988). Illusion and well being: Some social psychological contributions to a theory of mental health. *Psychological Bulletin, 103*(3), 193–210.

Taylor, S. E., & Schneider, S. K. (1989). Coping and the simulation of events. *Social Cognition, 7,* 174–194.

Thorne, A. (1987). The press of personality: A study of conversations between introverts and extraverts.

Journal of Personality and Social Psychology, 53, 718–726.

Thorne, A. (1989). Conditional patterns, transference, and the coherence of personality across time. In D. M. Buss & N. Cantor (Eds.), *Personality psychology: Recent trends and emerging directions* (pp. 149–159). New York: Springer-Verlag.

Tomkins, S. S. (1979). Script theory: Different magnification of affects. In H. E. Howe, Jr., & R. A. Dienstbier (Eds.), *Nebraska Symposium on Motivation* (Vol. 26). Lincoln: University of Nebraska Press.

Trope, Y. (1986). Self-enhancement and self-assessment in achievement behavior. In Sorrentino & E. Higgins (Eds.), *Handbook of motivation and cognition: Foundations of social behavior* (pp. 350–378). New York: Guilford Press.

Vallacher, R. R., & Wegner, D. M. (1987). What do people think they're doing? Action identification and human behavior. *Psychological Review, 94,* 3–15.

Veroff, J. (1982). Assertive motivations: Achievement versus power. In A. J. Stewart (Ed.), *Motivation and society* (pp. 99–132). San Francisco: Jossey-Bass.

Veroff, J. (1983). Contextual determinants of personality. *Personality and Social Psychology Bulletin, 9,* 331–344.

Wegner, D. M., Guiliano, T., & Hertel, P. T. (1985). Cognitive interdependence in close relationships. In W. Ickes (Ed.), *Compatible and incompatible relationships* (pp. 253–276). New York: Springer-Verlag.

Wilson, T. (1985). Strangers to ourselves: The origins and accuracy of beliefs about one's own mental states. In J. H. Harvey & G. Weary (Eds.), *Attribution in contemporary psychology* (pp. 9–23). New York: Academic Press.

Winter, D. G. (1973). *The power motive.* New York: Free Press.

Witkin, H., Dyk, R. B., Faterson, H. F., Goodenough, D. R., & Karp, S. A. (1962). *Psychological differentiation.* Potomac, MD: Erlbaum.

Wright, J. C. (1989). An alternative paradigm for studying the accuracy of person perception: Simulated personalities. In D. M. Buss & N. Cantor (Eds.), *Personality psychology; Recent trends and emerging directions* (pp. 61–81). New York: Springer-Verlag.

Wright, J. C., & Mischel, W. (1987). A conditional approach to dispositional constructs: The local predictability of social behavior. *Journal of Personality and Social Psychology, 53*(6), 1159–1177.

Wurf, E. (1988). *Negativity in the self-concept: Self-construal and feedback-seeking.* Unpublished doctoral dissertation, University of Michigan.

Zirkel, S., & Cantor, N. 1990. Personal construal of life tasks: Those who struggle for independence. *Journal of Personality and Social Psychology, 58* (1), 172–185.

Chapter 7

Cognitive–Experiential Self-Theory

Seymour Epstein
University of Massachusetts—Amherst

This chapter presents a summary of cognitive–experiential self-theory (CEST), including new developments and a review of the research stimulated by the theory. Several studies on a new construct, "constructive thinking," are described for the first time. Since its introduction (Epstein, 1973), CEST has undergone considerable development and has generated a considerable body of research, much of it recent and not yet published. It is beyond the scope of this chapter to review the theory and research in detail. The interested reader can find additional information in a number of publications, most of which provide an overview of the theory plus a detailed elaboration of selected aspects (Epstein, 1973, 1976, 1980, 1981, 1983, 1985, 1987, 1990 a, b; Epstein & Erskine, 1983; Epstein & Meier, 1989).

THE BASIC THEORY

The Nature of Personal Theories of Reality

According to CEST, everyone develops an implicit theory of reality that contains subdivisions of a self-theory, a world theory, and propositions connecting the two. A personal theory of reality is a hierarchically organized set of schemas and networks of schemas. The most basic schemas in a personal theory of reality are referred to as "postulates." Among the most important postulates are four derived from the basic functions of a personal theory of reality, which are discussed later. The four basic postulates include the degree to which the world is regarded as benign versus malevolent; the degree to which it is regarded as meaningful (including predictable, controllable, and just); the degree to which others are regarded favorably rather than as a source of threat; and the degree to which the self is regarded as worthy. Because the basic postulates represent the highest constructs in the hierarchy of a personal theory of reality, to invalidate any one of them would have a profoundly destabilizing effect on the entire personality structure. As one descends the hierarchy, schemas become narrower in scope and more closely related to direct experience. The very lowest-order schemas are situation-specific cognitions, which are not very informative about a person's personality in the absence of knowledge about their connections to higher-order constructs. Relatedly, lower-order constructs can readily change without affecting the higher-order structure. Thus, the upper structure is able to maintain a considerable degree of stability while allowing for a high degree of flexibility at the lower levels.

Basic beliefs are of two kinds: "descriptive" and "motivational" beliefs or schemas. Descriptive schemas are beliefs about what the self and the world are like, as in the four basic postulates described above. Motivational schemas are beliefs about what one has to do to obtain what one desires and avoid what one dislikes. Motivational beliefs, like other schemas in the experiential system, are derived primarily from emotionally significant experiences, and are thus emotionally charged (i.e., they are "hot," not "cold," cognitions about how to act in the world). Consider the case of a child with a rejecting mother. Such a child may develop the descriptive beliefs that the world is malevolent and untrustworthy, and the motivational beliefs that the only way to get by is to take what one wants and avoid attachments. (Unless stated otherwise, it should be understood that I am referring to beliefs in the experiential system, which may be quite different from a person's conscious beliefs.) Motivational schemas, like descriptive schemas, exist at various levels of generality and complexity, and subsume constructs such as values, goals, and plans.

Personal theories of reality, in common with scientific theories, serve the purposes of organizing the data of experience and directing behavior. In the case of scientific theories, the data that are organized constitute the subject matter of the science, and the behavior that is directed is the scientist's pursuit of understanding. In the case of personal theories of reality, the data that are organized are the experiences of everyday living, and the behavior that is directed is how the individual goes about living his or her daily life. Whereas the scientist is motivated only to understand the phenomena he or she wishes to study, the person in everyday life is motivated to live his or her life in an emotionally satisfying way.

The Four Basic Functions of a Personal Theory of Reality

Personal theories of reality have four basic functions: to assimilate the data of reality (which subsumes the need to maintain the conceptual system that does the assimilating); to maintain a favorable pleasure–pain balance; to maintain relatedness to others; and to maintain a favorable level of self-esteem. It is noteworthy that different personality theories emphasize one or another of these functions, but none, with the exception of CEST, attributes a central role to all. According to learning theory and psychoanalysis, the most important motive in human behavior is seeking pleasure and avoiding pain. This is referred to as the "pleasure principle" in psychoanalysis and is regarded as the source of reinforcement, and therefore of learning, in learning theory. The assimilation of the data of reality, and, relatedly, the maintenance of the stability of the conceptual system, are emphasized in phenomenological self-theories (e.g., Lecky, 1945/1969; Rogers, 1951; Snygg & Combs, 1949) and in Kelly's (1955) theory of constructive alternativism. The importance of maintaining relationships with others is emphasized in Bowlby's (1973) theory and in object relations theory (Cashdan, 1988). The need to enhance self-esteem is regarded as a primary motive by Allport (1927/1961) and Rogers (1951), and in Kohut's psychoanalytic self-theory (Cashdan, 1988). According to CEST, these motives are all of central importance, and any one of them can dominate the others, depending on the individual and circumstances.

Behavior, from the perspective of CEST, is a compromise among the four basic motives. The four basic motives thus serve as checks and balances against one another. For example, the need to enhance the self is normally kept from producing delusions of grandeur because of the needs to realistically assimilate the data of reality and to maintain relatedness with others. Given the simultaneous operation of the four basic motives, it follows that most people will exhibit a modest self-enhancing bias as the result of a compromise between the motive for self-enhancement and the other motives, particularly the motive to realistically assimilate the data of reality. This inference is supported by a considerable body of research that demonstrates self-serving biases in self-evaluation (Taylor & Brown, 1988). Contrary to how these findings have sometimes been interpreted, they do not indicate that reality awareness is an unimportant criterion of mental health, but only that it is not the only one.

An imbalance among the four basic functions is characteristic of maladaptive behavior. Such an imbalance can be produced by a threat to any of the functions. Thus, a serious threat to self-esteem can produce overcompensation to the point that the need to enhance the self overwhelms the other functions, resulting in, for example, a delusion of grandeur. Different disorders are associated with dominance by different basic functions (Epstein, 1980).

The Four Basic Beliefs Associated with the Four Basic Functions

Associated with the four basic functions are four basic beliefs. In order for the experiential system to allocate resources to the fulfillment of the four basic functions, it is necessary for it to assess their status. It follows that there are four basic assessments, or belief dimensions, about the fulfillment of the four basic functions. Accordingly, it can be assumed that every person has intuitive assessments in his or her personal theory of reality of the degree to which the world is (1) benign and (2) meaningful (including predictable, controllable and just); the degree to which (3) people are considered to be worth relating to; and the degree to which (4) the self is viewed as worthy (including competent, good, and lovable).

The Three Conceptual Systems

Modern cognitive personality theorists (e.g., Markus, 1977; Mischel, 1973) typically assume there is a single conceptual system. Although they sometimes speak of hot and cold cognitions, they view emotions as modifiers of the parameters in a single system. Emotions, for example, have been regarded as amplifiers of response tendencies (Tomkins, 1980). According to CEST, on the other hand, there are three conceptual systems: a rational conceptual system that operates primarily at the conscious level; an experiential conceptual system that operates primarily at the preconscious level; and an associationistic conceptual system that operates primarily at the unconscious level. In this respect, CEST has more in common with psychoanalytic theory, which assumes at least two separate systems, a conscious and an unconscious one. Although psychoanalytic theory recognizes the existence of a preconscious level of functioning, it does not view the preconscious as a separate system with its own rules of operation. Rather, it regards it as merely a way station between the conscious and unconscious systems, and it is assumed to operate by the same rules as the conscious system. CEST,

on the other hand, accords a central role to the preconscious level of awareness, for it is here that the experiential system—the system that automatically interprets reality and directs thought and behavior in everyday life—primarily operates.

The rational conceptual system operates predominantly at the conscious level, where it functions according to socially prescribed rules of communication and inference. CEST has nothing new to say about this system. The experiential and associationistic systems have their own rules of operation. Since the experiential system is the system of greatest concern to CEST, it is described in detail shortly. The associationistic system corresponds to a state of altered consciousness and is viewed as similar to Freud's unconscious system, which operates according to the rules of primary-process thinking. However, in common with Jung's views, it is also regarded as a source of creativity, as making inferences about the future as well as the past, and in general as a more sophisticated system than the Freudian unconscious. This is not the place for a detailed discussion of the associationistic system. Further discussion of the rational and associationistic systems, including their topographical representation, can be found in a previous article (Epstein, 1983). Let us turn to an indepth consideration of the experiential system.

The Experiential System

Attributes of the Experiential System

Unlike the rational system, which guides behavior by direct assessment of stimuli, the direction of behavior by the experiential system is mediated by feelings, or "vibes"; these include vague feelings of which individuals are normally unaware, as well as full-blown emotions of which they usually are aware. The experiential system is assumed to operate in the following manner. When an individual is confronted with a situation that requires some kind of response, depending on past emotionally similar experiences, the person experiences certain feelings. The feelings, or vibes, which can be very subtle, motivate action tendencies to seek to further the state if the vibes are pleasant and to reduce the state if they are unpleasant. The whole process occurs extremely rapidly, so that to all appearances the behavior is an immediate reaction to the eliciting stimulus. In the case of humans, the vibes produce not only tendencies to act in certain ways, but also tendencies to think in certain ways.

Table 7.1 contrasts the rules of operation of the rational and experiential systems. The list is a tentative one, derived from an analysis of people's thinking when they discuss highly charged emotional issues in comparison to their thinking when they discuss impersonal issues. It has also been influenced by an analysis of the nature of the appeals made in advertising and in politics and by findings from the Constructive Thinking Inventory, to be discussed later.

Several of the features in Table 7.1 contribute to a major characteristic of the system, which is to assess events rapidly and promote immediate decisive action. Included among such features are the holistic and categorical appraisal of events and the experience of the outcome of the appraisal process as self-evidently valid.

The experiential and rational systems both have advantages and disadvantages. The rational system is better suited for analytic analysis and consideration of long-term consequences. However, without the experiential system, the rational system is devoid of passion and commitment. Moreover, an analytic approach is not necessarily the best approach for solving all problems. For example, a holistic approach is less likely to be unable to see the forest for the trees. Moreover, a rational, analytic approach is apt to overlook significant sources of data that may be attended to by a more intuitive, holistic approach. Thus, a rational approach may arrive at solutions that, although reasonable from an external frame of reference, are counterproductive because they fail to take into account the emotional consequences of a decision. Given that each system has its advantages and limitations, the most adaptive solution is to employ both systems; this requires awareness of and respect for the operation of the experiential system.

Although the rational and experiential systems are independent, they are capable of communicating with and otherwise influencing each other. For example, the rational system can employ metaphor and imagery, which are more commonly the domain of the experiential system, and the experiential system can employ words, which are more commonly the domain

TABLE 7.1. A Comparison of the Attributes of the Experiential and Rational Systems

Experiential system	Rational system
1. Holistic	1. Analytic
2. Emotional: Pleasure- vs. pain-oriented (what feels good)	2. Logical: Reason-oriented (what is sensible)
3. Behavior mediated by "vibes" from past experiences	3. Behavior mediated by conscious appraisal of events
4. Encodes reality in concrete images and metaphors	4. Encodes reality in abstract symbols: Words and numbers
5. Rapid processing: Oriented toward immediate action	5. Slower processing: Oriented toward delayed action
6. Slow to change: Changes with repetitive experience, direct or vicarious	6. Changes rapidly: Changes with speed of thought
7. Learns directly from experience	7. Learns from symbolic representations of experience
8. Crudely differentiated and integrated: Associationistic, categorical, and organized into emotional complexes	8. More highly differentiated and integrated
9. Experienced passively and preconsciously: We are seized by our emotions	9. Experienced activity and consciously: We are in control of our thoughts
10. Self-evidently valid: "Experiencing is believing"	10. Requires justification via logic and evidence

Note. From "Cognitive-Experiential Self-Theory: Implications for Developmental Psychology" by S. Epstein, 1990b. In M. R. Gunnar (Ed.), *Minnesota Symposium on Child Psychology*, Hillsdale, NJ: Erlbaum. Copyright by Lawrence Erlbaum Associates. Reprinted by permission.

of the rational system. Words, of course, can be used to paint word pictures and pictures can be used to present analytical material, as in pictures in anatomy textbooks.

As has already been noted, the experiential system influences the rational system by producing feelings, or vibes, which guide thought as well as action. It is when its operation is not recognized that the experiential system is most likely to unreasonably dominate and influence the rational system. For its part, the rational system, by becoming aware of the experiential system, can often override its influence, as indicated in resolutions of conflicts between the heart and the mind in favor of the mind. The rational system can also influence the experiential system by providing the person with experiences, direct or vicarious, from which the experiential system can learn.

Evidence for an Independent Experiential System

Is there a need to postulate separate experiential and rational systems, when the view that there is but one system would be more in accord with the thinking of others and would be more parsimonious? The evidence for two systems is so great as to make it difficult to deny. First, there are the ubiquitous conflicts observed in everyday life between the heart and the mind. Obviously the heart cannot have desires; it can only beat. The conflict must reside between different construals in the brain. When a person buying a car says, "My reason told me to buy the Volkswagen, but my heart told me to buy the Stingray," he or she is describing a conflict between competing cognitions about a desirable course of action arrived at through different operations. When a student says, "I did not feel like studying, but I made myself do so," who is the self who did not feel like studying, and who is the self who made the other self do it? According to CEST, the first self is the self in the experiential system, and the second self is the one in the rational system. Parenthetically, it is noteworthy that people tend to view the rational system as a taskmaster that forces the experiential part of oneself to do unpleasant tasks and to forego immediate pleasure.

Irrational fears provide additional evidence of a system that operates independently of the rational system. There are many people who, despite knowing that it is far safer to travel by air than by automobile, elect to do the latter

because being on the ground "feels" safer, meaning that it is experientially judged to be safer. The difference between insight and intellectual knowledge provides another example of the difference between the two systems. Therapists know that it is often worse than useless to provide a client with intellectual information about his or her difficulties. On the other hand, providing knowledge through an emotionally meaningful experience, such as a transference relationship, can profoundly influence behavior. Apparently, there are intellectual knowledge and experiential knowledge, and experiential knowledge has different consequences with respect to feelings and behavior than intellectual knowledge does. Cigarette advertisments provide further evidence of the two systems: Advertisers are intuitively aware that a message in a picture directed to the experiential system can override a written message directed to the rational system, even if the latter contains threats to life itself.

A particularly compelling example of two separate systems is provided by an informal experiment described by Piaget (1973). Young children were given the task of hitting a target with a tetherball by releasing the string at the appropriate moment. With some practice, they succeeded. However, when asked to explain how, they incorrectly said that they released the ball when it was pointing at the target. If they did, it would, of course, have hit the wrong wall. Older children correctly reported that they released the ball when it was at a right angle to the target. Piaget's point in citing the experiment was that unless a child has an appropriate conscious schema for assimilating information, he or she is unable to report the nonverbal knowledge that he or she apparently has acquired. For present purposes, the example well illustrates the existence of two different ways of knowing.

Resistance to Acknowledging the Existence of an Experiential Conceptual System

If the experiential system is as important and evident as I have claimed it to be, how is it possible that it has been overlooked for so long? There are several reasons for this. One is that the experiential system provides the background of mental activity, whereas conscious thinking is in the foreground. One is reminded of Thomas Carlyle's thought that if a fish had an inquiring mind, the last thing it would discover would be water. People look out onto reality, and not reflexively back onto how they construct it.

A second reason why people are able to avoid awareness of the experiential system is that, no matter what the actual cause of their behavior, they are usually able to attribute it to conscious adaptive thinking (i.e., they can "rationalize" it).

A third reason why people resist awareness of their experiential system is because awareness is burdensome. One is reminded of the centipede who, when asked to describe the order in which it moved its many feet, became so confused that it could no longer walk. Yet, something more is involved in resistance to awareness of the experiential system than simply the effort that is required. Becoming aware of the preconscious thoughts that structure emotions confronts people with the role they play in producing their emotions, which has implications for responsibility. Many people would prefer to believe that they are passive victims of their emotions than to assume responsibility for them.

A final reason for resistance to acknowledging the existence of a preconscious system that influences behavior below the threshold of awareness is that there are already well-established theories that emphasize unconscious processes. Most psychologists are satisfied with their explanations of irrational behavior and thus see no reason to adopt a new system. As Kuhn (1970) has pointed out, old paradigms are not easily displaced.

Emotions and Moods

Emotions and moods are of particular interest to CEST for two reasons. First, most schemas in the experiential system have been inductively derived from emotionally significant experiences. Second, emotions provide a royal road to a person's preconscious schemas. That is, emotions are indicators, *par excellence,* of the cognitions in the experiential system. The greater the emotional reaction a person exhibits to a stimulus, the more it can be assumed that a significant belief in the person's theory of reality has been implicated. Thus, if one wishes to map the important schemas in a personal theory of reality, a useful procedure is to note the situations that cause the person to react emotionally. Of particular interest, in this respect, is the fact that emotional responses often belie conscious statements; thus, emotions provide a way of acquiring information about schemas in the experiential system that are distinguishable from beliefs in the rational system.

Let us examine the manner in which cognition influences emotions. If someone preconsciously interprets an injury as undeserved and believes that the perpetrator should be punished, the person will feel angry. If a person regards the same event as an example of humankind's destructive nature about which nothing can be done, he or she will most likely feel sad. Someone may even feel sympathy if he or she considers the perpetrator of the injury to be a maladjusted person who, because of an unbearable degree of frustration, has behaved unreasonably and needs help, not punishment.

The recognition that preconscious thoughts are normally the effective stimuli that elicit emotions has important implications for the control of emotions, for it follows that by altering one's preconscious cognitions it is possible to change one's emotions. That this relation has important implications for behavior change has not been lost on cognitive therapists, such as Beck (1976) and Ellis (1962).

What has been said of emotions is also true of moods. Emotions are cognitive–affective structures, somewhat like multiple personalities. The same is true of moods. They differ in that emotions are episodic reactions that occur in response to specific stimuli, whereas moods are more enduring states that often occur in the absence of identifiable stimuli. Thus, emotions may be superimposed on moods. A person in a sad mood may experience an emotion of joy when given pleasant news, only to have the affect shortly return to the baseline of the more enduring mood. In time, of course, moods also shift, but they do not do so as readily as emotions. It has been said, in this respect, that emotions are to moods as the waves are to the tides.

From the perspective of CEST, a basic difference between moods and emotions is that emotions are produced by preconscious appraisals of the momentary implications of a particular stimulus, whereas moods are produced by preconscious appraisals on a much larger scale (namely, where one currently stands in life and what one's future prospects are). This is not meant to deny that moods can also be influenced by other factors, including biological ones. Nor is it meant to deny that the influence between cognitions and feeling states goes in both directions. A depressed person is apt to interpret a particular stimulus in a different manner from the way he or she would in a happier frame of mind. Thus, it is obvious that feeling states can influence cognitions, as well as the other way around.

THE MAINTENANCE OF MALADAPTIVE SCHEMAS

As noted previously, the schemas in a personal theory of reality are derived primarily from emotionally significant experiences. If an individual has experienced the world as malevolent and unpredictable, it is understandable that the individual will develop a schema of the world as malevolent and unpredictable. On the face of it, encoding emotionally significant experiences veridically would seem to be highly adaptive, and in most circumstances, of course, it is. However, a problem arises when individual's develop beliefs that accurately describe the world of their early experience, but that are inaccurate with respect to the broader world and, relatedly, to later experience. This raises an extremely important question: Why do people then not accommodate their maladaptive schemas to conform to the new reality? There are at least four reasons why maladaptive beliefs are maintained despite conditions that would seem to favor their modification or abandonment: repression; insulation of higher-order schemas from immediate experience; the need to maintain the stability of the conceptual system; and the development of what I refer to as "sensitivities" and "compulsions."

Repression

In Freudian theory, the concept of repression carries almost the entire burden of accounting for why maladaptive reactions acquired in childhood are retained in adulthood despite a major shift in circumstances. As a result of repression, unacceptable memories and impulses become unavailable for correction by conscious reappraisal and learning. For this reason, a major aim of psychoanalysis is to make the unconscious conscious.

There is nothing magical about repression. All that is involved is that individuals have learned to direct their thinking away from a direction that, if pursued, would lead to uncovering the repressed material. The diversion is mediated by twinges of anxiety, referred to in psychoanalysis as "signal anxiety," that are instigated when thoughts approach an area of sensitivity. CEST accepts the psychoanalytic concept of repression, but believes that its range of application as well as that of the related concept of unconscious conflict have been overextended, and that there are other, equally important explanatory concepts overlooked by psychoanalysis. Moreover, CEST views repression in a somewhat different light from that of Freudian theory. According to psychoanalytic theory, once material is repressed into the unconscious, it is governed by primary-process thinking. Thus, all repressed material is viewed as similar to dream material and is presumably influenced by the same mechanisms that convert forbidden wishes (mainly sexual ones) into dream symbols; these include condensation, displacement, concrete imagery, associationistic thinking, and an absence of the constraints of time, place, and logic.

According to CEST, repression simply removes material from the rational conscious system. As a result, it is governed by the rules of the untempered experiential system (see Table 7.1). It is important to recognize that the repressed material, however, is not simply like other material in the experiential system: Its accessibility is constrained by the signal anxiety it elicits when stimulated, which causes its direct expression to be actively avoided. The most manifest symptom of repression is thus displacement, because what is avoided is direct expression of responses to the salient end of a generalization gradient, and what are expressed are responses to the more remote end of the dimension (Dollard & Miller, 1950; Epstein, 1982). A further maladaptive consequence of repression stems from the experiential system generalizing in a cruder, more stimulus-bound manner than the rational system (see Table 7.1).

In addition to displacement, symptoms of repression include avoidance reactions, resistance to extinction, and a discrepancy between beliefs in the rational and experiential system, all of which can be important sources of emotional disturbance and problems in living.

Insulation of Higher-Order Schemas from Immediate Experience

Given a hierarchically organized conceptual system in which lower-order schemas are situation-specific and higher-order constructs are broad generalizations, specific events, unless of overwhelming emotional significance, are apt to have little effect on higher-order constructs. Because beliefs acquired early in life are apt to become higher-order postulates, they can be expected to be resistant to modification. This is not to say that they cannot be changed, but that, to the extent that they have become higher-order constructs, they are difficult to change.

Maintenance of the Stability of the Conceptual System

People have a vested interest in maintaining the stability of their personal theories of reality, because these theories are necessary for making sense of the world and guiding behavior. As threat to the stability of their conceptual system mounts, people experience increasing anxiety and a tendency for their conceptual system to become disorganized. When disorganization is imminent, the anxiety becomes overwhelming, and people will do whatever they can to reduce its intensity and prevent disorganization (for a discussion of anxiety and disorganization as related to schizophrenia, see Epstein, 1976, 1979).

There are several strategies that can be used to maintain the integrity of basic beliefs despite disconfirming evidence. Three basic ones are framing the beliefs in an untestable manner; selectively perceiving and interpreting events to support current beliefs; and selectively seeking out experiences and shaping events so that they confirm extant beliefs (Epstein & Erskine, 1983; Swann, 1983). It is important to realize that the need to maintain basic beliefs applies to beliefs recognized to be maladaptive, as well as to beliefs considered desirable. The decision to maintain a destructive belief is not made consciously, but occurs at the preconscious level, where it is mediated by anxiety signals that arise whenever the stability of the conceptual system is threatened. A woman who was battered as a child, and who later falls in love with a man who batters her, does not make a deliberate choice to do so. Rather, the choice is made for her by the vibes elicited by her preconscious cognitions.

Sensitivities and Compulsions

"Sensitivities" refer to experientially derived generalizations that certain kinds of situations or events are dangerous. "Compulsions" refer to experientially derived generalizations that certain kinds of behaviors are effective ways of reducing threat. Both are resistant to extinction or modification because they have been learned under conditions of high emotional arousal and have, over time, become nuclei of perceptual and behavioral networks. Sensitivities correspond to preconscious descriptive beliefs, and compulsions correspond to preconscious motivational beliefs. Sensitivities and compulsions, as the terms are used in CEST, differ from their diagnostic use in clinical psychology in one very important respect. When used to describe abnormal behaviors, they refer to narrowly defined classes of stimuli and behavior. Thus, individuals are diagnosed as having a hand-washing compulsion or a compulsion to engage in certain other private rituals. In CEST, the meaning of the terms is expanded to include more complex patterns of behavior that, although maladaptive, are not abnormal in the usual sense of the term because they are relatively common, often defining the most salient characteristics of people.

The hallmark of a sensitivity is that whenever certain stimuli or situations arise, the individual becomes excessively distressed. Sensitivities can be identified by situations that "get to people," that "bug them," that their friends recognize they must avoid if they wish to maintain peace. The hallmarks of a compulsion are as follows: (1) The person acts in a rigid way across a variety of situations, such as always having to be dominant or always having to be ingratiating; (2) the person experiences distress whenever he or she is unable to behave in a manner consistent with the compulsion; (3) the compulsion become exaggerated when the person is threatened, particularly when the threat involves a relevant sensitivity. It is assumed that sensitivities are learned under conditions of high threat and that compulsions are learned as ways of coping with sensitivities. In order to understand the fundamental nature of sensitivities and compulsions, it is helpful first to consider the nature of anxiety.

Anxiety became established as part of the inherited repertoire of higher-order species because of its adaptive significance. When an animal, such as a rabbit, has a threatening experience, such as being attacked by a hawk, it experiences anxiety. From that point on, whenever a stimulus that is reminiscent of the original threat appears, the anxiety alarm sounds and the animal automatically responds with whatever actions it previously made that were followed by a reduction in anxiety. Normally, the anxiety and the responses to it are adaptive, because they provide the animal with an automatic warning signal and an automatic response for escaping from the danger. In time, if similar stimuli are experienced in the absence of real danger, the anxiety subsides; this, of course, is also adaptive. The greater the initial anxiety, the broader the gradient of generalization, and the more resistant the responses that reduced the anxiety are to extinction. The stimuli that evoke anxiety as a result of having been associated with the stressor are sensitivities. The automatic responses that are produced to these stimuli as a way of reducing anxiety are compulsions.

From the viewpoint of CEST, sensitivities and compulsions, not unconscious conflict and repression, are the most fundamental sources of maladaptive behavior. Unconscious conflict and repression are simply complications that make the sources and sometimes the nature of the sensitivities and compulsions unavailable to awareness. Accordingly, in many cases, removing repression (i.e., making the unconscious conscious) is not enough to correct maladaptive behavior, because the initial sensitivities and compulsions remain. All that may be accomplished by such a procedure is to transform a neurotic person without insight into one with insight.

As already noted, sensitivities correspond to descriptive schemas that identify sources of danger. Compulsions correspond to motivational schemas about how to avoid or escape from danger. The maladaptiveness of these schemas depends on how general, inflexible, and resistant to modification they are. Moreover, the earlier such cognitions are acquired and the greater the intensity and repetition of the emotional experiences on which they are

based, the more likely they are to be incorporated as central postulates in a personal theory of reality; this provides an additional reason as to why they are self-maintaining.

The acquisition of sensitivities and compulsions can account for many of the phenomena that psychoanalysts attribute to unconscious conflict. There is thus the danger that behavior will be diagnosed and treated by psychoanalysts as if unconscious conflict is present, when in fact it is not. To state this is not to deny the importance of unconscious conflict, but to suggest that it is less general than psychoanalysts assume, and to draw attention to another kind of unconscious (or, more accurately, preconscious) behavior with which it is often confused. To make the distinction clear, it is helpful to consider a specific case.

Some time ago, a young woman graduate student made repeated negative remarks or snickered whenever I spoke up in public. (Details in the story that follows have been altered to preserve anonymity.) I called her to my office after one such incident and asked her what about my behavior distressed her so. She looked astonished, and said that she was not aware of reacting negatively to me; in fact, she liked and admired me.

How is one to explain such a gross lack of awareness? A psychoanalyst would most likely say that she had unconscious hostile feelings toward someone, perhaps a parent or authority figure, and that she was displacing these on me. I suggested a little experiment to her: I asked her whether she would be willing to monitor her "vibes" whenever I spoke in public. The idea of an experiment appealed to her, and she agreed to do so. Two weeks later she came to my office with the results. After some practice, she had learned to detect her vibes, and it became apparent to her that they were not very good when she heard me speak. They made her want to defend her autonomy by putting me down. She recognized that they were the same feelings she had toward her father, toward whom she was consciously hostile. Since the hostility toward her father was conscious, the case for displacement of unconscious conflict is not tenable. The behavior can more simply be explained by assuming that the young woman had become sensitized to her father's voice and that the sensitivity had generalized to my voice. Because the generalization occurred at a preconscious level in the experiential system, there was no reason for her to be consciously aware of her reaction. In fact, since the negative reaction to me was inconsistent with her conscious thinking about me, there was reason for her not to recognize her aggressive behavior consciously, because it made no sense. As a further indication that unconscious conflict was not involved, she experienced no resistance when she detected the vibes. All that was necessary for her to become aware of the vibes and the thoughts with which they were associated was an act of attention. This case well illustrates the manner in which vibes control thought and behavior in the absence of awareness; according to CEST, this is the way in which most behavior is controlled in everyday life.

That behavior such as in the case above can be a source of serious problems in living is suggested by the following thought experiment. Imagine that I embarrassed the graduate student in public by responding in kind to her negative comments. This would have provided her with an objective reason for being hostile to me, which could have easily escalated into an ongoing conflict between us. Such conflicts regularly occur between spouses, between parents and children, between friends, and in the workplace, where they can have devastating consequences. It follows that unconscious conflict is not the *sine qua non* of maladaptive behavior, as psychoanalysts maintain.

THE CONSTRUCT OF CONSTRUCTIVE THINKING

Up to this point, maladaptive behavior has been discussed in terms of how such behavior is acquired and how it is maintained through the use of a variety of cognitive strategies. I wish now to introduce a new construct, "constructive thinking," that provides an additional perspective for viewing maladaptive behavior—one that is particularly suited to understanding success in living.

The logic behind constructive thinking is as follows. If emotions and, to a large extent, behavior are determined by the functioning of the experiential system, then the effectiveness of the experiential system should play an important role in a person's success in everyday living. This raises the question of whether it is possible to obtain a measure of the effectiveness of the experiential system in a manner analogous to the measurement of intellectual ability by intelligence tests. If so, what are the kinds of items that would have to be included? The answer is that one would need items that sample a person's automatic thinking in coping with the kinds of problems that arise in everyday living.

There are two aspects of automatic thinking that require consideration: content and process. "Content" refers to the specific beliefs in a personal theory of reality, such as whether the world is viewed as benign or malevolent or whether people are considered to be trustworthy or not. "Process" refers to the manner of functioning of the system. It includes variables such as overgeneralization, categorical thinking, and magical thinking. To illustrate these two classes of variables, let us consider some specific examples. The item "When I fail a test, I feel that I am a total failure and that I will never amount to anything," is a poor response with respect to both content and process. At the content level, it is unduly pessimistic; at the process level, it is characterized by gross overgeneralization. Contrast this item with the following: "When I do very well on an important test, I feel that I am a total success and that I will succeed in whatever I undertake." Here the content is positive, but the process is again indicative of gross overgeneralization. Now consider an item describing a constructive response in both ways: "When I fail a test, I realize it is only a single test, and I learn what I can from the experience without getting upset." This item illustrates positive content and process.

It is assumed that there are individual differences in preconscious thinking along a dimension that varies from extremely constructive to extremely destructive automatic thinking. The level of constructive thinking on this dimension corresponds to the intelligence of the experiential system, and is referred to as "constructive thinking." Good constructive thinking is defined as automatic thinking that facilitates coping with problems in living in a manner that maximizes the likelihood of an effective solution at a minimum cost in stress to oneself and distress to others. Poor constructive thinking consists of preconscious, automatic thinking that results in a relatively high cost in stress to oneself and distress to others, relative to the adequacy of the solutions achieved.

It is assumed that constructive thinking is more influenced by nurture and less by nature than rational intelligence. Relatedly, it is

UNIVERSITY OF WOLVERHAMPTON
Harrison Learning Centre

ITEMS ISSUED:

Customer ID: WPP62927740X

Title: Individual differences and personality
ID: 7622771115
Due: 17/11/2017 23:59

Title: Personality theories : basic assumptions,
research, and applications
ID: 7608624046
Due: 17/11/2017 23:59

Title: Handbook of personality : theory and
research
ID: 7620146671
Due: 03/11/2017 23:59

Total items: 3
Total fines: £7.60
27/10/2017 13:55
Issued: 3
Overdue: 0

Thank you for using Self Service.
Please keep your receipt.

Overdue books are fined at 40p per day for
1 week loans, 10p per day for long loans.

assumed that early experiences in childhood, particularly those that evoke strong emotions, initiate automatic coping reactions that tend over time to become strong habits. Consequently, although constructive thinking is, in all likelihood, more susceptible to change than rational intelligence, it is nevertheless not easy to change, and it is more responsive to direct or indirect experience than to rational discourse.

RESEARCH

Research on Basic Beliefs

How is one to study the basic beliefs in the experiential system? Basic beliefs are not easily influenced by events, and therefore are not easily studied in the laboratory. However, there are natural "experiments" of such intensity that they can shatter personalities and produce enduring changes in beliefs about the self and the world. These include traumatic events, such as criminal assault, natural disasters, warfare, and incapacitating illness.

According to CEST, the essence of the traumatic neurosis is the invalidation of basic postulates in a personal theory of reality, which results in the destabilization of the personality structure (Epstein, 1976). This is followed by attempts to establish a new integration, which can be accomplished either by finding new ways to assimilate the traumatic experience into the old structure (which is usually not possible), by modifying the old structure, or by establishing a radically new structure. Although a great deal of interesting research has been done on the relation of traumatic events to social attributions (e.g., Bulman & Wortman, 1977; Wortman, 1976), to social comparisons (e.g., Taylor, Wood, & Lichtman, 1983) and to interpersonal interactions (e.g., Wortman & Dunkel-Schetter, 1979), with rare exceptions this work has not focused on the concept of basic beliefs. An exception is the research of Janoff-Bulman, who, using concepts influenced by CEST, has examined the relation of extreme life events to changes in basic beliefs.

Based on a review of the literature on traumatic events, Janoff-Bulman (1989) concluded that following such events there is a widespread change in feelings of vulnerability. People, at the experiential level, recognize for the first time how vulnerable they actually are.

Accompanying the change in perceptions of vulnerability are the following changes in basic assumptions about the self and the world: The world is perceived as less benevolent and less meaningful (including predictable, controllable, and just), and the self is perceived as less worthy. It is noteworthy that these three basic beliefs correspond to three of the four basic beliefs in CEST. The fourth belief in CEST concerns relatedness. Interestingly, Janoff-Bulman includes this belief as a subcategory of the belief in the benevolence of the world, because it appears in the same factor when a factor analysis is done of the beliefs. However, she notes that it should not simply be merged with the belief in the impersonal world as benevolent, because it produces distinct correlations with other variables. In sum, then, a review of the research on trauma provides striking confirmation of the basic beliefs postulated by CEST.

In a study designed to examine the influence of traumatic events on basic beliefs, Janoff-Bulman (1989) investigated the relation between basic beliefs and reported events such as death of a parent, rape, and a disabling illness. The main finding was that the current views of victims of traumatic events were significantly more negative than those of nonvictims with respect to beliefs in the benevolence of the impersonal world, in their own self-worth, and in the predictability of significant events. The strongest findings were those with regard to self-worth. Different traumas had similar effects. There was no evidence that different traumas influenced different beliefs.

The Catlin and Epstein Study of the Relation of Significant Life Events to Current Basic Beliefs

In an elaboration of the Janoff-Bulman study, Catlin and Epstein (1990) examined current beliefs as a function of emotionally significant events, the age at which the events occurred, and the quality of the subjects' childhood relationships with their parents.

Subjects were 305 undergraduates who filled out a Major Life Events Schedule, in which they reported whether they had experienced any of the following events, and, if so, at what age: an emotionally significant move to another environment; death of a loved one; a major success, such as winning a prize in an athletic contest; a significant rejection; a significant love relationship outside of the family;

parental divorce; a significant immoral act; an accident that was one's own fault; an accident that was someone else's fault; sexual abuse (as a victim); a violent crime (as a victim); a non-violent crime (as a victim); or a natural disaster, such as a fire or a hurricane. Subjects also rated the immediate and long-term influence of each of the events on their self-esteem and on their attitude toward others. In addition, they completed the Mother–Father–Peer Inventory (MFP), which includes scales on childhood relationships with parents, and the Basic Beliefs Test, which provides scales on the following current beliefs: Benign World (e.g., "By and large, I feel that my personal world is a reasonably safe and secure place"), Meaningful World (e.g., "My life is lacking in purpose and meaning"), Predictable–Controllable World (e.g., "I feel that I have little control over the important events in my life"), Just World (e.g., "I feel I get a raw deal out of life"), Valuation of Relationships (e.g., "I like people and believe

in giving them the benefit of the doubt"), Global Self-Esteem (e.g., "I nearly always have a highly positive opinion of myself"), Competence (e.g., "I am often lacking in self-confidence"), and Lovability (e.g., "There are times when I have doubts about my capacity for maintaining a close love relationship").

The findings for the ratings of the immediate and enduring effects of events on attitudes toward the self and others are presented in Table 7.2. Similar results were obtained when current basic beliefs were correlated with reports of events. The overall results indicate both general and specific effects of events on beliefs. All basic beliefs tended to be affected by a significant life event, but, depending on the nature of the event, some beliefs were affected more than others.

The findings in the Catlin and Epstein (1990) study are consistent with those in the Janoff-Bulman (1989) study, as far as earlier events' being associated with current beliefs is

TABLE 7.2. Comparison of Initial and Lasting Effects of Major Life Events on Self- and Other-Acceptance ($n = 305$)

Event	No. of occurrences	Mean initial effect			Mean lasting effect		
		Self-acceptance	Other-acceptance	t	Self-acceptance	Other-acceptance	t
Move	153	−0.17*	−0.04	1.96	0.59***	0.25**	5.16***
Death	202	−0.50***	−0.11*	7.15***	0.07	0.06	0.32
Major success	241	1.45***	0.60***	15.71***	1.00***	0.38***	13.61***
Rejection	148	−1.38***	−0.85***	8.22***	0.22***	−0.30***	1.21
Love	222	1.43***	1.07***	7.81***	1.08***	0.77***	5.67***
Immoral act	140	−1.13***	−0.43***	9.40***	−0.34***	−0.20***	2.33*
Divorce	67	−0.54***	−0.62***	0.87	0.14	−0.22**	5.07***
Accident (own responsibility)	44	−1.04***	−0.24*	5.64***	−0.24*	0.02	3.08***
Accident (other's responsibility)	56	−0.34***	−0.37***	0.70	−0.02	−0.09	0.85
(Victim of) sexual abuse	45	−1.24***	−1.24***	0	−0.57***	−0.76***	2.28*
(Victim of) violent crime	25	−0.46**	−1.17***	2.13*	−0.04	−0.54**	3.61**
(Victim of) nonviolent crime	88	−0.93***	−1.27***	7.57***	−0.09	−0.44***	9.05***
Natural disaster	18	−0.21	−0.11	1.00	0.10	0.05	1.00

Note: A positive score signifies a favorable reaction and a negative score an unfavorable reaction. Asterisks next to means indicate significance of mean in comparison to no effect of event. Asterisks next to t indicate significance of difference between effect on self-acceptance and other-acceptance.
*$p < .05$. **$p < .01$. ***$p < .001$.
From *The Relation of Basic Beliefs to Extreme Life Events and Childhood Relationships with Parents* by G. Catlin and S. Epstein, 1990. Manuscript submitted for publication. Reprinted by permission of the authors.

concerned. However, there are also some differences. The finding of more specific effects than in the Janoff-Bulman study may be a consequence of the different way of measuring basic beliefs in the two studies. In the Janoff-Bulman study, with the exception of self-worth, beliefs were measured by abstract statements. In our study, with its emphasis on the experiential system, beliefs were measured by more personal, experiential descriptions.

The results are consistent with the conclusion that, following an extremely negative event, all basic beliefs tend to change in an unfavorable direction, but that some beliefs change more than others, depending on the event. Assimilation of the meaning of significant events continues over time and is associated with a tendency for the events to become less significant and to be reinterpreted in a more favorable way, at least for many negative events that have less than traumatic impact. As will be seen in the discussion below of the Fletcher (1988) study, traumatic events, such as combat, can induce a downward spiral; under such circumstances, negative beliefs, instead of rebounding after the negative event, become increasingly negative.

Of particular interest was the observation that the effect of significant life events on beliefs did not simply reflect the operation of a veridical generalization process. Rather, the effect was determined by the interaction of the external event and individual differences in the cognitive processing of the event. There appear to be at least three kinds of important individual-difference variables that determine the effect of an event on a person's beliefs about self and world: the cognitive ability of the individual; the degree to which self-serving strategies, such as ones that enhance self-esteem and facilitate the maintenance of an optimistic orientation, are used; and the automatic rules for interpreting events that are employed, such as whether loss of love signifies personal inadequacy and criticism signifies attack (Beck, 1976).

There were a number of interesting findings concerning childhood relationships. Reported favorable relationships with parents were highly reliably associated with favorable views on all basic beliefs. Although parental acceptance and encouragement of independence were associated much more strongly than single life events with current basic beliefs, a composite score of overall favorability of multiple life events was as strongly associated with current beliefs as was favorability of relationships with parents.

There was evidence of a specific relationship between certain kinds of child-rearing practices and basic beliefs, just as there was between certain kinds of significant life events and basic beliefs. Acceptance was more strongly associated with the current belief that one is love-worthy than that one is competent, and encouragement of independence exhibited the reverse pattern. Of particular interest was the finding that reported relationships with parents in childhood moderated the relation between events and beliefs. For subjects who reported a high level of acceptance by parents, there was a highly significant positive relation between favorability of multiple life-events and current beliefs in the areas of Meaningful World and Predictable–Controllable World, whereas for a group who reported low parental acceptance, the relation was nonsignificant.

Figure 7.1 presents the results for Meaningful World; the results for Predictable–Controllable World were similar. One interpretation of these findings is that for those with low parental acceptance, parental acceptance is the dominant influence on their views of the world as meaningful, predictable, and controllable; specific events, therefore, have relatively little influence. On the other hand, these same beliefs for people who report high parental acceptance are sensitive to environmental influence. For these individuals, if the world provides experiences that are consonant with relationships with their parents, this strongly confirms their belief that the word is meaningful, predictable, and controllable. Should the world, however, provide experiences that are contrary to their experiences in the family, a contrast effect results, and they view their world as more meaningless, unpredictable, and uncontrollable than before. It is noteworthy that these conclusions run counter to the psychoanalytic view that a positive relationship with parents fosters the development of ego strength, thereby contributing to the ability of people to cope emotionally with the vicissitudes of life. The results of this study suggest that such a view needs to be qualified by considering that experiences in or out of the family establish expectancies; when these expectancies are violated, the world is viewed as more capricious and uncontrollable than it would have been if there were less favorable expectations to begin with.

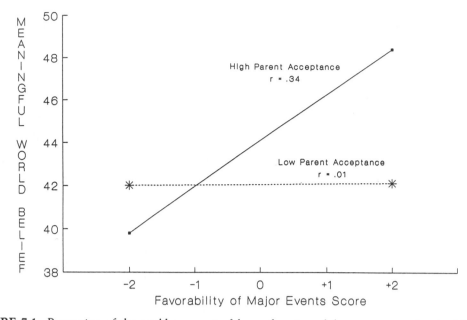

FIGURE 7.1. Perception of the world as meaningful as a function of the occurrence of major life events (favorable–unfavorable) for subjects reporting high and low levels of parent acceptance. From *The Relation of Basic Beliefs to Extreme Life Events and Childhood Relationships with Parents* by G. Catlin and S. Epstein, 1990, manuscript submitted for publication. Reprinted by permission of the authors.

Basic Beliefs and Posttraumatic Stress Disorder in Vietnam Veterans

In a doctoral dissertation that examined the influence of posttraumatic stress disorder (PTSD) on basic beliefs, Fletcher (1988) gave a battery of specially designed questionnaires to 214 veterans of the Vietnam war. Information was obtained on the veterans' experiences in Vietnam, including amount and kind of combat experience. Tests included scales for measuring symptoms of PTSD and for measuring various beliefs, including the four basic beliefs emphasized in CEST as well as lower-order beliefs (e.g., attitudes about the war, about authority figures, and about the policies of the U.S. government). Most items referring to beliefs were responded to for four time periods: before Vietnam; during Vietnam; 6 months after discharge; and the current period, which for most was about 15 years after discharge. To control for biased ratings, items from a scale of defensiveness were embedded among the other items for each time period. When the data were analyzed, defensiveness was partialed out of the relations between basic beliefs reported for a particular period and other variables.

It was hypothesized that basic beliefs would change in a negative direction following exposure to combat, and that the change would be greater and more enduring in those suffering from PTSD than in others. Interest also was in whether the effect of traumatic events would be general across all basic beliefs or whether certain beliefs would change more than others, depending on kind of combat experience.

The data were statistically analyzed in two main ways. First, correlations within each of the four periods were computed for the total group between beliefs and symptoms of PTSD. Second, so that changes over time could be examined, the veterans were divided into three groups—a noncombat control group, a combat control group without symptoms of PTSD, and a combat group with symptoms of PTSD—and repeated measurements of beliefs over periods were investigated in an ANOVA design.

In support of the hypothesis, there were highly reliable differences among the groups on the four basic beliefs following, but not preceding, Vietnam. Since the results, to a large degree, were similar across the four basic beliefs, and since the four basic beliefs were moderately highly correlated, an overall score of favorability of beliefs was obtained by combining the four beliefs. In Figure 7.2, it can be seen that favorability of beliefs decreased for all groups during Vietnam, but that the decrease was greatest for the PTSD group. For the two control groups, the decline continued up to the 6-month period after discharge, after which it reversed, although it never recovered to the prewar baseline. For these veterans, the bloom of youthful optimism was apparently replaced by a sadder but wiser view of life. The PTSD group exhibited a continuous decline up to the period of the study.

Although the strongest associations were with overall favorability of beliefs, there was some evidence that specific kinds of experiences were more strongly associated with some basic beliefs than with others. For example, amount of exposure to combat was most strongly negatively associated with the belief, Benign World, and least strongly negatively associated with Valuation of Relationships, whereas exposure to poor leadership was most strongly associated with Predictable–Controllable World and Valuation of Relationships and least strongly associated with Global Self-Esteem. There was even stronger evidence of relations between specific lower-order beliefs and events. For example, amount of exposure to combat was significantly associated with hardened beliefs about war and the enemy but not with attitudes toward authority or the U.S. government, whereas exposure to poor leadership was most strongly associated with attitudes toward authority and the U.S. government, but was not significantly associated with hardened beliefs about war and the enemy.

How is one to account for the continuous downward spiral in favorability of beliefs and symptoms in veterans with symptoms of PTSD? Why, when they returned to the more benign conditions of civilian life, did not the favorability of their beliefs increase? Although every effort was made to find evidence of prewar personality differences between the PTSD group and the combat control group, no such evidence was forthcoming; this is consistent with findings from other studies of Vietnam veterans. The only variables that differentiated the groups were ones relating to environmental conditions, such as amount and kind of combat, poor leadership, and exposure to conditions of uncertainty.

A possible explanation for the downward

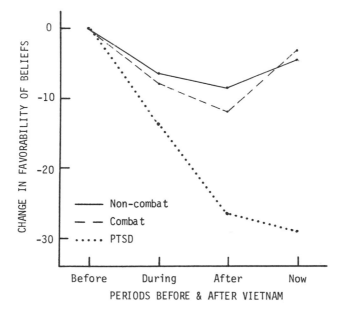

FIGURE 7.2. Change in overall favorability of basic beliefs from a pre-war baseline for Vietnam combat veterans with symptoms of PTSD, for a combat control group, and for a noncombat control group. From *Belief Systems, Exposure to Stress, and Posttraumatic Stress Disorder in Vietnam Veterans* by K. E. Fletcher, 1988, unpublished doctoral dissertation, University of Massachusetts at Amherst. Reprinted by permission of the author.

spiral is that following sufficient exposure to traumatic conditions, a new theory of reality becomes stabilized—one that includes a warrior identity. The new theory of reality then assimilates and seeks out experiences in a self-sustaining manner. As a result, a new benign environment is not perceived as such at all, because it is interpreted in ways that maintain the trauma-induced negative belief system. Despite its punishing consequences, there are adaptive advantages to such an orientation, for it ensures that the individual will never again be surprised and overwhelmed in the way he or she was by the initial trauma. It is beyond the scope of this presentation to pursue this issue further. Further discussion of this issue is available in Fletcher's (1988) dissertation and in an article on the traumatic neurosis (Epstein, 1990a).

Research on Constructive Thinking

The Construction and Structure of the Constructive Thinking Inventory

In order to facilitate research on constructive thinking, the Constructive Thinking Inventory (CTI) was constructed. As a full description of the inventory is provided elsewhere (Epstein & Meier, 1989), it will suffice to provide a brief description of the construction and structure of the scales. A large sample of items descriptive of constructive and destructive thoughts in everyday life was factor-analyzed. A global factor and the following six group factors were found: Emotional Coping, Behavioral Coping, Categorical Thinking, Superstitious Thinking, Naive Optimism, and Negative Thinking. The factors were converted to scales by selecting items with loadings greater than .30 and using standard psychometric procedures to winnow the items further.

The Global scale is composed entirely of items from the other scales; it includes items from all scales except Naive Optimism. The scales of Emotional Coping and Behavioral Coping account for more than half of the total variance of all six factors; this indicates that the domain of coping can be largely divided into coping with the inner world of emotions and thoughts and the outer world of events. This distinction is similar to one made by Folkman and Lazarus (1980; Lazarus & Folkman, 1984) between emotion-focused and problem-focused coping. The Emotional Coping scale includes items that refer to worrying, to taking things

personally, and to being sensitive to failure and disapproval. The Behavioral Coping scale contains items that refer to thinking in ways that facilitate effective action. The items refer to being action-oriented, to planning, and to being optimistic within reason.

Items in the Naive Optimism scale refer to stereotyped, simplistic ways of thinking (e.g., "I believe that people can accomplish anything they want to if they have enough willpower") and to overgeneralization following the occurrence of positive events. Unlike the optimistic items in the Behavioral Coping scale, those in the Naive Optimism scale are grossly unrealistic and have a Pollyanna-ish quality about them. An example of such an item is "If I were accepted at an important job interview, I would feel very good and think that I would always be able to get a good job." Naive Optimism is the only scale that is not significantly correlated with the Global scale or with any of the other scales. The Negative Thinking scale is the negative counterpart of Naive Optimism. Whereas naive optimists unrealistically overemphasize the positive, negative thinkers equally unrealistically overemphasize the negative. If the phrase were not awkward, Negative Thinking could be called "Naive Pessimism." Although Negative Thinking is conceptually related to Emotional Coping, the negative items in the Emotional Coping scale refer to taking things personally and worrying about what others think, whereas the Negative Thinking items refer to a pervasive doom-and-gloom orientation, suspiciousness of others, and emotions that interfere with performance. Nevertheless, recent research has demonstrated considerable overlap between the two scales, so it has been decided to merge them in the latest version of the CTI.

Categorical Thinking and Superstitious Thinking, unlike the other scales, refer to processes rather than content. They describe two fundamental processes that are necessary for developing an accurate model of the world—namely, cognitive differentiation and reality orientation. Most of the items in the Categorical Thinking scale are direct examples of categorical thinking, such as "There are basically two kinds of people in this world, good and bad," and "I tend to classify people as either for me or against me." However, the scale also includes items that refer to overgeneralizing and overreacting following failure and rejection (e.g., "When someone I know is rejected by a person they love, I feel they are inadequate and will never be able to accomplish anything"). The inclusion of such items should not be surprising, as unmodulated reactions of any kind are indications of categorical thinking. A third kind of item refers to being judgmental and intolerant of self and others. A possible explanation of why these items were psychometrically included is that they suggest a rigid and authoritarian manner of upbringing that may foster categorical thinking (Adorno, Frenkel-Brunswik, Levinson, & Sanford, 1950).

The scale of Superstitious Thinking initially included formal superstitions (e.g., "Black cats are bad luck"), private superstitions, and beliefs in esoteric and questionable phenomena, such as astrology and the existence of ghosts. It was found that private superstitions were much more strongly associated with pathology, particularly feelings of helplessness and depression, than were the other kinds of items. As a result, in the most recent version of the CTI, separate subscales have been created for Private Superstition and Esoteric Thinking. Examples of Private Superstition are "I sometimes think that if I want something to happen too badly, it will keep it from happening," and "When something good happens to me, I believe it will be balanced by something bad."

The Relation of the Constructive Thinking Inventory to Emotions

It follows from CEST that the CTI scales should be closely associated with emotions; in fact, this has been found to be the case. When the CTI scales were correlated with the Primary Emotions and Traits Scales (PETS), an adjective checklist that contains bipolar scales of the basic emotions plus higher-order scales of Positivity, Extraversion, Neuroticism, and Ego Strength, highly reliable, coherent relations were found. For example, the CTI Global scale was most highly correlated ($r = .59$) with the bipolar Positivity scale of the PETS, which is its most general scale. It was also highly correlated with Ego Strength (.55), Neuroticism (−.54), Anxiety (−.50), Depression (−.48), and Self-Esteem (.50). The only PETS scales with which it was not significantly correlated were Vigor and Caring. Examples of some other relations with the PETS attesting to the discriminant validity of the CTI are as follows: Anxiety was more highly correlated with Emotional Coping than with Behavioral Coping, whereas the opposite was true for Vigor; Categorical Thinking was more highly directly

associated with Anger than with any other emotion and was only weakly associated with Depression. Superstitious Thinking, on the other hand, was most strongly associated with Depression and was not significantly associated with Anger. Naive Optimism was significantly associated (positively) with only one variable, Positivity. In general, Naive Optimism has been found to be not at all or weakly associated with measures of adjustment. Possibly the low-reality component of the scale cancels out the positive-thinking component.

The Relation of the Constructive Thinking Inventory to Intelligence

In a study (reported in Epstein & Meier, 1989) designed to test the hypothesis that constructive thinking identifies a broad coping ability that is independent of intelligence as measured by intelligence tests, a group of college students was administered the CTI, the Shipley–Hartford Intelligence Test, the Seligman Attributional Style Questionnaire (ASQ), the Sarason Social Support Questionnaire (SSQ), and the Rotter Internal–External (I-E) Scale. The results of a factor analysis of the two best scales in each test (with the exception of the I-E, which has only one scale) are presented in Table 7.3. In support of the hypothesis, all the non-intelligence-related measures loaded exclusively on one factor, whereas the

TABLE 7.3. Factor Analysis of Two Most General Scales per Test (Study 2)

Variable	Factor 1	Factor 2
CTI Emotional Coping	.66	−.11
CTI Behavioral Coping	.72	−.06
ASQ Negative Composite	−.41	−.03
ASQ Positive Composite	.41	.05
I-E Scale[a]	−.50	−.18
SSQ Satisfaction with Support	.35	−.09
SSQ Quantity of Support	.31	−.05
Vocabulary IQ	.04	.46
Abstract IQ	.03	.70

Note. From "Constructive Thinking: A Broad Coping Variable with Specific Components" by S. Epstein and P. Meier, 1989, *Journal of Personality and Social Psychology.* Copyright 1989 by the American Psychological Association. Reprinted by permission.
[a]The I-E Scale provides scores on only a single scale.

two IQ measures, Abstract Thinking and Vocabulary, loaded on another. It is noteworthy that the highest loadings on the first factor were obtained by the two CTI scales.

The Relation of the Constructive Thinking Inventory to Success in Living

A study was conducted to determine how strongly the CTI, relative to other measures of coping style, is related to a variety of criteria of success in living (Epstein & Meier, 1989). Indices of success in living were obtained for success in the workplace, for success in social relationships, for love relationships, for academic achievement, and for mental and physical health.

Subjects were 181 undergraduate volunteers. The indices of success were composites of objective and subjective items. For example, success in work was measured by a scale of four items that included hours of work during the past year, rate of pay during the last job, total earnings during the past year, and estimation of employer satisfaction (as indicated by invitations to return, bonuses, promotions, being fired, salary increases, and estimated favorableness of the letter of recommendation the em-

ployer would write if asked to do so). Items were included in a scale if they contributed to an increase in the internal-consistency reliability (coefficient alpha) of the scale.

Table 7.4 presents the correlations of the best scales from the various tests of coping style with the criterion measures. It can be seen that the CTI scales correlated significantly with all criteria other than academic achievement. The measures of IQ, on the other hand, correlated most strongly with academic achievement and with little else. The scales from other inventories correlated with some of the criteria, but, overall, less widely and less strongly than the CTI scales. Different CTI scales produced different patterns of relations among the criteria, thereby providing evidence of discriminant validity.

Given the broad pool of items from which the CTI was constructed, it is not surprising that it overlaps with all of the domains represented by the other inventories of coping style that were investigated. The question remains as to what, if anything, the other inventories contribute beyond the contribution of the CTI. To answer this question, a series of stepwise multiple regression analyses was conducted that included the single best predictor variable from each of the measures of coping style (CTI, I-E,

TABLE 7.4. Correlations between Major Scales and Criteria of Success in Living

Scale	Work	Love	Social relationships	Academic achievement	Psychological symptoms	Physical symptoms	Self-discipline problems	Alcohol and drug problems
CTI Global Scale	.19*	.26***	.36***	.14	−.39***	−.22**	−.25***	−.22**
CTI Emotional Coping	.15*	.26***	.30***	.01	−.46***	−.28***	−.11	−.23**
CTI Behavioral Coping	.26***	.25***	.27***	.11	−.31***	−.18*	−.25***	−.15*
I-E Scale[a]	−.05	−.04	−.22**	−.04	.21**	.17*	.15	.09
ASQ Overall Composite	−.01	.16*	.34***	.16*	−.05	−.02	−.13	−.06
ASQ Negative Composite	.09	−.21**	−.25**	−.09	.16*	.13	−.12	.15
ASQ Positive Composite	.06	.04	.23**	.14	.07	.09	−.07	.05
SSQ Overall Support	.07	.32***	.62***	−.06	−.09	.01	.00	−.14
SSQ Satisfaction w/Support	.00	.31***	.43***	−.07	.03	.17*	−.04	−.18*
SSQ Quantity of Support	.10	.16*	.49***	.04	−.04	−.02	−.01	−.15
Total IQ	.11	−.04	−.10	.43***	.17*	−.04	−.14	−.02
Vocabulary IQ	.10	−.07	−.15	.30***	.14	−.08	−.22**	−.02
Abstract Thinking IQ	.07	−.02	−.05	.39***	.11	−.01	−.02	−.03

Note. From "Constructive Thinking: A Broad Coping Variable with Specific Components" by S. Epstein and P. Meier, 1989, *Journal of Personality and Social Psychology.* Copyright by the American Psychological Association. Reprinted by permission.
[a]Scored in the direction of "externality."
*p < .05. **p < .01. ***p < .001.

ASQ, and SSQ). Each of the criterion variables (work, love, social relationships, psychological symptoms, physical symptoms, self-discipline problems, alcohol and drug problems), in turn, was treated as the variable to be predicted. With few exceptions, the CTI scales were the only ones that remained in the equation. In other words, in almost all cases the other scales contributed nothing beyond the contribution of the CTI to the prediction of any of the criterion variables. The only exceptions involved the SSQ. In the prediction of Social Relationships and Love, the SSQ and the CTI made independent contributions. In the prediction of physical symptoms, both variables made independent contributions, but, ironically, the SSQ predicted in the opposite direction of what had been expected. Rather than producing an inverse relation with symptoms, which would have suggested that social support had a buffering effect, it produced a direct relation. Those with more symptoms than others reported that they were more satisfied with the support they received. The possibility is worth considering that the symptoms served to elicit support from others and therefore may have been acquired or maintained, in part, because of the secondary gain they provided.

In a study just completed (S. Epstein & L. Katz unpublished results), the Kobasa Hardiness scale was compared to the CTI. The criterion variables consisted of emotional well-being, several measures of physical well-being, and productive load. Emotional well-being was measured by reports of feelings of depression, anxiety, and irritability over the past year. Physical well-being was measured by reports of a variety of common physical symptoms, such as stomach aches, backaches, headaches, and colds over the past year, and productive load was measured by the total constructive effort subjects were expending, including the number of course credits they were taking, the amount of outside work they were performing, the organized social activities in which they were engaged, and their athletic and exercising activities. The CTI scales were significantly more strongly associated with all criteria than the Hardiness scales. When the best predicting CTI scales and Hardiness scales were entered into regression equations, the CTI scales completely displaced the Hardiness scales. In the prediction of emotional well-being, the Hardy Commitment scale by itself accounted for 4% of the variance (significant at the .01 level);

the CTI Emotional Coping scale by itself accounted for 17% of the variance; and both together accounted for 17% of the variance. In the prediction of physical well-being, the Hardy Control scale by itself accounted for 2% of the variance (significant at the .05 level); the CTI Emotional Coping scale by itself accounted for 5% of the variance (significant at the .01 level); and both together accounted for 5% of the variance. In the prediction of productive load, the Hardy Control scale by itself accounted for 1% of the variance (not significant); the CTI Behavioral Coping scale by itself accounted for 9% of the variance (significant at .001 level); and both together accounted for 9% of the variance. The only criterion variable with which the Hardiness scales produced as strong a relation as the CTI scales was Satisfaction with Health, where both produced correlations of .26 (significant at the .001 level). It is noteworthy that Satisfaction with Health was the most subjective of all of the criteria investigated.

In summary, the CTI was demonstrated to subsume, with one exception, the other measures of coping style to which it was compared, which included the ASQ, the I-E, the SSQ, and the Hardiness scales. The only exception was that the SSQ made an independent contribution to the prediction of social variables and to physical symptoms, although the latter was in the opposite direction of what was expected.

Green (1988) conducted a study under the supervision of Epstein, on coping with job-related stress in 92 public school administrators. An inventory was constructed that contained items describing the various kinds of stressful events that occur in the life of a public school administrator. Subjects responded to the inventory by noting how often they experienced each of the events and how stressful they found each to be.

The following terms were defined: "sensitivity," degree to which an event is regarded as stressful when it occurs; "load," job-related tasks with which an individual must cope; "stress," sum of products of load × sensitivity for all events. Factor analysis of the items indicated that there were two types of stress, "administrative" (impersonal tasks, such as making out budgets) and "interpersonal." Accordingly, separate scores on sensitivity, load, and stress were obtained for each type of stress. Interpersonal situations were generally found to be associated with higher levels of reported sensitivity and stress than were impersonal ones.

The CTI Global scale was strongly associated with sensitivity but unrelated to load. A significant relation between the CTI Global scale and stress could be accounted for almost exclusively by the relation of the CTI Global scale to sensitivity. In other words, people who were poor constructive thinkers were sensitive to many job-related events, particularly interpersonal ones, and therefore were likely to experience a great deal of stress. Constructive thinking was also found to be positively associated with job satisfaction and to be negatively associated with self-reported symptoms of mental distress and physical illness during the past year. In summary, the study indicated that what is experienced as stressful lies more in the eyes of the beholder than in the objective occurrence of events, and that those who experienced job-related events as more stressful than others were lower in job-satisfaction and in mental and physical well-being than others.

A Laboratory Study of Coping with Stress

In a recently completed study (Katz & Epstein, 1990) subjects who were among the upper and lower 5% of constructive thinkers as measured by the CTI were exposed to two laboratory stress tests: counting backwards by sevens and mirror tracing. The object of the study was to examine the thoughts, emotions, and physiological reactions of good and poor constructive thinkers when confronted with stressful tasks.

Measures of spontaneous thoughts, self-reported emotions on an adjective checklist, and physiological reactions (pulse rate, systolic and diastolic blood pressure, finger and wrist temperature) were taken at four points in time: before the stress period, immediately after the stress period, after a first recovery period, and after a second recovery period. Subjects also rated the degree of stress they experienced, their sources of concern, and their performance. At the end of the experiment, interviewers rated their impressions of the subjects on a number of variables. Self-report measures were obtained of mental well-being and physical illness during the past 4 months.

We were particularly interested in the kinds of destructive thoughts that poor constructive thinkers have when confronted with a known

stressor, and in the relation of constructive thinking to physiological and self-reported emotional reactivity. We also wished to verify previous findings that poor constructive thinkers have poorer mental and physical health than good constructive thinkers, and to fill in some of the links in the causal chain of inferences on why this may be so. Our reasoning was that the reduced level of mental and physical well-being in poor constructive thinkers is a result of the greater stress they experience because of the way in which they construe potentially stressful events.

When self-reported negative thoughts related and unrelated to the experiment were examined, highly significant group differences were found. It can be seen in Figure 7.3 that poor constructive thinkers had uniformly more negative thoughts unrelated to the experiment than good constructive thinkers did over all four periods. As for negative thoughts related to the experiment, both the main effect for groups and the interaction of groups × period were highly significant. Poor constructive thinkers had more negative thoughts at all periods, but the difference was greatest in the stress period. It may be concluded that, compared to good constructive thinkers, poor constructive thinkers have more negative thoughts in general than good constructive thinkers, and that they react to a stressor with a greater increase in negative thoughts.

When positive and neutral thoughts were examined as a function of periods, no group differences emerged either as a main effect or in interaction with period. Thus, it appears that poor constructive thinking is specifically associated with negative construals, and is unrelated to other kinds of thoughts.

In order to examine the effect of stress on emotions, the emotion variables were factor-analyzed. Two broad factors were obtained, one for Negative Emotions and one for Positive Arousal, or "Engagement". The results for Negative Emotions paralleled those for frequency of negative thoughts related to the experiment. (see Figure 7.4). As in the case of positive thoughts, the groups did not differ in positive arousal. However, there was an increase in positive arousal during the stress period for both groups, indicating that subjects in general felt more alert, energetic, and challenged during that period.

There were significant group differences on two physiological measures: diastolic blood

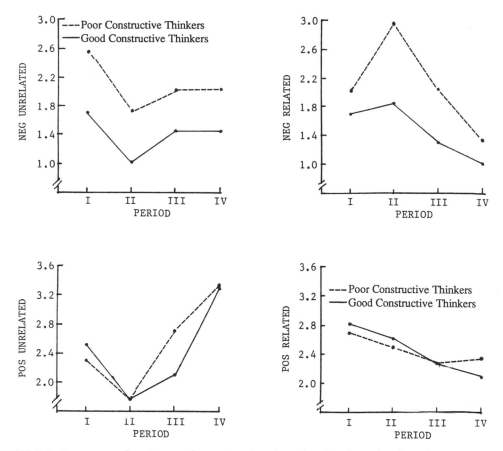

FIGURE 7.3. Frequency of positive and negative thoughts related and unrelated to the experiment for subjects high and low in constructive thinking at four periods: I, prestress; II, stress; III, first recovery period; IV, second recovery period. From *Constructive Thinking and Coping with Laboratory-Induced Stress* by L. Katz and S. Epstein, 1990, manuscript submitted for publication. Reprinted by permission of the authors.

pressure and finger temperature. Surprisingly, the differences were not associated with the stress period, but with the second recovery period. Poor constructive thinkers exhibited a greater increase in physiological arousal in this period than good constructive thinkers, as indicated by a greater increase in diastolic blood pressure and a greater decrease in finger temperature (see Figure 7.5). This finding is in particular need of replication as it was unanticipated. Assuming the finding holds up, one possible explanation is that it is the result of an after-discharge of anxiety following greater inhibition by the poor constructive thinking group. Another possibility is that the poor constructive thinkers became more distressed than the good constructive thinkers after negatively evaluating their constructive thinking and per-

formance in the interview period, which preceded the second recovery period.

Poor constructive thinkers rated the experiment as more stressful than good constructive thinkers. They also reported that they were more distressed about their performance than the good constructive thinkers reported. This was because of the high standards they set for themselves and because they were more concerned about the impression they made on the examiner, although they actually performed as well as the good constructive thinkers. The examiner, who was unaware of the groups to which the subjects belonged, rated poor constructive thinkers as less confident and more self-conscious than good constructive thinkers.

There were highly reliable differences on the measures of physical and mental well-being

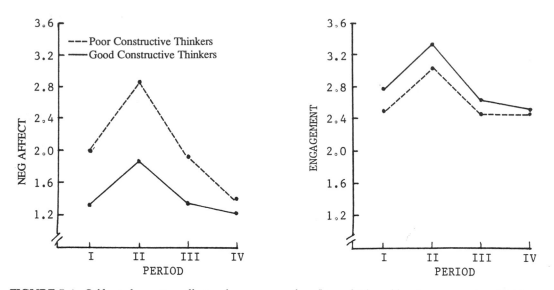

FIGURE 7.4. Self-rated negative affect and engagement for subjects high and low in constructive thinking at four periods: I, prestress; II, stress; III, first recovery period; IV, second recovery period. From *Constructive Thinking and Coping with Laboratory-Induced Stress* by L. Katz and S. Epstein, 1990, manuscript submitted for publication. Reprinted by permission of the authors.

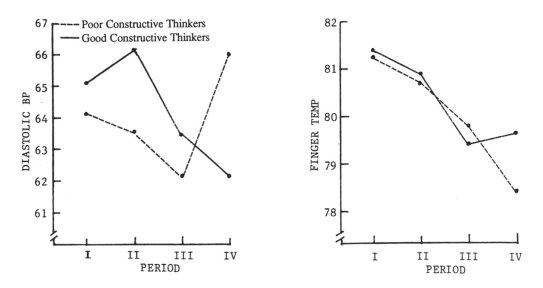

FIGURE 7.5. Physiological reactions for subjects high and low in constructive thinking at four periods: I, prestress; II, stress; III, first recovery period; IV, second recovery period. From *Constructive Thinking and Coping with Laboratory-Induced Stress* by L. Katz and S. Epstein, 1990, manuscript submitted for publication. Reprinted by permission of the authors.

during the past 4 months. Poor constructive thinkers reported a greater incidence of emotional distress and physical illnesses, such as stomachaches and headaches, than good constructive thinkers. In order to determine whether the kinds of negative thoughts a person had in the experiment were related to proneness to have physical symptoms, a regression analysis was conducted that included sex of the subject as a control variable, negative thoughts related to the experiment, negative thoughts unrelated to the experiment (both recorded during the experiment), and negative emotions during the experiment as predictor variables. The predicted variable was number of physical symptoms reported during the past 4 months. The only variable that was significant (.01 level) was negative thoughts related to the experiment ($r = .35$).

It will be recalled that negative thoughts about the experiment included thoughts about poor performance relative to one's own high standards, thoughts about having made a poor impression on the examiner, and the belief that one did poorly compared to others, despite actually having performed as well. The results, therefore, indicate that people who engaged in negative thinking directed against themselves, as opposed to other kinds of negative thinking, such as thinking about chores they had to do, were particularly prone to have stress-produced physical symptoms. Whatever the explanation, the finding of differential relations for two kinds of negative thinking and an absence of a negative emotions effect is important because it indicates that the results cannot be explained away by a general negativity factor (Costa & McRae, 1987; Watson & Pennebaker, 1989).

The Investigation of Constructive Thinking in Everyday Life

So far, all of the studies reported investigated constructive thinking with a self-report inventory, the CTI. To determine whether a similar structure of constructive thinking would emerge in records of everyday behavior, a study was conducted in which 40 college students kept daily records of their most stressful experience for 30 days. They first recorded the events in narrative form and then used a standard system for scoring the amount of stress they experienced, the ways in which they construed the situations, their mental and behavioral coping reactions, and whether they had any symptoms either before or after the event. They also took a battery of personality inventories that included the CTI.

Space limitations permit only a limited review of the extensive findings from this study. It is planned to analyze the data idiographically as well as nomothetically (see Epstein, 1983), but so far only the nomothetic analyses have been completed.

Factor analyses were conducted of the everyday mental and behavioral coping reactions. Two factors were found for mental coping: Adaptive Mental Coping, which included the variables Perspective Taking, Positive Thinking, Realistic Thinking, Exhortation, and Negative Thinking (scoring reversed); and Unrealistic Mental Coping, which included the variables Unrealistic Thinking, Denial, and Withdrawal. Two factors were also obtained from the factor analysis of behavioral coping: Adaptive Behavioral Coping, which included the variables Assertion, Achievement, Helpfulness, Instrumental Action, and Support Seeking; and Maladaptive Behavioral Coping, which included the variables Attack, Uncontrolled Expression of Emotions, Support Seeking, and Self-Punishment. It is noteworthy that Support Seeking was represented in both the adaptive and maladaptive factors. This can be attributed to the difference in degree and manner in which support was sought. In the first case, it represented the constructive use of social resources, whereas in the second it involved dependent attachment.

The structure of constructive thinking in daily life clearly does not correspond on a one-to-one basis with the factors in the CTI. One reason for this is that the coping variables in the study of daily stress did not lend themselves to the same kind of categorization as the items in the CTI. For example, there were no items in the list of everyday variables that were exemplars of superstitious thinking, categorical thinking, or naive optimism. The kinds of items that could be reasonably included in one format were simply not appropriate for inclusion in the other. Nevertheless, there were important areas of correspondence. For example, both methods provided evidence of a global coping factor. When the four coping factors in the data from the everyday behavior were correlated, there was enough commonality to justify combining them into a single measure. At the same time, there was sufficient independence to justify retaining them as independent scales. The strongest factors in the CTI, by far, were Emotional Coping and Behavioral Coping. These were replicated in the two major daily-stress factors, Adaptive Mental Coping and Adaptive Behavioral Coping. The scales (also factors) in the CTI other than Emotional Coping and Behavioral Coping refer to maladaptive ways of coping that are consolidated in the daily-stress factor of Unrealistic Mental Coping, as indicated by its significant correlations with the CTI scales Categorical Thinking, Superstitious Thinking, and Negative Thinking. The daily-stress factor of Maladaptive Behavioral Coping was not significantly correlated with any CTI scale, but was significantly correlated with scales in other inventories, such as the Neuroticism scale in the PETS. It may be concluded that although there is not a direct correspondence between all of the CTI scales and all of daily-stress factors, there is an impressive degree of correspondence between the larger factors, and there is coherence among the remaining factors.

Among other findings of interest, the daily-stress factors were coherently and differentially associated with daily moods and with a variety of personality inventories. For example, the factors of Adaptive Mental Coping and Adaptive Behavioral Coping were most strongly associated with positive daily moods, whereas the factors of Unrealistic Mental Coping and Maladaptive Behavioral Coping were most strongly associated with negative daily moods. Adaptive Mental Coping was positively associated with ego strength, agreeableness, and satisfaction with love life. It was also significantly positively associated with chronological age, suggesting that it, like the CTI scales, improves with experience in living. The factor of Unrealistic Mental Coping was associated with depression, anxiety, guilt over hostility, low ego strength, low self-esteem, and serious family problems in childhood (e.g., death, divorce, and institutionalization of a parent for mental illness). The factor of Adaptive Behavioral Coping was associated with high ego strength, extraversion, integration, caring, and age. The factor of Maladaptive Behavioral Coping was associated with guilt over hostility, neuroticism, and high arousal.

In conclusion, there is evidence in the records of daily living, as in the CTI, of a global coping factor and of group coping factors that are associated with daily moods, personality variables, early environmental influences, and mental health.

Parental Influence on the Development of Constructive Thinking

The relation between the constructive thinking of parents and their children was investigated in a recently completed study by S. Epstein and M. Lee (1988). A revised version of the CTI was administered to 79 college students and their parents. The students took the CTI as if they were their parents. They also took the MFP inventory, which, it will be recalled, provides information on relationships with parents during childhood.

It was found that the constructive thinking of the parents was significantly better than that of their children, which is consistent with previous findings that constructive thinking improves with experience in living. There were no sex differences on global constructive thinking. College men and women had nearly identical means, and the same was true of their mothers and fathers. Almost all the students were between 18 and 22 years old; the age range of their parents was 36–72. To determine whether constructive thinking continues to improve with age into the later years, correlations between age and constructive thinking were computed for the parents. A nonsignificant correlation close to zero was found. To test the possibility of an increase in constructive thinking followed by a decrease in old age, the scattergram was inspected. There was no evidence of a curvilinear relation. It may be concluded that constructive thinking increases sharply from late adolescence to adulthood, but does not continue to increase through the adult years.

Correlations were computed between the CTI scores of sons and daughters and their fathers and mothers. For both sons and daughters, correlation with fathers' but not with mothers' global constructive thinking was significant. On only two scales, Categorical Thinking and Esoteric Thinking, was there a significant correlation between mothers' and daughters' scores. (Esoteric Thinking, a new scale in the revised CTI, includes items such as believing in ghosts, flying saucers, astrology, and conventional superstitions.)

The finding that global constructive thinking for children of both sexes was more similar to that of their fathers than their mothers was unexpected. This raises the question of why the daughters modeled their constructive thinking after their fathers when the constructive thinking of their mothers was just as good. A clue is provided by the results on the children's perception of their parents' constructive thinking. When the daughters simulated their fathers' and mothers' responses, the mean for their fathers' perceived global constructive thinking was significantly higher than for their mothers'. Thus, the daughters had the mistaken belief that their fathers were better constructive thinkers than their mothers. It is noteworthy that the sons did not show the same bias, but evaluated their parents as equal in constructive thinking. Why the daughters modeled the poorer qualities of their mothers' constructing thinking, such as their esoteric and categorical thinking, and the better qualities of their fathers' constructive thinking is an interesting puzzle that will have to await future research to solve.

Correlations of CTI scores with MFP scores indicated that for male students global constructive thinking was significantly associated with encouragement of independence by fathers and acceptance by mothers. For female students, global constructive thinking was significantly associated with encouragement of independence and acceptance by both mothers and fathers. The strongest correlations of constructive thinking for sons were with fathers' child-rearing practices and for daughters with mothers' child-rearing practices. Regression analysis revealed that the strongest overall combination of mothers' and fathers' child-rearing practices predicting the constructive thinking of their children consisted of an independence-encouraging father and an accepting mother.

In summary, the results indicated that the college students of both sexes tended to model their constructive thinking after that of their fathers. They did this despite the fact that their fathers' constructive thinking was no better than their mothers'. That parental rearing practices play a role in the development of constructive thinking was indicated by the finding that an accepting mother and an independence-encouraging father were the conditions most conducive to high levels of constructive thinking in children of both sexes. An additional finding of interest was that a condition particularly conducive to the development of poor constructive thinking was having two parents who were categorical thinkers. When only one was, the influence of that one was moderated by the influence of the other.

The Influence of Deception on Constructive Thinking Inventory Scores

An obvious problem with self-report inventories is that they can easily be falsified. This is certainly true for many of the items in the CTI, where it is obvious what a good response is. Yet it is conceivable that there are several items that are not transparent, and that these could be used to construct a "lie-free" scale. Moreover, whether or not such a scale could be constructed, it is of interest to determine what kinds of attributes people think are most admired by others. With these considerations in mind, a study was conducted by S. Epstein and P. Bonneau (1988) to determine how falsifiable the CTI is.

The most recent version of the CTI contains an experimental scale that it was hoped would prove to be less susceptible to faking than other scales. The scale is composed of items that were found to be significantly correlated with the CTI Global scale but were not significantly correlated with a social desirability, or "lie," scale.

The latest version of the CTI and the Seligman ASQ were administered to 79 college students under two conditions, once with instructions to be honest and the other with instructions to make the best impression possible, as if applying for a job that they desperately wanted to obtain. The ASQ was selected because it is a novel test of coping style that may be difficult to fake: Instead of responding to standard questions, subjects respond in an open-ended way to vignettes, in the manner of a projective test. They then score their own responses for the degree to which their responses refer to attributes that are internal, general, and stable in themselves.

Under the faking condition, the means of most scales in the CTI changed significantly (.001 level) in a more favorable direction. The following did not change significantly: The Lie-Free scale, the Polarized Thinking scale (a facet of Categorical Thinking), the Thought Influence scale (a facet of Esoteric Thinking), and the Simplistic Thinking scale (which combines positive and negative overgeneralization). All 12 ASQ scales changed in a favorable direction at the .001 level of significance.

It is possible, of course, for scale means to remain the same in two conditions and yet for the position of individuals within conditions to shift radically. If this were the case in the present situation, the scales with means that did not change would be useless under conditions of deception. To examine this possibility, correlations were computed between the honest and faked conditions of the scales for which the means remained stable, to determine whether the rank order of individuals also remained stable. The following correlations were obtained: .54 for the Lie-Free scale, .47 for Polarized Thinking, .47 for Major Occult Beliefs, and .38 for Simplistic Thinking. When these correlations were corrected for attenuation, they increased, respectively, to .98, .61, .64, and .54. Adding sufficient items should therefore make it possible to construct a Lie-Free scale that, when faked, almost perfectly reproduces the score that would be obtained if the same scales were responded to honestly. Apparently the Lie-Free scale contains items that people do not know how to fake, and they assume that their honest responses to these items are the best ones.

Of course, even if future research verifies that the Lie-Free scale is immune from deception, if cannot be assumed that it is a necessarily useful measure of constructive thinking. The possibility would remain that in the process of making the scale lie-free, items were selected that are inadequate measures of overall constructive thinking. A critical step that remains to be taken is to demonstrate that the Lie-Free scale correlates significantly with appropriate criteria of success in living under conditions of deception. At this point, all that can be said is that the Lie-Free scale is highly promising.

In addition to contributing to the development of a deception-proof scale, the findings from this study have substantive contributions to make about the nature of constructive thinking. They indicate that people who overgeneralize broadly, who think in a polarized way, and who maintain strange beliefs generally do not view these ways of thinking as undesirable, but regard them as the most sensible way to think.

FUTURE DIRECTIONS

What are the most important implications of CEST? None has more far-reaching consequences than the assumption that there are separate experiential and rational systems. If there are two systems, as proposed, then the usual practice of referring to "*the* conceptual system" is clearly misguided. The fact that the two systems often overlap to a considerable extent is very likely a major reason why the distinction has been overlooked. Given sufficient overlap, it is possible to get by, within limits, by measuring either system and ignoring

the other. The price for doing so, however, is conceptual confusion and a loss of precision. If one is to take the viewpoint of CEST seriously, it is important to devise means of measuring cognitions in the two systems separately, to examine the role that each has in predicting behavior, and to treat the discrepancy between them as important data in its own right.

As in almost everything else, there are undoubtedly important individual differences in the degree to which people's behavior is determined by the rational system relative to the experiential system. Undoubtedly some people have a predominantly rational orientation, and others a predominantly experiential one. It would be useful to construct a measure of such individual differences. Such a measure would be useful in determining what kinds of messages are most effective with what kinds of people. It would also be useful for predicting behavior from attitudes and for examining the question of whether a balance between the two orientations is associated with better adjustment than an extreme orientation in either direction.

Another important topic for future research is the course of development of constructive thinking over the lifespan. What are the factors in child rearing and in other environmental influences that determine the level of a child's constructive thinking? What subtle influences in socialization differentially influence the development of constructive thinking in boys and girls? What is the normal course of development of constructive thinking over the entire lifespan, and how stable is a person's relative position? How, if at all, is constructive thinking related to that elusive concept called "wisdom"? To examine constructive thinking in young children, it will be necessary to devise measures other than self-report inventories. Developing such tests is an important challenge for the future.

An important implication of CEST is that the Freudian conceptualization of the unconscious leaves much to be desired and should be replaced by a more comprehensive model. An adequate theory of the unconscious must recognize that a failure to assimilate information occurs not only because of guilt over taboo thoughts and impulses, but also because people need to maintain the coherence and stability of their conceptual systems. It also should be recognized that not all that is unconscious was learned before language was available or was repressed after it was; most behavior is unconscious because that is the natural mode of operation of the human mind, as it is more efficient for behavior to be directed automatically than to require conscious reflection. Given the assumption that there is a separate experiential system that automatically assimilates experience and directs behavior, two important lines of inquiry are suggested. One is to establish the rules of inference of the experiential system. In this regard, a useful beginning would be to test the tentative model proposed by CEST. The second is to conduct research on the implications of harmony versus disharmony between the two systems.

Another important implication concerns the development of remedial procedures for improving constructive thinking. It follows from the nature of the experiential system that imagery should be an important vehicle for influencing the experiential system. It thus becomes important to conduct research on the use of imagery for changes in maladaptive beliefs in the experiential system. Research should also be conducted on the supplementary use of didactic procedures. It may be useful, for example, to instruct individuals on the nature of the experiential system and on how to use their rational systems to provide corrective experiences for their experiential systems. It may be particularly useful to teach people about the influence of the experiential mind on the rational mind, so that they can identify self-serving appeals by politicians and advertisers for short-term solutions to problems that require more complex long-term solutions.

Finally, it should be considered that it is no less important to train the experiential mind than the rational mind. Considering the importance of the experiential system, it is ironic, indeed, that our society requires 12 years of compulsory education for training its citizens' rational minds and none for training their experiential minds. A particularly important challenge for the future is to devise procedures for educating the experiential mind. Such programs need to be introduced into the school system, not as frills, but as serious programs for improving the functioning of the entire mind.

ACKNOWLEDGMENTS

Preparation of this chapter and the research reported in it were supported by Research Grant No. MH01293 and Research Scientist Award No. K05 MH00363 from the National Institute of Mental Health. I wish to acknowledge the contributions of Carolyn Holstein, who did the computing on most of the studies reported here, and of Alice Epstein, who critically reviewed previous drafts of the chapter.

REFERENCES

Adorno, T. W., Frenkel-Brunswik, E., Levinson, D. J., & Sanford, R. N. (1950). *The authoritarian personality.* New York: Harper.

Allport, G. W. (1961). *Pattern and growth in personality.* New York: Harcourt, Brace & World. (Original work published 1927)

Beck, A. T. (1976). *Cognitive therapy and the emotional disorders.* New York: International Universities Press.

Bowlby, J. (1973). *Attachment and loss: Vol. 2. Separation, anxiety, and anger.* New York: Basic Books.

Bulman, R. J., & Wortman, C. B. (1977). Attributions of blame and coping in the "real world": Severe accident victims react to their lot. *Journal of Personality and Social Psychology, 35,* 351–363.

Cashdan, S. (1988). *Object relations therapy: Using the relationship.* New York: Norton.

Catlin, G., & Epstein, S. (1990). *The relation of basic beliefs to extreme life events and childhood relationships with parents.* Unpublished manuscript.

Costa, P. T., & McRae, R. R. (1987). Hypochondriasis, neuroticism, and aging: When are somatic complaints unfounded? *American Psychologist, 40,* 19–28.

Dollard, J., & Miller, N. E. (1950). *Personality and psychotherapy: An analysis in terms of learning, thinking, and culture.* New York: McGraw-Hill.

Ellis, A. (1962). *Reason and emotion in psychotherapy.* New York: Lyle Stuart.

Epstein, S. (1973). The self-concept revisited, or a theory of a theory. *American Psychologist, 28,* 404–416.

Epstein, S. (1976). Anxiety, arousal, and the self-concept. In I. G. Sarason & C. D. Spielberger (Eds.), *Stress and anxiety* (Vol. 3, pp. 183–224). Washington, DC: Hemisphere.

Epstein, S. (1979). Natural healing processes of the mind: I. Acute schizophrenic disorganization. *Schizophrenia Bulletin, 5,* 313–321.

Epstein, S. (1980). The self-concept: A review and the proposal of an integrated theory of personality. In E. Staub (Ed.), *Personality: Basic issues and current research* (pp. 82–132). Englewood Cliffs, NJ: Prentice-Hall.

Epstein, S. (1981). The unity principles versus the reality and pleasure principles, or the tale of the scorpion and the frog. In M. D. Lynch, A. A. Norem-Hebeisen, & K. J. Gergen (Eds.), *Self-concept: Advances in theory and research* (pp. 27–37). Cambridge, MA: Ballinger.

Epstein, S. (1982). Conflict and stress. In S. Breznitz & L. Goldberger (Eds.), *Handbook of stress* (pp. 49–68). New York: Free Press.

Epstein, S. (1983). The unconscious, the preconscious and the self-concept. In J. Suls & A. Greenwald (Eds.), *Psychological perspectives on the self* (Vol. 2, pp. 219–247). Hillsdale, NJ: Erlbaum.

Epstein, S. (1985). The implications of cognitive–experiential self-theory for research in social psychology and personality. *Journal for the Theory of Social Behavior, 15*, 283–310.

Epstein, S. (1987). Implications of cognitive self-theory for psychopathology and psychotherapy. In N. Cheshire & H. Thomas (Eds.), *Self-esteem and psychotherapy* (pp. 43–58). New York: Wiley.

Epstein, S. (1988). *The measurement of drive and conflict in humans.* Progress report for the National Institute of Mental Health.

Epstein, S. (1990a). The self-concept, the traumatic neurosis, and the structure of personality. In D. Ozer, J. M. Healy, Jr., & A. J. Stewart (Eds.), *Perspectives on personality* (Vol. 3). Greenwich, CT: JAI Press.

Epstein, S. (1990b). Cognitive-experiential self-theory: Implications for developmental psychology. In M. R. Gunnar (Ed.). *Minnesota symposium on child psychology series.* Hillsdale, NJ: Erlbaum.

Epstein, S., & Bonneau, P. (1988). *Faking the Attribution Style Questionnaire and the Constructive Thinking Inventory.* Unpublished manuscript, University of Massachusetts at Amherst.

Epstein, S., & Erskine, N. (1983). The development of personal theories of reality. In D. Magnusson & V. L. Allen (Eds.), *Human development: An interactional perspective* (pp. 133–147). New York: Academic Press.

Epstein, S., & Lee, M. (1988). *The relation between college students' and parents' constructive thinking.* Unpublished manuscript, University of Massachusetts at Amherst.

Epstein, S., & Meier, P. (1989). Constructive thinking: A broad coping variable with specific components. *Journal of Personality and Social Psychology, 57*, 332–350.

Fletcher, K. E. (1988). *Belief systems, exposure to stress, and posttraumatic stress disorder in Vietnam veterans.* Unpublished doctoral dissertation, University of Massachusetts–Amherst.

Folkman, S., & Larzarus, R. S. (1980. An analysis of coping in a middle-aged community sample. *Journal of Health and Social Behavior, 21*, 219–239.

Green, M. (1988). *Occupational stress: A study of public school administrators in southeast Massachusetts.* Unpublished doctoral dissertation, University of Massachusetts at Amherst.

Horney, K. (1945). *Our inner conflicts.* New York: Norton.

James, W. (1910). *Psychology: The briefer course.* New York: Holt.

Janoff-Bulman, R. (1989). Assumptive worlds and the stress of traumatic events: Applications of the schema construct. *Social Cognition, 7*, 113–136.

Katz, L., & Epstein, S. (1990). *Constructive thinking and coping with laboratory-induced stress.* Manuscript submitted for publication.

Kelly, G. A. (1955). *The psychology of personal constructs* (2 vols). New York: Norton.

Kuhn, T. S. (1970). *The structure of scientific revolutions* (rev. ed.). Chicago: University of Chicago Press.

Lazarus, R. S., & Folkman, S. (1984). *Stress, appraisal, and coping.* New York: Springer Publishing Co.

Lecky, P. (1945/1969). *Self-consistency: A theory of personality.* Garden City, New York: Doubleday.

Markus, H. (1977). Self-schemata and processing information about the self. *Journal of Personality and Social Psychology, 35*, 63–78.

Mischel, W. (1973). Toward a cognitive social learning reconceptualization of personality. *Psychological Review, 80*, 252–283.

Piaget, J. (1973). The affective unconscious and the cognitive unconscious. *Journal of the American Psychoanalytic Association, 21*, 249–261.

Rogers, C. R. (1951). *Client-centered therapy.* Boston: Houghton Mifflin.

Snygg, D., & Combs, A. W. (1949). *Individual behavior.* New York: Harper & Row.

Swann, W. B., Jr. (1983). Self-verification: Bringing social reality into harmony with the self. In J. Suls & A. G. Greenwald (Eds.). *Psychological perspectives on the self* (Vol. 2, pp. 33–66). Hillsdale, NJ: Erlbaum.

Taylor, S. E., & Brown, J. D. (1988). Illusion and well-being: A social psychological perspective on mental health. *Psychological Bulletin, 103*, 193–210.

Taylor, S. E., Wood, J. V., & Lichtman, R. R. (1983). It could be worse: Selective evaluation as a response to victimization. *Journal of Social Issues, 39*(2), 19–40.

Tomkins, S. S. (1980). Affect as amplification: Some modifications in theory. In R. Plutchik & H. Kellerman (Eds.), *Emotion: Theory, research and experience, Vol. 1, Theories of emotion* (pp. 141–164). New York: Academic Press.

Watson, D., & Pennebaker, J. W. (1989). Health complaints, stress, and distress: Exploring the central role of negative affectivity. *Psychological Review, 96*, 234–254.

White, R. W. (1959). Motivation reconsidered: The concept of competence. *Psychological Review, 66*, 297–333.

Wortman, C. B. (1976). Causal attributions and personal control. In J. H. Harvey, W. J. Ickes, & R. F. Kidd (Eds.), *New directions in attributions research* (Vol. 1, pp. 23–52). Hillsdale, NJ: Erlbaum.

Wortman, C. B., & Dunkel-Schetter, C. (1979). Interpersonal relationship and cancer: A theoretical analysis. *Journal of Social Issues, 3*(5), 120–155.

Chapter 8

Personality Development from an Interactional Perspective

David Magnusson
University of Stockholm, Sweden

THE NEED TO INTEGRATE PERSPECTIVES AND APPROACHES IN PSYCHOLOGY

The overriding goal for psychological theorizing and research can be said to be understanding and explaining why individuals think, feel, act, and react as they do in real life (Magnusson, 1988). In order to achieve this, theory and research must address various molecular and molar aspects of individual functioning.

In order to understand and explain individuals' functioning at certain stages of development, as well as individual differences in this respect, it is necessary to distinguish between theories and models that discuss this issue in a *current* perspective and those that cover it in a *developmental* perspective. Models that are restricted to the current perspective analyze and explain why individuals function as they do in terms of their current psychological and biological dispositions, independently of the developmental process that might have led to the present state of affairs. Developmental models analyze and explain current functioning

in terms of an individual's developmental history; they are concerned with those aspects of the individual and his or her environment that are involved in the individual's developmental history, and the ways in which they have operated in the process leading to the present way of functioning. The current and the developmental perspectives on individual functioning are complementary; we need both of them.

Fragmentation: An Impediment to Real Progress

Many of those who have been interested in what hampers and what promotes progress in psychology as a science agree that one of the main impediments is the fragmentation of the field. It has been compartmentalized into subareas, each with its own concepts, methods, and research strategies (see, e.g., Staats, 1981; Toulmin, 1981). One implication of this fragmentation is that empirical research is not planned, implemented, and interpreted in one general frame of reference. Thus we lack a common language for the interpretation of empirical results and for the exchange of ideas. As a result, much psychological theorizing goes in a circle instead of moving forward. Psychological research thus runs the risk of being caught in what is the trend of the day, rather than being based on accumulated knowledge and real progress in theory. What we need is a common "model of the person" as a framework for planning, implementation, and interpretation of empirical research.

Metatheoretical Approaches to the Study of Individual Functioning

At a metatheoretical level, it is possible to distinguish three main approaches to the study of individual functioning, the identification of which contributes to placing the interactional approach within a total perspective. Few researchers adhere strictly to only one approach; it is a matter of where the researcher places the "center of gravity." The main distinction lies in each approach's interpretation of the main factors presumed to guide individual functioning, in terms of both the current perspective and the developmental process.

The first approach may be designated "mentalistic"; it emphasizes mental factors as the central ones for understanding why individuals function and develop as they do. According to this view, the main explanation for an individual's current functioning and development is to be found in the functioning of the brain, which can be analyzed in terms of intrapsychic processes of perceptions, thoughts, emotions, values, goals, plans, conflicts, and so forth.

The second approach identifies biological factors as having a primary influence on individual functioning. Thus various aspects of functioning and individual differences in this respect can be traced back to individual differences in biological factors. When biological models for current functioning are applied, an individual's thoughts, feelings, actions, and reactions are assumed to be determined basically by his or her biological equipment and its way of functioning. Primary determining factors are assumed to be found in the physiological system, in the brain, and in the autonomic

nervous system. An important aspect of the traditional application of this view is the assumption that there is a unidirectional causality between biological factors, on the one hand, and mental factors and conduct, on the other. Biology comes first; thinking, emotion, and action come as results.

When biological models of individual development are applied, the major determining guiding factors are genetic and maturational. In its extreme version, this model implies that individual differences in the course of development have their roots in genes, with only a minor role (if any) played by environmental and mental factors. This view was characterized by Cairns (1979a) in terms of the organism as a "gene machine." The view was discussed and criticized by Hunt (1961), who characterized the main elements of it in terms of "predetermined development" and "fixed intelligence."

The third approach locates the main causal factors for individual functioning in the environment. It is reflected in theories and models of human behavior at all levels of generality for environmental factors: macrosocial theories, theories about the role of the "sick family," and stimulus–response (S-R) models for various aspects of individual functioning, to give a few examples. A representative expression of an environmental approach to current functioning is to be found in traditional experimentally oriented personality research. Within this orientation, laws and principles for individual functioning are studied in terms of reactions to variation in the intensity of one or several aspects of the physical environment, most often in a laboratory setting. The trend in personality research to assign the dominating determinant of behavior to situations and situational conditions has been discussed and criticized in terms of "situationism" (Bowers, 1973).

In research on developmental psychology, various environmental streams can be identified. The behavioristic model gives the environment a strong determining role in the development process (Skinner, 1978). The most extreme environmental view on development was expressed by Watson (1930):

Give me a dozen healthy infants, well-formed, and my own specified world to bring them up in and I'll guarantee to take any one at random and train him to become any type of specialist I might select—doctor, lawyer, artist, merchant, chief—and, yes, even beggarman and thief, regardless of his talents, penchants, tendencies, abilities, vocations, and race of his ancestors. (p. 104)

An additional influential line, which had a strong impact on developmental psychology during the 1960s and 1970s, is rooted in sociology. The sociological influence is reflected in the vast amount of research on children growing up in environments differing with respect to general geographical or social characteristics (e.g., rural vs. urban cultures and various levels of social class) or with respect to more specific characteristics (e.g., one- vs. two-parent families, home vs. day care, mother's employment status, etc.). (See Bronfenbrenner & Crouter, 1983, for a discussion of "the new demography.")

As in the biological model, an essential characteristic of the environmental model is the assumption, most often implicit, of unidirectional causality—in this case, between environmental factors and individual functioning. This characteristic is reflected in the planning of research as well as in the interpretation of empirical results, which frequently involves the presentation of numerous correlations between characteristics of the environment and individual factors.

An old controversy in developmental research is that between a biological and an environmentalistic view. The debate can be traced back to the early times of Western civilization. Plato, in his *Republic*, discussed the central issue of justice in the perspective of human character as determined by nature *(physis)* and nurture *(trophe)*. In the modern history of psychology, the biological view was formulated and strengthened by the work of Galton and the publication of his book *Hereditary Genius* (1869). With respect to intelligence, his line of reasoning was followed in the beginning of this century by Terman, Goddard, and Yerkes, among others, all of whom believed that the intelligence tests that had been constructed at that time actually measured fixed and innate intelligence. As pointed out by Eccles and Robinson (1985), it was chiefly in the 18th century that the thesis of environmentalistic determinism became "official," much influenced by the empiricist psychology presented by John Locke.

A view emphasizing the role of environment and the possibilities of influencing individual development by environmental factors was advocated by Binet (1910). He strongly argued against the view of intelligence as an inherited, fixed quantity. He proposed that with practice, encouragement, and methods of instruction geared to the child's type of intelligence, one could succeed in increasing the child's attention, memory, and judgment. Through this process, the child's demonstrated intelligence would actually increase. Consequently, Binet developed a program of "mental orthopedics" as a method to improve the intelligence of mentally retarded children. Indications that the nature–nurture issue is still alive can be found in the works by Kamin (1974), representing an environmentalistic position, and by Jensen (1981), advocating a hereditarian view.

A somewhat younger controversy is that between the mentalistic and the environmentalistic perspective, which is reflected in the debate between proponents of a cognitive approach (see Piaget, 1948; Vygotsky, 1962) and proponents of a socialization approach (see Miller & Dollard, 1941) to social development and behavior. An example drawn from theories of moral development may illustrate the issue. For Kohlberg (1969), moral development is closely related to cognitive development. In contrast, both Marx and Freud, from very different perspectives, believed that conscience as the basis for moral choice is instilled from the outside through a process of socialization beyond the individual's control.

Consequences of Different Approaches

The distinction among the three approaches is not merely one of theoretical interest. It has important implications for planning and performing personality and developmental research; it also carries essential consequences for psychological application in the treatment of individual maladjustment, and for political and administrative decisions and actions in the society at large.

This point can be illustrated by the current discussion concerning the appropriate treatment of mental problems and mental illness. Each approach recommends different methods for curing patients and for forestalling the development of maladaption. The mentalistic approach sees the main cause of an individual's suffering—from depression or schizophrenia, for example—as the malfunctioning of thought processes. The natural treatment is then psychological therapy. According to the biological approach, an individual's thoughts, emotions, and actions can be influenced basically by changing his or her biological processes, and the appropriate therapy is therefore psychopharmacological treatment. The environmental approach holds that the genesis and development of various aspects of mental illness can be influenced and prevented by changing the environment through the removal, addition, or improvement of external conditions.

THE INTERACTIONAL PERSPECTIVE

The fragmentation of theorizing and empirical research, as discussed above, has been a main impediment to real progress in psychology in general and in the field of personality in particular. Even a superficial analysis of the object of interest in personality development—the individual as a totality, with respect to the personal and environmental factors that influence current functioning and development—leads to the conclusion that none of the three metatheoretical approaches to understanding the current and developmental processes of individual functioning is sufficient by itself to cover the essential features of these processes.

On the other hand, each of these approaches covers important elements among the phenomena that must be considered in a comprehensive framework or perspective for the study of individual functioning. Thus, any such perspective has to incorporate all three views and integrate them into a common framework. A modern version of what has come to be designated "interactionism" meets this requirement.

Definition and Basic Propositions

"Interaction," in the sense in which the term is used here, is a central principle of open systems at all levels, from the macrocosmos to the microcosmos (see Bertalanffy, 1968; Miller, 1978). Specific components of open systems do not function in isolation from one another, and they usually do not function interdependently in a linear way. The interaction process of individual functioning is much more complex, particularly for the biological and psychological

aspects. Within the biological system, interdependence and nonlinear interrelationships reflect a fundamental principle. The same is true for the relationship among the various aspects of the mental system and this system's interaction with biological factors. Interaction is also a fundamental principle underlying the relationship between the individual and the environment.[1]

The basic view of an interactional perspective for individual functioning can be summarized in three propositions that should be considered simultaneously (see Magnusson, 1988):

1. An individual develops and functions as a total, integrated organism; current functioning and development do not take place in single aspects per se, in isolation from the totality.
2. An individual develops and functions in a dynamic, continuous, and reciprocal process of interaction with his or her environment.
3. The characteristic way in which an individual develops and functions, in interaction with the environment, depends on and influences the continuous reciprocal process of interaction among subsystems of mental and biological factors.

To a casual observer, these propositions may seem obvious, even trivial. This chapter demonstrates, however, that when seriously considered together, the propositions have far-reaching and important implications for planning, implementing, and interpreting psychological research in general and personality and developmental research in particular.

At the metatheoretical level, two basic models of the person that are of particular interest as a background for the presentation of an interactionistic perspective can be distinguished: a "mechanistic" and a "dynamic" model. The two models use different root metaphors as concepts for explaining human behavior (Pepper, 1942).

The mechanistic model takes the machine as the basic metaphor. In this representation of psychological functioning, the individual is seen as passive and reactive rather than as an active agent. Complex psychological phenomena are regarded as being reducible to simpler elements and operations; analogously, qualitative changes are reducible to quantitative changes. Laws remain constant and invariant over time, and strict determinism is assumed. Thus dependent and independent variables can be clearly identified. Even though a mechanistic model of the person in its extreme formulations may no longer be explicitly accepted by psychologists as a basic metaphor, it still exerts a strong influence even on developmental research.

As a contrast, an interactional perspective reflects a dynamic model of the person. It views the person as being inherently active and as acting upon the environment, rather than as being only a passive recipient of external stimuli. The model emphasizes that all parts of an ongoing system are interrelated in a complex way. Therefore, it is not always meaningful to maintain the distinction between dependent and independent variables, since an element may be related to other elements in the process both as a cause and as an effect. Moreover, the individual is an organized configuration of parts, with the whole being greater than the sum of the parts and giving meaning to the constituent parts.

A Holistic Approach to Individual Functioning

An interactional view emphasizes an approach to the individual as an organized whole, functioning as a totality and characterized by the partially specific patterning of relevant aspects of structures and processes involved. The totality has properties beyond those belonging to the parts. It gets its characteristic features and properties from the interaction among the operating elements involved, not from the effect of each part on the totality.

Thus, an important point of departure for an interactional view on individual functioning is that an individual functions as a totality at each stage of development and that each aspect of the structures and processes that are operating (perceptions, plans, values, goals, motives, biological factors, conduct, etc.) takes on meaning from the role it plays in the total functioning of the individual. The whole picture has an information value beyond what is contained in the separate parts. This implies that the individual as a whole must be considered as the framework for planning, implementing, and interpreting empirical research on specific aspects of individual functioning in both a current perspective and a developmental perspective.

As is the case with many basic propositions in psychology, the emphasis on a holistic approach to individual functioning is not new. It was discussed early and at length by prominent researchers interested in psychological phenomena in a current perspective (e.g., Allport, 1937; Angyal, 1941; Lewin, 1935; Stern, 1911). More recent it has been applied by researchers mainly interested in a developmental perspective (e.g., Block, 1971; Cairns, 1979b; Sameroff, 1983; Wapner & Kaplan, 1983). (See also a recent review of Soviet psychology by Asmolov, 1984.)

PERSON–ENVIRONMENT INTERACTION

The second of the three propositions underlying the interactional approach emphasizes the dynamic, continuous, and reciprocal process of interaction between the individual and the environment. This is the fundamental feature of what might be called "classic interactionism" (for reviews, see Ekehammar, 1974; Endler, 1984; Endler & Magnusson, 1976; Magnusson & Endler, 1977; Pervin & Lewis, 1978). The view reflected in this proposition has been advocated and discussed by many researchers over the years under various headings. For example, Pervin (1968) adapted the term "transactional" (cf. Sameroff, 1975), and Bandura (1978) used the term "reciprocal determinism" for individual functioning in current terms. Reykowski's "regulative theory of personality" and Strelau's "regulative theory of temperament" also stress person–environment interaction (Strelau, 1983). For individual functioning in a developmental perspective, Baltes, Reese, and Lipsitt (1980) have used the term "dialectic–contextualistic"; Bronfenbrenner and Crouter (1983) have used the term "process–person–context model" (see also Bronfenbrenner, 1989); and Lerner and Kauffmann (1985) have employed the term "developmental contextualism." Likewise, Cicchetti and Sroufe (1978) have presented what they call an "organizational approach" to the study of development.

A Current Perspective

The debate about person–environment interaction during the last decades has been mostly concerned with individual functioning in a current perspective. The main points of such a view have been summarized (Endler & Magnusson, 1976) as follows:

1. Actual behavior is a function of a continuous process of multidirectional interaction of feedback between the individual and the situations he or she encounters.
2. The individual is an intentional, active agent in this interaction process.
3. On the person side of the interaction, cognitive and motivational factors are essential determinants of behavior.
4. On the situation side, the psychological meaning of situations for the individual is the important determining factor. (p. 1)

That behavior cannot be understood in isolation from the environmental conditions in which it occurs is a conclusion that can be drawn from everyday observations. Naturally, this proposition has long been advocated and elaborated by researchers with very different perspectives: behaviorists, phenomenologists, personologists, social psychologists, trait psychologists, and those advocating a psychodynamic view. One of the most explicit of these formulations was that of Brunswik (1952), who suggested that psychology be defined as the "science of organism—environment relationships." The importance of considering the role of environmental factors in models of behavior has also been underscored by researchers in neighboring disciplines, such as sociology and anthropology. Extensive reviews and discussions of the importance of situational conditions for individual functioning have been presented (Argyle, Furnham, & Graham, 1981; Magnusson, 1981b).

The view that environmental factors, particularly those in the immediate situation, influence behavior and should be considered in models for individual functioning has to be qualified by a distinction between *general* situational effects and *differential* situational effects (Magnusson, 1984b). General situational effects are the same for all individuals. It takes longer for all individuals to climb a high mountain than a low one, and most individuals would react more strongly if they met a tiger than if they met a house cat. The notion of differential situational effects is that, in addition to the general situational effects, there are also effects that are specific for individuals or groups of individuals. The individual differences in this respect are assumed to be dependent on the individuals' partially specific interpretations of stimuli and events in the environment. For example, some people experience situations characterized by strong demands for achievement as threatening and react negatively, psychologically and/or physiologically; others experience such demands as challenging in a positive sense and react accordingly. On the other hand, the latter group may become threatened and react with anxiety to situations involving expectation of separation or physical pain.

Even researchers who refer to themselves as interactionists in their formulations have not always been clear about the distinction between general and differential situational effects and about the consequences of this distinction for methodology and research strategy. However, if the strong theoretical formulations concerning the role of environmental conditions for individual functioning are to have meaning beyond the obvious and trivial, particularly with respect to implications for psychological research, they must imply the operation of differential situational effects, as reflected in Lewin's well-known formula: $B = f(P,E)$. However, it is interesting to note the limited impact that interactional formulations have had on empirical research, despite the strong emphasis on environmental factors by most researchers and the very important theoretical, methodological, and strategical consequences of the existence of differential situational effets. The following two examples illustrate this fact.

First, much research using the dominant "measurement" model (as distinguished from *theories* about psychological phenomena), frequently applied in personality and in much developmental research, regards variation in a certain aspect of individual functioning across situations as errors. This measurement model and the methods closely connected with it have had a strong impact on personality research during the last 30 to 40 years. (For further discussion of the consequences of the application of this measurement model, see Magnusson, 1976, 1984b.)

Second, in research on stress and anxiety, the integral role of environmental situational conditions has been particularly emphasized and incorporated into theoretical models (Endler, 1975; Lazarus & Launier, 1978; Spielberger, 1977). Thus, one would expect this to be a field in which differential situational factors are particularly taken into account in empirical research. However, an analysis of empirical research presented in two leading journals, *Psychosomatic Medicine* and *Psychophysiology,* during the period 1970–1980 showed that the strong theoretical formulations had almost no impact (Magnusson, 1984a).

A Developmental Perspective

The current functioning of individuals reflects the influence of their past course of development. An individual's readiness to interpret and respond to a certain situation has been formed by continuous interaction with various situations in the past. In the development process, the environment provides information to process and offers necessary feedback for the building of valid conceptions of the outer world as a basis for interaction. In this continuous interaction with the environment in its physical, cultural, and social manifestations, individuals develop a total integrated system of mental structures and contents that shape and constrain their modes of functioning. On the basis of and within the limits of inherited dispositions, affective tones become attached to specific contents and actions, and strategies are developed for coping with various kinds of environments and situations (Magnusson, 1980a).

The fact that the course of individual development with respect to functioning is dependent on the person's past experiences of physical, social, and cultural environmental characteristics is common knowledge. This second proposition of the interactional perspective was emphasized by early researchers interested in the issue of individual development. As Cairns (1980) reports, Baldwin (1897) explicitly discussed ontogenetic and evolutionary development in interactional terms. And, as suggested by Cairns and Cairns (1985), there is a direct line from Baldwin to Piaget's work on language and thought, Kohlberg's studies on ethical development, and the work of others who have influenced various areas of developmental research. During the last decade, interactional formulations of individual development that stress the role of environmental conditions for the developmental process have been presented in cognitive development, in cognition and motivation, in behavior genetics, in social development, in psychobiology,

and in temperament, among other areas (see Magnusson, 1988). A further contribution to the unification of developmental research in interactional terms was Sameroff's (1982) application of a systems theory (see also Hettema, 1979, and Urban, 1978). These examples demonstrate that the interactional approach to development has been more widely accepted as a framework for research on individual development than for research on personality in a current perspective. Nevertheless, the important theoretical, methodological, and strategical implications for developmental research of an interactional perspective have not yet been realized to the extent they deserve. There has been more talk than real scientific contributions.

Person–Environment Interaction as a Reciprocal Process

A central aspect of the interactional perspective is the reciprocal character of the person–environment interaction process. Reciprocity implies that the individual both influences and is influenced by the environment at each stage of development. The individual influences the environment according to his or her own goals, motives, and plans, seeking some situations and avoiding others. An important role in the person–environment interaction process is thus played by the meaning that the individual assigns to the environment. But the individual does not act upon a passive environment, as is implicit in some influential developmental theories. Rather, the environment acts on the individual in a way that is often initiated and maintained by the actions of the individual (Lerner & Busch-Rossnagel, 1981; Stattin & Magnusson, 1990).

The best illustration of the reciprocity in person–environment interactions can be drawn from person–person interaction, particularly parent–child interaction (see Bell, 1968; Davis & Hathaway, 1982; Hartup, 1978; Murphy, 1983; Parke, 1978; Peterson, 1968, 1979; Sears, 1951). To a certain extent, the behavior of one individual influences the behavior of others, whose behavior in turn will affect the reactions and actions taken by the first, and so on. A child influences the behavior of the parents and other family members who form an important aspect of its own developmental environment; the child is both the creation of and the creator of his or her environment.

THE PERSON IN THE INTERACTION PROCESS

An Active, Purposeful Agent

As indicated earlier, an important aspect in the interactional view of individual functioning is that individuals are not mainly passive receivers of stimulation from the environment to which they react; they are active, purposeful agents who interpret information from the environment about conditions and events and who act in the frame of their own systems of thoughts, values, goals, and emotions. One implication of this facet of interactionism is that when the process underlying individual functioning and development is described in terms of person–situation or person–environment interaction, the central issue for psychological theorizing and research is not how the person and the environment, as two separate parts of equal importance, interact. Rather—and this is essential—it is how individuals by their perceptions, thoughts, and feelings function in relation to an environment that, to some extent, they have purposefully erected, and how these aspects of individual functioning develop through the course of an ongoing interaction process (Bandura, 1978).

For the view presented here, the recent development in research on sensory perception and the functioning of the brain in the interpretation of information from the external world is of central interest. In contrast to the mainstream, traditional position, input into sensory processes is regarded as information that is interpreted and used in coping with internal and external problems, rather than viewed as stimulation of the sensory organs. The sensory organs function more as sensory systems than as independent sensory structures, and the brain as a whole works as a pattern recognizer rather than as an absolute-magnitude measuring device (see Popper & Eccles, 1977). In individuals' dealings with the external world, a fundamental role is played by the integrated system of their structured cognitions and conceptions of the external world (including their self-perceptions), their way of processing information, their emotions, their goals and values, and their coping strategies.

"Our experienced world is an organized world" (Krech & Crutchfield, 1948, p. 84). The structure and functioning of an individual's cognitive–emotional system is formed and changes slowly in a process of maturation and experience that takes place through the continuous, bidirectional interaction between the individual and the environment.

It is the perceptual–cognitive–emotional system with its connected physiological system that determines which situations individuals seek and which they avoid (as far as they have options); which situational conditions they attend to; how they interpret single stimuli and patterns of stimuli and events; and how they transform the information that the environment offers into inner and outer actions. Understanding the lawfulness of how subsystems of perceptions, cognitions, goals, plans, values, emotions, coping strategies, and physiological processes function in interaction with one another and as an integrated total system in current situations, and how these subsystems develop during the process of maturation and experience in development, therefore becomes a central task for theorizing and research in the field of personality development.

Various models for dealing with problems in the fields of perception, cognition, information processing, and decision making from a contemporary perspective have been presented. They include such different concepts as "categories," "dimensions," "schemas," "plans," "programs," "semantic networks," and "coping strategies" (Anderson, 1985). From an interactional perspective, it is important to observe that, with few exceptions, these models have concentrated on the organization and functioning of the cognitive system as it deals with information only; this has resulted in the neglect of other significant aspects, such as emotions, values, and goals (see, e.g., Zajonc & Markus, 1984). Broughton (1984) notes that those adapting a Piagetian view have contributed to the false dichotomy of cognition versus emotion. The limitations of such a pure informational approach cannot be emphasized too strongly. Emotions and values, which are closely attached to the perception of specific aspects of the environment and which are bound to specific cognitive contents, play a crucial role in determining how an individual selects, interprets, and treats information from the external world. The central role of goals in the perceptual–cognitive system and in dealing with internal and external problems has been discussed and elaborated by Pervin (1983b), and Bower (1981) has presented research showing the importance of emotions for cognitive processes.

The main elements in the view advocated here have their roots early in the history of psychology. The act psychologists in Europe, such as Brentano (1874/1924) and Stumpf (1883; one of the founders of the Berlin Verein für Kinderpsychologie), stressed the dynamic, active conception of the mind and mental processes as activities, rather than seeing the brain as only a receiving and interpreting organ. In the United States, James (1890) was a proponent of the same view. The functionalists, with Angell (1907) as the main leader, also emphasized mind in action and the role of the active mind in the individual's coping with the environmental conditions in an adaptation process (see also Carr, 1925; Thorndike, 1903; Woodworth, 1918). Of particular interest here is the role that the functionalists assigned to biological factors in their model for individual functioning—an issue that is dealt with in a later section.

Conceptions of the World and the Self

An important aspect of the perceptual–cognitive system—which, along with its affective tones and coping strategies, plays such a crucial role in the total functioning of the individual in the person–environment interaction process—is the person's conception of the total external world, including himself or herself (see Epstein & Erskine's [1983] discussion of "personal theories of reality" from an interactional perspective). Thomae (1988) argues that the individual's world is mainly a world of social situations cognitively represented. At each stage of development, the total system of conceptions about the outer world is influential in a person's inner thoughts as well as in his or her actual behavior. To a considerable degree, one's conceptions of the world determine which kind of environments and situations one seeks and avoids, which situational cues and events one attends to, and how one interprets them. These interpretations and the experiences gained by them form the main basis for a person's actual manifest behavior, and also contribute to successive changes in the cognitive–emotional system.

An individual's view of himself or herself, both with respect to self-image (i.e., cognitive–affective beliefs with respect to specific areas, such as status, mental capacity, practical skills, appearance, etc.) and with respect to self-evaluation (overall approval and acceptance of himself or herself), plays a central role in the process of interaction with the environment (see Burns, 1979; Markus & Wurf, 1987). This is particularly true when an individual is involved with others. In 1890, James devoted a whole chapter to this issue. Self-images and self-evaluations develop as one aspect of the individual's total conception of the world. In a current perspective, these self-images and self-evaluations play an important role in the selection and interpretation of information from the outer world, in the individual's sense of control of the environment, in his or her conduct in current situations, in the way he or she relates to others, and so forth.

In a developmental perspective, self-images and self-evaluations are formed through a continuous interaction with the environment as an element in the process through which the individual learns to predict and control external conditions (Brandstädter, 1984; Cairns & Cairns, 1988; Harter, 1983). The role of the social environment in this process, with its values, norms, rules, rewards, and punishments, has been emphasized by many researchers over the last century (see Baldwin, 1897, who proposed that the self in its various aspects is essentially a product of social process). Lewis and Brooks-Gunn (1979) stated that the self "is developed from the consistency, regularity, and contingency of the infant's action and outcome in the world" (p. 9). Central to the discussion regarding the development of self-perceptions and their role in current functioning are intelligence and mental capacity in its various aspects (Gardner, 1983), self-efficacy (Bandura, 1986), subjective competence (Heckhausen, 1983), inner and outer control (Rotter, 1955), predictive and behavior control (Mineka & Kihlstrom, 1978), motivation (McClelland, 1955), and learned helplessness (Seligman, 1975). One aspect of this process of self-perception and self-evaluation is the effect on the individual's sense of control over the environment—for example, one's ability to influence the direction of one's future educational and vocational career (Gustafson, Stattin, & Magnusson, 1989).

Individual Functioning: A Dynamic Process of Interaction among Subsystems

As emphasized earlier, the first two propositions of the interactional perspective have old roots. This is not the case for the third proposition, which says that the characteristic functioning of an individual in the dynamic person–environment interaction process depends on and influences the continuous reciprocal process of interaction among psychological and biological subsystems. This proposition forms a cornerstone in modern interactionism. It incorporates biological factors in the general model for individual functioning in a new way.

The role of biological factors in psychological phenomena was recognized early in the history of psychology. For example, in 1883, when Wundt made a plea for psychology as an independent scientific discipline, he emphasized the biological base for psychological phenomena (Wundt, 1948). Since the beginning of the history of differential psychology, the role of genetic factors in the course of individual development has been a main issue (see, e.g., Galton, 1869). However, in spite of these early formulations, until recently the role of biological factors in the development process has not been considered to the extent it deserves. With a few exceptions (see, e.g., Bronfenbrenner & Crouter, 1983; Cairns, 1979a; Cicchetti & Aber, 1986; Gottlieb, 1983; Kalverboer and Hopkins, 1983; Lerner, 1984; Levine, 1982; Rutter, 1989a), those who have discussed development as a dynamic person–environment interaction process have not included or discussed the possible role of biological factors in the process (cf. Susman, 1989). The neglect of the role of biological factors as a basis for understanding the psychological processes in the total functioning of individuals has been a major drawback and an impediment for further progress; consequently, the change of direction in this respect that has become apparent lately means an important contribution to the field.

The renewed strong interest in the role of biological aspects of individual functioning has been fostered by rapid developments in neuropsychology, endocrinology, and pharmacology, which have illuminated the continuous interplay among biological brain processes, other physiological processes, mental processes (thoughts and emotions), behavior, and environmental conditions. These findings contribute to bridging the gap between biological and psychological sciences and help us to a better understanding of psychological processes.

The interaction process in which an individual is involved with the environment can be described in terms of an active adaptation process. In this adaptation process, biological factors in constant interaction with cognitive–emotional factors play a key role. On the biological side of this internal process, the endocrine system—in particular, the sympathetic–adrenal and pituitary–adrenal subsystems—is of special importance. Cannon (1914) pointed to the role of the sympathetic–adrenomedullary system in emergency situations; he demonstrated that epinephrine and norepinephrine are released as an effect of sympathetic innervation in response to threatening stimuli, as an adjustment mechanism to prepare the body for fight or flight. The adaptive role of the adrenal cortex, which produces corticosteroids such as cortisol through release of adrenocorticotropic hormone (ACTH) from the pituitary in response to stress, was described by Selye (1950).

The relation of thoughts, emotions, and behavior to physiological processes has been elucidated in much recent empirical research (see Gunnar, 1986, for a review). As indicated above, the relationship between biological and mental factors is not generally unidirectional in the sense that biological factors determine individuals' thoughts, feelings, and actions, as is assumed in the traditional biological approach to individual functioning. Biological and perceptual–cognitive–emotional factors are in constant and reciprocal interaction. Physiological processes can be evoked by cognitive–affective events and are maintained in a continuous process of interaction between mental and biological factors (see, e.g., Krantz, Lundberg, & Frankenhaeuser, 1987).

Of particular interest for an interactional model of individual functioning is the essential role played by the individual's interpretation of the environment. The appraisal of external information guides thoughts and actions and evokes physiological systems, which in turn influence psychological events, thoughts, and emotions. A good illustration is the reaction of individuals to situations appraised as threatening, as emphasized above. Such an appraisal leads, among other things, to the activation of the autonomic nervous system and the excretion of epinephrine from the adrenal medulla. The activation of this physiological system influences other bodily processes, and the effect of these changes is to influence the individual's emotions and thoughts (Öhman & Magnusson, 1987). Experiments on monkeys by McGuire and his coworkers have demonstrated how social factors—for example, the status of the leader in the group and the leader's interpretation of the behavior of other group members—affect the leader's level of serotonin and 5-hydroxyindoleacetic acid (5-HIAA), which, among other things, are important regulators of individual mood (Raleigh, McGuire, Brammer, & Yuwiler, 1984). The influence of social factors on biological functions was also empirically shown by McClintock (1971), who found that the menstruation cycle in female students who shared dormitory rooms was synchronized within the course of one study year. In many cases, it coincided totally before the end of the school year. These examples illustrate the limitations of the traditional unidirectional view in which biological factors are considered as the cause of psychological effects.

Of further interest in this connection is the gender difference found in epinephrine excretion in situations involving stress and anxiety (see review by Frankenhaeuser, 1983). In situations where stress reactions are induced by demand for achievement, males excrete significantly more epinephrine than females, whereas the opposite is the case in situations involving a possible threat to a parent's child. A reasonable interpretation of this empirical finding is that gender differences in the interpretation of the two situations are responsible for the different reactions.

Psychologists who are opposed to the position advocated here may argue that they are psychologists, not physiologists. Of course, the central issue for psychology is not to understand physiological processes. When mental and biological factors are discussed in terms of reciprocal and dynamic interaction processes, the contention is similar to that made earlier concerning the interaction between the individual and the environment. In psychology, the concern is not with two subsystems of equal interest; rather, the main focus is on why individuals think, feel, act, and react as they do. But to say that this focus implies that biological processes should not be considered in the search for an explanation of individual functioning is an analogous to a meteorologist's

claiming lack of interest in how the landscape is shaped, since he or she is only dealing with the climate.

Structures and Processes

A "structure" is defined here as a functional organization of biological or mental elements, and a "process" as activated structures in operation.

According to the interactional perspective, an individual develops and functions as an integrated psychological and biological being in a continuous reciprocal interaction with the environment. In this process of interaction, both the biological and psychological subsystems of the individual and the environment are in a process of transition into new states during the course of development, at a pace and to an extent that varies over time but continues across the whole lifespan. In the individual, this development occurs as a result of maturation and experience.

The current functioning of an individual in the interaction process is determined by the character and properties of existing mental and biological structures. However, the end result of the process may be a change in the structures made use of. For example, an individual's self-perceptions, which play a strong role in the interpretation of a certain situation and in the actions based on this interpretation, may change as a result of the individual's participation in the situation. The rate at which structures change as a result of processes varies across time and with the character of the structures. Some structures are very resistant to change. In Bell's (1971) terms, we have "a moving bidirectional system" (p. 822). This implies a spiral-like individual development in terms of person–environment interaction and in terms of interactions among the subsystems of an individual: it is continuously growing and changing (see Langer, 1969).

Levels of Structures and Processes

The interaction processes take place at various levels of the person–environment system, from the interaction between a cell and its environment in the early stage of development of the fetus, up to the interaction between a person and the macroenvironment and between generations and their environments (Featherman & Lerner, 1985; Raush, 1977; Schneirla, 1972). The character of the interactional process varies with the level of complexity in the hierarchy of the total system. For example, the character of the interaction process in which neurotransmitters and cognitive factors are involved is different from the character of the interaction process between individuals and their environments as reflected in changes across generations or in the evolution of the human species.

A Temporal Perspective

The formulations representing development as a spiraling process bring the temporal perspective of the interaction process into focus. This perspective will vary with the character of the system under consideration, in the sense that processes in systems at a micro level generally are characterized by a shorter time perspective than processes in systems at a macro level. For example, the interaction process between neurotransmitters takes place at a faster speed than the interaction process between generations and environments. This implies that the pace at which the structures in the individual and the environment change as a result of maturation, learning, and experiences varies with the character of the systems, especially the level of the subsystems. The anatomical structure of the fetus changes (as a result of the cell–environmental context interaction) much faster than the individual changes in the process of aging. Since systems at various levels are embedded in each other and are involved in a constant, dynamic, reciprocal interaction, the temporal perspective does not apply only to one subsystem at a time. The important implication of this view is that each subsystem must be analyzed in terms of its context in the total person–environment system and the manner in which it affects and is affected by other subsystems.

Over time, the relative role of various factors may change. For example, a certain interaction process leading to psychosomatic problems can be studied in terms of what triggers, directs, strengthens, and maintains it, as well as in terms of its outcomes. Vulnerability factors may vary in significance across age levels. A certain factor—say, a physiological or somatic factor— or a certain set of such factors may start a process that is later strengthened, directed, and maintained mainly by other factors, such as cognitive–affective factors.

Readiness

In the developmental person–environment interaction process, the individual's readiness to respond to various aspects of the environment is a concept of central importance. It is well known from research using a number of species that a given aspect of the environment may have a strong effect at one age, but will be ineffective (or show a marked attenuation of impact) if presented either prior to or subsequent to this particular time period (Rasmuson, 1983). The concept of "readiness to respond," then, refers to the condition of the organism at a particular age period with respect to optimal responsiveness to a certain element in the environment. A well-known example is the phenomenon of "imprinting" in certain bird species, as demonstrated by Lorenz (1965) and others. Hubel and Wiesel (1970) showed that the ocular system of kittens does not develop adequately, and will not recover later, if the necessary patterned stimulation is not available during the first period of life. It is an issue for discussion whether and to what extent analogous "critical periods" (in the strong sense of the concept) exist with regard to the effect of environmental stimuli at the human level (see Bernstein, 1987; Cairns, 1979a). In the important area of language acquisition, Snow (1987) has questioned the widely accepted nation of a critical period. However, it is clear that at particular age periods during development the individual has a greater sensitivity and responsiveness to some aspects of the environment than to others.

Subsystems within the person are constantly changing during developmental phases from infancy into aging. Changes occurring in either the biological system or the perceptual– cognitive system (including the individual's world conceptions and self-conceptions) may be responsible for creating a state of heightened readiness to respond to aspects of the environment that were not previously observed. As an example, consider changes in the biological (hormonal) system and the self-subsystem during the teenage years, and their contribution to the increased readiness of such individuals to attend to appropriate cues and to respond to members of the opposite sex (see Magnusson, Stattin, & Allen, 1985; Stattin & Magnusson, 1990).

The Role of Genetic Factors

The course of individual development takes place in a body whose main characteristics are inherited—that is, determined by the gene combinations whose properties originate from the characteristics of the parents. (The role of genetic factors is extensively discussed by Plomin, Chipuer, & Loehlin, Chapter 9, this volume.)

The traditional view of the role of genetic factors has been one of a unidirectional cause–effect relation. At a most basic level, the onset and course of certain developmental sequences may be determined genetically, to the extent that they are common to all individuals. However, even such developmental sequences as the onset of the menstrual cycle in girls, and the regulation of growth in height, are modifiable by environmental factors to some extent. In most aspects, individual development takes place in a process of maturation and experiences in the interaction with the environment, on the basis of and within the limits set by inherited factors.

The interactive process in which genetic and environmental factors are involved in individual development has been discussed by Plomin (1989) and Scarr and McCartney (1983). Plomin, De Fries, and Loehlin (1977) examined the issues of interaction and correlation between genetic and environmental influences on human behavior, which complicate genetic analyses (see Plomin & Daniels, 1984). That there is a hereditary predisposition toward a certain type of behavior does not imply that it cannot be changed by environmental inferences (see Angoff, 1988). In his evaluation of the role of heredity and environment in individual differences in aggression, Cairns (1979a) drew the conclusion that the differences obtained by selective breeding show a strong environmental specificity and can be modified by environmental social conditions to such an extent that the inherited differences can be eradicated. The process by which the individual develops in interaction with the environment within the boundaries and the potentialities offered by inherited properties

was discussed by Lerner (1984) in terms of plasticity of the organism.

The characteristic of individual development as a process of continuous interaction between genetically determined and environmental factors was emphasized by Scarr (1981):

> Probabilistic models do not expect any one-to-one correspondence between genotype and phenotype. Rather, they emphasize the interplay of untold numbers of genes and developmental events that shape the course of phenotypic development with a cetain range of possible outcomes. Developmental change, not causal connections, is the focus. (pp. 155–156)

Thus, from the time of conception there is an interaction between the fetus and the environment—an interaction that goes on through the lifespan. The stage for individual development is set by inherited factors, but many different "plays" are possible.

Within the limits set by inherited factors, there are large potentalities for change, due to the interplay with environmental factors.

> To put it more plainly, the science of behavior from the epigenetic point of view is not a "psychology without heredity", but a science based on the idea that heredity means merely the fact that the zygote starts to develop with an extremely wide (especially in higher vertebrates), but not unlimited, range of behavior potentials, only a very small fraction of which can be realized during its developmental history. (Kuo, 1967, p. 128)

Underscoring his standpoint with empirical examples, the Nobel laureate Medawar (1984) strongly emphasized the meaninglessness of trying to "attach exact percentage figures to the contributions of nature and nurture (Shakespeare's terminology) to differences of intellectural capacities":

> The reason, which is, admittedly, a difficult one to grasp, is that the contribution of nature is a function of nurture and nurture a function of nature. The one [varies] in dependence on the other, so that a statement that might be true in one context of environment and upbringing would not necessarily be true in another. (p. 171)

Even in the etiology of the major psychoses, for which a strong heredity component is suggested by empirical studies, it is less clear how genes are involved. Neither manic–depressive illness nor schizophrenia show tidy segregation patterns within families that would suggest a simple Mendelian transmission. Day, Zubin, and Steinhauer (1987) have discussed the occurrence of schizophrenic episodes in an interactional perspective as the result of individual vulnerability in interaction with environmental stressors. In this perspective, the challenging question for developmental research is not how much of individual development is determined genetically, but how the process of interaction between genes and environment proceeds (Anastasi, 1958; Eysenck & Eysenck, 1985; Hofer, 1981).

Traits and States in Individual Functioning

Individual functioning and interindividual differences in this respect can be analyzed and discussed at two levels: (1) in terms of momentary states of structures and processes at a certain moment in time under certain external conditions (i.e., in terms of states), and (2) in terms of enduring features of the way individuals function (i.e., in terms of traits). The enduring characteristics of an individual's functioning can be identified for manifest behavior (cf. Cattell's [1965] definition of "surface traits" as "a bunch of behavior elements cluster[ing] together," p. 67). Of more interest for a discussion of the role of traits in an interactionistic view of personality is the identification of enduring dispositions of the perceptual–cognitive–emotional system to function in a coherent, consistent way (cf. Allport's [1937] definition of a "trait" as "a generalized and focalized neuropsychic system (peculiar to the individual) with the capacity to render many stimuli functionally equivalent and to initiate and guide consistent (equivalent) forms of adaptive and expressive behavior," p. 295).

The state–trait distinction is an old one. As Eysenck (1983) pointed out, Cicero made the distinction between an anxious temperament and state anxiety, and between the trait of irascibility and the state of anger. The distinction has played a central role in the history of personality. It was emphasized by Allport and Odbert (1936) in their monograph on personality labels and was reiterated by Allport (1937) in his plea for an idiographic approach to personality.

For the present discussion of an interactional view on individual functioning, the trait concept is of particular interest, since at a superficial level the interactional view has been interpreted as denying the existence of individual characteristics in terms of traits. A common reaction to interactional formulations was expressed by Plomin (1986): "If interactionism were to be believed, it would imply that 'main effects' cannot be found because everything interacts with everything else" (p. 249).

The trait concept per se and its relation to the state concept have been the subjects of much debate. Traits have been discussed, defended, and criticized with reference to different types of instruments for the collection of data (e.g., Zuckerman, 1983), to empirical evidence (see, e.g., Epstein, 1979; Vagg, Spielberger & O'Hearn, 1980), to different types of data (Nesselroade, 1988), and to the problems of labeling (Allen & Potkay, 1981). These discussions demonstrate the need for some clarifications of the conceptual distinction between states and traits and of the trait concept as it is used here.

It must first be emphasized that the distinction between states and traits is a conceptual one. As such, it need not and cannot be verified or rejected by reference to empirical results or the use of various types of instruments (Magnusson, 1980b). The fact that the concepts are fuzzy and sometimes even overlap cannot be used as an argument against the distinction.

As noted above, an interactional view of individual functioning has sometimes been regarded as opposing what has been designated "trait psychology." This is true as long as trait psychology claims that individual functioning in specific natural situations can be understood and explained solely with reference to traits. However, it is certainly not true if the question is whether an interactional view implies the existence of enduring aspects of individual functioning, which can be identified and discussed in terms of traits. In an interactional view, what Allport (1937) defined as "bona fide structures in each personality that account for the consistency of its behavior" (p. 37) play a central role.

Most of the discussion of traits during the last two decades has referred to empirical data for manifest behavior (see Magnusson, 1980a). However, a particular interest are the enduring characteristics of an individual's perceptual–cognitive system, guiding his or her choice of situations (as long as there are options), the situational conditions to attend to, and the interpretation of information from the environment. The existence of enduring dispositions enabling the individual to function in a lawful, consistent way across time and across situations provides the basis for purposeful interaction with the environment. The coherent functioning of the perceptual–cognitive system with its attached emotions explains the coherence and lawful adaptation of manifest behavior to varying environmental conditions (Mischel, 1973).

Individual Development: A Lifespan Process

Traditional developmental psychology has concentrated primarily on description and understanding of development during infancy and childhood. During the last decade, increasing attention has been devoted to research on adolescence (Petersen, 1988), and recently also to research on adult development and aging (Datan, Rodeheaver, & Hughes, 1987). This change of focus reflects an orientation of theorizing and research on individual development that was fostered by the introduction of the concept of lifespan development, emphasizing development as a lifelong process that begins at conception and ends at death (see, e.g., Baltes et al., 1980; Filipp & Olbrich, 1986).

THE ENVIRONMENT: THE EXTRAINDIVIDUAL SIDE OF THE OPEN SYSTEM

Individuals meet their environment most directly in specific situations. In actual physical terms, a "situation" can be defined as the part of the environment that is accessible for sensory perception on a certain occasion (Magnusson, 1981a). Within the frame of each situation, stimuli and events that influence an individual's behavior and that are influenced by the individual change constantly. The actual situation and the specific situational stimuli, cues, and events are interpreted by the individual; the meaning assigned to the total situation, as a frame of reference, and to specific stimuli and events within that frame provides the main basis for the interaction with the environment. As has been stressed by many researchers, the environmental influence on individual current functioning and development is not limited to the immediate situation.

Instead, the immediate situation is embedded in a larger environment, with physical, social, and cultural properties operating both directly and indirectly at all levels of specificity–generality in the person–environment interaction (Barker, 1965; Bronfenbrenner, 1989; Magnusson, 1981a; Pervin, 1978).

At all levels, aspects of the environment can influence the individual's current behavior and developmental life course. The environment may have profound importance for functioning in current situations as well as for the total life course of an individual, is, for example, whether or not he or she grows up in an urban instead of a rural area, in the mountains instead of the plains, or in a Christian instead of a Hindu family (cf. Silbereisen, Boehnke, & Reykowski, 1986; Törestad, Olah, & Magnusson, 1989). This circumstance naturally has to be considered when one is interpreting results from single studies performed in a certain culture under that culture's particular conditions. It restricts to some extent the generalizations that can be made from such studies. At the same time, it emphasizes the need for cross-cultural research, in order to determine what is variant and what is invariant across cultures in individuals' current functioning and development (see Lonner, 1980). Such research contributes additional essential knowledge for the understanding of the lawful principles underlying individual development.

The Environment as a Source of Stimulation versus a Source of Information

When we discuss environmental influences on the development of the individual, an important distinction should be made between the environment as a source of sensory stimulation and the environment as a source of information. This discussion relates to the old distinction between the external world "as it is" and as it is perceived and subjectively interpreted to be. For the environment as it is, Koffka (1935) introduced the term "geographical environment" and Murray (1938) talked about "alpha situations." The perceived environment was referred to by Koffka (1935) as the "behavioral environment," by Lewin (1935) as "life space," by Murray (1938) as "beta situations," by Tolman (1951) as "the immediate behavior space," and by Rotter (1955) as "the psychological situation." (See also Wohlwill's [1973a] distinction between the environment as a source of active stimulation and as a "context of behavior.")

The actual physical environment acts upon the individual in important respects that can be reacted to without an intermediate process of interpretation. For example, this effect occurs for some biological reactions to environmental stimulation, as well as for fear reactions to physical stimuli (as suggested by Zajonc & Markus, 1984) and for the organism's reactions to certain viruses. The view of the environment as a source of stimulation that elicits and releases individual responses was bluntly expressed by Skinner (1971): "A person does not act upon the world, the world acts upon him" (p. 211). It has been influential in respected fields of psychology for decades, with far-reaching consequences both for theory about psychological phenomena and for planning and interpreting empirical research.

The assumption that the environment essentially serves as a source of information contributes to understanding the way an individual interacts with the environment at various levels of complexity. This view is reflected in modern social learning theory, which assumes that an individual's way of dealing with the external world develops in a learning process in which two types of perceived contingencies are formed. These are (1) situation–outcome contingencies (implying that certain situational conditions will lead to certain outcomes), and (2) behavior–outcome contingencies (implying that certain actions by the individual will have certain predictable consequences) (see Bolles, 1972). The formation of situation–outcome and behavior–outcome contingencies constitutes one source for the stability and continuity of the individual's functioning in relation to the environment.

The extent to which the social environment is meaningfully structured, as well as *how* it is structured—that is, the system of values, norms, rules, and roles guiding the behavior of significant persons in the environment—is essential in the development of the child's conceptions of the external world and his or her role in it. The patterning and consistency of other people's behaviors, such as their demands and their rewards and punishments, are what help the child develop a sense of order and lawfulness, which can be used to assign meaning to the environment and to make valid predictions about situation–outcome contingen-

cies and behavior–outcome contingencies in the external world. Such valid contingencies enable the individual to make predictions about the external world—in other words, to exert predictive control. In addition, the formation of such contingencies allows the individual to foresee the outcomes of different lines of action and to use that knowledge as a basis for effective purposive action—in other words, to exert action control. The individual's ability to predict and take active control of the environment forms the fundamental basis for goal-directed activity and for the experience of meaningfulness. An important aspect of this view was well formulated by Sells (1966):

> Adaptive function of an organism also implies the existence of feedback mechanisms. The posture of the organism at any moment is in effect the expression of an intrinsic (and not necessarily consciously experienced) *hypothesis* concerning the nature of the environment. Every response is similarly an *interrogation* of the environment and the resulting feedback provides information (also not necessarily conscious) that enables adaptive response. The existence of biologic and neurophysiological feedback systems is a necessary assumption about adaptive organisms. (p. 133)

The view just described can resolve the dispute between Emmanuel Kant's idealistic idea that our consciousness is not shaped by reality, but reality is shaped by our consciousness, and Karl Marx's materialistic standpoint that reality is not shaped by our consciousness, but our consciousness is shaped by reality. According to the view advocated here, both are right: Consciousness is formed in a continuous process of interaction with reality and is thus dependent on it; at the same time, consciousness defines, at each moment and stage of the course of development, the reality that forms the basis for individuals' purposive dealing with the environment.

Optimal Environments

An example of the importance of person–environment interaction in development is the fact that individual readiness for a certain type of change is not enough for development to take place. Optimal development also presupposes the occurrence of appropriate environmental conditions (Hebb, 1955; Leuba, 1955). Optimal environmental conditions vary among individuals and with time and age for the same individual; they also vary between the sexes (see Uzgiris, 1977; Wachs, 1977). The extent to which changes in optimal environmental conditions take place depends, among other things, on the types of persons and kinds of environmental factors that are involved. The optimal level of external conditions will vary depending upon each individual's own adaptation level, which is based on prior experience, learning, and maturational factors.

As emphasized by Wohlwill (1973a), much research on the role of environmental conditions in individual development seems to imply a monotonic relation between the amount of diversity of external stimulation and optimal development. However, there is enough empirical evidence to suggest that there is an optimal level of stimulation with respect to both preference (the preferred level of stimulation) and enhancement (the developmentally optimal level of stimulation) (see Wachs, 1977). Either too little or too much stimulation will result in less satisfaction and less adequate development than occur with intermediate stimulation. Examples can be found in empirical research on stress, in which too high and too low demands on activity both lead to the same kind of and amount of physiological and psychological stress reactions, and in aging, where the optimal level of stimulation seems to be of particular importance.

Environmental Change

An individual's life course does not take place in an environment that is stable in its physical, social, or psychological properties. During the lifetime of an individual, the environment that confronts him or her and influences the course of development changes as well. The existence of environmental changes at different levels has consequences for both cross-sectional and longitudinal research on development, in that factors in the individual that determine maturation and learning in the course of development are nested within factors in a changing environment. These changes occur both at a macro level and at a micro level.

The macroenvironment undergoes constant change. Compare, for example, the situation today with the situation only 50 years ago with respect to our possibilities for travel, communication, and exchange of information.

Ideological and political movements influence and change educational opportunities, educational systems, and societal norms, rules, and roles. The implication of this is that even persons who grow up and stay in the same geographical environment may die in quite another environment than the one into which they were born. Constant change also means that different generations are born into different environments with different norms, value systems, and demands (see Elder, Caspi, & Downey, 1986). Methodologically, these circumstances raise the issue of separating generation effects from age effects in empirical research on individual development. Nor are the aspects of the total environment that directly confront the individual stable across the lifespan. Changes of various types may occur for various reasons:

1. As emphasized above, the individual changes his or her own environment by direct action. A baby who is crying night after night and does not eat regularly may influence the behavior of the parents, and a rebellious teenager may affect the emotional climate of the family (see Davis & Hathaway, 1982).

2. The individual may actively seek new situations and avoid earlier ones. The reason may be, for example, psychological and biological maturation, which leads to new interests (Magnusson et al., 1985; Stattin & Magnusson, 1990). Sometimes actively seeking new situations may imply moving to totally new environments.

3. Role transitions often lead to new kinds of situations. This is the case, for example, when one is advancing to new jobs, marrying, or becoming a parent. Many of these roles are normative and common to most people in a society, whereas others are specific to groups and individuals (see Baltes, 1978).

4. Specific "life events"—for example, birth of a new child in the family, death of a close relative, losing a job, and "chance events" (Bandura, 1982)—may change the character of the microenvironment (see Hultsch & Plemons, 1979).

Individuals who grow up and live in similar environments will develop and function with more similar conceptions of the world, more similar interpretations of external information, and more similar ways of coping with the environment in all its aspects than individuals who grow up and live in more varied environments. Such changes in the environment during the lifespan as those described above may have profound effects on an individual's course of development. Some changes occur as the result of actions by the individual himself or herself. Others are due to factors in the environment over which the individual does not exert any control; life events and chance events are good examples. The implications of such changes in the environment for an individual's life course make the traditional discussion about stability and change in single aspects of individual functioning per se complicated.

INDIVIDUALITY AND CONTINUITY IN PERSONALITY DEVELOPMENT: IMPLICATIONS FOR EMPIRICAL RESEARCH

A heatedly debated issue in the field of personality during the last two decades has been the one under the general heading of "personality consistency." This issue has primarily been discussed from a cross-sectional perspective— that is, whether and to what extent individuals function in a stable way across situations (see Endler, 1983, and Pervin, 1985, among others). Also, a central issue for development theory and empirical research is that of consistency and continuity in the structures and processes involved in the course of development, both with respect to specific aspects of individual functioning and with respect to the total functioning of the individual. This issue raises many theoretical and methodological problems (see Magnusson, 1988). A recent, comprehensive review of the debate on continuity and change in personality development and of new trends in this debate has been presented by Datan et al. (1987).

A cornerstone of an interactional view on development is that an individual functions and develops as a totality. Both in current functioning and in the transition to new stages in development, each aspect of individual functioning has no role independent of other elements; each specific aspect gets its functional meaning from the role it plays for the totality.

As a result of maturation and experience in the process of interaction with the environment and among subsystems of mental and biological factors, individuals change, across

time, their way of coping with the external world. The essential role in this process of individuals' own active construction of their lives has been emphasized by Carlson (1981) and Tomkins (1986) in their discussion of "script theory." In the process of transition into new stages, the nature of specific aspects of the coping process, as well as the role they play in the total pattern of operating factors, may change. Among the important characteristics of the developmental process are the individual differences that occur with respect to the pace and patterning of factors in the development process (Bateson, 1978; Hinde & Bateson, 1984; Uzgiris, 1977). Individual differences in this respect are partly genetically determined and partly influenced by environmental factors, as discussed in earlier sections.

Much of the theoretical debate and empirical research on developmental consistency has been characterized by (1) the use of the concepts of stability and change, connected with an interest in prediction; (2) empirical research focusing on single aspects of individual functioning, which are regarded as objectively measurable traits and studied as nomothetic variables that do not change across age levels; and (3) the application of linear regression models for the treatment of data. In the interactional perspective discussed here, this traditional approach to research on stability and change does not seem appropriate. The problems connected with this approach are further discussed in the next section. Here, it is essential to emphasize that the whole developmental process of an individual is lawful, coherent, and consistent. There is continuity and coherence across time in the patterns of individual functioning; it is individuals who are stable across time, not variables. Development is essentially a dynamic process, characterized by reorganization and adaptation. The changes that take place in the individual from one stage to another across time do so in a lawful and consistent way (see Sroufe & Rutter, 1984). As emphasized by Kagan (1978), this does not mean that one state can be predicted from an earlier one or that there need to be "closely dependent relations between all the successive stages" (p. 72). The essence of this view is that everything happens within an individual whose current functioning takes place against a personal history of mental and biological processes.

As emphasized by many researchers in the

field, the debate over personality consistency has not contributed much to a better understanding of individual functioning, largely because clear conceptualizations and problem specifications have been lacking. This conclusion is valid for research on personality consistency in both a cross-sectional and a developmental perspective. Any fruitful discussion of the issue of continuity and change must rely on (1) an analysis of the concepts used; (2) a specification of the levels of structures and processes in individual functioning that are covered by and reflected in the data used as a basis for discussions of appropriate models; (3) explication of the measurement model applied (relating data to the phenomena) and its basic assumptions; and (4) an appropriate strategy for empirical research. These and some related issues are discussed here with reference to the interactional view on individual development discussed above.

Hypothetical and Nonhypothetical Aspects of Individual Functioning in Developmental Research

For data to be meaningful and useful in elucidating a developmental problem, a fundamental prerequisite is that the data must be valid; that is, they must reflect the aspect of individual functioning that they are expected to reflect, and not something else. When we deal with basic somatic data—data for height, weight, pulse rate, excretion of catecholamines in the blood, and blood pressure, for example—the validity of the data does not cause any serious problems in most cases. Such data have the following characteristics, which are of basic importance for the application of most traditional measurement models and methods for data treatment:

1. Somatic variables can be unequivocally defined and operationalized with sufficient precision for most purposes. This precision in definition implies that the data for such variables directly reflect the individual characteristics in which we are interested. For practical purposes, such data can be interpreted straightforwardly without the use of a theory that explicates the nature of the phenomena or posits intervening variables.

2. Data for somatic variables reflect interindividual differences in *quantity* for a certain variable, without confounding quantitative differences with qualitative change. The same attribute is measured along a continuum; for instance, data for height refer to the same quality, independent of the quantitative level.

3. Data for such variables retain their qualitative meaning across age levels. Height is the "same" variable at the age of 8, at the age of 18, and at the age of 70. This property makes data for various ages comparable and meets the important and necessary prerequisite for meaningful longitudinal studies of single variables.

When a developmental issue can be elucidated by data of the kind just discussed, the situation offers no major problems in the application of traditional models and methods for treatment of data, as long as other conditions (e.g., representativeness) are met.

The situation becomes quite different and much more problematic when our interest is in "hypothetical variables"—that is, variables that are derived constructs, the operationalization of which is not clear-cut but must be chosen by the researcher (see Bergman & Magnusson, 1990). A certain hypothetical variable is assumed to reflect a certain aspect of the total functioning of an individual. Such abstractions—intelligence, aggressiveness, hyperactivity, attachment, independence, anxiety, mobility, social class, and many, many others—are the most common and are central in developmental research, both when the interest is in normal development (such as in the areas of cognition and social development), and when it is in the developmental background of adult problems (such as health problems, criminal behavior, and alcohol abuse). (For recent discussions of hypothetical constructs, see Hyland, 1981, and Kagan, 1984, among others. Methodological problems have been analyzed by Bookstein, 1986, among others.)

Before applying any measurement model using data for hypothetical variables, researchers must consider the fact that they do not have the properties summarized above for nonhypothetical variables. In contrast, the following characteristics are valid for such variables:

1. Hypothetical variables rely on verbal formulations and are "fuzzy"; they are not unequivocally delineated, and thus are not unequivocally defined theoretically in a manner that leads to one and only one measurement

method. In the beginning of this century, much energy was expended in discussions regarding what intelligence "really is." Of course, intelligence "isn't"; it does not exist as a unity, the boundaries of which can be delimited once and for all. It is an abstraction aimed at delineating a certain aspect of the total functioning of an organism. What is actually assessed by a certain measure of this aspect of individual functioning is, of course, defined by the properties of the instrument used for data collection, independently of the wording of the theoretical definition. Maintaining strict definitions of hypothetical constructs in terms of operationalization was stressed by early investigators as a means of avoiding confusion in the interpretation of results of empirical research. In this perspective, intelligence was defined in the following way: "Intelligence is what intelligence tests measure" (cf. Bridgeman, 1927). In the extreme case, this demand led to "operationalism," pure operationalization without a solid basis in theory—a movement that has been strongly criticized. However, there are strong reasons to emphasize the need for operational definitions again. The lack of adherence to such definitions has caused much confusion in the interpretation of the vast amount of empirical research in such important areas as social class, stress and anxiety, intelligence, and others.

2. Data for hypothetical variables often cannot be assumed to reflect only quantitative differences; rather, such measures are frequently confounded, since they may also reflect related qualitative differences. For example, a low aggressiveness score may not only reflect less of the "same" kind/quality of aggressiveness than does a high aggressiveness score. Rather, data for the hypothetical variable "aggressiveness" may well reflect both quantitative and qualitative differences at various levels, and the two cannot always be separated from each other.

3. Data for hypothetical variables that are assumed to reflect the same aspect of individual functioning across age levels may reflect qualitatively different aspects even if they are measured by the same instrument (see, e.g., Wohlwill, 1973b). An aspect that is covered by a certain type of data may change across age levels with respect to its very nature and with respect to the role it plays in the total functioning of the individual (see Kagan, 1971, for a discussion of homotypic and heterotypic stability; Emmerich, 1964, on what constitutes

"sameness"; and Brandstädter, 1988, on "functional equivalences").

Data Appropriate to the Level of Structures and Processes

One central aspect of the validity of data used in personality research is that they must be appropriate to the level of structures and processes under investigation (Magnusson, 1988).

The starting point for the choice of method for data collection and the type of data to be processed must be a substantive analysis of the character of these structures and processes. Data that are appropriate for the elucidation of structures and processes at one level of complexity can yield meaningless results if applied to problems at other levels. Ajzen and Fishbein (1977) presented empirical support for this statement in their studies of attitude–behavior correlations, showing that a prerequisite for a high correlation was that data must refer to targets and actions at corresponding levels of specificity. The point that data most effective for the description of the outcomes of developmental processes may not be effective for the analysis of the processes by which social patterns arise and are maintained or eliminated was made long ago by Binet (see Cairns & Ornstein, 1979).

The same point is valid for methods and procedures concerning data treatment. A primary requirement for effective research on developmental problems is that the instruments and procedures for data collection and treatment, as well as the data per se, must be appropriate to the character of the problem under consideration—in particular, to the level of complexity of the structures and processes. The neglect of this critical issue is a cause of much confusion and misunderstanding in the fields of personality and development. Since this distinction has important methodological implications for the interpretation of the results aimed at elucidating the issue of stability and change, it is dealt with here at some length.

The formulations above stress that for any meaningful interpretation of empirical data as a basis for description and explanation of continuity and lawfulness in the development process, researchers must be aware of and make explicit the level of complexity and generality at which they are working, with respect to the structure(s) and process(es) under consideration. The weather can serve as a useful analogy to make the point clear.

The appropriate data for studying inter-seasonal variations in temperature are aggregate data for seasons, obtained (1) on the basis of observations all days of the year or (2) on the basis of observations of a representative sampling of days for each season. Means for seasonal temperatures will be consistent and show, among other things, that most regions of the globe have higher temperatures in the summer than in the winter. The seasonal curves will reflect, in descriptive terms, perfect consistency from one year to another. This implies that there is perfect predictability concerning the difference in mean temperature between summer and winter. The descriptive lawfulness in seasonal variations can be explained in relation to the amount of sunshine, among other factors.

If we then direct our interest to the varieties in temperature at a lower level of the process, the variation from day to day, we will find that the descriptive curves for temperature from day to day show very little conspicuous lawfulness. And predictability, particularly of change in the weather, is surprisingly low, despite the high standard of meterorological research. In order to understand and explain day-to-day changes in temperature, the researcher has to analyze the processes, define all relevant factors, and plan and implement more finely graded analyses of the dynamic, reciprocal process of interaction among factors that contribute to determine changes in the daily temperature. (A meteorologist is in a more favorable position than a psychologist, since he or she can at least sometimes simulate conditions in the laboratory, without too much distortion of the real conditions under which the temperature changes.)

Data aggregated across days over one season can be regarded as measures of temperature as a "trait," a stable characteristic of the weather. Nevertheless, such aggregate data (even aggregations of observations across days within a week) do not help to improve day-to-day prediction of changes in the temperature or to demonstrate any lawfulness in the changes from day to day. Rather, if the two levels of analysis are not clearly distinguished but are mixed in the interpretation, the picture can be described (as it is in many reviews on important issues in psychology) as "confusing," since the temperature on a certain day in the winter may be warmer than on a certain day in the summer. This example demonstrates clearly one misunderstanding about the central problem in the discussion of personality consistency and person–situation interaction, and the misuse of results from empirical research as a basis for various interpretations of that issue.

Two essential conclusions for developmental research follow. First, the level of the structures and the process that are under consideration must be clearly distinguished. Second, the empirical data must be appropriate to the level of the process at which the problem is defined. The debate on personality consistency both in a current and in a developmental perspective becomes meaningless and fruitless when these two criteria are not met—for example, when consistency in aggregate data at the trait level is used as an argument against the existence of person–situation interactions, and when individual differences in cross-situational profiles, based on situation-specific data, are used as an argument against the existence of personality traits. Situation-specific data cannot be used without aggregation to elucidate the role of traits in individual functioning, and data aggregated in one way or another across situations and time cannot be used for the study of stability and change as a function of changes in situational conditions. Or, to take another example, data for frequency of a certain aspect of individual functioning cannot be interchanged with data for intensity, as has sometimes been done in research on anxiety (see Törestad & Magnusson, 1982).

Chronological Age as the Marker of Development: Interindividual Differences in Growth Rate

In biological and psychological research on developmental phenomena, the central marker of development is chronological age. It may be used as a dependent variable (e.g., when the age at which the menarche occurs is studied), but in most cases it serves as the main independent variable or as a control variable (e.g., when abstract thinking is studied as a function of chronological age). The main stages of development are discussed almost exclusively with reference to chronological age; this is true for research on phenomena at all age stages, from infancy to aging. Using chronological age as the marker of development is, however, connected with serious problems, which are too often overlooked. The problems have their basis in the existence of strong individual differences in growth rate, demonstrated for psychological as well as for biological aspects of individual functioning (see Bateson, 1978; Ljung, 1965; Loevinger, 1966).

The existence of individual differences in maturational tempo has far-reaching methodological consequences (see Magnusson, 1985, 1988). The general consequences for research design have been extensively discussed (Baltes, 1968; Nesselroade, 1988; Schaie, 1965; Wohlwill, 1970). However, the consequences for the choice of appropriate methods of data treatment and studies of individual development have been appreciated only to a very limited extent. Two empirical examples may serve as an illustration of the effect of neglecting individual differences in growth rate in developmental research. First, in an empirical study of sex differences in spatial ability, Waber (1977) found that the existence of such differences at a certain age was an effect of differences in maturational rate rather than of gender per se. Second, in a cross-sectional study of girls at the age of 14–15 years that was part of a longitudinal research program, we (Magnusson et al., 1985) observed a strong negative relation between the age at menarche and norm-related behaviors such as drinking, breaking parents' rules, sexual relations, and the like. If chronological age were used as the marker of development, the behaviors of early-maturing girls could be viewed as norm-breaking and deviant. However, in relation to the maturational level of the girls, the behaviors of early-maturing girls were normal and appropriate. In a follow-up at adulthood, the relation between age at menarche and social behaviors had totally disappeared. This example can serve as a basis for some important conclusions:

1. In all matrices of data for various aspects of individual functioning that are related systematically to biological maturation, a portion of the variance will be determined by individual differences with respect to biological growth rate. This is also true for data sets in which all subjects are of the same chronological age (i.e., in cross-sectional matrices where chronological age is controlled for). Thus, for example, coefficients reflecting relationships among variables will be partly determined by individual

differences in biological maturity. This effect, of course, will occur even if data for biological maturation are not included in a matrix of data.

2. Most discussions of models for development have focused on early development. What has been said here about the problems connected with using chronological age as a marker for development is not only applicable to research on early stages of individual development. It is equally important for research across the lifespan—for example, to the study of aging (see Johansson & Berg, 1989). The use of chronological age as the main marker of development in traditional research on aging is a major limitation in that type of research, since individual differences in biological age may be even greater in older age than in infancy, childhood, and/or adolescence. Using biological age as a central marker of development in research on aging—for example, standardizing data with reference to the endpoint of life or to the total length of life—would certainly contribute to more effective empirical research and to a fuller comprehension of the psychological and biological processes involved in the process of aging.

Interaction among Variables

An interactional view emphasizes individual functioning as a process of continuous interaction among systems of psychological and biological factors in the individual, and among systems of physical, social, and cultural factors in the environment. As discussed in the foregoing sections, these systems per se, as well as the character of their interplay, change across time in important ways (e.g., with respect to the specific factors operating in each subsystem and to their role in the subsystem, and thereby with respect to the functioning of the totality). The characteristic of the developmental process has effects that are reflected in statistical interactions of data for central aspects of individual functioning. This issue has been discussed and elaborated by Hinde and Dennis (1986) and Rutter (1983).

The importance of considering the existence of statistical interactions in data for essential aspects of individual functioning, when statistical methods are applied, becomes clear when we look at the basic assumptions made in the traditional measurement model.

Assumptions made in the Traditional Measurement Model

For the study of stability and change of various aspects of individual functioning in the course of development, an arsenal of methods for data treatment is available. Many of them are statistically highly sophisticated and very useful when they are applicable. However, they have been applied too often without due consideration to the underlying requirements that must be met if the outcome of the process of data analysis is to yield psychologically relevant results, not just numbers.

Among the most frequently used methods for the study of stability and change are linear regression methods (e.g., product–moment correlation, multiple correlation, cross-lagged correlation, path analysis) and linear models with latent variables (e.g., LISREL). The basic requirements for the appropriate application of these methods are the following:

1. The relation among the variables under study should be linear.
2. All variables in the equation should be relevant for all individuals.
3. Each specific variable must have the same weight for all individuals (i.e., it must play the same role for all individuals in the total functioning of the individuals).
4. Regardless of the quantitative *level* on a certain dimension, all data should reflect the same qualitative *aspect* of individual functioning.

When these requirements are seen in the light of (1) the properties of data for hypothetical variables, (2) the existence of sometimes strong interactions among developmental factors, and (3) the existence of sometimes strong interindividual differences in growth rate discussed in earlier sections, it becomes clear that the applicability of the linear regression methods for data treatment is more limited than would seem to be the case, given today's empirical developmental research. (For a more elaborate presentation and discussion of models and methods suitable to handle the complex situations being dealt with, the reader is referred to von Eye & Brandstädter, 1988.) The proliferation of linear regression methodology is particularly surprising, since the limitations of these methods were emphasized early for example, by Lewin (1931) and Allport (1966). Lewin argued strongly against the unsophisticated use of linear regression models, because they yield results that are valid for an "average" person, and such a person seldom exists.

A Variable versus a Person Approach

In previous sections of this chapter, certain methodological issues for the study of individual development have been discussed. An interactionistic, holistic view also has research strategy consequences with respect to a duality that has been the object of much discussion over decades; it is reflected in the debate over idiographic versus nomothetic, typological versus dimensional, and clinical versus statistical approaches. Pervin (1985) has recently presented a review of the issues and viewpoints in this debate (see also Pervin, 1983a). With reference to the interactional perspective presented in this chapter, two complementary research strategies for the study of developmental issues are contrasted here: a "variable" approach and a "person" approach (see Magnusson, 1985). In the variable approach, the central interest is in single variables or relations among them; problems are formulated in variable terms, and generalizations on the basis of empirical results are made in such terms (intelligence, aggressiveness, attachment, hyperactivity, etc.). In a person approach, the person is the central unit of analysis. Problems for investigation are formulated in person terms, and operationalization is made in terms of individual *patterns* of variables relevant for the problem under study. The results of studies grouping individuals on the basis of similarities in their characteristic patterns of relevant factors are interpreted in person terms. It should be observed that the variable and person approaches are conceptually distinct. The appropriateness of each of them cannot be determined once and for all; it depends upon the character of the problem under investigation and of the phenomena involved.

Though the debate about the appropriateness of the two basic approaches has gone on for a long time under various headings, there is no doubt that the variable approach has dominated developmental and personality research for decades. This approach is characteristic of research in the following areas:

1. The study of the stability of person factors. Most of the time, developmental consistency is studied in terms of rank-order stability.

2. Studies of the relation between environmental factors (e.g., various aspects of upbringing) and personality factors and behavior (e.g., antisocial behavior), both in a cross-sectional and in a developmental perspective. Most of the time, environmental factors are treated as independent variables.

3. The study of relations among person factors in the search for basic developmental factors using a factor-analytic approach. Most of the time, factor analysis employs matrices based on cross-sectional data.

4. Construct validation of personality traits. The basic assumption has been that high coefficients for the stability across ages of a certain variable are a prerequisite for claiming that the variable can be regarded as a trait (se Mischel, 1968).

The frequent application of linear regression models for data analysis in developmental research is closely connected with the variable approach. The reasons for underlining the limitations of such models for the appropriate treatment of data are also germane to a discussion of the variable approach. Two points are of particular importance with reference to the interactional view of individual functioning. First, many (not to say most) of the central factors operating in the individual development process are hypothetical constructs, as defined earlier. The problems involved in operationalizing such abstractions raise problems for studying them as nomothetical variables. Second, a basic proposition in the interactional view is that an individual functions as a totality and that each aspect of the structures and processes involved derives its functional meaning through its role in the totality. From this standpoint, studies of single aspects seen in isolation from other, interacting aspects can be expected to make only limited contributions to an understanding of individual functioning.

An analysis of the phenomena under consideration in the developmental process and of the assumptions made by a variable approach applying linear regression models leads to the conclusion that we need complementary approaches. To some extent, the problems arising from the use of linear regression models in a variable approach can be overcome by the application of other models for data treatment. However, with reference to an interactional view on individual development, a natural complement for the study of central developmental problems is a person approach, in which the course of development is studied in terms of patterns of variables relevant to the issue under consideration. The appropriate application of pattern analyses to the study of developmental issues is full of problems for research strategy, methodology, and theory (see, e.g., Bergman, 1988). For empirical illustrations, the reader is referred to Bergman & Magnusson (1984a, 1984b) and Magnusson and Bergman (1988, 1990).

Of course, under certain conditions a variable approach is appropriate and should be used in developmental research. Research on single variables that can be defined objectively and studied in isolation—for example, studies on development of height—demonstrates this (Garn, 1980; Tanner, 1978). What is argued here is the necessity of seriously considering the factors discussed above, which are relevant for the choice between a variable approach and a person approach to the study of developmental issues.

The Need for Longitudinal Research

An important consequence of an interactional view is that we need to follow the same individuals across time and to do this with a broad set of data covering relevant aspects of individual functioning, if we really want to come to grips with and be able to understand and explain the development process of individuals. Thus, a major implication of the interactional view for research strategy is that longitudinal research must be conducted if the development of individuals as totalities is to be understood as a process of maturation and experience in continuous interaction with the environment. There is no adequate alternative to longitudinal research for the study of important aspects of developmental issues (see, e.g., Baltes et al., 1980; Cairns, 1979a; de Ribaupierre, 1989; Livson & Peskin, 1980; Magnusson, 1988; McCall, 1977; Rutter, 1989a; 1989b; Wohlwill, 1970).

In order to understand the lawful patterning of developmental stability and change in individuals by discovering the distinct configurations of psychological and biological factors that characterize each person's course of development, there is a need to cover a broad spectrum of psychological, biological, and social aspects of individual functioning. To give one example: In our recent study, the range and restrictions of long-term consequences of early biological maturation among girls could be successfully investigated only by examining a wide range of factors for a representative group of girls followed from an early age to adulthood (Magnusson et al., 1985; Stattin & Magnusson, 1990).

FINAL COMMENTS

The complexity of the phenomena that must be considered in order to understand and explain why individuals think, feel, act, and react as they do in real life, and how they change over time in these respects, makes the psychologist's task exceedingly difficult. This complexity has led some researchers to take a pessimistic view of the future of psychology as a science. In the past, Kant questioned whether psychology would ever reach the status of a science (Cofer, 1981); a similar pessimism has been expressed by more contemporary psychologists (Cronbach, 1975; Gergen, 1973). It should be emphasized, however, that the litmus test of a scientific discipline cannot be whether or not its phenomena are complex and hard to analyze. Had such a criterion been applied in the natural sciences from the beginning of their history, physics and chemistry would never have been regarded as scientific disciplines. The only criterion for a science is the appropriateness of its methods in dealing with relevant questions. Whenever processes display order and regularity on the basis of given structures, it is a scientific challenge to map the lawfulness of this order and regularity.

The point of departure for an interactional perspective of individual functioning is that the life course of each individual takes place in a dynamic, reciprocal interaction process in which both the person and the environment change across time in a way that is characterized by order and regularity. There is, in principle, nothing mysterious or incomprehensible about the process—at least no more so than about phenomena investigated by other scientific disciplines. Therefore, if research stays within the boundaries of natural limitations and does not extend the discipline to include existential problems, research should move forward. Of course, this does not imply that scientific methods will ever reveal the final truth about why individuals think, feel, act, and react as they do; what can be done is to take steps in the direction of a better understanding of these phenomena. What is more important then than anything else is that we "use our brains" (Cronbach, 1975).

NOTE

1. This use of the term "interaction" should be distinguished from its use as a statistical term. The various ways in which the term "interaction" is used have been discussed by Olweus (1977).

REFERENCES

Ajzen, J., & Fishbein, M. (1977). Attitude–behavior relations: A theoretical analysis and review of empirical research. *Psychological Bulletin, 84,* 888–918.

Allen, B. P., & Potkay, C. R. (1981). On the arbitrary distinction between states and traits. *Journal of Personality and Social Psychology, 41,* 916–928.

Allport, G. W. (1937). *Personality: A psychological interpretation.* New York: Holt, Rinehart & Winston.

Allport, G. W. (1966). Traits revisited. *American Psychologist, 21,* 1–10.

Allport, G. W., & Odbert, H. S. (1936). Trait-names: A psycholexical study. *Psychological Monographs, 47*(Whole No. 211).

Anastasi, A. (1958). Hereditary, environment and the question "How"? *Psychological Review, 65,* 197–208.

Anderson, J. R. (1985). *Cognitive psychology and its implications.* New York: W. H. Freeman

Angell, J. R. (1907). The province of functional psychology. *Psychological Review, 14,* 61–91.

Angoff, W. H. (1988). The nature–nurture debate, aptitudes, and group differences. *American Psychologist, 43,* 713–720.

Angyal, A. (1941). *Foundations for a science of personality.* Cambridge, MA: Harvard University Press.

Argyle, M., Furnham, A., & Graham, J. A. (1981). *Social situations.* Cambridge, England: Cambridge University Press.

Asmolov, A. G. (1984). The subject matter of psychology of personality. *Soviet Psychology, 4,* 23–43.

Baldwin, J. M. (1897). *Social and ethical interpretations of mental development: A study in social psychology* (3rd ed.). New York: Macmillan.

Baltes, P. B. (1968). Longitudinal and cross-sectional sequences in the study of age and generation effects. *Human Development, 11,* 145–171.

Baltes, P. B. (1978). *Life span development and behavior* (Vol. 1). New York: Academic Press.

Baltes, P. B., Reese, H. W., & Lipsitt, L. P. (1980). Life-span developmental psychology. *Annual Review of Psychology, 31*, 65–110.

Bandura, A. (1978). The self system in reciprocal determinism. *American Psychologist, 33*, 344–358.

Bandura, A. (1982). The psychology of chance encounters and life paths. *American Psychologist, 37*, 747–755.

Bandura, A. (1986). *Social foundations of thought and action: A social cognitive theory.* Englewood Cliffs, NJ: Prentice-Hall.

Barker, R. G. (1965). Exploration in ecological psychology. *American Psychologist, 20*, 1–14.

Bateson, P. P. G. (1978). How does behavior develop? In P. P. G. Bateson & P. H. Klopfer (Eds.), *Perspectives in ethology: Vol. 3. Social behavior.* New York: Plenum Press.

Bell, R. Q. (1968). Reinterpretation of the direction of effects in studies of socialization. *Psychological Review, 75*, 81–95.

Bell, R. Q. (1971). Stimulus control of parent or caretaker by offspring. *Developmental Psychology, 4*, 63–72.

Bergman, L. R. (1988). You can't classify all of the people all of the time. *Multivariate Behavioral Research, 23*, 425–441.

Bergman, L. R., & Magnusson, D. (1984a). *Patterns of adjustment problems at age 10: An empirical and methodological study* (Report No. 615). Stockholm: Department of Psychology, University of Stockholm.

Bergman, L. R., & Magnusson, D. (1984b). *Patterns of adjustment problems at age 13: An empirical and methodological study* (Report No. 620). Stockholm: Department of psychology, University of Stockholm.

Bergman, L. R., & Magnusson, D. (1990). General issues about data quality in longitudinal research. In D. Magnusson & L. R. Bergman (Eds.), *Data quality in longitudinal research.* New York: Cambridge University Press.

Bernstein, M. H. (Ed.). (1987). *Sensitive periods in development: Interdisciplinary perspectives.* Hillsdale, NJ: Erlbaum.

Bertalanffy, L. von. (1968). *General system theory: Foundations, development, applications.* New York: Braziller.

Binet, A. (1910). *Les idées modernes sur les enfants [Modern ideas about children].* Paris: Ernest Flammarion.

Block, J. (1971). *Lives through time.* Berkeley, CA: Bancroft Books.

Bolles, R. C. (1972). Reinforcement, expectancy, and learning. *Psychological Review, 79*, 394–409.

Bookstein, F. L. (1986). The elements of latent variable models: A cautionary lecture. In M. Lamb, A. L. Brown, & B. Rogoff (Eds.), *Advances in developmental psychology* (Vol. 4). Hillsdale, NJ: Erlbaum.

Bower, G. H. (1981). Mood and memory. *American Psychologist, 36*, 129–148.

Bowers, K. S. (1973). Situationism in psychology: An analysis and a critique. *Psychological Review, 80*, 307–336.

Brandstädter, J. (1984). Personal and social control over development: Some implications of an action perspective in life-span developmental psychology. In P. B. Baltes & O. G. Brim (Eds.), *Life-span development and behavior* (Vol. 6). New York: Academic Press.

Brandstädter, J. (1988). Continuity, change and context: Poetics today. *Journal for Theory and Analysis of Literature and Communication, 9*, 187–204.

Bridgeman, P. W. (1927). *Logic of modern physics.* New York: Harper.

Brentano, E. (1924). *Psychologie vom empirischen Standpunkte.* Leipzig: F. Meiner. (Original work published 1874)

Bronfenbrenner, U. (1989). Ecological systems theory. *Annals of Child Development, 6*, 185–246.

Bronfenbrenner, U., & Crouter, A. C. (1983). The evolution of environmental models in developmental research. In W. Kessen (Vol. Ed.), *Handbook of child psychology* (4th ed.): *Vol. 1. History, theory, and methods.* New York: Wiley.

Broughton, J. M. (1984). Not beyond formal operations but beyond Piaget. In M. L. Commons, F. A. Richard, & C. Armon (Eds.), *Beyond formal operations: Late adolescent and adult cognitive development.* New York: Praeger.

Brunswik, E. (1952). *The conceptual framework of psychology.* Chicago: University of Chicago Press.

Burns, R. B. (1979). *The self-concept: In theory, measurement, development and behavior.* London: Longman.

Cairns, R. B. (1979a). *Social development: The origins and plasticity of interchanges.* San Francisco: Freeman Cooper.

Cairns, R. B. (1979b). Toward guidelines for interactional research. In R. B. Cairns (Ed.), *The analysis of social interactions: Methods, issues and illustrations.* Hillsdale, NJ: Erlbaum.

Cairns, R. B. (1980). Developmental theory before Piaget: The remarkable contribution of James Mark Baldwin. *Contemporary Psychology, 25*, 438–440.

Cairns, R. B., & Cairns, B. D. (1985). The developmental–interactional view of social behavior: Four issues of adolescent aggression. In D. Olweus, J. Block, & M. Radke-Yarrow (Eds.), *The development of antisocial and prosocial behavior.* New York: Academic Press.

Cairns, R. B., & Cairns, B. D. (1988). The sociogenesis of self concepts. In A. Bolger, A. Caspi, G. Downey, & M. Moorehouse (Eds.), *Persons in social context: Developmental processes.* Cambridge, England: Cambridge University Press.

Cairns, R. B., & Ornstein, P. A. (1979). Developmental psychology. In E. Hears (Ed.), *The first century of experimental psychology.* Hillsdale, NJ: Erlbaum.

Cannon, W. B. (1914). The emergency function of the adrenal medulla in pain and the major emotions. *American Journal of Physiology, 33*, 356–372.

Carlson, R. (1981). Studies in script theory: I. Adult analogs of a childhood nuclear scene. *Journal of Personality and Social Psychology, 40*, 501–510.

Carr, H. (1925). *Psychology.* New York: Longman-Green.

Cattell, R. B. (1965). *The scientific analysis of personality.* Chicago: Aldine.

Cicchetti, D., & Aber, J. L. (1986). Early precursors of later depression: An organizational perspective. In B. Lipsitt & C. Covee-Collier (Eds.), *Advances in infancy* (Vol. 4). Norwood, NJ: Ablex.

Cicchetti, D., & Sroufe, L. A. (1978). An organizational view of affect: Illustration from the study of Down syndrome infants. In M. Lewis & L. Rosenblum (Eds.), *The development of affect.* New York: Plenum Press.

Cofer, C. N. (1981). Introduction: Enduring issues and the nature of psychology. In R. A. Kasschau & C. N. Cofer (Eds.), *Psychology's second century: Enduring issues.* New York: Praeger.

Cronbach, L. J. (1975). Beyond the two disciplines of scientific psychology. *American Psychologist, 30*, 116–127.

Datan, N., Rodeheaver, D., & Hughes, F. (1987). Adult development and aging. *Annual Review of Psychology, 38*, 153–180.

Davis, A. J., & Hathaway, B. K. (1982). Reciprocity in parent–child verbal interactions. *Journal of Genetic Psychology, 140*, 169–183.

Day, R., Zubin, J., & Steinhauer, S. R. (1987). Psychosocial factors in schizophrenia in light of vulnerability theory. In D. Magnusson & A. Öhman (Eds.), *Psychopathology: An interactional perspective.* New York: Academic Press.

de Ribaupierre, A. (Ed.). (1989). Transition mechanism in child development: The longitudinal perspective. New York: Cambridge University Press.

Eccles, J., & Robinson, D. N. (1985). *The wonder of being human.* Boston: New Science Library.

Ekehammar, B. (1974). Interactionism in personality from a historical perspective. *Psychological Bulletin, 81*, 1026–1048.

Elder, G. H., Jr., Caspi, A., & Downey, G. (1986). Problem behavior and family relationships: Life course and intergenerational themes. In A. B. Sörensen, F. E. Weinhart, & L. R. Shervod (Eds.), *Human development and the life course.* Hillsdale, NJ: Erlbaum.

Emmerich, W. (1964). Continuity and stability in early social development. *Child Development, 35*, 311–332.

Endler, N. S. (1975). A person–situation interaction model of anxiety. In C. D. Spielberger & J. G. Sarason (Eds.), *Stress and anxiety* (Vol. 1). Washington, DC: Hemisphere.

Endler, N. S. (1983). A personality model, but not yet a theory. In M. M. Page (Ed.), *Nebraska Symposium on Motivation.* Lincoln: University of Nebraska Press.

Endler, N. S. (1984). Interactionism. In N. S. Endler & J. M. Hunt (Eds.), *Personality and the behavioral disorders* (Vol. 1). New York: Wiley.

Endler, N. S., & Magnusson, D. (1976). Toward an interactional psychology of personality. *Psychological Bulletin, 83*, 956–979.

Epstein, S. (1979). The stability of behavior: On predicting most of the people much of the time. *Journal of Personality and Social Psychology, 37*, 1097–1126.

Epstein, S., & Erskine, N. (1983). The development of personal theories of reality from an interactional perspective. In D. Magnusson & V. L. Allen (Eds.), *Human development: An interactional perspective.* New York: Academic Press.

Eysenck, H. J. (1983). Is there a paradigm in personality research? *Journal of Research in Personality, 17*, 369–397.

Eysenck, H. J., & Eysenck, M. W. (1985). *Personality and individual differences: A natural science approach.* New York: Plenum Press.

Featherman, D., & Lerner, R. M. (1985). *Ontogenesis and sociogenesis: Problematics for theory and research about development and socialization across the life span* (Scholarly Report Series No. 6). University Park: Center for the Study of Child and Adolescent Development, Pennsylvania State University.

Filipp, S.-H., & Olbrich, E. (1986). Human development across the life-span: Overview and highlights of the psychological perspective. In A. B. Sörensen, F. E. Weinart, & L. R. Sherrod (Eds.), *Human development and the life.* Hillsdale, NJ: Erlbaum.

Frankenhaeuser, M. (1983). The sympathetic–adrenal and pituitary adrenal response to challenge: Comparison between the sexes. In T. M. Dembroski, T. H.

Schmidt, & G. Blümchen (Eds.), *Biobehavioral bases of coronary heart disease.* Basel: S. Karger.

Galton, F. (1869). *Hereditary genius: An inquiry into its laws and consequences.* London: Macmillan.

Gardner, H. (1983). *Frames of mind.* New York: Basic Books.

Garn, S. H. (1980). Continuities and change in maturational timing. In O. G. Brim & J. Kagan (Eds.), *Constancy and change in human development.* Cambridge, MA: Harvard University Press.

Gergen, K. J. (1973). Toward generative theory. *Journal of Personality and Social Psychology, 26*, 309–320.

Gottlieb, G. (1983). The psychobiological approach to developmental issues. In M. M. Haith & J. J. Campos (Vol. Eds.), *Handbook of child psychology* (4th ed.): *Vol. 2. Infancy and developmental psychobiology.* New York: Wiley.

Gunnar, M. R. (1986). Human developmental psychoendocrinology: A review of research on neuroendocrine responses to challenge and threat in infancy and childhood. In M. E. Lamb, A. L. Brown, & B. Rogoff (Eds.), *Advances in developmental psychology* (Vol. 4). Hillsdale, NJ: Erlbaum.

Gustafson, S., Stattin, H., & Magnusson, D. (1989). *Aspects of the development and moderation of sex role orientation among females: A longitudinal study.* (Report No. 694). Stockholm: Department of Psychology, University of Stockholm.

Harter, S. (1983). Developmental perspectives on the self system. In E. M. Hetherington (Vol. Ed.), *Handbook of child psychology* (4th ed.): *Vol. 4. Socialization, personality, and social development.* New York: Wiley.

Hartup, W. W. (1978). Perspectives on child and family interaction: Past, present and future. In R. M. Lerner & G. B. Spanier (Eds.), *Child influences on marital and family interaction.* New York: Academic Press.

Hebb, D. O. (1955). Drives and the CNS (conceptual nervous system). *Psychological Review, 62*, 243–254.

Heckhausen, H. (1983). Concern with one's competence: Developmental shifts in person–environment interaction. In D. Magnusson & V. L. Allen (Eds.), *Human development: An interactional perspective.* Hillsdale, NJ: Erlbaum.

Hettema, P. J. (1979). *Personality and adaptation.* Amsterdam: North-Holland.

Hinde, R. A., & Bateson, P. (1984). Discontinuities versus continuities in behavioral development and the neglect of process. *International Journal of Behavioral Development, 7*, 129–143.

Hinde, R. A., & Dennis, A. (1986). Categorizing individuals: An alternative to linear analysis. *International Journal of Behavioral Development, 9*, 105–119.

Hofer, M. A. (1981). *The roots of human behavior: An introduction to the psychobiology of early development.* San Francisco: W. H. Freeman.

Hubel, D. H., & Wiesel, T. N. (1970). The period of susceptibility to the physiological effects of unilateral eye closure in kittens. *Journal of Physiology, 206*, 419–436.

Hultsch, D. F., & Plemons, J. K. (1979). Life events and life-span development. In P. B. Baltes & O. G. Brim (Eds.), *Life-span development and behavior* (Vol. 2). New York: Academic Press.

Hunt, J. M. (1961). *Intelligence and experience.* New York: Ronald Press.

Hyland, M. (1981). *Introduction to theoretical psychology*. London: Macmillan.

James, W. (1890). *The principles of psychology*. New York: Holt.

Jensen, A. R. (1981). *Straight talk about mental tests*. London: Methuen.

Johansson, B., & Berg, S. (1989). The robustness of the terminal decline phenomena: Longitudinal data from the digit-span memory test. *Journal of Gerontology; Psychological Sciences, 44*, 184–186.

Kagan, J. (1971). *Change and continuity in infancy*. New York: Wiley.

Kagan, J. (1978). Continuity and change in human development. In P. P. G. Bateson & P. H. Klopfer (Eds.), *Perspectives in ethology: Vol. 3. Social behavior*. New York: Plenum Press.

Kagan, J. (1984). The idea of emotion in human development. In C. E. Izard, J. Kagan, & R. B. Zajonc (Eds.), *Emotions, cognition and behavior*. Cambridge, England: Cambridge University Press.

Kalverboer, A. F., & Hopkins, B. (1983). General introduction: A biopsychological approach to the study of human behavior. *Journal of Child Psychology and Psychiatry, 24*, 9–10.

Kamin, L. J. (1974). *The science and politics of IQ*. Harmondsworth, England: Penguin Books.

Koffka, K. (1935). *Principles of gestalt psychology*. New York: Harcourt.

Kohlberg, L. (1969). Stage and sequence: The cognitive-developmental approach to socialization. In D. A. Goolin (Ed.), *Handbook of socialization theory and research*. Chicago: Ran McNally.

Krantz, D. S., Lundberg, U., & Frankenhaeuser, M. (1987). Stress and Type A behavior: Interactions between environmental and biological factors. In A. Baum & J. E. Singer (Eds.), *Handbook of psychology and health: Vol. 5. Stress and coping*. Hillsdale, NJ: Erlbaum.

Krech, D., & Crutchfield, R. S. (1948). *Theories and problems of social psychology*. New York: McGraw-Hill.

Kuo, Z.-Y. (1967). *The dynamics of behavior development: An epigenetic view*. New York: Random House.

Langer, J. (1969). *Theories of development*. New York: Holt, Rinehart & Winston.

Lazarus, R. S., & Launier, R. (1978). Stress-related transactions between person and environment. In L. A. Pervin & M. Lewis(Eds.), *Perspectives in interactional psychology*. New York: Plenum Press.

Lerner, R. M. (1984). *On the nature of human plasticity*. Cambridge, England: Cambridge University Press.

Lerner, R. M., & Busch-Rossnagel, N. A. (1981). Individuals as producers of their development: Conceptual and empirical bases. In R. M. Lerner & N. A. Busch-Rossnagel (Eds.), *Individuals as producers of their development: A life-span perspective*. New York: Academic Press.

Lerner, R. M., & Kauffman, M. B. (1985). The concept of development in contextualism. *Developmental Review, 5*, 309–333.

Leuba, C. (1955). Toward some integration of learning theories: The concept of optimal stimulation. *Psychological Reports, 1*, 27–33.

Levine, S. (1982). Comparative and psychobiological perspectives on development. In W. A. Collins (Ed.), *The Minnesota Symposium on Child Psychology: Vol. 15. The concept of development*. Hillsdale, NJ: Erlbaum.

Lewin, K. (1931). Environmental forces. In C. Murchison (Ed.), *A handbook of child psychology*. Worcester, MA: Clark University Press.

Lewin, K. (1935). *A dynamic theory of personality*. New York: McGraw-Hill.

Lewis, M., & Brooks-Gunn, J. (1979). *Social cognition and the acquisition of self*. New York: Plenum Press.

Livson, N., & Peskin, H. (1980). Perspectives on adolescence from longitudinal research. In J. Adelson (Ed.), *Handbook of adolescent psychology*. New York: Wiley.

Ljung, B.-O. (1965). *The adolescent spurt in mental growth*. Stockholm: Almqvist & Wiksell.

Loevinger, J. (1966). Models and measures of developmental variation. *Annals of the New York Academy of Sciences, 134*, 585–590.

Lonner, N. (1980). The search for psychological universals. In H. Triandis, W. Lambert, J. Berry, W. Lonner, A. Heron, R. Briolin, & J. Dragerns (Eds.), *Handbook of cross-cultural psychology* (Vol. 6). Boston: Allyn & Bacon.

Lorenz, K. (1965). *Evolution and the modification of behavior*. Chicago: University of Chicago Press.

Magnusson, D. (1976). The person and the situation in an interactional model of behavior. *Scandinavian Journal of Psychology, 17*, 253–271.

Magnusson, D. (1980a). Personality in an interactional paradigm of research. *Zeitschrift für Differentielle und Diagnostische Psychologie, 1*, 17–34.

Magnusson, D. (1980b). Trait–state anxiety: A note on conceptual and empirical relationships. *Personality and Individual Differences, 1*, 215–217.

Magnusson, D. (1981a). Problems in environmental analyses—an introduction. In D. Magnusson (Ed.), *Toward a psychology of situations: An interactional perspective*. Hillsdale, NJ: Erlbaum.

Magnusson, D. (Ed.). (1981b). *Toward a psychology of situations: An interactional perspective*. Hillsdale, NJ: Erlbaum.

Magnusson, D. (1984a). On the situational context. In K. M. J. Lagerspetz & P. Niemi (Eds.), *Psychology in the 1990's*. Amsterdam: Elsevier.

Magnusson, D. (1984b). The situation in an interactional paradigm of personality research. In V. Sarris & A. Parducci (Eds.), *Perspectives in psychological experimentation: Toward the year 2000*. Hillsdale, NJ: Erlbaum.

Magnusson, D. (1985). Implications of an interactional paradigm for research on human development. *International Journal of Behavior Development, 8*, 115–137.

Magnusson, D. (1988). Individual development from an interactional perspective: A longitudinal study. In D. Magnusson (Ed.), *Paths through life* (Vol. 1). Hillsdale, NJ: Erlbaum.

Magnusson, D., & Bergman, L. R. (1988). Individual and variable-based approaches to longitudinal research on early risk factors. In M. Ruther (Ed.), *Studies of psychosocial risk: The power of longitudinal data*. Cambridge, England: Cambridge University Press.

Magnusson, D., & Bergman, L. R. (Eds.). (1990). *Data quality in longitudinal research*. New York: Cambridge University Press.

Magnusson, D., & Endler, N. S. (Eds.). (1977). *Personality at the crossroads: Current issues in interactional psychology*. Hillsdale, NJ: Erlbaum.

Magnusson, D., Stattin, H., & Allen, V. (1985). Biological maturation and social development: A longitudinal study of some adjustment processes from mid-adolescence to adulthood. *Journal of Youth and Adolescence, 14*, 267–283.

Markus, H., & Wurf, E. (1987). The dynamic self-concept: A social psychological perspective. *Annual Review of Psychology, 38,* 299–337.

McCall, R. B. (1977). Challenges to a science of developmental psychology. *Child Development, 48,* 333–344.

McClelland, D. C. (1955). *Studies in motivation.* New York: Appleton-Century-Crofts.

McClintock, M. K. (1971). Menstrual synchrony and suppression. *Nature, 229,* 224–225.

Medawar, P. (1984). *Pluto's republic.* Oxford: Oxford University Press.

Miller, J. G. (1978). *Living systems.* New York: McGraw-Hill.

Miller, N. E., & Dollard, J. (1941). *Social learning and imitation.* New Haven, CT: Yale University Press.

Mineka, S., & Kihlstrom, J. F. (1978). Unpredictable and uncontrollable events: A new perspective on experimental neurosis. *Journal of Abnormal Psychology, 87,* 256–271.

Mischel, W. (1968). *Personality and assessment.* New York: Wiley.

Mischel, W. (1973). Toward a cognitive social learning reconceptualization of personality. *Psychological Review, 80,* 252–283.

Murray, H. A. (1938). *Explorations in personality.* New York: Oxford University Press.

Murphy, L. B. (1983). Issues in the development of emotion in infancy. In R. Plutchite & H. Kellerman (Eds.), *Emotion: Theory, research, and experience. Vol. 2. Emotions in early development.* New York: Academic Press.

Nesselroade, J. R. (1988). Some implications of the trait–state dysfunction for the study of development over the life span: The case of personality. In P. B. Baltes, D. L. Featherman, & R. L. Lerner (Eds.), *Life span development* (Vol. 8). Hillsdale, NJ: Erlbaum.

Öhman, A., & Magnusson, D. (1987). An interactional paradigm for research on psychopathology. In D. Magnusson & A. Öhman (Eds.), *Psychopathology: An interactional perspective.* New York: Academic Press.

Olweus, D. (1977). A critical analysis of the "modern" interactionist position. In D. Magnusson & N. S. Endler (Eds.), *Personality at the crossroads: Current issues in interactional psychology.* Hillsdale, NJ: Erlbaum.

Parke, R. D. (1978). Parent–infant interaction: Progress paradigms and problems. In G. P. Sackett (Ed.), *Theory and applications in mental retardation: Vol. 1. Observing behavior.* Baltimore: University Park Press.

Pepper, S. C. (1942). *World hypotheses: A study in evidence.* Berkeley: University of California Press.

Pervin, L. (1968). Performance and satisfaction as a function of individual environment fit. *Psychological Bulletin, 69,* 56–68.

Pervin, L. A. (1978). Definitions, measurements, and classifications of stimuli, situations, and environments. *Human Ecology, 6,* 71–105.

Pervin, L. A. (1983a). Idiographic approaches to personality. In N. S. Endler & J. M. Hunt (Eds.), *Personality and the behavioral disorders* (Vol. 1). New York: Wiley.

Pervin, L. (1983b). The stasis and flow of behavior: Toward a theory of goals. In M. M. Page (Ed.), *Nebraska Symposium on Motivation.* Lincoln: University of Nebraska Press.

Pervin, L. A. (1985). Personality: Current controversies, issues and directions. *Annual Review of Psychology, 36,* 83–114.

Pervin, L. A., & Lewis, M. (Eds.). (1978). *Perspectives in interactional psychology.* New York: Plenum Press.

Petersen, A. (1988). Adolescent development. *Annual Review of Psychology, 39,* 583–607.

Peterson, D. R. (1968). *The clinical study of social behavior.* New York: Appleton.

Peterson, D. R. (1979). Assessing interpersonal relationships by means of interaction research. *Behavioral Assessment, 1,* 221–276.

Piaget, J. (1948). *The moral judgment of the child.* Glencoe, IL: Free Press.

Plomin, R. (1986). Behavioral genetic methods. *Journal of Personality, 54,* 226–261.

Plomin, R. (1989). Environment and genes. Determinants of behavior. *American Psychologist, 4,* 105–111.

Plomin, R., & Daniels, D. (1984). The interaction between temperament and environment: Methodological considerations. *Merrill–Palmer Quarterly, 30,* 149–162.

Plomin, R., De Fries, J. C., & Loehlin, J. (1977). Genotype–environment interaction and correlation in the analysis of human behavior. *Psychological Bulletin, 84,* 309–322.

Popper, K. R., & Eccles, J. C. (1977). *The self and its brain.* Berlin: Springer-Verlag.

Raleigh, M. J., McGuire, M. T., Brammer, G. L., & Yuwiler, J. (1984). Social and environmental influences on blood serotonin concentrations in monkeys. *Archives of General Psychiatry, 41,* 405–410.

Rasmuson, M. (1983). The role of genes as determinants of behavior. In D. Magnusson & V. L. Allen (Eds.), *Human development: An interactional perspective.* New York: Academic Press.

Raush, H. L. (1977). Paradox levels and junctures in person–situation systems. In D. Magnusson & N. S. Endler (Eds.), *Personality at the crossroads: Current issues in interactional psychology.* Hillsdale, NJ: Erlbaum.

Rotter, J. B. (1955). The role of the psychological situation in determining the direction of human behavior. In M. R. Jones (Ed.), *Nebraska Symposium on Motivation.* Lincoln: University of Nebraska Press.

Rutter, M. (1983). Statistical and personal interactions: Facets and perspectives. In D. Magnusson & V. L. Allen (Eds.), *Human development: An interactional perspective.* New York: Academic Press.

Rutter, M. (1989a). Pathways from childhood to adult life. *Journal of Child Psychology and Psychiatry, 30,* 23–51.

Rutter, M. (Ed.). (1989b). *Studies of psychosocial risk: The power of longitudinal data.* Cambridge, England: Cambridge University Press.

Sameroff, A. L. (1975). Transactional models in early social relations. *Human Development, 18,* 65–79.

Sameroff, A. J. (1982). Development and the dialectic: The need for a systems approach. In W. A. Collins (Ed.), *The concept of development.* Hillsdale, NJ: Erlbaum.

Sameroff, A. J. (1983). Developmental systems: Contexts and evolution. In W. Kessen (Vol. Ed.), *Handbook of child psychology* (4th ed.): *Vol. 1. History, theory, and methods.* New York: Wiley.

Scarr, S. (1981). Comments on psychology: Behavior genetics and social policy from an antireductionist. In R. A. Kasschan & C. N. Cofer (Eds.), *Psychology's second century: Enduring issues.* New York: Praeger.

Scarr, S., & McCartney, K. (1983). How people make their own environments: A theory of genotype–

environment effects. *Child Development, 54,* 424–435.

Schaie, K. W. (1965). A general model for the study of developmental problems. *Psychological Bulletin, 64,* 92–107.

Schneirla, T. C. (1972). Levels in the psychological capacities of animals. In L. R. Aronson, E. Tobach, J. S. Rosenblatt, D. S. Lehrman (Eds.), *Selected writings of T. C. Schneirla.* San Francisco: Freeman Cooper.

Sears, R. R. (1951). A theoretical framework for personality and social behavior. *American Psychologist, 6,* 476–483.

Seligman, M. E. P. (1975). *Helplessness: On depression, development and death.* San Francisco: Freeman Cooper.

Sells, S. B. (1966). Ecology and the science of psychology. *Multivariate Behavioral Research, 1,* 131–144.

Selye, H. (1950). *Stress: The physiology and pathology of exposure to stress.* Montreal: Acta.

Silbereisen, R. K., Boehnke, K., & Reykowski, J. (1986). Prosocial motives from 12 to 18: A comparison of adolescents from Berlin (West) and Warsaw. In R. K. Silbereisen, K. Eyforth, & G. Rudinger (Eds.), *Development as action in context.* Berlin: Springer-Verlag.

Skinner, B. F. (1971). *Beyond freedom and dignity.* New York: Knopf.

Skinner, B. F. (1978). *Reflections on behaviorism and society.* Englewood Cliffs, NJ: Prentice-Hall.

Snow, C. (1987). Relevance of the notion of a critical period to language acquisition. In M. H. Bernstein (Ed.), *Sensitive periods in development: Interdisciplinary perspectives.* Hillsdale, NJ: Erlbaum.

Spielberger, C. D. (1977). State–trait anxiety and interactional psychology. In D. Magnusson & N. S. Endler (Eds.), *Personality at the crossroads: Current issues in interactional psychology.* Hillsdale, NJ: Erlbaum.

Sroufe, L. A., & Rutter, M. (1984). The domain of developmental psychopathology. *Child Development, 55,* 17–29.

Staats, A. W. (1981). Paradigmatic behaviorism, unified theory, unified theory construction, methods and the zeitgeist of separatism. *American Psychologist, 36,* 239–256.

Stattin, H., & Magnusson, D. (1990). Pubertal-maturation in female development. In D. Magnusson (Ed.), *Paths through life* (Vol. 2). Hillsdale, NJ: Erlbaum.

Stern, W. (1911). *Die differentielle Psychologie in ihrem methodischen Grundlagen.* Leipzig: Verlag von Johann A. Barth.

Strelau, J. (1983). *Temperament–personality–activity.* New York: Academic Press.

Stumpf, C. (1883). *Tonpsychologie* (Vol. 1). Leipzig: S. Hirzel.

Susman, L. (1989). Biology–behavior interactions in behavioral development. *ISSBD Newsletter,* No. 15, pp. 1–3.

Tanner, J. M. (1978). *Foetus into man: Physical growth from conception to maturity.* London: Open Books.

Thomae, H. (1988). *Das Individuum und seine Welt: Eine Persönlichkeitstheorie.* Göttingen, West Germany: Hogrefe.

Thorndike, E. L. (1903). *Educational psychology.* New York: Columbia University Press.

Tolman, E. C. (1951). A psychological model. In T. Parsons & E. A. Shils (Eds.), *Toward a general theory of action.* Cambridge, MA: Harvard University Press.

Tomkins, S. S. (1986). Script theory. In J. Aronoff, R. A. Zucker, & A. J. Rabin (Eds.), *Structuring personality.* New York: Academic Press.

Törestad, B., & Magnusson, D. (1982). *Frequency and intensity of anxiety reactions* (Report No. 593). Stockholm: Department of Psychology, University of Stockholm.

Törestad, B., Olah, A., & Magnusson, D. (1989). Individual control, intensity of reactions, and frequency of occurrence: An empirical study of cross-culturally invariant relations. *Perceptual and Motor Skills, 68,* 1139–1150.

Toulmin, S. (1981). Toward reintegration: An agenda for psychology's second century. In R. A. Kasschau & C. N. Cofer (Eds.), *Psychology's second century: Enduring issues.* New York: Praeger.

Urban, H. B. (1978). The concept of development from a systems perspective. In P. Baltes (Ed.), *Life-span development and behavior* (Vol. 1). New York: Academic Press.

Uzgiris, I. C. (1977). Plasticity and structure: The role of experience in infancy. In I. C. Uzgiris & F. Weizmann (Eds.), *The structuring of experience.* New York: Plenum Press.

Vagg, P. R., Spielberger, C. D., & O'Hearn, T. P. (1980). Is the state–trait anxiety inventory multidimensional? *Personality and Individual Differences, 1,* 207–214.

von Eye, A., & Brandstädter, J. (1988). Evaluating developmental hypothesis using statement calculus and nonparametric statistics. In P. B. Baltes, D. L. Featherman, & R. L. Levarer (Eds.), *Life-span development and behavior* (Vol. 8). New York: Academic Press.

Vygotsky, L. (1962). *Thought and language.* Cambridge, MA: MIT Press.

Waber, D. P. (1977). Sex differences in mental abilities, hemispheric lateralization, and rate of physical growth at adolescence. *Developmental Psychology, 13,* 29–38.

Wachs, T. D. (1977). The optimal stimulation hypothesis and early development: Anybody got a match? In I. C. Uzgiris & F. Weizmann (Eds.), *The structuring of experience.* New York: Plenum Press.

Wapner, S., & Kaplan, B. (Eds.). (1983). *Toward a holistic developmental psychology.* Hillsdale, NJ: Erlbaum.

Watson, J. B. (1930). *Behaviorism* (2nd ed.). New York: Norton.

Wohlwill, J. F. (1970). The age variable in psychological research. *Psychological Review, 77,* 49–64.

Wohlwill, J. F. (1973a). The concept of experience: S or R? *Human Development, 16,* 90–107.

Wohlwill, J. F. (1973b). *The study of behavioral development.* London: Academic Press.

Woodworth, R. S. (1918). *Dynamic psychology.* New York: Columbia University Press.

Wundt, W. (1948). Principles of physiological psychology. In W. Dennis (Ed.). *Readings in the history of psychology.* New York: Appleton-Century Crofts.

Zajonc, R. B., & Markus, H. (1984). Affect and cognition: The hard interface. In C. E. Izard, J. Kagan, & R. B. Zajonc (Eds.), *Emotions, cognition, and behavior.* Cambridge, England: Cambridge University Press.

Zuckerman, M. (1983). The distinctions between trait and state scales is not arbitrary: Comment on Allen and Potkay's "On the arbitrary distinction between traits and states." *Journal of Personality and Social Psychology, 44,* 1083–1086.

PART III
INTERFACE WITH OTHER FIELDS

Chapter 9

Behavioral Genetics and Personality

Robert Plomin and Heather M. Chipuer
Pennsylvania State University
John C. Loehlin
University of Texas

Shakespeare first brought the words "nature" and "nurture" together in *The Tempest* (1611/1974), when Prospero, speaking of Caliban says:

> A devil, a born devil, on whose nature
> Nurture can never stick; on whom my pains
> Humanely taken, all, all lost, quite lost . . .
> (IV.i.188–190)

This example of nurture in conflict with nature provided the impetus for the alliterative phrase "nature–nurture," coined by Francis Galton (1865) over 100 years ago. Joining these two words created a fission that exploded into the longest-lived controversy in the social and behavioral sciences. As in Shakespeare, the hyphen in nature–nurture connoted the implicit conjunction "versus." The appropriate conjunction is "and."

Behavioral genetics uses methods derived from quantitative genetic theory (Falconer, 1981) to ascribe observed differences among individuals to genetic and environmental sources. Until recently, these methods have mostly been used merely to demonstrate that genetic factors are important in the origins of individual differences in personality. However, the term "behavioral genetics" can be misleading, in that the theory and its methods are as informative about environmental components of variance as they are about genetic factors. For example, in addition to documenting the influence of heredity, behavioral genetic data provide the best available evidence for the importance of nongenetic factors in the etiology of individual differences in personality. Although it may seem obvious to most personality researchers that environmental influences have effects, good quantitative estimates of their importance are not easily achieved. Despite the reluctance of the behavioral sciences to acknowledge genetic influences even through the 1970s, genetic influence has become increasingly accepted during the 1980s. It is good for the field of personality that it has moved away from simple-minded environmentalism. The danger now, however, is that the rush from environmentalism will carom too far—to a view that personality is almost completely biologically determined. This tendency seems especially pronounced in research on psychopathology, where the search is on for single genes and simple neurochemical triggers. Although it would be splendid if simple biochemical answers could be found, this happy outcome seems unlikely, because psychopathology is at least as much influenced by environmental factors as it is by heredity (Plomin, DeFries, & McClearn, 1990). This also appears to be the case for normal personality.

The primary goal of this chapter is to provide an overview of some current areas of interest in behavioral genetic research on personality. We hope to illustrate what is known, what needs to be learned, and what new methods will shape research in the future. We assume that the reader has some general acquaintance with the methods of human behavioral genetics—family, twin, adoption, and combination designs. These methods are described in several textbooks (Dixon & Johnson, 1980; Falconer, 1981; Fuller & Thompson, 1978; Hay, 1985; Plomin, DeFries, & McClearn, 1990), as well as in an article specifically focused on behavioral genetic methods in personality research (Plomin, 1986a) and in two books on behavioral genetic research in personality (Cattell, 1982; Eaves, Eysenck, & Martin, 1989).

The chapter begins with a detailed discussion of two emerging findings in behavioral genetic research on personality: Identical-twin correlations are often more than twice as large as fraternal-twin correlations, and heritability estimates from twin studies often exceed estimates from adoption studies. The rest of the chapter consists of very brief overviews of other advances in behavioral genetic research on personality, with references that provide additional discussion. These issues include understanding the polygenic nature of genetic influence on personality; model-fitting analyses of behavioral genetic data; analysis of covariance among traits using multivariate techniques; exploration of long- and short-term personality change; and new behavioral genetic techniques that can explore links between the normal distribution of personality and its abnormal extremes. Although these advances are helpful in understanding nurture as well as nature, two new advances in this direction are especially relevant for the study of environmental influences in personality. The first in-

volves the possibility of genetic mediation of associations between environmental measures and personality. The second may be the most important finding in behavioral genetic research on personality: Environmental influences that affect personality do not make children in the same family similar to one another.

At the outset, it should be noted that all but a few behavioral genetic studies of personality rely on self-report personality questionnaires for adolescents and young adults, and on parental ratings for children. Very few behavioral genetic studies have used other methods, such as direct observations (Plomin, 1981). Moreover, behavioral genetic research has scarcely begun to be incorporated in the "New Look" in personality research that emerged after the 1970s, the "decade of doubt" (West, 1983). The methods of behavioral genetics are waiting to be applied to issues raised by advances in personality theory and measurement such as those described in this volume: social cognition (Cantor & Zirkel, Chapter 6, and Mischel, Chapter 5); approaches to the unconscious (Kihlstrom, Chapter 17); emotional expression and stress (Smith & Lazarus, Chapter 23); interactional approaches (Magnusson, Chapter 8); the self (Markus & Cross, Chapter 22); and attribution theory (Weiner, Chapter 18).

GENETIC INFLUENCE

As indicated in several reviews (Goldsmith, 1983; Loehlin, Willerman, & Horn, 1988; Plomin, 1986b), genetic influence on self-report measures of personality is nearly ubiquitous. Much of this evidence relies on comparisons between correlations for identical, or monozygotic (MZ), and fraternal, or dizygotic (DZ), twins. On average across diverse personality dimensions, MZ correlations are about .50, and DZ correlations are about .30 (Loehlin & Nichols, 1976). These twin correlations suggest that genetic influence on personality is not only significant but substantial. Doubling the difference between the two correlations results in an estimate that heritability, the proportion of phenotypic variance explained by genetic variance, is 40%.

The plot of this simple story has thickened as the field has advanced in two ways. First, very large twin studies have been reported. The low standard errors in these studies make it possible to believe in a finding that had begun to emerge from earlier, smaller, studies. The usual twin model assumes that MZ correlations can be no more than twice the magnitude of DZ correlations, because MZ twins are only twice as similar as DZ twins in terms of additive genetic variance. That is, the MZ:DZ ratio should be less than 2. On the contrary, for some traits, the MZ:DZ ratio substantially exceeds 2. The second complication is that adoption studies of personality have appeared in recent years, and these suggest less genetic influence than do the twin studies.

The purpose of this section is to document these two new findings and to explore possible explanations.

Monozygotic:Dizygotic Ratios Greater Than 2

Despite the average MZ and DZ correlations of .50 and .30, which yield an MZ:DZ ratio of 1.7, some personality traits—notably extraversion—yield DZ correlations that are consistently less than half the MZ correlations. A review of twin studies of extraversion and neuroticism concluded, "Of the 30 recent large sample MZ-DZ comparisons available, the DZ correlation was less than half that of the corre-

sponding MZ correlation in all cases for extraversion and in 22 cases for neuroticism" (Henderson, 1982, p. 419).

Four large twin studies of extraversion and neuroticism totaling over 23,000 pairs of twins have recently been reviewed (Loehlin, 1989). Table 9.1 reprints this summary of twin correlations. For extraversion, the weighted average MZ and DZ correlations are .51 and .18, respectively. For neuroticism, the corresponding average MZ and DZ correlations are .48 and .20. Thus, instead of the MZ:DZ ratio being less than 2, it is 2.8 for extraversion and 2.4 for neuroticism. For both traits, the MZ:DZ ratio exceeded 2 for both males and females in each of the four studies, conducted in four different countries. Doubling the difference between the MZ and DZ correlations yields heritability estimates of .65 for extraversion and .54 for neuroticism, but these are clearly overestimates of heritability because they exceed the MZ correlation itself, which is an upper-limit estimate of heritability.

Twin data are not available on anything like this scale for other personality traits. In the literature, MZ:DZ ratios greater than 2 are frequently reported for personality inventory scales, as are MZ:DZ ratios less than 2, but without enough consistency across studies to justify firm conclusions. Part of the problem is that the same measures are rarely included in

TABLE 9.1. Four Twin Studies of Neuroticism and Extraversion

	Neuroticism				Extraversion			
Samples	MZ-F	MZ-M	DZ-F	DZ-M	MZ-F	MZ-M	DZ-F	DZ-M
U.S. adolescents	.48	.58	.23	.26	.62	.57	.28	.20
Swedish adults	.54	.46	.25	.21	.54	.47	.21	.20
Australian adults	.52	.46	.26	.18	.53	.50	.19	.13
Finnish adults	.43	.33	.18	.12	.49	.46	.14	.15
Numbers of pairs								
United States	284	197	190	122	284	197	190	122
Sweden	2,720	2,279	4,143	3,670	2,713	2,274	4,130	3,660
Australia	1,233	566	751	351	1,233	566	751	351
Finland	1,293	1,027	2,520	2,304	1,293	1,027	2,520	2,304

Note. MZ, monozygotic; DZ, dizygotic; F, female; M, male. Studies: United States, Loehlin & Nichols (1976); Sweden, Floderus-Myrhed, Pedersen, & Rasmuson (1980); Australia, Martin & Jardine (1986); Finland, Rose, Koskenvuo, Kaprio, Sarna, & Langinvainio (1988). The table is from "Environmental and Genetic Contributions to Behavioral Development" by J. C. Loehlin, 1989, *American Psychologist, 44*, 1285–1292. Copyright 1989 by American Psychological Association.

more than one study. Another part of the problem is that twin sample sizes are often small.

In infancy and early childhood, twin data rely primarily on parental ratings, and these typically result in an extreme pattern of MZ:DZ ratios greater than 2. For example, the Emotionality, Activity, and Sociability (EAS) questionnaires of Buss and Plomin (1984) yield MZ correlations of about .60 and DZ correlations near zero during childhood. Simply doubling the difference between the MZ and DZ correlations implies a heritability greater than 1.0, whereas the MZ correlation itself suggests an upper-limit heritability estimate of .60.

Twin Heritability Estimates Greater Than Adoption Heritability Estimates

In addition to MZ correlations that are greater than twice DZ correlations, another finding that has recently emerged is that adoption studies of personality indicate less genetic influence than do the twin studies (Loehlin et al., 1988).

As just mentioned, parental rating data in childhood suggest very high heritability estimates, because MZ correlations are high whereas DZ correlations tend to be near zero. By contrast, adoption data using parental ratings of personality in childhood suggest low or even negligible heritability. Longitudinal data have been obtained yearly from 1 to 7 years of age in the Colorado Adoption Project (CAP; Plomin, Coon, Carey, DeFries, & Fulker, 1989; Plomin, DeFries, & Fulker, 1988). The CAP included 245 adoptive families and 245 matched nonadoptive families—biological parents and their adopted-away children, adoptive parents and their adopted children, matched nonadoptive parents and their children, and adopted and nonadopted siblings in these families. The average personality correlations in the CAP were .00 for biological mothers and their adopted-away offspring, .05 for adoptive parents and their adopted children, .10 for nonadoptive parents and their children, .07 for nonadoptive siblings, and .05 for adoptive siblings. This pattern of correlations provides little or no evidence for hereditary influence on personality at these ages—a conclusion supported by model-fitting analyses of the CAP parent–offspring and sibling data.

Similarly, little effect of heredity was found somewhat later in childhood in two other adop-

tion studies of families that included both adopted and natural children: the Minnesota transracial adoption study of 101 adoptive families (Scarr, Webber, Weinberg, & Wittig, 1981), and the Texas Adoption Project of 300 adoptive families (Loehlin, Horn, & Willerman, 1981; Loehlin, Willerman, & Horn, 1982). The average ages of the children were about 7 years for adoptees and about 10 years for natural children, with a wide age range. Across the two studies, the average weighted correlation for personality was .05 between parents and their natural children (340 pairings), and the correlation between parents and their adopted children was .07 (501 pairings). No sign of genetic influence can be found in these results. In the Texas study, estimates of genetic influence were also available from comparisons between biological mothers and their adopted-away offspring. The adjusted R^2 for regressions of adoptees' personality ratings on biological mothers' Minnesota Multiphasic Personality Inventory (MMPI) scales was .02, again suggesting negligible genetic influence.

Nonadoptive and adoptive siblings were also studied in the Texas and Minnesota projects. In the Texas study, the sibling adoption design again yielded no evidence for genetic influence: Average correlations were .05 for 24 pairs of nonadoptive siblings and .04 for 109 pairs of adoptive siblings. The Minnesota study suggested some genetic influence, in that the nonadoptive sibling correlation (.19 for 40 pairs) exceeded the adoptive sibling correlation (.01 for 66 pairs). However, the difference between the nonadoptive and adoptive sibling correlations is not nearly significant for samples of this size.

Adoption studies of self-reported personality in late adolescence or early adulthood have found evidence for genetic influence, but substantially less than heritabilities from twin studies at comparable ages (Scarr et al., 1981; Loehlin, Willerman, & Horn, 1985, 1987). Nonadoptive parents and offspring as well as nonadoptive siblings correlate about .15 on average, and adoptive relatives correlate about .05; these correlations suggest heritabilities on the order of 20%, in contrast to heritabilities of about 40% usually found in twin studies. These adoption study results agree with results from the Hawaii Family Study of adults, which found average parent–offspring and sibling correlations of .12 for 54 scales from five personality questionnaires administered to subsamples of

100 to 669 families (Ahern, Johnson, Wilson, McClearn, & Vandenberg, 1982).

Nonadditive Genetic Variance

Why is the MZ:DZ ratio greater than 2, and why are heritability estimates from twin studies greater than estimates from adoption studies? Nonadditive genetic variance could be the answer to both questions. It has traditionally been assumed that genetic influences on personality are inherited in an additive manner, as appears to be the case for physical characteristics such as height and weight. "Additivity" implies that the effect of a particular allele (an alternate form of a gene) is not influenced by other alleles at that locus (place on a chromosome) or at other loci. In other words, alleles and loci add up linearly in their effect on the phenotype and thus "breed true." Nonadditive genetic variance includes two types of interactive effects of genes, dominance and epistasis. "Dominance" involves interactive effects of alleles at a single locus; "epistasis" refers to interactive effects of alleles across different loci.

In terms of additive genetic variance, MZ twins are identical, whereas DZ twins, like other first-degree relatives, resemble each other 50% on average. For this reason, differences between MZ and DZ correlations are doubled to estimate heritability. However, DZ twins and nontwin siblings share only a quarter of genetic variance that is due to interactions between alleles at a locus (dominance) and very little genetic variance that is due to interactions among alleles at different loci (epistasis). Neither dominance nor epistasis contributes at all to genetic resemblance between parents and their offspring. That is, if genetic effects are due to particular combinations of alleles at the same locus or to special combinations of alleles at different loci, children will not inherit these combinations from their parents. Children inherit only one of two alleles at a locus from each parent, and the inheritance from a given parent of an allele at one locus is usually independent of inheritance of an allele at another locus. MZ twins, however, are identical for all genes and hence for all genetic effects, nonadditive as well as additive. (For details, see Plomin, DeFries, & McClearn, 1990.) Lykken (1982) has proposed the use of the word "emergenesis" to emphasize higher-order epistatic interactions that lead to high correlations for MZ twins and low correlations for DZ twins, nontwin siblings, and parents and offspring.

It follows that if nonadditive genetic variance is important for personality, twin study estimates of heritability that double the difference between MZ and DZ correlations will be inflated. For example, as noted earlier, doubling the difference between the average MZ and DZ correlations for extraversion yields a heritability estimate of .65. Heritability, however, can be no greater than the MZ correlation itself, which is .51. Because this twin estimate is inflated, it will exceed estimates based on parent–offspring and sibling adoption designs, which are little affected by the presence of nonadditive genetic variance.

Assortative mating, the tendency for spouses to be similar, must also be considered in this context because it works against the "MZ:DZ ratio > 2" pattern of twin correlations. Assortative mating increases the genetic resemblance between first-degree relatives. Identical twins, however, are already identical genetically, and their genetic similarity cannot be increased by assortative mating. Thus, in the presence of assortative mating, the twin method underestimates genetic influence because assortative mating adds to the correlation for DZ twins and thereby reduces the difference between MZ and DZ correlations. For IQ, which shows substantial assortative mating, nonadditive genetic variance is shown only when assortative mating is taken into account (Chipuer, Rovine, & Plomin, in press). However, assortative mating is much lower for personality than for IQ. The largest study on this topic found average spouse correlations of only .08 (Ahern, Johnson, Wilson, McClearn, & Vandenberg, 1982). Thus, assortative mating would be expected to have a negligible effect toward masking nonadditive genetic variance in twin studies. However, assortative mating is somewhat greater than average for extraversion (.12) and considerably greater for neuroticism (.22). Assortative mating of .22 could increase a "true" DZ correlation of .16 to .20, the average DZ correlation for neuroticism. Although this represents an increase of only .04 for the DZ correlation for neuroticism, if the true DZ correlation is .16 rather than .20, this raises the MZ:DZ ratio for neuroticism to 2.9.

Violations of the Equal-Environments Assumption

Although both of the problems described above are predicted by nonadditive genetic variance, they can be explained, at least post hoc, by environmental factors. The essence of the twin method is to compare the phenotypic similarities of MZ and DZ twins, and to ascribe greater MZ similarity to their greater genetic similarity. This assumes that the degree of environmental similarity is the same for the two types of twins.

Violations of the equal-environments assumption could explain the two problems. Both problems would occur if environmental factors increase MZ similarity relative to DZ similarity or decrease DZ similarity relative to MZ similarity. These two types of violations of the equal-environments assumption have been called "assimilation" and "contrast," respectively (Loehlin & Nichols, 1976). Either violation of the equal environments assumption would lead to MZ:DZ ratios greater than 2. This could inflate heritability estimates from twin studies, resulting in their being higher than adoption heritability estimates.

Some evidence exists indicating that the equal-environments assumption of the twin method is reasonable in terms of specific measures of environmental factors, such as time spent together (Plomin, DeFries, & McClearn, 1990). Nonetheless, even if certain measures of the environment show no effect, it is possible that other aspects of the environment (perhaps many environmental factors, each with small effect) lead in concert to a violation of the equal-environments assumption. Additional light can be shed on the issue of the equal-environments assumption by designs that combine adoption and twin studies—most notably, comparing reared-apart and reared-together MZ and DZ twins.

Combined Adoption—Twin Studies

The relevance of the combined adoption—twin design was noted in a recent review:

> Personality scale correlations for DZ twins often are less than half those for MZ twins. Such a phenomenon is ambiguous. It might reflect nonadditive genetic variance shared by MZ twins or it might reflect one or another environmental mechanism, such as an unusual degree of com-

monality of MZ twin environments, contrast or competition between DZ twins, or the like. One group that can help resolve such ambiguities is twins reared apart. For such twins, presumably, the special environmental mechanisms mentioned do not come into play, and if DZ *r*s are still less than half MZ *r*s, some direct or indirect genetic explanation would be required. (Loehlin et al., 1988, p. 110)

Two ongoing studies of adults employ the adoption—twin design. The Minnesota Study of Twins Reared Apart (MSTRA) includes 44 MZ and 27 DZ reared-apart twin pairs whose median age in 1988 was 41, as well as twins reared together whose average age in 1988 was 22 (Tellegen et al., 1988). The Swedish Adoption/Twin Study on Aging (SATSA) was derived from the Swedish Twin Registry, which contains information on both members of nearly 25,000 pairs of same-sex twins (McClearn et al., 1989; Pedersen, Friberg, Floderus-Myrhed, McClearn, & Plomin, 1984). SATSA personality data are available from 99 pairs of MZ twins reared apart (MZA), 229 pairs of DZ twins reared apart (DZA), 160 matched pairs of MZ twins reared together (MZT), and 212 matched pairs of DZ twins reared together (DZT). The average age of the SATSA twins in 1984 was 59 years, which makes the SATSA the first behavioral genetic study of personality in the last half of the life course.

SATSA results for 19 personality scales are summarized in Table 9.2. Model-fitting analyses indicate that genetic variance (additive plus nonadditive) on average accounts for 29% of the total variance for the scales listed in Table 9.2 (McClearn et al., 1989). Age at separation and degree of separation had little effect on the twin correlations: The number of significant effects of these two variables was no more than expected on the basis of chance alone (Pedersen, McClearn, Plomin, Nesselroade, & Friberg, in press). In SATSA as well as studies of twins reared together (Rose, Koskenvuo, Kaprio, Sarna, & Langinvainio, 1988), degree of contact in adulthood appears to be related somewhat to twin similarity in personality, although the direction of effects in interpreting this association is unclear.

Instead of average correlations of about .50 for MZT and .30 for DZT, SATSA correlations average .40 for MZT and .17 for DZT. The lower correlations for the MZT-DZT design may reflect a decline in the influence of shared

TABLE 9.2. Summary of SATSA Personality Correlations for Twins Reared Apart and Twins Reared Together

	MZ twins		DZ twins	
	Apart	Together	Apart	Together
Extraversion[a,f]	.30	.54	.04	.06
Neuroticism[a]	.25	.41	.28	.24
EAS[b]				
Emotionality—Distress	.30	.52	.26	.16
Emotionality—Fear[f]	.37	.49	.04	.08
Emotionality—Anger	.33	.37	.09	.08
Activity[f]	.27	.38	.00	.18
Sociability	.20	.35	.19	.19
Type A[c]				
Framingham	.23	.37	.19	.23
Pressure	.20	.42	.29	.23
Hard-Driving[f]	.39	.47	.10	.00
Ambitious[f]	.40	.30	.08	.11
Hostility	.21	.33	.21	.40
Assertiveness[f]	.16	.32	−.08	.20
Locus of control[d]				
Luck	.02	.28	.18	.32
Responsibility	.36	.30	.30	.18
Life Direction	.32	.30	.23	.15
NEO[e]				
Openness	.43	.51	.23	.14
Conscientious[f]	.15	.41	−.03	.23
Agreeableness	.19	.47	.10	.11

[a] The data are from Pedersen, Plomin, McClearn, and Friberg (1988).
[b] The data are from Plomin, Pedersen, McClearn, Nesselroade, and Bergeman (1988).
[c] The data are from Pedersen, Lichtenstein, et al. (1989).
[d] The data are from Pedersen, Gatz, Plomin, Nesselroade, and McClearn (1989).
[e] The data are from Bergeman et al. (1989).
[f] Model-fitting results indicate significant nonadditive genetic variance.

environment during the last half of the life course. Nonetheless, the average difference between the MZT and DZT correlations in SATSA is similar in magnitude to those obtained in other studies. The few exceptions to the rule of significant genetic influence are noteworthy: Hostility and Assertiveness scales from a measure of Type A behavior, a Luck factor (beliefs concerning the role of luck in determining people's outcomes) from a locus-of-control measure, and the Agreeableness scale from Costa and McCrae's (1985) NEO measure.

The results in Table 9.2 confirm the problem that MZ:DZ ratios are greater than 2. If only the classical twin comparison of MZT and DZT is considered, the average MZ:DZ ratio (.40/.17) is 2.4. For extraversion, the MZ:DZ ratio (.54/.06) is 9. Similarly, MSTRA results (Tellegen et al., 1988) suggest that MZ:DZ ratios are greater than 2 on average (MZT/DZT = .52/.22 = 2.4), and especially for a component of extraversion called Social Potency (MZT/DZT = .65/.08 = 8.1) and for a second-order extraversion-like factor called Positive Emotionality (MZT/DZT = .63/.18 = 3.5). In both SATSA and MSTRA, several other scales also show this pattern of twin correlation.

Table 9.2 also corroborates the problem that

twin heritability estimates exceed adoption heritability estimates. That is, the MZT-DZT part of the adoption–twin design suggests greater heritability than the MZA-DZA comparison. The average correlations in Table 9.2 are .27 for MZA and .14 for DZA. Three heritability estimates can be derived from these correlations: 27% from the MZA correlation, 28% from doubling the DZA correlation, and 26% from doubling the difference between the MZA and DZA correlations. Thus, the MZA-DZA adoption data in SATSA clearly suggest lower heritability than the MZT-DZT classical twin estimate of 46% (doubling the difference between the MZT and DZT average correlations of .40 and .17). The MSTRA results show only a slight tendency in this direction. Doubling the average MZA-DZA difference yields a heritability estimate of .58; the MZT-DZT data suggest a heritability estimate of .61. However, both MSTRA estimates are substantially greater than other twin estimates of heritability. This discrepancy might be a result of the small sample size, especially of the DZA group. On the other hand, it might be a result of the fact that MSTRA twins reared together are on average 20 years younger than the twins reared apart. The SATSA heritability estimates of about 27% based on MZA and DZA correlations are compatible with estimates from recent adoption studies.

In addition to confirming that MZ:DZ ratios are greater than 2 and that twin heritability estimates exceed adoption heritability estimates within the same study, the adoption–twin design is valuable because it can explore the extent to which the competing hypotheses of nonadditive genetic variance and violations of the equal-environments assumption are responsible for the two problems. If assimilation or contrast is important, we would expect to find that the MZ:DZ ratio is lower for reared-apart twins than for twins reared together, because reared-apart twins are not as subject to assimilation and contrast effects as are twins reared together. In terms of nonadditive genetic variance, however, expectations would be the same for twins reared apart and twins reared together. Thus, violations of the equal-environments assumption are at fault to the extent that the MZT:DZT ratio is greater than the MZA:DZA ratio; nonadditive genetic variance is the culprit to the extent that the MZA:DZA ratio is greater than 2.

The data in Table 9.2 suggest that, for the average twin correlations, the environmental explanation seems more appropriate. As expected, if the equal-environments assumption is violated, the MZT:DZT ratio (2.4) is greater than the MZA:DZA ratio (1.9). These data also suggest that the violation of the equal-environments assumption involves an MZ assimilation effect rather than a DZ contrast effect. MZT correlations are substantially greater than MZA correlations (.40 vs. .27, on average). DZT correlations are not much greater than DZA correlations (.17 vs. .14). Unfortunately, the MSTRA results do not confirm either of these findings, although it is not clear that the small sample size for twins reared apart in that study justifies such fine-grained comparisons. It is clear that more data on this point would be valuable.

The SATSA findings suggest that nonadditive genetic variance may not be important on average across personality traits. For extraversion, however, both the genetic hypothesis and the environmental hypothesis are supported. The MZT:DZT ratio (9.0) is greater than the MZA:DZA ratio (7.5), as predicted by the environmental hypothesis. However, the MZA:DZA ratio of 7.5 is substantially greater than 2, as predicted by the genetic hypothesis. Indeed, nonadditive genetic variance may account for most of the genetic variance for extraversion. Doubling the DZA correlation estimates narrow heritability—that is, additive genetic influence (plus half of the variance due to dominance, but little of the variance due to epistatic interactions). This estimate of 8% is substantially less than the MZA correlation of .30, which estimates broad heritability (additive plus nonadditive genetic variance). The difference between narrow and broad heritability indexes nonadditive genetic variance. In the case of extraversion in SATSA, nonadditive genetic variance may thus account for nearly three-quarters of the genetic variance.

By these criteria, violations of the equal-environments assumption are also indicated for the Emotionality—Distress and Emotionality—Anger components of the EAS, the Hard-Driving Type A factor, and the Openness and Agreeableness NEO scales. Nonadditive genetic variance is suggested for the Emotionality—Fear and Activity EAS scales, the Hard-Driving and Ambitious Type A scales, and possibly for Type A Assertiveness and NEO Conscientious. In Table 9.2, these latter scales are marked with an asterisk because SATSA maximum-likelihood, model-fitting analyses detected significant nonadditive genetic variance for them, even though the SATSA model had not taken into account the possibility of violations of the equal-environments assumption. A revised SATSA model incorporates violations of the equal-environments assumption by allowing separate estimates of the shared environment parameter for MZT and DZT twins (Bergeman et al., 1989).

In summary, SATSA results suggest that the general reason why twin studies yield greater estimates of heritability than adoption studies involves a violation of the equal-environments assumption of the twin method—specifically, an assimilation effect for MZT. However, evidence for nonadditive genetic variance remains for some traits such as extraversion, as seen in MZA-DZA comparisons.

On average, the assimilation effect inflates classical twin heritability estimates by as much as a factor of 2. The "true" typical heritability estimate for self-reported personality is closer to the adoption study estimate of 20% than to the twin study estimate of 40%. The MZ assimilation effect needs to be considered in future classical twin analyses of personality; in particular, more research is needed to explore the processes involved in this effect. For one thing, is it mostly a phenomenon of self-perceptions, or is it also reflected in actual behaviors?

Conclusions

We offer three conclusions by way of summary and as hypotheses for future research:

1. Twin study estimates of heritability tend to exceed estimates from adoption studies of first-degree relatives, primarily because of an assimilation effect that increases the correlation for MZT and thus inflates heritability estimates from classical twin studies.
2. The "true" heritability estimate for self-reported personality is closer to the adoption study estimate of 20% than to the twin study estimate of 40%.
3. However, nonadditive genetic variance is substantial for some personality traits such as extraversion.

The rest of the chapter consists of brief overviews of other issues and advances in behavioral genetic research on personality.

POLYGENIC INFLUENCE

It seems likely that genetic influence on personality involves many genes, each with small effects. Four lines of evidence support this hypothesis. First, selection studies of behavior of mice and rats, including temperamental characteristics such as emotionality, yield slow, continuous progress after many generations of selection, suggesting that many genes are involved (Plomin, DeFries, & McClearn, 1990). Second, unlike certain medical disorders such as Huntington disease, which have long been known to be single-gene characteristics, segregation analyses have yielded no clear evidence for single-gene or major-gene influences in personality. Third, the recent production of nearly complete linkage maps for human chromosomes makes it possible to detect single-gene linkage with a probability exceeding 95%. Evidence for linkage to a genetic marker provides the best evidence that a single or major gene affects a trait. However, no linkages have as yet been reported for personality, other than as concomitants of neurological disorders (McKusick, 1986). It should be noted that recent reports of linkage for manic–depressive disorder and for schizophrenia have failed to replicate (Plomin, Rende, & Rutter, in press). Fourth, recent research in plant genetics provides strong evidence that complex characteristics are typically influenced by many genes (e.g., Edwards, Stuber, & Wendel, 1987). Human personality is not likely to be less complex genetically.

A similar conclusion emerges from research on chromosomal effects. No consistent personality differences specific to a particular chromosomal disorder have been documented, even though very small deletions and translocations of chromosomes can now be detected, in addition to abnormalities involving entire extra or missing chromosomes (Valentine, 1986). Most notably, an extra Y chromosome in males is *not* related to aggressiveness, contrary to earlier claims (Schiavi, Theilgaard, Own, & White, 1984). There may be some general negative effects of chromosomal abnormalities on personality, such as lower self-esteem and maturity (Robinson, Bender, Borelli, Puck, & Salenblatt, 1983), but the mechanisms involved appear to be indirect (Gath, 1985). A new structural feature of chromosomes called "fragile sites" has attracted considerable interest (Nussbaum & Ledbetter, 1986). A fragile site on the X chromosome is importantly related to mental retardation and possibly autism, but no associations with personality have as yet been established.

It has been suggested that previous research has sometimes sketched unrealistic caricatures of individuals with chromosomal abnormalities—for example, that trisomy-21 children are unemotional and sociable, and that males with extra X chromosomes are passive and reclusive (Smith, 1977). Prospective studies of newborns show markedly less abnormality and greater individual variability than older studies of institutionalized individuals (Netley, 1986).

Even though genetic influence on personality appears to be polygenic, molecular genetic techniques will eventually contribute to our understanding of the genetics of personality. Molecular genetic approaches are likely to be more useful than studies of chromosomal disorders, because the resolving power of molecular genetic techniques is a single nucleotide base of deoxyribonucleic acid (DNA), whereas even the small chromosomal abnormalities involve millions of DNA bases. As more and more genetic markers are found using the powerful techniques of recombinant DNA, it should be possible to identify some of the genes responsible for polygenic variability in personality. Although it may be difficult to pin down the physiological functions of genes that account only for small amounts of variance, the value of this knowledge is that it will enable us to begin to make genetic predictions for a single individual rather than relying on familial resemblance.

MODEL FITTING

A major advance in genetic research on personality is the development of techniques to test explicit models of genetic and environmental influence. Single correlations, such as the correlation for MZ twins reared apart or the correlation for genetically unrelated children adopted together, may be quite sufficient for many purposes for estimating quantitative genetic parameters. Other behavioral genetic designs involve the comparison of two correlations, such as the twin method that compares correlations for MZ and DZ twins. The results of these studies can also be interpreted by examining the correlations and calculating quantitative genetic parameters directly.

However, even for such simple designs, fitting an explicit quantitative genetic model to observed data has many advantages over just calculating quantitative genetic parameters. Models make assumptions explicit; model fitting tests the fit of a particular model with its set of assumptions; it provides a means to analyze data for several different familial relationships or data sets simultaneously; it provides appropriate estimates of quantitative genetic parameters and errors of estimate given the assumptions of the model; and it makes it possible to compare the fit of alternative models.

Model fitting becomes particularly critical for the interpretation of data from different designs and samples—for example, when family, twin, and adoption data from several studies are included in the same analysis. Cattell (1953, 1960) has long argued for the need for this multimethod approach, which he calls "multiple abstract variance analysis" (MAVA). A model-fitting analysis of the largest twin and adoption data sets for extraversion and neuroticism illustrates the value of this approach (Loehlin, 1988).

An introduction to model fitting that includes behavioral genetic analyses of personality is available (Loehlin, 1987). A special issue of the journal *Behavior Genetics* has recently been devoted to model-fitting applications to twin analyses (Boomsma, Martin, & Neale, 1989). In quantitative genetics, model fitting basically involves solving a series of simultaneous equations in order to estimate genetic and environmental parameters that best fit observed familial correlations (Jinks & Fulker, 1970). The equations describe the model's genetic and environmental components of variance that contribute to each familial correlation. For example, a model of transmission from parents to offspring assumes that genetic and environmental parameters contribute to parent–offspring resemblance. The correlation between the adoptive parent and adopted child estimates the proportion of variance due to shared environmental influences, whereas the correlation between the biological parent and adopted-away child estimates half of the additive genetic influence. This simple model implies that the expected parent–child correlation in nonadoptive families is due to both shared environment and heredity. Thus, the three correlations are functions of only two parameters, which means that the equations can be solved and one degree of freedom remains to test the fit of the model to the data. More complex models are needed to incorporate assortative mating, selective placement, and genotype–environment correlation (Plomin, DeFries, & Fulker, 1988).

When the set of equations becomes large, the equations can be solved by iterative computer programs that adjust arbitrary values of the unknowns until the values implied by the equations match the observed values as closely as possible, according to a maximum-likelihood or weighted-least-squares criterion. Chi-square indexes the lack of fit between the model and the data. The difference in chi-square between appropriately nested models can itself be tested as a chi-square, which makes it possible to compare the fit of simpler models.

Model fitting is now nearly *de rigueur* in reporting behavioral genetic results. Four examples of model-fitting analyses of personality data follow. Cattell (1982) has applied his approach to the analysis of twin, biological sibling, and adoptive sibling personality data in adolescence for questionnaire and objective test results. Twin, adoptive, and biological relationships for three traits in the extraversion domain were fit separately for males and females (Carey & Rice, 1983). Combinations of twin, adoption, and family data for the California Psychological Inventory and the Thurstone Temperament Schedule have also been subjected recently to model fitting (Loehlin, 1985, 1986). Finally, Eaves et al. (1989) have reported numerous examples of model fitting for personality data.

Although model fitting represents the state of the art in behavioral genetic analysis, it has the disadvantage of being complex and sometimes seems to be a black box from which parameter estimates magically appear. We should not stand too much in awe of model fitting or allow it to obfuscate the basic simplicity of most behavioral genetic designs. For example, the twin design estimates genetic influence on the basis of the difference between MZ and DZ correlations. If the MZ correlation does not exceed the DZ correlation for a particular trait, there is no genetic influence (unless assortative mating approaches unity), and model-fitting analyses must come to that conclusion or there is something wrong with the model. Model fitting can be best viewed as providing refined analyses of the basic data of behavioral genetics—resemblance for relatives

who vary in genetic and environmental relatedness.

MULTIVARIATE ANALYSIS

As fields mature, they move from univariate analysis to multivariate analysis. A major methodological advance in behavioral genetic research during the past decade has been the extension of univariate analysis of the variance of traits considered one at a time to the multivariate analysis of genetic and environmental contributions to the covariance among traits (DeFries & Fulker, 1986). That is, phenotypic covariance between two traits may be mediated by genes that affect both traits (pleiotropy) or by common environmental factors. A multivariate approach is important because "it is unlikely that our convenient phenotypic trait measures are aligned in a simple one-to-one fashion with either the genetic or the environmental sources of influence upon them" (Loehlin & Nichols, 1976, p. 75). Any behavioral genetic analysis of the variance of a single trait can be applied to the correlations between traits (Plomin & DeFries, 1979).

Some of the earliest multivariate behavioral genetic research focused on personality (Loehlin, 1965). An example of an early bivariate analysis asked whether the sociability and impulsivity components of extraversion covary for genetic or environmental reasons; the answer was both (Eaves & Eysenck, 1976). A recent multivariate analysis of items on Eysenck's Psychoticism scale indicated genetic heterogeneity (Heath & Martin, in press).

A multivariate analysis makes it possible to approach a causal understanding of personality structure. That is, just as we study the phenotypic factor structure of personality traits, we can also study genetic and environmental factor structures that provide the foundation for the phenotypic factor structure. One surprising result is forming that was noted first in animal research on temperament: Genetic correlations and environmental correlations appear to be correlated (Hegman & DeFries, 1970). That is, the factor structure of genetic correlations among traits and the structure of environmental correlations are similar, and both are similar to the phenotypic factor structure. A similar finding was noted for human personality in 1976 by Loehlin and Nichols. Reasons for this intriguing finding are not yet clear. One possibility is that phenotypic structuring may reflect an underlying physiological structuring that mediates the influence of both genetic and environmental factors.

CHANGE

Longitudinal behavioral genetic data can be used to address a key issue in the development of personality: the genetic and environmental etiology of variability in age-to-age change as well as continuity (Plomin, 1986b). Multivariate concepts and methods are just as relevant to the study of the covariance between the "same" behavior at two occasions of measurement as they are to the analysis of the covariance between two behaviors at a single measurement occasion. For longitudinal data, age-to-age genetic change is seen as the extent to which genetic factors that affect the trait at one age are not correlated with genetic factors that affect the trait at another age. Several model-fitting approaches to the analysis of longitudinal data have been proposed (Boomsma & Molenaar, 1987; Eaves, Long, & Heath, 1986; Loehlin, Horn, & Willerman, in press; McArdle, 1986; Plomin, DeFries, & Fulker, 1988).

Although few longitudinal behavioral genetic analyses of personality are as yet available, genetic factors appear to be substantially involved in age-to-age change in personality during childhood (Plomin & Nesselroade, in press). In adulthood, however, two short-term longitudinal twin studies have found no evidence for genetic change (Eaves & Eysenck, 1976; Pogue-Geile & Rose, 1985). Personality changes that occur during adulthood appear largely to be due to nonshared environmental influences (Loehlin, Horn, & Willerman, in press).

Changes across occasions could involve 10, 20, and 30 years for the lifespan developmentalist; 1, 2, and 3 years for the child psychologist; 1, 2, and 3 days (or even 1, 2, and 3 minutes) for researchers interested in state; or situations 1, 2, and 3 for researchers interested in situational interactions with personality. Conceptually, the genetic issue is the same: Genes can contribute to change across occasions as well as to continuity. That is, these techniques indicate the extent to which genetic effects at one occasion are correlated with genetic effects at the other occasion, regardless

of whether the interval between occasions is years or minutes.

Short-term changes are the topic of state as compared to trait—a distinction that was emphasized by Cattell over 40 years ago (e.g., Cattell, Cattell, & Rhymer, 1947) and has received increasing attention in recent years (Nesselroade, 1988, in press). Both personality research and behavioral genetics research have historically tended to be trait-oriented. Both will profit by considering states as well as traits in trying to understand the variance of personality. However, the study of short-term change may require research strategies that differ from the traditional trait-oriented approach (Plomin & Nesselroade, in press). One way to begin to address states rather than traits is to study short-term change across situations that vary systematically. Some evidence already exists that such short-term changes in personality may be influenced by genetic factors (Dworkin, 1979; Matheny, in press; Matheny & Dolan, 1975). Although we are a long way from definitive answers to questions about the genetics of states and situations, the study of short-term change represents an exciting new direction for personality genetics.

THE ABNORMAL AND THE NORMAL

One of the most important issues at the interface between personality and disorders of clinical relevance is the extent to which behavioral disorders are part of the continuum of dimensions of personality. Although the relationship between the normal and the abnormal can be studied at the descriptive level of analysis, a new behavioral genetic technique can be used to investigate the extent to which the magnitude of genetic and environmental factors that affect the disorder is similar to the magnitude of effects on normal variability. In other words, the procedure assesses the extent to which a disorder is etiologically the extreme of a normal distribution of variability.

An analogous intuitive approach was taken by Nichols (1984) in an analysis of IQ scores for mildly and severely retarded individuals and their siblings. Siblings of severely retarded children (IQs less than 50) had an average IQ of 103, and none was retarded. In contrast, the average IQ of siblings of mildly retarded children (IQs from 50 to 69) was 85, and one-fifth of the siblings were retarded. This research yields two important results: (1) Severe retardation shows no familiality and is thus etiologically distinct from the rest of the IQ distribution, which, as shown in numerous studies, is familial; and (2) mild retardation is familial and is thus etiologically connected with the rest of the IQ distribution.

The technique used by DeFries and Fulker (1985, 1988; DeFries, Fulker, & LaBuda, 1987) in a study of reading disability yields an estimate of "group heritability"—the extent to which the difference between the extreme group and the unselected population is heritable—and compares it to the usual individual heritability. If group heritability is similar to individual heritability, it suggests that, in terms of genetic influences, the disorder is the extreme of the normal distribution. The method requires that quantitative data (e.g., reading scores) be obtained, rather than merely qualitative data (e.g., a diagnosis of reading disability).

The approach of DeFries and Fulker basically examines differential regression to the mean for MZ and DZ twins; it yields quantitative estimates of group heritability and individual heritability, and standard errors of these estimates. When these authors applied their approach to reading scores, they found a group heritability of about 30% and concluded that, in terms of genetic influence, reading disability represents the extreme on a normal distribution of reading ability. The power of their method to detect group heritability is impressive (DeFries & Fulker, 1988). For example, with 50 pairs of MZ twins and 50 pairs of DZ twins, a group heritability of 30% could be detected with 74% power ($p = .05$, one-tailed).

Stock in personality research will increase in value if it can be shown that some facets of psychopathology are indeed etiologically the extreme of normal personality dimensions. The first application of this approach to personality suggests that this might be the case (Plomin, in press).

GENETIC INFLUENCE ON ENVIRONMENTAL MEASURES

Recent behavioral genetic research suggests that measures usually assumed to be measures of the environment may show genetic influence. For example, in three twin studies, perceptions of parental affection indicated significant ge-

netic influence, whereas perceptions of parental control did not (Rowe, 1981, 1983a; Plomin, McClearn, Pedersen, Nesselroade, & Bergeman, 1988). Even reports of life events appear to be influenced genetically, especially reports of controllable life events (Plomin, Lichtenstein, Pedersen, McClearn, & Nesselroade, in press). Genetic influence has also been found in comparisons between nonadoptive and adoptive siblings for videotaped observations of maternal behavior (Dunn & Plomin, 1986) and for a widely used observation–interview measure of the home environment (Plomin, DeFries, & Fulker, 1988).

If environmental measures show genetic influence, associations between environmental measures and psychopathology may also be mediated genetically. This issue is conceptually similar to the multivariate analyses discussed earlier, in that the goal is to decompose the covariance between an environmental measure and personality into genetic and environmental components. One approach to disentangling genetic and environmental components of covariance between environmental measures and personality is to compare environment–development associations in nonadoptive families and adoptive families (Plomin, Loehlin, & DeFries, 1985). Analyses of this type suggest that fully half of environment–development associations in infancy and early childhood may be mediated genetically (Plomin, DeFries, & Fulker, 1988). For example, genetic mediation was found for associations between measures of parental "warmth" (cohesiveness and expressiveness) and infant "easiness" (low emotionality and difficultness, and high sociability and soothability). Evidence of genetic mediation is found longitudinally as well as contemporaneously—for example, when environmental measures at 12 months are used to predict personality at 3 and 4 years.

One implication of this research is that environmental measures and their association with personality cannot be assumed to be environmental in origin. Environmental measures need to be incorporated into behavioral genetic studies of personality, in order for us to assess genetic involvement in associations between environmental measures and personality. One specific direction for future research is to identify parental and child characteristics responsible for genetic mediation of environment–personality associations. Preliminary analyses along these lines suggest that traditional measures of parental personality are not the answer. It has been suggested that such measures do not capture the genetically influenced concomitants of environmental measures in the intense, emotion-laden context of familial relationships (Plomin, DeFries, & Fulker, 1988).

THE IMPORTANCE OF NONSHARED ENVIRONMENT

One of the most important discoveries in behavioral genetics involves nurture rather than nature: Environmental factors important in the development of personality are experienced differently by children growing up in the same family. Siblings resemble each other in personality, but mostly because of shared DNA, not shared experiences. Nonetheless, as we have seen, nongenetic factors account for the large majority of the variance of personality. The implication is that environmental variation lies in experiences *not* shared by siblings. This category of environmental influence has been called "nonshared," "E_1," "within-family," "individual," "unique," or "specific." An article in *Behavioral and Brain Sciences* discusses evidence for the importance of nonshared environment and implications of this finding (Plomin & Daniels, 1987). The article is followed by 32 commentaries and a response to the commentaries.

The importance of nonshared environment for personality was first emphasized in a 1976 study of highschool twins:

> Thus, a consistent—though perplexing—pattern is emerging from the data (and it is not purely idiosyncratic to our study). Environment carries substantial weight in determining personality—it appears to account for at least half the variance—but that environment is one for which twin pairs are correlated close to zero. . . . In short, in the personality domain we seem to see environmental effects that operate almost randomly with respect to the sorts of variables that psychologists (and other people) have traditionally deemed important in personality development. (Loehlin & Nichols, 1976, p. 92)

Data from family, twin, and adoption research converge on this conclusion. Family data indicate that sibling differences in personality are far greater than their similarities. As noted earlier, the average sibling correlation

in the largest sibling study is only .12 (Ahern et al., 1982). Although some sibling differences are presumably due to genetic differences, twin and adoption heritability estimates suggest that most of the differences between siblings are not genetic in origin.

Particularly impressive evidence for nonshared environment comes from MZ twins, because differences within pairs of MZ twins can only be due to nonshared environment and error of measurement. That is, genetic factors cannot explain differences within pairs of genetically identical individuals. The average correlation for MZT twins is about .50 for self-report personality questionnaires. Moreover, as discussed earlier, this correlation is inflated by a special MZ twin assimilation effect. This suggests that more than half of the variance of personality is due to nonshared environment and error. Model-fitting analyses of twin data consistently conclude that environmental influence is nearly all of the nonshared variety (Loehlin et al., 1988).

A direct test of the extent to which shared experiences make children in the same family similar is provided by adoptive siblings—genetically unrelated children adopted into the same families early in life. Because these siblings are not genetically related, their similarity can be caused only by shared family environment. The correlation between adoptive siblings indexes the total impact of all shared environmental factors that make individuals growing up in the same family similar to one another. For self-report personality questionnaires, the average correlation for adoptive siblings is only .05, suggesting that growing up in the same family accounts for only about 5% of the variance of personality traits. Another indication of the negligible influence of shared environment from adoption studies is that relatives reared apart—biological parents and their adopted-away offspring, for example—are no less similar than relatives living in the same family (Plomin, 1986b). If shared environment is only of minor importance but environmental variance is important, it follows that the environmental influence is largely of the nonshared variety.

The combined twin–adoption data summarized in Table 9.2 are also consistent with the conclusion that most environmental influence is nonshared. Model-fitting analyses that take into account nonadditive genetic and selective placement indicate that nonshared environment and error of measurement account for 62% of the variance on average for the 19 scales; the range of variance is only from 52% to 69% for the 19 scales. In contrast, shared environment accounts for 9% of the variance on average. Shared environment is negligible for most scales, although substantial for a few— 20% for Type A Hostility, 19% for Type A Assertiveness, 31% for Luck on the locus-of-control measure, and 21% for NEO Agreeableness.

When applied to adults as in SATSA, the twin–adoption design also makes it possible to differentiate shared rearing environment and shared postrearing environment. Shared rearing environment, which has been the focus of our attention to this point, can be detected by the comparison between twins reared together and twins reared apart. As seen in Table 9.2, DZT twins are no more similar than DZA twins. Although MZT twins are more similar than MZA twins, as explained earlier, this can be attributed to an assimilation effect unique to MZ twins. Postrearing shared environment occurs because possible effects of the family do not end when children leave home. Such postrearing shared environment effects can be detected in the SATSA design as twin resemblance not explained by heredity or by shared rearing environment (Plomin, McClearn, Pederson, Nesselroade, & Bergeman, 1988). For example, if twin correlations for all four groups in SATSA were .30, this pattern of correlations would indicate no genetic influence (MZ twins are no more similar than DZ twins) and no shared rearing environment (twins reared together are no more similar than twins reared apart). Twin resemblance in this case would be due to postrearing shared environment. Although selective placement could also contribute to this pattern of correlations, there is no evidence in the adoption literature for selective placement of adopted children for personality traits. Model-fitting analyses in SATSA have shown a significant effect for shared postrearing environment for only two (Neuroticism and Type A Hostility) of the 19 scales listed in Table 9.2.

Two exceptions to the rule of nonshared environment are conservatism and juvenile delinquency, for which both MZ and DZ twin resemblance is very high. In the case of conservatism, it has been suggested that the apparent shared environmental factor may be spurious—an artifact of strong assortative mating,

which raises the DZ correlation but not the MZ correlation (Martin et al., 1986). Assortative mating does not appear to explain the results for juvenile delinquency, which in six studies yield concordances of 87% and 72% for MZ and DZ twins, respectively (Gottesman, Carey, & Hanson, 1983). However, it has been suggested that this apparent shared environmental effect may be specific to twins because twins tend to be partners in delinquent acts (Rowe, 1983b).

The conclusion that environmental factors affecting personality operate primarily in a nonshared manner opens new opportunities for the study of environmental influences in personality. It suggests that instead of thinking about environmental influences on a family-by-family basis, we need to think on an individual-by-individual basis. The critical question is this: Why are children in the same family so different? The key to solving this puzzle is to study more than one child per family. The message is not that family experiences are unimportant; rather, the argument is that environmental influences in individual development are specific to each child, rather than general to an entire family.

Any environmental construct can be reconceptualized in terms of experiential differences between children in the same family. Even prototypical between-family variables such as socioeconomic status can be studied in terms of differences from one sibling to the next as family fortunes go up and down. Within the family, likely candidates for nonshared environment are differential parental treatment and differential sibling interactions, in addition to the well-studied family structure variables such as family size and composition (birth order, sibling age spacing, and gender differences). Differential experiences beyond the family also need to be examined, including relationships with teachers, friends, and peers. It is also possible that nonsystematic factors (e.g., accidents, illnesses, or other idiosyncratic experiences) initiate differences between siblings that, when compounded over time, make children in the same family different in unpredictable ways. A broad view of such accidents needs to be taken—for example, some might occur during prenatal development.

Differences within pairs of MZ twins provide an important tool to search for specific sources of nonshared environment, because their differences are entirely due to nonshared environment; DZ twins or nontwin siblings, by contrast, may also differ for genetic reasons. Studies relating MZ differences in personality to differences in their experiences have not yet been reported.

Although the MZ difference approach provides the most straightforward method of searching for specific sources of nonshared environment, this may not be the strategy of choice to start the search. As discussed earlier, an MZ assimilation effect is generally found for personality for MZ twins reared together, which means that they share environmental influences to a greater extent than other relatives. For this reason, it will be more difficult to find nonshared environmental influences using the MZ difference approach. An alternative first step in the search for specific sources of nonshared environment is to study nontwin siblings, even though sibling differences in personality may be due to genetic factors as well as nonshared environment. When nonshared environmental associations are found with sibling differences in personality, issues of cause and effect, including possible genetic mediation of the association, can be worked out in a second step.

Two studies have been reported that relate sibling differences in delinquent behavior to differences in their experiences. A study of siblings discordant for antisocial behavior found that delinquent boys experienced less positive interactions with their mothers and fewer close relationships with adults than did their brothers (Reitsma-Street, Offord, & Finch, 1985). Similarly, another study found that sibling differences in delinquency were related to differences in maternal closeness as rated both by parents and by children (Daniels, Dunn, Furstenberg, & Plomin, 1985). The possibility that genetic differences between siblings are responsible for these associations could be pinned down with a study of MZ twins, although delinquency is one of the few traits that shows little evidence of genetic influence (Gottesman et al., 1983). Two studies are underway to begin to search systematically for environmental factors responsible for nonshared environment, one in childhood (Plomin & Dunn, 1988) and one in adolescence (Reiss, Plomin, & Hetherington, 1987). These studies consider the role of genetics by comparing nonadoptive and adoptive siblings. The limiting factor in research of this type is likely to lie with the paucity of environmental measures specific to a child.

CONCLUSIONS

Although most attention has been paid to the nature–nurture question, one goal of this chapter has been to show that behavioral genetics has much more to offer the field of personality than heritability coefficients. In terms of genetics, recent developments include consideration of nonadditive genetic variance, model-fitting and multivariate analyses, the study of genetic change, the distinction between the normal and abnormal, and exploration of molecular genetic techniques in a quantitative genetic framework. As emphasized at the outset, behavioral genetics can advance the study of nurture as well as nature. The techniques mentioned as genetic advances—model fitting, multivariate analysis, behavioral genetic approaches to change—are just as relevant to the study of environmental influences. Examples of substantive advances in exploring the environment include the MZ assimilation effect, genetic influence on environmental measures, and nonshared environment.

Although the ratio of what is known to what can be learned remains small, the past decade has seen some substantial increases in the numerator of this ratio. We predict that when observers look back at the turn of the century, they will see behavioral genetics as a key player in advancing knowledge in the field of personality.

ACKNOWLEDGMENTS

Preparation of this chapter was supported in part by grants supporting the Swedish Adoption/Twin Study on Aging (SATSA), from the Successful Aging program of the John D. and Catherine T. MacArthur Foundation; the Colorado Adoption Project (CAP), from the National Science Foundation (No. BNS-86-04692) and the National Institute of Child Health and Human Development (Nos. HD-10333 and HD-18426); and a project on nonshared environment, from the National Institute of Mental Health (No. MH-43373).

REFERENCES

Ahern, F. M., Johnson, R. C., Wilson, J. R., McClearn, G. E., & Vandenberg, S. G. (1982). Family resemblances in personality. *Behavior Genetics, 12*, 261–280.

Bergeman, C. S., Chipuer, H. M., Plomin, R., Pedersen, N. L., McClearn, G. E., Nesselroade, J. R., Costa,

P., Jr., & McCrae, R. R. (1989). *Openness to experience, agreeableness, and conscientiousness assessed separately by age and gender: An adoption/twin study.* Manuscript submitted for publication.

Boomsma, D. I., Martin, N. G., & Neale, M. C. (Eds.). (1989). Genetic analysis of twin and family data: Structural modeling using LISREL [Special issue]. *Behavior Genetics, 19,* 3–161.

Boomsma, D. I., & Molenaar, P. C. M. (1987). The genetic analysis of repeated measures: I. Simplex models. *Behavior Genetics, 17,* 111–124.

Buss, A. H., & Plomin, R. (1984). *Temperament: Early-developing personality traits.* Hillsdale, NJ: Erlbaum.

Carey, G., & Rice, J. (1983). Genetics and personality/temperament: Simplicity or complexity? *Behavior Genetics, 8,* 299–313.

Cattell, R. B. (1953). Research designs in psychological genetics with special reference to the multiple variance analysis method. *American Journal of Human Genetics, 5,* 76–93.

Cattell, R. B. (1960). The multiple abstract variance analysis, equations and solutions: For nature–nurture research on continuous variables. *Psychological Bulletin, 67,* 353–372.

Cattell, R. B. (1982). *The inheritance of personality and ability.* New York: Academic Press.

Cattell, R. B., Cattell, A., & Rhymer, R. M. (1947). P-technique demonstrated in determining psychophysical source traits in a normal individual. *Psychometrika, 12,* 267–288.

Chipuer, H. M., Rovine, M., & Plomin, R. (In press). LISREL modelling: Genetic and environmental influences on IQ revisited. *Intelligence.*

Costa, P. T., Jr., & McCrae, R. R. (1985). *The NEO Personality Inventory manual.* Odessa, FL: Psychological Assessment Resources.

Daniels, D., Dunn, J. F., Furstenberg, F. F., Jr., & Plomin, R. (1985). Environmental differences within the family and adjustment differences within pairs of adolescent siblings. *Child Development, 56,* 764–774.

DeFries, J. C., & Fulker, D. W. (1985). Multiple regression analysis of twin data. *Behavior Genetics, 15,* 467–473.

DeFries, J. C., & Fulker, D. W. (1986). Multivariate behavioral genetics and development: An overview. *Behavior Genetics, 16,* 1–10.

DeFries, J. C., & Fulker, D. W. (1988). Multiple regression analysis of twin data: Etiology of deviant scores versus individual differences. *Acta Geneticae Medicae et Gemellologiae, 37,* 205–216.

DeFries, J. C., Fulker, D. W., & LaBuda, M. C. (1987). Evidence for a genetic aetiology in reading disability in twins. *Nature, 329,* 537–539.

Dixon, L., & Johnson, R. C. (1980). *The roots of individuality: A survey of human behavior genetics.* Belmont, CA: Wadsworth.

Dworkin, R. H. (1979). Genetic and environmental influences on person–situation interactions. *Journal of Research in Personality, 13,* 279–293.

Dunn, J. F., & Plomin, R. (1986). Determinants of maternal behaviour toward three-year-old siblings. *British Journal of Developmental Psychology, 57,* 348–356.

Eaves, L. J., & Eysenck, H. J. (1976). The nature of extraversion: A genetical analysis. *Journal of Personality and Social Psychology, 32,* 102–112.

Eaves, L. J., Eysenck, H. J., & Martin, N. G. (1989). *Genes, culture and personality: An empirical approach.* London: Academic Press.

Eaves, L. J., Long, J., & Heath, A. C. (1986). A theory of developmental change in quantitative phenotypes applied to cognitive development. *Behavior Genetics, 16,* 143–162.

Edwards, M. D., Stuber, C. W., & Wendel, J. F. (1987). Molecular-marker-facilitated investigations of quantitative-trait loci in maize. I. Numbers, genomic distribution and types of gene action. *Geneticae, 116,* 113–125.

Falconer, D. S. (1981). *Introduction to quantitative genetics* (2nd ed.). London: Longman.

Floderus-Myrhed, B., Pedersen, N., & Rasmuson, I. (1980). Assessment of heritability for personality based on a short form of the Eysenck Personality Inventory: A study of 12,898 twin pairs. *Behavior Genetics, 10,* 153–162.

Fuller, J. L., & Thompson, W. R. (1978). *Foundations of behavior genetics.* St. Louis: C. V. Mosby.

Galton, F. (1865). Hereditary talent and character. *Macmillan's Magazine, 12,* 157–166, 318–327.

Gath, A. (1985). Chromosomal abnormalities. In M. Rutter & L. Hersov (Eds.), *Child and adolescent psychiatry: Modern approaches* (2nd ed., pp. 118–128). Oxford: Blackwell Scientific.

Goldsmith, H. H. (1983). Genetic influence on personality from infancy to adulthood. *Child Development, 54,* 331–355.

Gottesman, I. I., Carey, G., & Hanson, D. R. (1983). Pearls and perils in epigenetic psychopathology. In S. B. Guze, E. J. Earls, & J. E. Barrett (Eds.), *Childhood psychopathology and development* (pp. 287–300). New York: Raven Press.

Hay, D. A. (1985). *Essentials of behaviour genetics.* Oxford: Blackwell.

Heath, A. C., & Martin, N. G. (in press). P as a dimension of personality: A multivariate genetic test of the Eysencks' psychoticism construct. *Journal of Personality and Social Psychology.*

Hegman, J. P., & DeFries, J. C. (1970). Are genetic correlations and environmental correlations correlated? *Nature, 226,* 284–286.

Henderson, N. D. (1982). Human behavior genetics. *Annual Review of Psychology, 33,* 403–440.

Jinks, J. L., & Fulker, D. W. (1970). Comparison of the biometrical genetical, MAVA, and classical approaches to the analysis of human behavior. *Psychological Bulletin, 75,* 311–349.

Loehlin, J. C. (1965). A heredity–environment analysis of personality inventory data. In S. G. Vandenberg (Ed.), *Methods and goals in human behavior genetics* (pp. 163–170). New York: Academic Press.

Loehlin, J. C. (1985). Fitting heredity–environment models jointly to twin and adoption data from the California Psychological Inventory. *Behavior Genetics, 15,* 199–221.

Loehlin, J. C. (1986). Heredity, environment, and the Thurstone Temperament Schedule. *Behavior Genetics, 16,* 61–73.

Loehlin, J. C. (1987). *Latent variable models: An introduction to factor, path, and structural analysis.* Hillsdale, NJ: Erlbaum.

Loehlin, J. C. (1989). Partitioning environmental and genetic contributions to behavioral development. *American Psychologist, 44,* 1285–1292.

Loehlin, J. C., Horn, J. M., & Willerman, L. (1981). Personality resemblance in adoptive families. *Behavior Genetics, 11,* 309–330.

Loehlin, J. C., Horn, J. M., & Willerman, L. (in press).

Heredity, environment, and personality change: Evidence from the Texas Adoption Project. *Journal of Personality.*

Loehlin, J. C., & Nichols, R. C. (1976). *Heredity, environment and personality.* Austin: University of Texas Press.

Loehlin, J. C., Willerman, L., & Horn, J. M. (1982). Personality resemblances between unwed mothers and their adopted-away offspring. *Journal of Personality and Social Psychology, 42,* 1089–1099.

Loehlin, J. C., Willerman, L., & Horn, J. M. (1985). Personality resemblance in adoptive families when the children are late adolescents and adults. *Journal of Personality and Social Psychology, 48,* 376–392.

Loehlin, J. C., Willerman, L., & Horn, J. M. (1987). Personality resemblance in adoptive families: A 10-year follow-up. *Journal of Personality and Social Psychology, 53,* 961–969.

Loehlin, J. C., Willerman, L., & Horn, J. M. (1988). Human behavior genetics. *Annual Review of Psychology, 39,* 101–133.

Lykken, D. T. (1982). Research with twins: The concept of emergenesis. *Psychophysiology, 19,* 361–373.

Martin, N. G., Eaves, L. J., Heath, A. C., Jardine, R., Feingold, L. M., & Eysenck, H. J. (1986). Transmission of social attitudes. *Proceedings of the National Academy of Sciences USA, 83,* 4364–4368.

Martin, N., & Jardine, R. (1986). Eysenck's contributions to behaviour genetics. In S. Modgil & C. Modgil (Eds.), *Hans Eysenck: Consensus and controversy* (pp. 13–61). London: Falmer.

Matheny, A. P., Jr. (in press). Children's behavioral inhibition over age and across situations: Genetic similarity for a trait during change. *Journal of Personality.*

Matheny, A. P., Jr., & Dolan, A. B. (1975). Persons, situations, and time: A genetic view of behavioral change in children. *Journal of Personality and Social Psychology, 144,* 224–234.

McArdle, J. J. (1986). Latent variable growth within behavior genetic models. *Behavior Genetics, 16,* 163–200.

McClearn, G. E., Plomin, R., Nesselroade, J. R., Pedersen, N., Friberg, L., & de Faire, U. (1989). *The Swedish Adoption/Twin Study on Aging: Individual differences in personality.* Manuscript submitted for publication.

McKusick, V. A. (1986). *Mendelian inheritance in man* (8th ed.). Baltimore: Johns Hopkins University Press.

Nesselroade, J. R. (1988). Some implications of the trait-state distinction for the study of development across the life-span: The case of personality research. In P. B. Baltes, D. L. Featherman, & R. M. Lerner (Eds.), *Life-span development and behavior* (Vol. 8, pp. 163–189). Hillsdale, NJ: Erlbaum.

Nesselroade, J. R. (in press). Issues in assessing constancy and change in adult personality development. In A. I. Rabin (Ed.), *Studying persons and lives.* New York: Springer Publishing Co.

Netley, C. (1986). Summary overview of behavioural developments in individuals with neonatally identified X and Y aneuploidy. *Birth Defects: Original Article Series, 22,* 293–306.

Nichols, P. L. (1984). Familial mental retardation. *Behavior Genetics, 14,* 161–170.

Nussbaum, R. L., & Ledbetter, D. H. (1986). Fragile X syndrome: A unique mutation in man. *Annual Review of Genetics, 20,* 109–145.

Pedersen, N. L., Friberg, L., Floderus-Myrhed, B., McClearn, G. E., & Plomin, R. (1984). Swedish early separated twins: Identification and characterization. *Acta Geneticae Medicae et Gemellologiae, 33,* 243–250.

Pedersen, N. L., Gatz, M., Plomin, R., Nesselroade, J. R., & McClearn, G. E. (1989). Individual differences in locus of control during the second half of the life span for identical and fraternal twins reared apart and reared together. *Journal of Gerontology 44,* 100–105.

Pedersen, N. L., Lichtenstein, P., Plomin, R., de Faire, U., McClearn, G. E., & Matthews, K. (1989). Genetic and environmental influences for the Type A behavior pattern and related traits: A study of twins reared apart and twins reared together. *Psychosomatic Medicine, 51,* 428–440.

Pedersen, N. P., McClearn, G. E., Plomin, R., Nesselroade, J. & Friberg, L. (in press). Effects of early rearing environment on twin similarity later in life: The Swedish Adoption/Twin Study on Aging. *Acta Geneticae Medicae et Gemellologiae.*

Pedersen, N. L., Plomin, R., McClearn, G. E., & Friberg, L. T. (1988). Neuroticism, extraversion, and related traits in adult twins reared apart and reared together. *Journal of Personality and Social Psychology, 55,* 950–957.

Plomin, R. (1981). Heredity and temperament: A comparison of twin data for self-report questionnaires, parental ratings, and objectivity assessed behavior. In L. Gedda, P. Parisi, & W. E. Nance (Eds.), *Twin research 3: Intelligence, personality, and development* (pp. 269–278). New York: Alan R. Liss.

Plomin, R. (1986a). Behavioral genetic methods. *Journal of Personality, 54,* 226–261.

Plomin, R. (1986b). *Development, genetics, and psychology.* Hillsdale, NJ: Erlbaum.

Plomin, R. (in press). Genetic risk and psychosocial disorders: Links between the normal and abnormal. In M. Rutter & P. Casaer (Eds.), *Biological risk factors for psychosocial disorders.*

Plomin, R., Coon, H., Carey, G., DeFries, J. C., & Fulker, D. W. (1989). *Parent–offspring and sibling adoption analyses of parental ratings of temperament in infancy and childhood.* Manuscript submitted for publication.

Plomin, R., & Daniels, D. (1987). Why are children in the same family so different from each other? *Behavioral and Brain Sciences, 10,* 1–16.

Plomin, R., & DeFries, J. C. (1979). Multivariate behavioral genetic analysis of twin data on scholastic abilities. *Behavior Genetics, 9,* 505–517.

Plomin, R., DeFries, J. C., & Fulker, D. W. (1988). *Nature and nurture during infancy and early childhood.* New York: Cambridge University Press.

Plomin, R., DeFries, J. C., & McClearn, G.E. (1990). *Behavioral genetics: A primer* (2nd ed.). New York: W. H. Freeman.

Plomin, R., & Dunn, J. F. (1988). *Genetics and family relationships* (National Science Foundation Grant No. BNS-88-06589). University Park: Pennsylvania State University.

Plomin, R., Lichtenstein, P., Pedersen, N., McClearn, G. E., & Nesselroade, J. R. (in press). Genetic influence on life events. *Psychology and Aging.*

Plomin, R., Loehlin, J. C., & DeFries, J. C. (1985). Genetic and environmental components of "environmental" influences. *Developmental Psychology, 21,* 391–402.

Plomin, R., McClearn, G. E., Pedersen, N. L., Nesselroade, J. R., & Bergeman, C. S. (1988). Genetic influence on childhood family environment perceived retrospectively from the last half of the life span. *Developmental Psychology, 24,* 738–745.

Plomin, R., & Nesselroade, J. R. (in press). Behavioral genetics and personality change. *Journal of Personality.*

Plomin, R., Pedersen, N. L., McClearn, G. E., Nesselroade, J. R., & Bergeman, C. S. (1988). EAS temperaments during the last half of the life span: Twins reared apart and twins reared together. *Psychology and Aging, 3,* 43–50.

Plomin, R., Rende, R. D., & Rutter, M. L. (in press). Quantitative genetics and developmental psychopathology. In D. Cicchetti (Ed.), *Rochester Symposium on Developmental Psychopathology.* Hillsdale, NJ: Erlbaum.

Pogue-Geile, M. F., & Rose, R. J. (1985). Developmental genetic studies of adult personality. *Developmental Psychology, 21,* 547–557.

Reiss, D., Plomin, R., & Hetherington, E. M. (1987). *Non-shared environment in adolescent development* (National Institute of Mental Health Grant No. MH-43373). Washington, DC: George Washington University.

Reitsma-Street, M., Offord, D. R., & Finch, T. (1985). Pairs of same-sexed siblings discordant for antisocial behaviour. *British Journal of Psychiatry, 146,* 415–423.

Robinson, A., Bender, B., Borelli, J., Puck, M., & Salenblatt, J. (1983). Sex chromosomal anomalies: Prospective studies in children. *Behavior Genetics, 13,* 321–329.

Rose, R. J., Koskenvuo, M., Kaprio, J., Sarna, S., & Langinvainio, H. (1988). Shared genes, shared experiences, and similarity of personality. *Journal of Personality and Social Psychology, 54,* 161–171.

Rowe, D. C. (1981). Environmental and genetic influences on dimensions of perceived parenting: A twin study. *Developmental Psychology, 17,* 203–208.

Rowe, D. C. (1983a). A biometrical analysis of perceptions of family environment: A study of twin and singleton sibling kinships. *Child Development, 54,* 416–423.

Rowe, D. C. (1983b). Biometrical genetic models of self-reported delinquent behavior: A twin study. *Behavior Genetics, 13,* 473–489.

Scarr, S., Webber, P. I., Weinberg, R. A., & Wittig, M. A. (1981). Personality resemblance among adolescents and their parents in biologically related and adoptive families. *Journal of Personality and Social Psychology, 40,* 885–898.

Schiavi, R. C., Theilgaard, A., Own, D. R., & White, D. (1984). Sex chromosome anomalies, hormones and aggressivity. *Archives of General Psychiatry, 41,* 93–99.

Shakespeare, W. (1974). The Tempest. In G. B. Evans (Textual Ed.), *The Riverside Shakespeare* (pp. 1606–1638). Boston: Houghton Mifflin. (Original work performed 1611)

Smith, D. W. (1977). Clinical diagnosis and nature of chromosomal abnormalities. In J. J. Yunis (Ed.), *New chromosomal abnormalities* (pp. 55–117). New York: Academic Press.

Tellegen, A., Lykken, D. T., Bouchard, T. J., Jr., Wilcox, K. J., Segal, N. L., & Rich, S. (1988). Personality similarity in twins reared apart and together. *Journal of Personality and Social Psychology, 54,* 1031–1039.

Valentine, G. H. (1986). *The chromosomes and their disorders: An introduction for clinicians.* London: Heinemann Medical.

West, S. G. (1983). Personality and prediction: An introduction. *Journal of Personality, 51,* 275–285.

Chapter 10

Biological Dimensions of Personality

Hans J. Eysenck
Institute of Psychiatry, University of London

TAXONOMIC THEORIES, CAUSAL THEORIES, AND THEIR HAZARDS

The Taxonomy of Personality

The term "biological dimensions of personality" has many different meanings in psychology, and a brief introduction is necessary to make clear how it is used in this chapter. There is no implication that other uses than the one here adopted may not be fruitful, but personality as conceived by Freud, Allport, or Guilford has little relevance to a chapter dealing essentially with the *biological* substratum of behaviorally defined dimensions of personality. Clearly, the study of personality has two interlocking aspects that nevertheless require to be kept distinct. The first is the descriptive or taxonomic aspect, dealing with the ways in which the holistic concept of "personality" can be split up into traits, dimensions, types, or whatever. The other aspect of personality study is more concerned with *causal* elements, including genetics, as well as environmental factors. Biological phenomena can help in the testing of taxonomic theories, and may also be able to test causal theories. It is perhaps in the latter capacity that they are most useful for the

development of a scientific psychology of personality (Eysenck, 1985). The importance of developing such a theory is emphasized by the fact that without it psychology as a whole lacks a vital link between traditional experimental psychology and the wide field of social psychology (Eysenck, 1984).

It is now widely agreed that a model for personality must be *hierarchical*, as I have argued from the beginning (Eysenck, 1947). Such a system has been envisaged to have four levels, at the bottom of which are singly occurring acts or cognitions. At the second level we have habitual acts or cognitions (e.g., an individual has frequent headaches, or is frequently unpunctual). The third level is that of traits, defined in terms of significant intercorrelations between different habitual behaviors. Thus a trait of "sociability" embraces such activities as going to parties, liking to talk to other people, being bored when alone, and preferring listening to reading. The fourth and final level is that of types, higher-order factors, or dimensions of personality. These are defined in terms of observed intercorrelations between traits; thus "extraversion" is defined by the observed correlations between sociability, liveliness, activity, assertiveness, dominance, surgency, and so on. Data used for assessment may be observations of actual behaviors, ratings by friends or relatives, self-ratings on personality questionnaires, behavior in miniature situations, or behavior in experimental situations (Eysenck & Eysenck, 1985).

Such a hierarchical system clearly entails a number of deductions that have only recently been brought to the center of attention. Thus a distinction between traits and states is implicit in the distinction between Stage 1 and Stage 2 of the model; lower stages deal with states, higher stages with traits. Similarly, the notion of "aggregation" (i.e., the increase in reliability of measurement when many instances are averaged) is clearly implicit in the model (Angleitner & Wiggins, 1986).

The multiplicity of traits and dimensions emerging from numerous factor-analytic studies might seem to render illusory the possibility of arriving at an agreed-upon paradigm (Eysenck, 1983b). This is not so. As Royce and Powell (1983) made clear after an exhaustive examination of all the published evidence, there is clear proof for the idea of a system of correlated personality traits, and at the type level for three major dimensions that may be labeled "introversion extraversion," "emotional independence," and "emotional stability." Royce and Powell subsume these dimensions under the general title of "affective types," to distinguish these aspects of personality from cognitive aspects.

These three major dimensions are very similar to those that have emerged from my 40 years of research in this field, although the names given to the dimensions are different. Extraversion–introversion (here abbreviated as E) retains its name, but emotional stability is labeled "neuroticism" (N), stressing the opposite end of the same continuum. Emotional independence in the Royce and Powell system becomes "psychoticism" (P), as opposed to what might be called "superego control." We (Eysenck & Eysenck, 1985) have reviewed the literature exhaustively, and have shown that these same factors emerge from many studies employing a great variety of questionnaires, including the Minnesota Multiphasic Personality Inventory (MMPI), the Sixteen Personality Factors Questionnaire (16 PF), the California Psychological Inventory (CPI), and others.

Figures 10.1, 10.2, and 10.3 show the hierarchical structure of P, E, and N, respectively, spelling out the nature of the traits that have

been found to intercorrelate positively to define the three superfactors or dimensions. The constructs of E and N are too well known to require much discussion; detailed evidence for the P factor has been given elsewhere (Eysenck & Eysenck, 1976).

There has for a long time been considerable argument about the number of dimensions needed to define personality. Some of these arguments clearly disregard the model (Eysenck, 1981). Thus to argue that the model I have proposed has 3 factors and that Cattell's (Cattell, Eber, & Tatsuoka, 1970) has 16 is meaningless: The Cattell factors are at the third level of the hierarchy proposed above, whereas my factors are at the fourth level. As McKenzie (1988) has shown, when the intercorrelations between Cattell's 16 factors are themselves submitted to factor analysis, three superfactors or dimensions emerge that are very similar to (if not identical with) P, E, and N.

An alternative model that has been frequently adopted is that of the "Norman Big 5" (Norman, 1963)—a five-factor model that, apart from E and N, includes "conscientiousness," "reasonableness," and "culture" (or "openness to experience" in McCrae & Costa, 1985). This model seems to combine type factors such as E and N with trait factors lying at the lower level, such as conscientiousness and agreeableness; it also includes a cognitive factor that does not seem to fit in with the dimensions of personality here discussed. Zuckerman et al. (1988) studied the intercorrelations between 46 scales and concluded that the best solution was a three-factor one (which approximates the model I have proposed); their own scales provide excellent markers for the three factors. Correlations of factors "derived from data for men and women and applied to data for the opposite sex show very good correspondence of factors at the 3-factor level" (Zuckerman et al., 1988, p. 96).

All these observations and conclusions are based on observed or self-rated behaviors and their intercorrelations; there is no implication in these data regarding biological causation. A number of findings, however, strongly suggest that biological factors play an important part in the genesis of personality differences on P, E, and N. The first of these is the fact that identical factors have been found cross-culturally in over 35 different countries covering most of the globe, from Uganda and Nigeria to Japan and mainland China, from the capitalist countries

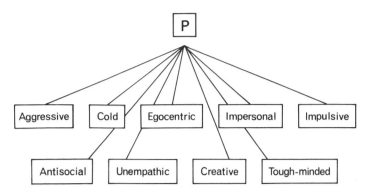

FIGURE 10.1. The hierarchical structure of psychoticism (P).

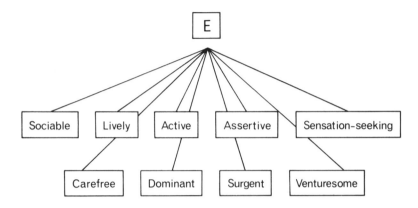

FIGURE 10.2. The hierarchical structure of extraversion–introversion (E).

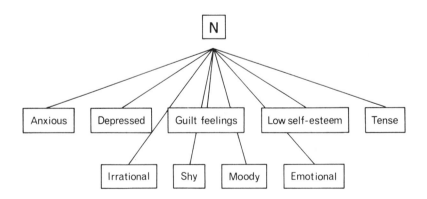

FIGURE 10.3. The hierarchical structure of neuroticism (N).

of the West and the American continent to Eastern-bloc countries such as the Soviet Union, Hungary, Czechoslovakia, Bulgaria, and Yugoslavia (Barrett & Eysenck, 1984). Such cross-cultural unanimity would be unlikely if biological factors did not play a predominant part; the great differences in culture, education, and environment generally would be expected to produce a variety of different personality dimensions.

The second important indicator is the fact that individuals tend to retain their position on the three major dimensions of personality over long periods of time (Conley, 1984a, 1984b,

1985). Such consistency in the face of changing environments points strongly to a biological basis for individual differences.

Last but not least, there is good evidence, much of which is reviewed in another chapter of this handbook (see Plomin, Chipuer, & Loehlin, Chapter 9), that genetic factors play a predominant part in the causation of individual differences in personality, with particular reference to P, E, and N. There are now some six studies of the genetics of personality, using large numbers of monozygotic and dizygotic twins, and employing the most advanced methods of analysis, all agreeing on the major findings (Eaves, Eysenck, & Martin, 1989). Genetic factors cannot directly influence behavior or cognitions, of course, and the intervening variables must inevitably be physiological, neurological, biochemical, or hormonal in nature.

Biological Theories of Personality

In what follows, special attention has been given to a particular set of theories (Eysenck, 1967, 1981), although alternative systems have been put forward and linked with biological modalities. One example is the work of Cloninger (1986), who postulates three uncorrelated dimensions of adaptive personality traits, which he links with differences in motivation and learning. He postulates that these are regulated by an interacting set of neurochemically specific adaptive neuronetworks, which modulate the activation, maintenance, and inhibition of behavioral responses to experience. Each of these three higher-order neuroadaptive systems is complex and involves communication among multiple brain areas via several neurotransmitters and comodulatory peptides and hormones. He postulates, however, that in spite of such interaction, each specific monoamine seems to have a principal neuromodulatory role in only one system (dopamine in activation, serotonin in inhibition, and norepinephrine in maintenance). Interesting as this set of postulates is, it seems extremely unlikely that individual differences in behavior can be reduced in such simplistic fashion to the actions and interactions of three monoamines, and the evidence is certainly not sufficient to make the system likely to be widely accepted.

The Pavlovian school has also developed a systematic framework linking personality, behavior, and biological factors. A detailed exposition of the many studies conducted in this field can be found in Mangan (1982) and Strelau (1983). There are two reasons for not going into details about this system here, and possibly a third. In the first place, descriptions of Russian work are usually not such as to make detailed replication possible, and the terms used are too imprecise to render easy an understanding of the theoretical models involved. In the second place, different investigators adopt different models, using the same nomenclature; this makes an understanding and a testing of these theories hazardous, particularly as the same authors (including Pavlov himself) frequently change their models and their use of terms. The possible third reason is that there are considerable similarities between the Pavlovian system and the model presented in this chapter, which would suggest favoring the latter in view of its greater specificity, and the much larger volume of work that has been devoted to it.

Rather separate from the psychological systems elaborated in the tradition of Pavlov is the work of Simonov (1981), which is relatively specific and based on physiological studies of animals. He specifies that the Pavlovian "strong" type (choleric) is produced by the predominance of the hypothalamus–frontal cortex system, whereas the "weak" type (melancholic) is characterized by the dominance of the amygdala–hippocampus system. Individual dominance of the hypothalamus–amygdala system is typical of the introvert; in extraverts, the frontal cortex–hippocampus system is predominantly developed. The system, in spite of lacking extensive studies with humans, is testable, and some of the studies to be reviewed presently are relevant to it.

Of particular interest for this chapter is the work of Gray (1964, 1970, 1972, 1981, 1982). Gray has attempted to formulate a general theory of biological determination of personality, and to reinterpret the descriptive aspects of the theory I have proposed by means of rotating the factors of N and E to 45°. Instead of E and N, therefore, Gray suggests two factors named, respectively, "anxiety" (N+,E−) and "impulsivity" (N+,E+). He has postulated that increasing levels of anxiety reflect increasing levels of sensitivity to signals of punishment, signals of nonreward, and novelty. Increasing levels of impulsivity reflect increasing levels of sensitivity to signals of reward and signals of nonpunishment. In thus relating signals of reward and punishment to personality, Gray has performed an important service, although the evidence suggests that both are in fact related to the E dimension, with extraverts responding more to signals of reward, introverts to signals of punishment (Eysenck & Eysenck, 1985).

Gray postulates an underlying physiological system, which he calls the "behavioral inhibition system" (BIS), the activity of which controls the level of anxiety. This system consists of an interacting set of structures comprising the "septo-hippocampal system," its monoaminergic afferents from the brain stem, and its neocortical projection in the frontal lobe (Gray, 1982). There is an underlying physiological system for the impulsivity dimension too, independent of that which underlies anxiety; activity in this system controls the level of impulsivity. However, little progress has been made in describing the structures that go to make up this system.

Interesting and important as Gray's contributions have been on the physiological side, they have certain important limitations. Practically all of the work has been done with animals, thus making the extension to humans essentially conjectural. Evidence from numerous correlational studies suggest that the picture Gray gives is essentially wrong. Measures of anxiety correlated very highly with N and only very little with E−, so that it is impossible to rotate anxiety into a factor equidistant from N and E−. Impulsivity according to the majority of empirical studies is most highly related to P, and thus lies outside the plane of the figure. Thus on the whole it would seem more appropriate to relate the BIS to E−, rather in line with my own earlier theories (Eysenck, 1957b), which relied on Pavlovian conceptions of inhibition and excitation rather than on arousal.

The various theories described above may be said for the most part to derive from the original theory linking cortical arousal with the E dimension (Eysenck, 1967). It is based essentially on the findings of Moruzzi and Magoun (1949) regarding the ascending reticular activating system (ARAS), a system activation of which elicited a general activation pattern in the cortical electroencephalogram (EEG). Collaterals from the ascending sensory pathways produce activity in the ARAS, which subsequently relays the excitation to numerous sites in the cerebral cortex. It was this excitation that produced the EEG synchronization observed by Moruzzi and Magoun. Much research has since shown that the reticular formation is implicated in the initiation and maintenance of motivation, emotion, and conditioning by way of excitatory and inhibitory control of autonomic and postural adjustments, and by way of cortical coordination of activity serving attention, arousal, and orienting behavior.

The link I suggested (Eysenck, 1967) between personality and the ARAS amounted to the suggestion that the E dimension is identified largely with differences in level of activity in the cortico-reticular loop, introverts being characterized by higher levels of activity than extraverts, and thus being chronically more cortically aroused than extraverts. In addition, I suggested that N is closely related to the activity of the visceral brain, which consists of the hippocampus−amygdala, singulum, septum, and hypothalamus. These two systems are independent: hence we have an orthogonal relation between E and N. However, this independence is only partial. One of the ways in which cortical arousal can be produced is through activity in the visceral brain, which reaches the reticular formation through collaterals. Activity in the visceral brain produces autonomic arousal, and I have used the term "activation" to distinguish this form of arousal from that produced by reticular activity. Thus in a condition of high activation, we would expect high arousal; a person who is strongly affected by anger, fear, or some other emotion will certainly also be in a state of high cortical arousal. Fortunately such states of strong emotional involvement are relatively rare, but they do indicate that the independence of the two systems is only relative (Routtenberg, 1966).

A detailed discussion of the concept of arousal by many authors is given in a recent edited book (Strelau & Eysenck, 1987). Clearly, the concept of general physiological arousal, which was a core construct in Duffy's (1957) early theory and Hebb's (1955) optimal arousal approach, does not seem viable any longer. The reticulo-cortical system of Moruzzi and Magoun (1949) now appears to be only one of several arousal systems (Zuckerman & Como, 1983). These probably include the limbic arousal system (suggested by recent work; Aston-Jones & Bloom, 1981), as well as a monoamine oxidase system, the diffuse thalamo-cortical system, and the pituitary−adrenocortical system (Zuckerman, 1984). This apparent diversity may not prevent the systems from operating in a relatively unitary fashion. Clearly, the way from the "conceptual nervous system" of Hebb to the "central nervous system" (CNS) of the neurosciences is a hard one!

The discrimination between an arousal system and an activating system that I have suggested has found strong empirical support in the work of Thayer (1978a, 1978b, 1986). He constructed an Activation–Reactivation Adjective Check List, which resulted in two major factors. The first of these is "general activation" (energetic, vigorous, lively, full of "pep," active, happy, and activated); this corresponds to the notion of "arousal" as defined above. The second factor is "high activation" (tense, anxious, jittery, clutched up, fearful, intense, and stirred up); this corresponds to the notion of "activation" as presented above. Thayer's concepts differ from my own in the sense that Thayer is dealing with states and I am dealing with traits; one would expect that in specific studies a combination of the two might be most highly correlated with psychophysiological measures (i.e., adding E scores to general arousal, and N scores to high activation).

The theory linking arousal with the E dimension is relatively novel, whereas that linking N and the limbic system has a long history, told in some detail elsewhere (Eysenck, 1970). Whether the attempt to get away from the conceptual nervous system and to reach some specific relationship with the CNS and the autonomic nervous system has been successful or not is a question to be discussed in the following sections. Before I go into details, it may be useful to note some of the difficulties standing in the way of testing theories such as those outlined briefly above.

Problems of Testing Biological Theories

There are very real problems posed by attempts to link behavior with neurophysiological functioning. At first sight, it might seem easy to obtain a measure of arousal or activation, and correlate it with a measure of E or N. But note the following:

1. There is no single measure of arousal or excitation in the neurophysiological field. As Lacey and Lacey (1958) have emphasized repeatedly, the underlying systems show "response specificity," in that different systems are primarily activated by suitable stimulation in different people. Thus one person may react to emotional stimuli primarily through an increase in heart rate, another through increase in the conductivity of the skin, a third through more rapid breathing, and so forth. No single measure is adequate to portray the complexity of reactions; the recommended solution is to take measures of as many systems as possible, and score changes in the system maximally involved. But few experimenters have followed this advice, so that failure to support the theory may be due to faulty or too restricted choice of measuring instrument.

2. There is also "stimulus specificity," in the sense that different people may be sensitive to different stimuli. Saltz (1970) has shown that failure, or the threat of failure, produces more anxiety among N+ subjects than among N− subjects, whereas shocks generate greater anxiety among N− than among N+ subjects. Genetic factors predispose individuals to condition anxiety responses to quite specific stimuli (Eysenck, 1987). Thus the usual stimuli chosen by experimenters (e.g., shocks) may result in quite different relationships between stimulus and response than some other stimuli.

3. Relations between stimulus and response are usually nonlinear. Both the Yerkes–Dodson law (Yerkes & Dodson, 1908) and Pavlov's (1927) law of transmarginal inhibitions show that as stimuli get stronger, responses at first increase in strength and then decline, producing a curvilinear regression. This leads to complex theoretical formulations that make precise prediction difficult. We can predict that the high arousal of introverts will lead to a reversal of the stimulus–response correlation at a lower point of stimulus intensity than would be true of extraverts, but the precise point is difficult to establish. Nevertheless, these two laws have shown impressive predictive powers in relation to a variety of behavioral responses (Eysenck, 1976; Eysenck & Eysenck, 1985).

4. Threshold and ceiling effects may make choice of measure difficult. If we take the electrodermal response (EDR) as a measure of N, we could use as our response measure (a) size of response, (b) latency of response, or (c) duration of response (i.e., time to return to baseline). Only c seems to give useful correlations, but that could not have been predicted from what little we know of the EDR.

5. Resting levels are ill defined, and are in-

fluenced powerfully by uncontrolled pre-experimental variables. Subjects coming into our laboratories may have suffered an emotional shock quite recently, may have smoked or drunk alcohol heavily, may have been frightened by rumors about the experiments to be performed, or may have been annoyed by being kept waiting; these and many other factors may determine decisively their reactions in the test. Elsewhere (Eysenck, 1981), I have discussed in detail how anticipation in subjects produced quite contradictory results in two series of experiments. Spence had postulated and found that eyeblink conditioning was correlated with N, but not E. I had postulated and found that eyeblink conditioning was correlated with E, but not N. Kimble visited both laboratories and discovered that whereas my subjects were reassured by the experimenter, were told explicitly that they would not receive electric shocks, did not see any of the threatening apparatus, and were not subjected to mechanical links with the eyelid, Spence went to the opposite extreme: His subjects were thoroughly frightened by the experimenter. As a consequence, N played an important part in Spence's experiments, differences in activation drowning out differences in arousal. By contrast, activation played no part in my experiment, allowing arousal to determine the observed correlations. Note that these pre-experimental conditions were not discussed in the presentation of the experiments in question!

6. Neurological and hormonal systems interact in complex ways, and so do the dimensions of personality; it is never safe to assume that E+ and E− subjects are not influenced in their reactions by differences in P, N, intelligence, or whatever. At best these extraneous influences balance out, but they obviously constitute a goodly background of noise against which the signal may not be all that strong. The effects of such interactions deserve more detailed study than they have received hitherto.

These problems should illustrate the difficulties of establishing the truth of a theory such as that considered in this chapter. We are dealing with a *weak* theory (Eysenck, 1960), as opposed to the *strong* theories often found in physics and other hard sciences. As Cohen and Nagel (1936) pointed out, in order to deduce the proposition P from our hypothesis H, and in order to be able to test P experimentally, many

other assumptions, K, must be made (about surrounding circumstances, instruments used, mediating concepts, etc.). Consequently it is never H alone that is being put to the test by the experiment—it is H and K together. In a weak theory, we cannot make the assumption that K is true, and consequently failure of the experiment may be due to wrong assumptions concerning K, rather than to H's being false (Eysenck, 1985). In a strong theory, enough is known about K to render empirical failure more threatening for H. This argument suggests that positive outcomes of testing H are more meaningful than negative ones. The former imply that both H and K are true; the latter that *either* H, or K, or both are false. In other words, failure does not lead to any certain conclusion. These considerations should be borne in mind when evaluating the material presented here. Even strong theories, such as Newton's theory of gravitation, were full of anomalies that occupied experimenters for 300 years in an attempt to strengthen K. Psychology also needs a similar concentrated effort involving what Kuhn (1970) calls "the ordinary business of science," in order to resolve the many anomalies still remaining.

At the beginning of this section, I have explained that I only deal implicitly in this chapter with certain other theories, such as those briefly described earlier. Equally, I concentrate here on the three major dimensions of personality, and only deal with individual traits insofar as the studies are relevant to the investigation of biological factors affecting P, E, and N. Books such as Zuckerman's (1983) edited volume *Biological Bases of Sensation-Seeking, Impulsivity, and Anxiety* are clearly relevant because sensation seeking and impulsivity share part of the variance with P and E (and to some extent with N). However, the literature concerning isolated traits is too large to be considered here if these traits do not form part of the major dimensions of personality.

EXTRAVERSION–INTROVERSION

Electroencephalography

The most direct physiological index of cortical arousal has often been assumed to be the EEG. High levels of arousal are usually assumed to be associated with low-amplitude, high-frequency activity in the alpha range of 8–13 Hz. There are, of course, serious criticisms of using the

EEG as an indicator of brain activity; being recorded from the outside of the skull, it represents a kind of composite or amalgam of electrical energy generated from different parts of the cortex, and may thus produce a misleading impression of the actual activity in any specific area of the brain. Nevertheless, if it were found that extraverts showed low-amplitide and high-frequency alpha activity, this would certainly speak very strongly against the theory.

Gale (1983) has reviewed 33 studies containing a total of 38 experimental comparisons. Extraverts were less aroused than introverts in 22 comparisons; introverts were less aroused than extraverts in 5 comparisons; and no significant effects of the E dimension were reported in the remaining comparisons. The ratio of 22 to 5 is certainly in favor of the hypothesis, but there still appears to be a good deal of inconsistency. There are a number of possible reasons for this. In the first place, hand-scoring techniques, which may be unreliable and subject to systematic errors, were used in some of the studies; standards of analysis are much higher now than they were when some of the early studies were done, and hand scoring would not now be considered admissible. In the second place, there were considerable variations from one study to another with respect to technical details, such as electrode placements and the ways in which alpha activity was defined. However, the third reason for inconsistency is probably the most relevant: The tasks performed by the subjects during the EEG recordings varied considerably, ranging from reclining in a semisomnolent state with eyes closed, to sitting upright and attempting to solve complex arithmetical problems.

Gale suggested that the effects of E on the EEG are influenced by the level of arousal induced by the experimental conditions. In particular, he suggested that introverts are most likely to be more aroused than extraverts in moderately arousing conditions, with the differences between introverts and extraverts either disappearing or being reversed with conditions producing either very low or very high levels of arousal. These suggestions follow from the general theory, with high levels of arousal in introverts producing the paradoxical lowering of arousal postulated by Pavlov's law of transmarginal inhibition. Conditions of very low arousal would paradoxically produce strong feelings of boredom in extraverts, which have been shown to lead to attempts at disinhibition.

Gale classified all the relevant EEG studies according to whether the test conditions were minimally, moderately, or highly arousing; he found that introverts appeared to be more aroused than extraverts in all 8 of the studies using moderately arousing conditions that reported significant effects of E, but the expected result was found in only 9 out of 12 significant studies using low-arousal conditions and 5 out of 7 using high-arousal conditions. This result certainly suggests that in testing the hypothesis we should avoid extreme low-arousal and high-arousal situations, although even under such conditions likely to produce failure of the hypothesis, we still have 14 experiments supporting it and only 5 giving the opposite result.

Gale's hypothesis was tested twice (O'Gorman & Lloyd, 1987; O'Gorman & Mallise, 1984), using testing with eyes open and eyes shut as the two conditions. The earlier study found a correlation between E as measured on the Eysenck Personality Questionnaire (EPQ) and the EEG, whereas the later study only found correlations between EEG and narrow impulsivity. This would suggest the possibility that P may also be characterized by low arousal, impulsivity being strongly correlated with P.

Venturini, Pascalis, Imperiali, and Martini (1981) found no significant differences in basic alpha rhythms between extraverts and introverts, but did find such differences in the alpha attenuation response: Extraverted subjects habituated to the auditory stimuli, whereas introverts did not; simply put, introverts were generally more responsive to stimulation. These new measures could with advantage be included in future studies.

Cortical evoked potentials (EPs) have also been used in attempts to relate EEG activity and personality. Two early studies (Hendrickson, 1973; Rust, 1975) gave inconclusive results, but more recently Stelmack, Achorn, and Michaud (1977) have reported a methodologically more adequate study. They found that introverts obtained greater amplitude of the average evoked response (AER) than extraverts with low-frequency stimulation (500 Hz) at 55 dB for one group of 30 subjects and 80 dB for another group of 30 subjects. No differences between groups were observed with high-frequency stimulation (1,000 Hz). Subjects were required to count a series of high- and low-frequency tones to increase the level of attention required. The authors argue that the determination of differences between introverts and extraverts may have been facilitated by employing low-frequency auditory stimulation. There is evidence that interindividual variability of the AER is greater at low frequency than at higher frequencies (Davis & Zerlin, 1966; Rothman, 1970), and an increase in variance would obviously increase the possibility of obtaining significant covariance.

Pascalis and Montirosso (1988) used a somewhat different rationale by eliciting event-related potentials (ERPs) in response to task-irrelevant tone pips, giving meaningful and meaningless speech passages for extraverts and introverts. They argued that the meaningful task would be more interesting and would be expected to have a higher arousal potential than the meaningless task; they also predicted that the differential arousal effects of the meaningful and nonmeaningful tasks would be expected to be greater for the extraverts than for the introverts, who might be expected to maintain a relatively high level of arousal or task engagement across both conditions. They accordingly predicted that extraverts would show larger ERP peak amplitude in the meaningful condition than in the meaningless one, but that introverts would not exhibit differences in the ERP peak amplitudes between conditions. They found that extraverts reported higher ratings of subjective engagement in the meaningful condition than in the meaningless one, whereas the reverse trend was exhibited by the introverts. A similar interaction was observed for N2 peak amplitude: The extraverts showed a larger N2 amplitude in the meaningful condition than in the meaningless one, while the reverse was found to be true for introverts. Studies by Ritter and colleagues (Ritter, Simpson, Vaughan, & Friedman, 1979; Ritter, Vaughan, & Simpson, 1983) suggest the hypothesis that N2 reflects a decision process in sensory discrimination tasks; in the case of the verbal stimuli, the N2 reflects a classification of words. From this perspective, it seems reasonable that the N2 component is indicative of differences in cognitive engagement between the two groups.

Stelmack and Wilson (1982) extended research on evoked responses to the brain stem (auditory brain stem evoked response, or BER). They found that E+ was positively correlated with the latency of Wave I of the BER at intensities of 75, 80, and 85 dB. Extraverts also tended to display longer latency for Wave V than introverts to high-frequency, 80-dB tone

bursts and to click stimuli at intensity levels ranging from 55 to 85 dB. As they point out, these results provide some evidence of individual differences in physiological responsiveness at the level of the auditory nerve and the brain stem. The findings are not easy to explain in terms of a simple arousal theory, and the authors argue that their findings may require the development of new conceptions of the neurophysiological bases of individual differences in E to accommodate differences in exonal or synaptic transmission, instead of a focus on differences in cortical reticular arousal systems.

More readily intelligible in terms of the theory described in this chapter are EP augmenting–reducing effects (Buchsbaum & Haier, 1983); the measurement of these effects is based on the construct of sensory modulation. The EP technique assesses cortical response to stimuli of varying intensities. Increasing intensity of stimulation may produce corresponding increases or decreases in the amplitude of particular EP components recorded from different subjects. "Augmenters" are so called because the stimulus–response slope is positive (i.e., increased stimulation produces increased amplitude), whereas for "reducers" the slope is negative (i.e., the increased stimulation produces decreased amplitude). In the study to be discussed, Haier, Robinson, Braden, and Williams (1984) studied 120 subjects, of whom 12 extreme augmenters and 13 extreme reducers completed the rest of the tests in the study. The test of augmenting–reducing was repeated, and 4 cases failing to reproduce a previous status were excluded, so that the final sample contained 11 augmenters and 10 reducers. Reducers had very significantly higher scores than augmenters on the EPQ E scale. Reducers also endured pain on a pressure device longer than augmenters, in accordance with previous findings that extraverts in general endure pain better (Eysenck & Eysenck, 1985). Sensation seekers on the Zuckerman Sensation-Seeking Scale were also significantly more likely to be reducers than augmenters.

These results are exactly the opposite of what one would have expected in terms of the theory I have proposed. According to this theory, we would expect an increase in amplitude with increases in stimulus intensity, up to a point where transmarginal inhibition would set in to lead to a reduction in amplitude. Furthermore, the point where reduction would be expected to set in should occur at *lower* levels of stimulus intensity for introverts than for extraverts. Thus introverts should be the reducers, extraverts the augmenters. This, indeed, had been the pattern in earlier EP studies (Friedman & Mears, 1979; Soskis & Shagass, 1974) and in studies using sensation-seeking measures, especially measures of disinhibition, which is most closely related to E (Knorring, 1980; Zuckerman, Murtaugh, & Siegal, 1974). Indeed, Buchsbaum and Silverman (1968) had postulated that a mechanism for regulation of the sensory input was at work in reducers, analogous to or identical with Pavlovian transmarginal inhibition. Thus, clearly, the Haier et al. (1984) hypothesis is rather out of line. More analytical studies are required to give us more information.

Two such studies have appeared recently. The first is by Lukas (1987), who used a Maxwellian-View Optical System for precise control of retinal illuminance, and carried out two studies comparing augmenting–reducing at O_z and C_z brain locations and their correlations with two personality measures—namely, Zuckerman's Sensation-Seeking Scale and Vando's Reducer–Augmenter Scale (Vando, 1974). The occipital potential showed no correlation with the personality measures, but the vertex potentials, which are known to be affected by nonsensory factors such as cortical arousal and attention, were significantly correlated with personality. Lukas concluded that vertex augmenters are sensation seekers, but that this relationship is true only for augmenting–reducing slopes to more intense light flashes. Lukas concluded further that how the brain responds to intense sensory stimulation as measured by augmenting–reducing determines how people respond behaviorally to intense sensations. Interestingly enough, Lukas extended his work to cats (Saxton, Siegel, & Lukas, 1987) and found that feline augmenters at a high intensity range were likewise more active and exploratory. This suggests that the relationship between sensory modulation and behavior is not confined to humans.

The most complete study of the augmenting/arousing effects in relation to personality has been done by Stenberg, Rosen, and Risberg (1988). They used six intensities of visual and six intensities of auditory stimuli, arguing that a superimposed mechanism of transmarginal or protective inhibition can account for the relationship with personality only if it generalizes across different modality and response definitions. They found that for the visual stimuli, the slope of the P90–N120 amplitude at the vertex correlated significantly with both the EPQ E Scale and the Disinhibition subscale of the Zuckerman Sensation-Seeking Scale in the way that augmenting –reducing theory would predict. However, over the primary visual area, no component showed the same personality relationship as the vertex wave, and one early component showed the opposite. This result, they argue, suggests that personality differences in visual EPs may reflect different ways of allocating processing resources between primary and association areas, rather than a general tendency to inhibit strong stimuli. In the auditory modality, personality differences were not apparent in the amplitude slopes, possibly due to the confluence from primary and association areas in auditory EPs in the vertex lead. The authors finally state that "there was a general tendency for latencies to correlate positively with extraversion and disinhibition, in congruence with Eysenck's theory on the biological basis of extraversion" (Stenberg et al., 1988, p. 571.) These results powerfully indicate the need for very detailed and specific studies to look at the precise relationships involved, using different stimulus modalities and different recording areas; only by thus enlarging our understanding will we be able to arrive at a more all-embracing theoretical formulation than is available at present. Perhaps an explanation will be found along these lines for the curious and unusual results of the Haier et al. (1984) study.

How do EEG measures of stimulus modulation relate to peripheral responses? Zuckerman, Simons, and Como (1988) studied 54 male subjects, scoring high or low on the Disinhibition subscale of the Sensation-Seeking Scale (high disinhibitors show extraverted behavior). They were exposed to four intensities of auditory stimuli on one occasion, and visual stimuli on another. Two interstimulus intervals (ISIs) were used for each set of stimuli: first a 17-second series, and then a 2-second series. High disinhibitors showed EP augmenting, and low disinhibitors showed EP reducing, on three of the four series; differences were significant on two of them. High disinhibitors also showed stronger orienting heart rate responses to visual and auditory stimuli, whereas low disinhibitors showed stronger defensive (acceleratory) heart rate responses. Heart rate responses were significantly correlated across stimulus modalities. Auditory and visual EP slope measures were correlated only for the long-ISI series. No differences were found for EDRs.

A final set of studies relates to the use of contingent negative variation (CNV), a technique in which EEG changes are observed between a warning signal and an effector signal. Dincheva, Piperova-Dalbokova, and Kolev (1984) showed that introverts are less distractible, in terms of CNV changes, than extraverts; Werre (1983) reported that distraction smoothed the differences in CNV between extraverts and introverts. Piperova-Dalbokova, Dinchava, and Urgelles (1984) thought that this might be due to the greater effect of distraction on extraverts. They argued that the effect of distraction on CNV depended on the stability of the CNV: The more stable or strong the CNV "modeling system" (Sokolov, 1963), the more difficult it would be to effect changes in it. To test this assumption, they investigated the ability to pass from one task to another in extraverted and introverted subjects. The results supported the assumption that in introverts the CNV is more stable, so that the original modeling system is still active after the paradigm is changed. Thus a greater "changeability" of extraverts, already postulated by Wundt (1903), is also apparent in the electrophysiological phenomena of the CNV. (Wundt had argued that the four temperaments of the ancient Greeks could be conceived of as being produced by two orthogonal factors—the cholerics and the sanguines being "changeable," the melancholics and phlegmatics being "unchangeable." This corresponds to the E dimension. Cholerics and melancholics were emotional, sanguines and phlegmatics nonemotional; this corresponds to the N dimension.)

O'Connor (1980) studied the effects of smoking and personality on the CNV (Eysenck & O'Connor, 1979). He found that for all latencies, extraverts showed an increase in latency and introverts a decrease in latency during smoking. Thus, personality differences are particularly marked in producing changes in opposite directions on the CNV.

The latest summary and report of research on the CNV comes in a chapter by Werre (1986). He found correlations with E, but not with N. The clearest differential effect on the CNV occurred when isolated, motivated young adult students performed a constant four-period reac-

tion time task, which was novel to them, in the morning. Under those conditions, there was a positive correlation between mean CNV amplitude and E. Conditions not producing personality differences were those that existed when the students were repeating the standard task, and when they were performing a second task in addition to the standard one. This study is notable for varying conditions under which subjects performed, so that the author could clarify the relationship between conditions and personality in effects on the CNV.

Most of the studies so far reviewed have been lacking in any sophisticated theoretical underpinning. The same cannot be said of a study by Robinson (1982), which tested some very specific theoretical conceptions. In this work, visual stimuli were sinusoidally modulated, and the relative amplitudes of these sinusoidal EEG responses were measured for each stimulus frequency. The resulting data were analyzed in a complex manner that produced measures of inductance (L) and capacitance (C). The C measure was regarded as an index of the inhibitory process, the L measure as an index of the excitatory process. Individuals in whom the excitatory and inhibitory processes where of comparable strength were regarded as balanced. Robinson combined theoretical ideas from Pavlov and myself, and argued that stable extraverts are strongly balanced individuals, whereas neurotic introverts are weakly balanced individuals. When only those individuals whose N and E scores were comparable, and whose C and L scores were also similar, were considered, a remarkably high correlation of .95 between personality and an EEG measure was obtained. Even when the total sample was included in the correlation, a correlation coefficient of .63 was still obtained. These are the strongest relationships between personality and the EEG to emerge from what is now quite a large body of data. If the findings can be replicated, we would be well on the way to understanding the underlying physiological basis of individual differences in the E dimension. One can only express the hope that such a replication will soon be forthcoming.

In a somewhat later study, Golding and Richards (1985) also used photic driving, but their results are difficult to evaluate. The number of significant correlations obtained was only just about what would have been expected by chance from the large number of correlations calculated (about 100, of which 12 were significant). They also reported a factor analysis of electrocortical measures, but the number of subjects was rather small for such an exercise. They found little by way of correlation with E, but their most convincing conclusions are that P is related to low arousability and that N is positively related to one factor of electrocortical arousability. It is unfortunate that many experimental studies using the EEG employ relatively few subjects. This is a hangover from the old tradition of experimental psychology, which combines complex apparatus and methodology with a small subject group; correlational studies involving individual differences require relatively large numbers of subjects.

Electrodermal Responses

A large amount of work has been done on the relationship between the E dimension and the EDR, usually in relation to the orienting response (OR) and its habituation. Most of the concern with the OR goes back to Sokolov's (1963) model, in which characteristics of stimulus input, such as intensity, frequency, and duration, are stored in a neuronal comparator. An OR should be elicited when the neuronal model of previous stimulation and that of currently occurring stimulation do not match. Habituation is said to occur on subsequent presentation of the stimulus when there is a match between current and previous stimulation. As Lynn (1966) has shown and documented, cortical excitatory impulses are contingent on changes in sensory stimulation in the ascending sensory tract and collaterals to the reticular formation, which in turn activate the hypothalamic sites that initiate the autonomic components of the OR. When repetitive sensory stimuli are received, cortical inhibitory impulses travel by way of the collaterals that transmit impulses from the ascending sensory tracts to the reticular formation, causing the diminution and eventual abandonment of the autonomic responses, and thus producing habituation.

The theory I have set forth would predict that introverts would show a stronger OR and slower habituation. These predictions have been very widely studied, and excellent reviews of the whole processes are available (Eysenck & Eysenck, 1985; Graham, 1973; O'Gorman, 1977; Stelmack, 1981). Because of these widely available summaries, I concentrate here on

more recent work, and discuss the earlier studies in less detail. The first point to be made is that there is a great deal of evidence consistent with the hypothesis of greater cortical arousal in introverts; this includes the work of Mangan and O'Gorman (1969), Crider and Lunn (1971), Wigglesworth and Smith (1976), Smith and Wigglesworth (1978), Stelmack, Bourgeois, Chain, and Pickard (1979), Gange, Geen, and Harkins (1979), Nielsen and Petersen (1976), Fowles, Roberts, and Nagel (1977), and Desjardin (1976). There are, however, also negative findings, usually consisting of failures to find differences rather than of contradictory findings of greater arousal in extraverts. Such reports have been published by Coles, Gale, and Kline (1971), Siddle & Heron (1976), Sadler, Melford, and Hanck (1971), Krupski, Rankin, and Bakens (1971), Bohlin (1972), Koriat, Averill, and Molenstram (1973), Bartol and Martin (1974), and Mangan (1974).

How can we account for these differences? The majority of studies certainly favor the hypothesis, but the number of failures to replicate is too large to be dismissed. It can be noted that greater intensity of stimulation tends to produce differences, whereas less intense stimulation does not. Thus, as far as auditory stimulation (which has been most widely used) is concerned, studies using sounds in the region of 60–75 dB typically fail to differentiate introverts and extraverts, whereas stimuli in the range of 75–90 dB tend to do so. Again, interindividual variability of the auditory ER has been found to be greater under low-frequency conditions, which also favor the differentiation of extraverts and introverts; similarly, low-frequency stimulation seems to be more effective in differentiating extraverts and introverts in the OR paradigm.

On the whole, it appears that conditions favoring differentiation between extraverts and introverts with the electrodermal measures of the OR can be described as moderately arousing, very much as in the case of the EEG. As Stelmack (1981) points out, "From among the stimulus conditions in the studies reviewed here, low frequency tones in the 75–90 dB intensity range and visual stimuli provide the base from which such an enquiry would commence" (p. 51). The recommendation for visual stimuli rests on the fact that these have been found more likely to produce a differentiation.

In considering these studies, we should also

remember the notion of autonomic response specificity mentioned earlier. An important study demonstrating the importance of this principle is that by Stelmack et al. (1979). This study was devoted to the habituation to neutral and affective words; multiple autonomic measures were recorded. A multiple-regression analysis was carried out, and this showed that a conjoint influence of cardiac, electrodermal, and vasomotor OR components accounted for 54% of the variation in E, which corresponds to a multiple correlation of .73; no single component accounted for more than 24%. As Stelmack (1981) points out, "The mechanism of the kind implied by the notion of autonomic response stereotypy can account for such an increase in prediction and suggests that the consideration of the individual autonomic response preference of subjects merits deliberate mention and that the application of multiple autonomic measurements may be worthwhile" (p. 32).

Another point of difference between studies relates to the different measures that have been taken. The technical points involved have been discussed in detail by Stelmack (1981). Differences in *phasic* response have been more frequently recorded than differences in *tonic* levels. Stelmack concludes his review as follows:

> A cautious optimism which O'Gorman (1977) expressed regarding the relation of extraversion and electrodermal habituation is supported by the additional work which has appeared since the application of his review. There is also some evidence that introverts demonstrate higher skin conductance levels and greater frequency of nonspecific responses than extraverts. These observations imply differences in basic arousal processes and suggest that the effect is not exclusively stimulus bound. (p. 53)

Another study using more than one measure for the determination of arousal level was reported by Matthews (1987). His work dealt with the interrelationships of various dimensions of E, self-reported arousal, and physiological arousal. A composite measure of skin conductance and heart rate was significantly positively correlated with a self-report General Arousal Measure; E as measured by the 16 PF, and two primary E factors (F and H), were significantly correlated with physiological arousal and/or one dimension of self-reported arousal. The relationship between E and arousal was not affected by the time of day. This study again emphasizes the importance of having more than one physiological index of arousal.

I now turn to more recent developments. One of the most important papers to be noted here is one by Wilson (1990), which is innovative in several different ways. The most important point to note is that the 61 men and 50 women who measured their own skin conductance did so hourly throughout one working day, as well as recording drug intake and activities. Thus the study attempts to deal directly with a point originally raised by Blake (1967), who found that body temperature, which he and others considered an index of arousal, was higher for introverts in the morning but higher for extraverts in the evening. Several recent studies have shown similar crossover in the relative performance of introverts and extraverts, according to whether the task is done in the morning or the evening (Colquhoun, 1960, 1971; Horne & Ostberg, 1975; Knorring, Mornstad, Forsgren, & Holmgren, 1986; Revelle, Anderson, & Humphrey, 1987). Generally, it has been found that introverts show superior performance in the morning and extraverts in the evening; this, too, has been interpreted in terms of differential arousal levels, the suggestion being that introverts are high in arousal in the morning, whereas in the afternoon or evening the arousal of extraverts overtakes that of introverts. Gray (1981) has made this the major point of his critique of the theory I have set forth, pointing out that it cannot be meaningful for people to be introverts in the morning, but extraverts in the evening!

Figure 10.4 shows Wilson's (1990) major results. We should look at the age-corrected figures for introverts; there was a difference in age between introverts and extraverts, and it is well known that as people get older, the number of sweat glands decreases. It is clear from the figure that introverts throughout the day showed higher skin conductance (were more aroused) than extraverts, with the difference being smaller in the evening and disappearing at midnight.

Why do the two groups come closer together in the evening? Examination of the particular aspects of the E dimension that are critical has suggested to Wilson that sociability is more instrumental than impulsiveness. This, he argues, is probably due to the fact that the

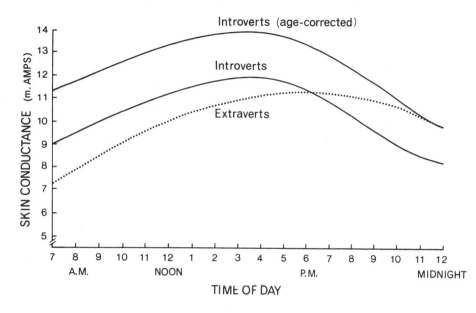

FIGURE 10.4. Changes in skin conductance over one working day for introverts (both raw and age-corrected figures) and extraverts. From "Personality, Time of Day and Arousal" by G. Wilson, 1990, *Personality and Individual Differences, 11,* 153–168. Copyright 1990 by Pergamon Press. Reprinted by permission.

activities attracting extraverts are more readily available in the evening, whereas the interests of introverts (e.g., task-oriented work in solitary activity) are more readily accommodated in the daylight hours. Supporting this idea is the fact that extraverts are more active, both generally and socially, in the evening, whereas introverts are more active in the morning.

The finding that extraverts also smoke and drink more than introverts in the evening may or may not be connected to the self-manipulation of arousal. It may simply reflect the fact that smoking and drinking are social activities. Smoking provides an opportunity for offering small gifts (cigarettes) to other people, helping them (striking the match), and generally establishing common ground by sharing the experience. Drinking alcohol is a notorious way of reducing social anxiety and facilitating companionship.

Wilson (1990) concludes: "Overall, our results suggest that the evening activity of extraverts is responsible for the higher arousal in the evening. Apparently, vigorous activity leads to higher levels of arousal as indexed by skin conductance (p. 167)." These results show the great importance of recording not only physiological measures of arousal, but also the activity preceding or accompanying the mea-

surement. Neglect to do so is one of the major criticisms of many of the studies summarized in this chapter.

Another interesting approach to the measurement of arousal levels in extraverts and introverts is to examine the differential effects on the two personality groups of systematic arousal manipulation (Smith, Rhypma, & Wilson, 1981). They used caffeine to increase arousal level, and followed up their original study in a more sophisticated one that gives a detailed discussion of methodology (Smith, Wilson, & Davidson, 1984). In addition to studying the effects of caffeine, Smith et al. (1984) also introduced a preparatory signal, which was expected to reduce the responses to the stimulus following it. Extraverts and introverts were randomly assigned to receive low, medium, or high doses of caffeine or a placebo. Each subject then received two sets of tones, with the tones in one set preceded by a preparatory signal. These signals reduced phasic amplitudes only at the highest level of stimulus intensity. Overall, introverts had higher overall skin conductance levels and response magnitudes. In addition, the preparatory signal had little effect on extraverts, but reversed dosage-related response patterns in introverts. Caffeine, as expected, produced an overall increase in both tonic and phasic measures of electrodermal activity. The introduction of manipulation of stimulus intensity, degree of arousal, and attention introduces a much more detailed and theory-oriented approach to the topic, and thus promises a much better understanding of the underlying variable. It is interesting that the use of caffeine was pioneered, in connection with personality variables, by Pavlov himself. It has also been used in a study of the effects of caffeine on personality in conditions of overhabituation and dishabituation (Smith, Wilson, & Jones, 1983).

These studies have been followed up by Smith, Rockwell-Tischer, and Davidson (1986). Special attention was paid to a dimensional variation, using signal and nonsignal conditions to study the effects on introverts and extraverts. Half of each personality group was randomly assigned to a distraction condition, the other half to an attending condition. Each subject received two blocks of 19 habituation trials, one involving a test stimulus and the other involving a dishabituation stimulus. In one of the two trial blocks, each stimulus was preceded by an auditory preparatory signal. Results showed that introverts gave larger skin conductance responses, and higher skin conductance levels, and showed greater dishabituation than extraverts. The signal reduced responding significantly more in introverts than in extraverts, and introverts were less affected by the distraction condition than were extraverts. Finally, extraverts showed more rapid habituation under nonsignal conditions, and the signal produced a greater increase in habituation rate for introverts than for extraverts. The effects noted are quite large for the most part, and illustrate the contention of the present chapter that more detailed theoretical attention, leading to greater complexity of methodology, is likely to repay the investigator by producing more clear-cut and interpretable results.

Miscellaneous Measures

There are large numbers of studies using the EEG OR EDR; by contrast, the measures used in this section have only been employed in a small number of cases, so that they are thrown together here under the heading of "miscellaneous."

The first set of studies to be described concerns stimulated salivation and its relation to the E dimension. The salivary glands are ideally suited to the investigation of physiological correlates of personality, because they are easily accessible and their secretion is almost exclusively under CNS control. The central salivation center is situated in the lateral reticular formation of the medulla at the level of the olive. Parasympathetic innervation of the parotid comes from the inferior salivary nucleus, and stimulation produces a profuse, watery parotid saliva of low organic content (Ganong, 1979). When subjects are stimulated by drops of lemon juice (preferably natural), the theory I have presented would predict that introverts would react more strongly than extraverts, producing a greater flow of saliva.

Deary, Ramsay, Wilson, and Riad (1988) summarized details of nine studies. Their findings were as follows:

> The negative correlation between extraversion and acid-stimulated salivation holds: for both male and female Ss with different saliva collection procedures; whether fresh or synthetic lemon juice or citric acid is used as a stimulus (although fresh lemon juice appears to be the most reliable); whether the stimulus is dropped or swabbed on to the tongue and whether the saliva is collected for 10 sec or 10 min. There is, however, some evidence that the correlation is more robust when testing is performed in the morning when arousal differences are at their greatest. Swallowing the stimulus also appears to reduce the correlation. (p. 906)

We (S.B.G. Eysenck & Eysenck, 1967) tested the hypothesis that swallowing the stimulus (and thus increasing its intensity) would evoke transmarginal inhibition preferentially in introverts, and found that it in fact reversed the correlation. Overall results are certainly favorable to the hypothesis.

Deary et al. (1988) tested 24 subjects, and reported a replication of the findings outlined above. They also corroborated the impression that the correlation holds in the morning ($r = .74$) but not in the afternoon. Furthermore, they found that stimulated salivation correlated with P ($r = -.58$) and with sensation seeking ($r = -.58$), but again only in the morning. "The salivation results suggest that extraversion and sensation-seeking (and perhaps also psychoticism) share a physiological basis. The time of day effects reported for the personality variable correlations are novel but require further study in a larger population" (p. 903).

The results follow from the hypothesis that greater arousal in introverts produces greater and more intense reaction to the stimulus (i.e., the lemon juice). However, as Corcoran (1981) has argued, it is not yet possible to decide whether the lemon juice test is an index of cortical or reticular activating system arousal, or whether it is rather a performance measure. Furthermore, there are two possibilities concerning cortical arousal differences. It is possible that introverts are more sensitive to incoming stimuli and become more aroused as a result of stimulation; or they may have high tonic arousal anyway, and their response to lemon juice may reflect this basic arousal difference. Deary et al. (1988) urge that "the integration of neural and anatomical, psychophysiological and personality data will be required to advance our understanding of this promising research tool" (p. 909).

As a footnote, it is interesting to note that Knorring, Knorring, Mornstad, and Nordlund (1987) suggested that because of the lower salivary rate in extraverts following stimulation (and also in unstimulated salivary secretion rate; Frith, 1968), there may be a greater rate of dental caries in extraverts; reduced salivary secretion is known to cause a number of dental disorders, including caries. They also argued that extraverts and high P scorers show more pronounced risk-taking behavior, possibly including a tendency to neglect health care programs. Thus they hypothesized that extraverts, and possibly also subjects with high P scores, would have an increased risk of caries. They examined 101 adolescents (15-year-olds) and found that extraverts had significantly more earlier caries and significantly more total caries, and a tendency toward higher values in initial and manifest caries. Subjects with high P scores were found to have significantly more manifest caries.

I next turn to a study of biochemical influences on personality—a group of determinants that has been studied more and more frequently in recent years. A good summary of work in this field is given by Zuckerman, Ballinger, and Post (1984). The first variables to be considered are the gonadal hormones, particularly testosterone. It is well known that P in particular, and also E and sensation seeking, are more prominent in males than in females; this suggests the involvement of testosterone in producing these behaviors. It is of course *prenatal* androgenization that has been

shown to be particularly effective in producing masculine-type behaviors (Eysenck & Wilson, 1979), and there are obvious problems with correlational studies of testosterone and behavior, as well as with other biochemicals that show day-to-day fluctuations in level. Testosterone in particular is subject to vagaries of sexual behavior and successful or unsuccessful attempts at dominance. Nevertheless, Daitzman, Zuckerman, Sammelwitz, and Ganjam (1978) found significant correlations between plasma androgen levels and the Disinhibition subscale of the Sensation-Seeking Scale (i.e., the scale most closely related to E). Estrogen correlated significantly with sensation seeking.

In a later and much more comprehensive study, Daitzman and Zuckerman (1980) used male subjects who scored in the high and low ranges of the Disinhibition scale, also including a variety of other personality scales. Again, they found high scorers on the Disinhibition scale to have higher levels of testosterone, estradiol, and estrogen than those with low scores. A factor analysis resulted in two factors, labeled "Stable Extraversion versus Neurotic Introversion" and "Social Deviancy versus Social Conformity." Estradiol had a high loading on Social Deviancy, testosterone on Stable Extraversion. These results, although awaiting replication, are in good agreement with a wide range of studies in male–female differences (Maccoby & Jacklin, 1974). Zuckerman et al. (1984) point out that the gonadal hormones play an important role in regulating the metabolism of several central neurotransmitters and that this may account for their role in increasing activity or general drive level. One influence is on the monoamine systems through their inhibitory effect on monoamine oxidase (MAO).

The enzyme MAO is present in all tissues including brain, with the highest brain concentrations being found in the hypothalamus. MAO plays a role in the degradation of the monoamines norepinephrine, dopamine, and serotonin. Studies of humans have largely relied on measurement of MAO from blood platelets, which are believed to have some significant relationship to brain MAO. Females have higher levels of MAO than males at all ages between 18 and 60 (Murphy et al., 1976), suggesting that the relations of MAO to personality would be similar to those found for testosterone.

The review of earlier studies by Zuckerman

et al. (1984) indicates that MAO levels related *negatively* to E and sensation seeking; these findings are consistent with behavioral observations of high- and low-MAO monkeys and humans (Coursey, Buchsbaum, & Murphy, 1979). High-MAO monkeys in a colony tended to be solitary, inactive, and passive; low-MAO monkeys tended to be active, to make many social contacts, and to engage frequently in play. In rodents, too, MAO inhibitors produce hyperactivity and increase activity in a novel environment. Coursey et al. (1979), in their human studies, found that low-MAO college students of both sexes reported spending more time in social activities than high-MAO subjects did; they were also more likely to use drugs, smoke cigarettes, and have a record of conviction for a criminal offense.

Low MAO levels are found in patients suffering from bipolar affective disorders, and are also found in chronic schizophrenics; there has been no direct study of P in this connection, but MAO has been connected with impulsivity, which is an important constituent of P.

Schalling, Edman, Asberg, and Oreland (1988) studied 58 male subjects and found that impulsivity and aggressiveness were negatively correlated with platelet MAO activity; detachment and E– were correlated with high MAO activity. Low-MAO subjects also showed a much higher degree of suspicion than high-MAO subjects—another link with P. However, the major link was with impulsiveness, some of the observed relations being surprisingly close. Thus, the question " Do you often do things on the spur of the moment?" produced 83% "yes" answers in low-MAO subjects, 41% in intermediate-MAO subjects, and 8% in high-MAO subjects. Not all the questions, of course, gave similarly high agreement.

Other recent studies in this field bear out these major findings (Calhoon, 1988; Klinteberg, Schalling, Edman, Oreland, & Asberg, 1987; Knorring, Oreland, & Wimblad, 1984). Correlations have also been found between measures of impulsivity and cerebrospinal fluid (CSF) levels of the serotonin metabolite 5-hydroxyindoleacetic acid (5-HIAA) (Schalling, Asberg, Edman, & Lavender, 1984). (This particular finding is interesting in view of the associations assumed to exist between low platelet MAO activity and central serotonergic hypoactivity.) These results form a fairly congruent whole centering on the concept of impulsivity, and hence implicating P (and E, in a rather less direct fashion).

I next discuss some studies involving the monoamine systems. The first of these was carried out by Ballinger et al. (1983), who studied the relationships between a number of biochemical measures and personality traits in a normal sample consisting of 43 male and female volunteers. The study is too complex to be described in detail, and I concentrate here on the major findings. CSF calcium correlated positively with E and negatively with neurotic E– and general N. Calcium ions are found throughout the nervous system and seem to facilitate the release of all types of neurotransmitters. Zuckerman et al. (1984) have argued:

> Although the relation between CSF calcium levels in brain are not known, the data suggest that CSF and possible blood levels in calcium may be involved in the generalized arousal or arousability that is essential to Eysenck's theory of personality. In theory, both introverts and neurotics are thought to be hyperaroused, the former because of low thresholds for arousal in the CNS, and the latter because of instability of the autonomic nervous system. (p. 420)

Another interesting finding from the Ballenger et al. (1983) study is that cortisol assayed from CSF correlated negatively with P and with the Disinhibition subscale of the Sensation-Seeking Scale. Low levels of CSF cortisol were found in individuals scoring high on these measures of non-neurotic impulsivity. One further interesting finding is that 3-methoxy-4-hydroxyphenethyleneglycol (MHPG), which is a major metabolite of norepinephrine, was negatively related to the N dimension. On the whole, this is a very important and path-breaking study, although the small number of subjects and the large number of correlations calculated make interpretation difficult. Replication with a large number of subjects would be very much in order.

The next topic is the sedation threshold. Elsewhere (Eysenck, 1957a), I have suggested two ways in which we can study the biology of personality through the administration of drugs. These are shown in Figure 10.5. In A, we give to a random sample of people a stimulant or depressant drug, and test behavioral consequences; the depressant drug should lead to more extraverted behavior, the stimulant drug to more introverted behavior. This prediction has been tested in a large number of studies (Eysenck, 1963, 1983c); the great majority of these have given positive results.

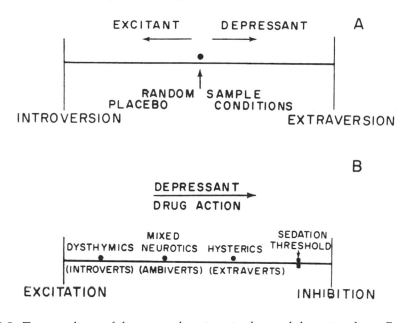

FIGURE 10.5. Two paradigms of drug research, using stimulant and depressive drugs. From "Drugs and Personality: I. Theory and Methodology" by H. J. Eysenck, 1957, *Journal of Mental Science, 103,* 119–131. Copyright 1957 by H. Eysenck. Reprinted by permission.

An alternative method is that shown under B in Figure 10.5. Here we start out with groups of introverts, ambiverts, and extraverts who are administered some form of depressant or sedative drug; also defined is a "sedation threshold" (i.e., a point at which qualitative differences in behavior occur as a function of drug administration). Because extraverts are characterized by low arousal (or higher inhibition) than introverts, according to the theory, they should require less of the drug to reach the threshold. This is the general theory underlying the studies to be now reviewed.

The sedative drug used is usually one of the barbiturates, which is administered by intravenous injection. The sedation threshold itself has been defined in different ways, usually involving physiological changes and unresponsiveness to verbal stimuli. The early studies involving this prediction all had positive results. Laverty (1958) found that the amount of sodium amytal needed to produce slower speech was greater for introverts than for extraverts. Similarly, Shagass and his colleagues discovered that the sedation threshold tended to be higher in introverts than in extraverts (Krishnamoorti & Shagass, 1964; Shagass & Jones, 1958; Shagass & Kerenyi, 1958). They also found that manifest anxiety was

associated with increased tolerance of barbiturates, which is not incompatible with the theory.

Later studies show a slightly more complicated picture. Rodnight and Gooch (1963) found that a tolerance of nitrous oxide was not related to E or N considered separately, but that E was negatively correlated with tolerance among subjects high in N, whereas there was a positive correlation between E and tolerance among those low in N. Claridge and Roth (1973), in a study of tolerance of amylobarbitone sodium, and Claridge, Donald, and Birchall (1981), using thyopentone, found very similar results. When Claridge et al. (1981) combined their thyopentone data with earlier data collected by Claridge (1967) and by Claridge and Roth (1973), and assigned their 126 subjects to nine groups on the basis of low, medium, or high E and low, medium, or high N, they found a highly significant interaction between E and N. The highest drug tolerance was shown by introverts with modest N and the lowest drug tolerance occurred among extraverts with high N. Thus, the hypothesis that introverts should have higher sedation thresholds than extraverts was supported among those of medium N, whereas the opposite tendency was present among those of low N.

Thus, although on the whole the data support the hypothesis, it clearly requires amplification.

Pupillometry is the next topic to be discussed in this section. In recent years there has been an increased interest in the use of the pupillary response as a psychophysiological measure relating to personality. Pupillary dilation is due primarily to sympathetic activity, whereas constriction reflects parasympathetic activity. We can thus use pupillometry to measure individual differences in responsiveness to stimulation, and tonic pupil size in the absence of specific stimulation can provide an index of general or autonomic arousal. In the first of this line of studies, Holmes (1967) measured speed of pupillary dilation to the offset of a light, and pupillary constriction to the onset of a light. The fast dilators tended to be extraverted, whereas the fast constrictors were introverted. Holmes argued that the rapid pupillary constriction of introverts indicated that they had greater amounts of acetylcholine at cholinergic synapses than extraverts.

Frith (1977) confirmed some of Holmes's findings, reporting that high scorers on the impulsivity component of E showed less pupillary constriction than low impulsives in responses to a light flash, perhaps because they were less reactive to stimulation. He also found that impulsivity was negatively correlated with pupil size during an initial interval of no stimulation. This suggests that the more impulsive subjects (those high in P?) were less aroused than the less impulsive subjects.

The most important study in this field was reported by Stelmack and Mandelzys (1975); they also found that introverts had larger pupils than extraverts in the absence of specific stimulation, suggesting that the introverted subjects were more aroused throughout the experiment. They tested phasic pupillary responses to auditorily presented neutral, affective, and taboo words; they found that introverts showed significantly more pupillary dilation to these stimuli than extraverts, especially in response to taboo words. In other words, introverts responded more strongly than extraverts to the auditory stimuli. Altogether this line of research seems promising, and should be pursued in the future.

What can we conclude from the data surveyed in this section? It will be clear that deductions from the general arousal theory tested in relation to psychophysiological measures present greater complexities than results of behavioral measures deduced from the general theory (Eysenck & Eysenck, 1985). Nevertheless, for the EEG, the EDR, and the miscellaneous measures discussed in this last subsection, the results are much more frequently positive and in line with prediction than negative; indeed, negative findings are usually simply failures to discover significant results, rather than results going in the direction opposite to that predicted. Many anomalies and problems remain, and certainly future research should be informed by past results in order to avoid some of the errors into which researchers have fallen. Nevertheless, when all is said and done, the data on the whole seem to support the general proposal that extraverts normally work at a lower level of arousal and are less easily aroused than introverts, except when transmarginal inhibition interferes.

Studies of Physique and Constitution

Another group of studies that deserves to be included in this chapter relates to physique and factors associated with body build generally; these factors are often labeled "constitutional." In the 1930s and 1940s there was a good deal of interest in this topic, particularly because of the work of Sheldon and his associates, who transplanted and revived the earlier work of Kretschmer (Kretschmer, 1948; Sheldon, Hartl, & McDermott, 1949; Sheldon & Stevens, 1940, 1942). Exhaustive reviews of this very large literature are given elsewhere (Eysenck, 1970; Rees, 1973); the fairly close relationship between physique and delinquency has also been documented (Eysenck & Gudjonsson, 1989). Most workers have used a three-dimensional scheme of description of human body build, but factorial studies (e.g., Rees & Eysenck, 1945) make it clear that in the main two factors are involved—namely, height and width. This is certainly true of males, for females; (for obvious reasons), a slightly more complex scheme is involved.

Interest in body build as a concomitant of personality has flagged in recent years, largely because of Sheldon's exaggerated claims, and perhaps also because of the *Zeitgeist* that betrayed more interest in environmental than in constitutional factors. However that may be, I may in this connection quote an earlier conclusion of mine:

On the whole the work reviewed would . . . support the proposition that there exists a correlation of the order of .3 to .5 between (a) ectomorph body-build and introversion, and (b) ectomorph body-build and neuroticism. Both these relationships work in the direction of making the dysthymic individual particularly ectomorph and the normal extravert particularly eurymorph. (Eysenck, 1970, p. 346)

Ectomorph body build is defined as having a high Rees–Eysenck index, which essentially uses height as a measure of the length factor and transverse chest width as a measure of a width factor; the former is then divided by the latter to give the index. Ectomorphs and eurymorphs are defined as lying one standard deviation above or below the mean of the population for this index—ectomorphs having greater height, eurymorphs having greater width. Neurotics are characterized by greater height, criminals by greater width of bodybuild.

One of the reasons why overall physique has ceased to be of interest is perhaps the fact that there seems to be little theoretical foundation for the observed findings. Rather more interesting are recent developments, such as the relationship among personality; pelvic outlet, size, and shape; and antenatal masculinization of the brain. As already mentioned, testosterone acts on certain brain centres during a short period of antenatal development, and as a consequence these diencephalic centers tend to dispose the individuals toward certain types of behavior—either typically male, typically female, or in between the two. It is not possible to index the imprinting of the diencephalic centers related to male and female sexual behavior by any obvious bodily indices or by stature. Schlegel (1983) suggested the use of the pelvic shape, using for the purpose the diameter of the pelvic outlet, indexed by the distance between the ischemic tuberosities. The reason for doing so was the simple fact that this index is largely determined by antenatal imprinting, and may hence be used as an index for that event. In an impressive series of studies, Schlegel managed to show very significant correlations between sexual and social behavior typical of females, on the one hand, and distance between the ischemic tuberosities, on the other. Thus leadership among friends and peers correlated −.43 with the index, preference for younger sex partners −.77, and preference for a more active sexual role −.90. Positive correlations were obtained for the need for social intercourse (.38), emotional reactivity and openness to human feelings (.35), ability to establish contact (.31), and suggestibility (.31). These correlations were obtained from 200 male subjects, and were derived from a detailed exploration in the form of a medical interview lasting 1 hour, based on a questionnaire, a brief biographical anamnesis, and a medical anamnesis. Again, it would seem that theory-oriented explorations have greater interest and predictive value than heuristic studies. It would seem justifiable to suggest other indices of antenatal imprinting.

An interesting aspect of physique that has not received as much attention as it deserves is blood group polymorphism. Its relevance to personality traits was originally suggested by Cattell, Young, and Hundleby (1964); Angst and Maurer-Groeli (1974) and Maurer-Groeli (1974a, 1974b) laid a solid foundation for this study when they discovered that there were significant differences in the frequency of blood groups found in Europe between introverts and extraverts and between highly emotional and relaxed persons. E− was found to be significantly more frequent among persons having the AB blood group. "Emotionality," or N, was significantly more frequent in persons having blood group B than in persons having blood group A. If we can interpret these findings as evidence for some pleiotropic mechanism linking blood groups and personality, then the importance of such a link is obvious.

Jogawar (1983) has recently tested a sample of 590 students, matching subjects in the different blood antigen groups for socioeconomic status and other variables. Using the 16 PF, he found that A groups were emotionally more stable than B groups; that B groups were more apprehensive that A groups; that A groups were more self-sufficient than B groups; and that B groups were more tense than AB groups. The original findings linking B blood groups with N, and A groups with emotional stability, were confirmed in this study; there is no evidence concerning the E dimension. The work of Lester and Gatto (1987) was based on only 92 students, which is too small a number to produce significant results where the differences are as small as they are in this field. It was found, however, that the AB and the O groups had higher E scores than the A or the B groups, which is not in accord with earlier work.

Some years ago (Eysenck, 1977), I attempted to extend these studies by making cross-cultural comparisons. These comparisons produced evidence that the Japanese score significantly lower on E and higher on N than do British groups (Barrett & Eysenck, 1984); accordingly, it might be predicted that the ratio A:B is larger in England than in Japan, and that the percentage of persons with blood group AB should be larger in Japan than in England. Using the averages derived from very large groups cited in the Mourant, Kopek, and Domaniewska-Sobezak (1976) book, I found that the percentage of persons with blood group AB was 3.01% in England and 8.98% in Japan—a very sizable difference in the predicted direction concerning the E dimension. The ratio A:B was, as predicted, larger in England than in Japan; the mean values were 4.54 and 1.64, respectively. When it is remembered that the total of the two samples amounts to over a million people, these differences are significant without any doubt.

I later (Eysenck, 1982) extended this study to a large number of different countries, for whom blood group frequencies and personality mean scores were known. When these countries were divided into "anxiety+," average, and "anxiety−" groups, it was found that the percentages with the B blood group were 14.60%, 12.71%, and 9.91%, respectively; these figures support the hypothesis. When extraverted countries were compared with introverted countries regarding the average AB proportion, the percentages found were 4.79% and 6.68%, respectively—again in line with the hypothesis. In a similar way, P+ and P− countries were compared; it was found that P+ groups had a much higher proportion with blood group B than P− groups, and also a much higher proportion with the AB blood group. These data thus give cross-cultural support for the hypothesis of a link between blood group polymorphism and personality.

Two recent studies (Boyer, 1986; Rinieris, Rabavilas, Lykouras, & Stefanis, 1983) have provided some information on the relation between blood groups and neurosis. Rinieris et al. (1983) studied 72 patients with obsessive−compulsive neurosis and 73 phobics, and compared them with 600 normal controls. Obsessive−compulsive neurosis was characterized by the A blood group, as was hysteria; in both cases, blood group O showed a negative relationship. Phobics, on the other hand, had a positive relationship with O and a negative one with A. Boyer studied two independent samples of psychiatric outpatients (n's = 52 and

60) with blood group A or O who filled in symptom questionnaires. In both samples, patients with blood group A scored significantly higher than those with blood group O on the obsessive−compulsive P factors. These results should be viewed in the light of earlier work on psychiatric patients, suggesting that blood group A is overrepresented in schizophrenia (Czechowicz & Pamnany, 1972; Masters, 1967; Mendlewicz, Massart-Guiot, Willmotte, & Fleiss, 1974). Blood group O occurs more often than expected in bipolar illness (Mendlewicz et al., 1974; Parker, Theilie, & Spielberger, 1961; Shapiro, Rafaelsen, Ryder, Svejgaard, & Sorensen, 1977). McKeon and McColl, 1982, failed to find differences according to blood group.

Many of these data are contradictory as far as studies of normals are concerned. It is doubtful to what extent they can be taken seriously, because of the well-known unreliability and lack of validity of psychiatric diagnosis. Furthermore, the concepts of N and P refer to *dispositional* states; diagnosed neurosis and psychosis refer to specific developed illnesses. Clearly, the field is an interesting and important one, but still in an early stage of development.

NEUROTICISM AND PSYCHOTICISM

This section must inevitably be a good deal shorter than the preceding, for the very good reason that there is much less work reported on N and P than on E. The reasons are not far to seek. It is relatively easy to change conditions of arousal in the laboratory; loud noise, novelty, repetition, strong visual stimuli, and many other sources of arousal can be produced and quantified, and do not raise ethical objections. On the other hand, it would be difficult if not impossible to produce strong emotional states in the laboratory; not only do we not know how to do this, but if we could do it there would be obvious ethical objections. Similarly, we simply do not know how to generate psychotic-like states through laboratory stimulation, and this too would be ethically objectionable.

Likewise, it is relatively simple to use drugs such as caffeine, nicotine (through cigarette smoking), or alcohol to produce extraverted and introverted behavior patterns. Elsewhere (Eysenck, 1983a, c), I have produced a taxonomy of drugs based on their effects on behavior and personality; this shows how personality differences can be produced by drug administration. Clearly, it would not be permissible to give hallucinogens or other psychoticizing dipsychotic drugs, or adrenergic or anxiolytic drugs, in the laboratory, simply for the purpose of carrying out research on personality. The main effects, the side effects, and the danger of addiction would make such use impossible.

As a consequence of these difficulties, most authors have relied on very weak emotional and sensory stimuli that, according to the study by Saltz (1970) mentioned earlier, would not be expected to produce emotional reactions similar to those of neurosis. Nevertheless, the early work along these lines (summarized in detail in Eysenck, 1970) seemed quite promising. In a pioneer study notable for its careful methodology and excellent statistical analysis, Darrow and Heath (1932) isolated groups of intercorrelated personality traits and psychophysiological reactions. They found a group of traits similar to N, which correlated quite highly with the following group of psychophysiological measures: (1) the recovery–reaction quotient; (2) the resistance rise during 2 minutes of rest after stimulation; (3) the percentage of association of the condition with the conditioning stimuli; and (4) the conditioned blood pressure rise. They called this group of personality constellations, all relating more or less to the same physiological measures, the "neurotic" constellation, because it comprised the larger part of what they judged to be the truly "neurotic" tendencies. Correlations between this constellation and the various physiological measures were in the .30–.40 region.

Many of the investigators at this time took their clue from the Eppinger and Hess (1917) theory of "vagotonia," based on the alleged physiological antagonism of the adrenergic and cholinergic branches of the autonomic nervous system. Predominance of one or the other was thought to explain personality and behavioral differences, and various investigators searched for such predominance. Darling (1940) was relatively unsuccessful, but the work of Wenger (1942, 1948, 1957) appeared at first very significant in its support of the theory, particularly as some of the work was done on quite large groups (he studied almost 500 normal cadets and aviation students as a control group, and 289 patients suffering from operational fatigue as an experimental group). Others following this line were Theron (1948), van der Merwe

(1948), and van der Merwe and Theron (1947).

Jost (1941) also reported positive results. In contrast to Wenger, Jost used physiological measures of a resting organism. Freeman (1948) laid special stress on physiological recovery after stress. He based this notion on the concept of "homeostasis" and the restoration of the original state after disturbance. Accordingly, he defined the physiological recovery quotient: $(B - C)/A$, in which B is arbitrarily defined as the level reached on the GSR 30 seconds after stimulation; C is the level reached 5 minutes after peak mobilization (B); and A is the level at which the stimulus is applied. This seems to be a valuable notion, which unfortunately has not been widely used. It is relatively free of the difficulties attaching to measuring *disturbances* of neuromuscular homeostasis, which are constrained by threshold and ceiling effects, and difficulties in measuring the resting state.

In direct contrast to these early and relatively promising studies, usually carried out on relatively small groups of subjects, stand the very large-scale, carefully organized, and minutely analyzed studies of Fahrenberg, Walschburger, Foerster, Myrtek, and Muller (1979) and Myrtek (1980). These two studies were undertaken on 125 male students who were administered many different psychophysiological tests, as well as personality and other questionnaires. They were also given interviews and asked questions concerning their individual reactions to the various tests. The stress tests used included mental arithmetic under noisy conditions, free speech, interview reactions, and the taking of blood samples. Ten separate psychophysiological measures were recorded: (1) electrodermal activity, (2) electrocardiogram, (3) blood pressure, (4) pulse frequency and amplitude, (5) skin temperature, (6) a pneumogram, (7) an electromyogram from forehead and arm, (8) eye movement, (9) eyelid movement, and (10) EEG. The resulting relationships were presented in many detailed tables, and a number of different types of statistical analyses were reported, including correlational analysis, factor analysis, item analysis, multitrait–multimethod analysis, and so on. It is difficult to fault either the experimental or the analytical methods used, although it must be said that there is too little explanation of the rotation methods used for the factor analysis to make judgment of the results possible.

Essentially, the findings of the Fahrenberg

et al. (1979) study were negative in the sense that all the different modalities, in relation to the different stresses, gave results incompatible with the function of the single activation factor, or even a small number of activation factors. Nor was there much evidence of any relationship between personality factors and the activation indices derived from all the different types of investigation. Something like eight independent psychophysiological activation factors had to be posited, although it might have been possible with the aid of oblique factor analysis to arrive at some form of higher-order activation and/or arousal factor (S). The results essentially confirm Lacey and Lacey's (1958) specificity hypothesis, with respect to both autonomic innovation and stress reaction. Myrtek's (1980) work confirms these results. The amount of information contained in the two books is truly phenomenal, and it will remain for many years a source of reference for students of this field.

Some recent studies are a little more positive. Maushammer, Ehmer, and Eckel (1981) examined the relationship of EEG, sensory EPs, and personality. Thirty subjects were used, and pain threshold and tolerance were observed. It was found that anxiety was positively correlated with peak latencies of the sensory EP, and so was N. For the latter, correlations depended on the stimulus and intensities; these correlations ranged from .54 to .73, with a significance level better than .001. No correlations were found for the E dimension. These very positive results certainly invite replication.

Heart rate reactions also show a significant relationship to N, and also to E (Harvey & Hirschmann, 1980). These authors studied defensive reactions and ORs following visual stimuli showing color slides of people who had died violently. Forty subjects with the most extreme scores on the EPQ E and N scales were selected from 300 females, and their heart responses were recorded. Beat-by-beat heart rate analyses revealed that initial accelerative responses, indicative of defense, were elicited from subjects scoring low on E and high on N. In contrast, initial decelerative responses, indicative of orienting, were elicited by subjects scoring high on E and low on N. These results are highly significant statistically, and in good agreement with the theory.

Using a rather less stressful task (performance on the Stroop test), Roger and Jamieson (1988) failed to find any differences in delayed heart rate recovery following stress for either E

or N. It is very doubtful whether the Stroop task really constitutes a stressful event, so the results do not contradict the theory to any strong degree.

Rather more relevant is a study by Naveteur and Baque (1987) looking at the relationship between electrodermal activity and anxiety in an attention-demanding task. A total of 24 subjects having extreme scores on the Cattell Anxiety Scale were tested. A variety of EDRs were assessed in relation to a cognitive task. Highly anxious subjects showed significantly lower skin conductance levels, lower skin conductance response amplitudes, fewer interstimuli spontaneous fluctuations, and longer latencies than subjects with low anxiety. These results certainly go directly counter to the theory, and it is also notable that they are in the opposite direction to results obtained for state anxiety, which were more in line with expectations. The authors list some 50 studies in a summary table that clearly indicates the contradictory results, making interpretation very difficult.

Of some interest in directing future research is a study by Lolas (1987), who argues that several convergent lines of evidence, both clinical and experimental, suggest that the right hemisphere may be more involved in processing, determining, and expressing emotional stimuli and states. From this, Lolas argues that persons differing in their degree of emotionality may show a differential activation and/or performance of one or the other hemisphere. It was found that N was significantly related to right-hemisphere negative-slope potential amplitudes at central leads; the author interprets this finding as suggesting a relatively higher right-hemisphere activation during a classical fixed four-period reaction time task. Again, these results are certainly worth following up, but are based on too few subjects to be definitive.

A series of other studies is reviewed elsewhere and (Eysenck & Eysenck, 1985; Stelmack, 1981). As these reviews indicate, studies within the normal population have not been successful in giving strong support to the theory linking N with psychophysiological measures of activation. Much more successful have been studies contrasting neurotics and normals. The account by Lader and Wing (1966) of their own and previous studies adequately surveys the field. The theory linking activation with N finds its strongest support in these studies, as far as tonic differences are concerned at least;

phasic differences are more difficult to establish because of differences in resting levels.

There is a large body of literature documenting the association of Type A behavior patterns and psychophysiological activity in response to stress (Wright, Contrada, & Glass, 1985). Studies using a Structured Interview have produced impressive evidence of Type A–Type B differences, in the direction of greater sympathetic activity of Type A probands following stress (there are no resting-state differences). Studies using questionnaires have given few positive results, possibly because subjects have generally been students rather than adults, or possibly because less relevant stressors have been used. The data are relevant because Type A behavior is closely related to N (Eysenck & Fulker, 1983), so that the positive association with psychophysiological indices may be counted as favoring the theory I have been discussing. What is important is that the stressors used in these studies are much more likely to produce relevant semineurotic reactions than are those usually employed in typical N-type research. Perhaps psychological researchers might achieve more positive results if they employed social stressors of the kind used in the studies summarized by Wright et al. (1985). These included, for instance, a competition, with a $25 prize, between the subject of the experiment and another apparent subject who was really a confederate of the experimenter; he was also an expert on the computer game in question, and practically unbeatable. In the course of the game he would rile the true subject of the experiment, teasing and taunting him, and generally "taking the mickey." He would also "win" the prize, thus adding injury to insult! Such elaborate tests are apparently needed to get proper emotional reactions in psychological experiments.

P has also attracted less research than E, partly because the concept of P is much newer, and partly because there does not exist a clear-cut theory that can be tested directly. Although originally suggested as a third basic dimension of personality in 1952 (Eysenck, 1952a), little work was done on the concept until much later (Eysenck & Eysenck, 1976). Earlier work on P has been reviewed by Claridge (1981, 1983), and more recent work by Zuckerman (1989). The Zuckerman review is particularly concerned with biological correlates of P.

It may be useful first to look at biological studies supporting the general theory that "psychoticism" is indeed correctly named; critics have often suggested that the P should stand for "psychopathy" rather than "psychoticism." The strongest evidence for the hypothesis that the P factor is indeed related at one end to psychotic behavior comes from studies using a variant of "criterion analysis" (Eysenck, 1950, 1952b), which may suitably be called the "proportionality criterion." The argument here is that if P is a genuine measure of psychoticism, then a test (or group of tests) that differentiates between psychotics and normals should equally distinguish between high- and low-P-scoring normals and high- and low-P-scoring psychotics. As an example, let us take work on HLA-B27. It has been found that certain specificities of the human leukocyte antigen system (HLA) are associated with particular diseases; in particular, HLA-B27 was strikingly increased in a group of chronic paranoid schizophrenics with poor prognostic features, as compared with the control group (McGuffin, 1979). Gattaz (1981) and Gattaz, Seitz, and Beckman (1985) have shown that high scorers on P constituted a significantly higher proportion of a subgroup of patients showing HLA-B27, when compared with patients without HLA-B27, than low scorers on P.

Similarly, in a group of psychiatrically healthy probands, those bearing HLA-B27 were found to have significantly higher P scores as compared with a group not having this antigen. P may be seen as a trait of the personality in someone at high risk for schizophrenia. When it is remembered that some HLA types have an influence upon neuronal postsynaptic membrane sensitivity to central neurotransmitters such as dopamine, the relationship may appear more than heuristic.

Even more important is the work of Claridge (1985), who has described psychopathology as being based on a failure of modulation of CNS arousal. According to this theory, psychosis does not involve a simple shift in, say, emotional arousal, but represents instead a much more complex dissociation of CNS activity. Claridge suggested that in the schizophrenic, physiological mechanisms that are normally congruent in their activity and thereby maintain integrated CNS function become uncoupled and dissociated. He concentrated on two aspects of CNS functioning that he considered to be particularly involved in this uncoupling process: (1) emotional arousal, and the mechanism concerned with the regulation of (2) sensory input, including variations in perceptual sensitivity and in the broadening and narrowing of tension. He called this the "phenomenon of reverse covariation" (Claridge, 1981). The theory was originally developed and tested by Venables (1963) and is reviewed, together with some new results, in a series of studies by Claridge and Brooks (1984), Brooks (1984), Rawlings and Claridge (1984), and Claridge, Robinson, and Birchall (1985).

More precisely, it was proposed that the nervous system in psychosis shows a strong tendency toward altered homeostasis, implicating the mechanisms of arousal and selective attention. It was found, using the EPQ P scale, that high P scorers closely resembled schizophrenics in showing the same profile of psychophysiological response, suggesting a similar style of CNS organization (Claridge, 1983; Claridge & Birchall, 1978; Claridge & Chappa, 1973). What was done in these studies was to compare sensory sensitivity and arousal. Sensory sensitivity might be measured by means of the two-flash threshold, or by examining the degree of "augmenting" or "reducing" in the EEG when the intensity of the single flash was varied. Generally, the sensory responses related to background arousal in a predictable and intuitively sensible way, but in schizophrenics the opposite was true: When physiological arousal was very low, sensitivity to environmental stimuli seemed to be much increased. This phenomenon, which was also shown to be producible by the psychedelic drug LSD, seemed to be a uniquely "psychotic" configuration of brain responses. That it should also be shown in normal individuals scoring high on P seems a powerful confirmation of the general theory of P. The fact that the same "psychotic" profile could be shown in first-degree relatives of schizophrenics, compared with a sample of neurotics' relatives, increases the power of the demonstration (Claridge, Robinson, & Birchall, 1983).

A similar strategy to that of Claridge was adopted by Robinson and Zahn (1985): They used two postural conditions (standing and reclining) to induce high and low activation levels in normal subjects divided into high- and low-P groups. Electrodermal and heart rate measures were recorded during each of these activation conditions, which included instructions, an initial rest period, a series of tones, a two-flash threshold task, and a final rest period. It was found that P+ subjects tended to display significantly lower autonomic arousability and poorer two-flash performance while undergoing the low-activation (reclining) condition. There was a reliable tendency for P+ subjects to evidence significantly slower recovery and rise time and to manifest significantly lower response criterion and sensory sensitivity. Robinson and Zahn compared the performance of P+ and P− groups to findings reported previously for schizophrenics and psychopaths for these tasks; although there was similarity to the behavior of schizophrenics in P+ scorers, they suggested a greater similarity to that of psychopaths. As psychopathy is postulated to be on the same continuum as schizophrenia (the P+ to P− continuum), this may simply indicate that the performance of schizophrenics may be disturbed to some degree by extraneous factors (their illness, hospitalization, drug treatment, etc.).

These and similar studies tend to support the interpretation of P as a measure of psychoticism, but they do little to advance our understanding of the causal relations involved. There are two major candidates (which may not be independent of each other, of course), but in each case we are dealing with one of the major traits underlying psychoticism, rather than with psychoticism itself. These two traits are aggressiveness and impulsivity. Some of the evidence for the relationship among P, testosterone, and MAO has already been given. Taking aggressiveness first, we may refer to an excellent summary by Olweus (1986), who not only reviews the evidence, but also provides some independent support.

I have already noted, of course, that present levels of testosterone and other androgens are not very reliable or valid measures of masculinity produced by antenatal masculinization through gonadal hormones; one would nevertheless be surprised if there were no differences at all in high-P and low-P subjects, or in aggressive and peaceful subjects, respectively. Some of the studies giving positive results for P have been reviewed elsewhere (Eysenck & Eysenck, 1976), and some of the striking differences are certainly significant in the expected direction. Because aggressivity and masculinity are such potent factors in high-P individuals (it will be remembered that males score almost twice as high as females on P), one would expect positive results from a study of these hormones. Olweus (1986) summarizes these results as follows:

Recent studies of the relationship between plasma testosterone levels and aggressive and antisocial behavior in the human male have yielded somewhat conflicting results. When combined with findings from animal studies . . . the studies with human males suggest that there may be a positive relationship between plasma and testosterone levels and one or more aspects of aggressive, impulsive, and antisocial behavior patterns. For animals, the findings also indicate that testosterone may have a causal influence on some forms of aggressive behavior. This, of course, does not preclude the possibility that an individual's testosterone level is at the same time affected by environmental and experiential factors (including the individual's own behavior). (p. 51)

The studies reviewed by Olweus were studies of males, using blood platelet techniques. Dabbs, Ruback, Frady, Hopper, and Sgoutas (1988), measuring testosterone concentrations in the saliva of 84 female prison inmates and 15 female college students, found that testosterone was highest in females guilty of unprovoked violence and lowest in those guilty of defensive violence, where inmates had reacted violently after being physically assaulted. Testosterone was also related to a number of prior charges and to parole board decisions about length of time to serve before being released on parole. These authors also give a good review of much of the evidence suggesting a close relationship between P-type behavior and testosterone. Work on impulsivity and MAO, as already reported, has shown a significant relationship.

Zuckerman (1989) has given a detailed discussion of the way in which the monoamine transmitters, enzymes, and metabolites are related. This is shown in Figure 10.6. On the left are shown the catecholamines, on the right the indoleamines; the biosynthesis of the neurotransmitters is regulated by enzymes that convert precursor compounds along a number of steps to the final form of the neurotransmitter. Other enzymes are involved in the degradation of the neurotransmitters, yielding metabolites, or breakdown products, which are eventually eliminated from the body. Shown in the figure are the primary steps in the biosynthesis and breakdown of norepinephrine and serotonin.

From what we know about the relationship between the neurotransmitters (e.g., dopamine, serotonin) to schizophrenia and psychosis generally, the observed relationships between impulsivity and MAO, 5-HIAA, and so on appear to make some sense; the theories are spelled out in detail by Zuckerman (1989). What is now needed, more than anything, is more clear-cut evidence that the relationship between these enzymes and personality implicates not only impulsivity, but also the more general higher-order concept of P. Until this is done, we must regard the evidence as insufficient to support a more general theory linking P with hormones such as testosterone and enzymes such as MAO.

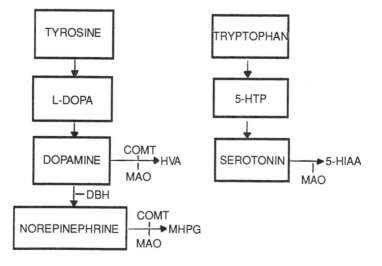

FIGURE 10.6. Steps in the biosynthesis and breakdown of norepinephrine (left) and serotonin (right). From "Personality in the Third Dimension: A Psychobiological Approach" by M. Zuckerman, 1989, *Personality and Individual Differences*, 10, 391–418. Copyright 1989 by Pergamon Press. Reprinted by permission.

SUMMARY AND CONCLUSIONS

It is clear from this account that although there are intriguing and instructive findings in the general field of the relationship between personality and psychobiology, there are also many anomalies, failures to replicate, and areas with insufficient data. The relationship between some form of arousal and the E dimension seems to be the most firmly established, although here also predictions made to experimental psychological findings seem to be more frequently validated than are similar deductions in the psychophysiological field. However, overall the evidence is sufficiently positive to suggest that the theory is along the right lines, although clearly much work remains to be done to clear up the remaining anomalies.

As regards the N construct, the position is clearly unsatisfactory. We have to consider the reasons why this might be so; perhaps future research, taking into account the objections to current methodologies, will give more positive results than are available at present.

Regarding the P dimensions, a relatively clear-cut theory is available along the lines advocated by Venables and Claridge, showing a reversal for P scorers in the areas of arousal and sensory reaction–interaction. Underlying this may be differences in MAO enzymatic activity and/or testosterone. What is clearly needed in this field is some more inclusive theory; however, there is already sufficient evidence to indicate the lines along which such a theory might be phrased.

All in all, considering the youth of the subject and the comparatively small amount of effort that has gone into its investigation until quite recently, results are not too disappointing. Future work can certainly be based with some confidence on the results that have been reported so far. What cannot be doubted is that such future work will lead to a revamping and improvement of grand theories; it may, of course, also produce entirely novel theories that are able to encompass the positive findings outlined in this chapter. This of course is the fate of most theories in science, and we should not cling too long to outmoded theories, just as we should not abandon theories, however weak, until better theories are forthcoming.

It may be useful to end this chapter by referring readers to sources that take the topic further in various directions, or contain useful summaries in greater detail than was possible here. Williams (1956) contributed an interesting early overview of *Biochemical Individuality*. Hartlage and Telzrov (1985) have edited an overview of *The Neuropsychology of Individual Differences*. Janke (1983) has edited a book titled *Response Variability to Psychotropic Drugs*. Prentley (1979) has written on *The Biological Aspects of Normal Personality*. Howard, Fenton, and Fenwick (1982) have produced a volume titled *Event-Related Brain Potentials in Personality and Psychopathology: A Pavlovian Approach*. These may usefully be consulted, in addition to the summaries already mentioned in the text.

REFERENCES

Angleitner, A., & Wiggins, J. S. (1986). *Personality assessment via questionnaires*. New York: Springer.

Angst, J., & Maurer-Groeli, Y. (1974). Blutgruppen und Personlichkeit. *Archiv für Psychiatrie und Nervenkrankheiten, 218,* 291–300.

Argue, J. M., Unzeba, M., & Torrubia, R. (1988). Neurotransmitter systems and personality measurements: A study in psychosomatic patients and healthy subjects. *Neuropsychobiology, 19,* 149–157.

Aston-Jones, G., & Bloom, F. E. (1981). Norepinephrine-containing locus coeruleus neurons in behaving rats exhibit pronounced responses to non-noxious environmental stimuli. *Journal of Neuroscience, 8,* 887–900.

Ballenger, J. C., Post, R. M., Jimmerson, D. C., Lake, C. R., Murphy, D. L., Zuckerman, M., & Cronin, C. (1983). Biochemical correlates of personality traits in normals: An exploratory study. *Personality and Individual Differences, 4,* 615–625.

Barrett, P., & Eysenck, S. B. G. (1984). The assessment of personality factors across 25 countries. *Personality and Individual Differences, 5,* 615–632.

Bartol, C. R., & Martin, R. B. (1974). Preference for complexity as a function of neuroticism, extraversion and amplitude of orienting response. *Perceptual and Motor Skills, 38,* 1155–1160.

Blake, M. F. (1967). Relationship between circadian rhythm of body temperature and introversion–extraversion. *Nature, 215,* 896–897.

Bohlin, G. (1972). Susceptibility to sleep during a habituation procedure as related to individual differences. *Journal of Experimental Research in Personality, 6,* 248–254.

Boyer, W. F. (1986). Influence of ABO blood type on symptomatology among outpatients: Study and replication. *Neuropsychobiology, 16,* 43–46.

Brooks, P. (1984). Schizotypy and hemisphere function: II. Performance asymmetry as a verbal divided visual-field task. *Personality and Individual Differences, 5,* 649–656.

Buchsbaum, M. S., & Haier, R. Z. (1983). Individual differences in augmenting/reducing evoked potentials.

In A. Gale & J. Edwards (Eds.), *Physiological correlates of human behavior* (Vol. 3). London: Academic Press.

Buchsbaum, M. S., & Silverman, J. (1968). Stimulus intensity control and the cortical evoked response. *Psychosomatic Medicine, 30,* 12–22.

Bull, R., & Gale, A. (1973). The reliability and interrelationships between various measures of electrodermal activity. *Journal of Experimental Research in Personality, 6,* 300–306.

Bullen, J. G., & Hemsley, D. R. (1984). Psychoticism and visual recognition thresholds. *Personality and Individual Differences, 5,* 735–739

Calhoon, L. L. (1988). Explorations into the biochemistry of sensation-seeking. *Personality and Individual Differences, 9,* 941–949.

Casey, J., & McManis, D. L. (1971). Salivary response to lemon juice as a measure of introversion in children. *Perceptual and Motor Skills, 33,* 1059–1065.

Cattell, R. B., Eber, H. W., & Tatsuoka, M. M. (1970). *Handbook for the Sixteen Personality Factors Questionnaire.* Champaign, IL: Institute for Personality and Ability Testing.

Cattell, R. B., Young, H., & Hundleby, J. (1964). Blood groups and personality traits. *American Journal of Human Genetics, 16,* 397–402.

Claridge, G. S. (1967). *Personality and arousal.* Oxford: Pergamon Press.

Claridge, G. S. (1981). Psychoticism. In R. Lynn (Ed.), *Dimensions of personality* (pp. 79–109). Oxford: Pergamon Press.

Claridge, G. S. (1983). The Eysenck Psychoticism scale. In J. P. Butcher & C. D. Spielberger (Eds.), *Advances in personality assessment* (Vol. 2, pp. 71–114). Hillsdale, NJ; Erlbaum.

Claridge, G. S. (1985). *Origins of mental illness.* Oxford: Blackwell.

Claridge, G. S., & Birchall, P. M. J. (1978). Bishop, Eysenck, Block and psychoticism. *Journal of Abnormal Psychology, 87,* 604–668.

Claridge, G., & Brooks, P. (1984). Schizotypy and hemisphere function: I. Theoretical considerations and the measurement of schizotypy. *Personality and Individual Differences, 5,* 633–648.

Claridge, G. S., & Chappa, H. J. (1973). Psychoticism: A study of its biological nature in normal subjects. *British Journal of Social and Clinical Psychology, 12,* 175–187.

Claridge, G. S., Donald, J., & Birchall, P. M. (1981). Drug tolerance and personality: Some implications for Eysenck's theory. *Personality and Individual Differences, 2,* 153–166.

Claridge, G., Robinson, D. L., & Birchall, P. (1983). Characteristics of schizophrenics' and neurotics' relatives. *Personality and Individual Differences, 4,* 651–664.

Claridge, G., Robinson, D. L., & Birchall, P. (1985). Psychophysiological evidence of "psychoticism" in schizophrenics' relatives. *Personality and Individual Differences, 6,* 1–10.

Claridge, G., & Roth, E. (1973). Sedative drug tolerance in twins. In G. S. Claridge, S. Carter, & W. Hume (Eds.), *Personality difference and biological variations.* Oxford: Pergamon Press.

Cloninger, C. R. (1986). A unified biosocial theory of personality and its role in the development of anxiety states. *Psychiatric Developments, 3,* 167–226.

Cohen, M. R., & Nagel, V. (1936). *An introduction to logic and scientific method.* New York: Harcourt, Brace.

Coles, M. G., Gale, A., & Kline, P. (1971). Personality and habituation of the orienting reaction: Tonic and response measures of electrodermal activity. *Psychophysiology, 8,* 54–63.

Colquhoun, W. P. (1960). Temperament, inspection efficiency and time of day. *Ergonoms, 3,* 377–378.

Colquhoun, W. P. (1971). *Biological rhythms and human performance.* London: Academic Press.

Conley, J. J. (1984a). The hierarchy of consistency: A review and model of longitudinal findings on adult individual differences in intelligence, personality and self-opinion. *Personality and Individual Differences, 5,* 11–26.

Conley, J. J. (1984b). Longitudinal consistency of adult personality: Self-reported psychological characteristics across 45 years. *Journal of Personality and Social Psychology, 47,* 1325–1333.

Conley, J. J. (1985). Longitudinal stability of personality traits: A multitrait–multimethod–multioccasion analysis. *Journal of Personality and Social Psychology, 49,* 1260–1282.

Corcoran, D. W. (1964). The relation between introversion and salivation. *American Journal of Psychology, 77,* 298–300.

Corcoran, D. W. (1981). Introversion–extraversion, stress and arousal. In R. Lynn (Ed.), *Dimensions of personality.* Oxford: Pergamon Press.

Costa, P. T., Chauncey, H. H., Rose, C. L., & Kapur, K. (1980). Relationship of paratid saliva flow rate and composition with personality traits in healthy men. *Oral Surgery and Medical Pathology, 50,* 416–422.

Coursey, R. D., Buchsbaum, M. S., & Murphy, D. C. (1979). Platelet MAO activity and evoked potentials in the identification of subjects biologically at risk for psychiatric disorders. *British Journal of Psychiatry, 194,* 372–381.

Crider, A., & Lunn, R. (1971). Electrodermal lability as a personality dimension. *Journal of Experimental Research in Personality, 5,* 145–150.

Czechowicz, A. S., & Pamnany, L. (1972). ABO blood groups and the aetiology of schizophrenia. *Medical Journal of Australia, 1,* 1252–1254.

Dabbs, J. M., Ruback, R. B., Frady, R. Z., Happer, C. H., & Sgoutas, D. S. (1988). Saliva testosterone and criminal violence among women. *Personality and Individual Differences, 9,* 269–275.

Daitzman, R., & Zuckerman, M. (1980). Disinhibitory sensation seeking personality and gonadal hormones. *Personality and Individual Differences, 1,* 103–110.

Daitzman, R., & Zuckerman, M., Sammelwitz, P., & Ganjam, V. (1978). Sensation seeking and gonadal hormones. *Journal of Biosocial Sciences, 10,* 401–408.

Darling, R. P. (1940). Autonomic action in relation to personality traits of children. *Journal of Abnormal and Social Psychology, 35,* 246–260.

Darrow, C. W., & Heath, L. C. (1932). Reaction tendencies relating to personality. In K. S. Lashley (Ed.), *Studies of the dynamics of behavior.* Chicago: University of Chicago Press.

Davis, H., & Zerlin, S. (1966). Acoustic relations of the human vertex potential. *Journal of the Acoustical Society of America, 39,* 109–116.

Deary, I. J., Ramsay, H., Wilson, J. A., & Riad, M. (1988). Stimulated salivation: Correlations with personality and time of day effects. *Personality and Individual Differences, 9,* 903–909.

Desjardin, E. C. (1976). *The effects of denotative and correla-*

tive linguistic meaning and word concreteness on the habituation of the skin conductance response: Extraversion and neuroticism as subject variables. Unpublished doctoral dissertation, University of Ottawa.

Dincheva, E., & Piperova-Dalbokova, D. C. (1982). Differences in contingent negative variation (CNV) related to extraversion–introversion. *Personality and Individual Differences, 3,* 447–451.

Duffy, E. (1957). The psychological significance of the concept of "arousal" or "activation." *Psychological Review, 64,* 265–275.

Eaves, L., Eysenck, H. J., & Martin, N. (1989). *Genes, culture and personality: An empirical approach.* New York: Academic Press.

Eppinger, H., & Hess, W. R. (1917). Vagotonia. *Nervous and Mental Disease Monographs, 20.*

Eysenck, H. J. (1947). *Dimensions of personality.* London: Routledge & Kegan Paul.

Eysenck, H. J. (1950). Criterion analysis: An application of the hypothetico-deductive method to factor analysis. *Psychological Review, 57,* 38–53.

Eysenck, H. J. (1952a). Schizophrenia–cyclothymia as a dimension of personality. *Journal of Personality, 20,* 345–384.

Eysenck, H. J. (1952b). *The scientific study of personality.* London: Routledge & Kegan Paul.

Eysenck, H. J. (1957a). Drugs and personality: I. Theory and methodology. *Journal of Mental Science, 103,* 119–131.

Eysenck, H. J. (1957b). *The dynamics of anxiety and hysteria.* London: Routledge & Kegan Paul.

Eysenck, H. J. (1960). The place of theory in psychology. In H. J. Eysenck (Ed.), *Experiments in personality* (Vol. 2, pp. 303–315.). London: Routledge & Kegan Paul.

Eysenck, H. J. (Ed.). (1963). *Experiments with drugs.* Oxford: Pergamon Press.

Eysenck, H. J. (1967). *The biological basis of personality.* Springfield, IL: Charles C Thomas.

Eysenck, H. J. (1970). *The structure of human personality* (3rd ed.). London: Methuen.

Eysenck, H. J. (Ed.) (1976). *The measurement of personality.* Lancaster, England: MTP.

Eysenck, H. J. (1977). National differences in personality as related to ABO blood groups polymorphism. *Psychological Reports, 41,* 1257–1258.

Eysenck, H. J. (Ed.). (1981). *A model for personality.* New York: Springer.

Eysenck, H. J. (1982). The biological basis of cross-cultural differences in personality: Blood group antigens. *Psychological Reports, 51,* 531–540.

Eysenck, H. J. (1983a). Drugs as research tools in psychology: Experiments with drugs in personality research. *Neuropsychobiology, 10,* 29–43.

Eysenck, H. J. (1983b). Is there a paradigm of personality research? *Journal of Research in Personality, 17,* 369–397.

Eysenck, H. J. (1983c). Psychopharmacology and personality. In W. Janke (Ed.), *Response variability to psychotropic drugs* (pp. 127–154). Oxford: Pergamon Press.

Eysenck, H. J. (1984). The place of individual differences in a scientific psychology. *Annals of Theoretical Psychology, 1,* 233–2286.

Eysenck, H. J. (1985). The place of theory in a world of facts. *Annals of Theoretical Psychology, 3,* 17–72.

Eysenck, H. J. (1987). The role of heredity, environment and "preparedness" in the genesis of neurosis. In H. J.

Eysenck & I. Martin (Eds.), *Theoretical foundations of behavior therapy* (pp. 379–402). New York: Plenum.

Eysenck, H. J., & Eysenck, M. W. (1985). *Personality and individual differences: A natural science approach.* New York: Plenum.

Eysenck, H. J., & Eysenck, S. B. G. (1967). Salivary response to lemon juice as a measure of introversion. *Perceptual and Motor Skills, 24,* 1047–1053.

Eysenck, H. J., & Eysenck, S. B. G. (1976). *Psychoticism as a dimension of personality.* London: Hodder & Stroughton.

Eysenck, H. J., & Fulker, D. (1983). The components of Type A behavior and its genetic determinants. *Personality and Individual Differences, 4,* 499–505.

Eysenck, H. J., & Gudjonsson, G. (1989). *Causes and cures of delinquency.* New York: Plenum.

Eysenck, H. J., & O'Connor, K. (1979). Smoking, arousal and personality. In J. Remond & J. Tizard (Eds.), *Electrophysiological effects of nicotine.* Amsterdam: Elsevier.

Eysenck, H. J., & Wilson, G. (1979). *The psychology of sex.* London: Dent.

Eysenck, S. B. G., & Eysenck, H. J. (1967). Physiological reactivity to sensory stimulation as a measure of personality. *Psychological Reports, 20,* 45–46.

Fahrenberg, J., Walschburger, P., Foerster, M., Myrtek, M., & Muller, W. (1979). *Psychophysiologische Aktivierungsforschung.* Munich: Minerva.

Fowles, D. C., Roberts, R., & Nagel, K. (1977). The influence of introversion–extraversion in the skin conductance responses to stress and stimulus intensity. *Journal of Research in Personality, 11,* 129–146.

Freeman, G. L. (1948). *The energetics of human behavior.* Ithaca, NY: Cornell University Press.

Friedman, J., & Meares, R. (1979). Cortical evoked potentials and extraversion. *Psychosomatic Medicine, 41,* 279–286.

Frith, C. D. (1968). Personality, nicotine and the salivary response. *Life Sciences, 7,* 1151–1156.

Frith, C. D. (1977). *Habituation of the pupil size and light responses to sound.* Paper presented at the meeting of the American Psychological Association, San Francisco.

Gale, A. (1983). Electroencephalographic studies of extraversion–introversion: A case study in the psychophysiology of individual differences. *Personality and Individual Differences, 4,* 371–380.

Gange, J. J., Geen, R. G., & Harkins, S. G. (1979). Autonomic differences between extraverts and introverts during vigilance. *Psychophysiology, 16,* 392–397.

Ganong, W. F. (1979). *Review of medical physiology.* Palo Alto, CA: Lange.

Gattaz, W. F. (1981). HLA-B27 as a possible genetic marker of psychoticism. *Personality and Individual Differences, 2,* 57–60.

Gattaz, W. F., Seitz, M., & Beckman, H. (1985). A possible association between HLA B-27 and vulnerability to schizophrenia. *Personality and Individual Differences, 6,* 283–285.

Golding, J. F., & Richards, M. (1985). EEG spectral analysis, visual evoked potential and photic-driving correlates of personality and memory. *Personality and Individual Differences, 6,* 67–76.

Graham, F. K. (1973). Habituation and dishabituation of responses innervated by the autonomic nervous system. In H. Peeke & M. Herz (Eds.), *Habituation* (Vol. 1, pp. 163–218). London: Academic Press.

Gray, J. A. (Ed.). (1964). *Pavlov's typology.* Oxford: Pergamon Press.

Gray, J. A. (1970). The psychophysiological basis of introversion – extraversion. *Behaviour Research and Therapy, 8,* 249–266.

Gray, J. A. (1972). The psychophysiological basis of introversion – extraversion: A modification of Eysenck's theory. In V. D. Nebylitsyn & J. A. Gray (Eds.), *The biological basis of individual behavior* (pp. 182–205). New York: Academic Press.

Gray, J. A. (1981). A critique of Eysenck's theory of personality. In H. J. Eysenck (Ed.), *A model for personality* (pp. 246–276). New York: Springer.

Gray, J. A. (1982). *The neuropsychology of anxiety: An enquiry into the functions of the septo-hippocampal system.* New York: Oxford University Press.

Haier, R. J., Robinson, D. L., Braden, W., & Williams, D. (1984). Evoked potential augmenting – reducing and personality differences. *Personality and Individual Differences, 5,* 293–301.

Hartlage, L. C., & Telzrov, C. F. (Eds.). (1985). *The neuropsychology of individual differences.* New York: Plenum.

Harvey, F., & Hirschmann, R. (1980). The influence of extraversion and neuroticism on heart rate responses to aversive visual stimuli. *Personality and Individual Differences, 1,* 97–100.

Hebb, D. O. (1955). Drives and the CNS (conceptual nervous system). *Psychological Review, 62,* 243–259.

Hendrickson, B. E. (1973). *An examination of individual differences in cortical evoked response.* Unpublished doctoral dissertation, University of London.

Holmes, D. S. (1967). Pupillary response, conditioning and personality. *Journal of Personality and Social Psychology, 5,* 95–103.

Horne, J., & Ostberg, O. (1975). Time of day effects on extraversion and salivation. *Biological Psychology, 3,* 301–307.

Horne, J. A., & Ostberg, O. (1976). A self-assessment questionnaire to determine morningness – eveningness in human circadian rhythms. *International Journal of Chronobiology, 4,* 97–110.

Howard, R. C., Fenton, G. W., & Fenwick, P. (1982). *Event-related brain potentials in personality and psychopathology: A Pavlovian approach.* New York: Research Studies Press.

Irmis, F. (1985). EEG and autonomic correlates of extraversion and neuroticism. *Archives of Neurology, 27* (Suppl.), 221–223.

Janke, W. (1983). *Response variability to psychotropic drugs.* Oxford: Pergamon Press.

Jogawar, V. V. (1983). Personality correlates of human blood groups. *Personality and Individual Differences, 4,* 215–216.

Jost, H. (1941). Some physiological changes during frustration. *Child Development, 12,* 9–15.

Klinteberg, B., Schalling, D., Edman, G., Oreland, L., & Asberg, H. E. (1987). Personality correlates of platelet monoamine oxidase (MAO) activity in female and male subjects. *Neuropsychobiology, 18,* 89–96.

Knorring, L. von. (1980). Visual averaged evoked responses and platelet monoamine oxidase in patients suffering from alcoholism. In H. Begleiter (Ed.), *Biological effects of alcoholism* (pp. 649–660). New York: Plenum.

Knorring, L. von, Knorring, A.-L. von, Mornstad, H., & Nordland, A. (1987). The risks of dental caries in extraverts. *Personality and Individual Differences, 8,* 343–346.

Knorring, L. von, Mornstad, H., Forsgren, L., & Holmgren, S. (1986). Saliva secretion rate and saliva composition in relation to extraversion. *Personality and Individual Differences, 7,* 38.

Knorring, L. von, Oreland, I. F., & Wimblad, B. (1984). Personality traits related to monoamine oxidase activity in platelets. *Psychiatric Research, 12,* 11–26.

Koriat, A., Averill, J. R., & Molenstram, E. (1973). Individual differences in habituation. Some methodological and conceptual issues. *Journal of Research in Personality, 7,* 88–101.

Kretschmer, E. (1948). *Korperban und Charakter.* Berlin: Springer-Verlag.

Krishnamoorti, S. P., & Shagass, C. (1963). Some psychological test correlates of sedation threshold. In J. Wortis, (Ed.), *Recent advances in biological psychiatry.* New York: Plenum.

Krupski, A., Rankin, D., & Bakens, P. (1971). Physiological and personality correlates of commission errors in an auditory vigilance task. *Psychophysiology, 8,* 304–311.

Kuhn, T. S. (1970). *The structure of scientific revolutions* (rev. ed.). Chicago: University of Chicago Press.

Lacey, J. I., & Lacey, B. C. (1958). Verification and extension of the principle of autonomic response-stereotype. *American Journal of Psychology, 71,* 50–73.

Lader, M., & Wing, L. (1966). *Physiological measures, sedative drugs and morbid anxiety* (Maudsley Monograph No. 14). Oxford: Oxford University Press.

Laverty, S. G. (1958). Sodium amytal and extraversion. *Journal of Neurology, Neurosurgery and Psychiatry, 21,* 50–54.

Lester, D., & Gatto, J. L. (1987). Personality and blood groups. *Personality and Individual Differences, 6,* 267.

Lolas, F. (1987). Hemispheric asymmetry of slow brain potentials in relation to neuroticism. *Personality and Individual Differences, 8,* 969–971.

Lolas, F., & Aquilera, N. (1982). Extraversion and inhibitions: A slow-potential study. *Biological Psychiatry, 17,* 963–969.

Lukas, J. N. (1987). Visual evoked potential augmenting – reducing and personality: The vertex augmenter is a sensation seeker. *Personality and Individual Differences, 8,* 385–395.

Lynn, R. (1966). *Attention, arousal and the orienting reaction.* New York: Pergamon Press.

Maccoby, E. E., & Jacklin, C. V. (1974). *The psychology of sex differences.* Stanford, CA: Stanford University Press.

Mangan, G. J. (1974). Personality and conditioning: Some personality and cognitive and psychophysiological parameters of classical appetitive (sexual) GSR conditioning. *Pavlovian Journal of Biological Psychology, 9,* 125–135.

Mangan, G. (1982). *The biology of human conduct.* Oxford: Pergamon Press.

Mangan, G. L., & O'Gorman, J. G. (1969). Initial amplitude and rate of habituation of orienting reaction in relation to extraversion and neuroticism. *Journal of Experimental Research in Personality, 3,* 275–282.

Masters, A. B. (1967). The distribution of blood groups in psychiatric illness. *British Journal of Psychiatry, 113,* 1309–1315.

Matthews, G. (1987). Personality and multidimensional arousal: A study of two dimensions of extraversion. *Personality and Individual Differences, 8,* 9–16.

Maurer-Groeli, Y. (1974a). Blutgruppen, Personlichkeit und Schulabschluss: Eine Untersuchung mittels FPI. *Schweizerische Zeitschrift für Psychologie, 33*, 407–410.

Maurer-Groeli, Y. (1974b). Blutgruppen und Krankheiten. *Archiv für Psychiatrie und Nervenkrankheiten, 218,* 301–318.

Maushammer, C., Ehmer, G., & Eckel, K. (1981). Pain, personality and individual differences in sensory evoked potentials. *Personality and Individual Differences, 2,* 335–336.

McCrae, R. R., & Costa, P. T. (1985). Updating Norman's "adequate taxonomy": Intelligence and personality dimensions in natural languages and in questionnaires. *Journal of Personality and Social Psychology, 49,* 710–721.

McGuffin, P. (1979). Is schizophrenia an HLA-associated disease? *Psychological Medicine, 9,* 721–728

McKenzie, J. (1988). Three superfactors in the 16PF and their relation to Eysenck's P, E and N. *Personality and Individual Differences, 9,* 843–850.

McKeon, J. P., & McColl, D. (1982). ABO blood groups in obsessional illness—state and trait. *Acta Psychiatrica Scandinavica, 65,* 74–78.

Mendlewicz, J., Massart-Guiot, T., Willmotte, J., & Fleiss, J. Z. (1974). Blood groups in manic–depressive illness and schizophrenics. *Diseases of the Nervous System, 35,* 39–41.

Moruzzi, G., & Magoun, H. W. (1949). Brain stem reticular formation and activation of the EEG. *Electroencephalography and Clinical Neurophysiology, 1,* 455–473.

Mourant, A. E., Kopek, S. C., & Domaniewska-Sobezak, K. (1976). *The distribution of the human blood groups.* London: Oxford University Press.

Muntaner, C., Garcia-Sevilla, L., Fernandez, A., & Torrubia, R. (1988). Personality dimensions, schizotypal and borderline personality traits and psychosis proneness. *Personality and Individual Differences, 9,* 257–268.

Murphy, D. L., Wright, L., Buchsbaum, M. S., Nichols, A., Costa, J. L., & Wyatt, R. Z. (1976). Platelet and plasma amino oxidase activity in 680 normals: Sex and age differences and stability over time. *Biochemical Medicine, 16,* 254–265.

Myrtek, M. (1980). *Psychophysiologische Konstitutionsforschung.* Göttingen, West Germany: Hogrefe.

Naveteur, L. J., & Baque, E. F. (1987). Individual differences in the electrodermal activity as a function of subjects' anxiety. *Personality and Individual Differences, 8,* 615–626.

Nielsen, T. L., & Petersen, K. E. (1976). Electrodermal correlates of extraversion, trait anxiety and schizophrenia. *Scandinavian Journal of Psychology, 17,* 73–80.

Norman, W. T. (1963). Toward an adequate taxonomy of personality attributes: Replicated factor structure. *Journal of Abnormal and Social Psychology, 66,* 574–583.

O'Connor, K. (1980). The contingent negative variation and individual differences in smoking behavior. *Personality and Individual Differences, 1,* 57–72.

O'Gorman, J. (1977). Individual differences in habituation of human physiological responses: A review of theory, method and findings in the study of personality correlates in non-clinical populations. *Biological Psychology, 5,* 257–318.

O'Gorman, J. G., & Lloyd, J.E.M. (1987). Extraversion, impulsiveness, and EEG alpha activity. *Personality and Individual Differences, 8,* 169–174.

O'Gorman, J. G., & Mallise, L. R. (1984). Extraversion and the EEG: II. A test of Gale's hypothesis. *Biological Psychology, 19,* 113–127.

Olweus, D. (1986). Aggression and hormones. In C. Olweus, J. Block, & M. Radke-Yarrow (Eds.), *The development of antisocial and prosocial behavior: Research, theories and issues* (pp. 51–74). New York: Academic Press.

Parker, J. B., Theilie, A., & Spielberger, C. D. (1961). Frequency of blood types in a homogeneous group of manic–depressive patients. *Journal of Mental Science, 107,* 936–942.

Pascalis, V. de, & Montrirosso, R. (1988). Extraversion, neuroticism and individual differences in event-related potentials. *Personality and Individual Differences, 9,* 353–360.

Pavlov, F. P. (1927). *Conditioned reflexes.* London: Oxford University Press.

Piperova-Dalbokova, D., Dincheva, E., & Urgelles, L. (1984). Stability of contingent negative variation (CNV) and extraversion–introversion. *Personality and Individual Differences, 5,* 763–766.

Prentley, R. A. (Ed.). (1979). *The biological aspects of normal personality.* Lancaster, England: MTP.

Raina, M. R., & Vats, A. (1982). Serum uric acid, serum cholesterol and personality. *Journal of Psychosomatic Research, 20,* 291–299.

Ramsey, R. W. (1969). Salivary response and introversion–extraversion. *Acta Psychologia, 29,* 181–187.

Rawlings, D., & Claridge, G. (1984). Schizotypy and hemisphere function: III. Performance asymmetries on tasks of letter recognition and local–global processing. *Personality and Individual Differences, 5,* 657–663.

Rees, L. (1973). Constitutional factors and abnormal behaviour. In H. J. Eysenck (Ed.), *Handbook of abnormal psychology* (pp. 487–539). London: Pitman.

Rees, L., & Eysenck, H. J. (1945). A factorial study of some morphological and psychological aspects of human constitution. *Journal of Mental Science, 91,* 8–21.

Revelle, W., Anderson, K. J., & Humphreys, M. S. (1987). Empirical tests and theoretical extensions of arousal-based theories of personality. In J. Strelau & H. J. Eysenck (Eds.), *Personality dimension and arousal* (pp. 17–36). New York: Plenum.

Rinieris, P., Rabavilas, A., Lykouras, E., & Stefanis, L. (1983). Neuroses and ABO blood types. *Neuropsychobiology, 9,* 16–18.

Ritter, W., Simpson, R., Vaughan, H. G., & Friedman, D. (1979). A brain event related to the making of a sensory discrimination. *Science, 203,* 1358–1361.

Ritter, W., Vaughan, H. G., & Simpson, R. (1983). On relating event-related potential components to stages of information processing. In A.W.K. Gaillard & W. Ritter (Eds.), *Tutorials in event-related potential research: Endogenous components.* Amsterdam: Elsevier/North-Holland.

Robinson, D. L. (1982). Properties of the diffuse thalamo-cortical system of human personality: A direct test of Pavlovian/Eysenckian theory. *Personality and Individual Differences, 3,* 1–16.

Robinson, T. N., & Zahn, T. P. (1985). Psychoticism and arousal: Possible evidence for a linkage of P and psychopathy. *Personality and Individual Differences, 6,* 47–66.

Rodnight, E., & Gooch, R. A. (1963). A new method for the determination of individual differences in susceptibility to a depressant drug. In H. J. Eysenck (Ed.), *Experiments with drugs* (pp. 169–193). Oxford: Pergamon Press.

Roger, D., & Jamieson, J. (1988). Individual differences in delayed heart-rate recovery following stress: The role of extraversion, neuroticism and emotional control. *Personality and Individual Differences, 9,* 721–726.

Rothman, H.V.L. (1970). Effects of high frequencies and intersubject variability on the auditory-evoked cortical response. *Journal of the Acoustical Society of America, 47,* 569–573.

Routtenberg, A. (1966). Neural mechanisms of sleep: Changing view of reticular formation function. *Psychological Review, 73,* 481–499.

Royce, J. R., & Powell, A. (1983). *Theory of personality and individual differences: Factors, systems and processes.* Englewood Cliffs, NJ: Prentice-Hall.

Rust, J. (1975). Cortical evoked potential, personality, and intelligence. *Journal of Comparative and Physiological Psychology, 89,* 1220–1226.

Sadler, T. G., Melford, R. B., & Hanck, R. L. (1971). The interaction of extraversion and neuroticism in orienting response habitation. *Psychophysiology, 8,* 312–318.

Saltz, E. (1970). Manifest anxiety: Have we misread the data? *Psychological Review, 77,* 568–573.

Saxton, P. M., Siegel, J., & Lukas, J. H. (1987). Visual evoked potential augmenting/reducing slopes in cats: 2. Correlations with behavior. *Personality and Individual Differences, 8,* 511–519.

Schalling, D. (19). Personality correlates of plasma testosterone levels in young delinquents: An example of person–situation interaction? In S. Mednick & T. Moffit (Eds.), *Biosocial bases of antisocial behavior.*

Schalling, D., Asberg, M., Edman, G., & Levander, S. (1984). Impulsivity, non-conformity, and sensation-seeking as related to biological markers for vulnerability. *Clinical Neuropharmacology, 7*(Suppl. 1), 746–747.

Schalling, D., Edman, G., Asberg, M., & Oreland, L. (1988). Platelet MAO activity associated with impulsivity and aggressivity. *Personality and Individual Differences, 9,* 597–606.

Schlegel, W. S. (1983). Genetic foundations of social behaviour. *Personality and Individual Differences, 4,* 483–490.

Shagass, L., & Jones, A. L. (1958). A neurophysiological test for psychiatric diagnosis: Results in 750 patients. *American Journal of Psychiatry, 114,* 1002–1009.

Shagass, L., & Kerenyi, A. B. (1958). Neurophysiologic studies of personality. *Journal of Nervous and Mental Disease, 126,* 141–147.

Shapiro, R., Rafaelsen, O., Ryder, L., Svejgaard, A., & Sorensen, H. (1977). ABO blood groups in unipolar and bipolar manic–depressive patients. *American Journal of Psychiatry, 134,* 197–200.

Sheldon, W. H., Hartl, E. M., & McDermott, E. (1949). *Varieties of delinquent youth.* New York: Harper.

Sheldon, W. H., & Stevens, S. S. (1940). *The varieties of human physique.* New York: Harper.

Sheldon, W. H., & Stevens, S. S. (1942). *The varieties of temperament.* New York: Harper.

Siddle, D., & Heron, A. (1976). Reliability of electrodermal habituation measures under two conditions of stimulus intensity. *Journal of Research in Personality, 10,* 195–200.

Simonov, P. V. (1976). Function of limbic structures

according to the information theory of emotions. *Acta Physiologica Hungarica, 48,* 363–366.

Simonov, P. V. (1980, February). *Neurosis as pathology of brain's limbic system.* Paper presented at the Symposium on Experimental and Clinical Neurosis, Havana, Cuba.

Simonov, P. V. (1981). Role of limbic structures in individual characteristics of behavior. *Acta Neurobiologiae Experimentalis, 41,* 473–582.

Smith, B. D., Rhypma, C., & Wilson, R. J. (1981). The electrodermal OR: Effects of caffeine, extraversion and impulsivity on dishabituation and spontaneous recovery. *Journal of Research in Personality, 15,* 233–290.

Smith, B. D., Rockwell-Tischer, S., & Davidson, R. (1986). Extraversion and arousal: Effects of attentional conditions on electrodermal activity. *Personality and Individual Differences, 7,* 293–303.

Smith, B. D., & Wigglesworth, M. Z. (1978). Extraversion and neuroticism on orienting reflex dishabituation. *Journal of Research in Personality, 12,* 284–296.

Smith, B. D., Wilson, R. J., & Davidson, R. (1984). Electrodermal activity and extraversion: Caffeine, preparatory signals and stimulus intensity effects. *Personality and Individual Differences, 5,* 59–65.

Smith, B. D., Wilson, R. J., & Jones, B. E. (1983). Extraversion and multiple levels of caffeine-induced arousal: Effects of overhabituation and dishabituation. *Psychophysiology, 20,* 29–34.

Sokolov, E. N. (1963). *Perception and the conditioned reflex.* Oxford: Pergamon Press.

Soskis, D. A., & Shagass, L. (1974). Evoked potential tests of augmenting–reducing. *Psychophysiology, 11,* 175–190.

Stelmack, R. M. (1981). The psychophysiology of extraversion and neuroticism. In H. J. Eysenck (Ed.), *A model for personality* (pp. 38–64). New York: Springer.

Stelmack, R. M., Achorn, E., & Michaud, A. (1977). Extraversion and individual differences in auditory evoked responses. *Psychophysiologogy, 14,* 368–374.

Stelmack, R. M., Bourgeois, R. P., Chain, J., & Pickard, L. W. (1979). Extraversion and the orienting reaction habituation rate to visual stimuli. *Journal of Research in Personality, 13,* 49–58.

Stelmack, R. M., & Mandelzys, (1975). Extraversion and pupillary response to affective and taboo words. *Psychophysiology, 12,* 536–546.

Stelmack, R. M., & Wilson, K. G. (1982). Extraversion and the effects of frequency and intensity on the auditory brain stem evoked response. *Personality and Individual Differences, 3,* 373–380.

Stenberg, G., Rosen, I., & Risberg, J. (1988). Personality and augmenting/reducing in visual and auditory evoked potentials. *Personality and Individual Differences, 9,* 571–579.

Strelau, J. (1983). *Temperament, personality, activity.* New York: Academic Press.

Strelau, J., & Eysenck, H. J. (Eds.). (1987). *Personality dimensions and arousal.* New York: Plenum.

Thayer, R. E. (1978a). Factor analytic and reliability studies on the Activation–Deactivation Adjective Check List. *Psychological Reports, 42,* 747–756.

Thayer, R. E. (1978b). Toward a psychological theory of multidimensional activation (arousal). *Motivation and Emotion, 2,* 1–34.

Thayer, R. E. (1986). Activation (arousal): The shift from

a single to a multidimensional perspective. In J. Strelau, F. Farley, & A. Gale (Eds.), *The biological basis of personality and behavior* (Vol. 1, pp. 115–127). London: Hemisphere.

Thayer, R. E., Takatashi, P. J., & Pauli, S. (1988). Multidimensional arousal states, diurnal rhythms, cognitive and social processes, and extraversion. *Personality and Individual Differences, 9,* 15–24.

Theron, P. A. (1948). Peripheral vasomotor reactions as indices of basic emotional tension and lability. *Psychosomatic Medicine, 10,* 335–346.

van der Merwe, A. B. (1948). The diagnostic value of peripheral vasomotor reactions in the psychoneuroses. *Psychosomatic Medicine, 10,* 347–354.

van der Merwe, A. B., & Theron, P. A. (1947). A new method of measuring emotional stability. *Journal of Genetic Psychology, 37,* 109–116.

Vando, A. (1974). The development of the R-A scale: A paper-and-pencil measure of pain tolerance. *Personality and Social Psychology Bulletin, 1,* 28–29.

Venables, P. (1963). The relationship between level of skin potential and fusion of paired light flashes in schizophrenic and normal subjects. *Journal of Psychiatric Research, 1,* 279–287.

Venturini, R., Pascalis, V. de, Imperiali, M. G., & Martini, P. S. (1981). EEG alpha reactivity and extraversion–introversion. *Personality and Individual Differences, 2,* 215–220.

Wenger, M. A. (1942). The stability of measurement of autonomic balance. *Psychosomatic Medicine, 4,* 94–95.

Wenger, M. A. (1948). Studies of autonomic balance in Army Air Forces personnel. *Comparative Psychology Monographs, 19,* 1–111.

Wenger, M. A. (1957). Pattern analyses of autonomic variables during rest. *Psychological Medicine, 19,* 240–244.

Werre, P. P. (1983). Contingent negative variation and interindividual differences. In R. Sinz & M. K. Rosenzweig (Eds.), *Psychophysiology, memory, motivation and event-related potentials in mental operations* (pp. 337–342). Amsterdam: Elsevier.

Werre, P. F. (1986). Contingent negative variation: Relation to personality, and modification by stimulation and sedation. In J. Strelau, F. Farley, & A. Gale (Eds.), *The biological basis of personality and behavior* (Vol. 2, pp. 77–90). London: Hemisphere.

Wigglesworth, M., & Smith, B. (1976). Habituation and dishabituation of the electrodermal orienting reflex in relation to extraversion and neuroticism. *Journal of Research in Personality, 10,* 437–445.

Williams, R. J. (1956). *Biochemical individuality.* New York: Wiley.

Wilson, G. (1990). Personality, time of day and arousal. *Personality and Individual Differences, 11,* 153–168.

Wright, R. A., Contrada, R. J., & Glass, D. C. (1985). Psychophysiological correlates of Type A behaviour. In E. S. Rabbin & S. B. Manuck (Eds.), *Advances in behavioural medicine* (pp. 39–88). London: JAI Press.

Wundt, W. (1903). *Grundzuge der physiologischen Psychologie* (5th ed., Vol. 3). Leipzig: W. Engelmann.

Yerkes, R. M., & Dodson, J. D. (1908). The relation of strength of stimulus to rapidity of habit formation. *Journal of Comparative Neurology and Psychology, 18,* 459–482.

Zuckerman, M. (Ed.). (1983). *Biological bases of sensation-seeking, impulsivity, and anxiety.* Hillsdale, NJ: Erlbaum.

Zuckerman, M. (1984). Sensation-seeking: A comparative approach to a human trait. *Behavioral and Brain Sciences, 7,* 913–971.

Zuckerman, M. (1989). Personality in the third dimension: A psychobiological approach. *Personality and Individual Differences, 10,* 391–418.

Zuckerman, M., Ballinger, J. C., & Post, R. M. (1984). The neurobiology of some dimensions of personality. *International Review of Neurobiology, 25,* 391–436.

Zuckerman, M., & Como, P, (1983). Sensation-seeking and arousal systems. Personality and Individual Difference, 4, 381–386.

Zuckerman, M., Kuhlman, D. M., & Camac, C. (1988). What lies beyond E and N? Factor analyses of scales believed to measure basic dimensions of personality. *Journal of Personality and Social Psychology, 54,* 96–107.

Zuckerman, M., Murtaugh, T., & Siegel, J. (1974). Sensation-seeking and cortical augmenting/reducing. *Psychophysiology, 11,* 535–542.

Zuckerman, M., Simons, R. E., & Como, P. (1988). Sensation-seeking and stimulus intensity as modulators of cortical, cardiovascular, and electrodermal response: A cross-modality study. *Personality and Individual Difference, 9,* 361–372.

Chapter 11

Self-Knowledge and Social Development in Early Life

Michael Lewis

University of Medicine and Dentistry of New Jersey,
Robert Wood Johnson Medical School

This chapter focuses on early social development and the role of cognition in it. Although the literature covering early social development is extensive, relatively little attention has been given to the role of cognition. This is not surprising, considering that social (and emotional) development has been accorded little importance in the development of cognition. Nevertheless, it seems reasonable to believe that social and emotional development require certain cognitive structures without which children are unlikely to develop into social beings.

In arguing for the role of cognition in social development, I do not wish to imply that social or emotional behavior is an epiphenomenon of cognitive behavior. Social and emotional behavior and development deserve the same status afforded to cognitive behavior and development. Besides this status differential, it is often assumed that cognitive development is dominant over social development. Here, too, I wish to take exception. There is no reason to believe that because certain social behaviors require certain cognitive capacities, cognitive development controls or orders social development. It is just as likely that particular social capacities give rise to particular cognitive behaviors and that cognitive development is as dependent on social development as the reverse. Consider, for example, the theories of Piaget (1952, 1954) and before him Baldwin (1899/1973). For both, a given level of cognitive ability becomes disorganized as the organism becomes less capable of coping with its interactions with the environment. This disorganization allows (or requires) the child to construct new structures. In this sense, it is the environment—social in nature—that causes cognitive change and growth. Although a focus on the nature of the environment has not been the central feature of the description of development, it must play a critical role. Gibson (1966), for one, found the nature of the environment to be central to any theory of an organism's adaptive growth. In his theory, the term "affordance" plays a critical role, as it is used to describe the influence of the environment (in interaction with the structures of the organism). More recently, Reigel (1976) and others have emphasized the role of the environment in children's development. For Reigel, much of the pressure to change (to develop) is to be found in the structure of the environment. Luria (1976) has also described how the structure of the social environment determines and alters the nature of the cognitive structures that develop.

However, neither the dominance of the social environment over cognition nor the dominance of cognitive structures over social development fully captures the developmental process. As in Werner's (1961) organismic approach, we must understand social development as taking place within the organism. It is within the child that a variety of processes and activities are found. Although it is convenient to differentiate the activities and development of the child into neat categories and taxonomies, the child itself develops, and these various actions and functions remain integrated, interdependent, and multiply caused. No simple linear model will do, whether it be cognitive → social or social → cognitive. Alternative ways of conceptualizing development are needed. Our attempt to utilize the "strange loop" or "fugue" of Hofstadter (1980) is one attempt at coming to understand the interdependence of the developmental process as it takes place within the child (Lewis, Sullivan, & Michalson, 1984; Sullivan, Lewis, & Alessandri, in press).

Having explicitly stated my belief in the interaction between social and cognitive behavior, I must now show how social development, especially in the opening years of life, is dependent upon and integrated with the development in other domains. I focus here upon self-schema development as the major cognitive attainment affecting social development. This focus is taken because of the belief that the self-schema or what has been called self-awareness or self-consciousness, both from an ontogenetic and phylogenetic point of view, is critical for understanding social development. This is so because self-development allows for the development of social relationships and of particular emotional states; these two tasks constitute the content of social life and development (Campos, Campos, & Barnett, 1989; Lewis, 1987).

In this chapter, I conceptualize social development as a set of three tasks over the life course: identity, culturation, and reproductive success. These are tasks in which all social creatures need to engage. Identity is the most relevant task for infancy, and this task receives the most attention. Identity, or what is called "self-schema," bears upon three important questions of social life: (1) Who am I? (2) What is my relationship to others? and (3) How do I feel about them? Each of these questions is considered in turn.

SOCIAL TASKS OVER THE LIFE COURSE

There are three overarching tasks that *any* social creature needs to accomplish. These three tasks I have labeled identity, culturation, and reproductive success. Each of these tasks can be achieved at different levels of complexity, both phylogenetically and ontogenetically. Because these tasks are to be found across all social creatures regardless of species, they can be viewed as biological necessities.

Identity

The first task, identity, refers to the development of a self. Its function is to connect an individual to a particular set of conspecifics. There are multiple levels of identity, which can be discussed from both an ontogenetic and a phylogenetic perspective. For present purposes in mapping the tasks, a phylogenetic approach is used; however, in the detailed discussion of the development of identity, I present an ontogenetic approach. At the simplest phylogenetic level, no experience is necessary for identity to occur. For cells, there are schemas of interconnectedness that bind particular member cells to each other. The resulting formations are symbiotic structures or more complex organizations made up of sets of separate but connected cells. The process of this type of identity is found in the basic message of the genetic material; the problem of identity, therefore, is based on necessity.

In a more complex organism, identity is established through experience. In the case of imprinting, for example, the baby chick or lamb identifies with other conspecifics through the early experience of physically following another. The process of identity here is located in the nature of the experience. Should the experience result in following a "not-like" species, the animal will become imprinted on another species. Thus, the identity of the chick as a chick will not be established. As in the well-known nursery rhyme "Mary Had a Little Lamb," we can see that the animal's identity process, although written into the genetic material, is dependent on the nature of the early experience. An animal's failure to identify with its own species has critical consequences for the animal. In particular, its social life and reproductive success are altered.

In the case of the most phylogenetically advanced organisms, and humans can be characterized as such, the process of identity is quite different. For humans, the identity process is mostly cognitive—a set of beliefs about oneself that we refer to as a "self-schema." Identity, for the mature human, refers to our beliefs about ourselves, including consciousness and our similarity to and difference from other humans and nonhumans around us. Whatever the level and process of identity, the achievement of it allows the organism to determine "who it is and where it belongs." The acquisition of this ability places the organism within a particular social setting of similar organisms.

Culturation

The second major task is culturation, although for some species the process involved in the acquisition of this ability does not include cultural experiences. This second overarching task refers to the organism's acquiring of particular abilities that allow it to function within the social group of conspecifics. For some species, the particular abilities—or what might be called "being competent"—involve little culturation, since the abilities emerge without learning or experiential impact. We usually refer to such development as "maturation" and ascribe the acquisition of these abilities as instinctual and innate (as in innate releasing mechanisms). For some other species, the acquisition of these abilities involves learning, although the abilities that emerge are generally similar regardless of the nature of the experience. Thus, for example, play behavior in nonhuman primates requires learning, although the types of play behaviors that emerge are similar.

In humans, not only are the abilities acquired through learning for the most part, but the learning is specific to particular groups. Thus, for example, the infant learns how to exhibit particular social behaviors under particular situations, even though the behaviors themselves are unlearned. Crying behavior is a good example of this, since crying in the human infant is genetically programmed. What appears to be learned is when to cry or not to cry. Whether it is more or less appropriate to cry is also learned as a function of the culture or the historical time in which one is raised. For example, there are no sex differences in crying in the newborn period (up to 3 months). Thereafter, however, girls cry more than boys, and there is every reason to believe that this is so because the social environment negatively reinforces crying in boys (Brooks-Gunn & Lewis, 1982).

Besides learning about social behavior, humans need to learn about social roles. Roles provide the social scripts that define one's behavior vis-à-vis other social conspecifics (Lewis, 1989b). Some learned roles are constant over the lifespan; others vary in dimensions and change over time. Sex roles, for example, emerge early and appear to remain constant over development (Weinraub et al., 1984), even though the specific behaviors that define the roles change as a function of age. Age roles, on the other hand, change over time, so that the roles we have as children differ both in behavior and type from the roles we have as adolescents or adults (Lewis, 1987). However these abilities are acquired, or by what process they undergo change, humans can act through their acquisition as members of the social network to which they belong. Without these abilities, humans might identify with a particular group, but would be unable to act as members of that group.

Reproduction

The last major task for any social organism is the acquisition of abilities associated with reproduction. Two separate skill areas are pertinent: (1) making friends, especially with members of the opposite sex, and physically mating; and (2) raising the resultant offspring. As with the other two major tasks, the process by which these abilities are acquired and the levels reached vary from those programmed directly into the genetic material to those acquired through learning and through culturation. Although we rarely consider the outcomes of early social development, in an evolutionary context successful reproduction, including the raising of offspring, constitutes the most important consequence.

The Sequelae of Social Tasks

Identity, culturation, and reproduction can be thought of as a time-locked sequence of social behaviors: The first leads to the second, the second to the third. It might be argued that identity requires culturation. Such a view holds that identity is an identity of something, this something being that acquired by culturation. Although this may be true, I prefer to hold to the proposition that identity, independent of the *context* of identity, occurs first. Piaget (1954) also believed that the first feature of objects that children learn is identity (object permanence). This is acquired prior to the learning of all other features.

This sequence of three tasks appears ontogenetically linked; however, its sequential character refers to the final or mature level of each task. Thus, the highest level of identity is reached before the highest level of culturation, and the highest level of culturation is reached before the highest level of reproductive success. It is possible that the lower levels of the later tasks can appear before the completion of the highest level of the earlier ones. In this way, it is possible that the completion of an earlier task (reaching its highest level) is helped by the acquisition of a lower level of a later task. There is no reason to believe that abilities that contribute to the second and third tasks cannot be found in the life of the child long before these tasks emerge in mature form.

In this perspective, then, infancy not only is the period for the emergence of identity, but also may have significance for the tasks of culturation and reproductive success. For example, data on maltreated human infants and nonhuman primates suggest that how a child is treated in infancy may have an important impact on its reproductive success. Harlow and Harlow (1969), for example, argued that poor parenting in infancy leads to poor parenting as an adult. Thus, even though these three major tasks have a developmental sequence and are related to one another, their malfunctioning in later life may have its origin in the earliest developmental period. Although this appears reasonable, it remains an assumption, and in general an unfulfilled promise of infancy re-

search (see Lewis, 1989a, 1989c). Whatever the developmental origin and connection of these tasks, they constitute one way of organizing the information achieved and that which still needs to be obtained in regard to the beginning of social development.

An analysis of all three tasks would enable us to examine the entire area of social development. In this chapter, I focus mainly on the first task, that of identity, because it is understudied and because many of the issues surrounding the topic bear on broader problems of social development. Before I do so, however, it is necessary to deal with an important issue: the meaning of a behavior over time.

This problem is not unique to the study of development, but is very much a part of the problem of understanding change. For mature creatures, we often assume that a particular behavior has a particular meaning. Moreover, the meaning of the behavior, the mechanisms that produce it, and the behavioral system in which it is embedded, for the most part, are the same. Although anthropology recognizes that the same behavior may have different meanings depending on the particular culture, this problem is of less concern for the understanding of social behavior within a culture. Moreover, though clinicians appreciate that particular behaviors may be caused by different and often competing mechanisms, this concept also plays a relatively small role in the understanding of social behavior. In the study of development, however, this problem of equivalence over time is a major issue, especially since similar behaviors are often, indeed usually, caused by and embedded in different processes. In fact, one cannot hope to understand social development without an appreciation of this problem.

LEVELS OF BEHAVIOR

It is clear that in the study of developmental processes and social development in particular, the issue of equivalence or the meaning of behavior becomes important to discuss (Lewis, 1967). Take, for example, the issue of depression in children. Until recently, it was thought that children under 8 years of age are not developmentally capable of being depressed. This was based on particular beliefs. Children younger than 8 years do not have certain cognitive capacities; it was therefore assumed that they cannot be depressed, since it was also thought that depression requires, among other abilities, the anticipation of future events (Rehm, Leventon, & Ivens, 1987). More to our point is the problem of equivalence. If depression is defined as a set of behaviors, and these behaviors are found only in adults, by definition children cannot be depressed (Malmquist, 1977). However, now that it has been acknowledged that depression in children is manifested by different symptoms from those found in adults, we can easily identify depressed children. This example, as well as many more, points out the need for a developmental perspective—one that is prepared to (1) locate the same structure as supported by different behaviors, and/or (2) locate different structures as supported by the same behavior.

I should like to argue that certain overarching tasks exist for all social creatures, and that social organisms differ from one another with respect to the level of the ability that is reached for each task. Human organisms achieve the most complex level of each social task when compared to most other mammals (even primates—excluding, perhaps, the chimpanzee). Moreover, levels vary within the human organism, such that social task achievement may be at one level in infants but at another level in adulthood. Such a "levels" analysis has been undertaken by others (Fischer, 1980; Mounoud, 1976) for cognitive development, but it is particularly useful for understanding social development.

It also is likely to be the case that different levels of an ability require different degrees of experiential interaction. The lowest levels of an ability may require almost no experience for their emergence, or, in fact, may exist at or prior to birth. Without the organism, higher levels of skill may require more experience or may be totally dependent on learning and culture. Such a view of levels allows for both a nativistic and a culturational world view. It may be the case that, across organisms, the same level of an ability may be achieved through different means. As such, one should be wary of concluding that similar abilities across species have similar histories. Werner (1961) considered this problem in his analysis of the equivalence of behaviors, and called this conclusion the "constancy fallacy."

This level-of-ability approach touches upon an issue that remains a considerable problem in social development. This is, as noted above, the notion of equivalence in behaviors across

age. One can often observe that a very young infant can perform some action that, when performed at an older age, would be considered to represent some underlying complex structure. Take, for example, the problem of imitation. Imitation is particularly important, since the establishment of a true imitative response heralds the development of a child's understanding of itself (Baldwin, 1899/1973).

The newborn infant will imitate certain body movements. For example, a tongue protrusion by an adult will produce a tongue protrusion in the infant (Meltzoff & Moore, 1977). Other forms of imitative behavior have been reported (Field, Woodson, Greenberg, & Cohen, 1982). Although there may be some question as to the reliability of this behavior (Anisfeld, in press), such actions have been called "imitation." "Imitation" has a particular meaning, usually implying some intentionality on the part of the imitator (Piaget, 1954). The finding that matching behavior exists in the newborn constitutes a challenge for developmental theory. We could claim that intentional behavior exists in the newborn, and therefore that imitation takes place. However, this is a nativistic explanation, implying that there is no development in the process of intention or in imitation. Alternatively, the same behavior can be said to have different meanings. We can say that the behavior at Time 1 is called X, whereas at Time 2 it is called Y. This solution has the effect of saying that Y, the more mature behavior, does not exist until Time 2. Thus, for example, imitation in the newborn is called "matching behavior," whereas in the 8-month-old it is called "imitation" (Jacobson, 1979). It is much like s stage theory notion, since X at Time 1 is not Y, nor is it Y-like.

Another way of handling this problem of the meaning of behavior is to consider that X and Y are functionally similar, but that they represent different levels of the same meaning. In this case, X and Y could be called the same behavior, but it would be acknowledged that X represents a lower level of the behavior than Y. In the imitation example, we may call both behaviors "imitation," but we recognize that newborn "imitation" is a lower level of imitation than is 8-month-old "imitation." This position requires us to consider that a particular ability may have multiple levels. These levels are ordered and may be controlled by different processes. Moreover, the level of the ability may be found as both a phylogenetic and an ontogenetic function. Thus, from a phylogenetic perspective, a nonhuman animal (e.g., a rat) may imitate, but this imitation is at a different level (and, we would assume, a lower level) than that of a 1-year-old child. Likewise, from an ontogenetic perspective, a newborn human may imitate, but this imitation is at a different and lower level than the imitation of a 2-year-old. Whether the levels found phylogenetically match those found ontogenetically is unknown, although there is every reason to assume that they do.

Such a view of levels allows for the development of an ability, while at the same time allowing for its existence across the entire span of development. Moreover, this developmental process may be seen both within and across species. The problem of equivalence is especially relevant to the understanding of social development. It is useful to use the level-of-ability approach in the study of social behavior and development. This involves the perspective that an ability may exist across species and age but may differ in the level achieved. In the social realm, humans differ from other animals,

and adult humans differ from infants in terms of levels achieved. For some abilities, the movement to the adult human level may occur within the first 2 years of life; for others, achieving the adult human level may require development over many years.

There are various levels of identity, three of which I will describe: self–other differentiation, self-conservation and interaction, and self-awareness (see Table 11.1). From a phylogenetic point of view, almost all social animals are capable of reaching the first two levels; however, only humans, and possibly chimpanzees, are capable of reaching the third level. Within humans there is an ontogenetic progression across levels, with the third level reached by approximately 15–18 months of age, although it does not stop at this point but continues to be elaborated. In fact, all three levels continue to be elaborated over the life course. Thus not only do they not replace one another; they each continue to develop!

Table 11.1 also indicates that each of these three levels of identity is associated with different aspects of the child's social life, including

TABLE 11.1. The Growth of Identity and Its Relationship to Other Aspects of Social Life

Identity level	Phylogenetic level	Ontogenetic level	Social relationships	Social–emotional behavior	
				Imitation	Emotional
I. Self–other differentiation	All social creatures	3 months	Interactions	Matching reflex	Primary emotions
					Empathic reflexive distress
II. Conservation of self across time and place	All social creatures	Starting at 8 months	Interactions	Matching reflex	Primary emotions
					Empathic reflexive distress
III. Self-awareness	Humans (and possibly chimpanzees)	Starting at 15–18 months	Relationships	Imitation	Self-conscious emotions: Embarrassment Shame Pride Guilt
					Empathic behavior

the infant's commerce with others and the infant's emotional behavior. The analysis to follow demonstrates that social and emotional behavior have different levels of complexity, and that these levels are associated with, if not caused by, the level of identity attained and used at any particular time. For example, imitation in its mature form cannot exist without self-awareness, but matching as a reflexive behavior can exist at a lower level of identity. Likewise, for social relationships, relationships can exist only after identity is established; before this level is reached, social interactions only are possible. The same type of analysis holds for emotional behavior. As I hope to show in the discussion to follow, the relation between the unfolding of diverse social and emotional behaviors can be understood best from a levels approach that involves the development of self-identity.

THE TASK OF IDENTITY

In this discussion, I first address the ontogenetic issue of the development of identity. Though the focus here is on a single cognitive aspect, that of identity, I use it to explore both social relationships and emotional behavior. The development of identity is essential for the understanding of social relationships, since relationships are themselves a product of development, with the mature level of relationship being possible *only* when the mature level of identity has been established. Emotional behavior, the content of social life, also has a developmental course, which also is dependent upon the level of identity.

The primary task for the human infant is the development of identity. The issue of identity is central to social life. Without some schema of physical place in time, space, and the social network, any action by an organism remains impossible. The task of identity is not restricted to the human infant, but exists for all living creatures. The level of cognition used (what I call "level" from this point on) needs to differ between organisms (phylogenetic comparison) and cultures, as well as over an organism's life (ontogenetic comparison). Once the mature level is reached, it may even vary over different situations.

What is human identity, and does it differ from that of other species? How does the human infant gain identity? What is its developmental course and mature level? And, finally, how does the issue of self-identity pertain to other social behaviors? These are the questions that need to be addressed.

Levels of Identity

In order to understand and answer these questions, we need first to address a more general question: What is meant when we use the term "human identity"? In order to consider this concept, it is necessary to make use of a variety of terms that appear in the literature. These include the development of a "self-schema," "self-awareness," and "self-reference" or "consciousness." For my purposes here, I will use the term "self-schema" as synonymous with "identity"; both terms refer to the total knowledge that one has pertaining to the self. "Self-awareness" and "consciousness" refer only to the final cognitive level associated with identity. To anticipate some of the detail to follow, identity or self-schema and self-awareness or consciousness are not the same. Some knowledge pertaining to the self is known by the self; some is not known but can be known; and some is not known and may not be known.

When organisms are preverbal (infants) or unable to speak (nonhuman primates), it is not possible to explore the issue of awareness, because the organism cannot be easily questioned and because the self as a phenomenological event is not easily studied without access to the internal processes of the organism. As a result, we must make inferences about infants' self-knowledge; although we can study self-knowledge, we cannot explore, at least in infancy, the epistemological issue of knowledge of the knowledge of self. Moreover, self-knowledge can precede the knowledge of self-knowledge. For example, by 8 months infants know something about objects (e.g., they will search for a hidden object), but they cannot tell us whether they have awareness of their knowledge of object permanence. We can accept their behavior as demonstrating knowledge, but we cannot ask about knowledge of knowledge. In the same way, we may speak of a cat's knowledge of spatial properties when it goes around an object rather than trying to go through it. Although we have no idea as to the form this knowledge takes (what the nature of thought is in the young infant or cat), we do infer that their knowledge exists.

In discussing self-awareness, we have a similar problem: Self-awareness is equivalent to knowledge of the knowledge of self. By referring to adult behavior in this regard, we may be able to discuss this issue more clearly. We agree that adults have knowledge of themselves, citing as evidence their use of self-referents, their ability to recognize themselves, and their use of self-directed behavior. Although adults have self-knowledge, they do not *always* have self-awareness. Many thoughts and actions do not involve any consideration of self. Moreover, much adult behavior occurs rapidly, with little or no reflective thought. During times of decision-making, when action does not have to be carried out quickly, when we have made an error and need to rethink an action, or when we violate some social rule and feel guilty or embarrassed, self-awareness is obvious (Lewis & Brooks-Gunn, 1979a).

Lack of self-awareness does not reflect the absense of self-involvement in ongoing behavior, but it suggests that the self has no executive role, leaving for other processes the mechanics of action. The self sets goals, has intentions, and evaluates, but specific behaviors are executed through simpler processes of associations and learned or overlearned response patterns. Abelson (1976) has linked these lower-level processes to scripts that guide behavior. Scripts, as a metaphor, are useful because they assume the organization and maintenance of complex behavior without evoking such executive functions as awareness, thinking, or planning. Recently, there has been a renewed interest in goals. Goals are like scripts because they are action plans as well as mental representations (Pervin, 1989). In brief, self-knowledge and self-awareness may be considered as at least somewhat distinct from each other.

Two major cognitive features of identity and several levels of cognitive complexities of self-development have been distinguished. We have called the first feature "existential identity" and the second "categorical identity" (Lewis & Brooks-Gunn, 1979a). This is the same distinction others have made—for example, James's distinction between the "me" and the "I" (James, 1890/1950). Wylie (1961) refers to this distinction as the "self as subject" and the "self as object." It is this first feature, existential identity, that I explore here, referring to the various cognitive levels in terms of the infant's ability (1) to distinguish self from others,

(2) to engage in self-conservation and interaction (what I have called the beginning of self-permanence), and (3) to attain self-awareness or consciousness. The second feature, categorical identity, refers to the particular aspects that children use to define themselves (e.g., gender, age, role, etc.). This distinction parallels that of other forms of knowledge—for example, of objects. As Piaget (1954) has pointed out, the knowledge of the existence of objects is acquired prior to an understanding of the various features of the object. In like fashion, the infant first comes to understand that its self exists (the existential self) prior to understanding the features of that existence (the categorical self). My colleagues and I have observed infant development in terms of self-schema; only a brief description of these findings is presented here.

Period 1: 0–3 Months

The first period can be characterized chiefly by a biological determinism. There exist both simple and complex reflexes, including responses to others that enhance interactions with caregivers. Reflexive behavior, at first predominant, declines over this period as early schemas and learning begin to predominate (Lewis & Brooks-Gunn, 1979a; Lipsitt, 1980; Papousek, 1981). The infant differentiates among social objects, and simple circular reactions with objects or people can be observed. Through both social and object interactions, self–other differentiation begins to occur.

Period 2: 3–8 Months

During the second period, but especially toward its end, active learning takes precedence over a waning reflex system. Object interactions and social behavior are facilitated by the development of more elaborate schemas. Complex action–outcome pairings occur, along with the beginning of means–ends relationships, in both the social and object domains. Primary and some aspects of secondary circular reactions are developed as the child learns of its effect on the world; the beginning of agency and intention can be inferred. The distinction between self and other is consolidated, but cannot be conserved over changes in the nature of the interaction, in terms of either people or objects. Reflected surfaces become of interest, due to the contingency between the child's action and the action in the mirror (Dixon, 1957; Rheingold, 1971). Although there is little evidence of self-recognition, children are able to adjust their bodies when placed in a room where visual cues give the appearance that the room is tilted. Such findings would appear to indicate elaborate visual–body schemas in spatial knowledge at this age.

Period 3: 8–15 Months

The third period is characterized by two important features. First, at the beginning of this period, infants show general response inhibition when presented with new information or stimuli. Unlike the younger child, the 8-month-old does not respond immediately to the stimulus event; that is, the infant is no longer stimulus-bound. This general inhibition—most often observed in one of its manifestations, that of stranger wariness or fear (Schaeffer, 1975)—allows the child to think about the stimulus before acting on it. This inhibition of action allows for the rapid development of additional schemas. Moreover, at about the last quarter of the first year, cognitive growth (in particular, memory development) allows the child to make comparisons. It is not possible to compare two events located in different spaces and/or times without being able to remember the first while experiencing the second. From this new ability, the child is able to respond differentially to familiar (family members) and strange people. In addition, memory capacity allows for an enduring pattern of social exchange with particular people. One consequence of these enduring social exchange patterns is the emergence of self-permanence. Like Cooley's (1909/1962) "looking-glass" theory, the permanence of social exchanges affects the self-schema. Moreover, this enduring interactive patterning will give rise to the third level, self-awareness or consciousness. We have stated "that any knowledge gained about the other (through interaction) also must be gained about the self" (Lewis & Brooks-Gunn, 1979b, p. 8). Baldwin (1899/1973) understood this when he wrote that "my sense of self grows by imitation of you, and my sense of yourself grows in terms of my sense of self. Both ego and alter are thus essentially social; each is a socius, and each is an imitative creation" (p. 338).

The second most critical accomplishment of this later period is the final establishment of self–other differentiation. This differentiation, which has been developing through the earlier periods, results in the conservation of the self as distinct from the other across a variety of different situations. This conservation of self represents the first important conservation task and is parallel to the child's growing understanding of object existence. Indeed, object permanence and self-permanence are viewed as part of the same process (Jackson, Campos, & Fischer, 1978). Feature recognition does not exist in any appreciable way, and self-recognition has not yet occurred (Lewis & Brooks-Gunn, 1979a). The emergence of self as agent facilitates more complex means–ends relationships, and with growing cognitive ability more elaborate plans can be observed.

Period 4: 15–24 Months

The 15- to 24-month period can be characterized as the emergence of self-awareness or consciousness. During this period, self-recognition becomes less dependent on contingency and increasingly dependent on feature analysis. The self as object becomes more evident in this feature recognition. Pointing behavior emerges, and self-recognition is evidenced through pointing to pictures of the self and through pointing to marks on the nose seen in reflecting surfaces. This action we have called "self-awareness," and it marks the mature level of human identity. At this time infants are able to consider themselves as among the social objects in their world and become conscious; that is, they can reflect on themselves—their actions, thoughts, and feelings.

The child's emerging sense of self results in a set of emotional states that can be characterized by self-awareness; that is, children's response in front of mirrors is embarrassment if they show self-recognition. Dixon (1957) calls this the "coy stage," and my colleagues and I (Lewis & Brooks-Gunn, 1979a; Lewis, Sullivan, Stanger, & Weiss, 1989) refer to this as the beginning of "self-conscious emotions." Not only does embarrassment become increasingly apparent, but fear of the loss of the mother also becomes intense. At this point empathic behavior emerges (Halperin, 1989; Zahn-Waxler & Radke-Yarrow, 1981), as the child is able to utilize the self to understand that (1) there are other selves and (2) these selves may have similar feelings and thoughts.

Period 5: 24–30 Months

At about 24 months, simple language knowledge—the mapping of the lexicon on some features—occurs and allows children to demonstrate knowledge of features of social objects, including themselves. These features include gender and age (Edwards & Lewis, 1979; Lewis & Feiring, 1978). Such knowledge supports the belief that the self as object emerges at this time and possesses a number of attributes, including goodness–badness and efficacy, as well as age and gender. At this point, children have knowledge about their own production and show anxiety over their failure (Kagan, 1984). Also at this point, self-conscious evaluative emotions emerge; these include pride, shame, and guilt (Lewis, in press; Lewis et al., 1989).

Although more empirical exploration is necessary, this mapping of the critical periods of self-development may be useful as an outline for the emergence of this cognitive capacity. It is interesting to note that Sanders (1964, 1980), using a more clinical approach, arrived at a similar sequence. More recently, Emde (1983) and Stern (1985) also have tried to articulate the levels or stages of development of the sense of self. The first level Stern calls a "core self." This occurs earliest in life and encompasses the basic features, including the physical and affective self. The second level is the "subjective self." The third is a "verbal self," which appears at about 15–18 months. This verbal self, if not the others, is clearly a cognitive milestone. It marks both the cognitive ability to use language and more, since it makes references to the self's ability to consider itself. Emde's (1983) analysis is even more cognitively based: He makes a distinction between a "prerepresentational" and a "representational" self. Again, a representational self has to have those features associated with language—representation and reference. It is what I have called "consciousness" (Lewis, in press). In general, then, there is some agreement as to the levels involved and the cognitive features necessary when we speak of the highest level of a mature self-identity—at least that part related to the existential self. The difficulties that exist, and that are addressed next, have to do with the problem of equivalence and mixing of levels of identity. As we will see, identity does not mean the same, nor are the processes the same, over earlier levels of the child's development.

Self-Awareness as the Mature Level of Identity

While recognizing that identity exists at the lowest level and therefore at an early age, it is not until self-consciousness evolves that I can speak of the human infant as acquiring the mature level of identity. For me, it is very important to differentiate the skill levels of identity. The highest level of identity for humans is achieved with the appearance of self-consciousness. For example, although an infant may be able to differentiate itself from others or may have knowledge of its location in space vis-à-vis other objects, and thus may be able to reach for and obtain objects, these features do not constitute the equivalence of what we mean by mature identity for humans. The skill of uniquely human identity (its mature form) can be said to exist only when awareness of the self occurs. This is a metacognition; that is, it is knowledge of knowing (Harre, 1984). Until such time, the child certainly has a level of identity. However, we would maintain that this level of identity is in no way different from that level found in any living organism capable of interactive behavior. It is not the mature form for our species.

The white rat shares with the human infant some levels of identity, certainly the ability to differentiate self from others. The white rat knows its location in space/time and therefore can move from one place in space/time to another in order to retrieve objects it desires—a fact we observe when the rat moves around objects rather than crashing into them. Rats are capable of engaging in fairly elaborate self-regulatory behavior; in fact, so are cells. What a rat or cell cannot do and a human infant can, sometime during the second half of the second year of life, is to make reference to itself. It is this level of identity, self-consciousness, that is the final skill of identity for the human infant. Unlike most other creatures whose identity resides at lower levels, human identity cannot be said to occur until this last level is reached. This level is captured first in the use of personal pronouns such as "me" or "mine" and in self-recognition (Levine, 1983; Lewis & Brooks-Gunn, 1979a). More complicated forms of self-consciousness are referenced by sentences that reflect the species' capacity (1) to consider itself as existing ("I am"); (2) to consider aspects of itself ("I am hungry" or "I am thinking"); and (3) to consider aspects of itself in interaction with other selves ("I am thinking about what you are thinking") (Lewis, in press).

The problem of knowledge and knowledge of knowledge has received considerable attention (Harre, 1984; Piaget, 1976). The problem, simply put, is this: "When you know X, do you know you know X?" The two variants of this proposition are "When you know X, *must* you know you know X?" and "When you know X, *can* you know you know X? If so, When do you know you know X?" It is clear that when an 8-month-old reaches for a toy and puts the toy into its mouth, it knows something about how to obtain the toy, about the toy's existence in a certain time/place, and about the pleasant sensation of the toy in the mouth. However, knowing X and knowing you know X are not necessarily identical. Indeed, it seems reasonable to assume that knowing about knowing X is an ontogenetic achievement that is not likely to occur prior to the stage of symbolic operations.

For human adults, it is also the case that there are occasions when they know X, but do not know that they know X. At other times, knowing about knowing X does occur. We save the terms "knowing" or "knowledge" for knowing X, and "consciousness" for knowing about knowing X. Under what conditions consciousness occurs or does not occur in adult humans is an important problem (Mandler, 1975). Such a discussion also leads us into a consideration of the concept of the unconscious, for this concept rests on the belief that we may know we know X, but not be aware of that knowledge. The belief in an unconscious is predicated on the notion that some of these recursive knowledge statements have a "not" statement embedded within them—for example, "I do not know that I know I know." This issue is not further explored here, since the problem we seek to investigate has to do with the emergence of consciousness. Nevertheless, such an analysis is incomplete unless we can deal with the concept of an unconscious. It seems reasonable to imagine, for example, that the emergence of consciousness must have as its complementary the emergence of an unconscious, yet no serious work as to the development of an unconscious has been undertaken.

Existential Anxiety Prior to Identity

Until consciousness emerges, it would seem illogical to ascribe to the human infant abilities that depend on this level. The human infant

may have earlier abilities that are related to this later level, although this is yet not known. That is, we do not know the connection between the earlier levels and those of self-awareness. Moreover, these earlier abilities may be similar to those inherent in other species. However, these earlier abilities are not awareness itself. Because of this, it is difficult to see how we can ascribe to the infant states dependent on awareness. For example, theorists such as Kernberg (1976, 1980), Stern (1985), and Lacan (1968) have claimed that the young infant is capable of experiencing anxiety over its own nonexistence. Another example of this problem is Rank's (1929) notion of birth anxiety; Freud (1936), in his critique, pointed out the difficulty of such views. Anxiety is a signal and as such has to be experienced. Only the ego can experience it: "The id cannot be afraid, as the ego can; it is not an organization, and cannot estimate situations of danger" (Freud, 1936, p. 80). Since the ego emerges only slowly, certainly not at birth, there can be no experience. From our perspective, the lack of logic resides in the fact that any anxiety over nonexistence, as an adult might experience it, cannot occur to an organism that has no consciousness of self or awareness of its existence. It is not possible for an organism to be anxious about its existence prior to the capacity to think about itself as existing—that is, prior to being able to experience itself and prior to being able to imagine its nonexistence.

Intersubjectivity Prior to Identity

This problem of levels of awareness leads to other difficulties as well. "Intersubjectivity," as has been defined in early infancy (see Emde, 1988; Stern, 1985), cannot be possible from the adult perspective, since it too depends on self-awareness. For example, interactive behavior between a 3- to 6-month-old infant and its mother may be viewed as an early example of intersubjectivity—the ability of the members to share experiences, to match, align, or attune their behavior to each other. Although such interactive behaviors may reflect intersubjectivity, they may also reflect much simpler processes. These do not involve intersubjectivity, but instead, for example, simple rules or contagious behaviors of holding and getting attention. For example, it is more efficient to stop moving (or talking) when someone else is talking if the goal is to attend. Thus, the onset of the action of one member of a dyad may terminate the action of another member for reasons other than those implied by intersubjectivity. Contagious behavior also appears similar to intersubjectivity (e.g., the organization of menstruation times of women living together).

It is only in the final stage of self-development, when the infant already has acquired self-awareness or consciousness, that intersubjectivity logically can be said to occur. Intersubjectivity between a mother and her 8-month-old child can take place as a function of a complex patterned system, one that may be present in any species; however, intersubjectivity that involves human awareness should not be possible at this age. This, of course, depends on how intersubjectivity is defined. If children's ability to share experiences and to match, align, or attune their behavior is based on their knowledge of themselves and others' selves, then intersubjectivity at this age is not possible. It is possible, however, to think of intersubjectivity as simply a statement of knowledge, or even as reflexive—for example, smiling when another smile appears. Under such a definition, intersubjectivity becomes simply a set of complex behavioral patterns that are triggered by other behaviors. Therefore, they are controlled less by complex cognitions and more by simple rules such as circular reactions. They do not have intentions in terms of a complex means–ends representation, but are more like automatic social responses. If we accept this definition as intersubjectivity, we find that a levels analysis of this concept also is possible; that is, like imitation, intersubjectivity has various levels, each of which is associated with a different level of identity.

I mention these problems in detail because they are related to many social abilities. Imitation, as I have already indicated, is another example of the levels problem in social development. Imitation in the newborn or very young infant reflects a reflex capacity to respond with stimulus matching to certain classes of events. The abilities necessary for this behavior need to be quite different for imitation in the older child and adult. It appears reasonable to argue that the abilities necessary for human existential identity appear only after a sequence of other levels has been ascended: Many of these are shared with other species. Once the human existential self, or awareness, emerges, the second feature of identity, categorical self, also emerges. In fact, I have argued that aspects of this categorical self emerge at about the same time as or soon after existential awareness (Lewis & Brooks-Gunn, 1979b). Such features as gender (Money & Ehrhardt, 1972), age (Lewis, 1985), and success or failure (Kagan, 1984; Lewis et al., 1989)—that is, knowledge of self and others—begin to make their appearance by the end of the second year of life.

The Emergence of Self-Awareness

The methodological procedure which I have used extensively in order to measure the onset of self-awareness is self-referential behavior, or what has more commonly been called "mirror-directed" behavior toward the self (Lewis & Brooks-Gunn, 1979a). This procedure has confirmed that the infant first appears capable of recognizing itself at about 15–18 months of age. I see the emergence of this skill as mostly dependent on biological programming related to the emerging cognitive maturational capacities of the organism. Thus, for example, a mental age of 15–18 months, rather than experience, is the critical feature (Lewis, 1986). Down syndrome children, as well as other handicapped children, who do not have a mental age of 15–18 months do not show this self-referential behavior and, we are inclined to believe, have not yet acquired self-awareness.

Although maturational features appear to play a large part in the development of this existential feature, there are some data indicating that the child's early social interactions affect the emerging of awareness within the envelope of a maturational period. Unfortunately, the two studies reported in the literature suggest alternative findings. In one (Lewis, Brooks-Gunn, & Jaskir, 1985), children who had poorer parent–child interactions developed self-awareness somewhat earlier than children who did not; in the other, Schneider-Rosen and Cicchetti (1984) found the reverse.[1]

The first task of any social organism is the establishment of identity. I have indicated that for the human infant the mature form of this ability does not emerge until the last and perhaps species-specific behavior emerges, that of awareness. Given the importance of the topic of identity, more research is clearly called for—research having to do with such issues as (1) the invariance of sequences and levels, (2) the relation between earlier levels and later ones, (3) individual differences, and (4) the role of experience in relationship to the emergence of awareness. In this regard, another important question raised for social development is the role of experience in level attainment. We recognize that experience may play a greater role in some levels than in others and may also play a greater role for some species than for others. The final issue raised here is the question of whether development can be facilitated by degrees of adversity as well as competency.

THE ROLE OF SELF-AWARENESS IN RELATIONSHIPS

Earlier, I have argued that identity, at any level, is necessary for the social life of organisms. Self-awareness, the highest level for the human child, plays an important role in social life—in particular, in social relationships. This topic has ramifications for a theory of social development. To anticipate my discussion somewhat, social relationships themselves have a developmental sequence of an ordered series of levels. At the highest level, social relationships are dependent upon the acquisition of self-awareness; thus, only upon the achievement of this intraorganismic capacity can the highest level of interorganismic capacity emerge. If such an analysis is correct, it calls into question some of the underlying assumptions about early social relationships as currently proposed in our theories of development.

Levels of Social Relationships

A social relationship requires a variety of abilities that have not been well studied. Hinde (1976, 1979) has articulated six dimensions that can be used to characterize a relationship: (1) goal structures, (2) diversity of interactions, (3) degree of reciprocity, (4) meshing of interactions, (5) frequency, (6) patterning and multidimensional qualities of interactions.

These six features of interaction define a lower level of relationships. Young human infants and their mothers, as well as other social creatures, can be said to have acquired this lower level. However, a human adult relationship needs to be characterized by a higher level. I, for one, find it difficult to accept that a rat

mother and her pups have a relationship of the same level as that of a human mother and her 3-year-old child. Hinde suggests two further features of a relationship that allow us to conceptualize a higher-level relationship for the human child and mother and that allow us to differentiate relationships of humans from those of animals. These features are (7) cognitive factors, or those mental processes that allow each member of an interaction to think of the other member as well as of himself or herself; and (8) something Hinde calls "penetration," which I would interpret as something having to do with ego boundaries.

Notice, then, that interactions alone (the first six features) are insufficient to describe a higher-level human relationship. Although interactive patterns may describe a nonhuman relationship or a relationship between a human mother and a very young infant, they are not descriptive of a higher-level relationship unless these patterns also have something to do with awareness of self. Indeed, we would argue that the highest level in the development of a relationship in humans can only occur with the development of self-identity. In other words, uniquely human relationships require identity (Lewis, 1987). Such a view was suggested by Sullivan (1953). For him, a relationship is by necessity the negotiation of at least two selves. Higher-level abilities are vital for a relationship, since without two selves (one has only an "I–it," not an "I–thou") there can be no relationship (Buber, 1958). Emde (1988) makes reference to the "we" feature of relationships, and, in support of the timetable of consciousness, points to the second half of the second year of life for its appearance.

Interactions and Relationships

The model of mature human relationships I have set forth requires us to consider levels in the development of a relationship over time, rather than seeing it as existing in its adult form from the first. Uniquely mature human relationships arise from interactions only after the development of identity. An interaction can lead to a relationship through the mediation of cognitive structures—in particular, the development of awareness (Lewis, 1987). Only after the acquisition of self-identity can a higher-level, specifically human relationship occur. Higher-level human relationships require self-awareness. Animal relationships do not need this skill; neither may relationships in infancy that occur prior to the acquisition of awareness. The meaning of the term "relationship," therefore, is not the same across levels. As with the problem of identity or imitation, the meanings of the terms we use (even when we use the same term) are not necessarily equivalent if the issue of level is not considered.

In fact, a relationship in the first year of human life may be at some level between a relationship of nonhuman animals and one of adults, since in the former case neither member of the dyad possesses identity, and in the latter both have identity. What I mean when I refer to "a mature human relationship" is the level that usually includes what the organism thinks about the self and other, the desire to share, and the use of empathy to regulate the relationship. Moreover, the issue of ego boundaries, as discussed by Hinde, also needs to be considered. When we consider ego boundaries, we need to make reference to the child's growing understanding of privacy, as well as its need to become a "we." Without these skills we may talk about a lower-level relationship, but not a mature human one.

From this point of view, the achievement of adult human relationships has a developmental progression. This progression involves, first, interactions (which may be similar to those shown by all social creatures); second, cognitive structures, including identity and such skills as empathy (the ability to place the self in the role of others); and, finally, the mature human form of relationships (Lewis, 1987). The relationships of 1-year-olds do not contain cognitive structures, and therefore may resemble those of other nonhuman animals. By 2 years of age, most children have identity and the beginnings of such skills as empathy (Borke, 1971; Zahn-Waxler & Radke-Yarrow, 1981). Their relationships now more closely approximate those at the mature level. Mahler's concept of individuation is relevant here, for, as she has pointed out, only when the child is able to individuate can it be said that a more mature relationship exists (Mahler, Pine, & Bergman, 1975). Prior to this point in time, the relationship between parent and child is more patterned and has the appearance of an automatic process.

Such an analysis raises the question of the nature of the child's relationships prior to identity. For me, a pre-identity-level relationship is a complex, social, species-patterned process. This level may be wired into the human species. In fact, it may be wired into other social animals, since work with animals supports the belief that these patterns (lower-level relationships) exist. For most other species, this complex, patterned interactive system decays with time; it either is replaced with more complex role interactions or disappears altogether. In humans, this early, complex, patterned system—a lower-level relationship—gives way to a mature relationship. The nature of the higher-level relationship is dependent on many factors. These include the nature of the complex interactions themselves and cognitions of these interactions—that is, the meaning given to them by the selves involved (Bowlby, 1982). Since adults already possess identity, their interactions with their children are already a part of their relationships with them. As such, the developmental process is mainly located in the infant. It is the developing member of the dyad who moves from lower-level (interactions) to higher-level relationships. The adult already has a higher-level relationship with the child; in part, this relationship may be based on the adults' constructed model of their relationship with their own mothers (Main, Kaplan, & Cassidy, 1985). From this point of view, the consistency in the relationship of the dyad must be found in the world of the adult, since the world of the child is undergoing much change and transformation. How then does such an analysis affect attachment relationships?

Attachment Relationships

Because of the central role attachment plays in the early social life of the child, I begin with a brief history of the concept. This is followed by a statement of its basic tenets. Finally, I show how the concept of identity affects our ideas about attachment.

Historical View

The mother, through her unique biological relationship, holds a special role vis-à-vis her child. Soon after the turn of the century, psychoanalytic theory began to describe the importance and central role of the mother in affecting and controlling the child's instinctual drives (Freud, 1915/1959). The current theory of attachment as it affects social development is an extension of this instinctual-drive theory, but even more an extension of object relations theory (Fairbairn, 1952; Klein, 1964). The attachment relationship, as the current important object relations model, has an epigenetic point of view. It specifies that the mother is the first and primary factor in the child's social life and that all subsequent relationships are affected by this early and unique dyadic interaction. Thus, if the mother–child relationship is a good one, the child will have a healthy social development; conversely, if the mother–child relationship is poor, the child will have poor social relationships and psychopathology. As we shall see, this theory relies on three critical features: its fixed sequence, its determinism, and its trait or structural quality.

Proof for the effect of the mother (or, in this case, her absence) on the child's development was offered in a dramatic fashion soon after World War II by the work of Spitz (1945, 1946; Spitz & Wolff, 1946). In a series of papers on institutionalized children, Spitz showed that children raised in such settings did not develop as normal children. Moreover, children who were separated from their mothers showed what Spitz termed "anaclitic depression" and, following this, the syndrome of "hospitalism." Anaclitic depression, as Spitz described it, was the deep depression that children exhibited when left for long periods of time without their mothers. This depression, Spitz believed, developed into hospitalism. Hospitalism was a synonym for the phrase "failure to thrive," which describes a condition observed in some home-reared children. Spitz's observations on institutional children were supported by Dennis (1960), working in orphanages in Tehran, Iran, and subsequently by Provence and Lipton (1962) in their book on institutionalized infants. Spitz's pioneer work offered proof of the importance of the mother in the child's development.

Even though Spitz's demonstrations were quite dramatic and indicated the failure to thrive of children placed in institutions, there remained some concern as to the possible variables that might account for this finding. First, of course, was the absence of a consistent and caring mother. Nevertheless, observation of the environments of these children indicated that not only were the children maternally deprived; in fact, they were deprived of many other aspects of an ideal environment. For example, the children were placed in environments whose physical surroundings (objects, etc.) were less than optimal for providing stimulation levels necessary for development. Moreover, the interaction with the available caregivers was minimal. The issue of general deprivation was raised as an alternative to Spitz's view. The argument took the form that the children's failure to thrive was due not only to absence of their mothers, but to a general absence of all those features of the environment that are necessary to provide optimal development. Thus, although it was true that the mothers were absent, it was also true that the children had few toys and few opportunities to engage other adults or even other children in meaningful interaction.

By the late 1950s, Harlow's work with motherless monkeys supported the object relations/attachment proposition that the absence of maternal contact irrevocably leads to poor development. Harlow (1958) demonstrated that rhesus monkey babies reared alone without their mothers showed poor social and emotional development as adults, both in terms of their own behavior and in terms of peer interactions. They appeared autistic, had stereotypic behavior, and did not show normal adult behavior in general. They had difficulty mating with peers; once the females became mothers, they were abusive to their babies, often killing them.

Such experimental evidence by Harlow seemed to revive the Spitz demonstration of the effect of mother's absence. With hindsight, we now know that Harlow's experiments with motherless monkeys presented us with the same conflicting findings that were found in Spitz's work. In the Harlow work, baby monkeys were raised without their mothers and in isolation. Thus, not only did they not have the presence of their mothers, but they did not interact with any other monkeys, including peers; like Spitz's institutionalized children, they were also object-deprived. In the case of nonhuman primates, subsequent work has pointed to the factor of general deprivation as being at least as important as the absence of the mother. For example, when monkeys were raised without their mothers but in the company of peers, few of the effects reported by Harlow were observed (Rosenblum, 1961). By 1960, the role of the mother as the most important factor in the child's subsequent social development was still controversial. Indeed, Yarrow (1963), in a review of the deprivation literature, pointed out many of the conflicting pieces of evidence that made it difficult to reach conclusions concerning the specific consequences of maternal deprivation.

About this time, Bowlby (1951), writing for the World Health Organization, demonstrated the high mortality rate of motherless infants. Bowlby concluded in this early report that mothers played a central role in their children's development and that their absence was likely to contribute to biological risk (i.e., risk of death). One of Bowlby's major contributions derived from his incorporation of ethology with object relations and drive theory. He introduced the notion that as part of the human condition, infants were capable of forming (indeed, needed to form) attachments to other humans. Using imprinting as a model, Bowlby argued that as part of the human need (or drive) condition, infants early in life become attached to other social objects (in particular, the mother); once attached, the social object then becomes the focus of the young organism's social and affective activities. Thus, as Hess (1959) and Scott (1962) argued for animals, Bowlby argued that humans, having become attached early in life to social objects, thus imitate and identify with these same social objects. In this way, Bowlby was able to integrate his biological/ethological perspective with that of the object relations view from which his primary assumptions sprung.

Still to be questioned were the degree and number of attachments of which the organism is capable. This question has been left for the most part unanswered, although it seems likely that if the human infant has as its biological imperative the capacity to attach itself to other social objects, that this attachment should be extended to a variety of objects. Bowlby's (1969) theory spoke to species behavior, in that all human organisms were thought to be endowed with a capacity to attach themselves to others. Nevertheless, the issue of multiple attachments, including those to fathers, grandparents, siblings, and others, has not been explored (Lewis, 1987). Because of this limit, attachment theory remains a theory about the child–mother relationship, and as such restricts our understanding of peer (Dunn & Kendrick, 1979) as well as father (Lamb, 1981) relationships.

The theory did not address individual differences in this capacity or ability. Working

with Bowlby, both Schaeffer (Schaeffer & Emerson, 1964) and Ainsworth (1964) were led to explore the possibility of how this theory of species attachment might be applied to individual differences in object relations. It was Ainsworth who devised a measurement system to observe individual dyadic differences in type of attachment. Ainsworth's quest for a paradigm or definition of the behaviors constituting attachment is an important part of the story of attachment theory as it evolved from the 1960s to the 1980s. In her work in Uganda, Ainsworth (1967) first thought to define attachment by proximity seeking and maintenance behavior. Her observations, as well as those of others, indicated that children from approximately 1 year of age on become distressed when removed from their mothers. In subsequent work Ainsworth explored not only proximity seeking and maintenance behavior, but also children's reaction to separation. Finally, the measurement procedures were altered to examine children's responses to reunion with their mothers after the mothers left the children alone for a few minutes. Within the measurement system used, the premise remains the following: There is a species need, derived from biological imperatives, that causes children to become attached to others, and individual dyadic differences in the nature of this attachment have profound effects on subsequent social and emotional development. Bowlby's species theory became Ainsworth's individual-dyad-difference theory. A unique and specific experimental paradigm was developed to measure individual differences in attachment; it is called the Strange Situation (see Ainsworth, Blehar, Waters, & Wall, 1978, for more details).

Once this paradigm was established, individual differences in attachment were related to subsequent development; research also related earlier behavior to the type of attachment displayed at 1 year of age. Three types of dyads were described: securely attached children (Type B; 70% of middle-class samples), insecurely attached children (avoidant; Type A; 20% of the samples), and ambivalent children (Type C; 10% of the samples). During the course of the three decades of research since the concept was articulated and described by Bowlby and Ainsworth, much work on attachment has been conducted (see Bretherton, 1987, and Lamb, Thompson, Gardner, & Charnov,

1985, for reviews of different aspects). The research work was first related to issues of definition and measurement; then work was conducted on the origins of differences in attachment as seen at 1 year of age; finally, the relationship of individual differences in the first year of life to subsequent development was examined (Ainsworth et al., 1978; Sroufe, 1979). All of this work rested on the premise that this early relationship not only is important in its own right, but affects subsequent social and emotional behavior.

At the same time that work on human attachment proceeded, work on attachment in nonhuman primates also was undertaken (Harlow, 1958; Suomi, 1978). This work rested on the same assumptions. Thus, attachment as a species concept was seen as extending beyond humans into all primates and possibly to all mammals as well (Cairns, 1966). So pervasive is this view of early social experience and the importance of infant object relations that it has now become the dominant theory of social development. There is no question of the power of this theory in understanding and explaining early social development, although its usefulness for explaining adult differences has yet to be demonstrated. Attachment theory rests on three features: fixed sequence, determinism, and trait or structural quality. These are described next.

Features of Attachment Theory

Fixed Sequence. Attachment in particular, and object relations in general, argue for a linear progression in which the infant first adapts to one person within the family network, usually the mother. From this basic adaptation, all subsequent social relationships follow. Although some continue to believe in the unique biological relation between mother and infant as the origin of subsequent social adaptation, others subscribe to a more general formulation, which specifies that attachment is a natural consequence of the infant's early interactions with others and that multiple attachments and multiple paths of social development are possible (Lewis, 1984). Thus, the model of adaptation stressing that the child first develops a relationship with the mother, then with the father and siblings, and then with others (e.g., peers) is a somewhat modified view of the biological nature of attachment. Although a

sequence still exists, it may be a series of sequences. That is, the child's initial attachment relationship can be viewed as plural, with there being a number of others to whom the infant may form an attachment relationship. Even so, a fixed-sequence argument still holds, in that all subsequent relationships (such as those with peers) will follow and be a consequence of the earlier attachment relationship(s).

Determinism. Not only do the object relations and attachment theories postulate a fixed sequence in the development of relationships; they also assume that later social experiences are determined by early ones, particularly the relationship between mother and child. This view is still widely held: Many investigators see the mother–infant attachment as determining the child's later peer relationships (Ahrend, Gove, & Sroufe, 1979; Matas, Ahrend, & Sroufe, 1978; Waters, Wippman, & Sroufe, 1979), as well as all other relationships (Sroufe, 1979). Although much has been made of the deterministic effects of early relationships on subsequent social relationships, the data are rather limited and the various alternative explanations are unexplored (see Lamb et al., 1985; Weinraub, Brooks, & Lewis, 1977).

Trait Quality. The issue and controversy surrounding the nature of a trait or an enduring aspect of personality have dominated much contemporary thinking (Pervin, 1978). The issue is raised again when we consider the effect of one relationship upon another. In the epigenetic view, the mother–infant or earliest attachment relationship endows the infant with a trait or characteristic that is located within the organism. This trait or its absence then determines subsequent relationships. Although the nature of the trait has not been clarified, Sroufe (1979) and Block and Block (1979) have associated it with ego skills; however, it could be a trait such as self-esteem, self-efficacy, or some combination of the two. Whatever its nature, it is the presence or absence of this trait that is thought to influence other relationships. An often-used metaphor is that the child is like an empty vessel that needs filling. Once filled, the child can move on to new relationships; if the child is not filled, movement will be inhibited, or the new relationships will be different in their nature or degree than if the child had been filled. The task of the earliest attachment relationship is to fill the vessel. Thus, the explanation for the establishment of relationships rests with a mechanism that resides in the organism.

Also related to this trait issue is the notion of a "critical period." Although this is seldom made explicit, it is assumed that the mother–infant relationship in the opening months of life is critical; if this relationship is inadequate, then the subsequent attachment relationships will be affected, and these in turn will affect all other relationships. Thus, there is assumed to be a critical period with a beginning and an end after which later experience has little effect. This we now know is not so, since even attachment relationships change as a function of the environment of the child (e.g., see Thompson & Lamb, 1984).

The notion of a trait provides a mechanism for the deterministic nature of the epigenetic model. One relationship can affect another through the creation of a trait in the child. The child then brings this trait to bear in its next relationship. Moreover, this trait or its absence, based on the outcome of the first relationship, is not easily affected by experience. This notion concerning early attachment relationships is troubling, given the problems associated with traits. The need to consider the environment of the child over the course of development, not only at the beginning, presents an alternative to this model and has begun to receive some attention (Lewis & Feiring, in press).

Attachment, Relationships, and Identity

Since the human infant's attachment relationship has received so much attention in the social development literature, my theoretical perspective on social relationships has important implications here as well. Recall the analysis presented earlier. By 1 year of age, when attachment relationships are reported to occur, we hold that the infant is not yet capable of adult human relationships. The 1-year-old child's attachment relationship is not a higher-level relationship, since the child does not possess identity. If there is a higher-level attachment relationship, it is located in the adult, since it is the adult who possesses identity. Although it is recognized that the attachment relationship exists for both mother and child, it would appear to be primarily the parent's relationship (see also Bowlby, 1982).

Why the attachment literature in general ascribes the classification mostly to the child rather than to the mother is unclear. For example, children, but not mothers, are usually called "Type A," "Type B," or "Type C" (see Lamb et al., 1985).

Since I have suggested that a higher-level human relationship exists for the adult but not the infant (at least not before the child's identity emerges), there is every reason to believe that the observed consistency in social development over time is promoted by environmental consistency rather than by the consistency located within the child. As others have shown, as long as the environment remains consistent, the child's attachment relationship remains consistent (Thompson & Lamb, 1984). Such findings support the view that attachment classifications in the 1-year-old are predictive of subsequent social development, because, to a large degree, they characterize the parent's environment rather than the child's. This is not to say that a child's complex interaction relationship, prior to identity relationship, does not affect subsequent relationships; it only means that a child's relationships within the first 2 years undergo a major transformation, whereas in this 2-year period those of the adult do not. For this reason, one might expect consistency to be more readily observed by focusing on the adult's relationship to the child rather than the reverse (Lewis & Feiring, in press; Sameroff, 1983).

Attachment as Representation

Recently, Main et al. (1985) have returned to a more cognitive view of attachment as suggested by Bowlby (1982)—that of a "working model." By a "working model," these authors mean a schema concerning the mother as a secure base. By focusing attention on the child's cognitive construction rather than just the interactive patterns of the dyad, the theory of attachment and relationships moves toward a greater realization that an attachment relationship involves the self and the representation of the self—what I have called identity. For example, Bowlby (1973) states,

The model of the attachment figure and the model of the self are likely to develop so as to be complementary and mutually nonconforming. Thus an unwanted child is likely not only to feel unwanted by his parents but to *believe that he is essentially unwanted.* (p. 208; emphasis added)

Such a view of relationships is much more similar to the one we posit as assuming an adult-like form. The level of representation of the relationship, including the self, is far different than it is for relationships formed by simple interactions. Notice that in Bowlby's view, the child believes that he, his self, is unwanted. Such a representation must mean that the child is capable of self-reflection. Moreover, it may even be the case that the simple interactions themselves may not be the only material on which the representation of a relationship is based. Other forms of knowledge may affect these representations. For example, two fathers have little interactive time with their children—one because he likes to play golf with his friends, the other because he works all the time to earn a living for his family. The children's representation of their fathers should differ, since it will be based upon both the interactive time and the reasons for that time.

Representations may have only a limited association with past events for a number of reasons. First, memory of past events has been shown to be poor (Hale, 1979); this is especially true for young children. Thus, the maintenance of the representation is difficult and is likely to undergo change. Second, memories of past events are influenced by variables intervening between those events and now (Rovee-Collier & Fagen, 1981). A set of positive past events is likely to be remembered differently, depending upon whether there has been a set of positive or negative intervening events. For example, I recently asked a group of 13-year-old children to describe their early childhood. There was no relation between their attachment classifications at 1 year and their descriptions of their early childhoods. Moreover, using a working-model hypothesis, I found no relation between the children's working models and their actual attachment classifications 12 years earlier. To find out what was determining their working models, I obtained data on their current lives by asking the children and their teachers to describe the children at this point in time. The data showed that the 13-year-old children's working models were dependent upon the nature of their current lives, rather than on what their attachment relationships were really like. Finally, there was no relation between their attachment classifications at 1 year and their current lives. Thus, I have some reason to believe that representations of early relationships may bear only slight resemblance to what actually happened. This should not be surprising, given the fact that memories are constructions and not exact representations of past events (Neisser, 1967).

As soon as we come to consider relationships in terms of representations (something also suggested by Hinde), we need to return to the child's capacity for self-reference. This, we believe, occurs after the first year of life, somewhere toward the middle of the second. If this is so, then the attachment relationship at 1 year reflects (1) the interactions that the child will subsequently use to form a working model of the relationship, and (2) the adult caregivers' relationship, including their working models of the attachment relationship with their parents.

To summarize, the extension of the issue of identity and its development into the realm of social life leads us to reconsider what it is that we mean by an infant–mother relationship. My suggestion is that this relationship, prior to identity attainment by the child, is not the same as a relationship between two adults. Although this appears obvious, it has important implications, the most important of which are as follows: (1) It is the adult who supports the relationship; and (2) these early exchanges become the material for the relationship, and as such bear no one-to-one relation to it. This is not to lessen their importance in the life of the developing child, but rather to suggest that there are levels of relationships that develop over time. This development has a phylogenetic, as well as an ontogenetic, character.

The issue of identity also requires that we reconsider what is meant by an attachment relationship and to whom we refer when we speak of an insecure or secure attachment. For us, an attachment relationship, as a relationship, refers more to the adult member of the dyad than to the infant. This leads to the possibility that the consistency found when looking at the effects of this early pattern of interactions are caused more by the adult (parent) than by the infant. What is clear is that this analysis forces us to consider the environment in more detail and makes us aware of the need to measure the environmental consistency in social development, rather than only the intraorganism consistency.[2]

SELF-AWARENESS AND EMOTIONAL LIFE

I have alluded to one other feature of social life that is affected by identity: the affective life of the child. Recently, I have suggested that identity has an impact upon the child's emotional development (Lewis, 1989a, 1989b; Lewis et al., 1989; Lewis & Michalson, 1983). The development of emotions necessitates identity in at least two ways. First, identity allows the child to become aware of the attained emotional states. Second, identity allows for the attainment of new emotional states.

Identity and Emotional Experience

Prior to identity, children have "primary emotional states"—for example, joy, fear, interest, disgust, sadness, and anger. Although children have these states, they are unaware of them (Lewis & Michalson, 1983). Such cognitions as "I am happy" require that the organism be capable of reflecting on its own inner states.

This awareness of one's internal emotional state I have labeled "emotional experience" in order to distinguish it from the emotional state itself. It is possible for adults to have an emotional state but to be unaware of it. For example, if I am driving a car and there is a sudden tire blowout, I may have an emotional state of fear. However, because I am so busy trying to bring the car under control, I may not be attending to (or experiencing) this state. Not until the car stops can I turn my attention to the internal state and then experience the fear. As I have pointed out elsewhere (Lewis, in press), the term "feeling" has been used to mean both the internal state and the experience of that state. This double usage is unfortunate, since it serves to confuse two probably separate features of emotional life.

From an ontogenetic perspective, the infant has emotional states from birth onward. However, only when self-awareness emerges can it logically be said that the child can experience these states. It is important to keep in mind that although the child may not be able to experience the state, the child *does* have that state. Thus, the child *is* in a state of pain, even though he or she may not be able to reflect upon that state. Moreover, and most importantly, this state of pain can and does affect

concurrent and subsequent states. This view is consistent with the analysis I have suggested for social relationships. Emotional states, like social interactive patterns, have an effect. They influence concurrent and subsequent emotional states and social interactions. They are stored and utilized, especially after 8 months of age, when memory becomes active and complex. Moreover, both social interactions and emotional states are likely to affect the development of self-awareness. Once self-awareness or consciousness emerges, these emotional states and social interactions become the basis of emotional experiences and social relationships. This position allows for the development of certain aspects of emotional life at the same time that it allows for the primary emotional states to be wired into the structures of the infant.

Identity and Attainment of Secondary Emotions

The development of identity provides the cognitive underpinning for the emergence of emotional states that are absent in the young child in the first year and a half of life. Although the child exhibits the primary emotions, including joy, anger, sadness, interest, disgust, and fear, it is not until the acquisition of identity that the child acquires such emotions as embarrassment, envy, empathy, pride, guilt, and shame (Lewis, in press; Lewis et al., 1989) These latter emotions, often called "secondary emotions" (as opposed to the primary ones), should be relabeled as "self-conscious emotions." We (Lewis et al., 1989), have presented a model of development of emotional states. Primary emotions occur early and, as states, are independent of self-awareness. Secondary emotions occur later and *only after* the attainment of self-awareness. Let us consider the emotions of embarrassment, pride, shame, and empathy.

Embarrassment occurs first as a consequence of self-consciousness or exposure (Buss, 1980; Lewis et al., 1989). Pride and shame occur when children evaluate their own actions against a standard and find them successful (as in pride) or lacking (as in shame). Notice that in each of these cases, self-reference relative to something is necessary for the emotional state to occur. As Kagan (1984) has pointed out, it is not until the end of the second year that standards appear and that anxiety centering around potential failure emerges.

The consideration of empathy as a final example brings together both the role of identity and the issue of levels. As in the earlier analysis, I see both a phylogenetic and an ontogenetic basis to this emotion, which is dependent upon the acquisition of identity. It is only a human relationship that is based upon empathy. Taking the role of the other through the extension of the self allows for a relationship uniquely different from one that is not based on such ability or based on an empathic reflex response. Sympathy, however, has a developmental history, or what I have referred to as levels (see Table 11.1). The lowest level of empathy is a reflex-like response to other's emotional expression. Infants crying in response to the sound of other infants' crying is an example of this reflex-like response. The highest level of empathy is based upon the organism's capacity to consider and understand how it might feel to be in the other's place. Empathy of this type cannot exist until the human child has attained identity (Halperin, 1989; Radke-Yarrow, Zahn-Waxler, & Chapman, 1983; Zahn-Waxler & Radke-Yarrow, 1981). Moreover, it is only an adult human relationship that is based upon this highest level.

What is important for our consideration here is that these self-conscious emotions have an impact on the nature of the child's social life, perhaps even more so than the primary ones. Clearly, social behavior is possible without these self-conscious emotions. Nonhuman animals engage in social behavior but do not have emotions requiring this level of identity. The issue, once again, has to do with levels and the ways in which we are to understand uniquely human social and emotional behavior.

SUMMARY

The domain of infant social development has been studied seriously for over 40 years, and much has been learned. Unfortunately, the theories governing research have been limited; because of this, the organization of the information acquired has been difficult. All social creatures need to acquire identity, learn social competencies, and reproduce. The analysis undertaken here claims that the tasks that organisms need to solve are the same across species;

however, the levels of ability underlying the tasks differ. Infants need to acquire identity that is human-specific—here, called "self-awareness" or "consciousness." The acquisition of this ability provides the basis for the other social tasks. In all cases, the tasks are uniquely different from both a phylogenetic and an ontogenetic point of view. The equivalence of behaviors and the meanings assigned to them are dependent upon an analysis of level of ability. In the discussion of these topics, I have described a number of problems that are common across many issues related to social development. In a broad sense, what I have tried to do in these comments is to reintroduce the importance of cognition into the study of social life. Although social life exists in the very young child, it is supported by the cognitions of adults and is based on processes different from the social life of adults. The fact that they look similar should not beguile us into believing that they are the same. To do so may simplify our task, but it has the unfortunate consequence of denying the role of developmental processes and cognitive structures in social life.

ACKNOWLEDGMENT

This chapter was supported by a grant from the W. T. Grant Foundation.

NOTES

1. The results of the Lewis et al. (1985) study raise several questions related to the rate of social development. The theoretical question has to do with the issue of whether faster social development—that is, development leading to a higher function—must be facilitated always by positive earlier experiences. In general, our theories of social development argue for the proposition that advances take place most quickly in "positive" environments as opposed to "negative" ones. Although this leaves open the question of the definition of "positive" and "negative," it seems reasonable to imagine that some development can be facilitated by "negative" experiences as well as by "positive" ones. For example, certain stress factors have been shown to facilitate some aspects of development (Rutter, 1981). In this particular case, self-awareness may be facilitated

by less interaction and positive responsivity of the caregiver. Mahler, Pine, and Bergman (1975) have suggested that individuation may be more difficult in an overly responsive environment. Freud (1920/1955) suggested that ego development is facilitated by the need for the child to formulate plans rather than receiving all outcomes automatically. Similar results have been reported as pseudoprecocity in the context of child maltreatment and maternal depression (see Radke-Yarrow, Zahn-Waxler, & Chapman, 1983). It is important to consider how the experiences of the child affect social development, keeping in mind that the effects may vary as a function of the type of outcome.

2. Another source of consistency, located in the child, may be temperament differences rather than relationships. Thus, although intraorganism consistency may be found, it may be related to other factors beside attachment.

REFERENCES

Abelson, R. (1976). Script processing in attitude formation and decision making. In J. S. Carroll & J. Payne (Eds.), *Cognition and social behavior* (pp. 33–47). Hillsdale, NJ: Erlbaum.

Ahrend, R., Gove, F. L., & Sroufe, L. A. (1979). Continuity of individual adaptation from infant to kindergarten: A predictive study of ego-resilience and curiosity in preschoolers. *Child Development, 50,* 950–959.

Ainsworth, M. D. S. (1964). Pattern of attachment behavior shown by the infant in interaction with his mother. *Merrill–Palmer Quarterly, 10,* 51–58.

Ainsworth, M. D. S. (1967). *Infancy in Uganda: Infant care and the growth of love.* Baltimore: Johns Hopkins University Press.

Ainsworth, M. D. S., Blehar, M. C., Waters, E., & Wall, S. (1978). *Patterns of attachment: A psychological study of the Strange Situation.* Hillsdale, NJ: Erlbaum.

Anisfeld, M. (in press). The question of early imitation of facial gestures: An historical–theoretical perspective and a meta-analysis.

Baldwin, J. M. (1973). *Social and ethical interpretations in mental development.* New York: Arno. (Original work published 1899)

Block, J., & Block, T. H. (1979). The role of ego control and ego-resiliency in the organization of behavior. In W. A. Collins (Ed.), *Minnesota Symposium on Child Psychology* (Vol. 13, pp. 229–239). Hillsdale, NJ: Erlbaum.

Borke, H. (1971). Interpersonal perception of young children: Egocentrism or empathy? *Developmental Psychology 5,* 263–269.

Bowlby, J. (1951). *Maternal care and mental health.* New York: Columbia University Press.

Bowlby, J. (1969). *Attachment and loss: Vol. 1. Attachment.* New York: Basic Books.

Bowlby, J. (1973). *Attachment and loss: Vol. 2. Separation.* New York: Basic Books.

Bowlby, J. (1982). Attachment and loss: Retrospect and prospect. *American Journal of Orthopsychiatry, 52*(4), 664–678.

Bretherton, I. (1987). New perspectives on attachment relations: Security, communication, and internal working models. In J. D. Osofsky (Ed.), *Handbook of infant development* (2nd ed., pp. 1061–1100). New York: Wiley.

Brooks-Gunn, J., & Lewis, M. (1982). Affective exchanges between normal and handicapped infants and their mothers. In T. Field & A. Fogel (Eds.), *Emotions and early interaction* (pp. 161–188). Hillsdale, NJ: Erlbaum.

Buber, M. (1958). *I and thou* (2nd ed., R. G. Smith, Trans.). New York: Scribner's.

Buss, A. H. (1980). *Self-consciousness and social anxiety.* San Francisco: Freeman Cooper.

Cairns, R. B. (1966). Attachment behavior of mammals. *Psychological Review, 73,* 409–426.

Campos, J., Campos, R. M., & Barnett, K. (1989). Emergent themes in the study of emotional development and emotion regulation. *Developmental Psychology, 25*(3), 394–402.

Cooley, C. H. (1962) *Social organization: A study of the larger mind.* New York: Schocken. (Original work published 1909)

Dennis, W. (1960). Causes of retardation among institutional children: Iran. *Journal of Genetic Psychology, 96,* 47–59.

Dixon, J. C. (1957). Development of self recognition. *Journal of Genetic Psychology, 91,* 251–256.

Dunn, J., & Kendrick, C. (1979). Interaction between young siblings in the context of family relationships. In M. Lewis & L. A. Rosenblum (Eds.), *The genesis of behavior: Vol 2. The child and its family* (pp. 143–168). New York: Plenum.

Edwards, C. P., & Lewis, M. (1979). Young children's concept of social relations: Social functions and social objects. In M. Lewis & L. A. Rosenblum (Eds.), *The genesis of behavior: Vol. 2. The child and its family* (pp. 245–266). New York: Plenum.

Emde, R. N. (1983). The prerepresentational self and its affective core. *Psychoanalytic Study of the Child, 38,* 165–192.

Emde, R. N. (1988). Development terminable and interminable: II. Recent psychoanalytic theory and therapeutic considerations. *International Journal of Psycho-Analysis, 69,* 283–296.

Fairbairn, W. R. D. (1952). *Object-relations theory of the personality.* New York: Basic Books.

Field, T. M., Woodson, R., Greenberg, R., & Cohen, O. (1982). Discrimination and imitation of facial expression by neonates. *Science, 218,* 179–181.

Fischer, K. (1980). A theory of cognitive development: The control and construction of hierarchies of skills. *Psychological Review, 87,* 477–531.

Freud, S. (1936). *The problem of anxiety.* New York: Norton.

Freud, S. (1955). Beyond the pleasure principle. In J. Strachey (Ed. and Trans.), *The standard edition of the complete psychological works of Sigmund Freud* (Vol. 18, pp. 4–67). London: Hogarth Press. (Original work published 1920)

Freud, S. (1959). Instincts and their vicissitudes. In *Collected papers.* New York: Basic Books. (Original work published 1915)

Gibson, J. J. (1966). *The senses considered as perceptual systems.* Boston: Houghton Mifflin.

Hale, G. A. (1979). Development of children's attention to stimulus components. In G. A. Hale & M. Lewis (Eds.), *Attention and cognitive development* (pp. 43–64). New York: Plenum.

Halperin, M. (1989, April). *Sympathy and self awareness.* Paper presented at the meeting of the Society for Research on Child Development, Kansas City, KS.

Harlow, H. F. (1958). The nature of love. *American Psychologist, 13,* 573–585.

Harlow, H. F., & Harlow, M. D. (1969). Effects of various mother–infant relationships on rhesus monkey behaviors. In B. M. Foss (Ed.), *Determinants of infant behavior* (Vol. 4, pp. 15–36). New York: Wiley.

Harre, R. (1984). *Personal being.* Cambridge, MA: Harvard University Press.

Hess, E. H. (1959). Imprinting. *Science, 130,* 133–141.

Hinde, R. A. (1976). Interactions, relationships, and social structure. *Man, 11,* 1–17.

Hinde, R. A. (1979). *Towards understanding relationships.* London: Academic Press.

Hofstadter, D. (1980). *Godel, Escher, Bach. An eternal golden braid.* New York: Random House.

Jackson, E., Campos, J. J., & Fischer, K. W. (1978). The question of decalogue between object permanence and person permanence. *Developmental Psychology, 14,* 1–10.

Jacobson, S. W. (1979). Matching behavior in young infants. *Child Development, 50,* 425–430.

James, W. (1950). *The principles of psychology.* New York: Holt. (Original work published 1890)

Kagan, J. (1984). *The nature of the child.* New York: Basic Books.

Kernberg, O. F. (1976). *Object relations theory and clinical psychoanalysis.* New York: Jason Aronson.

Kernberg, O. F. (1980). *Internal world and external reality: Object relations theory applied.* New York: Jason Aronson.

Klein, M. (1964). *Contributions to psychoanalysis, 1921–1945.* New York: McGraw-Hill.

Lacan, J. (1968). *Language of the self.* Baltimore: Johns Hopkins University Press.

Lamb, M. (1981). *The role of the father in child development* (2nd ed.). New York: Wiley.

Lamb, M., Thompson, R., Gardner, W., & Charnov, E. (1985). *Infant–mother attachment: The origins and developmental significance of individual differences in strange situation behavior.* Hillsdale, NJ: Erlbaum.

Levine, L. E. (1983). Mine: Self-definition in 2-year-old boys. *Developmental psychology, 19,* 544–549.

Lewis, M. (1967). The meaning of a response, or why researchers in infant behavior should be Oriental metaphysicians. *Merrill–Palmer Quarterly, 13*(1), 7–18.

Lewis, M. (1984). Social influences in development. In M. Lewis (Ed.), *The genesis of behavior: Vol. 4. Beyond the dyad* (pp. 1–12). New York: Plenum.

Lewis, M. (1985). Age as a social dimension. In T. Field & N. Fox (Eds.), *Social perception in infants* (pp. 299–319). New York: Academic Press.

Lewis, M. (1986). Origins of self-knowledge and individual differences in early self-recognition. In A. G. Greenwald & J. Suls (Eds.), *Psychological perspective on the self* (Vol. 3, pp. 55–78). Hillsdale, NJ: Erlbaum.

Lewis, M. (1987). Social development in infancy and early childhood. In J. D. Osofsky (Ed.), *Handbook of infant development* (2nd ed., pp. 419–493). New York: Wiley.

Lewis, M. (1989a). Challenges to the study of developmental psychopathology. In M. Lewis & S. Miller (Eds.), *Handbook of developmental psychopathology.* New York: Plenum.

Lewis, M. (1989b). Cultural differences in children's knowledge of emotional scripts. In P. Harris & C. Saarni (Eds.), *Children's understanding of emotion* (pp. 350–373). New York: Cambridge University Press.

Lewis, M. (1989c). Models of developmental psychopathology. In M. Lewis & S. Miller (Eds.), *Handbook of developmental psychopathology.* New York: Plenum.

Lewis, M. (in press). Thinking and feeling: The elephant's tail. In C. A. Maher, M. Schwebel, & N. S. Fagley (Eds.), *Thinking and problem solving in the developmental process: International perspectives.* New Brunswick, NJ: Rutgers University Press.

Lewis, M., & Brooks-Gunn, J. (1979a). *Social cognition and the acquisition of self.* New York: Plenum.

Lewis, M., & Brooks-Gunn, J. (1979b). Toward a theory of social cognition: The development of self. In I. Uzgiris (Ed.), *New directions in child development: Social interaction and comunication in infancy* (pp. 1–20). San Francisco: Jossey-Bass.

Lewis, M., Brooks-Gunn, J., & Jaskir, J. (1985). Individual differences in early visual self-recognition. *Developmental Psychology, 21,* 1181–1187.

Lewis, M., & Feiring, C. (1978). The child's social network: Social objects, social functions and their relationship. In M. Lewis & L. A. Rosenblum (Eds.), *The genesis of behavior: Vol. 2. The child and its family.* New York: Plenum.

Lewis, M., & Feiring, C. (in press). Attachment as personal characteristic or a measure of the environment. In J. Gerwitz & B. Kurtines (Eds.), *Intersections with attachment.* Hillsdale, NJ: Erlbaum.

Lewis, M., & Michalson, L. (1983). *Children's emotions and moods: Developmental theory and measurement.* New York: Plenum.

Lewis, M., Sullivan, M., & Michalson, L. (1984). The cognitive–emotional fugue. In C. E. Izard, J. Kagan, & R. Zajonc (Eds.), *Emotions, cognition, and behavior* (pp. 264–288). New York: Cambridge University Press.

Lewis, M., Sullivan, M. W., Stanger, C., & Weiss, M. (1989). Self-development and self-conscious emotions. *Child Development, 60,* 146–156.

Lipsitt, L. (1980). *The enduring significance of reflexes in human infancy: Developmental shifts in the first month of life.* Paper presented at the meeting of the Eastern Psychological Association, Hartford, CT.

Luria, A. R. (1976). *Cognitive development: Its cultural and social foundations.* Cambridge, MA: Harvard University Press.

Mahler, M. S., Pine, F., & Bergman, A. (1975). *The psychological birth of the infant.* New York: Basic Books.

Main, M., Kaplan, K., & Cassidy, J. (1985). Security in infancy, childhood and adulthood: A move to the level of representation. In I. Bretherton & E. Waters (Eds.), *Growing points of attachment theory and research. Monographs of the Society for Research in Child Development, 50*(1–2, Serial No. 209), 66–104.

Malmquist, C. P. (1977). Childhood depression: A clinical and behavioral perspective. In J. G. Schulterbrandt & A. Raskin (Eds.), *Depression in childhood: Diagnosis, treatment and conceptual models* (pp. 33–59). New York: Plenum.

Mandler, G. (1975). *Mind and emotion*. New York: Wiley.

Matas, L., Ahrend, R. A., & Sroufe, L. A. (1978). Continuity of adaptation in the second year: The relationship between quality of attachment and later competence. *Child Development, 49,* 547–556.

Meltzoff, A. N., & Moore, M. K. (1977). Imitation of facial and manual gestures by human neonates. *Science, 198,* 75–78.

Money, J., & Ehrhardt, A. (1972). *Man and woman, boy and girl*. Baltimore: Johns Hopkins University Press.

Mounoud, P. (1976). Les revolutions psychologiques de l'enfant. *Archives de Psychologie, 44,* 103–114.

Neisser, E. (1967). *Cognitive psychology*. New York: Appleton-Century-Crofts.

Papousek, H. (1981). The common in the uncommon children: Comments on the child's integrative capacities and on initiative parenting. In M. Lewis & L. Rosenblum (Eds.), *The uncommon child* (pp. 317–328). New York: Plenum.

Pervin, L. A. (1978). *Current controversies and issues in personality*. New York: Wiley.

Pervin, L. A. (Ed.). (1989). *Goal concepts in personality and social psychology*. Hillsdale, NJ: Erlbaum.

Piaget, J. (1952). *The origins of intelligence in children*. New York: International Universities Press.

Piaget, J. (1954). *Construction of reality in the child*. Paterson, NJ: Littlefield, Adams.

Piaget, J. (1976). *The grasp of consciousness*. Cambridge, MA: Harvard University Press.

Provence, S., & Lipton, R. C. (1962). *Infants in institutions*. London: Bailey & Swinger.

Radke-Yarrow, M. R., Zahn-Waxler, C. J., & Chapman, M. (1983). Children's prosocial dispositions and behavior. In E. M. Hetherington (Vol. Ed.), *Handbook of child psychology (4th ed.): Vol 4. Socialization, personality, and social development* (pp. 469–546). New York: Wiley.

Rank, O. (1929). *The trauma of birth*. London: Kegan, Paul, Trench & Trubner.

Rehm, L. P., Leventon, B., & Ivens, C. (1987). Depression. In C. L. Frame & J. L. Matson (Eds.), *Handbook of assessment in childhood psychopathology: Applied issues in differential diagnosis and treatment evaluation* (pp. 341–371). New York: Plenum.

Reigel, K. (1976). *Psychology of development and history*. New York: Plenum.

Rheingold, H. (1971). *Some visual determinants of smiling infants*. Unpublished manuscript.

Rosenblum, L. A. (1961). *The development of social behavior in the rhesus monkey*. Unpublished doctoral dissertation, University of Wisconsin.

Rovee-Collier, C. K., & Fagen, J. W. (1981). The retrieval of memory in early infancy. In L. P. Lipsett (Ed.), *Advances in infancy research* (Vol. 1, pp. 226–254). Norwood, NJ: Ablex.

Rutter, M. (1981). Stress, coping and development: Some issues and some questions. In N. Garmezy & M. Rutter (Eds.), *Stress, coping and development in children* (pp. 250–271). New York: McGraw-Hill.

Sameroff, A. J. (1983). Developmental systems: Contexts and evolution. In W. Kessen (Vol. Ed.), *Handbook of child psychology (4th ed.): Vol. 1. History, theory, and methods* (pp. 237–294). New York: Wiley.

Sanders, L. W. (1964). Adaptive relationships in early mother–child interactions. *Journal of the American Academy of Child Psychiatry, 3,* 231–264.

Sanders, L. W. (1980). New knowledge about the infant from current research: Implications for psychoanalysis. *Journal of the American Psychoanalytic Association 28,* 181–198.

Schaeffer, H. R. (1975). Cognitive components of the infant's response to strangeness. In M. Lewis & L. Rosenblum (Eds.), *The origins of fear* (pp. 11–24). New York: Wiley.

Schaeffer, H. R., & Emerson, P. E. (1964). The development of social attachments in infancy. *Monographs of the Society for Research in Child Development, 29* (Serial No. 94).

Schneider-Rosen, K., & Cicchetti, D. (1984). The relationship between affect and cognition in maltreated infants: Quality of attachment and the development of self-recognition. *Child Development, 55,* 648–658.

Scott, J. P., (1962). Genetics and the development of social behavior in mammals. *American Journal of Orthopsychiatry, 32,* 878–893.

Spitz, R. A. (1945). Hospitalism: An inquiry in the genesis of psychiatric conditions in early childhood. *Psychoanalytic Study of the Child, 1,* 53–73.

Spitz, R. A. (1946). Anaclitic depression: An inquiry into the genesis of psychiatric conditions in early childhood, II. *Psychoanalytic Study of the Child, 2,* 313–342.

Spitz, R. A., & Wolf, K. M. (1946). The smiling response: A contribution to ontogenesis of social relations. *Genetic Psychology Monographs, 34,* 57–125.

Sroufe, L. A. (1979). Socioemotional development. In J. D. Osofsky (Ed.), *Handbook of infant development*. New York: Wiley.

Stern, D. N. (1985). *The interpersonal world of the infant*. New York: Basic Books.

Sullivan, H. S. (1953). *The interpersonal theory of psychiatry*. New York: Norton.

Sullivan, M., Lewis, M., & Alessandri, S. (in press). Interface between emotion and cognition. In *Visions of development, environment and aesthetics: The legacy of J. F. Wohlwill*.

Suomi, S. J. (1978). Maternal behavior by socially incompetent monkeys: Neglect and abuse of offspring. *Journal of Pediatric Psychology, 3,* 28–34.

Thompson, R. A., & Lamb, M. E. (1984). Infants, mothers, families and strangers. In M. Lewis (Ed.), *The genesis of behavior: Vol. 4. Beyond the dyad*. New York, Plenum.

Waters, E., Wippman, J., & Sroufe, L. A. (1979). Attachment, positive effect, and competence in the peer group: Two studies in construct validation. *Child Development, 50,* 821–829.

Weinraub, M., Brooks, J., & Lewis, M. (1977). The social network: A reconsideration of the concept of attachment. *Human Development, 20,* 31–47.

Weinraub, M., Clemens, L. P., Sockloff, A., Ethridge, T., Facely, E., & Myers, B. (1984). The development of sex role stereotypes in the third year: Relationships to gender labeling, gender identity, sex typed toy preferences and family characteristics. *Child Development, 55,* 1493–1503.

Werner, H. (1961). *Comparative psychology of mental development*. New York: Science Editions.

Wylie, R. C. (1961). *The self concept*. Lincoln: University of Nebraska Press.

Yarrow, L. (1963). Research in dimensions of early maternal care. *Merrill–Palmer Quarterly, 9,* 101–104.

Zahn-Waxler, C. J., & Radke-Yarrow, M. R. (1981). The development of prosocial behavior: Alternative research strategies. In N. Eisenberg-Berg (Ed.), *The development of prosocial behavior* (pp. 109–138). New York: Academic Press.

Chapter 12

Personality, Social Psychology, and Person–Situation Relations: Standards and Knowledge Activation as a Common Language

E. Tory Higgins
Columbia University

> In "action" is included all human behaviour when and in so far as the acting individual attaches a subjective meaning to it. . . . Action is social in so far as, by virtue of the subjective meaning attached to it by the acting individual (or individuals), it takes account of the behaviour of others and is thereby oriented in its course.
>
> Max Weber (1967, pp. 156–157)

What is the relation between personality and social psychology? For those who identify with both areas, this is an important professional question. But it is also a central theoretical issue in the social science of psychology. How do the variables of concern to personality psychologists relate to the variables of concern to social psychologists? How might these areas function together so that greater progress would be made in identifying, studying, and understanding basic social phenomena? There are, of course, many possible answers to these questions. The purpose of this chapter is to suggest one possible approach by proposing a common language for personality and social psychology.

Personality psychologists have been traditionally concerned with distinguishing individuals in terms of regularities and consistencies in each person's orientations and responses. In contrast, social psychologists have been concerned with distinguishing situations (e.g., experimental vs. control conditions) in terms of regularities and consistencies in each situation's impact on the orientations and responses of people in general. Thus, the issue of how to integrate personality and social psychology can be, and historically has been, addressed in terms of understanding the nature of the "person × situation interaction" or person–situation relations. The present chapter also addresses this issue in these terms.

Although there has been considerable debate and controversy surrounding the nature of the person–situation relation, a review of the literature reveals a surprising amount of agreement over the years concerning how best to approach this issue (see, e.g., Allport, 1966; Bandura, 1986; Cantor & Kihlstrom, 1987; Endler, 1982; Kelly, 1955; Kenrick & Funder, 1988; Lewin, 1935; Marlowe & Gergen, 1969; Mischel, 1968, 1973; Murphy, 1954; Pervin, 1985; Rotter, 1954, 1955; Synder & Ickes, 1985). The following postulates for a "good" theory of the person–situation relation have been commonly suggested:

1. *The psychological significance of an event is a critical determinant of how a person responds to the event.* A fundamental characteristic of people is that they assign meaning to the events in their lives and then respond to those meanings. This insight into the nature of people has a long history in Western thought, but was most clearly developed at the turn of the century in the work of Weber (illustrated in the quotation above), Durkheim, Malinowski, Freud, James, Cooley, and others. Thomas and Thomas (1928) expressed the essence of this insight as follows: "If men define situations as real, they are real in their consequences." In the areas of personality and social psychology as well, Kelly (1955), Lewin (1935), Murray (1938), Sherif (1936), Rotter (1955), and other early theorists emphasized the importance of the psychological situation in determining people's motivations and actions. Social objects and events not only have meaning: they also have importance. The term "significance" refers to both the quality of conveying meaning and the quality of being important. Thus the concept "psychological significance" captures both the meaning and importance aspects of subjective experience.

2. *The psychological significance of an event is a product of both the person and the situation.* Those theorists who have emphasized the importance of the psychological significance of an event have typically also emphasized the joint influence of person and situation factors on the construction of an event's psychological significance. Lewin (1935), Murray (1938), and Rotter (1954) were especially influential proponents of the notion that behavior is a function of both the person and the psychological environment. In their review of personality and social psychology, Marlowe and Gergen (1969) concluded that "the consideration of situational variables alone, without respect to the interaction of situation and personality, is a

rather fruitless quest" (p. 645). In the same period, Mischel (1968) also concluded that the consideration of personality variables alone (and especially traits alone), without considering how the situation affects individuals, is rather futile. As Endler (1982) has recently pointed out, interactionism is not a new idea, but it is an idea whose time has come.

3. *Standards are a major determinant of the psychological significance of an event.* A "standard" is a criterion or rule established by experience, desires, or authority for the measure of quantity and extent or quality and value. Both people and situations can be differentiated in terms of the standards associated with them that influence the psychological significance of events. It is well recognized that the valued end states, reference points, and rules underlying responses are different for different people and at different phases of social development (for reviews, see Cantor & Kihlstrom, 1987; Higgins, 1989a; Higgins, Strauman, & Klein, 1986; Pervin, 1985). The importance of personal standards for individual differences in motivation and self-regulation has been emphasized in both psychodynamic models (e.g., Adler, 1929/1964; Freud, 1923/1961; Horney, 1950; Rogers, 1961; Sullivan, 1953) and social learning models (e.g., Bandura, 1977, 1986; Kanfer, 1971; Mischel, 1973; Rotter, 1954), as well as in models of achievement motivation and life tasks (e.g., Atkinson, 1964; Cantor & Kihlstrom, 1987; Klinger, 1975; Kuhl, 1978; Lewin, 1951; McClelland, 1961). Early on, James (1890/1948) emphasized that standards can function both as a basis for self-regulation and as a basis for self-evaluation (see also Carver & Scheier, 1981; Duval & Wicklund, 1972). It has also been recognized that the impact of situations on people's orientations and actions can vary because of differences in situational standards, such as differences in normative pressures and constraints, rules, and role and goal assignments (see e.g., Bandura, 1986; Barker, 1968; Endler, 1982; Mischel, 1973; Pervin, 1985; Synder & Ickes, 1985; Stryker & Statham, 1985).

4. *Within social knowledge, self-beliefs play a special role in the psychological significance of events.* Self-beliefs are just a subset of people's social knowledge, and thus cannot fully account for the person-situation relation. Nevertheless, self-beliefs include self-standards (e.g., self as a reference point; valued end

states for the self), the self-concept, self-expectancies, and perceived self-efficacy, and such self-beliefs have been assigned a central mediating role in various models of motivation and regulation (for reviews, see Bandura, 1986; Breckler & Greenwald, 1986; Dweck & Elliot, 1983; Harter, 1983; Markus & Wurf, 1987; Raynor & McFarlin, 1986; Tesser, 1986; Trope, 1986). Self-beliefs have also been considered a critical variable interrelating individuals and society (see Higgins, 1989a; Mead, 1934; Secord & Backman, 1965; Stryker & Statham, 1985; Swann, 1983). Indeed, it has even been suggested that an adequate theory of self-beliefs and the self-system may provide the key to integrating personality and social psychology (e.g., Greenwald, 1982; Markus, 1983; Marlowe & Gergen, 1969; Snyder & Ickes, 1985).

An integration of these four postulates yields the following general guiding proposition: Standards and social knowledge (especially self-beliefs), which are a function of both the person and the situation, are basic determinants of the psychological significance of events and thus strongly influence how people respond to events.

In addition to this general guiding proposition, the literature suggests that a "good" theory of the person–situation relation should also be directed by the following key principles:

1. There is a need for a common language of description for both persons and situations—for the person and the situation to be analyzed in terms of the same psychological variables (see Bem, 1982; Bem & Funder, 1978; Cantor & Kihlstrom, 1987; Greenwald, 1982; Markus, 1983; Mischel & Peake, 1982; Murray, 1938).

2. An account of nomothetic psychological processes interrelating persons and situations must be provided (see Cantor & Kihlstrom, 1987; Endler, 1982; Mischel, 1977; Pervin, 1985). Process models rather than strictly content models are needed (see Kruglanski, 1980).

3. The process models must take into account variations that arise from differences in content. Within a science of nomothetic psychological principles or processes, idiographic variables must also be included (see Bem, 1983; Bem & Allen, 1974; Hermans, 1988; Kelly, 1955; Mischel, 1973).

The purpose of the present chapter is to propose a theoretical perspective on person–situation relations that is directed by each of these key principles as well as the general guiding proposition. It is not possible within the limits of this chapter to provide a comprehensive exposition of this theoretical perspective. Instead, this perspective is illustrated by focusing on knowledge activation as a general nomothetic process variable and types of social standards as one type of idiographic content variable. Although I believe that these two variables are necessary components in any complete model of person–situation relations, they are clearly not sufficient. The chapter examines various forms of person–situation relations by considering individual and situational variability in knowledge activation as a process, and individual and situational variability in social categories and social standards as the content involved in the process of knowledge activation. The first section begins with a general process model of knowledge activation that incorporates the first two of the four postulates given above (i.e., psychological significance as a product of both the person and the situation) and contains some idiographic assumptions (i.e., individual differences in knowledge availability and accessibility). The next section expands the model by incorporating the second two postulates and introducing further idiographic assumptions (i.e., a typology of social standards). The third section describes multiple stages and types of person–situation relations in the common language of knowledge activation and standards. The final section describes patterns of person–situation relations within so-called "personality" and "social psychology" phenomena that allow such phenomena to be studied from either a personality or a social-psychological orientation.

KNOWLEDGE ACTIVATION AND SUBJECTIVE MEANING

The significance of objects and events derives in part from the meaning of their inherent properties or "affordances" to humans in general (see Gibson, 1979; McArthur & Baron, 1983). Data-driven effects on people's representations also include accommodation and novel representations constructed from novel input (see Piaget, 1952). But people's representations are not just data-driven. Much of the significance of objects and events derives from how individuals represent and categorize them. There has long been a recognition that knowledge structures built up from past experiences are a major determinant of how people represent and categorize external stimuli (e.g., Bartlett, 1932; Bruner, 1957a; Hebb, 1949; Kelly, 1955; Wertheimer, 1923). Rather than being either data-driven or theory-driven, however, people's constructed representations are best conceptualized in terms of theory–data relations (see Higgins & Bargh, 1987; Wyer & Srull, 1986)

Theory–data relations comprise one form of person–situation relations that contributes to subjective meaning. But they are not the only form. Data or input is only one aspect of a perceiver's situation. A perceiver's exposure to input also occurs within a context of perception that influences the theory-data constructions. In this way, subjective meaning is context-driven as well as theory-driven and data-driven (see Higgins & Stangor, 1988). *The situation contributes both data-driven and context-driven effects.* During dyadic interaction, for example, one's interaction partner provides both target data and a social context for one's perception of the partner.

Thus, a model of the impact of person–situation relations on subjective meaning must take into account theory–context relations as well as theory–data relations. Moreover, as discussed earlier, a common language for describing both person and situation effects on subjective meaning is needed. One approach to this issue that meets both of these criteria is to consider person–situation relations and subjective meaning in terms of knowledge accessibility and activation (see Higgins, 1989b).

Knowledge Accessibility as a Function of Persons and Situations

The "New Look" in perception that emerged in the 1940s proposed that needs, values, attitudes, and expectancies determine perception and result in people "going beyond the information given" (Bruner, 1957a). To capture the general role of expectancies and motivational states on perception, Bruner (1957b) introduced the notion of category "accessibility," which denoted "the ease or speed with which a given stimulus input is coded in terms of a given category under varying conditions." Two general sets of conditions were proposed to affect accessibility: expectancies (subjective probability estimates of the likelihood of a given event) and motivational states (certain kinds of search sets induced by needs, task goals, etc.). The model postulated that expectancies and motivational states momentarily increase the accessibility of stored categories, which in turn increases the likelihood that a stimulus input will be perceived in terms of that category rather than a competing alternative category.

A significant implication of the notion of accessibility is that people will apply a particular category to an input not solely because of the match between the features of the input and those of the category. Instead, other factors, such as expectancies and need states, can increase the *prior* likelihood that a particular category rather than an alternative will be applied to the input. And, once a particular category is applied to an input, features missing in the input that are part of the category will tend to be filled in (i.e., people will "see what isn't there").

This consequence of accessibility, however, is not restricted to momentary increases in accessibility from the relatively strategic, stimulus-orienting variables described by Bruner (e.g., instructional sets, stimulus-related goals). It can also occur as a result of momentary increases in accessibility from extraneous variables and as a result of chronic accessibility.

With respect to momentary increases in accessibility, activation of a construct from recent or frequent "contextual priming" is capable of increasing the accessibility of a construct. The importance of recency and frequency of exposure as variables influencing subsequent performance has been recognized for a long time. In the early 19th century, Thomas Brown proposed recency and frequency as basic conditions under which the general principle of association operates (see Heidbreder, 1933). And in the late 19th century, Edward Lee Thorndike (1898) proposed in his law of exercise that the more recently and frequently a stimulus–response bond is exercised, the more effectively it is stamped in.

In social psychology, a series of studies beginning in the late 1970s demonstrated that simply activating a construct in one task was capable of increasing the accessibility of the construct sufficiently to give it precedence when subjects categorized a target person's behavior in a subsequent, unrelated task (see Higgins, 1981; Higgins & Bargh, 1987; Wyer & Srull, 1981, 1986). For example, in one study (Higgins, Rholes, & Jones, 1977), subjects were initially exposed to one or another set of trait constructs ("adventurous" vs. "reckless") as an extraneous aspect of a supposed study on perception, and later participated in an "unrelated" study on reading comprehension where they were asked to characterize the behaviors of a target person whom they read about. The study found that the subjects were much more likely to use the constructs activated or primed in the "perception" study than alternative constructs when they later categorized the target person in the "comprehension" study. This basic finding that recent activation increases the likelihood of a construct's being used in subsequent judgments has been replicated in many subsequent studies (e.g., Bargh, Bond, Lombardi, & Tota, 1986; Carver, Ganellen, Froming, & Chambers, 1983; Erdley & D'Agostino, 1988; Fazio, Powell, & Herr, 1983; Herr, 1986; Herr, Sherman & Fazio, 1983; Higgins, Bargh, & Lombardi, 1985; Higgins & Chaires, 1980; Martin, 1986; Rholes & Pryor, 1982; Sinclair, Mark, & Shotland, 1987; Smith & Branscombe, 1987; Srull & Wyer, 1979, 1980). There is also evidence that frequent activation of a construct increases how long the construct will remain predominant in subsequent categorization (e.g., Higgins et al., 1985; Lombardi, Higgins, & Bargh, 1987; Srull & Wyer, 1979, 1980).

Other results of these studies suggest that the *assimilation* effect of recent and frequent activation is more likely to occur when the priming events are unconscious than when they are conscious (see Lombardi et al., 1987). Thus, this effect does not require that subjects be aware of (i.e., remember) the primed construct at the point when the construct is to be used in categorization (see Higgins & Chaires, 1980). Indeed, experimental conditions that increase the likelihood of such awareness, as by using highly memorable priming stimuli or actually reminding subjects of the priming events, are more likely to produce a "contrast" effect on judgment than an assimilation effect (see Herr, 1986; Herr et al., 1983; Lombardi et al., 1987; Martin, 1986; Neuman & Uleman, in press; Strack, Schwarz, Bless, Kubler, & Wanke, 1988). Conversely, experimental conditions that increase the likelihood that subjects will

suppress awareness of a priming event, as when remembering a priming event would be unpleasant, increase the likelihood that an assimilation effect will be produced (e.g., Martin, 1986).

With respect to chronic accessibility, Kelly (1955) pointed out early on that "construct systems can be considered as a kind of scanning pattern which a person continually projects upon his world. As he sweeps back and forth across his perceptual field he picks up blips of meaning" (p. 145). Mischel (1973) suggested that individual differences in the subjective meaning of social events may be especially evident in the personal constructs individuals employ, and that these personal constructs may show the greatest resistance to situational presses. More generally, it has been proposed that there are individual differences, including cross-cultural differences, in the "theories" or viewpoints that people have about human nature and personality (e.g., Kelly, 1955; Sarbin, Taft, & Bailey, 1960; Tagiuri, 1969; Tajfel, 1969).

These early accounts of personal constructs or viewpoints did not specify whether the individual differences involved the *availability* or the *accessibility* of constructs. In discussing individual differences in constructs, Higgins, King, and Mavin (1982) pointed out that there can be both individual differences in the particular kinds of constructs that are present in memory for potential use in processing social input (differences in the kind of stored knowledge that is available for use) and individual differences in the readiness with which available constructs are actually used (differences in the likelihood of using available constructs).

There is now considerable evidence that individual differences in the chronic accessibility of alternative constructs can influence person perception and social behavior (e.g., Bargh & Pratto, 1986; Bargh & Thein, 1986; Fazio, 1986; Higgins et al., 1982; King & Sorrentino, 1988; Lau, 1989; Strauman & Higgins, 1987). For example, in one study (Higgins et al, 1982), subjects' chronically accessible constructs were measured by asking them to list the traits of a type of person that they liked, that they disliked, that they sought out, that they avoided, and that they frequently encountered. Chronic accessibility was defined in terms of output primacy—those traits a subject listed first in response to the questions. About 1 week later, subjects participated in an "unrelated" study conducted by a different experimenter. Each subject read an individually tailored essay containing some behavioral descriptions of a target person that moderately exemplified the subject's accessible trait constructs, and other behavioral descriptions that moderately exemplified trait constructs that were not chronically accessible for the subject but were for some other subject. (This "quasi-yoking" design controlled for the content of the descriptions that were related vs. unrelated to the chronically accessible constructs.)

On both a measure of subjects' impressions of the target person and a measure of their recall of the behavioral descriptions, the study found that subjects were significantly more likely to exclude information that was unrelated to their chronically accessible constructs than information that was related to them. These basic effects were also found in another study (Higgins et al, 1982) in which chronic accessibility was defined in terms of the frequency of output to different questions rather than the primacy of output. Moreover, there was evidence from a 2-week delay measure included in this second study that the effects persisted or even increased over time.

There is also evidence that chronic knowledge accessibility is an important factor in relation to personal attitudes and opinions. Fazio (1986), for example, reports a series of studies suggesting that the chronic accessibility of object–evaluation associations influences the likelihood that people's attitudes about objects will guide their behaviors toward the objects. Most recently, Lau (1989) conducted a set of studies using an alternative operationalization of individuals' chronically accessible constructs, and found (1) that chronically accessible constructs are relatively stable even over years and (2) that they guide the processing of information about a wide variety of political objects.

Chronic individual differences in the availability of constructs have little obvious relation to temporary changes in people's expectancies or goals. Perhaps this is why Bruner's (1957b) category accessibility and Kelly's (1955) personal constructs were treated as completely distinct phenomena in the traditional literature. By distinguishing between individual differences in the accessibility of constructs and individual differences in the availability of constructs, we (Higgins et al, 1982) proposed a basic conceptual link between the phenomena of temporary category accessibility and chronic personal constructs. First contextual priming can be conceptualized as a situational factor that creates momentary individual differences in construct accessibility. Second, if frequent priming increases how long a construct will remain accessible or predominant, then long-term individual differences across many situations in the frequency with which different kinds of constructs are activated (e.g., differences in parental instructions) may be expected to lead to chronic individual differences in construct accessibility. If there is no exposure to a particular construct at all, then the construct will not even be available (i.e., it will have zero accessibility). Thus, chronic individual differences in construct accessibility should function like temporary individual differences in construct accessibility. The "synapse" model of knowledge accessibility was developed in order to account for differences in subjective meaning from both momentary context (i.e., situation) and chronic individual (i.e., person) sources of variation in accessibility.

The "Synapse" Model of Knowledge Accessibility

We (Higgins & King, 1981) suggested an energy cell metaphor for construct accessibility, in which the energy or action potential of a construct (i.e., the cell) is increased whenever the construct is excited or activated, and the energy slowly dissipates over time. It was assumed that as the energy level of a construct increased, the likelihood of its utilization increased (for an alternative model of knowledge accessibility and activation, see Wyer & Srull, 1981, 1986). Higgins et al (1985) elaborated the Higgins and King (1981) energy cell metaphor into a "synapse" model in which it was suggested that perhaps, as for synapses, the decay over time of the excitation level of a construct following its last activation is slower when the construct has been frequently activated than when it has been activated only once. In the "synapse" model, then, frequent and recent activation are distinguished in terms of the differences in their decay functions following final activation.

We (Higgins et al., 1985) tested the "synapse" model's conceptualization of accessibility effects by exposing subjects to two alternative constructs for characterizing subsequent input, one being primed more frequently and the other being primed only once but most recently. Immediately following the last prime, the most recently activated construct would be at its maximum level of excitation, whereas the excitation level of the frequently primed construct would already be below maximum because its final activation occurred earlier. At this point, then the "synapse" model would predict that the recently primed construct would be predominant in categorization. However, the excitation level of the frequently activated construct was expected to decay more slowly than that of the recently activated construct. Thus, it was predicted that with sufficient delay between final priming and the input to be categorized (filled with a counting-backwards task that taxes subjects' working memory), the frequently activated construct would predominate in categorization. This predicted crossover pattern was obtained.

If chronic accessibility functions like temporary accessibility, as the synapse model predicts, then combining in the same study chronic individual differences in construct accessibility (as measured by the primacy-of-output measure used in Higgins et al., 1982) and temporary differences in construct accessibility (as produced by a priming manipulation) should yield enhanced effects of construct accessibility. In a direct test of this implication, Bargh et al. (1986) found that the chronic and temporary sources of a construct's accessibility combined additively to increase the likelihood that the construct would be used to interpret behavioral descriptions of a target person.

Bargh and Pratto (1986) used the Stroop color-naming paradigm to test another implication of the proposed similarity between chronic and temporary accessibility—that a chronically accessible construct, like a temporarily accessible construct, should be at a higher level of readiness to be activated by a stimulus input to which it is related. Bargh and Pratto (1986) found that subjects' chronically accessible constructs were indeed at a higher level of activation readiness than their inaccessible constructs (as revealed by greater interference on the color-naming task from the chronically accessible constructs). And in an important test of the proposal that chronic accessibility is likely to be associated with automatic or passive processing (see Bargh, 1984; Higgins & King, 1981), Bargh and Thein (1985) found evidence of the processing efficiency expected with automatic processing for subjects' impressions and recall of a target person's behaviors when the processing involved subjects' chronically accessible constructs and not when it involved their inaccessible constructs.

The proposal that chronic and temporary accessibility may function similarly was based on generalizing from relatively prolonged differences in temporary accessibility produced by frequent priming in a single experimental session to chronic differences in accessibility from frequent activation across the many natural situations associated with an individual's socialization experiences (Higgins et al., 1982). This analysis suggests that individual differences in chronic accessibility should function like differences in temporary accessibility produced by frequent priming. As described earlier, we (Higgins et al., 1985) found a recency/frequency × brief-delay/long-delay interaction in a study involving contextual priming. In a later study (Bargh, Lombardi, & Higgins, 1988), subjects' chronically accessible constructs were substituted for the frequently primed constructs in the design, and the same crossover pattern was found. The similarity in pattern of results between the Higgins et al. (1985) and Bargh et al. (1988) studies supports our (Higgins et al., 1982) suggestion that chronic accessibility may function like momentary accessibility from frequent activation.

The results of these various studies are consistent with the basic assumption of the synapse model that temporary (situation) and chronic (person) sources of accessibility function similarly. They both contribute to the current level of excitation of available knowledge. The temporary sources include momentary contextual priming as well as situationally induced expectancies and goals (e.g., task goals). The chronic sources include chronic contextual activation as well as long-term expectancies (e.g., stereotypes) and goals (e.g., life tasks). The synapse model proposes that for available knowledge, knowledge-related expectancies and goals combine additively with chronic accessibility and contextual priming to increase the excitation level of the knowledge (Higgins, 1989). The knowledge can be general declarative knowledge, episodic knowledge, or procedural knowledge (see Higgins, 1989b; Smith, 1989). With respect to episodic knowledge, for example, there are studies suggesting that activating people's past life experiences can influence their subsequent behaviors and judgments (see Clark & Isen, 1982; Salancik & Conway, 1975; Schwarz & Clore, 1987; Strack, Schwarz, & Gschneidinger, 1985). There are also studies suggesting that contextually priming alternative orientations and procedures for dealing with a task can influence how people respond to the task, whether the task is creative problem solving or administering rewards and punishments (e.g., Carver et al., 1983; Higgins and Chaires, 1980).

Thus far, two knowledge accessibility contributors to knowledge excitation levels have been considered: the person variable of chronic individual differences in knowledge accessibility, and the situation variable of temporary increases in knowledge accessibility from contextual priming. Let us turn now to the third major contributor to knowledge excitation levels—the situation variable of data or input.

Input as a Situational Source of Activation: The Role of Applicability

As discussed earlier, subjective meaning is constructed from previously stored knowledge and current informational input from the situation (i.e., a theory–data relation). When the input is sufficiently detailed, elaborate, and salient, and the basic knowledge is available to everyone (as is typically the case in studies with undergraduates), then individual differences in knowledge accessibility contribute little to variation in subjective meaning compared to differences in the input (e.g., in the instructions or target person). This is often the case in social psychology experiments. Indeed, social psychology experiments, such as dissonance or conformity experiments, often are designed or tuned specifically to contain properties (i.e., input) that would lead all subjects to construct the same subjective meaning (see Snyder & Ickes, 1985). When the input is less detailed, elaborate, and salient, or the basic knowlege is not available to everyone (as is typically the case in developmental studies), then individual differences in knowledge availability and accessibility can contribute significantly to variation in subjective meaning. This has been the case in most studies of knowledge accessibility and has been demonstrated in a couple of different ways.

One method, exemplified by the Higgins et al. (1977) study, has been to construct each behavioral description (i.e, input) so that its

features are roughly equal in similarity or overlap to the features of two alternative constructs that could be used to characterize it (e.g., "adventurous" and "reckless"). That is, each behavioral description is constructed so that two alternative constructs are equally applicable for characterizing it. This method involves exposing all subjects to the same *ambiguous* input. The other method, exemplified by the Srull and Wyer (1979) studies, has been to construct a set of behavioral descriptions that together has enough features associated with a particular trait construct (e.g., "hostile") that the construct is applicable to the set, but does not possess so many of the features associated with the construct that the set would require characterization in terms of the construct. This method involves exposing all subjects to the same *vague* input.

In both of these methods, the input has features that are similar to the features of some stored knowledge. The synapse model assumes that when there is an overlap of features between input and stored knowledge, the excitation level of the stored knowledge increases (see Higgins, 1989b). Indeed, the model assumes that normally it is the addition to the excitation level of stored knowledge contributed by the input that causes the knowledge to reach the threshold level for activation and utilization. Otherwise, people would literally lose touch with reality. As the prior accessibility of the stored knowledge increases, however, the amount of contribution by the input necessary to reach threshold decreases. Thus, even impoverished input (i.e., few input features similar to the stored knowledge) may be sufficient to cause stored knowledge to be utilized when accessibility from both person and context sources is high.

Knowledge accessibility effects are different for vague input than for ambiguous input. Higher knowledge accessibility influences responses to vague input by providing the higher prior level of excitation needed for the small additional amount of excitation contributed by the input to be sufficient to activate the knowledge and have it applied to the input. Without the high prior level of knowledge accessibility, the vague input would not be sufficient to activate the knowledge. In the case of ambiguous input, however, the input can have high feature similarity to two or more knowledge structures, and thus can contribute a large additional amount of excitation. Thus, high prior levels of knowledge accessibility are not required to activate the knowledge structures. The issue in this case is which knowledge structure will be utilized, which will predominate. For ambiguous input, then, higher knowledge accessibility influences responses by allowing one of the alternative knowledge structures to predominate, because its higher prior level produces a higher resultant level when combined with the input.

The synapse model proposes that the combination of the prior level of excitation of stored knowledge (i.e., accessibility) and its applicability to the input is what determines the likelihood that the knowledge will be used in judging the input. Early support for this proposal was provided in the Higgins et al. (1977) study described earlier. The subjects were randomly assigned to four priming conditions: applicable, positive priming (e.g., "adventurous"); applicable, negative priming (e.g., "reckless"); nonapplicable, positive priming (e.g., "neat"); and nonapplicable, negative priming (e.g., "disrespectful"). The constructs in the applicable conditions were both denotatively and connotatively related to the stimulus description, whereas the constructs in the nonapplicable conditions were only connotatively related. Only the applicable priming influenced subjects' later categorizations of the stimulus person's behaviors.

The proposal that the combination of accessibility and applicability to input is what determines the likelihood of knowledge's being used in judging the input has a number of implications. First, it implies that for the same input, increasing the prior accessibility of stored knowledge should increase the likelihood that it will be used to judge the input. Second, it implies that for the same prior accessibility of stored knowledge, an increase in the applicability of the knowledge to the input should increase the likelihood that it will be used to judge the input. Applicability can be increased by selecting knowledge to prime whose features are more similar to the input features than alternative knowledge structures, or by selecting an input whose features are more similar to the primed knowledge than an alternative input. Applicability of stored knowledge (e.g., stereotypes) to input can also be increased by contextually increasing the salience of those features of an input that are most similar to the stored knowledge (see McArthur, 1981; Taylor & Fiske, 1978).

The synapse model further distinguishes between the extent to which the features of the stored knowledge and the input overlap (which defines the applicability factor in the synapse model of accessibility) and the extent to which the perceiver considers the stored knowledge to be applicable to the data. The latter involves the factor of "perceived applicability." This factor can have independent effects on how information is used (e.g., Ajzen, 1977; Kruglanski, Friedland, & Farkash, 1984; Trope & Ginossar, 1988; see Higgins & Bargh, 1987, for a review). Perceived applicability concerns both the *perceived relevance* of some information for use in a current task and the *perceived appropriateness* of using it. Even when stored information is activated because of its applicability to the input, it will not be consciously used if it is perceived as being either irrelevant or inappropriate.

When knowledge is available, the synapse model proposes that the various sources of excitation combine additively (except under certain conditions discussed in Higgins, 1989b). Most importantly, the model proposes that different combinations of sources of excitation that yield the same final level of excitation are not distinguishable. That is, as in misattribution and excitation transfer effects (see, e.g., Zillman, 1978), people do not know the source of their excitation levels. When stored knowledge is activated and applied to input to provide subjective meaning, the perceiver does not know to what extent the subjective meaning derived from his or her past knowledge, the momentary context, or the features of the input. The person source of chronic knowledge accessibility and the situation sources of contextual priming and input applicability combine to produce a final level of excitation that is experienced only as an outcome.

A synapse model account of the person–situation relation in terms of person and situation sources of knowledge activation is not restricted to any single "interaction" assumption (see Endler, 1982; Olweus, 1977). The model could be either considered mechanistic/unidirectional because the joint effects of the sources are described as a linear combination, or considered dynamic/interdependent because the explanation of the combination is process-oriented and emphasizes interrelations between person and situation sources. If availability or perceived applicability of stored knowledge is manipulated, moreover, statistical interaction effects rather than additive main effects of the person and situation sources should be found (see Higgins, 1989b).

Thus far, the proposed theory of the person–situation relation in terms of knowledge activation has incorporated the first two postulates outlined earlier (i.e., subjective meaning as a product of both person and situation sources) and contains some idiographic assumptions (i.e., individual differences in knowledge availability, accessibility, and applicability). It is time to add the importance element of psychological significance, as well as to expand the model by incorporating the second two postulates and further idiographic assumptions. This will involve proposing typologies of standards and self-belief patterns, and discussing how activation of such knowledge structures influences people's social information processing and emotional–motivational states.

SOCIAL STANDARDS AND PSYCHOLOGICAL SIGNIFICANCE

Any model of person–situation relations has a special interest in predicting social action. And, as noted by Weber in the quotation at the beginning of the chapter, action is social insofar as its psychologial significance derives from and takes into account other people. A standard, as stated earlier, is a criterion or rule established by experience, desires, or authority for the measure of quantity and extent or quality and value. Social standards are those standards that are established by past interpersonal experiences, knowledge of self and others, and current social contexts. Action that occurs in relation to social standards, therefore, is social action. Thus, a model of person–situation relations will be enhanced by considering the nature of social standards and their impact on both the meaning and the importance of social events.

A typology of social standards has been proposed (Higgins, Strauman, & Klein, 1986). The following description of social standards expands and somewhat modifies this typology. Table 12.1 provides a summary of the proposed classification of different types of social standards.

Factuals

"Factuals" are standards that involve a person's beliefs about the actual attributes (e.g., traits,

appearance, performance, outcomes, opinions) of one or more persons. Users subjectively experience such standards as real entities (i.e., as having actually occurred or existed). Of course, the user's belief that the standard is factual need not be objectively accurate. As outlined in Table 12.1, there are four basic kinds of factual standards:

1. *Social category factuals.* A "social category factual" is a person's representation of a factual standard defined by the "average" (e.g., mean, median, modal, prototypical) attributes of the members of some social category or group. The perceiver may or may not be a member of the social category or group in question. Many studies have found that changes in the social category standard to which a perceiver compares a target person (self or other) influence

TABLE 12.1. A Classification of Types of Social Standards

A. Factuals
  1. Social category factuals
  2. Meaningful-other factuals
  3. Biographical factuals
  4. Social context factuals
B. Guides
  1. Self-guides
    a. Ideal/own self-guide
    b. Ideal/other self-guide
    c. Ought/own self-guide
    d. Ought/other self-guide
  2. Other-guides
    a. Ideal other-guide
    b. Ought other-guide
  3. Normative guides
    a. Ideal normative guide
    b. Ought normative guide
  4. Social context guides
    a. Ideal social context guide
    b. Ought social context guide
C. Possibilities
  1. Self-possibilities
    a. Can self-possibility
    b. Future self-possibility
    c. Counterfactual self-possibility
  2. Other-possibilities
    a. Can other-possibility
    b. Future other-possibility
    c. Counterfactual other-possibility
  3. Social context possibilities
    a. Can social context possibility
    b. Future social context possibility
    c. Counterfactual social context possibility

---

the perceiver's evaluative and regulatory responses to the target (see Higgins, Strauman, & Klein, 1986). Reference groups, for example, can function as sources of information about the modal attributes or outcomes of members of a social group that serve as points of comparison or reference points in social evaluation (see Hyman, 1942; Kelley, 1952).

2. *Meaningful-other factuals.* A "meaningful-other factual" is a person's representation of a factual standard defined by the attributes of another individual who is meaningful to the perceiver, either because of the appropriateness or *relevance* of the individual's attributes for social comparison (Bernstein & Crosby, 1980; Festinger, 1954; Goethals & Darley, 1977), or because of his or her personal *importance* to the perceiver. The meaningful other may or may not be a personal acquaintance of the perceiver (e.g., a movie star) and may or may not be currently living (e.g., a deceased older brother). Merton and Kitt (1952) describe such meaningful others to whom soldiers in World War II may have idiosyncratically compared their lot—a civilian friend in a "cushy" job back home, a cousin enjoying life as a war correspondent, an undrafted movie star described in a magazine. Reference to a meaningful other can also influence judgments of others (Nisbett & Ross, 1980; Sarbin et al., 1960). Indeed, reference to self as a meaningful other has been described as a major determinant of people's judgments of others (see Higgins, 1981; Markus & Smith, 1981; Ross, 1977).

3. *Biographical factuals.* A "biographical factual" is a person's representation of a factual standard defined by the target's own past attributes (i.e., a temporal comparison). Children, especially, have been described as judging their current performance by comparing it to their past performance (see Ruble, 1983; Suls & Mullen, 1982; Veroff, 1969), but adults do so as well. And either recent or remote past performances or attributes can be used as reference points (see Brickman, Coates, & Janoff-Bulman, 1978).

4. *Social context factuals.* A "social context factual" is a person's representation of a factual standard defined by the attributes of the immediate context of people to whom the perceiver is currently exposed (and notices). The social context can include one or more people. Social category factuals, meaningful-other factuals, and biographical factuals are person variables because they are relatively chronic standards that people bring into immediate situations (where they may or may not be activated). In contrast, social context factuals are situation variables.

The developmental literature reports that children begin by early elementary school age to evaluate a target's performance (self or other) by comparing the target's performance to the performance of other children in their immediate context (see Dweck & Elliot, 1983; Ruble, 1983). For adults as well, when there is a salient immediate context of other people, the reference point is often given by the context (e.g., Manis & Armstrong, 1971; Morse & Gergen, 1970; Sherman, Ahlm, Berman, & Lynn 1978; see Higgins & Stangor, 1988, for a review). Manis and Armstrong (1971), for example, found that subjects evaluated neutral faces more positively when they appeared within a context of unpleasant faces than when they appeared within a context of pleasant faces. And Sherman et al. (1978) found that subjects judged the importance of recycling to be greater when it was judged in the context of relatively unimportant social issues than when it was judged in the context of relatively important social issues.

Guides

"Guides" are standards that involve representations of those attributes that, from the standpoint of some social appraiser (self, specific other, or social group), are valued or preferred for some social target (self, specific other, or social group). As outlined in Table 12.1, people represent valued end states for themselves that are associated with beliefs about and responses to them as individual targets ("self-guides"), and they represent valued end states for specific other people that are associated with their own beliefs about and responses to these people as individual targets ("other-guides"). People also represent attributes valued by some group for those who enact or participate in socially defined roles or situations ("normative guides"). Finally, people represent the valued attributes communicated and emphasized by others in specific momentary contexts ("social context guides").

Much of the literature on guides has been concerned with chronic self-regulatory and self-evaluative processes. Thus, the focus has been on self-guides and normative guides. The traditional self and psychodynamic literatures suggest a variety of such guides that people use. James (1890/1948) distinguished between the "spiritual" self, which resembles Kelley's (1952) normative reference group as a standard representing moral and religious social expectations, and the "ideal social" self, which involves a person's representation of others' hopes and aspirations for him or her and beliefs about his or her potential. Cooley (1902/1964) similarly described a social "ideal" self built up by imagining how a "better I" would appear in the minds of admired others. The literature also describes a standard involving what a person would like to be (e.g., Allport, 1955; Lewin, 1935; Rogers, 1961). Both Rogers (1961) and Lewin (1935) distinguished between a person's own hopes about what he or she would like to be and the expectations of authority figures concerning what a person should be. Heider (1958) described the disharmony that can occur when people's personal wishes are in conflict with ought prescriptions. Freud's "ego ideal" also involved both imaginary ideal possibilities and a representation of societal moral and ethical standards (see Cameron, 1963; Freud, 1923/1961).

The literature has suggested a variety of different types of guides that influence self-regulation and self-evaluation, but has not provided a consistent or systematic framework for distinguishing among them. Nor has the literature been explicit about distinguishing among self-guides, other-guides, and normative guides. The following typology is an initial attempt to do so.

1. *Self-guides.* To begin with, my colleagues and I (see Higgins, 1987; Higgins, Strauman, & Klein, 1986) attempted to organize self-guide distinctions in terms of two dimensions—domains of the self (i.e., "ideal" and "ought") and standpoints on the self (i.e., "own" and "significant other"). This yielded the following four basic kinds of self-guides:

a. *Ideal/own self-guide*—a person's representation of the attributes that he or she would ideally like to possess; a person's own hopes, wishes, and aspirations for himself or herself.

b. *Ideal/other self-guide*—a person's representation of the attributes that some significant other (e.g., mother, father, spouse, boss) or reference group would ideally like him or her to possess; a person's beliefs concerning the hopes, wishes, and aspirations held for him or her by some significant other or reference group.

c. *Ought/own self-guide*—a person's representation of the attributes that he or she ought to possess; a person's own beliefs about his or her duty, obligations, and responsibilities.

d. *Ought/other self-guide*—a person's representation of the attributes that some significant other or reference group believes he or she ought to possess; a person's beliefs about a significant other's or reference group's sense of his or her duty, obligations, and responsibilities.

2. *Other-guides.* People not only represent the end states that they and others value for themselves as targets; they also represent the end states they personally value for other individuals as targets. Other-guides involve the perceiver's own standpoint on a specific other person as target and can involve either the ideal or ought domain as follows:

a. *Ideal other-guide*—a person's representation of the attributes that he or she would ideally like some specific person to possess; a person's hopes, wishes, and aspirations for a specific person.

b. *Ought other-guide*—a person's representation of the attributes that he or she believes that a specific other person ought to possess; a person's beliefs about a specific other person's duty, obligations, and responsibilities.

3. *Normative guides.* Self-guides and other-guides involve representations of valued end states for oneself as target or for another person as target. Thus, self-guides and other-guides are individual standards in the sense that they apply to some individual as target. In contrast, normative guides involve representations of the attributes that some group prefers or demands that others possess when engaging in particular roles and situations. Such guides are perceived as being shared by members of the group (which may or may not be true). The group could be very large, such as "people in general," or quite small, such as "people like me." The perceiver may or may not be a member of the group. In any case, normative guides are subjectively perceived as *social* standards rather than as individual standards.

Earlier, I have discussed the function of reference groups as providing social category factuals or points of comparison in social evaluation. As Kelley (1952) pointed out, a reference group can also function to provide a person with a set of norms or values that he or she believes is shared by members of the reference group (see also Merton & Kitt, 1952;

Newcomb, 1952; Sherif, 1948). Normative guides pertain to this second function of reference groups.

Often the same normative guides are available to most members of a community. In this sense they are unlike the personality variable of self-guides. Nevertheless, as reflected in the personality variable of "social desirability" or the "need for approval" (see, e.g., Crowne & Marlowe, 1964), there can still be differences in the extent to which people are regulated by the same normative guides. In addition, normative guides can vary across people when the people come from different cultures or subcultures. Moreover, even in the same subculture, there can be individual differences in the chronic accessibility of the different normative guides associated with different reference groups. And individuals with different values can have different normative guides if each believes that others generally, or at least similar others, share his or her values (i.e., the different normative guides are associated with different perceived in-groups).

The applicability of different normative guides varies across situations, because different normative guides are associated with different roles and situations. In addition, the accessibility of normative guides can vary as a result of contextual priming. Hornstein, Lakind, Frankel, and Manne (1975), for example, report that subjects who had been previously exposed to a news broadcast describing a charitable person were more likely to behave cooperatively and expect others to behave cooperatively than subjects who had not heard the news broadcast. (See also Wilson & Capitman, 1982, for evidence of a decay in such prosocial effects of contextual priming when there is a delay between priming and exposure to the social input.) In another study of prosocial behavior by Harvey and Enzle (1981), subjects were or were not exposed to rules that varied in their association to the normative guide of helping others (e.g., "People should not harm others" vs. "People should obey the speed limit"). Subjects were most likely to help another person subsequently in those conditions in which the helping normative guide was made more accessible from exposure to a highly associated rule.

Normative guides, then, have the interesting property of varying across both people and situations. As discussed by Pool, Shweder, and Much (1983; see also Much & Shweder, 1978; Nucci & Turiel, 1978), normative guides also vary in their prescriptivity (i.e., the degree of cultural preference that conduct proceed in one way or another), their obligation (i.e., the extent to which the rule is binding or required regardless of what anyone wants to do), and their importance. Morals (ethics) differ from conventions (customs) in these respects. Whereas moral have a clear "ought" characteristic, conventions can have more of an "ideal" characteristic, in the sense that they represent attributes that are preferred and considered desirable but are not considered obligatory. For example, many Americans understand that the larger society considers eating turkey on Thanksgiving to be desirable but does not demand that everyone do so. More generally, there are cultural goals that function more as frames of aspirational reference or cultural preferences than as prescriptions or obligations (see Merton, 1957). In addition, attributes can be perceived as ideal because they are perceived as the usual way of being or doing things. They are normative in the sense that they occur most frequently. As such, they become highly familiar and in turn preferred (see Zajonc, 1968).

Thus, two basic types of normative guides can be distinguished as follows:

a. *Ideal normative guide*—a person's representation of the attributes that some group would ideally like people to possess in particular roles and situations; the attributes (perceived as) wanted and preferred in socially defined roles and situations.

b. *Ought normative guide*—a person's representation of the attributes that some group believes people ought to possess in particular roles and situations; the attributes (perceived as) demanded and prescribed in socially defined roles and situations.

4. *Social context guides.* Self-guides, other-guides, and normative guides are chronic representations of valued attributes for specific target individuals (self or other) or for socially defined roles or situations. Such chronic guides constitute general goals, rules, and orientations for self or others that a person brings into a particular momentary context. As such, they are person variables (although normative guides also contain general situational information). But any specific context also has its own momentary set of goals, rules, and constraints that are emphasized and communicated by the participants in the immediate situation. Such context-specific guides are situation variables.

Indeed, social control is the process by which

participants in a context press for obedience to
their rules, which may or may not be the same
as an individual's chronic guides (see Homans,
1950). The participants in a particular context
can also emphasize social interaction goals and
task goals that differ from the individual's
chronic guides. In experimental, studies, for
example, the experimenter often gives instructions to subjects that communicate both
particular rules that each subject should follow
and specific goals that the experimenter wants
each subject to pursue. In his classic book on
social structure and personality, Parsons (1964)
distinguishes orientations to normative patterns (i.e., normative guides) from orientations
to the urgent, immediate demands belonging to
the occasion, the exigencies of a particular context.

Two basic types of contextual guides can be
distinguished as follows:

a. *Ideal social context guide*—a person's representation of the attributes that the participants
in the current context would ideally like other
participants (including him or her) to possess;
the attributes (perceived as) wanted and preferred by the context participants.

b. *Ought social context guide*—a person's
representation of the attributes that the participants in the current context believe other participants (including him or her) ought to possess; the attributes (perceived as) demanded
and prescribed by the context participants.

Guides represent valued attributes or end
states. A fuller account of the role of guides in
social behavior must also consider the means
that people use to attain their valued ends.
Although there is a clear recognition of the
importance of strategies, procedures, programs,
and scripts in self-regulation (see, e.g., Cantor
& Kihlstrom, 1987; Carver & Scheier, 1981;
Markus & Wurf, 1987; Showers & Cantor,
1985; Smith, 1984), there has generally been
less consideration of means than of ends in
personality and social psychology (but see Kanfer, 1971; Kuhl, 1984; Merton, 1957; Mischel
& Patterson, 1978; Schank & Abelson, 1977;
Spivak, Platt, & Shure, 1976). Different types
of guide procedures could be and need to be
distinguished, including self-guide procedures,
other-guide procedures, normative guide procedures, and social context guide procedures.
But such a discussion is beyond the scope of this
chapter.

Possibilities

"Possibilities" are standards involving representations of the attributes of a target person
(self or other) that are perceived to be nonfac-
tual (i.e., to have never actually existed for the
target) but are perceived as possible (i.e., will
exist, could or might exist, could have or might
have existed). As possibilities, they may be
perceived to be either realistic or unrealistic.
Table 12.1 outlines the different types of
possibilities.

1. *Self-possibilities.* The bulk of the literature
has been concerned with possibilities for the
self. The following basic types of self-
possibilities have been described in the literature:

a. *Can self-possibility*—a person's representation of the attributes that someone (own or
other standpoint) believes he or she can possess; beliefs about one's capabilities or potential. James (1890/1948) described a potential
self as a standard to which people compare their
actual selves. More recently, a number of motivational models have emphasized the importance of the potential self, or people's representation of the type of person they believe
they are capable of becoming (see Bandura,
1982, 1986; Cantor, Markus, Niedenthal, &
Nurius, 1986; de Charms, 1968; Deci & Ryan,
1985; Higgins, Tykocinski, & Vookles, in
press; Markus, 1983; Markus & Nurius, 1986)
or would both like to be and think they really
can be (Schlenker, 1985).

b. *Future self-possibility*—a person's representation of the attributes that someone (own or
other standpoint) believes he or she is likely to
possess in the future; expectations about the
type of person one will become. There is a long
history of theories in personality and social psychology that emphasize the influence of people's outcome expectancies on their motivation
and behavioral intentions (e.g., Ajzen & Fishbein, 1970; Atkinson, 1964; Kelly, 1955;
Lewin, 1935; Rotter, 1954). Some of the outcome expectancies discussed in these models,
however, derive from the immediate context
rather than from a person's chronic expectancies about his or her future attributes or end
states. More recent models explicitly propose
that people are motivated by representations of
a future self or probable possible self (e.g., Higgins et al., in press; Markus & Nurius, 1986).

c. *Counterfactual self-possibility*—a person's

representation of the actual self-attributes that he or she might have possessed in the past or present, as alternatives to the actual self-attributes that he or she did and does possess. Counterfactual selves include fantasies and dreams (or nightmares) about oneself (see, e.g., Freud, 1923/1961; Horney, 1950; Levinson, 1978; Singer, 1976), others' viewpoint on one's actual self that differs from one's own viewpoint (see, e.g., Erikson, 1963; Mead, 1934; Stryker, 1980), and mental simulations of possible self-states that differ from the actual state of affairs (see Kahneman & Miller, 1986; Kahneman & Tversky, 1982; Miller, Turnbull, & Farland, 1989).

2. *Other-possibilities.* Other-possibilities include the same three basic types as self-possibilities, as shown in Table 12.1.

3. *Social context possibilities.* Self-possibilities and other-possibilities constitute a person's chronic beliefs about the attributes that he or she or another person can, will, or might possess (person variables). Such chronic beliefs are representations of possibilities that the person brings into a particular context. But the momentary context may also provide input concerning a target person's possibilities (a situation variable). In experimental studies of achievement motivation, for example, "false feedback" manipulations often convey information about subjects' capabilities (i.e, *can* possibilities) and "task difficulty" manipulations often convey information about the likelihood of future success or failure (i.e., *future* possibilities). Dissonance studies examining postdecisional regret may make salient the positive attributes of the forsaken alternative that a subject might have possessed (i.e., *counterfactual* possibilities). Social context possibilities, then, include the same three basic types as self- and other-possibilities as shown in Table 12.1.

General Comments

This section has presented a typology of social standards. Three major types of standards have been described—factuals, guides, and possibilities—along with a variety of subtypes. The psychological significance of a behavior–standard match, mismatch, or nonmatch is different for different types of standards. For example, a mismatch between the actual self and an ideal self-guide signifies "the absence of positive outcomes," whereas a mismatch between the ac-

tual self and an ought self-guide signifies "the (expected) presence of negative outcomes" (Higgins, 1987). Indeed, even the psychological significance of a mismatch between the actual self and an ideal self-guide is different for different relations between the ideal self-guide and the can and future self-possibilities. For instance, when the ideal self-guide matches the can self-possibility, the self-discrepancy pattern as a whole signifies "chronic failure to meet one's positive potential" (Higgins et al., in press). These differences in psychological significance, moreover, are associated with distinct emotional vulnerabilities (see Higgins, 1987; Higgins et al., in press). In a later section, the psychological significance of different social-psychological situations, such as "cognitive dissonance" and "obedience to authority," is also shown to involve distinct patterns of relations to different kinds of standards.

This section has emphasized the phenomenological differences among the various types of standards. It should be noted, however, that standards also have a common feature—their *multifunctionality*. Standards can function either as reference points or as regulatory criteria. Vulnerability to emotional problems, for example, may be associated with a general tendency to use self-guides not only as valued end states in self-regulation, but also as reference points in self-evaluation, such as when people judge their performance to be a "success" or a "failure" depending on whether it matches their high personal ideal rather than a more objective, factual criterion (see Higgins & Moretti, 1988). It is also possible for a factual standard to function as a regulatory criterion. For example, a competitively oriented person may be motivated to surpass the performance of another person. Indeed, the same information may function as a reference point or as a self-regulatory criterion for different people in the same context. In Asch's classic study of social influence (see Asch, 1952), for example, the judgments of the other group members could have functioned either as a reference point for subjects to interpret whether or not their own judgment was "correct" (i.e., informational conformity) or as an end state defining the "right" judgment (i.e., normative conformity; see Deutsch & Gerard, 1955).

In addition to being multifunctional, standards also constitute different kinds of knowledge—general declarative knowledge (e.g., social category standards), episodic knowledge (e.g., autobiographical standards), and procedural knowledge (e.g., normative guides). Therefore, the person–situation relations involved in knowledge activation described earlier occur for standards as well. It is time now to consider how knowledge activation and social standards as variables in a common language of personality and social psychology can be used to examine the complexities of person–situation relations in more detail. To begin with, person–situation relations at various stages of information processing are considered.

MULTIPLE FORMS OF PERSON–SITUATION RELATIONS

The personality and social psychology literature has provided examples of different kinds of "person × situation interactions" involving various kinds of personalities interacting with various kinds of situations. However, less attention has been paid to the nature of the interaction itself—to distinguishing among different *forms* of interaction. From an information-processing perspective, one would expect there to be different forms of "person × situation interactions" associated with different kinds of social information processing. Endler (1982) has emphasized the need to distinguish between perception of and reaction to situations when considering forms of person × situation interactions. From an information-processing perspective, other stages need to be distinguished as well.

When one begins to consider all the person–situation relations that occur in ongoing social interactions, one despairs of describing them intelligibly. It is not my purpose to be exhaustive (or to exhaust the reader), however. Rather, the purpose of this section is to combine an information-processing perspective and the common language of standards and knowledge activation in order to illustrate some of the multiple kinds of person–situation relations that are possible.

Exposure to Input

Before information processing begins, a person is typically exposed to some input information. Experimental studies in personality and social psychology are designed to control subjects' ex-

posure to input. Yet, as Snyder and Ickes (1985) point out, individuals in the natural course of their lives also have some control both over the situations they enter and over the input to which they expose themselves (see also Buss, 1987; Merton, 1957; Olweus, 1977; Wachtel, 1973). People may prefer some situations over others because the social context guides of the participants or the normative guides associated with the role and situation allow them to fulfill their self-guides. For example, participating in a particular situation may pressure or permit them to be the kind of person they want to be or believe they ought to be.

When people expose themselves to input, they may also select one kind of "data" rather than another because the personal significance of each alternative has a different relation to their standards. From the perspective of cognitive dissonance and selective exposure (Festinger, 1957), for example, people may avoid input that they believe would suggest that they have acted inconsistently with their self-guides (see, e.g., Aronson, 1969; Deutsch, Krauss, & Rosenau, 1962). Experimental studies may also manipulate momentary social context guides that influence the kinds of data a person is motivated to seek. Kruglanski and Mayseless (1988), for example, found that subjects asked an interviewee different questions about himself or herself, depending on whether they believed the purpose of the interview was to be accurate or to make quick decisions. Although these different epistemic motivations (i.e., need to avoid closure vs. need for closure) were situation variables in this study, they can also be person variables (see Kruglanski, 1989).

Given that different situations have different input (e.g., context guides, target person data), and that the significance of this input varies for different individuals (e.g., it matches, mismatches, or is irrelevant to self-guides), the control that people have over exposing themselves to input creates an important and early form of person–situation relation. For example, people's choices of entertainment have been found to be a joint function of differences in people's sensation-seeking motivation and differences in the stimulation level of various entertainment alternatives (see Zuckerman, 1988). This form of person–situation relation nicely exemplifies the interaction between personal need and situational press, emphasized by Murray (1938).

People not only have control over the input to which they expose themselves; when they do expose themselves to the input, they often change the input by their presence (see Bowers, 1973; Buss, 1987). This can occur because the behaviors of the entrant unintentionally influence the behaviors of the situation participants, as when aggressive children elicit aggressive responses in other children (e.g., Rausch, 1977) or highly active children elicit competitive and angry responses in their parents (Buss, 1987). (The phenomenon of an entrant's intentionally attempting to change or control the behavior of context participants in order to meet his or her needs is considered an output strategy and is discussed later.) Kelley and Stahelski (1970), for example, found that people whose goal choice and behavior were competitive caused a cooperative partner to become competitive. Moreover, they judged their partner to be competitive without being aware of their role in producing their partner's competitive behavior. More generally, the expectancies of perceivers concerning their interactive partner can cause them to behave toward their partner in such a way as to confirm those expectancies (e.g., Synder, Tanke, & Berscheid, 1977; Word, Zanna, & Cooper, 1974; see Darley & Fazio, 1980; Miller & Turnbull, 1986).

It is not only the behaviors of entrants that can unintentionally influence the situation participants. An entrants' social status, demographic status, or attributes (e.g., attractiveness or emotional state) can also modify the situation and its participants. Goffman (1959) has noted that information about an entrant helps to define the situation, including what is expected of the situation participants. That is, the entrant influences the context guides. The individual attributes of the entrant can also change which attributes of the other participants become salient and accessible. For example, the accessibility of gender and gender-related constructs will vary, depending on whether it is a male or a female who enters a context that currently contains only females or only males (see Higgins & King, 1981; McGuire, McGuire, & Winton, 1979). The effect of the entrant on the input depends on both the attributes of the entrant and the attributes of the context. Thus, as this case exemplifies, the change that people can produce in the input to which they expose themselves constitutes another form of person–situation relation.

Identification of Input

Once perceivers are exposed to the input, they represent the stimulus details contained in the input and then designate each stimulus as being a particular type of entity. Identification involves recognizing that the stimulus is an instance of some previously established class of actions, events, or objects (see Higgins, Strauman, & Klein, 1986; Trope, 1986). If they are unable to identify the stimulus, they may construct a new category or go to another stage to judge its significance. Identification is a process in which the perceiver's system responds to the extent of similarity or overlap in the features of the stimulus and the features in each of a set of alternative knowledge structures that can be used to characterize the stimulus (see Rosch, 1978; Tversky & Gati, 1978).

The identification stage involves knowledge activation (and construction), but does not yet involve the use of standards. Standards, as discussed earlier, are criteria for the measure of quantity and quality. Before such measurement is possible, however, one must know *what* is being measured. For example, before determining the magnitude or significance of an aggressive act, one must first judge the act to be aggressive (see Higgins, Strauman, & Klein, 1986; Trope, 1986). It is by applying stored knowledge to input, the identification stage, that such initial judgments are made. At this stage, then, the various forms of person–situation relations concern person and situation sources of knowledge accessibility and activation.

One form of person–situation relation at this stage is individual variability in which features are contained in a person's alternative knowledge structures and situational variability in which features are contained in the data (i.e., differences in applicability). This form of person–situation relation is especially likely when people from different cultures interact. For example, in identifying an "agreement," American and Japanese executives may differ both in their agreement-related behaviors and in their beliefs about the features that define an agreement.

Applicability of alternative knowledge structures to data as a form of person–situation relation provides a partial answer to a classic issue in personality: When are individual differences revealed (see Epstein, 1983; Pervin, 1985; Snyder & Ickes, 1985)? It has been suggested in the literature that individual differences are most likely to be revealed when situations are "weak" (see Snyder & Ickes, 1985). One way in which situations can be weak is for the data to be either ambiguous (e.g., the Thematic Apperception Test) or vague (e.g., the Roschach). The impact of individual differences in chronic knowledge accessibility on identification of input is likely to be greater when the data is ambiguous or vague, because the relative contribution to the excitation level of a particular stored construct from prior accessibility (as a person variable), compared to the input's feature overlap with the construct (as a situation variable), is greater. Moreover, as discussed earlier, the effects of chronic knowledge accessibility on identification are different for ambiguous and vague input. Thus, there are different forms of person–situation relations and different ways to reveal individual differences, depending on the type of "weak" data used.

Applicability of alternative knowledge structures to the data is one determinant of identification. Another determinant is knowledge accessibility. As discussed earlier, the sources of accessibility include expectancies, motivational orientations, and prior activation. Momentary contexts (as a situation variable) via each of these sources can modify the relative accessibility of individuals' alternative knowledge structures (a person variable), thereby influencing identification (for a review, see Higgins & Stangor, 1988).

First, momentary contexts can induce different expectancies in more or less subtle ways. In a class example of a more subtle manipulation. Bruner and Minturn (1955) first showed subjects a series of either letters or numbers, and then presented the subjects with a "broken" capital B, which had a small separation between the vertical and the curved part of the letter such that it could be identified either as a "B" or as a "13." Subjects identified the figure as a "B" when they had been previously exposed to letters, but identified it as a "13" when they had been previously exposed to numbers. In another classic study involving a less subtle manipulation, Kelley (1950) gave students an expectancy that their new instructor was either a "warm" person or a "cold" person prior to the instructor's arrival. This contextual set had a significant impact on the students' judgments of the new instructor.

Momentary contexts can also influence motivational orientation by inducing specific emotional/arousal states or goals. Clark, Milberg, and Erber (1984), for example, found that aroused subjects were more likely than nonaroused subjects to identify positive facial expressions as a high-arousal expression (joy) than a low-arousal expression (serenity) (see also Stangor, 1986, reported in Higgins & Stangor, 1988). Cohen and Ebbesen (1979) found that subjects even attended to different behavioral features of a target person, as measured by Newtson's (1973) unitizing measure, depending on whether they were given the goal to form an impression of the target or to remember the target's behaviors (for a review of the information-processing effects of contextually induced goals, see Wyer & Srull, 1986).

Contextual priming is another way in which momentary contexts can influence identification. As discussed earlier, recent and frequent prior activation of stored knowledge increases the likelihood that the stored knowledge will be used subsequently to identify stimuli to which it is applicable (e.g., Higgins et al., 1977; Srull & Wyer, 1979, 1980). Carver et al. (1983), for example, first had subjects view a videotape portrarying either a hostile or a neutral employer interacting with his secretary as part of a supposed study on long-term memory. Then, in an "unrelated" study during the same session, the subjects were asked to make judgments of the vaguely hostile behaviors of a target person. Subjects identified the target person as being more hostile when "hostility" had been previously primed by observing a hostile model on the videotape. Thus, contextual priming can occur simply from prior observation of models of different types of attributes. Indeed, Bargh and Pietromonaco (1982) showed that it was not even necessary for people to be aware of the contextual priming event when it occurred in order for priming to influence subsequent judgments.

Prolonged situational determinants of long-term expectancies, motivational orientations, and frequent activation (e.g., socialization background) are also sources of chronic individual differences in accessibility (see Higgins & King, 1981). An especially important type of long-term expectancy is the stereotypic belief. Stereotypic beliefs are especially likely to influence social judgments when there is little direct information about the target (i.e., vague or impoverished data) and when the judgment is not based directly on the data (see Higgins & Bargh, 1987). Nevertheless, even when there is direct information about the target and the judgment is presumably based on the data, stereotypic beliefs can influence judgments as long as the data are not highly diagnostic. In a study by Darley and Gross (1983), for example, subjects viewed a videotape of a fourth-grade female child that portrayed her performance on a variety of achievement test problems in an inconsistent or ambiguous manner. The same target information was used to identify the target as possessing high or low abilities, depending on whether the subjects believed that the child was from a high or a low socioeconomic background, respectively.

Stereotypic beliefs as a person variable can interact with contextual variables (e.g., target data, contextual priming) to produce another form of person–situation relation. In one study (Higgins & King, 1981, Study 1), for example, subjects read about a target person who ostensibly was either male or female and whose behavior exemplified both stereotypically male traits (e.g., ambitious, selfish) and stereotypically female traits (e.g., polite, dependent). The other experimental manipulation was the sex composition of the group in which a subject performed the person perception task. Some subjects were the solitary member of their gender in the group, whereas other subjects were the same gender as all but one of the other members of the group (e.g., a female majority/ solo male group consisting of a female experimenter, two or three female subjects, and one solitary male subject). All subjects performed the task independently, and no talking was permitted. Encoding and identification of the target person information was measured indirectly through subjects' recall of the target information. A three-way interaction among sex of target, sex-relatedness of stereotypic information, and subject group sex composition was found. The pattern of results suggested that when a subject's gender was in the minority, thus making the subject more conscious of gender as a person attribute, the subject inhibited using stereotypic beliefs when encoding the target person.

A recent study by Devine (1989, Study 3) also found that low-prejudice subjects inhibited expressing stereotypic beliefs about a group (black Americans) when the context of the person perception task made the subjects conscious of group membership as a person characteristic. All subjects in the study of group sex composition were likely to have been relatively low-prejudice in regard to gender. In Devine's study, however, half of the white subjects were low-prejudice and half were high-prejudice in regard to black Americans. Although both groups of subjects had equal knowledge of black American pejorative stereotypes, low-prejudice subjects apparently inhibited applying pejorative traits to black Americans. One explanation for this finding is that the chronic personal guides of the low-prejudice subjects (e.g., self-guides valuing liberality and tolerance) and the social context guide introduced by the experimenter (which raised conscious concerns with applying stereotypic beliefs) combined to lower the perceived applicability of the accessible pejorative traits to the target. (See the earlier discussion of "perceived applicability" as a knowledge activation variable.) Interpreted in this way, this study demonstrates a new form of person–situation relation in which the perceived applicability of stored knowledge to a target, which is itself a person–situation relation (i.e., a theory–data relation), is influenced by both perceivers' chronic orientations to some target (a person variable) and the extent to which the momentary context makes the perceivers conscious of the issue of applicability (a situation variable).

Perceivers' chronic interpersonal orientations (a person variable) can also interact with contextually induced differences in interpersonal orientation (a situation variable) to influence how a target person is encoded. In a study by Battistich and Aronoff (1985), for example, subjects who were either high on dominance or high on dependency expected to interact either cooperatively or competitively with a target person whom they saw on videotape performing a combination of assertive-related and affiliative-related behaviors. The subjects' descriptions and judgments of the target person after viewing the tape reflected the impact of both the person-related and situation-related interpersonal orientations, as well as the particular target behaviors that were observed (another situation variable).

Yet another form of person–situation relation has been mentioned briefly earlier—the interaction of individual differences in the chronic accessibility of alternative constructs (a person variable) and contextual differences in the temporary accessibility of alternative constructs produced by priming (a situation variable). This form of person–situation relation was examined in a recent study by Bargh, Lombardi, and Higgins (1988). All subjects were primed by recent exposure to a trait construct that could be used to characterize the behavior of a target person in a subsequent task. The subjects were preselected so that the alternative trait construct for categorizing the behavioral description was a chronically accessible construct for half of the subjects but was not for the other half of the subjects. As in the study by Higgins et al. (1985) that compared the effects of recent versus frequent priming, the delay between the priming task and the categorization task was either short or long. When the alternative trait construct was chronically accessible for subjects, a crossover pattern was found: Subjects tended to use the recently primed construct to categorize the target's behavior after the short delay, but to use the chronically accessible construct after the long delay.

Interpretation and Appraisal of Input

After perceivers identify what a stimulus is, they typically move to determining its magnitude and significance. At this stage, then, an identified stimulus (as one mental element) may be related to a standard (another mental element) as a criterion for judging or inferring the relative quantity or quality of the stimulus. Thus, standards will now function as a major type of content in the process of knowledge activation.

Interpretation involves inferring or construing the meaning or implications of a stimulus, and appraisal involves an overall estimation of the worth or value of the stimulus. Given the multifunctionality of standards discussed earlier, the same standard can be used for both interpretation and appraisal. It is probably more common, however, for different standards to be used at the interpretation and appraisal stages (see Higgins, Strauman, & Klein, 1986).

It is often difficult to distinguish between identification and interpretation of an event, especially when they are linguistically encoded. For example, the statement "Tom was helpful" may refer either to a recognition that Tom's act was an instance of the "helpful" performance class (i.e., identification) or to a judgment that Tom's helpful act was more helpful than the acts of the other people in the situation (i.e.,

interpretation of an identified act in relation to a social context factual standard). It is also difficult to know when an interpretation involves a causal attribution rather than simply a judgment relative to some standard. It should be noted, however, that at least some variables in attribution theory, such as "consensus," "consistency," or "social desirability" (e.g., Heider, 1958; Jones & Davis, 1965; Kelley, 1967), could be described in terms of variables in standard theory, such as social category factuals, biographical factuals, and normative guides (see Higgins, Strauman, & Klein, 1986). In any case, for the purpose of describing additional forms of person–situation relations, what is most important about interpretation and appraisal processes is that they often (if not typically) involve the use of some standard of evaluation.

Experimenter-provided information about the performance of others can strongly influence people's interpretation of a target person's performance (for reviews, see Higgins & Stangor, 1988; Ruble, 1983). In a series of studies, for example, my colleagues and I have found that subjects' initial judgments of a target judge's sentencing decisions vary as a function of the harshness or leniency of the sentencing decisions of other trial judges that they read about at the same time (see Higgins & Stangor, 1988). This variation in initial judgments resulted from subjects' using the context information as a factual standard rather than from a perceptual, adaptation-level effect, because subjects' judgments and memory of the input were initially independent. These studies demonstrated another form of person–situation relation. In addition to manipulating the social context factual in the first session, we created an individual difference in the subjects' available knowledge of trial judges' sentencing decisions by exposing different groups of subjects to different instances of trial judges' sentencing decisions across the two sessions of the study. The studies found that subjects' initial judgment based on the immediate social context factual provided in the first session (a situation variable) and the social category factual acquired by subjects across the two sessions (a person variable) functioned together to determine subjects' subsequent recall of the target judge's behavior.

An interaction of social context factuals and social category factuals is only one way in which person and situation factuals may interact. Many other versions of this form of person–situation relation are possible. For instance, people's judgments may be influenced by a combination of a social context factual and an available biographical factual. Austin, McGinn, and Susmilch (1980), for example, found that subjects' satisfaction with their reward for performing a task was influenced in an additive manner by both the level of reward received by another person for performing the same task (i.e., a social context factual as a situation variable) and the level of reward that they had previously received (i.e., an autobiographical factual as a person variable).

A related form of person–situation relation involves the interaction of guides. One version of this form of relation would be the interaction of normative guides and social context guides. The values and preferences of a particular group can have an impact on a person through the person acquiring them as normative guides (e.g., socialization into the group) and by being exposed to them as social context guides when interacting with members of the group. When people are members of a group they frequently encounter, their normative guides (a person variable) and the social context guides (a situation variable) are likely to be the same. But when people are not members of a group they frequently encounter, their normative guides and the social context guides may be different, which is likely to produce self-regulatory and self-evaluative conflict and emotional distress (see Van Hook & Higgins, 1988). One might expect, for example, that people who are not members of the cultural community in which they live would be more vulnerable to emotional distress than people who are members. Consistent with this expectation, Rosenberg (1962) found that people have more emotional problems when they live in a neighborhood where the predominant religion is different from their own than when they live in a neighborhood where their own religion is the predominant one, especially when the other religion values different personal qualities from those valued by their own religion.

Another form of person–situation relation involves individual differences in self-guides interacting with contextual differences in input. Indeed, Atkinson's (1964) classic account of achievement motivation can be understood in this way. As we have suggested (Higgins, Strauman, & Klein, 1986), ideal self-guides may be the basis for high-need achievers' self-

regulation, whereas ought self-guides may be the basis for low-need achievers' self-regulation (a person variable). Information about task difficulty, on the other hand, is typically provided by the experimenter, by properties of the task itself, or by exposure to the performance of others on the task (a situation variable). Thus, the classic interaction between high-need versus low-need achievers and high versus low task difficulty in regard to achievement motivation reflects another form of person–situation relation.

There are other cases of contextual differences in input interacting with individual differences in self-guides. In one study (Higgins, Bond, Klein, & Strauman, 1986, Study 1), for example, undergraduates listed their actual self-attributes (their self-concept), their ideal self-attributes (their ideal/own and ideal/other self-guides), and their ought self-attributes (their ought/own and ought/other self-guides). For each subject, an actual–ideal self-discrepancy score and an actual–ought self-discrepancy score were obtained. Two types of individuals were then identified—those with a high actual–ideal discrepancy score but a low actual–ought discrepancy score, and those with a high actual–ought discrepancy score and a low actual–ideal discrepancy score (a person variable). In the experimental session a few weeks later, the subjects were asked to imagine either a positive or a negative event (a situation variable). A self-discrepancy, like any other available knowledge structure, should only be activated when the input is applicable. Thus, it was predicted that the individual difference in which type of self-guide was part of the discrepancy would only produce differences in emotional responses when subjects imagined a negative event (e.g., receiving a grade of "D" on an important exam). As expected, there was no difference between the actual–ideal discrepancy subjects and the actual–ought discrepancy subjects when a positive event was the input. But when a negative event was the input, the actual–ideal discrepancy subjects became more dejected (e.g., discouraged, sad), whereas the actual–ought subjects became more agitated (e.g., afraid, tense).

A related form of person–situation relation consists of individual differences in types of self-discrepancies as the person variable and type of contextual priming (rather than type of input) as the situational variable. Another study (Higgins, Bond, et al, 1986, Study 2) exemplifies this form of relation. In this study, two new types of individuals were identified—those who possessed both an actual–ideal discrepancy and an actual–ought discrepancy, and those who possessed neither discrepancy. Like any other knowledge structure, a self-discrepancy cannot be activated if it is not available. Therefore, contextual priming of self-guides should have little effect on those individuals without any discrepancy. But contextual priming should have an effect on those individuals with discrepancies. In addition, the effect on these individuals should depend on the type of priming involved. If the ideal self-guide is primed, then individuals who possess both types of discrepancies should experience an increase in dejection. If the ought self-guide is primed, then such individuals should experience an increase in agitation. Type of contextual priming was manipulated in this study by having subjects think about either their own and their parents' hopes and aspirations for them (ideal self-guide priming) or their own and their parents' beliefs about their duties and obligations (ought self-guide priming). As expected, ideal priming produced increases in dejection and ought priming produced increases in agitation, but only for those individuals who had both types of discrepancies available.

If one assumes that increasing self-focused attention increases the accessibility of self-guides (see Duval & Wicklund, 1972, and Carver & Scheier, 1981, for similar proposals), then increasing self-focused attention should produce emotional problems in people who possess self-discrepancies (i.e., people with low self-esteem). As with any other knowledge structure, however, active attention to an alternative, competing standard should reduce the effects of chronically accessible self-guides (see Higgins et al., 1982), thus reducing the emotional problems of people with self-discrepancies. Both of these forms of person–situation relations were demonstrated in a study by Brockner (1979; Study 2). Subjects high and low in self-esteem (a person variable) performed a task either in the presence of a mirror and a video camera (contextual priming of self-guides), or instead with instructions to maintain undivided attention to the task at all times (a competing contextual guide: both manipulations of a situation variable). In the former condition, the high-self-esteem subjects performed much better than the low-self-esteem subjects, whereas there was, if anything, a slight reversal in the latter condition.

As discussed earlier, the literature has suggested that personality differences are more likely to be revealed when situations are "weak" (see Snyder & Ickes, 1985). The earlier discussion has identified one way for situations to be weak—to have ambiguous or vague data. Another way is for social context guides as a situational variable to be low in number, salience, or potency. The weaker the social context guides associated with a particular situation, the stronger will be the influence of personal guides on social evaluation processes. To the extent that these personal guides vary in strength and in type (e.g., ideal/own vs. ought/other self-guides), individual differences in appraisal and emotional–motivational responses will be revealed. Moreover, different forms of person–situation relations may be revealed by varying the relative strength of different social context guides as the situational variable.

Output

After people have been exposed to input, identified it, and assigned it some psychological significance, they respond to it in some manner. Experimental studies in personality and social psychology typically attempt to constrain the range of possible responses to those dimensions of interest to them; dissonance studies, for example, typically limit the possible modes of dissonance resolution to attitude change. Studies concerned with the earlier stages of processing, such as identification or interpretation, also use subjects' responses on particular measures to examine the person–situation relations involved at these stages. To this extent, we have already considered the output stage. But people's output in everyday life is rarely a direct reflection of the earlier processing stages. People who have processed the input information in the same way may nevertheless respond to it differently because of person differences (e.g., differences in procedural knowledge), situation differences (e.g., differences in contextual guides), and new forms of person–situation relations.

When we consider the output stage, the first issue is what determines how much a person responds to input that has been processed. One major determinant of the extent of responding is self-control (see, e.g., Bandura, 1986; Kanfer, 1971; Meichenbaum, 1977; Mischel, 1983; Mischel & Patterson, 1978; Spivak et al.,

1976). One kind of self-control that has received considerable attention concerns resistance to temptation or distraction. The classic paradigms for studying this kind of self-control involve presenting children with a conflict. For instance, there may be a conflict between waiting only a brief period to receive a small reward and waiting a long period to receive a large reward. Alternatively, there may be a conflict between taking time now to look at an interesting object and working within a time limit in order to receive an attractive reward later. There is considerable evidence that young children are not as effective as older children in resisting temptation or distraction (a person variable). This developmental difference has been explained in terms of younger children not having available the effective self-control procedures that older children possess (see, e.g., Mischel & Patterson, 1978). Contextual instruction, however, can make procedures for effective resistance available and accessible to young children (a situational variable), and this greatly increases young children's successful resistance. Mischel and Patterson (1978), for example, report that whereas the correlation between age and resistance to distraction was .45 without contextual instruction, the correlation was only .20 with contextual instruction for the younger children.

Counteracting individual differences in the availability of self-control procedures through exposure to contextual input for learning the procedures is one form of person–situation relation that can influence how much a person responds to stimuli. Another form of person–situation relation that can influence extent of responding involves an interaction between individual differences in response orientation from varying self-guides (a person variable) and environmental press differences from varying contextual guides (a situation variable). For instance, a social context guide can have a disinhibiting effect on eating behavior for people who have been socialized to inhibit food consumption (see Woody & Costanzo, 1981). In a study on eating behavior, for example, Herman and Mack (1975) selected subjects who were either restrained eaters (dieters) or unrestrained eaters (nondieters). Restrained eaters possess self-guides that inhibit their food intake, especially in the presence of others. Because of their dieting, restrained eaters also tend to be hungry or deprived (Nisbett, 1972). Thus, they are motivated to eat, but their self-guides inhibit consumption. When their self-

guides are accessible, then, restrained eaters should eat less than unrestrained eaters. But if there is a contextual guide that competes with and inhibits their self-guides, then unrestrained eaters may eat more because their motivation to reduce their hunger by eating is no longer inhibited by their self-guides. Herman and Mack (1975) provided such a contextual guide by requiring some subjects to eat a preload of milkshake prior to eating ice cream as part of a supposed study on the effect of one taste experience on a subsequent taste experience. When there was no preload, the restrained eaters consumed considerably less ice cream than the unrestrained eaters. But when there was a preload, the restrained eaters actually consumed more ice cream than the unrestrained eaters.

Another form of person–situation relation that influences the quantity of output responses involves individual differences in attitudes or self-guides (a person variable) that are made accessible or salient by a momentary context (a situation variable). In a study by Carver (1975), for example, some subjects condoned and some subjects opposed the use of punishment in learning situations. The presence or absence of a mirror was used to manipulate subjects' self-awareness (i.e., to manipulate the temporary accessibility of self-guides concerning use of punishment). When subjects were assigned the teacher role in a "learning experiment," the subjects' personal attitudes toward punishment influenced their use of punishment as a teacher when the mirror was present but not when the mirror was absent (see also Fazio, Chen, McDonel, & Sherman, 1982; Snyder & Kendzierski, 1982; Wicklund, 1982).

Person–situation relations not only influence the *quantity* of output responding; they also influence the *quality* of responding. People will modify their output responses to suit the social situation, especially their immediate audience. Perhaps the best-known example of this is people varying their behaviors to enhance or control others' impressions of them (see, e.g., Goffman, 1959; Jones, 1964; Snyder, 1979). People also tune their communicative behaviors to suit their audience in order to attain a variety of goals. Higgins and Rholes (1978), for example, found that when subjects were asked to communicate to an audience about the same target person, their descriptions were tailored to be more positive when the audience supposedly liked the target person than when the audience supposedly disliked the target person (the "audience-tuning" effect). One form of person–situation relation that influences output quality involves individual differences in interpersonal orientation (a person variable) interacting with the attributes of the interaction partner (a situation variable). In an extension of the Higgins and Rholes (1978) study, for example, subjects high and low in authoritarianism were led to believe that their audience was either of higher status than they were or of the same status as they were (Higgins & McCann, 1984). When the interaction partner was supposedly equal in status, the high and low authoritarians displayed the audience-tuning effect to the same degree. But when the interaction partner was supposedly higher in status, the high authoritarians displayed the audience-tuning effect to a much greater degree than the low authoritarians.

Not only do people modify their output responses to suit their immediate social situation; they also modify their output responses to change their immediate social situation in order to meet their needs. Buss (1987) describes the mechanism of "manipulation" as involving tactics that individuals use intentionally to alter and shape the social environments they inhabit. There are both individual and situational determinants of the use of such procedural knowledge. An especially interesting form of person–situation relation involving manipulation tactics is described by Buss, Gomes, Higgins, and Lauterbach (1987). They found for couples that using a given tactic, especially charm and coercion, tended to be associated with receiving that tactic in turn. One explanation for such reciprocity of tactics is that exposure to the use of a tactic by one's partner increases the accessibility of one's available procedural knowledge for the tactic, thus increasing the likelihood of using the tactic oneself. The reciprocity relation for charm and coercion may be especially high, because the procedural knowledge for these tactics is more generally available than for other tactics (e.g., debasement). The results of this study suggest that the use of a particular tactic is a function of both individual differences in the availability and chronic accessibility of different tactics (a person variable) and contextual differences in the priming of tactics by the behavior of one's partner (a situation variable).

Another important form of person–situation relation that influences output responses involves people's strategies for dealing with stressful events and the discomfort they produce. There has been a long history of interest in individual differences in coping styles and defense mechanisms (e.g., A. Freud, 1937; Lazarus, 1966). If one considers *stress control strategies* as procedural knowledge, then one form of person–situation relation would involve individual differences in stress control strategies (a person variable) interacting with input that activates the strategies (a situation variable). One would expect stress control strategies, like any knowledge structure, to be utilized only when they are applicable to the input. Consistent with this expectation, Mischel, Ebbesen, and Zeiss (1973) found that individual differences between repressors and sensitizers in considering their own personal liabilities was greater when the input involved a failure experience (a stressful event) than when it involved a success experience (a nonstressful event).

People typically have alternative stress control strategies for dealing with particular events. For any particular event, most people may use the same optimal strategy. But some people may not have the optimum strategy available to apply to a particular event. Such people may have to resort to a less optimal strategy. This individual difference is most likely to be revealed when events demand more than the usual range of alternative strategies (see Wright & Mischel, 1987). Wright and Mischel (1987), for example, report a form of person–situation relation involving individual differences in nonoptimal stress control strategies (a person variable) and differences in environmental press (a situational variable). They found that individual differences in the use of aggression or in the use of withdrawal as stress control strategies were more evident in high-demand than in low-demand contexts. The use of a nonoptimal strategy by certain individuals in a high-demand context presumably occurs because a more optimal alternative strategy that is applicable to this situation is not available to them, thus leaving the nonoptimal strategy as the most accessible strategy by default.

This section has distinguished among multiple kinds of "person × situation interactions" by describing some distinct forms of person–situation relations at various stages of information processing, including exposure to input, identification of input, interpretation and appraisal of input, and output. These descriptions of various forms of person–situation relations suggests that the nature of the so-called "person × situation interaction" is more complex than has been suggested by the previous literature. Classic issues in personality and social psychology may be fruitfully reconsidered in light of this complexity. The next section briefly considers some of these issues.

PATTERNS OF PERSON–SITUATION RELATIONS

Personality and social psychologists have long recognized that social behavior is influenced by both person and situation variables. The issue has not been whether there are person × situation interactions, but how best to conceptualize or investigate them. The most common approach historically has been to identify those situations when a particular type of person will or will not behave in a certain way, and those people in a particular type of situation who will or will not behave in a certain way—the "moderating-variable" perspective (see Bem & Allen, 1974; Endler, 1982; Snyder & Ickes, 1985). This perspective holds that person–situation relations are formed by personality variables and social-psychological variables, each functioning as a moderator for the other.

The moderating-variable perspective has been very useful in delineating a wide variety of factors that increase or decrease the power of standard personality measures or standard social-psychological manipulations to predict particular social behaviors. The disadvantage of this perspective is that it maintains—indeed, reifies—the notion that personality and social-psychological variables involve different kinds of psychological factors. By contrast, the perspective taken here is that personality and social-psychological variables involve the same basic underlying factors and differ simply in the source of variation in these factors. If personality and social psychology involve the same basic factors, and these factors involve person–situation relations, then personality and social psychology should *each* involve person–situation relations. A close examination of personality and social-psychological variables reveals that this is indeed the case.

Person–Situation Relations in Personality and in Social Psychology

Let us begin by considering the following classic examples of personality types:

1. *High achievement motivation* (see Atkinson, 1964; McClelland, 1961). High (resultant) achievers have been described as having high standards of excellence, wanting to reach an achievement goal, deriving pleasure from success, having high expectations for success, and seeking challenging tasks. Such individuals can be characterized as possessing both high ideal/own self-guides and high future self-possibilities as standards for self-regulation and self-evaluation. Self-regulation and self-evaluation also require accurate assessment of current actual selves, which is maximally accomplished by engaging in tasks of moderate difficulty (see Trope, 1986). Thus, this personality orientation constitutes a person–situation relation between particular self-guides and self-possibilities (a person variable) and particular self-assessment tasks (a situation variable).

2. *High authoritarianism* (see Adorno, Frenkel-Brunswik, Levinson & Stanford, 1950). High authoritarians have been described as having a rigid adherence to conventional values; obedience to and respect for moral authority; a tendency to submit to and identify with high-status/high-power figures; and a tendency to condemn, criticize, and punish low-status/low-power individuals. Such individuals can be characterized as possessing high ought guides as evaluative standards for both self and others, and as perceiving matches versus mismatches to standards differentially, depending on the status and power of the target person. Thus, this personality orientation constitutes a person–situation relation between particular self- and other-guides (a person variable) and particular targets of application (a situation variable).

3. *High self-monitoring* (see Snyder, 1979). High self-monitors have been described as being highly motivated to adhere to the different social roles and social expectancies associated with different kinds of situations and to behave in a manner that is appropriate to a specific context, and as using cues of relevant others in social situations as guidelines for controlling their verbal and nonverbal self-presentations. Such individuals can be characterized as possessing strong normative guides (ideals and oughts), and as being strongly oriented to using social context guides (ideals and oughts) for self-regulation. Thus, this personality orientation constitutes a person–situation relation between particular normative guides (a person variable) and particular social context guides (a situation variable).

Each of these personality types, then, can be conceptualized as constituting in itself a person–situation relation, and each type constitutes a different kind of relation. Indeed, if one accepts these conceptualizations, it is somewhat misleading to describe these personality types as being "high" achievers, authoritarians, and self-monitors, as if there were some dimension of achievement motivation, authoritarianism, and self-monitoring that individuals can possess "high" or "low" values along. What would it mean to be "low" in these cases? In terms of the present model, it could mean that the person–situation relation possessed by those who are "high" in a type of personality is unavailable or low in chronic accessibility to those who are "low." But this is not typically how individuals low in a personality type have been described. Low achievers, for example, have been described as having high expectations for failure, as anticipating much displeasure from failure, as attributing failure to a lack of ability, and as being oriented to easy or difficult tasks for self-assessment. Thus, rather than possessing a "low" amount of the same person–situation relation as high achievers, low achievers are better characterized as possessing a different person–situation relation—ought/other self-guides as standards for self-regulation and self-evaluation, and an orientation to nonchallenging self-assessment tasks (see Higgins, Strauman, & Klein, 1986). In many cases, then, individuals "high" or "low" in some personality dimension may actually exhibit qualitatively different person–situation relations that reflect qualitatively different orientations and expectancies. Indeed, the "mysterious moderates" of various personality dimensions (see Sorrentino & Short, 1977) may be mysterious precisely because they constitute a variety of alternative person–situation relations that have yet to be identified.

As suggested earlier, it is not just personality phenomena that involve person–situation relations; social-psychological phenomena do so as well. Consider the following classic examples of social-psychological phenomena:

1. *Cognitive dissonance* (see Aronson, 1969; Deutsch et al., 1962; Festinger, 1957). In the classic "insufficient-justification" paradigm of cognitive dissonance, an experimenter induces (indeed, seduces) experimental subjects to behave in a manner that is incompatible with their personal values under the illusion of free choice. This psychological situation, artfully crafted by the experimenter, can be characterized as involving the experimenter's priming situationally appropriate normative guides in the subject (e.g., "Good experimental subjects help out the experimenter") that motivate the subject to behave in a manner that the experimenter knows is discrepant from the subject's self-guides (e.g., "Thou shalt not lie"), while making explicit the absence of any social context guide demanding the behavior (e.g., "Of course, you do not have to engage in this behavior; it is up to you"). This *pattern* of standard matches, mismatches, and nonmatches— normative guide matches (a person variable), self-guide mismatches (a person variable), and social context guide nonmatches (a situation variable)—constitutes the psychological situation of "cognitive dissonance" that people feel a need to resolve. This analysis is compatible with Cooper and Fazio's (1984) recent characterization of dissonance as "feeling responsible for an aversive event," since perceiving a mismatch between a behavior and a self-guide is aversive, and perceiving a nonmatch between a behavior and a social context guide (i.e., perceiving the behavior as uninfluenced by situational forces) produces a feeling of personal responsibility. The social-psychological condition of dissonance, then, involves the contextual construction and activation of a particular pattern of person and situation elements.

2. *Obedience to authority* (see Milgram, 1974). In Milgram's paradigm, an experimenter orders subjects to behave in a manner that is incompatible with their personal values, while emphasizing that they have no choice but to follow his or her instructions. This psychological situation could be characterized as involving the experimenter's both priming situationally appropriate normative guides in the subject (e.g., the subject is assigned the role of teacher, and in that role is expected to deliver punishment to a learner) and, when necessary, constructing particular social context guides for the subject (e.g., "The experiment requires that you continue [punishing the learner]"; "You have no other choice, you *must* go on"). Both of these experimenter actions pressure subjects to behave in a manner that is discrepant from the subjects' self-guides (e.g., "One should not inflict suffering on a helpless person who is neither harmful nor threatening to oneself"). This pattern of standard matches and

mismatches—normative guide matches (a person variable), self-guide mismatches (a person variable), and social context guide matches (a situation variable)—constitutes the psychological situation of "obedience to authority." This social-psychological condition again involves the contextual construction and activation of a particular pattern of person and situation elements.

When social-psychological conditions are characterized in terms of a common language of person and situation elements, any similarities and differences between conditions are more readily revealed. Consider, for example, the social-psychological conditions of "cognitive dissonance" and "obedience to authority" just described. The patterns of these two conditions are similar in that they both involve normative guide matches and self-guide mismatches. The critical element that distinguishes these two conditions is that the pattern of "obedience to authority" involves a social context guide match (i.e., the experimenter explicitly introduces a social context guide that presses for the behavior), whereas the pattern of "cognitive dissonance" involves a social context guide nonmatch (i.e., the experimenter removes any explicit social context guide that presses for the behavior).

This analysis suggests that changing this critical element in the two patterns should transform these social-psychological conditions. In the "cognitive-dissonance" paradigm, for example, creating a social context guide match should transform the pattern into an "obedience-to-authority" pattern and thus remove dissonance effects. Indeed, a social context guide match is created in the "low-choice" condition of dissonance experiments in which the experimenter requires subjects to perform the discrepant act, and in this condition dissonance effects are typically not found (see Wicklund & Brehm, 1976).

The alternative possibility is to create a social context guide nonmatch in the "obedience-to-authority" paradigm by explicitly telling subjects that it is their choice how much to punish the learner. This change should transform the pattern into a "cognitive-dissonance" pattern and create dissonance effects in subjects who punish the learner. Some subjects may create this condition on their own by believing that, regardless of what the experimenter has said, it is their choice to punish the learner. These subjects should experience cognitive dissonance. Cognitive dissonance in this paradigm may be resolved by reducing attention to or minimizing the negative consequences of punishing the learner, or by derogating the experimenter or the learner. Milgram (1974) reports that such resolutions were evident among subjects who experienced strain in his study, although the role of perceived choice in these resolutions was not directly examined. Milgram (1974) does report, however, that subjects who experienced strain attempted frequently to make the experimenter take full responsibility for their actions; this could have been an attempt to establish or re-establish a perception of "no choice."

"Cognitive dissonance" and "obedience to authority" are not the only psychological situations in which normative guides, self-guides, and social context guides constitute the elements in an overall pattern. "Resistance to social influence," for example, can also be characterized as involving a pattern comprised of these elements. In Asch's (1952) classic studies of resistance to group influence (where the groups are composed of one subject and a set of experimental stooges), the subjects are given a discrimination task in which they are asked, "Please be as accurate as possible." After a couple of normal trials, the subjects are confronted with a majority judgment that is incorrect prior to giving their own judgment. At this stage there is a conflict between subjects' self-guide to be truthful (e.g., a belief that it is their obligation to respond as they perceive) and the social context guide of accuracy given by the experimenter and associated with the majority opinion (see Asch, 1952). "Resistance to social influence" is most likely to occur when another member of the group also makes a judgment different from the majority's (Asch's "introducing a partner"), even if this judgment is also different from the subject's judgment (see Allen & Levine, 1968).

One interpretation of this situation is that the partner functions as a salient exemplar of "independent people," which activates subjects' normative guides to be independent. The normative guide, then, counteracts the social context guide sufficiently for the self-guide to become the predominant influence on behavior (i.e., telling the truth)—a pattern of normative guide matches, self-guide matches, and social context guide mismatches.

If this interpretation of "resistance to persuasion" is reasonable, then it should not be necessary to reduce the "unanimous majority" by introducing a dissenting partner in order to activate this pattern. It should be sufficient to activate a normative guide for independence. For example, simply reminding a subject of a positive reference group that values independent behavior should be enough; this could be accomplished rather subtly through a priming manipulation. Indeed, a less subtle technique of increasing subjects' awareness of normative guides by vivid reminders of their group membership (i.e., increasing the salience of subjects' religious affiliation) has been shown to increase resistance to persuasive messages that conflict with the normative guides (e.g., Kelley, 1955).

These various examples illustrate how personality and social-psychological variables both involve patterns of person and situation elements. Given this, it should be possible to consider social-psychological variables in terms of the role of person variability (i.e., from a "personality" perspective) and personality variables in terms of the role of situational variability (i.e., from a "social-psychological" perspective). As an example of a social-psychological variable, consider how cognitive dissonance might be studied from a personality perspective. It should first be noted that cognitive-dissonance experiments are typically designed to minimize any effects from individual-difference variables. For instance, subjects are preselected in order to assure that the induced behavior will be discrepant from their personal standards (e.g., to assure that the position they agree to advocate is discrepant from their personal beliefs). If this were not done, the *extent* of self-guide mismatch as an element in the pattern would vary, and this would produce individual differences in the *magnitude* of dissonance. Another possibility would be to select individuals who vary in the type of self-guide from which their act is discrepant (e.g., ideal/own discrepant vs. ought/other discrepant); this might produce individual differences in the *quality* of dissonance (e.g., disappointed in oneself vs. tense). These differences, in turn, could produce differences in modes of resolving dissonance.

It is also possible that there are individual differences in how often the dissonant pattern has been experienced in the past, and thus individual differences in the chronic accessibility of this pattern (as measured, perhaps, by the frequency and ease with which individuals remember occasions when they freely chose to behave in a role-appropriate but value-discrepant manner). As the chronic accessibility of this pattern increases, the magnitude of dissonance produced by a dissonance manipulation should increase, and the strength of the manipulation needed to produce dissonance should decrease. Finally, it may be that different dissonance paradigms vary in which type of self-guide (i.e., which personality) is most relevant to the situation involved in the paradigm. For instance, ideal self-guides may be more relevant or applicable to the paradigm of "free choice" (e.g., deciding which desirable product to buy), whereas ought self-guides may be more applicable to the paradigm of "counterattitudinal behavior" (e.g., deciding whether to act contrary to one's beliefs.)

It is also possible to consider personality variables from a "social-psychological" perspective by examining situational variability in pattern activation. As an example of a personality variable, consider how high or low achievement motivation might be studied from a social-psychological perspective. If different types of contextual priming are introduced into the achievement situation (i.e., ideal priming vs. ought priming), situational differences in the type of achiever engaged by a task may be found. For instance, prior to a task subjects may be asked either what score they hope or wish to attain (ideal priming) or what score they believe they should or ought to attain (ought priming). High achievers should be engaged by the task more than low achievers when the situation involves ideal priming and less than low achievers when the situation involves ought priming. Such differences in task engagement may also be found by introducing different types of social context guides (i.e., an ideal social context guide vs. an ought social context guide), such as having subjects work in teams with partners who discuss the score they hope the team will attain or the score they believe the team ought to attain.

In order to fully appreciate the extent to which person–situation relations are involved in personality and social psychology, one must also consider the role of person–situation relations in the acquisition of social knowledge and social standards. That is, one must take a developmental perspective on person–situation relations. It is not possible to review here all the developmental person–situation relations that affect motivation and action. Even a brief discussion, however, reveals how developmental variables contribute to the underlying complexity of person–situation relations in personality and social psychology.

Person–Situation Relations in the Developmental Underpinnings of Personality and Social Psychology

Although personality and social psychology differ in whether variation across individuals or variation across situations is of special interest, a major concern of both areas is to understand social action. As Max Weber pointed out many years ago (see the quotation at the beginning of the chapter), action is social insofar as the acting individual attaches a subjective meaning to it that takes account of the behavior of others and is thereby oriented in its course. Both the meaning and importance of the social world depend on individuals' representations of their social interactions and interpersonal experiences. When people behave in terms of such representations, then, their behavior is social action (see Mead, 1934; Stryker & Statham, 1985). Thus, to the extent that the acquisition of such representations involves person–situation relations, person–situation relations underlie social action regardless of whether one examines individual or situational variability in social action.

The present chapter has emphasized the role of standards, and especially self-guides, in social motivation and action. For the purpose of illustration, then, the person–situation relations involved in acquiring self-guides are briefly considered. (For a fuller discussion of the development of the self-system more generally, see Harter, 1983; Higgins, 1989a.)

Children's representations of their social world depend both on the social information to which they are exposed and on their mental representational capacity. Not until they are between 1½ and 2 years of age are children capable of representing the interrelation between two relations (see Case, 1985; Fischer, 1980; Piaget, 1952), such as the relation between a particular kind of self-feature (e.g.,

response, appearance) and a particular kind of response to them, and the relation between this kind of response to them and their experiencing a particular kind of psychological situation. For the first time, children can respresent self–other contingencies (e.g., "When I do X, Mother does Y; and when Mother does Y, I feel Z)". At this stage, then, children are capable of anticipating the consequences of their own actions. The significant others in the child's life respond to the child's features, thus linking the child to the larger society and providing the social meanings of the child's features. The psychological situations produced in the child by the responses of significant others are represented as the social consequences of the child's features, thus providing the social importance of the features. In representing self–other contingencies, then, children's self-features acquire psychological significance. These psychologically significant representations of self–other contingencies are the precursors of self-guides.

Between 4 and 6 years of age, children become capable of inferring the thoughts, expectations, motives, and intentions of others (see Shantz, 1983). This new inferential ability can be applied to self–other contingency knowledge. Children are motivated to learn what kinds of self-features are expected, valued, and preferred by the significant others in their lives, in order to produce those self-features that others respond to positively and avoid producing those self-features that others respond to negatively. Children at this stage, then, have both the ability and motivation to acquire self-guides. Children now not only anticipate others' responses to their features, but also represent others' valued end states for them. It is these representations of others' valued or preferred end states for them—self-guides—that now provide the social meanings of their self-features. And children's representations of the consequences for them of others' standpoints on them—their representations of the psychological situations they will experience by meeting or failing to meet others' valued end states for them—are what provide the importance of their self-features. At this stage, then, the psychological significance of children's self-features can become tied to their self-guides.

Later stages of the development of mental representational capacity have further implications for the psychological significance of the self and for self-evaluative and self-regulatory processes (see Higgins, 1989a). The present account is sufficient, however, to illustrate a critical person–situation relation underlying social action. As children's mental representational capacities change, their representations of the social world can change. As these representations change, the social meaning of their self-features changes, which in turn influences their self-evaluative and self-regulatory processes. Thus, the person variable of mental representational capacity is an essential factor in social action.

On the other hand, what is being represented is information about social interactions—how and why others respond in particular ways to particular features that one displays (and later, to particular traits that one possesses). This self–other contingency knowledge defines the psychological significance of one's actions. The situation variable of exposure to self–other contingent interactions becomes a person variable that plays an essential role in the self-regulatory and self-evaluative processes underlying social action.

Thus, both the person variable of mental representational capacity and the situation variable of exposure to self–other contingency interactions are essential for the acquisition of self-contingency knowledge, which is a person variable that plays an important role in regulating social action. Moreover, the variables of personal capacity and situational exposure do not function independently of each other. It is the *relation* between these variables, the person–situation relation, that is critical to the acquisition of self–other contingency knowledge. In addition, the self-other contingency knowledge is *itself* a person–situation relation: The mental representation includes person information about one's own self-features, situation information about how other people respond to those features, and the relation between them.

Although exposure to a self–other contingency interaction is a situation variable, there are individual differences in the nature of the self–other contingencies to which people are exposed. Some of these differences are age-related because normative guides vary as a function of the social life phase of a child (see Higgins & Eccles-Parsons, 1983). Other differences arise from differences in modes of caretaker–child interaction. Caretaker–child interactions vary in their frequency, consistency, and so on, as well as in the type of psychological situation involved in the interaction (see Higgins, 1989a). For example, if a child's behavior is perceived by his or her mother as failing to fulfill the mother's hopes for the child, the mother is likely to feel disappointed in the child and to withdraw love and attention from the child. If such a "love withdrawal" mode occurs often, then the child is likely to acquire an ideal self-guide and be vulerable to experiencing the absence of positive outcomes (i.e., dejection-related emotions). In contrast, if a child is perceived by his or her mother as violating what the mother believes the child ought to do, the mother is likely to feel angry at the child and to criticize or punish the child. If such a "punitive/critical" mode of interaction occurs often, then the child is likely to acquire an ought self-guide and be vulnerable to experiencing the (expected) presence of negative outcomes (i.e., agitation-related emotions).

Such socialization differences in modes of caretaker–child interaction constitute yet another form of person–situation relation. In this case, a prolonged difference in a situation variable produces an individual difference in self-guides. This form of person–situation relation is quite common. As discussed in an earlier section, prolonged differences in exposure to social knowledge can produce individual differences in knowledge availability. In addition, prolonged differences in the frequency with which available social knowledge is activated can produce individual differences in the chronic accessibility of knowledge.

It is inherent to the nature of social learning that individual differences often reflect prolonged situational differences. As Murray (1938) pointed out, "much of what is now *inside* the organism was once *outside*" (p. 40). In this sense, one might describe a "person × situation" interaction as a relation between two kinds of situations—the prior prolonged situations represented in the person and the current momentary situation. But given that exposure to and representation of these situations typically vary across individuals, "person × situation" interactions are more accurately described in terms of relations between prior person–situation relations and current person–situation relations.

SUMMARY AND CONCLUDING REMARKS

This chapter has explored the relation between personality and social psychology by reconsidering the nature of person–situation relations. First, a set of commonly held postulates for constructing a "good" theory of person–situation relations has been identified. An integration of these postulates yields the following general guiding proposition: Standards and social knowledge (especially self-beliefs), which are a function of both the person and the situation, are basic determinants of the psychological significance of events and thus strongly influence how people respond to events. An illustrative model of person–situation relations has been constructed following this guiding proposition. In line with additional key principles suggested in the literature, the model has been constructed to have a common language of description for both persons and situations, to provide an account of the psychological processes underlying the interrelations of persons and situations, and to include idiographic assumptions within a science of nomothetic processes.

The illustrative model includes a general account of how knowledge availability, accessibility, and activation assign subjective meaning to social events and how the use of different types of person and situation standards determines the psychological significance of these events. This model permits multiple kinds of person–situation relations to be identified at various stages of social information processing. Patterns composed of both person and situation elements within personality and within social psychology have also been described; these suggest how personality and social psychological phenomena could be translated into a common language for study. Further commonalities and complexities concerning person–situation relations in personality and social psychology have been revealed by considering how social knowledge and standards are acquired developmentally.

The general objective of the chapter has been to illustrate how personality and social psychology can be theoretically integrated to create, along with developmental psychology, a general social science of psychology. The proposed common language of social standards and knowledge activation will undoubtedly need to

be supplemented by other idiographic content variables and nomothetic process variables. We may hope that a common language of manageable size will be able to account for the bulk of person–situation relations in personality and social psychology. But it is clear that a common language combining nomothetic processes and idiographic typologies is needed if progress is to be made in integrating personality and social psychology.

Without such a common language, personality and social psychology will continue to characterize the social world of experience with their own distinct labels as if there were different underlying social phenomena. For example, "social desirability" (or the "approval motive") is a label for a personality determinant of action, whereas "social norm" is a label for a social-psychological determinant of action. In both cases, however, the phenomenon of interest concerns the impact of normative guides on behavior. It is not the phenomenon that differs, but rather the orientation to the the phenomenon—a greater concern with either individual or situational variability in the phenomenon. Greater progress will be made by combining these orientations so as to consider the multiple person–situation relations underlying the phenomenon.

I am not suggesting that one can easily map personality and social-psychological phenomena onto each other, as with "social desirability" and "social norm." Indeed, this is precisely the major drawback of personality and social psychology as separate areas that have labeled and continue to label their own social worlds. Proceeding in this manner has produced little consensus concerning what *are* the basic phenomena of the social world. Instead, many different phenomena in each area will continue to be studied with little contribution from the other area. Historically, this approach has led to a proliferation of phenomena in personality and social psychology, with little sense of which phenomena are central to either area or how the phenomena are interrelated across areas. It is a great advantage to any science to identify basic phenomena that need to be studied. This can be accomplished more readily if personality and social psychologists recognize that they are studying different sources of variability in the same social phenomena and thus should work together to identify those phenomena that are basic. For example, the impact of Freud's "ego-state conflicts" in personality and abnormal psychology and of Festinger's "cognitive dissonance" in social psychology suggests that the resolution of discrepancies and conflicts involving guides is a basic phenomenon for both personality and social psychologists. The historical interest of personality and abnormal psychologists in personal constructs (including irrational beliefs and negative cognitions), and the recent interest of social psychologists in contextual priming, suggest that subjective meaning from knowledge accessibility may be another basic phenomenon for personality and social psychologists.

It would be an exciting endeavor for personality and social psychologists to identify (and discover) basic social phenomena and then to work together on these phenomena from converging orientations. Even though the personality and social psychologists may focus on different sources of variability in such collaborative work, it should be understood that they are both studying complex person–situation relations underlying the same basic phenomena. Moreover, the different sources of variability examined by personality and social psychologists should then be combined through the use of a common process language, just as the contributions of the personality variable of personal constructs and the social-psychological variable of contextual priming can be combined in the language of knowledge accessibility. In this way, personality and social psychology will no longer function simply as moderators of each other's effects, but will combine to create an integrated social science of psychology.

ACKNOWLEDGMENTS

Preparation of this chapter was supported by Grant MH 39429 from the National Institute of Mental Health. I would like to thank Susan Andersen, Arie Kruglanski, Diane Ruble, Yaacov Trope, Jim Uleman, and Mark Zanna for helpful comments and suggestions at various stages of this project.

REFERENCES

Adler, A. (1964). *Problems of neurosis.* New York: Harper & Row. (Original work published 1929)

Ajzen, I. (1977). Intuitive theories of events and the effects of base rate information on prediction. *Journal of Personality and Social Psychology, 35,* 303–314.

Ajzen, I., & Fishbein, M. (1970). The prediction of behavior from attitudinal and normative variables. *Journal of Experimental Social Psychology, 6,* 466–487.

Adorno, T. W., Frenkel-Brunswik, E., Levinson, D. J., & Sanford, R. N. (1950). *The authoritarian personality.* New York: Harper.

Allen, V. L., & Levine, J. M. (1968). Social support, dissent, and conformity. *Sociometry, 31,* 138–149.

Allport, G. W. (1955). *Becoming.* New Haven, CT: Yale University Press.

Allport, G. W. (1966). Traits revisited. *American Psychologist, 21,* 1–10.

Aronson, E. (1969). The theory of cognitive dissonance: A current perspective. In L. Berkowitz (Ed.), *Advances in experimental social psychology* (Vol. 4, pp. 1–34). New York: Academic Press.

Asch, S. E. (1952). *Social psychology.* Englewood Cliffs, NJ: Prentice-Hall.

Atkinson, J. W. (1964). *An introduction to motivation.* Princeton, NJ: Van Nostrand.

Austin, W., McGinn, N. C., & Susmilch, C. (1980). Internal standards revisited: Effects of social comparisons and expectancies on judgments of fairness and satisfaction. *Journal of Experimental Social Psychology, 16,* 426–441.

Bandura, A. (1977). *Social learning theory.* Englewood Cliffs, NJ: Prentice Hall.

Bandura, A. (1982). The self and mechanisms of agency. In J. Suls (Ed.), *Psychological perspectives on the self* (Vol. 1, pp. 3–39). Hillsdale, NJ: Erlbaum

Bandura, A. (1986). *Social foundations of thought and action: A Social cognitive theory.* Englewood Cliffs, NJ: Prentice-Hall.

Bargh, J. A. (1984). Automatic and conscious processing of social information. In R. S. Wyer, Jr., & T. K. Srull (Eds.), *Handbook of social cognition* (Vol. 3, pp. 1–43). Hillsdale, NJ: Erlbaum.

Bargh, J. A., Bond, R. N., Lombardi, W. J., & Tota, M. E. (1986). The additive nature of chronic and temporary sources of construct accessibility. *Journal of Personality and Social Psychology, 50,* 869–878.

Bargh, J. A., Lombardi, W. J., & Higgins, E. T. (1988). Automaticity of chronically accessible constructs in person × situation effects on person perception: It's just a matter of time. *Journal of Personality and Social Psychology, 55,* 599–605.

Bargh, J. A., & Pietromonaco, P. (1982). Automatic information processing and social perception: The influence of trait information presented outside of conscious awareness on impression formation. *Journal of Personality and Social Psychology, 43,* 437–449.

Bargh, J. A., & Pratto, F. (1986). Individual construct accessibility and perceptual selection. *Journal of Experimental Social Psychjology, 22,* 293–311.

Bargh, J. A., & Thein, R. D. (1985). Individual construct accessibility, person memory, and the recall–judgment link: The case of information overload. *Journal of Personality and Social Psychology, 49,* 1129–1146.

Barker, R. G. (1968). *Ecological psychology.* Stanford, CA: Stanford University Press.

Bartlett, F. C. (1932). *Remembering.* Cambridge, England: Cambridge University Press.

Battistich, V. A., & Aronoff, J. (1985). Perceiver, target, and situational influences on social cognition: An interactional analysis. *Journal of Personality and Social Psychology, 49*, 788–798.

Bem, D. J. (1982). Persons, situations, and template matching: These and variations. In M. P. Zanna, E. T. Higgins, & C. P. Herman (Eds.), *The Ontario Symposium: Vol. 2. Consistency in social behavior* (pp. 173–186). Hillsdale, NJ: Erlbaum.

Bem, D. J. (1983). Constructing a theory of the triple typology: Some (second) thoughts on nomothetic and idiographic approaches to personality. *Journal of Personality, 51*, 566–577.

Bem, D. J., & Allen, A. (1974). On predicting some of the people some of the time: The search for cross-situational consistencies in behavior. *Psychological Review, 81*, 506–520.

Bem, D. J., & Funder, D. C. (1978). Predicting more of the people more of the time: The search for cross-situational consistencies in behavior. *Psychological Review, 85*, 485–501.

Bernstein, M., & Crosby, F. (1980). An empirical examination of relative deprivation theory. *Journal of Experimental Social Psychology, 16*, 442–456.

Breckler, S. J., & Greenwald, A. G. (1986). Motivational facets of the self. In R. M. Sorrentino & E. T. Higgins (Eds.), *Handbook of motivation and cognition: Foundations of social behavior* (pp. 145–164). New York: Guilford Press.

Brickman, P., Coates, D., & Janoff-Bulman, R. (1978). Lottery winners and accident victims: Is happiness relative? *Journal of Personality and Social Psychology, 36*, 917–927.

Brockner, J. (1979). Self-esteem, self-consciousness, and task performance: Replications, extensions, and possible explanations. *Journal of Personality and Social Psychology, 37*, 447–461.

Bruner, J. S. (1957a). Going beyond the information given. In H. Gruber et al. (Eds.), *Contemporary approaches to cognition*. Cambridge, MA: Harvard University Press.

Bruner, J. S. (1957b). On perceptual readiness. *Psychological Review, 64*, 123–152.

Bruner, J. S., & Minturn, A. L. (1955). Perceptual identification and perceptual organization. *Journal of General Psychology, 53*, 21–28.

Bowers, K. S. (1973). Situationism in psychology: An analysis and critique. *Psychological Review, 80*, 307–336.

Buss, D. M. (1987). Selection, evocation, and manipulation. *Journal of Personality and Social Psychology, 53*, 1214–1221.

Buss, D. M., & Craik, K. H. (1981). The act frequency analysis of interpersonal dispositions: Aloofness, gregariousness, dominance, and submissiveness. *Journal of Personality and Social Psychology, 49*, 175–192.

Buss, D. M., Gomes, M., Higgins, D. S., & Lauterbach, K. (1987). Tactics of manipulation. *Journal of Personality and Social Psychology, 52*, 1219–1229.

Cameron, N. (1963). *Personality development and psychopathology*. Boston: Houghton Mifflin.

Cantor, N., & Kihlstrom, J. F. (1987). *Personality and social intelligence*. Englewood Cliffs, NJ: Prentice-Hall.

Cantor, N., Markus, H., Niedenthal, P., & Nurius, P. (1986). On motivation and the self-concept. In R. M. Sorrentino & E. T. Higgins (Eds.), *Handbook of motivation and cognition: Foundations of social behavior* (pp. 96–121). New York: Guilford Press.

Carver, C. S. (1975). Physical aggression as a function of

objective self-awareness and attitudes toward punishment. *Journal of Experimental Social Psychology, 11*, 510–519.

Carver, C. S., Ganellen, R. J., Froming, W. J., & Chambers, W. (1983). Modeling: An analysis in terms of category accessibility. *Journal of Experimental Social Psychology, 19*, 403–421.

Carver, C. S., & Scheier, M. F. (1981). *Attention and self-regulation: A control-theory approach to human behavior*. New York: Springer.

Case, R. (1985). *Intellectual development: Birth to adulthood*. New York: Academic Press.

Clark, M. S., & Isen, A. (1982). Toward understanding the relationship between feeling states and social behavior. In A. H. Hastorf & A. M. Isen (Eds.), *Cognitive social psychology* (pp. 73–108). New York: Elsevier.

Clark, M. S., Milberg, S., & Erber, R. (1984). Effects of arousal on judgments of others' emotions. *Journal of Personality and Social Psychology, 46*, 551–560.

Cohen, C. E., & Ebbesen, E. B. (1979). Observational goals and schema activation: A theoretical framework for behavior perception. *Journal of Experimental Social Psychology, 15*, 305–329.

Cooley, C. H. (1964). *Human nature and the social order*. New York: Schocken Books. (Original work published 1902)

Cooper, J., & Fazio, R. H. (1984). A new look at dissonance theory. In L. Berkowitz (Ed.), *Advances in experimental social psychology* (Vol. 17, pp. 229–265). New York: Academic Press.

Crowne, D. P., & Marlowe, D. (1964). *The approval motive: Studies in evaluative dependence*. New York: Wiley.

Darley, J. M., & Fazio, R. H. (1980). Expectancy confirmation processes arising in the social interaction sequence. *American Psychologist, 35*, 867–881.

Darley, J. M., & Gross, P. H. (1983). A hypothesis-confirming bias in labeling effects. *Journal of Personality and Social Psychology, 44*, 20–33.

DeCharms, R. (1968). *Personal causation*. New York: Academic Press.

Deci, E. L., & Ryan, R. M. (1985). *Intrinsic motivation and self-determination in human behavior*. New York: Plenum.

Deutsch, M., & Gerard, H. B. (1955). A study of normative and informational social influences upon individual judgment. *Journal of Abnormal and Social Psychology, 51*, 629–636.

Deutsch, M., Krauss, R. M., & Rosenau, N. (1962). Dissonance or defensiveness? *Journal of Personality, 30*, 16–28.

Devine, P. G. (1989). Stereotypes and prejudice: Their automatic and controlled components. *Journal of Personality and Social Psychology, 56*, 5–18.

Duval, S., & Wicklund, R. A. (1972). *A theory of objective self-awareness*. New York: Academic Press.

Dweck, C. S., & Elliot, E. S. (1983). Achievement motivation. In E. M. Hetherington (Vol. Ed.), *Handbook of child psychology* (4th ed,): Vol. 4. Socialization, personality, and social development (pp. 643–691). New York: Wiley.

Endler, N. S. (1982). Interactionism comes of age. In M. P. Zanna, E. T. Higgins, & C. P. Herman (Eds.), *The Ontario Symposium: Vol. 2. Consistency in social behavior* (pp. 209–249). Hillsdale, NJ: Erlbaum.

Epstein, S. (1983). Aggregation and beyond: Some basic

issues on the prediction of behavior. *Journal of Personality, 51*, 360–392.

Erdley, C. A., & D'Agostino, P. R. (1988). Cognitive and affective components of automatic priming affects. *Journal of Personality and Social Psychology, 54*, 741–747.

Erikson, E. H. (1963). *Childhood and society* (rev. ed.). New York: Norton.

Fazio, R. H. (1986). How do attitudes guide behavior? In R. M. Sorrentino & E. T. Higgins (Eds.), *Handbook of motivation and cognition: Foundations of social behavior* (pp. 204–243). New York: Guilford Press.

Fazio, R. H., Chen, J., McDonel, E. C., & Sherman, S. J. (1982). Attitude accessibility, attitude–behavior consistency, and the strength of the object–evaluation association. *Journal of Experimental Social Psychology, 18*, 339–357.

Fazio, R. H., Powell, M. C., & Herr, P. M. (1983). Toward a process model of the attitude–behavior relation: Accessing one's attitude upon mere observation of the attitude object. *Journal of Personality and Social Psychology, 44*, 723–735.

Festinger, L. (1954). A theory of social comparison processes. *Human Relations, 1*, 117–140.

Festinger, L. (1957). *A theory of cognitive dissonance.* Evanston, IL: Row, Peterson.

Fischer, K. W. (1980). A theory of cognitive development: The control and construction of hierarchies of skills. *Psychological Review, 87*, 477–531.

Freud, A. (1937). *The ego and the mechanisms of defense.* New York: International Universitie, Press.

Freud, S. (1961). The ego and the id. In J. Strachey (Ed. and Trans.), *The standard edition of the complete psychological works of Sigmund Freud* (Vol. 19, pp. 3–66). London: Hogarth Press. (Original work published 1923)

Gibson, J. J. (1979). *The ecological approach to visual perception.* Boston: Houghton Mifflin.

Goethals, G. R., & Darley, J. M. (1977). Social comparison theory: An attributional approach. In J. M. Suls & R. L. Miller (Eds.), *Social comparison processes: Theoretical and empirical perspectives* (pp. 259–278). Washington, DC: Hemisphere.

Goffman, E. (1959). *The presentation of self in everyday life.* Garden City, NY: Doubleday.

Greenwald, A. G. (1982). Ego task analysis: An integration of research on ego-involvement and self-awareness. In A. H. Hastorf & A. M. Isen (Eds.), *Cognitive social psychology* (pp. 109–147). New York: Elsevier.

Harter, S. (1983). Developmental perspectives on the self-system. In E. M. Hetherington (Vol. Ed.), *Handbook of child psychology (4th ed.) Vol. 4. Socialization, personality, and social development* (pp. 275–385). New York: Wiley.

Harvey, M. D., & Enzle, M. E. (1981). A cognitive model of social norms for understanding the transgression–helping effect. *Journal of Personality and Social Psychology, 41*, 866–875.

Hebb, D. O. (1949). *The organization of behavior.* New York: Wiley.

Heidbreder, E. (1933). *Seven psychologies.* New York: Appleton-Century-Crofts.

Heider, F. (1958). *The psychology of interpersonal relations.* New York: Wiley.

Herman, C. P., & Mack, D. (1975). Restrained and unrestrained eating. *Journal of Personality, 43*, 647–660.

Hermans, H. J. M. (1988). On the integration of nomothesic and idiographic research methods in the study of personal meaning. *Journal of Personality, 56*, 785–812.

Herr, P. M. (1986). Consequences of priming: Judgment and behavior. *Journal of Personality and Social Psychology, 51*, 1106–1115.

Herr, P. M., Sherman, S. J., & Fazio, R. H. (1983). On the consequences of priming. Assimilation and contrast effects. *Journal of Experimental Social Psychology, 19*, 323–340.

Higgins, E. T. (1981). Role-taking and social judgment: Alternative developmental perspectives and processes. In J. H. Flavell & L. Ross (Eds.), *Social cognitive development: Frontiers and possible futures* (pp. 119–153). Cambridge, England: Cambridge University Press.

Higgins, E. T. (1987). Self discrepancy: A theory relating self and affect. *Psychological Reiew, 94*, 319–340.

Higgins, E. T. (1989a). Continuities and discontinuities in self-regulatory and self-evaluative processes: A developmental theory relating self and affect. *Journal of Personality, 57*, 407–444.

Higgins, E. T. (1989b). Knowledge accessibility and activation: Subjectivity and suffering from unconscious sources. In J. S. Uleman and J. A. Bargh (Eds.) *Unintended thought* (pp. 75–123). New York: Guilford.

Higgins, E. T., & Bargh, J. A. (1987). Social cognition and social perception. *Annual Review of Psychology, 38*, 369–425.

Higgins, E. T., Bargh, J. A., & Lombardi, W. (1985). The nature of priming effects on categorization. *Journal of Experimental Psychology: Learning, Memory, and Cognition, 11*, 59–69.

Higgins, E. T., Bond, R. N., Klein, R., & Strauman, T. (1986). Self-discrepancies and emotional vulnerability: How magnitude, accessibility, and type of discrepancy influence affect. *Journal of Personality and Social Psychology, 51*, 5–15.

Higgins, E. T., & Chaires, W. M. (1980). Accessibility of interrelational constructs: Implications for stimulus encoding and creativity. *Journal of Experimental Social Psychology, 16*, 348–361.

Higgins, E. T., & Eccles-Parsons, J. E. (1983). Social cognition and the social life of the child: Stages as subcultures. In E. T. Higgins, D. N. Ruble, & W. W. Hartup (Eds.), *Social cognition and social development: A sociocultural perspective* (pp. 15–62). New York: Cambridge University Press.

Higgins, E. T., & King, G. (1981). Accessibility of social constructs: Information processing consequences of individual and contextual variability. In N. Cantor & J. Kihlstrom (Eds.), *Personality cognition, and social interaction* (pp. 69–121). Hillsdale, NJ: Erlbaum.

Higgins, E. T., & King, G. A., & Mavin, G. H. (1982). Individual construct accessibilty and subjective impressions and recall. *Journal of Personality and Social Psychology, 43*, 35–47

Higgins, E. T., & McCann, C. D. (1984). Social encoding and subsequent attitudes, impressions, and memory: "Context-driven" and motivational aspects of processing. *Journal of Personality and Social Psychology, 47*, 26–39.

Higgins, E. T., & Moretti, M. M. (1988). Standard utilization and the social-evaluative process: Vulnerability to types of aberrant beliefs. In T. F. Oltmanns and B. A. Maher (Eds.), *Delusional beliefs* (pp. 110–137). New York: John Wiley & Sons.

Higgins, E. T., & Rholes, W. S. (1978). "Saying is believing": Effects of message modification on memory and liking for the person described. *Journal of Experimental Social Psychology, 14,* 363–378.

Higgins, E. T., Rholes, W. S., & Jones, C. R. (1977). Category accessibility and impression formation. *Journal of Experimental Social Psychology, 13,* 141–154.

Higgins, E. T., & Stangor, C. (1988). Context-driven social judgment and memory: When "behavior engulfs the field" in reconstructive memory. In D. Bar-Tal & A. W. Kruglanski (Eds.), *The social psychology of knowledge* (pp. 262–298). New York: Cambridge University Press.

Higgins, E. T., Strauman, T., & Klein, R. (1986). Standards and the process of self-evaluation: Multiple affects from multiple stages. In R. M. Sorrentino & E. T. Higgins (Eds.), *Handbook of motivation and cognition: Foundations of social behavior* (pp. 23–63). New York: Guilford Press.

Higgins, E. T., Tykocinski, O., & Vookles, J. (in press). Patterns of self-beliefs: The psychological significance of relations among the actual, ideal, ought, can, and future selves. In J. M. Olson & M. P. Zanna (Eds.), *The Ontario Symposium: Vol. 6. Self-inference processes.* Hillsdale, NJ: Erlbaum.

Homans, G. C. (1950). *The human group.* New York: Harcourt, Brace & World.

Horney, K. (1950). *Neurosis and human growth.* New York: Norton.

Hornstein, H. A., Lakind, E., Frankel, G., & Manne, S. (1975). Effects of knowledge about remote social events on prosocial behavior, social conception, and mood. *Journal of Personality and Social Psychology, 32,* 1038–1046.

James, W. (1948). *Psychology.* New York: World. (Original work published 1890)

Jones, E. E. (1964). *Ingratiation: A social psychological analysis.* New York: Appleton-Century-Crofts.

Jones, E. E., & Davis, K. E. (1965). From acts to dispositions: The attribution process in person perception. In L. Berkowitz (Ed.), *Advances in experimental social psychology* (Vol. 2, pp. 219–266). New York: Academic Press.

Kahneman, D., & Miller, D. (1986). Norm theory: Comparing reality to its alternatives. *Psychological Review, 93,* 136–153.

Kahneman, D., & Tversky, A. (1982). The simulation heuristic. In D. Kahneman, P. Slovic, & A. Tversky (Eds.), *Judgment under uncertainty: Heuristics and biases* (pp. 201–208). New York: Cambridge University Press.

Kanfer, F. H. (1971). The maintenance of behavior by self-generated stimuli and reinforcement. In A. Jacobs & L. B. Sachs (Eds.), *Psychology of private events* (pp. 39–59). New York: Academic Press.

Kelley, H. H. (1950). The warm-cold variable in first impressions of persons. *Journal of Personality, 18,* 431–439.

Kelley, H. H. (1952). Two functions of reference groups. In G. E. Swanson, T. M. Newcomb, & E. L. Hartley (Eds.), *Readings in social psychology* (2nd ed., pp. 410–430). New York: Holt, Rinehart & Winston.

Kelley, H. H. (1955). Salience of membership and resistance to change of group-anchored attitudes. *Human Relations, 8,* 275–289.

Kelley, H. H. (1967). Attribution theory in social psychology. In D. Levine (Ed.), *Nebraska Symposium on Motivation* (Vol. 15, pp. 192–238). Lincoln: University of Nebraska Press.

Kelley, H. H., & Stahelski, A. J. (1970). The social interaction basis of cooperators' and competitors' beliefs about others. *Journal of Personality and Social Psychology, 16,* 66–91.

Kelley, G. A. (1955). *The psychology of personal constructs.* New York: Norton.

Kenrick, D. T., & Funder, D. C. (1988). Profiting from controversy: Lessons from the person–situational debate. *American Psychologists, 43,* 23–34.

King, G. A., & Sorrentino, R. M. (1988). Uncertainty orientation and the relation between individual accessible constructs and person memory. *Social Cognition, 6,* 128–149.

Klinger, E. (1975). Consequences of commitment to and disengagement from incentives. *Psychology Review, 82,* 1–25.

Kruglanski, A. W. (1980). Lay epistemo-logic—process and contents: Another look at attribution theory. *Psychological Review, 87,* 70–87.

Kruglanski, A. W. (1989). *Lay epistemics and human knowledge: Cognitive and motivational bases.* New York: Plenum.

Kruglanski, A. W., Friedland, N., & Farkash, E. (1984). Laypersons' sensitiviy to statistical information: The case of high perceived applicability. *Journal of Personality and Social Psychology, 46,* 503–518.

Kruglanski, A. W., & Mayseless, O. (1988). Contextual effects in hypothesis testing: The role of competing alternatives and epistemic motivations. *Social Cognition, 6,* 1–20.

Kuhl, J. (1978). Standard setting and risk preference: An elaboration of the theory of achievement motivation and an empirical test. *Psychological Review, 85,* 239–248.

Kuhl, J. (1984). Volitional aspects of achievement motivation and learned helplessness: Toward a comprehensive theory of action control. In B. A. Maher (Ed.), *Progress in experimental personality research* (Vol. 12, pp. 99–170). New York: Academic Press.

Lau, R. R. (1989). Construct accessibility and electoral choice. *Political Behavior, 11,* 5–32.

Lazarus, R. S. (1966). *Psychological stress and the coping process.* New York: McGraw-Hill.

Levinson, D. J. (1978). *The seasons of a man's life.* New York: Ballantine Books.

Lewin, K. (1935). *A dynamic theory of personality.* New York: McGraw-Hill.

Lewin, K. (1951). *Field theory in social science.* New York: Harper.

Lombardi, W. J., Higgins, E. T., & Bargh, J. A. (1987). The role of consciousness in priming effects on categorization. *Personality and Social Psychology Bulletin, 13,* 411–429.

Manis, M., & Armstrong, G. W. (1971). Contrast effects in verbal output. *Journal of Experimental Social Psychology, 7,* 381–388.

Markus, H. (1983). Self-knowledge: An expanded view. *Journal of Personality, 51,* 543–565.

Markus, H., & Nurius, P. (1986). Possible selves. *American Psychologist, 41,* 954–969.

Markus, H., & Smith, J. (1981). The influence of self-schema on the perception of others. In N. Cantor & J. F. Kihlstrom (Eds.), *Personality, cognition, and social interaction* (pp. 233–262). Hillsdale, NJ: Erlbaum.

Markus, H., & Wurf, E. (1987). The dynamic self-concept: A social psychological perspective. *Annual Review of Psychology, 38,* 299–337.

Marlowe, D., & Gergen, K. J. (1969). Personality and social interaction. In G. Lindzey & E. Aronson (Eds.), *Handbook of social psychology,* (2nd ed., Vol. 3, pp. 590–665). Reading, MA: Addison-Wesley

Martin, L. L. (1986). Set/reset: Use and disuse of concepts in impression formation. *Journal of Personality and Social Psychology, 51,* 493–504.

McArthur, L. Z. (1981). What grabs you? The role of attention in impression formation and causal attribution. In E. T. Higgins, C. P. Herman, & M. P. Zanna (Eds.), *Social cognition: The Ontario symposium* (Vol. 1, pp. 201–246). Hillsdale, NJ: Erlbaum.

McArthur, L. Z., & Baron, R. M. (1983). Toward an ecological theory of social perception. *Psychological Review, 90,* 215–235.

McClelland, D. C. (1961). *The achieving society.* Princeton, NJ: Van Nostrand.

McGuire, W. J., McGuire, C. V., & Winton, W. (1979). Effects of household sex composition on the salience of one's gender in the spontaneous self-concept. *Journal of Experimental Social Psychology, 15,* 77–90.

Mead, G. H. (1934). *Mind, self, and society.* Chicago: University of Chicago Press.

Meichenbaum, D. (1977). *Cognitive-behavior modification: An integrative approach.* New York: Plenum.

Merton, R. K. (1957). *Social theory and social structure.* Glencoe, IL: Free Press.

Merton, R. K. & Kitt, A. S. (1952). Contributions to the theory of reference-group behavior. In G. E. Swanson, T. M. Newcomb, & E. L. Hartley (Eds.), *Readings in social psychology* (2nd ed, pp. 430–444). New York: Holt, Rinehart & Winston.

Miller, D. T., & Turnbull, W. (1986). Expectancies and interpersonal processes. *Annual Review of Psychology, 37,* 233–256.

Miller, D. T., Turnbull, W., & McFarland, C. (1989). Counterfactual thinking and social perception: Thinking about what might have been. In M. P. Zanna (Ed.), *Advances in experimental social psychology* (Vol. 23). New York: Academic Press.

Milgram, S. (1974). *Obedience to authority.* New York: Harper & Row.

Mischel, W. (1968). *Personality and assessment.* New York: Wiley.

Mischel, W. (1973). Toward a cognitive social learning reconceptualization of personality. *Psychological Review, 80,* 252–283.

Mischel, W. (1977). The interaction of person and situation. In D. Magnusson & N. Endler (Eds.), *Personality at the crossroads: Current issues in interactional psychology* (pp. 333–352). Hillsdale, NJ: Erlbaum.

Mischel, W. (1983). Delay of gratification as process and as person available in development. In D. Magnusson & V. P. Allen (Eds.), *Human development: An interactional perspective* (pp. 149–165). New York: Academic Press.

Mischel, W., Ebbesen, E. B., & Zeiss, A. R. (1973). Selective attention to the self: Situational and dispositional determinants. *Journal of Personality and Social Psychology, 27,* 129–142.

Mischel, W., & Patterson, C. J. (1978). Effective plans for self-control in children. In W. A. Collins (Ed.), *Minnesota Symposia on Child Psychology* Vol. 11, pp. 199–230). Hillsdale, NJ: Erlbaum.

Mischel, W., & Peake, P. K. (1982). Beyond deja vu in the search for cross-situational consistency *Psychological Review, 89,* 730–755.

Morse, S. J., & Gergen, K. J. (1970). Social comparison, self-consistency, and the concept of self. *Journal of Personality and Social Psychology, 16,* 148–156.

Much, N. C., & Shweder, R. A. (1978). Speaking of rules: The analysis of culture in the breach. In W. Damon (Ed.), *New directions for child development: Vol. 2. Moral development* (pp. 19–39). San Francisco: Jossey-Bass.

Murphy, G. (1954). Social motivation. In G. Lindzey (Ed.), *Handbook of social psychology* (Vol. 2, pp. 601–633). Reading, MA: Addison-Wesley.

Murray, H. A. (1938). *Explorations in personality.* New York: Oxford University Press.

Newcomb, T. M. (1952). Attitude development as a function of reference groups: The Bennington study. In G. E. Swanson, T. M. Newcomb, & E. L. Hartley (Eds.), *Readings in social psychology* (2nd ed., pp. 420–430). New York: Holt, Rinehart & Winston.

Newman, L. S., & Uleman, J. S. (in press). Assimilation and contrast effects in spontaneous trait inference. *Personality and Social Psychology Bulletin.*

Newtson, D. (1973). Attribution and the unit of perception of ongoing behavior. *Journal of Personality and Social Psychology, 28,* 28–38.

Nisbett, R. E. (1972). Hunger, obesity, and the ventromedial hypothalamus. *Psychological Review, 79,* 433–453.

Nisbett, R. E., & Ross, L. D. (1980). *Human inference: Strategies and shortcomings of social judgment.* Englewood Cliffs, NJ: Prentice-Hall.

Nucci, L. P., & Turiel, E. (1978). Social interactions and the development of social concepts in preschool children. *Child Development, 49,* 400–407.

Olweus, D. (1977). Aggression and peer acceptance in preadolescent boys: Two short-term longitudinal studies of ratings. *Child Development, 48,* 1301–1313.

Parsons, T. (1964). *Social structure and personality.* Glencoe, IL: Free Press.

Pervin, L. A. (1985). Personality: Current controversies, issues and directions. *Annual Review of Psychology, 36,* 83–114.

Piaget, J. (1952). *The origins of intelligence in children.* New York: International University Press.

Pool, D. L., Schweder, R. A., & Much, N. C. (1983). Culture as a cognitive system: Differentiated rule understandings in children and other savages. In E. T. Higgins, D. N. Rubie, & W. W. Hartup (Eds.), *Social cognition and social development: A sociocultural perspective* (pp. 193–213). New York: Cambridge University Press.

Rausch, M. L. (1977). Paradox, levels, and junctures in person–situation systems. In D. Magnusson & N. S. Endler (Eds.), *Personality at the crossroads: Current issues in interactional psychology* (pp. 287–304). Hillsdale, NJ: Erlbaum.

Raynor, J. O., & McFarlin, D. B. (1986). Motivation and the self-system. In R. M. Sorrentino & E. T. Higgins (Eds.), *Handbook of motivation and cognition: Foundations of social behavior* (pp. 96–121). New York: Guilford Press.

Rholes, W. S., & Pryor, J. B. (1982). Cognitive accessibility and causal attributions. *Personality and Social Psychology Bulletin, 8,* 719–727.

Rogers, C. R. (1961). *On becoming a person.* Boston: Houghton Mifflin.

Rosch, E. (1978). Principles of categorization. In E. Rosch

& B. B. Lloyd (Eds.), *Cognition and categorization* (pp. 27–48). Hillsdale, NJ: Erlbaum.

Rosenberg, M. (1962). The dissonant religious context and emotional disturbance. *American Journal of Sociology, 68*, 1–10.

Ross, L. (1977). The intuitive psychologist and his shortcomings: Distortions in the attribution process. In L. Berkowitz (Ed.), *Advances in experimental social psychology* (Vol. 10, pp. 173–220). New York: Academic Press.

Rotter, J. B. (1954). *Social learning and clinical psychology.* Englewood Cliffs, NJ: Prentice-Hall.

Rotter, J. B. (1955). The role of the psychological situation in determining the direction of human behavior. In M. R. Jones (Ed.), *Nebraska Symposium on Motivation* (Vol. 3, pp. 245–269). Lincoln: University of Nebraska Press.

Ruble, D. N. (1983). The development of social comparison processes and their role in achievement-related self-socialization. In E. T. Higgins, D. N. Ruble, & W. W. Hartup (Eds.), *Social cognitions and social development: A sociocultural perspective* (pp. 134–157). New York: Cambridge University Press.

Salancik, G. R., & Conway, M. (1975). Attitude inferences from salient and relevant cognitive content about behavior. *Journal of Personality and Social Psychology, 32*, 829–840.

Sarbin, T. R., Taft, R. & Bailey, D. E. (1960). *Clinical inference and cognitive theory.* New York: Holt, Rinehart & Winston.

Schank, R. C., & Abelson, R, P. (1977). *Scripts, plans, goals, and understanding: An inquiry into human knowledge structures.* Hillsdale, NJ: Erlbaum.

Schlenker, B. R. (1985). Identity and self-identification. In B. R. Schlenker (Ed.), *The self and social life* (pp. 65–100). New York: McGraw-Hill.

Schwarz, N., & Clore, G. L. (1987). How do I feel about it? The informative function of affective states. In K. Fiedler and J. Forgas (Eds.), *Affect, cognition and social behavior.* (pp. 44–62). Toronto: C. J. Hogrefe.

Secord, P. F., & Backman, C. W. (1965). An interpersonal approach to personality. In B. Maher (Ed.), *Progress in experimental personality research* (Vol. 2, pp. 91–125). New York: Academic Press.

Shantz, C. U. (1983). Social cognition. In J. H. Flavell & E. M. Markman (Vol. Eds), *Handbook of child psychology* (4th ed. Vol. 3. *Cognitive development* (pp. 495–555). New York: Wiley.

Sherif, M. (1936). *The psychology of social norms.* New York: Harper.

Sherif, M. (1948). *An outline of social psychology.* New York: Harper.

Sherman, S. J., Ahlm, K., Berman, L., & Lynn, S. (1978). Contrast effects and their relationship to subsequent behavior. *Journal of Experimental Social Psychology, 14*, 340–350.

Showers, C. J., & Cantor, N. (1985). Social cognition: A look at motivated strategies. *Annual Review of Psychology, 36*, 275–305.

Sinclair, R. C., Mark, M. M., & Shotland, R. L. (1987). Construct accessibility and generalizability across response categories. *Personality and Social Psychology Bulletin, 13*, 239–252.

Singer, J. L. (1976). *Daydreaming and fantasy.* London: George Allen & Unwin.

Smith, E. R. (1984). A model of social inference processes. *Psychological Review, 91*, 392–413.

Smith, E. R. (1989) Content and process specificity in the effects of prior experiences. In R. S. Wyer, Jr., & T. K. Srull (Eds.), *Advances in social cognition* (Vol. 3). Hillsdale, NJ: Erlbaum.

Smith, E. R., & Branscombe, N. R. (1987). Procedurally mediated social inferences: The case of category accessibility affects. *Journal of Experimental Social Psychology, 23*, 361–382.

Snyder, M. (1979). Self-monitoring processes. In L. Berkowitz (Ed.), *Advances in experimental social psychology* (Vol. 12, pp. 85–128). New York: Academic Press.

Snyder, M., & Ickes, W. (1985) Personality and social behavior. In G. Lindzey & E. Aronson (Eds.), *Handbook of social psychology* (3rd ed., Vol. 2, pp. 883–948). New York: Random House.

Snyder, M., & Kendzierski, D. (1982). Choosing social situations: Investigating the origins of correspondence between attitudes and behavior. *Journal of Personality, 50*, 280–295.

Snyder, M., Tanke, E. D., & Berscheid, E. (1977). Social perception and interpersonal behavior: On the self-fulfilling nature of social stereotypes. *Journal of Personality and Social Psychology, 35*, 656–666.

Sorrentino, R. M., & Short, J. A. C. (1977). The case of the mysterious moderates: Why motives sometimes fail to predict behavior. *Journal of Personality and Social Psychology, 35*, 478–484.

Spivak, G., Platt, J., & Shure, M. (1976). *The problem-solving approach to adjustment.* San Francisco: Jossey-Bass.

Srull, T. K., & Wyer R. S., Jr. (1979). The role of category accessibility in the interpretation of information about persons: Some determinants and implications. *Journal of Personality and Social Psychology, 37*, 1660–1672.

Srull, T. K., & Wyer, R. S., Jr. (1980). Category accessibility and social perception: Some implications for the study of person memory and interpersonal judgments. *Journal of Personality and Social Psychology, 38*, 841–856.

Strack, F., Schwarz, N., Bless, H., Kubler, A., & Wanke, M. (1988). *Remember the priming events! Episodic cues may determine assimilation vs. contrast effects.* Unpublished manuscript. University of Mannheim, West Germany.

Strack, F., Schwartz, N., & Gschneidinger, E. (1985). Happiness and reminiscing: The role of time perspective, affect, and mode of thinking. *Journal of Personality and Social Psychology, 49*, 1460–1469.

Strauman, T. J., & Higgins, E. T. (1987). Automatic activation of self-discrepancies and emotional syndromes: When cognitive structures influence affect. *Journal of Personality and Social Psychology, 53*, 1004–1014.

Struker, S. (1980). *Symbolic interactionism.* Menlo Park, CA: Benjamin/Cummings.

Stryker, S., & Statham, A. (1985). Symbolic interaction and role theory. In G. Lindzey & E. Aronson (Eds.), *Handbook of social psychology* (3rd ed., Vol. 1, pp. 311–378). New York: Random House.

Sullivan, H. S. (1953). *The interpersonal theory of psychiatry.* New York: Norton.

Suls, J., & Mullen, B. (1982). From the cradle to the grave: Comparison and self-evaluation across the lifespan. In J. Suls (Ed.), *Psychological perspectives on the self* (Vol. 1, pp. 97–125) Hillsdale, NJ: Erlbaum.

Swann, W. B., Jr. (1983). Self-verification: Bringing social reality into harmony with the self. In J. Suls and

A. G. Greenwald (Eds.), *Social psychological perspectives on the self* (Vol. 2, pp. 33–66). Hillsdale, NJ: Erlbaum.

Tagiuri, R. (1969). Person perception. In G. Lindzey & E. Aronson (Eds.), *The handbook of social psychology*, (2nd ed., Vol. 3, pp. 395–449). Reading, Ma: Addison-Wesley.

Tajfel, H. (1969). Social and cultural factors in perception. In G. Lindzey & E. Aronson (Eds.), *Handbook of social psychology* (2nd ed., Vol. 3, pp. 315–394). Reading, MA:: Addison-Wesley.

Taylor, S. E., & Fiske, S. T. (1978). Salience, attention, and attribution: Top of the head phenomena. In L. Berkowitz (Ed.), *Advances in experimental social psychology* (Vol. 11, pp. 249–288). New York: Academic Press.

Tesser, A. (1986). Some effects of self-evaluation maintenance on cognition and action. In R. M. Sorrentino & E. T. Higgins (Eds.), *Handbook of motivation and cognition: Foundations of social behavior* (pp. 435–464). New York: Guilford Press.

Thomas, W. I., & Thomas, D. S. (1928). *The child in America*. New York: Knopf.

Thorndike, E.L. (1898). Animal intelligence: An experimental study of the associative processes in animals. *Psychological Review, 5* (Monograph Suppl. 2, No. 8)

Trope, Y. (1986). Self-enhancement and self-assessment in achievement behavior. In R. M. Sorrentino & E. T. Higgins (Eds.), Handbook of motivation and cognition: *Foundations of social behavior* (pp. 350–378). New York: Guilford Press.

Trope, Y., & Ginossar, Z. (1988). On the use of statistical and nonstatistical knowledge: A problem-solving approach. In D. Bar-Tal & A. W. Kruglanski (Eds.), *The social psychology of knowledge* (pp. 209–230). New York: Cambridge University Press.

Tversky, A., & Gati, I. (1978). Studies of similarity. In E. Rosch & B. B. Lloyd (Eds.), *Cognition and categorization* (pp. 79–98). Hillsdale, NJ: Erlbaum.

Van Hook, E., & Higgins, E. T. (1988). Self-related problems beyond the self-concept: The motivational consequences of discrepant self-guides. *Journal of Personality and Social Psychology, 55,* 625–633.

Veroff, J. (1969). Social comparison and the development of achievement motivation. In C. P. Smith (Ed.), *Achievement-related motives in children* (pp. 46–101). New York: Russell Sage Foundation.

Wachtel, P. (1973). Psychodynamics, behavior therapy, and the implacable experimenter: An inquiry into the consistency of personality. *Journal of Abnormal Psychology, 82,* 323–334.

Weber, M. (1967). Subjective meaning in the social situation. In G. B. Levitas (Ed.), *Culture and consciousness: Perspectives in the social sciences* (pp. 156–169). New York: Braziller.

Wertheimer, M. (1923). Untersuchunger zur Lehre van der Gestalt: II. *Psychologische Forschung, 4,* 301–350.

Wicklund, R. A. (1982). Self-focused attention and the validity of self-reports. In M. P. Zanna, E. T. Higgins, & C. P. Herman (Eds.), Consistency in social behavior: The Ontario symposium (Vol. 2, pp. 149–172). Hillsdale, NJ: Erlbaum.

Wicklund, R. A., & Brehm, J. W. (1976). *Perspectives on cognitive dissonance.* Hillsdale, NJ: Erlbaum.

Wicklund, R. A., & Gollwitzer, P. M. (1982). *Symbolic self-completion.* Hillsdale, NJ: Erlbaum.

Wilson, T. D., & Capitman, J. A. (1982). Effects of script availability on social behavior. *Personality and Social Psychology Bulletin, 8,* 11–19.

Woody, E. Z., & Costanzo, P. R. (1981). The socialization of obesity-prone behavior. In S. S. Brehm, S. M. Kassin, & F. X. Gibbons (Eds.), *Developmental social psychology* (pp. 211–234). New York: Oxford University Press.

Word, C. O., Zanna, M. P., & Cooper, J. (1974). The nonverbal mediation of self-fulfilling prophecies in interracial interaction. *Journal of Experimental Social Psychology, 10,* 109–120.

Wright, J. C., & Mischel, W. (1987). A conditional approach to dispositional constructs: The local predictability of social behavior. *Journal of Personality and Social Psychology, 53,* 1159–1177.

Wyer, R. S. & Srull, T. K. (1981). Category accessibility: Some theoretical and empirical issues concerning the processing of social stimulus information. In E. T. Higgins, C, P. Herman, & M. P. Zanna (Eds.), *Social cognition: The Ontario symposium* (Vol. 1, pp. 161–197). Hillsdale, NJ: Erlbaum.

Wyer, R. S., Jr., & Srull, T. K. (1986). Human cognition in its social context. *Psychological Review, 93,* 322–359.

Zajonc, R. B. (1968). Attitudinal effects of mere exposure. *Journal of Personality and Social Psychology, 9,* 1–27.

Zillmann, D. (1978). Attribution and misattribution of excitatory reactions. In J. H. Harvey, W. J. Ickes, & R. F. Kidd (Eds.), *New directions in attribution research* (Vol. 2, pp. 335–368). Hillsdale, NJ: Erlbaum.

Zuckerman, M. (1988). Behavior and biology: Research on sensation seeking and reactions to the media. In L. Donohew, H. E. Syphar, & E. Tory Higgins (Eds.), *Communication, social cognition, and effect* (pp. 173–194). Hillsdale, NJ: Erlbaum.

Chapter 13

The Disorders of Personality

Theodore Millon

Harvard Medical School and University of Miami

As should be evident to those reading this handbook, opinions differ concerning how best to define personality. There is general agreement, however, that it is an inferred abstraction rather than a tangible phenomenon with material existence. Problems inevitably arise, however, when professionals reify these conceptual constructs into substantive entities. To paraphrase Kendell (1975), "familiarity leads us to forget their origins in human imagination." Certainly, the disorders of personality should not be construed as palpable "diseases." They are constructions invented to facilitate scientific understanding and professional communication. Should these constructs fail to achieve these aims, they should be recast or discarded. Unfortunately, most are likely to fade slowly, like old generals, receding all too slowly into the dustbins of history.

PERSONALITY AND PERSONALITY DISORDERS

From the viewpoint of psychopathology, what should the construct "personality" represent?

It may best be conceived as the psychological equivalent of the body's biological system of structures and functions. To elaborate: The human body as a whole comprises a well-organized yet open system of relatively stable structures that interconnect functionally as they process a wide range of both internal and external events in a coherent and efficient manner. The diversity of functions carried out by the body is awesome in its complexity and efficacy, as is the internal organization of structures impressively elaborate in its intricacy and articulation. The distinctive configuration of structures and functions that have evolved ensures that the system as a whole remains both viable and stable. This is achieved by processes that maintain internal cohesion and by actions that utilize, control, or adapt to external forces. A biological disorder arises when one or several of the following occurs: The balance and synchrony among internal components go awry; a particular structure is traumatized or deteriorates, with the result that it repetitively or persistently malfunctions; foreign entities such as bacteria or viruses intrude themselves, either overwhelming or insidiously undermining the system's integrity.

The construct "personality" may be conceived as a psychic system of structures and functions paralleling those of the body. It is not

339

a potpourri of unrelated traits and miscellaneous behaviors, but a tightly knit organization of stable structures (e.g., internalized memories and self-images) and coordinated functions (e.g., unconscious mechanisms and cognitive processes). Given continuity in one's constitutional equipment and a narrow band of experiences for learning behavioral alternatives, this "system" develops an integrated pattern of characteristics and inclinations that are deeply etched, cannot be easily eradicated, and pervade every facet of life experience. This system *is* the sum and substance of what the construct "personality" would "mean." Mirroring the body's organization, it would be a distinctive configuration of interlocking perceptions, feelings, thoughts, and behaviors that provide a template and disposition for maintaining psychic viability and stability. From this perspective, mental disorders would be best conceived as stemming from failures in the personality system's dynamic pattern of adaptive competencies. Just as physical ill health is never a simple matter of an intrusive alien virus, but reflects also deficiencies in the body's capacity to cope with particular physical environments, so too is psychological ill health not merely a product of psychic stress alone, but represents deficiencies in the personality system's capacity to cope with particular psychosocial environments.

Personality—Environment Interaction

Implied in the preceding paragraph is the assertion that adequate clinical analyses of both physical and mental disorders require data beyond those that inhere in the individual alone. In the biological realm, it must encompass knowledge of relevant features of the physical environment; in the psychological domain, it calls for an awareness of the character of the psychosocial environment. Kendell (1975) points to the reciprocal nature of this person—environment field in the following example:

A characteristic which is a disadvantage in one environment may be beneficial in another. The sickle cell trait is a deviation from the norm which in most environments produces a slight but definite biological disadvantage. In an environment in which malaria is endemic, however, it is positively beneficial. . . . This is a particularly serious matter where mental illness if concerned because here the environment, and especially its social aspects, is often of paramount importance. Quali-

ties like recklessness and aggressiveness, for example, may lead a man to be regarded as a psychopath in one environment and to be admired in another. (p. 15)

For the greater part of our psychodiagnostic history, attention has been focused on the patient's internal characteristics alone. When one moves to a systems perspective, external social and interpersonal dynamics are given equal status. As noted in Kendell's illustration, it may be clinically impossible to disentangle these elements when appraising the clinical consequences of an internal characteristic—for example, whether the sickle cell trait is advantageous or disadvantageous. For diagnostic purposes, internal and external factors are inextricably linked elements. Intrapsychic structures and dispositions are essential, but they will prove functional or dysfunctional according to their efficacy in specific interpersonal, familial, or social contexts. (It should be noted parenthetically that to assert that internal and external factors are interdependent and reciprocal is *not* to say that they contribute equal shares to the variance or prevalence of a particular pathology.)

The rationale for broadening the notion of a "disorder" to include the interplay of both internal and external systems is especially appropriate when evaluating personality pathology. Not only does personality express itself in everyday, routine interactions within group and familial settings, but the ordinary characteristics that comprise the patient's personality will elicit reactions that feed back to shape the future course of whatever impairments the person may already have. Thus, the behaviors, mechanisms, and self-attitudes that individuals exhibit with others will evoke reciprocal responses that influence whether their problems will improve, stabilize, or intensify. It is not only how experiences are processed intrapsychically, therefore, but also how social and familial dynamics unfold, that will determine whether the patient functions in an adaptive or maladaptive manner.

On the Nature of Personality Disorders

Historically, personality disorders have been in a tangential position among psychopathological syndromes, never having achieved a significant measure of recognition in the literature of either abnormal psychology or clinical psychiatry. Until recently they have been categorized in the official nomenclature with a melange of other, miscellaneous, and essentially secondary syndromes. The advent of the American Psychiatric Association's (1980) *Diagnostic and Statistical Manual of Mental Disorders*, third edition (DSM-III) has changed this status radically. Personality disorders now not only hold a place of prominence among syndromal groups, but have become central to the diagnostic schema. With the DSM-III multiaxial format—a significant breakthrough in its own right (Strauss, 1975; Williams, 1985a, 1985b)—personality pathologies comprise, by themselves, one of only two required "mental disorder" axes. Henceforth, diagnoses assess not only the patient's current symptom picture, via Axis I, but also those pervasive features that characterize the enduring personality pattern, recorded on Axis II. In effect, the revised multiaxial format requires that symptom states no longer be diagnosed as clinical entities isolated from the broader context of the patient's lifelong style of relating, coping, behaving, thinking, and feeling—that is, his or her personality.

This conception of personality breaks the long-entrenched habit of considering syndromes of psychopathology as one or another variant of a disease—in other words, some "foreign" entity or lesion that intrudes insidiously within the person to undermine his or her so-called normal functions. The archaic notion that all metal disorders represent external intrusions or internal disease processes is an offshoot of prescientific ideas, such as the concept of demons or spirits that ostensibly "possess" or cast spells on the person. The role of infectious agents and anatomical lesions in physical medicine reawakened this archaic view. Of course we no longer see demons, but many still see some alien or malevolent force as invading or unsettling the patient's otherwise healthy status. This view is an appealing simplification to the layperson, who can attribute his or her irrationalities to some intrusive or upsetting agent. It also has its appeal to the less sophisticated clinician, for it enables him or her to believe that the insidious intruder can be identified, hunted down, and destroyed.

Such naive notions carry little weight among modern-day medical and behavioral scientists. Given our increasing awareness of the complex nature of both health and disease, we recognize, for example, that most physical disorders result from a dynamic and changing interplay between individuals' capacities to cope and the environment within which they live. It is the patients' overall constitutional makeup—their vitality, stamina, and immunologic system—that serves as a substrate inclining them to resist or to succumb to potentially troublesome environmental forces. To illustrate: Infectious viruses and bacteria proliferate within the environment; it is the person's immunologic defenses that determine whether or not these microbes will take hold, spread, and ultimately be experienced as illness. Individuals with robust immunologic capacities will counteract the usual range of infectious microbes with ease, whereas those with weakened systems (e.g., those with acquired immune deficiency syndrome [AIDS]) will be vulnerable, fail to handle these "intrusions," and quickly succumb. Similarly, structural disorders such as coronary artery disease are not merely a consequence of the stress on one's life, but reflect each individual's metabolic capacity to break down cholesterol and lipoprotein intake; it is the body's ability to process nutritional and adrenergic excess that is the major determinant of whether arterial disease does or does not occur. Those with balanced enzymatic functions will readily transform and dispose of excess lipids, whereas those with less adequate equipment will accumulate arterial plaques that gradually develop into disease. Psychopathologic disorders should be thought of as reflecting the same interactive pattern. Here, however, it is not the immunologic defenses or enzymatic capacities but the patient's personality pattern—that is, coping skills and adaptive flexibilities—that will determine whether or not the person will master or succumb to his or her psychosocial environment. Just as physical ill health is likely to be less a matter of some alien virus than it is a dysfunction in the body's capacity to deal with infectious agents, so too is psychological ill health likely to be less a product of some intrusive psychic strain than it is a dysfunction in the personality's capacity to cope with life's difficulties. Viewed this way, the structure and characteristics of personality become the foundation for the individual's capacity to function in a mentally healthy or ill way.

Differentiating "Normal" from "Disordered" Personalities

No sharp line divides normal from pathological behavior; they are relative concepts representing arbitrary points on a continuum or gradient. Not only is personality so complex that certain areas of psychological functioning operate normally while others do not, but environmental circumstances change, so that behaviors and strategies that prove adaptive at one time fail to do so at another. Moreover, features differentiating normal from abnormal functioning must be extracted from a complex of signs that not only wax and wane, but often develop in an insidious and unpredictable manner.

Pathology results from the same forces that are involved in the development of normal functioning. Important differences in the character, timing, and intensity of these influences will lead some individuals to acquire pathological structures and functions, whereas others develop adaptive ones. When an individual displays an ability to cope with the environment in a flexible manner, and when his or her typical perceptions and behaviors foster increments in personal satisfaction, then the person may be said to possess a normal or healthy personality. Conversely, when average or everyday responsibilities are responded to inflexibly or defectively, or when the individual's perceptions and behaviors result in increments of personal discomfort or curtail opportunities to learn and to grow, then we may speak of a pathological or maladaptive pattern.

Numerous attempts have been made to develop definitive criteria for distinguishing psychological normality from abnormality. Some of these criteria focus on features that characterize the so-called "normal," or "ideal," state of mental health, as illustrated in the writings of Shoben (1957), Jahoda (1958), and Offer and Sabshin (1974); others have sought to specify criteria for concepts such as abnormality or psychopathology, as exemplified in the work of Scott (1958) and Buss (1966). The most common criterion employed is a statistical one, in which normality is determined by those behaviors that are found most frequently in a social group, and pathology or abnormality by features that are uncommon in that population. Among diverse criteria used to signify normality are a capacity to function autonomously and competently, a tendency to adjust to one's environment effectively and efficiently, a subjective sense of contentment and satisfaction, and the ability to self-actualize or to fulfill one's potentials. Psychopathology is noted by deficits among the preceding.

Despite the problematic nature of drawing sharp boundaries within the normality–disorder continuum, three features may be extracted to serve as differentiating criteria: a functional inflexibility, a tendency to foster vicious or self-defeating circles, and a tenuous stability under conditions of stress (Millon, 1969).

In the case of "functional inflexibility," the alternative strategies the individual employs for relating to others, for expressing feelings, and for resolving conflict and stress are not only few in number, but appear to be practiced rigidly—that is, imposed upon conditions for which they are ill suited. The individual not only is unable to adapt effectively to the circumstances of life, but arranges his or her environment to avoid neutral events that are experienced as conflictual or stressful. As a consequence, opportunities for learning new, more adaptive behaviors are reduced, and life becomes ever more narrowly circumscribed.

What distinguishes disordered from normal personality functioning is not only its rigidity and inflexibility, but its tendency to foster "vicious circles." What this means is that the person's habitual cognitions, mechanisms, and behaviors perpetuate and intensify pre-existing difficulties. Maneuvers such as reaction formation, cognitive constriction, and behavioral arrogance are processes by which individuals restrict their opportunities for new learning, misconstrue essentially benign events, and provoke reactions from others that reactivate earlier problems. In effect, personality disorders are themselves pathogenic; that is, they generate and perpetuate existent dilemmas, provoke new predicaments, and set into motion self-defeating sequences that cause their already established difficulties not only to persist, but to be further aggravated.

The third feature that distinguishes the disordered from the normal end of the continuum is what I prefer to term "structural instability"—that is, a fragility or lack of resilience under conditions of subjective stress. Given the ease with which troubled personalities are vulnerable to the reactivated past, and given their paucity of alternative coping mechanisms, they are extremely susceptible to the impact of new difficulties. Faced with recurrent failures, anxious lest old, unresolved conflicts re-emerge, and unable to recruit new functional strategies, these persons are likely to revert to increasingly pathological coping, to less adequate cognitive and emotional controls, to a loss of psychic cohesion, and ultimately to confused and erratic transactions with "reality."

PERSONALITY DISORDERS AND PSYCHOPATHOLOGY

Although the term "disorder" is employed as a label for all of the major syndromes of the official nosology, the current revision of DSM-III (DSM-III-R: American Psychiatric Association, 1987), classification systems can go awry if their categories encompass too wide a range of clinical conditions. There is a need to subdivide the subject of psychopathology along useful points of distinction. As discussed elsewhere (Millon, 1987b), a logical framework for a taxonomy of mental disorders would be one based on quantitative dimensions such as space and time. In nosological terms, space would translate into the degree to which the manifestation of a pathological process falls on a continuum from "circumscribed" (focal) to "pervasive" (systemic). Time would represent the duration of the psychopathology—that is, where it falls on a continuum from "transient" (acute) to "enduring" (chronic). It is largely on these grounds that distinctions should be made among "personality disorders," "clinical syndromes," and "adjustment reactions."

Differentiating Personality Disorders, Clinical Syndromes, and Adjustment Reactions

In addition to the two dimensions of circumscribed–pervasive and transient–enduring, the primary basis for distinguishing the DSM's concepts of "disorder," "syndrome," and "reaction" is the extent to which the observed pathology can be attributed to ingrained or internal characteristics versus external stressors or precipitants. As previously discussed, pathology always reflects a person–environment interaction. Nevertheless, it is useful to distinguish types of pathology in terms of the extent to which their determinants derive from personological versus situational forces—an issue evoking considerable debate in our field these past two decades.

Personality disorders (Axis II) are best conceived as those conditions that are "activated" primarily by internally embedded structures and pervasive ways of functioning. At the opposite end of this person–situation or internal–external continuum are the adjustment reactions, best construed as specific pathological responses attributable largely to circumscribed environmental precipitants. Between these polar extremes lie what have been termed clinical syndromes (Axis I), categories of psychopathology that are anchored more or less equally and simultaneously to internal personal attributes and external situational events. Exhibited as intensifications of a patient's characteristic style of functioning or as disruptions in his or her underlying psychic makeup, clinical syndromes are conceived of as responses to situations for which the individual's personality structure is notably vulnerable.

Viewed from a different perspective, the attributes that comprise personality have an inner momentum and autonomy; they are expressed with minimal inducement or external provocation. In contrast, the responses comprising adjustment reactions are conceived of as stimulus-specific. They not only operate independently of the individual's personality, but are elicited by events that are apt to be judged consensually as "objectively" troublesome. Clinical syndromes are similar to adjustment reactions (both compose Axis I of the DSM) in that they are prompted also by external events, but their close connection to inner personality traits results in the intrusion of memories and affects that complicate what might otherwise be a simple response to the environment. Hence, they often fail to "make objective sense," appearing irrational and strangely complicated. To the knowledgeable clinician, however, these syndromes signify the presence of an unusual vulnerability on the part of the patient; in effect, a seemingly neutral stimulus has reactivated a painful hidden memory or emotion. Viewed in this manner, clinical syndromes arise in individuals who are encumbered with notably adverse biological dysfuctions or early experiences. The upsurge of deeply rooted feelings presses to the surface, overrides present realities, and becomes the prime stimulus to which the individual responds. It is this flooding into the present of the reactivated past that gives the clinical syndromes much of their symbolic, bizarre, and hidden meaning.

In contrast to the clinical syndromes, adjustment reactions are simple and straightforward. They do not "pass through" a chain of complicated internal structures and circuitous functional transformations before emerging in manifest form. Uncontaminated by the intrusion of distant memories and intrapsychic processes, adjustment reactions tend to be rational and understandable in terms of precipitating stimuli. Isolated from past emotions and defensive manipulations, they are expressed in an uncomplicated and consistent fachion, unlike clinical syndromes, whose features are highly fluid, wax and wane, and take different forms at different times.

Unfortunately, the rather neat conceptual distinctions I have just drawn are not readily observed in the "real" world of clinical conditions. Interaction and overlap will almost always blur these boundaries, given that psychopathologies are rarely qualitatively distinct "disease entities." It would be a most naive clinician who asserted that his or her troubled patients invariably exhibited distinct personality disorders.

The subject areas that subdivide the clinical world differ in the degree to which their phenomena are inherently differentiated and organized. Some areas are "naturally" more articulated and quantifiable than others. To illustrate with an example from other sciences: The laws of physics relate to highly probabilistic processes in many of its most recondite spheres, but the features of our everyday physical world are highly ordered and predictable. Theories in this latter realm of physics (e.g., mechanics, electricity) serve largely to *uncover* the lawful relationships that do, in fact, exist in nature; it was the task of turn-of-the-century physicists to fashion a network of constructs that faithfully mirrored the universal nature of the phenomena they studied. By contrast, probabilistic realms of physical analysis (e.g., short-lived elementary particles) or systems of recent evolutionary development (e.g., psychosocial interactions) are inherently weakly organized, lacking either articulated or invariant connections among their constituent elements. In knowledge domains that relate to these less ordered spheres of nature (the "softer" sciences), classifiers and theorists find it necessary to *impose* a somewhat arbitrary measure of order; in so doing, they construct a degree of clarity and coherence that is not fully consonant with the "naturally" unsettled and indeterminate character of their subject.

Rather than equivocate strategically, or succumb to the "futility of it all," noble or pre-tentious efforts are made to arrange and categorize these inexact and probabalistic elements so that they simulate a degree of precision and order transcending that which they intrinsically possess. To illustrate: In fields such as economics and psychopathology, categories and classifications are, in considerable measure, splendid fictions, compelling notions, or austere formulas devised to give coherence to their inherently imprecise subjects.

Interrelationships Among Personality Disorders and Clinical Syndromes

The view that mental disorders are composed of distinct entities reflects our field's level of scientific development rather than the intrinsic nature of psychopathological phenomena. Hempel (1961), for example, has noted that in their early stages all sciences tend to order their variables into separate or discrete classes. As progress occurs, advanced methods of analysis become available to enable scientists to deal with the interplay of elements comprising their field, and thereby to specify how formerly unconnected characteristics overlap and interrelate. It would appear, then, that as personologic and psychopathologic sciences progress, syndromes are likely to be conceived less as discrete and independent, and more as converging and reciprocal, exhibiting both interconnected and distinct features.

A step toward the twin goals of differentiation and coordination was taken in the DSM-III, where the two major axes are separate yet interrelated. Axis I consists of the clinical syndromes—those symptom states that wax and wane in their severity over time, and that display themselves as the more acute and dramatic forms of psychopathology. On Axis II are found the personality disorders, which represent the more enduring and pervasive characteristics that often underlie and provide a context for understanding the more florid and transient Axis I symptomatologies. Each axis is recorded separately, yet they are conceived as representing interrelated clinical features. In its multiaxial construction, the DSM-III sought to encourage clinicians to explore relationships among diagnostic categories. It was hoped that clinical syndromes would no longer be seen as standing on their own as discrete entities; rather, they would be viewed as either precursors, extensions, or substrates for one another. More specifically, the clinical syndromes would be understood, at least in part, to be disruptions of functioning among the personality disorders—springing forth, so to speak, to dominate the clinical picture under stressful or otherwise vulnerable circumstances. Envisioned in this fashion, clinical syndromes are not distinct diagnostic entities, but are interrelated with complex personality characteristics.

How are these two elements of clinical psychopathology likely to be related (Docherty, Feister, & Shea, 1986)? Of the numerous explanations offered to account for these relationships, the most widely held possibility is that personality is etiological—that is, that personality disorders precede the onset of the clinical syndrome, and therefore establish a vulnerability to symptom formation (Klerman, 1973). This viewpoint, most heavily supported by psychoanalytic theorists, emphasizes the developmental history and early family environment as factors that shape individuals and predispose them to the clinical states of anxiety, worthlessness, or dejection (McCranie, 1971).

A related explanation of the connection between the two axes is that certain personalities may repeatedly create stressful life circumstances that precipitate development of clinical episodes (Akiskal, Khani, & Scott-Strauss, 1979). Illustrative of this are borderline personalities, with their erratic lifestyles and propensity toward tumultuous relationships and self-destructive behaviors.

In a related hypothesis, characterologic features may render an individual vulnerable to certain psychosocial stressors. The growing body of research on stress events, anxiety, and depression reflects the mounting interest in this theory. Studies have shown that depressions are frequently preceded by stressful events associated with separation or loss (Paykel, Myers, & Dienelt, 1970). Since not all people who experience stress become anxious or depressed, it is felt that either a genetic predisposition and/or life history factors (e.g., personality style, effectiveness of coping mechanisms, or available supports) may predispose certain individuals toward a clinical outcome (Becker, 1977). The dependent individual, for example, tends to be quite susceptible to feelings of anxiety and depression under the conditions of interpersonal loss, abandonment, or rejection.

Another explanatory approach suggests that many personality disorders may actually represent subclinical manifestations of major clinical syndromes (Akiskal, et al., 1979; Akiskal. Hirschfield, & Yerevanian, 1983). From this perspective, lifelong affective traits or "affective personalities" (e.g., the cyclothymic personality) may represent gradual stages of transition to full syndromic affective episodes (e.g., manic–depressive illness). Similarly, the schizotypal personality may be a dilute form of schizophrenia, and the avoidant personality may be a chronic, milder variant of clinical anxiety or phobia.

It has also been argued that rather than increasing vulnerability to a clinical state such as depression, personality may exert a "pathoplastic" effect; that is, it colors and molds the particular expression of the clinical symptoms (Paykel, Klerman, & Prusoff, 1976). Depending on the premorbid personality, symptoms such as hopelessness, anxiety, or self-deprecation may serve a variety of goals. In this thesis, the secondary gains of certain clinical states may elicit nurturance from others, excuse the avoidance of unwanted responsibilities, rationalize poor performance, or safely permit the expression of anger toward others. Partly determined by the gains received, clinical syndromes may take the form of dramatic gestures, irritable negativism, passive loneliness, or philosophical intellectualization.

Docherty et al. (1986) offer another possible basis for the comorbidity of certain Axis I and Axis II disorders—one they term the "coeffect" thesis. As they state it:

> This model proposes that the personality disorder and the syndrome disorder are separate psychobiological structures. However, it is proposed that they both arise from a common cause or third factor, a single disease process that generates both entities. In this model, neither the personality disorder nor the syndrome disorder is causative of the other. They are simply correlates. Each is caused by a common third variable. For example, a particular form of child-raising experience may give rise to dependent personality and also, independently, to vulnerability to depressive episodes. (p. 317)

Not to be overlooked in these patterns of relationship is the evidence that personality characteristics may influence a clinically disturbed individual's response to both psychopharmacological and psychotherapeutic treatment (Akiskal et al., 1980; Charney, Nelson, & Quinlan, 1981).

CONCEPTUAL AND CLASSIFICATION ISSUES

Humans developed reliable and useful classifications long before the advent of modern scientific thought and methods. Information, skill, and instrumentation were achieved without "science" and its symbolic abstractions and techniques of research. If useful classifications may be acquired by intelligent observation and common sense alone, what special values are derived by applying the complicated and rigorous procedures required in developing explicit criteria, categorical homogeneity, and diagnostic efficency? Do rigor, clarity, precision, and experimentation represent more than a compulsive and picayunish concern for details, more than the pursuit for the honorific title of "science"? Are the labors of differentiating clinical attributes or exploring assessment cutting scores in a systematic fashion worth the time and effort involved?

There is little question in this "age of science" that the answer would be yes. But why? What are the distinguishing virtues of precision in one's terminology, the specification of observable conceptual referents, the analysis of covariant attribute clusters? What sets these procedures apart from everyday methods of categorizing knowledge? Most relevantly, are conceptual definition and classification possible in the domain of personologic disorders? Can these most fundamental of scientific activities be achieved in a subject that is inherently inexact, one that possesses only modest levels of intrinsic order, one in which even the very slightest variations in context or antecedent conditions (often of a minor or random character) produce highly divergent consequences (Bandura, 1982)? Because this "looseness" within the network of variables in psychic pathology is unavoidable, are there any grounds for believing that such endeavors can prove more than illusory? Persuasive answers to this question of a more philosophical nature must be bypassed in this all-too-concise chapter; those who wish to pursue this line of analysis would gain much by reading, among others, Pap (1953), Hempel (1965), and Meehl (1978). Let us touch, albeit briefly, on a more tangible and psychologically based rationale for believing that formal classification in personality pathology may prove to be at least a moderately fruitful venture.

Can Personality Disorders Be Classified?

There is a clear logic to classifying "syndromes" in medical disorders. Bodily changes wrought by infectious diseases and structural deteriorations repeatedly display themselves in a reasonably uniform pattern of signs and symptoms that "make sense" in terms of how anatomic structures and physiological processes are altered and dysfunction. Moreover, these biological changes provide a foundation not only for identifying the etiology and pathogenesis of these disorders, but also for anticipating their course and prognosis. Logic and fact together enable us to construct a rationale to explain why most medical syndromes express themselves in the signs and symptoms they do, as well as the sequences through which they unfold.

Can the same be said for personologic and psychopathological classifications? Is there a logic, perhaps evidence, for believing that certain forms of clinical expression (e.g., behaviors, cognitions, affects, mechanisms) cluster together as do medical syndromes—in other words, that they not only covary frequently, but "make sense" as a coherently organized and reasonably distinctive group of characteristics? Are there theoretical and emprical justifications for believing that the varied features of personality display a configurational unity and expressive consistency over time? Will the careful study of individuals reveal congruency among attributes such as overt behavior, intrapsychic functioning, and biophysical disposition? Is this coherence and stability of psychological functioning a valid phenomenon—that is, not merely imposed upon observed data by virtue of clinical expectation or theoretical bias?

There are reasons to believe that the answer to each of the preceding questions is yes. Stated briefly and simply, the observations of covariant patterns of signs, symptoms, and traits may be traced to the fact that people possess relatively enduring biophysical dispositions that give a consistent coloration to their experience, and that the range of experiences to which people are exposed throughout their lives is both limited and repetitive (Millon, 1969, 1981). Given the limiting and shaping character of these biogenic and psychogenic factors, it should not be surprising that individuals develop clusters of prepotent and deeply ingrained behaviors, cognitions, and affects that clearly distinguish them from others of dissimilar backgrounds. Moreover, once a number of the components of a particular clinical pattern are identified, knowledgeable observers are able to trace the presence of other, unobserved, but frequently correlated features comprising that pattern.

If we accept the assumption that most people do display a pattern of internally consistent characteristics, we are led next to the question of whether groups of patients evidence commonality in the patterns they display. The notion of clinical categories rests on the assumption that there exist a limited number of such shared covariances—for example, regular groups of diagnostic signs and symptoms that can confidently be used to distinguish certain classes of patients. (It should be noted that because patients can profitably be classified into categories does not negate the fact that patients so classified display considerable differences as well—differences we routinely observe with medical diseases.)

Another question that must be addressed concerning the nature of personological categories may be phrased best as follows: Why does the possession of characteristic A increase the probability, appreciably beyond chance, of also possessing characteristics B, C, and so on? Less abstractly, why do particular behaviors, attitudes, mechanisms, and so on covary in repetitive and recognizable ways, instead of exhibiting themselves in a more or less haphazard fashion? And even more concretely, why should, say, behavioral defensiveness, interpersonal provocativeness, cognitive suspicion, affective irascibility, and excessive use of the projection mechanism co-occur in the same individual, instead of being uncorrelated and randomly distributed among different individuals?

The "answers" are, first, that temperament and early experience simultaneously affect the development and nature of several emerging psychological structures and functions; that is, a wide range of behaviors, attitudes, affects, and mechanisms can be traced to the same origins, leading thereby to their frequently observed covariance. Second, once an individual possesses these initial characteristics, they set in motion a series of derivative life experiences that shape the acquisition of new psychological attributes causally related to the characteristics that preceded them in the sequential chain. Common origins and successive

linkages increase the probability that certain psychological characteristics will frequently be found to pair with specific others, resulting thereby in repetitively observed symptom or trait clusters. Illustrations of these reciprocal covariances and serially unfolding concatenations among longitudinal influences (e.g., etiology) and concurrent attributes (e.g., signs, traits) are provided elsewhere (Millon, 1969, 1981).

Grievances itemizing the inadequacies of both our current and historic systems of classification have been voiced for years, as have suggestions that endeavors to refine these efforts are fussy and misdirected, if not futile and senseless pretensions that should be abandoned. However, the presence of such systems is both unavoidable (owing to our linguistic and attribution habits) and inevitable (owing to our need to differentiate and to record, at the very least, the most obvious of dissimilarities among the psychologically impaired). Given the fact that one or another set of classes is inevitable—or, as Kaplan (1964, p. 279) once phrased it, "it is impossible to wear clothing of no style at all"—it would appear both sensible and fitting that we know the explicit basis upon which such distinctions are to be made, rather than have them occur helter-skelter in nonpublic and nonverifiable ways. Furthermore, if personality pathology is to evolve into a true science, its diverse phenomena must be subject to formal identification, differentiation, and quantification procedures. Acts such as diagnosis and assessment presupppose the existence of discernable phenomena that can be recognized and measured. Logic necessitates, therefore, that psychopathologic states and processes be distinguished from one another, being thereby classified or grouped in some manner, *before* they can be subjected to identification and quantification.

Whatever data are included to provide the substantive body of a classification system, decisions must be made concerning the structural framework into which the groupings will be fit, the rules that will govern the clinical attributes and defining features selected, and the compositional properties that will characterize these attributes. Here we are dealing with the overall architecture of the classification—whether its constituents should be conceived as categories or dimensions, as well as a host of other differentiating characteristics from which one may choose. A number of the more signifi-cant of these structural elements, and the choices to be made among them, are discussed in this section. This is a task of no simple proportions, since there is nothing logically self-evident, nor is there a traditional format or contemporary consensus, to guide selections among these alternatives (see Millon, 1987a, and Frances & Widiger, 1986, for fuller discus-sion of this topic).

Categorical Types versus Dimensional Traits

An important issue separates medical from psy-chological traditions in the classification of their primary subject domains. Psychology's primary subjects have been especially well un-derstood by methods of dimensional analysis and quantitative differentiation (e.g., in-telligence measures, aptitude levels, trait mag-nitudes, etc.). By contrast, medicine has made its greatest progress by increasing its accuracy in identifying and categorizing discrete "disease" entities. The issue separating these two historic approaches may be best stated in the form of a question: Should personality pathology by con-ceived and organized as a series of dimensional traits that combine to form a unique profile for each individual, or should certain central char-acteristics be selected to exemplify and categorize personality types found commonly in clinical populations?

The view that personality pathology might best be conceived as dimensional traits has only recently begun to be taken as a serious alterna-tive to the more classic categorical approach. Certain trait dimensions have been proposed in the past as relevant to these disorders (e.g., dominance–submission, extraversion–intro-version, and rigidity–flexibility), but these have not been translated into the full range of personality syndromes. Some traits have been formulated so that one extreme of a dimension differs significantly from the other in terms of their clinical implications; an example here would be emotional stability versus emotional vulnerability. Other traits are psychologically curvilinear, so that both extremes have nega-tive implications; an example of this would be an activity dimension such as listlessness versus restlessness.

There are several advantages to dimensional models that should be noted. Most important is that they combine several clinical features or personality traits into a single profile. By their

comprehensiveness, little information of po-tential significance is lost, nor is any single trait given special attention, as when only one dis-tinctive characteristic is brought to the fore-ground in a categorical typology. Furthermore, a trait profile permits the inclusion of unusual or atypical cases; in typologies, odd, infre-quent, or "mixed" conditions often are excluded, since they do not fit the prescribed categories. Given the diversity and idiosyncratic character of many clinical personalities, a dimensional system encourages the representation of individuality and uniqueness, rather than "forcing" patients into categories for which they are ill suited. Another advantage of a dimensional format is that the strength of traits is gauged quantitatively, and therefore each characteristic extends into the nor-mal range; as a consequence, normality and ab-normality are merely arranged as points on a continuum rather than as distinct and separable phenomena.

Despite their seeming advantages, di-mensional systems have not taken strong root in the formal diagnosis of personality patholo-gy. Numerous complications and limitations have been noted in the literature, and these are recorded briefly here.

First is the fact that there is little agreement among dimensional theorists concerning the number of traits necessary to represent per-sonality. For example, Menninger (1963) con-tended that a single dimension would suffice; Eysenck (1960) asserted that three are needed (see also Chapter 10, this volume); by contrast, Cattell (1965) claimed to have identified as many as 33 and believes there are many more (see also Chapter 4, this volume). Recent mod-els have not achieved a notable level of con-sensus either. It appears, in fact, that theorists invent dimensions in accord with their ex-pectations, rather than "discovering" them as if they were intrinsic to nature, merely awaiting scientific detection. The number of traits re-quired to assess personality is not determined by the ability of our research to disclose some inherent truth, but rather by our predilections for conceiving and organizing our observations.

Second, describing personality with more than a few trait dimensions produces such com-plex and intricate schemas as to require geometric or algebraic representation. There is nothing intrinsically wrong with such quantita-tive formats, but they do pose considerable dif-ficulty both in comprehension and in com-munication among clinicians. Most mental health workers are hesitant about working with complex multivariate statistics, and the consequent feeling that one is lost in one's own professional discipline is not likely to make such schemas attractive, let alone practical for everyday use. Apart from matters of convenience and comfort, algebraic representations must be grouped into categories before the information they contain can be communicated. In effect, once a population has been identified as possessing a similar profile or dimensional pattern, it comprises a category. Thus, although the original format may have been dimensional, those who are grouped within it invariably are spoken of as constituting a "type."

Categorical models have been the preferred schemas for representing both clinical syndromes and personality disorders. It should be noted, however, that most contemporary categories neither imply nor are constructed to be all-or-none typologies. Although singling out and giving prominence to certain features of behavior, they do not overlook the others, but merely assign them lesser significance. It is the process of assigning centrality or relative dominance to particular characteristics that distinguishes a schema of categories from one composed of trait dimensions. Conceived in this manner, a type simply becomes a superordinate category that subsumes and integrates psychologically covariant traits, which in turn represent a set of correlated habits, which in their turn stand for a response displayed in a variety of situations. When this superordinate type is found with some frequency in clinical populations, we have reason to conclude that it may be useful as a concept that gives coherence to seemingly diverse symptoms.

Among the advantages of categorical typologies is their ease of use by clinicians who must make relatively rapid diagnoses with large numbers of patients whom they see briefly. Although clinical attention in these cases is drawn to only the most salient features of the patient, a broad range of traits not directly observed is strongly suggested. It is this capacity to suggest characteristics beyond the immediately observed that adds special value to an established system of types. For example, let us assume that an individual is diagnosed as a histrionic personality, following the observation that his or her behaviors are seductive and dramatic; although the data base is limited, there is reason to believe that the person is likely to be characterized also as stimulus-seeking, needful of attention, interpersonally capricious, emotionally labile, and so on. In effect, assignment to a particular type or category often proves useful by alerting the clinician to a range of unobserved but frequently correlated behaviors. This process of extending the scope of associated characteristics contrasts with the tendency of dimensional schemas to fractionate personality into separate and uncoordinated traits. Typologies restore and recompose the unity of personality by integrating seemingly diverse elements into a single coordinated syndrome. Moreover, the availability of well-established syndromes provides standard references for clinicians, who would otherwise be faced with repeated analyses and *de novo* personality constructions.

There are, of course, objections to the use of categorical typologies in personality. They contribute to the fallacious belief that psychopathological syndromes are discrete entities, even medical "diseases," when in fact they are merely concepts that help focus and coordinate observations. Furthermore, categories often fail to identify and include important aspects of behavior, since they reflect a decision to narrow the list of characteristics that are considered primary. Of course, the discarding of information is not limited to categories; dimensional schemas also choose certain traits to the exclusion of others. The problem, however, is that categorical types tend to give primacy to only a single characteristic. Another criticism is that the number and diversity of types are far less than the individual differences observed in clinical work. Not only are there problems in assigning many patients to the limited categories available, but clinicians often claim that the better they know a patient, the greater the difficulty they have in fitting him or her into a single category. A final criticism reflects the diversity of competing systems available: Numerous classifications have been formulated in the past century, and one may question whether any system is worth utilizing if there is so little consensus among categorists themselves. Is it possible to conclude from this review whether categorical or dimensional schemas are potentially the more useful for personality classifications? An illuminating answer may have been provided by Cattell (1970), who wrote:

> The description by attributes [traits] and the description by types must . . . be considered face and obverse of the same descriptive system. Any object whatever can be defined either by listing measurements for it on a set of [trait] attributes or

by sequestering it to a particular named [type] category. (p. 40)

In effect, Cattell has concluded that the issue of choosing between dimensional traits and categorical types is both naive and specious, since they are two sides of the same coin. The essential distinction to be made between these models is that of comprehensiveness. Types are higher-order syntheses of lower-order dimensional traits; they encompass a wider scope of generality. For certain purposes, it may be useful to narrow attention to specific traits; in other circumstances, a more inclusive level of integration may be appropriate. Is there another solution to the question of how the data of personality pathology might best be organized? Two newer approaches to this question have been proposed; they are touched on briefly next.

The Prototypal Model

The construct "prototype" has a long history, but only recently has it been introduced as a potentially useful option for classifying psychopathology. As presently formulated, it appears to meld several attributes of both categorical and dimensional schemas. It may prove especially apt as we seek to develop a format for representing both the composite of diverse elements comprising personality (the multidimensional aspect) and the features that distinguish personality from other forms of psychopathology—namely, durability and pervasiveness (the categorical aspect).

How has the concept of prototype been defined? Horowitz, Post, French, Wallis, and Siegelman (1981) describe the construct succinctly:

> A prototype consists of the most common features or properties of members of a category and thus describes a theoretical ideal or standard against which real people can be evaluated. All of the prototype's properties are assumed to characterize at least some members of the category, but no one property is necessary or sufficient for membership in the category. Therefore, it is possible that no actual person would match the theoretical prototype perfectly. Instead, different people would approximate it to different degrees. The more closely a person approximates the ideal, the more the person typifies the concept. (p. 575)

Mischel (1984) characterizes the prototypal approach as useful in recognizing the especially "fuzzy" nature of natural categories along the lines articulated by Wittgenstein. Category knowledge about persons and situations is represented by a loose set of features that are correlated, but only imperfectly, with membership in that category. The approach implies that categorization decisions (e.g., about who is a prototypic extrovert or used car salesman type) will be probabilistic and that the members of a category will vary in degree of membership. There will be many ambiguous borderline cases that yield overlapping, fuzzy boundaries between the categories. To study such fuzzy sets, one seeks the clearest and best exemplars (the most prototypic members), omitting the less prototypic, borderline instances. The prototype approach both to persons and to situations lends itself readily to the construction of orderly taxonomies containing categories at different levels of abstraction or inclusiveness. (p. 356)

Cantor, Smith, French, and Mezzich (1980) note that the "classical" approach to diagnosis depends on the identification of singly necessary or jointly sufficient features. By contrast, the prototypal view merely requires that sets be comprised of correlated features. As a result of this conceptual openness,

> prototypes permit extensive heterogeneity of category instances. Thus, one instance may contain most of the correlated features of the prototype and another may contain hardly any at all . . . prototypes make sense out of variations in typicality, where typical instances are simply those that share many correlated features with the category prototype. . . . The higher the overlap, the faster, more accurately, and more confidently the instance can be classified. An immediate consequence of this prototype-matching process is that typical instances will by categorized more efficiently than atypical ones, because typical instances have greater featural overlap with their prototypes. . . . To the degree that the prototypes for two categories have many common features and few distinctive ones, the categorizer may have difficulty distinguising between members of these categories. . . . There is one more factor that must be considered in a prototype-matching process. This factor reflects the degree of richness of a category prototype (as measured by the total number of its features) as well as the distinctiveness of the prototype (as measured by the number of its features that are not shared by rival categories). (pp. 184–185)

It is evident that the prototype approach shares many of the attributes associated with the dimensional approach—notably the diversity of correlated traits and symptoms involved, and hence the heterogeneity found among similarly diagnosed patients.

Frances and Widiger (1986) elaborate some of the advantages to be gained by the introduction of a prototypal format, especially as it may apply to the personality disorders:

> A number of practical implications follow from a prototypic orientation. Diagnostic categories are defined by polythetic (multiple and optional) criteria sets rather than monothetic criteria sets (that is, membership will require only the satisfaction of five of eight criteria and not five of five). This means that the diagnosis can be met by many (in this case 93) different combinations of individual criteria items. A measure of prototypicality for each patient can be established by simply identifying the number of criteria items possessed by the patient, with the patient who meets all eight of eight being considered the most prototypic. A prototypal model also acknowledges that some symptoms or combinations of symptoms are more important to the diagnosis than others and should therefore be given greater weight. One can do this by having the essential symptoms be necessary while the rest are optional. (p. 251)

Albeit implicitly, the prototype model guided the thinking of several DSM-III Task Force members who formulated both the rules and diagnostic criteria of the manual—for example, the opportunity to select only a subset of the criteria that make up a category, the presence of "mixed" syndromes, even the encouragement of multiple diagnoses. Cantor et al. (1980) record that these DSM-III changes

> help to emphasize, rather than obscure, the probabilistic nature of diagnostic categorizations. On the basis of the new manual, clinicians can now be trained to expect heterogeneity among patients and to recognize the probabilistic nature of diagnostic categorizations. Also, utilization of confidence/typicality ratings in diagnosis can be encouraged, and diagnoses can be made on the basis of degree of fit between the patient's cluster of symptoms and the prototypes for various different categories. (p. 192)

Diverging from the single, overarching attribute that characterizes a categorical typology, the prototype concept appears well suited to represent the pervasive and durable features that distinguish personality disorders from the frequently transient and narrowly circumscribed expressive sphere of the clinical syndromes.

Prototypal Domain Traits

The fact that some diagnostic classes in contemporary nosologies (e.g., DSM-III, the ninth edition of the *International Classification of Diseases* [ICD-9]) are composed essentially of a single clinical feature (e.g., depression), whereas others encompass several mixed features (e.g., histrionic personality), has not only confounded discussions of categoricality versus dimensionality, but has contributed a share of confusion to theory, research, and practice as well.

Skinner (1986) has elaborated several "hybrid models" that seek to integrate elements of a number of divergent schemas. In what he terms the "class–quantitative" approach, efforts are made to synthesize quantitative dimensions and discrete categories. Likewise, Livesley (1986a, 1986b) has formulated a schema to bridge both conceptual models. I have described an endeavor of a similar nature in earlier reports (Millon, 1984, 1986). My approach involves what I have termed "prototypal domain traits," which mix categorical and dimensional elements in a personological classification. The approach is essentially a refinement and more detailed specification of the prototypal model described above; it also broadens and makes more comparable the diagnostic criteria employed in the formulations of the DSM-III. As in the official schema, several criteria are specified for each disorder, but these criteria encompass a large set of clinical domains (e.g., mood/temperament, cognitive style). It is the diagnostic criterion that is conceived to be prototypal, not the personality as a whole. Each specific domain is given a prototypal standard for each personality. To illustrate: If the clinical attribute "interpersonal conduct" were to be deemed of diagnostic value in assessing personality disorders, then a specific prototypal criterion would be identified to represent the characteristic or distinctive manner in which individuals with each type of personality disorder ostensibly conduct their interpersonal life.

If a classification schema were to be composed that includes all relevant clinical domains (e.g., self-image, expressive acts, interpersonal conduct, cognitive style), and that specifies a prototypal feature for every domain for each of the personality disorders, the proposed format would then be fully comprehensive in its clinical scope and would possess directly comparable prototypal features for its parallel diagnostic categories. A schema of this nature would furnish both detailed substance and clinical symmetry to its taxonomy.

To enrich its qualitative categories (the several prototypal features comprising the clinical range seen in each domain) with quantitative discriminations (numerical intensity ratings), clinicians would not only identify which prototypal feature or features (e.g., distraught, hostile, labile) in a clinical domain (e.g., mood/temperament) best characterize a patient, but would record a rating or number (e.g., from 1 to 10) to represent the degree of prominence or pervasiveness of the chosen feature(s). Clinicans would be encouraged in such a prototypal schema to record and quantify more than one feature per clinical domain (e.g., if suitable, to note both "distraught" and "labile" moods, should their observations lead them to infer the presence of two prototypal characteristics in that domain).

The prototypal domain model illustrates that categorical (qualitative distinction) and dimensional (quantitative distinction) approaches need not be framed in opposition, much less considered mutually exclusive. Assessments can be formulated, first, to recognize qualitative (categorical) distinctions in which prototypal features best characterize a patient (they would permit the multiple listing of several such features), and second, to differentiate these features quantitatively (dimensionally) so as to represent their relative degrees of clinical prominence or pervasiveness. To illustrate: In the "interpersonal conduct" domain, Patient A may be appraised as justifying quantitative ratings of 10 on an "aversive" prototypal feature, 6 on the "ambivalent" feature, and 4 on the "secretive" feature. Patient B may be assigned a rating of 9 on the "ambivalent" feature, 7 on "aversive," and 2 on "paradoxical." Both patients are characterized by the "aversive" and "ambivalent" prototypal features, but to differing extents. They are not only distinguishable quantitatively (dimensionally) on two of the same qualitative (categorical) features; they differ as well on qualitative grounds, one having been judged as exhibiting "secretive," the other as exhibiting "paradoxical" interpersonal conduct.

As may be evident, the prototypal domain approach includes the specification and use of categorical attributes in the form of distinct prototypal characteristics, yet allows for a result that permits the diversity and heterogeneity of a dimensional schema.

Clinical Domains of Personality

Individuals differ in the degree to which their behaviors are enduring and pervasive. Moreover, each individual displays this durability and pervasiveness only in certain of his or her characteristics; that is, each of us possesses a limited number of attributes that are resistant to changing times and situational influences, whereas other of our attributes are readily modified. Furthermore, it should be noted that the features exhibiting this consistency and stability in one person may not be the same features showing these qualities in others. These core qualities of persistence and extensiveness appear only in characteristics that have become crucial in maintaining the individual's structural balance and functional style. To illustrate: The "interpersonal" attribute of significance for some is being agreeable, never differing or having conflict; for another, it may be interpersonally critical to keep one's distance from people so as to avoid rejection or the feeling of being humiliated; for a third, the influential interpersonal characteristic may be that of asserting one's will and dominating others.

In the following paragraphs, I identify a number of the major domains of personality that possess clinical significance. More specifically, I outline a set of structural and functional prototypal domains that not only will aid us in differentiating among the pathological personalities, but will provide us with specific diagnostic criteria that typify each personality prototype.

Valuable though it may be to organize a schema of clinical domains which represents various historic models, it may be more useful to set them aside in favor of an arrangement, discussed in prior pages, that conceives of the personality system in a manner similar to that of the body system—that is, dividing its primary domains into "structural" and "functional" spheres. The biological subjects of anatomy and physiology, respectively, investigate embedded and essentially permanent structures, which serve as mechanisms for action, and functions, which regulate internal changes and external transactions.

In the psychological sphere, functional characteristics represent dynamic processes that transpire within the intrapsychic world and between the individual and his or her psychosocial environment. For definitional purposes, we might say that the functional domains represent "expressive modes of regulatory action"—that is, behaviors, cognitions, perceptions, and mechanisms that manage, adjust, transform, coordinate, balance, discharge, and control the give-and-take of inner and outer life.

Not only are there several modes of regulatory action (e.g., behavioral, cognitive), but there are numerous variations in the way each of these functional domains are manifested or expressed. Every individual employs every domain in the course of his or her life, but individuals differ with respect to which domains they enact most frequently, and diverge even more in which of the expressive variations of these functions they typically manifest. As Bowers (1977) has put it:

> The way a person performs a common behavior is sometimes quite revealing. One person ordinarily eats and makes love fastidiously; another person is given to gluttony in both circumstances. The more idiosyncratically expressive a common behavior is . . . [the more it is] attributable to a relatively stable personality and behavioral organization. (p. 75)

Particular domains and expressive variations—those I speak of as "prototypal"—characterize certain personalities best. However, even the most distinctive of personalities will display several variations within any specific domain. Furthermore, dissimilar individuals differ in which variations they express most often, but these differences are largely a matter of quantitative frequency (dimensionality) rather than qualitative distinctness (categorality).

Four *functional* clinical domains relevent to personality are briefly described here. Prototypal variations associated with each personality disorder are specified later in detailed tables and the Appendix to this chapter.

1. *Expressive acts.* These relate to the observables of physical and verbal behavior, usually recorded by noting what the patient does and how he or she does it. Through inference, observations of overt behavior enable us to deduce either what the patient unknowingly reveals about himself or herself, or (often conversely) what he or she wishes us to think or to know about him or her. Not only are the range and character of behavioral functions wide and diverse; they also convey both distinctive and worthwhile clinical information, from communicating a sense of personal

incompetence to exhibiting general defensiveness to demonstrating disciplined self-control, and so on.

2. *Interpersonal conduct.* A patient's style of relating to others may be captured in a number of ways, such as the manner in which his or her actions affect others (intended or otherwise); the attitudes that underlie, prompt, and give shape to these actions; the methods by which he or she engages others to meet his or her needs; or his or her way of coping with social tensions and conflicts. Extrapolating from these observations, the clinician may construct an image of how the patient functions in relation to others (antagonistically, respectfully, aversively, secretively, etc.).

3. *Cognitive style.* How the patient perceives events, focuses his or her attention, processes information, organizes thoughts, and communicates his or her reactions and ideas to others are among the most useful indices to the clinician of the patient's distinctive way of functioning. Synthesizing these signs and symptoms may make it possible to identify indications of what may be termed an impoverished style, distracted thinking, cognitive flightiness, constricted thought, or the like.

4. *Regulatory mechanisms.* Although "mechanisms" of self-protection, need gratification, and conflict resolution are consciously recognized at times, those that remain unconscious and thereby avoid reflective appraisal often begin a sequence of events that intensifies the very problems they were intended to circumvent. Mechanisms usually represent internal processes, and hence are more difficult to discern and describe than processes anchored closer to the observable world. Despite the methodological problems they present, the task of identifying which mechanisms are chosen (e.g., rationalization, displacement, reaction formation) and the extent to which they are employed is central to a comprehensive clinical personality assessment.

The *structural* domains represent a deeply embedded and relatively enduring template of imprinted memories, attitudes, needs, emotions, conflicts, and so on; these templates guide the experience and transform the nature of ongoing life events. Psychic structures have an orienting and pre-emptive effect, in that they alter the character of action and the impact of subsequent experiences in line with preformed inclinations and expectancies. By selectively lowering thresholds for transactions that are consonant with either constitutional proclivities or early learnings, these structures often cause future events to be experienced as variations of the past. The following describes both the character and persistence of these structural residues of early experience (Millon, 1969):

> Significant experiences of early life may never recur again, but their effects remain and leave their mark. Physiologically, we may say that we have etched a neurochemical change; psychologically, they are registered as memories, a permanent trace and an embedded internal stimulus. In contrast to the fleeting stimuli of the external world, these memory traces become part and parcel of every stimulus complex which activates behavior. Once registered, the effects of the past are indelible, incessant, and inescapable. They now are intrinsic elements of the individual's makeup; they latch on and intrude into the current events of life, coloring, transforming, and distorting the passing scene. Although the residuals of subsequent experiences may override them, becoming more dominant internal stimuli, the presence of earlier memory traces remain in one form or another. In every thought and action, the individual cannot help but carry these remnants into the present. Every current behavior is a perpetuation, then, of the past, a continuation and intrusion of these inner stimulus traces.
>
> The residuals of the past do more than passively contribute their share to the present. By temporal precedence, if nothing else, they guide, shape, or distort the character of current events. Not only are they ever present, then, but they operate insidiously to transform new stimulus experiences in line with past. (p. 200)

For purposes of definition, structural domains may be described as "cognitive–affective substrates and action dispositions of a quasi-permanent nature." Possessing a network of interconnecting pathways, these structures contain the internalized residues of the past in the form of memories and affects that are associated intrapsychically with conceptions of self and others.

Four structural domains relevant to clinical appraisal are next briefly described. Thirteen prototypic variations, one for each personality disorder, are specified in later tables and the Appendix.

5. *Mood/temperament.* Few observables are more relevant to clinical analysis than the predominant character of an individual's affect and the intensity and frequency with which he or she expresses it. The "meaning" of extreme emotions is easy to decode. This is not so with the more persistent temperaments and subtle moods that insidiously and repetitively pervade the patient's ongoing relationships and experiences. Not only are the expressive features of mood conveyed by terms such as "distraught," "labile," "fickle," or "hostile" communicated via self-report, but they are revealed as well (albeit indirectly) in the patient's level of activity, speech quality, and physical appearance.

6. *Self-image.* As the inner world of symbols is mastered through development, the "swirl" of events buffeting the young child gives way to a growing sense of order and continuity. One major configuration emerges to impose a measure of sameness upon an otherwise fluid environment—the perception of self-as-object, a distinct, ever-present, and identifiable "I" or "me." Self-identity provides a stable anchor to serve as a guidepost and to give continuity to changing experience. Most persons have an implicit sense of who they are, but differ greatly in the clarity and accuracy of their self-introspections. Few can articulate the psychic elements that comprise this image, such as stating knowingly whether they view themselves as primarily alienated, or inept, or complacent, or conscientious, and so on.

7. *Object representations.* As noted previously, significant experiences from the past leave an inner imprint—a structural residue composed of memories, attitudes, and images, which serves as a substrate of dispositions for perceiving and reacting to life's ongoing events. Analogous to the various organ systems of which the body is composed, both the character and substance of these representations of significant persons and events of the past can be differentiated an analyzed for clinical purposes. Variations in the nature and content of this inner world can be associated with one or another personality and lead us to employ descriptive terms to represent them, such as "shallow," "vexatious," "undifferentiated," "concealed," and "irreconcilable."

8. *Morphologic organization.* The overall architecture that serves as a framework for an individual's psychic interior may display weakness in its structural cohesion; exhibit deficient coordination among its components; and possess few mechanisms to maintain balance and harmony, regulate internal conflicts, or mediate external pressures. The concept of "morphologic organization" refers to the struc-

tural strength, interior congruity, and functional efficacy of the personality system. "Organization" is a concept akin to and employed in conjunction with current psychoanalytic notions such as "borderline" and "psychotic" levels, but this usage tends to be limited, relating essentially to quantitative degrees of integrative pathology, not to variations either in integrative character or configuration. "Prototypic" variants of this structural domain are associated with each of the 13 personality disorders; their distinctive organizational qualities are represented with descriptors such as "inchoate," "disjoined," and "compartmentalized."

Cumulative "scores" obtained by assessing the presence of prototypic features across multiple clinical domains will result in personality configurations composed of mixed diagnostic assignments—portrayals that depict, in fact, the natural or "real" compositional structure of patients. Such diagnostic mixtures are highly informative and can be especially useful in identifying which domain should serve as the initial focus of therapy: deciding to address the prototypic feature of interpersonal conduct that would benefit by group or family techniques, or pinpointing the feature of mood/temperament that would be especially responsive to psychopharmacologic treatment, or discerning the character and level of a patient's prototypic morphologic organization that may be conducive to psychodynamically oriented therapy, and so on.

THE DISORDERS

In this section, I describe the clinical features and note the history of each of five of the more recently formulated and clinically prevalent DSM-III-R's personality disorders. In addition, brief reference is made to current issues and the rather meager empirical literature gathered in recent decades on these five disorders. The prototypic domain schema discussed in the preceding pages is presented in a series of adjoining summary tables. The Appendix to this chapter presents comparable tables for the eight DSM-III-R personality disorders that have not been selected for discussion in the following pages. Reference to the Appendix will provide the reader with each disorder's prototypic features across both functional and structural clinical domains.

Narcissistic Personality Disorder

Clinical Features

The DSM-III and DSM-III-R describe the narcissistic personality as possessing a grandiose sense of self-importance. Notable are the individual's exhibitionism and desire to gain attention and admiration from others. Abilities or achievements are unrealistically exaggerated, and there is a tendency toward extreme self-absorption. A sense of entitlement—the expectation that others will bestow special favors and considerations without assuming reciprocal responsibilities—is also characteristic of the narcissist. This special status for self is taken for granted; there is little awareness that exploitative behavior is inconsiderate and presumptuous. Achievement deficits and social irresponsibilities are justified by a boastful arrogance, expansive fantasies, facile rationalizations, and frank prevarications. Marked rebuffs to self-esteem may provoke serious disruptions in the more characteristic unruffled composure. And despite the insouciant air of indifference and imperturbability, the individual is often quite preoccupied with how well he or she is regarded. When the person is faced with criticism or failure, there is either an attitude of cool disdain or feelings of intense rage, humiliation, or emptiness.

Historical Forerunners

Havelock Ellis, in his 1898 paper on autoeroticism, first gave psychological significance to the term "narcissism." Sigmund Freud's major contribution, "On Narcissism" (1914/1925), was devoted exclusively to development and pathology. He suggested that in cases of "perversion" and homosexuality, libidinal development has suffered disturbances that lead the individual to avoid the mother as the primary love object and to substitute the self instead. Another early and significant formulation from a psychoanalytic perspective was furnished by Wilhelm Reich in *Charakteranalyse* (1933). The major features of what he termed the "phallic–narcissistic" type, included such characteristics as being self-assured, arrogant, impressive in bearing, disdainful, and displaying airs of dignity and superiority.

More recent analytic conceptions include those of Otto Kernberg and Heinz Kohut. In *Borderline Conditions and Pathological Narcis-*

sism, Kernberg (1975) characterizes narcissistics as possessing an "unusual degree of self-reference in their interactions (p. 655)," as well as a great need to be admired, a shallow emotional life, and an exploitative and sometime parasitic relationship with others. Kohut's (1971) presentation of the narcissistic structure in *The Analysis of the Self* depicts the disorder as primarily following serious incursions into self-esteem; thus he stresses features such as hypochondriasis, depression, and feelings of emptiness and deadness. I have formulated an alternative social learning thesis concerning the origin of the narcissistic syndrome (Millon, 1969, 1981). According to this conception, the foundation of the disorder is best traced to excessive and unconditional parental valuation; this results in an unjustified sense of self-worth and a consequent vulnerability to objective inadequacies and failures.

Current Research and Issues

Other than theoretical and case studies, there has been minimal research concerning either the specific criteria for narcissistic personality disorder or whether they cohere into a meaningful pattern. Morey (1988a, 1988b) has carried out a series of studies examining the convergence and internal consistency of several of the DSM-III personality disorders, including the narcissistic; similar research with a more limited sample has been published by Pfohl et al. (1986). Both studies suggest that the narcissistic criteria show limited discriminability, with the possible exception of those related to feelings of grandiosity, fantasy preoccupations, and a sense of self-entitlement.

The decision to introduce the narcissistic disorder into DSM-III was not received in an entirely favorable manner. Gunderson (1983), Vaillant and Perry (1985), and Bursten (1982) raised questions concerning the evidence for the disorder, asserting that narcissistic elements exist in all patients who exhibit personality disorders. Problematic also was the view that its prime features are not readily observable—for example, that they must be inferred from nonstandard sources, such as the emerging of the transference relationship in analytic therapy. Developing and refining criteria that could be identified and reliably evaluated remain troublesome aspects of this disorder. Yet, as Lasch (1978) has noted, the narcissistic pattern may come close to characterizing our most recent generation of Americans, troubled or not.

Reference may be made to Table 13.1, in which the diagnostic features of this personality are framed in terms of broad trait domains.

Self-Defeating Personality Disorder

Clinical Picture

Self-defeating (masochistic) personality disorder, newly introduced in DSM-III-R, is a character type well described in the literature. Relating to others in an obsequious and self-sacrificing manner, these persons allow if not actually encourage others to exploit or take advantage of them. They seem to be drawn to situations or relationships in which they will suffer. Focusing on their very worst features, many assert that they deserve being shamed and humbled. To compound their pain and anguish—states that they experience as comforting and that they may strive to achieve—they actively and repetitively recall their past misfortunes, as well as transform otherwise fortunate circumstances into their potentially most problematic outcomes. Not untypically, they will incite rejecting responses from others, and then feel hurt or humiliated. Typically acting in an unpresuming and self-effacing ways, they will often intensify their deficits and place themselves in an inferior light or abject position.

Historical Forerunners

Although the concept of masochism was first formulated by Krafft-Ebing in his studies of psychopathologic sexual behavior in 1882, it was Freud and his disciples who developed a more contemporaneous explication. Prior to formulating his hypothesis that destructive behaviors are conceived best as derivatives of a death instinct, Freud referred to the masochist as like a child who is behaving with inexplicable naughtiness and is thereby "making a confession and trying to provoke punishment as a simultaneous means of setting his sense of guilt at rest and of satisfying his masochism" (1918/1925, p. 28). Reich (1933) identified the major traits as "chronic tendencies to inflict pain upon and to debase oneself ('moral masochism') and an intense passion for tormenting others, from which the masochist suffers no less than his object." (pp. 237–238) What appears to distinguish the genesis of the masochistic patterns, according to Reich, is the strategy the children acquire to spitefully "get back" at and

TABLE 13.1. Narcissistic Personality

Functional Domains

(a) BEHAVIORALLY ARROGANT (e.g., flouts conventional rules of shared social living, viewing them as naive or inapplicable to self; reveals a careless disregard for personal integrity and an indifference to the rights of others).

(b) INTERPERSONALLY EXPLOITIVE (e.g., feels entitled, is unempathic, and expects special favors without assuming reciprocal responsibilities; shamelessly takes others for granted and uses them to enhance self and indulge desires).

(c) COGNITIVELY EXPANSIVE (e.g., has an undisciplined imagination and exhibits a preoccupation with immature fantasies of success, beauty, or love; is minimally constrained by objective reality, takes liberties with facts, and often lies to redeem self-illusions).

(d) RATIONALIZATION MECHANISM (e.g., is self-deceptive and facile in devising plausible reasons to justify self-centered and socially inconsiderate behaviors; offers alibis to place oneself in the best possible light, despite evident shortcomings or failures).

Structural Domains

(e) INSOUCIANT MOOD (e.g., manifests a general air of nonchalance and imperturbability; appears coolly unimpressionable or buoyantly optimistic, except when narcissistic confidence is shaken, at which time either rage, shame, or emptiness is briefly displayed).

(f) ADMIRABLE SELF-IMAGE (e.g., confidently exhibits self, acting in a self-assured manner and displaying achievements; has a sense of high self-worth, despite being seen by others as egotistic, inconsiderate, and arrogant).

(g) CONTRIVED INTERNALIZATIONS (e.g., inner object representations are composed far more than usual of illusory ideas and memories, synthetic drives, conflicts, and pretentious, if not simulated, percepts and attitudes, all of which are readily refashioned as the need arises).

(h) SPURIOUS MORPHOLOGIC ORGANIZATION (e.g., coping and defensive strategies tend to be flimsy and transparent, appear more substantial and dynamically orchestrated than they are, regulating impulses only marginally, channeling needs with minimal restraint, and creating an inner world in which conflicts are dismissed, failures are quickly redeemed, and self-pride is effortlessly reasserted).

Note. From "Personality Prototypes and Their Diagnostic Criteria" by T. Millon, 1986, in T. Millon and G. L. Klerman (Eds.), *Contemporary Directions in Psychopathology* (p. 702), New York: Guilford Press. Copyright 1986 by The Guilford Press. Reprinted by permission.

torture their rejecting parents. According to Horney (1939),

> [T]he specifically masochistic way of expressing hostility is by suffering, helplessness, by the person representing himself as victimized and harmed. The hostility . . . is not altogether merely defensive. It often has a sadistic character. . . . [It] springs from the vindictiveness of a weak and suppressed individual . . . who craves to feel that he too can subject others to his wishes and make them cringe. (pp. 261–263)

Nonanalytic writers also characterized personality variants akin to the masochistic or self-defeating types. Thus, Schneider (1923/1950) spoke of the depressive psychopath in whom "suffering is taken as a mark of quality and there is a tendency to establish an aristocracy of discomfort (p. 81).

Current Research and Issues

The position that a "masochistic" character should be added to the DSM-III personality disorder section (Axis II) came too late in the committee's deliberations to be examined fully. Several analytically oriented authors made recommendations of this nature during the period prior to the development of the DSM-III-R (Frances, 1980; Gunderson, 1983; Kernberg, 1984). The decision to add the disorder to the appendix followed considerable controversy, however (Rosewater, 1987; Walker, 1987). Widiger and Frances (1988) summarize the issues well and succinctly in the following passage:

> The major empirical controversies are whether self-defeating personality disorder is biased against and/or harmful to women; whether it is a subaffective disorder, and whether it overlaps too much with the dependent and passive–aggressive personality disorders. There is some concern that the self-defeating personality disorder diagnosis may result in blaming the victim of abusive relationships, ignoring the threatening dominance of the spouse, and denigrating the loyalty and commitment of a wife to a marriage. Masochism was associated with "feminine nature" in the early

TABLE 13.2. Self-Defeating Personality

Functional Domains

(a) BEHAVIORALLY ABSTINENT (e.g., presents self as nonindulgent, frugal, and chaste, refraining from exhibiting signs of pleasure or attractiveness; acts in an unpresuming and self-effacing manner, preferring to place self in an inferior light or abject position).

(b) INTERPERSONALLY DEFERENTIAL (e.g., relates to others in a self-sacrificing, servile, and obsequious manner, allowing if not encouraging others to exploit or take advantage; is self-abasing and solicits condemnation by accepting undeserved blame and courting unjust criticism).

(c) COGNITIVELY INCONSISTENT (e.g., thinks and repeatedly expresses attitudes contrary to inner feelings; experiences contrasting emotions and conflicting thoughts toward self and others, notably love, rage, and guilt).

(d) DEVALUATION MECHANISM (e.g., repetitively recalls past injustices and anticipates future disappointments as a means of raising distress to homeostatic levels; misconstrues, if not sabotages, good fortune so as to enhance or maintain preferred suffering and pain).

Structural Domains

(e) DOLEFUL MOOD (e.g., is frequently forlorn and mournful; will intentionally display a plaintive and gloomy appearance, occasionally to induce guilt and discomfort in others).

(f) UNDESERVING SELF-IMAGE (e.g., focuses on the very worst features of self, asserting thereby that one is worthy of being shamed, humbled, and debased; feels that one has failed to live up to the expectations of others and, hence, deserves to suffer painful consequences).

(g) DEBASED INTERNALIZATIONS (e.g., inner object representations are composed of disparaged past memories and discredited achievements, of positive feelings and erotic drives transposed into their least attractive opposites, of internal conflicts intentionally aggravated, of mechanisms of anxiety reduction subverted by processes which intensify discomfort).

(h) INVERTED MORPHOLOGIC ORGANIZATION (e.g., owing to a significant reversal of the pain–pleasure polarity, structures have a dual quality—one more or less conventional, the other its obverse—resulting in a repetitive undoing of affect and intention, of a transposing of channels of need gratification with those leading to frustration, and of engaging in actions which produce antithetical, if not self-sabotaging, consequences).

Note. From "Personality Prototypes and Their Diagnostic Criteria" by T. Millon, 1986, in T. Millon and G. L. Klerman (Eds.), *Contemporary Directions in Psychopathology* (p. 707), New York: Guilford Press. Copyright 1986 by The Guilford Press. Reprinted by permission.

psychoanalytic literature. The DSM-III-R title was changed from masochistic to self-defeating in order to minimize the association of the diagnosis with this early literature. (p. 644)

As they go on to state, there are alternative explanations for this disorder that do not involve traditional analytic formulations. Numerous proposals of a more empirical and social learning character have begun to be published (Curtis, 1989) and provide reasonable explanations of the disorders.

Table 13.2 outlines several criteria for the disorder that seek to bridge some of the older and newer criteria.

Avoidant Personality Disorder

Clinical Picture

The diagnostic label "avoidant personality" is new, coined by me in *Modern Psychopathology* (Millon, 1969) as a designation for individuals distinguished best by their active, as opposed to passive, aversion to social relationships. Personality traits of a cast similar to the avoidant are scattered through the clinical literature, most frequently in conjunction with the schizoid personality. However, the social detachment of avoidants does not stem from deficient drives and sensibilities, as in the schizoid, but from an active and self-protective restraint. Avoidant personalities are acutely sensitive to social deprecation and humiliation. They feel their loneliness and isolated existence deeply, experience being out of things as painful, and have a strong (if often repressed) desire to be accepted. Despite their longing to relate and to be active participants in social life, they fear placing their welfare in the hands of others. Since their affective feelings cannot be expressed overtly, they are often directed toward an inner world of fantasy and imagination. Recurrent anxieties and a pervasive mood disharmony characterize their emotional life, however, and there is an overalertness to signs of potential social derogation that is intensified by

tendencies to distort events in line with anticipated rejection.

Historical Forerunners

The first portrayal that approximates the character of the avoidant pattern was described by
Eugen Bleuler (1911) in his classic text, *Dementia Praecox: Or the Group of Schizophrenias.*
Here, Bleuler depicted patients who "quite
consciously shun any contact with reality because their affects are so powerful that they
must avoid everything which might arouse
their emotions" (p. 65). Ernst Kretschmer
(1925) described the hyperaesthetic variant of
the schizoid temperament in his *Physique and
Character* as follows: "continual psychic conflict
. . . life is composed of a chain of tragedies . . .
sensitive susceptibility . . . behaves shyly, or
timidly, or distrustfully . . . seek as far as possible to avoid and deaden all stimulation from
the outside" (pp. 156–161).

In 1945 Karen Horney, drawing upon a neo-
Freudian orientation for her book *Our Inner
Conflicts,* characterized a pattern akin to the
avoidant, which she termed the "detached
type" and referred to as exhibiting a "moving
away from" interpersonal style. She notes that
for these personalities "there is intolerable
strain in associating with people and solitude
becomes primarily a means of avoiding it . . .
the underlying principle here is never to become so attached to anybody or anything so
that he or it becomes indispensable . . . better
to have nothing matter much" (Horney, 1945,
pp. 72–73).

As conceived in DSM-III, the avoidant personality had its origins in biosocial learning
theory (Millon, 1969) and was formulated as a
pattern that reflected an actively detached coping style. Prior to DSM-III, patients who were
anxiously withdrawn or exhibited social eccentricities were typically assigned the schizoid diagnosis; they now are likely to be diagnosed
as avoidant and schizotypal, respectively.
Whether all three disorders are merely minor
variants of the same basic syndrome has been
actively discussed in the literature (Frances,
1980; Livesley, Reiffer, Sheldon, & West,
1987; Millon, 1987b; Trull, Widiger, &
Frances, 1987).

Current Research and Issues

Widiger, Frances, Spitzer, and Williams (1988)
provide a succinct analysis of the major issues

associated with the avoidant personality disorder. As they state it:

> When it was introduced in DSM-III, avoidant
> personality disorder received considerable criti-
> cism for its deficient empirical support, lack of
> familiarity to clinicians, and close resemblance to
> the schizoid personality disorder. Some suggested
> that it was only narrowly relevant to the taxon-
> omy developed by Millon. However, avoidant
> personality disorder may actually have more util-
> ity than the schizoid diagnosis, as suggested by the
> fact that the prevalence rates in clinical settings
> for avoidant personality disorder are much higher
> than [those for] the rarely diagnosed schizoid per-
> sonality disorder. Many more persons appear to be
> socially withdrawn because of an anxious insecuri-
> ty than because of an apathetic indifference. . . .
> An important focus for future research will be the
> comorbidity and overlap of avoidant personality
> disorder with anxiety disorders, particularly social
> phobia. (p. 789)

There is logic to the view that the avoidant
disorder may be a complexly learned expression
of the single-dimension anxiety disorder. The
avoidant pattern may reflect the outgrowth of
secondary traits generated by the interaction of
a common strong biogenic disposition (e.g.,
the septohippocampal inhibition system;
Fowles, 1984; Millon, 1990) and broad-based,
interpersonal aversive learnings. This may give
rise to the avoidant's cluster of traits, such as
the anticipation of rejection, easy discourage-
ment, hypersensitivity to punishment, and
anxious withdrawal. The high comorbidity reported between the avoidant and dependent
personalities (Kass et al., 1985; Trull et al.,
1987) may also be traced in part to similar
biogenic sensitivities that evolve into somewhat different forms, owing to contrasting patterns of early experience and learning (Millon,
1981).

Table 13.3 provides a formal description of
the avoidant's characteristics.

Schizotypal Personality Disorder

Clinical Picture

Coined as a syndromal designation in the 1950s
by Sandor Rado, the schizotypal trait constellation had been described under a variety of other
terms for several prior decades. According to
DSM-III, where the label was assigned official
status, the prime characteristics of the disor-
order include various eccentricities in behavior,

thought, speech, and perception. Although it does not invariably occur, periodic and marked social detachment may be notable, often associated with either flat affect or severe interpersonal anxiety. There is a tendency to follow a meaningless, idle, and ineffectual life, drifting aimlessly and remaining on the periphery of normal societal relationships. Some schizotypal individual possess significant affective and cognitive deficiencies, appearing listless, bland, unmotivated, and obscure, and only minimally connected to the external world. Others are dysphoric, tense, and withdrawn; they are fearful and intentionally seclusive, inclined to damp down hypersensitivities and to disconnect from anticipated external threats. Notable also are their social attainment deficits—their repeated failure to maintain durable, satisfactory, and secure roles consonant with age. Many have experienced several brief and reversible periods in which either bizarre behaviors, extreme moods, irrational impulses, or delusional thoughts were exhibited. To many clinicians, the schizophrenic disorder is a syndromal prototype of which the schizotypal personality is a dilute and nonpsychotic variant.

Historical Forerunners

Although not labeled as such, the early history of the schizotypal concept may be traced in allusions found in the literature to dementia praecox and schizophrenia. A more recent parallel may be seen in the designation "ambulatory schizophrenics"—a term employed by Gregory Zilboorg (1941) to represent patients who "seldom reach the point at which hospitalization appears necessary . . . although they remain inefficient, peregrinatory, [and] casual in their ties to things and people." A similar formulation was presented by Roy Scharfer (1948) in his depiction of what he termed the "schizophrenic character." In 1949, Paul Hoch and Phillip Polatin proposed another variant in their conception of "pseudoneurotic schizophrenia." A major pathognomonic sign they noted was "the lack of inhibition in displaying certain emotions that is especially striking in otherwise markedly inhibited persons." To Sandor Rado (1956), who coined the schizotypal label, the primary defect is an "integrative pleasure deficiency," evident in the patient's lack of joy, love, self-confidence, and the capacity to engage in the "affectionate

---

TABLE 13.3. Avoidant Personality

Functional Domains

(a) BEHAVIORALLY GUARDED (e.g., warily scans environment for potential threats; overreacts to innocuous events and anxiously judges them to signify personal ridicule and threat).

(b) INTERPERSONALLY AVERSIVE (e.g., reports extensive history of social pan-anxiety and distrust; seeks acceptance, but maintains distance and privacy to avoid humiliation and derogation).

(c) COGNITIVELY DISTRACTED (e.g., is preoccupied and bothered by disruptive and often perplexing inner thoughts; the upsurge from within of irrelevant and digressive ideation upsets thought continuity and interferes with social communications).

(d) FANTASY MECHANISM (e.g., depends excessively on imagination to achieve need gratification and conflict resolution; withdraws into reveries as a means of safely discharging affectionate as well as aggressive impulses).

Structural Domains

(e) ANGUISHED MOOD (e.g., describes constant and confusing undercurrents of tension, sadness, and anger; vacillates between desire for affection, fear of rebuff, and numbness of feeling).

(f) ALIENATED SELF-IMAGE (e.g., sees self as a person who is socially isolated and rejected by others; devalues self-achievements and reports feelings of aloneness and emptiness, if not depersonalization).

(g) VEXATIOUS INTERNALIZATIONS (e.g., inner object representations are composed of readily reactivated, intense, and conflict-ridden memories, limited avenues of gratification, and few mechanisms to channel needs, bind impulses, resolve conflicts, or deflect external stressors).

(h) FRAGILE MORPHOLOGIC ORGANIZATION (e.g., a precarious complex of tortuous emotions depend almost exclusively on a single modality for its resolution and discharge, that of avoidance, escape, and fantasy; and hence when faced with unanticipated stress, there are few resources available to deploy and few positions to revert to, short of a regressive decompensation).

Note. From "Personality Prototypes and Their Diagnostic Criteria" by T. Millon, 1986, in T. Millon and G. L. Klerman (Eds.), *Contemporary Directions in Psychopathology* (p. 699), New York: Guilford Press. Copyright 1986 by The Guilford Press. Reprinted by permission.

give and take in human relationships." Elaborating on Rado's formulation, Paul Meehl (1962) presented an inventive neurologic–social learning thesis, seeking to elucidate the developmental origins of the schizotypal pattern.

Current Research and Issues

Considerable research has been undertaken in the relatively short period of time since the introduction of the schizotypal designation in DSM-III. Siever and Klar (1986) have provided a recent and exemplary review of the research literature, especially genetic and biologic studies connecting the personality disorder to its ostensible schizophrenic "parent." In evaluating the origins and evidence for this connection, Siever and Klar (1986) note:

> The Danish adoption studies of Kety and colleagues (1975) established that the diagnostic category of "borderline schizophrenia" and "latent schizophrenia", conceived of as a milder form of schizophrenia with social isolation, eccentricity, and transient psychotic-like symptoms, was more common in the biologic relatives of schizophrenics than in their adoptive relatives or in the biologic relatives of controls. The characteristics of the relatives with "borderline schizophrenia" generated the empirical basis for the criteria of schizotypal personality disorder. Several investigators applied the criteria for schizotypal personality disorder, or related criteria derived from descriptions of the borderline schizophrenics in the Danish adoption studies, to relatives of schizophrenics and found evidence for an association between schizophrenia and schizotypal characteristics. (p. 286)

Since the Danish studies were reported, questions have arisen as to whether the schizotypal pattern also occurs with disorders other than schizophrenia—that is, whether or not Kety et al. (1975) are correct in assuming that schizotypy is *specific* in its ability to identify relatives of patients with schizophrenia. Two recent reports raise serious questions as to this ostensible covariance (Coryell & Zimmerman, 1986; Squires-Wheeler, Skodol, Friedman, & Erlenmeyer-Kimling, 1988).

Another controversy surrounds the essential criterion that distinguishes the schizotypal disorder from other, similar disorders. Gunderson and Siever (1985) give primacy to the patient's social–interpersonal eccentricities, whereas Frances (1985) has argued that the evidence is stronger in the realm of cognitive–perceptual aberrations. For the present, the evidence is equivocal.

Suggestions concerning other criteria within the major realms of schizotypal pathology may be reviewed in Table 13.4.

Borderline Personality Disorder

Clinical Picture

Prior to the fashionable status it achieved in the 1970s, the label "borderline" was most often assigned when a clinician was uncertain about the diagnosis of a patient. Recognizing that many patients do exhibit mixed symptoms of indeterminant seriousness and changing character, certain theorists proposed that the borderline concept be formally employed to represent a midrange level of personality cohesion or prognostic severity (e.g., Kernberg, 1975; Millon, 1969). Although this view was that the borderline label is best used to designate a moderately decompensated level of functioning observable among different personality types and symptom constellations, the 1980 DSM-III characterized the syndrome as a discrete entity, a specific and identifiable disorder that possesses its own distinctive clinical features.

The most salient symptom ascribed to these personalities is the depth and variability of their moods. Borderlines typically experience extended periods of dejection and disillusionment, interspersed on occasion with brief excursions of euphoria and significantly more frequent episodes of irritability, self-destructive acts, and impulsive anger. Most individuals with this personality have had checkered histories either in personal relationships or in school or work performance. Few persevere to attain mature goals, and many exhibit an extreme unevenness in fulfilling normal social functions and responsibilities. Their histories show repeated setbacks, a lack of judgment and foresight, tendencies to digress from earlier aspirations, and failures to utilize their natural aptitudes. Most appear not to learn from their troubled experiences and involve themselves in the same imbroglios and quandaries as before. Disturbances in identity and goals are extremely common; these are evident in uncertainties regarding self-esteem, gender, and vocational aims. Their periodic moody contrariness often alternates with subjective feelings and complaints of isolation, emptiness, or boredom.

TABLE 13.4. Schizotypal Personality

Functional Domains	Structural Domains
(a) BEHAVIORALLY ABERRANT (e.g., exhibits socially gauche habits and peculiar mannerisms; is perceived by others as eccentric, disposed to behave in an unobtrusively odd, aloof, curious, or bizarre manner).	(e) DISTRAUGHT OR INSENTIENT MOOD (e.g., reports being apprehensive and ill-at-ease, particularly in social encounters; is agitated and anxiously watchful, distrustful of others and wary of their motives); or (e.g., manifests drab, apathetic, sluggish, joyless, and spiritless appearance; reveals marked deficiencies in face-to-face rapport and emotional expression).
(b) INTERPERSONALLY SECRETIVE (e.g., prefers privacy and isolation, with few, highly tentative attachments and personal obligations; has drifted over time into increasingly peripheral vocational roles and clandestine social activities).	(f) ESTRANGED SELF-IMAGE (e.g., possesses permeable ego-boundaries, exhibiting recurrent social perplexities and illusions as well as experiences of depersonalization, derealization, and dissociation; sees self as forlorn, with repetitive thoughts of life's emptiness and meaninglessness).
(c) COGNITIVELY AUTISTIC (e.g., mixes social communication with personal irrelevancies, circumstantial speech, ideas of reference, and metaphorical asides; is ruminative, appears self-absorbed and lost in daydreams with occasional magical thinking, obscure suspicions, and a blurring of fantasy and reality).	(g) CHAOTIC INTERNALIZATIONS (e.g., inner object representations consist of a jumble of piecemeal memories and percepts, random drives and impulses, and uncoordinated channels of regulation that are only fitfully competent for binding tensions, accommodating needs, and mediating conflicts).
(d) UNDOING MECHANISM (e.g., bizarre mannerisms and idiosyncratic thoughts appear to reflect a retraction or reversal of previous acts or ideas that have stirred feelings of anxiety, conflict, or guilt; ritualistic or "magical" behaviors serve to repent for or nullify assumed misdeeds or "evil" thoughts).	(h) FRAGMENTED MORPHOLOGIC ORGANIZATION (e.g., coping and defensive operations are haphazardly ordered in a loose assemblage, leading to spasmodic and desultory actions in which primitive thoughts and affects are discharged directly, with few reality-based sublimations, and significant further disintegrations of structure likely under even modest stress).

Note. From "Personality Prototypes and Their Diagnostic Criteria" by T. Millon, 1986, in T. Millon and G. L. Klerman (Eds.), *Contemporary Directions in Psychopathology* (p. 708), New York: Guilford Press. Copyright 1986 by The Guilford Press. Reprinted by permission.

Historical Forerunners

Because of its newness as a formal diagnostic designation, the label "borderline" has no historical tradition or clinical literature. Nevertheless, there are precursors that refer to essentially the same constellation of traits. Thus, in the eighth edition of his *Lehrbuch,* Emil Kraepelin (1921) described what he termed the "excitable personality" in the following manner: "[T]he coloring of mood is subject to frequent change . . . periods are interpolated in which they are irritable and ill-humored, also perhaps sad, spiritless, anxious; they shed tears without cause . . . they are mostly very distractible and unsteady in their endeavors" (p. 130). Kurt Schneider (1923) referred to a "labile personality" in *Psychopathic Personalities,* depicting such individuals as "characterized by the abrupt and rapid changes of mood . . . and [exhibiting] sporadic reactions of a morose and irritable character" (p. 116). Adolf Stern (1938) was the first among those of a psychoanalytic persuasion to apply the designation "borderline" to a group of treatment-resistant neuroses. Miletta Schmeideberg (1947), Arlene Wolberg (1952), and Robert Knight (1953) also presented thoughtful papers on borderline functioning from an analytic perspective. More recent is the work of Otto Kernberg (1975), who portrayed the syndrome in the following manner in *Borderline Conditions and Pathological Narcissism:* "Such patients . . . present . . . a lack of clear identity and lack of understanding in depth of other people . . . a lack of impulse control, lack of anxiety tolerance, [and a] lack of sublimatory capacity" (p. 161).

Current Research and Issues

The borderline disorder is perhaps the most commonly diagnosed of the personality disorders; likewise, it has become the disorder with the greatest number of publications in the past decade or so. From 1975 to 1988, there have been some 1,300 citations in the literature dealing with the epidemiology, course, characteristics, and treatment of the disorder. The range, diversity, and (unfortunately) the inconsistency of findings is impressive, if not heartening. Little can be said definitively concerning the pathogenesis of the condition, although there appears to be a growing consensus regarding its key features. The major etiological models center on early experience, especially as formulated by analysts such as Kernberg (1975, 1984), Stone (1980), and Gunderson (1984). More recent conceptions favoring the etiological role of contemporary social changes have been proposed (Millon, 1987b).

A breakdown of the major clinical features of this protean disorder may be found in Table 13.5.

Closing Comment

The introduction of DSM-III in 1980 provided a promising foundation for developing a systematic and empirically grounded schema for the personality disorders. Insufficent time has passed, however, to enable us to evaluate the particulars advanced in the DSM-III and its recent revision, DSM-III-R. What we have to work with is a promise, not a reality. Little empirical grounding exists for the criteria included in the manuals; it is the intent of the DSM-IV committee to provide this grounding, or to point to areas in which further work is mandatory. Many issues beyond those concerning the adequacy of the criteria must be faced—notably, whether these disorders are best conceived of as natural categories, quantitative dimensions, or conceptual prototypes. No less significant is the adequacy of the external validators used to determine the adequacy not only of each syndrome, but of the specific clinical features employed to define them. Last, but not least, are the theoretical assumptions and perspectives we bring to bear on the very nature of the subject itself: How we approach and conceive it will in great measure predetermine what we find.

TABLE 13.5. Borderline Personality

Functional Domains	*Structural Domains*
(a) BEHAVIORALLY PRECIPITATE (e.g., displays a desultory energy level with sudden, unexpected and impulsive outbursts; abrupt, endogenous shifts in drive state and in inhibitory control, places activation equilibrium in constant jeopardy).	(e) LABILE MOOD (e.g., fails to accord unstable mood level with external reality; has either marked shifts from normality to depression to excitement, or has extended periods of dejection and apathy, interspersed with brief spells of anger, anxiety, or euphoria).
(b) INTERPERSONALLY PARADOXICAL (e.g., although needing attention and affection, is unpredictably contrary, manipulative, and volatile, frequently eliciting rejection rather than support; reacts to fears of separation and isolation in angry, mercurial, and often self-damaging ways).	(f) UNCERTAIN SELF-IMAGE (e.g., experiences the confusions of an immature, nebulous, or wavering sense of identity; seeks to redeem precipitate actions and changing self-presentations with expressions of contrition and self-punitive behaviors).
(c) COGNITIVELY CAPRICIOUS (e.g., experiences rapidly changing, fluctuating, and antithetical perceptions or thoughts concerning passing events; vacillating and contradictory reactions are evoked in others by virtue of one's behaviors, creating, in turn, conflicting and confusing social feedback).	(g) INCOMPATIBLE INTERNALIZATIONS (e.g., rudimentary and expediently devised, but repetitively aborted, learnings have led to perplexing memories, enigmatic attitudes, contradictory needs, antithetical emotions, erratic impulses, and opposing strategies for conflict reduction).
(d) REGRESSION MECHANISM (e.g., retreats under stress to developmentally earlier levels of anxiety tolerance, impulse control, and social adaptation; among adolescents, is unable to cope with adult demands and conflicts, as evident in immature, if not increasingly infantile behaviors).	(h) DIFFUSED MORPHOLOGIC ORGANIZATION (e.g., inner object structures exist in a dedifferentiated configuration in which a marked lack of clarity and distinctness is seen among elements, levels of consciousness occasionally blur and an easy flow occurs across boundaries that usually separate unrelated percepts, memories, and affects, all of which results in periodic dissolution of what limited psychic order and cohesion is normally present).

Note. From "Personality Prototypes and Their Diagnostic Criteria" by T. Millon, 1986, in T. Millon and G. L. Klerman (Eds.), *Contemporary Directions in Psychopathology* (p. 709), New York: Guilford Press. Copyright 1986 by The Guilford Press. Reprinted by permission.

APPENDIX. PROTOTYPIC DOMAIN FEATURES OF OTHER DSM-III-R PERSONALITY DISORDERS*

Dependent Personality

Functional Domains

(a) BEHAVIORALLY INCOMPETENT (e.g., ill-equipped to assume mature and independent roles; is docile and passive, lacking functional competencies, avoiding self-assertion, and withdrawing from adult responsibilities).

(b) INTERPERSONALLY SUBMISSIVE (e.g., subordinates needs to stronger, nurturing figure, without whom feels anxiously helpless; is compliant, conciliatory, placating, and self-sacrificing).

(c) COGNITIVELY NAIVE (e.g., is easily persuaded, unsuspicious, and gullible; reveals a Pollyanna attitude toward interpersonal difficulties, watering down objective problems, and smoothing over troubling events).

(d) INTROJECTION MECHANISM (e.g., is firmly devoted to another to strengthen the belief that an inseparable bond exists between them; jettisons any independent views in favor of those of another to preclude conflicts and threats to the relationship).

Structural Domains

(e) PACIFIC MOOD (e.g., is characteristically warm, tender, and noncompetitive; timidly avoids social tension and interpersonal conflicts).

(f) INEPT SELF-IMAGE (e.g., views self as weak, fragile, and inadequate; exhibits lack of self-confidence by belittling own aptitudes and competencies).

(g) IMMATURE INTERNALIZATIONS (e.g., inner object representations are composed of unsophisticated ideas and incomplete memories, rudimentary drives, and childlike impulses, as well as minimal competencies to manage and resolve stressors).

(h) INCHOATE MORPHOLOGICAL ORGANIZATION (e.g., entrusts others with the responsibility to fulfill needs and to cope with adult tasks; thus there is both a deficit and lack of diversity in internal mechanisms and regulatory controls, leaving a miscellany of relatively undeveloped and undifferentiated adaptive abilities, as well as an elementary system for functioning independently).

Histrionic Personality

Functional Domains

(a) BEHAVIORALLY AFFECTED (e.g., is overreactive, stimulus-seeking, and intolerant of inactivity, resulting in impulsive, unreflected, and theatrical responsiveness; describes penchant for momentary excitements, fleeting adventures, and short-sighted hedonism).

(b) INTERPERSONALLY FLIRTATIOUS (e.g., actively solicits praise and manipulates others to gain needed reassurance, attention, and approval; is demanding, self-dramatizing, vain, and seductively exhibitionistic).

(c) COGNITIVELY FLIGHTY (e.g., avoids introspective thought and is overly attentive to superficial and fleeting external events; integrates experience poorly, resulting in scattered learning and thoughtless judgments).

(d) DISSOCIATION MECHANISM (e.g., regularly alters self-presentations to create a succession of socially attractive but changing facades; engages in self-distracting activities to avoid reflecting on and integrating unpleasant thoughts and emotions).

Structural Domains

(e) FICKLE MOOD (e.g., displays short-lived dramatic and superficial emotions; is overreactive, impetuous, and exhibits tendencies to be easily enthused and as easily angered or bored).

(f) SOCIABLE SELF-IMAGE (e.g., views self as gregarious, stimulating, and charming; enjoys the image of attracting acquaintances and pursuing a busy and pleasure-oriented social life).

(g) SHALLOW INTERNALIZATIONS (e.g., inner object representations are composed largely of superficial and segregated affects, memories, and conflicts, as well as facile drives and insubstantial mechanisms).

(h) DISJOINED MORPHOLOGICAL ORGANIZATION (e.g., there exists a loosely knit and carelessly united conglomerate in which processes of internal regulation and control are scattered and unintegrated, with few methods for restraining impulses, coordinating defenses, and resolving conflicts, leading to mechanisms that must, of necessity, be broad and sweeping to maintain psychic cohesion and stability, and, when successful, only further isolate and disconnect thoughts, feelings, and actions).

*From "Personality Prototypes and Their Diagnostic Criteria" by T. Millon, 1986, in T. Millon and G. L. Klerman (Eds.), *Contemporary Directions in Psychopathology* (pp. 698–710), New York: Guilford Press. Copyright 1986 by The Guilford Press. Reprinted by permission.

Antisocial Personality

Functional Domains

(a) BEHAVIORALLY IMPULSIVE (e.g., is impetuous and irrepressible, acting hastily and spontaneously in a restless, spur-of-the-moment manner; is short-sighted, incautious, and imprudent, failing to plan ahead or to consider alternatives, much less heed consequences).

(b) INTERPERSONALLY IRRESPONSIBLE (e.g., is untrustworthy and unreliable, failing to meet or intentionally negating personal obligations of a marital, parental, employment, or financial nature; actively violates established social codes through duplicitous or illegal behaviors).

(c) COGNITIVELY DEVIANT (e.g, construes events and relationships in accord with socially unorthodox beliefs and morals; is disdainful of traditional ideals and contemptuous of conventional values).

(d) ACTING-OUT MECHANISM (e.g., inner tensions the might accrue by postponing the expression of offensive thoughts and malevolent actions are rarely constrained; socially repugnant impulses are not refashioned in sublimated forms, but are discharged directly in precipitous ways, usually without guilt).

Structural Domains

(e) CALLOUS MOOD (e.g., is insensitive, unempathic, and cold-blooded, as expressed in a wide-ranging deficit in social charitableness, human compassion, or personal remorse; exhibits a coarse uncivility, as well as an offensive, if not ruthless, indifference to the welfare of others).

(f) AUTONOMOUS SELF-IMAGE (e.g., sees self as unfettered by the restrictions of social customs and the restraints of personal loyalties; values the image and enjoys the sense of being free, unencumbered, and unconfined by persons, places, obligations, or routines).

(g) REBELLIOUS INTERNALIZATIONS (e.g., inner object representations comprise an ungovernable mix of revengeful attitudes and restive impulses driven to subvert established cultural ideals and mores, as well as to debase personal sentiments and material attainments of society which were denied to the individual).

(h) UNBOUNDED MORPHOLOGICAL ORGANIZATION (e.g., inner defensive operations are noted by their paucity, as are efforts to curb refractory drives and attitudes, leading to easily transgressed controls, low thresholds for impulse discharge, few subliminatory channels, unfettered self-expression, and a marked intolerance of delay or frustration).

Aggressive/Sadistic Personality

Functional Domains

(a) BEHAVIORALLY FEARLESS (e.g., is unflinching, recklessly daring, thick-skinned, and seemingly undeterred by pain; is attracted to challenge, risk, and harm, as well as undaunted by danger and punishment).

(b) INTERPERSONALLY INTIMIDATING (e.g., reveals satisfaction in competing with, dominating, and humiliating others; regularly expresses verbally abusive and derisive social commentary, as well as exhibiting vicious, if not physically brutal behavior).

(c) COGNITIVELY DOGMATIC (e.g., is strongly opinionated and closed-minded, as well as unbending and obstinate in holding to one's preconceptions; exhibits a broad-ranging authoritarianism, social intolerance, and prejudice).

(d) ISOLATION MECHANISM (e.g., can be cold-blooded and remarkably detached from an awareness of the impact of one's destructive acts; views objects of violation impersonally, as symbols of devalued groups devoid of human sensibilities).

Structural Domains

(e) HOSTILE MOOD (e.g., has an excitable and pugnacious temper which flares readily into contentious argument and physical belligerence; is mean-spirited and fractious, willing to do harm, even persecute others to get one's way).

(f) COMPETITIVE SELF-IMAGE (e.g., is proud to characterize self as assertively independent, vigorously energetic, and realistically hard-headed; values aspects of self that present tough, domineering and power-oriented image).

(g) PERNICIOUS INTERNALIZATION (e.g., inner object representations are best distinguished by the presence of strongly driven aggressive energies and malicious attitudes, as well as by a contrasting paucity of sentimental memories, tender affects, internal conflicts, shame, or guilt feelings).

(h) ERUPTIVE MORPHOLOGICAL ORGANIZATION (e.g., despite a generally cohesive structure composed of routinely adequate modulating controls, defenses, and expressive channels, surging, powerful, and explosive energies of an aggressive and sexual nature produce precipitous outbursts that periodically overwhelm and overrun otherwise competent restraints).

Obessive–Compulsive Personality

Functional Domains

(a) BEHAVIORALLY DISCIPLINED (e.g., maintains a regulated, repetitively structured, and highly organized life pattern; is perfectionistic, insisting that subordinates adhere to personally established rules and methods).

(b) INTERPERSONALLY RESPECTFUL (e.g., exhibits unusual adherence to social conventions and proprieties; prefers polite, formal, and correct personal relationships).

(c) COGNITIVELY CONSTRICTED (e.g., constructs world in terms of rules, regulations, time schedules, and social hierarchies; is unimaginative, indecisive, and notably upset by unfamiliar or novel ideas and customs).

(d) REACTION FORMATION MECHANISM (e.g., repeatedly presents positive thoughts and socially commendable behaviors that are diametrically opposite one's deeper, contrary, and forbidden feelings; displays reasonableness and maturity when faced with circumstances that evoke anger or dismay in others).

Structural Domains

(e) SOLEMN MOOD (e.g., is unrelaxed, tense, joyless, and grim; restrains warm feelings and keeps most emotions under tight control).

(f) CONSCIENTIOUS SELF-IMAGE (e.g., sees self as industrious, reliable, meticulous, and efficient; fearful of error or misjudgment, and hence overvalues aspects of self that exhibit discipline, perfection, prudence, and loyalty).

(g) CONCEALED INTERNALIZATIONS (e.g., only those inner objects, affects, attitudes, and actions which are socially approved are allowed conscious awareness or behavioral expression, resulting in gratification being highly regulated, forbidden impulses sequestered and tightly bound, personal and social conflicts defensively denied and kept from awareness, and all maintained under stringent control).

(h) COMPARTMENTALIZED MORPHOLOGICAL ORGANIZATION (e.g., psychic structures are rigidly organized in a tightly consolidated system that is clearly partitioned into numerous, distinct, and segregated constellations of drive, memory, and cognition, with few open channels to permit interplay among these components).

Passive–Aggressive Personality

Functional Domains

(a) BEHAVIORALLY STUBBORN (e.g., resists fulfilling expectancies of others, frequently exhibiting procrastination, inefficiency, and erratic as well as other contrary and irksome behaviors; reveals gratification in demoralizing and undermining the pleasures and aspirations of others).

(b) INTERPERSONALLY CONTRARY (e.g., assumes conflicting and changing roles in social relationships, particularly dependent acquiescence and assertive independence; is concurrently or sequentially obstructive and intolerant of others, expressing either negative or incompatible attitudes).

(c) COGNITIVELY NEGATIVISTIC (e.g., is cynical, skeptical, and untrusting, approaching positive events with disbelief, and future possibilities with trepidation; has a misanthropic view of life, expressing disdain and caustic comments toward those experiencing good fortune).

(d) DISPLACEMENT MECHANISM (e.g., discharges anger and other troublesome emotions either indirectly or by shifting them from their instigator to settings or persons of lesser significance; expresses resentments by substitute or passive means, such as acting inept or perplexed, or behaving in a forgetful or indolent manner).

Structural Domains

(e) IRRITABLE MOOD (e.g., frequently touchy, obstinate, and resentful, followed in turn by sulky and moody withdrawal; is often fretful and impatient, reporting being easily annoyed or frustrated by others).

(f) DISCONTENTED SELF-IMAGE (e.g., sees self as misunderstood, unappreciated, and demeaned by others; recognizes being characteristically resentful, disgruntled, and disillusioned with life).

(g) OPPOSITIONAL INTERNALIZATIONS (e.g., inner object representations comprise a complex of countervailing inclinations and incompatible memories that are driven pervasively by strong dissident impulses designed to nullify the achievements and pleasures of others).

(h) DIVERGENT MORPHOLOGICAL ORGANIZATION (e.g., there is a clear division in the pattern of internal elements such that coping and defensive maneuvers are often directed toward incompatible goals, leaving major conflicts unresolved and psychic cohesion impossible by virtue of the fact that fulfillment of one drive or need inevitably nullifies or reverses another).

Schizoid Personality

Functional Domains

(a) BEHAVIORALLY LETHARGIC (e.g., appears to be in a state of fatigue, low energy, and lack of vitality; is phlegmatic, sluggish, displaying deficits in activation, motoric expressiveness, and spontaneity).

(b) INTERPERSONALLY ALOOF (e.g., seems indifferent and remote, rarely responsive to the actions or feelings of others, possessing minimal "human" interests; fades into the background, is unobtrusive, has few close relationships, and prefers a peripheral role in social, work, and family settings).

(c) COGNITIVELY IMPOVERISHED (e.g., seems deficient across broad spheres of knowledge and evidences vague and obscure thought processes that are below intellectual level; communication is easily derailed, loses its sequence of thought, or is conveyed via a circuitous logic).

(d) INTELLECTUALIZATION MECHANISM (e.g., describes interpersonal and affective experiences in a matter-of-fact, abstract, impersonal, or mechanical manner; pays primary attention to formal and objective aspects of social and emotional events).

Structural Domains

(e) FLAT MOOD (e.g., is emotionally impassive, exhibiting an intrinsic unfeeling, cold and stark quality; reports weak affectionate or erotic needs, rarely displaying warm or intense feelings, and apparently unable to experience pleasure, sadness, or anger in any depth).

(f) COMPLACENT SELF-IMAGE (e.g., reveals minimal introspection and awareness of self; seems impervious to the emotional and personal implications of everyday social life).

(g) MEAGER INTERNALIZATIONS (e.g., inner object representations are few in number and minimally articulated, largely devoid of the manifold percepts and memories, or the dynamic interplay among drives and conflicts that typify even well-adjusted persons).

(h) UNDIFFERENTIATED MORPHOLOGICAL ORGANIZATION (e.g., given an inner barrenness, a feeble drive to fulfill needs, and minimal pressures to defend against or resolve internal conflicts or to cope with external demands, internal structures may best be characterized by their limited coordination and sterile order).

Paranoid Personality

Functional Domains

(a) BEHAVIORALLY DEFENSIVE (e.g., is vigilantly alert to anticipate and ward off expected derogation and deception; is tenacious and firmly resistant to sources of external influence and control).

(b) INTERPERSONALLY PROVOCATIVE (e.g., displays a quarrelsome, fractious, and abrasive attitude; precipitates exasperation and anger by a testing of loyalties and a searching preoccupation with hidden motives).

(c) COGNITIVELY SUSPICIOUS (e.g., is skeptical, cynical, and mistrustful of the motives of others, construing innocuous events as signifying hidden or conspiratorial intent; reveals tendency to magnify tangential or minor social difficulties into proofs of duplicity, malice, and treachery).

(d) PROJECTION MECHANISM (e.g., actively disowns undesirable personal traits and motives, and attributes them to others; remains blind to one's own unattractive behaviors and characteristics, yet is overalert to, and hypercritical of, similar features in others).

Structural Domains

(e) IRASCIBLE MOOD (e.g., displays a cold, sullen, churlish, and humorless demeanor; attempts to appear unemotional and objective, but is edgy, envious, jealous, quick to react angrily, or take personal offense).

(f) INVIOLABLE SELF-IMAGE (e.g., has persistent ideas of self-importance and self-reference, asserting as personally derogatory and scurrilous, if not libelous, entirely innocuous actions and events; is pridefully independent and highly insular, experiencing intense fears, however, of losing identity, status, and powers of self-determination).

(g) UNALTERABLE INTERNALIZATIONS (e.g., inner object representations are precisely arranged in an unusual configuration of deeply held attitudes, unyielding percepts, and implacable drives which, in turn, are aligned in an idiosyncratic and fixed hierarchy of tenacious memories, immutable cognitions, and irrevocable beliefs).

(h) INELASTIC MORPHOLOGICAL ORGANIZATION (e.g., systemic constriction and inflexibility of coping and defensive methods, as well as rigidly fixed channels of conflict mediation and need gratification, creates an overstrung and taut frame that is so uncompromising in its accommodation to changing circumstances that unanticipated stressors are likely to precipitate either explosive outbursts or inner shatterings).

REFERENCES

Akiskal, H. S., Hirschfield, R., & Yerevanian, B. (1983). The relationship of personality to affective disorders. *Archives of General Psychiatry, 40,* 801–810.

Akiskal, H. S., Khani, M. K., & Scott-Strauss, A. (1979). Cyclothymic temperamental disorders. *Psychiatric Clinics of North America, 2,* 527–554.

Akiskal, H. S., Rosenthal, T. L., Haykal, R. F., Lemmi, H., Rosenthal, R. H., & Scott-Strauss, A. (1980). Characterological depressions: Clinical and sleep EEG findings separating "subaffective dysthymias" from "character-spectrum disorders." *Archives of General Psychiatry, 37,* 777–783.

American Psychiatric Association. (1980). *Diagnostic and statistical manual of mental disorders* (3rd ed.). Washington, DC: Author.

American Psychiatric Association. (1987). *Diagnostic and statistical manual of mental disorders* (3rd ed., rev.). Washington, DC: Author.

Bandura, A. (1982). The psychology of chance encounters and life paths. *American Psychologist, 37,* 747–755.

Becker, J. (1977). *Affective disorders.* New York: General Learning Press.

Bleuler, E. (1911/1950). *Dementia praecox: Or the group of schizophenias.* New York: International Universities Press.

Bursten, B. (1982). Narcissistic personalities in DSM-III. *Comprehensive Psychiatry, 23,* 409–420.

Buss, A. H. (1966). *Psychopathology.* New York: Wiley.

Contor, N., Smith, E. E., French, R. D., & Mezzich, J. (1980). Psychiatric diagnoses as prototype categorization. *Journal of Abnormal Psychology, 89,* 181–193.

Cattell, R. B. (1965). *The scientific analysis of personality.* Chicago: Aldine.

Cattell, R. B. (1970). The integration of functional and psychometric requirements in a quantitative and computerized diagnostic system. In A. R. Mahrer (Ed.), *New approaches to personality classification* (pp. 9–52). New York: Columbia University Press.

Charney, D. S., Nelson, J. C., & Quinlan, D. M. (1981). Personality traits and disorder in depression. *American Journal of Psychiatry, 138,* 1601–1604.

Coryell, W., & Zimmerman, M. (1986). The heritability of schizophrenia and schizoaffective disorder: A family study. *Archives of General Psychiatry, 45,* 323–327.

Curtis, R. (Ed.). (1989). *Self-defeating behaviors.* New York: Plenum.

Docherty, J. P., Feister, S. J., & Shea, T. (1986). Syndrome diagnosis and personality disorder. In A. Frances & R. E. Hale (Eds.), *American Psychiatric Association annual review* (Vol. 5, pp. 315–355). Washington, DC: American Psychiatric Association.

Ellis, H. (1898). Auto-erotism: A psychological study. *Alienist and Neurologist, 19,* 260–299.

Eysenck, H. J. (1960). *The structure of human personality.* London: Routledge & Kegan Paul.

Fowles, D. (1984). Biological variables in psychopathology. In H. Adams & P. Sutker (Eds.), *Comprehensive handbook of psychopathology* (pp. 77–110). New York: Plenum.

Frances, A. (1980). The DSM-III personality disorders section: A commentary. *American Journal of Psychiatry, 137,* 1050–1054.

Frances, A. (1985). Validating schizotypal personality disorders: Problems with the schizophrenia connection. *Schizophrenia Bulletin, 11,* 595–597.

Frances, A., & Widiger, T. (1986). The classification of personality disorders: An overview of problems and solutions. In A. Frances & R. E. Hale (Eds.), *American Psychiatric Association annual review* (Vol. 5, pp. 240–257). Washington, DC: American Psychiatric Association.

Freud, S. (1925). On narcissism: An introduction. In *Collected papers.* London: Hogarth Press. (Original work published 1914)

Gunderson, J. G. (1983). DSM-III diagnoses of personality disorders. In J. P. Frosch (Ed.), *Current perspectives on personality disorders.* Washington, DC: American Psychiatric Press.

Gunderson, J. G. (1984). *Borderline personality disorders.* Washington, DC: American Psychiatric Press.

Gunderson, J. G., & Siever, L. (1985). Relatedness of schizotypal to schizophrenic disorders: Editor's introduction. *Schizophrenia Bulletin, 11,* 532–537.

Hempel, C. G. (1961). Introduction to problems of taxonomy. In J. Zubin (Ed.), *Field studies in the mental disorders* (pp. 3–22). New York: Grune & Stratton.

Hempel, C. G. (1965). *Aspects of scientific explanation.* New York: Free Press.

Hoch, P. H., & Polatin, P. (1949). Pseudoneurotic form of schizophrenia. *Psychiatric Quarterly, 23,* 248–276.

Horney, K. (1939). *New ways in psychoanalysis.* New York: Norton.

Horney, K. (1945). *Our inner conflicts.* New York: Norton.

Horowitz, L., Post, D., French, R., Wallis, K., & Siegelman, E. (1981). The prototype as a construct in abnormal psychology: 2. Clarifying disagreement in psychiatric judgments. *Journal of Abnormal Psychology, 90,* 575–585.

Jahoda, M. (Ed.). (1958). *Current concepts of positive mental health.* New York: Basic Books.

Kaplan, A. (1964). *The conduct of scientific inquiry.* San Francisco: Chandler.

Kass, F., Skodol, A. E., Charles, E., et al. (1985). Scaled ratings of DSM-III personality disorders. *American Journal of Psychiatry, 142,* 627–630.

Kendell, R. E. (1975). *The role of diagnosis in psychiatry.* Oxford: Blackwell.

Kernberg, O. F. (1975). *Borderline conditions and pathological narcissism.* New York: Jason Aronson.

Kernberg, O. F. (1984). *Severe personality disorders.* New Haven, CT: Yale University Press.

Kety, S. S., Rosenthal, D., & Wender, P. H. (1975). Mental illness in families of adopted individuals who have become schizophrenic. In R. Fieve & D. Rosenthal (Eds.), *Genetic research in psychiatry.* Baltimore: Johns Hopkins University Press.

Klerman, G. L. (1973). The relationship between personality and clinical depressions: Overcoming the obstacles to verifying psychodynamic theories. *International Journal of Psychiatry, 11,* 227–233.

Knight, R. P. (1953). Borderline states. *Bulletin of the Menninger Clinic, 17,* 1–12.

Kohut, H. (1971). *The analysis of self.* New York: International Universities Press.

Kraepelin, E. (1913). *Psychiatrie: Ein Lehrbuch* (8th ed., Vol. 3). Leipzig: Barth.

Krafft-Ebing, R. (1882). *Psychopathia Sexualis* (English translation, 1937). New York: Physicians and Surgeons Books.

Kretschmer, E. (1925). *Physique and character.* London: Kegan Paul.

Lasch, C. (1978). *The culture of narcissism.* New York: Norton.

Livesley, W. J. (1986a). Theoretical and empirical issues in the selection of criteria to diagnose personality disorders. *Journal of Personality Disorders, 1,* 88–94.

Livesley, W. J. (1986b). Trait and behavior prototypes of personality disorder. *American Journal of Psychiatry, 43,* 1018–1022.

Livesley, W. J., Reiffer, L. I., Sheldon, A., & West, M. (1987). Prototypicality ratings of DSM-III criteria for personality disorders. *Journal of Nervous and Mental Disease, 175,* 395–401.

McCranie, E. J. (1971). Depression, anxiety and hostility. *Psychiatric Quarterly, 45,* 117–133.

Meehl, P. (1962). Schizotaxia, schizotypy, schizophrenia. *American Psychologist, 17,* 827–838.

Meehl, P. (1978). Theoretical risks and tabular asterisks: Sir Karl, Sir Ronald, and the slow progress of soft psychology. *Journal of Consulting and Clinical Psychology, 46,* 806–834.

Menninger, K. (1963). *The vital balance.* New York: Viking.

Millon, T. (1969). *Modern psychopathology: A biosocial approach to maladaptive learning and functioning.* Philadelphia: W. B. Saunders.

Millon, T. (1981). *Disorders of personality: DSM-III, Axis II.* New York: Wiley-Interscience.

Millon, T. (1984). On the renaissance of personality assessment and personality theory. *Journal of Personality Assessment, 48,* 450–466.

Millon, T. (1986). Personality prototypes and their diagnostic criteria. In T. Millon & G. L. Klerman (Eds.), *Contemporary directions in psychopathology: Towards the DSM-IV.* New York: Guilford.

Millon, T. (1987a). On the nature of taxonomy in psychopathology. In C. Last & M. Hersen (Eds.), *Issues in diagnostic research.* New York: Plenum.

Millon, T. (1987b). On the prevalence and genesis of the borderline personality disorder: A social learning thesis. *Journal of Personality Disorders, 1,* 354–372.

Millon, T. (Ed.). (1987c). Personality disorder criteria: Empirical or theoretical? *Journal of Personality Disorders, 1,* 71–112.

Millon, T. (1990). *Toward a new personology: An evolutionary model.* New York: Wiley-Interscience.

Mischel, W. (1984). Convergences and challenges in the search for consistency. *American Psychologist, 39,* 351–364.

Morey, L. C. (1988a). Personality disorders in DSM-III and DSM-III-R: An examination of convergence, coverage, and internal consistency. *American Journal of Psychiatry, 145,* 573–577.

Morey, L. C. (1988b). A psychometric analysis of the DSM-III-R personality disorder criteria. *Journal of Personality Disorders, 2,* 109–124.

Offer, D., & Sabshin, M. (1974). *Normality: Theoretical and clinical concepts of mental health* (rev. ed.). New York: Basic Books.

Pap, A. (1953). Reduction-sentences and open concepts. *Methods, 5,* 3–30.

Paykel, E. S., Klerman, G. L., & Prusoff, B. A. (1976). Personality and symptom pattern in depression. *British Journal of Psychiatry, 129,* 327–334.

Paykel, E. S., Myers, J. K., & Dienelt, M. N. (1970). Life events and depression. *Archives of General Psychiatry, 221,* 753–760.

Pfohl, B., Coryell, W., Zimmerman, W., et al. (1986).

DSM-III personality disorders: Diagnostic overlap and internal consistency of individual DSM-III criteria. *Comprehensive Psychiatry, 27,* 144–155.

Rado, S. (1956). Schizotypal organization: Preliminary report on a clinical study of shcizophrenia. In S. Rado & G. E. Daniels (Eds.), *Changing concepts of psychoanalytic medicine.* New York: Grune & Stratton.

Reich, W. (1933). *Charakteranalyse.* Leipzig: Sexpol Verlag.

Rosewater, L. B. (1987). A critical analysis of the proposed self-defeating personality disorder. *Journal of Personality Disorders, 1,* 190–196.

Schafer, R. (1948). *The clinical application of psychological tests.* New York: International Universities Press.

Schmeideberg, M. (1947). The treatment of psychopaths and borderline patients. *American Journal of Psychotherapy, 1,* 45–55.

Schneider, K. (1923/1950). *Psychopathic personalities.* London: Cassell.

Scott, W. A. (1958). Social psychological correlates of mental illness and mental health. *Psychological Bulletin, 55,* 65–87.

Shoben, E. J. (1957). Toward a concept of the normal personality. *American Psychologist, 12,* 183–189.

Siever, L. J., & Klar, H. (1986). A review of DSM-III criteria for the personality disorders. In A. Frances & R. E. Hale (Eds.), *American Psychiatric Association annual review* (Vol. 5). Washington, DC: American Psychiatric Association.

Skinner, H. (1986). Construct validation approach to psychiatric classification. In T. Millon & G. L. Klerman (Eds.), *Contemporary directions in psychopathology: Toward the DSM-IV.* New York: Guilford.

Squires-Wheeler, E., Skodol, A. E., Friedman, D., & Erlenmeyer-Kimling, L. (1988). A preliminary report of the specificity of DSM-III schizotypal personality traits. *Psychological Medicine, 18,* 757–765.

Stern, A. (1938). Psychoanalytic investigation of and therapy in the borderline group of neuroses. *Psychoanalytic Quarterly, 7,* 467–489.

Stone, M. H. (1980). *The borderline syndromes.* New York: McGraw-Hill.

Strauss, J. S. (1975). A comprehensive approach to psychiatric diagnosis. *American Journal of Psychiatry, 132,* 1193–1197.

Trull, T., Widiger, T., & Frances, A. (1987). Covariation of avoidant, schizoid, and dependent personality disorder criteria sets. *American Journal of Psychiatry, 144,* 767–771.

Vaillant, G., & Perry, J. (1985). Personality disorders. In H. Kaplan (Ed.), *Comprehensive textbook of psychiatry IV* (4th ed.). Baltimore: Williams & Wilkins.

Walker, L (1987). Inadequacies of the masochistic personality disorder diagnosis in women. *Journal of Personality Disorders, 1,* 183–189.

Widiger, T., & Frances, A. (1985). The DSM-III personality disorders: Perspectives from psychology. *Archives of General Psychiatry, 42,* 615–523.

Widiger, T., & Frances, A. (1988). The personality disorders. In J. A. Talbot, R. E. Hales, & S. C. Yudofsky (Eds.), *Textbook of psychiatry* (pp. 621–648). Washington, DC: American Psychiatric Press.

Widiger, T., Frances, A., Spitzer, R. L., & Williams, J.B.W. (1988). The DSM-III-R personality disorders: An overview. *American Journal of Psychiatry, 145,* 786–795.

Williams, J.B.W. (1985a). The multiaxial system of

DSM-III: Where did it come from and where should it go? I. Its origins and critiques. *Archives of General Psychiatry, 42,* 175–180.

Williams, J.B.W. (1985b). The multiaxial system of the DSM-III: Where did it come from and where should it go? II. Empirical studies, innovations, and recom-

mendations. *Archives of General Psychiatry, 42,* 181–186.

Wolberg, A. (1952). The "borderline patient." *American Journal of Psychotherapy, 6,* 694–701.

Zilboorg, G. (1941). Ambulatory schizophrenia. *Psychiatry, 4,* 149–155.

Chapter 14

Personality Change and Psychotherapy

Stanley B. Messer
Rutgers University
Seth Warren
Rutgers University

Not all theories of personality explain the process of personality change, nor are all efforts to effect psychological change supported by a personality theory. There is a venerable tradition of conceptualizing personality in terms of traits, for example, with no corresponding theory of the change process. Likewise, there are attempts within the domain of behavior therapy to bring about change in such troublesome behaviors as smoking, overeating, or compulsions, with no corresponding theory of personality. The purpose of this chapter is to review those theories providing explanations both of personality and of how personality change comes about. The theories we address here are further defined by the following four characteristics:

1. They recognize that personality is structured and organized. Personality is not merely a collection of individual traits, nor is it made up of atomistic bits of disconnected behavior. Personality is patterned. Not only are

there parts; there is also a piecing together of the parts in such a way that they comprise an integrated structure (Pervin, 1989). Thus, a collection of individual variables or traits does not constitute a theory of personality unless it is ordered hierarchically and interrelated in a holistic fashion. This structural criterion also implies a degree of consistency in personality functioning, even if the behavioral manifestations of that structure differ in varying situations.

2. They include the concept of development. There is a recognition that personality emerges over time out of a matrix of biological and social factors, and these factors are specified in the theory.

3. They articulate the conditions or mechanisms that bring about change in personality in the terms defined by the theory.

4. They can be subjected to empirical proof. Although there may be more than one kind of evidence allowable as proof, the theory can be and has been researched in accordance with prevailing scientific and scholarly standards.

371

Four major theories fulfill the conditions specified above: psychoanalysis, the phenomenological/experiential model, cognitive theory, and intersubjective/self-psychological approaches. These theories are not unimodal, of course. There are variations on each one, with significant differences in outlook. Within psychoanalysis, for example, there is a drive/structural model, an ego/adaptive model, and an object relations/interpersonal model, each of which focuses on somewhat different features of human personality. However, each variation also possesses a degree of overlap with its close kin. They all posit unconscious processes, view conflict as central in personality functioning, and employ the concepts of transference and resistance in the conduct of psychotherapy.

Following a brief presentation of the models and examples, illustrating ways of assessing their terms, we turn to the major factors each model credits with bringing about personality change. These include interpretation, relationship factors, cognitive re-education, and empathic inquiry. We then consider several current topics and trends in psychotherapy: the failure of clients to change, or the problem of resistance; the movement to integrate techniques from different therapies or to discern their common elements; and a new approach to process research in psychotherapy. Finally, we take up the thorny problem of assessing personality change or psychotherapy outcome, including the source of outcome ratings, the procedures used to collect the information, and the kinds of goals that a theory defines. Throughout, our emphasis is on maladaptive aspects of personality and on the link among a personality theory, its view of psychopathology, and therapeutic modalities of change.

An attitude pervading this chapter is that the terms of a personality theory and the goals of its related system of psychotherapy are not neutral (cf. London, 1986). They are embedded in a value structure that determines what is most important to know about and change in an individual. In addition, the terms of the theory dictate the method to be used in its evaluation, and the results obtained are necessarily determined by that method (Messer, 1985). In this sense, the modes of assessment are also value-laden. If the theory focuses on unconscious factors, for example, collecting dreams and early memories or analyzing transcripts from psychoanalytic psychotherapy may be a more fertile mode of assessment and source of information than responses to a questionnaire or other forms of conscious self-report may be. As we try to demonstrate below, there is a necessary link among the nature of the theory, the kind of change one hopes to bring about by psychotherapy, and the measures employed to assess that change. We begin with psychoanalysis, historically the earliest and clinically the most influential of the therapies.

PSYCHOANALYTIC MODELS OF PERSONALITY AND CHANGE

Theory and Assessment

Drive/Structural Theory

The basic model of human functioning proposed by Freud and elaborated upon particularly by Arlow and Brenner (1964) is a conflict model of personality. Fueling human behavior in all its forms are the sexual and aggressive drives (part of the id), which are modulated by the mechanisms of defense (part of the ego). In addition, typically serving as aids to the ego are the dictates of conscience and ideals (the superego). When things go well, a dynamic balance is maintained among these functions, and a person achieves both some drive satisfaction and a suitable adaptation to reality; in such a case the drive energy is said to have been neutralized. For example, underlying the seemingly straightforward act of reading this chapter may be the wish for power over others through knowledge acquisition (derivative of the aggressive drive) and/or the wish to win the approval, admiration, or even love of a professor or colleague (derivative of the sexual drive). In addition, it may satisfy one's ego ideal of being the best-informed student or psychologist one can be (superego function). Defenses such as sublimation and intellectualization enable one to read and learn relatively smoothly and comfortably, in spite of one's unconscious wishes.

When an internal or external stressor arises that upsets the drive–defense balance, however, symptoms or maladaptive behaviors of some kind occur. It is the strength of the conflict model to be able to describe and explain the resultant psychopathology or maladaptive behavior. (See Westen, Chapter 2, this volume, for a fuller treatment of Freudian drive theory.) In the current example, because of a conflict over power or competition, or as a displaced reaction (defense) to ambivalent feelings toward a parent, one may procrastinate or avoid reading this chapter in spite of (or because of) a deadline imposed by a professor or publisher. Alternatively, one may develop anxiety, attentional deficits, or a headache (symptom) whenever one begins to read it, or even thinks about having to read it.

There are two research programs currently underway that aim to measure the major constructs of the drive/structural model, in order to achieve a better understanding of psychopathology and psychotherapy. The Idiographic Conflict Formulation (ICF) method (Perry, Augusto, & Cooper, 1987, pp. 8–10) calls for two experienced clinicians to view a videotape of an unstructured psychodynamic interview and to discuss and formulate the subject's conflicts on the following dimensions: (1) Wishes (which are the observable counterpart of drives); (2) countervailing Fears; (3) resultant Symptomatic and Avoidant Outcomes (such as defenses). In order to make the ICF useful in assessing change in psychotherapy, also measured are (4) vulnerability to Specific Stressors and (5) the Best Level of Adaptation to Conflicts. Here is an abbreviated example involving a 23-year-old divorced woman, condensed from Perry, Luborsky, Silberschatz, and Popp (1989, pp. 313–315):

Wish: The subject has a wish that someone help her to express her own anger and sexual needs, from which she otherwise distances herself. This wish is often expressed through victimization rather than direct expression of her own needs. She is seeking the affirmation of her own emotional life.

Fear: The subject has a fear of her own hostility, sexuality, and emotionality in general, which includes a fear of seeing herself as the aggressor in many social situations.

Symptomatic Outcomes: Victimization by others' aggression and inability to stand up for herself against verbal abuse.

Avoidant Outcomes: Her primary mechanism for avoidance involves the minimization and suppression of affects that might provide protective internal cues. She avoids asking directly for what she needs by

taking the position of being a healer for others.

Specific Stressors: Any situation that requires her to say directly what she needs.

Best Level of Adaptation: Her behavior now appears to involve fewer counterphobic and masochistic mechanisms for dealing with her rage and disappointment than her behavior at previous points in her life.

Two raters are required to agree on their formulation and to support their assertions with the available evidence. The final product is four to eight pages in length; most of it consists of a presentation of the evidence. To assess reliability, the original formulations on 20 cases were compared with a second set of 20 formulations of the same cases, composed by a second independent team of clinician/judges (Perry et al., 1987). Two independent teams of similarity raters considered correctly matched pairs and two types of wrongly matched pairs of formulations, and rated them by consensus for similarity on a scale of 1 (no overlap) to 7 (complete overlap). The reliability of the two consensus ratings was moderately high: Intraclass correlations ranged from .54 to .75. In addition, the mean overall similarity rating for the three core components for correctly matched formulation pairs was significantly higher than for either type of mismatch.

Another way of preparing psychodynamic formulations in an objective fashion was developed at the University of Pennsylvania and is known as the Core Conflictual Relationship Theme (CCRT) method (Luborsky & Crits-Christoph, 1988; Luborsky, Crits-Christoph, & Mellon, 1986). It is actually a blend of the drive/structural model and the object relations/interpersonal model described below. The data used are Wishes (narratives about wishes, intentions, needs, and so on); Responses from (important) Others (RO), including the therapist; and the Response of Self (RS). All data are extracted from transcripts of early psychoanalytic therapy sessions. Positive ROs refer to gratification of the Wish, and negative ROs refer to lack of its gratification. These Relationship Episodes (REs) are identified by one set of judges and then given to a second set of judges, who rate the REs for completeness on a scale of 1–5. Those REs with an average of two judges' ratings equal to 2.5 or better are retained. A minimum of 10 REs are used; an average RE usually comprises from half a page to three pages of double-spaced type. An example of an RE, condensed from Perry et al. (1989, p. 304–308) follows:

> *Wish:* Conscious: to resist and overcome domination or exploitation.
> Unconscious: to submit, to go along, not to resist domination.
> *Response from Other:* Dominating, exploiting, forceful.
> *Response of Self:* Feels helpless, weak, submissive, nonresistant.

In narrative form, it reads as follows (Perry et al., 1989):

> I wish to resist domination and not to be forced to submit or to be overpowered. But the other person dominates, takes control and overpowers me (after some initial help, support and guidance to tempt me into submission). Then I feel dominated, submissive, helpless, and victimized. (p. 304)

The Wish category corresponds to the psychoanalytic id impulse. The RO and RS are conceived as resultants of ego and superego functions, mobilized to cope with the Wish, and conflicting with it maladaptively (Luborsky, 1984, p. 19). Because the level of inference must be limited to achieve reliability, CCRT Wishes are viewed as only derivatives of id impulses, and ROs and RSs are those responses capable of being observed and reported by the subject.

In a recent article (Crits-Christoph, Luborsky, et al., 1988), two methods were employed to measure reliability of CCRTs. In the first method, tailor-made CCRTs of two judges were compared using a paired-comparison method. In a second approach, the tailor-made CCRTs were coded into ready-made or standard categories (e.g., Wishes for closeness, independence; ROs such as dominates, rejects; RSs such as dependent, angry). This allowed the judges to pick the standard category that was closest in meaning to the tailor-made wording, and also to put the data in a form that could be analyzed by measures of interjudge agreement for nominal data. When the method of mismatched cases on the tailor-made CCRTs was used, the pooled judges' reliability was .79. In addition, the mean difference between matched and mismatched cases was highly statistically significant. When the standard categories were used, the weighted kappa for the Wish and negative RS was .61, and for the negative RO it was .70—all highly significant.

It should be noted that from a traditional psychoanalytic viewpoint, this method sacrifices some of the intrapsychic and unconscious material that is favored by psychoanalytic theorists and therapists and that is captured by Perry's ICF method (Collins, 1989). Luborsky and his colleagues are now at work on a refinement of the CCRT method that will allow for the recording of unconscious as well as conscious wishes. Reliability of such unconscious wishes has not yet been demonstrated.

The Ego/Adaptive Model

Whereas in the drive/structural model the drives are the fueling mechanisms for behavior, in the ego/adaptive model the ego is viewed as having its own source of energy and its own set of motives, wishes, and values, which derive from the person's need to adapt to and live in the real world (Hartmann, 1964). Adaptive tendencies and ego interests are motivational forces in their own right (Greenberg & Mitchell, 1983). Pleasure comes not just from drive satisfaction but from ego satisfaction—that which the ego chooses to do, regardless of drive considerations. Ego functions can include perception, memory, affect, action, thinking, and considerations of reality. "Competence motivation" (White, 1959) and the wish to master a situation need not be reduced to drive imperatives, but constitute a "conflict-free ego sphere" present from birth (Hartmann, 1939). To return to our earlier example, reading this chapter need not be analyzed into drive-derivative components as we have done above, but can constitute an ego activity performed for the sheer pleasure of reading, for the satisfaction of professional success, or for the challenge of mastering new material in the interests of adapting to external requirements. Of course, the ego itself may contain irrational beliefs that may curtail the pleasure involved in reading the chapter or may lead to its avoidance entirely. Although this would constitute conflict, it would not be *inter*systemic (between id and ego) as in the drive/structural model, but *intra*systemic (between different functions of the ego alone).

A current program of research that operates within an ego psychological model is that of

Weiss, Sampson, and the Mount Zion Psychotherapy Research Group (1986). It is grounded in what the authors call the hypothesis of "higher mental functioning," which postulates that people can exert some control over their unconscious mental life, including their repressed beliefs. The authors refer to Freud's later work, in which he "assigned a much greater part to those agencies of the mind that are acquired by learning from experience, that think and anticipate, make decisions and plans, and direct criticism against the self" (Weiss et al., 1986, p. 31). Thus, people develop pathogenic beliefs by drawing inferences from the frightening, grim or traumatic aspects of their childhood. Examples of such beliefs are "If I succeed too well, my sister will look bad," and "If I separate from my mother, she will be devastated." The theory places less emphasis on anxiety as a motivator than on unconscious guilt—survivor guilt in the former example, separation guilt in the latter (Messer, 1989). According to Weiss and colleagues, a patient enters psychotherapy with a plan for solving problems. The patient's plan may be thought of as a strategy, with conscious and unconscious elements, for disconfirming pathogenic beliefs by developing greater understanding of them in therapy and by testing them in the relationship with the therapist (Silberschatz, Fretter, & Curtis, 1986).

In order to capture the relevant psychodynamic and cognitive features of an individual seeking therapy and to assess them in a reliable way, the Mount Zion group developed the Plan Diagnosis Method (Caston, 1986; Curtis, Silberschatz, Weiss, Sampson, & Rosenberg, 1988), which has demonstrated excellent reliability (Rosenberg, Silberschatz, Curtis, Sampson, & Weiss, 1986) and which has since been superseded by the Plan Formulation Method (PFM; Curtis & Silberschatz, 1989). In both versions, the Plan consists of four components: Goals that the patient would like to achieve; Obstructions, which are the irrational pathogenic beliefs and associated guilt and fears that prevent the patient from achieving the goals; Tests, which are actions of patients in therapy by means of which they attempt to disconfirm their pathogenic beliefs; and Insights into the nature and origins of the patient's pathogenic beliefs that would help him or her achieve therapeutic goals (Curtis et al., 1988). Here are sample items taken from the latter article describing the case of Myra, a 32-year-old single woman who described her problem as a fear of commitment in relationships (pp. 261–262):

> *Goals:* To feel less responsible for her mother and exert greater control over her relationship with Paul.
> *Obstructions:* She believes that she would be disloyal and abandoning of her mother if she developed new relationships.
> *Tests:* She will see if the therapist feels left out when she discusses her work, as she imagines her mother and Paul would feel left out.
> *Insights:* To become aware that she inhibits herself from developing and enjoying relationships with others because she feels guilty allowing herself more than her mother has.

The construction of a Plan, according to the PFM, involves five steps (Curtis & Silberschatz, 1989):

1. Clinical judges independently review one to three transcripts of early interviews and create lists of items they believe are relevant for the case under the Goals, Obstructions, Tests, and Insights headings, along with plausible but less relevant items.
2. These lists are combined and randomly distributed under the four headings of the PFM.
3. The list is returned to the judges, each of whom rates each item for degree of relevance to the case on a 5-point Likert scale.
4. Reliability is measured for each of the four components by means of an intraclass correlation for pooled judges.
5. Items falling below the median of the items in each category are dropped, redundancies are eliminated, and the remaining items then constitute the final Plan formulation.

In a study of five cases from four different settings on which Plans were formulated in this manner, intraclass correlations (coefficient alpha) for groups of three to eight judges ranged from .72 to .95, indicating very satisfactory levels of reliability for the PFM (Curtis & Silberschatz, 1989). In addition, the stability of the PFM is very good across a 3-month time lapse (Pearson correlations of .94–.98), and the PFM has been shown to be applicable to a different theoretical perspective—namely, object relations (Collins & Messer, in press).

The Object Relations/Interpersonal Model

Unlike the drive model, which emphasizes aggressive and sexual drives pressing for expression, and the ego model, which stresses a person's adaptive capacities, the object relations/interpersonal model posits an innate propensity of the individual to relate to others and form attachments to them. Current relationships are ultimately understood in terms of past relationships from any developmental period, insofar as the latter have become patterned and predictable ways of interacting with others. In psychotherapy, as in life outside the consulting room, people will re-enact these organized interpersonal schemas, unconsciously playing out roles and putting others into counter-roles (Strupp & Binder, 1984). They may, for example, enact the role of the needy child and see others and act toward them as the ungiving parents. They may expect others to be seducers, and see themselves as victims and as helpless to resist.

In terms of our ongoing example, they may view the professor who assigns this chapter as an authoritarian and insensitive taskmaster and themselves as the unfortunate ones being forced to submit to his or her unreasonable demands. They will then act toward the professor in light of this interpersonal expectation, attempting to get him or her to enact the counter-role to confirm their expectations. Alternatively, they may see themselves as favored students and the professor as an admiring parent. Whereas the more purely interpersonal model stresses the social nature of this interaction, the object relations approach also posits the concomitant formation of internal images of self and others; in this way, it maintains more of a link with the intrapsychic models described above.

Working within this model, Strupp and his associates (Butler & Binder, 1987; Schacht & Henry, in press; Strupp & Binder, 1984) have developed an empirically based approach to assessment and psychotherapy. They conceptualize the therapist–client relationship in general, and transference in particular, as operating within an interactive field that does not stem from the client alone. Therapists must discern the role into which clients place them (transference) without falling too deeply into it, in order to interpret the enactment to the clients.

The patterned Dynamic Focus (Schacht, 1984) or Cyclical Maladaptive Pattern (Butler & Binder, 1987) describing the interpersonal scenario is the equivalent of the ICF, the CCRT, or the PFM described above. It consists of four elements: Acts of Self, which include domains of private and public action such as affect and motives; Expectations of Others' Reactions, which are the imagined anticipations of what others may do or think; Acts of Others toward Self, including the observed acts of others that are viewed as occurring in specific relation to acts of self and are often evoked by the client's own actions; and Acts of Self toward Self (the Introject), referring to how one treats oneself. Here is an example of a woman complaining of depression and marital difficulties (condensed from Schacht, 1984, p. 50):

Acts of Self: The patient assumes a passive interpersonal position in which she refrains from disclosing her inner self, withdraws or procrastinates, defers and submits to others' wishes, and spends much time in private thinking and wondering rather than in communication.

Expectation of Others' Reactions: She expects that other people will ignore and/or reject her.

Observed Reactions of Others: The patient observes that others do not spontaneously recognize her distress and rescue her; she interprets this as evidence that they are unwilling to examine relationships or make changes.

Introject: The patient berates herself for feeling helpless and experiences significant associated depression. She imagines negative responses from others, and consequently she stifles and controls herself, refraining from asserting her desires or complaints.

A videotape of a semistructured interview serves as the source of the raw data for generating the Dynamic Focus. Interpersonal transactions are isolated with high levels of interjudge agreement ($>.90$) and are assembled into short elements in the fourfold scheme above, which in turn are organized into a coherent narrative. These are coded into the very sophisticated and psychometrically sound system known as the Structural Analysis of Social Behavior (SASB; Benjamin, 1982). This circumplex model allows object relations events to be described from the points of view of Self, Other, and Introject. (We cannot do justice to its complexity here.) The elements of the Dynamic Focus have been reliably coded onto the SASB axes of Affiliative versus Disaffiliative Behaviors (ranging from tender sexuality to murderous attack) and the dimension of Interdependence versus Autonomy. This coding allows changes in patients' core object relations patterns to be tracked in a quantified way.

Another ambitious attempt to develop a method for identifying sources of interpersonal distress has been made by L. Horowitz and his associates (Horowitz et al., 1988). Their new method for aggregating psychodynamic formulations of independent clinicians is called the Consensual Response Method. In one study, clinical raters read the consensual formulations and judged whether each problem on an inventory of interpersonal problems was likely to be distressing for each patient. The raters were very successful in predicting which problems were actually discussed in treatment, lending initial validity to this promising method (Horowitz, Rosenberg, Ureño, Kalehzan, & O'Halloran, 1989).

Interpretations as the Agent of Change

Each of the four theories of personality described in this chapter highlights different kinds of curative factors as a natural derivative of the way in which it formulates normal personality and psychopathology. Even the vocabulary of change—what is viewed as in need of change and how that change is to be brought about—differs from one approach to another. (Note that even the terms "curative factors" and "psychopathology" reveal a value-laden attitude—in this case, the use of a medical vocabulary to describe problematic or disordered behavior and ways of altering or influencing it.)

Within the psychoanalytic model, including each of the three variants, the fundamental mode of operation is interpreting unconscious material—be it fantasies, wishes, ego defenses, early memories and dreams, interpersonal patterns, or self- and object representations. Given the emphasis in psychoanalytic therapy on unconscious factors determining behavior, it is perhaps not surprising that expanding awareness of that which is hidden should be considered so prominent a factor in bringing

about change. The object is to increase self-understanding, and thereby to strengthen the ego's capacity for more adaptive and creative activity. Many psychoanalytic writers acknowledge, however, that interpretation must take place within a good working relationship with a client who has the capacity and willingness to profit from the experience (Strupp, 1989).

What is interpretation? It is an explanatory statement that helps to bring meaning and understanding to a person's behavior, thoughts, or actions. It may refer to a defense or to the relation of drive (impulse, feeling, wish) to a defense against it (repression, reaction formation, etc.); to feelings toward the therapist, which are said to be transferred from other important figures; to the perception of people or events in the client's current life; or to figures from the past. Interpretations may also refer to perceived parallels between the client's psychological experience of past or present figures and the way in which the therapist is viewed. For example, at the right moment and following the relevant behavior or associations in therapy, a therapist might say the following to one of the students mentioned above, who is procrastinating over reading this chapter assigned by the professor because he or she resents the professor's authority: "You are afraid to acknowlege directly your anger toward me for setting the time and the fee. Instead, you avoid coming to a session—your assignment here—or you come late, just as you procrastinate about doing your professor's assignments."

Malan (1980) was one of the first to test empirically the relationship between interpretation and outcome in brief psychoanalytic therapy. He found that the more frequently a therapist interpreted the link between clients' feelings toward the therapist and their feelings toward their parents (transference–parent link) or other persons, the more favorable the outcome of therapy. In a methodologically more sophisticated study, which employed audiotapes rather than therapist notes, Marziali (1984) partially replicated these results. A more recent study, however, failed to find a direct linear relationship between interpretations pertaining to particular persons and outcome (Piper, Debbane, Bienvenu, Carufel, & Garant, 1986). In a review of 22 findings evaluating the impact of interpretations on outcome, Orlinsky and Howard (1986) reported that 11 supported the effect, 8 showed no association, and 3 showed a negative impact.

They concluded (quite rightly, in our view) "that other important factors act to neutralize or potentiate the impact of interpretation on patient outcome" (p. 324).

Just what those mediating factors may be has been the object of a fruitful line of inquiry begun by the Penn and Mount Zion psychotherapy research groups. A major limitation of all the studies just described is the lack of attention to the *content* of the interpretation, as opposed to its form or its object (person) focus. What seemed to be needed was a way of evaluating the *accuracy or suitability* of the interpretations for the particular clients to whom they were addressed. According to the theory of psychoanalytic therapy, an interpretation must speak to the specific issues and concerns of the client if it is to have mutative power (Strachey, 1934). The development of the CCRT method described above allowed Crits-Christoph, Cooper, and Luborsky (1988) to develop such a measure of the accuracy of therapist interpretations. The latter was defined as the degree of congruence between the content of the client's CCRT and the content of the therapist's interpretations. A moderately strong relationship was found between accuracy of interpretations of the Wish and RO components of the CCRT (derived from early therapy sessions) and treatment outcome. Partial correlations also showed that the predictive power of these CCRT components was not due to other factors, such as the quality of the therapeutic alliance.

In a similar vein, Silberschatz et al. (1986) assessed the suitability of therapist interpretations by evaluating their compatibility with the client's Plan (Goals, Obstructions, Tests, and Insights, as described above) in three cases. How would interpretations judged as highly compatible with the Plan stack up against transference interpretations in predicting client progress in therapy? Results showed that the suitability of interpretations was a better predictor of patients' immediate progress (measured by the Experiencing Scale) than whether the interpretations were transference or nontransference. Furthermore, the percentage of Plan-compatible interpretations in the two cases with good outcomes was far higher than the percentage of interpretations that were not compatible with the clients' Plans, whereas the opposite was true in the poor-outcome case. The authors concluded that interpretations may be helpful or harmful, depending on their meaning to a particular patient.

Recently, attempts have been made to use the mode of assessing personality problems to gauge the nature of the outcome achieved in psychoanalytic therapy. For example, when the problems are defined by means of the PFM (Silberschatz, Curtis, & Nathan, 1989), the related Plan Attainment Scale measures clients' progress in terms of the degree to which they (1) achieve the Goals set for therapy in the Plan, (2) overcome the Obstructions to attaining these goals, and (3) develop the relevant Insights as specified in the Plan. Similarly, the CCRT was measured early and late in treatment to discover whether components of the CCRT change over the course of therapy (Crits-Christoph, Luborsky, Dahl, & Friedman, in press). Changes were small but statistically significant for four of the five measures of relationship patterns. Furthermore, the size of the correlations with change in symptom patterns indicated that the CCRT provides extra information not assessed by symptom ratings. We regard such attempts to provide theory-relevant measures of change—linking assessment, process, and outcome—as an important new direction in psychotherapy research.

PHENOMENOLOGICAL/ EXPERIENTIAL MODELS OF PERSONALITY AND CHANGE

Rogers's Client-Centered Theory as Exemplar

Whereas Freud's model of personality is strongly biological, with clear connections to natural science, phenomenological models are more purely psychological in thrust. They are concerned with the phenomenology of consciousness and the organization and function of subjective experience. In the words of the Gestalt psychologist Koffka (1935), "For us phenomenology means as naive and full a description of direct experience as possible" (p. 73). Carl Rogers's client-centered theory is one of the best examples of a phenomenologically oriented personality theory that also has strong and direct links to clinical practice. Its philosophical and psychological wellsprings lie especially in Husserl's phenomenological psychology, Kant's transcendental phenomenology, and the Gestaltists' notions of the holistic nature of phenomena (Rychlak, 1973).

According to client-centered theory, the

core tendency of human beings is to actualize their potentialities (Rogers, 1959), which are all in the service of the maintenance and enhancement of life. The most important form of this tendency is actualizing the self, with concomitant needs for positive regard and positive self-regard. The former refers to the person's satisfaction at receiving the approval of others and frustration at receiving disapproval; the latter refers to approving or disapproving of oneself. The concept of "self," which is central in Rogers's theory, is an organized pattern of perceptions referred to by the person as "me" or "I." It is a conscious or potentially conscious portion of a person's psychological makeup. Although the self changes, it retains pattern, coherence, and organization, and hence is a personality structure (Pervin, 1984). Related to it is the "ideal self," or the self-concept a person aspires to and values.

Rogers specified three characteristics of the fully functioning person. The first is "openness to experience," in which the person is both emotional and reflective; the opposite is defensiveness. A second characteristic is "existential living," which involves fully experiencing life in a here-and-now, moment-to-moment way. A person living in this manner is flexible, adaptable, and spontaneous. The third characteristic is "organismic trusting." Such a person, in Rogers's (1961) words, allows himself or herself "to consider each stimulus, need and demand, its relative intensity and importance, and out of this complex weighing and balancing, discover that course of action which would come closest to satisfying all his [or her] needs in the situation" (p. 190). Two auxiliary features of the fully functioning person are "experiential freedom"—the feeling of being free to choose between alternative courses of action—and "creativity." The maladaptive person as described by Rogers is defensive, lives according to a preconceived plan, disregards inner needs and outer stimuli, feels manipulated, and is conventional and conforming. By contrast, the adjectives he uses to describe the lived experience of the fully functioning person are "exciting, rewarding, challenging, meaningful" (1961, p. 196).

The Therapeutic Relationship as Change Agent

Psychoanalysis, as described previously, views interpretations of the tranferential elements of the relationship between therapist and client and its link to others as constituting the primary mechanism of personality change. The relationship is regarded as an important focus of exploration, which is enhanced by the relative neutrality of the therapist. In the cognitive therapies described below, a positive client–therapist relationship is prescribed to gain the client's cooperation with the recommended regimen for change. Client-centered therapy, by contrast, emphasizes the quality of the relationship itself as the most powerful locus of personality change. It highlights the realistic aspects of the relationship, and not its projected or transferential features. Optimally, an accepting and egalitarian relationship is achieved. Rogers (1957, 1959) has spelled out the qualities a therapist should bring to the relationship, referring to them as the necessary and sufficient conditions of therapeutic personality change. They include (1) empathy, (2) unconditional positive regard or nonpossessive warmth, and (3) congruence or genuineness.

"Empathy," always the "first among equals" of desirable therapeutic conditions in client-centered therapy, is the therapist's ability to understand what clients are experiencing and to convey that understanding to them. Such close tracking enables clients to appreciate their inner experience as an important source of information for guiding their own lives (Rice, 1988). "Unconditional positive regard" refers to a therapeutic attitude of caring and prizing of clients—not because of their desirable characteristics such as high intelligence or physical attractiveness, but as unique human beings, warts and all. Rogers also used the term "nonpossessive warmth" to describe this attitude. "Congruence" or genuineness requires that therapists be aware of their own feelings in relation to clients and that they be willing to share these feelings with clients without burdening them. To Rogers (1980), this means not hiding behind a mask of professionalism.

Research in Client-Centered Therapy

How have the terms of Rogers's personality theory been adapted to measures of change in psychotherapy research? One aspect of the fully functioning person that received early research attention was organismic trusting, which implies a compatibility between people's perception of self as it is and as they would like it to be. Using a variant of the Q-sort technique, Butler and Haigh (1954) assessed the size of the discrepancy between the perceived actual self and the ideal self to evaluate how this gap was affected by a course of client-centered therapy. Results revealed that whereas a control group showed no change in the actual–ideal discrepancy from before to after therapy and at follow-up, the client group showed a marked decrease in the discrepancy, accounted for by self-descriptions' becoming more like the ideal self. Supporting the value of the measure of actual–ideal congruence are several studies indicating that those high in actual–ideal congruence are the better adjusted (e.g., Brophy, 1959; Turner & Vanderlippe, 1958). It is noteworthy that in a meta-analysis of psychotherapy outcomes, the one area in which client-centered therapy produced greater improvement relative to other approaches was in self-esteem (Smith, Glass, & Miller, 1980).

Let us turn now to the "necessary and sufficient" conditions of personality change. To what extent have research studies backed up Rogers's claims? A thorough review of these three process variables as they relate to therapy outcome was conducted recently by Orlinsky and Howard (1986). They uncovered 86 findings on empathic receptiveness, 94 on unconditional positive regard, and 53 on therapist genuineness, remarking that these were among the most intensively researched variables in the process–outcome literature. About 40–60% of the findings were positive and significant, and only one or two were mildly negative. Of the three variables, therapist genuineness correlated less frequently and somewhat more weakly with outcome than the other two.

The authors further analyzed these results according to whether process and outcome were judged by an observer, by objective indices, by the client, or by the therapist. The frequency of significant positive findings across all outcome categories was much greater when therapist conditions were gauged from the client's rather than the therapist's perspective. It should be noted that Rogers (1957), in an elaboration of the necessary conditions of change, specified that communication to the client of the therapist's empathy, genuineness, and regard must be achieved. The findings where clients rated the presence of the conditions, therefore, are the most crucial, and they tend to support Rogers's hypothesis most strongly.

These data and others pertaining to features of the therapeutic bond, such as therapist engagement with and attunement to the client, led Orlinsky and Howard (1986) to conclude that a good therapeutic bond contributes strongly to positive outcomes across all forms of psychotherapy. Following Frank (1974), they hypothesized that such a bond strengthens client morale and conveys a positively toned affective message to clients that is relevant to their self-evaluation. They also pointed out, however, that little is yet known about how micro-outcomes (changes that occur along the way in therapy) contribute to macro-outcomes. In this connection, there are some interesting new lines of research originating largely within the experiential therapies, which are described below.

It is worth pausing to ask whether the conditions for constructive personality change as posed by Rogers truly have been assessed by the many studies summarized by Orlinsky and Howard (1986). In a sharply critical review, Watson (1984) claims that they have not. He points out, for example, that if any one of the conditions is absent, then no relationship is predicted by client-centered therapy between any of the other conditions and client improvement. As such, he regards most of the findings cited above as irrelevant. In addition, he does not accept that just any definition of therapist warmth taps unconditional positive regard unless it is shown to remain constant even under changes in the content of the client's experience. Furthermore, he emphasizes that, from a phenomenological standpoint, the client must be the source of the ratings, as Orlinsky and Howard's findings bear out.

Of the 15 studies Watson reviewed, all of which used the client as the source of measured outcome, only 2 assessed all the hypothesized conditions, including client incongruence (i.e., the client's being in a vulnerable or anxious state). (Client incongruence as specified by Rogers was absent in many analogue studies, which therefore were excluded from Watson's review.) The results of the two studies that met all the conditions supported Rogers's hypotheses. However, since these two studies were correlational in design, even they did not adequately address the issue of the conditions as *causal* factors, as Rogers hypothesized. For causation to be determined, either a path analysis or an experimental design is called for. What can be concluded from these reviews is that there is moderately strong evidence for the potency of the individual conditions of personality change as set out by Rogers, but more sophisticated studies have yet to be performed, particularly on the effects of their combination.

We turn now to the cognitive therapies, which derive from a distinctly different tradition than do the psychoanalytic and phenomenological/experiential approaches, and which historically are of more recent origin.

COGNITIVE THEORIES OF PERSONALITY AND CHANGE

Over the past two decades, cognitive theories of personality have become a major influence on clinical psychologists interested in personality change, as well as on developmental, social, and cognitive psychologists studying personality and its development. Most generally, such theories share an emphasis on internal, inferred mental structures that are understood to be closely related to the experience and behavior of individuals.

Cognitive theories of personality are relatively recent, although their antecedents can be traced throughout the 20th century (Leahey, 1980). Their chief influences were Piaget's structuralist developmental theory (Piaget with Inhelder, 1969), Bandura's (1973) social learning theory, and the advent of computers along with the notion of artificial intelligence in the 1950s. It may be argued, however, that cognitive clinical theories have origins independent of the cognitive tradition in general psychology: Clinical practice often reflects applied and systematic "common-sense" notions such as "the power of positive thinking," and techniques of persuasion are certainly not limited to academic psychology. Nonetheless, the "cognitive revolution" that may be said to have taken place during the 1960s and 1970s stimulated new thinking about the nature of personality; it provided a basis for theorizing about personality and change outside the psychoanalytic, experiential, and trait theories, which have dominated personality theory throughout much of the past 50 years.

Cognitive Models of Personality

An important precursor to current cognitive models was Kelly's (1955) construct theory, which presented the idea of the individual construing the world in relatively enduring ways. It was a theory with clinical relevance, as it included a developmental framework and had implications for change. In particular, the notion of the complexity of individuals' systems of constructs was related to both their intelligence and their psychological functioning. Progressive change was seen as taking place in the direction of increased differentiation of constructs; thus, people, events, and experience of the world could be perceived in greater detail and richness as the result of psychological growth. (For further elaboration, see Kelly, 1958; Maher, 1969.)

Cognitive theories of personality are based on the assumption that there are structures of cognition that determine how an individual comes to evaluate, interpret, and organize the large and complex bodies of information related to the self and others. In particular, these theories share the idea that there are mental structures such as "scripts" that organize and determine individuals' behavior, affect, and experience (Abelson, 1981; Tomkins, 1979). Carlson (1981), for example, has examined such organizing structures, which she refers to as "nuclear scenes," in a manner also relevant to psychoanalytic theory. A related idea is that of "schemas" (Neisser, 1967); this concept is rooted in the cognitive tradition of Piaget and his work on the evolution and development of thinking, and in Bartlett's (1932) famous studies of memory. Of particular interest from the point of view of personality change are self-schemas, which organize experience, feelings, judgments, and perceptions of self and others (Markus, 1983; Markus & Nurius, 1986). Safran (1990) summarizes recent theoretical work on schemas, presenting the notion of the "interpersonal schema," which he defines as a "generalized representation of self–other relationships." This appears to be very similar to Stern's (1985b) concept of "representations of interactions that have been generalized," to be discussed below under the topic of intersubjective theories of personality.

Also relevant to cognitive theories of personality and cognitive therapy is the body of literature on attribution theory, which attempts to explain the way individuals attribute causality to themselves or others (Försterling, 1985, 1986). Similarly, research on the concepts of social judgment, "person perception" (how people know about others), and "implicit personality theories" examines the ways in which people look at themselves, others, and the world, and how interpersonal information is encoded, organized, and utilized (Cantor &

Kihlstom, 1987; Cantor & Mischel, 1979; Fiske & Taylor, 1984; Higgins & Bargh, 1987).

Cognitive Therapies

The work of Beck and his colleagues (Beck, 1976; Beck, Rush, Shaw, & Emery, 1979; Emery, Hollon, & Bedrosian, 1981) represents one of the more significant attempts to apply cognitive concepts to clinical problems. The model is based on the notion that certain distortions or biases in attribution and information processing lead to maladaptive patterns of behavior and mood disorders. Thus, specific cognitive errors, if made persistently, cause depression and other psychopathology. For example, "catastrophizing" is the term for the error of overstating consequences or defining as catastrophic some anticipated event. Another example is "personalizing," which is the error of interpreting negative events as directed at the individual or caused by the individual. Compared to nondepressed individuals, depressed people tend to see themselves as responsible for problems and frustrations, and to see situations as unchanging and globally negative. As such, the attributions made by persons who are depressed are significantly different from those made by "normal" individuals (see also Försterling, 1986). A meta-analytic study of outcome research on the efficacy of cognitive therapy for depression suggests that this treatment may be more effective than pharmacotherapy, behavior therapy, and other psychotherapies (Dobson, 1989).

Another cognitive model of psychopathology, developed by Ellis (1970; Ellis & Harper, 1975), is joined to a corresponding treatment he calls "rational–emotive therapy." Ellis believes that people's difficulties in living arise from irrational beliefs, and the treatment focuses directly on changing or eliminating them. Examples are the beliefs that "I must be loved by everyone," and "The past irrevocably and completely determines my present experience and behavior."

A third major cognitive model has evolved from the work of Bandura (1977, 1982) and his associates, and forms the theoretical basis of much of the cognitive–behavioral treatment that has developed over the past 15 years. A central concept in Bandura's (1973) social learning theory is "self-efficacy," or the belief people have about their ability or competence to accomplish some behavior or attain a par-

ticular goal. Research in cognitive–behavioral therapy has shown that the initial level of self-efficacy is significantly correlated with therapy outcome; this suggests that self-efficacy functions as a mediating variable of the individual's behavior. Treatment is focused on influencing the client's self-efficacy regarding the target behavior, both through cognitive means (such as persuasion or logic) and through more traditional behavioral techniques.

All three examples illustrate cognitive therapists' emphasis on cognitive variables that mediate or influence affects and behaviors—in particular, faulty attribution, irrational beliefs, and self-efficacy. Each theorist suggests that certain beliefs about the self, others, or the nature of the world will influence feelings, relationships, and performance. Therefore, these beliefs or cognitions are seen as causally important aspects of personality functioning. They are also viewed as open to intervention or change, the topic to which we now turn.

Cognitive Re-education as the Mechanism of Change

There are two basic processes that underlie all cognitive approaches to personality change: the modification of existing maladaptive beliefs, and the acquisition of needed or absent mediating cognitions. The overall agent of change is cognitive re-education, in the course of which old, destructive cognitions are unlearned and replaced by new, more adaptive ones, and areas of deficiency are remedied by the learning of new cognitive skills.

The first process, the correction of cognitive distortions, is central to the approaches of cognitive therapy (Beck, 1976), rational–emotive therapy (Ellis, 1970), and systematic rational restructuring (Goldfried, DeCenteceo, & Weinberg, 1974). In each, personality change is understood to be the result of persuasion, logic, and instruction, as clients' irrational or distorted beliefs are systematically brought out and challenged. Beck and his colleagues also emphasize clients' use of experience and experimentation to "disprove" invalid ideas; this makes the treatment behavioral as well as cognitive. However, the mediating variables are understood to be mental contents or cognitions, and the focus is on changing how clients think about themselves and their environment.

The process of learning new cognitions, rather than correcting existing, distorted ones, is illustrated by the cognitive technique of "problem-solving training," which focuses on helping clients develop more effective coping and decision-making skills (Goldfried & Goldfried, 1975). The steps of problem solving are formalized and taught, as the client is helped to internalize the problem-solving process so that the training can be applied to any situation. Another example of learning new cognitions is "stress inoculation training" (Meichenbaum, 1985), which involves teaching clients to approach and anticipate the requirements of feared or problematic situations. The focus here is on teaching adaptive, anticipatory responses using cognitive techniques and mediators. Other techniques are "thought stopping" for intrusive, obsessive, or psychotic thoughts, and "self-instructional training" (Meichenbaum, 1977), in which overt problem-solving procedures are transformed into covert self-verbalizations to enable clients to accomplish previously problematic behaviors.

In contrast to the situation with psychoanalytic and phenomenological/experiential therapies, there is virtually no research from a cognitive point of view specifically into the process of psychotherapy and its relationship to change. For example, although persuasion is a key technique of cognitive therapy, it is not a focus of study among cognitive therapists. In the traditions of pragmatism and functionalism, upon which cognitive therapies draw, the emphasis is on techniques and demonstrations of efficacy (Hollon & Beck, 1986). Thus, a typical study may compare two or more cognitive or cognitive–behavioral techniques in the treatment of a particular emotional or behavioral disorder. For many of the cognitive approaches, a general study of the process of therapy would be impossible or irrelevant, because the change agents (such as learning or persuasion) are understood to be folded into the specific techniques or procedures—be they teaching coping skills or disproving invalid ideas—and are not separable from them. Instead, cognitive therapists seem to rely on existing bodies of experimental research in areas such as social and personality psychology, particularly social cognition, although even in these instances the connection between experimental research and cognitive therapy is tenuous (Brewin, 1989).

The importance of such research notwithstanding, we believe that it does not fully address the nature of therapeutic process and change. It is clear, however, that as the cognitive therapies have been maturing, the theories of change upon which they rely are becoming more sophisticated and elaborate. Their assimilation of available traditions in psychology, such as constructivism, systems theory, and structural developmental models, have led to significant refinements of the bases of cognitive treatments and the corresponding conceptions of change (Brewin, 1989; Guidano & Liotti, 1985; Joyce-Moniz, 1985; Mahoney, 1985, 1988; Neimeyer, 1988; Safran, 1990). As cognitive therapists hone their theories of the change process, we believe that they will increasingly turn to the study of that process in its own right.

A criticism that may be made of cognitive theories is that they are not really theories of personality at all, but rather groups of theoretical statments about cause-and-effect relationships between specific internal mental events and behaviors. The models lack comprehensiveness, failing to address a full range of important psychological dimensions such as development, subjective experience, and phenomena related to the idea of the "whole person." Regarding the last-mentioned of these, many cognitive views, in part reflecting their roots in behaviorism, tend to be atomistic, conceptualizing personality as a collection of "cognitions" in a metaphorical basket; the nature of the basket is not examined, nor is the relationship among the cognitions. Some advocates of cognitive theories would do away with the notion of personality altogether, preferring to address specific cognitive constructs rather than theorize about structure. These criticisms, however, are now being addressed by cognitive theorists and therapists (e.g., Dobson, 1988; Mahoney, 1985, 1988). To the extent that cognitive therapy begins to examine developmental questions, applies structural models of growth and change, and develops more highly refined conceptions of the change process, it will become an increasingly adequate framework for personality theory and research.

We turn now to the intersubjective/self-psychological approach to personality and change, which does address these important dimensions.

INTERSUBJECTIVE THEORIES OF PERSONALITY AND CHANGE

Intersubjective theories of personality regard the relationship between the person and the surrounding psychological or interpersonal environment as one of figure and ground. They emphasize the contextual nature of personality, locating personality variables within the constantly shifting and temporally bounded interpersonal milieu. The person is not viewed as residing in a vacuum, as an entirely separate entity, but rather as a dynamic and responsive being always affected by and affecting the continuous psychological field.

Intersubjective theories can be related to "interactionist" ideas in personality psychology. These ideas developed in response to dissatisfaction with trait theories, which locate the determinants of behavior and experience in the individual alone, as well as to situationist theories, which view the environment as the primary determinant. (See Pervin, 1985, and Higgins, Chapter 12, this volume, for a discussion of the status of the "person–situation controversy" and issues of interactionism.)

Another related tradition is the school of "interpersonal psychiatry," originating in the work of Harry Stack Sullivan (1953). Sullivan reframed psychoanalytic notions of personality functioning and psychopathology in terms of the interpersonal milieu of the individual. Of particular interest here is his notion of the self as arising developmentally from the "reflected appraisals" of parenting figures, highlighting the essentially social and interactive quality of personality. Although Sullivan developed his views independently of psychoanalytic theories evolving in Europe, some of his ideas are mirrored in the developments attributed to the British school of object relations theory, which in turn constitute the historical foundation for more contemporary intersubjective personality theories (Greenberg & Mitchell, 1983). The work of D. W. Winnicott, an important figure in the British psychoanalytic tradition, can be cited as an example.

Winnicott (1958, 1965), who drew on his experience as a pediatrician observing mothers and their infants, developed concepts stressing the interdependent and interactive nature of the developing personality and its environment. He viewed the psychological world of the infant as inextricably bound up with the responsiveness of the environment, as represented by the quality of the mothering provided. (Mothering, in Winnicott's theory, is not restricted to the actual mother.) The notions of the "true self" and the "false self," which Winnicott viewed as the poles of a dimension of personality functioning that he ul-

timately came to view as a primary diagnostic dimension, point to the importance of what he called the "good-enough mother." By meeting the psychic needs of the infant repeatedly and consistently, the good-enough mother enables the infant to develop an authentic and realistic sense of its own efficacy and experience. Winnicott's perspective leads to an emphasis on the "boundary conditions" or psychic borders between the relatively vulnerable and undifferentiated infant and the more differentiated mother, who provides the responses needed to regulate the infant's fluctuating inner, affective states. Thus, personality in this view is grounded in developmental and interpersonal contexts. However, although Winnicott pointed to the historical importance of the interpersonal and intersubjective domains, it is only in the "self psychology" of Heinz Kohut that the centrality of the adult's *current* intersubjective field is fully addressed.

Self Psychology as Distinct from Psychoanalysis and Client-Centered Therapy

Psychoanalytic self psychology is presented separately from the main discussion of psychoanalytic models of personality change for three reasons. First, self psychology is based upon fundamentally different assumptions about the nature of personality. Although the structures it posits are related to those of psychoanalysis, it pays far less attention to biologically based drives and subsequent mental conflict. Instead of drives, defenses, and conflicts, Kohut addresses the cohesiveness, temporal stability, and affective qualities of self-experience in the context of the perceived characteristics of the environment.

A second justification for separate treatment is that self-psychological clinical practice is organized around a distinctive notion of what is therapeutic—a notion arising directly from the intersubjective conceptualization of personality, which in many respects is more akin to the clinical theories of phenomenological and humanistic therapies (Kahn, 1985). This point is discussed at greater length below.

A third important difference between self psychology and psychoanalysis may be described as methodological: The idea of an "intersubjective" approach reflects a notion of knowledge, data, and evidence that is decidedly different from the natural science view of method taken by traditional psychoanalytic theorists. Most critically, the intersubjective approach takes the context of knowledge to be a determinant of that knowledge; what can be learned of the personality is bound by the particular context of the inquiring relationship and its intentions.

> The varied patterns of meaning that emerge in psychoanalytic research are brought to light within a specific psychological field located at the point of intersection of two subjectivities. Because the dimensions and boundaries of this field are intersubjective in nature, the interpretive conclusions of every case study must be understood as *relative* to the intersubjective context of their origin. (Atwood & Stolorow, 1984, p. 6)

This represents a substantial and significant shift away from the natural science epistemology of Freud, which permits observations to be made of the individual without reference to the context or the environment.

There is also a significant relationship between the clinical theories of Kohut and of Rogers (Kahn, 1985), whose work has been discussed earlier in this chapter. Kohut's theories are presented separately from those of the experiential therapists for several reasons. First, historically, Kohut's work arises from the psychoanalytic tradition, and he does not seem to have been significantly influenced by the work of humanistic, phenomenological, and experiential theorists. His theories are far more attentive to issues of development and of the individual's personal history, reflecting their basically psychoanalytic origins. Along these lines, in self psychology the therapeutic process is understood to require accurate reconstruction of the patient's past experience, and it places less emphasis on here-and-now experience (except as these are related to transference phenomena). Finally, although both Rogers and Kohut make empathy a central therapeutic technique, Kohut alone views empathy as a means of finding out about the subjective experience of the other.

The Self Psychology of Heinz Kohut

Kohut is the central figure in what now appears to be a major historical branching of the psychoanalytic mainstream. The evolution of his thinking (Kohut, 1959, 1971, 1977, 1984) has

generated much interest among psychoanalysts and psychotherapists, and it may be said that the work of Kohut and his followers is transforming the theory and practice of psychotherapy (Wolf, 1988), as have ego psychology and object relations theory before it. Kohut's revised theory of narcissism, and his central concept of the "selfobject," provides a clear illustration of intersubjective theories of personality structure and change.

Kohut came to view narcissism as underlying a distinct and separate line of psychological development (Kohut, 1977, 1984) in addition to the psychosexual and psychosocial stages. At one end of the dimension, there are infantile fantasies about the self and others, which tend to reflect grandiose and idealized fantasies of the omnipotence of the self or the other, or fantasies of extreme helplessness and powerlessness. At the other end, developmentally advanced and psychologically "healthier" narcissism prevails, allowing for interdependent attachment to others; stable self-esteem and confidence; and investment in relationships, work, and personal convictions.

Central to Kohut's theory is the notion that individuals, throughout their lives, exist within the psychological context of a "selfobject matrix," the intrapsychic representation of the self-sustaining functions of the environment. Wolf (1988) defines "selfobject" as "neither self nor object, but the *subjective* aspect and a self-sustaining function performed by a relationship of self to objects who by their presence or activity evoke and maintain the self and the experience of selfhood" (p. 184). What is of importance here is the idea that the "self" is constantly embedded in the context of the experienced responsiveness of others, and that no internal state can be posited without explicit reference to the quality of the responsiveness of the environment. Thus, affective states always are related to the changing selfobject milieu, which either adequately provides needed empathic attunement or fails to do so. Empathic failure results in narcissistic rage, fragmentation, and depletion of the self—leading to chronic feelings of emptiness—or in overstimulation of the self (Kohut, 1977, 1984).

An important aspect of Kohut's model is that it is emphatically developmental. The evolution and development of the personality is determined in large part by the nature of the surrounding environment. This in itself is not so different from Freud's thinking about psychosexual development, but it places much less emphasis on internal drive states, and much more on the quality of the actual interaction between the child and its caretakers. In fact, Kohut's view was that the nature of this interaction is both the driving force behind, and the determinant of the success of, the formation of the adult personality.

> What creates the matrix for the development of a healthy self in the child is the self-object's capacity to respond with proper mirroring at least some of the time; what is pathogenic is not the occasional failure of the self-object, but his or her chronic incapacity to respond appropriately. (Kohut, 1977, p. 187n)

Also illustrated in this passage is Kohut's notion of "transmuting internalizations," a structure-building process resulting from the "optimal frustration" of the child's narcissistic needs, which leads to the "consolidation of the self" (Kohut, 1977).

A distinctive feature in Kohut's theory is that although the events of a person's early years are seen as crucial for the formation of a stable self, the individual's narcissistic needs are understood to continue throughout the life cycle. The psychologically healthy adult also needs the "mirroring of the self by self-objects . . . and he continues to need targets for his idealization. . . . [S]elf-object relations occur on all developmental levels and in psychological health as well as in psychological illness" (Kohut, 1977, p. 188n). Because individuals remain within the dynamic field of a "selfobject matrix" throughout their lives, Kohut's personality theory is thoroughly contextual, permitting understanding of the subjective experience of the adult as well as of the child only by including reference to the relevant selfobject milieu.

Research on Intersubjectivity

This last point, emphasizing the importance of context, creates difficulties for the empirical researcher, as may be surmised. Although the clinical and theoretical literatures of self psychology have grown exponentially during the past decade, very little research has been done to examine the constructs and hypotheses of self psychology using traditional empirical methods. One reason is that the exploration of personality is considered possible only in the interpersonal context of an empathically attuned relationship. Thus, the investigative method of choice among self psychologists is "sustained empathic inquiry" into the subjective world of the individual (Stolorow, Brandschaft, & Atwood, 1987). The notion that the observer influences and shapes the observed has plagued a modern psychology intent on objective knowledge. It is in the realm of subjective experience, however, that this idea takes on particular importance. It is the hypothesis of Kohut and his followers that the condition and state of the self, a psychological structure, can be understood only through the singular juncture of patient and psychoanalytic therapist. That is to say, for self psychologists, the psychoanalytic method, as an "empathic–introspective" method, is the method *par excellence* for the study of subjective experience and its structures (Stolorow et al., 1987). From this point of view, there can be no possibility of applying objective methods to discover universal facts or principles in regard to the subjective domain of the self.

This having been said, it nonetheless appears possible and desirable to develop research projects that would enable systematic and rigorous examination of the theoretical and clinical postulates of intersubjective theories of personality. The potential exists for methods to be developed that are applicable to the clinical setting, but that also satisfy the need for public and systematic investigation (American Psychoanalytic Association, 1988; Spence, 1988). Such methods, however, including those deriving from hermeneutic theory, may require revision of the notions of scientific validity that currently prevail among behavioral scientists (Messer, Sass, & Woolfolk, 1988). In addition, research in nonclinical areas of psychology may be brought to bear on the theories described above. The following brief discussion of the applicability of current developmental research to self psychology will serve as an illustration.

A number of researchers have been working on the way in which representations of self and others develop, and such studies are directly applicable to psychoanalytic theory and practice. Specifically, this work suggests that the representations of self and others that arise in infancy and evolve throughout development are the result of particular patterns of interaction with significant figures (Beebe, 1986; Beebe & Lachman, 1988a, 1988b; Sander, 1983; Stern, 1983, 1985a, 1985b). These empirical studies, typically based on microanalyses of mother–infant interactions, provide a growing body of support for the ideas that infants have a presymbolic representational capacity; that they have expectations about relationships; that mothers and infants mutually influence each other's internal affective states; and that failures of "matching," or failures of attunement on the part of mothers, have observable effects on their infants. (See Beebe & Lachman, 1988a, for a more systematic review.)

Beebe and Lachman (1988a, 1988b) suggest that because interaction structures are represented more or less permanently, persistent failures of attunement on the part of a parent will be incorporated into an infant's representations of self and others; this closely parallels Kohut's ideas about falures in the self-object milieu of the infant. Stern (1985b) has developed a concept he calls "representations of interactions that have been generalized" (RIGs), which arise in the infant from the accumulated experience of episodes of interpersonal interaction. These RIGs are essentially prototypic or schematic structures that are evoked out of memory by certain conditions of a current situation, which in turn help the infant structure and anticipate aspects of that situation. It follows that the quality of early interactions will come to shape and thereby determine the nature of the child's sense of self and others and the relationships between the two. Stern (1985b) elaborates on some of the clinical implications of his empirical work with mothers and infants, suggesting that psychoanalytic theory must accommodate the findings of empirical research taking place in various adjacent or contiguous fields.

As developmental researchers explore the origins of structures of selfhood and internalized representations of others, they provide data that are relevant to psychoanalytic theories of personality development and psychopathology. In particular, it appears that such recent work, focusing on affect regulation and the effects of interaction, attunement, and failures of attunement between mothers and their infants, tends to complement the clinical theories of self psychology, with their corresponding attention to attunement and the vicissitudes of the self.

Sustained Empathic Inquiry as the Mechanism of Personality Change

As noted above, self psychology is distinct from traditional psychoanalysis, not only in its theory of personality, but also in its conceptualization of the change process. Kohut's views evolved steadily over the years (Kohut, 1971, 1977, 1984), from the conventional psychoanalytic view that interpretation leads to the illumination of unconscous conflict and an increase of consciousness, toward a novel conception of therapeutic action. As the self, along with the nature of selfobject relations, became the central organizing structures in his theory of personality, Kohut focused more and more on the role of empathic inquiry in promoting the resumption of thwarted developmental processes.

As elucidated by Wolf (1988), the therapeutic process consists of the awakening or stimulating of previously warded-off selfobject needs or wishes as the therapist, through an empathic stance, creates conditions of safety for the patient. Patients' wishes to be understood inevitably encounter failures on the part of the analyst, who cannot be in perfect attunement all the time. Such empathic failures result in a disruption of the needed selfobject bond with the therapist, followed by the defensive regression to more archaic modes of relating, such as detachment or overly sexualized or aggressive verbalizations or behavior (Wolf, 1988). As the therapist maintains a respectful, inquiring, and accepting stance, interpretation of the rupture, its causes, and its origins in the patient's personal history becomes possible, enabling the restoration of the needed selfobject tie with the therapist. As this process repeats itself over and over again during the course of therapy, the patient, through "transmuting internalizations," comes to develop a less vulnerable self, with greater capacity for relationships and for investment in work and playful activity. By "transmuting internalizations," Kohut means the internalization of structures and functions previously provided by the environment, such as the affect-regulating function of the mother.

As Stolorow et al. (1987) point out, there seem to be two processes of change occurring simultaneously. One is the structure building of the self through the process of internalization described above. The other is the resumption of developmental processes that have been interfered with in the individual's development. These authors suggest that the establishment of a needed relationship that sustains the self is in itself curative, by providing a medium in which growth and maturation may occur. They further suggest that the "optimal frustration" implied in Kohut's cycle of rupture and restoration of the empathic bond may not be necessary for growth; on the contrary, they say that growth occurs only when the needed selfobject tie is intact. The assumption here is that humans naturally have narcissistic needs, such as needs for approval, attention, and validation. Pathology is thought to result from the failure of the environment to provide needed responses, leading to various pathological formations of the self. Therapy provides the ambiance in which the original, unmet needs can be re-experienced, recognized, and appropriately responded to by the analyst, freeing the patient from defensive structures of character or behavior. Being understood is the central mechanism of change.

The relation of this paradigm to client-centered theory and therapy is readily apparent. In fact, in the absence of any empirical research investigating the clinical hypotheses of self psychology, it is possible to turn to research into the therapy relationship arising from the work of Rogers (1959) and other experiential therapists. There is also a growing body of literature that, although not derived from self psychology, points to the importance of the "therapeutic alliance"—a term originally used by Zetzel (1956). Although the terms are not identical, the therapeutic alliance is very likely to overlap significantly with what has been referred to here as the presence of a self-sustaining "selfobject tie" with the therapist. Both refer to the atmosphere of trust, comfort, safety, and acceptance that evolves in a satisfactory treatment relationship. Therefore, the results of research supporting the role of the alliance provide a measure of support for Kohut's conception of therapeutic change. For example, Luborsky, McLellan, and Woody (1985) found that a measure of the therapeutic alliance was the strongest predictor of therapy outcome in three different types of psychotherapy. In their review of "therapist attunement" as a factor in therapy outcome and process, Orlinsky and Howard (1986) reported that a majority of 86 studies surveyed, and especially those reflecting the patient's view of the relationship, found a positive relationship between therapist attunement and outcome. About two-thirds of the 31 findings they reviewed also reflected an association between "reciprocal attunement" and positive therapy outcome. The Vanderbilt Project (Hartley & Strupp, 1983; Strupp, 1980a, 1980b) has identified aspects of the therapeutic relationship

associated with good outcome. The Center for the Study of Neuroses (Horowitz, Marmar, Weiss, DeWitt, & Rosenbaum, 1984; Jones, Cumming, & Horowitz, 1988) has also presented work clarifying the nature of the therapeutic alliance and factors that contribute to its strength.

CURRENT TOPICS AND TRENDS IN PERSONALITY CHANGE AND PSYCHOTHERAPY

Several issues cut across the four theories of personality change discussed above, and deserve separate treatment: the problem of client resistance to change; the movement to combine theories or techniques of change, or to seek common factors operating in psychotherapy; new approaches to psychotherapy process research; and assessing psychotherapy outcome.

Resistance or Failure to Change

The fact that people at times do not progress in therapy is often conceptualized as the problem of "client resistance"; predictably, however, the explanation of it varies from one psychotherapy to another. Within psychoanalysis, resistance is viewed as an expectable and integral part of therapy. It is one of the ways in which clients repeat their difficulties in the transference, and it is analyzed accordingly. A client who continually comes late to sessions or is silent for long periods, for example, may be trying to avoid intimacy with the therapist just as he or she is doing with the partner or spouse. Such resistance, from an interpersonal or object relations outlook, is an enactment of a maladaptive way of relating to others (Blatt & Erlich, 1982) and presents a special opportunity to explore these interpersonal problems in the therapist–client relationship. Stagnation in therapy may also result if the therapist's interpretations are frequently inaccurate. This situation requires the therapist to think carefully about how countertransference issues may be contributing to the problem, and how to formulate the client's issues in alternative ways.

In contrast to the psychoanalytic conceptualization of resistance as an inevitable prelude to change, cognitive–behavioral therapists often view it as the enemy of progress, a self-defeating way in which clients throw up barriers to therapeutic movement. In this guise, resistance is noncompliance with the advice of the therapist. It calls for further cognitive–

behavioral analysis of the causes of the impasse, such as improperly conceived homework assignments (Meichenbaum & Gilmore, 1982), which the cognitive therapist must correct so that the business of therapy—behavioral or cognitive change—can proceed apace. However, akin to the psychoanalytic view, resistance is also seen by cognitive therapists as the appearance in therapy of the same dysfunctional cognitions manifested in daily life. Clients may make negative attributions about their capacity to be helped, much as they complain in a pessimistic manner to others of their failings. Cognitive therapists may then challenge these distorted cognitions with the expectation that their amelioration in therapy will generalize to other situations.

Within client-centered therapy, the causes of resistance are placed squarely at the therapist's doorstep. In some way, the therapist is not providing the necessary and sufficient conditions for change to come about. He or she is being detached or cold rather than warm and accepting, false or overly "professional" rather than genuine, and insufficiently empathic in not conveying an understanding of the client's subjective experience. In a similar vein, within the intersubjective approach, client resistance is viewed as resulting from either inevitable, small failures of therapist empathy, such as an occasional lateness or an impending vacation, or major ruptures of empathy in which the therapist grossly misunderstands the patient. In either case, to express the consequence in Kohut's language, there is a rupture of the self-object transference tie, which may lead to resistance in the form of increased symptomatic behavior, less coherence in the client's sense of self, aggressive outbursts, or other forms of decompensation. The therapist's task is to explore the client's reaction to empathic failure, or to understand his or her own lack of attunement and, in a sensitive way, to repair the selfobject tie. Clearly, resistance to change is an issue for all therapies, but the ways of defining, understanding, and treating it are closely linked to the associated theories of personality and change.

Integration and Eclecticism in Theories of Psychotherapy

Many experienced psychotherapists regard themselves as eclectic in practice (Smith, 1982), even while maintaining allegiance predominantly to one theory of change. If evidence indicates that each approach is to some extent effective, the argument goes, why not add one to the other to create a repertory that will be more substantial and enduring than any one alone? Wachtel (1977), for example, has proposed an integration of psychoanalytic and behavioral approaches, with an accompanying theory of change based on an interpersonal–dynamic outlook. Psychoanalytic theory can provide an understanding of the unconscious meaning of symptoms (e.g., anxiety), whereas behavior therapy can address the underlying problem directly (e.g., by systematic desensitization and assertiveness training to learn to approach the underlying fear). Wachtel has proposed a positive feedback loop in which change resulting from behavioral interventions can facilitate insight, which in turn can lead to further behavioral change.

Another approach to eclecticism argues that underlying the manifest differences in mechanisms of change are fundamental common factors that constitute the true agents of change, divergent theoretical rationales notwithstanding. Goldfried (1980), for example, has suggested that fruitful common ground which he terms "clinical strategy," lies between the nitty-gritty of specific techniques and the more abstract theoretical explanations of their effectiveness. One such strategy that he proposes is "having the patient/client engage in new, corrective experiences" (p. 94), which can come about either through cognitive–behavioral homework assignments or through the attainment of insight in the context of the client–therapist relationship. Other proposed common factors include the amelioration of demoralization (Frank, 1974), feedback about client feelings and behavior, and therapist qualities such as respectful attentiveness and trustworthiness.

Orlinsky and Howard (1987), in their generic model of psychotherapy, have provided "a single frame of reference within which the varied species of therapy can be described without distortion and can by systematically compared" (p. 7). They list five components of the therapeutic process that they view as active in any therapy and discuss their social, cultural, and psychological aspects and implications. In a sophisticated transtheoretical approach, Prochaska and DiClemente (1986) have proposed a stage theory of change, in which different levels of problems (symptoms; maladaptive cognitions; and interpersonal, family/systems, and intrapersonal conflicts) are seen as taking priority at different stages of therapy (precontemplation, contemplation, action, and maintenance). They view one or another therapy system (psychoanalytic, experiential, cognitive, etc.) as having a predominant role at a particular level of problem and stage of therapy.

These examples are illustrations of current efforts to break out of traditional molds and to range across therapies in the service of clinical utility and theoretical comprehensiveness. However, in spite of their obvious appeal, attempts at integration and eclecticism are not without their problems. On the clinical level, let us take the nature of the therapist–client relationship as an example. How can one simultaneously be neutral in the service of promoting transference, as psychoanalytic therapy requires; real and genuine in the service of authenticity, as phenomenological/experiential therapy prescribes; and didactic in the service of guiding clients' cognitions or behavior, as cognitive therapy dictates? In terms of psychotherapy process, is the feedback obtained from self-monitoring of cigarette smoking really comparable to learning about one's character defenses or unconscious conflicts in the transference? The theoretical foundations (or, on a larger scale, the visions of reality) underlying each approach can be irreparably compromised in the attempt to find a common ground (Messer & Winokur, 1980, 1984).

Furthermore, by endorsing eclecticism or integration, we lose our grip on the nomological net of research corroboration that the individual theories of personality and change have achieved painstakingly over time. The established structure of observation, fact, and theory is at least partially vitiated when therapeutic change agents are combined in a new format (Messer, 1986b).

Notwithstanding these difficulties, we believe that the judicious assimilation by one therapy of features from another is inevitable and desirable (Messer, 1986a). For example, the variants of psychoanalysis, such as ego psychology and self psychology, bring psychoanalytic therapy closer in its outlook and practice to both cognitive and phenomenological/experiential therapy. Similarly, client-centered therapy has been broadened and deepened by the inclusion of cognitive concepts (Wexler & Rice, 1974) and the use of interpretation (Ivey & Simek-Downing, 1980), even though accurate empathy remains its central mechanism of change. It is through dis-

course and dialogue among proponents of different, even opposing, viewpoints that new concepts and research directions are developed.

A New Paradigm for Psychotherapy Research

In recent years there has been an attempt to assess the efficacy of psychotherapy by meta-analyses of hundreds of outcome studies (e.g., Shapiro & Shapiro, 1982; Smith et al., 1980). The findings support the value of psychotherapy compared to no therapy or to placebos. Comparing treated and untreated groups, the average effect size is about one standard deviation, which means that the average treated person is better off than 80% of those not treated (Lambert, Shapiro, & Bergin, 1986). Furthermore, improvement lasts (e.g., Nicholson & Berman, 1983). However, meta-analytic comparisons of different psychotherapies reveal little superiority of one treatment over another. This is surprising, in light of the fact that most studies of the process of psychotherapy demonstrate systematic and substantial differences in the techniques of therapists of different theoretical persuasions (e.g., Luborsky, Woody, McLellan, O'Brien, & Rosenzweig, 1982; Stiles, 1979). Among the factors posited to account for this paradox are the presence of a common core of therapeutic processes across treatments despite apparent technical diversity (Stiles, Shapiro, & Elliott, 1986), as discussed above, and the lack of differentiated outcome measures, which is discussed below.

The traditional group comparison method sheds little light on the effects of specific interventions within sessions, the study of which is necessary to understand the active ingredients of psychotherapy. Although the correlation of process with outcome measures provides some of that information, many of the moderator and contextual variables that are in play are lost or ignored, leading only to moderate effect sizes or variable results, as we have shown above. For example, some of the equivocal findings regarding empathy, warmth, and genuineness may be due to a disregard for the role of the context in which this triad occurs (Rice & Greenberg, 1984). Problems like these have led recently to the endorsement of a new paradigm for psychotherapy research, which has been variously called "events or task analysis" (Rice & Greenberg, 1984), "discovery-oriented" research (Elliott, 1984; Mahrer, 1988), or "subprocess or microprocess research" (Gendlin, 1986). The basic purpose of all these approaches, which have been developed by the more experientially oriented psychotherapy researchers, is to study particular patterns of client or therapist events and their immediate antecedents or effects, as a way of better understanding what brings about change. As an example of this paradigm, we describe Mahrer's (1988) discovery-oriented approach, followed by a clinical example of Greenberg's task analysis method.

Mahrer's first step is to select a target of investigation, such as a client's expressing intense affect or describing a memory from early childhood. The second step is to collect as many instances as possible of this focal event by perusal of audio recordings, videotapes, or transcriptions of therapy sessions. Third, an instrument is selected or developed to provide a means of looking more closely at the phenomenon—for example, interviewing client and therapist about the event (Elliott, 1984) or developing a category system that allows a detailed analysis of it. Fourth, the instrument is applied to all instances of the targeted behavior. Fifth, the data are scanned for patterns that reveal something new about the phenomenon under investigation, which might lead to the development of theories to explain it.

The kinds of questions one can then pose are as follows: (1) Given a certain therapist operation carried out under this condition, what are the consequences? (2) Given this client consequence, what therapist operations under what conditions can achieve this consequence? (3) Given this condition, what operation can achieve this consequence? The results of this analysis should provide the therapist with specific guidelines as to what to do under defined conditions. It should be noted that verification of what emerges in this five-step discovery-oriented process requires confirmation and validation in later stages of the research.

Employing the method of task analysis, Greenberg (1984) has constructed a model for conflict resolution that makes use of the Gestalt two-chair dialogue. In this technique, based in experiential therapy, the therapist has the client experience two parts of the conflict (or "split") in two different chairs and then helps to create contact between them. Greenberg and Dompierre (1981) first determined

that this technique was likely to contain some active ingredients of therapy by demonstrating that it was more effective in resolving conflict than was empathic reflection. Greenberg then proposed a preliminary model of conflict resolution through analysis of the literature and clinicians' ideas of how the process worked. Subsequently, he studied events in therapy sessions that began with a "client marker"—namely, a statement indicating that the client was experiencing a conflict.

Based on his observations, Greenberg altered the original model of successful resolution in Gestalt therapy of the split. His final model of the process of conflict resolution has three components: criticizing the self from one side of the conflict (in one chair), expressing a felt desire from the opposite side (in the second chair), and then experiencing a softening attitude of the "critic" toward the self. In an attempt to verify this model, Greenberg (1984) compared resolvers and nonresolvers of the conflict and found that if one or more of the three components were missing, positive outcomes were not obtained. All resolvers showed the softening pattern, whereas none of the nonresolvers did so.

Evaluation of this vein of research depends on the worth one ascribes to the study of fairly circumscribed events in therapy. From a contextualist viewpoint, one could argue that what happened 20 minutes prior to the marker event, or even in previous sessions, may be more influential than proximal therapist or client behaviors. The narrowing of perspective can skew the understanding of such events taken out of their larger psychological context. Furthermore, one cannot readily assume that all events beginning with a particular client or therapist marker are identical in psychological meaning. Quite different therapeutic interventions may be needed for apparently similar events such as conflicts, dreams, and strong affect, depending on such factors as the state of the client, the nature of the working alliance, and the phase of therapy. However, despite these limitations, we endorse the principle of microanalytic research, as it holds promise for establishing a firmer scientific base for the practice of psychotherapy.

Traditionally, research in psychotherapy is divided into the study of process and outcome. Having described the new discovery-oriented/task-analytic approach to process, we turn our attention to psychotherapy outcome.

The Outcome Problem in Psychotherapy Research

What exactly do we mean when we claim that psychotherapy has brought about personality change? According to whom? By what measures? Along what dimensions? To restate these questions: Does it matter who should be doing the assessing, how they should be doing it, and what personality concepts should be guiding them? Surely the answers to these questions will determine in what respect we consider a person changed as a result of a psychotherapy experience. We examine each of these three closely related factors in turn to determine how they might influence our evaluation of change.

Who Should Assess Change?

The major evaluators of outcome are typically the client, the therapist, and/or the researcher. Occasionally relatives, friends, hospital personnel, insurance providers, or employers are involved in judging improvement. The problem, however, is that client, therapist, and researcher ratings correlate only moderately well, especially when one gets beyond measures of global adjustment. How are we to determine whose judgment is most accurate, true, or essential? Our contention is that there is no one correct answer to this question, but that one's choice of evaluator is closely linked to the theory with which one is working.

With a Rogerian account, as we have noted above, clients must be the principal arbiters of change, since it is they who are most in touch with their own experience. From a psychoanalytic perspective, however, to rely mainly on clients' accounts may be to ignore transference feelings, which can distort their responses. For example, clients may wish to please the therapist in order to maintain his or her love, leading to an overly positive evaluation, or they may be angry or frustrated, resulting in an overly critical or disparaging evaluation.

Perhaps the therapist who has gotten to know the client well over a period of time, and who can better sense the client's need to answer in a favorable way, is the best arbiter of true change. But therapists, too, have a stake in the outcome; furthermore, they can be overly influenced by their idiosyncratic reactions to clients based on their relationship to them over time.

An outside observer would not have the subjective and emotional investment of either the therapist or the client, and hence might be the evaluator of choice. Supporting such thinking are the findings that observer ratings are usually less positive than client or therapist ratings (e.g., Garfield, Prager, & Bergin, 1971; Green, Gleser, Stone, & Seifert, 1975). But will clients expose themselves as fully to an outside evaluator who, in addition, will be lacking the privileged information of the therapist? Luborsky (1971) has pointed out that the ratings of clients and therapists reflect the specific areas needing change in a way that other measures cannot. Clearly, choice of rating source involves tradeoffs, and psychotherapy researchers must always ask themselves what individuals are in the best position to assess the particular constructs of interest to them. Currently, the preferred approach among researchers is to include all three sources of assessment; of course, this does not resolve the problem of how to interpret lack of agreement among these several sources. There is no escaping the need for interpretation of the data of personality and change (Messer et al., 1988).

How Should Change Be Assessed?

At one time, projective techniques were commonly used to assess change in psychotherapy, especially when most psychotherapy was largely psychoanalytically derived. However, both their psychometric limitations and the ascendence of other theories of psychotherapy that do not emphasize intrapsychic change have led to a decline in their use. Objective personality measures deriving from a trait approach to personality, such as Cattell's Sixteen Personality Factors Questionnaire, were also found wanting as outcome measures because they are not sensitive to change in personality from before to after therapy. However, other kinds of objective measures have been employed successfully. Client-centered therapists found Q-sort methodology to be compatible with their theory of change, and cognitive therapists devised instruments such as the Automatic Thoughts Questionnaire (Hollon & Kendall, 1980) to assess negative self-statements that are accessible to the individual. These kinds of instruments have the advantages of high reliability and focused purpose. Obviously, they are closely tied to particular views of what constitutes personality and psychopathology;

in fact, cognitive therapists Segal and Shaw (1988) point out that choosing a particular mode of cognitive assessment is best conceived of as a theory-guided process.

Another mode of assessment is the structured or semistructured interview. Such an interview has the merits of allowing the client to speak freely and of covering a wide domain. However, problems of interviewer influence and low reliability have always plagued this method. (See Lambert, Christensen, & DeJulio, 1983, for a fuller treatment of the topic of outcome assessment.) Our major point is that the kind of outcome measure one chooses—be it the Minnesota Multiphasic Personality Inventory or the Rorschach, depression inventories or Q-sort, psychophysiologial or anxiety scales, or some form of clinical interview—has a decisive influence on what aspects of change one captures.

Furthermore, one cannot separate the study of personality or change from the context in which the data are gathered. Unlike the typical subject in a laboratory-based personality experiment, clients come to clinical psychologists with problems they want to resolve. This prompts them to share intimate matters in a different way than they would as subjects in an experiment—embarrassment, guilt, and shame notwithstanding. To paraphrase Bronfenbrenner (1977), psychologists too often study how adults behave in strange situations, doing strange things with strange people. In contrast, the clinician gets a view of personality as it emerges in an intense two-person situation over time. This view will change as clients becomes more able and willing to relate aspects of their experience and personality functioning not readily shared or known at the beginning of therapy. One learns about clients' personalities through empathy and introspection even more surely than through questionnaires and inventories. We believe that one of the reasons for the decline of psychoanalytic theory among personality researchers is the difficulty they experience in assessing, in an objective manner, the fullness of personality that is apparent in the intimate relationships upon which psychoanalytic observations and theory rely. The changes that take place in psychotherapy are often subtle and not easily measured; hence, there is a pressing need for measures like the CCRT, the ICF, and the Plan Attainment Scale. The gain in scientific exactitude of typical personality studies is too often bought at

the expense of a full-bodied understanding and assessment of personality and change.

In addition, usual research methods do not allow for the possibility that knowledge of personality may be more a dynamic unfolding than a static state—the result of a dialectical process of observing, interpreting, and then modifying one's observations and interpretations as a result of feedback (Steele, 1979). In this account, one never arrives at a final truth or certainty about an individual's personality, but only a time- and context-bound understanding that is singularly shaped by the very process through which it was attained (Packer, 1985; Woolfolk, Sass, & Messer, 1988). The importance of interpretive perspectives in psychology becomes apparent when considering assessment of change, and argues for a method of investigating personality and change that is dialectical, empathic, and clincially meaningful. If data are emergent, and not simply "there" to be tapped, then the process by which they are obtained is a crucial determinant of their form and meaning.

What Kinds of Change Should Be Assessed?

Closely connected to the source of evaluation and the techniques employed to assess change are the nature of the constructs measured and the way in which they decisively influence outcome measurement. These are not scientific matters alone, but, more fundamentally, issues of theory and value. One's theoretical beliefs will determine the choice of personality domain assessed, the techniques used in the attempt to change it, and the evaluation of whether that attempt has been successful. For example, if one decides, as do Rogerians, that the discrepancy between the client's perceived actual self and ideal self is of prime importance, then one adopts a measure of self-esteem. Similarly, if self-schemas of depressed clients are the constructs of interest, then the Dysfunctional Attitude Scale (Weissman & Beck, 1978) is appropriate. If one is psychoanalytically oriented and believes that transference manifestations, or the form and content of sadomasochistic and other fantasies, are the surest means of gauging change in interpersonal or intrapsychic patterns, a semistructured or unstructured interview will be the method of choice. And if the claims of one's guiding personality theory are such that several aspects of personality are expected to change, one must take a multidimensional approach to evaluation. It must be remembered, however, that the percentage of clients considered changed or improved will probably vary with the instrument employed. Mintz, Luborsky, and Christoph (1979), for example, reported effect sizes of different change measures ranging from .52 to .93.

Another way of addressing what dimensions of change are assessed following psychotherapy is to ask what the goals are. If we are treating a depressed person, are we aiming at a decrease in the symptoms of depression, such as sadness or withdrawal; a change in irrational beliefs or negative self-statements; a resolution of underlying conflicts over unfulfilled dependency needs; or a change in the construal of self- and object representations, which refers to nothing less than clients' ways of construing their world? Do we believe that the absence of depression and other negative affects is possible and desirable (Lazarus, 1976) or rather that the best that clients can hope for is the exchange of neurotic misery for everyday unhappiness (Breuer & Freud, 1893–1895/1955)? The comic view of life, which describes conflict as centered in situations, allows for the former, whereas a tragic outlook, which considers conflict to arise from inner forces beyond awareness and control, posits the latter (Messer, 1986b; Messer & Winokur, 1984). Or perhaps we expect that a successful therapeutic experience will lead to greater autonomy, differentiation, and maturation, and not merely to a decrease in negative affect.

Such value-laden choices cannot be avoided, but they can be made explicit, so that our outcome measures reflect what we believe is important in human functioning. In fact, different psychotherapies may open up different kinds of options for clients: "Each therapy may offer a different choice of paths which lead away from psychopathology (however defined), but which lead toward different destinations" (Stiles, 1983, p. 187). Outcome, says Stiles, may be construed as divergence rather than convergence on a common definition of normality.

SUMMARY

In this chapter, we have attempted to show how four prominent approaches to understanding personality—psychoanalytic, phenomeno-logical/experiential, cognitive, and intersubjective—are all closely interwoven with their modes of assessment, the nature of the change process they posit, and the kinds of outcomes they seek. Each proposes a different principal mechanism of change: interpretation, the therapeutic relationship, cognitive re-education, and sustained empathic inquiry, respectively. We have discussed four additional topics, including client resistance, psychotherapy integration, new directions in psychotherapy process research, and psychotherapy goals and outcomes. Although we have striven to maintain a scientific outlook in assessing the claims of the four theories of personality change, we end by reiterating that personality theory and change exist within a value framework that is closely bound up within the sociohistorical context in which we live. In this sense, the study of personality and psychotherapy are necessarily interpretive disciplines in which matters of ultimate truth are forever elusive.

ACKNOWLEDGMENT

We acknowledge with appreciation the editorial assistance of Laura McCann.

REFERENCES

Abelson, R. P. (1981). Psychological status of the script concept. *American Psychologist, 36,* 715–729.

American Psychoanalytic Association, Committee on Scientific Activities. (1988, January). *How can we best share our clinical experience? Suggestions for alternative methods of case reporting.* Paper presented at the meeting of the American Psychoanalytic Association, New York.

Arlow, J., & Brenner, C. (1964). *Psychoanalytic concepts and the structural theory.* New York: International Universities Press.

Atwood, G. E., & Stolorow, R. D. (1984). *Structures of subjectivity.* Hillsdale, NJ: Analytic Press.

Bandura, A. (1973). *Aggression: A social learning analysis.* Englewood Cliffs, NJ: Prentice-Hall.

Bandura, A. (1977). Self-efficacy: Toward a unifying theory of behavioral change. *Psychological Review, 84,* 191–215.

Bandura, A. (1982). Self-efficacy mechanism in human agency. *American Psychologist, 37,* 122–147.

Bartlett, F. C. (1932). *Remembering.* Cambridge, England: Cambridge University Press.

Beck, A. T. (1976). *Cognitive therapy and the emotional disorders.* New York: International Universities Press.

Beck, A. T., Rush, A. J., Shaw, B. F., & Emery, G. (1979). *Cognitive therapy of depression.* New York: Guilford Press.

Beebe, B. (1986). Mother–infant mutual influence and precursors of self- and object representations. In J. Masling (Ed.), *Empirical studies of psychoanalytic theories* (vol. 2, pp. 27–48). Hillsdale, NJ: Analytic Press.

Beebe, B., & Lachman, F. M. (1988a). The contribution of mother–infant mutual influence to the origins of self- and object representations. *Psychoanalytic Psychology,* 5, 305–337.

Beebe, B., & Lachman, F. M. (1988b). Mother–infant mutual influence and precursors of psychic structure. In A. Goldberg (Ed.), *Frontiers of self psychology: Progress in self psychology* (vol. 3, pp. 3–26). Hillsdale, NJ: Analytic Press.

Benjamin, L. S. (1982). Use of Structural Analysis of Social Behaviors (SASB) to guide interventions in psychotherapy. In D. Keisler & J. Anchin (Eds.), *Handbook of interpersonal psychotherapy* (pp. 190–212). New York: Pergamon Press.

Blatt, S. J., & Erlich, H. S. (1982). Level of resistance in the psychotherapeutic process. In P. Wachtel (Ed.), *Resistance: Psychodynamic and behavioral approaches* (pp. 69–91). New York: Plenum.

Breuer, J., & Freud, S. (1955). Studies on hysteria. In J. Strachey (Ed. and Trans.), *The standard edition of the complete psychological works of Sigmund Freud* (vol. 2, pp. 1–309). London: Hogarth Press. (Original work published 1893–1895)

Brewin, C. R. (1989). Cognitive change processes in psychotherapy. *Psychological Bulletin,* 96, 379–394.

Bronfenbrenner, U. (1977). Toward an experimental ecology of human development. *American Psychologist,* 32, 513–531.

Brophy, A. L. (1959). Self, role, and satisfaction. *Genetic Psychology Monographs,* 59, 236–308.

Butler, J. M., & Haigh, G. V. (1954). Changes in the relation between self-concepts and ideal concepts consequent upon client centered counseling. In C. R. Rogers & R. F. Dymond (Eds.), *Psychotherapy and personality change* (pp. 55–75). Chicago: University of Chicago Press.

Butler, S. F., & Binder, J. L. (1987). Cyclical psychodynamics and the triangle of insight: An integration. *Psychiatry,* 50, 218–231.

Cantor, N., & Kihlstrom, J. F. (1987). *Personality and social intelligence.* Englewood Cliffs, NJ: Prentice-Hall.

Cantor, N., & Mischel, W. (1979). Prototypes in person perception. In L. Berkowitz (Ed.), *Advances in experimental social psychology* (vol. 12, pp. 3–52). New York: Academic Press.

Carlson, R. (1981). Studies in script theory: I. Adult analogues of a childhood nuclear scene. *Journal of Personality and Social Psychology,* 40, 501–510.

Caston, J. (1986). The reliability of the diagnosis of the patient's unconscious plan. In J. Weiss, H. Sampson, & the Mount Zion Psychotherapy Research Group, *The psychoanalytic process* (pp. 241–255). New York: Guilford Press.

Collins, W. D. (1989). *The reliability, stability and theoretical adaptability of the Plan Diagnosis Method.* Unpublished doctoral dissertation, Rutgers University.

Collins, W. D., & Messer, S. B. (in press). Extending the Plan Formulation Method to an object relations perspective: Reliability, stability, and adaptibility. *Psychological Assessment: A Journal of Consulting and Clinical Psychology.*

Crits-Christoph, P., Cooper, A., & Luborsky, L. (1988). The accuracy of therapists' interpretations and the outcome of dynamic psychotherapy. *Journal of Consulting and Clinical Psychology,* 56, 490–495.

Crits-Christoph, P., Luborsky, L., Dahl, L., & Friedman, S. (in press). Measuring the outcome of dynamic psychotherapy using the Core Conflictual Relationship Theme method. In J. Ghannam (Ed.), *Psychoanalytic research methods.* New York: Guilford Press.

Crits-Christoph, P., Luborsky, L., Dahl, L., Popp, C., Mellon, J., & Mark, D. (1988). Clinicians can agree in assessing relationship patterns in psychotherapy. *Archives of General Psychiatry,* 45, 1001–1004.

Curtis, J. T., & Silberschatz, G. (1989). *The Plan Formulation Method: A reliable procedure for case formulation.* Manuscript submitted for publication.

Curtis, J. T., Silberschatz, G., Weiss, J., Sampson, H., & Rosenberg, S. (1988). Developing reliable psychodynamic case formulations: An illustration of the Plan Diagnosis Method. *Psychotherapy,* 25, 256–265.

Dobson, K. S. (1988). The present and future of the cognitive–behavioral therapies. In K. S. Dobson (Ed.), *Handbook of cognitive–behavioral therapies* (pp. 387–414). New York: Guilford Press.

Dobson, K. S. (1989). A meta-analysis of the efficacy of cognitive therapy for depression. *Journal of Consulting and Clinical Psychology,* 57, 414–419.

Elliott, R. (1984). A discovery-oriented approach to significant events in psychotherapy: Interpersonal process recall and comprehensive process analysis. In L. N. Rice & L. S. Greenberg (Eds.), *Patterns of change* (pp. 249–286). New York: Guilford Press.

Ellis, A. (1970). *The essence of rational psychotherapy: A comprehensive approach to treatment.* New York: Institute for Rational Living.

Ellis, A., & Harper, R. A. (1975). *A new guide to rational living.* North Hollywood, CA: Wilshire Books.

Emery, G., Hollon, S. D., & Bedrosian, R. C. (Eds.), (1981). *New directions in cognitive therapy: A casebook.* New York: Guilford Press.

Fiske, S. T., & Taylor, S. E. (1984). *Social cognition.* New York: Random House.

Försterling, F. (1985). Attributional retraining: A review. *Psychological Bulletin,* 98, 495–512.

Försterling, F. (1986). Attributional conceptions in clinical psychology. *American Psychologist,* 41, 275–285.

Frank, J. D. (1974). Psychotherapy: The restoration of morale. *American Journal of Psychiatry,* 131, 271–274.

Garfield, S. L., Prager, R. A., & Bergin, A. E. (1971). Evaluation of outcome in psychotherapy. *Journal of Consulting and Clinical Psychology,* 37, 307–313.

Gendlin, E. T. (1986). What comes after traditional psychotherapy research? *American Psychologist,* 41, 131–136.

Goldfried, M. R. (1980). Toward the delineation of therapeutic change principles. *American Psychologist,* 35, 991–999.

Goldfried, M. R., DeCenteceo, E. T., & Weinberg, L. (1974). Systematic rational restructuring as a self control technique. *Behavior Therapy,* 5, 247–254.

Goldfried, M. R., & Goldfried, A. P. (1975). Cognitive change methods. In F. H. Kanfer & A. P. Goldstein (Eds.), *Helping people change* (pp. 89–116). New York: Pergamon Press.

Green, B. L., Gleser, G. C., Stone, W. N., & Seifert,

R. F. (1975). Relationships among diverse measures of psychotherapy outcome. *Journal of Consulting and Clinical Psychology, 43,* 689–699.

Greenberg, L. S. (1984). A task analysis of intrapersonal conflict resolution. In L. N. Rice & L. S. Greenberg (Eds.), *Patterns of change* (pp. 67–123). New York: Guilford Press.

Greenberg, L. S., & Dompierre, L. (1981). Differential effects of Gestalt two-chair dialogue and empathic reflection at a split in counseling. *Journal of Counseling Psychology, 28,* 288–294.

Greenberg, J. R., & Mitchell, S. A. (1983). *Object relations in psychoanalytic theory.* Cambridge, MA: Harvard University Press.

Guidano, V. F., & Liotti, G. (1985). A constructivistic foundation for cognitive therapy. In M. J. Mahoney & A. Freedman, (Eds.), *Cognition and psychotherapy* (pp. 101–142). New York: Plenum.

Hartley, D. E., & Strupp, H. H. (1983). The therapeutic alliance: Its relationship to outcome in brief psychotherapy. In J. Masling (Ed.), *Empirical studies of psychoanalytic theories* (Vol. 1, pp. 1–38). Hillsdale, NJ: Analytic Press.

Hartmann, H. (1939). *Ego psychology and the problem of adaptation.* New York: International Universities Press.

Hartmann, H. (1964). *Essays on ego psychology.* New York: International Universities Press.

Higgins, E. T., & Bargh, J. A. (1987). Social cognition and social perception. *Annual Review of Psychology, 38,* 364–426.

Hollon, S. D., & Beck, A. T. (1986). Cognitive and cognitive–behavioral therapies. In S. L. Garfield & A. E. Bergin (Eds.), *Handbook of psychotherapy and behavior change* (3rd ed., pp. 443–482). New York: Wiley.

Hollon, S. D., & Kendall, P. C. (1980). Cognitive self-statements in depression: Development of an Automatic Thoughts Questionnaire. *Cognitive Therapy and Research, 4,* 383–396.

Horowitz, L. M., Rosenberg, S. E., Baer, B. A., Ureño, G., Kalehzan, B. M., & Villseñor, V. S. (1988). Inventory of interpersonal problems: Psychometric properties and clinical applications. *Journal of Consulting and Clinical Psychology, 56,* 885–892.

Horowitz, L. M., Rosenberg, S. E., Ureño, G., Kalehzan, B. M., & O'Halloran, P. (1989). The psychodynamic formulation, the consensual response method, and interpersonal problems. *Journal of Consulting and Clinical Psychology, 57,* 599–606.

Horowitz, M. J., Marmar, C., Weiss, D. S., DeWitt, K. N., & Rosenbaum, R. (1984). Brief psychotherapy of bereavement reactions. *Archives of General Psychiatry, 41,* 438–448.

Ivey, A. E., & Simek-Downing, L. (1980). *Counseling and psychotherapy: Skills and practice.* Englewood Cliffs, NJ: Prentice-Hall.

Jones, E. E., Cumming, J. D., & Horowitz, M. J. (1988). Another look at the nonspecific hypothesis of therapeutic effectiveness. *Journal of Consulting and Clinical Psychology, 56,* 48–55.

Joyce-Moniz, L. (1985). Epistemological therapy and constructivism. In M. J. Mahoney & A. Freedman (Eds.), *Cognition and psychotherapy* (pp. 143–179). New York: Plenum.

Kahn, E. (1985). Heinz Kohut and Carl Rogers: A timely comparison. *American Psychologist, 40,* 893–904.

Kelly, G. (1955). *The psychology of personal constructs.* New York: Norton.

Kelly, G. (1958). The theory and technique of assessment. *Annual Review of Psychology, 9,* 323–352.

Koffka, K. (1935). *Principles of gestalt psychology.* New York: Harcourt, Brace.

Kohut, H. (1959). Introspection, empathy, and psychoanalysis. *Journal of the American Psychoanalytic Association, 5,* 389–407.

Kohut, H. (1971). *The analysis of the self.* New York: International Universities Press.

Kohut, H. (1977). *The restoration of the self.* New York: International Universities Press.

Kohut, H. (1984). *How does analysis cure?* New York: International Universities Press.

Lambert, M. J., Christensen, E. R., & DeJulio, S. S. (1983). *The assessment of psychotherapy outcome.* New York: Wiley-Interscience.

Lambert, M. J., Shapiro, D. A., & Bergin, A. E. (1986). The effectiveness of psychotherapy. In S. L. Garfield & A. E. Bergin (Eds.), *Handbook of psychotherapy and behavior change* (3rd ed., pp. 311–381). New York: Wiley.

Lazarus, A. A. (1976). *Multimodal behavior therapy.* New York: Springer.

Leahey, T. H. (1980). *A history of psychology.* Englewood Cliffs, NJ: Prentice-Hall.

London, P. (1986). *The modes and morals of psychotherapy* (2nd ed.). Washington, DC: Hemisphere.

Luborsky, L. (1971). Perennial mystery of poor agreement among criteria for psychotherapy outcome. *Journal of Consulting and Clinical Psychology, 37,* 316–319.

Luborsky, L. (1984). *Principles of psychoanalytic psychotherapy.* New York: Basic Books.

Luborsky, L., & Crits-Christoph, P. (1988). Measures of psychoanalytic concepts—the last decade of research from "The Penn Studies." *International Journal of Psychoanalysis, 69,* 75–85.

Luborsky, L., Crits-Christoph, P., & Mellon, J. (1986). The advent of objective measures of the transference concept. *Journal of Consulting and Clinical Psychology, 54,* 39–47.

Luborsky, L., McLellan, A. T., & Woody, G. E. (1985). Therapist success and its determinants. *Archives of General Psychiatry, 42,* 602–611.

Luborsky, L., Woody, G. E., McLellan, A. T., O'Brien, C. P., & Rosenzweig, J. (1982). Can independent judges recognize different psychotherapies? An experience with manual-guided therapies. *Journal of Consulting and Clinical Psychology, 30,* 49–62.

Maher, B. (1969). (Ed.). *Clinical psychology and personality: Selected papers of George Kelly.* New York: Wiley.

Mahoney, M. J. (1985). Psychotherapy and human change processes. In M. J. Mahoney & A. Freedman, (Eds.), *Cognition and psychotherapy* (pp. 3–48). New York: Plenum.

Mahoney, M. J. (1988). The cognitive sciences and psychotherapy: Patterns in a developing relationship. In K. S. Dobson (Ed.), *Handbook of cognitive–behavioral therapies* (pp. 357–386). New York: Guilford Press.

Mahrer, A. R. (1988). Discovery-oriented psychotherapy research: Rationale, aims, and methods. *American Psychologist, 43,* 604–702.

Malan, D. H. (1980). *Toward the validation of dynamic psychotherapy.* New York: Plenum.

Markus, H. (1983). Self-knowledge: An expanded view. *Journal of Personality, 51,* 543–565.

Markus, H., & Nurius, P. (1986). Possible selves. *American Psychologist, 41,* 954–969.

Marziali, E. A. (1984). Prediction of outcome of brief psychotherapy from therapist interpretive interventions. *Archives of General Psychiatry, 41,* 301–304.

Meichenbaum, D. (1977). *Cognitive-behavior modification.* New York: Plenum.

Miechenbaum, D. (1985). *Stress inoculation training.* New York: Pergamon Press.

Meichenbaum, D., & Gilmore, J. B. (1982). Resistance from a cognitive–behavioral perspective. In P. Wachtel (Ed.), *Resistance: Psychodynamic and behavioral approaches* (pp. 133–156). New York: Plenum.

Messer, S. B. (1985). Choice of method is value-laden too. *American Psychologist, 40,* 1414–1415.

Messer, S. B. (1986a). Behavioral and psychoanalytic perspectives at therapeutic choice points. *American Psychologist, 41,* 1261–1272.

Messer, S. B. (1986b). Eclecticism in psychotherapy: Assumptions, problems and tradeoffs. In J. C. Norcross (Ed.), *Handbook of eclectic psychotherapy* (pp. 379–397). New York: Brunner/Mazel.

Messer, S. B., (1989). [Review of *The psychoanalytic process*]. Psychoanalytic Psychology, 6, 111–114.

Messer, S. B., Sass, L. A., & Woolfolk, R. L. (Eds.). (1988). *Hermeneutics and psychological theory: Interpretive perspectives on personality, psychotherapy and psychopathology.* New Brunswick, NJ: Rutgers University Press.

Messer, S. B., & Winokur, M. (1980). Some limits to the integration of psychoanalytic and behavior therapy. *American Psychologist, 35,* 818–827.

Messer, S. B., & Winokur, M. (1984). Ways of knowing and visions of reality in psychoanalytic therapy and behavior therapy. In H. Arkowitz & S. B. Messer (Eds.), *Psychoanalytic therapy and behavior therapy: Is integration possible?* (pp. 63–100). New York: Plenum.

Mintz, J., Luborsky, L., & Christoph, P. (1979). Measuring the outcomes of psychotherapy: Findings of the Penn Psychotherapy Project. *Journal of Consulting and Clinical Psychology, 47,* 319–334.

Neimeyer, R. A. (1988). Integrative directions in personal construct theory. *International Journal of Personal Construct Psychology, 1,* 283–297.

Neisser, U. (1967). *Cognitive psychology.* New York: Appleton-Century-Crofts.

Nicholson, R. A., & Berman, J. S. (1983). Is follow-up necessary in evaluating psychotherapy? *Psychological Bulletin, 93,* 261–278.

Orlinsky, D. E., & Howard, K. I. (1986). Process and outcome in psychotherapy. In S. L. Garfield & A. E. Bergin (Eds.), *Handbook of psychotherapy and behavior change* (3rd ed., pp. 311–381). New York: Wiley.

Orlinsky, D. E., & Howard, K. I. (1987). A generic model of psychotherapy. *Journal of Integrative and Eclectic Psychotherapy, 6,* 6–27.

Packer, M. J. (1985). Hermeneutic inquiry in the study of human conduct. *American Psychologist, 40,* 1081–1093.

Perry, J. C., Augusto, F., & Cooper, S. H. (1987). *The assessment of psychodynamic conflicts: I. Reliability of the idiographic conflict formulation method.* Unpublished manuscript, The Cambridge Hospital, Cambridge, MA.

Perry, J. C., Luborsky, L., Silberschatz, G., & Popp, C. (1989). An examination of three methods of psychodynamic formulations based on the same videotaped interview. *Psychiatry, 52,* 302–323.

Pervin, L. A. (1984). *Personality: Theory and research* (4th ed.). New York: Wiley.

Pervin, L. A. (1985). Personality: Current controversies, issues and directions. *Annual Review of Psychology, 36,* 83–114.

Pervin, L. A. (1989). Psychodynamic–systems reflections on a social intelligence model of personality. In R. S. Wyer & T. K. Srull (Eds.), *Advances in social cognition* (vol. 2, pp. 153–161). Hillsdale, NJ: Erlbaum.

Piaget, J., with Inhelder, B. (1969). *The psychology of the child.* London: Routledge & Kegan Paul.

Piper, W. E., Debbane, E. G., Bienvenu, J., Carufel, F., & Garant, J. (1986). Relationship between the object focus of therapist interpretations and outcome in short-term individual psychotherapy. *British Journal of Medical Psychology, 59,* 1–11.

Prochaska, J. O., & DiClemente, C. C. (1986). The transtheoretical approach. In J. C. Norcross (Ed.), *Handbook of eclectic psychotherapy* (pp. 163–200). New York: Brunner/Mazel.

Rice, L. N. (1988). Integration and the client-centered relationship. *Journal of Integrative and Eclectic Psychotherapy, 7,* 268–277.

Rice, L. N., & Greenberg, L. S. (Eds.). (1984). *Patterns of change.* New York: Guilford Press.

Rogers, C. R. (1957). The necessary and sufficient conditions of therapeutic personality change. *Journal of Consulting Psychology, 21,* 95–103.

Rogers, C. R. (1959). A theory of therapy, personality, and interpersonal relationships, as developed in the client-centered framework. In S. Koch (Ed.), *Psychology: The study of a science. Vol. 3. Formulations of the person and the social context* (pp. 184–256). New York: McGraw-Hill.

Rogers, C. R. (1961). *On becoming a person.* Boston: Houghton Mifflin.

Rogers, C. R. (1980). *A way of being.* Boston: Houghton Mifflin.

Rosenberg, S. E., Silberschatz, G., Curtis, J. T., Sampson, H., & Weiss, J. (1986). A method for establishing reliability of statements from psychodynamic case formulations. *American Journal of Psychiatry, 143,* 1454–1456.

Rychlak, J. F. (1973). *Introduction to personality and psychotherapy.* Boston: Houghton Mifflin.

Safran, J. D. (1990). Towards a refinement of cognitive therapy in light of interpersonal theory: I: Theory. *Clinical Psychology Review, 10,* 87–105.

Sander, L. (1983). To begin with: Reflections on ontogeny. In J. Lichtenberg & S. Kaplan (Eds.), *Reflections on self psychology* (pp. 85–104). Hillsdale, NJ: Analytic Press.

Schacht, T. (1984). *Toward operationalizing the transference: A research method for identifying a focus in time limited dynamic psychotherapy.* Unpublished manuscript, Vanderbilt University Center for Psychotherapy.

Schacht, T. E., & Henry, W. P. (in press). Modeling recurrent relationship patterns with Structural Analysis of Social Behavior: The SASB-CMP. In N. Miller, J. Docherty, & L. Luborsky (Eds.), *Handbook of psychodynamic treatment research.* New York: Basic Books.

Segal, Z. V., & Shaw, B. F. (1988). Cognitive assessment: Issues and methods. In K. S. Dobson (Ed.), *Handbook of cognitive–behavioral therapies* (pp. 39–81). New York: Guilford Press.

Shapiro, D. A., & Shapiro, D. (1982). Meta-analysis of

comparative therapy outcome studies: A replication and refinement. *Psychological Bulletin, 92,* 581–604.

Silberschatz, G., Curtis, J. T., & Nathan, S. (1989). Using the patient's plan to assess progress in psychotherapy. *Psychotherapy, 26,* 40–46.

Silberschatz, G., Fretter, P. B., & Curtis, J. T. (1986). How do interpretations influence the process of psychotherapy? *Journal of Consulting and Clinical Psychology, 54,* 646–652.

Smith, D. (1982). Trends in counseling and psychotherapy. *American Psychologist, 37,* 802–809.

Smith, M. L., Glass, G. V., & Miller, T. I. (1980). *The benefits of psychotherapy.* Baltimore: Johns Hopkins University Press.

Spence, D. (1988). *Rhetoric versus evidence as a source of persuasion.* Unpublished manuscript, Robert Wood Johnson Medical School, University of Medicine and Dentistry of New Jersey.

Steele, R. S. (1979). Psychoanalysis and hermeneutics. *International Review of Psychoanalysis, 6,* 389–411.

Stern, D. N. (1983). The early development of schemas of self, of other, and of "self with other." In J. Lichtenberg & S. Kaplan (Eds.), *Reflections on self psychology* (pp. 49–84). Hillsdale, NJ: Analytic Press.

Stern, D. N. (1985a). Affect attunement. In J. D. Call, E. Galenson, & R. L. Tyson (Eds.), *Frontiers of infant psychiatry* (Vol. 2). New York: Basic Books.

Stern, D. N. (1985b). *The interpersonal world of the infant.* New York: Basic Books.

Stiles, W. B. (1979). Verbal response modes and psychotherapeutic technique. *Psychiatry, 42,* 49–62.

Stiles, W. B. (1983). Normality, diversity and psychotherapy. *Psychotherapy, 20,* 183–189.

Stiles, W. B., Shapiro, D. A., & Elliott, R. (1986). "Are all psychotherapies equivalent?" *American Psychologist, 41,* 165–180.

Stolorow, R. D., Brandschaft, B., & Atwood, G. E. (1987). *Psychoanalytic treatment: An intersubjective approach.* Hillsdale, NJ: Analytic Press.

Strachey, J. (1934). The nature of the therapeutic action of psychoanalysis. *International Journal of Psycho-Analysis, 15,* 127–159.

Strupp, H. H. (1980a). Success and failure in time-limited psychotherapy: Comparison 1. *Archives of General Psychiatry, 37,* 595–603.

Strupp, H. H. (1980b). Success and failure in time-limited psychotherapy: Comparison 2. *Archives of General Psychiatry, 37,* 708–716.

Strupp. H. H. (1989). Psychotherapy: Can the practitioner learn from the researcher? *American Psychologist, 44,* 717–724.

Strupp, H. H., & Binder, J. L. (1984). *Psychotherapy in a new key.* New York: Basic Books.

Sullivan, H. S. (1953). *The interpersonal theory of psychiatry.* New York: Norton.

Tomkins, S. S. (1978). Script theory: Differential magnification of affects. In R. A. Dienstbier (Ed.), *Nebraska Symposium on Motivation* (Vol. 26, pp. 201–236). Lincoln: University of Nebraska Press.

Turner, R. H., & Vanderlippe, R. H. (1958). Self–ideal congruence as an index of adjustment. *Journal of Abnormal and Social Psychology, 57,* 202–206.

Wachtel, P. (1977). *Psychoanalysis and behavior therapy: Toward an integration.* New York: Basic Books.

Watson, N. (1984). The empirical status of Rogers' hypotheses of the necessary and sufficient conditions for effective psychotherapy. In R. F. Levant & J. M. Shlien (Eds.), *Client-centered therapy and the person-centered approach: New directions in therapy, research and practice* (pp. 17–40). New York: Praeger.

Weiss, J., Sampson, H., & the Mount Zion Psychotherapy Research Group. (1986). *The psychoanalytic process.* New York: Guilford Press.

Weissman, A. N., & Beck, A. T. (1978). *Development and validation of the Dysfunctional Attitude Scale: A preliminary investigation.* Paper presented at the annual meeting of the American Educational Research Association, Toronto.

Wexler, D. A., & Rice, L. N. (Eds.). (1974). *Innovations in client-centered therapy.* New York: Wiley.

White, R. W. (1959). Motivation reconsidered: The concept of competence. *Psychological Review, 66,* 297–333.

Winnicott, D. W. (1958). *Through paediatrics to psychoanalysis.* London: Hogarth Press.

Winnicott, D. W. (1965). *The maturational process and the facilitating environment.* New York: International University Press.

Wolf, E. S. (1988). *Treating the self.* New York: Guilford Press.

Woolfolk, R. L., Sass, L. A., & Messer, S. B. (1988). Introduction to hermeneutics. In S. B. Messer, L. A. Sass, & R. L. Woolfolk (Eds.), *Hermeneutics and psychological theory: Interpretive perspectives on personality, psychotherapy and psychopathology* (pp. 2–26). New Brunswick, NJ: Rutgers University Press.

Zetzel, E. R. (1956). Current concepts of transference. *International Journal of Psycho-Analysis, 4,* 77–105.

Chapter 15

The Semiotic Subject of Cultural Psychology

Richard A. Shweder and Maria A. Sullivan
University of Chicago

During the 1970s and 1980s, the "person" or the "subject" re-emerged as a prominent topic of investigation within anthropology, and as the core concept for a field of investigation known as "cultural psychology." Cultural psychology is the study of the way in which culture and consciousness make each other up. It is a basic tenet of cultural psychology that the processes of consciousness may not be uniform across the cultural regions of the world.

The "person" re-emerged in cultural psychology as a "semiotic subject," for whom the historically acquired meaning of a situation or stimulus event is the major constraint on his or her response to it, and for whom different situations elicit different responses because they activate differing locally rational response sets. In this chapter, we examine the semiotic subject of cultural psychology and contrast it with two other conceptions of the person, which have until recently dominated the intellectual landscape in psychology and anthropology. The first is the conception of the person as a central processing mechanism. The second is the conception of the person as a vessel for autonomous mental states. The semiotic person of cultural psychology is presented as an alternative to both.

THE RETURN OF THE "PERSON" IN ANTHROPOLOGY

To gain a general acquaintance with recent cross-cultural research on the "person," the reader might review, selectively, the volumes edited by Heelas and Lock (1981); Marsella and White (1982); Levy and Rosaldo (1983); Shweder and LeVine (1984); Kleinman and Good (1985); White and Kirkpatrick (1985); Holland and Quinn (1987); Stigler, Shweder, and Herdt (1990); D'Andrade (in press); and Shweder (in press). The reader might also wish to examine the review articles by Fogelson (1979) and Lutz and White (1986), as well as issues of the budding journals *Ethos: Journal of the Society for Psychological Anthropology* and *Culture, Medicine and Psychiatry.*

The "person" or "subject" first returned to anthropology under the banner of person-centered ethnography, with its focus on the everyday *experiences*—in particular, the emotional feelings (anger, sadness, embarrassment) and the nonemotional feelings (chest pains, anxiety, depersonalization *cum* spirit possession)—of individuals in different cultures of the world (Csordas, 1983, 1988; Fiske, in press; Herdt, 1981; Kakar, 1982; Kleinman, 1986;

LeVine, 1983; Levy, 1973, 1984; Myers, 1979, 1988; Obeyesekere, 1981; Rosaldo, 1980; Scheper-Hughes, 1985; Seymour, 1983; Spiro, 1983; Super & Harkness 1986; Weisner & Gallimore, 1977; Whiting & Edwards, 1985; Whiting & Whiting, 1975).

Then the "person" or "subject" resurfaced in the "ethnopsychological" study of regional variations in text-centered and discourse-centered *conceptions* of mind, self, body, motivation, and emotion (D'Andrade, 1965, 1974, 1987; Foucault, 1980; see Gaines, 1982; Geertz, 1973; Lakoff & Kovecses, 1987; Lutz, 1988; Mageo, 1989; Marriott, 1989; Myers, 1979; Rosaldo, 1984; Shweder, 1981; Shweder & Bourne, 1984; Shweder & D'Andrade, 1980; Straus, 1977; Weiss et al., 1986; Weiss et al., 1988; Wierzbicka, 1986; Wikan, 1987, 1989a, 1989b).

For example, to select a recent study (Wikan, 1989a, 1989b), the Balinese have the idea that anger, sadness, and envy are "hot" emotions destructive of the vitality of the breast milk that a mother feeds to her infants. There is also among the Balinese a related idea, reminiscent of the views of some of our Hindu informants in Orissa, India, that "strong life forces" and bodily fluids are protective shields against sorcery. With regard to sorcery, Wikan reports that "on the evidence of the souls of the dead themselves" (1989b, p. 295), 50% of all deaths in Bali are thought to be caused by black magic or poison from an intimate other. It is noteworthy that in many parts of Southeast Asia, including Bali, interpersonal anxieties prevail in indigenous explanations of suffering. It is also noteworthy that in other regions of the world, other orders of reality (e.g., moral transgression, "stress," or sociopolitical exploitation) are far more salient in local accounts of the causes of illness, misery, and death. Such ethnopsychological findings suggest that, on a worldwide scale, meaning systems and the patterns of inferential reasoning they support may become differentiated, stabilized, and densely packed into a limited number of "ideological regions" (see Gaines, 1982; Kleinman, 1986; Murdock, 1980). For example, under circumstances of premature death, it is primarily in the circum-Mediterranean region of the world (which includes, of course, Europe in the 16th and 17th centuries and today) that the folk go hunting for a witch.

Or, to select a second example of ethnopsychological research (in this case, research on emotional functioning), there is that divide or fault line made famous by Max Weber (1930) between those regions of the world (e.g., Northern Europe) where it is believed that "you are not going to be happy in life unless you are working hard on something," and those regions (e.g., Southern Europe or, as the stereotype goes, Southern California) where it is believed that "you are not going to be happy in life unless you are *not* working hard on something."

It should be noted that ethnopsychological research grants no privilege to academic social science conceptions of mind, self, and emotion. Ethnopsychologists believe in a spirit of fair play. Thus social science conceptions of things—for example, the idea that all feeling states should be reduced to only two parameters, "pleasantness" and "arousal"; or the currently fashionable notion of personality dispositions as fixed forces that go around self-selecting their own environments, as if they were shoppers picking out consumer products in a marketplace—are viewed as extensions of (in this case, "Western" or "secular humanist" or "Protestant individualist") folk categories, values, and beliefs.

Most recently, the "person" or "subject" has also reappeared in various manifestos, programmatic essays, or demonstration studies calling explicitly or implicitly for a "cultural psychology" to examine regional and cultural differentiations of human nature, with special reference to the way in which person-based processes of consciousness (including reasoning processes, learning processes, self-maintenance processes, emotion processes, and nonemotional feeling processes) are altered by the meaning systems and conceptual frameworks within which they are embedded (Cole, 1989; D'Andrade, 1981, 1986; Howard, 1985; Kleinman, 1986; Marriott, 1989; Miller, 1984; Peacock, 1983; Rosaldo, 1984; Shweder, 1986, 1990).

Although many anthropologists continue to be quite pious about the "principle of psychic unity" (a principle that they often mistakenly believe to be an essential debating point in the battle against racism, thereby overlooking the fact that homogeneity is too great a price to pay for equality), it has today become thinkable that the processes of consciousness may not be uniform across the cultural regions of the world. After all, the idea of psychic pluralism is not really radical. For example, there are among learning theorists (see Bitterman, 1975) some who are willing to entertain the possibility that the "laws of learning" are not invariant across animal species. To cite one instance, partial or intermittent reward (in contrast to consistent reward) produces greater resistance to extinction in rats and pigeons, but not in certain species of turtles or fish. And even among "hard-nosed" cognitive psychologists, it is no longer bold or reckless to imagine that the processes of human category learning (e.g., feature frequency processes, exemplar comparison processes, prototype comparison processes) may be diverse, and may vary in response to task demands (see Estes, 1986). If the processes of digestion (e.g., lactose intolerance) and the causes of heart attacks (Marmot, Kogevinas, & Elston, 1987; McKeigue et al., 1988) can vary across human populations, why should anthropologists and psychologists be unwilling to entertain the possibility that across cultural traditions the processes of consciousness diverge and then settle into a stable yet distinctive equilibrium with the cultural meaning systems of which they are a part?

Far better data are needed than we currently have on the processes of consciousness in the different traditions of the world. The current lack of a rich corpus of relevant data on the topic suggests that the "principle of psychic unity" has been assumed more than it has been scrutinized. (However, among cross-cultural psychologists there does seem to exist a fair amount of skepticism about the universality of social psychological processes; see, e.g., Pepitone & Triandis, 1987.)

As we design more sophisticated studies of psychological functioning in other cultural traditions, there is reason enough to leave open the possibility that, for instance, within the terms of this or that meaning system anger is typically transformed into sadness, while in other meaning systems the opposite may be true (sadness may be transformed into anger); that drive arousal (e.g., fasting and sexual abstinence) rather than drive reduction may be rewarding; that the feelings that are differentiated as "emotional feelings" versus "non-emotional feelings" (e.g., for most Americans, anger, sadness, guilt, and disgust vs. cleanliness, boredom, tiredness, and horniness) are not the same around the world; and so forth.

CULTURAL PSYCHOLOGY: A ROSE BY ANY OTHER NAME . . . ?

It should be noted at once that although there exists today within anthropology a flourishing discipline committed to the study of the "person" or the "subject," there has yet to develop complete consensus about what it should be called. Throughout this chapter we use the expression "cultural psychology" to refer to the discipline, although it should be understood that other designations ("ethnopsychology," "folk psychology," "person-centered ethnography," "psychological anthropology") are in use as well.

There are several reasons why we prefer the expression "cultural psychology" to the others. First, the problem with the old standard expression "psychological anthropology," which replaced the even older expression "culture and personality," is its lingering association with certain forms of psychological reductionism (of culture to psychic universals) that are no longer dominant within anthropology (see Shweder, 1990).

Second, the problem with the expression "ethnopsychology" is that it suggests the study of understanding rather than of experience. Thus the expression "ethnopsychology" has come to suggest the study of received doctrines about consciousness rather than the study of consciousness itself. (How to characterize regional differentiations within human psychological nature still remains an open question, of course, and it is by no means apparent that regional variations in the organization of consciousness are the products of the subset of cultural doctrines concerned with psychological functioning per se.)

Third, the problem with the expression "folk psychology" is that, despite its continental roots reminiscent of Dilthey and Wundt (20th-century psychology has not been even-handed in its mythic treatment of Wundt's work, and most psychologists seem unaware of his extensive work on folk psychology), the expression connotes a false contrast between folk and scientific psychology. This carries with it the unfortunate and questionable implication that through social science one can be lifted out of tradition, custom, and folk belief. By means of the forms of systematic inquiry that we honor with the label "science," we may, of course, be lifted out of error, ignorance, and confusion. Yet "error," "ignorance," and "confusion" are not proper synonyms for "folk belief."

Finally, the expression "person-centered ethnography" is fine as far as it goes, but it does not go far enough. "Person-centered ethnography" is only one item on our intellectual agenda, and there is some danger that the expression may direct our attention away from the task of theory construction and of theory-driven empirical research. "Have no hypothesis, will travel" is a calling card that can take you only just so far.

That leaves us with "cultural psychology," which is itself not entirely free of excess connotative baggage. The expression "cultural psychology" is intended to designate the study of the way culture and consciousness make each other up (see Putnam, 1987, for a discussion of the way in which mind and world "make each other up"; see also Stigler et al., 1990). The problem with the expression is that it may adventitiously suggest a disciplinary location within psychology. The proper place for the study of "cultural psychology" is some kind of interdisciplinary location within anthropology and within psychology, with collaborative efforts stretching across the open borders of these two now very fragmented disciplines.

Nevertheless, the expression "cultural psychology" does have the advantage of provoking the right questions: Do the processes of consciousness vary in proportion to variations in the historically and culturally constituted stimulus environments of which the processes of consciousness are an essential part? How do these alterations in the processes of consciousness take place? Within what constraints or boundary conditions do the processes of consciousness operate, anyway?

Another reason why "cultural psychology" seems appropriate as a label for anthropology's person-centered research agenda goes to the heart of the present chapter: The person re-emerged within anthropology as a semiotic subject. This is hardly surprising. For some time, a personless anthropology of symbolic forms (Lévi-Strauss, 1963, 1966, 1969) stood in desperate theoretical need of a "subject" with the right psychological capacities to be the agent for those stored-up "symbols and meanings" that define a cultural tradition (see Geertz, 1973; Shweder & LeVine, 1984).

A semiotic subject is a person for whom the meaning of a situation is the major determinant of his or her response to it. Consequently, the intellectual agenda of cultural psychology is defined by the following four questions:

1. What is meaning such that a situation can have it?
2. What is a person such that what something means can determine his or her response to it?

3. What meanings or conceptions of things have been stored up (e.g., in texts and narratives) and institutionalized (e.g., in practices and everyday discourse) in various regions of the world?
4. What effect, if any, have those stored-up and institutionalized meanings had on the organization and operations of individual consciousness?

To date, the third of these questions has received the most explicit attention among anthropologists. There have been studies of the implications of displaying various emotions (anger, envy, sadness) in various cultural contexts (Abu-Lughod, 1986; Miller & Sperry, 1987; Wellencamp, 1988); of the difference between sociocentric and egocentric (or individualistic) conceptions of self (Dumont, 1970; Miller, 1984; Miller & Luthar, 1989; Mines, 1988; Noricks et al., 1987; Read, 1955; Shweder & Bourne, 1984; Shweder & Miller, 1985; Triandis, 1989); and of similarities and differences in folk classifications of reality and subjective states (Coleman & Kay, 1981; D'Andrade, 1987; Lakoff, 1987; Luhrmann, 1989; Sweetser, 1987).

Answers to the first two questions, concerning meaning and personhood, are usually implicit in the anthropological and psychological literature and are sometimes explicitly offered there (e.g., D'Andrade, 1984), although they have been more central concerns in the literatures of linguistics, literary criticism, and philosophy (e.g., Fish, 1980; Labov & Fanischel, 1977; Parfit, 1986; Rescher, 1988; Scruton, 1986; Searle, 1979; Taylor, 1989). The fourth question, concerning regional variations in the processes of consciousness, defines an empirical agenda for the next decade and points to an inviting terrain for collaborative investigation between anthropologists and psychologists.

In this chapter, we focus on the conception of the person (the second question above) most suitable for a cultural psychology. Along the way we consider briefly some answers to the third question, with special attention to conceptions of personal identity in Bali as described by Geertz (1973), and problems in the cross-cultural study of affective functioning. The distinction between "emotional feelings" and "nonemotional feelings" figures centrally in various person-centered ethnographic accounts, especially in those person-centered ethnographies where the native informant's experience of headaches, chest pains, tiredness, dizziness, and loss of appetite is interpreted as the somatization of sadness, or where his or her experience of ancestral spirit attack or other possessive states is interpreted as a transformation of hostility (see Levy, 1973; Kleinman, 1986; Obeyesekere, 1981; Shweder, 1987, 1988). The cognitive and cultural basis of the distinction between emotional and nonemotional feelings, and some problematic aspects of interpreting subjective states, are briefly addressed.

We discuss some of the assumptions about meaning (the first question) and personhood (the second question) that answers to the third question presuppose. We leave for another occasion a more detailed consideration of the effects on the organization and functioning of individual consciousness that one might expect if it is indeed true that one cannot be indifferent to cultural meaning systems and still understand how consciousness works (the fourth question).

Each of those topics is enormous; within the limits of a single chapter, we can treat them in only the most cursory fashion.

THE SEMIOTIC SUBJECT

As a first step, let us define the notion of "meaning" broadly, as all the implications and probable inferences that are gotten across to a "person" when a "text" or "symbol" is lit up by a "conceptual scheme." Let us define a "text" or "symbol" as anything (an object, an experience, an event, a sound pattern, a setting, a visual sensation) that is a vehicle for meaning. Let us define a "conceptual scheme" as the intellectual apparatus that explains how this or that person, a member of this or that interpretive community, draws this or that implication or probable inference from this or that text.

Our definition of a "conceptual scheme" is broad enough to include both so-called "concepts" or "propositions" (semantic meanings that are "necessary" and cannot be "canceled" without contradiction—e.g., a "dog" is an "animal"), as well as so-called "conceptions" or "beliefs" (pragmatic meanings, which are noncriterial even though they may be deeply entrenched in one community or another—e.g., the idea that a "dog" makes a suitable "pet").

Two peoples can have different "conceptions" of things (e.g., one but not the other may believe that dogs are "polluted" animals that are cursed to mate in public). Two peoples can differ in the "concepts" that are important in their lives (e.g., in one culture but not another, whole sections of the economy may be given over to the breeding, grooming, feeding, maintenance, and display of dogs). Nevertheless, there is one way in which two peoples cannot differ: Two peoples cannot have a different concept of the same idea. This is merely a logical (and perhaps trivial) point, yet it is still worth making. A "dog that is not an animal" is not a dog. It is not a different concept of a dog; it is not a concept of a dog at all. Our definition of a "conceptual scheme" is meant to include more than just those necessary or incorrigible truths that are (semantically) definitive of concepts; it includes all the causal knowledge, presuppositions, and beliefs that justify and explain an inference from a text.

For example, the verbal utterance or sound pattern "Roger is so lonely" is a "text" or "symbol." In some interpretive communities (between spouses in our own subculture), said under the right circumstances, this text will invite the inference "Let's set him up with one of our single female friends"; the intellectual apparatus or conceptual scheme supporting that inference will include ideas about the institution of dating, about feeling states and the projects they motivate, about interpersonal attraction, about "middlemen" and "matchmaking," and so on.

Or, to cite a somewhat more exotic example, the event "the death of a husband" is a "text." In some interpretive communities (rural Hindu communities in India), this will invite the inference "I must now absolve myself of sin"; the conceptual scheme supporting that inference is a vast network of propositions, presuppositions, and beliefs definitive of traditional Hinduism's moral world. Indeed, many widows in India do spend the balance of their lives cleansing and unburdening themselves of sin by fasting, praying, avoiding all "hot foods" (meat, fish, onions, garlic, spices of all kinds), withdrawing from the world, reading scriptural texts, feeding Brahman priests, and so on.

The conceptual scheme lending rational support to these activities of traditional Hindu widows includes the ideas that the material world and its natural processes are imbued with divinity; that a divine world is a just world governed by laws of retributive causation for past transgressions; that while souls are immortal, they are reincarnated into the material world in forms (animal vs. human, female vs. male, deformed vs. well-formed, widowed vs. unwidowed) that are proportionate to the quality of the souls' previous moral career; that in a just world, widowhood is punishment for past transgressions; and that the obdurate fact that a woman's husband died before she did is an undeniable sign indicating that the woman should now undertake to absolve herself of guilt, for the sake of her next reincarnation on earth. (See Shweder, in press, for an expansion of these notions as they might be used to provide a reasoned moral defense of the practice of suttee—the immolation of a widow on her deceased husband's funeral pyre.)

There are two defining features of the semiotic person: intentional consciousness and rationality. Another way to say this is that because the activities of semiotic persons are the activities of intentional beings using conceptual schemes to draw inferences from texts, those activities invite rational reconstruction in a language of intentional consciousness. The idea of a semiotic person is a rather ancient idea (Aristotle had much to say about it), even though the locution "semiotic" is rather new. The semiotic person is an agent endowed with the powers of intentional consciousness, for whom rational self-regulation is a telos.

The power of "intentional" consciousness is a god-like endowment, which, just like the idea of "God," is difficult to define and easy to misunderstand. Persons endowed with intentionality have the following faculty: Their actions and reactions are directed at and responsive to what texts or symbols mean or imply, as defined above. Texts are always "about" (aimed at, responsive to, depicting of) something else, and this is so even in those special (and astonishing) cases when texts are "about" themselves—for example, when language is used to talk about language.

Here is another way to put the point: Texts or symbols are vehicles for the acts of consciousness of intentional beings, who create, take an interest in, and understand texts by virtue of their own god-like (or "magical") capacity to "see through" the textual or symbolic object (the print on the page, the shape of the letter or of the sound, etc.) to what it signifies or represents. It is the power of intentional consciousness that makes it possible for the semiotic subject to react to any and every situation or object as a text or a symbol.

Yet the semiotic person not only constructs meanings by drawing inferences from symbols and texts; the semiotic person also monitors the inferences that he or she draws, constrained by the terms of some conceptual scheme and by his or her own powers of rationality. So, along with the powers of intentional consciousness, rationality is the other quality definitive of the semiotic subject. Persons for whom rationality is a telos strive to control or regulate their own involvement with meanings in three primary ways: by optimizing the fit or seeking proportionality (1) between their desires and their real interests; (2) between their means and their ends; and (3) between their responses to reality and the descriptions under which reality has been put by them.

In other words, the successful semiotic person, conceptualized as an intentional rational agent, is moral, practical, and scientific. In a constructed world made up of meanings, he or she tries to pursue worthy ends, and to do so efficiently and with an accurate grasp of things. (For a discussion of the three aspects of rationality—moral, practical, and scientific— see Rescher, 1988.)

The anthropological literature offers many semiotic accounts of the meaning and rationality of the stable, local, repetitive, and (to outsiders) "apparently" bizarre behavior of members of different cultural communities. For example, Spiro (1966) provides us with an account of Burmese religious spending. He begins with the observation that the Burmese spend a very large proportion of their income on such expensive and (from a Western observer's point of view) inconsequential religious activities as the feeding of monks, the financing of pagodas, the ordination of a son into a monastic order, and the like. In other words, to many Western observers, Burmese religious spending appears to be a wasteful and irrational squandering of family income.

Spiro's semiotic strategy in rationalizing those activities is to represent for us the Burmese behavioral environment or life space as a historically constructed stimulus situation, which includes a specification of the moral, practical, and scientific aspects of the Burmese life space. According to the Burmese, "the duration of 'life' is not confined to the mere 60 or 70 years of this existence, but extends over an incalculable duration of tens of thousands of years" (Spiro, 1966, pp. 1166–1167). Rebirth as a wealthy man is a worthy end in life, and the most effective and realistic means to achieve that end is through the accumulation of "merit" through acts of "charity."

Many anthropologists have been guided in their research by the idea of a historically constructed stimulus situation. Their tenet is that stimulus situations do not exist independently of our involvements with them and interpretations of them, and that behavior cannot be properly understood without a conception of the way in which historically constructed stimulus situations and semiotic persons make each other up. Full-blooded semiotic researchers refuse to separate their descriptions of the stimulus situation from the meanings and conceptions of things that have been stored up and institutionalized in this or that region of the world.

During the past 20 years, perhaps the most full-blooded, widely discussed and hotly debated (see Shweder & LeVine, 1984, pp. 12–17; Wikan, 1987, 1989a,b) description of a historically constructed stimulus environment has been Geertz's (1973) semiotic analysis of the ways in which the Balinese grasp and socially construct the relevant facts of personal identity. In Bali, according to Geertz, the inventory of culturally available labels by which an individual may be uniquely identified consists of the following: (1) personal names; (2) birth order names; (3) kinship terms; (4) teknonyms ("father of _____" "grandmother of _____"); (5) status designators; and (6) public titles. These various symbol systems for labeling persons represent different orders of self-conception; they highlight and they obscure different aspects of the self.

It is noteworthy that personal names are for the Balinese the least important order among the symbolic orders of names. Personal names exist, but they are arbitrarily coined nonsense syllables that convey no information at all about family or group membership. Moreover, a person's personal name is considered intensely private. It is seldom used to address another person, nor is it used as a means of self-reference. Indeed, one's personal name is known by increasingly fewer people throughout one's lifetime. According to Geertz, this cultural dwarfing of a symbolic code for personal naming reflects (and dialectically helps create) the fact that for the Balinese personal, idio-

syncratic, or biographic truths about personality are muted, devalued, and kept out of sight.

In contrast, the symbolic codes for expressing the generic and enduring aspects of human community and one's place in it (e.g., status designators and public titles) are highly elaborated in Bali and receive cultural emphasis. (See also Shweder & Bourne, 1984; Shweder, Mahapatra, & Miller, 1987; Shweder & Miller, 1985; and Shweder, Much, Pool & Dixon, 1990 for a detailed discussion of cross-cultural variations in egocentric rights-based vs. sociocentric duty-based conceptions of the person.)

According to Geertz, the Balinese preference (in representations of the person) for status designators and public titles has the effect of keeping personal individualistic qualities out of consciousness and of hiding the transitory and impermanent material and biographical aspect of the self. Balinese status designators are inherited caste names, which derive from the Indian Hindu *varna* system. They designate relative degrees of prestige in a hierarchical ordering of groups stratified by distance from divinity. Such caste names are blind to individual talent; they function instead to prescribe appropriate forms of decorum among people of disparate rank.

Similarly, public titles have the effect of focusing consciousness on a person's eligibility for occupying public roles. In many settings people are addressed by public title, which emphasizes their community station or social position as the essence of their personal identity. As a result, not only is everyday social interaction highly ceremonialized; individual character is systematically relegated to a secondary position or kept backstage.

The symbolic life of the Balinese has affective consequences. One consequence is that with the symbolic muting of the personal, the idiosyncratic, and the individual, "stage fright" (*lek*, a variant of "shame") has become a salient emotion in Balinese life. As Geertz suggests, in a culture that stresses the role-based or station-based presentation of self, each time a man plays *Hamlet* he worries that there may be a failure in representation and of aesthetic distance. He is anxious lest his audience may perceive his idiosyncratic personality through the role, and apprehend him as an ego struggling to stage the part properly.

It is tempting in the context of summarizing Geertz's brief discussion of *lek* to develop a full-blown semiotic theory of the emotions. Although space limitations do not permit this, we would argue for the fruitfulness of a conception of the "emotions" as a subclass of the intentional states of rational human beings.

As intentional states, the different emotions can be identified by their aims or projects (e.g., the aim of fear is "to flee," of shame "to hide," of happiness "to celebrate," of remorse "to undo and redo," and of sadness "to die"). Moreover, as intentional states, each emotion can be rationally evaluated or justified by reference to some set of validity conditions (e.g., danger, insult, loss, transgression, etc.). A distinctive feature of "emotional" states as a subclass of intentional states is that they are *experienced by the body* (e.g., as pleasant or unpleasant, as arousing or calming, as tightening or relaxing, etc.) in ways that may serve to motivate the aim. Not *all* intentional states (e.g., knowing that Billings is a city in Montana) implicate the phenomenological qualities of somatic experience as a motivational system, but the "emotions" do.

Emotions can also be viewed, conversely, as a subset of feelings: Just as not all intentional states are emotional states, not all feeling states are emotional feeling states, which means that not all feeling states are intentional states. There are nonemotional feelings (e.g., cleanliness, thirst, tiredness, horniness, numbness, an itch), which may motivate human behavior but are not symbolic of or about anything.

Someone who feels guilty, afraid, or angry feels it *about*, *of*, or *at* something. Because those particular emotional feelings are acts of intentional consciousness directed at an intentional object, they can be justified or criticized in rational terms. It is not quite the same with nonemotional feelings. Thirst, tiredness, and other nonemotional feelings are certainly experienced and motivating, and they can even be explained (they may be highly correlated with other events). Nevertheless, even when we are baffled by such feelings (e.g., someone is tired all the time, even after much sleep), there is no rational warrant for criticizing a person for being tired on grounds that his or her exhaustion is unjustified by some set of eliciting conditions. Nonemotional feelings lack an intentional object (they are mere somatic events); emotional feelings, being both feelings and intentions, are precisely designed to symbolically bridge the gaps among psyche, soma, and the world, and to be topics for evaluation, approbation, and rational debate. It is wrong

for someone to be angry at or to wish to attack people who intend him or her no harm. It is not reprehensible for someone to feel hungry after feasting for hours, even though it may be bizarre (unless his hunger is itself constructed as an act of intentional consciousness.)

One of the relatively well-documented observations in the cross-cultural study of experience is the observation that loss, insult, and abuse are experienced with emotional feelings (sadness or anger) by some peoples of the world and with nonemotional feelings (chest pains, tiredness, headaches) by others (see, e.g., Kleinman, 1986; Levy, 1973; Shweder, 1985). A typical observation might concern the experiences of an infertile woman who is abandoned by her husband. For those who imagine that they would react to this validity condition (abandonment because of infertility) with an emotional feeling (e.g., anger or sadness), it is quite surprising to note that such an abandoned woman may express no emotional feelings whatsoever, but rather complains of aches, pains, and exhaustion and seeks the help of a medium or exorcist to help her get rid of an invading demonic spirit. As surprising as it may seem, on a worldwide scale this woman's response to abandonment appears to be a common one.

At the moment it is difficult to know what to make of such cases. One interpretation is that the cunning of intentionality should never be underestimated. To the very extent that nonemotional feelings such as headaches, chest pains, and exhaustion are not proper topics for criticism and moral evaluation, a nonemotional response to insult, loss, and rejection may serve an intentional aim—namely, to avoid the appraisal process. A second interpretation is that the supposed headaches, chest pains, and tiredness are really just indigenous somatic metaphors (e.g., "my heart is breaking") for true emotional feelings (e.g., sadness). A third interpretation, perhaps the most provocative, is that there are cross-cultural variations in the construction of emotional feelings. In other words, in our cultural tradition headaches, chest pains, and tiredness (along with honor, purity, solemnity, loyalty, and many other candidate "emotions") have not been constructed as emotional feelings; however, perhaps in other traditions they have been constructed as emotional feelings that are responsive to and directed at intentional objects, and this construction makes those feelings in those traditions proper topics of criticism and debate.

Other interpretations are possible. Because research on the cultural psychology of the semiotic person is still in its infancy, almost everything interesting has yet to be done.

THE PERSON AS A CENTRAL PROCESSING MECHANISM

Our foregoing account of the person as a rational intentional agent (a semiotic subject) differs considerably from two other conceptions of the person that have dominated the intellectual scene in psychology and anthropology for many years: (1) the idea of the person as a central processing mechanism; and (2) the idea of the person as a vessel for autonomous mental states. The first idea is a rather ancient one, but it was revivified during the "cognitive revolution" of the 1960s. The second idea is also ancient, but is well known as a product of classical culture and personality theory and of contemporary nomothetic and idiographic, psychometric and so-called interactionist approaches to the subject in personality psychology (e.g., as described by Cattell, 1957, and Child, 1968). (For a "deconstruction" of autonomous mental states, see Mischel, 1968, 1973; see also Shweder, 1979a, 1979b, 1980). For a full discussion of the person as a central processing mechanism, see Shweder, 1990; the present discussion recapitulates aspects of that essay.)

The "cognitive revolution" of the 1960s was initially welcomed by many scholars (Shweder counts himself as one of them) as the obvious corrective to the radical behaviorism that preceded it. The revolution seemed to address a serious limitation in psychology—in particular, the absence of a notion of meaning, symbolism, and intentional consciousness in theories of the person. A look back over general psychology of the past 30 years now suggests that, unfortunately, the "cognitive revolution" turned out to be far less than a rediscovery of intentional consciousness and far more than the displacement of behaviorism. Along with "cognitivism" came a spirit of Platonism, which aroused an ancient fascination (perhaps even an obsession) with formal or structural models, with abstract criteria, and with the bewitching idea of a central processing mechanism of the mental life.

The basic idea of a central processing mechanism is that deep within all human beings is an inherent processing device, which enables us to think (classify, remember, infer, imagine), experience (feel, need, desire), act (strive, choose, evaluate), and learn. Not only is the central processing mechanism presumed to be an abstract, fixed, and universal property of human mental life; it is also presumed that this abstract, fixed, and universal form transcends and is sealed off from all the concrete, variable, and particular stuff, substance, or content upon which it operates.

For those who conceive of the person as a central processing mechanism, it is a necessary step to draw a fundamental distinction between intrinsic (internal) psychological structures and processes (assumed to be abstract, fixed, and universal) and extrinsic (external) environmental content (assumed to be concrete, variable, and task-specific); to analytically withdraw the knower from what he or she knows and the person from what he or she pursues; and to insist on a basic division between the central processing mechanism of the person and his or her personal or group history, context, stimulus environment, institutional setting, resources, beliefs, values, knowledge, or any other kinds of extrinsic stuff. All this stuff—historically constructed stimuli, resources, values, meanings, knowledge, language, technologies, institutions (including, e.g., everything that makes up the intentional consciousness of traditional Hindu widows or Balinese "actors," as described above)—is conceived to be external to or outside of the central processing mechanism.

The idea of the person as a central processing mechanism has had an enormous impact on "mainstream" psychology. Under its influence during the 1960s and 1970s, high-status research in psychology came to be guided by a small set of research heuristics, which had the effect of directing research away from the study of the intentional consciousness of rational agents. Those heuristics have been discussed on other occasions (Shweder, 1984, 1990; see also Fiske & Shweder, 1986); four of them are listed below.

Heuristic 1. Search for a central processing mechanism and represent it as an abstract structure or pure mathematical form; mere "content" should play no part in psychological explanation.

Heuristic 2. Language meanings (semantics) and language use (pragmatics) are epiphenomenal to the true causes of behavior; what people mean by their words and do with their words in specific situations can be ignored.

(Syntax and phonology, of course, remain legitimate topics of investigation within the central processing mechanism framework, for they are thought to be abstract and structural and perhaps even deep; see Heuristic 1.)

Heuristic 3. What is really real (the central processing mechanism) is interior and exists sealed off inside the skin of individuals. The exterior stimulus situation and historically constructed sociocultural environment are extrinsic to the person and must be controlled or avoided—by moving into the lab, by using meaning-free stimulus materials, by standardizing the context, and so on.

Heuristic 4. Search for timeless and spaceless laws of nature. The organization of knowledge in 19th-century Newtonian physics is the ideal form for all true understanding.

One quick and dirty (and striking) indicator of the influence of those heuristics on personality research is the strong inclination among social-psychological researchers to move very quickly—indeed, to rush—from the discovery of some local, context-specific, meaning-saturated regularity (e.g., an audience facilitation effect or a dissonance reduction effect) to the representation of it in the literature as a fundamental law or basic process. We suspect that this "presumption of basic process" is so commonplace because of the hegemony of the central processing mechanism as an idea. For those who think of the person as a central processing mechanism, the whole point of personality research is to get behind the "superficial" and local content of things, to isolate the presumed mechanism of the mental life, and to describe the invariant laws of its operation. It then takes about a decade for the latest "fundamental" or "basic" process to be unmasked as a "mere" local regularity. It is a measure of the influence of the central processing mechanism idea on the field of psychology that the discovery of a fascinating, stable, replicable, but "mere" local regularity is usually associated with feelings of despair!

THE PERSON AS A VESSEL FOR AUTONOMOUS MENTAL STATES

The second conception of the person that has dominated the intellectual scene is the idea of the person as a vessel for enduring mental states acting from within ("endogenously") as autonomous causal forces. It should be noted that from the point of view of those who advocate

this conception of the person, the mental states contained within the vessel can be either global and general (e.g., "anxiety") or specific and conditionalized (e.g., a "fear of flying"), as long as they are enduring and autonomous.

The idea of the person as a vessel for autonomous mental states has prevailed in trait psychology (Cattell, 1957). Yet it is also pervasive among scholars who have come to terms with the so-called "consistency" debate of the 1970s and 1980s (Magnusson & Endler, 1977) and have gone beyond it in very creative ways (e.g., Caspi, 1987). These days one of the "hot" and exciting areas of personality research is concerned with documenting the disposition-guided selection of real-world environments (e.g., early marriage for dependent females) and with tracing lines of continuity over the lifespan in other people's reactions to noteworthy mental states (e.g., downward mobility for hostile males). Nevertheless, some of the very best researchers in the field (even some of our admired friends) continue to talk about persons as though they were vessels for autonomous mental states, such as shyness, hostility, or dependency (e.g., Caspi, Elder, & Bem, 1987).

Because the cultural psychology of the semiotic subject rests on the complete rejection of autonomous mental states as the basic causal entities of personality, and because mental state language plays a part in personal descriptions in everyday life, it is important for us to examine this presemiotic concept in some detail and to be clear about the hazards of appropriating the mental state concepts of everyday life as a causal theory of action. What people are disposed to do as viewed from the outside (e.g., to be honest, to seek attention from members of the opposite sex) is not a causal explanation for why they do it.

To speak from the vantage point of cultural psychology, there are two good reasons for rejecting the presemiotic idea of the person as a vessel for autonomous mental states acting as causal forces: (1) the doubtful dualistic assumption presupposed by the idea; and (2) the bizarre empirical findings that result when the world is studied in the terms suggested by that idea. First, however, we describe the idea in somewhat more detail.

The Idea of Autonomous Mental States

Relatively enduring, autonomous, and individuating mental states are the basic constitutive elements used in personality psychology for constructing a representation of a person. In the English language, those mental states are labeled with everyday locutions such as "hostility," "self-confidence," "dependency," "fearfulness," or "timidity." Many psychologists believe that the thousands of mental states lexicalized in the English language are ultimately reducible to a simple pentad of psychometrically constructed traits, the "Big Five": surgency (or extraversion), agreeableness, conscientiousness, emotional stability (or neuroticism), and culturedness (or intelligence). (See Digman & Inouye, 1986; John, Chapter 3, this volume; Norman, 1963; for an analysis of the "Big Five" as a conceptual structure, see D'Andrade, 1985.)

In this imaginative construction of the subject, enduring mental states are said to be autonomous in the following sense: They possess "the capacity of directing responses to stimuli into characteristic channels" (Allport, 1960, p. 132). As Allport notes in his presemiotic rendition of a person, "the stimulus is not the crucial determinant in behavior that expresses personality; the trait itself is decisive" (p. 132).

It is important to notice that (with all due respect to the "consistency" debate of the past 20 years), Allport's idea of his subject is utterly neutral with respect to the issue of the causal breadth of autonomous mental states. In constructing a presemiotic account of personality it matters not at all whether the attributed mental state is broad ("anger-prone") or narrow ("tends to get angry when contradicted by an 'alpha' male in an argument at a scientific meeting"), qualified or unqualified, general or specific, dynamic or static, libidinous or otherwise. It matters not at all whether the locution used to characterize or symbolize the mental state is an adjective ("friendly"), a noun ("an extravert") or a verb phrase ("likes to party a lot"). What does matter for a presemiotic reading of the subject is that his or her activities in the world (i.e., his or her "responses" or "reactions" or "behaviors") are interpreted as products of the autonomous influence of some set of (narrow or broad, qualified or unqualified) mental states.

The First Problem: The Doubtful Dualistic Presupposition

Presupposed by the idea of autonomous mental states as causes of behavior is the assumption of an untroubled division of all things into two categories: "things of the subjective world" (mental states) and "things of the objective world" (stimulus situations). The assumption is that these two categories (subject vs. object) and their analogues (inside vs. outside, trait vs. stimulus, mind vs. matter, person vs. world, gene vs. environment, etc.) are mutually exclusive of each other, and jointly exhaustive of all causes. In other words, it is assumed that every causal force is either inside the person in the mental state *or* outside the person in the stimulus situation, and that there is no cause that has the property of being simultaneously *both* inside the person *and* in the stimulus situation, or of being *neither* subjective *nor* objective.

The presemiotic assumption of subject–object, inside–outside, person–situation, mind–world dualism—that there are only two fundamental kinds of causes (subjective mental states and objective stimulus situations), and that they are mutually exclusive and exhaustive causes—has had major implications for the definition of personality, for the definition of a stimulus situation, and for the measurement of both.

Here is how things went from bad to worse. First, researchers interested in personality-expressive behavior presupposed the validity of the dualistic assumption. Then, reasoning from that (dubious) assumption, they drew the impeccable deductive conclusion that if one could only standardize or control for the influence of outside ("exogenous") stimulus variables, then all variations in behavior *must* be due to the influence of autonomous ("endogenous") mental states. Finally, a certain (misleading) methodological warning was institutionalized in the discipline: At all costs, one must avoid observing different persons in different stimulus situations (the so-called hazard of "noncomparable" stimulus events). Why? Because if one observes different persons in different stimulus situations, then all one can infer is that different stimulus situations elicit different responses, which (given the dubious dualistic assumption) leaves nothing to say about the autonomous mental states of the person per se. (Of course, from the semiotic point of view of cultural psychology, that is precisely the point—to deconstruct autonomous mental states into the intentional activities of rational agents.)

In practice, the stricture that one must standardize or control for exogenous or stimulus-based influences on behavior was achieved by taking note of differences in the way different persons responded (e.g., anxiously vs. calmly) to the *same* stimulus situation (e.g., "standing in a crowded elevator") or to an identical set of stimulus situations (e.g., "standing in a crowded elevator," "sitting in a dentist's chair," "preparing for an examination," "landing at an airport"). Ultimately, in line with Allport's ideas, the presemiotic subject came to be defined as the residual variance left over after one had controlled for the (rational or normative) demands of exogenous stimulus variables. In other words, the person was defined in terms of postulated subjective, mental, or internal states that were supposed to cause one person's responses to the world to be different from the responses others would manifest *in the same or comparable stimulus situations* (see Child, 1968, p. 83.)

There was yet another conclusion that seemed logical enough, given the dubious dualistic presupposition of presemiotic personality research. This conclusion was that stimulus situations ought to be defined, described, or specified (and judgments of "sameness" or "comparability" made) independently of the subject's interpretation of them. It was reasoned that if stimulus situations are objective things outside the person then they cannot be subjective things inside the person too. Stimulus situations, it was argued, should be described in a "third-person" language.

In principle, the demand for an objective or "third-person" specification of the stimulus situation meant that stimulus situations ought to be defined using a language uncontaminated with "first-person" subjective predicates; the stimulus situation should ideally be described only in a language of time, spatial location, mass, and volume. In practice, this "in-principle" demand was impossible to believe in, because objective "third-person" specifications of relevant stimulus situations seemed so ludicrous when achieved; for example, just try "objectively" specifying the stimulus situation "preparing for an examination," without any reference to human purposes and institutions. "Preparing for an examination" cannot be translated into pure objective predicates. To paraphrase Wittgenstein, trying to do so is like searching for the real artichoke by divesting it of its leaves.

Since pure objectivity was impossible to achieve, the "in-principle" demand for an objective or "third-person" specification of the stimulus situation was assimilated to a far weaker criterion—namely, that stimulus situations

should be defined from the socialized perspective of the researcher, using setting and event descriptors (e.g., "crowded," an "elevator," an "examination") assumed to have a *common* or *shared* meaning for all the subjects in the study (which, of course, is not quite the same thing as translating all stimulus situations into pure objective predicates such as time, location, mass, and volume, or into predicates with a *de facto* "universal" meaning). This weaker demand, that the stimulus situation must be described from the socialized perspective of the researcher using predicates whose meanings were shared with one's subjects, was introduced for two reasons: (1) to create a unitary frame of reference (the "comparable" stimulus situation) as the background against which to figure individual variations in response; and (2) to create a standard frame of reference (the "commensurate" stimulus situation) so as to be able to attribute all *variations* in behavioral outcome to the causal influences of subjective or endogenous mental states.

Within the constraints of the dubious dualistic framework of presemiotic personality theory the subject's "interpretation" of the stimulus situation (which plays such a central part in semiotic research) was split up into two parts. The part of the subject's interpretation that was not shared with the experimenter or with all other subjects (e.g., "My parents stop speaking to me when I do not do well on exams") was simply classified as yet one more autonomous mental state. It was treated as an "inside-the-head" or subjective variable, as a cognitive scheme mediating the relationship between the "objective" stimulus situation and the subject's response. The part of the subject's interpretation that was shared with other subjects (e.g., "Examinations are used as measures of success") was treated as a property of the "objective" stimulus situation (where "objective" now meant little more than the stimulus situation as represented from the socialized point of view of the researcher, on the presumption of observer–subject and subject–subject intersubjectivity). The distinction between subject and object, person and situation was transformed into the difference between interpretations that varied from person to person and those that did not.

Despite this surreptitious collapse of a real distinction between subject and object or person and situation it nevertheless continued to be assumed by presemiotic researchers that somehow the stimulus situation existed prior to and independently of the "interpretations" that subjects "imposed" on it. It continued to be assumed that interpretations were subjective autonomous things and that situations were not.

Almost no one seemed prepared to entertain a semiotic point of view, such as the one advocated by Fish (1980), from which it might be argued that *any* representation of a stimulus situation (whether it is the subject's or observer's, whether it is shared with all, with some or with none) is "an interpretive act performed at so deep a level that it is indistinguishable from consciousness itself" (1980, p. 272; however, see Gergen, 1986). Almost no one seemed prepared to argue, as did Fish (fighting other battles), that the very idea of cognitive "mediation" or "interpretation" is quite wrong "because it suggests an imposition upon raw data of a meaning not inherent in them" (1980, p. 270). No one seemed prepared to adopt the following semiotic point of view: Precisely because there is no such thing as a raw stimulus situation that exists independently of someone's interpretive assumptions, it is not Allport's trait but rather Fish's stimulus situation—a stimulus situation *already* saturated with our consciousness—"that is the crucial determinant in behavior that expresses personality" (Allport, 1960, p. 132).

The dualistic (subjective vs. objective, inside vs. outside, person vs. stimulus situation) supposition of presemiotic personality research was quite convenient for constructing a world in which individual differences in personality could be conceived in terms of autonomous mental states; however, it was also quite hazardous. For what if it is not possible to divide the world up into two mutually exclusive and exhaustive things (subjective mental states vs. objective stimulus situations)? What if the stimulus situation does not exist independently of some person's definition of it, and mental states do not exist autonomously, independently of the intentional objects (the constructed situations) that engage them? Mischel's (1968) famous critique of personality trait psychology made everyone aware of the hazards.

Mischel's Critique of Autonomous Mental States

The presemiotic conception of the subject, as a selection of autonomous enduring mental states, nearly collapsed in the late 1960s. In 1968 Walter Mischel published his provocative volume *Personality and Assessment,* which suggested that the abstract locutions of personality language are not labels for autonomous or free-floating causal forces. Mischel's book was preceded and followed by several analysis-of-variance studies supportive of the same point (e.g., Endler, 1969; Endler & Hunt, 1966; Moos, 1969; see also D'Andrade, 1965). Although it can be argued that Mischel's position in 1968 was somewhat ambiguous (did he reject autonomous mental states or did he just reject abstract ones?), it still seems to us when we look back on the consistency debates initiated by Mischel's book that the conception of the subject in presemiotic personality research is especially vulnerable on one fundamental point—the assumption of subject–object dualism.

All the fun began, for those for whom it was fun, when Mischel and others started advertising the following pattern of effects, which seemed to hold true across a broad range of mental states (anxiety, hostility, dependency, etc.): The person who felt, for example, more anxious than others while sitting in the dentist's chair was not *typically* the person who felt more anxious than others while standing in a crowded elevator or while preparing for an exam. In other words, the stimulus situations that were most anxiety-provoking for some persons were not *typically* the most anxiety-provoking stimulus situations for other persons. Or, to put it another way, *neither* the mental states (e.g., anxiety) lexicalized as abstract terms in the English language, *nor* the stimulus situations (e.g., sitting in a dentist's chair), *as described or constructed from the socialized point of view of the researcher,* were generally decisive as determinants of behavior. The answer to the "causal" modeler's question "How much of each?" (autonomous mental states vs. objective stimulus situations) was "Not much of either" (see Lachman, 1989). Something else— something more, something less, something neither purely subjective nor purely objective—seemed to be going on.

It is not our aim to review the various reactions among personality researchers to Mischel's critique of the presemiotic subject or to write about personality research from the perspective of the history of ideas (see Alston, 1975; Bem, 1974; Shweder, 1979a, 1979b, 1981; Shweder & D'Andrade, 1980; see also Cronbach, 1975, 1986, on the problems of a world without main effects). We would simply note that although Mischel's critique arrived with great force, the presemiotic conception of the person as a vessel for autonomous mental states still seems to live on happily among many taxonomically oriented personality psychologists.

In some circles the presemiotic subject has been preserved by reconceptualizing the subject as a psychometric person, by reducing the goals of science to actuarial prediction, and by avoiding explanatory worries about what else might be going on. The presemiotic subject became a statistical aggregate, an average across occasions, a place holder for some set of dispositions or inclinations (expressed in probabilistic terms) to respond in certain ways in certain situations (e.g., Buss & Craik, 1983; Epstein, 1979). (This position is defensible within its own very narrow limits, because it merely acknowledges those stabilities that exist in a subject's patterns of involvement with the world, without trying to understand or explain them; advocates of this position recognize that a disposition is not a causal agent.)

Even those personality researchers who worried a lot about what else might be going on were not prepared to radically revise their conception of the subject. There was a time in the early 1970s when the slogan "interactionism" was the rage (see, e.g., Magnusson & Endler, 1977; see also Magnusson, Chapter 8, this volume). "Interactionism," properly used, referred to the massive statistical interaction effects discovered in person × situation × response mode analysis-of-variance designs; it meant that a great deal of the variance in human behavior was yet to be explained.

Yet "interactionism" offered no fundamentally new explanations for behavior, and it went nowhere. Interactionists continued to presuppose that all causes could be classified as either subjective or objective, as either mental or stimulus-bound. They then drew the "radical" conclusion that, somehow, subjective states and objective conditions were both decisive for behavior. This is quite different from drawing the conclusion that *neither* autonomous mental states *nor* objective stimulus conditions are determinants of behavior, and it falls far short of rejecting the presemiotic presupposition that all causes of behavior must be analytically separable into subjective causes (autonomous mental states) and objective causes (external stimulus situations). (See

Mischel, 1973, for a noble and insufficiently appreciated attempt to spell out various ways to develop such a conclusion.)

The Second Problem: When "Findings" Start to Seem Bizarre

In order to make a rhetorical point, let us divide research scholars into two types: Type 1, those scholars who believe in the reality of any findings generated within the terms of some conceptual framework that is assumed to be secure; and Type 2, those scholars who become insecure about their conceptual framework because of the irreality of the findings that it generates. We believe that there is something "irreal" about some of the findings generated within the framework of the presemiotic idea of the person.

In particular, let us consider the following robust finding, repeatedly generated within the terms of the presemiotic personality research paradigm: If one presupposes that the person is a vessel for autonomous mental states and then studies the distribution of those mental states, *within-unit variance overwhelms between-unit variance, whatever the unit—individual, family, or culture.* It is almost as if the full range of human diversity reproduces itself at every level of organization. Thus, if one presupposes a presemiotic conception of the person, one discovers that within-culture variation in individual mental states is greater than between-culture variation (see, e.g., Kaplan, 1954). At a different level of analysis, one discovers that within-family variation in individual mental states is comparable to between-family variation (Plomin & Daniels, 1987). And finally, as Mischel has made us so well aware, one even discovers that within-individual variation in mental states across situations or response modes keeps pace with between-individual variation (Mischel, 1968, 1973; Mischel & Peake, 1982).

Consider, for example, recent findings of massive within-family variations in individual mental states (see Plomin & Daniels, 1987). It has been discovered that identical twins *reared together* (in other words, subjects with identical "insides" who are exposed to apparently similar "outside" stimulus conditions) are often quite different from each other in their reactions to the world (e.g., one but not the other becomes depressed), and that full siblings who grow up in the same family (in other words, subjects with similar "insides" who are exposed to apparently similar "outside" stimulus conditions) are not much more like each other in mental dispositions than are random pairs of people from the general population.

As Type 2 scholars, we think that these findings are bizarre. Because we do not believe the world is *that* strange and noisy, we believe there is something wrong with the paradigm (the conception of the person as a vessel for autonomous mental states and the presemiotic division of things into autonomous mental states and objective stimulus conditions) that produces a methodology resulting in such findings. We think that this is one of those times in the history of a science when the "facts" are what we should doubt, for the sake of progress in our field.

The standard presemiotic interpretation of these findings in terms of "nonshared environmental effects" is that the mental dispositions of children in a typical family are so different because the children do not really share the same history of exposure to objective (read "observer-defined") stimulus situations. The interpretation is that different stimulus situations produce different responses; that stimulus conditions are not always the same, or even similar, for different members of the family; and that through differential exposure to decisively different stimulus situations, different members of the same family become vessels for different autonomous mental states. This interpretation is presemiotic because it does not challenge the assumption of subject–object, inside–outside, mind–world dualism. Instead, it presupposes a fundamental division of things into autonomous interior states and exterior stimulus conditions, and then tries to derive autonomous interior states from an idiosyncratic or unique history of exposure to exterior stimulus conditions. It assumes that what is common in the exposure histories and genetic inheritance of members of the same family is overwhelmed by what is idiosyncratic. The interpretation is inventive, yet it seems ad hoc.

An entirely different approach is suggested by the semiotic conception of the person. What members of the same family, community, or culture share are not autonomous mental states, but rather the conceptual schemes that are the instruments of their intentional consciousness. The various stimulus situations in a life space possess their evocative potentials by virtue of the way in which persons with intentional consciousness get involved with them—define them, classify them, tell stories about them, hold beliefs about them, reason about them, evaluate them, and appropriate them to some purpose—which is what the rationality of the semiotic subject is all about. What members of localized subgroups share are those definitions, classifications, stories, reasons, and evaluations. Those are the theoretical terms in which functioning in a life space should be understood. Those are the terms in which unsurprising family-specific, community-specific, culture-specific, or ideological-region-specific patterns of within-unit sharing ought to be discovered.

Thus, we conclude this chapter with a semiotic interpretation of the Plomin and Daniels (1987) findings. From a semiotic perspective those findings represent a *reductio ad absurdum* of the presemiotic conception of the person, as well as of the things that it measures and its measure of things. Indeed, one might propose as a test for the plausibility of any conception of the person (semiotic or presemiotic) that members of the same stable community turn out more like each other than like random members of other communities, that members of the same family turn out more like each other than like random members of other families, and that single persons turn out more like themselves from moment to moment than like random others at the same point in time. Where the presemiotic language of autonomous mental states has failed to discover significant levels of within-culture, within-family, or within-individual sharing, it is our wager that the language of intentional consciousness will succeed. With luck, if collaborative research in cultural psychology takes off during the next decade (as we hope it will), by the turn of the century we should be in a position to collect on our bet or to pay up.

REFERENCES

Abu-Lughod, L. (1986). *Veiled sentiments: Honor and poetry in Bedouin society.* Berkeley: University of California Press.

Allport, G. (1960). *Personality and social encounter.* Boston: Beacon Press.

Alston, W. P. (1975). Traits, consistency and conceptual alternatives for personality theory. *Journal for the Theory of Social Behavior, 5,* 17–48.

Bem, D. I. (1974). On predicting some of the people some of the time. *Psychological Review, 81*, 506–520.

Bitterman, M. E. (1975). The comparative analysis of learning. *Science, 188*, 699–709.

Buss, D. M., & Craik, K. H. (1983). The act frequency approach to personality. *Psychological Review, 90*, 105–126.

Caspi, A. (1987). Personality and the life cycle. *Journal of Personality and Social Psychology, 53*, 1203–1213.

Caspi, A., Elder, G. H., Jr., & Bem, D. J. (1987). Moving against the world: Life course patterns of explosive children. *Developmental Psychology, 22*, 303–308.

Cattell, R. B. (1957). *Personality and motivation: Structure and measurement.* Yonkers-on-Hudson, NY: World.

Child, I. L. (1968). Personality in culture. In E. F. Borgatta & W. W. Lambert (Eds.), *Handbook of personality theory and research* (pp. 82–145). Chicago: Rand McNally.

Cole, M. (1989). *Cultural psychology: A once and future discipline?* Unpublished manuscript, University of California–San Diego.

Coleman, L., & Kay, P. (1981). Prototype semantics: The English verb "lie." *Language, 57*, 26–34.

Cronbach, L. J. (1975). Beyond the two disciplines of scientific psychology. *American Psychologist, 30*, 116–127.

Cronbach, L. J. (1986). Social inquiry by and for earthlings. In D. W. Fiske & R. A. Shweder (Eds.), *Metatheory in social science: Pluralisms and subjectivities* (pp. 83–107). Chicago: University of Chicago Press.

Csordas, T. J. (1983). The rhetoric of transformation in ritual healing. *Culture, Medicine, and Psychiatry, 7*, 333–375.

Csordas, T. J. (1988). Elements of charismatic persuasion and healing. *Medical Anthropology Quarterly, 2*, 121–142.

D'Andrade, R. (1965). Trait psychology and componential analysis. *American Anthropologist, 67*, 215–228.

D'Andrade, R. (1974). Memory and the assessment of behavior. In T. Blalock (Ed.), *Social measurement* (pp. 139–186). Chicago: Aldine-Atherton.

D'Andrade, R. (1981). The cultural part of cognition. *Cognitive Science, 5*, 179–185.

D'Andrade, R. (1984). Cultural meaning systems. In R. A. Shweder & R. A. LeVine (Eds.), *Culture theory: Essays on mind, self, and emotion* (pp. 88–122). New York: Cambridge University Press.

D'Andrade, R. (1985). Character terms and cultural models. In J. Dougherty (Ed.), *Directions in cognitive anthropology* (pp. 88–119). New York: Cambridge University Press.

D'Andrade, R. (1986). Three scientific world views and the covering law models. In D. W. Fiske & R. A. Shweder (Eds.), *Metatheory in social science: Pluralisms and subjectivities.* (pp. 19–41). Chicago: University of Chicago Press.

D'Andrade, R. (1987). A folk model of the mind. In D. Holland & N. Quinn (Eds.), *Cultural models in language and thought* (pp. 112–148). New York: Cambridge University Press.

D'Andrade, R. (Ed.). (in press). *Culture and motivation.* Cambridge, England: Cambridge University Press.

Digman, J. M., & Inouye, J. (1986). Further specification of the five robust factors of personality. *Journal of Personality and Social Psychology, 50*, 116–123.

Dumont, L. (1970). *Homo hierarchicus.* Chicago: University of Chicago Press.

Endler, N. S. (1969). Generalizability of contributions from sources of variance in the S-R inventories of anxiousness. *Journal of Personality, 37*, 1–24.

Endler, N. S., & Hunt, J. M. (1966). Sources of behavioral variance as measured by the S-R inventory of anxiousness. *Psychological Bulletin, 65*, 336–346.

Epstein, S. (1979). The stability of behavior: I. On predicting most of the people most of the time. *Journal of Personality and Social Psychology, 37*, 1097–1126.

Estes, W. (1986). Array models for category learning. *Cognitive Psychology, 18*, 500–549.

Fish, S. (1980). *Is there a text in this class?* Cambridge, MA: Harvard University Press.

Fiske, A. (in press). *The elementary forms of sociality.* New York: Free Press.

Fiske, D. W., & Shweder, R. A. (Eds.). (1986). *Metatheory in social science: Pluralisms and subjectivities.* Chicago: University of Chicago Press.

Fogelson, R. D. (1979). Person, self and identity: Some anthropological retrospects, circumspects, and prospects. In B. Lee (Ed.), *Psychological theories of the self.* New York: Plenum.

Foucault, M. (1980). *The history of sexuality.* New York: Random House.

Gaines, A. D. (1982). Cultural definitions, behavior and the person in American psychiatry. In A. Marsella & G. White (Eds.), *Cultural conceptions of mental health and therapy* (pp. 167–191). Dordrecht, The Netherlands: D. Reidel.

Geertz, C. (1973). Person, time and conduct in Bali. In *Interpretation of cultures: Selected essays of Clifford Geertz* (pp. 360–411). New York: Basic Books.

Gergen, K. J. (1986). Correspondence versus autonomy in the language of understanding human action. In D. W. Fiske & R. A. Shweder (Eds.), *Metatheory in social science: Pluralisms and subjectivities* (pp. 136–162). Chicago: University of Chicago Press.

Heelas, P., & Lock, A. (Eds.). (1981). *Indigenous psychologies: The anthropology of the self.* London: Academic Press.

Herdt, G. (1981). *The guardians of the flute.* New York: McGraw-Hill.

Holland, D., & Quinn, N. (Eds.). (1987). *Cultural models in language and thought.* Cambridge, England: Cambridge University Press.

Howard, A. (1985). Ethnopsychology and the prospects for a cultural psychology. In G. M. White & J. Kirkpatrick (Eds.). *Person, self and experience.* Berkeley: University of California Press.

Kakar, S. (1982). *Shamans, mystics and doctors.* Boston: Beacon Press.

Kaplan, B. (1954). A study of the Rorschach responses in four cultures. *Papers of the Peabody Museum of American Archaeology and Ethnology, 42*(2).

Kleinman, A. (1986). *Social origins of distress and disease.* New Haven, CT: Yale University Press.

Kleinman, A., & Good, B. (Eds.). (1985). *Culture and depression: Towards an anthropology of affects and affective disorders.* Los Angeles: University of California Press.

Labov, W., & Fanischel, D. (1977). *Therapeutic discourse.* New York: Academic Press.

Lachman, M. E. (1989). Personality and aging at the crossroads: Beyond stability versus change. In K. W. Schaie & C. Schooler (Eds.), *Social structure and aging: Psychological processes.* Hillsdale, NJ: Erlbaum.

Lakoff, G. (1987). *Women, fire and dangerous things.* Chicago: University of Chicago Press.

Lakoff, G., & Kovecses, Z. (1987). The cognitive model of anger inherent in American English. In D. Holland & N. Quinn (Eds.), *Cultural models in language and thought* (pp. 195–221). Cambridge, England: Cambridge University Press.

Lévi-Strauss, C. (1963). *Structural anthropology.* New York: Doubleday.

Lévi-Strauss, C. (1966). *The savage mind.* Chicago: University of Chicago Press.

Lévi-Strauss, C. (1969). *The raw and the cooked.* New York: Harper & Row.

LeVine, R. A. (1983). *Culture, behavior and personality.* Chicago: Aldine.

Levy, R. I. (1973). *Tahitians: Mind and experience in the Society Islands.* Chicago: University of Chicago Press.

Levy, R. I. (1984). Emotion, knowing, and culture. In R. A. Shweder & R. A. LeVine (Eds.), *Culture theory: Essays on mind, self, and emotion* (pp. 214–237). New York: Cambridge University Press.

Levy, R. I., & Rosaldo, M. Z. (Eds.). (1983). Self and emotion [Special issue]. *Ethos: Journal of the Society for Psychological Anthropology, 11.*

Luhrmann, T. M. (1989). *Persuasion of the witch's craft.* Cambridge, MA: Harvard University Press.

Lutz, C. (1988). *Unnatural emotions.* Chicago: University of Chicago Press.

Lutz, C., & White, G. (1986). The anthropology of emotions. *Annual Review of Anthropology, 15,* 405–436.

Mageo, J. M. (1989). Aga, Amio, Loto: Perspectives on the structure of the self in Samoa. *Oceania, 59,* 181–199.

Magnusson, D., & Endler, N. S. (Eds.). (1977). *Personality at the crossroads: Current issues in interactional psychology.* Hillsdale, NJ: Erlbaum.

Marmot, M. G., Kogevinas, M., & Elston, M. A. (1987). Social economic status and disease. *Annual Review of Public Health, 8,* 111–135.

McKeique, P. M., et al. (1988). Diabetes, hyperinsulinaemia and coronary risk factors in Bangladeshis in East London. *British Heart Journal, 60,* 390–396.

Marriott, M. (1989). Constructing an Indian ethnosociology. *Contributions to Indian Sociology, 23,* no. 1.

Marsella, A. J., & White, G. (Eds.). (1982). *Cultural conceptions of mental health and therapy.* Dordrecht, The Netherlands: D. Reidel.

Miller, J. G. (1984). Culture and the development of everyday explanation. *Journal of Personality and Social Psychology, 46,* 961–978.

Miller, J. G., & Luthar, S. (1989). Issues of interpersonal responsibility and accountability: A comparison of Indians' and Americans' moral judgments. *Social Cognition, 7,* 237–261.

Miller, P. J., & Sperry, L. L. (1987). The socialization of anger and aggression. *Merrill–Palmer Quarterly, 33,* 1–31.

Mines, M. (1988). Conceptualizing the person: Hierarchical society and individual autonomy in India. *American Anthropologist, 90,* 568–579.

Mischel, W. (1968). *Personality and assessment.* New York: Wiley.

Mischel, W. (1973). Towards a cognitive social learning reconceptualization of personality. *Psychological Review, 80,* 252–283.

Mischel, W., & Peake, P. (1982). In search of consistency: Measure for measure. In M. Zanna, E. T. Higgins, &

C. P. Herman (Eds.), *Consistency in social behavior: The Ontario Symposium of Personality and Social Psychology* (Vol. 2). Hillsdale, NJ: Erlbaum.

Moos, R. H. (1969). Sources of variance in responses to questionnaires and in behavior. *Journal of Abnormal Psychology, 74,* 405–412.

Murdock, G. P. (1980). *Theories of illness.* Pittsburgh: University of Pittsburgh Press.

Myers, F. R. (1979). Emotions and the self: A theory of personhood and political order among Pintupi aborigines. *Ethos: Journal of the Society for Psychological Anthropology, 7,* 343–370.

Myers, F. R. (1988). The logic and meaning of anger among Pintupi aborigines. *Man (N.S.), 23,* 589–610.

Noricks, J. S., et al. (1987). Age, abstract thinking and the American concept of the person. *American Anthropologist, 89,* 667–675.

Norman, W. T. (1963). Toward an adequate taxonomy of personality attributes: Replicated factor structure in peer nomination personality ratings. *Journal of Abnormal and Social Psychology, 67,* 574–583.

Obeyesekere, G. (1981). *Medusa's hair.* Chicago: University of Chicago Press.

Parfit, D. (1986). *Reasons and persons.* Oxford: Oxford University Press.

Peacock, J. L. (1983). Religion and life history: An exploration in cultural psychology. In E. M. Bruner (Ed.), *Text, play and story: The construction and deconstruction of self and society.* Washington, DC: American Ethnological Society.

Pepitone, A., & Triandis, H. C. (1987). On the universality of social psychological theories. *Journal of Cross-Cultural Psychology, 18,* 471–498.

Plomin, R., & Daniels, D. (1987). Why are children in the same family so different from one another? *Behavioral and Brain Sciences, 10,* 1–16.

Putnam, H. (1987). *The many faces of realism.* LaSalle, IL: Open court.

Read, K. E. (1955). Morality and the concept of the person among the Gahuku-gama. *Oceania, 25,* 233–282.

Rescher, N. (1988). *Rationality.* Oxford: Oxford University Press.

Rosaldo, M. Z. (1980). *Knowledge and passion: Ilongot notions of self and social life.* Cambridge, England: Cambridge University Press.

Rosaldo, M. Z. (1984). Toward an anthropology of self and feeling. In R. A. Shweder & R. A. LeVine (Eds.), *Culture theory: Essays on mind, self, and emotion.* New York: Cambridge University Press.

Scheper-Hughes, N. (1985). Culture, scarcity and maternal thinking: Maternal detachment and infant survival in a Brazilian shantytown. *Ethos: Journal of the Society for Psychological Anthropology, 13,* 291–317.

Scruton, R. (1986). *Sexual desire.* New York: Free Press.

Searle, J. (1979). *Expression and meaning.* Cambridge, England: Cambridge University Press.

Seymour, S. (1983). Household structure and states and expressions of affect in India. *Ethos 11,* 263–277.

Shweder, R. A. (1979a). Rethinking culture and personality theory: Part 1. A critical examination of two classical postulates. *Ethos: Journal of the Society for Psychological Anthropology, 7,* 255–278.

Shweder, R. A. (1979b). Rethinking culture and personality theory: Part 2. A critical examination of two more classical postulates. *Ethos: Journal of the Society for Psychological Anthropology, 7,* 279–311.

Shweder, R. A. (1980). Rethinking culture and personality

theory: Part 3. From genesis and typology to hermeneutics and dynamics. *Ethos: Journal of the Society for Psychological Anthropology, 8,* 60–94.

Shweder, R. A. (1981). Fact and artifact in trait perception: The systematic distortion hypothesis. In B. A. Maher & W. B. Maher (Eds.), *Progress in Experimental personality research* (Vol. 11, pp. 65–99). New York: Academic Press.

Shweder, R. A. (1984). Anthropology's romantic rebellion against the enlightenment: Or, there's more to thinking than reason and evidence. In R. A. Shweder & R. A. LeVine (Eds.), *Culture theory: Essays on mind, self, and emotion* (pp. 27–66). New York: Cambridge University Press.

Shweder, R. A. (1985). Menstrual pollution, soul loss and the comparative study of emotions. In A. Kleinman & B. J. Good (Eds.), *Culture and depression: Towards an anthropology of affects and affective disorders* (pp. 184–213). Los Angeles: University of California Press.

Shweder, R. A. (1986). Divergent rationalities. In D. W. Fiske & R. A. Shweder (Eds.), *Metatheory in social science: Pluralisms and subjectivities* (pp. 163–196). Chicago: University of Chicago Press.

Shweder, R. A. (1987). How to look at Medusa without turning to stone. *Contributions to Indian Sociology, 21,* 37–56.

Shweder, R. A. (1988). Suffering in style. *Culture, Medicine and Psychiatry, 12,* 479–497.

Shweder, R. A. (1990). Cultural psychology: What is it? In J. Stigler, R. A. Shweder, & G. Herdt (Eds.), *Cultural psychology: Essays on comparative human development.* New York: Cambridge University Press.

Shweder, R. A. (in press). *Thinking through cultures: Expeditions in cultural psychology.* Cambridge, MA: Harvard University Press.

Shweder, R. A., & Bourne, E. J. (1984). Does the concept of the person vary cross-culturally? In R. A. Shweder & R. A. LeVine (Eds.), *Culture theory: Essays on mind, self, and emotion* (pp. 158–199). New York: Cambridge University Press.

Shweder, R. A., & D'Andrade, R. G. (1980). The systematic distortion hypothesis. In R. A. Shweder (Ed.), *Fallible judgement in behavioral research: New directions for methodology of behavioral science* (pp. 37–58). San Francisco: Jossey-Bass.

Shweder, R. A., & LeVine, R. A. (Eds.). (1984). *Culture theory: Essays on mind, self, and emotion.* New York: Cambridge University Press.

Shweder, R. A., Mahapatra, M., & Miller, J. G. (1987). Culture and moral development. In J. Kagan & S. Lamb (Eds.), *The emergence of morality in young children* (pp. 1–83). Chicago: University of Chicago Press. Reprinted in J. Stigler, R. A. Shweder, & G. Herdt (Eds.), *Cultural psychology.* New York: Cambridge University Press, 1990.

Shweder, R. A., & Miller, J. G. (1985). The social construction of the person: How is it possible In K. J. Gergen & K. Davis (Eds.), *The social construction of the person* (pp. 41–69). New York: Springer.

Shweder, R. A., Much, N. C., Pool, D., & Dixon, S. (1990). *Moral discourse realms.* Manuscript in preparation.

Spiro, M. E. (1966). Buddhism and economic action in Burma. *American Anthropologist, 68,* 1163–1173.

Spiro, M. E. (1983). *Oedipus in the Trobriands.* Chicago: University of Chicago Press.

Stigler, J., Shweder, R. A., & Herdt, G. (Eds.) (1990). *Cultural psychology: Essays on comparative human development.* New York: Cambridge University Press.

Straus, A. S. (1977). Northern Cheyenne ethnopsychology. *Ethos: Journal of the Society for Psychological Anthropology, 5,* 326–357.

Super, C. M., & Harkness, S. (1986). The developmental niche: A conception at the interface of child and culture. *International Journal of Behavioral Development, 9,* 545–569.

Sweetser, E. E. (1987). The definition of *lie:* An examination of the folk models underlying a semantic prototype. In D. Holland & N. Quinn (Eds.), *Cultural models in language and thought* (pp. 43–66). Cambridge, England: Cambridge University Press.

Taylor, C. (1989). *Sources of the self.* Cambridge, MA: Harvard University Press.

Triandis, H. (1989). The self and social behavior in differing cultural contexts. *Psychological Review, 96,* 506–520.

Weber, M. (1930). *The Protestant ethic and the spirit of capitalism.* London: Allen & Unwin.

Weisner, T. S., & Gallimore, R. (1977). My brother's keeper: Child and sibling caretaking. *Current Anthropology, 18,* 169–190.

Weiss, M. G. et al. (1986). Traditional concepts of mental disorder among Indian psychiatric patients: Preliminary report of work in progress. *Social Science and Medicine, 23,* 379–386.

Weiss, M. G. et al. (1988). Humoral concepts of mental illness in India. *Social Science and Medicine, 27,* 471–477.

Wellencamp, J. C. (1988). Notions of grief and catharsis among the Toraja. *American Ethnologist, 15,* 486–500.

White, G., & Kirkpatrick, J. (Eds.). (1985). *Person, self, and experience: Exploring Pacific ethnopsychologies.* Berkeley: University of California Press.

Whiting, B. B., & Edwards, C. P. (1985). *Children of other worlds.* Cambridge, MA: Harvard University Press.

Whiting, J. W. M., & Whiting, B. B. (1975). *Children of six cultures.* Cambridge, MA: Harvard University Press.

Wierzbicka, A. (1986). Human emotions: Universal or culture specific? *American Anthropologist, 88,* 584–594.

Wikan, U. (1987). Public grace and private fears: Gaiety, offense and sorcery in Northern Bali. *Ethos: Journal of the Society for Psychological Anthropology, 15,* 337–365.

Wikan, U. (1989a). Illness from fright or soul loss: A north Balinese culture-bound syndrome? *Culture, Medicine, and Psychiatry, 13,* 25–80.

Wikan, U. (1989b). Managing the heart to brighten face and soul: Emotions in Balinese morality and health care. *American Ethnologist, 16,* 294–312.

PART IV
RESEARCH TOPICS: INTRAPERSONAL AND INTERPERSONAL, PRIVATE AND PUBLIC ASPECTS OF PERSONALITY

Chapter 16

Personality and Private Experience: Individual Variations in Consciousness and in Attention to Subjective Phenomena

Jerome L. Singer and George A. Bonanno
Yale University

> The subjective factor is as ineluctable a datum as the extent of the sea and the radius of the earth.
>
> —CARL G. JUNG (1921/1971, p. 375)

To be human implies that we vary along with others of our species on a dimension of experience that is private. We sustain a possession-like belief in a secret independence, what William James (1890/1952) called "my thoughts." Our memories; our day or night dreams; our aesthetic, spiritual, or sensual absorptions; and our projected futures all seem to us capable of remaining hidden from the scrutiny or even awareness of others. Perhaps an omniscient deity, if we are believers, can penetrate this veil of inner experience. But our thoughts are known to our fellow humans only if we choose to share them. Like the spies in John le Carré's novels, we need reveal our hidden secrets only under special forms of compulsion—the ritual of the confessional, the voluntary contract with a psychoanalyst or a hypnotist, the mutual self-disclosure that strengthens the bonds of an intimate friendship or sexual relationship.

Many of the world's great literary personages have shared their imaginative constructions publicly in novels, stories, essays, and abundant private correspondence. Such material must ultimately stem from their own recollections and fantasies. But what of the rest of the population, who have little enough opportunity or occasion for sharing their memories, daydreams, or night dreams, let alone their "secrets," with others? The vast range of human subjective experience and its variations in the degree to which there is conscious awareness of its facets, involvement in its working, and playful or tormented extension of its properties in daydreams or fantasies thus offer a challenge for exploration to the personality theorist and researcher. The way for such exploration was opened to psychology by William James's accounts of the stream of consciousness and by Sigmund Freud's exploration of the influences on conscious thought and action of presumed unconscious wishes.

To Carl G. Jung we acknowledge a debt for formulating in great detail a theory of those personality variations in awareness and emphasis on private experience, which he called "introversion." This model laid the basis for the systematic study of individual differences in what we can call the "private personality." Jung's distinction between a public "persona" and a private subjective "ego" (used differently from Freud's more popular term) encapsulates the issues we are addressing herein. We put some stress on Jung's model because, more than Freud's, it lends itself to an examination of individual differences in both public and private representations of the organism. We would propose, contrary to Jung, that the personal unconscious is probably overemphasized; it is more likely that "shadow" experiences are functionally likely to come to awareness in the stream of thought, in passing fantasies or daydreams that may be quickly dismissed in some circumstances or cherished in others. We are more willing to view the relationship of conscious and unconscious processes to the information-processing models, which involve procedural and content-oriented cognitive structures (Kihlstrom, 1987; see Kihlstrom, Chapter 17, this volume). The stance we take in our review of the relevant literature in this chapter is that consciousness is more extensive than the models of Jung or Freud might suggest. We carry on a continuous stream of thought, anticipating or fantasizing a vast range of possible situations or self-representations and trying out mentally a considerable repertory of possible actions. For example, unless we are suddenly asked to report, we often may not recall how many times we have consciously thought about "possible selves" (Markus & Nurius, 1986), both positive or acceptable (Jung's "ego") and unacceptable (Jung's "shadow"). We propose that the thinking introversion pole of the introvert–extravert dimension of personality (as distinct from social introversion)[1] reflects relatively greater interest in and awareness of these ongoing thoughts and, thus, in a sense, a more differentiated consciousness. Our objective in this chapter is to review a range of phenomena that characterize relatively conscious thought and to examine some of the major methodologies for exploring individual variations in such private experiences.

THE SPECIAL ROLE OF PRIVACY OR PERSONAL AUTONOMY IN THE HUMAN CONDITION

For much of the first 60 years of this century personality theorists in particular and psychologists in general placed greatest emphasis on the specific, presumably biologically derived drives that were thought to serve as motivators of thought and action. A major shift in our conception was signaled in 1959 with the publication of Robert White's (1959) paper on competence and Ernst Schachtel's (1959) book *Metamorphosis*. These were soon followed by Tomkins and Messick's (1962) *Computer Simulation of Personality;* Tomkins's seminal two-volume work *Affect, Imagery and Consciousness* (1962–1963); Fritz Heider's *The Psychology of Interpersonal Relations* (1958); and Nebraska Symposium contributions such as those by J. M. Hunt (1965), White (1960), Neal Miller (1963), and Karl Pribram (1963). These works reflected a confluence of data and theory from (1) research on the sleep cycle; (2) the field of artificial intelligence and computer programming; (3) the shift in experimental psychology away from stimulus–response sensation and perception models toward broader cognitive conceptions; and (4) Hebb's brain models. These developments eventuated in what was initially termed a "cognitive revolution" (Dember, 1974) but which with more recent attention to emotion might best be called a "cognitive–affective" perspective on human thought and action (Singer, 1966, 1974, 1984).

The present chapter assumes such a cognitive–affective point of view. We propose that human beings are best regarded as creatures who are biologically endowed with the necessary capacities and motivated from birth to explore their environments and to move gradually toward labeling and assigning meaning to their experiences. The human information-processing systems are closely tied to the separate, differentiated affective system, so that we are aroused, frightened, angered, or depressed by large degrees of sudden or persisting incongruity between our expectancies (plans, goals, or wishes) and the information presented in a given situation. Likewise, we are moved to laughter and joy when incongruities are resolved, or to interest and to exploration when the novelty we confront is at a moderate level rather than an extreme one (Mandler, 1984; Singer, 1974, 1984; Tomkins, 1962). If there is an overarching human motive from this perspective it is to assign meaning, to make sense of the world. The theorizing and empirical research of the Kreitlers points up the heuristic value of such an approach for personality study (Kreitler & Kreitler, 1976, 1990). The unexpectedly discrepant or the ambiguous may in moderate doses be positively reinforcing, but in large or persisting amounts may evoke unpleasant affects such as terror, anxiety, anger, or sadness, and distress and thus prove negatively reinforcing.

If we are indeed "wired" to make sense of our environment—to select, to identify, to label, to encode and to schematize new stimulation—what are the sources of this information? We propose that for human beings (as far as we can tell), our stimuli derive either from the "objective" world, the consensually measurable physical and social stimuli in our milieu, or from the "subjective" or private world of our memories and ongoing mental processes (Cartwright, 1981; Pope & Singer, 1978). At any given moment the human being must assign a priority to responding either to those stimuli that come from exodermic sources (sounds, light patterns, smells, touches, or tastes) or to those that appear to be "internal" (the recollections, associations, images, interior monologues, wishful fantasies, or ruminative worries that characterize consciousness). Bodily sensations or signals of pain or malfunction from our organ systems represent a kind of intermediary source of stimulation, although we propose that such experiences often appear to us to have an "objective" quality, despite their inherent embeddedness within our physical selves. We must generally give greater weight in our instantaneous assignments of priority to externally derived stimuli, or else we are likely to be hit by cars, to bump into poles, or to step into ditches. But human environments are characterized by sufficient redundancy, and our motor skills and cognitive plans for specific situations generally are so overlearned and well differentiated, that we have ample opportunity to engage in elaborate memories, planful thought, or fantasies even while driving cars or participating in business meetings.

We further propose that our human condition is such that we are forever in the situation of deciding how much attention to give to self-generated thought and how much to information from the external social or physical environment. This dilemma represents, we believe, a way of formulating the introversion–extraversion dimension of human experience. It may be seen as one manifestation of, or perhaps even as the prototype for, the major existential dilemma of the human being—the persisting dialectical struggle between what David Bakan (1966) called "communion and

agency" or Andras Angyal (1965) termed "homonymy versus autonomy." Within the umbrella of the overarching motive for meaning we humans are always seeking on the one hand to be part of someone or some system beyond ourselves—to feel loved, admired, or respected, to feel close to an individual or a group—and, on the other, to sustain a sense of autonomy and individuality, of self-direction, privacy in thought, or uniqueness in competence and skill. The extensive analysis of psychopathological conditions presented by Blatt and Schichman (1983) has shown how depression and psychotic patterns can be delineated along what they term "introjective" and "anaclitic" dimensions. Piaget's (1951) developmental conception of accommodation and assimilation is just one other example of the widespread reliance by theorists on a fundamental distinction between "looking without and looking within."

We have elsewhere (Bonanno & Singer, 1990) attempted to integrate these diverse strands of theorizing into what we hope can become a heuristic model of personality variation, as illustrated in Figure 16.1. The triangular shape allows for one to estimate potential pathological or maladaptive implications of extreme positions on the dimensions. The sloping sides of the triangle represent the relative emphasis on seeking to enhance self-esteem versus simply preferring the social context. The domain of one's uniqueness, as represented by the autonomy of private thoughts and the development of one's special skills, is reflected on the right. The left half of the triangle characterizes efforts to seek affiliation or attachment, intimacy, group membership—perhaps even what Schachtel (1959) termed the "embeddedness affect," the sense of loss of selfness through the communion or intimacy often symbolized in passionate sexuality. If we bisect the triangle from apex to base and then imagine horizontal lines from side to side, these represent dimensions along which individuals can vary with respect to relative psychological investment in individuation and privacy (right) or in attachment and communion (left). Nearer the apex, where the horizontal dimensions are shorter, we propose that individuals located on those lines have attained a better balance in the existential struggle between the dual polarities. Thus, even someone located close to the triangle edge near the apex may still function adaptively while showing an introverted or extraverted personality style, or a field-independent or field-dependent cognitive style. Similarly, near the apex one may find individuals who at one pole of the horizontal may be more inclined to experience shame emotions (socially oriented), at the other pole a more individualized emphasis may heighten a private sense of guilt (Lewis, 1990). In general, our assumption or article of faith is that persons located nearer the center horizontally and higher vertically are more likely to function effectively and adaptively, with better physical and mental health and with less inflexible reliance on particular defense mechanisms. As the sides widen and closer to the base, we find various diagnosable pathological groups—some more oriented to exaggerated autonomy and privacy in personality, others more to issues of attachment and social investment.

Elsewhere (Bonanno & Singer, 1990), we have explored the left-hand side of our model, which represents relatedness to others and movement away from private experience. For our purposes in this chapter we are, in effect, emphasizing the upper right-hand quadrant— the relatively "normal" or adaptive human var-

iations in emphasis upon private, autonomous experience and self-differentiation and actualization. We further delimit our review by focusing upon the more private experiential components of this quadrant, since other chapters deal with overt "acts" and individualized skills and competencies.

THE VARIETIES OF HUMAN CONSCIOUS EXPERIENCE

Extensive recent analyses of consciousness are available in the work of Natsoulas (1978, 1983, 1986–1987), Baars (1986–1987), Marsh (1977), and Ornstein (1977). A useful organizational structure has been described by Fromm (1979). As represented in Figure 16.2, one can conceptualize consciousness or awareness as ranging from normal waking alertness (in which processing presumably includes both active sensitivity to external cues and a somewhat lesser attentiveness to material generated by long-term memory) through certain Buddhist and Hindu Yogic meditative states or psyche-

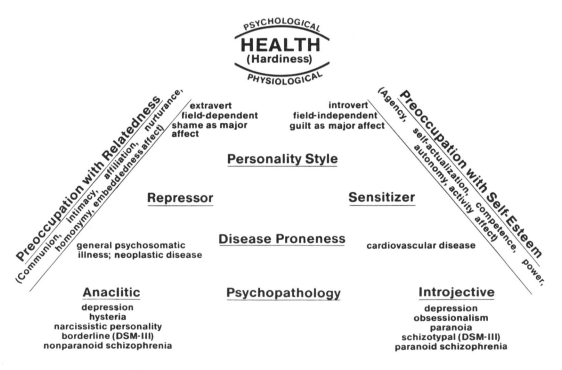

FIGURE 16.1. A model of psychological and physiological health as a function of the balance of interpersonal relatedness and self-esteem. From "Repressive Personality Style: Theoretical and Methodological Implications for Health and Pathology" by G. A. Bonanno and J. L. Singer (1990), in J. L. Singer (Ed.), *Repression and Dissociation*. Chicago: University of Chicago Press. Copyright by the University of Chicago Press. Reprinted by permission.

delic drug conditions. Fromm employed the term "ego activity–receptivity," which we assume represents a sense of self-awareness, self-directedness, and a self-conscious executive orientation that can take the form of a receptive, "watching-the-movie" quality or the form of an action-oriented, change-producing response pattern.

As can be seen from Figure 16.2 the continuum from secondary process to primary process orders the states reasonably well. We would propose, however, a broader use of the terms "primary process" and "secondary process" to indicate that the lower end of the continuum is characterized not only by more undefended drive activity or egocentricity in the Freudian sense, but also by much greater attention to stimulation generated by long-term memory, without much responsiveness to current external stimulation (see Antrobus, 1986, and discussion later in this chapter). The "waking entranced" state seems to us an intense absorption that can be directed to external stimuli or to some combination of internal and external, such as observing a play or sporting event or being "lost in a book" (Nell, 1988). This absorption may be closer to the various states of hypnosis than Fromm would suggest.

For the balance of this chapter, we examine some characteristics of the various manifestations of consciousness and relate these to some of the types of individual-difference measures that make for variations in private experience. First, however, we must confront the problem of measurement and operationalization. What methods can we use to sustain these phenomena as problems for scientific study? Then we must consider some of the substantive, theoretical issues and some research directions for exploring the private personality as reflected in these differing manifestations of conscious experience.

Most cognitive theories tend to emphasize consciousness as a feature of the private personality. They do not preclude, however, the possibility that many of our plans and anticipations may have become so automatic that they unroll too rapidly for us to notice them in the flurry of events. As an analogy, when we first learn to drive an automobile we must consciously think of each step to be taken: "Depress the clutch, shift the gear, gradually release the clutch, slightly feed the gas by stepping on the gas pedal." When we have carried out a squence like this often enough, we can

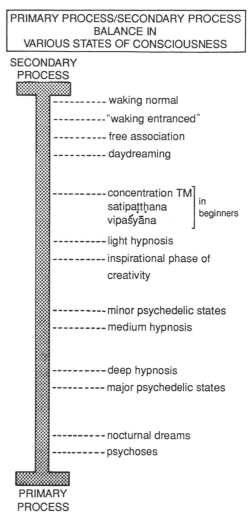

FIGURE 16.2. Fromm's (1979) model of the range of consciousness. From "Primary and Secondary Process in Waking and in Altered States of Consciousness," by E. Fromm, 1978–1979, *Journal of Altered States of Consciousness*, 4, 115–128. Copyright 1978 by Baywood Press. Reprinted by permission.

then engage in the complex motor and perceptual acts necessary for driving a car, and can simultaneously talk, think of other events, listen to music, or observe the scenery. Langer's (1983) notion of "mindlessness," or overlearned mental action sequences, is relevant here. Meichenbaum and Gilmore (1984) have further developed the viewpoint that unconscious processes reflect well-established or overlearned constructs, schemas, or metacognitions (e.g., rules of memory retrieval and various biasing rules about material accepting or threatening to self-beliefs)—a position similar to Tomkins's (1979) theory of nuclear scenes and scripts.

Private experiences such as conscious thoughts, fantasies, or images provide an alternative environment to the continuous processing of material from the external world (Singer, 1974). Thoughts may be reshaped, reorganized, and acted on by further thought in much the same way as our experience is modified by new inputs fom the physical or social environment. Thus, there is a constant restructuring of material in the memory system; memory is never simply a process of passive storage (Bonanno, 1990).

In addition, cognitive theories assume that certain attitudes, beliefs, or pattens of information are more central or self-oriented than others and are more likely to evoke complex affective responses. In this view the self can be regarded as an object of cognition or as a part of perceived experience rather than as an agent. Because our most personal schemas are associated both with a long background of memories from childhood and with our most recent experiences, they are linked to the most complex network of related images, memories, and anticipations. Novel material that does not fit in with beliefs about the self will generate a sense of incongruity. In the face of persisting incongruity, an experience relating to the self will evoke greater intensities of distress or anger than will a thought that relates to other persons or stems from news of other countries.

In summary, the human being is regularly confronted by two major sources of stimulation: the complex physical and social characteristics of the surrounding environment, which make demands for "channel space" on one's sensory system; and an alternative, competitive set of stimuli (some form of "recycled" memory material) generated by the brain, which may also have an impact on the sensory system. Such centrally generated stimulation may have somewhat less urgency when one is in the highly activated and aroused condition of wakefulness. A third source of stimulation (weaker in its demand for conscious processing, but often no less important) is the signaling system from the ongoing machinery of our bodies—a system of great importance in health, but not yet well enough researched and certainly, except under great pain or fatigue, often ignored. Later, we consider some of the implications of the link between bodily cues and the stream of consciousness. As far as we can tell, most people are carrying on some kind of ongoing interior monologue, a kind of gloss on immediately occurring events that also engages in associations of these events. Under circumstances in which the external stimulus field involves sufficient redundancy or familiarity that one can draw on automatized cognitive and motor processes, one may become aware of the continuing array of memories or fantasies unrelated to the immediate environment. Since much of our stream of thought is made up of unfinished intentions of long-standing as well as current concerns, the attention to such stimulation often provokes negative emotions of fear, sadness, shame/guilt, or anger and has generally a mildly aversive quality. Thus we often prefer to turn on the radio or television, do crossword puzzles, or (if in an elevator with a stranger) to talk about the weather, rather than to stay with the thought sequence.

METHODS FOR STUDYING DAYDREAMS AND ONGOING THOUGHT

How can we accumulate systematic data on the private experiences we have so far emphasized? Let us begin by concentrating on those ongoing conscious thought processes that make up the first two or three categories at the top of Fromm's list. Simple reflection suggests that we carry on relatively continuous inner monologues or simulated dialogues with ourselves or significant others, as well as becoming aware of recurring memories, anticipations of upcoming events, and more extended fantasies and daydreams. Defining daydreams as shifts of attention away from immediate tasks or immediate goal-directed problem-solving thought (Klinger, 1971, 1978; Singer, 1966, 1975, 1978), we can identify a whole range of approaches to studying such processes and the individual differences in attending to or assigning priority to them. Indeed, the whole shift of modern psychoanalysis toward an object relations perspective implies that much conscious (and, presumably, unconscious) mental activity is oriented to private simulated dialogues with the internalized mental representations of fathers, mothers, other relatives, or caregivers (Kohut, 1984; Mitchell, 1984; Singer, 1985). The increasing interest of social psychologists in cognitive processes has forced upon these investigators a heightened awareness that much human thought is addressed to "possible selves" (Markus & Nurius, 1986) and to "anticipatory coping" in the form of mental simulations (Taylor & Schneider, 1989). Although the anecdotal reports of psychoanalysts continue to be suggestive in this field, the past quarter of a century has witnessed considerable development of methods for addressing these phenomena in a measurable, replicable fashion that meets reasonable standards of scientific inquiry.

Patterns of Daydreaming: Early Studies with the Rorschach Inkblots

Among attempts to assess individual differences in awareness of or response to private experiences, a fruitful suggestion emerged from Hermann Rorschach's early explorations with inkblot associations (Rorschach, 1942). He proposed on the basis of his observations that persons who were inclined to "see" human figures as associations to the blots, especially those associations involving humans in action, were also more likely to be individuals who showed a rich fantasy life and engaged in much daydreaming. Rorschach also proposed that the persons who provided more of such Human Movement (usually abbreviated in English as M) responses were on the one hand likely to be imaginative, but also on the other hand more susceptible to motoric inhibition or controlled behavioral motion. Research attention has focused chiefly upon linking the M response frequency to measures of fantasy, motor control, creativity, self-awareness, and planfulness (Moise, Yinon, & Rabinowitz, 1988–1989; Singer & Brown, 1977). Dozens of individual-difference and factor-analytic studies consistently show that persons who give more M associations to inkblots (especially responses that are well formed in relation to the blot shapes) are also more likely to tell rich and varied stories to Thematic Apperception Test (TAT) pictures, to score higher on questionnaire measures of daydreaming frequency, and to provide more varied and cognitively complex free associations and person descriptions to tests and in psychoanalytic sessions. They are also more likely to sit quietly in waiting rooms, to inhibit writing speed, to resist laughing if so instructed when listening to a "laughing" record, to show fewer impulsive responses in problem-solving tasks, to be more accurate in time estimates, to manifest less open aggression, and

so forth (Singer & Brown, 1977). The recent studies by Blatt and various colleagues have provided some evidence for separating hospitalized neurotic patients along the dimensions of "anaclitic" and "introjective" (or "attachment-related" vs. "self-esteem-related" conflict focuses). The former group, more like hysteric or repressive patients, show fewer or more poorly formed M responses; the latter show more of such responses with better-developed shapes (M+ or H+). The anaclitic patients respond better to support-expressive or direct therapies, whereas the introjectives do better in more psychoanalytic types of therapy, where imaginative productivity and free associations are critical (Blatt, 1990; Blatt & Schichman, 1983).

Patterns of Daydreaming: The Imaginal Processes Inventory

Although Rorschach inkblots may have some continuing value clinically, investigators have come to recognize that direct inquiries about people's fantasies and daydreams do evoke useful responses and avoid the cumbersome inferential structure necesssary for dealing with Rorschach data. Following some of the early questionnaire approaches for estimating daydream frequency introduced by Page (1957) and Singer and Schonbar (1961), Singer and Antrobus (1963, 1972) developed a series of 22 scales of 12 items, each designed to measure a wide range of patterns of inner experience and types of daydreams. This Imaginal Processes Inventory (IPI) has been factor-analyzed in a number of different studies with varying samples across the age spectrum (Singer, 1978). More recently, a very extensive new analysis of the IPI with large college samples has led to a shortened 45-item version, the SIPI. Based on a comprehensive factor analysis of the scales, three second-order factors—Positive–Constructive Daydreaming, Guilty-Dysphoric Daydreaming, and Poor Attentional Control— have been identified and formed into three 15-item scales with good internal consistency (Huba, Singer, Aneshensel, & Antrobus, 1982b; Segal, Huba, & Singer, 1980). From the varied uses of the IPI, some generalizations are possible about the normative role of daydreams.

Briefly, a large number of studies indicate that most people report being aware of at least some daydreaming every day, and that their daydreams vary considerably from obvious wishful thinking or "castles in Spain" to elaborate and complex visions of frightening or guilty encounters. Cultural differences in frequency and patterning of daydreaming as reported on these questionnaires also emerge (Singer & McCraven, 1961, 1962). As noted above, a series of factor-analytic studies indicates that, at least for the scales of the IPI, the data yield three major factors that characterize ongoing thought: a Positive–Constructive Daydreaming style, a Guilty–Dysphoric Daydreaming style, and a Poor Attentional Control pattern that is generally characterized by fleeting thoughts and an inability to focus on extended fantasy (Giambra, 1974; Huba, Segal, & Singer, 1977; Isaacs, 1975; Segal & Singer, 1976; Singer & Antrobus, 1963, 1972; Starker, 1973;). Giambra (1977a, 1977b) not only found evidence for factor patterns similar to those reported in these studies, but also tracked these across an extensive age range; in addition, he checked the test–retest reliability of daydreaming reports in response to this set of scales and found them to be surprisingly high.

We are left, however, with the question as to whether self-report responses to highly structured questionnaires of the type employed can be truly reflective of persisting behavior patterns in other situations. This is not easy to demonstrate. There are, however, indications from a series of studies that individuals who report a good deal of daydreaming on such questionnaires are also more likely to report a good many task-irrelevant thoughts of a daydream-like nature while they are engaged in a laboratory experiment involving the detection of signals (Antrobus, Coleman, & Singer, 1967). They are also more likely to report that their images are vivid or to fail to detect externally flashed signals when they are engaged in imaging (Fusella, 1972). High Positive–Vivid daydreamers are more likely to show a leftward shifting of their eyes during reflective thought, presumably indicating greater activation of the right side of the brain, which is usually associated with image production (Meskin & Singer, 1974); they are also more likely to report certain kinds of positive content in their recalled nocturnal dreams (Starker, 1978). Isaacs (1975), in a very careful and extensive analysis of the language usage of subjects who reported on their thoughts during signal detection tasks under controlled conditions, found that subjects high on the Positive–Constructive Daydreaming scale of the IPI also were more likely to show stimulus-independent mentation occurring during the task. Their language usage also made more reference to analogies and phrases of a "this is like that" nature, reflecting a more metaphoric or elaboration-oriented turn of mind. Rodin and Singer (1977) found that overweight subjects reported less visual content in their daydreams than did normal-weight subjects. These differences between the weight groups were also reflected in the fact that the overweight subjects were inclined to shut their eyes when presented with a reflective question that involved some need to engage in imagery (presumably in order to shut out the impact of the external cues). The overweight participants also were more inclined to be rightward eye shifters during reflective thought—that is, emphasizing verbal rather than imagery forms of thinking. Differences in the effects of rapid eye movement (REM) deprivation and in the relationship between stimulus-independent thought in a laboratory setting and questionnaire responses of daydreaming were also found by Feldstein (1972).

A series of studies by Segal et al. (1980) has also indicated systematic differences in resorting to drugs and alcohol by subjects who differ in their patterns of daydreaming style. In general, these data (based on more than 1,000 college students at Yale University and at Murray State University in Kentucky) indicate that drug users, particularly those who resort to hallucogenics or heroin and cocaine, tend to be rather externally oriented individuals, seeking external sensations and experiences and not much given to developing or elaborating inner fantasy. Drinking patterns seem somewhat more related to the Guilty–Dysphoric style of daydreaming. Presumably, for some individuals whose predominant ongoing inner experience has a negative, hostile, or self-recriminatory tone, drink seems to obliterate self-awareness and thought more effectively.

The use of questionnaires, also checked by systematic interview of smaller subsamples, has proven to be helpful in examining special ways in which daydreaming is reflected in daily life. Hariton and Singer (1974) explored the use by a group of suburban married women of a variety of fantasies while the women were actually engaged in sexual intercourse with their husbands. The results indicated in general that daydreaming frequency of a more general kind was likely to be linked to resorting to day-dreaming during sex itself. Specific differences in styles of daydreaming during the coital act, and the relationship of such thoughts to relative satisfaction and dissatisfaction in the marriage, were also explored.

Campagna (1985–1986) made use of the IPI as part of a study of masturbatory fantasies in college freshmen. His results generally did not indicate much relationship between the more general daydreaming patterns and the specific form that masturbatory fantasy took, although there was some tendency for those subjects who showed high scores on the Positive–Constructive Daydreaming factor to be inclined to have more story-like and fanciful masturbation fantasies (e.g., "I am a sultan who has a harem available for my every whim").

Although it has often been believed that psychotic individuals, particularly schizophrenics, are likely to show excessive fantasizing, most of the evidence available from Rorschach reports (Singer & Brown, 1977) and from questionnaire studies seems to contradict this expectation. If anything, comparative studies of normal and disturbed individuals, while indicating some specialized patterns of fantasy for the psychotics, do not indicate any greater frequency or indeed do not indicate that the overall nature of daydreaming is at the heart of the psychotic process (Giambra & Traynor, 1974; Schultz, 1976; Starker & Singer, 1975a, 1975b; Streissguth, Wagner, & Weschler, 1969).

A series of studies by Starker and collaborators has examined the links between psychopathological patterns ranging from sleep disturbances, dysphoric dreams, the flashbacks and nightmares of combat-exposed Vietnam veterans, and the hallucinations of schizophrenics to scores on the daydreaming scales of the IPI (Starker, 1974, 1984–1985; Starker & Hasenfeld, 1976; Starker & Jolin, 1982–1983, 1983–1984). These studies indicate, for example, that IPI patterns of Guilty–Dysphoric Daydreaming and Poor Attentional Control characterize the thought patterns of combat-exposed (in contrast to non-combat-exposed) Vietnam veterans. Such daydream styles are also associated with nightmares in the veterans. Starker's work also suggests that a dysphoric daydreaming style is associated with unpleasant night dreams and with sleep disturbance in normal as well as pathological respondents.

For normal samples, we can cite a few instances suggesting convergent validity of the daydream patterns. For example, Positive–Constructive Daydreaming has been associated with vividness of visual imagery, hypnotizability, and absorption (Crawford, 1982). Golding and Singer (1983) factor-analyzed the IPI, along with the Depressive Experiences Questionnaire (Blatt, Quinlan, Chevron, McDonald, & Zuroff, 1982) and the Bem Sex-Role Inventory (Bem, 1974), and again produced a factor solution representing three fundamental characteristics of inner experience. Two of these factors suggest the dual poles represented in our triangular proposal represented in Figure 16.1: One factor matches the Poor Attentional Control factor of the IPI with a dependency-oriented depressive experience and psychological femininity; another factor matches the Guilty–Dysphoric Daydreaming factor of the IPI with a self-critically oriented depressive experience. A third factor, reflecting perhaps an optimal balance between the attachment and self-esteem poles, may be regarded as the ideal of psychological and physiological health (Bonanno & Singer, 1990). Here Positive–Constructive Daydreaming loaded on the factor, with a negative loading for inefficacy-oriented depressive experience and with both psychological masculinity and femininity loading positively.

Two rather sophisticated psychometric analyses suggest that the three dimensions of inner experience emerging from the development of the shorter version of the IPI (the SIPI) can be replicated with new samples and that the factor scale scores show reasonable reliability across time (Huba & Tanaka, 1983–1984, Tanaka & Huba, 1985–1986). The questionnaire data seem consistent in suggesting three major variations in the form taken by the ongoing waking thoughts of the individual—that is, three major dimensions characterizing the private personality. One of these, the Positive–Constructive Daydreaming pattern, seems to reflect normal, wishful, playful, and also planful daydreaming tendencies. And, indeed, this pattern does not correlate with measures of psychopathology as a rule. It may, however, occasionally play a role similar to repression as an escape that may have negative health consequences, as an important study by Jensen (1987) suggests. The second dimension can be characterized as Guilty–Dysphoric Daydreaming or unpleasant, emotionally toned fantasies. Scales such as Guilty Content in Daydreams,

Hostile–Aggressive Daydreams, Fear-of-Failure Fantasies, and so forth load highest on this factor. The third pattern that we identify really represents a negation of an extended, elaborated inner experience. It reflects Poor Attentional Control and is characterized by high loadings of such scales as Distractibility, Susceptibility to Boredom, and other scales suggesting an inability to sustain an extended skein of private imagery or, for that matter, to maintain a prolonged internally oriented concentration without reacting to the continuous stimulation in the physical environment.

Some other examples of correlates of these daydreaming styles can be cited briefly. In a study employing Fenigstein, Scheier, and Buss's (1975) scales of Public and Private Self-Consciousness and Tellegen and Atkinson's (1974) Absorption Scale, a distinct cluster emerged including positive–constructive daydreaming, guilty–dysphoric daydreaming, private self-consciousness, and absorption—a dimension suggestive of thinking introversion. Poor attentional control, public self-consciousness, and social anxiety formed a separate cluster reflecting something more like an emotional instability dimension (Barrios & Singer, 1981–1982). In studies of hypnotic susceptibility or of the use of daydreaming scales to predict waking imagery methods of helping people to overcome creative blocks, there is further evidence that a predisposition to positive, planful daydreaming is consistently tied to measures of absorption, imagery vividness, and hypnotic responsiveness (Barrios & Singer, 1981–1982; Crawford, 1982).

Recent studies by McIlwraith and Schallow (1983a, 1983b) found that adults and children who were heavy viewers of television, especially of the more violent programming, where also characterized by higher scores on the Guilt–Dysphoric Daydreaming dimension. The data are correlational and cross-sectional, but other evidence suggests that persons with unpleasant and distressing inner experiences may seek distraction and passive escapes from such thoughts in television (Csikszentmihalyi & Kubey, 1981). Once exposed to the violence and disaster that characterize daily television fare, they may find their later conscious experience increasingly characterized by frightening, hostile, or fearful fantasies (Kubey, 1982).

QUESTIONNAIRE MEASURES OF INTROVERSION–EXTRAVERSION

In his seminal work *Psychological Types,* Jung (1921/1971) defined the attitude types of introversion–extraversion as products of basic human "processes of adaptation" that regulate the direction of attention. The introvert, according to Jung, "interposes a subjective view" between response to the environment and the objective details of the environment, thus maintaining a primary attentional focus inward toward ongoing thought and experience rather than outward toward situational constraints and variations. Jung also postulated the function types of thinking–feeling and sensing–intuiting to articulate further individual differences and more "pure" types within the global introversion–extraversion dimension. A thinking introvert differs from a feeling introvert, for example, in that the former is strongly influenced by subjective ideas and the latter by subjective images and feelings.

The primary research tool for investigating the attitude and function types has been the Myers–Briggs Type Inventory (MBTI).[2] The MBTI was developed as an operationalization and extension of Jung's theory into four unique dimensions of human variation (Briggs-Myers & Myers, 1980). However, in contrast to Jung's emphasis on "pure" types within the introversion–extraversion framework, the MBTI is based on the notion that individuals vary on each dimension, including the preference for judging versus perceiving, with the result that 16 unique personality types are scorable.

A good many studies have been carried out in recent years using the MBTI. The general profile emerging from these studies appears to support the reliability and validity of the basic introversion–extraversion dimension, and to a lesser degree of the function types; however, little or no support has appeared for their hypothesized interrelations. Test–retest reliability for the MBTI has recently been established for periods of 1–2 years (Leiden, Veach, & Herring, 1986) and 10–12 years (Levy & Ridley, 1987). In addition, validity has been suggested by studies demonstrating general correlations between the MBTI and predicted patterns of natural language (Seegmiller & Epperson, 1987), styles of handling conflict (Mills, Robey, & Smith, 1985), attendance at sociopolitical events (Greer, Ridley &

Roberts, 1984), attraction and maintenance of relationship patterns (Vinacke, Shannon, Palazzo, & Balsavage, 1988), and overall Minnesota Multiphasic Personality Inventory (MMPI) scores (Linton, Kuechenmeister, Kuechenmeister, & White, 1982). McCrae and Costa (1989) recently investigated the relationship of the various dimensions and found little evidence to support the hypothesized interactions derived from Jung's formulations. Instead, their data showed only main effects and thus suggest that the MBTI measures several independent dimensions.

The MBTI has, however, provided empirical support for the basic bipolar dimension of introversion–extraversion. For example, when compared to extraverts, introverts have been found to be more focused on specific problems during free conversation (Thorne, 1987), more likely to accept misleading information about an automobile accident (Ward & Loftus, 1985), and more likely to provide ongoing thought reports including words denoting internal processes or awareness (Davis & Johnson, 1983–1984). In addition, introverts were more common among physicians who relied on the information provided by diagnostic tests (Ornstein, Johnson, Markert, & Afrin, 1987). Introverts were less frequent among bipolar, mania, and drug abuse patients (Bisbee, Mullaly, & Osmond, 1983). Finally, Kreienkamp and Luessenheide (1985) found that pilot training was briefer and more efficient when flight instructors and their students were matched for MBTI introversion–extroversion scores. Contrary to the predictions of our model (Bonanno & Singer, 1990), no relationship has been found between introversion–extaversion and field dependence–independence (Lusk & Wright, 1983; Thomas, 1983). Field dependence–independence was measured, however, by the Embedded Figures Test. This estimate has been shown to be associated with IQ measures and is not a measure of style unless statistical removal of the intelligence element is carried out.

In summary, the extension of Jung's theory of attitude and function types into a complex matrix of 16 unique psychological types, as operationalized by the MBTI, has failed to generate the requisite empirical support. The MBTI has, however, demonstrated relationships between the basic dimension of introversion–extraversion and predicted behavioral and personality-related variables; as such, it indicates the validity of Jung's more global and theoretically appealing formulation. In keeping with our examination of the private personality, the introverted or internally directed pole of human experience, we next review recent attempts to assess inwardly directed self-focus or self-awareness by other questionnaire measures.

PUBLIC AND PRIVATE SELF-CONSCIOUSNESS

The notion of self-awareness as a psychological state characterized by attention directed inwardly toward the self became a topic of importance to experimental psychologists in the early 1970s. Duval and Wicklund (1972) developed a theoretical framework of self-awareness that spawned a host of creative manipulations, such as the use of mirrors or cameras, to induce self-awareness experimentally in the laboratory. The potential of this paradigm led Fenigstein et al. (1975) to operationalize the construct of self-awareness for a questionnaire measure as a trait-like aspect of personality, which they termed "self-consciousness." The factor-analytic methodology employed by Fenigstein et al. in the development of the Self–Consciousness Scale (SCS) resulted in the further dissection of self-consciousness into public and private aspects. The Private Self-Consciousness subscale consists of items suggesting a responsivity or direction of attention toward self-generated thoughts, feelings and fantasies, whereas the Public Self-Consciousness subscale consists of items suggesting a disposition toward the self as perceived by others (e.g., appearance, self-presentation style).

The SCS has produced a large and consistent body of literature with both related questionnaire measures and more critical performance manipulations. Using a technique borrowed from the earlier self-awareness literature, Carver and Scheier (1978) showed that participants responded to a sentence completion task with significantly more self-focused responses when they sat before a mirror. Additional analyses, however, indicated that the mirror manipulation only influenced those participants who were low scorers in Private Self-Consciousness. Participants scoring high in Private Self-Consciousness, who were presumably already self-focused, were virtually unaffected by the mirror use. Subsequent studies have associated high scorers on Private Self-Consciousness with less likelihood of being suggestible regarding assessment of their own internal state (Scheier, Carver, & Gibbons, 1979). Such persons also were characterized by greater concern with self-assessment following initial performance on intelligence-related measures, and, interestingly, by a more positive response from others following brief "get-acquainted" situations (Lloyd, Paulsen, & Brockner, 1983). Franzoi (1983) compared participants' self-evaluations on questionnaries with the evaluations that their close friends had made of them on the same measures, and found that individuals scoring high in Private Self-Consciousness evaluated themselves more consistently in comparison to their friends' ratings than did those scoring low in Private Self-Consciousness. Fenigstein (1984) found that high scorers in Public Self-Consciousness, on the other hand, showed a greater propensity to "overperceive" themselves as the target of a hypothetical social situation. Plant and Ryan (1985) also found Public Self-Consciousness to be associated with less intrinscially motivated behavior as measured in a laboratory setting.

Studies employing questionnaire measures have also produced evidence consistent with the notion of stable patterns of internal or external self-attention. Cheek and Briggs (1982) found that participants who scored high in Private Self-Consciousness exhibited a greater tendency to endorse items on a scale related to personal aspects of identity, such as feelings and emotions, whereas participants scoring high in Public Self-Consciousness endorsed items related to social identity, such as popularity and attractiveness to others. High Private Self-Consciousness scorers also reported themselves to be more self-disclosive (Franzoi & Davis, 1985; Franzoi, Davis, & Young, 1985).

A CONTINUUM OF SELF-AWARENESS

Elsewhere (Bonanno & Singer, 1990), we have outlined in greater detail the model displayed here as Figure 16.1 and emphasized another questionnaire-based personality dimension, repression–sensitization. We have proposed that repressors are typified by a focus away from inner experience, which may include defensive operations and an avoidant style of information

processing, whereas sensitizers show the opposite pattern and a possible overfocus on inner experience. A cursory glance at the literature on public versus private self-consciousness suggests an immediate compatibility with the repression–sensitization continuum. Yet public and private self-consciousness pertain not to public and private aspects of experience, but to different components of inner experience. In other words, public and private self-consciousness both lie at the inner-focused pole of the bipolar continuum, but describe different contents of inner experience. Wicklund, whose work on self-awareness was instrumental in the development of the SCS, has criticized the Public Self-Consciousness subscale of the SCS as not concerning the focus of attention at all, but rather as reflecting "social dependency" (Wicklund & Gollwitzer, 1987). Although this is too lengthy a debate to review here, what is important is that in defense of the Public Self-Consciousness scale, Fenigstein (1987) and Carver and Scheier (1987) explicitly define public self-consciousness not as a focus of attention away from the self, but instead as a reflection of "self-focused attention, bearing on the public aspects of oneself." Public and private self-consciousness are seen as "one process of self-focus, and two different domains of content illuminated by that process" (Carver & Scheier, 1987, p. 538).

A recent study by Nasby (1989) illustrates this point. He had participants study lists of trait adjectives by considering how accurately they described either a private or a public view of the self. They also rated the adjectives for private or public self-descriptiveness and then completed a recognition test that included distractor trait items not previously studied. The number of false alarms ("new" distractor items incorrectly identified as "old" on the recognition test) was predicted by the descriptiveness of the trait and the component of self-consciousness that matched the self-schema activated during the study phase. When participants studied the traits in relation to their private self-schemas (Experiment 1), distractor items that were high in private self-descriptiveness were more often incorrectly endorsed as "old" (i.e., assimilated to the private self-schema), and this effect was greater for participants high in private self-consciousness. Similarly, when trait adjectives were studied in relation to subjects' public self-schemas (Experiment 2), distractor items that were high in public self—descriptiveness were more often incorrectly endorsed as "old," and this effect was greater for participants high in public self-consciousness.

EXPERIMENTAL APPROACHES TO THOUGHT SAMPLING

As we have suggested, questionnaire approaches—whether measuring daydreaming patterns, vividness and control of imagery (Tower & Singer, 1980), introversion, or self-consciousness—assume that respondents can make reasonably accurate assessments of their accumulated frequencies of private experiences. As an alternative to questionnaire measures, many investigators have invested in the more labor-intensive approaches involving the correlation of actual daydream and fantasy reports with other self-report and questionnaire variables (Gold, Gold, Milner & Robertson, 1986–1987; Gold & Reilly, 1985; Starker & Jolin, 1982–1983, 1983–1984). Such practices heed Craik's (1986) call for a "methodological pluralism" in which multiple research paradigms are concurrently employed and evaluated in the investigation of any single personality issue. Craik encouraged the combined use of as many of the following methods as possible: field studies (which would include thought and daydream self-reports), projective techniques, observer judgments, biographical and archival analyses, self-characterizations via personality scales and inventories, and laboratory measurements of behavior in standardized conditions.

Andersen and her colleagues have provided a nice illustration of Craik's point by investigating the role of self-knowledge in the social inference process across several studies, using a combination of self-report questionnaires, ratings of private thoughts or feelings, recollections of reactions to specified situations, manipulations of the context of recollections as either privately rehearsed or publicly expressed, structured interviews, and ratings by hidden observers (Andersen, 1984; Andersen & Ross, 1984; Andersen & Williams, 1985). But more direct methods of thought sampling do exist and are probably still underrepresented as approaches to personality assessment. More extensive reviews of such approaches are available elsewhere; here, we only highlight the possibilities and theoretical relevance of sampling ongoing thoughts and affective reactions (Quattrone, 1985; Singer, 1978; Singer & Kolligian, 1987).

One approach that affords maximum "control" over extraneous stimulation (at the cost of some artificiality or possibly reduced "ecological validity") is the use of prolonged signal detection "watches" by participants seated in soundproof, reduced-stimulation booths. Since the amount of external stimulation can be controlled, it remains to be determined to what extent individuals will shift their attention away from processing external cues (by which they earn money for accurate signal detection) toward the processing of material that is generated by the presumably ongoing activity of their own brains. Can we ascertain the conditions under which participants, even with high motivation for external signal processing, will still show evidence that they are carrying on task-unrelated thoughts and imagery (TUITs)?

Thus, if while detecting auditory signals an individual is interrupted periodically (say, every 15 seconds) and questioned about whether any stimulus-independent thoughts occurred, a "yes" response is scored as a TUIT. If the participant and experimenter have agreed in advance on a common definition of what constitutes a task-irrelevant thought, the experimenter has at least some reasonable assurance that reports are more or less in keeping with the operational definition established. A thought such as "Is that tone louder than the one before it? It sounded like it was" is considered stimulus-dependent or task-relevant and elicits a "no" response, even though it is, of course, a thought. A response such as "I've got to remember about picking up the car keys for my Saturday night date" is scored as a TUIT. A thought about the experimenters in the next room ("Are they trying to drive me crazy?"), even though in some degree generated by the circumstances in which the subject finds himself or herself, is nevertheless scored as a TUIT because it is not directly relevant to the processing of the signals, which has been defined for the respondent as his or her main task. However, it may considered an *experiment-related* TUIT.

In this research paradigm, keeping the subjects in booths for a fairly lengthy time and obtaining reports of the occurrence of stimulus-independent thought after each 15 seconds of signal detection (with tones presented at rates of about one per second) have made it possible to build up rather extensive information on the frequency of occurrence of TUITs, as well as their relationship to the speed of signal presentation, the complexity of the task, and other characteristics of the subjects' psychological situation.

In addition to generalizations about the nature of cognitive processing (Singer, 1988), the signal detection model also permits the study of some degree of individual differences. Antrobus et al. (1967) were able to show that participants, already by self-report predisposed to be imaginative, were more likely as time went on to report stimulus-independent thoughts than individuals who had reported on a questionnaire that they were little given to daydreaming. The differences between the two groups increased over time, as did the number of errors. Initially, the high daydreamers reported a considerable number of TUITs, without differing in the level of errors from the low daydreamers. As time went on, however, there were indications that the high daydreamers seemed to be preferring to respond to stimulus-independent mentation; error rate increased significantly, compared with the relatively stable rate of errors for the subjects who showed relatively little stimulus-independent mentation.

Controlled studies of ongoing thought during signal detection watches afford a rich opportunity for estimating the determinants of the thought stream. We know that the introduction of unusual or alarming information prior to entry into the detection booth (overhearing a broadcast of war news) can increase the amount of stimulus-independent thought, even though accuracy of detections may not be greatly affected (Antrobus, Singer, & Greenberg, 1966). A series of studies directed by Mardi Horowitz (1978) has demonstrated that specific emotional experiences of an intense nature prior to engaging in signal detection lead to emergence of material in the form of stimulus-independent ideation when thought is sampled during the detection period. Such findings have suggested a basis for understanding clinical phenomena such as "unbidden images" (Horowitz 1978) or "peremptory ideation" (Klein, 1967). We can go even further with such a procedure and begin to develop a systematic conceptualization of the determinants of the stream of consciousness and their relationship to personality.

Some methods that sacrifice the rigid controls of the signal detection booth for greater ecological relevance have been increasingly employed in the development of an approach to determining the characteristics and determinants of waking conscious thought. These involve (1) asking participants to talk out loud over a period of time while in a controlled environment, and then scoring the verbalization along empirically or theoretically derived categories; (2) allowing the respondent to sit, recline, or stand quietly for a period of time and interrupting the person periodically for reports of thought or perceptual activity; or (3) requiring the person to signal by means of a button press whenever a new chain of thought begins, and then to report verbally in retrospect or to fill out a prepared rating form characterizing various possible features of ongoing thought.

Klinger (1977a, 1977b, 1978, 1981) has employed thought sampling in the forms described above to test a series of hypotheses about ongoing thought. He has made a useful distinction between "operant" and "respondent" thought processes. The former category includes thoughts that have a conscious instrumental property—the solution of a specific problem, analysis of a particular issue presently confronting one, examination of the implications of a specific situation in which one finds oneself at the moment. Operant thought is active and directed, and has the characteristics of what Freud called "secondary-process" thinking. As Klinger (1978) has noted, it is volitional; it is checked against new information concerning its effectiveness in moving toward a solution or the consequences of a particular attempted solution; and there are continuing efforts to protect such a line of thought from drifting off target or from being distracted either by external cues or by extraneous, irrelevant thought. Operant thought seems to involve a greater sense of mental and physical effort, and it probably has the property that the neurologist Head (1926) called "vigilance," Goldstein (1940) the "abstract attitude," and Pribram and McGuinness (1975) "effort"—a human capacity especially likely to suffer from massive frontal brain damage. Klinger's (1978) research involving thought-sampling methods has suggested that operant thought is correlated to some degree with external situation-related circumstances. It involves higher rates of self-reports about progress toward the goal of the thought sequence, as well as of efforts to resist drift and distraction.

Respondent thought, in Klinger's terminology, involves all other thought processes. These are nonvolitional in the sense of conscious direction of a sequence, and most are relatively noneffortful (Bowers, 1982–1983). Respondent processes include seemingly unbidden images (Horowitz, 1978) or peremptory thought (Klein, 1967); they are the mental distractions one becomes aware of when trying to sustain a sequence of operant thought (e.g., analyzing the logic of a scientific or legal argument) or simply trying to concentrate on writing checks to pay bills. Most of what we consider daydreams and fantasies (and, of course, nighttime dreams) are instances of respondent thought.

One can, of course, further classify ongoing thought as stimulus-dependent or stimulus-independent (Singer, 1966); thought identifiably relevant to external cues or to processing environmentally operated cues is, at least to some degree, stimulus-dependent. In a sample of 285 reports from a dozen subjects, Klinger (1978) reported a significant correlation between the environmental setting and reports of operant or directed thought, but a goodly percentage of the variance of both operant and respondent thought seemed independent of the physical or social milieu.

The use of thought sampling in a reasonably controlled environment also permits evaluation of a variety of conditions that may influence or characterize ongoing consciousness. One can score the participants' verbalizations on dimensions such as (1) organized, sequential versus degenerative, confused thought; (2) use of imagery, related episodes, or event memory material versus logical–semantic structures; (3) reference to current concerns and unfulfilled intentions; (4) reminiscence of past events versus orientation toward the future; and (5) realistic versus improbable content. A study by Pope (1978) demonstrated that longer sequences of thought with more remoteness from the participants' immediate circumstances were obtained when the respondents were reclining rather than walking freely and when they were alone rather than in an interpersonal situation. Zachary (1983) evaluated the relative role of positive and negative emotional experiences just prior to a thought-sampling period. He found that intensity of experience rather than its emotional nature and, to a lesser extent, the relative ambiguity versus clarity of the material, determined recurrence in the thought stream.

Studies reviewed by Klinger, Barta, and Maxeiner (1981) point to the relative importance of current concerns as determinants of the material that emerges in thought sampling. "Current concerns" are defined as "the state of an organism between the time one becomes committed to pursuing a particular goal and the time one either consummates the goal or abandons its objective and disengages from the goal" (Klinger et al., 1981, p. 162). Such concerns, as measured by a well-thought-out psychometric procedure, make up a useful operationalization of the Freudian wish in its early (prior to libido theory) form (Holt, 1976). They may range from unfulfilled intentions (e.g., to pick up a container of milk on the way home) to long-standing unresolved desires (e.g., to please a parent or to settle an old score with a parent or sibling). In estimating current concerns at a point in time prior to thought-sampling sessions, one obtains scale estimates of the valences of the goals, the relative importance of intentions in some value and temporal hierarchy, the person's perception of the reality of goal achievement, and so on. It seems clear that only after we have explored the range and influence of such current consciously unfulfilled intentions in a sampling of the individual's thoughts, emotions, and behavioral responses can we move to infer the influence of unconscious wishes or intentions.

The possibilities for controlled, hypothesis-testing uses of laboratory thought sampling are exemplified in a study of determinants of adolescents' ongoing thought following simulated parental confrontations (Klos & Singer, 1981). In this study, a hierarchy of experimental conditions was set up prior to a thought-sampling procedure that was expected to yield differential degrees of recurrence in the consciousness of the participants. It was proposed that even for beginning college students, parental involvements were likely to prove especially provocative of further thought. Klos and Singer chose to evaluate the relative role of (1) generally fulfilled versus unresolved situations (the old Zeigarnick effect; Lewin, 1935); (2) a mutual nonconflictual parental interaction; (3) a confrontation or conflict with a parent that involved, however, a collaborative stance by the adult; and (4) a comparable confrontation in which the parent's attitude was clearly coercive rather than collaborative. It was proposed that exposure (through a simulated interaction) to each of these conditions would yield differences in the later recurrence of simulation-relevant thoughts in the participants' consciousness.

The data provided clear support for the major hypotheses. The frequency of thoughts' recurrences occurred in the predicted order, with the effects clearly amplified by a history of longstanding interpersonal stress with a parent. The incompletion effect was a modest one, mainly in evidence in the nonconflictual situation. It was overriden to some degree by the increasing coerciveness of the imaginary conflict situations. Of special interest is the fact that, once exposed to a simulated parent conflict, young people with a history of stress reflected this brief, artificial incident in as many as 50% of their later thoughts. If we tentatively generalize from these results, the thought world of adolescents who have had long-standing parent difficulties may be a most unpleasant domain, since many conflictual chance encounters or even film or television plots may lead to a considerable degree of thought recurrence. The implications of a method of this kind (combined with estimates of personality variables or of other current concerns) for studying various groups (e.g., clinical patients, postsurgical patients, hypertensives, etc.) seem very intriguing.

THOUGHT-SAMPLING METHODS IN NATURAL SETTINGS

It is obvious that laboratory-based methods present some difficulties. Because of the artificiality of the situation—the controls on physical movement and restrictions on novel sensory input that are necessary for their effectiveness—laboratory methods may yield overestimations of naturally occurring fantasy and daydreaming. An approach to thought sampling that circumvents some of these problems calls for participants to carry signaling devices in pockets, in purses, or on pants belts as physicians do. These "beepers" go off at random during the ordinary activities of participants, and they at once fill out a special card that asks for reports of activity just prior to the signal, the environmental setting, their current thoughts, and their emotional state. Typically, these beepers are carried for a week and go off at 2-hour intervals on the average, permitting an accumulaton of about 50–60 reports per participant. Studies by Klinger (1978), Hurlburt (1979, 1980, 1990), and McDonald (1976), and a whole series directed by Csiks-

zentmihalyi (1982; Csikszentmihalyi & Graef, 1980; Csikszentmihalyi & Kubey, 1981; Csikszentmihalyi & Larson, 1984) all demonstrate the feasibility of this method, its potential for reliable results, and its suitability for hypothesis testing as well as for accumulation of normative data.

An example of this approach is found in a study where participants whose TAT results pointed to greater motivation for intimacy showed more interpersonal thoughts and more positive emotional responses in interpersonal situations than did low-intimacy-motive scorers, based on a week-long accumulation of eight daily reports (McAdams & Constantian, 1983). The relationship between accumulated daily reports about thought patterns and a self-report questionnaire, the IPI (Singer & Antrobus, 1972; see earlier discussion) was evaluated by Hurlburt (1980). He reported significant correlations between the retrospective questionnaire scales for frequent daydreaming, acceptance of daydreaming, and low distractibility, and the accumulated daily reports of daydreaming, based on 2 days of dozens of interruptions. The IPI scale of Sexual Daydreams was significantly correlated ($r = +.40$) with the accumulated record of sexual fantasies. Similarly, those persons who had higher Future-Oriented Daydreaming or the IPI were significantly more likely to be engaging in fantasies of the future ($r = +.39$) when interrupted by the electronic pager during the 2 days sampled.

Added to this collection are accumulated samples of ongoing thought garnered from clinical populations. These studies have provided some useful and often unexpected results (Hurlburt, 1990; Hurlburt & Melancon, 1987; Johnson & Larson, 1982; Margraf, Taylor, Ehlers, Roth, & Agras, 1987). Although validity and reliability data have supported this approach (Csikszentmihalyi & Larson, 1987), it remains to be seen whether scores based on such labor-intensive accumulations will yield data superior to those obtained via relatively simple questionnaire methods. Thought reports collected in laboratory settings, as a case in point, have been found to vary with different instructions regarding the intent of the experiment and the possible risks of self-disclosure (Bonanno, 1988–1989). Further reseach is needed, then, to elucidate the influences of situational constraints on naturalistic thought reports, independent of the variables under study.

THE PRIVATE PERSONALITY AS REFLECTED IN HYPNOTIC SUSCEPTIBILITY AND MEDITATIVE STATES

We have chosen to place our greatest emphasis on the private personality as reflected in ongoing normal waking thought, because we believe that such processes must form a normative baseline for the more "glamorous" phenomena such as hypnosis, the various meditative states, or the parameters of nocturnal dreaming and sleep mentation. Let us now turn to some other lines of research that exemplify the "deeper" levels reflected in Fromm's categorization of states of consciousness as shown in Figure 16.2 above.

The phenomenon of hypnosis is far too extensive in its implications and in the research literature exploring its physiological, clinical, and cognitive implications to permit a thorough review here. Of particular relevance for the private personality are two facets of the research literature: (1) the use of hypnotic states or approximations thereof (Barber, 1981; Lynn & Rhue, 1988; Wilson & Barber, 1978, 1983) to study processes of imagery and fantasy; and (2) the question of hypnotic susceptibility as a special personality trait that may have significant implications for private experience.

There is a persisting controversy as to whether the phenomenon of hypnosis is indeed a unique state of consciousness with special properties that can be delineated from other waking states where individuals voluntarily engage in behaviors or thought patterns reflecting great suggestibility or intense absorption (Barber, 1981; Fromm & Shorr, 1979; Sarbin & Coe, 1972; Spanos, 1982). The question of whether the hypnotic situation is better interpreted in terms of social-psychological role playing or of an unconscious dissociated state goes beyond the scope of this chapter. What is relevant is that hypnosis is generally accepted as an extreme example of those states of intense absorption in either private thought, reading, movie watching, or reminiscence that we can all identify as occurring with more or less regular frequency in our ordinary waking lives. Under such conditions we may also engage in relatively automatic processes of a goal-directed nature with little conscious attention to them, much as a hypnotic subject, seemingly asleep, still carries out motor acts suggested by the hypnotist. Dissociations of this type are easily

recognizable by scientists, scholars, and artists who can resonate to the many occasions when, absorbed in reading or thought, they continued to walk or drive long distances or, indeed, even to simulate interest in some social situation. In this sense one might hypothesize that persons especially susceptible to absorption in private processes may prove to be good hypnotic subjects. A factor as yet relatively unstudied, however, is that introverts may also, in the interest of their autonomy, resist the submissiveness implicit in the hypnotist–subject relationship and use their own capacity for self-absorption to resist the instructions. With the widespread application of hypnosis for research introduced by Ernest Hilgard (1965), participants have increasingly come to see the hypnotic performance in a more positive light, and we may soon see the term "hypnotic susceptibility" replaced by "hypnotic capability."

The findings of Josephine Hilgard (1979) have opened a stimulating path to the linking of hypnosis to individual differences in private experience. She found evidence that hypnotically susceptible respondents were more likely to have been daydreamers in childhood and to become absorbed in reading or movie viewing. Results on a questionnaire developed by Tellegen and Atkinson (1974) that measures susceptibility to absorption have been shown to correlate consistently with hypnotic susceptibility as well as with daydreaming (Barrios & Singer, 1981–1982; Crawford, 1982). Wilson and Barber (1978, 1983), employing a form of a waking imagery scale that followed the form of the standard hypnotic susceptibility measures without reference to "sleep," were able to identify individuals whom they termed "fantasy-prone" personalities. Lynn and Rhue (1988) screened 6,000 college students to produce five samples of 156 fantasy-prone subjects and then looked at differences on various dimensions between those with extremely high and extremely low scores on fantasy proneness. In general, the fantasizers differed from the low scorers in hypnotizability, waking-imagery-induced suggestibility, absorption, vividness of imagery, and creativity. Although there were some suggestions that some of the fantasy-prone subjects were likely to have histories of child abuse and to score higher on some MMPI scales of psychopathology, the fantasizers on the whole seemed to fall within normal limits on most measures. Hypnotizable respondents not measured for fantasy proneness did show a much greater tendency to report early child-hood abuse (Nash & Lynn, 1985–1986), but much more extensive work not relying solely on retrospective self-report is necessary to clar-ify this result. If fantasy proneness is a viable dimension we need more studies linking the measure used by Nash and Lynn to measures of the other constructs cited in this chapter, such as introversion, daydreaming styles, and self-consciousness, all of which have broader corre-lates.

If hypnotizability alone is viewed as a sepa-rate trait one can identify a considerable num-ber of studies reporting interesting performance differences within situations occurring during and after hypnosis, or with tasks that are closely similar to hypnosis. For example, a series of studies by Spanos and colleagues (see Spanos, Bridgman, Hendrikus, Gwynn, & Saad, 1982–1983) suggests that the phenomena reported in hypnosis may be more determined by social demand characteristics than by the establish-ment of a separate brain state, of the type proposed by investigors such as Raikov (1983–1984). That hypnotic susceptibility has trait-like properties is suggested by other studies, whether or not the hypnotic performance is attributed to a special state or simply to an intense form of social role taking that may characerize highly susceptible individuals (Gorassini, Hooper, & Kitching, 1987–1988; Kunzendorf & Benoit, 1985–1986; Spanos, Ollerhead, & Gwynn, 1985–1986; Spanos & Radtke, 1981–1982).

An intriguing theory proposed by Kunzen-dorf (1985–1986a, 1985–1986b) may link the issue of hypnosis back to the properties of ongo-ing waking consciousness and to the issue of the repressive style we have already discussed. Kun-zendorf proposes that a major characteristic of waking consciousness (and a function we sug-gest is better developed in persons who put greater emphasis on self-awareness) is that of carefully distinguishing externally generated perceptions from the images generated from long-term memory. This "monitoring" of per-ceptions and images in waking consciousness contrasts with the behavior of hypnotic sub-jects, who, as part of their trance state or absorbed role playing, eschew such activity and are thus more susceptible to at least some hallu-cination-like responses. Dreaming is presum-ably a state in which this monitoring function is drastically reduced, although not completely absent as lucid dreaming data suggest (Gacken-

bach, 1985–1986). Kunzendorf further pro-poses that repressors are characterized by assigning higher priorities to monitoring imag-ery than to monitoring percepts, and presum-ably by trying to avoid these images. Thus, in a study using hypnosis, Kunzendorf found that hypnotized repressors showed heightened imag-ery, whereas sensitizers showed no effect of the suggestions on imagery. This contrasted with their performance in the waking state, where represors showed much less vividness in imag-ery than did sensitizers (Kunzendorf, 1985–1986a, 1985–1986b). Kunzendorf, Brown, and McGee (1983) have also reported correla-tions between daydreaming, sleep time, and hypnotizability. Thus, higher hypnotizability was associated with fewer hours of sleep and more likelihood of daydreaming during the day. Daydreaming frequency was negatively corre-lated ($r = -.53$, $p < .001$) with hours of sleep.

In summary, a private personality character-ized by greater emphasis on one's own thoughts and fantasies, and by absorption in personal thought or its vicarious form in reading, may make one more capable of participating in the contract between hypnotist and subject or even in self-hypnosis (Singer & Pope, 1981). Whether introversion may also make it possible to resist hypnosis if one's attitude is negative to the process remains to be tested. Considerably more research is needed yet to bring fantasy proneness, absorption, Kunzendorf's percep-tion and imagery monitoring, private self-consciousness, daydreaming, and hypnotic capability into some more systematic relation-ship.

Following the general outlines of Fromm's ordering of states of consciousness we may touch briefly on meditative states. In contrast to the other features of private experience we have reviewed or to dreaming, meditative states are usually attained through instructed special practice leading to a defined skill. Even hypnosis, although usually a voluntary con-tractual occurrence, is on a natural continuum (as we have suggested), with states accessible to all persons at various times in their lives, such as intense absorption in thought or in reading or film watching. Meditation, by contrast, is a learned skill that requires months or years of practice and is often closely tied to particular bodies of religious lore (Goleman, 1977). The best available empirical research has focused primarily on the development of measurement tools (self-report questionnaires of varying degrees of psychometric sophistication) that can assist in delineating the variations in private experience that characterize different forms of meditation. Daniel Brown and various collaborators have developed questionnaires that can differentiate among self-hypnotic, imagery, and meditative experiences or between novices and experienced meditators (Brown, Forte, Rich, & Epstein, 1982–1983; Forte, Brown, & Dysart, 1987–1988). Pekala and Levine (1982–1983) have devised a Phenomenology of Consciousness questionnaire, which has shown considerable stability in reports of various meditation-like states across time and which has implications for uses comparable to the Profile of Trance, Imaging and Meditation Experience (TIME) developed by Brown's group.

The availability of reasonably reliable instruments opens the way for future research on the relations between such measures of variations in conscious experience, including meditative states, and measures of introversion, self-consciousness, reality monitoring, daydreaming styles, or hypnotic susceptibility. Intriguing possibilities for study beckon. Are introverts, individuals high in private self-consciousness, and certain types of daydreamers more likely to be adept at acquiring meditative skills? And what types of meditation—Zen Buddhist, Hindu Yogic, Tibetan, or Burmese—would be attractive to various personalities?

DREAMING

Space limitations preclude any examination of those features of conscious experience specifically attributable to drug use, alcohol inebriation, or toxic effects of disease such as delirium. We turn, finally, just briefly to a consideration of the phenomenon of sleep mentation or dreaming. Dreams are so private and personal, so filled with the seeming novelty of travel to far-off realms, encounters with long-dead or faraway relatives and friends, and narrow escapes from strangers or monsters, that they not only seem the epitomes of privacy but often take on a sense of mysterious religiosity.

A review of the vast literature on dreams is beyond the scope of this chapter (or volume). Sophisticated accounts of the current state of theory and research on the relation of dreaming to the sleep stages are widely available and need not be reviewed here (Arkin, Antrobus, &

Ellman, 1978; Cohen, 1979; Globus, 1987; Hobson, 1988; Hunt, 1989).

Of special relevance to our discussion of the private personality is the generally consistent finding that night dreams—although perhaps more strikingly visual, usually believed in as "real" while they are ongoing, and often more bizarre or apparently metaphoric or symbolic—are generally found to be continuous with the waking thought styles and daydream content of normal persons (Antrobus, 1978; Breger, Hunter, & Lane, 1971; Cohen, 1979; Starker, 1974). Cohen (1979) has reviewed his own and others' studies of dream reports in the sleep laboratory, which indicate how presleep ratings of self-confidence and personality styles of repression or sensitization interact to produce very different patterns of dream content, affect, and structure. Singer and Schonbar (1961) found that persons showing more self-awareness and daydreaming also seemed to recall more dreams, as evidenced from a collection of daily dream logs.

Perhaps the most sophisticated current theory of the continuity between daytime thought and nocturnal dreaming has been proposed by Antrobus (1986). The psychoanalytic model of Freud and the much more recent neurochemical–physiological and cognitive model of Hobson and McCarley (1977) both assume that dreaming occurs when one's cognitive system is fundamentally changed from its normal waking state. "Since none of the models is explicit about how this system produce[s] thought and imagery in the waking state, the models are less than clear concerning how the waking system is altered to produce sleep mentation such as dreaming" (Antrobus, 1986, p. 193). What Antrobus proposes is that one must first describe normal waking thought, consider daydreaming and wandering of the mind as baseline phenomena of human experience, and then consider what neurocognitive events are necessary to produce dreamlike thought.

By reviewing relevant studies of sleep and wakefulness, Antrobus proposes that two processes—cortical activation and heightened sensory threshold—are sufficient to modify both waking and sleeping thought. The so-called Stage 1 phase of the electroencephalographic sleep cycle, where longer and often more "dreamlike" or bizarre reports are obtained upon awakenings in the laboratory, is characterized by a stage of high activation but also by a high threshold for awareness of externally generated sensory phenomena. The high activation leads to brain activity characterized by searches of material from long-term memory, since little competing external stimulation can penetrate the high sensory threshold. This accounts for the interesting story-like quality or the lengthy content properties of dreams, *and* for their believability (since no external stimuli need be processed). But, as Antrobus shows, similar conditions often prevail in the waking state. And, indeed, his data suggest that when thought reports are obtained under conditions of wakefulness (high activation) but also of reduced sensory stimulation, these reports are rated as "dreams" by outside judges. Such thought reports are often even rated as more dreamlike than Stage 2 sleep and even some Stage 1-REM reports. Thus, night dreams turn out to be largely indistinguishable from the waking thoughts we experience when we let our minds wander in understimulated conditions, or even in the informationally overfamiliar environments common enough during a normal day.

This type of analysis suggests that our dreams may well be relatively similar to the free-ranging daydreams that many people experience throughtout the day but that (because external events interfere, or because people have no reason to rehearse such thoughts or to label the process) are often forgotten. Thought sampling or studies of presleep or sleep onset thought point to the great frequency of such dreamlike experiences, once attention is paid to the process (Foulkes & Vogel, 1965; Singer, 1966). We also remember as a rule only one dream a night, usually the one associated with awakening in the morning. The remembered dream seems more vivid because there has been less interference from processing external stimuli during the night. It is a figural experience against a dark background, in contrast with waking fantasies, which often are more like a ground against a figure of directed thoughts or externally derived information processing. Nor are nocturnal dreams so much more bizarre or creative on the whole than waking thought, as Cohen's (1979) analyses have shown. Rather, sleep mentation as collected from laboratory reports of awakenings during various sleep stages is relatively mundane—full of relatively practical issues, immediate family concerns, and the like. Repressors do show more present-related content, while sensitizers' content

roams more freely across time dimensions, but on the whole it cannot be shown that laboratory-derived dream reports are as glamorous as the clinical literature suggests (Cohen, 1979). Is this a constraint imposed by the laboratory setting? Without much more extensive studies of individual patients' dreams before, during, and after a laboratory sleep period, we cannot be sure whether demand characteristics are at work.

What of the determinants of dream content? Despite Freud's original emphasis on the content as a disguised attempted wish fulfillment (and, later, more specifically, a childhood sexual or aggressive wish), the most recent theories posed by investigators working from a research-derived framework are inclined to put more emphasis on day residues, current concerns, unfulfilled intentions, and general unfinished business (Antrobus, 1978; Breger et al., 1971; Cohen, 1979; Hoelscher, Klinger, & Barta, 1981; Hunt, 1989; Klinger, 1978; Singer, 1984, 1988). Singer (1988) has elsewhere proposed that many of the images, symbols, and metaphors that characterize our more interesting dreams can be detected in advance of the dream in waking thought samples collected during the prior few days from the dreamer. Supportive data are as yet available only from some individual cases. A study employing a larger sample and using multiple-regression analysis of thought content and of the structure of waking daydreams to predict the images and content of subsequent night dreams is planned to address this proposal.

This brief summary cannot do justice to the complex and intriguing process of dreams as perhaps among the most precious "possessions" of our private personality. The sharing of one's dreams may represent a special cultural ritual, an act of intimacy with a lover or friend, a determination to obtain help by exposing one's dreams to a psychoanalyst, or a special act of scientific courage, as Freud showed in his classic book. With the heightened knowledge we have of the concurrent psychophysiology of sleep mentation, we can begin to look more deeply into the special properties of the waking states as well, and at continuities for individuals and groups across times and situation. We need much more research on personality variables as they intersect with both waking and nocturnal dream content. It is clear from some studies that variables such as psychological-mindedness, daydreaming styles, repressor styles, Rorschach measures of fantasy prone-ness, and other estimates of inner experience correlate with frequency of recall, dream content and structural qualities, the effects of deprivation of sleep, and Stage 1-REM cycles (Cartwright, 1977; Cohen, 1979; Hoyt & Singer, 1978). But most studies are cross-sectional and rely on single variables, or, at best, one mediating variable. The way remains open for much greater exploration of this key sphere of the private personality.

We have begun this chapter by talking of the secrecy and privacy of experiences such as thoughts, fantasies, and dreams. Our review, however, points to the emergence of an array of methods by which scientific research can be carried out to explore these seemingly ephemeral or hidden facets of the human personality. Although theory may not yet be fully developed, we can go on in the future with an exploration of the phenomena of ongoing consciousness. As laboratory, questionnaire, and naturalistic data accumulate, we can expect the development of more sophisticated theoretical models to follow.

NOTES

1. Because Eysenck's extensive research on introversion involves a scale that seems to emphasize more the elements of social withdrawal, we do not deal with that body of literature in this chapter, as it is unclear what relevance it bears to private experience.

2. As indicated earlier, the very extensive literature on introversion–extraversion generated by Eysenck (1981) focuses on the correlates of the Eysenck Personality Inventory, in which introversion has a special meaning relating to social withdrawal and physiological inhibition. That valuable work is beyond the scope of the present chapter.

REFERENCES

Andersen, S. M. (1984). Self-knowledge and social inference: II, The diagnosticity of cognitive/affective and behavioral data. *Journal of Personality and Social Psychology, 46,* 294–307.

Andersen, S. M., & Ross, L. (1984). Self-knowledge and social inference: I. The impact of cognitive/affective and behavioral data. *Journal of Personality and Social Psychology, 46,* 280–293.

Andersen, S. M., & Williams, M. (1985). Cognitive/affective reactions in the improvement of self-esteem: When thoughts and feelings make a difference. *Journal of Personality and Social Psychology, 49,* 1086–1097.

Angyal, A. (1965). *Neurosis and treatment: A holistic theory.* New York: Wiley.

Antrobus, J. S. (1978). Dreaming for cognition. In A. M. Arkin, J. S. Antrobus, & S. Ellman (Eds.), *The mind in sleep* (pp. 569–581). Hillsdale, NJ: Erlbaum.

Antrobus, J. S. (1986). Dreaming: Cortical activation and perceptual thresholds. *Journal of Mind and Behavior, 7,* 63–82.

Antrobus, J. S., Coleman, R., & Singer, J. L. (1967). Signal detection performance by subjects differing in predisposition to daydreaming. *Journal of Consulting Psychology, 31,* 487–491.

Antrobus, J. S., Singer, J. L., & Greenberg, S. (1966). Studies in the stream of consciousness: Experimental enhancement and suppression of spontaneous cognitive processes. *Perceptual and Motor Skills, 23,* 399–417.

Arkin, A. M., Antrobus, J. S., & Ellman, S. M. (Eds.). (1978). *The mind in sleep.* Hillsdale, NJ: Erlbaum.

Baars, B. J. (1986–1987). What is a theory of consciousness a theory of? The search for critical constraints on theory. *Imagination, Cognition and Personality, 6,* 3–24.

Bakan, D. (1966). *The duality of human existence.* Chicago: Rand McNally.

Barber, T. X. (1981). *Hypnosis: A scientific approach.* South Orange, NJ: Power.

Barrios, M., & Singer, J. L. (1981–1982). The treatment of creative blocks: A comparison of waking, imagery, hypnotic dream and rational discussion techniques. *Imagination, Cognition and Personality, 1,* 89–116.

Bem, S. L. (1974). The measurement of psychological androgyny. *Journal of Consulting and Clinical Psychology, 42,* 155–162.

Bisbee, C., Mullaly, R. W., & Osmond, H. (1983). Temperament and psychiatric illness. *Journal of Orthomolecular Psychiatry, 12,* 19–25.

Blatt, S. (1990). Interpersonal relatedness and self definition: Two personality configurations and their implications for psychopathology and psychotherapy. In J. L. Singer (Ed.), *Repression and dissociation.* Chicago: University of Chicago Press.

Blatt, S. J., Quinlan, D. M., Chevron, E. S., McDonald, C., & Zuroff, D. (1982). Dependency and self-criticism: Psychological dimensions of depression. *Journal of Consulting and Clinical Psychology, 50,* 113–124.

Blatt, S. J., & Schichman, S. (1983). Two primary configurations of psychopathology. *Psychoanalysis and Contemporary Thought, 6,* 127–158.

Bonanno, G. A. (1988–1989). Sampling conscious thought: Influence of repression-sensitization and reporting conditions. *Imagination, Cognition and Personality, 8,* 293–306.

Bonanno, G. A. (1990). Remembering and psychotherapy. *Psychotherapy: Theory, Research, Practice, Training, 27,* 2.

Bonanno, G. A., & Singer, J. L. (1990). Repressive personality style. Theoretical and methodological implications for health and pathology. In J. L. Singer

(Ed.), *Repression and dissociation.* Chicago: University of Chicago Press.

Bowers, P. B. (1982–1983). On *not* trying so hard: Effortless experiencing and its correlates. *Imagination, Cognition and Personality, 2,* 3–14.

Breger, L., Hunter, I., & Lane, R. (1971). *The effect of stress on dreams.* New York: International Universities Press.

Briggs-Myers, I. B., & Myers, P. B. (1980). *Gifts differing,* Palo Alto, CA: Consulting Psychologists Press.

Brown, D. P., Forte, M., Rich, P., & Epstein, G. (1982–1983). Phenomenological differences among self-hypnosis, mindfulness meditation, and imaging. *Imagination, Cognition and Personality, 2,* 291–309.

Campagna, A. F. (1985–1986). Fantasy and sexual arousal in college men: Normative and functional aspects. *Imagination, Cognition, and Personality, 5,* 3–20.

Cartwright, R. D. (1977). *Night life.* Englewood Cliffs, NJ: Prentice-Hall.

Cartwright, R. D. (1981). The contribution of research on memory and dreaming to a twenty-four-hour model of cognitive behavior. In W. Fishbein (Ed.), *Sleep, dreams, and memory.* New York: SP Medical and Scientific Books.

Carver, C. S., & Scheier, M. F. (1978). Self-focusing effects of dispositional self-consciousness, mirror presence, and audience presence. *Journal of Personality and Social Psychology, 36,* 324–332.

Carver, C. S., & Scheier, M. F. (1987). The blind man and the elephant: Examination of the public–private literature gives rise to a faulty perception. *Journal of Personality, 55,* 525–541.

Cheek, J. M., & Briggs, S. R. (1982). Self-consciousness and aspects of identity. *Journal of Research in Personality, 16,* 401–408.

Cohen, D. B. (1979). *Sleep and dreaming: Origins, nature and functions.* New York: Pergamon Press.

Craik, K. H. (1986). Personality research methods: An historical perspective. *Journal of Personality, 54,* 18–51.

Crawford, H. J. (1982). Hypnotizability, daydreaming styles, imagery vividness and absorption: A multidimensional study, *Journal of Personality and Social Psychology, 42,* 915–926.

Csikszentmihalyi, M. (1982). Toward a psychology of optimal experience. In L. Wheeler (Ed.), *Review of personality and social psychology* (Vol. 3). Beverly Hills, CA: Sage.

Csikszentmihalyi, M., & Graef, R. (1980). The experience of freedom in daily life. *American Journal of Community Psychology, 8,* 401–414.

Csikszentmihalyi, M., & Kubey, R. (1981). Television and the rest of life: A systematic comparison of subjective experience. *Public Opinion Quarterly, 45,* 317–328.

Csikszentmihalyi, M., & Larson, R. (1984). *Being adolescent.* New York: Basic Books.

Csikszentmihalyi, M., & Larson, R. (1987). Validity and reliability of the experience-sampling method. *Journal of Nervous and Mental Disease, 175,* 526–536.

Davis, L. T., & Johnson, P. J. (1983–1984). An assessment of conscious content as related to introversion–extroversion. *Imagination, Cognition and Personality, 3,* 149–165.

Dember, W. (1974). Motivation and the cognitive revolution. *American Psychologist, 29,* 161–168.

Duval, S., & Wicklund, R. A. (1972). *A theory of objective self-awareness.* New York: Academic Press.

Eysenck, H. J. (Ed.). (1981). *A model for personality.* New York: Springer.

Feldstein, S. (1972). *REM deprivation: The effects on inkblot perception and fantasy processes.* Unpublished doctoral dissertation, City University of New York.

Fenigstein, A. (1984). Self-consciousness and the overperception of self as a target. *Journal of Personality and Social Psychology, 47,* 860–870.

Fenigstein, A. (1987). On the nature of public and private self-consciousness. *Journal of Personality, 55,* 543–554.

Fenigstein, A., Scheier, M. F., & Buss, A. H. (1975). Public and private self-consciousness: Assessment and theory. *Journal of Consulting and Clinical Psychology, 43,* 522–527.

Forte, M., Brown, D., & Dysart, M. (1987–1988). Differences in experience among mindfulness mediators. *Imagination, Cognition and Personality, 7,* 47–60.

Foulkes, D., & Vogel, G. (1965). Mental activity at sleep onset. *Journal of Abnormal and Social Psychology, 70,* 231–243.

Franzoi, S. L. (1983). Self-concept differences as a function of private self-consciousness and social anxiety. *Journal of Research in Personality, 17,* 275–287.

Franzoi, S. L., & Davis, M. H. (1985). Adolescent self-disclosure and loneliness: Private self-consciousness and parental influences. *Journal of Personality and Social Psychology, 48,* 768–780.

Franzoi, S. L., Davis, M. H., & Young, R. D. (1985). The effects of private self-consciousness and perspective taking on satisfaction in close relationships. *Journal of Personality and Social Psychology, 48,* 1584–1594.

Fromm, E. (1978–1979). Primary and secondary process in waking and in altered states of consciousness. *Journal of Altered States of Consciousness, 4,* 115–128.

Fromm, E. (1979). The nature of hypnosis and other altered states of consciousness: An ego psychological theory. In E. Fromm & R. E. Shor (Eds.), *Hypnosis: Developments in research and new perspectives* (2nd ed., pp. 81–103). Chicago: Aldine.

Fromm, E., & Shorr, R. E. (Eds.). (1979). *Hypnosis: Developments in research and new perspectives* (2nd ed.). Chicago: Aldine.

Fusella, V. (1972). *Blocking of an external signal through self-projected imagery: The role of inner acceptance, personality style, and categories of imagery.* Unpublished doctoral dissertation, City University of New York.

Gackenbach, J. I. (1985–1986). A survey of considerations for inducing conscious awareness of dreaming while dreaming. *Imagination, Cognition and Personality, 5,* 41–56.

Greer, C., Ridley, S. E., & Roberts, A. (1984). Jungian personality types as a predictor of attendance at a Black College Day march. *Psychological Reports, 54,* 887–890.

Giambra, L. M. (1974). Daydreaming across the life span: Late adolescent to senior citizen. *International Journal of Aging and Human Development, 5,* 115–140.

Giambra, L. M. (1977a). Adult male daydreaming across the life span: A replication, further analyses, and tentative norms based upon retrospective reports. *International Journal of Aging and Human Development, 8,* 197–228.

Giambra, L. M. (1977b). Daydreaming about the past: The time setting of spontaneous thought intrusions. *The Gerontologist, 17*(a), 35–38.

Giambra, L. M., & Traynor, T. D. (1977). Depression and

daydreaming: An analysis based on self-ratings. *Journal of Clinical Psychology, 34,* 14–25.

Globus, G. (1987). *Dream life, wake life.* Albany: State University of New York Press.

Gold, S. P., Gold, R. G., Milner, J. S., & Robertson, K. R. (1986–1987), Daydreaming and mental health. *Imagination, Cognition and Personality, 6,* 67–74.

Gold, S. R., & Reilly, J. P., III. (1985). Daydreaming, current concerns and personality. *Imagination, Cognition, and Personality, 5,* 117–125.

Golding, J. M., & Singer, J. L. (1983). Patterns of inner experience: Daydreaming styles, depressive moods, and sex roles. *Journal of Personality and Social Psychology, 45,* 663–675.

Goldstein, K. (1940). *Human nature in the light of psychopathology.* Cambridge, MA: Harvard University Press.

Goleman, D. (197). *The varieties of meditative experience.* New York: Dutton.

Gorassini, D. R., Hooper, C. L., & Kitching, K. J. (1987–1988). The active participation of highly susceptible hypnotic subjects in generating their hypnotic experiences. *Imagination, Cognition and Personality, 7,* 215–226.

Hariton, E. B., & Singer, J. L. (1974). Women's fantasies during sexual intercourse: Normative and theoretical implications. *Journal of Consulting and Clinical Psychology, 42,* 313–322.

Head, H. (1926). *Aphasia and kindred disorders of speech* (2 vols.). Cambridge, England: Cambridge University Press.

Heider, F. (1958). *The psychology of interpersonal relations.* New York: Wiley.

Hilgard, E. R. (1965). *Hypnotic susceptibility.* New York: Harcourt Brace Jovanovich.

Hilgard, J. R. (1979). Imaginative and sensory–affective involvements in everyday life and in hypnosis. In E. Fromm & R. E. Short (Eds.), *Hypnosis: Developments in research and new perspectives* (2nd ed.). Chicago: Aldine.

Hobson, J. A. (1988). *The dreaming brain.* New York: Basic Books.

Hobson, J. A., & McCarley, R. W. (1977). The brain as a dream state generator: An activation–synthesis hypothesis of the dream process. *American Journal of Psychiatry, 134,* 1335–1348.

Hoelscher, T., Klinger, E., & Barta, S. G. (1981). Incorporation of concern and nonconcern-related verbal stimuli into dream content. *Journal of Abnormal Psychology, 90,* 88–91.

Holt, R. R. (1976). Drive or wish? A reconsideration of the psychoanalytic theory of motivation. In M. M. Gill & P. S. Holzman (Eds.), Psychology versus metapsychology: Psychoanalytic essays in memory of George S. Klein. *Psychological Issues, 9*(4), Monograph No. 36).

Horowitz, M. (1978). *Image formation and cognition* (2nd ed.). New York: Appleton-Century-Crofts.

Hoyt, M., & Singer, J. L. (1978). Psychological effects of REM ("dream") deprivation upon waking mentation. In A. M. Arkin, J. S. Antrobus, & S. Ellman (Eds.), *The mind in sleep* (pp. 459–486). Hillsdale, NJ: Erlbaum.

Huba, G. J., Segal, B., & Singer, J. L. (1977). The consistency of daydreaming styles across samples of college male and female drug and alcohol users. *Journal of Abnormal Psychology, 86,* 99–102.

Huba, G. J., Singer, J. L., Aneschensel, C. S., & Antrobus, J. S. (1982). *The short imaginal processes inventory.* Port Huron, MI: Research Psychologists Press.

Huba, G. J., & Tanaka, J. S. (1983–1984). Confirmatory evidence for three daydreaming factors in the Short Imaginal Processes Inventory. *Imagination, Cognition and Personality, 3,* 139–148.

Hunt, H. T. (1989). *The multipicity of dreams.* New Haven, CT: Yale University Press.

Hunt, J. M. (1965). Intrinsic motivation and its role in psychological development. In D. Levine (Ed.), *Nebraska Symposium on Motivation* (Vol. 13). Lincoln: University of Nebraska Press.

Hurlburt, R. T. (1979). Random sampling of cognitions and behavior. *Journal of Research in Personality, 13,* 103–111.

Hurlburt, R. T. (1980). Validation and correlation of thought sampling with retrospective measures. *Cognitive Therapy and Research, 4,* 235–238.

Hurlburt, R. T. (1990). *Sampling normal and schizophrenic inner experience.* New York: Plenum.

Hurlburt, R. T., & Melancon, S. M. (1987). Single case study. "Goofed-up" images: Thought-sampling with a schizophrenic woman. *Journal of Nervous and Mental Disease, 175,* 575–578.

Isaacs, D. (1975). *Cognitive styles in daydreaming.* Unpublished doctoral dissertation, City University of New York.

James, W. (1952). *The principles of psychology* (2 vols.). New York: Dover. (Original work published 1890)

Jensen, M. R. (1987). Psychological factors in the prognosis and treatment of neoplastic disorders. *Journal of Personality, 55,* 317–342.

Johnson, C., & Larson, R. (1982). Bulimia: An analysis of mood and behavior. *Psychosomatic Medicine, 44,* 341–351.

Jung, C. G. (1971). *Psychological types* (H. G. Baynes, Trans.: revised by R. F. C. Hull). Princeton, NJ: Princeton University Press. (Original work published 1921)

Kihlstrom, J. F. (1987). The cognitive unconscious. *Science, 237,* 1445–1452.

Klein, G. S. (1967). Peremptory ideation: Structure and force in motivated ideas. In R. R. Holt (Ed.), Motives and thought: Psychoanalytic essays in honor of David Rapaport. *Psychological Issues, 5*(2–3, Monograph No. 18/19).

Klinger, E. (1971). *The structure and functions of fantasy.* New York: Wiley.

Klinger, E. (1977a). The nature of fantasy and its clinical uses. *Psychotherapy: Theory, Research, and Practice, 14,* 223–231.

Klinger, E. (1977b). *Meaning and void: Inner experience and the incentives in people's lives.* Minneapolis: University of Minnesota Press.

Klinger, E. (1978). Modes of normal conscious flow. In K. S. Pope & J. L. Singer (Eds.), *The stream of consciousness.* New York: Plenum.

Klinger, E. (1981). The central place of imagery in human functioning. In E. Klinger (Ed.), *Imagery: Vol. 2. Concepts, results and applications* (pp. 187–225). New York: Plenum.

Klinger, E., Barta, S., & Maxeiner, M. (1981). Current concerns: Assessing therapeutically relevant motivation. In P. Kendall & S. Hollon (Eds.), *Assessment strategies for cognitive–behavioral interventions.* New York: Academic Press.

Klos, D. S., & Singer, J. L. (1981). Determinants of the adolescent's ongoing thought following simulated parental confrontations. *Journal of Personality and Social Psychology, 41,* 975–87.

Kohut, H. (1984). *How does analysis cure?* Chicago: University of Chicago Press.

Kreienkamp, R. A., & Luessenheide, H. D. (1985). Similarity of personalities of flight instructors and student pilots: Effect of flight training time. *Psychological Reports, 57,* 465–466.

Kreitler, H., & Kreitler, S. (1976). *Cognitive orientation and behavior.* New York: Springer.

Kreitler, S., & Kreitler, H. (1990). *The cognitive foundations of personality traits.* New York: Plenum.

Kubey, R. (1982). *Recuperative leisure and the psychic economy: The case of television.* Unpublished doctoral dissertation, University of Chicago.

Kunzendorf, R. G. (1985–1986a). Hypnotic hallucinations as "unmonitored" images: An empirical study. *Imagination, Cognition and Personality, 5,* 255–270.

Kunzendorf, R. G. (1985–1986b). Repression as the monitoring and censoring of images: An empirical study. *Imagination, Cognition and Personality, 5,* 31–40.

Kunzendorf, R. G., & Benoit, M. (1985–1986). Spontaneous post-hypnotic amnesia and spontaneous rehypnotic recovery in repressors. *Imagination, Cognition and Personality, 5,* 303–310.

Kunzendorf, R. G., Brown, C., & McGee, D. (1983). Hypnotizability: Correlations with daydreaming and sleeping. *Psychological Reports, 53,* 406.

Langer, E. (1983). *The psychology of control.* Beverly Hills, CA: Sage.

Leiden, L. I., Veach, T. L., & Herring, M. W. (1986). Comparison of the abbreviated and original versions of the Myers–Briggs Type Indicator personality inventory. *Journal of Medical Education, 61,* 319–321.

Levy, N., & Ridley, S. E. (1987). Stability of Jungian personality types within a college population over a decade. *Psychological Reports, 60,* 419–422.

Lewin, K. (1935). *A dynamic theory of personality.* New York: McGraw-Hill.

Lewis, H. B. (1990). Shame, repression, field dependence and psychopathology. In J. L. Singer (Ed.), *Repression and dissociation.* Chicago: University of Chicago Press.

Linton, P. H., Kuechenmeister, C. A., Kuechenmeister, S., & White, H. (1982). Personality type and symptom formation. *Research Communications in Psychology, Psychiatry and Behavior, 7,* 463–476.

Lloyd, K., Paulsen, J., & Brockner, J. (1983). The effects of self-esteem and self-consciousness on interpersonal attraction. *Personality and Social Psychology Bulletin, 9,* 397–403.

Lusk, E. J., & Wright, H. (1983). Relation of scores on group Embedded Figures Test and Myers–Briggs Type Indicator. *Perceptual and Motor Skills, 57,* 1209–1210.

Lynn, S. J., & Rhue, J. W. (1988). Fantasy proneness: Hypnosis, developmental antecedents and psychopathology. *Amerian Psychologist, 43,* 35–44.

Mandler, G. (1984). *Mind and body.* New York: Norton.

Margraf, J., Taylor, C. B., Ehlers, A., Roth, W. T., & Agras, W. S. (1987). Panic attacks in the natural environment. *Journal of Nervous and Mental Disease, 175,* 558–565.

Markus, H., & Nurius, P. (1986). Possible selves. *American Psychologist, 41,* 954–969.

Marsh, C. (1977). A framework for describing subjective states of consciousness. In N. Zinberg (Ed.), *Alternate states of consciousness* (pp. 121–144). New York: Free Press.

McAdams, D., & Constantian, C. A. (1983). Intimacy and affiliation motives in daily living: An experience sampling analysis. *Journal of Personal and Social Psychology, 4,* 851–861.

McCrae, R. R., & Costa, P. T., Jr. (1989). Reinterpreting the Myers–Riggs Type Indicator from the perspective of the five-factor model of personality. *Journal of Personality, 57,* 17–40.

McDonald, C. (1976). *Random sampling of cognitions: A field study of daydreaming.* Unpublished master's dissertation, Yale University.

McIlwraith, D., & Schallow, J. (1983a). Adult fantasy life and patterns of media use. *Journal of Communication, 33,* 78–91.

McIlwraith, D., & Schallow, J. (1983b). Television viewing and styles of children's fantasy. *Imagination, Cognition and Personality, 2,* 323–333.

Meichenbaum, D., & Gilmore, J. B. (1984). The nature of unconscious processes: A cognitive–behavioral perspective. In K. Bowers & D. Meichenbaum (Eds.). *The unconscious reconsidered.* New York: Wiley.

Meskin, B. B., & Singer, J. L. (1974). Daydreaming, reflective thought, and laterality of eye movements. *Journal of Personality and Social Psychology, 30,* 64–71.

Miller, N. E. (1963). Some reflections on the law of effect produce a new alternative to drive reduction. In M. R. Jones (Ed.), *Nebraska Symposium on Motivation* (Vol. 11). Lincoln: University of Nebraska Press.

Mills, J., Robey, D., & Smith, L. (1985). Conflict-handling and personality dimensions of project-management personnel. *Psychological Reports, 57,* 1135–1143.

Mitchell, S. A. (1984). Object relations theory and the developmental tilt. *Contemporary Psychoanalysis, 20,* 473–499.

Moise, F., Yinon, Y., & Rabinowitz, A. (1988–1989). Rorschach inkblot Movement Response as a function of motor activity or inhibition. *Imagination, Cognition and Personality, 8,* 39–48.

Nasby, W. (1989). Private and public self-consciousness and articulation of the self-schema. *Journal of Personality and Social Psychology, 56,* 117–123.

Nash, M. R., & Lynn, S. J. (1985–1986). Child abuse and hypnotic ability. *Imagination, Cognition and Personality, 5,* 211–218.

Natsoulas, T. (1978). Consciousness. *American Psychologist, 33,* 906–914.

Natsoulas, T. (1983). A selective review of concepts of consciousness with special reference to behavioristic interpretations. *Cognition and Brain Theory, 6,* 417–447.

Natsoulas, T. (1986–1987). The six basic concepts of consciousness and William James's stream of thought. *Imagination, Cognition and Personality, 4,* 289–320.

Nell, V. (1988). *Lost in a book.* New Haven, CT: Yale University Press.

Ornstein, R. E. (1977). *The psychology of consciousness* (2nd ed.). New York: Harcourt Brace Jovanovich.

Ornstein, S., Johnson, A., Markert, G., & Afrin, L. (1987). Association between family medical residents' personality and laboratory test-ordering for hypertensive patients. *Journal of Medical Education*, 62, 603–605.

Page, H. A. (1957). Studies of fantasy-daydreaming and Rorschach scoring categories. *Journal of Consulting Psychology*, 21, 111–114.

Pekala, R., & Levine, R. (1982–1983). Quantifying states of consciousness via an empirical–phenomenological approach. *Imagination, Cognition and Personality*, 2, 51–71.

Piaget, J. (1951). *Play, dreams, and imitation in childhood.* New York: Norton.

Plant, R. W., & Ryan, R. M. (1985). Intrinsic motivation and the effects of self-consciousness, self-awareness, and ego-involvement. An integration of internally controlling styles. *Journal of Personality*, 53, 435–449.

Pope, K. S. (1978). *The flow of consciousness.* Unpublished doctoral dissertation, Yale University.

Pope, K. S., & Singer, J. L. (1978). Regulation of the stream of consciousness: Toward a theory of ongoing thought. In G. E. Schwartz & D. Shapiro (Eds.), *Consciousness and self-regulation* (Vol. 2.). New York: Plenum.

Pribram, K. H. (1963). Reinforcement revisited: A structural view. In M. R. Jones (Ed.), *Nebraska Symposium on Motivation* (Vol. 11), Lincoln: University of Nebraska Press.

Pribram, K. H., & McGuinness, D. (1975). Arousal, activation and effort in the control of attention. *Psychological Review*, 82, 116–149.

Quattrone, G. A. (1985). On the congruity between internal states and action. *Psychological Bulletin*, 98, 3–40.

Raikov, V. L. (1983–1984). EEG recordings of experiments in hypnotic age regression. *Imagination, Cognition and Personality*, 3, 115–132.

Rodin, J., & Singer, J. L. (1977). Eyeshift, thought, and obesity. *Journal of Personality*, 44, 594–610.

Rorschach, H. (1942). *Psychodiagnostics.* New York: Grune & Stratton.

Sarbin, T. R., & Coe, W. C. (1972). *Hypnosis: A social psychological analysis of influence communication.* New York: Holt, Rinehart & Winston.

Schachtel, E. G. (1959). *Metamorphosis.* New York: Basic Books.

Scheier, M. F., Carver, C. S., & Gibbons, F. X. (1979). Self-directed attention, awareness of bodily states, and suggestibility. *Journal of Personality and Social Psychology*, 37, 1576–1588.

Schultz, K. D. (1976). Imagery and the control of depression. In J. L. Singer & K. S. Pope (Eds.), *The power of human imagination* (pp. 281–308). New York: Plenum.

Segal, B., Huba, G., & Singer, J. L. (1980). *Drugs, daydreaming and personality.* Hillsdale, NJ: Erlbaum.

Segal, B., & Singer, J. L. (1976). Daydreaming, drug and alcohol use in college students: A factor analytic study. *Addictive Behaviors*, 1, 227–235.

Seegmiller, R. A., & Epperson, D. L. (1987). Distinguishing thinking–feeling preferences through the content and analysis of natural language. *Journal of Personality Assessment*, 51, 42–52.

Singer, J. L. (1966). Daydreaming and planful thought: A note on Professor Stark's conceptual framework. *Perceptual and Motor Skills*, 23, 113–114.

Singer, J. L. (1974). Daydreaming and the stream of thought. *American Scientist*, 62, 417–425.

Singer, J. L. (1975). Navigating the stream of conscious-

ness: Research in daydreaming and related inner experience. *American Psychologist*, 30, 727–738.

Singer, J. L. (1978). The constructive potential of imagery and fantasy processes. In E. Witenberg (Ed.), *Recent developments in interpersonal psychoanalysis.* New York: Gardner Press.

Singer, J. L. (1984). *The human personality.* New York: Harcourt Brace Jovanovich.

Singer, J. L. (1985). Transference and the human condition: A cognitive–affective perspective. *Psychoanalytic Psychology*, 2, 189–219.

Singer, J. L. (1988). Sampling ongoing consciousness and emotional experience: Implications for health. In M. J. Horowitz (Ed.), *Psychodynamics and cognition* (pp. 297–346). Chicago: University of Chicago Press.

Singer, J. L., & Antrobus, J. S. (1963). A factor-analytic study of daydreaming and conceptually-related cognitive and personality variables. *Perceptual and Motor Skills*, (Monograph Supplement No. 3-V17).

Singer, J. L., & Antrobus, J. S. (1972). Daydreaming, imaginal processes, and personality: A normative study. In P. Sheehan (Ed.), *The function and nature of imagery.* New York: Academic Press.

Singer, J. L., & Brown, S. L. (1977). The experience-type: Some behavioral correlates and theoretical implications. In M. A. Rickers-Orsiankina (Ed.), *Rorschach psychology* (pp. 325–374). Huntington, NY: Krieger.

Singer, J. L., & Kolligian, J., Jr. (1987). Personality: Developments in the study of private experience. *Annual Review of Psychology*, 38, 533–574.

Singer, J. L., & McCraven, V. (1961). Some characteristics of adult daydreaming. *Journal of Psychology*, 51, 151–164.

Singer, J. L., & McCraven, V. (1962). Patterns of daydreaming in American subcultural groups. *International Journal of Social Psychiatry*, 8, 272–282.

Singer, J. L., & Pope, K. S. (1981). Daydreaming and imaging skills as predisposing capacities for self-hypnosis. *International Journal of Clinical and Experimental Hypnosis*, 29, 271–281.

Singer, J. L., & Schonbar, R. (1961). Correlates of daydreaming: A dimension of self-awareness. *Journal of Consulting Psychology*, 25, 1–17.

Spanos, N. P. (1982). A social psychological approach to hypnotic behavior. In G. Weary & H. Mirels (Eds.), *Integrations of clinical and social psychology* (pp. 231–271). Oxford: Oxford University Press.

Spanos, N. P., Bridgeman, M., Hendrikus, J. S., Gwynn, M., & Saad, C. L. (1982–1983). When seeing is not believing: The effects of contextual variables on the reports of hypnotic hallucinators. *Imagination, Cognition and Personality*, 2, 195–210.

Spanos, N. P., Ollerhead, V. G., & Gwynn, M. I. (1985–1986). The effects of three instructional treatments on pain magnitude and pain tolerance: Implications for theories of hypnotic analgesia. *Imagination, Cognition and Personality*, 5, 321–338.

Spanos, N. P., & Radtke, H. L. (1981–1982). Hypnotic visual hallucinations as imaginings: A cognitive–social psychological perspective. *Imagination, Cognition and Personality*, 1, 147–171.

Starker, S. (1973). Aspects of inner experience: Autokinesis, daydreaming, dream recall and cognitive style. *Perceptual and Motor Skills*, 36, 663–673.

Starker, S. (1974). Two modes of visual imagery. *Perceptual and Motor Skills*, 38, 649–650.

Starker, S. (1978). Dreams and waking fantasy. In K. S. Pope & J. L. Singer (Eds.), *The stream of consciousness*. New York: Plenum.

Starker, S. (1984–1985). Daydreams, nightmares, and insomnia: The relation of waking fantasy to sleep disturbances. *Imagination, Cognition, and Personality, 4,* 237–248.

Starker, S., & Hasenfeld, R. (1976). Daydream styles and sleep disturbance. *Journal of Nervous and Mental Disease, 163,* 391–400.

Starker, S., & Jolin, A. (1982–1983). Imagery and fantasy in Vietnam veteran psychiatric inpatients. *Imagination, Cognition and Personality, 2,* 15–22.

Starker, S., & Jolin, A. (1983–1984). Occurrence and vividness of imagery in schizophrenic thought: A thought-sampling approach. *Imagination, Cognition and Personality, 3,* 49–60.

Starker, S., & Singer, J. L. (1975a). Daydreaming and symptom patterns of psychiatric patients: A factor analytic study. *Journal of Abnormal Psychology, 84,* 567–570.

Starker, S., & Singer, J. L. (1975b). Daydream patterns and self-awareness in psychiatric patients. *Journal of Nervous and Mental Disease, 161,* 313–317.

Streissguth, A. P., Wagner, N., & Weschler, J. D. (1969). Effects of sex, illness and hospitalization on daydreaming. *Journal of Consulting and Clinical Psychology, 33,* 218–225.

Tanaka, J. S., & Huba, G. J. (1985–1986). Longitudinal stability of three second-order daydreaming factors. *Imagination, Cognition, and Personality, 5,* 231–238.

Taylor, S. E., & Schneider, S. K. (1989). Coping and the simulation of events. *Social Cognition, 7,* 174–194.

Tellegen, A., & Atkinson, G. (1974). Openness to absorbing and self-altering experiences ("absorption"), susceptibility. *Journal of Abnormal Psychology, 83,* 268–277.

Thomas, C. R. (1983). Field independence and Myers–Briggs thinking individuals. *Perceptual and Motor Skills, 57,* 790.

Thorne, A. (1987). The press of personality: A study of conversations between introverts and extraverts. *Journal of Personality and Social Psychology, 53,* 718–726.

Tomkins, S. S. (1962–1963). *Affect, imagery, consciousness* (2 vols.). New York: Springer.

Tomkins, S. S. (1979). Script theory: Differential magnification of affects. In H. E. Howe, Jr., & R. A. Dienstbier (Eds.), *Nebraska Symposium on Motivation* (Vol. 26). Lincoln: University of Nebraska Press.

Tomkins, S. S., & Messick, S. (1962)., *Computer simulation of personality*. New York: Wiley.

Tower, R. B., & Singer, J. L. (1980). The measurement of imagery: How can it be clinically useful? In P. C. Kendall & S. Holland (Eds.), *Cognitive–behavioral interventions: Assessment methods*. New York: Academic Press.

Vinacke, W. E., Shannon, K., Palazzo, V., & Balsavage, L. (1988). Similarity and complementarity in intimate couples. *Genetic, Social and General Psychology Monographs, 114,* 51–76.

Ward, R. A., & Loftus, E. F. (1985). Eyewitness performance in different psychological types. *Journal of General Psychology, 112,* 191–200.

White, R. W. (1959). Motivation reconsidered: The concept of competence. *Psychological Review, 66,* 297–333.

White, R. W. (1960). Competence and the psychosexual stages of development. In M. R. Jones (Ed.), *Nebraska Symposium on Motivation* (Vol. 8). Lincoln: University of Nebraska Press.

Wicklund, R. A., & Gollwitzer, P. M. (1987). The fallacy of the public–private self-focus distinction. *Journal of Personality, 55,* 497–523.

Wilson, S. C., & Barber, T. X. (1978). The Creative Imaginative Scale as a measure of hypnotic responsiveness: Applications to clinical and experimental hypnosis. *American Journal of Clinical Hypnosis, 20,* 235–249.

Wilson, S. C., & Barber, T. X. (1983). The fantasy-prone personality: Implications for understanding imagery, hypnosis and parapsychological phenomena. In A. A. Sheikh (Ed.), *Imagery: Current theory research and application* (pp. 133–149). New York: Wiley.

Zachary, R. (1983). *Cognitive and affective determinants of ongoing thought*. Unpublished doctoral dissertation, Yale University.

Chapter 17
The Psychological Unconscious

John F. Kihlstrom
University of Arizona

Non amo te, Sabidi, nec possum dicere quare:
hoc tantum possum dicere, non amo te.
Marcus Valerius Martialis
Epigrammata, I, 32 *

The doctrine of mentalism states that mental states are to actions as causes to effects. When classifying the mental states that are causally implicated in behavior, philosophers and psychologists have generally taken refuge in the threefold "trilogy of mind" proposed initially by Kant, and later adopted by the German and Scottish philosophers: cognition, emotion, and motivation (Hilgard, 1980b). As psychology developed as an empirical science, research focused on those mental states that were accessible to consciousness. Thus, Wundt, Titchener, and other structuralists who founded the earliest psychological laboratories generally assumed that the mind is able to observe its own inner workings. Their research relied on the method of introspection, by which trained observers attempted to analyze their own percepts, memories, and thoughts into elementary sensations, images, and feelings. This line of scientific inquiry on

conscious mental life was interrupted by the radical behaviorism of Watson and his followers, who argued that consciousness was nonexistent, epiphenomenal, or irrelevant to behavior. One of the most salutary by-products of the "cognitive revolution," and the subsequent development of an interdisciplinary cognitive science, has been the revival of interest in consciousness (Hilgard, 1977, 1980a, 1987).

This is fine so far as it goes, but even the 19th-century psychologists recognized that the mental structures and processes underlying experience, thought, and action were not completely encompassed within the span of conscious awareness. That is to say, consciousness is not all there is to the mind. For example, Helmholtz concluded that conscious perception was the product of unconscious inferences based on the individual's knowledge of the world and memories of past experience. Somewhat later, Freud asserted that our conscious mental lives were determined by unconscious ideas, impulses, and emotions, as well as defense mechanisms unconsciously arrayed against them (see Bowers & Meichenbaum, 1984; Ellenberger, 1970;

*Many readers will be familiar with the following free translation by the 18th century English poet Thomas Brown (Howell, 1980):

I do not love you Dr Fell, but why I cannot tell;
But this I know full well, I do not love you, Dr. Fell.

Klein, 1977; Perry & Laurence, 1984; Whyte, 1960). Ever since that time, investigators have explored the dynamic and the cognitive unconscious in separate, largely independent lines of inquiry (Burston, 1986).

THE DYNAMIC UNCONSCIOUS IN PSYCHOANALYSIS

The dynamic unconscious is sometimes considered to be the intellectual property of psychodynamic approaches to personality and psychopathology that evolved beginning in the 19th century (Ellenberger, 1970; Macmillan, 1989), and especially of the psychoanalytic tradition initiated by Sigmund Freud. As defined by Shevrin and Dickman (1980), the dynamic unconscious is psychological, meaning that the terms applied to conscious experience ("perception," "affect," "motive," etc.) are also applicable to unconscious mental life; it is active, meaning that unconscious processes affect ongoing behavior and experience; and it is different, meaning that unconscious processes are organized differently, and follow different procedural rules, than their conscious counterparts. In the clinical theory of psychoanalytic psychology, the psychological unconscious is manifest in the formation of symptoms—bothersome ideas, impulses, and behaviors for which the patient cannot account, and over which he or she has no control. It should be noted that Shevrin and Dickman (1980) actually use the term "*psychological* unconscious," as opposed to unconscious brain events and other physiological processes (see also Kihlstrom, 1984). Because their discussion is explicitly framed by psychoanalytic theory, it seems appropriate to introduce it here. However, it should be noted that except for certain implications concerning the drive-relatedness of unconscious processes, and the unconscious origins of dreams and symptoms, their treatment applies equally well to the cognitive and dynamic views of the psychological unconscious.

Based on his observations of hysterical patients, and his analysis of such phenomena as dreams, errors, and jokes, Freud (1900/1953, Ch. 7) initially proposed a topographical division of the mind into three mental compartments, or "systems," which he called Cs, Pcs, and Ucs. The system Cs, or conscious mind, contains those thoughts, feelings, mo-

tives, and actions of which we are phenomenally aware at the moment. Freud explicitly likened consciousness to a sensory organ capable of perceiving other mental contents. The system Pcs, by contrast, contains mental contents that are not currently in conscious awareness, but that are available to consciousness, and that can be brought into awareness under certain conditions. Finally, the system Ucs contains mental contents that are unavailable to consciousness—that cannot enter awareness under any circumstances. According to Freud, contents are exchanged between the systems Pcs and Cs by virtue of "cathexis"—by having attention paid to, or withdrawn from, them; contents residing in the system Ucs are kept out of (or expelled from) the system Pcs by means of repression. As others (e.g., Erdelyi, 1985) have noted, this topographical model, with its spatial metaphors, may be read as an anticipation of modern multistore models of human information processing.

Freud maintained this account of the vicissitudes of consciousness for approximately two decades (Freud, 1912/1958, 1915/1957, 1917/1961), but then introduced a wholesale revision of his view, shifting from a topographical to a functional analysis of the mind (Freud, 1923/1961, 1940/1964). This new account postulated three different types of mental activity, rather than three different storage structures: the "id," "ego," and "superego." The id was described as the seat of the instincts, which are expressed through either the automatic discharge of reflex action, or the hallucinatory wish-fulfillment of primary-process thought. The ego is concerned with the external physical environment, and discovers reality by means of the logical operations of secondary-process thought. The superego, similarly, is concerned with the constraints on instinctual expression imposed by the moral values of the external social environment.

Although it might seem natural to graft the topographical model onto the functional one, such a connection proved untenable. The id is strictly unconscious, and except in cases of psychosis can be known only through inference. By the same token, consciousness is necessarily a quality of the ego—after all, the ego functions expressly to permit us to become aware of external reality. At the same time, however, the defense mechanisms are also part of the ego, and their operations are not accessible to consciousness; and since the ego cannot be conscious of all of external reality at once, some of its contents (and, correspondingly, of the superego) must necessarily be preconscious.

The problem of reconciling the two different divisions of the mind, topographic and functional, was not solved by Freud before he died. Nevertheless, his assignment of some nonconscious mental functions to the ego, in both its defensive and nondefensive spheres, initiated an important research tradition within post-Freudian psychoanalysis. Beginning with the work of Anna Freud, and especially in the hands of Heinz Hartmann, David Rapaport, and George Klein, psychoanalytic ego psychology focused on the nondefensive, reality-oriented tasks of the ego (Kihlstrom, 1988). The research of the ego psychologists dealt with conventional topics of perception, memory, and thinking, and in many respects it resembled that being performed elsewhere in academic laboratories. In other respects, however, their work was quite different: For example, it favored prose over nonsense syllables as stimulus materials; took images and dreams seriously; and emphasized the interplay of emotional, motivational, and cognitive processes. The tradition of psychoanalytic ego psychology was linked most closely with mainstream experimental psychology by the work of Bruner, Klein, and others on the "New Look" in perception and attendant research on such topics as subliminal perception, perceptual defense and vigilance, and repression–sensitization (Bruner & Klein, 1960; Erdelyi, 1974, 1985).

In the present context, the most important feature of psychoanalytic ego psychology is that it took seriously the question of the psychological unconscious, and of the relations between conscious and nonconscious mental processes, at a time when most academic psychologists had difficulty taking consciousness itself seriously. A sort of manifesto for this viewpoint has been offered by Shevrin and Dickman (1980), who review a number of studies of selective attention, subliminal perception, and event-related potentials (ERPs) in support of two broad propositions: (1) that the initial stage of human information processing is outside of consciousness, is psychological in nature, is active in its effect on consciousness, and operates on principles that are qualitatively different from those governing conscious cognition; and (2) that representation of a mental event in consciousness is jointly determined by stimulus, state, and motivational factors.

At the same time, it should be noted that although Shevrin and other ego psychologists locate their research and theorizing squarely within the Freudian tradition, little if any of their evidence bears directly on the propositions of classical psychoanalysis—a point made by Shevrin and Dickman themselves (1980). In the first place, most work on selective attention and ERPs bears on mental states and processes that are preconscious, and does not address questions of nonconscious mental life (to adopt Freud's usage of these terms). For example, demonstrations of parallel processing at early stages of perception, while arguably evidence for qualitative differences between conscious and nonconscious cognition, do not perforce support a distinction between primary- and secondary-process thinking. Even research on perceptual defense and repression, while clearly relevant to the effects of emotion and motivation on cognition, rarely go beyond events that are merely unpleasant to tap the primitive sexual and aggressive contents that Freud attributed to the id—a criticism offered by Rapaport (1942) almost a half-century ago.

The undoubted success of ego-psychological research on preconscious (and even unconscious) mental life, while having its origins in neo-Freudian psychoanalysis, does not thereby support the essential propositions of psychoanalytic theory. This is because precisely the same propositions are offered, implicitly or explicitly, by cognitive theories that evolved independently of, and owe no intellectual allegiance to, the psychoanalytic tradition. To put it another way, research on subliminal perception, motivated forgetting, and the like offers little support for the Freudian conception of nonconscious mental life because the propositions that have been tested are rarely unique to Freudian theory. Such support can only be provided by research that tests those hypotheses that are unique to Freudian theory—for example, that unconscious contents are sexual and aggressive in nature, and that unconscious processes are primitive and irrational. Such experiments are hard to come by, and positive findings rarer still.

THE PSYCHOLOGICAL UNCONSCIOUS IN COGNITIVE THEORY

Within 19th-century academic psychology, perhaps the most forceful advocate of nonconscious mental life was William James (1890; see also Hilgard, 1969; Kihlstrom & Tobias, 1989; Myers, 1986; Taylor, 1983). James held that mental states can be unconscious in at least two different senses. First, a mental event can be excluded from attention or consciousness: "We can neglect to attend to that which we nevertheless feel" (1890, p. 201; see also pp. 455–458). These unattended, unconscious feelings are themselves mental states. Second, and more important, James drew on the clinical observations of cases of hysteria and multiple personality—some made by others, some by himself (Taylor, 1983)—to argue for a division of consciousness into primary and secondary (and, for that matter, tertiary and more) consciousnesses (sic), only one of which is accessible to phenomenal awareness at any point in time. To avoid a possible oxymoron in the negation of consciousness, which was what really bothered him, James preferred to speak of "co-conscious" or "subconscious" mental states, rather than "unconscious" ones.

The radical behaviorists were no more interested in nonconscious than in conscious mental life, so empirical interest in the kinds of problems that interested Helmholtz and James (not to mention Freud) declined precipitously in the years after World War I. Serious theoretical interest in nonconscious mental life had to wait for the triumph of the cognitive revolution (Hilgard, 1980a, 1987). For example, the classic multistore model of information processing, of the sort proposed by Atkinson and Shiffrin (1968), implicitly makes consciousness coterminous with attention and primary memory. In this way, the model seems to identify nonconscious mental life with early, "preattentive" mental processes, such as feature detection and pattern recognition, that occur prior to the formation of a mental representation of an event in primary memory. By regarding attention and rehearsal as prerequisites for a full-fledged cognitive analysis of an event, and by implicitly identifying consciousness with higher mental processes, the classic multistore model leaves little or no room for the *psychological unconscious*—complex mental structures and processes that influence experience, thought, and action, but that are nevertheless inaccessible to phenomenal awareness.

A rather different perspective on nonconscious mental life is provided by Anderson's (1983) ACT* model of the architecture of cognition. ACT* holds that people can become aware of declarative knowledge (about themselves, their environments, their processing goals, and other relevant information), and that this awareness depends on the amount of activation possessed by the representations in question. However, it also holds that procedural knowledge is not available to introspection under any circumstances. Thus, procedural knowledge appears to be unconscious in the strict sense of the term. Because unconscious procedural knowledge is the cognitive basis for all higher thought processes, ACT* and similar revisionist models afford a much wider scope for the cognitive unconscious than did the classic statements.

An even larger place for nonconscious mental structures and processes has been created by a recent variant on information-processing theory known as "connectionism" or "parallel distributed processing" (PDP; McClelland, Rummelhart, & the PDP Research Group, 1986; Rummelhart, McClelland, & the PDP Research Group, 1986). PDP models postulate the existence of a large number of interacting processing units, or "modules," each devoted to a specific task. Because the activation of individual processing units can vary continuously as opposed to discretely, it is not necessary for an object to be fully represented in consciousness before information about it can influence other units. In addition, only some modules are assumed to be accessible to awareness and subject to voluntary control. Finally, PDP models assume parallel rather than serial processing, which permits a large number of activated units to influence each other at any particular moment in time. The number of simultaneously active processing units, and the speed at which they pass information among themselves, both may exceed the span of conscious awareness. Thus, in contrast to multistore information-processing theories that restrict the cognitive unconscious to elementary sensory–perceptual operations, PDP models seem to consider almost all information processing, including the higher mental functions involved in language, memory, and thought, to be unconscious.

Consciousness and Automaticity

Theories aside, it is clear that a good deal of mental activity is unconscious in the strict sense of being inaccessible to phenomenal awareness under any circumstances. Although some unconscious procedural knowledge appears to be innate, other cognitive and motoric skills that are acquired through experience may become routinized through practice, and their operations thereby rendered unconscious. In a metaphor derived from computer science, this process is described as "knowledge compilation," suggesting that the format in which the knowledge is represented has been changed (Anderson, 1982). In this way, both innate and acquired cognitive procedures may be unconscious in the strict sense of the term (Nisbett & Wilson, 1977). Unconscious procedural knowledge has also been described as "automatic," as opposed to "controlled" or "effortful" (for reviews, see Kahneman & Triesman, 1984; Shiffrin & Schneider, 1984). Automatic processes are so named because they are inevitably engaged by the presentation of specific stimulus inputs, regardless of any intention on the part of the subject. In addition, automatic processes consume few or no attentional resources, permitting us to perform two or more complex tasks simultaneously so long as at least one of them is routinized.

All theorists appear to be united about these two features of automatic processes (Anderson, 1982; Hasher & Zacks, 1979, 1984; LaBerge, 1975; Logan, 1980; Posner & Snyder, 1975; Schneider & Shiffrin, 1977; Shiffrin & Schneider, 1977, 1984). The first criterion, of course, represents the defining feature of automaticity: To put it bluntly, automatic processes are those that are executed automatically. Set down this way, of course, the definition of automaticity is circular. Thus the second criterion seems to have been adopted in part to escape tautology, and perhaps because of difficulties in objectively measuring or controlling subjects' intentions as well (though this does not seem to be an insurmountable obstacle; see Peterson & Hochberg, 1983). But it should be noted that the concept of automaticity does not *require* anything other than independence from intention. It is certainly possible to conceive of automatic processes that, once invoked by appropriate stimulus conditions, consume attentional resources—just as a room heater, automatically activated by a thermostat, consumes electricity.

Even if the lack of intention and attention (together or separately) were to be accepted as criteria for automaticity, there are still procedural difficulties involved in documenting them in any particular case. Consider, for example, an experiment on spatial location in which word pairs are presented in one of four

quadrants of a computer screen (e.g., Fleeson & Kihlstrom, 1988). In a "true incidental" condition, subjects are asked to make a judgment about the word pairs, but not instructed to remember them or where they occurred. In an "item-only/intentional" condition, subjects are asked to remember the words, but not the locations in which they were presented. In an "item-plus-context/intentional" condition, subjects are asked to remember both the words and their locations. Suppose that subsequent testing shows that memory for spatial location does not differ between the two intentional conditions, but is diminished in the true incidental condition. The first result indicates that the processing of spatial location is automatic, while the second indicates that it is intentional. Which comparison is relevant to the question of intentionality?

Hasher and Zacks (1979, 1984) have offered four additional criteria for defining a process as automatic. In their formulation, information is automatically processed if the following conditions hold:

1. The information is processed independent of the subject's intention (this is the first of the consensus criteria).
2. The mental representation of information processed automatically does not differ from that of the same information processed in an effortful manner.
3. Training and feedback do not improve processing.
4. There are no individual differences in processing.
5. There are no age differences in processing.
6. Arousal, stress, or simultaneous task performance have no effect on processing (this is a variant on the second of the consensus criteria).

These additional criteria have formed the foundation for a number of interesting lines of research. For example, Hasher and Zacks's (1979) proposal that information pertaining to the temporal and spatial context of events is automatically encoded, coupled with the assumption that automatic processes are age-invariant, has led to a number of studies comparing memory for context in children, young adults, and the elderly. Although comparisons of intentional versus incidental encoding conditions sometimes support the conclusion that context is encoded automatically (Hasher & Zacks, 1984), other evidence indicates that the elderly have special difficulty encoding context (Burke & Light, 1984; Schacter, Kaszniak, & Kihlstrom, in press)—a finding that violates the criterion of invariance of automatic processes with age. Under these circumstances, it seems better for the present to decouple Hasher and Zacks's (1979) additional criteria from the concept of automaticity, and to treat the effects of such factors as training, age, and individual differences as empirical questions, as opposed to a priori assumptions.

A further quandary concerns the proper name for the opposite of "automaticity." Posner and Snyder (1975) and Bargh (1984) contrast "automatic" processes with "conscious" ones; Schneider and Shiffrin (e.g., Shiffrin & Schneider, 1984) with "controlled"; Logan (1980) and Bargh (1984) with "attentional"; and Hasher and Zacks (1979, 1984) with "effortful." Each of these contrasts captures something about automaticity, but some seem to represent a priori theoretical commitments that should be expressed as empirical questions. It is not necessarily the case that automatic processes should be unconscious, and that intentional ones should be conscious—or even that automatic processes should consume no attentional resources. Thus, the implicit opposition of automatic, involuntary, unconscious, and effortless processes against those that are controlled, conscious, and effortful leads to a certain amount of uncertainty when classifying particular mental processes. To take an example, posthypnotic suggestions are (in the classic case) executed outside of conscious awareness, but they are not automatic in the sense of either being invariant across conditions (Spanos, Menary, Brett, Cross, & Ahmed, 1987) or requiring no attentional resources (Hoyt & Kihlstrom, 1989). For the present, it seems best to contrast automatic processes with those that are controlled or intentional.

Implicit Perception and Memory

Although the procedural knowledge structures guiding thought and action may be unconscious, the declarative knowledge structures on which they operate are ordinarily thought to be available to conscious awareness. Thus, we generally assume that people notice and can describe the salient features of an object or event, even if they cannot articulate the way in which those features have been integrated to form certain judgments made about it. However, another implication of automatization is that the processes in question may operate on structures of declarative knowledge that are not themselves fully conscious. This raises the question of subliminal perception—the possibility that events that are not consciously detected may nonetheless have an impact on perceptual and cognitive functioning (Dixon, 1971, 1981).

Ever since the first demonstration of subliminal perception, by Peirce and Jastrow (1884), various methodological critiques have sought to demonstrate that events cannot be analyzed for meaning unless they have been consciously identified and attended to (for a recent review, see Holender, 1986). Recently, however, a number of compelling demonstrations of preconscious processing have appeared in the literature. For example, Marcel (1983a, 1983b) employed a lexical decision task in which one stimulus word (the prime) is followed by another word (the target), and the subject has to decide whether the target is a meaningful word. Such judgments are facilitated when the prime is also a word, and especially when the prime and target are from the same taxonomic category; however, most of these demonstrations have involved primes that could be consciously detected by the subject. Marcel followed his primes with masking stimuli, with the result that subjects were unable to detect the primes reliably. Nevertheless, such primes facilitated performance on the lexical decision task. Since semantic priming obviously requires some degree of semantic processing, it appears that meaning analyses can be performed on stimuli that are themselves outside of conscious awareness. Marcel's essential findings have since been confirmed by a number of investigators (e.g., Fowler, Wolford, Slade, & Tassinary, 1981; Greenwald, Klinger, & Liu, 1989; Reingold & Merikle, 1989). Despite persisting methodological critiques (e.g., Cheesman & Merikle, 1985, 1986; Erickson, 1960; Holender, 1986), the available literature clearly supports the proposition that certain aspects of semantic processing can occur in the absence of conscious awareness.

Preconscious processing appears to be mediated by the activation of relevant mental representations already stored in memory. Are analogous effects observed in memory itself? Just as there are palpable effects on experience, thought, and action of events that cannot be consciously perceived, so there may be similar effects of events that cannot be consciously remembered. An early demonstration along these lines was provided by Nelson (1978), whose subjects showed significant savings in relearning paired associates that they were unable to recall or even to recognize from a previous learning experience. Other demonstrations have made use of repetition priming effects, in which the processing of an unremembered item is facilitated by the fact that it was encountered previously. Similarly, studies of priming in tests involving lexical decision or word identification (e.g., Jacoby & Dallas, 1981), or completion of word fragments (e.g., Tulving, Schacter, & Stark, 1982), have shown that the magnitude of the priming effect is independent of the subject's ability to recognize the item as having been presented in a previous study session (see Schacter, 1987, for a review).

Relearning and priming effects such as these show that task performance may be affected by available memories of prior experiences, even though those experiences are not accessible to conscious recall. On the basis of results such as these, Schacter (Graf & Schacter, 1985; Schacter, 1987) has drawn a distinction between "explicit" and "implicit" memory. Explicit memory involves the conscious re-experiencing of some aspect of the past, whereas implicit memory is revealed by a change in task performance that is attributable to information acquired during a prior episode. An increasingly large literature from both patient and nonpatient populations indicates that people can display implicit memory without having any conscious recollection of the experiential basis of the effect.

The effects of implicit memory are conceptually similar to the effects of subliminal perception, in that both reveal the impact on experience, thought, and action of events that are not accessible to conscious awareness. The term "implicit" perception might be offered as an alternative to "subliminal" perception, in an attempt to get away from the unfortunate psychophysical implications of the concept of the "limen." However, in contrast to implicit perception, the events contributing to implicit memory effects are clearly detectable by the subject at the time they occur, attention is devoted to them, and they are at least momen-

tarily represented in phenomenal awareness. Arguably, "implicit memory" should be reserved for those situations where a consciously perceived event is subsequently lost to conscious recollection, leaving "implicit perception" for instances where stimulus information in the current (or immediately past) environment affects ongoing experience, thought, and action. Since memory is the residual trace of perceptual activity, it stands to reason that implicit percepts can reveal themselves in memory—even if it should turn out that implicit percepts produce only implicit memories. Still, both sets of phenomena illustrate the cognitive unconscious, by showing perception and memory outside of phenomenal awareness.

One thorny theoretical issue in studies of implicit memory is whether priming effects can reflect the acquisition of new knowledge, or only the activation of pre-existing information. Consider, for example, the case where subjects study paired associates such as "sour–grapes" or "small–potatoes," and are then asked to give the first word that comes to mind when cued with "sour" or "small." Subjects will show priming of the targeted responses—a classic manifestation of implicit memory—independently of their ability to explicitly recall the word pairings on the study list. Because phrases such as "sour grapes" and "small potatoes" are common English idioms, the priming seems to reflect the activation of knowledge already stored in semantic memory. The question is whether completely novel pairings, such as "sour–potatoes" and "small–grapes," would have the same effect. The answer is affirmative (e.g., Schacter & Graf, 1989), but it appears that although implicit memory for pre-existing knowledge is independent of encoding conditions, implicit memory for new associations occurs only if the subject engages in some degree of deep processing at the time of presentation.

It seems likely that implicit perception is subject to the same sorts of constraints. That is, events in the current environment may actively influence mental functioning outside of conscious awareness, but only under conditions where (1) the event activates pre-existing knowledge or (2) the subject devotes active attention to the segment of the stimulus field where the event occurs. These conjectures remain to be tested. However, it is clear that the positive evidence for implicit perception and memory should not be taken as grounds for concluding that *all* current and past events, regardless of whether they are consciously attended, are encoded in memory and influence ongoing experience, thought, and action—as implied, for example, by the specter of subliminal advertising (Moore, 1982) or subliminal persuasion (Merikle, 1988). On the contrary, a major task for future research is to discover the conditions under which implicit percepts and memories are formed, and those in which they are expressed.

Implicit Thought and Learning

Implicit perception and memory do not exhaust the domain of the psychological unconscious. For example, it appears that we can also have implicit *thought,* as revealed in some recent experiments by Bowers and his associates (Bowers, 1984, 1987; Bowers, Regehr, Balthazard, & Parker, in press). In these experiments, subjects are presented with word triads patterned after those of the remote-associates test, and are instructed to think of a word that they all have in common. Some of the triads are soluble, but others are not. Subjects are presented with both kinds of triads simultaneously, and must indicate which is which. An example is provided below:

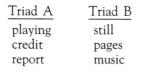

Triad A	Triad B
playing	still
credit	pages
report	music

Bowers finds that subjects can perform this task with considerable accuracy, even though they cannot solve the soluble triad. They seem to be responding to some vague "feeling of knowing" analogous to that observed in episodic and semantic memory. But the point is that the correct solution influences the subjects' choice behavior, even though they are not consciously aware of it, in much the same manner as in implicit perception and memory.

A rather different line of research has sought to document the conceptually related phenomenon of implicit *learning*—as demonstrated by subjects' ability to use rules acquired through experience, in the absence of awareness of the rules themselves. In some ways, of course, implicit learning is demonstrated in language acquisition, where speakers acquire the ability to distinguish grammatical from ungrammatical utterances, even though they cannot articulate the grammatical rules underlying the judgments. Reber (1976, 1989) has attempted to model this process in the laboratory by developing artificial grammars whose rules control the construction of well-formed strings of letters. One such grammar runs approximately as follows:

A1. The first letter of the string can be either P or T.

B1. If the first letter was T, the next letter must be S.
B2. If the next letter was S, it can be repeated an infinite number of times.
B3. If S was not repeated, the next letter must be X.
B4. If the next letter was X, then the next letter can be either X or S.
B5. If the next letter was S, the string ends.
B6. If the next letter was X, the next letter must be T.
B7. If the next letter was T, go to C2.

C1. If the first letter is P, the next letter must be T.
C2. If the next letter was T, it may be repeated an infinite number of times.
C3. If T was not repeated, the next letter must be V.
C4. If the next letter was V, the next letter must be P or V.
C5. If the next letter was V, the string ends.
C6. If the next letter was P, the next letter may be X or S.

D2. If the next letter is S, the string ends.
D3. If the next letter is X, the next letter must be T.
D4. If the next letter was T, go to C2.

In Reber's procedure, subjects are asked to memorize a set of (perhaps) 20 grammatical letter strings (e.g., PVPXVPS or PTTTVPS). They are then tested with a number of new strings, some of which (e.g., PTTTTVPS) conform to the rule, while others (e.g., PTVPXVSP) do not. Interestingly, subjects are able to distinguish grammatical from nongrammatical letter strings at better than chance levels, even though none of them are able to give a full and accurate account of the grammatical rule that they have clearly induced from the study set. Other investigators have produced similar sorts of demonstrations (e.g., Broadbent, FitzGerald, & Broadbent, 1986; Lewicki, 1986; Razran, 1961). Although their interpretation is somewhat controversial (Brewer, 1974), it seems plausible to conclude that these experiments do show the acquisition of new knowledge in the absence of either conscious intent to learn, or conscious awareness of what is learned.

IMPLICIT COGNITION IN NEUROPSYCHOLOGY AND PSYCHOPATHOLOGY

The reference experiments just described give us *prima facie* evidence for four different aspects of the cognitive unconscious. In Schacter's (1987) work, we have implicit memory: a change in task performance attributable to some past event, but in the absence of conscious recollection of that event. In Marcel's (1983a, 1983b) research, we have implicit perception: a change in task performance attributable to some *current* event, but in the absence of conscious perception of that event. Bowers's (1984, 1987) studies reveal implicit thought—reflections in behavior of problem-solving activity outside phenomenal awareness. And Reber's (1976, 1989) experiments reveal implicit learning—the acquisition of knowledge in the absence of reflective awareness of the knowledge itself. It should be noted that these sorts of implicit cognition effects are produced under conditions that might be described as "degraded:" stimulus presentations that are too brief to be consciously perceived; encoding conditions, or retention intervals, that produce memories too weak (in some sense) to be retrieved; problems that are too difficult to be solved except by crossword mavens; grammars that are fiendishly complex. But it turns out that consciousness does not depend on stimulus features alone.

Thus, in other cases, the problem is not in the task environment imposed on the subjects, but rather with the subjects themselves. For example, some of the most dramatic demonstrations of the effects of implicit memory come from studies by Schacter (1987) and his associates, among others, on cases of the amnesic syndrome resulting from bilateral damage to the medial temporal lobe (including the hippocampus) and diencephalon (including the mammillary bodies). These patients display a gross anterograde amnesia, meaning that they cannot remember events that occurred since the onset of the brain damage; other intellectual functions remain relatively intact. When they study a list of familiar words, and are asked to recall them shortly thereafter, they show gross impairments in memory compared to controls. But quite different results are obtained when they are asked to identify briefly presented words, or to complete a word stem or other fragment with a meaningful word. Not surprisingly, intact subjects show superior performance on trials where the correct response is a word that had appeared on the previously studied list, compared to those where the correct response is an entirely new word. This advantage of old over new items reflects a sort of priming effect of the previous learning experience. However, amnesic subjects also show normal levels of priming, despite the fact that they cannot remember the words they studied.

Although the available evidence is somewhat controversial, some phenomena analogous to implicit cognition appear to be observed in a variety of other neuropsychological syndromes as well. For example, Weiskrantz and his colleagues (Weiskrantz, 1980; Weiskrantz, Warrington, Sanders, & Marshall, 1974) have reported a patient who had extensive damage to the striate cortex of the occipital lobes. Although the patient reported an inability to see, he was nonetheless able to respond appropriately to some visual stimuli—a phenomenon called "blindsight" (for a review, see Campion, Latto, & Smith, 1983, and commentaries). Similarly, patients with bilateral lesions to the mesial portions of the occipital and temporal cortex are unable to recognize previously encountered faces as familiar—a condition known as "prosopagnosia." Nevertheless, there are now several reports indicating that prosopagnosic patients show differential behavioral responses to old and new faces (e.g., deHaan, Young, & Newcombe, 1987; Tranel & Damasio, 1985); this dissociation is similar to the implicit memory seen in the amnesic syndrome.

Even in the absence of demonstrable brain insult, injury, or disease, conceptually implicit cognition effects have been reported in the conversion disorders, once labeled "conversion hysteria" (for reviews, see Hilgard, 1977; Kihlstrom, 1984, in press; Kihlstrom & Hoyt, 1988). For example, Hilgard (cited in Hilgard

& Marquis, 1940) demonstrated that a patient with functional anesthesia and paralysis could acquire a conditioned finger withdrawal response in the affected arm; similarly, Brady and Lind (1961) showed that a functionally blind patient nonetheless displayed discriminative responses to visual stimulation. More recently, Sackeim, Nordlie, and Gur (1979) and Bryant and McConkey (1989) have reported cases of visual conversion disorder in which choice behavior was influenced by visual cues, even though the patients reported that they were unaware of the visual stimuli in question. The outcomes of these clinical case studies, then, parallel those of modern, well-controlled studies of implicit perception in intact subjects. The difference is that the stimuli shown to influence behavior are not degraded, but are clearly perceptible in terms of intensity, duration, and other characteristics.

In much the same way, studies of the memory disorders affecting patients with limited amnesia, fugue, and multiple personality reveal phenomena paralleling implicit memory (Kihlstrom, in press; Schacter & Kihlstrom, 1989). A number of case studies of functional retrograde amnesia show the likely influence of implicit memories for events that are otherwise inaccessible to conscious awareness. For example, a rape victim studied by Gudjonsson (1979; Gudjonsson & Taylor, 1985) showed electrodermal responses to stimuli related to events that she could not remember. And a case of fugue was solved by asking the patient to dial numbers randomly on a telephone: she unknowingly dialed her mother, who subsequently provided an identification (Lyon, 1985). And in a case of amnesia following homosexual rape, the patient experienced an increase in subjective distress when presented with Thematic Apperception Test (TAT) cards depicting one person attacking another from behind (Kaszniak, Nussbaum, Berren, & Santiago, 1988; see also Schacter, Wang, Tulving, & Freedman, 1982).

The most dramatic evidence along these lines comes from cases of multiple personality disorder (Schacter & Kihlstrom, 1989). Although a symmetrical or asymmetrical amnesia between personalities is commonly considered to be a cardinal symptom of this syndrome (Bliss, 1986; Kihlstrom, in press), some interpersonality transfer may be observed on tests of implicit as opposed to explicit memory. For example, Ludwig, Brandsma, Wilbur, Bend-

feldt, and Jameson (1972), in the first experimental study of memory in multiple personality, found a number of instances in which information acquired by one personality influenced the performance of another personality on various learning and conditioning tasks, despite an apparent amnesic barrier between these same alter egos. Similarly, Nissen, Ross, Willingham, MacKenzie, and Schacter (1989) found some evidence of implicit memory shared by eight alter egos that were mutually amnesic on tests of explicit memory. However, such priming and transfer were not obtained between all the personalities, or on all the experimental tasks.

DISSOCIATION AND NEODISSOCIATION

The differences between explicit and implicit perception seen in conversion disorder, and between explicit and implicit memory seen in the functional amnesias, suggest that they share underlying mental processes in common (Kihlstrom, in press). In the late 19th and early 20th centuries, Freud's rival Pierre Janet (1889, 1907) described this process as one of dissociation (actually, his term was *désagrégation*). Janet's work on hysteria was overshadowed by Freud's (Perry & Laurence, 1984), and his magnum opus *Psychological Automatisms* (1889) unfortunately has gone untranslated. For these reasons, Janet's theoretical ideas are known primarily through secondary sources (Ellenberger, 1970; Hilgard, 1977), and only the briefest account of them can be given here.

Janet's theoretical work was predicated on Claude Bernard's paradigm of analysis followed by synthesis: the study of elementary psychological functions taken separately, and then the reconstruction of the whole mind based on knowledge of these parts. The elementary mental functions were labeled "psychological automatisms"; far from the elementary sensations, images, and feelings of the structuralists, they were construed as complex intelligent acts, adjusted to their circumstances, and accompanied by a rudimentary consciousness. Each automatism unites cognition, emotion, and motivation with action. Thus, automatisms resemble what some contemporary theorists (e.g., Anderson, 1983) would call "productions" (or "production systems")—condition–action units that are executed in response to appropriate contextual cues.

Janet held that under normal circumstances, all psychological automatisms are bound together into a single stream of consciousness, each accessible to introspection and susceptible to voluntary control. However, the occurrence of mental trauma, especially in a vulnerable individual, may result in the splitting off of one or more psychological automatisms from conscious monitoring and control. Under these circumstances, there exist two or more streams of mental functioning (consciousness, in James's broad sense), each of which processes inputs and outputs, but only one of which is accessible to phenomenal awareness and voluntary control. The dissociated automatisms constitute "fixed ideas" (*idées fixes*), which possess some degree of autonomy with respect to their development and effects on ongoing experience, thought, and action. The operation of these dissociated (as opposed to integrated or synthesized) psychological automatisms provides the mechanism for the major symptoms of hysteria: They produce the ideas, images, and behaviors that intrude, unbidden, on the stream of conscious thought and action; and their capacity to process information is responsible for the paradoxical ability of the hysterically blind or deaf to negotiate their environments successfully. Janet described these dissociated automatisms as "*sub*conscious" as opposed to "*un*conscious," and considered repression as just one possible mechanism for dissociation.

Janet's ideas were championed by the American psychologist Morton Prince (1906), and more recently by E. R. Hilgard (1977), who proposed a "neodissociation" theory of divided consciousness (see also Kihlstrom, 1984). Neodissociation theory assumes that the mental apparatus consists of a set of cognitive structures similar to Janet's automatisms and Bartlett's (1932) schemata, which monitor, organize, and control both thought and action in various domains. Each of these structures can seek or avoid inputs, or facilitate or inhibit outputs. The structures are arranged hierarchically, are normally in communication with each other, and are linked to a superordinate structure that provides for executive monitoring and control.

As the ultimate endpoint for all inputs, and the ultimate starting point for all outputs, the executive control structure provides the psychological basis for the phenomenal experiences of awareness and intentionality. However, certain conditions can alter the integration and organization of these structures, breaking the links between one or more subsystems or between a subsystem and the executive. Such a situation results in a condition of divided consciousness, in which percepts, thoughts, feelings, and actions are processed without being represented in phenomenal awareness. Such circumstances, of course, can lead to phenomena of implicit cognition, and to behaviors that are perceived as involuntary.

Whether in its original or its updated form, dissociation theory provides a rather different view of nonconscious mental functioning than does psychoanalytic theory (Hilgard, 1977; Kihlstrom, 1984). In the first place, dissociation theory holds that nonconscious mental contents are not necessarily restricted to primitive sexual and aggressive ideas and impulses, nor are nonconscious mental processes necessarily irrational, imagistic, or in any other way qualitatively different from conscious ones; they are simply not consciously accessible. In the second place, dissociation theory holds that the restriction of awareness need not be motivated by purposes of defense, nor need it necessarily have the effect of reducing conflict and anxiety; rather, it can occur simply as a consequence of particular psychological operations. Although largely compatible with the principles of contemporary cognitive psychology, dissociation theory also offers a somewhat different perspective on the cognitive unconscious. Thus, nonconscious mental processes are not restricted to automatized procedural knowledge, and nonconscious mental contents are not limited to unattended or degraded percepts and memories. These differences suggest that dissociative processes deserve more attention from both cognitive and clinical psychologists than they have received in the recent past.

IMPLICIT COGNITION IN SPECIAL STATES OF CONSCIOUSNESS

Setting aside the neurological and psychiatric syndromes, even normal subjects in special states of consciousness can give evidence of perception, memory, and thought outside of awareness. An especially interesting vehicle for such research is hypnosis, a social interaction in which one person (the hypnotist) gives suggestions to another (the subject) for experiences involving alterations in perception, memory, and voluntary action. For example, it may be suggested that the subject: cannot see a particular object in his or her visual field; will forget the events that transpired during hypnosis; or will execute a suggestion after hypnosis has been terminated (Kihlstrom, 1984, 1985a, 1985b, 1987; Kihlstrom & Hoyt, 1988). In highly hypnotizable individuals, responses to these suggestions seem to involve alterations in the accessibility to consciousness of relevant percepts, memories, and thoughts.

Consider an experiment (Kihlstrom, 1980, 1985b) that was originally construed as bearing on the episodic–semantic distinction in memory. The subjects memorized a list of unrelated words to a strict criterion of learning, and then received a suggestion that they would not be able to remember the words they had learned. On an initial test of recall, the hypnotic virtuosos showed a very dense posthypnotic amnesia, remembering virtually none of the words they had previously memorized. Nevertheless, these amnesic subjects were significantly more likely to give list items as responses on a word association test, compared to carefully matched control items—a kind of priming effect.

These priming results show an effect of episodic memory for a prior experience on subjects' performance on a semantic memory task, despite the fact that the subjects could not remember the experience that was the source of the priming effect. In other words, the hypnotic subjects displayed implicit memory for their earlier experience, just as amnesic patients do. The big difference is that amnesic patients do not encode these memories particularly well, as evidenced by the fact that there are no known circumstances under which they can display explicit memory for them. By contrast, posthypnotically amnesic subjects are able to recall their experiences perfectly following administration of the prearranged reversibility cue. Thus, for hypnotic subjects the episodic memories remain available for conscious retrieval, by virtue of having been adequately encoded at the outset, even if they are temporarily inaccessible.

Although the most extensive evidence for implicit cognition in special states of awareness comes from research on hypnosis (e.g., Kihlstrom, 1984, 1985a; Kihlstrom & Hoyt, 1988), hints of similar effects may also be found elsewhere. For example, upon awakening, individuals rarely report any memory for events that transpired while they were asleep—dreams and reveries, brief awakenings, episodes of sleepwalking or sleep talking, presentation of instructional materials, and the like (Arkin, Antrobus, & Ellman, 1978). In fact, such a lack of explicit memory is one of the subjective criteria by which sleep is diagnosed, and constitutes the main evidence against the efficacy of sleep learning (Aarons, 1976). Nevertheless, there is some evidence of implicit memory for sleep experiences (Eich, in press; Schacter & Kihlstrom, 1989). The most dramatic example is provided by Evans's (1979) studies of sleep suggestion. In these studies, subjects were found to respond about 20% of the time to suggestions for simple motor behaviors administered during Stage REM sleep. Although they were unable to remember suggestions, cues, or responses upon awakening, they continued to respond to appropriate cues on subsequent nights—clear evidence for the behavioral influence of memory outside of awareness.

In a similar vein, the adequacy of general anesthesia is assessed, in large part, by the surgical patient's inability to remember his or her surgery (Rosen & Lunn, 1987). Although it is extremely rare for surgical patients to remember details of their operations, conversations among members of the medical team, and the like, there is some evidence for implicit as opposed to explicit memory for surgical events (e.g., Bennett, 1988; Kihlstrom & Schacter, in press). For example, Bennett (1988) has found evidence of postanesthetic suggestion effects, similar to those obtained by Evans (1979) in sleeping subjects. Furthermore, a recent experiment found significant priming effects on a word association task similar to the one described earlier (Kihlstrom, 1980), in patients who were presented with a list of paired associates during surgery (Kihlstrom, Schacter, Cork, Hurt, & Behr, 1989).

A TAXONOMY OF THE COGNITIVE UNCONSCIOUS

These sorts of clinical and experimental studies, conducted in a wide variety of domains and with many different types of subjects, seem to lead to two general types of conclusions. First, consciousness is not to be identified with any particular perceptual–cognitive functions, such as discriminative response to stimulation, perception, memory, or the higher mental processes involved in judgment or problem solving. All of these functions can proceed outside of phenomenal awareness. Rather, consciousness is an experiential quality that may accompany any of these functions. The fact of conscious awareness may have particular consequences for psychological function: It seems necessary for voluntary control, for example, as well as for communicating one's mental states to others and for sponsored teaching. But it is not necessary for many forms of complex psychological functioning. Second, they lead to a provisional taxonomy of nonconscious mental structures and processes constituting the domain of the cognitive unconscious.

There are, within the domain of procedural knowledge, a number of complex processes that are unconscious in the proper sense—unavailable to introspection, in principle, under any circumstances. By virtue of routinization (or perhaps because they are innate), such procedures operate on declarative knowledge without either conscious intent or conscious awareness, in order to construct the person's ongoing experience, thought, and action. Execution of these mental processes, which can be known only indirectly through inference, is inevitable and consumes no attentional capacity. They may be described as unconscious in the strict sense of that term—in short, they comprise the "unconscious proper."

In principle, declarative knowledge is available to phenomenal awareness, and can be known directly through introspection or retrospection. However, it is now clear that procedural knowledge can interact with and utilize declarative knowledge that is not itself accessible to conscious awareness. The phenomena of implicit perception and memory suggest a category of "preconscious" declarative knowledge structures. Unlike truly unconscious procedural knowledge, these percepts and memories are available to awareness under ordinary circumstances. Although activated to some degree by current or prior perceptual–cognitive activity, and thus able to influence ongoing experience, thought, and action, they do not cross the threshold required for representation in working memory, and thus for conscious awareness. These representations, which underlie the phenomena of implicit perception and memory, reside on the fringes of consciousness, and changed circumstances can render them consciously accessible—at least in principle.

The phenomena of hypnosis and related states seem to exemplify a category of "subconscious" declarative knowledge. These mental representations, which are fully activated by perceptual inputs or acts of thought, are above the threshold ordinarily required for representation in working memory, and are available to introspection and retrospection under some circumstances, seem nevertheless dissociated from phenomenal awareness (Hilgard, 1977). Dissociative phenomena are of theoretical interest because they cannot comfortably be classified as either unconscious or preconscious. They are not limited to innate or routinized procedural knowledge; their execution is not automatic, and it consumes cognitive capacity. The stimulus input has not been degraded in any way, and the resulting memory traces are fully encoded and available for explicit retrieval. From the point of view of activation notions of consciousness, these phenomena are theoretically interesting because they indicate that high levels of activation (supported by the active deployment of attention and complex mental processing), although presumably necessary for residence in working memory, are not sufficient for conscious awareness.

THE MECHANISM OF CONSCIOUSNESS

What is required in order to achieve conscious awareness? At a psychological level of analysis, it seems that conscious awareness requires that a mental representation of an event be connected with some mental representation of the self as agent or experiencer of that event (Kihlstrom, 1984, 1987, 1989; Kihlstrom & Tobias, 1989). In his discussion of the stream of consciousness, James (1890) wrote that "the first fact for . . . psychologists is that thinking of some sort goes on" (p. 219). He also wrote, immediately thereafter, that "thought tends to personal form" (p. 220)—that is, every thought (by which James meant every conscious mental state) is part of a personal consciousness: "The universal conscious fact is not 'feelings exist' or 'thoughts exist' but '*I* think' and '*I* feel,' " (p. 221, emphasis added).

In other words, an episode of ongoing experience, thought, and action becomes conscious if, and only if, a link is made between the mental representation of the event itself and some mental representation of the self as the agent or experiencer of that event. This mental representation of self, including the internal environment, resides in working memory as a memory structure, along with coexisting representations of the current external environment (Anderson, 1983; Kihlstrom & Cantor, 1984; Kihlstrom et al., 1988). Both self and context representations are necessary for the construction of a full-fledged conscious perception—which, following James, always seems to take this form: "*I see* (or hear, smell, taste, etc.) *this, now.*" And since memory is the residual trace of perceptual activity, these elements are necessary for the reconstruction of a full-fledged conscious recollections as well.

Within a generic associative-network theory of knowledge representation (e.g., Anderson, 1983), an episode of experience is represented by one node connecting three others: an "event" node, containing a raw description of an event; a "context" node, specifying the spatial and temporal (and perhaps emotional and motivational) context in which the event occurred; and a "self" node, indicating the person as the agent or the experiencer of the event. Conscious recollection of such an event occurs only when the representation of the self is retrieved along with some other information about the event. The inability to retrieve the links among all three types of propositions accounts for some of the peculiarities in conscious memory (Kihlstrom, 1984; Kihlstrom & Tobias, 1989; Reed, 1988). What unites the various phenomena of the cognitive unconscious—automatic processing and the various forms of implicit perception, memory, and thought—is that the link to self either does not get forged in the first place, or else it is subsequently lost. Thus, Claparede (1911/1951) wrote of the amnesic syndrome: "If one examines the behavior of such a patient, one finds that everything happens as though the various events of life, however well associated with each *other* in the mind, were incapable of integration with the *me* itself" (p. 71; emphasis in original).

Recently, Schacter (in press) has offered some provocative speculations concerning the neuropsychological foundations of conscious and nonconscious mental processes. A large number of neurological syndromes may be described as disorders of consciousness (for a review, see Schacter, McAndrews, & Moscovitch, 1988). For example, the dissociations between implicit and explicit memory seen in the amnesic syndrome suggest that the disorder reflects, in part, a failure to encode consciously accessible memories or to gain conscious access to memories, rather than a gross anterograde amnesia. Similarly, close examination of prosopagnosia yields evidence of discriminative response to old and new faces, even in the absence of conscious feelings of familiarity. And patients with cortical blindness show evidence of "blindsight" in their performance of visually guided responses. Evidence for disruptions in consciousness in the language disorders is tentative but also provocative (for a review, see Schacter et al., 1988). For example, patients with lesions in certain regions of the left occipital and temporal lobes, and adjacent areas, show an acquired dyslexia in which they cannot recognize whole words but must rely on a strategy of letter-by-letter decoding. Nevertheless, such patients can make correct lexical decisions concerning words presented too briefly to be decoded on a letter-by-letter basis, thus giving evidence of implicit *reading*. Within the broad class of aphasias, patients with lesions in Broca's area show disruptions in the use of Syntax, whereas those with lesions in Wernicke's area appear to lose semantic information. Even so, careful study sometimes reveals a selective disruption of explicit, but not implicit, linguistic knowledge. For example, patients with lesions in Broca's area can make accurate judgments of grammaticality, whereas their counterparts with lesions in Wernicke's area show semantic priming on lexical decision tasks. Finally, patients suffering many different neurological syndromes show symptoms of "anosognosia," meaning that they appear to be unaware of the extent of their psychological deficits (for a review, see McGlynn & Schacter, 1989).

Surveying this material, Schacter (in press) has proposed that the conscious experience of perceiving, remembering, and knowing reflects the operation of a hypothetical "conscious awareness system" (CAS), which is different from the executive system that initiates and monitors various cognitive–behavioral activities. The CAS normally interacts with the modules that regulate such operations as perception, memory, and language, and the product of such interaction is the conscious experience of perceiving, remembering, comprehending, or communicating. Thus, processing by one of the modules is not by itself sufficient to produce conscious experience. Consciousness requires some output from the module in question to the CAS. Certain forms of brain damage produce a breakdown in communication between, say, the module governing memory and that governing consciousness, without necessarily impairing the functions of the memory module per se, or the connections between CAS and modules for perception or language. Such a state of affairs would result in an impairment of explicit but not implicit memory, but no defects in explicit perception or language functioning.

Schacter (in press) has not gone so far as to locate the CAS at a specific cortical site, but he has described several possible neuropsychological mechanisms underlying the communication breakdown. Damage to the CAS itself, of course, would produce a general loss of explicit cognition across a wide variety of domains. The fact that such a syndrome has not been observed suggests that CAS is widely distributed across the cortical mass. Concerning the specific disorders of consciousness, one possibility is that a relatively intact cognitive module becomes functionally disconnected (Geschwind, 1965) from an intact CAS; another is that the damaged cognitive module sends degraded signals to an intact CAS. Although these and other possibilities remain to be explored, Schacter's (in press) ideas represent an important new direction in the study of the biological substrates of consciousness.

THE PSYCHOLOGICAL UNCONSCIOUS IN THE TRILOGY OF MIND

It should be noted that most experimental work on nonconscious processing has followed Helmholtzian rather than Freudian lines, in employing neutral stimulus materials and sterile laboratory procedures that effectively limit the role played by personality factors, or the influence of the psychological unconscious on interpersonal relations. Moreover, most of the work summarized here has been more or less exclusively cognitive in nature, and has deemphasized the rest of the trilogy of mind—the emotional and motivational factors that are of central interest to personality and social psychology. Even so, several recent lines of work indicate how the concepts and paradigms employed in the laboratory study of the cognitive conscious may be extended to these domains.

Some of this research has an explicitly psychodynamic flavor. For example, Shevrin and his colleagues (Shevrin & Dickman, 1980) have studied the ERPs evoked in neurotic patients by words theoretically related to their complaints. By means of a tachistoscope, the words are presented too briefly to be consciously recognized: nevertheless, the patients appear to give differential ERPs to stimuli, depending on whether they are relevant to their complaints. In another line of research, Silverman and his colleagues (Silverman, 1976, 1983; Silverman, Lachman, & Milich, 1982; Silverman & Weinberger, 1985) have reported that brief tachistoscopic presentations of "symbiotic" messages such as "Mommy and I are one," too brief to be consciously recognized, can have effects on the behavior of both psychiatric patients and normal subjects. Shevrin's work focuses on the intensive study of carefully selected cases. Silverman's work has been somewhat more nomothetic in character, but his theoretical predictions have been controversial even among psychoanalysts, and his observations have proved difficult to replicate (Balay & Shevrin, 1988). Nevertheless, the two lines of research are obviously related to nonpsychodynamic work on implicit perception, and serve to illustrate the possibilities afforded by the marriage of psychodynamic theory with experimental method (Horowitz, 1988).

Other investigators, not necessarily aligned with the psychodynamic tradition, have also effectively used paradigms of implicit perception. For example, Kunst-Wilson and Zajonc (1980) have shown that mere exposure to line drawings of polygons increases judgments of their attractiveness, even though the exposures themselves are too brief to be consciously perceived (see also Seamon, Brody, & Kauff, 1983; Seamon, Marsh, & Brody, 1984). Bornstein, Leone, and Galley (1987) replicated and extended this effect: Not only did subjects show more positive attitudes toward people depicted in tachistoscopically presented photographs, but they also interacted more positively with these same individuals when they later encountered them in a contrived social interaction. Zajonc (1980) has used these results to claim that affective responses are independent of, and perhaps even prior to, cognitive processing. However, Mandler, Nakamura, and Van Zandt (1987) showed that mere exposure, outside of awareness, also increased ratings of brightness, darkness, and *disliking*. Thus, the preference effect of Kunst-Wilson and Zajonc (1980) seems to be a specific instantiation of a more general principle that activation of an internal representation of an object affects judgment about any relevant dimension of that object (Mandler et al., 1987), and does not support specific claims concerning the priority of affect (Lazarus, 1984; Zajonc, 1984).

Nevertheless, the effects on preference judgments and other emotional responses set the stage for other analyses of unconscious influences on social cognition and interaction (Cantor & Kihlstrom, 1987, 1989; Kihlstrom & Cantor, 1989). Some early research along these lines was reported by Nisbett and Wilson (1977; see also Wilson, 1985; Wilson & Stone, 1985), who argued that people largely lack introspective access to the actual determinants of their judgments and other behaviors (for critiques, see Bowers, 1984; Smith & Miller, 1978). More recently, programmatic research by Bargh (1984, 1989) has explored the impact of unconscious, automatic processes on impression formation; and another program by Lewicki (1986; Lewicki & Hill, 1987) has shown that information about the features of social stimuli (and the covariations among them) can be acquired through implicit learning and can influence behavior, even though it is stored in a form that is inaccessible to conscious awareness.

The success and vigor of these lines of research is clear to all observers, and promises much to the personality and social psychologists of the future. A full century since the publication of Janet's (1889) *Psychological Automatisms* and James's (1890) *Principles of Psychology*, and five decades since the death of Freud, the study of nonconscious life has been completely revolutionized. For the first time, contemporary cognitive psychology has begun to offer a clear theoretical framework for studying the relations between conscious and nonconscious mental life. Along with the development of a new class of psychological theories has come a new set of observations, derived from sophisticated new experimental paradigms, including research in cognitive neuropsychology. Thus far, this body of research has revealed a view of nonconscious mental life that is more extensive than the unconscious inference of Helmholtz, but also quite different—kindler, gentler, and more rational—from the seething unconscious of Freud.

Still and all, it should be recognized that almost all of the work to date has been done within the confines of cognitive psychology and cognitive neuropsychology, with relatively little attention paid to the role of unconscious processes in personality and social interaction. Thus, it would seem that an important agenda item for the near future would be the deliberate adoption by personality and social psychologists of the concepts and principles that have served their cognitive colleagues so well, and the systematic extension of research on the psychological unconscious beyond words and polygons to people and actions, and beyond implicit cognition to implicit emotion and implicit motivation.

ACKNOWLEDGMENTS

The point of view represented herein is based in part on research supported by Grant Nos. MH-35856 and MH-44739 from the National Institute of Mental Health, and by Subcontract No. 1122SC from the Program on Conscious and Unconscious Mental Processes of the John D. and Catherine T. MacArthur Foundation, through the University of California–San Francisco. I thank Terrence L. Barnhardt, Lawrence J. Couture, Martha L. Glisky, Marcia K. Johnson, Susan M. McGlynn, Elizabeth Merikle, Paula M. Niedenthal, Mary A. Peterson, Daniel L. Schacter, Douglas J. Tataryn, and Betsy A. Tobias for their comments.

REFERENCES

Aarons, L. (1976). Sleep-assisted instruction. *Psychological Bulletin, 83*, 1–40.

Anderson, J. R. (1982). Acquisition of cognitive skill. *Psychological Review, 89*, 369–406.

Anderson, J. R. (1983). *The architecture of cognition.* Cambridge, MA: Harvard University Press.

Arkin, A. M., Antrobus, J. S., & Ellman, S. J. (1978). *The mind in sleep.* Hillsdale, NJ: Erlbaum.

Atkinson, R. C., & Shiffrin, R. M. (1968). Human memory: A proposed system and its control processes. In K. W. Spence & J. T. Spends (Eds.), *The psychology of learning and motivation* (Vol. 2, pp. 89–195). New York: Academic Press.

Balay, J., & Shevrin, W. (1988). The subliminal psychodynamic activation method: A critical review. *American Psychologist, 43*, 161–174.

Bargh, J. A. (1984). Automatic and conscious processing of social information. In R. S. Wyer and T. K. Srull (Eds.), *Handbook of social cognition* (Vol. 3, pp. 1–43). Hillsdale, NJ: Erlbaum.

Bargh, J. A. (1989). Conditional automaticity: Varieties of automatic influence in social perception and cognition. In J. S. Uleman & J. A. Bargh (Eds.), *Unintended thought* (pp. 3–51). New York: Guilford Press.

Bartlett, F. C. (1932). *Remembering: A study in experimental and social psychology.* Cambridge, England: Cambridge University Press.

Bennett, H. L. (1988). Perception and memory for events during adequate general anesthesia for surgical operations. In H. M. Pettinati (Ed.), *Hypnosis and memory* (pp. 193–231). New York: Guilford Press.

Bliss, E. L. (1986). *Multiple personality, allied disorders, and hypnosis.* New York: Oxford University Press.

Bornstein, R. F., Leone, D. R., & Galley, D. J. (1987). The generalizability of subliminal mere exposure effects: Influence of stimuli perceived without awareness on social behavior. *Journal of Personality and Social Psychology, 53,* 1070–1079.

Bowers, K. S. (1984). On being unconsciously influenced and informed. In K. S. Bowers & D. Meichenbaum (Eds.), *The unconscious reconsidered* (pp. 227–272). New York: Wiley-Interscience.

Bowers, K. S. (1987). Revisioning the unconscious. *Canadian Psychology, 28,* 93–104.

Bowers, K. S., & Meichenbaum, D. (Eds.). (1984). *The unconscious reconsidered.* New York: Wiley-Interscience.

Bowers, K. S., Regehr, G., Balthazard, C., & Parker, K. (in press). Intuition in the context of discovery. *Cognitive Psychology.*

Brady, J. P., & Lind, D. I. (1961). Experimental analysis of hysterical blindness. *Behaviour Research and Therapy, 4,* 331–339.

Brewer, W. F. (1974). There is no convincing evidence for operant or classical conditioning in adult humans. In W. B. Weimer & D. S. Palermo (Eds.), *Cognition and the symbolic processes* (pp. 1–42). Hillsdale, NJ: Erlbaum.

Broadbent, D. E., FitzGerald, P., & Broadbent, M. H. P. (1986). Implicit and explicit knowledge in the control of complex systems. *British Journal of Psychology, 77,* 33–50.

Bruner, J. S., & Klein, G. S. (1960). The function of perceiving: New Look retrospect. In S. Wapner & B. Kaplan (Eds.), *Perspectives in psychological theory.* New York: International Universities Press.

Bryant, R. A., & McConkey, K. M. (1989). Visual conversion disorder: A case analysis of the influence of visual information. *Journal of Abnormal Psychology, 98,* 326–329.

Burke, D. M., & Light, L. L. (1981). Memory and aging: The role of retrieval processes. *Psychological Bulletin, 90,* 513–546.

Burston, D. (1986). The cognitive and dynamic unconscious: A critical and historical perspective. *Contemporary Psychoanalysis, 22,* 133–157.

Campion, J., Latto, R., & Smith, Y. M. (1983). Is blindsight an effect of scattered light, spared cortex, and near-threshold vision? *Behavioral and Brain Sciences, 6,* 423–486.

Cantor, N., & Kihlstrom, J. F. (1987). *Personality and social intelligence.* Englewood Cliffs, NJ: Prentice-Hall.

Cantor, N., & Kihlstrom, J. F. (1989). Social intelligence and cognitive assessments of personality. In R. S. Wyer & T. K. Srull (Eds.), *Advances in social cognition* (Vol. 2, pp. 1–59). Hillsdale, NJ: Erlbaum.

Cheesman, J., & Merikle, P. M. (1985). Word recognition and consciousness. In D. Besner, T. G. Waller, & G. E., MacKinnon (Eds.), *Reading research: Advances in theory and practice* (Vol. 5, pp. 311–352). New York: Academic Press.

Cheesman, J., & Merikle, P. M. (1986). Distinguishing conscious from unconscious perceptual processes. *Canadian Journal of Psychology, 40,* 343–367.

Claparede, E. (1951). [Recognition and "me-ness"]. In D. Rapaport (Ed.), *Organization and pathology of thought* (pp. 58–75). New York: Columbia University Press. (Original work published 1911)

deHaan, E. H. F., Young, A., & Newcombe, F. (1987). Face recognition without awareness. *Cognitive Neuropsychology, 4,* 385–415.

Dixon, N. (1971). *Subliminal perception: The nature of a controversy.* London: McGraw-Hill.

Dixon, N. (1981). *Preconscious processing.* Chichester, England: Wiley.

Eich, E. (in press). Learning during sleep. In R. R. Bootzin, J. F. Kihlstrom, & D. L. Schacter (Eds.), *Sleep and cognition.* Washington, DC: American Psychological Association.

Ellenberger, H. F. (1970). *The discovery of the unconscious: The history and evolution of dynamic psychiatry.* New York: Basic Books.

Erdelyi, M. H. (1974). A new look at the New Look: Perceptual defense and vigilance. *Psychological Review, 81,* 1–25.

Erdelyi, M. H. (1985). *Psychoanalysis: Freud's cognitive psychology.* San Francisco: W. H. Freeman.

Erickson, C. W. (1960). Discrimination and learning without awareness: A methodological survey and evaluation. *Psychological Review, 67,* 279–300.

Evans, F. J. (1979). Hypnosis and sleep: Techniques for exploring cognitive activity during sleep. In E. Fromm & R. E. Shor (Eds.), *Hypnosis: Developments in research and new perspectives* (pp. 139–184). New York: Aldine.

Fleeson, W., & Kihlstrom, J. F. (1988). *Automatic and effortful encoding of episodic context.* Unpublished manuscript, University of Michigan.

Fowler, C. A., Wolford, G., Slade, R., & Tassinary, L. (1981). Lexical access with and without awareness. *Journal of Experimental Psychology: General, 110,* 341 362.

Freud, S. (1953). The interpretation of dreams. In J. Strachey (Ed. and Trans.), *The standard edition of the complete psychological works of Sigmund Freud* (Vol. 4, pp. 1–338; Vol. 5, pp. 339–621). London: Hogarth Press. (Original work published 1900)

Freud, S. (1957). The unconscious. In J. Strachey (Ed. and Trans.), *The standard edition of the complete psychological works of Sigmund Freud* (Vol. 14, pp. 159–215). London: Hogarth Press. (Original work published 1915)

Freud, S. (1958). A note on the unconscious in psychoanalysis. In J. Strachey (Ed. and Trans.), *The standard edition of the complete psychological works of Sigmund Freud* (Vol. 12, pp. 255–266). London: Hogarth Press. (Original work published 1912)

Freud, S. (1961). Introductory lectures on psycho-analysis. In J. Strachey (Ed. and Trans.), *The standard edition of the complete psychological works of Sigmund Freud* (Vol. 15, pp. 1–239; Vol. 16, pp. 243–463) London: Hogarth Press. (Original work published 1917)

Freud, S. (1961) The ego and the id. In J. Strachey (Ed.

and Trans.), *The standard edition of the complete psychological works of Sigmund Freud* (Vol. 19, pp. 1–66). London: Hogarth Press. (Original work published 1923)

Freud, S. (1964). An outline of psycho-analysis. In J. Strachey (Ed. and Trans.), *The standard edition of the complete psychological works of Sigmund Freud* (Vol. 23, pp. 139–207). London: Hogarth Press. (Original work published 1940)

Geschwind, N. (1965). Disconnexion syndromes in animals and man. *Brain, 88,* 237–294.

Graf, P., & Schacter, D. L. (1985). Implicit and explicit memory for new associations in normal and amnesic subjects. *Journal of Experimental Psychology: Learning, Memory, and Cognition, 11,* 501–518.

Greenwald, A. G., Klinger, M. R., & Liu, T. J. (1989). Unconscious processing of dichopatically masked words. *Memory and Cognition, 17,* 35–47.

Gudjonsson, G. H. (1979). The use of electrodermal responses in a case of amnesia. *Medicine, Science, and the Law, 19,* 138–140.

Gudjonsson, G. H., & Taylor, P. J. (1985). Cognitive deficit in a case of retrograde amnesia. *British Journal of Psychiatry, 147,* 715–718.

Hasher, L., & Zacks, R. T. (1979). Automatic and effortful processes in memory. *Journal of Experimental Psychology: General, 108,* 356–388.

Hasher, L., & Zacks, R. T. (1984). Automatic processing of fundamental information: The case of frequency of occurrence. *American Psychologist, 39,* 1372–1388.

Hilgard, E. R. (1969). Levels of awareness: Second thoughts on some of William James' ideas. In R. B. MacLeod (Ed.), *William James: Unfinished business.* Washington, DC: American Psychological Association.

Hilgard, E. R. (1977). Controversies over consciousness and the rise of cognitive psychology. *Australian Psychologist, 12,* 7–26.

Hilgard, E. R. (1980a). Consciousness in contemporary psychology. *Annual Review of Psychology, 31,* 1–26.

Hilgard, E. R. (1980b). The trilogy of mind: Cognition, affection, and conation. *Journal of the History of the Behavioral Sciences, 16,* 107–117.

Hilgard, E. R. (1987). *Psychology in America: A historical survey.* San Diego: Harcourt Brace Jovanovich.

Hilgard, E. R., & Marquis, D. G. (1940). *Conditioning and learning.* New York: Appleton-Century-Crofts.

Holender, D. (1986). Semantic activation without conscious identification in dichotic listening, parafoveal vision, and visual masking: A survey and appraisal. *Behavioral and Brain Sciences, 9,* 1–66.

Horowitz, M. J. (1988). *Psychodynamics and cognition.* Chicago: University of Chicago Press.

Howell, P. (1980). *A commentary on Book I of the epigrams of Martial.* London: Athlone.

Hoyt, I. P., & Kihlstrom, J. F. (1989). *Posthypnotic suggestion and waking instruction: Allocation of attentional resource in simultaneous tasks.* Unpublished manuscript, University of Wisconsin.

Jacoby, L. L., & Dallas, M. (1981). On the relationship between autobiographical memory and perceptual learning. *Journal of Experimental Psychology: General, 110,* 306–340.

James, W. (1890). *Principles of psychology.* New York: Holt.

Janet, P. (1889). [*Psychological automatisms*]. Paris: Alcan.

Janet, P. (1907). *The major symptoms of hysteria.* New York: Macmillan.

Kahneman, D., & Triesman, A. (1984). Changing views of attention and automaticity. In R. Parasuraman & D. R. Davies (Eds.), *Varieties of attention* (pp. 29–61). New York: Academic Press.

Kaszniak, A. W., Nussbaum, P. D., Berren, M. R., & Santiago, J. (1988). Amnesia as a consequence of male rape: A case report. *Journal of Abnormal Psychology, 97,* 100–104.

Kihlstrom, J. F. (1980). Posthypnotic amnesia for recently learned material: Interactions with "episodic" and "semantic" memory. *Cognitive Psychology, 12,* 227–251.

Kihlstrom, J. F. (1984). Conscious, subconscious, unconscious: A cognitive view. In K. S. Bowers & D. Meichenbaum (Eds.), *The unconscious reconsidered* (pp. 149–211). New York: Wiley-interscience.

Kihlstrom, J. F. (1985a). Hypnosis. *Annual Review of Psychology, 36,* 385–418.

Kihlstrom, J. F. (1985b). Posthypnotic amnesia and the dissociation of memory. In G. H. Bower (Ed.), *The psychology of learning and motivation* (Vol. 19, pp. 131–178). Orlando, FL: Academic Press.

Kihlstrom, J. F. (1987). The cognitive unconscious. *Science, 237,* 1445–1452.

Kihlstrom, J. F. (1988). Personality. In E. R. Hilgard (Ed.), *Fifty years of psychology: Essays in honor of Floyd Ruch* (pp. 139–152). Glenview, IL: Scott, Foresman.

Kihlstrom, J. F. (1989). Cognition, unconscious processes. In G. Adelman (Ed.), *Neuroscience year: The yearbook of the encyclopedia of Neuroscience* (pp. 34–36). Boston: Birkhauser Boston.

Kihlstrom, J. F. (in press). Dissociative disorders. In P. B. Sutker & H. E. Adams (Eds.), *Comprehensive handbook of psychopathology* (2nd ed.). New York: Plenum.

Kihlstrom, J. F., & Cantor, N. (1984). Mental representations of the self. In L. Berkowitz (Ed.), *Advances in experimental social psychology* (Vol. 17, pp. 1–47). Orlando, FL: Academic Press.

Kihlstrom, J. F., & Cantor, N. (1989). Social intelligence and personality: There's room for growth. In R. S. Wyer & T. K. Srull (Eds.), *Advances in social cognition* (Vol. 2, pp. 197–214). Hillsdale, NJ: Erlbaum.

Kihlstrom, J. F., Cantor, N., Albright, J. S., Chew, B. R., Klein, S. B., & Neidenthal, P. M. (1988). Information processing and the study of the self. In L. Berkowitz (Ed.), *Advances in experimental social psychology* (Vol. 21, pp. 145–178). San Diego: Academic Press.

Kihlstrom, J. F., & Hoyt, I. P. (1988). Hypnosis and the psychology of delusions. In T. F. Oltmanns & B. A. Maher (Eds.), *Delusional beliefs: Interdisciplinary perspectives* (pp. 66–109). New York: Wiley-Interscience.

Kihlstrom, J. F., & Schacter, D. L. (in press). Anesthesia, implicit memory, and the cognitive unconscious. In B. Bonke, W. Fitch, & K. Millar (Eds.), *Memory and awareness in anesthesia.* Rotterdam: Swets & Zeitlinger.

Kihlstrom, J. F., Schacter, D. L., Cork, R. C., Hurt, C., & Behr, S. E. (1989). *Implicit and explicit memory following surgical anesthesia.* Unpublished manuscript, University of Arizona.

Kihlstrom, J. F., & Tobias, B. T. (1989). Anosognosia, consciousness, and the self. In G. P. Prigatano & D. L. Schacter (Eds.), *Awareness of deficit following brain injury: Clinical and theoretical aspects* (in press). New York: Oxford University Press.

Klein, D. B. (1977). *The unconscious: Invention or discov-*

ery? *A historico-critical inquiry.* Santa Monica, CA: Goodyear.

Kunst-Wilson, W. R., & Zajonc, R. B. (1980). Affective discrimination of stimuli that cannot be recognized. *Science, 207,* 557–558.

LaBerge, D. (1975). Acquisition of automatic processing in perceptual and associative learning. In P. M. A. Rabbit & S. Dornic (Eds.), *Attention and performance V.* New York: Academic Press.

Lazarus, R. S. (1984). On the primacy of cognition. *American Psychologist, 39,* 124–129.

Lewicki, P. (1986). *Nonconscious social information processing.* New York: Academic Press.

Lewicki, P., & Hill, T. (1987). Unconscious processes as explanations of behavior in cognitive, personality, and social psychology. *Personality and Social Psychology Bulletin, 13,* 355–362.

Logan, G. D. (1980). Attention and automaticity in Stroop and priming tasks: Theory and data. *Cognitive Psychology, 12,* 523–.

Ludwig, A. J., Brandsma, J. M., Wilbur, C. B., Bendfeldt, E., & Jameson, D. H. (1972). The objective study of a multiple personality: Or, are four heads better than one? *Archives of General Psychiatry, 26,* 298–310.

Lyon, L. S. (1985). Facilitating telephone number recall in a case of psychogenic amnesia. *Journal of Behavior Therapy and Experimental Psychiatry, 16,* 147–149.

Macmillan, M. B. (1989). *Freud reevaluated: The completed arc.* Unpublished manuscript, Monash University, Melbourne, Australia.

Mandler, G., Nakamura, Y., & Van Zandt, B. J. S. (1987). Nonspecific effects of exposure on stimuli that cannot be recognized. *Journal of Experimental Psychology: Learning, Memory, and Cognition, 13,* 646–648.

Marcel, A. (1983a). Conscious and unconscious perception: Experiments on visual masking and word recognition. *Cognitive Psychology, 15,* 197–237.

Marcel, A. (1983b). Conscious and unconscious perception: An approach to the relations between phenomenal experience and perceptual processes. *Cognitive Psychology, 15,* 238–300.

McClelland, J. L., Rummelhart, D. E., & the PDP Research Group. (1986). *Parallel distributed processing: Explorations in the microstructure of cognition. Vol. 2. Psychological and biological models.* Cambridge, MA: MIT Press.

McGlynn, S. M., & Schacter, D. L. (1989). Unawareness of deficits in neuropsychological syndromes. *Journal of Clinical and Experimental Neuropsychology, 11,* 143–205.

Merikle, P. M. (1988). Subliminal auditory messages: An evaluation. *Psychology and Marketing, 5,* 355–372.

Moore, T. E. (1982). Subliminal advertising: What you see is what you get. *Journal of Marketing, 46,* 38–47.

Myers, G. E. (1986). *William James: His life and thought.* New Haven, CT: Yale University Press.

Nelson, T. (1978). Detecting small amounts of information in memory: Savings for nonrecognized items. *Journal of Experimental Psychology: Human Learning and Memory, 4,* 453–468.

Nisbett, R., & Wilson, T. D. (1977). Telling more than we can know: Verbal reports on mental processes. *Psychological Review, 84,* 231–259.

Nissen, M. J., Ross, J. L., Willingham, D. B., MacKenzie, T. B., & Schacter, D. L. (1989). Memory and awareness in a patient with multiple personality disorder. *Brain and Cognition, 8,* 117–134.

Peirce, C. S., & Jastrow, J. (1884). On small differences of sensation. *Memorials of the National Academy of Sciences, 3,* 73–83.

Perry, C., & Laurence, J.-R. (1984). Mental processing outside of awareness: The contributions of Freud and Janet. In K. S. Bowers & D. Meichenbaum (Eds.), *The unconscious reconsidered* (pp. 9–40). New York: Wiley-Interscience.

Peterson, M. A., & Hochberg, J. (1983). Opposed-set measurement procedure: A quantitative analysis of the role of local cues and intention in form perception. *Journal of Experimental Psychology: Human Perception and Performance, 9,* 183–193.

Posner, M. I., & Snyder, C. R. R. (1975). Attention and cognitive control. In R. L. Solso (Ed.), *Information processing and cognition: The Loyola Symposium.* Hillsdale, NJ: Erlbaum.

Prince, M. (1906). *The dissociation of a personality.* New York: Longmans, Green.

Rapaport, D. (1942). *Emotions and memory.* Baltimore: Williams & Wilkins.

Razran, G. (1961). The observable unconscious and the inferable conscious in current Soviet psychophysiology. *Psychological Review, 68,* 81–147.

Reber, A. S. (1976). Implicit learning of artificial grammars. *Journal of Verbal Learning and Verbal Behavior, 5,* 855–863.

Reber, A. S. (1989). Implicit learning and tacit knowledge. *Journal of Experimental Psychology: General, 118,* 219–235.

Reed, G. (1988). *The psychology of anomalous experience* (rev. ed.). Buffalo, NY: Prometheus Books.

Reingold, E. M., & Merikle, P. M. (1989). Using direct and indirect measures to study perception without awareness. *Perception and Psychophysics, 44,* 563–575.

Rosen, M., & Lunn, J. N. (1987). *Consciousness, awareness, and pain in general anaesthesia.* London: Butterworths.

Rummelhart, D. E., McClelland, J. L., & the PDP Research Group. (1986). *Parallel distributed processing: Explorations in the microstructure of cognition. Vol. 1. Foundations.* Cambridge, MA: MIT Press.

Sackeim, H. A., Nordlie, J. W., & Gur, R. C. (1979). A model of hysterical and hypnotic blindness: Cognition, motivation, and awareness. *Journal of Abnormal Psychology, 88,* 474–489.

Schacter, D. L. (1987). Implicit memory: History and current status. *Journal of Experimental Psychology: Learning, Memory, and Cognition, 13,* 501–518.

Schacter, D. L. (in press). Toward a cognitive neuropsychology of awareness: Implicit knowledge and anosognosia. *Journal of Clinical and Experimental Neuropsychology.*

Schacter, D. L., & Graf, P. (1989). Modality specificity of implicit memory for new associations. *Journal of Experimental Psychology: Learning, Memory, and Cognition, 15,* 3–12.

Schacter, D. L., Kaszniak, A. W., & Kihlstrom, J. F. (in press). Models of memory and the understanding of memory disorders. In T. Yanagihara & R. C. Peterson (Eds.), *Memory disorders in clinical practice.* New York: Marcel Dekker.

Schacter, D. L., & Kihlstrom, J. F. (1989). Functional amnesia. In F. Boller & J. Graffman (Eds.), *Handbook of neuropsychology* (Vol. 3, pp. 209–231). Amsterdam: Elsevier.

Schacter, D. L., McAndrews, M. P., & Moscovitch, M.

(1988). Access to consciousness: Dissociations between implicit and explicit knowledge in neuropsychological syndromes. In L. Weiskrantz (Ed.), *Thought without language* (pp. 242–278). Oxford: Oxford University Press.

Schacter, D. L., Wang, P. L., Tulving, E., & Freedman, M. (1982). Functional retrograde amnesia: A quantitative case study. *Neuropsychologia, 20,* 523–532.

Schneider, W., & Shiffrin, R. M. (1977). Controlled and automatic human information processing: I. Detection, search, and attention. *Psychological Review, 84,* 1–66.

Seamon, J. G., Brody, N., & Kauff, D. M. (1983). Affective discrimination of stimuli that are not recognized: Effects of shadowing, masking, and cerebral laterality. *Journal of Experimental Psychology: Learning, Memory, and Cognition, 9,* 544–555.

Seamon, J. G., Marsh, R. L., & Brody, N. (1984). Critical importance of exposure duration for affective discrimination of stimuli that are not recognized. *Journal of Experimental Psychology: Learning, Memory, and Cognition, 10,* 465–469.

Shevrin, H., & Dickman, S. (1980). The psychological unconscious: A necessary assumption for all psychological theory? *American Psychologist, 35,* 421–434.

Shiffrin, R. W., & Schneider, W. (1977). Controlled and automatic human information processing: II. Perceptual learning, automatic attending, and a general theory. *Psychological Review, 84,* 127–190.

Shiffrin, R. W., & Schneider, W. (1984). Automatic and controlled processing revisited. *Psychological Review, 91,* 269–276.

Silverman, L. H. (1976). Psychoanalytic theory: "The reports of my death are greatly exaggerated." *American Psychologist, 31,* 621–637.

Silverman, L. H. (1983). The subliminal psychodynamic activation method: Overview and comprehensive listing of studies. In J. Masling (Ed.), *Empirical studies of psychoanalytic theories* (pp. 69–100). Hillsdale, NJ: Erlbaum.

Silverman, L. H., Lachman, F. M., & Milich, R. H. (1982). *The search for oneness.* New York: International Universities Press.

Silverman, L. H., & Weinberger, J. (1985). Mommy and I are one: Implications for psychotherapy. *American Psychologist, 40,* 1296–1308.

Smith, E. R., & Miller, J. D. (1978). Limits on perception of cognitive processes: Reply to Nisbett and Wilson. *Psychological Review, 85,* 355–362.

Spanos, N. P., Menary, E., Brett, P. J., Cross, W., & Ahmed, Q. (1987). Failure of posthypnotic responding to occur outside the experimental setting. *Journal of Abnormal Psychology, 96,* 52–57.

Taylor, E. (1983). *William James on exceptional mental states: The 1896 Lowell Lectures reconstructed.* New York: Scribner's.

Tranel, D., & Damasio, A. R. (1985). Knowledge without awareness: An autonomic index of facial recognition by prosopagnosics. *Science, 228,* 1453–1454.

Tulving, E., Schacter, D. L., & Stark, H. A. (1982). Priming effects in word-fragment completion are independent of recognition memory. *Journal of Experimental Psychology: Learning, Memory, and Cognition, 8,* 336–342.

Weiskrantz, L. (1980). Varieties of residual experience. *Quarterly Journal of Experimental Psychology, 32,* 365–386.

Weiskrantz, L., Warrington, E. K., Sanders, M. D., & Marshall, J. (1974). Visual capacity in the hemianopic field following a restricted occipital ablation. *Brain, 97,* 709–728.

Whyte, L. L. (1960). *The unconscious before Freud.* New York: Basic Books.

Wilson, T. D. (1985). Strangers to ourselves: The origins and accuracy of beliefs about one's own mental states. In J. H. Harvey & G. Weary (Eds.), *Attribution: Basic issues and applications* (pp. 9–36). Orlando, FL: Academic Press.

Wilson, T. D., & Stone, J. I. (1985). Limitations of self-knowledge: More on telling more than we can know. *Review of Personality and Social Psychology, 6,* 167–183.

Zajonc, R. B. (1980). Feeling and thinking: Preferences need no inferences. *American Psychologist, 35,* 151–175.

Zajonc, R. B. (1984). On the primacy of affect. *American Psychologist, 39,* 117–123.

Chapter 18

Attribution in Personality Psychology

Bernard Weiner

University of California–Los Angeles

Attribution theory is concerned with causal inferences, or the perceived reason(s) why an event has occurred. Thus, attribution theorists attempt to resolve how individuals answer such questions as these: "Why has Mary rejected my proposal?" "Has Bill intentionally harmed me?" and so forth. The originator of this conceptual approach, Fritz Heider, and subsequent key contributors, including Edward Jones and Harold Kelley, are social psychologists. Their primary interests in interpersonal relations and social behavior were greatly illuminated when they took into account the replies to the queries posed above. However, causal issues are as much a concern to personality psychologists as to social psychologists. For instance, answers to a question such as "Why have I failed?" surely can affect self-esteem (consider the consequences of the answer "I am dumb"). In addition, self-esteem is likely to influence the answer to that question. In this example, the intersection of attribution theory and personality psychology is evident. My task in this handbook is to document that attributional analyses have contributed much to the understanding of problems that lie at the very heart of personality psychology. Indeed, it could readily be argued that attribution theory is as central to personality psychology as it is to social psychology.

To accomplish my goal, it is helpful to employ a time-honored distinction called upon by Kelley and Michela (1980) in their review of the attributional literature. They state that the linkage between antecedents and causal inferences, a stimulus–organism (S-O) connection, be labeled "the attribution process," and that the relation between causal inferences and the organism's responses to those constructions (O-R) be called "the attributional process." The attribution process pertains to how causal inferences are reached—that is, how one knows. As such, the attribution process relates to epistomology. Attributional processes, on the other hand, refer to "So what?" That is, given a causal inference, what are its implications for future thought and action? Attributional processes thus relate to function. Attribution theory, which includes both attribution and attributional processes, therefore may be considered a cognitive functionalism.

Guided by the S-O versus O-R distinction, this chapter is divided into two main sections. The first section considers the attribution process; the second section examines the attributional process. Three topics of interest to personality psychologists are addressed in the first section:

465

1. The effects of self-involvement on causal inferences. Inasmuch as the self may be perceived as a causal agent, biases are possible, and causal attributions become linked with mechanisms of defense.

2. The effects of the perspective of the person (actor or observer) on causal inferences. This issue has implications for the perceived normativeness of behavior and for conceptions of traits. The traits versus state distinction in personality theory also finds correspondence and empirical support in attribution language.

3. The existence of individual differences in causal inferences. It has been contended that there are enduring tendencies or inclinations toward particular causal perceptions. If so, then attributional predispositions may be considered cognitive traits.

The functional consequences of causal ascriptions are considered in the second section. It will be seen that behavioral dynamics are guided to a surprising extent by causal ascriptions. Behavioral dynamics are one of the main subthemes (along with structure and development) of the field of personality, so that any theory shedding light on the dynamics of behavior is also in part a theory of personality. The topics examined in the second section include the following:

1. The determinants of expectancy of success; relations between individual predispositions and the stability of causal ascriptions are emphasized.
2. Attribution–affect linkages and attributional approaches to emotion.
3. The mediating influence of causal ascriptions on the dynamics of achievement strivings.

In sum, attribution theorists have addressed a daunting array of topics that are pertinent to personality psychology. Because one of my aims in this chapter is breadth of coverage, each theme is examined, but in less depth than the cited authors would consider sufficient.

THE ATTRIBUTION PROCESS: THE DETERMINANTS OF CAUSAL PERCEPTIONS

One of the very early issues of concern to researchers in social cognition, and to attribution

theorists more specifically, was whether the perception of people obeys the same rules as the perception of objects. Heider (1958), for example, contended that "many of the principles underlying social perception have parallels in the field of nonsocial or thing perception" (p. 21). However, he and others certainly acknowledged some differences in perceptual rules, given that people but not objects are interactive with the perceiver, evaluate the perceiver, express emotions, and so on. In a similar vein, questions were raised about the similarity of the rules of other-perception and self-perception; again, there was recognition of differences but also of congruence. Differences are of particular interest to personality psychologists, whereas similarities may be of greater centrality to social psychologists.

The most influential and enduring conceptual approach to the formation of causal ascriptions has been offered by Kelley (1967, 1971). As a social psychologist, he is more concerned with general rules than with possible differences when judging the self as opposed to judging others. Kelley, like others before him, presumes that covariation is the foundation of the attribution process and likens the ascription of causality to the more formal statistical procedures employed by scientists. Assume, he writes, that an individual enjoys a movie. A question then raised is whether the enjoyment is to be attributed to the person (e.g., he or she is easily pleased) or to the perceived properties of the entity (it is a good movie). Kelley (1967) reasons that the responsible factor is primarily determined by examining the covariation of the effect and the causal factors over (1) entities (movies), (2) persons (other viewers of the movie), and (3) time (the same person on repeated exposures). Attribution of enjoyment to the entity rather than to the person (or self) is more likely if the individual responds differentially to movies, if the response to this movie is consistent over time, and if the response agrees with the social consensus of others. Thus, the probability of attribution to the movie is maximized when the individual enjoys only that movie, he or she enjoys it on repeated occasions, and others also like the movie. On the other hand, if the individual likes all movies (i.e., his or her response to the entity is not distinctive), and if no one else likes this particular movie (i.e., there is low consensus), then the person or others would ascribe the enjoyment to attributes of the viewer (e.g., he or she is a movie cultist). Another way of phrasing this process is that the causal factor is different or not part of the generalization being made. Hence, if only Person X likes a movie, or if Person X likes all movies except Film Y, then the perceived causal factors are the person and the movie, respectively (see Hewstone & Jaspars, 1987). These patterns, to which I return often during the chapter, have been for the most part empirically substantiated in many investigations (see Kelley & Michela, 1980). However, complex issues remain to be resolved (see, e.g., Hewstone & Jaspars, 1987; Hilton & Slugoski, 1986; Pruitt & Insko, 1980).

In other early formulations relating to the attribution process (say, during the 1970–1980 decade), the study of differences between self- and other-perception was dominant. The labels of two of the most popular topics stressing disparities are the "hedonic bias" and the "actor versus observer perspective." In this section on attribution processes, I examine these two topics in turn, and then consider individual differences in causal ascriptions.

The Hedonic Bias

The hedonic bias (or error) also is known as the "self-serving attribution bias," "ego enhancement," "ego defensiveness," and "beneffectance." The concept refers to the tendency to take credit for success and/or to attribute failure to factors external to the self (e.g., "I succeeded because I am smart but failed because the teacher is biased," or "I succeeded because I worked hard but failed because the economy is bad"). It is presumed that this pattern of ascriptions maximizes the pleasure linked with success and minimizes the pain generated by failure. Hence, the hedonic bias is one manifestation of the underlying pleasure–pain principle of personality and motivation most often associated with Freudian thinking and philosophers such as Bentham. Other hedonic attribution patterns also are possible, such as ascribing success to permanent (stable) factors and failure to temporary or unstable causes. However, differences in the perceived locus of causality (internal or external to the actor) have been the focus of attention in examinations of hedonic or motivational influences on perceived causality.

Many personality theorists have contended that we are motivated to see ourselves in a positive light. But Heider (1958) first applied this principle to the formation of causal ascriptions, suggesting that the perceived reasons for an event or outcome tend to "fit the wishes" of the person. In opposition to the cognitive antecedents outlined by Kelley and the presumed rationality of the attribution process, the hedonic bias intimates that causal beliefs also are determined by "irrational" forces, or by rationalization as well as rationality.

Dynamically oriented psychologists have embraced the idea of a self-serving bias, and a large experimental literature has emerged examining this phenomenon. Three questions can be raised in regard to hedonic biasing: (1) Is it true? (2) What accounts for such biases? and (3) What effects might this have on personality functioning?

Is It True?

The vast majority of self-serving bias investigations have taken place in achievement-related contexts, where success and failure can be manipulated or readily ascertained. The data convincingly document the existence of the proposed bias (see reviews by Bradley, 1978; Zuckerman, 1979). For example, prototypical studies in achievement-related contexts have revealed that in athletic settings, players in a competitive game attribute their wins to skill and effort and their losses to bad luck (Snyder, Stephan, & Rosenfield, 1976; see review in Mullen & Riordan, 1988); in school environments, teachers ascribe improved performance of students to good teaching, but lack of improvement to students' low ability and/or lack of effort (Beckman, 1970; Johnson, Feigenbaum, & Weiby, 1964); and in gambling situations, following a loss but not a win, gamblers search for possible external reasons (Gilovich, 1983). Similar findings also have been observed in the political arena. For example, politicians ascribe victories to personal characteristics but losses to party label (Kingdon, 1967).

So prevalent is this bias that at an earlier date (Weiner, 1980) I suggested that mere documentation may not be of great value. I stated, "[I]n the face of overwhelming evidence that behavior is a function of both the id and the ego (wishes and reality), it seems impossible that motivated inferential errors do not exist. And everyday observations often reveal instances of mass personal delusion!" (p. 297).

Other investigators had reached the same conclusions and therefore began to search for the conditions that maximize the hedonic bias. Bradley (1978) suggested that the bias is enhanced when (1) an individual's behavior is observed by others; (2) the individual had a free choice in deciding to act and feels responsible for the outcome of the action; (3) conditions of high ego involvement are present; and (4) conditions of high objective self-awareness are present. There is an insufficient body of evidence to feel confident about any of these proposed moderator variables, although all have been documented at one time or another by one investigator or another. Inasmuch as research on self-serving biases declined in the 1980s, it is unlikely that the importance of these moderators will be determined in the near future.

Why the Observed Hedonic Bias?

Three mechanisms have been proposed to account for the observed hedonic biasing of causal attributions. It is not possible to designate any one of these as most important; all have been documented at one time or another by one investigator or another. It is quite likely that all play some role in the observed bias, depending on the situational context in which the attribution is being made and on a host of other factors.

One postulated mechanism already has been introduced: Hedonic biasing is in service of the pleasure–pain principle. It is ego enhancing to take credit for success rather than to ascribe success externally, and it is ego-defensive to place fault externally rather than on the self. Of course, there may be independent attributional biases for success and failure, so that the observed bias could be due only to self-enhancement or only to ego defensiveness. This has not been determined.

A motivational interpretation of self-serving ascriptions therefore assumes that attributions influence emotions (see review in Weiner, 1986). That is, internal ascriptions for success enhance self-esteem more than external ascriptions, whereas external ascriptions for failure maintain self-worth relative to internal ascriptions. Note that given the latter mechanism, attributions function as defenses to protect the self from negative affect. Like other defenses, this bias certainly need not involve conscious alteration of perceived causality.

A second mechanism proposed to account

for hedonic biasing relies on principles of rational inference making (see Miller & Ross, 1975). It has been suggested that most individuals (and particularly the oft-tested college students) have had general success in life and expect further success. (This is akin to the "Lake Wobegon effect," where "all the children are above average.") If success is anticipated, then actual success will tend to result in an internal ascription, inasmuch as the behavior is consistent with the past. On the other hand, failure is inconsistent with prior outcomes and thus promotes an entity (external) attribution. In sum, the self-serving bias can be explained by using principles of attribution proposed by Kelley (1967) without postulating "irrational forces." Nevertheless, although not motivationally driven, the causal inferences have motivational consequences.

A second argument of the cognitivists is that some errors in causal ascription may result from ignorance or misuse of information. For example, Kelley (1967) notes that during periods of economic prosperity, business gains may be ascribed by an executive to personal acumen rather than to the favorable economic circumstances. This error is fostered by the likelihood that rewarded responses will be repeated, thus providing evidence of covariation and perceived self-responsibility. On the other hand, during a depression unfavorable economic circumstances are likely to be blamed for declining profits. Regardless of the individual's actions, profits decrease. Thus, there is no covariation of response and outcome, so that the consequences are externally ascribed.

In sum, cognitive processes may account for self-serving biases. When one is comparing motivational versus cognitive interpretations, some types of evidence are of particular importance in supporting one position over the other. The motivational but not the cognitive interpretation leads to the prediction that biasing will be exhibited in self-attributions, but not when attributions are being made about the success and failure of others (unless those others are pertinent to the self, such as one's family members). Some researchers do not find a self-serving pattern when attributions are made for the behaviors of others, or find it at a much moderated level in comparison to self-ascriptions (e.g., Beckman, 1970; Snyder et al., 1976; Taylor & Koivumaki, 1976; but see Frieze & Weiner, 1971, for nonsupporting data). A motivational but not a cognitive interpretation also suggests that there should be greater biasing given a highly ego-involving situation. As Bradley (1978) summarizes, there is some evidence supporting this hypothesis, although it is rather sparse.

Finally, still a third possible mechanism underlying self-serving biases is that the individual wants to "appear good." That is, attributions are conscious devices used to appear favorably in the eyes of others. Individuals do admit that they use impression management techniques and argue that they are "not to blame" more than they really believe (Orvis, 1977). Inasmuch as experimental investigations of biasing have taken place in the presence of others, impression management could account for some of the self-serving ascriptions. One implication of this position is that, if others think better of one who accepts personal blame for failure, then that pattern of attributions should be publicly displayed. It has been reported that teachers at times exhibit a reversal of the usual hedonic attributions, accepting more blame for the poor performance of students than credit for success (Ross, Bierbrauer, & Polly, 1974; but see Greenberg, Pyszczynski, & Solomon, 1982).

In sum, as indicated previously, the most viable current position is that there are many determinants of the observed pattern of attributions that has been designated as "self-serving," and it may not be possible to discover the mechanism underlying this response pattern (see Tetlock & Levi, 1982). Self-serving biases must be considered in the larger situational context and may be expressed in different ways in disparate environments, as well as mediated by different mechanisms.

Implications for Personality

The hedonic bias, particularly when mediated by motivational processes, has the function of maintaining a positive affective state for the individual. It is generally accepted that a positive view of the self and a positive mood state are necessary for adaptation and for persistence toward goals. Thus, this is a very central ego mechanism, deserving more study within the larger framework of other possible self-enhancing and self-protective mechanisms.

However, as with other defenses, the possibility exists of maladaptive use, so that the organism is ultimately more harmed than benefited. For example, Jones and Berglas (1978) have documented the existence of a dysfunc-

tional self-handicapping strategy to alter attributions (but see Baumeister and Scher, 1988, who refer to this as a "tradeoff" strategy). Jones and Berglas suggest that a student may go to a party the night before an exam, so that failure, if experienced, will be ascribed to external factors (also see Covington and Omelich, 1979, for a discussion of the positive attributional benefits of not expending effort). Unfortunately, these strategies promote failure. Jones and Berglas (1978) also reason that self-destructive behaviors such as alcoholism may in some instances be instigated by a self-handicapping strategy, protecting the person from an ascription for failure such as low ability. Although this phenomenon is not well documented, and one wonders about its pervasiveness (after all, most individuals prefer success to failure), the analysis by Jones and Berglas could provide novel insights into some apparently dysfunctional behaviors (see Arkin & Baumgardner, 1985).

Finally, if the perceived hedonic bias is cognitively mediated (i.e., it is the consequence of rational information processing), then the attributional consequences of failure could be very harmful for individuals who have a history of failure and anticipate future failures. Success, being inconsistent with the past, would then be externally ascribed, so that it would be difficult for these individuals to increase feelings of self-worth. That is, there would be a reversal of the hedonic bias (perhaps we shall call this a "self-destructive bias"). This possibility is explored in greater detail later in the chapter.

The Actor–Observer Perspective

The presumed contrast between the causal perceptions of actors and observers is traceable to an insight of Heider (1958), as so many other hypotheses about attributional processes are. Heider stated, "The person tends to attribute his own reactions to the object world, and [the reactions] of another . . . to personal characteristics [of that other]" (p. 157). This assumption was elaborated and formalized by Jones and Nisbett (1971). Their frequently cited contention is as follows: "There is a pervasive tendency for actors to attribute their actions to situational requirements whereas observers tend to attribute the action to stable dispositions" (p. 80). Both the actor and the observer are therefore presumed to be engaged in the same attributional endeavor—attempting to explain some observed behavior. The answers to the "why" question, however, are assumed to differ as a function of the perspective of the perceiver: Actors see the situation as causal (e.g., "I did it because I was provoked"), whereas observers perceive the person as causal (e.g., "He did it because he is aggressive").

Here again, three questions can be addressed regarding the hypothesized effects of viewer perspective on attributions: (1) Is it true? (2) If true, then why? and (3) What are the implications of this disparity for personality psychology?

Is It True?

Following the Jones and Nisbett (1971) publication, a plethora of studies were conducted to attempt to verify the suggested actor–observer attributional disparity (see review in Monson & Snyder, 1977). Typical among the types of investigations was a series of studies conducted by Nisbett, Caputo, Legant, and Maracek (1973). They asked male subjects to consider why they had chosen their girlfriends, as opposed to the reasons for an acquaintance's choice of a girlfriend. More trait attributions were made in the latter than in the former judgment (e.g., "He is the kind of person who likes . . .").

Unfortunately, such results are not always replicable (see review in Monson & Snyder, 1977). Monson and Snyder conclude that "in a variety of circumstances, actors attribute to themselves more responsibility for their own behaviors and the consequences of their actions than do observers" (p. 92). Furthermore, at times it is difficult to distinguish a person from a situation attribution, so that some reported findings regarding actor–observer differences are ambiguous. For example, choosing a girlfriend because she is tall implies a situation (entity) attribution, yet this is perhaps indistinguishable from an ascription "I like tall girls," which is a person attribution.

In their review, Monson and Snyder (1977) agree that the attributions of actors and observers differ. However, they instead argue that actors are more accurate in their causal inferences than are observers. To understand the origin of this hypothesis, it is necessary to examine why differences initially were expected between actors and observers.

Why the Presumed Actor–Observer Differences?

Two main hypotheses have been advanced to account for the suggested attribution disparities between actors and observers. First, it has been contended that actors know more about themselves and their personal histories than do observers. It is also argued that they have monitored themselves in a variety of situations and therefore recognize the variety of responses that they have displayed in these environments. Because of this perceived (and actual) cross-situational variability, they tend to make (accurate) attributions to the situation rather than to the person. That is, they perceive entity–behavior covariation rather than person–behavior covariation. Conversely, because observers primarily interact with actors in restricted settings, where behavioral consistency is likely, they have little information about behavioral variability across situations. Hence, they tend to make inaccurate person (trait) attributions for the behaviors of others.

Although this interpretation is apparently reasonable, there are numerous problems with it. First, the explanation presumes that persons in fact exhibit little cross-situational consistency. There is evidence that this is untrue, and even that there is differential consistency within an individual across different types of responses (Bem & Allen, 1974). Thus, the unequal information presumption seems unlikely to account for the majority of actor–observer differences in attributions. However, unequal knowledge certainly could contribute to the proposed greater accuracy among actors than observers, as postulated by Monson and Snyder (1977).

A second explanation for the hypothesized differences between actors and observers, also first mentioned by Heider (1958), relates to focus of attention. There is a great deal of evidence that behavior is attributed to what is visually salient (see Taylor & Fiske, 1978). For the actor, his or her behavior is salient, whereas for the observer, the actor is focal. Hence, there is differential salience of potential causal factors between actors and observers. In one early study supporting this line of reasoning, Storms (1973) videotaped and replayed a conversation so that actors viewed themselves as respondents, whereas observers viewed the environment from the perspective of the actor. Given these conditions, the "usual" actor–observer difference in causal inference was reversed. Note that this finding rules out attribution disparities due to unequal possession of information, which is unaffected by the perspective manipulation. However, given that this phenomenon itself is unreliably observed, it is unlikely that a single mediating process or mechanism will be identified.

Implications for Personality

Let us assume that there are differences between actors and observers in the tendency to make person versus situation attributions, even though this may occur only on some occasions in some settings. What consequences does this have for personal functioning and for issues germane to personality psychology?

If actors perceive that behavior is situationally determined, then others may be expected to behave in the same way as the actor when in those situations. To use Kelley's terms once more, situation–behavior covariation is anticipated, and ascriptions are then external for the action. Personal behavior therefore would be perceived as normative. This has implications for underrecognition of personal pathology and the uniqueness and distinctiveness of the self. Evidence supporting this deduction emerges from work related to the so-called "false-consensus effect." For example, Ross, Greene, and House (1977) report that students overestimate the commonness of their own responses; that is, they perceive that their own behavior is typical of what other students think and do (see Marks & Miller, 1987; Mullen et al., 1985).

On the other hand, if observers perceive that behavior is person-determined, then situational determinants of behavior may be discounted. That is, there is perceived person–behavior covariation, which results in internal ascriptions. The tendency to overattribute behavior to the person and underestimate the influence of the environment is captured with the oft-used (and too often accepted) label "the fundamental attribution error" (Ross, 1977). For example, it has been reported that even if individuals are forced to write an essay from a particular vantage point, the writer is thought to have the opinion expressed in the essay (Jones & Harris, 1967; but see Wright & Wells, 1988).

In sum, actor–observer attribution differences imply that actors subscribe to a theory of personality akin to that espoused by con-

tingency reinforcement theorists; that is, they believe that behavior is altered to fit the situation and the demands of the environment. On the other hand, the perspective hypothesis also implies that observers entertain naive theories of personality that are more consistent with the beliefs of "pure" trait theorists. The existence of these biases or errors in causal thinking has been suggested to be one reason why personality psychologists have pursued the discovery of traits. Some attribution theorists have contended that traits may exist more in the minds of perceivers, including perceiving psychologists, than in the actions of the actor. This error could be enhanced because trait ascriptions provide a mechanism to make predictions about actors across a variety of settings, including environments in which the person has not been observed. Of course, prediction is one of the main goals of psychologists.

Final Observations on Hedonic Biasing and Actor–Observer Differences

Hedonic biasing and actor–observer differences have been the focus of a great deal of research and are of manifest importance to the field of personality. It appears that the hedonic bias does indeed exist, but the mechanism responsible for this attributional pattern remains unclear. Conversely, it is not certain that there are disparities in attributions between actors and observers; however, if this were established, then one mechanism (salience) would be known. These two sources of error are not independent, and indeed may conflict with each other at times if one carries these hypotheses to their extreme, as is typically done in the psychological literature. In situations of success, the hedonic bias dictates that ascriptions will be to the self (e.g., ability and effort), whereas the perspective of the actor implies that ascriptions will be made externally. It is therefore of little wonder that some issues surrounding these two phenomena remain unresolved.

Trait–State Concepts from an Attribution Perspective

An important distinction made by personality psychologists, perhaps most fully examined in the study of anxiety, contrasts traits and states. This distinction has been justified on a variety of empirical criteria employed in test assessment. For example, measures of traits are expected to have higher test–retest reliability than measures of states. In addition, state indicators should change more in different situations than should trait indicators (see Chaplin, John, & Goldberg, 1988).

To examine some of the differential features discriminating traits and states, Chaplin et al. (1988) had subjects rate a series of acknowledged traits and states on a variety of characteristics, including stability, consistency over situations, source of causality, duration, intensity, and controllability. It was found that stability, consistency, and internal causality were linked with traits, whereas instability, inconsistency, and external causality were associated with states. As already discussed, consistency over time and lack of distinctiveness have been identified by Kelley (1967) as criteria for personal causality. On the other hand, inconsistency over time and distinctive responding are criteria for entity causality. In sum, the trait–state distinction finds correspondence in the analysis of causal attributions, and particularly with the distinction between internal and external causality.

Chaplin et al. (1988) also discuss the function or utility of the trait–state distinction. They reason:

> [W]e have suggested that traits and states serve people's needs to predict, explain, and control social behavior. The easiest way to accomplish this would be to have only two kinds of person characteristics. The first kind would include those that enable people to predict behavior reliably over time and situations and thus lead to social actions based on the person (e.g., to seek out or to avoid people with that characteristic). The second kind of characteristic, being unstable over time, cannot be predicted from past experience with the person, but may be controlled by manipulating the situation. (p. 555).

They conclude that the trait–state distinction therefore "organizes the layperson's understanding of human action" (p. 555). This statement certainly is in accord with the presumptions of attribution theorists.

Individual Differences in Causal Perceptions

For some psychologists, the actor–observer literature suggests that traits are not inherent in persons, but rather are causal inferences about others. Furthermore, these inferences are quite likely to be biased, inasmuch as they are derived from limited observations and information. Nonetheless, the conclusions (or presumptions) that others exhibit cross-situational consistency may have functional value and foster predictions about behavior without requiring a great deal of cognitive activity.

The position of most personality psychologists, on the other hand, is that traits are intrinsic or essential components of what it means to be a "person." These enduring structures are then manifested in a variety of situational contexts. One endeavor of attribution theorists consistent with this position has been the search for individual differences in causal perceptions. The question raised has been whether some persons are more likely to make certain types of causal inferences or particular attributional decisions than are others.

One can perceive of many potential individual difference tendencies that influence causal perceptions. For example, Cacioppo and Petty (1982) developed a Need for Cognition Scale, assessing the need to explain events in the world and the tendency to enjoy this type of cognitive activity. In a similar manner, Fletcher, Davilvocis, Fernandez, Peterson, and Reeder (1986) advanced an Attributional Complexity Scale, which is designed to predict the complexity of causal ascriptions that are made for behavioral events. They also present evidence that scores on this scale are only weakly related to the need for cognition.

The instruments of Cacioppo and Petty (1982) and Fletcher et al. (1986) relate to the process, rather than to the content, of causal thinking. That is, they do not focus on what specific causal ascriptions will be made, as opposed to the likelihood of making attributions and how many will be called forth. These individual-difference measures have only recently been proposed and have not (yet) spawned a large supporting literature. The more dominant individual-difference approach in attribution theory pertains to the content of causal ascriptions, or the tendency to perceive that particular causes or types of causes will have or have had an effect. Two scales and their derivatives dominate this research. One instrument was developed by Rotter (1966) and examines preferences for internal versus external causal beliefs. Although Rotter is associated with social learning theory, I consider this measuring device as part of attribution theory, inasmuch as it assesses beliefs about causality (or what is called "locus of control"). The second instrument, linked with Abramson, Teasdale, and Seligman (1978), contrasts internal, stable, and general (global) ascriptions and attributions that are external, unstable, and specific, or what is known as "attributional style." The Rotter inventory has been related to a wide array of cognitive and behavioral activities, whereas attributional style primarily has been restricted to the study of maladaptive behaviors and states, particularly depression.

Locus of Control

The concept of locus of control and the measurement instruments devised by Rotter and others have fostered a voluminous psychological literature, including numerous full-length books (e.g., Lefcourt, 1976, 1981; Phares, 1976). Perhaps what I can best do in this context is to provide some historical background that often is overlooked and to offer one interpretation of the empirical and theoretical legacy of this approach.

Rotter is identified with social learning and, as a clinician, wanted to create a conceptual system that would be useful in dealing with clinical problems while remaining true to the logical positivism represented in social learning theory. He also accepted expectancy–value theory, contending that the strength of motivation to perform an action is in part determined by the expectancy of attaining the desired goal. Clinical difficulties were anticipated when expectancies of success were nonveridical and when there was a low expectancy for a highly valued goal. Hence, one of Rotter's central quests was to identify the determinants of expectancy of success.

In a series of experimental studies, Rotter and his colleagues (e.g., James & Rotter, 1958) documented that performance at skill tasks results in different changes in expectancy of success than does performance at chance tasks. For example, following a loss at a skill task expectancy of future success frequently drops, whereas it remains the same or may even increase after a loss at a chance task (the "gambler's fallacy"). This laboratory experimental research suggested to Rotter that some individuals may perceive the world as if it were composed of skill tasks, whereas others perceive life outcomes as chance-determined. That is,

he suggested that there are individual differences in causal beliefs about the self-determination of outcomes; these, in turn, result in disparate subjective likelihoods of success and failure across a variety of situations.

The measure of locus of control, or the I-E Scale (I for Internal, E for External) was constructed to measure individual differences in personal construction of the world as skill-related (internal) or chance-related (external) (Rotter, 1966). To the best of my knowledge, however, the scale never has been successfully reported to relate to expectancy of success or to expectancy change. Rather, the I-E Scale took on a life of its own, divorced from expectancy–value theory and from social learning. And indeed it was a very active life. Scores on the scale were related to literally hundreds of different variables. There was also a strong impulse to consider the scores as evaluative: It was "good" to be an "internal," inasmuch as internality was associated with information processing, openness to experience, positive mental health, and so on. Correspondingly, it was "bad" to be an "external."

Even during the heyday of the I-E Scale (say, from 1967 to 1982), there were concerns about the breadth of personality traits, or their cross-situational generality. Such doubts also were raised about locus of control. For example, within the achievement domain, internality for success is uncorrelated with internality for failure (see Weiner, 1980). In response to this uncertainty, and to enhance predictive validity, specific locus-of-control scales began to be developed. For example, Lefcourt, von Baeyer, Ware, and Cox (1979) distinguished between locus for affiliative and achievement outcomes in their control scale. And health locus-of-control scales were constructed to examine whether individuals consider health-related outcomes as subject to personal or environmental control (e.g., Lau & Ware, 1981; Wallston & Wallston, 1980). The connection of internal locus of control with physical well-being further promoted the linkage between perceived personal control and positive adaptation and coping.

In sum, studies of individual differences in causal attributions began with the search by Rotter to understand the determinants of expectancy of success. This led to the study of skill and chance tasks and to the conception that individuals tend differentially to perceive the world as skill- or chance-governed. The I-E

Scale did not shed light on subjective expectancies; there is little theoretical legacy from this research, nor any solutions to the generality of this predisposition. But there is an empirical heritage: Perceiving control over life events appears to be an important correlate of physical and mental health. This principle has been demonstrated in a variety of contexts and is now being applied in schools, nursing homes, work environments, and other situations where there is a trend toward fostering personal freedom and responsibility.

Attributional Style

While the individual-difference studies were converging on the union between internal control and adaptation, another huge psychological literature was evolving that manipulated, rather than assessed, perceived control and examined the effects of these manipulations on a variety of cognitions and behaviors. An experimental manipulation of lack of control gave rise to the investigation of "learned helplessness," to subsequent speculations about the role of attributions in depression, and then to an individual-difference measure to assess these attributions.

As was true of locus of control, a formidable number of research studies were generated by the concept of learned helplessness and the Attributional Style Questionnaire. In the past few years numerous reviews of these topics have appeared (e.g., Brewin, 1985; Coyne & Gotlib, 1983; Peterson & Seligman, 1984; Robins, 1988; Sweeney, Anderson, & Bailey, 1986, to cite only a few published journal articles). Given this extensive area of research and the few pages I have to devote to this topic, it again seems prudent to provide some historical background and attempt briefly to clarify the current state of the literature.

Initial investigations by Seligman (1975) and others appeared to demonstrate that a variety of infrahumans, when first given uncontrollable or inescapable shock, exhibit little motivation to learn and act when these behaviors become instrumental to escaping. This syndrome of cognitive and motivational deficits was captured with the label "learned helplessness," and was compared to symptoms exhibited by depressed humans. More specifically, it was argued that if the probability of a desired outcome is perceived as not increased by one's actions (i.e., there is noncontingency between

response and outcome), then future noncontingency is anticipated and helplessness results.

Abramson et al. (1978) then gave attributions a central role in this conception: "We argue that when a person finds that he is helpless, he asks *why* he is helpless. The causal attribution he makes then determines the generality and chronicity of helplessness deficits as well as his later self-esteem" (p. 50). Thus, the theory was expanded as follows:

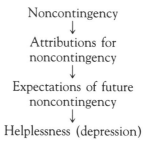

Noncontingency
↓
Attributions for
noncontingency
↓
Expectations of future
noncontingency
↓
Helplessness (depression)

As in the historical development of locus of control, from this experimental research the idea was generated that there might be characteristic attributional styles, or dispositions to perceive and/or judge particular causes as most salient across a variety of situations. What attributions might be dysfunctional? Abramson et al. suggested that attributing noncontingency (which they subsequently did not distinguish from failure) to the self is dysfunctional, inasmuch as this results in low self-esteem (note that this is the reverse hedonic bias mentioned earlier). In addition, attributions of failure to causes that do not change over time (causal stability) and to causes that appear in a variety of settings (causal globality) are also maladaptive. This pattern was anticipated to lead to the onset of depression or to be a precursor that, if combined with negative life events, would make individuals vulnerable to symptoms of helplessness (see Brewin, 1985, for the distinction between onset and vulnerability models). On the other hand, ascriptions of failure that are external, unstable, and specific were considered adaptive.

This thinking resulted in the development of the Attributional Style Questionnaire (Peterson et al., 1982). Scores on this measure have been related to depressive symptoms. The scale presents individuals with hypothetical positive or negative outcomes (e.g., "You go to a party and do not meet new friends"). The respondents then generate a causal explanation and rate that cause on the dimensions of locus, stability, and generality. This instrument has been marred by psychometric inadequacies (see Cutrona, Russell, & Jones, 1985), with the most typical problem related to a lack of cross-situational consistency. In discussing this issue, Anderson, Jennings, and Arnoult (1988) have concluded that the Attributional Style Questionnaire has a "moderate level of specificity." That is,

> [Scores are] cross-situationally consistent only across situations that are similar in psychologically meaningful ways, but not across very divergent types of situations. This view maintains that within situation types (e.g., interpersonal failure) the relative standing of individuals will remain fairly constant from one situation to another, but that between different situation types (e.g., interpersonal failure vs. noninterpersonal success) there will be little correspondence. (p. 980)

And what about the predictions of depression? There is a great deal of inconsistency in the literature: Some individual investigators and general reviews support the helplessness position, whereas others fail to find such support (see Robins, 1988, who attributes differences in part to the sample size and therefore to statistical power). The most recent summary articles are presenting evidence that attributional style does correlate weakly to moderately with depression, and that scores on the locus subscale are particularly predictive. There also is some evidence that attributional style precedes depression onset (rather than that depression causes alterations in perceived causality). However, the causation issue remains uncertain.

In sum, the issues are far from settled, and one can anticipate that research in this area will continue to flourish (as opposed to investigations using locus-of-control measures, which are abating). For the present, the conclusions and advice of Anderson et al. (1988) seem very wise. They conclude that both the extreme pessimism of some recent researchers and the broad, sweepingly optimistic claims of some proponents are unwarranted, and that further work on specifying the appropriate level of assessment for attributional style would be useful.

In addition, attributional style is now being conceived of as "explanatory style" and "optimism vs. pessimism." In a rather startling finding, Peterson, Seligman, and Vaillant (1988) report that explanatory style at age 25 (assessed by means of content analysis of available protocols of wartime experience) predicted health status at ages 45–60 (but *not* between the ages of 30 and 40). Hence, the focus of attributional style is broadening beyond depression and toward the study of general well-being.

THE ATTRIBUTIONAL PROCESS: THE CONSEQUENCES OF CAUSAL PERCEPTIONS

I now turn to the effects of causal ascriptions on the dynamics of behavior. This topic has not been totally neglected in the prior pages: The hedonic bias relates to experienced positive and negative affect; the actor–observer difference has implications for perceived normality and deviance; and both locus of control and attributional style have been associated with a variety of processes and states. Nonetheless, these consequences have up to this point been secondary to the issue of attributional selection or choice of causal ascriptions. That is, biases, perspectives, and individual differences have all been considered to be determinants or antecedents of causal ascriptions.

Another factor distinguishing the prior half of the chapter from this section is that the focus shifts away from locus of causality. Recall that the hedonic bias concerns self-blame versus environmental blame; the actor–observer effect pertains to self-ascription versus environmental ascription; and locus of control is defined as the perceived responsibility of self versus nonself. However, as revealed briefly in the examination of attributional style, there are properties or characteristics of perceived causality in addition to locus. Before I turn to specific attributional consequences, these other causal properties must be introduced, inasmuch as they are equal in importance to causal locus when considering behavioral dynamics. This hints that more attention should also be paid to the determinants of these causal perceptions.

Causal Dimensions (or Causal Properties)

Certainly two, and perhaps as many as four, properties of causes have been identified in addition to locus (see Weiner, 1985, 1986). Consider, for example, the two causal ascriptions of aptitude and effort, which are reported to be salient causes of achievement success and failure. These two are similar in that both causes are internal to the actor. However, effort is thought of as fluctuating more over time than is aptitude. The causes therefore differ in what is called "stability." Furthermore, effort is subject to volitional change, but aptitude is not. That is, causes also vary in perceived controllability. Controllability and locus are conceived as independent of causal stability.

Some investigators also distinguish between stability over time and stability over situations (or what is called "globality"). In addition, others distinguish between controllability and intentionality (consider the difference between manslaughter and murder). In the subsequent discussion of causal consequences, the properties of globality and intentionality are, for the most part, ignored.

Expectancy of Success

It is evident that some themes throughout the study of personality dynamics are considered more important or central than others and constantly reappear. One such focus is goal expectancy. A number of major theorists, including Atkinson, Lewin, and Rotter, include the expectancy of success among the determinants of aspiration level (goal selection). In criticizing the approach of psychoanalytic theory to goal seeking, Rotter and Hochreich (1975) stated:

> Simply knowing how much an individual wants to reach a certain goal is not sufficient information for predicting his behavior. A student may want very badly to finish school and qualify himself for a well-paying job. But his past experiences may have led him to believe that no amount of studying will result in a passing grade. . . . A fellow student may share the same strong goals and, as a result of a different set of past experiences in school, will have a high expectancy that studying will lead to academic success. . . . The goals in these two cases are identical, but the expectancies differ, and as a result, the behavior of the two students is likely to differ. (p. 95)

There have been numerous approaches to and theories about expectancy of success and expectancy change. One influential conception associated with Rotter and his colleagues has linked perceived locus of control to expectancy. As revealed earlier, it is known, for example, that following failure at a chance task (external causality) expectancies tend not to shift downward and may actually increase. On the other hand, following failure at a skill task (internal causality) there are downward shifts in expectation of future success.

In contrast to this "focus on locus," a second attributional position contends that the stability of a cause determines expectancy shifts. If conditions (the presence or absence of causes) are expected to remain the same, then the outcomes experienced on past occasions may be expected to recur. A success under these circumstances should produce relatively large increments in the anticipation of future success, and a failure should strengthen the belief that there will be subsequent failures (as in skill tasks). On the other hand, if the causal conditions are perceived as likely to change, then the present outcome may not be expected to be repeated in the future, or there may be uncertainty about subsequent outcomes. A success therefore should yield relatively small increments, if any, and perhaps decrements in the expectancy of subsequent success, whereas a failure need not necessarily intensify the belief that there will be future failures (as in chance tasks). This connection of causal stability with future expectancy is in accord with the logic of cause–effect associations and has received extensive empirical support (see review in Weiner, 1986).

For the personality theorist, the prior discussion intimates that when there is quitting in the face of nonattainment of a goal (task failure, social rejection, etc.), when expectancy of success appears to be low following failure, and when there is hopelessness about the future, then one should be alerted to find stable attributions for past failures. On the other hand, if there is persistence given failure, if expectancy of success remains reasonably high, and it there is optimism about the future, then one should be alerted to find unstable ascriptions for prior goal nonattainments. The reverse conditions characterize ascriptions for success (i.e., stable attributions result in more positive anticipations than do unstable ascriptions). A wide range of antecedents and consequences that involve causal stability and expectancy estimates have already been identified; these are pertinent for the study of personality.

Characterological versus Behavioral Self-Blame

A distinction that has been particularly useful to health psychologists contrasts characterological and behavioral self-blame. Janoff-Bulman

(1979) contends that the former is a "maladaptive, self-deprecating response" whereas the latter represents "an adaptive, control-oriented response" (p. 1799). Characterological blame faults personal traits for negative events (e.g., inability to stay out of trouble as a cause of rape), while behavioral blame faults a particular action (e.g., walking down the wrong street). Hence, characterological blame has the properties of stability and uncontrollability; behavioral blame is perceived as unstable and controllable. It has been found that depressed individuals are particularly susceptible to characterological blame and that this tendency relates to high expectations for future negative experiences, as compared with the behavioral blame responses of the nondepressed (see Janoff-Bulman, 1979).

A variety of negative events (rape, abortion, etc.) have been found to elicit more maladaptive negative reactions (time to recovery, fears about the future, etc.), given characterological rather than behavioral blame (see, e.g., Major, Mueller, & Hilderbrandt, 1985). It is apparent that positive coping requires some optimism about the future, and, according to this attributional analysis, positive expectancies are related to perceptions about causal instability for prior negative events.

Situational Determinants

It has been proposed that the stability of attributions for negative outcomes influence future expectancies which, in turn, affect persistence in the face of failure. Anderson (1983) and Anderson and Jennings (1980) documented that both dispositional and situational determinants of causal stability ascriptions affected persistence at an achievement-related task. They had subjects engage in telephone solicitations to donate blood to the Red Cross. The first call, however, was to a confederate who refused to donate. Prior to this rejection, the subjects were assessed for characterological versus behavioral self-blame with the Attributional Style Questionnaire. In addition, an experimental manipulation varied the perceived cause of the rejection. The instruction eliciting stable attributions stated that success was determined by a stable personality trait ("Some guys have it, some don't"); the instruction evoking unstable attributions indicated that strategy was the main outcome determinant ("Use different tactics . . . until finding one that works").

In these studies, it was found that both the dispositional tendency and the attributional manipulation influenced how many subsequent phone calls were made after the initial failure. Given no experimental manipulation, those high in behavioral blame persisted longer than subjects classified as high in characterological blame. But in the experimental conditions, the instructions overrode the individual-difference tendencies: Subjects given instructions that elicited unstable ascriptions made more phone calls than those ascribing rejection to a personality trait.

Prior Expectancies

There is a bidirectional relation between causal ascriptions and expectancy of success; that is, just as causal ascriptions influence subsequent expectancy, expectancy of success also has an effect on causal attributions. The logic of this argument is similar to that offered in the cognitive explanation of the hedonic bias. Specifically, if expectancy of success is high, then failure is nonconfirmatory and elicits an unstable ascription (e.g., bad luck). But if expectancy of success is low, then failure is consistent with the prior belief and elicits a stable attribution (e.g., low ability). Likewise, high expectancy followed by success results in a stable attribution (e.g., high ability), while low expectancy followed by success evokes an unstable ascription (e.g., good luck). This analysis is summarized in Table 18.1. Note, therefore, that low expectancies of success are difficult to alter, and a self-perpetuating cycle of pessimism is established.

Self-maintaining, dysfunctional belief systems have been identified for many groups and vulnerable individuals, including psychiatric

TABLE 18.1 Hypothesized Relations among Outcomes, Expectancy, Attributions, and the Subsequent Expectancy, Based on Attributional Principles

Independent variables		Dependent variables	
Outcome	Expectancy 1	Attribution	Expectancy 2
Success	High	Stable	High
Success	Low	Unstable	Low
Failure	High	Unstable	High
Failure	Low	Stable	Low

rehabilitees, lonely and depressed persons, the retarded, and those low in self-esteem. In addition, when failing at male-defined tasks, females exhibit this same pattern of expectations (see review in Weiner, 1986).

Emotion

Certainly the study of personality and personality processes must include an analysis of emotion. There have been two quite distinct attributional approaches to the study of emotion. The initial and more encompassing theory was proposed by Schachter and Singer (1962); their conception was in part responsible for the revival of the study of affective states in psychology. My colleagues and I developed a second, more limited approach (Weiner, Russell, & Lerman, 1978, 1979). I consider each conception rather briefly here.

The Schachter and Singer Theory of Emotion

The concept of "arousal," which refers to the intensity or state of activation of an individual, plays a central role in the Schachter and Singer (1962) conception. They specify two different ways in which an emotion can be generated. One is the usual, everyday experience; the second is more atypical but has been responsible for a number of oft-cited research studies. In everyday emotional states, external cues trigger physiological processes and serve as the label to which feelings are attached. For example, someone takes out a gun; this is appraised and interpreted as a threat; arousal increases; the arousal is linked with (attributed to) the gun; and an emotion is experienced. This is depicted in the top half of Figure 18.1. The second way in which an emotional state can be initiated is with the perception of "unexplained" arousal. In an experimental setting, this can be created by having the subjects unknowingly ingest an activating drug. The arousal theoretically generates a search to determine the source of the arousal, given that an instigating source is not immediately evident. Again, arousal and the attribution or inference about the arousal source then produce an emotional state. This process is depicted in the bottom half of Figure 18.1.

Perhaps the most influential research resulting from this conception has involved a "misattribution" paradigm. In these investigations, subjects may be provided with a false reason for an event, or they may experience arousal but misattribute its source. For example, in what is known as a transfer excitation paradigm, subjects may exercise or hear a loud noise at Time 1. They then experience another source of arousal at Time 2, such as an attractive member of the opposite sex. It has been reported that many emotional states (e.g., sexual excitement) and actions (e.g., aggression) are enhanced when the total arousal is a composite of the events experienced at Time 1 and Time 2, given that activation is attributed to only the Time 2 experience (see review in Reisenzein, 1983).

The Schachter and Singer (1962) formulation "has . . . become the most influential cognitive approach to emotions" (Reisenzein, 1983, p. 239). However, in the past few years this theory has met with many criticisms and its influence has been greatly reduced. There is evidence, for example, that unexplained arousal is in itself a negative affective state; that individuals do not necessarily search the environment for the source of their arousal; and that arousal is not necessary for an emotional experience. That is, "the role of arousal in emotion has been overstated" (Reisenzein, 1983, p. 239).

Cognition–Emotion Associations

My colleagues and I have also proposed an attributional framework for the study of emotions (Weiner et al., 1978, 1979). Moreover, we have assumed that cognitions of increasing complexity enter into the emotion process to further refine and differentiate affective experience. It is proposed that following the outcome of an event, there is initially a generally positive or negative reaction (a "primitive" emotion), based on the perceived success or failure of that outcome (the "primary" appraisal). For example, after receiving an A in a course, hitting a home run in a baseball game, or being accepted for a date, an individual will feel "happy." In a similar manner, after receiving an F in a course, failing to get a hit, or being rejected, the person will experience sadness. These emotions are labeled "outcome-dependent/attribution-independent," for they are determined by the attainment or nonattainment of a desired goal, and not by the cause of that outcome.

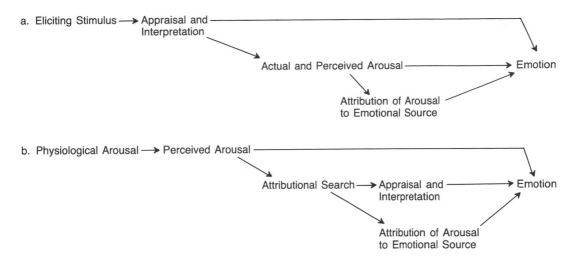

FIGURE 18.1. The process of emotion generation (a) in everyday life, and (b) in the case of unexplained arousal, as proposed by Schachter and Singer (1962). Adapted from Reisenzein (1983), p. 241.

Following the appraisal of the outcome, a causal ascription is sought. A different set of emotions is then generated by the chosen attribution(s). Each dimension of the ascription is uniquely related to a set of feelings. The cognition–emotion sequence proposed is depicted in Figure 18.2

Causal Locus and Self-Esteem (Pride). Locus of causality, the dimension of ascription first introduced by Rotter and initially thought to be linked with expectancy of success, influences self-esteem and self-worth. More specifically, successful outcomes that are ascribed to the self(e.g., personality, ability, effort) result in

greater self-esteem (pride) than success that is externally attributed (e.g., task ease, good luck). As Isenberg (1980) stated, "The definition of pride, then, has three parts. There is (1) a quality which (2) is approved and (3) is judged to belong to oneself" (p. 357). This quality is exemplified in self-statements such as "I succeeded because I [am smart, worked hard, etc.]."

The relation between self-ascription and pride is directly relevant to the hedonic bias, examined in the first section of this chapter. Indeed, the basic premise of hedonic bias research is that internal attributions for goal attainment, and external attributions for nonattainment of a goal, enhance and protect self-esteem. Thus, the documentation of the self-serving attributional bias can also be considered as evidence supporting the relation between locus of causality and self-esteem. In addition, numerous studies of excuses, rationalizations, self-handicapping strategies, and the like document clearly that self-esteem is a function fo causal locus (see review by Snyder & Higgins, 1988).

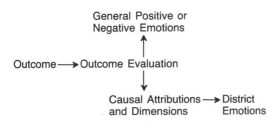

FIGURE 18.2. The cognition–emotion process according to Weiner, Russell, and Lerman (1978, 1979).

Causal Controllability and Social Emotions. A variety of salient emotions are associated with the concept of controllability, or whether one "could have done otherwise." These include anger, pity, guilt, and shame (see reviews in Weiner, 1986).

Anger. Anger is elicited by the violation of an "ought" or "should." Thus, anger is an attribution of blame (see Averill, 1983). Most instances of anger in everyday life involve a voluntary and unjustified act, such as telling a lie or being involved in a potentially avoidable accident.

Pity. In contrast to the linkage between controllability and anger, uncontrollable causes are associated with pity and sympathy. Thus, another's loss of a loved one because of an accident or illness, or failure by another because of a physical handicap, are prevalent situations that elicit pity.

Guilt. In their review of the guilt literature, Wicker, Payne, and Morgan (1983) concluded: "In general, guilt is said to follow from acts that violate ethical norms . . . or moral values. Guilt is accompanied by feelings of personal responsibility" (p. 26). Thus, if guilt is experienced, then perceived self-responsibility seems to be a necessary antecedent (Hoffman, 1975).

Shame. Shame often is indistinguishable from guilt in that both "involve negative self-evaluations that are painful, tense, agitating, real, present, and depressing" (Wicker et al., 1983, p. 33). However, shame and the related affect of humiliation seem to arise from uncontrollable causes, such as lack of aptitude. This contrasts with guilt, which is particularly elicited by lack of effort in achievement contexts.

The four affects examined above are interrelated in complex ways. Anger, for example, serves as a cue to others that a moral wrong has been committed. Hence, if this explanation is accepted, the targeted individual will experience guilt. Pity, on the other hand, conveys that the person "could not have done otherwise" and is "fundamentally different." Hence, if accepted from others, pity is a stimulus for feelings of shame and humiliation.

Causal Stability and Time-Related Emotions. Thus far, outcome-dependent emotions of happiness and sadness have been examined, as well as the attribution-dependent emotions of pride, anger, pity, guilt, and shame. The dimension–affect association yet to be discussed involves causal stability. Recall that causal stability in part determines future expectancy of success and failure. Thus, emotions such as hope and fear, which are influenced by future anticipations, are guided by perceived causal stability (see review in Weiner, 1986).

Summary of Emotional Antecedents

Attribution theorists have been concerned both with the emotional process and with specific emotions. Two processes have been proposed, one focusing on the concept of arousal, the other eschewing the need for arousal and assuming that cognitions are sufficient antecedents of emotional states. Both theories are able to address prevalent human emotions that lie at the very essence of personality.

The Dynamics of Behavior

Personality and motivational theorists, including Lewin, Rotter, and Atkinson, presume that behavior is a function of the likelihood of attaining a desired goal (the subjective expectancy of success) and the affective or incentive value associated with that goal. The essence of expectancy–value theory, which they espouse, is that behavior is governed by hedonic concerns and there is an attempt to maximize subjective expected utility. Inasmuch as causal ascriptions influence both expectancy of success and affect, attributional analyses have provided a theoretical vehicle for interpreting the dynamics of action.

Prior to considering a behavioral episode from an attributional perspective, it is first necessary to consider the directional cues of the affects that have been examined. The relations among thoughts about perceived control, emotional reactions, and subsequent behavioral tendencies are shown in Table 18.2. Table 18.2 reveals that anger tends to evoke "retaliation," or, in the words of Karen Horney (1937), going against others; pity and guilt tend to elicit "restitution," or going toward tasks or others. That is, pity and guilt give rise to "repayment," or the tendency to make a situation more equitable and in balance (see Trivers, 1971). Finally, shame tends to produce withdrawal and retreat. To use the vocabulary of Horney once more, a person who feels shame is inclined to go away from others. Note, then,

TABLE 18.2 Relations among Causal Thinking, Affect, and Action

Causal antecedent	Affect	Action tendency
Personal "failure," controllably caused by others	Anger	Retaliation (going against)
Failure of another, uncontrollable	Pity	Restitution (going toward)
Failure of self or another, controllably caused by actor	Guilt	Restitution (going toward)
Failure of self, uncontrollable	Shame	Retreat (going away from)

that each of these affects brings with it a program for action. Thus, affects summarize the past, providing an overall evaluation for what has occurred; they also prescribe for the future. Hence, they seem to provide the glue between thinking and acting, or between attributions and behavior.

Behavioral Sequences in the Achievement Domain

The analyses of expectancy and affect proposed by attribution theorists have been used to explain behavior in a variety of contexts. Here I explore only achievement strivings and use attributional language to account for two sequences that might be observed in everyday life.

The more traditional explanation of achievement strivings associated with personality theory rests on the belief that there are cross-situational traits leading individuals to approach or avoid achievement-related activities. Those called high in achievement concerns are thought to be attracted to achievement tasks, whereas those considered low in achievement concerns (or relatively high in anxiety about failure) are thought of as repelled by achievement activities. More complex theoretical analyses of achievement strivings have suggested that individuals high in achievement needs are particularly attracted to tasks of intermediate difficulty, whereas those low in achievement needs especially want to avoid tasks where the likelihood of success is at the intermediate level.

Rather than relying upon traits and level of task difficulty, attribution theorists focus on the role of causal ascriptions in augmenting or dampening achievement-related behavior. Let us consider how attribution theorists might explain the following two behavioral observations:

1. Jane fails her psychology exam and then seeks tutoring and increases her study time.
2. Mary fails her psychology exam and decides to drop out of school.

In the first scenario, a negative outcome (failure) is experienced. This should generate the outcome-related negative affects of frustration and sadness. Negative outcomes evoke search to understand why the goal was not attained. Let us assume that Jane has performed well in the past, but that on this particular test others do well but she does poorly. Because the outcome is at variance with the social norms, Jane attributes the failure to herself. And because the outcome also is at variance with her past behavior, the attribution is to an unstable factor—lack of adequate preparation and study time. As already intimated, these causes are perceived as internal and unstable, and also as controllable. Because the causes are unstable, Jane maintains a reasonable expectation of success in the future and is hopeful. Because the causes are controllable by Jane, she experiences guilt, while her teacher and parents are angry. High expectations of future success, along with hopefulness and guilt, are able to overcome her feelings of sadness and weakened self-esteem; they result in renewed goal strivings and an increase in motivation to perform better on the next exam.

In the second scenario, Mary also is described as failing her exam. This again elicits outcome-dependent emotions of sadness as well as causal search. Let us assume that Mary has failed exams in the past, while other students have been performing well. Hence, there is person–outcome covariation, and Mary ascribes failure to herself. She attributes the poor performance to lack of ability, which is internal, stable, and uncontrollable. Because the cause is internal, Mary's self-esteem is lowered; because the cause is stable, Mary anticipates future failure and feels hopeless; and because the cause is uncontrollable, Mary feels ashamed and humiliated. In addition, her parents and teachers feel sorry for her and communicate this, furthering her disbelief in her own competence. Thus, in this achievement situation, Mary has a low expectation of future success and is feeling sad (outcome-related affect), low in self-worth (locus-related affect), hopeless (stability-related affect), and ashamed (uncontrollability-related affect). These thoughts and affective states decrease achievement striving and result in withdrawal from the setting.

In research pertinent to these achievement-related sequences, Covington and Omelich (1984) examined the attributions, affects, and subsequent performance of students who described their midterm exam as a subjective failure. Lack-of-effort ascriptions were most highly correlated with guilt, whereas low-ability attributions were most positively correlated with shame. In addition, guilt and high expectancy were positively related to performance on the next exam, whereas humiliation was negatively related to subsequent school grade.

Attributional Therapy

In conjunction with the growth of an attributional approach to personality dynamics, there has been a growing field of attributional therapy (see Forsterling, 1985, 1986). Attributional therapies are guided by the fundamental principle that thoughts (in this case, causal ascriptions) guide behavior. It then follows that a change in thinking should produce a change in action. The goal of attributional therapies, therefore, has been to substitute adaptive causal ascriptions for those that are dysfunctional, with the anticipation that this alteration will produce changes in behavior.

Attributional therapies have been, for the most part, confined to achievement-related contexts. The researchers (change agents) have assumed that dysfunctional attributions have greater impact in situations of failure than of success, and that the most maladaptive causal ascription for achievement failure is lack of ability (as in the second scenario above, describing Mary). This logically follows inasmuch as lack of ability is conceived of as an internal, stable, and uncontrollable cause.

In the majority of experimental reports, the adaptive cause that the therapist or researcher has sought to substitute is lack of effort (see the

first scenario above, describing Jane). Lack of effort is considered an internal cause, just as is low ability. However, effort is conceived of as unstable and controllable. Less frequently, the designated causal attribution for achievement failure in the published literature has been bad luck or an overly difficult task. Because these are external causes for failure, self-esteem is maintained. Luck and task difficulty ascriptions do differ, however, in other respects. Luck is perceived as more unstable than is task difficulty, so that expectancies for success should be higher given a luck ascription rather than a difficulty ascription. It should be noted, therefore, that lack of effort, bad luck, and an overly difficult task are all specified to improve motivation and coping, relative to a low-ability ascription for failure. However, the variables mediating the hypothesized improvement are not identical for the three causal ascriptions. Effort attributions theoretically maintain expectancy and induce guilt (positive motivators), while still lowering self-esteem (a performance inhibitor); luck attributions theoretically maintain expectancy of success as well as self-esteem; and task difficulty attributions only maintain positive self-esteem, while lowering expectancy estimates. This analysis reveals some of the insights provided by attribution theory (see Weiner, 1988, for a fuller discussion of attributional therapy).

GENERAL CONCLUSIONS AND FUTURE THOUGHTS

In the very first paragraph of this Chapter I state that attribution theory is as central to personality psychology as it is to social psychology. I believe that this assertion has been documented in this chapter, which has examined attributions as defense mechanisms; attributions as determinants of trait inferences; individual differences in causal ascriptions (as assessed via measures of locus of control and attributional style); and attributional determinants of expectancy of success, affective experience, and the dynamics of behavior and behavioral change. I do not think that one can ask for a broader range of relevance from any extant theoretical system.

It is now worthwhile to ask, over 30 years after the publication of Heider's (1958) book *The Psychology of Interpersonal Relations*, about the future of attribution theory. Is this *Zeitgeist* over? To answer a question about the future, it is informative to turn back to the past and consider the precursors of attribution theory. Festinger's (1957) theory of cognitive dissonance provided the dominant research paradigm for social psychology in the 1960s. Dissonance theory offered a non-common-sense approach to attitude formation and change, based on the "fit" between cognitive elements. In part because of the intention of social psychologists in the 1950s to progress beyond what was known as "bubba" (grandmother) psychology, the dominance of dissonance is readily understood. But by the end of the 1960s dissonance had run its course. The many studies that were conducted left others to search for new places to leave their personal mark. Of equal importance, however, dissonance was linked to drive theory and mechanism; yet the conception of drive already had been discarded by most motivational theorists. And of perhaps greatest importance, dissonance theory was conceptually sparse, so that there were few new directions toward which the theory could turn.

Attribution theory replaced dissonance as the dominant paradigm within social psychology. Unlike dissonance, it grew from naive psychology and relied upon accessible, conscious experience. Unlike dissonance, it was not linked to drive theory, but rather to the emerging cognitive conceptions of action. And unlike dissonance, it was conceptually rich, with systems of interrelated concepts and many directions to explore.

The belief in the importance of conscious experience, and the ascendance of cognitive psychology, have not waned. In addition, attribution theory continues to incorporate new concepts. Hence, I suspect that it has a long future before it diminishes in centrality, as all conceptions in psychology eventually do. Attribution theory is now becoming an established part of psychotherapy (see Brewin, 1988; Forsterling, 1988); it is being applied to areas ranging from sports psychology to consumer behavior (see Graham & Folkes, in press); it has successfully addressed issues related to reactions to the stigmatized, excuse giving, and consequences of perceived responsibility (see review in Weiner, 1986); it is established in motivational and educational psychology; and on and on. I see the immediate future as including diversification and entry into ever-widening areas, each serving as a place for both specific modification and general theoretical

development. Certainly, with the ever-increasing interest in self-perception, affective experience, and construals of the environment, personality psychology will remain at the core of attributional concerns.

REFERENCES

Abramson, L. Y., Seligman, M. E. P., & Teasdale, J. (1978). Learned helplessness in humans: Critique and reformulation. *Journal of Abnormal Psychology, 87,* 49–74.

Anderson, C. A. (1983). Motivational and performance deficits in interpersonal settings: The effects of attributional style. *Journal of Personality and Social Psychology, 45,* 1136–1147.

Anderson, C. A., & Jennings, D. L. (1980). When experiences of failure promote expectations of success: The impact of attributing failure to ineffective strategies. *Journal of Personality, 48,* 393–407.

Anderson, C. A., Jennings, D. L., & Arnoult, L. H. (1988). The validity and utility of the attributional style construct at a moderate level of specificity. *Journal of Personality and Social Psychology, 55,* 979–990.

Atkin, R. M., & Baumgardner, A. H. (1985). Self-handicapping. In J. H. Harvey & G. Weary (Eds.), *Attribution: Basic issues and applications* (pp. 169–202.). New York: Academic Press.

Averill, J. R. (1983). Studies on anger and aggression. *American Psychologist, 38,* 1145–1160.

Baumeister, R. F., & Scher, S. J. (1988). Self-defeating behavior patterns among normal individuals: Review and analysis of common self-destructive tendencies. *Psychological Bulletin, 104,* 3–22.

Beckman, L. (1970). Effects of students' performance on teachers' and observers' attributions of causality. *Journal of Educational Psychology, 61,* 76–82.

Bem, D. J., & Allen, A. (1974). On predicting some of the people some of the time: The search for cross-situational consistencies in behavior. *Psychological Review, 81,* 506–520.

Bradley, G. W. (1978). Self-serving biases in the attribution process: A reexamination of the fact or fiction question. *Journal of Personality and Social Psychology, 36,* 56–71.

Brewin, C. R. (1985). Depression and causal attributions: What is their relation? *Psychological Bulletin, 98,* 297–309.

Brewin, C. R. (1988). *Cognitive foundations of clinical psychology.* Hillsdale, NJ: Erlbaum.

Cacioppo, J. T., & Petty, R. E. (1982). The need for cognition. *Journal of Personality and Social Psychology, 42,* 116–131.

Chaplin, W. F., John, O. P., & Goldberg, L. R. (1988). Conceptions of traits and states: Dimensional attributes with ideals as prototypes. *Journal of Personality and Social Psychology, 54,* 541–557.

Covington, M. V., & Omelich, C. L. (1979). Effort: The double-edged sword in school achievement. *Journal of Educational Psychology, 71,* 169–182.

Covington, M. V., & Omelich, C. L. (1984). An empirical examination of Weiner's critique of attributional research. *Journal of Educational Psychology, 76,* 1214–1225.

Coyne, J. C., & Gotlib, I. H. (1983). The role of cognition in depression: A critical appraisal. *Psychological Bulletin, 94,* 472–505.

Cutrona, C. E., Russell, D., & Jones, R. D. (1985). Cross-situational consistency in causal attributions: Does attributional style exist? *Journal of Personality and Social Psychology, 47,* 1043–1058.

Festinger, L. (1957). *A theory of cognitive dissonance.* Evanston, Ill: Row, Peterson.

Fletcher, G. J. O., Danilovics, P., Fernandez, G., Peterson, D., & Reeder, G. D. (1986). Attributional complexity: An individual difference measure. *Journal of Personality and Social Psychology, 51,* 875–884.

Forsterling, F. (1985). Attributional training: A review. *Psychological Bulletin, 98,* 495–512.

Forsterling, F. (1986). Attributional conceptions in clinical psychology. *American Psychologist, 41,* 275–285.

Forsterling, F. (1988). *Attribution theory in clinical psychology.* New York: Wiley.

Frieze, I. H., & Weiner, B. (1971). Cue utilization and attributional judgments for success and failure. *Journal of Personality, 39,* 591–606.

Gilovich, T. (1983). Biased evaluation and persistence in gambling. *Journal of Personality and Social Psychology, 44,* 1110–1126.

Graham, S., & Folkes, V. S. (Eds.). (in press). *Applications of attribution theory.* Hillsdale, NJ: Erlbaum.

Greenberg, J., Pyszczynski, T., & Solomon, S. (1982). The self-serving attributional bias: Beyond self-presentation. *Journal of Experimental Social Psychology, 18,* 56–67.

Heider, F. (1958). *The psychology of interpersonal relations.* New York: Wiley.

Hewstone, M., & Jaspars, J. (1987). Covariation and causal attribution: A logical model of the intuitive analysis of variance. *Journal of Personality and Social Psychology, 53,* 663–672.

Hilton, D. J., & Slugoski, B. R. (1986). Knowledge based causal attribution: The abnormal conditions focus model. *Psychological Review, 93,* 75–88.

Hoffman, M. L. (1975). Developmental synthesis of affect and cognition and its implications for altruistic motivation. *Developmental Psychology, 11,* 607–622.

Horney, K. (1937). *Neurotic personality of our times.* New York: Norton.

Isenberg, A. (1980). Natural pride and natural shame. In A. O. Rorty (Ed.), *Explaining emotions* (pp. 355–384). Berkeley: University of California Press.

James, W., & Rotter, J. B. (1958). Partial and 100% reinforcement under chance and skill conditions. *Journal of Experimental Psychology, 55,* 397–403.

Janoff-Bulman, R. (1979). Characterological versus behavioral self-blame: Inquiries into depression and rape. *Journal of Personality and Social Psychology, 37,* 1798–1809.

Johnson, T. J., Feigenbaum, R., & Weiby, M. (1964). Some determinants and consequences of the teacher's perception of causation. *Journal of Educational Psychology, 55,* 237–246.

Jones, E. E., & Berglas, S. (1978). Control of attributions about the self through self-handicapping strategies: The appeal of alcohol and the role of underachievement. *Personality and Social Psychology Bulletin, 4,* 200–206.

Jones, E. E., & Harris, V. A. (1967). The attribution of

attitudes. *Journal of Experimental Social Psychology, 3,* 1–24.

Jones. E. E., & Nisbett, R. E. (1971). The actor and the observer: Divergent perceptions of the causes of behavior. In E. E. Jones, D. E. Kanouse, H. H. Kelley, R. E. Nisbett, S. Valins, & B. Weiner (Eds.), *Attribution: Perceiving the causes of behavior* (pp. 79–94). Morristown, NJ: General Learning Press.

Kelley, H. H. (1967). Attribution theory in social psychology. In D. Levine (Ed.), *Nebraska Symposium on Motivation* (Vol. 15, pp. 192–238). Lincoln: University of Nebraska Press.

Kelley, H. H. (1971). Causal schemata and the attribution process. In E. E. Jones, D. E. Kanouse, H. H. Kelley, R. E. Nisbett, S. Valins, & B. Weiner (Eds.), *Attribution: Perceiving the causes of behavior* (pp. 151–174). Morristown, NJ: General Learning Press.

Kelley, H. H., & Michela, J. L. (1980). Attribution theory and research. *Annual Review of Psychology, 31,* 457–501.

Kingdon, J. W. (1967). Politicians' beliefs about voters. *American Political Science Review, 14,* 137–145.

Lau, R. R., & Ware, J. W., Jr. (1981). The conceptualization and measurement of a multidimensional health-specific locus of control scale. *Medical Care, 19,* 1147–1158.

Lefcourt, H. M. (1976). *Locus of control.* Hillsdale, NJ: Erlbaum.

Lefcourt, H. M. (Eds.). (1981). *Research with the locus of control concept* (Vol. 1). New York: Academic Press.

Lefcourt, H. M., von Baeyer, C. L., Ware, E. E., & Cox, D. J. (1979). The Multidimensional–Multiattributional Causality Scale: The development of a goal specific locus of control scale. *Canadian Journal of Behavioral Science, 11,* 286–304.

Major, B., Mueller, P., & Hilderbrandt, K. (1985). Attributions, expectations, and coping with abortion. *Journal of Personality and Social Psychology, 48,* 585–599.

Marks, G., & Miller, N. (1987). Ten years of research on the false-consensus effect: An empirical and theoretical review. *Psychological Bulletin, 102,* 72–90.

Miller, D. T., & Ross, M. (1975). Self-serving biases in the attribution of causality: Fact or fiction? *Psychological Bulletin, 82,* 213–225.

Monson, T. C., & Snyder, M. (1977). Actors, observers, and the attribution process: Toward a reconceptualization. *Journal of Experimental Social Psychology, 13,* 89–111.

Mullen, B., Atkins, J. L., Champion, D. S., Edwards, C., Hardy, D., Story, J. E., & Vanderklok, M. (1985). The false consensus effect: A meta-analysis of 115 hypothesis tests. *Journal of Experimental Social Psychology, 21,* 262–283.

Mullen, B., & Riordan, C. A. (1988). Self-serving attributions for performance in naturalistic settings: A meta-analytic review. *Journal of Applied Social Psychology, 18,* 3–22.

Nisbett, R. E., Caputo, C., Legant, P., & Maracek, J. (1973). Behavior as seen by the actor and as seen by the observer. *Journal of Personality and Social Psychology, 27,* 154–165.

Orvis, B. R. (1977). *The bases, nature, and affective significance of attributional conflict in young couples.* Unpublished doctoral dissertation, University of California–Los Angeles.

Peterson, C., & Seligman, M. E. P. (1984). Causal explanations as a risk factor for depression: Theory and evidence. *Psychological Review, 91,* 347–374.

Peterson, C., Seligman, M. E. P., & Vaillant, G. (1988). Pessimistic explanatory style is a risk factor for physical illness: A thirty-five year longitudinal study. *Journal of Personality and Social Psychology, 55,* 23–27.

Peterson, C., Semmel, A., von Baeyer, C., Abramson, L. Y., Metalsky, G. I., & Seligman, M. E. P. (1982). The Attributional Style Questionnaire. *Cognitive Therapy and Research, 6,* 287–299.

Phares, E. J. (1976). *Locus of control in personality.* Morristown, NJ: General Learning Press.

Pruitt, D. J., & Insko, C. A. (1980). Extention of the Kelley attribution model: The role of comparison object consensus, target object consensus, distinctiveness and consistency. *Journal of Personality and Social Psychology, 39,* 39–58.

Reisenzein, R. (1983). The Schachter theory of emotions: Two decades later. *Psychological Bulletin, 94,* 239–264.

Robins, C. J. (1988). Attributions and depression: Why is the literature so inconsistent? *Journal of Personality and Social Psychology, 54,* 880–889.

Ross, L. (1977). The intuitive psychologist and his shortcomings: Distortions in the attribution process. In L. Berkowitz (Ed.), *Advances in experimental social psychology* (Vol. 10, pp. 173–220). New York: Academic Press.

Ross, L., Bierbrauer, G., & Polly, S. (1974). Attribution of educational outcomes by professional and non-professional instructors. *Journal of Personality and Social Psychology, 29,* 609–618.

Ross, L., Greene, D., & House, P. (1977). The "false consensus effect": An egocentric bias in social perception and attribution processes. *Journal of Experimental Social Psychology, 13,* 279–301.

Rotter, J. B. (1966). Generalized expectancies for internal versus external control of reinforcement. *Psychological Monographs, 80*(1, Whole No. 609).

Rotter, J. B., & Hochreich, D. J. (1975). *Personality.* Glenview, IL: Scott, Foresman.

Schachter, S., & Singer, J. E. (1962). Cognition, social, and physiological determinants of emotional state. *Psychological Review, 69,* 379–399.

Seligman, M. E. P. (1975). *Helplessness: On depression, development and death.* San Francisco: W. H. Freeman.

Snyder, C. R., & Higgins, R. L. (1988). Excuses: Their effective role in the negotiation of reality. *Psychological Bulletin, 104,* 23–35.

Snyder, M. L., Stephan, W. G., & Rosenfield, D. (1976). Egotism and attribution. *Journal of Personality and Social Psychology, 33,* 435–441.

Storms, M. D. (1973). Videotape and the attribution process: Reversing actors' and observers' point of view. *Journal of Personality and Social Psychology, 27,* 165–175.

Sweeney, P., Anderson, K., & Bailey, S. (1986). Attributional style in depression: A meta-analytic review. *Journal of Personality and Social Psychology, 50,* 974–991.

Taylor, S. E., & Fiske, S. T. (1978). Salience, attention, and attribution: Top of the head phenomena. In L. Berkowitz (Ed.), *Advances in experimental social psychology* (Vol. 11, pp. 249–288). New York: Academic Press.

Taylor, S. E., & Koivumaki, J. H. (1976). The perception of self and others: Acquaintanceship, affect, and actor–observer differences. *Journal of Personality and Social Psychology, 33,* 403–408.

Tetlock, P. E., & Levi, A. (1982). Attribution bias: On the inconclusiveness of the cognition–motivation debate. *Journal of Experimental, Social Psychology, 18,* 68–88.

Trivers, R. L. (1971). The evolution of reciprical altruism. *Quarterly Review of Biology, 46,* 35–57.

Wallston, K. A., & Wallston, B. S. (1980). Health locus of control scales. In H. Lefcourt (Ed.), *Advances and innovation in locus of control research* (pp. 198–234). New York: Academic Press.

Weiner, B. (1980). *Human motivation.* New York: Holt, Rinehart & Winston.

Weiner, B. (1985). An attributional theory of achievement motivation and emotion. *Psychological Review, 92,* 548–573.

Weiner, B. (1986). *An attributional theory of motivation and emotion.* New York: Springer.

Weiner, B. (1988). Attribution theory and attributional therapy: Some theoretical observations and suggestions. *British Journal of Clinical Psychology, 27,* 93–104.

Weiner, B., Russell, D., & Lerman, D. (1978). Affective consequences of causal ascriptions. In J. H. Harvey, W. J. Ickes, & R. F. Kidd (Eds.), *New directions in attribution research* (Vol. 2, pp. 59–88). Hillsdale, NJ: Erlbaum.

Weiner, B., Russell, D., & Lerman, D. (1979). The cognition–emotion process in achievement-related contexts. *Journal of Personality and Social Psychology, 37,* 1211–1220.

Wicker, W. F., Payne, G. C., & Morgan, R. D. (1983). Participant descriptions of guilt and shame. *Motivation and Emotion, 7,* 25–39.

Wright, E. F., & Wells, G. L. (1988). Is the attitude-attribution paradigm suitable for investigating the dispositional bias? *Personality and Social Psychology Bulletin, 14,* 183–190.

Zuckerman, M. (1979). Attribution of success and failure revisited or: The motivational bias is alive and well in attribution theory. *Journal of Personality, 47,* 245–287.

Chapter 19

Sex, Gender, and the Individual

Richard D. Ashmore
Rutgers University

Since the dawn of recorded history, philosophers, poets, and others have articulated "theories" about the sexes; for the most part, these have been quite simple. During the relatively brief time since the advent of modern scientific psychology in the late 19th century, psychologists, too, have been drawn to this topic. And, although generally maintaining the caution necessitated by an empirical and inductive approach to truth (see, however, Morawski, 1985), they also pursued relatively simple explanations of sex and gender. One of the major lessons learned by researchers over the past decade and a half is that men and women are much more complicated and diverse than most past formulations would lead one to believe. However, this lesson should not lead to despair at understanding the sexes. In recent years (and, in most cases, with clues from earlier contributors), major conceptual and empirical tools for addressing the complexity of sex and gender have been made available.

Reflecting the broader nature–nurture divide, and consistent with the tendency to seek simple causal models, social scientists have tended to favor either biological and genetic or societal and learning accounts of the conduct of females and males. In recent years, biosocial interactionist models have been suggested as a way to merge these apparently conflicting causal paradigms. Although such models are desirable, especially in that they work against oversimplification, they are at this point not well developed (Adkins-Regan, 1989). An alternative strategy is to elaborate multifaceted explanations within a given level of analysis. (See Ashmore & Del Boca, 1986a, Chs. 1 and 8, on this basic idea, and the conceptual linking of adjacent levels of analysis to construct more comprehensive frameworks.) This chapter follows this within-level approach. At the outset, it is recognized that _Homo sapiens_ is both a biological beast and a social creature. The term "sex" is used to denote that large and diverse set of biological (e.g., anatomy, brain structure, hormones) and genetic/evolutionary factors that contribute to the ways in which women and men think, feel, and behave. "Gender" is used to acknowledge the fact that "male" and "female" are cultural constructions and that each person is brought up in a particular society with a rich set of beliefs and expectations about these social categories. The focus in this chapter is on the individual who must confront and come to terms with both sets of factors. Thus, the level of analysis is psychological. I leave to the biologists the explication of the precise functioning of the presumed biological inputs, and to sociologists and anthropologists the fine-grained analysis of the societal causes.[1]

To describe what psychologists have learned about sex, gender, and the individual and to set the stage for future work on this topic, this chapter adopts the following plan. First, a history of psychologists' efforts to understand sex and gender is offered. Second, I describe the major conclusion from this historical analysis (that three basic paradigms have guided the efforts of psychologists—"sex differences," "gender as a personality variable," and "sex as a social category"; see also Deaux, 1984) and identify several other trends in past theory and measurement (e.g., that conceptual analysis has lagged behind methods). Third, each of the three overarching perspectives is described in depth and critiqued. By way of preview, the paradigms of "sex differences" and "gender as a personality variable" are judged as unduly simplified and as not fitting well with the accumulated data, whereas the perspective of "sex as a social category" offers considerable promise in explicating sex, gender, and the individual. Within this general approach, I further suggest that the concept of self or identity is particularly useful for psychological-level analyses, and I describe a "multiplicity model of gender identity" to illustrate this assertion.

A HISTORY OF PSYCHOLOGISTS' CONCERN WITH SEX AND GENDER

What Has Been Done?

Although different purposes and perspectives would yield a somewhat different picture (compare, e.g., the present analysis with those by Carter, 1987b; Crawford & Marecek, 1989; Lewin, 1984a, 1984b; Morawski, 1985, 1987; Pleck, 1984; Rosenberg, 1982),[2] it is possible to identify six *relatively* distinct periods in the study of sex, gender, and the individual. With *approximate* starting and ending dates, and named in terms of the *predominant* focus of research during the period, these are as follows: (1) 1894–1936: "sex difference in intelligence"; (2) 1936–1954: "masculinity–femininity as a global personality trait"; (3)

1954–1966: "sex-role development"; (4) 1966–1974: "grand new theories of sex typing"; (5) 1974–1982: "androgyny as a sex-role ideal"; (6) 1982–present: "sex as a social category."

1894–1936: Sex Difference in Intelligence

The first period began with the publication of Ellis's (1894) *Man and Woman,* in which he urged a scientific approach to sex differences and reviewed the largely nonscientific literature that existed at the time he wrote. The ending point for this era has been selected because it marked the start of a new period with the publication of *Sex and Personality* by Terman and Miles (1936) and the approximate "close" of the sex-difference-in-intelligence issue. The next year, Terman and Merrill (1937) published a major revision of the Binet–Simon Intelligence Scale; one alteration was that sex differences in global intelligence were "controlled" out (Garai & Scheinfeld, 1968; Willerman, 1979, pp. 388–390). The primary aim of work during the period 1894 to 1936 was to determine empirically whether males are intellectually superior to females, and the scientific consensus by the early 1930s was that there is no sex difference in general mental ability.

Psychology emerged as a separate academic discipline and empirical science in the United States during the last decades of the 1800s. Almost from the outset of this fledgling field, sex and gender were issues that drew attention. Among the leaders in this effort were young females, some of whom were still graduate students (see Rosenberg, 1982), whose primary aim was to subject to objective scientific test what many laypeople of the time assumed to be a fact—that men and women are quite different with men superior, especially in intellectual ability. Scientists, inside and outside of psychology, cooperated in undergirding this ideology, primarily by attempting to show that this presumed sex difference in intelligence was rooted in female–male physical differences, especially in the brain (Shields, 1975, 1982). The underlying largely implicit causal model was as follows: biological sex → brain anatomy → intelligence → societal accomplishments (especially males' alleged greater contributions to politics, science, and the like) and societal arrangements (especially greater male power and prestige). Beginning with Thompson

(1903), attempts were made to test just one part of this chain, the correlation of sex with intellectual ability. The development of IQ measures and the rise of the testing movement helped address this issue, and by the early 1930s enough data had accumulated to lead most psychologists concerned with the issue to conclude that there are no general intelligence differences between the sexes (e.g., Miles 1935).

1936–1954: Masculinity–Femininity as a Global Personality Trait

The second period, from 1936 to 1954, is somewhat more difficult to label, since it involved several different trends and activities. The major and most revolutionary development was the introduction and dissemination within psychology of the notion of a pair of opposing and general personality traits, "masculinity" and "femininity." The seminal work was *Sex and Personality* by Terman and Miles (1936). Using intelligence tests as a model, these authors also introduced a self-report measure of masculinity–femininity (which, following a longstanding convention in the field, I abbreviate in this chapter, in regard to such measures and the research surrounding them, as "M-F"). This was followed by other similar instruments, and M-F scales became standard components in omnibus personality inventories (Pleck, 1984). Although Terman and Miles (1936) explicitly avoided explicating the origins of masculinity–femininity, the underlying implicit framework was as follows: nature and nurture → masculinity–femininity → individual differences in behavior and adjustment. It is important to emphasize the latter consequence, adjustment, because a major but tacit assumption of this line of work was that femininity is normal and natural in females (but not males), and that the parallel is true for masculinity.

During this same period, however, research into sex differences continued. Most such work was by developmentalists (Jacklin, 1989), and the focus was on more specific intellectual abilities (e.g., math) rather than general IQ, and on nonintellectual qualities (especially interests). The 1954 ending date for this period has been selected because in that year Terman and Tyler's *Manual of Child Psychology* chapter featured sex differences; this had been true in the two earlier editions (Terman, 1946; Wellman, 1933), but would not be the case in the next two (Mischel, 1970; Huston, 1983).

Although M-F tests proliferated and developmentalists continued to investigate sex differences, most researchers in social and personality psychology, influenced by the hypothetico-deductive *Zeitgeist* in the high-prestige area of animal learning, began to do research aimed at discovering general laws of human behavior. In this quest, sex differences were at best a complication, since they violated general principles. Many researchers "solved" this "problem" by using same-sex samples. In part guided by the cultural assumption that "man" is the generic case for humans in general, most often males only were used in research (e.g., early work on achievement motivation). Thus, an important but not explicit or conscious by-product of this avoidance of possible sex differences was that researchers tended to ignore females.

1954–1966: Sex-Role Development

From roughly 1954 to 1966, the new and primary focus was on sex-role development (Tyler, 1965). The question was this: How do little boys and girls become adult men and women? And the answer was sought either in the Freudian concept of "identification," according to which the child makes the same-sex parent part of himself or herself, or a notion borrowed from sociology, "sex role," according to which society has a set of prescriptions about how members of each sex should behave and children are taught these. Many researchers combined the two ideas into "sex-role identification," which indicated both what the child was to learn and how this was to be learned (Pleck, 1984).

During the same era, work on sex differences continued, and M-F measures remained popular. Regarding the latter, Goldberg (1971) wrote, "In the past 15 years, M-F has become the single most popular construct for inclusion in new personality inventories" (pp. 326–327). And yet the majority of social, personality, and other psychologists continued to ignore sex and especially females (cf. Carlson & Carlson, 1960; Carlson, 1971). The laboratory experiment was *the* scientific method (see Hendrick 1977, regarding social psychology), and sex was either tacked on as an uninteresting other variable or "controlled" by using participants of just one sex.

1966–1974: Grand New Theories of Sex Typing

The next major development in the field was the publication of Maccoby's (1966) *The*

Development of Sex Differences (Carter, 1987b), which included formal and detailed introductions of cognitive-developmental (Kohlberg, 1966) and social learning (Mischel, 1966) theories of sex-role identity and sex differences in behavior, respectively. This initiated a period during which a considerable amount of effort was devoted by developmentalists to testing the tenets of these formulations (Carter, 1987b). Work also continued on the themes already identified. Even more importantly, the movements for social change sweeping the United States led to calls for a "relevant" psychology and, most directly pertinent to the present topic, one sensitive to and not subjugating women. This set the stage for the subsequent period in work on sex, gender, and the individual.

1974–1982: Androgyny as a Sex-Role Ideal

The next watershed event was Bem's (1974) introduction of a new psychological construct, "androgyny," which was viewed as a blending of masculinity and femininity—something not possible under the earlier conceptual framework that viewed these as opposites. Even more radical in terms of past sex and gender work, but congruent with much feminist social and intellectual criticism of the time, was the proposal that androgyny, not masculinity in males and femininity in females, is "healthy," because it allows the individual to match his or her behavior to situational demands. Bem (1974) developed a self-report measure of androgyny, and its building blocks femininity and masculinity (I refer in this chapter to such measures as "M-F-A" measures). Other paper-and-pencil instruments were quickly developed, and there followed an explosion of research linking scores on these questionnaires to a wide variety of other variables, especially indices of self-esteem and psychological adjustment (Cook, 1985).

The year 1974 also witnessed the publication of another monumental book by Maccoby, this one coauthored by Jacklin. In *The Psychology of Sex Differences*, these authors reviewed a large number of studies concerned with female–male differences in a wide variety of domains, including intellectual, emotional, and social variables. Their general conclusion—that there are few documented sex differences, and that those that exist are small and qualified by statistical interactions with third variables—was quickly accepted by most workers in the field.

Thus, sex differences, which were generally thought to be widespread and large, were now "minimized" (Lorber, 1981).

1982–Present: Sex as a Social Category

Yet another period was inaugurated with the publication of Sherif's (1982) paper "Needed Concepts in the Study of Gender Identity." Sherif argued that the psychological analysis of sex and gender must begin with the recognition that gender is a societal-level social category system. This was followed by Deaux's (1984) identification of a sex-as-a-social-category approach as distinct from and in opposition to sex differences and masculinity–femininity, and by our (Ashmore & Del Boca, 1986a) suggestion that the female-male distinction be seen as an instance of intergroup relations.

As Sherif was introducing a new perspective, there were major changes in existing paradigms, signaled by Bem's (1981) initial piece on gender schema theory and Gilligan's (1982) *In a Different Voice*. The former publication proposed a new cognitive perspective on masculinity–femininity–androgyny, whereas the latter suggested that there are major sex differences and that women's attributes should be viewed as positive and not as deficits vis-à-vis men. In addition to Bem's cognitive restructuring, Spence (1985; Spence, Deaux, & Helmreich, 1985; Spence & Sawin, 1985) urged that masculinity–femininity not be viewed as a global and homogeneous construct. Concerning sex differences, the 1980s brought other "maximizing" theories of gender and also saw the development of meta-analytic techniques and their application to female–male differences. The results of these quantitative reviews have tended to support the general position implied by Gilligan—namely, that there are more meaningful sex differences than suggested by the Maccoby and Jacklin (1974) review (see especially Eagly, 1987, 1989a).

A Major Conclusion From This Look at The Past

If this history is viewed as a whole, the major conclusion is that the efforts of psychologists who are not biologically inclined have been guided by one of three basic paradigms—sex differences, gender as a personality variable, and sex as a social category. (There is a fourth, the developmental psychology of sex and gender; this is not, given my expertise and goals for this chapter, treated in depth here [see Carter, 1987a; Huston, 1983].) The sex-differences approach, situated within an individual-difference/differential psychology (e.g., Minton & Schneider, 1980) and closely aligned with the testing movement, was the earliest to be adopted, and the one with the most continuing interest and impact. According to this paradigm, the key to unlocking the "why" of sex and gender is to identify average differences in experience and action between the biological sex categories, female and male. The next framework to guide psychological inquiry was gender as a personality variable, which arose in the mid-1930s, and is generally part of a personality trait psychology. Androgyny-era variants, however, were inspired by feminist values (Bem, 1974, 1985), and the most recent form has a cognitive underpinning (Bem, 1981). Whatever the variant, however, this paradigm assumes that sex and gender are represented in the individual in terms of one or a small number of explicitly gendered trait-like qualities or essences (Morawski, 1985), and the measurement of these is the key task. The third general stance in the field, sex as a social category, was foreshadowed by earlier publications and trends; however, as a relatively explicit and generally applied perspective it is of quite recent origin, being most clearly evidenced only in works published in the last decade. This final paradigm assumes that what individual men and women think, feel, and do is crucially shaped by the fact that male and female are important social categories. Because sex differences, gender as a personality variable, and sex as a social category are the dominant approaches to sex, gender, and the individual, they are worth a closer look. Thus, these three paradigms are described in detail below. But first, what more can be learned from looking backward?

Hints From This Look Over the Shoulder

The historical review above suggests not only one major conclusion, but also several hints about what this upcoming in-depth analysis will reveal. First, the sex-differences and gender-as-a-personality-variable paradigms contain many implicit yet crucial assumptions and impose too simple a framework on the psychology of sex and gender. Second, under the

broad paradigms are more circumscribed theories and even more specific concepts.

In terms of theory, relatively general and explicit conceptual frameworks were slow to come to this field. Sex-difference work of the first period was very strictly empirical, with most researchers suggesting that either nature or nurture could account for the results (see, however, Morawski, 1985). Terman and Miles, in introducing masculinity–femininity in 1936, went out of their way to avoid a theoretical account and also invoked both heredity and environment as possible general causes. Although Freudian thought guided much theoretical work of the 1930s and 1940s, sex differences and M-F research remained atheoretical. Although sex role and identification became important explanatory concepts in the 1950s, it was not until 1966 that formal and grand sex-typing theories were articulated (see, however, Kagan, 1964). In light of the tremendous amount of published work that has appeared over the past two decades (Cook, 1985; Spence et al., 1985), there has been surprisingly little change in broad and general sex and gender theories. Roopnarine and Mounts (1987) cover the "traditional theories"—psychoanalytic, social learning, and cognitive-developmental—and they write basically the same things that were noted nearly two decades ago. (Granted, social learning theory has become more cognitive, and Chodorow, 1978, and others have introduced feminist psychoanalytic theories.) Certainly many midrange theories have been advanced, but it was not until Bem (1981) introduced gender schema theory that a grand explanatory model was put forth. Although the relative paucity of theory or conceptual analysis more generally is due to multiple factors, one important contributor is that much past work, especially that done by personality and social psychologists, tends to be method-driven (see Ashmore, Del Boca, & Wohlers, 1986, for a similar argument regarding research on sex stereotypes). Terman and Miles (1936) introduced not only the concepts of masculinity and femininity but also an easy-to-use M-F test; much sex-role development research of the 1950s employed the IT scale (Brown, 1956); and the large volume of research over the past decade and a half has relied heavily on a small number of self-report measures (Ashmore et al., 1986; Cook, 1985; Del Boca, Ashmore, & McManus, 1986; Katz, 1986).

Because of the apparent favoring of methods over conceptual analysis, it is necessary to look within theories (within paradigms) at hypothetical constructs, and especially at how these constructs are measured. Since concepts and measures are crucially intertwined, they are discussed together. It is impossible, given the space constraints and goals of this chapter, to fully describe and analyze the scientific vocabulary of sex and gender. Here only major constructs and measures are discussed. (For further and more in-depth analyses of concepts and their measurement, see Ashmore & Del Boca, 1979; Beere, 1979; Carter, 1987a; Cook, 1985; Del Boca & Ashmore, 1980a; Huston, 1983; Sedney, 1989; Sherif, 1982.)

In terms of disciplinary and subdisciplinary preferences, sociologists and anthropologists favor "sex role" (e.g., Giele, 1988). This term, in spirit, can be traced back to Mead (1935) and came to the fore in psychology with a push from Parsons (1942; Parsons & Bales, 1955; see Pleck, 1984). As even its supporters admit (Giele, 1988), "sex role" is a vague and general term (see Staines & Libby, 1986, and sources they cite), and is subject to many quite divergent operational definitions (Angrist, 1969). Within psychology, "identification," and later "identity" or "orientation," were added as suffixes to "sex role" (e.g., much M-F-A work is assumed to index "sex-role orientation"). In addition, the notion of "sex differences" has wide appeal, although strong criticisms of the term have been voiced, and suggested alternatives (e.g., "sex-related differences" [Jacklin, 1981], "sex similarities") have been proposed. One big problem with the concept of "sex differences" is that it is too simple, summing over interactions to come up with female–male main effects. By the time Mischel wrote his *Manual of Child Psychology* chapter in 1970, the focal concept was "sex typing," which in a sense replaces "sex differences" and "sex role." As Huston (1983) forcefully demonstrates in the next such chapter, one shortcoming of many earlier works is the failure to fully realize the multidimensionality of sex typing (which Huston treats as including both actual and expected sex differences).

To turn to gender as a personality variable, M-F work has been criticized for ignoring the relative independence of different facets of masculinity and femininity (e.g., Constantinople, 1973; Tyler, 1965) and for using a simple-minded and tautological sex-differences

item selection and validation procedure (Constantinople, 1973; Goldberg, 1971). In the mid-1970s, "androgyny" became the "salted peanuts" of many sex and gender workers. Many conceptual definitions have been offered, but there is a tenuous connection to operationalizations (Sedney, 1989), and the field is dominated by research using just a handful of paper-and-pencil questionnaires and a single scoring procedure (the median-split method; see below, and Cook, 1985). The cognitive revolution pervading psychology has also affected the present topic, especially in the form of the concept "gender schema," which has been central in the 1980s both for social and personality psychologists (e.g., Bem, 1981, 1985) and for developmentalists (e.g., Liben & Signorella, 1987; Martin & Halverson, 1981). Carter (1987b) believes that gender schema will offer the necessary basis for making substantial progress in the psychology of sex and gender in the future. I place my money on another concept, however. If this chapter achieves its goal, in combinaion with the earlier analyses by Sherif (1982) and Spence (1985) and current research and theory by Deaux (1989), a major concept for future work will be "gender identity," which is provisionally defined, in process terms, as how the individual takes the social construction of gender and the biological "facts" of sex and incorporates these into a multifaceted personal identity structure.[3]

SEX DIFFERENCES

Do women and men differ in thought, feeling, and behavior? This seems a simple question to answer. The "independent variable," biological sex of subject, is easy to measure, and psychology's statistical tools are designed to detect the presence of differences. The apparent simplicity of the scientific task may account in part for the early adoption of and the continuing interest in this type of research, but the accumulated work has not yielded simple answers. In fact, over the past several decades and still today, there are diverse and divergent conclusions to this question: Are there psychological sex differences? Although there is at present no clear overall consensus, it is becoming a bit easier to identify points of convergence and the bases for disagreement. Furthermore, it is possible to evaluate the sex-differences approach to the study of sex, gender, and the individual.

This section is organized as follows. First, within the history presented in the preceding section, a finer-grained look is taken at recent sex-differences work (see Rosenberg, 1982, and Morawski, 1985, 1987, for details on the earlier periods). This research illustrates the tension between minimizing and maximizing sex differences (Lorber, 1981) and provides a "mature" form of the sex-differences perspective for appraisal. First, the tendency to minimize sex differences during the 1974–1982 androgyny era is described. Next, two current trends (subthemes during the period of sex as a social category [1982–present]), both of which maximize sex differences, are covered in depth. The first movement, best illustrated by Gilligan's (1982) *In a Different Voice,* is based on a "soft" interpretive methodology; the second derives inspiration from the "hard" side of the discipline, using a recently developed set of statistical procedures known as "meta-analysis" to objectively and quantitatively summarize multiple studies of sex differences. This section concludes with an evaluation of the sex-differences paradigm. A major conclusion is that the paradigm is not a promising general approach, and yet that the issue of male–female differences cannot be ignored by sex and gender researchers.

Minimizing Sex Differences in the 1970s

Although the major theme in gender research of the 1970s was the construct "androgyny," there was an important revival of the sex-differences perspective. As noted above, the crucial publication in this regard was the book by Maccoby and Jacklin (1974). The authors' overall conclusion, based on a narrative review of a large and diverse collection of empirical studies, was that there are few sex differences and that even these are small in magnitude and overshadowed by interactions. This general assessment quickly became the wisdom in the field of psychology. The extensive and detailed critique of Maccoby and Jacklin by Block (1976) went almost unnoticed. (This point is documented by the *Social Science Citation Index:* From 1978 through 1987, the Maccoby and Jacklin book was cited 2,075 times, or 207.5 citations per year, while there were only 103 citations, 10.3 per year, of the Block article.)

This ignoring of Block, whose general point was that Maccoby and Jacklin may have underestimated the number and strength of sex differences, is particularly curious given that Maccoby and Jacklin's overall conclusions are at odds, *in this general sense,* with the many reviews of the sex-differences literature going back several decades (i.e., Anastasi, 1958; Garai & Scheinfeld, 1968; Maccoby, 1966; Miles, 1935; Scheinfeld, 1943; Terman, 1946; Terman & Tyler, 1954; Tyler, 1965; Wellman, 1933; see also Block, 1976, pp. 285–286). The rapid and widespread acceptance of Maccoby and Jacklin, given these apparently opposing forces, is a testimony to the quality of their scholarship and presentation. At the same time, the authors' conclusions may have been judged valid, in part, because they fit the tenor of the times in society and academia in terms of debunking the tacit assumption (in psychology and the broader American culture) that the sexes are quite different with males better (Eagly, 1989a). Thus, minimizing differences served to undermine the "business-as-usual" dominance of males.

Maximizing Sex Differences in the 1980s

During the present decade, the sex-differences issue has taken another turn—this time away from the minimizing position of the 1970s and toward maximizing female–male differences (see Lorber, 1981, and Hare-Mustin & Marecek, 1988). This has two primary manifestations, which, when considered together, constitute an odd couple: One involves an interpretive methodology and thus corresponds with the "soft" side of psychology as a science, whereas the other is based on meta-analytic procedures, which are "hard" statistical tools.

Listen to Women; Different Male and Female Selves; Accentuate the Positive

The three different headings contained in the title of this subsection serve to identify three major messages from recent interpretive work that emphasizes, rather than downplays, sex differences. The most influential contributor to this work is Gilligan (1982, 1986). Chodorow (1978) and Miller (1976) foreshadow Gilligan, and Belenky, Clinchy, Goldberger, and Tarule (1986) present an analysis of ways of knowing that parallels Gilligan's work on morality (Crawford, 1989).

The first message is that women need to be studied in their own right and in their own terms. Gilligan argues, as do many other academic feminists, that male scholars have taken male experience as human experience, and that when they have included women, it has been by comparing them to models developed by and on (or in terms of) males. This not only leads to the general denigration of women (they do not measure up according to male-derived standards), but also fundamentally distorts women's experience (since often the standards simply do not make sense for females). In large part, then, Gilligan's aim has been to include women's experience in the development of psychological theory. This helps explain the subtitle of her 1982 volume, *Psychological Theory and Women's Development* (see Gilligan, 1986). One implication of this first message of 1980s feminist maximizing scholarship, "Listen to women," is that Gilligan's primary sample for her work on moral development reported in *In a Different Voice* includes only women. (In parallel fashion, Belenky et al., 1986, only interviewed women.)

The use of females only is a strength with respect to the goal of listening to women and developing theories that can include women's experience, but it is a distinct weakness with regard to the second message—that men and women, on average, have fundamentally different global selves. Gilligan argues that the sexes develop different selves and different moral stances because of early learning experiences. Most importantly, little girls experience themselves as like their primary caregivers, their mothers, and as a result develop a personal identity based on connections to others; by contrast, boys' first major interpersonal task is to develop a self that is separate from their mothers, whom they see as fundamentally different from them. This early difference is amplified by later experiences such that, as adolescents and adults, men's selves and morality are characterized by separation, whereas women's are typified by connectedness. (Belenky et al., 1986, find that women's personal epistemologies are also different from men's, with women more often basing knowledge on intuitive and personal grounds.) Gilligan's methods and conclusions have been subjected to careful and detailed critical analysis (e.g., Kerber et al., 1986), as have those of Belenky et al. (Craw-

ford, 1989). One major criticism has been the use of single-sex samples—a charge used by minimizers in the 1970s, against earlier sex-differences research (e.g., Maccoby & Jacklin, 1974). In this regard, there are follow-ups to Gilligan's orginal work using both males and females (Gilligan, 1986). It is too early to know whether the sex differences that Gilligan and Belenky's group have proposed will stand up under further study by these authors and other investigators.

There are, however, two general criticisms that I think will be shown to be valid by subsequent research. First, Gilligan, and Belenky and her associates, posit very general and global differences between the sexes. A lesson from past sex-differences work (note the failure of overall IQ to differentiate the sexes, but the existence of differences on more specific types of intellectual ability, expecially math, verbal, and spatial; see below) and many other areas of psychology is the need to partition global constructs into more precise, content-specific concepts (regarding sex and gender see below and Spence et al., 1985). Second, Belenky's group and Gilligan implicitly lump all women and all men. Stack (1986) concerning Gilligan, and Crawford (1989) on Belenky et al., note that these maximizing analyses do not describe how women's voices or epistemologies vary as a function of social class, ethnicity, and related variables. Future work will probably show that the person variables of interest to Gilligan and to Belenky and colleagues vary considerably as a function of such variables. Quite simply, humans develop not just in a gendered world, but one that is structured in important and enduring ways by ethnicity, class, and other potent societal variables.

The final message of the 1980s feminist maximizing scholars is that differences need not be construed as deficits. Most particularly, women's moral stances and ways of knowing are not inferior forms of the way men in general approach these important human issues. This is a significant point, but one that, once said and even agreed to, is hard to maintain. Humans are almost by nature evaluative beings (cf. Ashmore, 1981; Osgood, 1969); particularly when it comes to societally important social categories, it is almost impossible to think about differences without attaching more value to one way of thinking, feeling, or behaving. This tendency can be seen even in the original authors themselves who at times elevate women's ways of moral decision making and thinking above the "different" modal approaches of men. And, in the reception of their work outside psychology, these ideas often are used to establish the superiority of women's nature or culture (see Crawford, 1989; Kerber et al., 1986). On the one hand, this can serve as leverage against the societally dominant patriarchal value system. On the other hand, there is the danger that others can use the same or apparently the same suggested difference and yet evaluate it negatively. For example, women's concern with basing moral decision making on maintaining interpersonal relations can be seen as bad in that it contradicts universalism and transpersonal rules (which are the hallmarks, according to Gilligan, of males' moral stance), and thus as a deficit.

Objectively Combine Effect Sizes to Distill Sex Differences

The late 1970s not only witnessed publications by Chodorow (1978) and Miller (1976) that foreshadowed current feminist scholarship accentuating sex differences; during this same period the groundwork was being established for a new method for summarizing research literatures. This procedure, meta-analysis, has been applied to sex differences and has fundamentally altered the scientific discourse on this topic. When Maccoby and Jacklin (1974) did their monumental survey of the sex-differences literature, they relied on an approach, the narrative review, that is as old as the field of psychology itself. To summarize the findings of multiple studies of the same topic, the reviewer collects all relevant studies, reads these, and somehow comes to a conclusion about the weight of the evidence. In the Maccoby and Jacklin review, such conclusions were reached by what has been termed the "box score" or "vote-counting" method. The reviewers tallied the studies showing statistically significant sex differences; where a substantial proportion showed a difference with one sex consistently exceeding the other on a particular variable (as was true, for example, of studies on aggression), the authors concluded that a sex difference had been empirically demonstrated. There are several problems with narrative reviews. Most important for the present purposes are these: (1) The box score method is conservative, in that it tends to underestimate or fails to detect actual differences (cf. Cooper &

Rosenthal, 1980; see Hyde, 1986, and Hedges & Olkin, 1980, for why this is the case). (2) Vote counting takes into account only part of the information available in most original reports. Most importantly, it fails to consider the size of the effect (in looking only at whether the difference in question achieved a particular significance level) and ignores sample size (e.g., treating a nonsignificant p in one study based on 20 males and females as equivalent in informativeness to a statistically significant p in a study involving thousands of participants of each sex).

Beginning in the late 1970s, meta-analytic techniques were developed as a means of quantitatively combining studies to summarize bodies of research; beginning with Hall (1978), such techniques have been applied increasingly to sex differences (Eagly, 1987, 1989a; Green & Hall, 1984; Hyde & Linn, 1986). The first step in a meta-analysis is similar to that in a narrative review, collecting the relevant studies. The subsequent steps, however, are quite different. Rather than focusing on whether the difference in question achieves a particular significance level, the meta-analyst tallies d, a measure of effect size in standard units. In sex-differences research, this is the difference between the means for male and female participants divided by the pooled within-sex standard deviation. These effect sizes are then combined across studies, measures of average effect size are calculated, and tests of significance are applied to these measues of central tendency. This process is not as easy as this brief description suggests; cautions have been voiced, and special procedures for combining effect sizes and testing significance have been developed and refined (cf. Hedges & Becker, 1986; Hedges & Olkin, 1985). Particularly important is the need to test for the homogeneity of effect sizes (see Hedges & Becker, 1986; Hyde, 1986).

What Meta-Analysis Can Do. Meta-analysis can simplify and objectively summarize large bodies of research. And, though this is not recognized by most critics *and some practitioners,* it can facilitate the testing of theories of sex and other differences (see, e.g., Eagly, 1987). Whether or not these are theory-derived, meta-analysis can also help identify moderating and mediating variables. Finally, it can aid in the critique of business as usual. That is, this procedure need not be a conservative tool, simply reinforcing the status quo in a particular research domain. Systematically recording attributes of studies in a particular research paradigm and analyzing these actually make it possible to test how general or nongeneral research procedures are (e.g., Eagly & Crowley, 1986, on helping). Thus, meta-analysis need not be as susceptible to the "garbage in, garbage out" problem identified by some critics (LaFrance, 1986).

What Meta-Analysis Cannot Do. Meta-analysis cannot provide a simple and quantitative answer to the overarching question: Are men and women different? It does yield important inputs to answering this question, but it does not give a definitive "yes–no" or "*p* less than" answer. There are three primary reasons: (1) The question cannot be answered at an overall level because sex differences vary as a function of type of dependent variable (see Table 19.1 and accompanying discussion below). (2) Interactions of sex with "third variables" are almost always present. (3) Even for statistically significant effect sizes for a sex main effect, a judgment is required as to whether a particular effect size is big or small, important or not.

Not only will meta-analysis not resolve the sex-differences controversy; like any tool, it can be abused by the analyst (Green & Hall, 1984) and misinterpreted by the consumer. It may be particularly easy to abuse and misinterpret because it is so seductive—it is a fancy tool. It fulfills a major and difficult need, the necessity to summarize large volumes of accumulated research. And, in so doing, it is "hard" and scientific (the combination of studies is based on statistical rules, and there is not much room for interpretation), and it provides simple and straightforward results (an average effect size). In this regard, meta-analysis is like factor analysis, multidimensional scaling, or causal modeling, all of which take large amounts of information and reduce these to simpler and quantitative forms, and, at the same time, all of which require care and skill to implement and interpret correctly.

An Illustrative Summary. Keeping in mind these plaudits and caveats about meta-analysis, the accumulated quantitative summaries of sex differences research still provide the best way to answer, albeit in a preliminary and not completely satisfactory way, the original question: Are the sexes different or similar? Table 19.1

presents an illustrative summary of sex differences and similarities as determined by meta-analytic procedures. This table is *not exhaustive* (not all meta-analyses of sex differences are included) and is *not in final form* (it does not fully convey the intricacies of meta-analysis as applied to the present topic). I hope, however, that even in such an unfinished form the table will nudge experts in the field to flesh out this table or something like it to give a needed summary of quantitative reviews of male–female comparisons. (Some steps have already been taken in this direction; see especially Eagly, 1987, 1989a; Hall, 1984). Such fleshing out should involve not only adding the results of more meta-analytic reviews on the same as well as new variables; in addition, *and more importantly*, the "Homogeneity" and "Moderator(s)" columns, which qualify sex-difference main effects, should be improved and made more precise. In addition, it would be desirable to add a new column called "Limits of primary research paradigm," which would indicate shortcomings and limitations of the way in which the variable in question is most often operationalized and sex differences assessed. An example: Eagly and Crowley (1986), in their meta-analysis of helping research, document that almost all published studies on this topic have been done in situations where a person is called upon to give or not to give aid to a stranger on a short-term basis. They note that this type of helping, what they term "heroic helping," is more congruent with the traditional male role than with the female role (which emphasizes helping within established relationships; e.g., a mother helping her daughter or husband). This "Limit of primary research paradigm" might be indicated in a revised Table 19.1 by something like "Heroic helping overrepresented; nurturant relationship helping underrepresented."

Sex differences in specific behaviors that have been summarized by means of meta-analytic procedures are organized in Table 19.1 as follows: (1) The primary row variable is "Domain of attribute." I have used the five general content areas of sex typing identified by Huston (1983) and somewhat modified by Ashmore and Ogilvie (1989; see below), and in some cases I have subdivided these. (2) The primary column variable is magnitude of "Effect Size" of difference. This utilizes the *rough* categorization suggested by Cohen (1977). Cohen based his benchmarks for small ($d = .20$), medium

TABLE 19.1. An Illustrative Summary of Sex Differences as Determined by Meta-Analytic Procedures: Domain of Attribute × Sex-Difference Effect Size

Domain of attribute	Negligible to "small" effect size (.00–.20)				"Small" to "moderate" effect size (.20–.50)				"Moderate" and "large" effect size (.50–.80 and larger)			
	Variable	Average effect size[1]	Homogeneity[2]	Moderator(s)[3]	Variable	Average effect size	Homogeneity	Moderator(s)	Variable	Average effect size	Homogeneity	Moderator(s)
Personal–social attributes												
Personality	Empathy, picture/story assessment[i]	-.10	—	—	Empathy, reflexive crying[j]	-.27	—	Sex of experimenter	Empathy, self-report[i]	-.99	—	—
Social behavior	Leadership emergence				Helping[j]	.34[5]	No	Danger; skill				
	Social leadership[o]	-.18	Yes	—	Aggression (adults)[k]	.29[5]	No	Physical vs. psychological aggression; beliefs (e.g., guilt)				
	Influenceability											
	Persuasion[m]	-.16	—	% male authors								
	Persuasion[n]	-.11	No	Subjects' nationality	Aggression (children)[l]	.50	No	Age; aggression type; method; measure				
	Other conformity[m]	-.28	—	% male authors	Influenceability							
	Other conformity[n]	-.13	No	% male authors; test length	Group pressure[m]	-.32	—	% male authors				
	Leadership style				Group pressure[n]	-.28	No	Outcome measure				
	Interpersonal vs. task[p]	.03	No	Organizational vs. assessment vs. laboratory	Leadership emergence[o]							
					Unspecified[o]	.29	No	Length of interaction; gender linkage of task				
					General	.32	No					
					Task	.41	No					
					Leadership style							
					Democratic vs. autocratic[p]	-.22	No	—				

Category	Variable	d	Sig	Moderators	Variable	d	Sig	Moderators	Variable	d	Sig	Type
Attitudes												
Causal attributions	Success–ability[r]	.13	Yes	Cause vs. info	Neg. attitude toward homosexuals[q]	.21	No	Target sex; year; sample size				
	Success–effort[r]	-.04	Yes	Cause vs. info								
	Success–task[r]	-.01	No	Cause vs. info								
	Success–luck[r]	-.07	No	Cause vs. info								
	Failure–Ability[r]	.16	No	Cause vs. info								
	Failure–effort[r]	.15	No	Cause vs. info								
	Failure–task[r]	-.08	No	Cause vs. info								
	Failure–Luck[r]	-.15	No	Cause vs. info								
Well-being	Overall well-being[s]	-.01	No	Marital status								
	Life satisfact.[s]	-.03	No	Marital status								
	Happiness[s]	-.07	No	Marital status								
	Positive affect[s]	-.07	No	Marital status								
	General evaluation[s]	.09	No	Marital status								
Social relationships	(None)				(None)							
Interests and abilities												
Interests	(None)				(None)							
Abilities												
Mental	Verbal[c]	-.02	—	Year	Verbal[e]	-.24[4]	No	Year; selectivity of sample	Visual–spatial perception[f]			
	Verbal[d]	-.11	No	Year; test type; first author's sex	Math[c]	.36	No	Year; selectivity; age	Spatial perception[f]			
					Math[e]	.43[4]	No	Year; selectivity	(Over 18)	.64	Yes	Age
	Visual-spatial				Visual-spatial[e]	.45[4]	No	Year; selectivity	(12–13)	.37	Yes	Age
	Spatial visualization[f]	.13	Yes	—					(Under 12)	.37	Yes	Age
									Mental rotation[f]			
									Shepard–Metzler	.94	Yes	Task
									Other	.26	Yes	Task
Social	Facial identification[h]				Nonverbal decoding[g]	-.43	—[6]					
	Hits	-.10	—		Face recognition[g]	-.34	—					
	Misses	-.08	—		Expression[g]	-.52	—					

(Continued)

497

TABLE 19.1. (Continued)

	Negligible to "small" effect size (.00–.20)				"Small" to "moderate" effect size (.20–.50)				"Moderate" and "large" effect size (.50–.80 and larger)			
Domain of attribute	Variable	Average effect size[1]	Homo-geneity[2]	Moderator(s)[3]	Variable	Average effect size	Homo-geneity	Moderator(s)	Variable	Average effect size	Homo-geneity	Moderator(s)
Symbolic and stylistic behaviors												
	Distance approach to others				Body involvement[g]	−.32	No[6]	Age (and others)	Social smiling[g]	−.63	Yes[6]	—
	Staged[g]	.12	Yes[6]	Age	Body self-consciousness[g]	−.45	Yes	Age	Gaze[g]	−.68	No	—
	Projective[g]	.14	—	—					Receipt of Gaze[g]	−.65	—	—
									Distance of approach to others, nat[g]	.56	—	—
									Body restlessness[g]	.72	—	—
									Facial expressiveness[g]	−1.01	—	—
									Distance of approach by others			
									Staged	.63	—	—
									Laboratory	.85	—	—
									Natural	.95	—	—
									Body expansiveness[g]	1.04	—	—
									Body expressiveness[g]	−.58	—	—
									Speech errors[g]	.70	—	—
									Vocal-filled pauses[g]	1.19	—	—
Biological/physical/material attributes												
	Vertical jump[a]	.18	Yes	Age	Activity level[b]	.49	No	Age (and others)	Throw velocity[a]	2.18	Yes	Age
	Reaction time[a]	.18	Yes	—	Catching[a]	.43	Yes	Age	Throw distance[a]	1.98	No	Age
	Tapping[a]	.13	Yes	Age	Anticipation timing[a]	.38	Yes	—	Throw accuracy[a]	.96	Yes	—
	Pursuit rotor[a]	.11	Yes	Age	Shuttle run[a]	.32	Yes	Age	Wall volley[a]	.83	Yes	—
	Balance[a]	.09	Yes	Age	Agility[a]	.21	Yes	—	Grip strength[a]	.66	Yes	Age
	Arm hang[a]	.01	Yes	—	Fine eye-motor coordination[a]	−.21	Yes	—	Sit-ups[a]	.64	No	Age
					Flexibility[a]	−.29	Yes	—	Dash[a]	.63	No	Age
									Long Jump[a]	.54	No	Age

Note. Sources of average effect size, homogeneity, and moderator(s) are indicated by alphabetic superscripts following each variable name. The sources are as follows:

[a]Thomas & French (1985)
[b]Eaton & Enns (1986)
[c]Feingold (1988; I calculated the above means of all effect sizes reported in his Table 3)
[d]Hyde & Linn (1988)
[e]Hyde (1981)
[f]Linn & Petersen (1986)
[g]Hall (1984; from Eagly, 1987, p. 104, Table 4.2)
[h]Shapiro & Penrod (1986)
[i]Eisenberg & Lennon (1983)
[j]Eagly & Crowley (1986)
[k]Eagly & Steffen (1986)
[l]Hyde (1986)
[m]Eagly & Carli (1981)
[n]Becker (1986)
[o]Eagly & Karau (1989)
[p]Eagly & Johnson (1989)
[q]Kite (1984)
[r]Whitley, McHugh, & Frieze (1986)
[s]Wood, Rhodes, & Whelan (in press)

[1]This is an average effect size; a positive value indicates that males' sex group mean exceeded that for females. All are central tendency of d's; some are mean, some are mean weighted by sample size (where possible this was used), some are median.

[2]Homogeneity is a statistical test of consistency of effect size across studies and is roughly analogous to within-condition variance in an analysis of variance (ANOVA). In terms of entries in this column: "—" means this was not tested for; "Yes" means that the gender effect size did not violate the assumption of homogeneity (for studies evaluating moderator variables, th s test was done with hypothesized moderators included); "No" means that the homogeneity assumption was tested and found to be violated.

[3]A moderator is a variable that affects the magnitude of the sex-difference effect size and is roughly analagous to a sex × — (moderator) interaction in an ANOVA.

[4]Based on Rosenthal & Rubin (1982) and Becker & Hedges (1984) reanalyses of Hyde (1981) data.

[5]Upper-bound estimate due to inability to estimate some effect sizes when on y "no difference" was reported in original study.

[6]Although Hall (1984) did not report formal tests of homogeneity, it is likely that all or most of the nonverbal sex differences reported are not homogeneous (Eagly, 1987, p. 105).

499

($d = .50$), and large ($d = .80$) effect sizes on his nonsystematic inspection of effect sizes in the behavioral sciences and argued that medium effect sizes are perceived in everyday life.

In response to the question of whether there are psychological sex differences, Table 19.1 suggests that the answer is "Yes, but . . ." or "Males and females are both similar and different." More specifically, the table speaks to the size and content of female–male average group differences. The average effect sizes for sex differences range from .01 (for the biological/ physical/material variable "arm hang" and the personal–social attribute of "overall well-being") to 2.18 for the biological/physical/ material variable "throw velocity." Many of the moderate-to-large sex differences are for the biological/physical/material category, and these emphasize strength and throwing. Even in this domain, however, the sexes are both similar and different (i.e., there are small and moderate, as well as large, differences indicated in the table). The greatest number of large average effect sizes are indicated for symbolic and stylistic behaviors, specifically some of the nonverbal behaviors summarized by Hall (1984). Showing predominately moderate average effect sizes are both mental and social abilities in the interests and abilities category, and the social behaviors studied meta-analytically under the personal–social attributes category. Thus, relatively large sex differences are demonstrated for physical abilities and for body use and positioning; more modest differences are shown in abilities and social behaviors; and many negligible sex differences are sprinkled across all domains.

To turn to the issue of content, the results presented in Table 19.1 indicate similarities with previous reviews, but also some differences. (It is not possible to compare the table fully with narrative reviews, because, first, meta-analyses have not been done on all the variables addressed in nonquantitative literature summaries; second, Table 19.1, since it is primarily intended to be illustrative, does not present all published meta-analyses of sex differences.) On the one hand, concerning physical and intellectual abilities, Table 19.1 is generally congruent with the conclusions reached in nonquantitative reviews from Wellman (1933) to Block (1976) and Minton and Schneider (1980). Concerning personal–social attributes, the Table 19.1 summary is somewhat more consistent with Block's than with

Maccoby and Jacklin's position. In regard to divergences with existing summaries, the most prominent is that past reviewers have all agreed that a clear and strong sex difference is shown for aggression, but the meta-analyses place it only in the small-to-moderate category. (This may in part be due to the paradigms used to assess this sex difference.) In addition, Hall's work shows nonverbal behavior to be an area of relatively sharp male–female differences, and this content area has not been featured in past reviews.

Table 19.1 also can be used to highlight several qualifications to the foregoing overall conclusions. Concerning the size of sex differences, the labels "small," "moderate," and "large" in the table are used according to Cohen's (1977) criteria. Eagly (1987, pp. 114–125) provides a detailed analysis of, and heuristics to help interpret, effect sizes. Here suffice it to say that no statistical technique by itself will answer the question of what sex differences are "real" or "meaningful." Such judgments require other considerations than average effect sizes.

The average effect sizes in Table 19.1 are importantly qualified both by the "Homogeneity" and "Moderator(s)" columns. As the numerous "Nos" in the former reveal, many of the documented differences are not statistically homogeneous (Hedges & Becker, 1986). This indicates that there is a great deal of within-sex variance unaccounted for. To state it somewhat differently, there is considerable variation among males and females on most dimensions studied. As the column "Moderator(s)" indicates, most sex differences are not simple main effects, but instead are qualified in important ways by interactions with third variables. For example, 12 of the 20 motor performance variables summarized by Thomas and French (1985) are moderated by age.

It is also necessary to note qualifications concerning the content of female–male differences. Table 19.1 does not represent a random selection of all important variables (however "important" is defined). It is, rather, the result of multiple forces. One is whether sufficient studies are available to do a quantitative review, and it is probable that more studies are available on topics that researchers have felt might yield sex differences. Thus, Table 19.1 as a gestalt overstates the degree to which the sexes are different versus similar. What Table 19.1 does not include is also important. To my knowledge, no meta-analyses have been done on sex differences in interests, even though this topic has been much researched since the 1930s.

The Sex-Differences Approach: A Critique

Is the sex-differences approach a coherent and productive strategy for seeking to understand sex, gender, and the individual? I think not. Should it be? Again, no. The reasons for these negative answers can be partitioned into two overall groupings. The first concerns the methodological soundness of individual studies and of the literature as a whole; the second has to do with the long-term scientific fruitfulness of this approach.

Methodological Soundness of Sex-Differences Research and Literature as a Whole

Since others have extensively reviewed the methodological and interpretational problems of sex-differences research (e.g., Crawford, 1989; Deaux, 1984; Jacklin, 1981; Maccoby & Jacklin, 1974), I highlight here just four basic issues that researchers, meta-analysts, and consumers should consider.

1. *Who gets studied?* All texts on differential psychology note that in order to establish average sex-group differences, it is necessary to use random or representative samples of males and females (e.g., Minton & Schneider, 1980), and yet in most studies sex is confounded with other potent variables or studied within just a single range of other important variables. For example, much sex-differences work is done on children, and sex differences are generally negligible in young children. Thus, as Block (1976) noted, Maccoby and Jacklin's (1974) conclusion that sex differences are minimal may have been due to their heavy reliance on one subset of males and females, those under the age of 7.

2. *How do they get studied?* The way in which a construct is assessed can also significantly influence the size of sex differences. This seems obvious, but is generally underappreciated. For example, the measures operationalizing most of the constructs in Table 19.1 are largely based on formal testing procedures and laboratory situations. With regard to the greater male ability in math, all of the meta-analyses are of formal nonclassroom tests. If instead one examines course grades, there is an overall tendency for females to get better math grades (Kimball, 1989). Although formal tests may come closer to being good measures of ability, they are not without biases (e.g., most such tests reward guessing, and males appear more willing to guess than females; Adler, 1989).

3. *What gets studied?* The crucial points are that (a) there is no one right set of variables and (b) the current set of topics has developed, in part, through accident and implicit forces. Regarding this second point, the existing set of sex-difference variables is not based on an overall formal analysis of sex and gender that specifies that particular variables should vary by sex and others should not.

4. *What do non-negligible sex differences mean?* This is almost impossible to answer at present. One major caution, however, can be advanced. Large differences, even those for biological/physical/material variables, are not necessarily caused solely or even primarily by genetic factors. In Table 19.1, the largest sex difference is for throw velocity. It is likely that this motor performance variable has a genetic underpinning. At the same time, however, throwing ability can be improved by practice, and boys, on average, participate in more competitive sports where such practice occurs (Thomas & French, 1985). That documented sex differences are not "fixed" by genetic factors is further illustrated by the mental abilities summarized in Table 19.1. As can be seen, "Year" (in which data were collected) is an important moderator variable. More specifically, it has been found that the differences between males and females on the "big three" mental abilities have been declining in recent years. As a consequence, the once clear superiority of females in verbal ability has essentially disappeared, and the "traditional" male superiority in math has greatly declined (Feingold, 1988; Jacklin, 1989).

Scientific Fruitfulness of the Sex-Differences Approach

Beyond the specific methodological and interpretational problems with sex-differences research, a sex-differences strategy does not promise to substantially further our understanding of sex, gender, and the individual. First and foremost, though easy to overlook, is the fact that this strategy is not a coherent and explicit scientific approach. Few psychologists define themselves as sex-differences researchers (though many may say they look at sex differences in their research on some substantive issue such as achievement or athletics), and fewer still argue that assessing sex differences is the best way to understand sex and gender. Rather, sex differences are accumulated most often in research directed at other ends. Sometimes these other goals are gender-linked (e.g., the work by Eccles, 1985, 1987, on math performance by boys and girls), but quite often the researcher doing primary sex-differences work is not at all concerned with female–male distinctions (as is true of much work by social psychologists on aggression, helping, leadership, and the like). Even when the researcher has male–female comparisons as a focal hypothesis, seldom is it thought that biological sex per se causes some action. In sum, the sex-differences approach is not a purposeful one, but instead a loose body of findings that is generally incidental to other interests.

Even if a coherent sex-differences strategy were to be articulated and implemented, it would not constitute an acceptable answer to why women and men think, feel, and behave as they do. On the "cause" side, biological sex, the key partitioning variable, is too simple. Sex and gender are each multifaceted and cannot be reduced to two categories, female and male. Furthermore, biological sex is confounded with many other variables—most importantly, the individuals' response to gender as a societal category system. On the "content" side, sex-differences research yields average sex-group differences; these do not necessarily fit any one individual. Moreover, one cannot simply "add up" a list of documented differences. Such summation ignores how the variables are configured, both at an aggregate level and more importantly within individuals (Carlson, 1972; Tyler, 1965).

In sum, sex-differences research is susceptible to methodological and interpretational problems and is not a coherent and fruitful research strategy. These general considerations, plus the recognition that reporting sex differences may give the impression that women and men are more different than the data allow, have led some psychologists to propose that the reporting of sex differences should be restricted (McHugh, Koeske, & Frieze, 1986) or eliminated (Baumeister, 1988). I would agree with Eagly (1989b), that such restriction would not be a good idea. To the reasons she adduces, I would add that sex-differences

work cannot be stopped (especially since a lot of it is not primarily concerned with sex differences), and it cannot be ignored. Better-constructed studies and quantitative reviews will improve the literature, and researchers and the profession as a whole need to be more mindful of how scientific sex differences reach the public at large (see Crawford, 1989). At the same time, this is not a strategy to be encouraged.

GENDER AS A PERSONALITY VARIABLE

The second major approach to sex and gender at the individual level has been to posit the existence of the general individual-difference constructs "masculinity" and "femininity," which somehow summarize one's psychological maleness or femaleness and guide overt action. As noted above, one version of this basic idea was first broached by Terman and Miles (1936), and the implicit framework underlying their research guided most subsequent such work for almost four decades.

In this section, a more detailed look is taken at recent work using a gender-as-a-personality-variable approach. First, the androgyny era (1974–1982) is described, with special attention to the contributions of Sandra Bem and Janet Spence, the leaders in the "new looks in masculinity–femininity," and to the concept of "androgyny" as a personality type combining masculine and feminine attributes. Next, I describe how, in the 1980s, they have taken divergent paths. Bem has moved on to the cognitive construct of "gender schema," which is conceived as a *generalized* predisposition to process information in gender-related terms and focuses attention on sex-typed (schematic) versus non-sex-typed (aschematic) individuals. Spence, on the other hand, has championed the idea that gender at the individual level is best conceived as a *multiplicity* of constructs, rather than in terms of one or even a small number of relatively global constructs. The concluding subsection involves an evaluation of the general approach of construing gender as a personality variable.

1974–1982: The Androgyny Era

In the early 1970s, the approach initiated by Terman and Miles was dealt a double whammy that swept it away. First, there appeared a detailed and well-reasoned critique of the approach (Constantinople, 1973). Second, within a year, two easy-to-use self-report measuring devices based on a new view of masculinity and femininity were proposed (Bem, 1974; Spence, Helmreich, & Stapp, 1974, 1975). These were soon followed by three similar paper-and-pencil questionnaires, and there ensued a large number of studies linking the reconceptualized masculinity and femininity, and especially an exciting new construct, "androgyny," to a wide variety of other variables (Cook, 1985).

Constantinople (1973) criticized the Terman and Miles approach for failing to come to grips with masculinity and femininity as abstract psychological concepts. In addition, a careful review of the empirical evidence revealed scant support for the validity of the major M-F scales. In particular, the two key assumptions of such scales were found to be suspect. First, the assumption that psychological femininity and masculinity are opposites was untestable, given scale construction and scoring. Second, the assumption that masculinity and femininity are homogeneous global categories was unsupported by quite variable and often low correlations between subscales within measures and by factor analyses revealing multiple underlying factors for individual instruments, as well as by variable and frequently low covariation across devices. As will be described, work in the androgyny era only really addressed the issue of masculinity and femininity as bipolar versus two separate dimensions, and did not fully come to grips with femininity and masculinity as theoretical constructs or with the question of how homogeneous these are.

The two major figures during the androgyny era were Janet Spence and Sandra Bem, and it is instructive to identify the similarities and differences in their "new looks." Bem, and Spence and her collaborators, agreed on the following four major points:

1. Femininity and masculinity can be assessed via self-reports concerning personality traits. Bem developed the Bem Sex Role Inventory (BSRI), and Spence et al. the Personal Attributes Questionnaire (PAQ). The use of a self-report method is similar to the work of Terman and Miles, but the focus on traits represents a significant narrowing of content focus.

2. Masculinity and femininity are not opposite ends of a single continuum, but rather are separate and independent. Thus, the BSRI and PAQ each had separate M and F scales, not a single M-F scale.

3. Femininity and masculinity are defined from the outside in (from gender at the societal level to the individual). This is in sharp contrast with the Terman and Miles framework, which implicitly assumed that masculinity and femininity are best specified from the inside out (sex from within the person). For the instrument developed by Terman and Miles, items were selected on the basis of average *sex-group differences in endorsement*. Thus, M was equated with what biological males report that they think, do, or feel more than biological females, and F was defined in a parallel fashion. According to Bem, Spence, and others during the androgyny era, femininity and masculinity are defined in terms of societal ideals and expectations. Thus, for example, the items for Bem's scales were picked on the basis of subjects' perceptions of *cultural norms concerning gender and personality* (e.g., M items were those judged as more socially desirable in a man than a woman). This is a subtle shift, but important.

4. Contrary to the majority of past M-F workers, Spence and Bem did not assume that it was healthy for people to be sex-typed.

Although they shared basic assumptions, the conceptual and empirical starting points for Bem and for Spence et al. were quite different. Bem's objective was as much political (in the sense of contributing to social change) as scientific (Bem, 1972, 1974). She viewed traditional sex roles as restricting individuals, with females limited to being feminine and males required to be masculine. As a new cultural ideal, she proposed the concept of "psychological androgyny" (as did others at about this same time, both in psychology [e.g., Block, 1973] and outside), which she regarded as a distinct and general gendered personality type based on the balancing of masculinity and femininity within the individual. According to Bem, this balance allowed the person to adapt to contextual demands, to act "like a woman (or man)" as the situation required. This flexibility would presumably make both men and women better adjusted psychologically. Thus, like Terman and Miles, Bem saw masculinity and femininity as linked to psychological health, but she did so in a quite different way from the originators of the gender-as-a-personality-variable paradigm.

To measure androgyny and its building blocks, Bem (1974) created a new scale. As noted, the F and M subscales were defined in terms of cultural ideals for males and females; the BSRI comprised trait adjectives judged to be substantially more desirable in females than males (F items) or much better for males than females to possess (M items).

Janet Spence came to the study of masculinity and femininity "almost by happenstance" (Spence, 1988, p. 199); although it is risky to divine others' motives, it appears that her work on the topic stemmed, in large part, from a desire to construct methodologically sound and standardized instruments to assess gender concepts. She began by developing the Attitudes Toward Women Scale (Spence & Helmreich, 1972). Spence and her colleagues (Spence et al., 1974) initially proffered the PAQ as an improvement and extension of an existing device to assess sex stereotypes, the Sex-Role Stereotype Questionnaire, and then adapted it to index masculinity and femininity. From the outset, Spence and her coworkers regarded androgyny as a descriptive label and a convenience for data analysis, not as a distinctive personality type. And Spence and Helmreich (see especially 1978, 1979) viewed their device for measuring masculinity, femininity, and androgyny as just assessing the personality trait aspect of gender at the individual level. Thus, the PAQ was just one instrument among a battery of questionnaires they developed for indexing various gender-related variables.

In terms of method, Spence et al. (1974, 1975) used consensual or cultural sex stereotypes (not sex-role ideals, as Bem did) as the vehicles for getting at masculinity and femininity. Thus, the items making up their F and M subscales were judged desirable in both men and women, but were seen by judges as more typical of one sex or the other. (Spence et al., 1974, 1975, also developed a third subscale for the PAQ. It comprised items that were not only seen as more typical of one sex or the other, but also were regarded as more desirable in that sex. This subscale [M-F] was bipolar.)

The late 1970s saw a boom in androgyny research, and such work continued into the 1980s. There exists, thus, a huge literature on the "new looks in masculinity–femininity" (now "masculinity–femininity–androgyny"). Unfortunately, this is not a neat and tidy body of work, with failures to replicate and inconsistent findings abounding (cf. Cook, 1985). Recognizing that this situation makes generalizations hazardous, I attempt the following summary and assessement; this is organized in terms of questions about the central concept, androgyny, and draws heavily from a major review by Cook (1985).

What Exactly Is Androgyny?

Many conceptual definitions of "androgyny" have been offered. To date, however, only the formulations of Bem and of Spence and her colleagues have drawn much empirical attention. Sedney (1989) has recently provided a framework for organizing the multiple theoretical views on androgyny and suggested ways in which the as-yet-unresearched formulations might be addressed empirically.

Bem (1974) began with a "balance" notion: An androgynous person is one who endorses as self-relevant both male and female qualities in roughly the same proportion or amount. In 1975, however, Spence and her colleagues demonstrated that individuals with one type of balance androgyny—those individuals with low M scores and low F scores—scored low on self-esteem. This challenged a basic assumption of androgyny as psychologically healthy and forced a redefinition *in operational terms* of androgyny as only high F–high M scores. This position, which was preferred by Spence et al. from the start and dubbed the "additive model," was accepted by Bem (1977, 1979).

The empirical identification of androgynous individuals as those with high M–high F scores was accomplished by simultaneous and independent median splits on the M and F subscales. This procedure creates a 2 × 2 table and partitions all participants in a study into one of four categories: high M–high F (androgynous), high M–low F (masculine; sex-typed males and cross-sex-typed females), low M–high F (feminine; sex-typed females and cross-sex-typed males), and low M–low F (undifferentiated). This classification system was quickly and widely adopted.

There are four major problems with this operational solution to what androgyny means: First, it was not accompanied by a thorough re-evaluation of the construct of androgyny. Second, it created a new concept, "undifferentiated," that also has remained unanalyzed as a theoretical term. Third, it is rough;

as a consequence, misclassification of those who score near the median is likely. It also throws away a lot of data, since two continuous variables are compressed into four discrete categories. (See Cook, 1985, especially pp. 104–105 and 135–136, on these and other criticisms.) Finally, it makes it difficult to answer this crucial question: Is androgyny a *special* combination of masculinity and femininity? Since androgyny is defined by "adding" F and M scores, it is not possible to test whether androgyny contributes to important dependent variables anything beyond its constituents. I return to this issue below, but first it is necessary to address the building blocks of androgyny, femininity and masculinity.

What Is the Content and Structure of the M and F Subscales That Go into the Defining of Androgyny?

There is now considerable evidence that the trait measures of F and M tap a pair of general personality constellations that have been labeled either "instrumental" and "expressive" or "agentic" and "communal" (Cook, 1985; see, however, Paulhus, 1987, for an alternative interpretation). The particular measures, however, vary widely in their degree of internal consistency. The PAQ subscales are nearly homogeneous, whereas the BSRI M and F subscales appear to contain multiple contents (Cook, 1985). There is also fairly good evidence that the subscales predict other instrumental and expressive actions (Taylor & Hall, 1982; see, however, Whitley, 1988).

Although these results support the validity of the M and F subscales, one major perplexity has arisen, and this concerns the specific traits "masculine" and "feminine." At first blush, it seems obvious that these would be the best markers of the constructs of psychological masculinity and femininity as assessed by the BSRI (they are not on the PAQ). In fact, they are not. In factor analyses of responses to the BSRI, masculine and feminine do not load with the other instrumental and expressive items, but instead form their own *bipolar* factor (Brown, 1986; Pedhazur & Tetenbaum, 1979; Spence, 1985; see also Storms, 1979). This anomaly was one input into Bem's (1979) decision to drop masculine and feminine from the BSRI, though she phrased her decision primarily in terms of degree of covariation of endorsement with biological sex. It may also be one

reason why Spence (1983) decided that scores on the PAQ should not be labeled masculine and feminine. Rather, she feels that the more descriptive and more specific rubrics "instrumental" and "expressive" are more appropriate. Whatever the status of these speculations, the fact that self-descriptions of "masculine" and "feminine" do not covary with scores on M and F subscales creates a conceptual problem that has yet to be fully addressed.

An important subquery regarding content is this: Do masculinity and femininity comprise just positive attributes? According to Bem, yes. According to Spence and her colleagues, no. Spence, Helmreich, and Holohan (1979) developed the Extended Personal Attributes Questionnaire (EPAQ) to assess the negative as well as positive side of masculinity and femininity. Positive M scores and negative F scores were found to be moderately negatively correlated, and the same pattern held true for positive F scores and negative M scores. This suggests some degree of bipolarity of psychological femininity and masculinity.

What Is the Relation Between Masculinity and Femininity?

Terman and Miles assumed a strong and negative correlation between masculinity and femininity and built this into their M-F measuring device. Androgyny researchers assumed that the constructs are essentially unrelated. In fact, the correlations between F and M measures from the BSRI, PAQ, and other androgyny measures range from $-.42$ to $+.47$ and vary as a function of specific instrument and sex composition of the sample (Cook, 1985, p. 77; see also Marsh & Myers, 1986). Although the overall average correlation of M and F across studies may be near zero, the range of r's suggests that it is incorrect to conclude that masculinity and femininity are unrelated; instead, the average correlation is low but highly variable. What contributes to this substantial variability beyond scale type and sex composition is an important issue for future work.

How Are Masculinity, Femininity, and Androgyny Related to Other Variables?

The question of how masculinity, femininity, and androgyny are related to other variables can be partitioned into two more specific yet in themselves broad queries: First, is androgyny a general sex-role trait? Second, what is the relationship of androgyny to psychological adjustment? The answer to the first question is probably no. Two literatures are pertinent to this summary answer: (1) Research examining the relation between gender-as-a-personality variable measures (especially the BSRI and PAQ) and indices of other gender constructs. As summarized by Cook (1985, pp. 87–90), the link of M-F-A measures to gender-related attitudes, sex stereotyping, and personal erotic preference is weak and inconsistent (see, however, Frable, 1989). (2) Research examining the relation of androgyny to behavioral measures of sex-role flexibility. Bem's (1974, 1975) initial claim was that androgyny allowed the individual to adapt her or his behavior to situational requirements, and she reported laboratory investigations lending credence to this claim. These early studies, however, did not test the hypothesis *directly*, since a between-subjects design was used. Thus, Bem did not demonstrate that the same person scoring as androgynous on the BSRI behaved differently across situations varying in sex-role demands (Cook, 1985, pp. 79–82). Later researchers were apparently more interested in testing the alleged goodness of androgyny, since there is much more research on the next question than on the issue of flexibility, which, on the basis of current data, must be judged as not proven.

What is the relationship of androgyny to psychological health? The starting point for Bem's (1974) analysis was the assumption that it is better for individuals to have in their behavioral repertoires both male and female propensities, so that they can adjust to varying situations. That is, flexibility of gendered personality leads to success in meeting contextual demands, which in turn fosters a positive view of self and good adjustment. This notion has been most often tested by assessing the covariation of the PAQ and BSRI with self-report measures of self-esteem and mental health. Androgyny (defined as high M–high F scores) does covary with high self-esteem and good adjustment. This is congruent with Bem's initial position, but a more detailed examination of the accumulated data does not support Bem's assumption that androgyny, as a special construct that emerges from a balance of masculinity and femininity, is *uniquely* associated with positive self-regard and personal adjustment. First, the demonstrated convergence may be artifactual. On the PAQ and BSRI, which contain only positive items, androgyny as high

M–high F means endorsing as self-descriptive many positive items, and most self-esteem measures boil down to very much the same thing. Thus, it has been suggested that the correlation between androgeny and self-esteem is due to shared method variance, and this position has received support (Brown, 1986; Carson, 1989, p. 234). Second, the documented covariation of androgyny with high self-esteem and positive mental health may involve confusing two main effects for an interaction. That is, is androgyny as a special combination of masculine and feminine responsible for higher self-esteem and better adjustment, or can the constituent constructs alone account for the variation in self-evaluation and adjustment? The existing data suggest that both M and F scores independently contribute to reported self-esteem and mental health, with M contributing more. The interaction of M and F, the special combination of these two factors, does not add much unique variance to that of the components acting alone (cf. Bassoff & Glass, 1982; Cook, 1985; Taylor & Hall, 1982; Whitley, 1983, 1985). (Concerning the apparent "superiority" of M, Bem, 1985, and others have countered that self-esteem and adjustment scales may be biased toward M. A recent study by Orlofsky & O'Heron, 1987, supports both sides of this argument: M is more strongly and consistently related to indices of adjustment, but F does best predict feminine measures of this construct.)

1982–Present: Broad (Bem) and Narrow (Spence) Perspectives on Femininity and Masculinity

Although research on androgyny continued in the 1980s, the two leaders during the androgyny era moved on to other topics. In so doing, however, each developed themes that were apparent in her earlier work. Bem (1985) stressed the "political" nature of her work, especially the dysfunctional aspect of society's insistence on the functional value of the male–female distinction, and sought an account of sex and gender at the individual level that was relatively unicomponented. Spence, on the other hand, moved even further in the direction of a multidimensional view of gender phenomena.

In 1981, Bem proposed a new psychological concept, "gender schema." (At about the same time, similar proposals were made by Martin &

Halverson, 1981, and by Markus, Crane, Bernstein, & Siladi, 1982.) Gender schema is a hypothetical cognitive construct that organizes a large body of diverse "knowledge" in terms of society's specification of what goes with the female–male distinction. Like other schemas, gender schema influences information processing. Furthermore, gender-schematic processing is, according to Bem (1981, 1985), one crucial input into the development of sex-typed individuals. That is, the child's self-concept can become assimilated to the gender schema, and the schema can take on prescriptive as well as descriptive functions. Thus, the child who is highly gender-schematic is predisposed to become sex-typed in personality and behavior because of a self-fulfilling prophecy. Bem (1981, 1985) used the BSRI to identify sex-typed and non-sex-typed individuals (androgynous and undifferentiated), and presented evidence that they differentially processed information in accordance with her theory.

Bem's gender schema theory has the distinct advantage of focusing attention on how the individual uses sex as a way to organize experience. At the same time, however, her formulation seems to require further clarification and development. To begin with, as is clearer in her later writing (Bem, 1985, 1987), her theory is as concerned with society's gender schema as with the individual's, if not more so. This raises at least three problems. First, Bem's research does not assess the cultural gender schema; thus, the key causal variable is not directly studied. Second, culture is treated as quite homogeneous. The possibility of significant subcultural variation (by race, region, and the like) is ignored, and implicitly it is assumed that all cultural media (e.g., television, schools), as well as all individuals who socialize children, pass on the same message about gender. Third, the individual is treated as a very passive recipient of societal forces. Bem allows the individual personal definitions of masculinity and femininity, but these are held to be irrelevant to gender-schematic processing and sex typing.

An additional point, not unrelated to the preceding, is that the notion of gender schema as an individual-level cognitive construct remains undeveloped both conceptually and empirically. Concerning theoretical vagueness, it is not entirely clear whether a gender schema has one component ("Males are ___ *and* females are ___"), which Bem believes; two

dimensions ("Males are___; females are ___"), a position favored by Markus and her colleagues; or multiple distinct facets with either one or two underlying second-order factors (see, e.g., Carver, 1989; Marsh & Myers, 1986). Regarding empirical development, it is a bit surprising and disorienting that there is no direct measure of individual-level gender schema. Bem does not view the BSRI as directly assessing gender schema, but instead sex typing (which is assumed to be, in part, due to gender-schematic processing). A combined conceptual and empirical loose end is the status of cross-sex-typed individuals. Bem (1985) admits that these individuals are not well accounted for by her current formulation. According to a strict rendition of gender schema theory, cross-sex-typed individuals should behave like sex-typed individuals, since they have the same information-processing apparatus. And sometimes they do, but at other times they are like non-sex-typed participants, and at still other times they are like neither group (Cook, 1985). Finally, although subsequent research has at times supported the gender schema theory (Cook, 1985), the basic information-processing studies proferred by Bem (1981) have not fared consistently well in either direct or conceptual replications (Carson, 1989).

At the same time that Bem has focused her attention on a cognitively mediated cultural account of sex typing as a homogeneous and unidimensional phenomenon, Spence has extended her thinking about gender as a multiplicity of elements. She has developed measures of the several different components. In addition, she has studied both lay and social scientists' definitions of masculinity and femininity (Spence & Sawin, 1985) and from this has constructed a theory of gender identity (Spence, 1985). She finds both the person in the street and the academic researcher to have vague understandings of these concepts. At the same time, each of us seems to regard our masculinity (or femininity) as important. This pair of apparently inconsistent facts has led Spence to propose that children learn their gender identity, narrowly defined as a fundamental sense of maleness or femaleness (see note 3), early in life when verbal labels that facilitate clear thinking are absent. And yet this sense of one's maleness or femaleness leads the child to take on interests and traits that, for him or her, define gender identity. Although Spence does not mention Kohlberg (1966), this process seems similar to that posited by cognitive-developmentalist accounts of sex typing. What is crucially different about Spence's theory is that each developing child is assumed to be exposed to many different definitions of maleness and femaleness, that the child puts these together for the self as masculinity and femininity, and that these become functionally autonomous of gender identity itself. Thus, masculinity and femininity are important, but they are many different things.

Spence's formulation has the ability to account not only for the paradox she began with (masculinity and femininity are personally important yet fuzzy concepts), but also for the lack of tight interrelationships among the various facets of gender at the individual level (see below and Downs & Langlois, 1988; Huston, 1983; Spence, 1985). Future work is needed to directly assess the hypothesized notion of gender identity and associated senses of femininity–masculinity and to test the development of these. One troublesome point for Spence's theory is that gender identity, which is a key construct, is nonproblematic for most people most of the time. That is, most people are certain of their biological sex, and gender identity (as narrowly defined) is highly correlated with biological sex. This suggests the need for a broader view of gender identity, which is proposed in the next major section of this chapter. First, however, a critical analysis of the gender-as-a-personality-variable perspective as a general strategy for seeking to understand sex, gender, and the individual is presented.

Evaluation of the Gender-as-a-Personality-Variable Paradigm

Although it is important to identify and rectify the measurement and procedural problems commonly found in research on gender as a personality construct, scientific understanding of sex, gender, and the individual will not be greatly advanced by simply conducting the same type of research in a more methodologically sound manner. Rather, what is needed is a critical analysis of basic conceptual issues underlying the gender-as-a-personality-variable perspective. Regarding methodological problems, the reader is referred to Beere (1979), Cook (1985, especially pp. 143–150), and Huston (1983, especially p. 395); here it is

simply noted that past work has too often been method-driven, with the BSRI and PAQ (in part because they are easy to administer and score) coming to "define" concepts rather than the other way around. As a step toward the needed conceptual analysis, and as a means of critiquing this approach, the following comments are offered. Content and process issues are treated separately, although they are certainly intertwined in actuality (cf. Ashmore et al., 1986).

Content Issues

Four interrelated criticisms are put forth about the content assumptions made in the major attempts to construe gender as a personality construct.

1. *Essentialism.* As Morawski (1985) has so clearly and cogently argued, the major problem of this area of work is the underlying assumption that masculinity and femininity are basic essences that have clear and separate identities and reside within individuals. A related assumption is that by following a physical science model, researchers can measure and study these essences. As Morawski has also noted, this search to locate psychological gender in personal essences stems, in part, from the American cultural value of individualism and from scientists' as well as laypersons' tendency to explain human experience and action in terms of stable qualities of individuals.

The guiding yet implicit assumption of essentialism may help account for the overemphasis of researchers on personality traits in measuring masculinity, femininity, and androgyny. Although Terman and Miles (1936) used items reflecting diverse content areas, most measures since, even and especially those developed during the androgyny era of the last decade and a half, have employed personality trait adjectives almost exclusively (Cook, 1985, Ch. 2). Except for Spence (1983, 1985), the tacit assumption of most researchers is that masculinity–femininity–androgyny (also termed more abstractly as "sex typing" or "sex-role identity/orientation") can be captured fully by self-ascription of stable internal dispositional qualities. Although this may turn out to be true (or, more likely, true for some people), there is now considerable evidence that sex and gender can be incorporated into one's self in multiple, not highly interconnected ways (see below and also Cook, 1985; Huston, 1983; Spence, 1985). The heavy reliance on personality traits as the key to a general individual-difference gender construct is especially puzzling, because these do not appear as general and robust as other male–female differences. Perhaps most importantly, sex differences in the structure and function of social relationships (particularly play groups) come much earlier developmentally and remain substantial throughout much of the life span (Huston, 1983; Maccoby, 1987). It is possible that the assumption of essentialism grounded in the core American value of individualism leads researchers toward personality traits and away from relationships.

2. *Failure to consider social and life-stage context.* Masculinity–femininity–androgyny formulations, from Terman and Miles through Bem's gender schema theory, have slighted the context in which the gendered individual exists and behaves. Certainly all models have assumed that, at least in part, children learn masculinity and femininity from culture. However, masculinity–femininity–androgyny and gender schema, as conceptualized and measured, are individual qualities that do not involve other people or relationships (Morawski, 1985), and these personality (or cognitive) variables are regarded as stable and predictive of behavior in the same manner across the lifespan of an individual, as well as from situation to situation at any one point of a single individual's life (Cook, 1985).

3. *Individual ignored.* In most gender-as-a-personality-variable formulations, the individual is pawn to genetic and biological factors and/or to societal prescriptions.

4. *Oversimplification.* Researchers during the androgyny era are to be congratulated for going beyond the assumption of earlier work that femininity and masculinity are opposite ends of a single continuum, and Bem's gender schema theory is a step forward in suggesting how cultural arrangements can foster information-processing structures in the heads of individuals that contribute to sex typing. Even the conceptual advances of the past decade and a half, however, treat sex and gender at the individual level as much too simple and unitary. As already noted at several points above, individual gender variables are only loosely intercorrelated; thus, seeking to explain gender at the level of the person in terms of one or even a small number of concepts is not likely to be successful.

Process Issues

Two criticisms are offered. First, the relation of causes to contents has not been well described. Most past work on gender as a personality variable has been too static and nondevelopmental (Del Boca & Ashmore, 1980b; Katz, 1986; Lewin, 1984b). Second, the relation of contents to consequences is likewise unclear. The link of masculinity–femininity–androgyny as well as gender schema to behavior is not well specified or empirically documented. Early workers apparently expected masculinity and femininity to predict almost any and all actions. Bem (1974) began by predicting that androgyny would enable individuals to behave flexibly across situations. One solution to the many failures to show M-F measures predictive of other social action is to recognize multiplicity. This is the tack Spence (1985) has taken, and it is explored more fully in the next section of this chapter. Another is to regard sex typing as indexed by M-F-A scales as related to some but not all other individual-level gender constructs. This is the view of Bem (1985) and Frable (1989), but they are not completely clear about how one identifies such other variables.

In sum, the gender-as-a-personality-variable perspective has the distinct advantage of moving analysis beyond biological sex as the independent variable in sex-differences work. In addition, the M-F-A work of the last decade and a half has pushed psychologists toward recognizing the importance of gender as a societal-level social category system, rather than focusing exclusively on sex as a simple set of biological and genetic causal factors. On the debit side, the criticisms above can be summarized as follows: The gender-as-a-personality-variable perspective oversimplifies sex, gender, and the individual by focusing on a small set of narrowly defined essences and treating these as linked in a simple and direct way to a small set of homogeneous antecedent variables (causes) and a broad range of outcome variables (consequences).

SEX AS A SOCIAL CATEGORY

The final major approach to sex, gender, and the individual stresses not average sex-group differences or gender as a global personality construct, but rather focuses on sex as a social category. This perspective is not a well-articulated and thoroughly researched paradigm, but instead has been proposed by a loose confederation of workers grappling with a common set of issues—how best to conceptualize and study the individual in relation to social contexts (from the broad societal setting to specific interpersonal encounters) containing gender-based expectations and prescriptions. My own working answers to these issues center on the individual's identity or self-concept and how this is formed, organized, and acted upon in gendered social contexts. This framework, featuring a multiple component view of "gender identity," is described in some depth in order to illustrate the more general and inclusive sex-as-a-social-category approach.

The first step in introducing my "multiplicity model of gender identity" (and the overall sex-as-a-social-category approach) is to describe the paradigm it seeks to replace. Next, three lines of work that were especially important to the emergence of this new model are described. Following this, the bulk of this section is used to describe my gender identity heuristic model and the type of research it generates.

Origins of the Multiplicity Model of Gender Identity

Current Personality and Social-Psychological Approaches to Sex, Gender, and the Individual

As the preceding critique of gender as a personality variable has suggested, the (generally implicit) causal model underlying this perspective, and much other nonbiological gender research of the past 15 years or so, can be summarized as follows: (1) Cause: Homogeneous culture. The media and other mediators of American culture persent a uniform set of messages about gender. → (2) Content: Globally gendered individual. The individual directly assimilates these and forms his or her "sex-role orientation" (masculinity–femininity–androgyny), sex stereotypes, and gender attitudes, each of which is assumed to be homogeneous and the three of which are presumed to be tightly interconnected. → (3) Consequences: Sex-typed behavior. A wide variety of specific acts are simply determined by this global individual propensity (labeled, for example, as "sex-typed vs. non-sex-typed" in Bem's [1981] gender schema theory).[4]

The criticisms of this extant guiding

framework can be partitioned into those concerning content and structure, and those having to do with process issues. The former can be summarized as follows:

1. The current model includes too narrow and restricted a set of contents, causes, and consequences. With regard to contents, this point has been made concerning (a) how the individual incorporates gender into self, of which only self-perceived traits are routinely considered (see above and Huston, 1983; Katz, 1986); (b) how gender influences perception of others, with only traits assigned to the superordinate gender categories assessed (Ashmore & Del Boca, 1979; Ashmore et al., 1986; Deaux, 1984); and (c) how individuals evaluate gender-related issues, with global sex-role attitude measures predominating (Brannon, 1978; Del Boca et al., 1986). On the causes side, American culture is not so homogeneous as it is portrayed, and the local interpersonal environments of individuals are also diverse and often contain conflicting "lessons" about the sexes (Sherif, 1982; Spence, 1985).

2. The assumption that gender-related thoughts and feelings are strongly interconnected generally remains untested, and the evidence that does exist suggests loose rather than tight interrelationships (Downs & Langlois, 1988; Huston, 1983; Spence, 1985; Spence et al., 1985; see, however, Frable, 1989).

3. Although the major content variables in this model are at the level of the individual, seldom is the individual the unit of analysis. Rather, aggregate data analysis is the rule, and seldom are attempts made to understand how individuals create their own personal views concerning sex and gender.

Critical analyses of the process elements in the model guiding much extant work suggest the following:

1. The content constructs are depicted as much too static. It is as if, for example, "sex-role orientation" is learned, and, once acquired, does not change much (Cook, 1985). As Katz (1986) has so clearly shown, "gender identity" varies considerably over the life course; at a more micro level, views of self in terms of gender can be revised as a result of interpersonal interactions (Deaux & Major, 1987).

2. The ways in which cultural portrayals and

interpersonal relationships shape thoughts and feelings about gender and how these, in turn, guide social action are seldom studied directly. For example, on the antecedent side, analyses of media content are made, and it is assumed that media consumers "absorb" this content (see Greenberg, 1988, on the "drip, drip drip" hypothesis), but how this absorption occurs is infrequently studied.

Setting the Stage for the Multiplicity Model

In addition to and partly overlapping the preceding critique of the current paradigm, three precursors to the multiplicity model can be identified. The first of these is the paradigm of sex as a social category. The multiplicity model is grounded in an intergroup relations perspective that contrasts sharply with the underlying models guiding the two general approaches discussed above—differential psychology (for sex differences) or trait psychology (for gender as a personality variable). The second precursor is the concept of gender as a multiplicity. This follows, in part, from the recognition that gender at the individual level derives from complex and multifaceted social contexts rather than being some unitary essence, as is assumed in most work on sex differences or gender as a personality variable. The third precursor is the idea of self or identity as the key concept for locating sex and gender at the individual level. This is necessary to bring a social category approach in to the realm of psychology. Without this focal concept, a social category perspective is susceptible to sociological reductionism (Crawford & Marecek, 1989). These three precursors are now considered in more detail.

The Sex-as-a-Social-Category Perspective. There were early calls to phrase sex and gender in terms of intergroup relations (e.g., Hacker, 1951), but there was no concerted and widespread movement in this direction until the 1980s. Work in the 1970s, however, set the stage for construing sex as a social category. The M-F-A measures of the androgyny era, which were based on socially desirable aspects of gender roles (BSRI) or of sex stereotypes (PAQ), focused attention on *society's* notions of male and female. Furthermore, during the same period that the concept of psychological androgyny flourished, a considerable amount of research was also conducted on sex stereotypes and gender-related attitudes (see Ash

more et al., 1986, and Del Boca et al., 1986, respectively, for summaries). These efforts crystallized in the 1980s as several independent proposals converged on the basic notion that a psychological analysis of sex and gender should begin with the recognition that sex/gender is a social category system (Deaux, 1984; Sherif, 1982) and that female–male relations parallel other forms of intergroup relations (Ashmore & Del Boca, 1986a). American society, like all other cultures, specifies that female-male is an important distinction (i.e., sex is a major social category) and associates men and women with different sets of descriptive expectations (stereotypes) and prescriptive expectations (roles). Furthermore, like other forms of intergroup relations (e.g., blacks and whites in the United States), the social categories "men" and "women" differ in societal-level power and prestige (e.g., men hold disproportionately more high-level political and economic positions). A sex as a social catgory or intergroup relations approach to sex, gender, and the individual assumes that these societal-level realities have a crucial impact on the individual's thoughts, feelings, and behaviors. Recently several different yet related attempts have been made to specify how this occurs. Two prominent examples are Eagly (1987), who emphasizes the power of social roles, and Deaux and Major (1987), who provide a detailed model of gender in interpersonal exchanges.

Gender as a Multiplicity. Although the assumption that sex and gender are relatively homogeneous phenomena has long been the predominant view, there have been dissenting voices (e.g., Mischel, 1970). The most prominent and influential person in calling for construing gender as a multiplicity has been Spence, who has repeatedly espoused the position that the individual's thoughts, feelings, and behaviors concerning sex and gender are only loosely interconnected (Spence, 1984, 1985; Spence & Helmreich, 1978, 1980; Spence et al., 1985). This multiplicity, or "separate-pie" (Downs & Langlois, 1988), or "loose-glue" perspective is, as noted above, most consistent with the accumulated data.

Self or Identity as the Key Concept for Locating Sex and Gender at the Individual Level. Here the crucial figure is Carolyn Sherif (especially 1982), who suggested that the notion of an organized self-system is the essential construct for developing an individual-level psychology of gender that is consistent with and responsive to both the intergroup and nonhomogeneous nature of female–male relations and, at the same time, allows for analysis at the individual level. At about this same time, outside the field of sex and gender, the notion of a multifaceted, socially derived personal identity, which had been central to turn-of-the-century psychologists (e.g., Baldwin, 1897/1973; James, 1890), was coming to the fore in social and personality psychology (Rosenberg, 1988; Rosenberg & Gara, 1985), psychological sociology (Weigert, 1983), and intergroup relations (Babad, Birnbaum, & Benne, 1983; Tajfel, 1981).

Gender Identity: Gendered Personal Identity in Social Contexts

A Multicomponent View of Sex, Gender, and the Individual

Together with Daniel M. Ogilvie (Ashmore & Ogilvie, 1989) and Frances K. Del Boca (Ashmore & Del Boca, 1986a, 1986b), I have been developing an alternative construal of sex, gender, and the individual that draws on the critique and stage-setting developments described above. This is a heuristic model; as such, it provides a general plan, but leaves many details to be worked out. The following assumptions guide the development of the alternative model:

1. Gender can and should be studied at multiple, complementary levels (Ashmore & Del Boca, 1986a, especially Chs. 1 and 8). A particularly important level is "social-psychological," since it is at the interface of the individual and the social (from society as a whole down to the people immediately surrounding the individual). At the social-psychological level, the focus is on the individual in social contexts. At this level, the model posits three key interrelated yet distinct general constructs: "gender identity" (the structured set of gendered personal identities that results when the individual takes the social construction of gender and the biological "facts" of sex and incorporates these into an overall self-concept), "thinking about the sexes" (beliefs about the attributes of men and women ["sex stereotypes"], of gender subtypes, and of specific women and men), and "gender-related attitudes" (evaluative orientations toward the

sexes and toward issues and targets associated with gender). With regard to social contexts, two general types are distinguished. Past social contexts are viewed as "causes" of current "contents." For the sake of analysis, the hypothesized antecedent variables are partitioned into three broad classes: "contact with culture," "relationships with specific individuals," and "self-guided activities." Current social contexts are assumed to be reciprocally linked to "contents." That is, it is predicted that gender identity, thinking about the sexes, and gender-related attitudes both shape and are shaped by current social stimuli, especially other people. The present framework is least developed concerning the contents–consequences interface. Deaux and Major (1987) have offered a detailed view of gender in social interaction that can provide a guide for fleshing out this portion of the present framework.

2. Sex and gender are extremely important inputs to the individual, and yet they do not (a) require "specialized" scientific concepts, or (b) speak with a single voice. "Sex" denotes a complex set of powerful biological variables, and "gender" is a highly significant social category system in all societies. Thus, it is assumed that sex and gender pervade most aspects of daily life and can shape many aspects of psychological structure and function. That sex and gender are potent inputs to individuals does not mean that they require a special set of constructs. Rather, it is proposed that basic research and theory in personality, social, and developmental psychology offer concepts that can be tailored to the undeniably unique aspects of gender (see, e.g., work construing sex stereotypes in terms of the basic social-psychological concept "implicit personality theory": Ashmore, 1981; Ashmore & Del Boca, 1979; Ashmore et al., 1986; Ashmore & Tumia, 1980; Del Boca & Ashmore, 1980a). Sherif (1982) has argued for the "self-system" (an important concept in basic social and personality psychology) as "necessary" for the construct of "gender identity." By suggesting that the inputs to the individual do not speak with a single voice, I intend to highlight the fact that the United States is a complex and heterogeneous society, and as such does not provide its citizens with one homogeneous "definition" of gender. Rather, multiple definitions are portrayed in the mass media, and children are exposed by the media and in their everyday

relationships to a wide variety of "models" of maleness and femaleness (Sherif, 1982; Spence, 1985).

3. (Wo)man is assumed to be both a cognitive creature and a social beast (Ashmore & Del Boca, 1986a, esp. Chap. 1). The former aspect of human nature means that attention must be paid to the manner in which individuals internally represent external reality. The social side of human nature suggests that "other people" are an especially important aspect of the contexts in which individuals develop and negotiate their personal gender-related beliefs and feelings. A concrete implication is the need to develop a model of personal identity that stresses "self in" social relationships (Ogilvie & Ashmore, 1990).

4. To understand the individual in a social context requires an integrated idiographic–nomothetic approach. Not only does society present a fragmented set of lessons about sex and gender; it is also the case that individuals creatively construct their own internal representations from the raw materials supplied by "culture" and specific others. They do not need to simply swallow whole or spit out cultural portrayals or personally salient role models. Spence (1985) argues that people use personal and, in some cases, idiosyncratic equations in calculating their masculinity and femininity. The proffered multiplicity model posits that this is true for all of the multiple contents of gender identity. This "personalizing" means that, whenever possible, it is desirable to assess gender thoughts and feelings in the individual's terms and to do within-person analyses (in order to avoid aggregating responses that may obscure personal perspectives). This does not mean that testing across-person generalizations are ruled out. Indeed, nomothetic properties of individual belief systems can be calculated in a manner that permits powerful comparisons across individuals, which in turn can be related to antecedents and consequences.

5. It is not assumed that children learn gender lessons and then that, once acquired, thoughts and feelings about sex and gender remain fixed. Instead, some contents of gender belief systems are regarded as quite stable (e.g., one's sense of being a biological male or female), whereas others are subject to considerable modification (Katz, 1986; Spence, 1985). Normative life stage events (e.g., becoming a parent) and personal experiences (e.g., breaking up with a long-time boyfriend or girlfriend) are particularly important causes of such modifications.

These assumptions lead to the alternative depicted in Figure 19.1. Since the key to the proposed framework is the notion of multiplicity, I begin with the hypothesized "contents" of

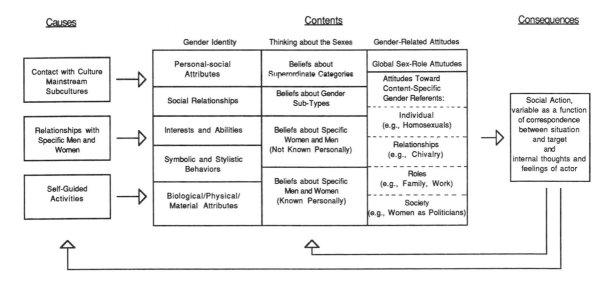

FIGURE 19.1 Multiplicity model for representing individual-level gender concepts. From *Gender Identity, Sex Stereotypes, and Social Action* by R. D. Ashmore and D. M. Ogilvie, 1989, grant proposal funded by the National Institute of Mental Health. Reprinted by permission of the authors.

gender at the level of the individual. The same three basic types of contents described above (i.e., sex-role orientation, sex stereotypes, gender attitudes) are posited; the crucial difference is that Figure 19.1 presents each as multicomponented. The multiple aspects of "thinking about the sexes" (which subsumes sex stereotypes) are described elsewhere (see Ashmore, 1981; Ashmore, Del Boca, & Titus, 1984; Ashmore et al., 1986) as are those of "gender-related attitudes" (Ashmore & Del Boca, 1989). The emphasis here is on "gender identity." First, a working definition of this term is offered. Then the hypothesized contents, causes, and consequences of gender identity are described. This section concludes by describing illustrative research directions suggested by this perspective.

Working Definition of Gender Identity

Although it is premature to set down a hard and fast specification of the meaning of this key concept, it is necessary to offer a provisional definition (see also above and note 3). Put most simply, *gender identity is an individual's structured set of gendered personal identities.* Personal identities are affective, cognitive, and behavioral links between an individual's self and biological/physical/material factors, interests and abilities, relationships with specific other people, social categories and dimensions of affect and personality, and styles of behaving. These links can be conscious, nonconscious (nonmotivated unawareness, often due to overlearning), or unconscious (motivated nonawareness, as in repression). Most people, most of the time, are not aware of the *structure* of their overall personal identity. "Gendered" refers to the sex/gender linkage of a personal identity. Two types of gender linkage can be distinguished: "consensual" (shared beliefs about what goes with male–female and how strongly) and "personal" (an individual's view of the direction and extent to which an identity element and sex/gender covary). An example will clarify this distinction: A woman may regard "aggressive" as a personality trait closely linked to her self. At a societal level in America, this characteristic is associated stereotypically with males. The hypothetical woman, however, need not personally subscribe to this consensual sex linkage. She may regard "aggressive" as something that is equally characteristic of women and men.

Contents of Gender Identity

The most crucial step for the present model, since it emphasizes the nonhomogeneity of gender identity, is to identify the possible content-specific components of thinking about, experiencing, and enacting self in terms of sex and gender. We (Ashmore & Ogilvie, 1989) build on Huston's (1983) delineation of five content areas of "sex typing": "biological gender," "activities and interests," "personal–social attributes," "gender-based social relationships," and "stylistic and symbolic content" (see Huston's Table 1).[5] As indicated in the earlier section on gender as a personality variable, only self-perceived personality traits have been studied in much depth with adults. To develop a more comprehensive picture of gender identity, it is necessary to assess other aspects of the "personal–social attributes" category (especially identities; Deaux, 1989), and, equally importantly, to explore the other four neglected or "new" content areas suggested by Huston. It is also necessary, we believe, to slightly modify and extend Huston's category system.

We (Ashmore & Ogilvie, 1989) propose as the first additional crucial content of gender identity "biological/physical/material attributes." We agree with Huston that biological factors must be considered in how the individual constructs a personal identity informed by sex and gender. However, we broaden her category somewhat by explicitly differentiating and adding "physical" and "material" aspects. The term "differentiating" should be highlighted, because not all of the ways in which men and women present themselves physically are clearly or neatly connected to "biological" factors, and yet they are or may be important "definitions" of one's sex or gender group membership (e.g., wearing high-heeled shoes). The importance of physical and material factors for gender identity is suggested by (1) Deaux and Lewis's (1984) work on sex stereotypes; physical appearance was the strongest component in terms of shaping inferences to other contents of beliefs about women and men. (2) Brownmiller's (1984) analysis of "femininity;" four of her eight content chapters concern biological/physical/material aspects of femininity (i.e., body, hair, clothes, skin). (3) Developing a unified overall personal identity is a crucial task in adolescence (Erikson, 1968), and this is a period marked by dramatic biological changes and heightened concern with physical appearance. (4) Establishing and maintaining intimate social relationships is a major concern of many adolescents and adults, and physical attractiveness is a key consideration in dating choices (Patzer, 1985).

The second proposed content area, "symbolic and stylistic behaviors," requires less justification. There is considerable research indicating aggregate-level sex differences in nonverbal behaviors (see Table 19.1, above), and theoretical attention to how nonverbal sex differences relate to relations between the sexes (e.g., Henley, 1977). As Huston (1983) notes, however, how nonverbal and extralinguistic behaviors, body carriage, and other symbolic and stylistic behaviors are implicated in one's sense of and experience of sex and gender have not been fully explored. That they are probably quite important is suggested by the fact that two of Brownmiller's (1984) femininity chapters (i.e., voice, movement) concern this category.

We (Ashmore & Ogilvie, 1989) slightly revised Huston's third category, from "interests and activities" to "interests and abilities." The rationale is as follows: Work and leisure are two major spheres of life, and thus it seems desirable to distinguish these, with "interests" denoting leisure orientations and "abilities" one's work-related capacities.[6] (It is recognized that ability is involved in leisure activities and that interests affect achievement.) This general category has been surprisingly neglected by researchers concerned with gender and the individual, even though "sex-role identity" in children is often assessed by toy preference (Beere, 1979); even though leisure activities are quite important in the social lives of adolescents (e.g., popular music and self-definition); and even though considerable research has shown that self-concept of ability is a crucial ingredient in the achievement behavior and career development of boys and girls (Eccles, 1985, 1987).

The fourth suggested "new content" for gender identity is "social relationships." There is evidence that boys and girls enact and experience social relationships differently (e.g., Maccoby, 1987; Schofield, 1982, Ch. 5), and that this is also true of adolescents' and young adults' close personal relationships (Huston & Ashmore, 1986; Peplau & Gordon, 1985). To date, however, these leads have not informed assessments of gender identity. We distinguish two crucial aspects of gender-based social relationships: (1) how one's relationships with men and women are differentially experienced and enacted; and (2) how one's sense of masculinity and femininity are differently organized and expressed in relationships with others.

Causes of Gender Identity

How do an individual's multiple personal identities become gendered? The major extant theories of sex and gender each point to one or a small set of causes for sex-role orientation, gender schema, or whatever is the preferred central construct. The present formulation in a sense subsumes these models by assuming that many different causal variables are important, that different individuals are more responsive to certain types of inputs than others, and that *different causes can shape different components of gender identity* (see also Spence, 1985).

As a simplifying device, we (Ashmore & Ogilvie, 1989) identify three general classes of inputs, and these causal factors are indicated at the left-hand side of Figure 19.1. The first, "contact with culture," includes exposure to the media, the educational system, and other sources of societal messages about maleness and femaleness. This first set of causal factors roughly corresponds to societal theories that stress socialization, and to such current psychological models as social role (e.g., Eagly, 1987) and gender schema formulations that emphasize culture as a major and compelling force (Bem, 1981, and especially 1985). My own view, however, is that most past theories centering on this class of inputs have overestimated the homogeneity of mainstream American culture's portrayals; especially in the 1980s, there has been an explosion of "alternative media," which are probably best illustrated by the growth of cable television at the expense of network (mainstream) channels. These theories have also ignored subcultures; although white English-speaking people dominate the mainstream media, subcultural messages are powerfully expressed via religious institutions (e.g., for many black Americans) and some branches of the media (e.g., Spanish-language radio and cable TV stations). Finally, these theories have assumed that consumers of culture are passive and isolated and simply "absorb" the lessons depicted; media researchers have found this image of the audience to be inaccurate, and it is being replaced by an "active audience" view (Hawkins & Pingree, 1986).

The second general category of inputs, "relationships with specific men and women," suggests that people learn about sex and gender by watching specific people around them and by forming and maintaining relationships with some of these individuals. This grouping roughly corresponds to psychoanalytic formulations, especially object relations versions thereof (e.g., Chodorow, 1978); to the symbolic-interactionist notion of the "looking-glass self"; and also to the modeling component of social learning theories (Mischel, 1970). Although we acknowledge the role that these mechanisms may play, we suggest, as an extension of the basic logic of the multiplicity perspective, that people (both knowingly and unwittingly) are different selves with different people, and that these multiple "self-withs" can be organized by sex/gender (e.g., a man may experience his self as open and relaxed with the specific important men in his life, but as emotionally restricted and tense in his relationships with women).

The third general set of factors contributing to gendered identities is "self-guided activities." This is a generally neglected (though there has been work on sex differences in skills; see Liss, 1983), but, I would argue, potent set of inputs into gender identity. Block (1984) described the important role that "doing" can play in creating sex differences. Quite simply, if boys are dressed in jeans and girls in dresses, then boys are more likely to engage in exploration (e.g., climbing trees), and this in turn may predispose men in general to be more exploratory in their interactions with the environment. Block also noted that children's self-guided activities are often done with tools supplied by and in environments shaped by adults. Thus, for example, boys are more often given heavy toy trucks and girls more often receive dolls as gifts. Heavy toy trucks can make noise, cause damage, and "have an effect," whereas dolls more often can be used to talk with and dress up. Playing with trucks, then, can contribute to an agentic (not always positive) orientation, whereas playing with dolls can foster a communal personal style.

In order to avoid the too general prescription "Study all causes in relation to all contents," our (Ashmore & Ogilvie, 1989) multiplicity model includes the following working principles:

1. *Content specificity.* The content of an input should most strongly shape the parallel content in gender identity. Thus, for example, exposure to cultural messages about the body (as in fashion magazines) should affect the biological/physical/material content of gender identity. Failure to attend to content specificity may help account for the weak and inconsistent relationship documented between television viewing and children's thoughts and feelings about gender (Huston, 1983).

2. *Referent specificity.* The referent of an input should most strongly shape the parallel individual-level gender concept. Not only do the hypothesized causal inputs involve a content (i.e., *what* they are about), but they also include a referent (i.e., *who* they are about). At the simplest level, contact with culture is about things and other people (not the individual himself or herself, or people who are important to the individual in a day-to-day sense). Thus, exposure to culture should have the most impact on beliefs about and evaluations of abstract issues and objects and general classes of people, which, in terms of Figure 19.1, includes the superordinate categories and gender subtypes portions of thinking about the sexes and most gender-related attitudes, *but not gender identity.* Relationships with specific men and women should have the strongest impact on thoughts and feelings about specific women and men (under thinking about the sexes) and the "self-with" aspect of the social relationships component of gender identity (since the referent is a relationship, or "me-with"). Self-guided activities should have the strongest impact on all gender identity components, since the referent is "self." That is, self-knowledge derives primarily from experiencing the process and observing the outcomes of one's own actions. In short, gender identity derives from doing, not listening or seeing.[7]

3. *Gender learning as an aspect of personal "tasks."* How an input becomes part of the self depends on the person's "task" (e.g., Cantor, Norem, Niedenthal, Langston, & Brower, 1987) or "goal" (Pervin, 1989). For certain age periods, sex and gender constitute a major personal task. Thus, in early school age, children (at least in this society) are motivated to learn what "boy" and "girl" are like and are concerned with fitting self into this system. Thus, for the modal child in this age period, Kohlberg (1966) is probably correct. However, my hunch is that for most people, most of the time,

gender learning is not the major personal task. (Much later in the life cycle, in adulthood, reassessment of one's self can lead to an identity organized around gender; see Stewart, 1989.) Rather, the person's task is to develop and maintain a sense of self that involves four basic considerations identified by a long line of self-theorists (such a long line that it is impossible to give credit in a fully appropriate manner): survival (e.g., D. M. Ogilvie, personal communication, July 7, 1989), evaluation (e.g., Tesser, 1988), control (e.g., Bandura, 1977), and consistency (e.g., Duval & Wicklund, 1972). How gender may enter into this is suggested by the following example. Although continuing to live is generally taken for granted, events can, in actuality or just in our minds and hearts, threaten our existence; according to Ogilvie (1987a, 1987b, personal communication), these can become anchored in us as an "undesired (or feared) self." Many people's undesired selves may be unrelated to sex and gender issues. However, it may be that fear of being feminine for some American males may result from a perceived threat to survival. The young boy who puts on his mother's dress and lipstick and is discovered by his father may experience the father's anger and shock as a threat to his very existence; if so, "being like a girl" (particularly dressing like females or having feminine play interests) may become an undesired or feared self.

Consequences of Gender Identity

The present formulation suggests a major shift in focus about the outcomes of gender at the individual level. Sex-differences workers began with the issue of whether men are smarter than women, and the focus continues to be on socially constructed good–bad abilities, especially intellectual abilities. Masculinity–femininity workers, both within the Terman and Miles perspective and during the androgyny era, sought evidence that one form of gendered personality caused positive psychological adjustment. The present multiplicity model, with an extension of the content specificity principle to the contents-to-consequences link, suggests that, instead of researching relatively general evaluative "dependent variables," it would be more productive to study how different contents are linked to particular social actions. (This crucial idea is an extension of Ajzen & Fishbein's [1977] correspondence

notion regarding the attitude–behavior link.) Content-specific gender-related attitudes should be predictive of positive versus negative social action (e.g., help–hinder) concerning the specific attitude object (e.g., attitude toward abortion and donating money to the National Abortion Rights League). Sex stereotypes (within the more general content category of thinking about the sexes) should most directly affect information processing about men and women in general. The various aspects of gender identity should each most immediately affect content-related self-relevant action, as in the following two examples. First, sense of self as having a masculine versus a feminine body and appearance should affect clothes selection, physical activities, and, where appearance is central to job definition, occupational choice. Second, one's belief in having high ability in the "male areas" of math and science should have an impact on course and major selection in school, as well as on the choice of careers seen to require such abilities.

Our model also recognizes that gender identity, thinking about the sexes, and gender-related attitudes are just one set of inputs to social action. As Cook and Selltiz (1964) noted about the relation of attitude to behavior, other aspects of the person and situational variables also shape action. The progress that social psychologists have made in recent years in understanding when, how, and why attitudes predict behavior can serve as a model for gender identity workers (see Del Boca et al., 1986, pp. 153–154).

Directions for Research

Of the many directions for research suggested by the multiplicity model of gender identity, two general strategies are of the highest priority—measuring all the parts and putting the pieces together. The first, measuring all the parts, involves developing procedures and (where possible) standardized instruments for assessing the multiple components of gender identity. The personality trait facet of the social relationships component is already well covered by the PAQ, BSRI, and related techniques (Cook, 1985). Deaux (1989) is developing methods for getting at the identities portion of social relationships. We (Weil & Ashmore, 1989) have constructed a self-report instrument, modeled after the PAQ, for indexing self-perceived ability in gender-related and non-gender-related areas.

As part of a longitudinal study, we (Ashmore & Ogilvie, 1989) are assessing most of the hypothesized components of gender identity. At this time, we have completed only those sessions concerned with the "self-with" portion of the social relationships component. Each participant (the group consisted of college juniors and seniors) generated a list of important people in his or her life and a set of words and phrases describing these people and "self-with" each person. By means of a computerized procedure, each participant described "self-with" each of 25 important others, using 42 of the most frequently used personal descriptors (the individual's own words and phrases) and 18 traits from the ACL having known consensual sex-stereotypic linkages (Williams & Best, 1982). The resulting "me-with"_____(25 important others) × personal and consensual features (60 descriptors) matrix was subjected to both multidimensional scaling and HICLAS (a hierarchical clustering algorithm that does not require strict set inclusion and that represents simultaneously both targets and features; cf. DeBoeck & Rosenberg, 1988; Rosenberg, 1988).

Figure 19.2 presents the HICLAS results for one male participant. In order to protect the participant's anonymity, names of specific others have been replaced by the nature of the relationship to the target and, where necessary, m (for male) or f (for female). Figure 19.2 shows how both the "self-withs" (at the top of the figure) and the features (at the bottom) are clustered (e.g., at the middle top of the figure, the grouping beginning with "m-ex-roommate" and ending with "uncle" indicates that the person experiences himself quite similarly with all these people). The figure also shows the superset–subset relations among the clusters. For example, "self with mom (now)" is a superset for the left-hand (begins with "f-friend") and middle (begins with "dad's mom") "self-with" subsets below it; thus, when with "mom (now)," the person sees himself as having attributes descriptive of both of these lower-order (in the sense of being more specific) groupings. Looking across the feature side of the figure makes it clear that this means that the person experiences quite different selves when with "mom (now)."

Regarding the multiplicity model of gender identity, Figure 19.2 illustrates two points.

First, our model specifies that individuals must be studied in their own right, and Figure 19.2 is a picture of one person's "self-with" structure. As can be seen by its placement at the top of the features clustering (and the bottom of the figure), this male sees self as masculine (as well as "a talker," active, and tough) with all the important people in his life. This would not surprise gender-as-a-personality-variable researchers, but the participant's personal definition of "masculine" would. In a follow-up interview, we showed the person the figure, and, among other things, asked: "What does being 'masculine' mean to you?" He responded: "I feel responsible to help other people." Second, even though the multiplicity model stresses the individual and the necessity of idiographic research methods, it does not eschew nomothetic analysis. Within each individual's gendered personal identity structure (or a portion of it, as in the present "self-with" structure), it is possible to construct nomothetic properties. For example, in the HICLAS diagrams it is possible to assess how high (how general, central) the labels "masculine" and "feminine" are or how mixed or separate the stereotypic male and female traits are in the clusters. These two examples could represent the personal salience of masculinity and femininity and the degree of self-gender schematicity, respectively. These indices (and others) can then be used in between-subjects analyses to link contents to either causes or consequences.

The second high-priority task the multiplicity model sets for researchers is putting the pieces together. Once measures of the various aspects of each content component are developed, the questions become these: How are they interrelated at both an individual and an aggregate level? Is it possible to identify types of individuals in terms of within- and between-content component covariation of gender-related nomothetic properties? (See Ogilvie & Ashmore, 1989, for one means of answering the second question.)

FINAL COMMENT

It is fitting that this chapter concludes with the very difficult issue of how to put the pieces together. At the outset it was noted that, as with poets and philosophers before them, most psychologists have sought to understand the sexes in very simple terms. Recent research has shown that women and men are multifaceted

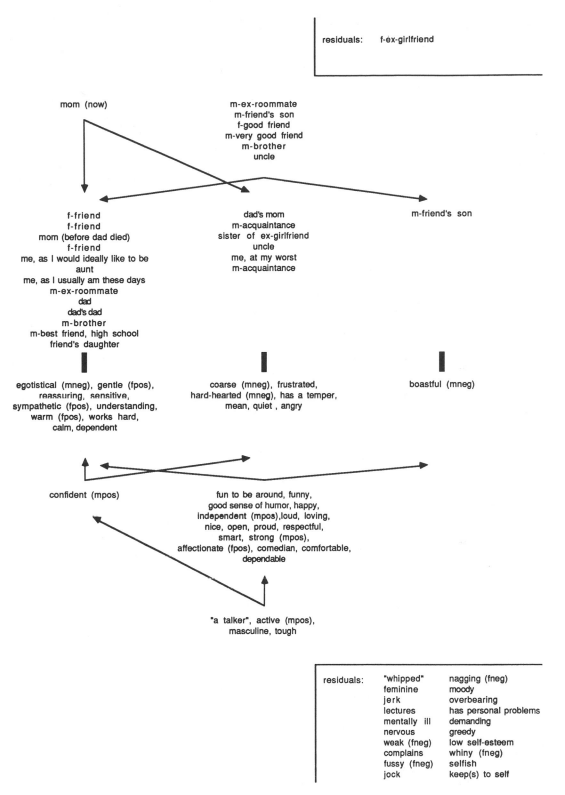

residuals: f-ex-girlfriend

mom (now)

m-ex-roommate
m-friend's son
f-good friend
m-very good friend
m-brother
uncle

m-friend's son

f-friend
f-friend
mom (before dad died)
f-friend
me, as I would ideally like to be
aunt
me, as I usually am these days
m-ex-roommate
dad
dad's dad
m-brother
m-best friend, high school
friend's daughter

dad's mom
m-acquaintance
sister of ex-girlfriend
uncle
me, at my worst
m-acquaintance

egotistical (mneg), gentle (fpos),
reassuring, sensitive,
sympathetic (fpos), understanding,
warm (fpos), works hard,
calm, dependent

coarse (mneg), frustrated,
hard-hearted (mneg), has a temper,
mean, quiet , angry

boastful (mneg)

confident (mpos)

fun to be around, funny,
good sense of humor, happy,
independent (mpos),loud, loving,
nice, open, proud, respectful,
smart, strong (mpos),
affectionate (fpos), comedian, comfortable,
dependable

"a talker", active (mpos),
masculine, tough

residuals: "whipped"   nagging (fneg)
feminine   moody
jerk   overbearing
lectures   has personal problems
mentally ill   demanding
nervous   greedy
weak (fneg)   low self-esteem
complains   whiny (fneg)
fussy (fneg)   selfish
jock   keep(s) to self

FIGURE 19.2 Hierarchical classes (HICLAS) representation of one male respondent's "self-with" facet of the social relationships component of gender identity. From *Gender Identity, Sex Stereotypes, and Social Action* by R. D. Ashmore and D. M. Ogilvie, 1989, grant proposal funded by the National Institute of Mental Health. Reprinted by permission of the authors.

519

and much more complicated than suggested by the sex-differences and gender-as-a-personality-variable paradigms. Researchers using a general sex-as-a-social-category perspective are attempting to understand this complexity. For them, the big challenge is to capture and represent in as simple a way as possible the multiple causes, contents, and consequences of sex, gender, and the individual.

ACKNOWLEDGMENTS

The preparation of this chapter was supported, in part, by National Institute of Mental Health Grant Nos. MH40871-01/02 (Richard D. Ashmore and Frances K. Del Boca, Co-Principal Investigators) and MH40871-03/04 (Richard D. Ashmore and Daniel M. Ogilvie, Co-Principal Investigators). Many individuals have helped bring this chapter to its final form. I particularly wish to thank Dan Ogilvie and Fran Del Boca. They each read and provided very useful comments on an earlier draft; more importantly, many of the ideas in this chapter are "ours" and not "mine." I also thank Lawrence A. Pervin for his patience and comments. Finally, I express my gratitude to Laura Kennedy and Scott Bilder for their help in conducting the research reported and in preparing tables and figures, as well as for their responses to an earlier draft of this chapter.

NOTES

1. The distinction made here between "sex" and "gender" is consistent with Unger's (1979) suggestions about these terms. (At points, however, "sex" and "gender" are both used to describe the societal categories "female" and "male.") The decision not to pursue a biosocial interactionist model is a necessary simplifying device, and does not mean that I regard biological and social variables as independent. Perhaps most importantly, and counter to many people's intuitions, biological factors do not act in a simple and direct way on human behavior; rather, they are subject to considerable cultural interpretation (e.g., see Kessler & McKenna, 1978, on the social definition of the "biological" categories female and male, and Tiefer, 1987, on the social construction of sexuality).

2. Two other caveats: I am not a historian, and the history I present is shaped by my personal and professional beliefs and values. I am a white, middle-class, middle-aged (I went to college and graduate school in the 1960s) male who is not afraid of the "L[iberal] word." I am also a psycho-

logical social psychologist whose specialty since deciding "what I want to do when I grow up" has been intergroup relations.

3. This working definition is quite general, and it is different from the way in which the term "gender identity" is used by some social scientists to refer to a much more specific phenomenon (i.e., the individual's fundamental sense of being a biological male or female). It is my view that the broader definition is preferable, in order to capture and reflect the multiple and diverse ways in which sex and gender influence self-relevant thoughts, feelings, and behaviors (for supportive arguments see Katz, 1986, and Sherif, 1982). I flesh out the general definition below by identifying the content categories of personal identity that are most likely to be affected by sex and gender.

4. This is admittedly oversimplified, and, as such, is not an accurate summary of all extant efforts in this field. It is most inaccurate in two ways: (a) With respect to contents, a number of writers have urged that gender thoughts and feelings are best construed as multiple and loosely interconnected rather than as of a single cloth (e.g., Spence, 1985). (b) Concerning causes, developmental psychologists have built and tested much more elaborate models than that suggested here. Although these two aspects of extant work are left out at this point, they are used below to develop an alternative framework.

5. There is no one correct way to partition the contents of gender identity. We began with the typology developed by Huston because it fully covered the domain of extant sex-typing work (which was the basis for Huston's constructing it) and because it fit well with the types of self-concept contents identified by social and personality psychologists (e.g., James's [1890] material, spiritual, and social selves) and developmental psychologists' work on understanding of self and other (e.g., Hart & Damon's [1985] physical, psychological, and social selves parallel those identified by James, plus the added active self [which is similar to Huston's "interests and activities" and the here suggested "interests and abilities"]).

6. In addition, we have removed "activities" from contents to both causes (to highlight that what one does [self-guided activities] is a determinant of what one is [gender identity contents]) and consequences (to emphasize that gendered contents are just one causal input into action). Concerning the latter, the activities in which men and women engage are determined not just by gender identity, thinking about the sexes, and

gender-related attitudes, but also by other personal qualities and by situational factors (Cook & Selltiz, 1964; see also below, "Consequences of Gender Identity").

7. The foregoing analysis does not mean that others are irrelevant to the development of gender identity. First and foremost, much self-guided activity takes place in environments and with implements provided by others. In addition, what one sees and hears assist in the interpretation of personal experiences. For example, a boy who wears his mother's clothes and likes doing this will still be affected by the fact that he sees very few similar enactments on television and receives a spanking from his father. Finally, personal action and gender identity developed from it are not unrelated to stereotype and attitude development, and stereotypes and evaluative orientations can have a direct impact on one's sense of self.

REFERENCES

Adkins-Regan, E. (1989). Genesis of gender [Review of *Masculinity/femininity: Basic perspectives*]. *Contemporary Psychology, 34*, 243–245.

Adler, T. (1989, March). Sex-based differences declining, study shows. *APA Monitor*, p. 6.

Ajzen, I., & Fishbein, M. (1977). Attitude–behavior relations: A theoretical analysis and review of empirical research. *Psychological Bulletin, 84*, 888–918.

Anastasi, A. (1958). *Differential psychology* (3rd ed.). New York: Macmillan.

Angrist, S. S. (1969). The study of sex roles. *Journal of Social Issues, 25*, 215–232.

Ashmore, R. D. (1981). Sex stereotypes and implicit personality theory. In D. L. Hamilton (Ed.), *Cognitive processes in stereotyping and intergroup behavior* (pp. 37–81). Hillsdale, NJ: Erlbaum.

Ashmore, R. D., & Del Boca, F. K. (1979). Sex stereotypes and implicit personality theory: Toward a cognitive–social psychological conceptualization. *Sex Roles, 5*, 219–248.

Ashmore, R. D., & Del Boca, F. K. (Eds.). (1986a). *The social psychology of female–male relations: A critical analysis of central concepts*. Orlando FL: Academic Press.

Ashmore, R. D., & Del Boca, F. K. (1986b). *Thinking about the sexes: Causes, contents, and consequences.* Grant proposal submitted to the National Institute of Mental Health.

Ashmore, R. D., & Del Boca, F. K. (1989). *The development and initial validation of a structured inventory to assess the multiple components of gender-related verbal attitudes.* Unpublished manuscript.

Ashmore, R. D., Del Boca, F. K., & Titus, D. (1984, August). *Types of women and men: Yours, mine and ours.* Paper presented at the annual meeting of the American Psychological Association, Toronto.

Ashmore, R. D., Del Boca, F. K., & Wohlers, A. J (1986). Gender stereotypes. In R. D. Ashmore & F. K. Del Boca (Eds.), *The social psychology of female–male relations: A critical analysis of central concepts* (pp. 69–119). Orlando, FL: Academic Press.

Ashmore, R. D., & Ogilvie, D. M. (1989). *Gender identity, sex stereotypes, and social action.* Grant proposal funded by the National Institute of Mental Health.

Ashmore, R. D., & Tumia, M. (1980). Sex stereotypes and implicit personality theory: I. A personality description approach to the assessment of sex stereotypes. *Sex Roles, 6*, 501–518.

Babad, E. Y., Birnbaum, M., & Benne, K. D. (1983). *The social self: Group influences on personal identiy.* Beverly Hills, CA: Sage.

Baldwin, J. M. (1973). *Social and ethical interpretations in mental development* (2nd ed.). New York: Arno Press. (Original work published 1897)

Bandura, A. (1977). *Social learning theory.* Englewood Cliffs, NJ: Prentice-Hall.

Bassoff, E. S., & Glass, G. V. (1982). The relationship between sex roles and mental health: A meta-analysis of twenty-six studies. *Counseling Psychologist, 10*, 105–112.

Baumeister, R. F. (1988). Should we stop studying sex differences altogether? *American Psychologist, 43*, 1092–1095.

Becker, B. J. (1986). Influence again: An examination of reviews and studies of gender differences in social influence. In J. S. Hyde & M. C. Linn (Eds.), *The psychology of gender: Advances through meta-analysis* (pp. 178–209). Baltimore: Johns Hopkins University Press.

Becker, B. J., & Hedges, L. V. (1984). Meta-analysis of cognitive gender differences: A comment on an analysis by Rosenthal and Rubin. *Journal of Educational Psychology, 76*, 583–587.

Beere, C. A. (1979). *Women and women's issues: A handbook of tests and measures.* San Francisco: Jossey-Bass.

Belenky, M. F., Clinchy, B. M., Goldberger, N. R., & Tarule, J. M. (1986). *Women's ways of knowing: The development of self, voice, and mind.* New York: Basic Books.

Bem, S. L. (1972). *Psychology looks at sex roles: Where have all the androgynous people gone?* Paper presented at the UCLA Symposium on Sex Roles, Los Angeles.

Bem, S. L. (1974). The measurement of psychological androgyny. *Journal of Consulting and Clinical Psychology, 42*, 165–172.

Bem, S. L. (1975). Sex role adaptability: One consequence of psychological androgyny. *Journal of Personality and Social Psychology, 31*, 634–643.

Bem, S. L. (1977). On the utility of alternative procedures for assessing psychological androgyny. *Journal of Consulting and Clinical Psychology, 45*, 196–205.

Bem, S. L. (1979). Theory and measurement of androgyny: A reply to Pedhazur–Tetenbaum and Locksley–Colten critiques. *Journal of Personality and Social Psychology, 37*, 1047–1054.

Bem, S. L. (1981). Gender schema theory: A cognitive account of sex typing. *Psychological Review, 88*, 354–364.

Bem, S. L. (1985). Androgyny and gender schema theory: A conceptual and empirical integration. In T. B. Sonderegger (Ed.), *Nebraska Symposium on Motivation* (Vol. 32, pp. 179–226). Lincoln: University of Nebraska Press.

Bem, S. L. (1987). Gender schema theory and the romantic tradition. In P. Shaver & C. Hendrick (Eds.), *Review of personality and social psychology: Vol. 7. Sex and gender* (pp. 251–271). Beverly Hills, CA: Sage.

Block, J. H. (1973). Conceptions of sex role: Some cross-cultural and longitudinal perspectives. *American Psychologist, 28,* 512–526.

Block, J. H. (1976). Issues, problems, and pitfalls in assessing sex differences: A critical review of *The psychology of sex differences. Merrill–Palmer Quarterly, 22,* 283–308.

Block, J. H. (1984). *Sex role identity and ego development.* San Francisco: Jossey-Bass.

Brannon, R. (1978). Measuring attitudes (toward women, and otherwise): A methodological critique. In J. A. Sherman & F. L. Denmark (Eds.), *The psychology of women: Future directions in research* (pp. 647–731). New York: Psychological Dimensions.

Brown, D. G. (1956). Sex role preferences in young children. *Psychological Monographs, 70* (Whole No. 421).

Brown, R. (1986). *Social psychology, the second edition.* New York: Free Press.

Brownmiller, S. (1984). *Femininity.* New York: Fawcett/Columbine.

Cantor, N., Norem, J. K., Niedenthal, P. M., Langston, C. A., & Brower, A. M. (1987). Life tasks, self-concept ideals, and cognitive strategies in a life transition. *Journal of Personality and Social Psychology, 53,* 1178–1191.

Carlson, R. (1971). Where is the person in personality research? *Psychological Bulletin, 75,* 203–219.

Carlson, R. (1972). Understanding women: Implications for personality theory and research. *Journal of Social Issues, 28,* 17–32.

Carlson, E., & Carlson, R. (1960). Male and female subjects in personality research. *Journal of Abnormal and Social Psychology, 61,* 482–483.

Carson, R. C. (1989). Personality. *Annual Review of Psychology, 40,* 227–248.

Carter, D. B. (Ed.). (1987a). *Current conceptions of sex roles and sex typing: Theory and research.* New York: Praeger.

Carter, D. B. (1987b). Sex role research and the future: New directions for research. In D. B. Carter (Ed.), *Current conceptions of sex roles and sex typing: Theory and research* (pp. 243–251). New York: Praeger.

Carver, C. S. (1989). How should multifaceted personality constructs be tested? Issues illustrated by self-monitoring, attributional style, and hardiness. *Journal of Personality and Social Psychology, 56,* 577–585.

Chodorow, N. (1978). *The reproduction of mothering: Psychoanalysis and the sociology of gender.* Berkeley: University of California Press.

Cohen, J. (1977). *Statistical power analysis for the behavioral sciences* (rev. ed.). New York: Academic Press.

Constantinople, A. (1973). Masculinity-femininity: An exception to a famous dictum. *Psychological Bulletin, 80,* 389–407.

Cook, E. P. (1985). *Psychological androgyny.* New York: Pergamon Press.

Cook, S. W., & Selltiz, C. (1964). A multiple-indicator approach to attitude measurement *Psychological Bulletin, 62,* 36–55.

Cooper, H. M., & Rosenthal, R. (1980). Statistical versus traditional procedures for summarizing research findings. *Psychological Bulletin, 87,* 442–449.

Crawford, M. (1989). Agreeing to differ: Feminist epistemologies and women's ways of knowing. In

M. Crawford & M. Gentry (Eds.), *Gender and thought: Psychological perspectives* (pp. 128–145). New York: Springer-Verlag.

Crawford, M., & Marecek, J. (1989). Psychology reconstructs the female: 1968–1988. *Psychology of Women Quarterly, 13,* 147–165.

Deaux, K. (1984). From individual differences to social categories. Analysis of a decade's research on gender. *Americal Psychologist, 39,* 105–116.

Deaux, K. (1989, May). *Identity and change.* Paper presented at Nags Head Conference on Sex and Gender, Nags Head, NC.

Deaux, K., & Lewis, L. L. (1984). The structure of gender stereotypes: Interrelationships among components and gender label. *Journal of Personality and Social Psychology, 46,* 991–1004.

Deaux, K., & Major, B. (1987). Putting gender into context: An interactive model of gender-related behavior. *Psychological Review, 94,* 369–389.

DeBoeck, P., & Rosenberg, S. (1988). Hierarchical classes: Model and data analysis. *Psychometrika, 53,* 361–381.

Del Boca, F. K., & Ashmore, R. D. (1980a). Sex stereotypes and implicit personality theory: II. A trait-inference approach to the assessment of sex stereotypes. *Sex Roles, 6,* 519–535.

Del Boca, F. K., & Ashmore, R. D. (1980b). Sex stereotypes through the life cycle. In L. Wheeler (Ed.), *Review of personality and social psychology* (Vol. 1, pp. 163–192). Beverly Hills, CA: Sage.

Del Boca, F. K., Ashmore, R. D., & McManus, M. A. (1986). Gender-related attitudes. In R. D. Ashmore & F. K. Del Boca (Eds.), *The social psychology of female–male relations: A critical analysis of central concepts* (pp. 121–163). Orlando, FL: Academic Press.

Downs, A. C., & Langlois, J. H. (1988). Sex typing: Construct and measurement issues. *Sex Roles, 18,* 87–100.

Duval, S., & Wicklund, R. R. (1972). *A theory of objective self-awareness.* New York: Academic Press.

Eagly, A. H. (1987). Reporting sex differences. *American Psychologist, 42,* 756–757.

Eagly, A. H. (1989a, March). *Gender and social behavior: Adventures in the study of sex differences.* Invited address presented at the meeting of the Association for Women in Psychology, Newport, RI.

Eagly, A. H. (1989b). *On the advantages of reporting sex comparisons.* Manuscript submitted for publication.

Eagly, A. H., & Carli, L. L. (1981). Sex of researchers and sex-typed communications as determinants of sex differences in influenceability: A meta-analysis of social influence studies. *Psychological Bulletin, 90,* 1–20.

Eagly, A. H., & Crowley, M. (1986). Gender and helping behavior: A meta-analytic review of the social psychological literature. *Psychological Bulletin, 100,* 283–308.

Eagly, A. H., & Johnson, B. T. (1989). *Gender and leadership style: A meta-analysis.* Manuscript submitted for publication.

Eagly, A. H., & Karau, S. J. (1989). *Gender and the emergence of leaders: A meta-analysis.* Manuscript submitted for publication.

Eagly, A. H., & Steffen, V. J. (1986). Gender and aggressive behavior: A meta-analytic review of the social psychological literature. *Psychological Bulletin, 100,* 309–330.

Eaton, W. O., & Enns, L. R. (1986). Sex differences in

human motor activity level. *Psychological Bulletin, 100,* 19–28.

Eccles, J. (1985). Sex differences in achievement patterns. In T. B. Sonderegger (Ed.), *Nebraska Symposium on Motivation* (Vol. 32, pp. 97–132). Lincoln: University of Nebraska Press.

Eccles, J. (1987). Gender roles and women's achievement related decisions. *Psychology of Women Quarterly, 11,* 135–172.

Eisenberg, N., & Lennon, R. (1983). Sex differences in empathy and related capacities. *Psychological Bulletin, 94,* 100–131.

Ellis, H. (1894). *Man and woman.* London: Scott.

Erikson, E. H. (1968). *Identity: Youth and crisis.* New York: Norton.

Feingold, A. (1988). Cognitive gender differences are disappearing. *American Psychologist, 43,* 95–103.

Frable, D. E. S. (1989). Sex typing and gender ideology: Two facets of the individual's gender psychology that go together. *Journal of Personality and Social Psychology, 56,* 95–108.

Garai, J. E., & Scheinfeld, A. (1968). Sex differences in mental and behavioral traits. *Genetic Psychology Monographs, 77,* 169–299.

Giele, J. Z. (1988). Gender and sex roles. In N. J. Smelser (Ed.), *Handbook of sociology* (pp. 291–323). Newbury Park, CA: Sage.

Gilligan, C. (1982). *In a different voice: Psychological theory and women's development.* Cambridge, MA: Harvard University Press.

Gilligan, C. (1986). Reply by Carol Gilligan. *Signs, 11,* 324–333.

Goldberg, L. R. (1971). A historical survey of personality scales and inventories. In P. McReynolds (Ed.), *Advances in psychological assessment* (Vol. 2, pp. 293–336). Palo Alto, CA: Science and Behavior Books.

Green, B. F., & Hall, J. A. (1984). Quantitative methods for literature reviews. *Annual Review of Psychology, 35,* 37–53.

Greenberg, B. S. (1988). Some uncommon television images and the drench hypothesis. In S. Oskamp (Ed.), *Applied social psychology annual: Vol. 8. Television as a social issue* (pp. 88–102). Newbury Park, CA: Sage.

Hacker, H. M. (1951). Women as a minority group. *Social Forces, 30,* 60–69.

Hall, J. A. (1978). Gender effects in decoding nonverbal cues. *Psychological Bulletin, 85,* 845–875.

Hall, J. A. (1984). *Nonverbal sex differences: Communication accuracy and expressive style.* Baltimore: Johns Hopkins University Press.

Hare-Mustin, R. T., & Marecek, J. (1988). The meaning of difference: Gender theory, postmodernism, and psychology. *American Psychologist, 43,* 455–464.

Hart, D., & Damon, W. (1985). Contrasts between understanding self and understanding others. In R. L. Leahy (Ed.), *The development of self* (pp. 151–178). Orlando FL: Academic Press.

Hawkins, R., & Pingree, S. (1986). Activity in the effects of television on children. In J. Bryant & D. Zillman (Eds.), *Perspectives on media effects.* Hillsdale, NJ: Erlbaum.

Hedges, L. V., & Becker, B. J. (1986). Statistical methods in the meta-analysis of research on gender differences. In J. Hyde & M. C. Linn (Eds.), *The psychology of gender: Advances through meta-analysis* (pp. 14–50). Baltimore: Johns Hopkins University Press.

Hedges, L. V., & Olkin, I. (1980). Vote-counting methods in research synthesis. *Psychological Bulletin, 88,* 359–369.

Hedges, L. V., & Olkin, I. (1985). *Statistical methods for meta-analysis.* Orlando, FL: Academic Press.

Hendrick, C. (1977). Social psychology as an experimental science. In C. Hendrick (Ed.), *Perspectives on social psychology* (pp. 1–74). Hillsdale, NJ: Erlbaum.

Henley, N. M. (1977). *Body politics: Power, sex, and nonverbal communication.* Englewood Cliffs, NJ: Prentice-Hall.

Huston, A. C. (1983). Sex-typing. In E. M. Hetherington (Vol. Ed.), *Handbook of child psychology* (4th ed): *Vol. 4. Socialization, personality, and social development* (pp. 387–467). New York: Wiley.

Huston, T. L., & Ashmore, R. D. (1986). Women and men in personal relationships. In R. D. Ashmore & F. K. Del Boca (Eds.), *The social psychology of female–male relations: A critical analysis of central concepts* (pp. 167–210). Orlando, FL: Academic Press

Hyde, J. S. (1981). How large are cognitive gender differences? A meta-analysis using ω^2 and d. *American Psychologist, 36,* 892–901.

Hyde, J. S. (1986). Gender differences in aggression. In J. S. Hyde & M. C. Linn (Eds.), *The psychology of gender: Advances through meta-analysis* (pp. 51–66). Baltimore: Johns Hopkins University Press.

Hyde, J. S., & Linn, M. C. (Eds.). (1986). *The psychology of gender: Advances through meta-analysis* Baltimore: Johns Hopkins University Press.

Hyde, J. S., & Linn, M. C. (1988). Gender differences in verbal ability: A meta-analysis. *Psychological Bulletin, 104,* 53–69.

Jacklin, C. N. (1981). Methodological issues in the study of sex-related differences. *Developmental Review, 1,* 266–273.

Jacklin, C. N. (1989). Female and male: Issues of gender. *American Psychologist, 44,* 127–133.

James, W. (1890). *Principles of psychology.* New York: Holt.

Kagan, J. (1964). Acquisition and significance of sex typing and sex-role identity. In M. L. Hoffman & L. W. Hoffman (Eds.), *Review of child development research* (Vol. 1, pp. 137–168). New York: Russell Sage Foundation.

Katz, P. A. (1986). Gender identity: Development and consequences. In R. D. Ashmore & F. K. Del Boca (Eds.), *The social psychology of female–male relations: A critical analysis of central concepts* (pp. 21–67). Orlando, FL: Academic Press.

Kerber, L. K., Greeno, C. G., Maccoby, E. E., Luria, Z., Stack, C. B., & Gilligan, C. (1986). On *In a different voice*: An interdisciplinary forum. *Signs, 11,* 304–333.

Kessler, S. J., & McKenna, W. (1978). *Gender: An ethnomethodological approach.* New York: Wiley.

Kimball, M. M. (1989). A new perspective on women's math achievement. *Psychological Bulletin, 105,* 198–214.

Kite, M. E. (1984). Sex differences in attitudes toward homosexuals: A meta-analytic review. *Journal of Homosexuality, 10,* 69–81.

Kohlberg, L. A. (1966). A cognitive-developmental analysis of children's sex-role concepts and attitudes. In E. E. Maccoby (Ed.), *The development of sex differences* (pp. 82–173). Stanford, CA: Stanford University Press.

LaFrance, M. (1986). Reading between the lines [Review of *Nonverbal sex differences: Communication accuracy and expressive style*]. *Contemporary Psychology, 31,* 793–794.

Lewin M. (1984a). "Rather worse than folly?" Psychology measures femininity and masculinity: I. From Terman and Miles to the Guilfords. In M. Lewin (Ed.), *In the shadow of the past: Psychology portrays the sexes* (pp. 155–178). New York: Columbia University Press.

Lewin, M. (1984b). Psychology measures femininity and masculinity: II. From "13 gay men" to the instrumental–expressive distinction. In M. Lewin (Ed.), *In the shadow of the past, Psychology portrays the sexes* (pp. 179–205). New York: Columbia University Press.

Liben, L. S., & Signorella, M. L. (Eds.). (1987). *Children's gender schemata.* San Francisco: Jossey-Bass.

Linn, M. C., & Peterson, A. C. (1986). A meta-analysis of gender differences in spatial ability: Implications for mathematics and science achievement. In J. S. Hyde & M. C. Linn (Eds.), *The psychology of gender: Advances through meta-analysis.* Baltimore: Johns Hopkins University Press.

Liss, M. B. (Ed.). (1983). *Social and cognitive skills: Sex roles and children's play.* New York: Academic Press.

Lorber, J. (1981). Minamalist and maximalist feminist ideologies and strategies for change. *Quarterly Journal of Ideology, 5,* 61–66

Maccoby, E. E. (Ed.). (1966). *The development of sex differences.* Stanford, CA: Stanford University Press.

Maccoby, E. E. (1987). The varied meanings of "masculine" and "feminine." In J. M. Reinisch, L. A. Rosenblum, & S. A. Sanders (Eds.), *Masculinity/femininity:Basic perspectives* (pp. 227–239). New York: Oxford University Press.

Maccoby, E. E., & Jacklin, C. N. (1974). *The psychology of sex differences.* Stanford, CA: Stanford University Press.

Markus, H., Crane, M., Bernstein, S., & Siladi, M. (1982). Self-schemas and gender. *Journal of Personality and Social Psychology, 42,* 38–50.

Marsh, H. W., & Myers, M. (1986). Masculinity, feminity, and androgyny: A methodological and theoretical critique. *Sex Roles, 14,* 397–430.

Martin, C. L., & Halverson, C. F., Jr. (1981). A schematic processing model of sex-typing and stereotyping in young children. *Child Development, 52,* 1119–1134.

McHugh, M. D., Koeske, R. D., & Frieze, I. H. (1986). Issues to consider in conducting non-sexist research: A guide for researchers. *American Psychologist, 41,* 879–890.

Mead, M. (1935). *Sex and temperament in three primitive socieities.* New York: Morrow.

Miles, C. C. (1935). Sex in social psychology. In C. Murchison (Ed.), *A handbook of social psychology* (Vol. 2, pp. 683–797). New York: Russell & Russell.

Miller, J. B. (1976). *Toward a new psychology of women.* Boston: Beacon Press.

Minton, H. L., & Schneider, F. W. (1980). *Differential psychology.* Monterey, CA: Brooks/Cole.

Mischel, W. (1966). A social-learning view of sex differences in behavior. In E. E. Maccoby (Ed.), *The development of sex differences* (pp. 56–81). Stanford, CA: Stanford University Press.

Mischel, W. (1970). Sex typing and socialization. In P. H. Mussen (Ed.), *Carmichael's manual of child psychology* (3rd ed., Vol. 2, pp. 3–72). New York: Wiley.

Morawski, J. G. (1985). The measurement of masculinity and femininity: Engendering categorical realities. *Journal of Personality, 53,* 196–223.

Morawski, J. G. (1987). The troubled quest for masculin-

ity, femininity, and androgyny. In P. Shaver & C. Hendrick (Eds.), *Review of personality and social psychology: Vol. 7. Sex and gender* (pp. 44–69). Beverly Hills, CA: Sage

Ogilvie, D. M. (1987a, December). *Dreaded states and cherished outcomes: Satisfaction across the life span.* Invited address at the Max-Planck-Institute, West Berlin.

Ogilvie, D. M. (1987b). Self structure and life satisfaction in late middle-aged men and women. *Psychology and Aging, 2,* 217–224.

Ogilvie, D. M., & Ashmore, R. D. (1990). Self with other representations as units of analysis in self-concept research. In R. P. Lipka & T. M. Brinkthoupt (Eds), *Studying the self: Perspectives across the life-span.* New York: Teachers College Press.

Orlofsky, J. L. & O'Heron, C. A. (1987). Stereotypic and nonstereotypic sex role trait and behavior orientations: Implications for personal adjustment. *Journal of Personality and Social Psychology, 52,* 1034–1042.

Osgood, C. E. (1969). On the whys and wherefores of E, P, and A. *Journal of Personality and Social Psychology, 12,* 194–199.

Parsons, T. (1942). Age and sex in the social structure of the United States. *American Sociological Review, 7,* 604–616.

Parsons, T., & Bales, R. F. (1955). *Family: Socialization and interaction process.* New York: Free Press.

Patzer, G. L. (1985). *The physical attractiveness phenomena.* New York: Plenum.

Paulhus, D. L. (1987). Effects of group selection on correlations and factor patterns in sex role research. *Journal of Personality and Social Psychology, 53,* 314–317.

Pedhazur, E. J., & Tetenbaum, T. J. (1979). Bem Sex Role Inventory: A theoretical and methodological critique. *Journal of Personality and Social Psychology, 37,* 996–1016.

Peplau, L. A., & Gordon, S. L. (1985). Women and men in love: Gender differences in close heterosexual relationships. In V. E. O'Leary, R. K. Unger, & S. B. Wallston (Eds.), *Women, gender, and social psychology* (pp. 257–291). Hillsdale, NJ: Erlbaum.

Pervin, L. A. (Ed.). (1989). *Goal concepts in personality and social psychology.* Hillsdale, NJ: Erlbaum.

Pleck, J. H. (1984). The theory of male sex role identity: Its rise and fall, 1936 to the present. In M. Lewin (Ed.), *In the shadow of the past: Psychology portrays the sexes* (pp. 205–225). New York: Columbia University Press.

Roopnarine, J. L., & Mounts, N. S. (1987). Current theoretical issues in sex roles and sex typing. In D. B. Carter (Ed.), *Current conceptions of sex roles and sex typing: Theory and research* (pp. 7–32). New York: Praeger.

Rosenberg, R. (1982). *Beyond separate spheres: Intellectual roots of modern feminism.* New Haven, CT: Yale University Press.

Rosenberg, S. (1988). Self and others: Studies in social personality and autobiography. In L. Berkowitz (Ed.), *Advances in experimental social psychology* (Vol. 21, pp. 57–95). San Diego: Academic Press.

Rosenberg, S., & Gara, M. A. (1985). The multiplicity of personal identity. In P. Shaver (Ed.), *Review of personality and social psychology: Vol. 6. Self, situations, and social behavior* (pp. 87–114). Beverly Hills, CA: Sage.

Rosenthal, R., & Rubin, D. B. (1982). A simple, general

purpose display of magnitude of experimental effect. *Journal of Educational Psychology, 74,* 166–169.

Scheinfeld, A. (1943). *Women and men.* New York: Harcourt, Brace.

Schofield, J. W. (1982). *Black and white in school: Trust, tension, or tolerance?* New York: Praeger.

Sedney, M. A. (1989). Conceptual and methodological sources of controversies about androgyny. In R. K. Unger (Ed.). *Representations: Social constructions of gender.* Amityville, NY: Baywood.

Shapiro, P. N., & Penrod, S. (1986). Meta-analysis of facial identification studies. *Psychological Bulletin, 100,* 139–156.

Sherif, C. W. (1982). Needed concepts in the study of gender identity. *Psychology of Women Quarterly, 6,* 375–398.

Shields, S. A. (1975). Functionalism, Darwinism, and the psychology of women: A study in social myth. *American Psychologist, 30,* 739–754.

Shields, S. A. (1982). The variability hypothesis: The history of a biological model of sex differences in intelligence. *Signs, 7,* 769–797.

Spence, J. T. (1983). Comment on Lubinski, Tellegen, and Butcher's "Masculinity, femininity, and androgyny viewed and assessed as distinct concepts." *Journal of Personality and Social Psychology, 44,* 440–446.

Spence, J. T. (1984). Masculinity, feminity and gender-related traits: A conceptual analysis and critique of current research. In B. A. Maher & W. B. Maher (Eds.), *Progress in experimental personality research* (Vol. 13, pp. 1–97). New York: Academic Press.

Spence, J. T. (1985). Gender identity and its implications for the concepts of masculinity and femininity. In T. B. Sonderegger (Ed.), *Nebraska Symposium on Motivation* (Vol. 32, pp. 59–96). Lincoln: University of Nebraska Press.

Spence, J. T. (1988). Janet Taylor Spence, 1923– . In A. N. O'Connell & N. F. Russo (Eds.), *Models of achievement: Reflections of eminent women in psychology* (Vol. 2, pp. 189–204). Hillsdale, NJ: Erlbaum.

Spence, J. T., Deaux, K., & Helmreich, R. L. (1985). Sex roles in contemporary American society. In G. Lindzey & E. Aronson (Eds.), *Handbook of social psychology* (3rd ed., Vol. 2, pp. 149–178). New York: Random House.

Spence, J. T., & Helmreich, R. L. (1972) The Attitudes towards Women Scale: An objective instrument to measure attitudes toward the rights and roles of women in contemporary society. *JSAS: Catalog of Selected Documents in Psychology, 2,* 66 (Ms. No. 153).

Spence, J. T., & Helmreich, R. L. (1978). *Masculinity and femininity: Their psychological dimensions, correlates, and antecedents.* Austin: University of Texas Press.

Spence, J. T., & Helmreich, R. L. (1979). On assessing "androgyny." *Sex Roles, 5,* 721–738.

Spence, J. T., & Helmreich, R. L. (1980). Masculine instrumentality and feminine expressiveness: Their relationships with sex role attitudes and behaviors. *Psychology of Women Quarterly, 5,* 147–163.

Spence, J. T., Helmreich, R. L., & Holahan, C. K. (1979). Negative and positive components of psychological masculinity and femininity and their relationships to self-reports of neurotic and acting-out behaviors. *Journal of Personality and Social Psychology, 37,* 1673–1682.

Spence, J. T., Helmreich, R. L., & Stapp, J. (1974). The Personal Attributes Questionnaire: A measure of sex-role stereotypes and masculinity–femininity. *JSAS: Catalog of Selected Documents in Psychology, 4,* 43. (Ms. No. 617)

Spence, J. T., Helmreich, R. L., & Stapp, J. (1975). Ratings of self and peers on sex-role attributes and their relation to self-esteem and conceptions of masculinity and femininity. *Journal of Personality and Social Psychology, 32,* 29–39.

Spence, J. T., & Sawin, L. L. (1985). Images of masculinity and femininity: A reconceptualization. In V. O'Leary, R. Unger, & B. Wallston (Eds.), *Sex, gender and social psychology* (pp. 35–66). Hillsdale, NJ: Erlbaum.

Stack, C. B. (1986). The culture of gender: Women and men of color. *Signs, 11,* 321–324.

Staines, G. L., & Libby, P. L. (1986). Men and women in role relationships. In R. D. Ashmore & F. K. Del Boca (Eds.), *The social psychology and female–male relations: A critical analysis of central concepts* (pp. 211–258). New York: Academic Press.

Stewart, A. J. (1989, May). *Social change and identity.* Paper presented at Nags Head Conference on Sex and Gender, Nags Head, NC.

Storms, M. D. (1979). Sex role identity and its relationships to sex role attributes and sex role stereotypes. *Journal of Personality and Social Psychology, 37,* 1779–1789.

Tajfel, H. (1981). Social stereotypes and social groups. In J. C. Turner & H. Giles (Eds.). *Intergroup behavior* (pp. 144–167). Chicago: University of Chicago Press.

Taylor, M. C., & Hall, J. A. (1982). Psychological androgyny: Theories, methods, and conclusions. *Psychological Bulletin, 92,* 347–366.

Terman, L. M. (1946). Psychological sex differences. In L. Carmichael (Ed.), *Manual of child psychology* (pp. 954–1000). New York: Wiley.

Terman, L. M., & Merrill, M. A. (1937). *Measuring intelligence.* Boston: Houghton Mifflin.

Terman, L. M., & Miles, C. C. (1936). *Sex and personality.* New York: McGraw-Hill.

Terman, L. M., & Tyler, L. E. (1954). Psychological sex differences. In L. Carmichael (Ed.), *Manual of child psychology* (2nd ed., pp. 1064–1114). New York: Wiley.

Tesser, A. (1988). Toward a self-evaluation maintenance model of social behavior. In L. Berkowitz (Ed.), *Advances in experimental social psychology* (Vol. 21, pp. 181–227). New York: Academic Press.

Thomas, J. R., & French, K. E. (1985). Gender differences across age in motor performance: A meta-analysis. *Psychological Bulletin, 98,* 260–282.

Thompson (Wooley), H. T. (1903). *The mental traits of sex: An experimental investigation of the normal mind in men and women.* Chicago: University of Chicago Press.

Tiefer, L. (1987). Social constructionism and the study of human sexuality. In P. Shaver & C. Hendrick (Eds.), *Review of personality and social psychology: Vol. 7. Sex and gender* (pp. 70–94). Beverly Hills, CA: Sage.

Tyler, L. E. (1965). *The psychology of human differences* (3rd ed.). New York: Appleton-Century-Crofts.

Unger, R. K. (1979). Toward a redefinition of sex and gender. *American Psychologist, 34,* 1085–1094.

Weigert, A. (1983). Identity: Its emergence within sociological psychology. *Symbolic Interaction, 6,* 183–206.

Weil, C. E., & Ashmore, R. D. (1989). *The construction and validation of a measure of self-perception of ability in gender-linked areas.* Unpublished manuscript.

Wellman, B. L. (1933). Sex differences. In C. Murchison (Ed.), *A handbook of child psychology* (Vol. 2, pp. 626–649). New York: Russell & Russell.

Whitley, B. E., Jr. (1983). Sex role orientation and self-esteem: A critical meta-analytic review. *Journal of Personality and Social Psychology, 44,* 765–778.

Whitley, B. E., Jr. (1985). Sex-role orientation and psychological well-being: Two meta-analyses. *Sex Roles, 12,* 207–225.

Whitley, B. E., Jr. (1988). Masculinity, femininity, and self-esteem: A multitrait–multimethod analysis. *Sex Roles, 18,* 419–431.

Whitley, B. E., Jr., McHugh, M. C., & Frieze, I. H. (1986). Assessing the theoretical models for sex differences in causal attributions of success and failure. In J. S. Hyde & M. C. Linn (Eds.), *The psychology of gender: Advances through meta-analysis.* (pp. 102–135). Baltimore: Johns Hopkins University Press.

Willerman, L. (1979). *The psychology of individual and group differences.* San Francisco: W. H. Freeman.

Williams, J. E., & Best, D. L. (1982). *Measuring sex stereotypes: A thirty-nation study.* Beverly Hills, CA: Sage.

Wood, W., Rhodes, N. & Whelan, M. (1989). Sex differences in positive well-being: A meta-analytic review of the effects associated with marital status. *Psychological Bulletin, 106,* 249–264.

Chapter 20

Perspectives on Competence Motivation

Richard Koestner
McGill University
David C. McClelland
Boston University

The study of motivation is concerned with how behavior is energized, sustained, directed, and stopped (Jones, 1955). Despite the fact that motivational questions dominated American psychology for the first half of this century, it has been noted that a comprehensive theoretical framework does not yet exist in the area of human motivation (Brody, 1980). For the purpose of this chapter, we employ the principle of "competence motivation" as our organizing theme. Although this concept is most closely associated with Robert White (1959), it is important to note that other significant motivation theorists such as Murray (1938), Lewin (1951), and Maslow (1943) shared his view of humans as proactive organisms who are motivated to extend their capabilities and to interact with their environment effectively. We briefly review the history of motivational concepts in general, and then go on to consider two bodies of literature that have extensively examined motivational processes related to competence. Specifically, we first outline social-psychological research that has examined

the impact of external events on people's natural tendency to pursue competence goals; this field of study is commonly designated "intrinsic motivation." Second, we review personality research that has examined the correlates of individual differences in achievement motives. Throughout these sections, we discuss other current theories of motivation that are relevant to issues of competence.

A BRIEF HISTORY OF MOTIVATION RESEARCH

Motivational Theories Built on Associative Bonds and Reinforcements

The dominant approaches to motivation during the 1940s and 1950s viewed behavior as regulated by stimulus–response associative bonds that develop through reinforcement processes. Clark Hull (1943) proposed that the occurrence of a particular response is a multiplicative function of drive and habit strength. "Drives" were viewed as the effects of tissue deficits that

527

central nervous system as a persist-
. Drive-related stimuli were said to
avior aimed at reducing the physiological imbalances. The end result of this
motivational sequence is a consummatory response that reduces the physiological need and
brings about learning. "Habits" were defined as
the amount of reinforced practice an animal
has had in making the response previously
(i.e., the strength of associations linking stimulus conditions to particular responses). Over
time, such drive-induced learning gradually
shapes behavior into an economical pursuit of
goal objects.

Operant behavior theory assigned an all-
important role to external stimuli as the key
determinants of behavior and, like Hullian
theory, rejected all explanations of action in
terms of internal forces such as thoughts and
feelings (Skinner, 1953). It was assumed either
that environmental events elicit actions directly as in a reflexive response, or that certain
actions are strengthened by environmental
events in the past (Mook, 1987). Thus, in
order to understand how a particular behavior
is energized and regulated, an operant behaviorist would focus on identifying the environmental conditions that are associated with
the enactment of the given behavior. For example, if an excellent student suddenly began
to achieve lower grades, an operant analysis
would probably examine whether the reinforcement contingencies surrounding school performance and success had been altered in some
way. This analysis would *not* be likely to include inquiries about the student's achievement
concerns or goals for the future.

Theories Focused on Psychological Needs and Goal Selection (Choices)

Drive-reduction-based theories of motivation
held a pre-eminent position in American psychology until critics took aim at their central
proposition: that drive reduction acts as a rein-
forcer and promotes learning. Harlow (1953)
assumed the role of primary antagonist when he
proclaimed that "internal physiological drives
are of little importance to learning and their
small importance steadily decreases as we
ascend the phyletic scale and as we investigate
problems of progressively greater complexity"
(p. 214). In fact, Harlow's experimental work
with monkeys convinced him that it was more

likely that drive state *inhibits* rather than facilitates learning. In place of the hypothesis that
learning is a means of drive reduction, Harlow
(1953) suggested that primate learning is primarily driven by curiosity. Support for this
proposition was provided by numerous studies
showing that monkeys learned to solve puzzles
when no internal drive was present and motivation to learn was provided simply by the presence of the puzzle.

Murray (1938) proposed a theory of motivation that highlighted the role of *psychological*
rather than physiological needs. He argued that
psychological needs (also called "motives")
function as organizing forces that guide mental,
verbal, and physical processes along a certain
course. He defined these psychological needs as
enduring features of personality that energize,
direct, and select behavior and experience.
Needs are triggered by environmental forces,
called "press," that can be real or perceived and
that have arousing properties (Murray &
Kluckhohn, 1953). Although Murray identified over 40 psychological needs, only 4 have
received extensive research attention—the
needs for achievement, power, affiliation, and
self-determination. Murray (1938) and others
who have followed in his tradition, such as
McClelland (1985) and White (1975), have
stressed that the role of stable underlying motive dispositions in guiding behavior can be
most clearly identified when one studies an
individual's behavior over an extended period
of time.

Robert White (1959) delivered the *coup de
grace* to orthodox drive-reduction-based theories of motivation in his classic paper, "Motivation Reconsidered: The Concept of Competence," where he identified two fatal flaws in
these theories: (1) Exploratory drives bear no
relation to tissue deficits; and (2) exploratory
behaviors do not lead to any consummatory
response. White offered a very different picture
of human motivation; he insisted that humans,
instead of seeking to reduce tension by satisfying physiological needs, cherish the experience
of raised tension and mild excitement. In fact,
he argued that humans have an innate tendency to strive to exercise and extend their
capabilities. White referred to the energy behind this tendency as "competence motivation"
and to the corresponding affect as "feelings of
efficacy." The paradigmatic example of com-
petence-motivated behavior is the play of
young children. This type of behavior serves a

useful adaptive function, because it enables the children to steadily build up their capacities in relation to the world.

Associative theories of motivation, as outlined by Hull and Skinner, were also assailed by theorists who emphasized the central role of cognition in the determination of behavior. Kurt Lewin (1935) argued that cognitions rather than "drive–response associative links" are the key building blocks of motivated behavior. He asserted that in order to understand the spontaneity and variability of human behavior, it is necessary to assume that internal forces, such as wishes, urges, and desires, play a significant role in the determination of action. Lewin (1951) was particularly struck by humans' capacity to engage in intentional, goal-directed action. He proposed that people behave when they have intentions or goals and that they persist until they have carried out their intentions, even trivial or nonsensical ones.

Lewin (1951) also noted that environmental events "are not neutral to us in our role as acting beings . . . they challenge us to certain activities" (p. 117). The intensity with which events challenge us varies from "irresistible attraction" to "mild inclination," depending on the internal situation of the person. This variation in challenge or attraction has commonly been referred to as the "valence" or "value" of an object or event. A number of motivational theories have employed the concepts of expectancies and valence as the fundamental principles of motivated behavior. Expectancy–value theories assume that one's tendency to perform a particular activity is a joint function of the strength of one's expectancies that these actions will lead to specific outcomes and the subjectively perceived values of these outcomes.

Social-cognitive approaches to motivation, as elaborated by Julian Rotter (1966), Walter Mischel (1973), and Albert Bandura (1977), argued that expectancies of future reinforcements rather than one's history of past reinforcements (as argued by Skinner, 1953) provide the motivational impetus for behavior. The central proposition of these approaches is that the regulation of behavior is guided by people's self-imposed goals and the consequences that ensue from them. Bandura (1977, 1982) also assigns a central role to efficacy beliefs in determining whether particular goals will be pursued and achieved. "Perceived self-efficacy" refers to judgments of how well one can perform actions required to deal with a prospective situation. In Bandura's view, it is not sufficient merely to expect that particular outcomes covary with particular behaviors; one must also believe that one is capable of carrying out the requisite instrumental actions

Current Approaches

A focus on psychological needs and/or goals has replaced the earlier emphasis on associative bonds and reinforcement processes in the study of human motivation. The focus on psychological needs derives primarily from Murray's seminal *Explorations in Personality*, whereas it can be suggested that current goal theories have their origins in the work of Kurt Lewin. Theories built on psychological needs and goals share a belief that people's thoughts, feelings, and desires play a dominant role in the regulation of behavior. The present chapter adopts a focus that highlights the role of psychological needs in the energization and maintenance of competence-related behaviors. For those readers who would like more information on goal theories of motivation we recommend a recent edited volume by Pervin (1989), which provides an excellent review of current theories in social and personality psychology that are built around goal concepts. Furthermore, for a more extensive historical review of motivational concepts, see Cofer (1985).

INTRINSIC MOTIVATION

Intrinsic motivation is based in innate, organismic needs for competence and self-determination (Deci & Ryan, 1985). These needs provide the impetus for an ongoing cyclical process of seeking out and attempting to master optimal challenges. This view of humans can be placed within a humanistic motivational tradition that emphasizes the person's being an active agent, oriented toward growth and toward choosing how to behave on the basis of evaluating both inner psychological needs and opportunities present in the environment (Mook, 1987). A central theme in humanistic theories is the idea that social and environmental forces may actually prevent the emergence of a person's human nature (Rogers, 1963). In this vein, early research on intrinsic motivation examined the thwarting effects of various forms of social control on people's natural tendency to persist at challenging and interesting activities. In this research, "intrinsically motivated behavior" has been operationally defined as those actions that are performed in the absence of any external contingencies. Stated differently, they include behaviors in which satisfaction is concurrent with one's involvement in the activity, rather than being linked to some separable effect of the activity.

The Effects of Rewards and Constraints

An early study by Deci (1971) showed that college student subjects who received a monetary reward for playing with an interesting puzzle subsequently displayed diminished levels of behavioral interest for the puzzles during a free-choice period, compared to subjects who were unrewarded. A parallel field study conducted at a school newspaper found similar undermining effects related to the administration of monetary rewards (Deci, 1971). It was soon shown that other forms of rewards, such as prizes or good-player awards, produced similar undermining effects (Harackiewicz, 1979; Lepper, Greene, & Nisbett, 1973). The negative effects of rewards were particularly pronounced when they were expected (Lepper et al., 1973), salient (Ross, 1975), and contingent on task engagement (Ryan, Mims, & Koestner, 1983). These results were originally explained by Deci (1975), who suggested that the experience of being rewarded led people to shift the perceived locus of causality for their puzzle playing from internal ("I played because I find these puzzles interesting") to external ("I played because I was being paid to do so"). Since people make choices about their behavior on the basis of perceptions, the person who has shifted to an external locus of causality will pursue the activity only when he or she thinks a reward will be forthcoming.

If rewards can undermine intrinsic motivation, it should follow that more blatant forms of social control will lead to an external perceived locus of causality and produce similar negative consequences. In fact, studies showed that threats (Deci, Cascio, & Krusell, 1975), deadlines (Amabile, DeJong, & Lepper, 1976), evaluation (Harackiewicz, Manderlink, & Sansone, 1984), surveillance (Lepper & Greene, 1975), and explicit competition (Deci, Betley, Kahle, Abrams, & Porac, 1981) all resulted in diminished intrinsic motivation. By contrast, providing subjects with choice about which activities to pursue led to enhanced intrinsic motivation (Zuckerman, Porac, Lathin, Smith, & Deci, 1978), presumably by facilitating a shift toward a more internal perceived locus of causality.

Cognitive-Evaluation Theory

Deci and Ryan (1980) proposed that intrinsic motivation is a function of the extent to which circumstances allow a person to experience feelings of challenge, competence, and self-determination. If a task is optimally challenging it should generally stimulate intrinsic motivation because it provides the person with the greatest opportunity to stretch his or her capacities (Csikszentmihalyi, 1975). If external events enhance feelings of competence, as when someone is told he or she has done a task very well, intrinsic motivation is likely to increase. By contrast, events that lead to feelings of incompetence are likely to undermine intrinsic motivation. It should be noted that Bandura's (1982) self-efficacy theory converges with cognitive-evaluation theory up to this point. Bandura (1989) suggests that motivation for an activity will be at its peak when strong self-efficacy beliefs are combined with some moderate uncertainty about the outcome (i.e., when a person feels competent and challenged). Cognitive-evaluation theory departs from Bandura's analysis in its assertion that feelings of self-determination are a *necessary* condition for intrinsic motivation to flourish. Thus, even if an activity is challenging and a person perceives himself or herself to be highly competent, the person will not display high levels of intrinsic motivation unless the performance of the activity is experienced as self-determined. For example, a child who has been pressured by demanding parents to master a challenging musical instrument is unlikely to continue playing the instrument when the external controls are removed (e.g., when he or she goes off to college and can no longer be closely observed by the parents).

Cognitive-evaluation theory also asserts that the way people interpret an external event, rather than its objective features, is the key determinant of how it will affect motivation.

This proposition suggests that personality factors may influence the relative salience of the competence-relevant and autonomy-relevant features of a particular external event. Thus, whereas one person might experience praise from a supervisor as a reflection of his or her own competence, another might view it as a form of interpersonal control that infringes on his or her self-determination. The emphasis on interpretation also implies that the nature of the interpersonal and intrapersonal context in which an external event is embedded will greatly affect whether it is perceived as supporting autonomy or controlling behavior (i.e., pressuring a person toward a specified outcome). Each of these hypotheses has received considerable empirical attention.

Competence Feedback and Intrinsic Motivation

Cognitive-evaluation theory (Deci & Ryan, 1980, 1985) and Bandura's self-efficacy theory both make the prediction that receiving competence feedback for one's performance serves to promote and maintain intrinsic motivation for an activity. Support for this prediction comes from several studies showing that positive competence feedback enhances intrinsic motivation relative to negative or neutral feedback (Boggiano & Ruble, 1979; Deci, 1972; Vallerand & Reid, 1984). However, the literature suggests that two personality factors may moderate the relation between performance feedback and intrinsic motivation: gender and attributional style.

Several studies have found that males respond more favorably to positive verbal feedback than do females (Deci, 1972; Deci, Cascio, & Krusell, 1975; Zinser, Young, & King, 1982). It has been suggested that because of traditional sex-role socialization practices, the competence aspect of praise may be more salient to males, whereas the controlling aspect is more salient to females (Deci & Ryan, 1985). This results in males' and females' often making different interpretations of the meaning of praise: Males view it as an affirmation of their competence at the activity, which translates into heightened intrinsic motivation; females understand the praise to mean that they are being controlled, which results in diminished feelings of self-determination, which in turn undermines their intrinsic motivation. More recent work suggests that the way in which feedback is delivered will determine whether sex differences will be found. Thus, Kast and Conner (1988) showed that ambiguous performance feedback, which contained *both* controlling and informational elements, led to diminished intrinsic motivation for females relative to males. When performance feedback was either clearly controlling or noncontrolling, no sex differences emerged (Ryan, 1982).

A person's attributions regarding performance outcomes may also moderate the relation between performance feedback and intrinsic motivation. Two studies showed that children with an internal locus of control responded more favorably to praise for their performance than did children with an external locus of control (Baron & Ganz, 1972; Danner & Lonky, 1981). Similarly, Zuckerman, Larrance, Porac, and Blanck (1980) found that following positive feedback, subjects who did not fear success displayed greater intrinsic motivation than did those who were afraid of success. Most recently, Koestner, Zuckerman, and Olsson (in press) showed that college students who customarily attributed their achievement successes to internal causes responded better to social comparison praise than to mastery-focused praise, whereas those subjects who were reluctant to take credit for their successes showed the reverse pattern. Thus, the degree to which people are comfortable with accepting credit for positive performance outcomes seems to exert considerable influence on the relation between competence feedback and intrinsic motivation.

Interpersonal Context and Intrinsic Motivation

Several studies have examined whether the interpersonal context in which external inputs are received will influence their motivational impact. For example, two studies showed that performance feedback administered in a noncontrolling interpersonal context led to greater intrinsic motivation than did similar feedback administered in a controlling context (Pittman, Davey, Alafat, Wetherill, & Kramer, 1980; Ryan, 1982). Similarly, Ryan et al. (1983) found that performance-contingent rewards delivered in a controlling interpersonal context diminished intrinsic motivation, relative to comparable rewards delivered in a more autonomy-supportive context. In each of these studies, a controlling context was created by having the experimenter emphasize that he had expectations concerning how the subject *should* perform. Finally, a study by Koestner, Ryan, Bernieri, and Holt (1984) showed that if behavioral limits minimized the use of controlling imperatives and also acknowledged children's conflicting feelings, they did not have a negative impact on the children's intrinsic motivation for a painting activity.

Intrapersonal Events and Intrinsic Motivation

Ryan (1982) proposed that the experience of being ego-involved with an activity causes people to pressure themselves in a way that is similar to the pressure exerted by external evaluation and surveillance. He followed deCharms (1968) in using the term "ego involvement" to refer to a condition in which a person's self-esteem evaluations hinge upon attaining a specified performance outcome. By contrast, a state of "task involvement" is said to exist when a person is absorbed in an activity because of its inherent qualities, such as its interest value or level of challenge. In one study, Ryan (1982) induced ego involvement by suggesting to subjects that some interesting hidden-figure puzzles were a test of creative intelligence." Subjects in a task-involving condition were merely given some information about how the puzzles were created. The results showed that ego-involved subjects reported significantly more pressure and tension than task-involved ones, and also subsequently displayed less free-choice intrinsic motivation. Two studies using nearly identical procedures replicated the undermining effect of ego involvement relative to task involvement (Koestner, Zuckerman, & Koestner, 1987; Plant & Ryan, 1985).

Nicholls (1984) proposed that the two types of involvement differentially affect the way in which a person thinks about his or her level of competence. He defines ego-involving situations as those where a person's goal is to demonstrate high competence relative to others and where mastery of the task is only a means to this end. Task-involving situations are those in which a person's concern is to learn to perform the activity and where mastery of the task is an end in itself. The way in which people use performance attributions to make judgments about their level of competence is dramatically different, depending on whether the person is ego-involved or task-involved. Jagacinski and Nicholls (1984) demonstrated that under task-involving conditions, self-perceptions of high effort led to positive affect and judgments of high competence; under ego-involving conditions, higher effort was associated with the experience of lower competence and more negative affect. Koestner et al. (1987) recently extended Nicholls's analysis to the realm of intrinsic motivation. Their results showed that the motivational impact of effort-focused praise depended on whether the person who received it was task-involved or ego-involved. Subjects who were task-involved interpreted effort praise as competence feedback and showed high levels of intrinsic motivation after receiving it. By contrast, if subjects approached the activity in an ego-involved manner, effort-focused praise had a substantially demotivating impact: The subjects displayed less intrinsic motivation, were reluctant to pursue challenge, and evidenced a marked performance decrement at a subsequent task.

Learning versus Performance Goals

Whereas Ryan (1982) distinguished ego and task involvement in terms of their differential impact on feelings of self-determination, thus incorporating them into the framework of cognitive-evaluation theory, an alternative theoretical account distinguishes the two types of involvement in terms of goals. Dweck and Leggett (1988) recently suggested that there are two important classes of goals in the achievement domain: (1) "performance goals," wherein an individual is concerned with gaining favorable judgments of his or her competence; and (2) "learning goals," wherein people are concerned with increasing their competence or mastery at an activity. Stated differently, people can be cued into either *proving* their ability or *improving* their ability. Within this framework, task involvement would be categorized as a special case of learning goals, whereas ego involvement is more representative of performance goals. Dweck and Leggett (1988) review evidence indicating that performance goals are likely to lead to a maladaptive pattern of achievement behavior when an individual is faced with difficult tasks. Specifically, children with a performance orientation have been shown to display a helpless motivational pattern, characterized by avoidance of challenges and markedly impaired performance, when confronted with obstacles. Learning goals, by contrast, lead people to assume a mastery-oriented pattern of thoughts, feelings, and behaviors, whereby challenge is pursued vigorously and obstacles to goal attainment are met with resilient and renewable effort. Dweck and Leggett (1988) provide further evidence that these two types of goal orientations are largely determined by children's implicit theories of intelligence. Conceptualizing intelligence as a fixed entity that cannot be changed leads to the adoption of performance goals, whereas viewing intelligence as a malleable, improvable characteristic is associated with the learning goal of developing that characteristic.

Processes Related to Intrinsic Motivation

Conditions that give rise to intrinsically motivated behavior also seem to promote adaptive functioning in a number of other ways. Studies typically show, for example, that people who behave in an intrinsically motivated fashion also report greater feelings of interest and enjoyment in their activities (Harackiewicz, 1979). People who are intrinsically motivated to perform an activity show the following distinctive characteristics: (1) They tend to prefer having a choice about what they will do next (Haddad, 1982); (2) when given a range of options, they will choose tasks that are challenging (Koestner et al., 1987; Shapira, 1976); (3) they respond with greater effort and persistence after failure (Boggiano & Barrett, 1985); (4) they show increased capacity for conceptual learning (Grolnick & Ryan, 1987); (5) they display greater cognitive flexibility in their problem-solving attempts (Condry, 1977; McGraw & McCullers, 1979); and (6) they display higher levels of creativity, spontaneity, and expressiveness (Amabile, 1983; Koestner et al., 1984).

The beneficial effects of maintaining an intrinsic motivational orientation toward one's activities have been demonstrated beyond the confines of the laboratory as well. Thus, conditions that give rise to an intrinsic motivational orientation have been shown to promote (1) feelings of self-esteem and perceived competence among schoolchildren (Deci, Nezlek,

& Sheinman, 1981); (2) the maintenance of treatment gains among weight loss patients (Dienstbier & Leak, 1976); and (3) psychological and physical well-being among elderly nursing home residents (Langer & Rodin, 1976; Rodin & Langer, 1977).

Motivational Orientation and Social Functioning

A handful of studies have applied the distinction between intrinsic and extrinsic motivational orientations to the study of personal relationships. Garbarino (1975) showed that fifth-grade girls who were promised a reward for tutoring a younger peer subsequently behaved in a more critical and demanding manner than girls who were not promised a reward. In another study, it was shown that children who were induced to interact with another child in order to gain access to an attractive game had a less positive impression of that child than did children who were not focused on an extrinsic incentive (Boggiano, Klinger, & Main, 1985). Motivational orientations may also play a significant role in the development and course of close relationships (Pittman & Heller, 1987). Two studies indicate that intrinsically motivated couples (where the relationship is perceived as chosen and as satisfying in and of itself) report greater feelings of love than couples who approach their relationship in a more extrinsic, utilitarian fashion (Rempel, Holmes, & Zanna, 1985; Seligman, Fazio, & Zanna (1980).

Applications to Education, Work, and Sports

A great deal of current research is aimed at applying principles drawn from research on intrinsic motivation to realms such as athletics, education, and work. For example, a number of studies suggest that athletes are more likely to persist at their sporting endeavors if they approach their training with an intrinsic rather than an extrinsic motivational orientation (Vallerand, Deci, & Ryan, 1987). Furthermore, employees of a large corporation were found to be more satisfied and trusting if their managers supported their autonomy (Deci, Connell, & Ryan, 1989). In the educational realm, studies indicate that teaching styles that encourage an intrinsic orientation are associated with superior school adjustment, compared to styles that make extensive use of controlling contingencies (deCharms, 1976; Ryan, Connell, & Deci, 1985). Similarly, parenting styles that are autonomy-oriented foster intrinsic motivation and promote superior school adjustment among grade-schoolers (Grolnick & Ryan, 1989). Most impressively, deCharms (1981) reported that inner-city boys whose teachers had emphasized self-direction in grade school were more likely than other such boys to graduate from high school.

Internalization Processes

Most teachers and parents would agree that promoting intrinsic motivation in children is a wonderful ideal; however, they will then quickly point out that there are many things a child must do that are neither interesting nor challenging (e.g., "How do I get Johnny intrinsically motivated to clean his room?"). Parents and teachers feel they are responsible for shaping children's behavior in a socially acceptable direction. Schools are expected to ensure that children follow rules and to work diligently at learning tasks that are patently uninteresting (e.g., multiplication tables). Ryan et al. (1985) have extended the theory of intrinsic motivation to a consideration of the processes by which extrinsic regulation of behavior can be gradually transformed into internalized forms of self-regulation. These authors define "internalization" as "an organismic process by which children assimilate the socializing environment and accommodate to its demands and affordances" (p. 33). The following internalization continuum is proposed (from the most external to the most fully internalized level): (1) "external regulation," in which prescribed behaviors are performed solely on the basis of extrinsic contingencies; (2) "introjected regulation," in which a person uses contingent self-approval or disapproval to regulate his or her behavior; (3) "identification," in which a formerly extrinsic regulation is experienced as one's own value or goal; and (4) "integration," in which one's various internalized goals are integrated with one another into a coherent hierarchy that is free of conflict. The internalization process is facilitated by interpersonal environments that provide structure while at the same time supporting feelings of autonomy and relatedness (Grolnick & Ryan, 1989).

INDIVIDUAL DIFFERENCES IN COMPETENCE MOTIVES

The preceding review suggests the importance of distinguishing between competence goals that arise within an intrinsic as opposed to an extrinsic motivational framework. This section considers the hypothesis that an individual's need for competence can develop over time in a predominantly intrinsic or extrinsic direction, and that these trends can be measured as stable individual differences. It is further assumed that these individual differences will largely determine the form and function of a person's competence behaviors.

The primary goals for intrinsically oriented competence motivation are to improve one's skills and to accomplish tasks more effectively. This form of competence motivation has the following characteristics: (1) It is energized by natural incentives for variety and challenge; (2) it is associated with the feelings of interest and surprise; and (3) it leads to a subjective state of feeling curious or exploratory (McClelland, 1985). Once a person is engaged with an activity, this intrinsic form of competence motivation is primarily guided by self-reactions (e.g., feelings of satisfaction as the person accomplishes, or anticipates accomplishing, the task successfully). We propose that the "implicit" need for achievement, as coded from associative thought content, is currently the best method for assessing individual differences in this form of competence motivation.

The second form of competence motivation is more extrinsic and outcome-focused in nature. Here the primary goal is to behave in a competent manner as defined by the particular situation or as accepted as a part of the person's self-image. Rather than cherishing the *process* of performing an activity, extrinsically oriented people behave as they believe they are supposed to. This extrinsic form of competence motivation is governed by an acquired desire to perform like an achiever, rather than by the natural incentives of challenge and variety. Instead of being associated with interest, the extrinsic form of competence motivation is likely to be associated with feelings of pressure and tension. Once a person is engaged with an activity, this extrinsic form of competence motivation is primarily guided by social reactions (e.g., feelings of pride when the person is recognized for one's accomplishment and of shame if recognition is not forthcoming).

We propose that this form of "self-attributed" achievement or competence motivation is best assessed via self-report inventories such as the Personal Preference Schedule (Edwards, 1954) or the Personality Research Form (Jackson, 1974). We now review what is known about individual differences in these two forms of motivation.

Achievement Motivation

McClelland, Atkinson, Clark, and Lowell (1953) sought to examine the unique effects on fantasy of arousing the motive to achieve. Attempts were made to arouse the achievement motive by telling young men that performance tests they were taking would yield information pertaining to their general intelligence and leadership abilities, and then by manipulating the amount of success and failure feedback they received. Shortly afterward, subjects were asked to write brief, 5-minute stories to a series of four to six Thematic Apperception Test (TAT) picture cues. Stories written under arousal conditions contained many more references to doing things better than did those written under nonarousal, neutral conditions. Further analysis revealed that the fantasies of aroused subjects were more likely to include details such as whether a character in the story anticipated positive feelings at success, behaved in a way to promote success, and showed the capacity to overcome obstacles on the road to accomplishment. These detailed differences were incorporated into an overall "need for achievement" (n Ach) score, which reflected the number of stories containing imagery about doing things better and the extent to which these images were elaborated into a sequence of achievement-related thoughts, feelings, and behavior by characters in the story.

Murray (1938) had originally defined the need for achievement as the desire "to overcome obstacles, to exercise power, to strive to do something difficult as well and as quickly as possible" (p. 49). His was a dictionary definition that included references to imagery such as "exercising power," which did not differentiate the stories of those in whom the achievement motive was aroused. In contrast, McClelland et al. (1953) offered a definition that was limited to summarizing the empirical differences obtained in stories written under aroused and neutral conditions: "a concern with doing

things better, with surpassing standards of excellence" (p. 228).

Further research on the fantasy measure of n Ach indicated that the scoring criteria were objective enough so that high levels of interrater agreement could be attained. Successful replications of the effect of achievement arousal on fantasy thought content have been obtained with female subjects (Stewart & Chester, 1982) and with people from countries as diverse as Germany (Heckhausen, 1967), Japan (Hayashi & Habu, 1962), Poland (Krol, 1981), India (Mehta, 1969), and Brazil (Angelini, 1959). From the theoretical point of view, successful cross-cultural replications are of crucial importance, since they show that the effects on associative thought of arousing the achievement motive are the same, regardless of social, cultural, or linguistic definitions of the concepts of "success" or "achievement."

The fantasy measure of n Ach has traditionally been used as an index of dispositional motivation rather than as a measure of aroused, state-like motivation. Although the psychometric credentials of fantasy-derived measures have frequently been criticized (e.g., Entwisle, 1972), a number of more recent, carefully conducted methodological studies have led to the following conclusions: (1) The test—retest reliability of TAT measures of social motives is acceptably high when these measures are administered under standardized conditions and the retest instructions explicitly state that subjects can tell stories similar to the ones they told their first time (Heckhausen, Schmalt, & Schneider, 1985; Lundy, 1985; McClelland, 1985; Winter & Stewart, 1977); and (2) TAT motive measures display excellent construct validity despite poor internal consistency (Atkinson, 1981). (For a full discussion of psychometric issues related to the fantasy assessment of motives, see Atkinson, Bongort, & Price, 1977; Lundy, 1988; McClelland, 1985.)

Characteristics of Achievement-Motivated Individuals

Initial validation studies focused on showing that the need for achievement functioned like a biological drive in the sense of energizing, directing, and selecting behavior (McClelland et al., 1953). That is, a strong achievement motive should make one active in pursuing achievement goals, sensitive to cues related to achievement, and quick to learn what is necessary to reach an achievement goal (Biernat, 1989). Early evidence provided support for each of these functions: (1) Individuals scoring high on n Ach were more physiologically aroused while concentrating at a task than were individuals with low n Ach scores (Mücher & Heckhausen, 1962); (2) achievement-motivated subjects identified tachistiscopically presented achievement-related words more quickly than their peers with low n Ach scores (McClelland & Liberman, 1949); (3) numerous studies showed that subjects with high n Ach scores outperformed those with low n Ach scores at a variety of activities (McClelland et al., 1953).

As support for our contention that the n Ach measure reflects an intrinsic form of competence motivation, we would like to focus attention on the many characteristics that individuals scoring high on n Ach share with people who are intrinsically motivated. Most strikingly, the three defining features of intrinsically motivated behavior have also been shown to characterize individuals who are high in achievement motivation: (1) They pursue optimal challenges (Atkinson, 1957; Cooper, 1983); (2) they prefer to function in a self-determined manner (Feld, 1967; McKeachie, 1961; Rokeach, 1973); and (3) they are very interested in receiving performance feedback (French, 1958; McClelland, 1961). Further similarities include the findings that individuals with high n Ach scores are likely to (1) display greater innovativeness in problem solving (Sinha & Mehta, 1972); (2) attribute their successes to ability factors (Heckhausen et al., 1985); and (3) energetically persist in the face of failure (French & Thomas, 1958; Weiner, 1966). Finally, there are some striking parallels between developmental factors found to promote achievement motivation and those that are hypothesized to foster the development of intrinsic motivation. Specifically, two types of parenting behaviors have been shown to lead to the development of achievement motivation: (1) placing an emphasis on independence training (especially in decision making), and (2) setting challenging standards for achievement (Heckhausen, 1982). Both of these parental characteristics have also been hypothesized to foster children's intrinsic motivation (Deci & Ryan, 1985; Grolnick & Ryan, in press).

Achievement Motivation and the Pursuit of Challenge

Of all of the characteristics associated with achievement motivation, challenge preferences have received the most extensive theoretical attention. The definition of n Ach implies that people who score high on this dimension will be drawn to activities that are moderately difficult. That is, if the incentive is "to do better," neither a very easy nor a very difficult task will offer much opportunity for gratification. A large number of studies indicate that the achievement motive influences difficulty preferences and goal aspirations. For example, in a study examining children's risk preferences at a variety of tasks (ring toss, mazes, dot connections), McClelland (1958) found that children with a strong achievement motive tended to take moderate risks, whereas children with a weak achievement motive preferred either very safe or very speculative enterprises. Several other studies have replicated these risk-taking patterns for high- and low-need achievers (Atkinson & Litwin, 1960; Clark, Teevan, & Ricciuti, 1956; Cooper, 1983). Furthermore, the relation of achievement motivation to risk preferences has also been demonstrated beyond the confines of the laboratory. Thus, young adults who are high in achievement motivation are especially likely to choose college majors of intermediate difficulty (Issaccson, 1964) and to aspire to vocations of moderate difficulty (Morris, 1966).

In a classic 1957 paper, Atkinson proposed a theoretical model to explain the relation of achievement motivation to risk preference. He suggested that the strength of preference for various activities is a joint function of the motive to achieve success (Ms), the expectancy or probability of success (Ps), and the incentive value of success (Is), where incentive value is defined as 1 minus the probability of success $(1 - Ps)$. In other words, it is assumed that the value of success is directly proportional to its difficulty. Using this formula, it can be seen that if the probability of success is moderate $(Ps = .50)$, the product of $Ps \times Is$ is maximal, explaining why moderately difficult tasks offer the largest incentive value. If the motive to achieve success is higher, as in those with high n Ach scores, the preference for moderately difficult tasks should be even greater.

It has been argued that other aspects of an

individual's personality need to be considered before accurate predictions can be made regarding the relation between *n* Ach scores and difficulty preferences. For example, Kuhl (1978) has emphasized the importance of considering *subjective* standards of difficulty. Such emphasis seems warranted, given the findings in several studies that achievement-motivated individuals initially estimate tasks as easier than people with low *n* Ach scores do (McClelland, 1985). Sorrentino and Short (1986) propose that a separate construct labeled "uncertainty orientation" should be used in conjunction with the traditional measure of *n* Ach. They theorized that need for achievement primarily reflects the affective value a person derives from success, whereas uncertainty orientation assesses the cognitive value people place on performance outcomes. Thus, people with high *n* Ach scores are expected to pursue moderately difficult tasks only if they are also oriented toward uncertainty rather than certainty—toward finding out what their abilities really are, rather than to confirming previously held beliefs about these abilities.

Achievement Motivation and Performance

The central proposition of early research was that individuals who are high scorers on the *n* Ach measure should generally perform better at achievement-oriented activities than those who are low scorers (Lowell, 1952). Numerous studies can be cited in support of this hypothesis (see Biernat, 1989 and Cooper, 1983, for recent examples). In fact, the support is so strong that Sorrentino and Higgins (1986) recently concluded that "the projective measure of *n* Ach continues to be the single best predictor of actual performance in achievement-oriented activity" (p. 16). Although we agree with this assessment, it is important to point out that the relationship between achievement motivation and performance is conditional on, or bounded by, other factors. Here we follow Wright and Mischel (1987) when they suggest that dispositional constructs should be viewed as clusters of if–then propositions, in which the contingency between the disposition (achievement motivation) and the disposition-relevant behavior (better performance) is conditional on certain factors in the situation. The interesting thing is that the conditional relationship between achievement motivation

and better performance hinges on precisely those situational factors that have been linked to intrinsic motivation—challenge, self-determination, and competence feedback. That is, in order for a person's achievement motivation to be aroused the person must consider himself or herself personally responsible for the outcome; must perceive some, but not too much, risk concerning chances of success; and must have some knowledge of the outcome (McClelland, 1961).

An early study by Clark and McClelland (1956) was designed to test the prediction that individuals with high *n* Ach scores would outperform those scoring low on *n* Ach at an anagrams task. Surprisingly, this prediction was confirmed only on those words that were moderately difficult. No performance differences due to *n* Ach scores were found on either the very easy or the very difficult anagrams. Another study by Karabenick and Youseff (1968) found that subjects with high *n* Ach scores outperformed those with low *n* Ach scores when learning moderately difficult paired associates, but not when performing either very easy or very difficult pairs. The moderating role of level of challenge on the relation between achievement motivation and performance has been confirmed in other studies (Atkinson, 1958; McClelland, Koestner, & Weinberger, 1989; Raynor & Entin, 1982).

With regard to the importance of self-determination in sustaining achievement motivation, it was quickly established that when extrinsic social controls were placed on individuals scoring high on *n* Ach, they no longer performed better than those scoring low on *n* Ach (McClelland et al., 1953). A variety of other controlling external contingencies have been shown to undermine the efforts of achievement-oriented individuals to perform well: (1) pressure to hurry (Schroth, 1988; Wendt, 1955); (2) an authoritarian organizational structure (Andrews, 1967); (3) extraneous incentives such as money (Atkinson, 1958; Douvan, 1956); and (4) a competitive goal structure (Groszko & Morgenstern, 1974). Such findings led McClelland (1985) to conclude that only if a person scoring high on *n* Ach feels personally responsible for a performance outcome is he or she likely to derive any satisfaction from doing something better.

The final boundary condition that moderates the relation between achievement motivation and performance is whether the situation provides competence feedback. For example, French (1958) showed that individuals with high n Ach scores performed more efficiently after receiving performance feedback rather than after receiving affiliative feedback, whereas subjects with low n Ach scores showed the reverse pattern. In a more applied setting, Bartmann (1965) found that children high on n Ach profited more than children low on n Ach from programmed instruction in which a teaching machine gave immediate feedback on the correctness of each step taken to learn something.

Why Has Need for Achievement Consistently Failed to Predict Performance in School?

The most damaging criticism of achievement motivation theory is that it has failed to predict school performance (Entwisle, 1972). It is rather surprising that prediction of school performance has been used as a litmus test of the utility of the "need for achievement" construct. After all, the original investigators of the achievement motive cautioned researchers against expecting a straightforward linear relationship between n Ach scores and school performance (McClelland et al., 1953): "The relation of n Ach scores to college grades is obviously of great practical importance. On the other hand, it is of dubious theoretical significance since grades are affected by so many unknown factors" (p. 237).

McClelland (1961) later made the point that the kind of motivation represented in a high n Ach score may not be particularly welcome in many academic settings. People with high n Ach scores like to solve problems set by themselves; high grades often require skill in taking exams, in following instructions, and in finding solutions set by others. It has been suggested that the need for affiliation and the need for power could just as easily be expected to promote excellent school performance, given certain conditions (Gallimore, 1981). The best empirical illustration of the fact that many different motives can lead to school success was provided by a study by McKeachie (1961) in which he showed that, given certain conditions, school performance could be predicted on the basis of high need for power (if the classroom setting provided the opportunity to talk), high need for affiliation (if the classroom climate was warm and friendly), or high need

for achievement (if the classroom setting was autonomy-supportive).

Why does the achievement motive construct continue to be excoriated for failing to directly predict something that it was never expected to predict? Perhaps, as Gallimore (1981) suggested, the label "achievement motivation" was poorly chosen because it so easily overgeneralizes to include all motivations to achieve. McClelland (1985) recently confessed that he wished he had used the label "efficiency motive," since the notion of doing things better involves efficiency calculations, whereas "achievement" is a more generic term that can be applied to achieving goals for any motive.

The analysis above gives some clear guidelines for investigators to follow when seeking to establish a relation between achievement motivation and performance in school. A positive relationship will be found only when the school context supports autonomy, provides challenge, and offers frequent performance feedback. The study by McKeachie (1961) described above, and another by O'Connor, Atkinson, and Horner (1966), provide support for the role of self-determination and challenge in facilitating the expression of achievement motivation in the direction of excellent school performance.

Achievement Motivation and Entrepreneurial Activities

The status of the achievement motive as an intrinsic competence motive is further supported by the role it plays in career choice and success. Although need for achievement has sometimes been associated with managerial and executive success, it is particularly in the realm of entrepreneurial activity that the achievement motivation construct has shown the greatest explanatory power. This is not surprising when one considers that operating a small business offers precisely those conditions under which people with high n Ach scores have been found to thrive: (1) the opportunity to take moderate risks while pursuing challenging activities; (2) responsibility for initiating actions; and (3) objective feedback on the success of decisions. Studies in several countries have shown that young men with high n Ach scores are more attracted to business occupations than their peers with low n Ach scores (McClelland, 1987). Furthermore, longitudinal studies have shown that college-age men who were high on *n* Ach were significantly more likely to be found in business occupations 14 years later, compared to men who were low on *n* Ach (McClelland, 1965).

Not only are achievement-motivated men drawn to business careers, they also seem to excel at them. The fantasy measure of *n* Ach has been shown to predict entrepreneurial activity over time in the United States (Durand, 1975; McClelland, 1965) and in India (McClelland, 1987). Studies with farmers (who can be classified as operators of small businesses) have shown that those with high *n* Ach scores are more likely to adopt innovative agricultural practices (Sinha & Mehta, 1972) and to show improved productivity over time (Singh, 1979). The relation between *n* Ach scores and entrepreneurial activity holds up even when the analysis is conducted at the level of cultural comparisons. Thus, McClelland (1961) showed that among preliterate tribes, 75% of those with high levels of achievement imagery in their folk tales were characterized as having at least some full-time entrepreneurs, as contrasted with only 38% of tribes with low levels of achievement imagery in their folk tales.

Further evidence of the strong association between the achievement motive and entrepreneurial success comes from several studies that have documented the positive effects of achievement motivation training in business and sales. These training programs led to increased productivity and effectiveness among operators of small businesses, particularly if they were in a position of authority where they could pursue their goals in a self-determined manner (McClelland & Winter, 1969). The benefits of achievement training for entrepreneurs have been confirmed in various countries around the world (McClelland, 1965; Miron & McClelland, 1979). Interestingly, one set of studies found that training programs were most successful over the long term if people's feelings of self-determination were simultaneously enhanced (McClelland & Winter, 1969).

Entrepreneurial talents of highly achievement-motivated individuals can be observed in non-business-related activities as well. Andrews (1966) found that college students with high *n* Ach scores were far more strategic about their schoolwork than were those with low *n* Ach scores: They were more likely to investigate course requirements before signing up for a class, to talk with teachers before an exam was given, and to contact the teacher about the exam after it was given. In a very different context, Sheppard and Belitsky (1966) showed that blue-collar workers with high *n* Ach scores displayed greater problem-solving initiative after they had been laid off: Compared to men with low *n* Ach scores, they started looking for work sooner and employed a greater variety of job-seeking techniques.

The Relation of Achievement Motivation to Social Adjustment

Although achievement motivation has generally been examined in relation to task-related outcomes, it can be hypothesized that a concern with standards of excellence may be translated into a variety of positive life outcomes that are not work-related. That is, a general concern with doing things better should affect not only the way a person goes about his or her work, but also the way in which the person seeks to get along with others. In fact, there have been assorted findings suggesting that achievement motivation is positively related to various indicators of social adjustment. For example, children with high *n* Ach scores were rated by their teachers as working well with others (Feld, 1967) and received higher sociometric ratings from their peers (Lifshitz, 1974; Teevan, Diffenderfer, & Greenfeld, 1986) than children with low *n* Ach scores. Similarly, adult men with high *n* Ach scores were especially likely to be nominated as successful in their life and work by a large sample of their peers (Kaltenbach & McClelland, 1958). Furthermore, two studies showed that achievement motivation is associated with better marital adjustment (McAdams & Vaillant, 1982; Veroff & Feld, 1970). The social success associated with high achievement motivation probably explains why people with high *n* Ach scores have been shown to possess a more positive and stable self-concept than individuals with low *n* Ach scores (Coopersmith, 1960; Hamm, 1977; Srivastava, 1979). It should be noted that these findings parallel the positive social consequences associated with an intrinsic motivational orientation.

Veroff (1982) has suggested that men and women high in achievement motivation are well-socialized people who have adopted ideal societal prescriptions of conduct, and as a consequence feel comfortable with themselves and get along well with others. In line with this reasoning there is evidence that n Ach scores are positively related (1) to the development of self-regulatory skills (Mischel, 1961; Skolnick, 1966); (2) to the adoption of a cooperative interpersonal style when working with others (Terhune, 1968); and (3) to higher levels of ego development (Lasker, 1978).

There is some evidence that achievement motivation may also be associated with better physical health. In a national survey, Veroff (1982) reported that men with high n Ach scores reported better health than those with low n Ach scores. In a longitudinal study, McClelland (1979) found that high n Ach scores in college men predicted to healthy cardiac functioning 30 years later. Koestner, Ramey, Kelner, Meenan, and McClelland (1989) recently showed that chronic illnesses such as rheumatoid arthritis and osteoarthritis can result in diminished levels of achievement motivation.

Factors That Influence the Expression of Achievement Motivation

Our review of research related to the achievement motive has glossed over a rather significant complication: There is considerable evidence that achievement motivation research does not provide an adequate explanation of females' competence behavior (Entwisle, 1972). Thus, a number of researchers have reported that females with high n Ach scores generate results that are dissimilar to those of males and that are also inconsistent with theory. The most plausible explanation for this apparent sex difference in the expression of the achievement motive is that in order to predict action consequences on the basis of motives, one must also consider the role of self-concept variables.

Cantor, Markus, Niedenthal, and Nurius (1986) proposed that self-knowledge serves to regulate ongoing behavior by providing a set of interpretive frameworks that make sense of past behavior and also provide means–end heuristics for new behavior. These authors make the interesting suggestion that a person's "possible selves" will function to give meaning to global motives. "Possible selves" are defined as aspects of one's self-concept that reflect one's perceived potential—the kind of person one would like to become, for example. As such, possible selves can be construed as representations of people's enduring goals, aspirations, and val-

ues. There is considerable evidence that a woman's possible selves will influence the way in which achievement motivation is expressed in action.

An early illustration of this point was provided in a study by French and Lesser (1964), in which they determined whether college women were oriented toward a career or toward a traditional role as a wife and mother (i.e. whether their dominant future self was the career woman or the family woman). They found that n Ach scores in career-oriented women were significantly associated with doing better at an academic task (anagrams), but not with doing better at a social task (which involved listing the number of different ways in which they could make friends if they moved into a new community). In contrast, among the women oriented toward the traditional women's role, those with higher n Ach scores performed better at the social task of how to make friends, but did not perform better at the anagrams task.

Two recent longitudinal studies have confirmed the important role played by women's self-conceptions as career-oriented versus family-oriented in determining the manner in which their achievement motive will be manifested. Jenkins (1987) reported that college women's level of achievement motivation predicted to their work values, job perceptions, and sources of satisfaction at age 32 only if they were career-oriented. Most strikingly, Elder and MacInnis (1983) were able to identify different "motivational trajectories" for young women with strong achievement motivation, depending on whether they placed an emphasis on family goals exclusively or on both family *and* work goals. For women whose orientation included an emphasis on work *and* family, high achievement motivation related to higher IQ scores, better grades, and completing school, as well as to marrying and starting families later than their peers who were low in achievement motivation. For women with an exclusively family-centered orientation, achievement motivation related to investment in activities that are part of the sequence of dating, courtship, and marriage (e.g., placing great emphasis on physical appearance as teenagers and talking about boys a great deal). Results such as these led Veroff (1986) to conclude that the clearest relation between women's achievement motivation and performance occurs in studies that account for women's orientation toward family versus career goals.

The channeling of the achievement motive in the direction of self-conceptions related to future possible selves can be viewed as a general phenomenon. Raynor (1969) suggested that in order to accurately predict the relation between achievement motivation and performance, it was necessary to take into account the importance of the activity in one's future plan. Thus, an achievement-motivated teenager who dreams of becoming a basketball star is likely to be more motivated in the gym than the classroom. In a study with college students, Raynor and Entin (1982) measured both performance on the n Ach measure and the extent to which the students saw doing well in a particular course as important because it was related to their future career success. That is, for some students but not others, doing well in the course was seen as a subgoal to later achievement. Students high on n Ach did better in the course than those low on n Ach only if they saw doing well in it as instrumental to reaching a long-term achievement goal. Thus, achievement motivation provided an impetus toward doing something well. The conscious self-conception in terms of future career identity defined the particular area in which this impetus expressed itself.

Another Kind of Achievement Motive

We have reviewed a great deal of evidence that indicates the utility of the fantasy-derived measure of n Ach as a measure of an intrinsic competence motive that orients people toward approaching achievement goals offering challenge, self-determination, and performance feedback. We have also shown that these same conditions are essential to creating a facilitating environment in which achievement-motivated individuals are likely to perform to their full capabilities. Despite the apparent usefulness of the fantasy measure of n Ach, a combination of trends in motivation research have led to its being used progressively less often. Three trends are particularly noteworthy.

The declining use of the TAT measure of n Ach can be partly attributed to the cognitive revolution in psychology, which turned attention away from the interest in unconscious and mechanistic models of motivation aroused by the earlier Freudian and Hullian conceptions, respectively. Current motivational investigators focus more on information processing—on how motivational tendencies become intentions and under what circumstances intentions are transformed into actions (e.g., Friese, Stewart, & Hannover, 1987; Heckhausen & Kuhl, 1985). It has been assumed that these processes could best be followed by asking subjects to report consciously on their desires, intentions, goals, and reasons for action (Kuhl, 1986). From this point of view, the problem was to explain the TAT-based motives in such cognitive terms, rather than to consider them to be separate and distinct.

The second reason why the fantasy measure of n Ach is in decline can be related to the barrage of psychometric criticisms that it and measures like it have received. It is very disconcerting to find that almost any undergraduate who has taken a course on tests and measurement glibly dismisses all fantasy-derived measures because he or she has been taught that they are unreliable. Clearly, the arguments of those who have defended the psychometric integrity of these measures have been drowned out.

The final reason for the diminished use of the fantasy measure of n Ach stems from the first two: It was believed that self-report measures could be easily constructed and could be used in place of the fantasy one. Such self-report measures are more in tune with the cognitive orientation and can more easily satisfy conventional psychometric standards. These measures have the added attraction of being quite easy to administer and score, in comparison to the fantasy-derived system, with its lengthy protocol and elaborate coding procedures. Given these three factors, it is little wonder that the following question arises: Why should anyone bother to use the fantasy measure of n Ach when there are such a wide variety of replacements to choose from?

We think the answer is quite straightforward: Self-report measures of n Ach do not reflect the same construct as the fantasy measure. This is one of those unfortunate cases that plague the field of personality in which researchers are using "the same term for different classes of data as if the theoretical meaning of the term were unaffected by the form of its evidence" (Kagan, 1988, p. 615). A sure sign of such identity confusion in the area of achievement motivation is the fact that n Ach scores derived from self-report measures bear no consistent relation to n Ach scores derived from coding fantasy thought content. This fact was reported first in 1953 by McClelland et al.; was replicated in

1956 by Child, Frank, and Storm; and has been confirmed many times since then (for a review, see McClelland et al., 1989). Few facts in psychology are as well established as this one, yet psychologists have had difficulty in dealing with it. The most common reaction to this failure has been to gloss over it and to treat the self-report measures as if they were assessing the same variables as the TAT-based measure, despite the lack of correlation between them.

It should not come as too much of a surprise that fantasy and questionnaire measures of the same motive do not correlate. Murray (1938) searched for motives in fantasy in the first place precisely because he felt investigators could not trust information about motives obtained through interviews or questionnaires. As Hogan and Nicholson (1988) point out, responses on questionnaires are not *self-reports;* they are *self-presentations.* Even the most caustic critic of fantasy measures of n Ach pointed out the fact that questionnaire measures of n Ach are highly vulnerable to self-presentational biases (Entwisle, 1972).

Another way to react to the lack of correlation between self-report and fantasy measures of n Ach is to take it seriously—to insist that, at a minimum psychologists should not call by the same name two measures that do not correlate with each other (McClelland, 1980). Perhaps there are two qualitatively different kinds of human motivation, both of which are important, and what needs explaining is how they differ and how they relate to each other. A number of theorists are offering similar proposals concerning multilevel motivational systems (see Brody, 1980; Buck, 1985; Pervin, 1983).

Breckler and Greenwald (1986) distinguish between private and public motivational aspects of the self. The private self is concerned with individual achievement and guides behavior by internal standards. These authors suggest that the fantasy measure of n Ach should be viewed as reflecting a private aspect of the self. The public aspect of the self is concerned with winning approval from other persons. This is supposedly most readily accomplished by conforming to the expectancies and requests of high-status others. Breckler and Greenwald conclude that it would be desirable to have measures that assess both the private and public aspects of self-related constructs. We suggest that self-report measures of n Ach capture the public motivational aspect of the self.

Wilson (1985) suggests that there are aspects of the self that one cannot talk about, that are not accessible to our introspections. He therefore distinguishes between two motivational systems that vary in terms of the extent to which they are governed by conscious processes: (1) a cognitive-motivational system that directs overt behavior and is partly, or even largely, unconscious; and (2) a conscious verbal explanatory system that seeks and reports explanations for actions (Wilson, 1985). Similarly, Raynor and McFarlin (1986) distinguish between a "behavioral system," for which phenomenal self-awareness is not a requirement of personality functioning, and a "self-system," which requires phenomenal awareness and is motivated to maximize positive value regarding one's self-image. We would place the construct reflected by fantasy measures of n Ach within the relatively nonconscious realm, whereas self-report measures of n Ach are more reflective of the conscious verbal explanatory system concerned with one's self-image.

We (McClelland et al., 1989) recently proposed that attitudinal or self-reported motives be referred to as "self-attributed" and the fantasy-derived motives be called "implicit" since a person is not explicitly describing himself or herself as having the motive. The self-attributed motives, derived from questionnaires, are expected to be (1) more cognitively elaborated; (2) tied less directly to natural incentives and emotions; and (3) more likely to function in a conscious, or even self-conscious, mode. This article summarizes research aimed at more clearly delineating the differences between these two kinds of motivation.

Three central differences between self-attributed and implicit motives have been identified. First, McClelland (1980, 1985) has reviewed a wealth of evidence indicating that measures of implicit motives are more effective in predicting behavior in relatively unconstrained situations, whereas conscious self-reports of motives more accurately predict restricted activities such as attitudes and choices.

Second, several studies have shown that the implicit motives tend to predict action trends over time better than the self-attributed measures. Thus, the TAT-derived measure of n Ach was shown to predict entrepreneurial activity over time (McClelland, 1965, 1987); the "inhibited power motive" syndrome was shown to predict managerial success over 16 years (McClelland & Boyatzis, 1982); and the intimacy motive was shown to predict marital satisfaction and psychosocial adjustment over 17 years (McAdams & Vaillant, 1982). In many of these studies, a variety of self-report motive measures showed no predictive validity.

The final difference between self-attributed and implicit motives is that they appear to be particularly responsive to different classes of environmental incentives. Recent studies (McClelland et al., 1989; Patten & White, 1977) suggest that self-attributed motives are most likely to affect performance when there are relevant social incentives present in the situation. Thus, a person who reports being high in achievement motivation is most likely to outperform someone who reports being low in achievement motivation when the two are in a performance setting in which an authority figure stresses the importance of working hard and doing well. On the other hand, the McClelland et al. (1989) study provides evidence that implicit motives as assessed by the fantasy method are primarily responsive to variations in the nature of task-inherent incentives. Thus, people who score high on the fantasy measure of n Ach will outperform low scorers on challenging tasks, but not on easy or difficult tasks. Importantly, this study showed that self-reported motives did not interact with task incentives, nor was the relation of fantasy motives to behavior influenced by manipulations of social incentives.

CONCLUSIONS

Research on intrinsic motivation has examined the impact of external events on people's natural tendency to pursue competence goals. This research has led to the conclusion that intrinsic motivation will be greatest under conditions that foster feelings of challenge, competence, and self-determination. The influence of external events upon a person's level of intrinsic motivation for an activity can be moderated by stable personality factors such as gender or attributional style, as well as by situationally induced intrapersonal processes such as ego involvement. The adoption of an intrinsic motivational orientation toward activities is associated with a variety of adaptive behaviors (e.g., improved conceptual learning and heightened creativity). Motivational processes uncovered

in the study of intrinsic motivation are being extended to explain the way in which external regulations gradually become internalized.

It has been proposed that an individual's innate need for competence can develop over time in a predominantly intrinsic or extrinsic direction. The primary goal of intrinsically oriented competence motivation is to improve one's skill and to accomplish tasks more effectively. The implicit need for achievement, as coded from associative thought content, appears to capture this intrinsic form of competence motivation. We have reviewed evidence indicating that people with high scores on n Ach measures are oriented toward approaching achievement goals offering challenge, self-determination, and performance feedback. These same conditions appear to be essential for creating a facilitating environment in which achievement-motivated individuals are likely to perform to their full capabilities.

The primary goal for the extrinsic form of competence motivation is to perceive oneself as behaving in a competent manner, as defined by the particular situation or as accepted as a part of one's self-image. Rather than cherishing the *process* of performing an activity, extrinsically oriented people behave as they believe they are supposed to. Instead of being associated with interest, the extrinsic form of competence motivation is likely to be associated with feelings of pressure and tension. We have proposed that this form of *self-attributed* achievement or competence motivation is best assessed via self-report inventories such as the Edwards Personal Preference Schedule (Edwards, 1954) or the Jackson Personality Research Form (Jackson, 1974). Empirical evidence suggests that the two kinds of competence motivation are independent of each other, appear to predict to different classes of behaviors, and appear to be responsive to different types of environmental incentives.

Future research in the area of competence motivation should continue to pay careful attention to whether competence activities are pursued from an intrinsic or extrinsic motivational orientation. Furthermore, we encourage researchers to continue to use the fantasy measures of n Ach, in light of the considerable evidence that it is measuring something quite different from self-report inventories that purport to assess the same construct. The most comprehensive understanding of motivational processes related to the pursuit of competence goals is likely to be attained when both implicit and self-attributed achievement motives are assessed and when external influences are carefully identified, as in research on intrinsic motivation.

ACKNOWLEDGMENTS

We would like to thank Edward Deci, Lawrence Pervin, and Joel Weinberger for their comments on earlier versions of the chapter. Preparation of this chapter was supported by a grant from the Fonds Pour la Formation de Chercheurs et l'Aide de la Recherche (FCAR-Quabec).

REFERENCES

Amabile, T. M. (1983). *The social psychology of creativity.* New York: Springer.

Amabile, T. M., DeJong, W., & Lepper, M. R. (1976). Effects of externally imposed deadlines on subsequent intrinsic motivation. *Journal of Personality and Social Psychology, 34,* 92–98.

Andrews, J. D. W. (1966). *The achievement motive in lifestyle among Harvard freshmen.* Unpublished doctoral dissertation, Harvard University.

Andrews, J. D. W. (1967). The achievement motive in two types of organizations. *Journal of Personality and Social Psychology, 6,* 163–168.

Angelini, A. L. (1959). Studies in projective measurement of achievement motivation of Brazilian students. *Acta Psychologia, 15,* 359–360.

Atkinson, J. W. (1957). Motivational determinants of risk-taking behavior. *Psychological Review, 64,* 359–372.

Atkinson, J. W. (1958). Toward experimental analysis of human motivation in terms of motives, expectancies and incentives. In J. W. Atkinson (Ed.), *Motives in fantasy, action, and society* (pp. 288–305). Princeton, NJ: Van Nostrand.

Atkinson, J. W. (1981). Studying personality in the context of an advanced motivational psychology. *American Psychologist, 36,* 117–128.

Atkinson, J. W., Bongort, K., & Price, L. H. (1977). Explorations using computer simulation to comprehend TAT measurement of motivation. *Motivation and Emotion, 1,* 1–27.

Atkinson, J. W., & Litwin, G. H. (1960). Achievement motive and test anxiety conceived as motive to approach success and motive to avoid failure. *Journal of Abnormal and Social Psychology, 60,* 52–63.

Bandura, A. (1977). Self-efficacy: Toward a unifying theory of behavioral change. *Psychological Review, 84,* 191–215.

Bandura, A. (1982). Self-efficacy mechanism in human agency. *American Psychologist, 37,* 122–147.

Bandura, A. (1989). Self-regulation of motivation and action through internal standards and goal systems. In L. Pervin (Ed.), *Goal concepts in personality and social psychology* (pp. 19–85). Hillsdale, NJ: Erlbaum.

Baron, R. M., & Ganz, R. L. (1972). Effects of locus of control and type of feedback on the task performance of lower class black children. *Journal of Personality and Social Psychology, 21,* 124–130.

Bartmann, T. (1965). *Denkerziehung im Programmierten Unterricht.* Munich: Manz.

Biernat, M. (1989). Motive and values to achieve: Different constructs with different effects. *Journal of Personality, 57,* 69–95.

Boggiano, A. K., & Barrett, M. (1985). Performance and motivational deficits of helplessness: The role of motivational orientations. *Journal of Personality and Social Psychology, 49,* 1753–1761.

Boggiano, A. K., Klinger, C. A., & Main, D. S. (1985). Enhancing interest in peer interaction: A developmental analysis. *Child Development, 57,* 852–861.

Boggiano, A. K., & Ruble, D. N. (1979). Competence and the overjustification effect: A developmental study. *Journal of Personality and Social Psychology, 37,* 1462–1468.

Breckler, S. J., & Greenwald, A. G. (1986). Motivational facets of the self. In R. M. Sorrentino & E. T. Higgins (Eds.), *Handbook of motivation and cognition* (pp. 145–164). New York: Guilford Press.

Brody, N. (1980). Social motivation. *Annual Review of Psychology, 31,* 143–168.

Buck, R. (1985). Prime theory: An integrated view of motivation and emotion. *Psychological Review, 92,* 389–413.

Cantor, N., Markus, H., Niedenthal, P., & Nurius, P. (1986). On motivation and the self concept. In R. M. Sorrentino & E. T. Higgins (Eds.), *Handbook of motivation and cognition* (pp. 96–121). New York: Guilford Press.

Child, I. L., Frank, K. F., & Storm, T. (1956). Self-ratings and TAT: Their relations to each other and to adulthood background. *Journal of Personality, 25,* 96–114.

Clark, R. A., & McClelland, D. C. (1956). A factor analytic integration of imaginative and performance measures of the need for achievement. *Journal of General Psychology, 55,* 73–83.

Clark, R. A., Teevan, R. C., & Ricciuti, H. N. (1956). Hope of success and fear of failure as aspects of need for achievement. *Journal of Abnormal Psychology, 53,* 182–86.

Cofer, C. N. (1985). Drives and motives. In G. A. Kimble & K. Schlesinger (Eds.), *Topics in the history of psychology* (Vol. 2, pp. 151–190). Hillsdale, NJ: Erlbaum.

Condry, J. (1977). Enemies of exploration: Self-initiated vs. other initiated learning. *Journal of Personality and Social Psychology, 35,* 459–477.

Cooper, W. H. (1983). An achievement motivation nomological network. *Journal of Personality and Social Psychology, 44,* 841–861.

Coopersmith, S. (1960). Self-esteem and need for achievement as determinants of selective recall and repetition. *Journal of Abnormal and Social Psychology, 60,* 310–317.

Csikszentmihalyi, M. (1975). *Beyond boredom and anxiety.* San Francisco: Jossey-Bass.

Danner, R. W., & Lonky, E. (1981). A cognitive-developmental approach to the effects of rewards on intrinsic motivation. *Child Development, 52,* 1043–1052.

deCharms, R. (1968). *Personal causation: The internal affective determinants of behavior.* New York: Academic Press.

deCharms, R. (1976). *Enhancing motivation: Change in the classroom.* New York: Academic Press.

deCharms, R. (1981). Origins of competence and achievement motivation in personal causation. In L. U. Fyans (Ed.), *Achievement motivation* (pp. 22–33). New York: Plenum.

Deci, E. L. (1971). Effects of externally mediated rewards on intrinsic motivation. *Journal of Personality and Social Psychology, 18,* 105–115.

Deci, E. L. (1972). Intrinsic motivation, extrinsic reinforcement and inequity. *Journal of Personality and Social Psychology, 22,* 113–120.

Deci, E. L. (1975). *Intrinsic motivation.* New York: Plenum.

Deci, E. L., Betley, G., Kahle, J., Abrams, L., & Porac, J. (1981). When trying to win: Competition and intrinsic motivation. *Personality and Social Psychology Bulletin, 7,* 79–83.

Deci, E. L., Cascio, W. F., & Krusell, J. (1975). Cognitive evaluation theory and some comments on the Calder, Staw critique. *Journal of Personality and Social Psychology, 31,* 81–85.

Deci, E. L., Connell, J. P., & Ryan, R. M. (1989). Self-determination in a work organization. *Applied Psychology, 74,* 580–590.

Deci, E. L., Nezlek, J., & Sheinman, L. (1981). Characteristics of the rewarder and intrinsic motivation of the rewardee. *Journal of Personality and Social Psychology, 40,* 1–10.

Deci, E. L., & Ryan, R. M. (1980). The empirical exploration of intrinsically motivated processes. In L. Berkowitz (Ed.), *Advances in experimental social psychology* (Vol. 13, pp. 39–80). New York: Academic Press.

Deci, E. L., & Ryan, R. M. (1985). *Intrinsic motivation and self determination in human behavior.* New York: Plenum.

Diensthier, R. A., & Leak, G. K. (1976, August). *Effects of monetary reward on maintenance of weight loss: An extension of the overjustification effect.* Paper presented at the annual convention of the American Psychological Association, Washington, DC.

Douvan, E. (1956). Social status and success strivings. *Journal of Abnormal and Social Psychology, 52,* 219–223.

Durand, D. E. (1975). Effects of achievement motivation and skill training on the entrepreneurial behavior of black businessmen. *Organizational Behavior and Human Performance, 14,* 76–90.

Dweck, C. S., & Leggett, E. L. (1988). A social cognitive approach to motivation and personality. *Psychological Review, 45,* 256–273.

Edwards, A. L. (1954). *Edwards Personal Preference Schedule manual.* New York: Psychological Corporation.

Elder, G. H., Jr., & MacInnis, D. J. (1983). Achievement imagery in women's lives from adolescence to adulthood. *Journal of Personality and Social Psychology, 45,* 394–404.

Entwisle, D. R. (1972). To dispel fantasies about fantasy-based measures of achievement motivation. *Psychological Bulletin, 77,* 377–391.

Feld, S. C. (1967). Longitudinal study of the origins of achievement strivings. *Journal of Personality and Social Psychology, 7,* 408–414.

French, E. G. (1958). Effects of the interaction of motivation and feedback on task performance. In J. W. Atkinson (Ed.), *Motives in fantasy, action, and society.* Princeton, NJ: Van Nostrand.

French, E. G., & Lesser, G. D. (1964). Some characteristics of the achievement motive in women. *Journal of Abnormal and Social Psychology, 68,* 119–128.

French, E. G., & Thomas, F. H. (1958). The relationship of achievement motivation to problem-solving effectiveness. *Journal of Abnormal and Social Psychology, 56,* 45–48.

Friese, M., Stewart, J., & Hannover, B. (1987). Goal orientation and planfulness: Action styles as personality concepts. *Journal of Personality and Social Psychology, 52,* 1181–1194.

Gallimore, R. (1981). Affiliation, social context, industriousness and achievement. In R. H. Munroe, R. L. Munroe, & B. B. Whiting (Eds.), *Handbook of cross-cultural human development* (pp. 689–715). New York: Garland/STPM.

Garbarino, J. (1975). The impact of anticipated reward upon cross-aged tutoring. *Journal of Personality and Social Psychology, 32,* 421–428.

Grolnick, W. S., & Ryan, R. M. (1987). Autonomy in children's learning: An experimental and individual difference investigation. *Journal of Personality and Social Psychology, 52,* 890–898.

Grolnick, W. S., & Ryan, R. M. (1989). Parent styles associated with children's self-regulation and competence: A social contextual perspective. *Journal of Educational Psychology, 81,* 143–154.

Groszko, M., & Morgenstern, R. (1974). Institutionalized discrimination: The case of achievement-oriented women in higher education. *International Journal of Group Tensions, 4,* 82–92.

Haddad, Y. S. (1982). *The effect of informational versus controlling verbal feedback on self-determination and preference for challenge.* Unpublished doctoral dissertation, University of Rochester, NY.

Hamm, R. J. (1977). Stability of self-concept and fear of failure. *Psychological Reports, 40,* 522.

Harackiewicz, J. (1979). The effects of reward contingency and performance feedback on intrinsic motivation. *Journal of Personality and Social Psychology, 37,* 1352–1363.

Harackiewicz, J., Manderlink, G., & Sansone, C. (1984). Rewarding pinball wizardry: Effects of evaluation and cue valence on intrinsic interest. *Journal of Personality and Social Psychology, 47,* 287–300.

Harlow, H. F. (1953). Mice, monkeys, men and motives. *Psychological Review, 60,* 23–32.

Hayashi, T., & Habu, K. (1962). Research on the achievement motive: An experimental test of the "thought sampling" method by using Japanese students. *Japanese Psychological Research, 4,* 30–42.

Heckhausen, H. (1967). *The anatomy of achievement motivation.* New York: Academic Press.

Heckhausen, H. (1982). The development of achievement motivation. In W. W. Hartup (Ed.), *Review of child development research* (Vol. 6, pp. 600–668). Chicago: University of Chicago Press.

Heckhausen, H., & Kuhl, J. (1985). From wishes to action: The deadends and short cuts on the long way to action. In M. Frese & J. Sabini (Eds.), *Goal-directed behavior: Psychological theory and research on action* (pp. 134–160). Hillsdale, NJ: Erlbaum.

Heckhausen, H., Schmalt, H. D., & Schneider, K. (1985). *Achievement motivation in perspective.* Toronto: Academic Press.

Hogan, R., & Nicholson, R. A. (1988). The meaning of personality test scores. *American Psychologist, 43,* 621–627.

Hull, C. L. (1943). *Science and human behavior.* New York: Macmillan.

Issaccson, R. L. (1964). Relation between n Achievement, test anxiety, and curricular choices. *Journal of Abnormal Psychology, 68,* 447–452.

Jackson, D. N. (1974). *Manual for the Personality Research Form.* Goshen, NY: Research Psychology Press.

Jagacinski, C. M., & Nicholls, J. G. (1984). Conceptions of ability and related affect in task involvement and ego involvement. *Journal of Educational Psychology, 76,* 909–919.

Jenkins, S. R. (1987). Need for achievement and women's careers over 14 years: Evidence for occupational structure effects. *Journal of Personality and Social Psychology, 53,* 922–932.

Jones, M. R. (Ed.). (1955). *Nebraska Symposium on Motivation (Vol. 3).* Lincoln, University of Nebraska Press.

Kagan, J. (1988). The meanings of personality predicates. *American Psychologist, 43,* 614–620.

Kaltenbach, J. E., & McClelland, D. C. (1958). Achievement and social status in three small communities. In D. C. McClelland, A. L. Baldwin, U. Bronfenbrenner, & F. L. Strodtbeck (Eds.), *Talent and society* (pp. 112–134). Princeton, NJ: Van Nostrand.

Karabenick, S. A., & Yousseff, Z. I. (1968). Performance as a function of achievement levels and perceived difficulty. *Journal of Personality and Social Psychology, 10,* 414–419.

Kast, A., & Conner, K. (1988). Sex and age differences in response to informational and controlling feedback. *Personality and Social Psychology Bulletin, 14,* 514–523.

Koestner, R., Ramey, A., Kelner, S., Meenan, R., & McClelland, D. C. (1989). Hidden motivational deficits among arthritic adults. *Motivation and Emotion, 12,* 20–27.

Koestner, R., Ryan, R. M., Bernieri, F., & Holt, K. (1984). Setting limits in children's behavior: The differential effects of controlling versus informational styles on intrinsic motivation and creativity. *Journal of Personality, 52,* 233–248.

Koestner, R., Zuckerman, M., & Koestner, R. (1987). Praise, involvement and intrinsic motivation. *Journal of Personality and Social Psychology, 53,* 383–390.

Koestner, R., Zuckerman, M., & Olsson, J. (in press). Attributional style, comparison focus of praise and intrinsic motivation. *Journal of Research in Personality.*

Krol, T. Z. (1981). Heckhausen's Thematic Apperception Test for measurement of achievement motivation. *Przeglad-Psychologiczny, 24,* 565–572.

Kuhl, V. (1978). Standard setting and risk preference: An elaboration of the theory of achievement motivation and an empirical test. *Psychological Review, 85,* 239–248.

Kuhl, J. (1986). Motivational and information processing: A new look at decision making, dynamic change and action control. In R. M. Sorrentino & E. T. Higgins (Eds.), *Handbook of motivation and cognition* (pp. 404–434). New York: Guilford Press.

Langer, E. J., & Rodin, J. (1976). The effects of choice and personal responsibility for the aged: A field experiment in an institutional setting. *Journal of Personality and Social Psychology, 34,* 191–198.

Lasker, H. M. (1978). *Ego development and motivation: A cross-cultural cognitive-developmental analysis of n Achievement.* Unpublished doctoral dissertation, University of Chicago.

Lepper, M. R., & Greene, D. (1975). Turning play into work: Effects of adult surveillance and extrinsic rewards on children's intrinsic motivation. *Journal of Personality and Social Psychology, 31,* 479–486.

Lepper, M. R., Greene, D., & Nisbett, R. E. (1973). Undermining children's intrinsic interest with extrinsic rewards: A test of the "overjustification" hypothesis. *Journal of Personality and Social Psychology, 28,* 129–137.

Lewin, K. (1935). *A dynamic theory of personality.* New York: McGraw-Hill.

Lewin, K. (1951). Intention, will, and need. In D. Rapaport (Ed.). *Organization and pathology of thought* (pp. 95–153). New York: Columbia University Press.

Lifshitz, M. (1974). Achievement motivation and coping behavior of normal and problematic preadolescent kibbutz children. *Journal of Personality Assessment, 38,* 138–143.

Lowell, E. L. (1952). The effect of need for achievement on learning and speed of performance. *Journal of Psychology, 33,* 1159–1177.

Lundy, A. C. (1985). The reliability of the Thematic Apperception test. *Journal of Personality Assessment, 49,* 141–145.

Lundy, A. C. (1988). Instructional set and thematic apperception test validity. *Journal of Personality Assessment, 52,* 309–320.

Maslow, A. H. (1943). A theory of human motivation. *Psychological Review, 50,* 370–396.

McAdams, D. P., & Vaillant, G. E. (1982). Intimacy motivation and psychosocial adaptation: A longitudinal study. *Journal of Personality Assessment, 46,* 586–593.

McClelland, D. C. (1958). Risk-taking in children with high and low need for achievement. In J. W. Atkinson (Ed.), *Motives in fantasy, action, and society* (pp. 306–327). Princeton, NJ: Van Nostrand.

McClelland, D. C. (1961). *The achieving society.* Princeton, NJ: Van Nostrand.

McClelland, D. C. (1965). N Achievement and entrepreneurship: A longitudinal study. *Journal of Personality and Social Psychology, 1,* 389–392.

McClelland, D. C. (1979). Inhibited power motivation and high blood pressure in men. *Journal of Abnormal Psychology, 88,* 182–190.

McClelland, D. C. (1980). Motive dispositions: The merits of operant and respondent measures. In L. Wheeler (Ed.), *Review of personality and social psychology* (Vol. 1, pp. 10–41). Beverly Hills, CA: Sage.

McClelland, D. C. (1985). *Human motivation.* Glenview, IL: Scott, Foresman.

McClelland, D. C. (1987). Characteristics of successful entrepreneurs. *Journal of Creative Behavior, 3,* 219–233.

McClelland, D. C., Atkinson, J. W., Clark, R. A., & Lowell, E. L. (1953). *The achievement motive.* New York: Appleton-Century-Crofts.

McClelland, D. C., & Boyatzis, R. E. (1982). The leadership motive pattern and long-term success in management. *Journal of Applied Psychology 67,* 737–743.

McClelland, D. C., & Liberman, A. M. (1949). The effect of need for achievement or recognition of need-related words. *Journal of Personality, 18,* 236–256.

McClelland, D. C., Koestner, R., & Weinberger, J. (1989). How do self-attributed and implicit motives differ? *Psychological Review, 96,* 690–702.

McClelland, D. C., & Winter, D. G. (1969). *Motivating economic achievement.* New York: Free Press.

McGraw, K. O., & McCullers, J. C. (1979). Evidence of a detrimental effect of extrinsic incentives on breaking a mental set. *Journal of Social Psychology, 15,* 285–294.

McKeachie, W. J. (1961). Motivation, teaching methods, and college learning. In M. R. Jones (Ed.), *Nebraska Symposium on Motivation* (Vol. 9, pp. 111–141). Lincoln: University of Nebraska Press.

Mehta, P. (1969). *The achievement motive in high school boys.* New Delhi: National Council of Educational Research and Training.

Miron, D., & McClelland, D. C. (1979). The impact of achievement motivation training on small business performance. *California Management Review, 21*(4), 13–28.

Mischel, W. (1961). Delay of gratification, need for achievement, and acquiescence in another culture. *Journal of Abnormal and Social Psychology, 62,* 543–552.

Mischel, W. (1973). Toward a cognitive social learning reconceptualization of personality. *Psychological Review, 80,* 252–283.

Mook, D. G. (1987). *Motivation: The organization of action.* New York: Norton.

Morris, J. C. (1966). Propensity for risk-taking as a determinant of vocational choice. *Journal of Personality and Social Psychology, 3,* 328–335.

Mücher, H., & Heckhausen, H. (1962). Influence of mental activity and achievement motivation on skeletal muscle tone. *Perceptual and Motor Skills, 14,* 217–218.

Murray, H. A. (1938). *Explorations in personality.* New York: Oxford University Press.

Murray, H. A., & Kluckhohn, C. (1953). Outline of a conception of personality. In C. Kluckhohn, H. A. Murray, & D. Schneider (Eds.) *Personality in nature, society and culture* (pp. 3–52). New York: Knopf.

Nicholls, J. G. (1984). Achievement motivation: Conceptions of ability, subjective experience, task choice, and performance. *Psychological Review, 91,* 328–346.

O'Connor, P. A., Atkinson, J. W., & Horner, M. (1966). Motivational implications of ability grouping in schools. In J. W. Atkinson & N. T. Feather (Eds.), *A theory of achievement motivation* (pp. 141–156). New York: Wiley.

Patten, R. L., & White, L. A. (1977). Independent effects of achievement motivation and overt attribution on achievement behavior. *Motivation and Emotion, 1,* 39–59.

Pervin, L. A. (1983). The stasis and flow of behavior: Toward a theory of goals. In M. M. Page (Ed.). *Personality: Current theory and research* (pp. 1–53). Lincoln: University of Nebraska Press.

Pervin, L. A. (Ed.). (1989). *Goal concepts in personality and social psychology.* Hillsdale, NJ: Erlbaum.

Pittman, R. S., Davey, M. E., Alafat, K. A., Wetherill, K. V., & Kramer, N. A. (1980). Informational versus controlling verbal rewards. *Personality and Social Psychology Bulletin, 6,* 228–233.

Pittman, R. S., & Heller, J. F. (1987). Social motivation. *Annual Review of Psychology, 38,* 461–489.

Plant, R., & Ryan, R. M. (1985). Intrinsic motivation and the effects of self-consciousness, self-awareness, and ego-involvement: An investigation of internally controlling styles. *Journal of Personality, 53,* 435–449.

Raynor, J. O. (1969). Future orientation and motivation of immediate activity: An elaboration of the theory of achievement motivation. *Psychological Review, 76,* 606–610.

Raynor, J. O., & Entin, E. E. (1982). Future orientation and achievement motivation. In J. O. Raynor & E. E. Entin (Eds.), *Motivation, career striving, and aging* (pp. 13–82). Washington, DC: Hemisphere.

Raynor, J. O., & McFarlin, D. (1986). Motivation and the self-system. In R. M. Sorrentino & E. T. Higgins (Eds.), *Handbook of motivation and cognition* (pp. 315–349). New York: Guilford Press.

Rempel, J. K., Holmes, J. G., & Zanna, M. P. (1985). Trust in close relationships. *Journal of Personality and Social Psychology, 49,* 95–112.

Rodin, J., & Langer, E. J. (1977). Long-term effects of control relevant intervention with the institutionalized aged. *Journal of Personality and Social Psychology, 35,* 897–902.

Rogers, C. (1963). The actualizing tendency in relation to "motives" and to consciousness. In M. R. Jones (Ed.), *Nebraska Symposium on Motivation* (Vol. 11, pp. 1–23). Lincoln: University of Nebraska Press.

Rokeach, M. (1973). *The nature of human values.* New York: Free Press.

Ross, M. (1975). Salience of reward and intrinsic motivation. *Journal of Personality and Social Psychology, 32,* 245–254.

Rotter, J. B. (1966). Generalized expectancies for internal versus external control of reinforcement. *Psychological Monographs, 80*(1, Whole No. 609).

Ryan, R. M. (1982). Control and information in the intrapersonal sphere: An extension of cognitive evaluation theory. *Journal of Personality and Social Psychology, 43,* 450–461.

Ryan, R. M., Connell, J. P., & Deci, E. L. (1985). A motivational analysis of self-determination and self-regulation in education. In C. Ames & R. E. Ames (Eds.), *Research on motivation in education: The classroom milieu* (pp. 13–51). New York: Academic Press.

Ryan, R. M., Mims, V., & Koestner, R. (1983). Relation of reward contingency and interpersonal context to intrinsic motivation: A review and test using cognitive evaluation theory. *Journal of Personality and Social Psychology, 45,* 736–750.

Schroth, M. L. (1988). Relationships between achievement related motives, extrinsic conditions, and task performance. *Journal of Social Psychology, 127,* 39–48.

Seligman, C., Fazio, R. H., & Zanna, M. P. (1980). Effects of salience of extrinsic rewards on liking and loving. *Journal of Personality and Social Psychology, 38,* 453–460.

Shapira, Z. (1976). Expectancy determinants of intrinsically motivated behavior. *Journal of Personality and Social Psychology, 34,* 1235–1244.

Sheppard, H. L., & Belitsky, A. H. (1966). *The job hunt.* Baltimore: Johns Hopkins University Press.

Singh, S. (1979). Personal characteristics of fast-progressing and slow-progressing farmers. *Indian Psychological Review, 18*(1–4), 9–19.

Sinha, B. P., & Mehta, P. (1972). Farmers' need for achievement and change-proneness in acquisition of information from a farm telecast. *Rural Sociology, 37,* 417–427.

Skinner, B. F. (1953). *Science and human behavior.* New York: Macmillan.

Skolnick, A. (1966). Motivational imagery and behavior over twenty years. *Journal of Consulting Psychology, 30,* 463–478.

Sorrentino, R. M., & Higgins, E. T. (1986). Motivation and cognition: warming up to synergism. In R. M.

Sorrentino & E. T. Higgins (Eds.), *Handbook of motivation and cognition* (pp. 3–20). New York: Guilford Press.

Sorrentino, R. M., & Short, J. C. (1986). Uncertainty orientation, motivation, and cognition. In R. M. Sorrentino & E. T. Higgins (Eds.), *Handbook of Motivation and Cognition* (pp. 379–403). New York: Guilford Press.

Srivastava, N. (1979). Achievement motivation and self concept in two settings. *Asian Journal of Psychology and Education, 4,* 5–9.

Stewart, A. J., & Chester, N. L. (1982). Sex differences in human social motives: Achievement, affiliation and power. In D. G. Winter & A. J. Stewart (Eds.), *Motivation and society.* San Francisco: Jossey-Bass.

Teevan, R. C., Diffenderfer, D., & Greenfeld, N. (1986). Need for achievement and sociometric status. *Psychological Reports, 58,* 446.

Terhune, K. W. (1968). Motives, situation and interpersonal conflict within prisoners' dilemma. *Journal of Personality and Social Psychology, 8*(3, Pt. 2).

Vallerand, R. J., Deci, E. L., & Ryan, R. M. (1987). Intrinsic motivation in sport. *Exercise and Sports Sciences Reviews, 15,* 389–425.

Vallerand, R. J., & Reid, G. (1984). On the causal effects of perceived competence on intrinsic motivation: A test of cognitive evaluation theory. *Journal of Sport Psychology, 6,* 94–102.

Veroff, J. (1982). Assertive motivations: Achievement versus power. In D. G. Winter & A. J. Stewart (Eds.), *Motivation and society* (pp. 99–132). San Francisco: Jossey-Bass.

Veroff, J. (1986). Contextualism and human motives. In D. R. Brown & J. Veroff (Eds.), *Frontiers of motivational psychology* (pp. 132–143). New York: Springer-Verlag.

Veroff, J., & Feld, S. (1970). *Marriage and work in America:*

A study of motives and roles. New York: Van Nostrand Reinhold.

Weiner, B. (1966). The role of success and failure in the learning of easy and complex tasks. *Journal of Personality and Social Psychology, 3,* 339–344.

Wendt, H. W. (1955). Motivation, effort and performance. In D. C. McClelland (Ed.), *Studies in motivation* (pp. 448–459). New York: Appleton-Century-Crofts.

White, R. W. (1959). Motivation reconsidered: The concept of competence. *Psychological Review, 66,* 297–333.

White, R. W. (1975). *Lives in progress.* New York: Holt, Rinehart & Winston.

Wilson, T. D. (1985). Strangers to ourselves: The origins and accuracy of beliefs about one's own mental states. In J. H. Harvey & G. Weary (Eds.), *Attribution: Basic issues and applications* (pp. 217–243). New York: Academic Press.

Winter, D. G., & Stewart, A. J. (1977). Power motive reliability as a function of retest instructions. *Journal of Consulting and Clinical Psychology, 45,* 436–440.

Wright, J. C., & Mischel, W. (1987). A conditional approach to dispositional constructs: The local predictability of social behavior. *Journal of Personality and Social Psychology, 53,* 1159–1177.

Zinser, O., Young, J. G., & King, P. E. (1982). The influence of verbal reward on intrinsic motivation in children. *Journal of General Psychology, 106,* 85–91.

Zuckerman, M., Larrance, D., Porac, J., & Blanck, P. D. (1980). Effects of fear of success on intrinsic motivation, causal attributions and choice behavior. *Journal of Personality and Social Psychology, 39,* 503–513.

Zuckerman, M., Porac, J., Lathin, D., Smith, R., & Deci, E. L. (1978). On the importance of self-determination for intrinsically motivated behavior. *Personality and Social Psychology Bulletin, 4,* 443–446.

Chapter 21

Personality Continuity and Change Across the Life Course

Avshalom Caspi
University of Wisconsin–Madison

Daryl J. Bem
Cornell University

In this chapter, we look at personality from a longitudinal perspective—the perspective uniquely suited to answering questions about continuity and change in personality over time. What types of continuity and change are observed? What are the factors mediating them? What processes or mechanisms promote, disrupt, or transform the continuity of personality across the life course? Our purpose here is to discuss the conceptual and methodological issues involved in answering such questions, not to provide an exhaustive review of longitudinal studies or their findings. (A review of longitudinal studies of personality development may be found in Moss & Susman, 1980.)

The longitudinal study of personality is also uniquely suited to be an interdisciplinary enterprise, engaging sociologists, anthropologists, and historians, as well as personality, social, and developmental psychologists. Although the fulfillment of this interdisciplinary promise remains largely in the future, we have found it useful to adopt a sociocultural perspective on the life course. (The term "life course" is itself a sociological alternative to the psychologists' more familiar "lifespan.") In particular, we conceive of the life course as a sequence of culturally defined, age-graded roles that the individual enacts over time. We further believe that transition points in the life course hold particular significance for the continuity and transformation of personality.

TYPES OF CONTINUITY AND CHANGE

The assertion that an individual's personality has changed or remained the same over time is ambiguous. The boy who has daily temper tantrums when he is 2 but weekly temper tantrums when he is 9 has increased his level of emotional control; he has changed in *absolute* terms. But if he ranks first in temper tantrums among his peers at both ages, he has not changed in *relative* terms. Further ambiguity arises if the form of the behavior changes. If this boy emerges into adulthood as a man who is irritable and moody, we may grant that the phenotype has changed but claim that the underlying genotype has not. A third ambiguity arises when a claim of continuity rests on observations not of an individual, but of a *sample* of individuals. The continuity of an attribute at the group level may be masking large but mutually canceling changes at the individual level.

There are, in short, several meanings denoted by the terms "continuity" and "change." The purpose of this section is to disentangle some of those meanings.

Absolute Stability

Absolute stability refers to the constancy in the quantity or amount of an attribute over time. Conceptually, it connotes the stability of an attribute within a single individual, but it is typically assessed empirically by examining group means. Absolute stability is frequently reported in longitudinal studies of personality traits in adulthood (Conley, 1985; Kelly, 1955; Schaie & Parham, 1976; Siegler, George, & Okun, 1979). For example, Costa and McCrae (1980) report that there is little evidence for maturational changes in personality during adulthood in their longitudinal studies. Working within a trait model of personality, they have based their research on factor-analytically derived measures of neuroticism, extraversion, and openness to experience. Cross-sectional and longitudinal analyses supplemented by cross- and time-sequential designs revealed few age differences and few age changes on these dimensions (Costa & McCrae, 1988; Costa et al., 1986).

Whereas some personality changes have been noted when subjects are first tested as late adolescents and young adults (Mortimore, Finch, & Kumka, 1982), evidence from other large-scale longitudinal surveys of youths during adolescence—an age period commonly characterized by rapid and dramatic change—have failed to reveal striking mean-level changes on personality trait measures (Nesselroade & Baltes, 1974) or on measures of the self-concept (Dusek & Flaherty, 1981).

Despite the absence of evidence for developmental changes in these studies, absolute changes have been observed when individuals cross important life course transitions. For example, a study of 30 primiparous couples from the third trimester of pregnancy to 6 months postpartum found dramatic mean-level shifts not just in role behaviors, but also in sex-typed personality and identity measures (Feldman & Aschenbrenner, 1983).

It is also important to note that the assessment of absolute stability requires that the same attribute be measured over successive occasions. Absolute stability has no meaning if the "same" attribute actually refers to different phenotypic expressions of a personality variable. Thus, absolute stability cannot be assessed over long time intervals where identical behaviors cannot be assessed. For example, it is not possible to assert that an individual who is irritable and moody as an adult is more or less ill-tempered in absolute terms than he or she was as a child who had weekly temper tantrums.

Differential Stability

Differential stability refers to the consistency of individual differences within a sample of individuals over time—in other words, the retention of an individual's *relative* placement within the group. This is the most common definition of continuity and is typically indexed by a correlation coefficient.

Longitudinal projects that were begun earlier in this century (e.g., the Berkeley Guidance and Oakland Growth Studies, Kelly's Longitudinal Study, Terman's Study of Gifted Children) have now spanned the lives of their participants; in conjunction with other, shorter-term investigations, they provide compelling evidence for the stability of individual differences. Differential stability is often observed on ability and intelligence tests (Schaie, 1983). In addition, evidence for the stability of personality characteristics has been marshalled with instruments such as the Sixteen Personality Factors Questionnaire (Siegler et al., 1979), the Guilford–Zimmerman Temperament Survey (Costa, McCrae, & Arenberg, 1980), the Minnesota Multiphasic Personality Inventory (MMPI; Finn, 1986), the Bernreuter Personality Inventory (Conley, 1984b), the Strong-Campbell Interest Inventory (Campbell, 1974), and the Study of Values (Kelly, 1955).

Although these are all self-report instruments, personality ratings by clinicians, acquaintances, and spouses also reveal impressive temporal continuities (Block, 1971; Conley, 1985; Costa & McCrae, 1988). Costa and McCrae (1988) conclude that maturational changes by themselves have little effect on the ordering of individual differences in adulthood, and Conley estimates that "twenty percent of the personality-trait variance is longitudinally consistent over a period of 40 years of adulthood" (1984a, p. 22).

Again, however, it is important to underscore the difference between differential and absolute continuity. Because correlation coefficients discard information related to the absolute level of scores, estimates of differential stability are nondevelopmental (Wohlwill, 1980). Thus, a sample of individuals may preserve their rank ordering across occasions, but show change in mean levels of the trait over time. Physical height is an obvious example. Another example is provided by the study of primiparous couples, cited earlier. Despite the absolute changes the subjects showed in their sex-typed personality characteristics across the transition from expectancy to parenthood, the *differential* stability displayed by the same attributes was quite high.

Although the distinction between absolute and differential indices is not difficult to grasp, it has often led to misinterpretations. For example, the observation that the correlation for estimates of intelligence between adopted children and their biological mothers is usually higher than that between these children and their adoptive mothers often leads to the incorrect inference that environment has little effect on IQ. In fact, the mean IQ scores of early-adopted children suggest that they can benefit from enriched family environments (Jensen, 1973; Scarr & Weinberg, 1983).

The interpretation of differential stability must also take into account extraneous sources of influence. For example, correlation coefficients depend on the amount of variability in the measures. Homogeneous populations will thus show less temporal stability than will unselected populations, because of a restricted range. Similarly, systematic attrition may alter the composition of longitudinal samples in ways that affect variability. For example, if more extreme individuals are unavailable for follow-up relative to less extreme individuals, the homogeneity of the sample will increase,

and the apparent temporal continuity of personality will be artifactually attenuated.

Changes in variability—and hence changes in estimates of differential stability—can also arise for more substantive reasons. The use of the correlation coefficient as an index of temporal stability implicitly assumes that variability remains constant across the period of development under study. But, as Wohlwill (1980) notes,

> Many dimensions conform to [a] model of individuation emerging at some point during development and increasing over a period of time, only to converge toward a terminal level at which differences are either eliminated . . . or greatly attenuated in amount . . . [Differential stability] must be considered in relation to the overall pattern of differentiation over the course of development characterizing a particular variable. (p. 408)

Gerontologists have repeatedly drawn attention to the possibility that interindividual variability may increase in later life, although the evidence is equivocal (Bornstein & Smircina, 1982). In the realm of personality development, Haan (1981) has suggested that increased heterogeneity may reflect individuated ways of meeting new, age-specific situational challenges, whereas increased homogeneity may indicate that individuals accommodate to common experiences with similar solutions. For example, she reports that women in the Oakland Growth and Berkeley Guidance Studies diverged from adolescence to midlife on a factor labeled Open/Closed to Self—a dimension reflecting "views of the self as self-guided or as regulated by external rules and standards" (p. 127). But they converged on a factor labeled Heterosexual Under/Overcontrol—a dimension reflecting "ways of openly expressing and indulging the self and sexual interests or guarding against interpersonal involvements" (p. 127). Over time, the women became more individualized in their openness to experience, but more alike in their sexual self-expressiveness.

Structural Stability

Structural stability refers to the persistence of correlational patterns among a set of variables across time. Typically, such stability is indexed by the similarity of factor-loading configurations between sets of identical attributes across repeated measurements. The amount of common variance accounted for by each dimension and the similarity of the interrelations among the dimensions across time are other possible indices (Emmerich, 1968).

Structural change may indicate a developmental transformation. For example, factor analyses of mental test items in infancy and early childhood point to important qualitative changes in the nature of intelligence. McCall, Eichorn, and Hogarty (1977) studied the Berkeley Growth Study children who were examined repeatedly from birth to age 5. Changes in the nature of the factors across this time period suggested that major stage transitions in cognitive development occur at about 2, 7, 8, 13, and 21 months of age. Some developmental psychologists believe that structural invariance should always be established before investigating other kinds of stability (Nesselroade, 1977)—a strategy employed by Haan (1981) and by Costa and McCrae (1980).

Although there do not appear to be qualitative structural shifts beyond adolescence in the personality variables examined in most studies, there may be qualitative shifts in other personality domains, such as in "theories of oneself" (Brim, 1976). Research employing spontaneously generated descriptions of the self points to qualitative changes in adolescents' self-conceptions, resulting, in part, from the development of formal operations (Livesley & Bromley, 1973). As in the example of the differentiation of abilities cited earlier, it is possible that the self-concept of young children, which is relatively simple and undifferentiated, may evolve to become more complex later in childhood (Harter, 1983). We may also expect greater structural complexity to occur because the person acquires an increasingly multifaceted set of roles and corresponding identities (Higgins & Eccles-Parsons, 1983; McGuire & McGuire, 1982).

Ipsative Stability

Absolute, differential, and structural stabilities are indexed by statistics that characterize a sample of individuals. As we have noted above, however, stabilities at the group level may not mirror stabilities at the individual level. For this reason, some theorists advocate the use of ipsative stability, which explicitly refers to continuity at the individual level. In particular, it

denotes continuity in the configuration of variables within an individual across time. Ipsative stability could also be called *morphogenic* stability (Allport, 1962) or *person-centered* stability. This latter term derives from Jack Block's (1971) distinction between a variable-centered approach to personality, which is concerned with the relative standing of persons across variables, and a person-centered approach, which is concerned with the salience and configuration of variables within the person. An ipsative approach to the study of development thus seeks to discover regularities involved in the course of development by identifying each person's salient attributes and their intraindividual organization (Emmerich, 1968).

Very little systematic longitudinal research has been conducted from an ipsative point of view. A major exception is Block's *Lives through Time* (1971), which employed the Q-sort technique of personality description to analyze personality continuity and change in the Berkeley Guidance and Oakland Growth Studies.

In the Q-sort technique, a sorter provides a description of an individual's personality by sorting a set of cards containing personality attributes into piles ranging from attributes that are least descriptive to those that are most descriptive of the individual. This produces an ipsative or person-centered description, because the sorter explicitly compares each attribute with other attributes within the same individual; for example, placing the item "is cheerful" in the most descriptive pile of cards implies that, compared with other traits, cheerfulness stands out as uniquely salient within this individual's personality. In contrast, standard rating scales produce variable-centered descriptions because the rater implicitly compares the individual with other individuals on each attribute; a rating of "very cheerful" implies that the individual is very cheerful compared with other individuals.

In his investigation, Block used the Q-sort technique to convert a bewildering variety of noncomparable data to a standardized ipsative or person-centered description of each individual. First, he had clinically trained judges examine the diverse data collected on an individual at one point in time (e.g., early adolescence); they then did independent Q-sorts of that individual, based on impressions they had formed from examining the folder of data. A different set of judges followed the same procedure for the data collected on that same individual during late adolescence and again in adulthood. In this way, the data were all expressed in the common language of the Q-sort, enabling Block to examine the continuity and change of personality over time, despite the fact that noncomparable kinds of data had originally been collected.

Continuity and change were indexed by computing correlations across the set of attributes—Q-correlations—between an individual's Q-sort profiles from different measurement occasions; the higher the correlation, the more the configuration of attributes within the individual remained stable across time. Block's analysis confirms that aggregate measures of stability can mask large individual differences in personality continuity. For example, the average Q-correlations between early and late adolescence exceeded .70 and those between late adolescence and adulthood exceeded .50, but the correlations ranged from moderately negative to the maximum imposed by measurement error. In a similar analysis of personality continuity and change between childhood and adolescence, Ozer and Gjerde (1989) report median Q-correlations ranging from .52 to .71, with considerable variability in the distribution of these scores.

Because Q-correlations are correlations between individuals rather than between variables, they can be subjected to cluster analysis or inverse factor analysis to produce groups of similar individuals an empirically derived typology of personality. Block (1971) extended this reasoning to construct a typology of personality changes over time. He first concatenated the adolescent and adult Q-sorts of each individual into a single string of variables and subjected these to inverse factor analysis, thereby treating two subjects as similar if and only if they were similar at both time periods. This produced a typology of developmental trajectories over the years, comprising five male and six female types. A similar analysis has recently identified trajectories across four age periods from childhood through adolescence (Ozer & Gjerde, 1989).

Coherence

The kinds of stability we have discussed so far refer to "homotypic continuity"—continuity of similar behaviors or phenotypic attributes over time. The concept of coherence enlarges the

definition of stability to include "heterotypic continuity"—continuity of an inferred genotypic attribute presumed to underlie diverse phenotypic behaviors. As Kagan and Moss (1962) suggest, a specific behavior in childhood may not be predictive of a phenotypically similar behavior later in adulthood, but may still be associated with behaviors that are conceptually consistent with the earlier behavior. Such phenotypically different but conceptually related responses may be derivatives of earlier behavior (Livson & Peskin, 1980; Moss & Susman, 1980). Kagan (1969) notes that heterotypic continuities are most likely to be found from the earlier years of life, when children go through numerous rapid changes. In contrast, homotypic continuities are more likely to be found after puberty, when psychological organization nears completion.

Examples of heterotypic continuities were reported by Ryder (1967), who re-examined the data from Kagan and Moss's longitudinal study at the Fels Research Institute. For example, childhood task persistence was related to adult achievement orientation. Similarly, childhood aggression, sociability, physical adventurousness, and nonconformity were related to adult sexual behavior.

Another example of personality coherence is provided in a study of men who had been highly dependent on adults in late childhood. As adults, they were characterized as calm, warm, giving, and sympathetic; they were more likely to seek reassurance from others, and others in turn felt nurturant toward them. They were also more likely than other men to have happy, intact marriages at midlife (Caspi, Bem, & Elder, 1989). There is thus

> Continuity in these men's lives, but the phenotypic interactional style of their childhood is not simply carried forward through the life course. Rather, these men seem to have transformed their childhood dependency into a mature, nurturant style in adulthood that serves them particularly well in the intimate interpersonal world of home and family. (p. 397)

Other examples of personality coherence include the finding that the developmental antecedents of adult Type A behavior may be found in phenotypically dissimilar temperamental attributes in childhood (MacEvoy et al., 1988; Steinberg, 1985, 1986). And Bronson (1966) has identified dimensions corresponding to the sociability and impulsiveness components of extraversion that show stability from middle childhood through adolescence, despite phenotypic discontinuities in their specific manifestations. The implied genotypic continuities thus exist in what she refers to as the individual's "central orientations."

It is important to emphasize that coherence and heterotypic continuity refer to a *conceptual* rather than a literal continuity among behaviors or attributes. Accordingly, the investigator who claims to have discovered coherence must necessarily have a theory—no matter how rudimentary or implicit—that specifies the "genotype" or provides the basis on which the diverse behaviors and attributes can be said to belong to the same equivalence class. In what sense is adult sexual behavior a "derivative" of childhood physical adventurousness? In what ways is adult nurturance the "same thing" as childhood dependency?

As these examples illustrate, the "theories" behind claims of coherence often amount to little more than appeals to the reader's intuitions. Often they are post hoc interpretations of empirical relationships discovered in large correlation matrices (Moss & Susman, 1980). With the notable exception of the psychoanalytic theory of psychosexual stages and their adult sequelae, most personality theories do not specify links between personality variables at different developmental periods. Nevertheless, a number of researchers have adopted a social–developmental approach that provides a general framework for understanding coherence. Such an approach focuses on the distinctive ways in which individuals organize their behavior in order to meet new environmental demands and developmental challenges.

For example, Sroufe (in press) suggests Anna Freud's (1980, Ch. 3) concept of "developmental lines" as a heuristic device for the study of personality coherence. By outlining the tasks and milestones that can be expected in the course of development, we can design assessment procedures that adequately capture the organization of behavior in different developmental periods. Continuity across development can then be discerned in children's adaptational profiles with respect to the challenges they face at each developmental phase (Sroufe, 1979, in press). This general approach enables Sroufe and his colleagues to confer conceptual coherency on their findings

that individuals who are securely attached as infants later explore their environments as toddlers (Matas, Arend, & Sroufe, 1978), are less dependent on their teachers in preschool (Sroufe, Fox, & Pancake, 1983), and attain higher sociometric status in late childhood (Sroufe, in press).

Invariant behavior patterns do not emerge in these findings. Instead, we see a predictable and meaningful way of relating to the environment in different social settings at different ages. The continuities of personality are thus expressed not through the constancy of behavior across time and in diverse circumstances, but through the consistency over time in the ways in which the person characteristically modifies his or her changing contexts as a function of his or her behavior.

Beyond childhood the search for genotypic continuities becomes somewhat more complicated, and it may be that a purely psychological approach may be inadequate for the analysis of personality continuity and change as the individual increasingly negotiates social roles defined by the culture. As we noted in the introduction, we have found it useful to adopt a sociocultural perspective in our own work and to conceive of the life course as a sequence of culturally defined, age-graded roles that the individual enacts over time (Caspi, 1987; Helson, Mitchell, & Moane, 1984). We describe the application of this approach below as we examine factors mediating continuity.

FACTORS MEDIATING CONTINUITY AND CHANGE

Methods of Assessment

Data on personality come in a variety of forms. Building on distinctions initially proposed by Cattell, Block (1977) identifies several sources of personality data. L-data come from the Life record and include family, educational, occupational, and marital histories; O-data are ratings or descriptions of the individual by peers and other Observers; S-data are Self-observations, ratings, and descriptions, including responses to personality inventories and interviews; and T-data are derived from performance Tests, behavior samplings, and objective laboratory measurements. (Note the mnemonic abbreviation LOST.)

In general, O- and S-data display strong continuities across time, correlate well with each other, and predict real-life outcomes (L-data). For example, peer ratings of aggression yield consistent predictions across assessment intervals of 22 years (Eron, Huesmann, Dubow, Romanoff, & Yarmel, 1987 Huesmann, Eron, Lefkowitz, & Walder, 1984; Huesmann, Eron, & Yarmel, 1987). Such ratings—and similar ratings of social withdrawal—also predict important life outcomes (Moskowitz & Schwartzman, 1989).

T-data tend to show lower stabilities across time than do O- or S-data. A study of infants and their mothers in the Strange Situation procedure is illustrative. The investigators compared time samples of discrete activities (e.g., looking, glancing, vocalizing, smiling, and touching the adult) with observer ratings of behaviors (e.g., proximity seeking and contact maintaining) (Waters, 1978). The time samples showed lower temporal stabilities than did the more global observer ratings.

In addition, T-data do not typically correlate highly with corresponding O- and S-data. Nevertheless, T-data can predict well in longitudinal studies if they are carefully conceived and operationalized. For example, laboratory assessments of children's ability to delay gratification during the preschool years predict attentiveness, planfulness, and ability to deal well with stress and frustration in adolescence (Mischel, Shoda, & Peake, 1988; see also Funder, Block, & Block, 1983).

Stability and predictive utility are not, of course, the only reasons for favoring particular kinds of data. Different kinds of data are also differentially suited for answering different questions (Moskowitz, 1986). Ratings may predict long-term outcomes in part because they tend to eliminate situational sources of variance. In making ratings, observers implicitly sum over situations while taking context into account in a way that behavior sampling ignores. As Sroufe (1979) has noted, "there is a logic and coherence to the person that can only be seen in looking at total functioning" (p. 835).

Observer ratings, of course, are often culturally biased. But in some instances, this may be precisely why they are more predictive of future outcomes than are more objective assessments. Future outcomes are themselves frequently the product of culturally conditioned reactions of others to the individual. For example, Carson (1969) has noted that personality disorders are diagnosed according to criteria of social convention. Accordingly, observer ratings—with their cultural biases—are the assessment method of choice for identifying such disorders (Harkness, 1989).

But such assessments are *not* the method of choice if one is interested in examining the functional relations between an individual's behaviors and other ongoing events in the situation. Despite their apparent lack of individual-difference stability, observational assessments that preserve the precise actions of individuals are better suited for analyzing how social behavior patterns are maintained and changed over time (Cairns & Green, 1979). The study of continuity and change must include both year-to-year assessments of individual differences and minute-to-minute assessments of social interaction. Each provides different but crucial information about stability and change in personality development.

Variables Assessed

In general, studies of individuals across the life course find that measures of intellectual performance show the strongest continuities; personality variables such as extraversion, emotional stability, and impulse control are next; and political attitudes and measures of self-opinions (e.g., self-esteem, life satisfaction) are last, showing correlations between .2 and .4 over 5- to 10-year intervals (Conley, 1984a).

It is unlikely that these differences are simply a function of the differential reliability of the three kinds of variables, because this hierarchy obtains even when the measures are corrected for unreliability. However, a related methodological consideration is that ability tests demand maximal performance, whereas personality and attitude questionnaires assess representative performance. Indeed, Willerman, Turner, and Peterson (1976) showed that a personality test modeled on an ability format predicted a laboratory assessment of behavior better than did a traditional personality test asking about typical performance.

It is also possible that consistencies in social behavior require environmental supports, whereas cognitive activities are less influenced by changes in social context and may be supported more by internal feedback systems (Cairns, 1979). This interpretation would seem to account for the relatively low consistencies observed among attitudes, which may be especially susceptible to changes in sociocultural context. Finally, it is noteworthy that this hierarchy of continuity roughly parallels the size of the heritability coefficients for the three kinds of variables, suggesting that genetic and genotype–environment processes may be helping to sustain the intellectual and personality characteristics across time.

We noted above that an investigator may choose a method of assessment for reasons other than its temporal stability or predictive utility. Similarly, an investigator may be interested in examining a particular set of personality variables longitudinally, whether or not they are the best candidates for continuity. Nevertheless, those whose goal is to construct a general theory of personality usually include temporal continuity and transsituational consistency among their criteria for "good" personality variables.

Recent research indicates that the "Big Five" personality factors—neuroticism, extraversion, openness to experience, agreeableness, and conscientiousness—may have the requisite longitudinal stabilities (e.g., Digman, 1989). These same five factors emerge from a variety of both O- and S-data, and they may well turn out to be the structural basis for a general theory of personality (Digman & Inouye, 1986; McCrae & Costa, 1985, 1987; Norman, 1963; Peabody & Goldberg, in press).

Our own preference is for personality variables that clearly refer to genotypic features of the human organism rather than to hybrid features of the person and the culture. An example of the latter is the trait of "honesty," which showed very little consistency in the classic study of children's character by Hartshorne and May (1928). Because such a trait is a creation of our culture, it existed as a coherent class of behaviors in the minds of adult investigators, but not in the behaviors of the children—who had yet to "learn" the trait (Bem & Allen, 1974). Similarly, the traits of "masculinity" and "femininity" refer to quite diverse responses that our culture has chosen to lump together into two mutually exclusive equivalence classes.

It seems to us that by keeping person variables and cultural variables "pure" and clearly distinct from each other, we will be better able to integrate them explicitly into an interactional theory of personality. We thus concur with those who would select personality variables that are genotypically rooted in our

biology as much as possible (Kagan, 1989). The variables of extraversion and neuroticism may qualify on this count because of their high heritabilities (Floderus-Myhred, Petersen, & Rasmuson, 1980), but it is not clear that the other members of the "Big Five" do.

A more promising domain is that of temperament (Chess & Thomas, 1987; Rothbart & Derryberry, 1981; Rothbart & Goldsmith, 1985). Buss and Plomin (1975, 1984) have proposed at least three criteria for defining a temperament: Heritability, stability, and evolutionary significance. Activity, sociability, and emotionality—and possibly impulsivity—appear to meet these criteria. It is now important to attempt to link the conceptual domain of temperament, which has been explored with infants and children, to the study of personality trait dimensions, which has been carried out with adults.

Variables that refer to an individual's stylistic way of processing information and interacting with the internal and external environment may also be a promising category for a general theory (Bem, 1983). Examples include cognitive styles such as field dependence–independence (Witkin & Goodenough, 1981); distinctions between levelers and sharpeners (Gardner, Holzman, Klein, Linton, & Spence, 1959); and categories of the Jungian typology, such as preferences for sensing versus intuition, thinking versus feeling, and so forth (Myers, 1976). The mechanisms of ego defense would fall into this category, and they seem to have enjoyed greater utility and longevity than those parts of psychoanalytic theory that seem more culture-bound. Mischel (1968) also notes that cognitive-style variables are second only to intellective ability in showing the temporal and cross-situational consistencies.

It also seems to us that a successful theory is likely to be morphogenic or person-centered, focusing on the salience and configuration of variables within the person rather than on the relative standing of persons across variables. This model of the person as an intrapsychic system of interacting components is still absent from most longitudinal studies of personality, although some investigators have called for approaches in which the person, not the variable, is the focus of analysis. The longitudinal projects that appear to come closest to our ideal in these respects are Magnusson's (1988) study of individual development and adjustment in Sweden, Pulkkinen's (1982, 1986, 1988) study of children in Finland, and Block and Block's (1980) study of ego development at the University of California–Berkeley.

Individual Differences

Different individuals show different degrees of personality continuity across the life course. For example, in his study of participants in the Berkeley Guidance and Oakland Growth Studies, Block (1971) reports that those whose personalities remained stable from adolescence to adulthood (nonchangers) were quite different from those whose personalities changed (changers). In particular, nonchangers of both sexes were more intellectually, emotionally, and socially successful as adolescents than the changers, and a Q-sort measure of adjustment also showed them to be better adjusted.

Why do changers change? Part of the answer may be maturation. The changers Block studied were less mature as adolescents than the nonchangers, and the changes they underwent as they reached adulthood may simply have reflected the further maturation of late bloomers. It also seems likely that the personalities of the adolescent changers were more aversive, causing others to pressure them to change. These explanations can only be part of the story, however, because the Q-sort descriptions show that male changers did not display more mature, pleasant, or adjusted personalities as adults than they had as adolescents.

Another possibility is the pressure of social norms. For example, Block found that female nonchangers were more conservative, submissive, and better adjusted in adolescence than the female changers, who were described in part as being rebellious. These subjects became adults between 1945 and 1960, a time of quite traditional sex roles in America. Clearly, conservative, submissive young women would fit better into the prescribed role than rebellious young women. (Those of us who are feminists can take heart that the female changers became as well adjusted in adulthood as the nonchangers, while remaining unconventional and rebellious.)

Further evidence for the influence of sex-role norms comes from the longitudinal study conducted at the Fels Research Institute from 1929 to 1954, and reported in the book *Birth to Maturity* (Kagan & Moss, 1962). A number of continuities were found from childhood to adulthood, but they were related to the sex of the individual and the sex-appropriateness of the behaviors being assessed. For example, passivity and dependency showed continuity for female subjects but not for male subjects; aggression showed continuity for male subjects but not for female subjects. These findings, too, suggest that individuals who do not conform to the culture's norms are likely to be pressured to change. Passivity is acceptable for females but not for males; aggression is acceptable for males but not for females.

There was also some evidence that behavior that is inconsistent with sex-role expectations in childhood may not be entirely suppressed, but may be expressed in adulthood in more socially acceptable ways. For example, boys who were passive during childhood became men who were noncompetitive in adulthood. Earlier, we noted that our own studies of the Berkeley archives showed that dependent boys became warm, nurturant men with happy marriages (Caspi et al., 1989). As Kagan and Moss (1962, p. 269) note, "the individual's desire to mold his overt behavior in accordance with the culture's definition of sex-appropriate response is a major determinant of the patterns of continuity and discontinuity in his development." More generally, deviant individuals are often disliked and are thus likely to be coerced into more modal patterns—what Cattell (1973) has called "coercion to the biosocial norm."

Age and Time Span

Two major conclusions about age and time span emerge from longitudinal research: (1) Stability coefficients tend to increase as the age of the subjects increases, and (2) they tend to decrease as the time interval between observations increases (Clarke & Clarke, 1984; Moss & Susman, 1980; Olweus, 1979).

The first conclusion is, in part, a concession to repeated failures to find meaningful behavioral continuities from infancy to later childhood and adulthood:

> Almost all investigators find some theoretically reasonable relations between variation in behavior during the years prior to adolescence and variation a decade later . . . [However] there is little firm evidence for the idea that individual differences in psychological qualities displayed

during the first two years of life are predictive of similar or theoretically related behaviors a decade hence. (Kagan, 1980, p. 63)

In general, differences between children in aggression, dominance, dependency, sociability, and shyness are preserved from middle and late childhood through adolescence and adulthood (Huesmann et al., 1984; Kagan & Moss, 1962; Olweus, 1979). Clinical observations similarly suggest that if children persist in problem behavior by age 10, it is more difficult to alter behavior patterns thereafter (Patterson, 1982).

A number of methodological explanations for the differences in age-to-age correlations are plausible, but do not appear to be operative. For example, they do not seem to be due to differences in measurement reliabilities. Highly reliable assessments of temperamental variables can be obtained in infancy (Bates, 1988). Nor do the differences seem to derive from developmental changes in variance. Although congntive measures may show variance changes from infancy to early childhood, temperamental attributes do not appear to conform to this pattern of differentiation (McDevitt, 1986; Plomin, DeFries, & Fulker, 1988). It is thus unlikely that the lower age-to-age correlations earlier in life are due to insufficient differentiation.

More substantively, Kagan (1981) has proposed that very early experiences may have few lasting effects because of the lack of self-awareness before the second year of life. The appearance of more stable individual differences beginning in middle and later childhood may be due to the associated emergence of belief systems and expectations that find continuous affirmation in an expanding and reactive social environment (Harter, 1983; Kagan, 1984).

Another possibility is that age-to-age correlations may be affected by differing rates of maturation (Bloom, 1964). According to McCall (1983),

> It is quite possible that individual differences become rearranged at the advent of new skills, a phenomenon that would be reflected in reduced cross-age stabilities at points in development where major discontinuities in the developmental function occur. Consequently, cross-age stabilities should be higher for periods that do not span a discontinuity, and lower for comparable periods that do embrace a discontinuity in developmental function. (p. 120)

Thus, stability may not emerge until infants experience the major qualitative stage transitions in the first few years of life. A related possibility is that much of the observed variation in infant behavior is due to transient conditions, such as temporary allergies. When these conditions disappear with growth, so do their associated behavioral tendencies (Kagan, 1984). Although this does not rule out the possibility of developmental discontinuities, it does suggest that temporary conditions may masquerade as more meaningful qualitative shifts in development and affect age-to-age correlations in a similar manner.

A final explanation for the observed changes in age-to-age correlations is that early behavioral differences are especially likely to be modified by the child's subsequent experiences with the environment (Chess & Thomas, 1987). For example, temperamental dimensions in infancy are the entire personality of the newborn, but as development proceeds, the expression of early temperamental differences is increasingly subject to new experiences. By later childhood and adulthood, temperamental dimensions are but a subset of personality (Goldsmith et al., 1987).

The conclusion that stability coefficients tend to decrease as the time interval between observations increases would seem to be primarily a methodological artifact: Error-caused attenuation should increase as the time interval between measurements increases. But real events can lie behind "error-caused" attenuation. Real people show real change over time, and the trajectories of real lives can be dramatically altered by both planned interventions and chance events. Accordingly, it is of special interest when this pattern is systematically violated.

This was illustrated in a longitudinal study by Livson and Peskin (1967), who correlated preadult personality variables with adult psychological health. They found that measurements from the early adolescent years (ages 11, 12, and 13) were more predictive of adult functioning than similar behaviors either earlier in childhood or later in the midadolescent years. They suggest that the way a particular child adapts to the transition between grade school and junior high school is predictive of how he or she will adapt to similar transitions in later life. It is not the time interval that matters, but the similarity of the environmental demands at the two measurement occasions that determines the magnitude of the stability coefficient.

Developmental Stages

The Livson–Peskin study raises a larger issue regarding the meaning of age: "Age itself is an empty variable, for it is not merely the passage of time, but the various biological and social events that occur with the passage of time that have relevance for personality change" (Neugarten, 1977, p. 633). Accordingly, stage theories of personality attempt to replace age with such events. After adolescence, most of these events are changes in role demands rather than the events of an internal biological clock. An example is provided by the couples, cited earlier, who showed sex-typed personality and identity changes as they made the transition from pregnancy to infant care (Feldman & Aschenbrenner, 1983).

More generally, Guttman (1975) has suggested that the requirements of parenthood establish sex-role distinctions in the early years of adulthood. Women need to suppress elements of aggressivity if they are to succeed in their roles as caretakers of children; men need to suppress elements of affiliation if they are to succeed in their roles as economic providers. After the demands of parenthood are over, the earlier-suppressed elements of personality can be expressed. Thus, men will move from active to passive modes of functioning over adulthood, whereas women will move in the opposite direction. A study by Helson and Moane (1987) is consistent with this speculation. They found that during their late 20s, women showed an increase in femininity and self-discipline. In their later years, however, they showed a decrease in femininity and an increase in confidence, dominance, and coping skills.

Helson and Moane's study was not designed to explore a specific stage model of personality development. Moreover, no comparable studies have been conducted on men across this time period, and there is currently no more empirical support for one stage model of personality development than for another.

Throughout this chapter, we have focused on continuities and changes in objective indices of personality. But there is also research that examines subjective or phenomenological continuity and change. For example, Woodruff and Birren (1972) retested a sample of middle-aged adults 25 years after they had originally completed the California Test of Personality. In addition to describing their current selves, they were asked to complete the same test as they thought they had answered it in adolescence. Although there were, in fact, very few age changes over the 25-year span, subjects perceived such changes, believing that their adolescent adjustment had been much worse than it actually was. Other studies have also shown perceptions of discontinuity, but not necessarily always in the direction of seeing improvement with age.

In a study examining subjective changes predicted by Erikson's (1950) stage theory of psychosocial development, subjects in early, middle, and later adulthood filled out rating scales as they would have at earlier ages, at the present time, and as they might in the future (Ryff, 1984). Subjects reported past and future changes that Erikson's theory predicts for the appropriate developmental dimensions (generativity and integrity); there were no reported changes on the nondevelopmental control scales.

The difference between perceived and actual discontinuities suggests the possibility that the flow of psychological time (subjective age) may be relatively independent of calendar time and may exert an effect on behavior that is similarly independent of chronological age (Riegel, 1972). Rossi (1980) reported that the correlations between desired age, subjective age, and chronological age in a sample of women between 36 and 51 years of age were quite low, ranging from $-.15$ to $.21$. Moreover, both desired and subjective ages had an effect on women's relationships with their children that was independent of chronological age. Women who wanted to be younger than they were reported greater difficulty rearing adolescent children than did women who accepted their age. Women who felt older than they were reported less emotional closeness to their children.

Time perspective itself may change in later years. Neugarten (1977) has suggested that people in midlife experience a gradual change in time perspective, in which life is structured in terms of time left to live rather than time since birth. This shift is accompanied by heightened introspection and interiority. A matched-pairs analysis of aged persons—half of whom were a year or less away from death—similarly suggested that a time line based on distance from death may be more useful than chronological age for understanding the psychological world of the very old (Lieberman & Coplan, 1970). Simonton (1988) has confirmed this point by examining the objective qualities of classical musical works from the starting point of the composers' death dates backwards.

In general, it appears that stage models of personality may prove more useful for phenomenological than for objective assessments of continuity and change. In the next section, we argue that an emphasis on social transitions may prove more profitable than a focus on stages defined either by "inner processes" (e.g., Kohlberg, 1966) or by broad psychosocial tasks (e.g., Levinson, 1986).

Social Transitions

Situations differ from one another in the degree to which they permit individual differences to manifest themselves. Some situations are weak, permitting a variety of responses and hence a variety of individual differences to flourish; other situations are strong, constraining behavioral choices and eliciting similar responses from most individuals (Mischel, 1977). In general, the influence of dispositional factors on behavior appears to be most pronounced in settings that are unstructured, where individuals are forced to rely primarily on their own internal traits to guide their behavior (Snyder & Ickes, 1985).

For example, individual differences in introversion–extraversion predict behavior better in situations that encourage neither one or the other (Monson, Hesley, & Chernick, 1982). Likewise, marked dispositional influences on social behaviors emerge more strongly from unstructured dyadic interactions than from more traditional, structured experimental paradigms (Ickes, 1982). Similar findings emerge from research in behavior genetics, where twin studies have shown that genetic effects are most pronounced in unstructured situations and in response to novel social encounters. For example, differences between monozygotic and dizygotic twin pairs are stronger in playroom settings, where the range of behavior reactions is less restricted, than in test-room settings that are highly structured (Matheny & Dolan, 1975). Monozygotic–dizygotic differences are also stronger when children are confronted by unfamiliar rather than familiar persons (Plomin & Rowe, 1979). Research further demonstrates that individual differences emerge strongly in settings that require individuals to master and negotiate new demands and tasks. For example, Wright and Mischel (1987) have shown that the social behaviors of children diverged as the competency requirements of the situations in which they were engaged increased.

This last finding reminds us that unstructured situations are also frequently characterized by uncertainty, ambiguity, novelty, and sometimes stress. We suggest that these several situational characteristics are precisely those that characterize transition events in the life course—going to school for the first time, launching a career, getting married, becoming a first-time parent, and so forth. Accordingly, we propose that dispositional factors should be most influential and individual differences should be most in evidence in the life course when individuals are required to enter new relationships and assume new roles. A corollary is that the crucial variables for understanding continuity in personality across the life course may well be those that characterize the ways in which different individuals negotiate such transitions. In other words, we believe that personality continuities are most likely to be evident during life course discontinuities.

This may seem paradoxical, because most theoretical perspectives on life discontinuities assume that these are times when major reorganizations of personality occur. Nevertheless, research on social transitions in the life course seems to indicate that pre-existing characteristics are actually likely to be accentuated during these times.

For example, irritable and explosive men became even more so during the severe economic setbacks of the Great Depression (Elder & Caspi, 1988), and the coping styles of entrepreneurs whose businesses suffered extensive damage during a natural disaster were accentuated during the recovery period (Anderson, 1977). Similar accentuation of pre-existing individual differences has been observed in children going off to school for the first time (Alexander & Entwistle, 1988), and among entering college students whose distinguishing attributes are likely to be reinforced and extended by their experience in selected settings (Feldman & Newcomb, 1969). Even catastrophic change has this effect. After analyzing experiences of individuals during the Nazi revolution, Allport, Bruner, and Jandorf (1941) concluded that "very rarely does catastrophic . . . change produce catastrophic alterations in personality. . . . Where change does take place it seems invariably to accentuate trends clearly present in the pre-[crisis] personality" (pp. 7–8).

Perhaps most pertinent is the finding by Livson and Peskin (1967), cited earlier, that children's adaptation during the transition years between grade school and junior high school predicted later life adjustment better than did earlier assessments taken in childhood and later assessments taken in adolescence. These investigators suggest that these transition years be viewed "as a microcosm of adult life, anticipating its requirements for active and effective adaptation" (1967, p. 517).

This possibility was addressed in some of our own recent research on the continuity of interactional styles across the life course (Caspi et al., 1989). In one study, we studied men who had been shy in late childhood, focusing on those points in their later lives when they would have to abandon familiar roles and enter new and unfamiliar social settings. We paid particular attention to the transition from youth to adulthood, when they would be called on to assume the new roles of marriage, parenthood, and career. Compared with men who had not been shy as children, these men significantly delayed their entry into these new roles, being 3–4 years older on the average than other men in marrying, becoming fathers, and establishing stable careers. In short, men who were reluctant to enter social settings as children appeared to have become adults who were more generally reluctant to enter the new and unfamiliar social settings required by important life course transitions (Caspi, Elder, & Bem, 1988).

We believe that studying individual differences at transition points in the life course provides a unique opportunity for discerning general principles that govern the functions and processes of personality.

Historical Factors

Most of what we know about personality development across the life course comes from people who spent their formative years during the Great Depression, went through World War II and the Korean conflict, and raised their own children either during the booming postwar era or in the tumultuous 1960s (Rossi, 1980). Accordingly, we do not know how much of our knowledge is culturally and historically specific. This is, of course, a problem in personality and social psychology generally, but it typically remains unacknowledged; both data and theory are presented as if they were necessarily transhistorically valid and culture-free (cf. Gergen, 1982). Those who deal with longitudinal data, however, have been somewhat more sensitive to the issue.

Methodologically, the problem is usually dealt with through some variation of cohort analysis, which seeks to disentangle cohort (year of birth), period (year of measurement), and age effects (Baltes, Cornelius, & Nesselroade, 1979). Cohort and period effects are historical in nature. Historical influences take the form of a cohort effect when social change differentiates the life patterns of successive cohorts. For example, members of relatively small birth cohorts may encounter more favorable employment opportunities than members of relatively large birth cohorts may (Glenn, 1980). Historical influences take the form of a period effect when specific influences, such as wars, exert a relatively uniform effect across successive birth cohorts. For example, secular trends in the timing of marriages and first births across the 20th century are largely an expression of massive period effects (Rodgers & Thornton, 1985). A third type of effect occurs through maturation or aging, as illustrated by a decline for most individuals on ability tests that involve speed of response (Horn & Donaldson, 1980).

Baltes (1987) has suggested that cohort differences are most pronounced in relation to those aspects of development that are not stabilized in the process of genetic and cultural evolution. For example, there are few observable historical effects on cognitive development among children in developed countries, but there are marked shifts in values, attitudes, and beliefs related to secular trends. Even when they do occur, historical changes tend to affect only the mean levels of cognitive and personality attributes; they seldom alter the ordering of individuals—differential stability remains high (McCall, 1977).

The promise of cohort analysis, however, remains unfulfilled until specific historical changes can be linked to specific changes in life patterns (Elder, Caspi, & Burton, 1988). The treatment of historical influences as cohort or period effects in itself provides no clues about such linkages. In that sense, a cohort difference is like a difference in an age or social class; it remains an empty finding until it can be translated into psychological processes and events.

One of the few research programs to provide

such an analysis is Elder's (1974, 1979) extended examination of two birth cohorts who lived through the Great Depression and World War II. With pre-Depression birth dates that differed by only 8 years, these cohorts experienced dramatically different historical times. Members of the Oakland cohort were young children during the prosperous 1920s. This stable childhood ensured a measure of security and developmental continuity when they entered the hard times of the Great Depression. In contrast, members of the Berkeley cohort encountered family hardships during the vulnerable years of early childhood, and the developmental tasks of adolescence were accompanied by the disruptions and pressures of homefront mobilization. Although economic deprivation produced similar changes in the family environments of children in both cohorts, the differential developmental effects of these changes on the two cohorts were still evident at midlife.

Analyses like Elder's raise the larger epistemological issue of how we can move from historically specific findings to a more general understanding of life course processes. Sometimes it is easy to extract the general finding behind relatively superficial historical differences. For example, a study of men born in the 1920s found that low ego control in adolescence predicted midlife drinking problems (Jones, 1981). A recent study of children born in the late 1960s found that low ego control at ages 3–4 predicted marijuana use at age 14 (Block, Block, & Keyes, 1988). Clearly, the historical change in the drug of choice is trivial; the general finding is obvious.

Sometimes the general finding is more obscure. For example, intellectual competence in a sample of women born in the 1920s was positively correlated with the number of children they had (during the postwar baby boom) (Livson & Day, 1977). But in both earlier and later samples of women, the correlation between tested intelligence and fertility was negative (Retherford & Sewell, 1988). As Livson and Day (1977) note, historically specific findings like these are useful

> only if they are interpreted not as direct if–then relationships, but as providing an understanding of the intrapsychic and interpersonal characteristics that mediate one's child-bearing response to a social context prevailing during the period in which fertility decisions are made. (p. 321)

This tension between historical specificity and transhistorical generality is directly analogous to the tension between idiographic and nomothetic approaches to personality, and the choice of strategy is largely a matter of the investigator's metatheoretical taste. The data themselves place no contraints on the specificity or universality of the inferences drawn or the theories constructed therefrom.

This is strikingly illustrated by comparing Elder's analysis with Jack Block's (1971) analysis of the same subjects. As we have seen, Elder's strategy was to compare the two cohorts with each other; Block combined the two cohorts into a single sample for analysis. Elder gave his 1974 book the title *Children of the Great Depression,* denoting that his subjects lived in a particular place and time. Block gave his book the title *Lives through Time.* His subjects might have lived anywhere, anytime.

Ultimately, of course, it would be desirable to have an account of life course continuity and change that would transcend the historical specificity of Elder's approach but would qualify the historical generality of Block's. As we imply in the following section, such an account would have to move beyond description to explanation, to provide a set of general mechanisms through which life course continuity is (or is not) achieved and consequential life outcomes are affected.

MECHANISMS OF CONTINUITY AND CHANGE

As we have seen in this chapter, there is an extensive data base of research documenting and describing continuity and change in personality across the life course. Efforts to go beyond description to the more difficult task of explanation are, however, far less developed. Nevertheless, recent attempts to integrate genetic, environmental, and interactional processes of personality functioning appear quite promising.

Genetic Influences

The quantitative methods that behavioral geneticists have traditionally employed to estimate the genetic and environmental components of phenotypic variance at a given point in time have now been extended to estimate genetic contributions to continuity and change across time (Plomin, 1986; Rowe, 1987).

One of the earliest attempts to do this examined a sample of twins who completed the California Psychological Inventory (CPI) and the MMPI at age 16 and again at age 28 (Dworkin, Burke, Maher, & Gottesman, 1976, 1977). The results showed that changes in trait levels (profile elevations) for both the CPI and the MMPI from adolescence to adulthood were influenced by genetic similarity. For the CPI, the trend correlations were .69 and .30 for monozygotic and dizygotic twins, respectively; for the MMPI, the corresponding correlations were .49 and .16. Changes in trait organization (profile contour) showed evidence of significant genetic influence for the CPI but not for the MMPI. Thus genetic factors were implicated not only in the expression of traits at both ages, but also in the process of personality change across time.

Similar genetic effects have been observed in infancy, a period of rapid developmental change during which it is difficult even to detect continuities within a single individual. For example, even though assessments of temperament across 6, 12, 18, 24, and 30 months of age showed low to modest stabilities, within-pair analyses revealed that monozygotic twins were more likely to change in concert than were dizygotic twins (Matheny, 1980, 1983, 1989). An earlier study of adaptability similarly showed only modest correlations between two laboratory settings and large mean-level changes in behavior across age, and yet monozygotic twin pairs remained more similar to one another across both settings and ages than did dizygotic twin pairs (Matheny & Dolan, 1975). And finally, monozygotic twin pairs are more concordant than dizygotic twin pairs in both the timing and patterning of ups and downs in intellectual functioning (Wilson, 1983).

Because longitudinal data on twins are not extensive, some investigators have turned to a methodology in which children in adoptive and nonadoptive families are compared with their biological parents. Longitudinal genetic correlations from infancy and early childhood to adulthood have now been modeled explicitly with data from the Colorado Adoption Project, an ongoing study of nearly 500 adoptive and nonadoptive families (Plomin & DeFries, 1985). The results suggest that much of the phenotypic stability for IQ is mediated genet-

ically; that is, genetic factors that produce individual differences in children correlate significantly with genetic factors that produce individual differences in adulthood (DeFries, Plomin, & LaBuda, 1987). In contrast, temperament variables show more evidence of change in the genetic components across time (Plomin et al., 1988).

Although the results of the several studies we have cited so far demonstrate that genetic factors can influence the continuity of personality across the life course, they still do not address the mechanisms by which they do so. Two research programs illustrate very different ways in which this more difficult task might be approached.

A study of common fears in twins suggests—albeit speculatively—that evolutionary theorizing might eventually be helpful in this regard. In a sample of several hundred twins ranging in age from 14 to 34, Rose and Ditto (1983) found that monozygotic twins became more similar across time on fear of death of a loved one and fear of one's own death, whereas dyzygotic twins became less similar. For example, the correlation on fear of death of a loved one between monozygotic twins under the age of 20 years was .45, but rose to .60 for monozygotic twins over the age of 20; the comparable correlations for dizygotic twins were .47 and .22. The authors conclude:

> Perhaps no event is more threatening, no fear more adaptive than the threatened elimination of one's genes from the species. . . . Untimely death or early loss of loved ones is intensely feared at all ages, and our results suggest that young twin siblings, regardless of genetic similarity, quite closely resemble one another in the intensity with which they experience such fears. With maturity, however, fears of death among [dizygotic] co-twins diverge, while those of monozygotes converge. Whatever the explanation, increased salience of shared genes in adult fear of death is an intriguing heuristic result of our analysis. . . . It provides the first demonstration of significant changes in heritability across age in social behaviors or attitudes. (p. 367)

An attempt to look at physiological mechanisms underlying genetic stability is illustrated by Kagan's work on shyness or "inhibition to the unfamiliar." Shyness appears to be one of the most heritable personality dimensions in infancy, childhood, and adulthood (Daniels & Plomin, 1985), and Kagan's earlier work showed modest stabilities from childhood to adulthood on measures of shy behavior (Kagan & Moss, 1962). Recently, Kagan, Reznick, and Snidman (1987, 1988) have suggested that inherited variations in threshold of arousal in selected limbic sites may be contributing to these findings.

Two samples of consistently inhibited or uninhibited children who were selected at either 21 or 31 months of age have now been followed up to the age of 7½ years. Peripheral physiological variables (e.g., heart rate, pupillary dilation, norepinephrine activity, cortisol levels) are consistenly correlated with indices of behavioral inhibition at every age. Kagan and his colleagues note that such findings are consonant with neurobehavioral studies of the amygdala and hypothalamus, and, when coupled with research on shy and introverted adults, point persuasively to the role of inherent individual differences in central nervous system functioning in producing longitudinal consistencies in this behavioral style.

Environmental Influences

One continuity-promoting mechanism is so mundane that it is often overlooked: Behavioral patterns may show stability across the life course because the environment remains stable. Social behavior theorists have been telling us this for years, of course, as have others (e.g., Bloom, 1964; Bradley, Caldwell, & Rock, 1988; Cairns & Hood, 1983; McCall, 1981). Whether one considers such behavioral stability an artifact or "real" personality continuity depends on one's theoretical predilections.

Few longitudinal studies, however, have actually assessed the stability and change of environment alongside the stability and change of behavior patterns. An approximation to this methodology was carried out by Hanson (1975), who re-examined the archives from the Fels Research Institute on which Kagan and Moss based their *Birth to Maturity* (1962). He found that 28 out of 30 environmental variables known to be related to IQ (e.g., parental involvement with the child, freedom to engage in verbal expression, direct teaching of language behavior) showed significant continuities from early to late childhood, with correlations corrected for attenuation ranging from .44 to .99.

Similar stabilities have also been found in parents' reports of child-rearing practices from childhood to adolescence (Roberts, Block & Block, 1984); in global observations of maternal sensitivity from infancy to the preschool years in high-risk samples (Pianta, Sroufe, & Egeland, 1989); and in parenting practices that correlate with children's aggressive acts (Patterson & Bank, in press).

Children's peer networks can also serve as a source of behavioral continuity. In a research program that explicitly adopts a social–ecological approach to the study of longitudinal continuity, Cairns and his colleagues identify children's social networks and attempt to determine how these affect the interpersonal behaviors that occur within them over time (Cairns & Cairns, 1988; Cairns, Perrin, & Cairns, 1985). In general, they find that children's social networks are quite stable over periods of at least 1 year, and that they serve as guides for norm formation and the consolidation of behavioral patterns.

If the environments of most children are as stable as all these data suggest, then the continuities observed in trait measures over time may simply reflect the cumulative and continuing continuities of those environments. Again, however, one person's phenomenon may be another's artifact.

The direct corollary of the assertion that behavioral continuities reflect environmental constancies is, of course, that environmental change will produce behavioral change. Here the evidence is abundant. For example, Rutter (1987) has noted that residential treatments have a marked influence on current behavior, but that these influences do not persist when youngsters return home to an environment that maintains its delinquency-promoting characteristics. Changes in the prosocial direction were shown by boys in England whose delinquent behavior diminished when their families moved out of London—a result that could not be attributed to selective migration (West, 1982). And finally, a longitudinal study of adolescent mothers shows that the sequelae of unplanned teen parenthood strongly depend on subsequent environmental events, such as further education, fertility control, marriage, and independence from the family of origin (Furstenberg, Brooks-Gunn, & Morgan, 1987).

It is important to note, however, that such environmental events are not random; they may themselves be a function of the individual's personality. Which women choose to return to school? Which choose to use contraception? Which are able to enter stable marriages? In short, the behavioral changes reported in many studies may derive from changes in environments that are themselves brought about by stable personality attributes. Clearly, we are dealing here with person–environment interactions—a topic to which we now turn.

Person–Environment Interactions

It is now widely acknowledged that personality and behavior are shaped in large measure by interactions between the person and the environment. There are many kinds of interaction, but we suggest that there are three that play particularly important roles both in promoting the continuity of personality across the life course and in controlling the trajectory of the life course itself (cf. Buss, 1987; Plomin, DeFries, & Loehlin, 1977; Scarr & McCartney, 1983). *Reactive* interaction occurs when different individuals exposed to the same environment experience it, interpret it, and react to it differently. *Evocative* interaction occurs when an individual's personality evokes distinctive responses from others. *Proactive* interaction occurs when individuals select or create environments of their own.

Reactive Interaction

Different individuals exposed to the same environment experience it, interpret it, and react to it differently. An anxious, sensitive child will experience and react to authoritarian parents in very different ways from a calm, resilient child. The person who interpets a hurtful act as the product of malice will react differently from one who interprets the same act as the product of incompetence. Each individual thus extracts a subjective psychological environment from the objective surroundings, and that subjective environment is what shapes both personality and subsequent interaction.

This is, of course, the basic tenet of the phenomenological approach historically favored by social psychology and embodied in the famous dictum that if people "define situations as real, they are real in their consequences"

(Thomas & Thomas, 1928). It is also the assumption that connects Epstein's (1980; Epstein & Erskine, 1983) writings on the development of "personal theories"; Tomkins's (1979, 1986) description of "scripts" about the self and interpersonal interactions; and Bowlby's (1973) analysis of "working models"—mental representations of the self and others—that develop in the context of interactional experiences.

All three theories assert that people continually revise their personal theories, scripts, and working models as a function of experience. But if these function as filters for social information, it is important to ask how revision occurs. In fact, social psychologists, who tend to focus on the cognitive rather than the motivational features of internal organizational structures, argue that "self-schemas"—psychological constructs of the self—screen and select from experience to maintain structural equilibrium (Greenwald, 1980). Once a schema becomes well organized, it filters experience and makes people responsive to information that matches their expectations and views of themselves (Markus, 1977). Cantor and Kihlstrom (1987) review a host of related cognitive processes that promote consistency and that may also impair people's ability to change.

As we indicate next, however, the use of existing structures to organize experience is not entirely unconscious. Persistent ways of perceiving, thinking, and behaving are not preserved simply by psychic forces, nor are they entirely attributable to features of the cognitive system; they are also maintained by the consequences of everyday action (Wachtel, 1977).

Evocative Interaction

Each individual evokes distinctive responses from others. An infant who squirms and fusses when picked up will evoke less nurturance from a parent than one who likes to be cuddled. Docile children will evoke a less controlling style of child rearing from parents than will aggressive children. The person acts, the environment reacts, and the person reacts back in mutually interlocking evocative interaction.

The ways in which evocative interaction can promote continuity has been elegantly shown by Patterson's (1982) work with aggressive boys. Such a boy's coercive behaviors initiate a cycle of parental anger and further aggression until the parents finally withdraw, thereby reinforcing the boy's initial aggression: "Family members and antisocial children alternate in the roles of aggressors and victims, each inadvertently reinforcing the coercive behavior of the other" (Patterson & Bank, in press). We noted above that stable environments can create stable behavioral patterns. Patterson's work shows that behavioral patterns can themselves create stable environments.

By extension, we have suggested that a child whose temper tantrums coerce others into providing such short-term payoffs in the immediate situation may learn an interactional style that continues to work in later years. The immediate reinforcement not only short-circuits the learning of more controlled interactional styles that might have greater adaptability in the long run; it also increases the likelihood that coercive behaviors will recur whenever similar interactional conditions arise later in the life course (Caspi et al., 1989; Caspi, Elder, & Bem, 1987).

It is also through evocative interaction that phenomenological interpretations of situations—the products of reactive interaction—are transformed into situations that are "real in their consequences." Early experiences can set up expectations that lead an individual to project particular interpretations onto new situations and relationships, and thence to behave in ways that corroborate those expectations (Wachtel, 1977). For example, because aggressive children expect others to be hostile (Dodge, 1986), they may behave in ways that elicit hostility from others, thereby confirming their initial suspicion and sustaining their aggression. Expectation-confirming interactions have also been demonstrated in the domains of extraversion–introversion (Snyder & Swann, 1978), physical attractiveness (Snyder, Tanke, & Berscheid, 1977), and racial stereotypes (Word, Zanna, & Cooper, 1974).

Individuals also elicit and selectively attend to information that confirms rather than disconfirms their self-concepts (Darley & Fazio, 1980; Snyder, 1984; Swann, 1983, 1985, 1987). This promotes stability of the self-concept, which in turn promotes the continuity of behavioral patterns that are congruent with that self-concept (Andrews, 1988; Backman, 1985, 1988; Secord & Backman, 1965; see also Carson, 1969, and Snyder & Ickes, 1985).

In these several ways, then, reactive and evocative interactions enable an ensemble of behaviors, expectations, and self-concepts to evoke maintaining responses from others; thereby, they promote continuity across time.

Proactive Interaction

As children get older, they can move beyond the environments imposed by their parents and begin to select and construct environments of their own. These environments, in turn, can promote the continuity of personality. For example, a sociable girl will choose to go to the movie with friends rather than stay home alone and watch television; her social personality thus selects her into an environment that further reinforces and sustains her sociability. And what she cannot select, she will construct: If nobody invites her to the movies, she will organize the event herself. As the name implies, proactive interaction is a process through which individuals become active agents in their own personality development (cf. Buss, 1987; Diener, Larsen & Emmons, 1984; Emmons, Diener, & Larsen, 1986; Plomin, 1986; Snyder & Ickes, 1985). Scarr and McCartney (1983) have proposed that this dispositionally guided selection and creation of environments becomes increasingly infuential in development as the child gains increased autonomy.

An example of the personality-sustaining effects of proactive interaction comes from Kohn's ambitious longitudinal work on personal values and the workplace. Men with intellectual flexibility and self-directedness move into complex jobs; the complexity of their work then continues, in turn, to enhance their flexibility and self-directedness (Kohn, 1977; Kohn & Schooler, 1978, 1983).

But the environments that are most consequential for personality are probably our interpersonal environments, and it is in friendship formation and mate selection that the personality-sustaining effects of proactive interaction are the most intriguing.

Friends tend to be similar with respect to values, attitudes, and personality characteristics (Kandel, 1978; Newcomb, 1961), and the similarity–attraction function appears to be continuous across the life-span (Byrne & Griffitt, 1966). The implications of homophyly for the stability of behavior are especially interesting with respect to problem behavior, where it appears that deviant activities need the support of the peer group not only for their initiation but for their sustenance as well. For example, it appears that aggressive children, although unpopular in the larger community of peers, are closely linked to particular subgroups. In particular, boys and girls tend to affiliate with friends who match their aggressive behavior (Cairns, Cairns, Neckerman, Gest & Gariepy, 1988; Giordano, Cernkovich, & Pugh, 1986). Consistent with the social learning formulation of differential association theory, Patterson (1988; Patterson & Bank, in press) has suggested that each individual shops for settings and people that maximize his or her positive payoffs. The trial-and-error process of shopping and being rejected inevitably leads problem children to identify groups of peers that will reinforce their behaviors. In turn, as Patterson notes, membership in a delinquent peer group is a key determinant of drift into subsequent delinquency (Matza, 1964). Thus, the social network, whose composition is in part determined by direct social preferences, may serve as a convoy through development, producing support for acts of increasing violence and deviance.

Research on marriage similarly indicates that people tend to choose partners who are similar to themselves; positive assortative mating has been well documented for physical characteristics, cognitive abilities, and personality dispositions (Epstein & Guttman, 1984; Jensen, 1978; Vandenberg, 1972). Moreover, similarities between spouses appear to be a function of personal preference rather than by-products of social homogamy (Mascie-Taylor & Vandenberg, 1988).

Using the archives of the Institute of Human Development, Caspi and Herbener (1990) sought to determine whether assortative mating of spouses on personality characteristics might promote personality continuity. When the original members of the Oakland Growth and Berkeley Guidance Studies were interviewed in 1970 and 1980, so were their spouses, thereby providing personality profiles (in the form of individual Q-sorts) of subjects and spouses that could be directly correlated with each other. Caspi and Herbener divided the 126 couples into three groups of equal size on the basis of the similarity between the spouses' 1970 Q-sorts, and then examined the continuity of each person's personality from 1970 to 1980.

They found that the least similar spouses showed individual continuities of .4 from 1970 to 1980; moderately similar spouses showed individual continuities of .5; and the most similar spouses showed continuities of .6. Further analyses demonstrated that these findings were not simply due to spouses' similarities in age, social class, or education, nor did stable people simply select more similar partners.

The proactive interactional process that promotes the continuity of personality has also been documented in the domain of political attitudes. Newcomb's classic study of students at Bennington College found that the political liberalism acquired by the women who attended Bennington in the 1930s was sustained over the subsequent 25 years of their lives, in part because they selected liberal friends and husbands who continued to provide social support for their politically liberal attitudes (Newcomb, 1943; Newcomb, Koenig, Flacks, & Warwick, 1967).

Life Course Consequences of Person–Environment Interactions

We have noted that the processes of reactive, evocative, and proactive interaction enable an individual's personality both to shape itself and to promote its own continuity through the life course. These same processes also enable an individual's personality to influence the life course itself. In particular, person–environment interactions can produce two kinds of consequences in the life course: cumulative consequences and contemporary consequences.

Consider again the boy who has temper tantrums. His ill temper may provoke school authorities to expel him (evocative interaction), or it may cause him to experience school so negatively (reactive interaction) that he chooses to quit as soon as he is legally permitted to do so (proactive interaction). In either case, leaving school may limit his future career opportunities, channeling him into frustrating, low-level jobs. This low occupational status may then lead to an erratic work life characterized by frequent job changes and bouts of unemployment, possibly disrupting his marriage and leading to divorce. In this hypothetical scenario, these occupational and marital outcomes are *cumulative* consequences of his childhood personality. Once set in motion by childhood temper tantrums, the chain of events takes over and culminates in the adult outcomes—even if he is no longer ill-tempered as an adult.

On the other hand, if this boy does carry his

ill temper into adulthood, then *contemporary* consequences are also likely to arise. He is likely to explode when frustrations arise on the job or when conflicts arise in his marriage. This can lead to an erratic work life, low-level occupational status, and divorce. In this scenario, the same occupational and marital outcomes are *contemporary* consequences of his current personality, rather than consequences of earlier events such as quitting school.

We have explored these two hypothetical scenarios in some of our own work, using the Institute of Human Development archives from the Berkeley Guidance Study to identify men and women who had a history of temper tantrums during late childhood (Caspi et al., 1987, 1989). We then traced the continuities and consequences of this personality style across the subsequent 30 years of the subjects' lives. Here we summarize the findings only for the male subjects.

We began with the continuity question: Do ill-tempered boys become ill-tempered men? Apparently so. Correlations between the temper tantrum scores in late childhood and Q-sort ratings 20 years later revealed that ill-tempered boys were later described as significantly more undercontrolled, irritable, and moody than their even-tempered peers.

We then examined the subjects' work histories. The major finding was that ill-tempered boys who came from middle-class homes suffered a progressive deterioration of socioeconomic status as they moved through the life course. They were somewhat more likely than their even-tempered peers to terminate their formal education earlier; the occupational sta-

tus of their first jobs was significantly lower, and by midlife (age 40) their occupational status was indistinguishable from that of men born into the working class. A majority of them held jobs of lower occupational status than those held by their fathers at a comparable age. They also had more erratic work lives, changing jobs more frequently and experiencing more unemployment between ages 18 and 40.

Did these men become occupationally disadvantaged because their earlier ill-temperedness started them down a particular path (cumulative consequences) or because their current ill-temperedness handicapped them in the world of work (contemporary consequences)? The path analysis displayed in Figure 21.1 reveals evidence—albeit indirect—for both kinds of consequences.

Cumulative consequences are implied by the effect of childhood ill-temperedness on occupational status at midlife: Tantrums predicted lower educational attainment ($\beta = -.34$, $p < .05$), and educational attainment in turn predicted occupational status ($\beta = .59$, $p < .001$). But there was no direct effect of ill-temperedness on occupational status ($\beta = -.10$). In other words, middle-class boys with a history of childhood ill-temperedness arrived at lower occupational status at midlife because they had truncated their formal education, not because they continued to be ill-tempered. (The subsequent link between occupational status and occupational stability cannot be interpreted unequivocally, because these are contemporaneous variables.)

Contemporary consequences are implied by the strong direct link between ill-temperedness

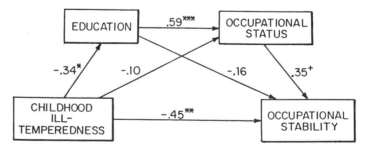

FIGURE 21.1. Midlife occupational status and stability of men with middle-class origins as a function of childhood ill-temperedness ($N = 45$). Adolescent IQ is included as an exogenous variable in this model; its correlation with temper tantrums was $-.09$ (n.s.). $+p < .10$; $^*p < .05$; $^{**}p < .01$; $^{***}p < .001$) From "Moving Against the World: Life-Course Patterns of Explosive Children" by A. Caspi, G. H. Elder, Jr., & D. J. Bem, 1987, *Developmental Psychology, 23*, pp. 308–313. Copyright 1987 by American Psychological Association. Reprinted by permission.

and occupational stability ($\beta = -.45$, $p <$ .01). Men with a childhood history of ill-temperedness continued to be ill-tempered in adulthood, where it got them into trouble in the world of work. (A history of childhood ill-temperedness also affected the domestic sphere. Almost half, or 46% of the men with histories of childhood ill-temperedness had divorced by age 40, compared with only 22% of other men.)

As we have noted earlier, the processes of reactive, evocative, and proactive interaction not only shape personality and mediate its continuity over time, but enable the personality to influence the trajectory of the life course itself.

THE CHALLENGE OF CHANGE

In the opening section of this chapter, we discussed the multiple meanings of the term "continuity." But both there and throughout this chapter, we have finessed the comparable problem involving the term "change." In particular, the term can denote some kind of systematic change (e.g., developmental maturation) or simply the absence of continuity. Conceptually, both continuity and systematic change are positive phenomena in their own right; both can be sought as figure against a background of randomness. But just as the claim of personality coherence requires a theory that specifies the basis on which the diverse phenotypic behaviors can be said to cohere, so a claim of systematic change requires a theory that specifies in what way the observed absence of continuity is "systematic." And just as it is more difficult to sustain a claim of coherence than to demonstrate one of the empirically simpler forms of continuity, so it is more difficult to sustain a claim of systematic change than to demonstrate a simple absence of continuity. Not surprisingly, then, when the term "change" appears in the literature, it most frequently denotes merely the absence of continuity. This chapter has reflected that same imbalance.

Moreover, we have implied that the most promising candidates for theories of systematic change do not seem to do the job. For example, we concluded our discussion of stage theories of adult development by noting that they seem to be more useful for predicting phenomenological changes than for predicting objectively assessed changes in personality. (Even the classic stage

theories of childhood cognitive development are currently under challenge, with the challengers claiming that children already possess the same cognitive competencies as adults but merely lack domain-specific knowledge; see S. L. Bem, 1989; Gelman & Baillargeon, 1983; Keil, 1989.) Finally, we suggested—perversely—that potentially disruptive social transitions in the life course produce personality continuity, not personality change.

In short, it is with some diffidence that we have included the word "change" in the title of this chapter. False advertising, perhaps; we prefer to think of it as a promissory note.

ACKNOWLEDGMENT

Preparation of this chapter was supported in part by a grant from the National Institute of Mental Health (MH-41827).

This chapter is dedicated to the pioneering researchers, past and present, of the Institute of Human Development, University of California at Berkeley. For over half a century, they have asked the critical questions and furnished the important answers. Their wisdom and efforts will continue to guide the longitudinal study of lives.

REFERENCES

Alexander, K. L., & Entwistle, D. S. (1988). Achievement in the first 2 years of school: Patterns and processes. *Monographs of the Society for Research in Child Development, 53*, (Ser No. 218).

Allport, G. W. (1962). The general and the unique in psychological science. *Journal of Personality, 30*, 405–422.

Allport, G. W., Bruner, J. S., & Jandorf, E. M. (1941). Personality under social catastrophe: Ninety life histories of the Nazi revolution. *Character and Personality, 10*, 1–22.

Anderson, C. R. (1977). Locus of control, coping behaviors, and performance in a stress setting: A longitudinal study. *Journal of Applied Psychology, 62*, 446–451.

Andrews, J. D. W. (1988). *The active self in psychotherapy: An integration of therapeutic styles.* New York: Gardner Press.

Backman, C. W. (1985). Interpersonal congruency theory revisited: A revision and extension. *Journal of Social and Personal Relationships, 2*, 489–505.

Backman, C. W. (1988). The self: A dialectical approach. In L. Berkowitz (Ed.), *Advances in experimental social psychology* (Vol. 21, pp. 229–260). New York: Academic Press.

Baltes, P. B. (1987). Theoretical propositions of life-span developmental psychology: On the dynamics between growth and decline. *Developmental Psychology, 23,* 611–626.

Baltes, P. B., Cornelius, S. W., & Nesselroade, J. R. (1979). Cohort effects in developmental psychology. In J. R. Nesselroade & P. B. Baltes (Eds.), *Longitudinal research in the study of behavior and development* (pp. 61–87). New York: Academic Press.

Bates, J. E. (1988). Temperament in infancy. In J. D. Osofsky (Ed.), *Handbook of infant development.* New York: Wiley.

Bem, D. J. (1983). Constructing a theory of the triple typology: Some (second) thoughts on nomothetic and idiographic approaches to personality. *Journal of Personality, 51,* 566–577.

Bem, D. J., & Allen, A. (1974). On predicting some of the people some of the time: The search for cross-situational consistencies in behavior. *Psychological Review, 81,* 506–520.

Bem, S. L. (1989). Genital knowledge and gender constancy in preschool children. *Child Development, 60,* 649–662.

Block, J. (1971). *Lives through time.* Berkeley, CA: Bancroft.

Block, J. (1977). Advancing the psychology of personality: Paradigmatic shift or improving the quality of research. In D. Magnusson & N. S. Endler (Eds.), *Personality at the crossroads: Current issues in interactional psychology* (pp. 37–63). Hillsdale, NJ: Erlbaum.

Block, J., & Block, J. H. (1980). The role of ego-control and ego-resilience in the organization of behavior. In W. A. Collins (Ed.), *Minnesota Symposium on Child Psychology* (Vol. 13, pp. 39–101). Hillsdale, NJ: Erlbaum.

Block, J., Block, J. H., & Keyes, (1988). Longitudinally foretelling drug usage in adolescence: Early childhood personality and environmental precursors. *Child Development, 59,* 336–355.

Bloom, B. S. (1964). *Stability and change in human characteristics.* New York: Wiley.

Bornstein, R., & Smircina, M. T. (1982). The status of the empirical support for the hypothesis of increased variability in aging populations. *The Gerontologist, 22,* 258–260.

Bowlby, J. (1973). *Attachment and loss:* Vol. 2. Separation. New York: Basic Books.

Bradley, R. H., Caldwell, B. M., & Rock, S. L. (1988). Home environment and school performance: A ten-year follow-up examination of three models of environmental action. *Child Development, 59,* 852–867.

Brim, O. G., Jr. (1976). Life span development of the theory of oneself: Implications for child development. In H. W. Reese (Ed.), *Advances in child development and behavior* (Vol. 11, pp. 242–253). New York: Academic Press.

Bronson, W. C. (1966). Central orientations: A study of behavior organization from childhood to adolescence. *Child Development, 37,* 125–155.

Buss, A. H., & Plomin, R. A. (1975). *A temperament theory of personality development.* New York: Wiley.

Buss, A. H., & Plomin, R. (1984). *Temperament: Early developing personality traits.* Hillsdale, NJ: Erlbaum.

Buss, D. M. (1987). Selection, evocation, and manipulation. *Journal of Personality and Social Psychology, 53,* 1214–1221.

Byrne, D., & Griffitt, W. (1966). A developmental investigation of the law of attraction. *Journal of Personality and Social Psychology, 4,* 699–702.

Cairns, R. B. (1979). *Social development.* San Francisco: Freeman.

Cairns, R. B., & Cairns, B. D. (1988). The sociogenesis of self concepts. In N. Bolger, A. Caspi, G. Downey, & M. Moorehouse (Eds.), *Persons in context: Developmental processes* (pp. 181–202). New York: Cambridge University Press.

Cairns, R. B., Cairns, B. D., Neckerman, H. J., Gest, S. D., & Gariepy, J.-L. (1988). Social networks and aggressive behavior: Peer support or peer rejection? *Developmental Psychology, 24,* 815–823.

Cairns, R. B., & Green, J. A. (1979). How to assess personality and social patterns: Observations or ratings? In R. B. Cairns (Ed.), *Analysis of social interaction.* Hillsdale, NJ: Erlbaum.

Cairns, R. B., & Hood, K. E. (1983). Continuity in social development: A comparative perspective on individual difference prediction. In P. B. Baltes & O. G. Brim, Jr. (Eds.), *Life-span development and behavior* (Vol. 5, pp. 301–358). New York: Academic Press.

Cairns, R. B., Perrin, J. E., & Cairns, B. D. (1985). Social structure and social cognition in early adolescence: Affiliative patterns. *Journal of Early Adolescence, 5,* 339–355.

Campbell, J. (1974). *Handbook for the Strong-Campbell Vocational Inventory.* Stanford, CA: Stanford University Press.

Cantor, N., & Kihlstrom, J. (1987). *Personality and social intelligence.* Englewood Cliffs, NJ: Prentice-Hall.

Carson, R. C. (1969). *Interaction concepts of personality.* Chicago: Aldine.

Caspi, A. (1987). Personality in the life course. *Journal of Personality and Social Psychology, 53,* 1203–1213.

Caspi, A., Bem, D. J., & Elder, G. H., Jr. (1989). Continuities and consequences of interactional styles across the life course. *Journal of Personality, 57,* 375–406.

Caspi, A., Elder, G. H., Jr., & Bem, D. J. (1987). Moving against the world: Life-course patterns of explosive children. *Developmental Psychology, 23,* 308–313.

Caspi, A., Elder, G. H., Jr., & Bem, D. J. (1988). Moving away from the world: Life-course patterns of shy children. *Developmental Psychology, 24,* 824–831.

Caspi, A., & Herbener, E. S. (1990). Continuity and change: Assortative marriage and the consistency of personality in adulthood. *Journal of Personality and Social Psychology. 58,* 250–258.

Cattell, R. B. (1957). *Personality and motivation structure and measurement.* Yonkers-on-Hudson, NY: World.

Cattell, R. B. (1973). *Personality and mood by questionnaire.* San Francisco: Jossey-Bass.

Chess, S., & Thomas, A. (1987). *Origins and evolution of behavior disorders.* Cambridge, MA: Harvard University Press.

Clarke, A. D. B., & Clarke, A. M. (1984). Constancy and change in the growth of human characteristics. *Journal of Child Psychology and Psychiatry, 25,* 191–210.

Conley, J. J. (1984a). The hierarchy of consistency: A review and model of longitudinal findings on adult individual differences in intelligence, personality, and self-opinion. *Personality and Individual Differences, 5,* 11–25.

Conley, J. J. (1984b). Longitudinal consistency of adult personality: Self-reported psychological characteristics across 45 years. *Journal of Personality and Social Psychology*, *47*, 1325–1333.

Conley, J. J. (1985). Longitudinal stability of personality traits: A multitrait–multimethod–multioccasion analysis. *Journal of Personality and Social Psychology*, *49*, 1266–1282.

Costa, P. T., Jr., & McCrae, R. R. (1980). Still stable after all these years: Personality as a key to some issues in aging. In P. B. Baltes & O. G. Brim, Jr. (Eds.), *Life-span development and behavior* (Vol. 3, pp. 65–102). New York: Academic Press.

Costa, P. T., & McCrae, R. R. (1988). Personality in adulthood: A six-year longitudinal study of self-reports and spouse ratings on the NEO personality inventory. *Journal of Personality and Social Psychology*, *54*, 853–863.

Costa, P. T., McCrae, R. R., & Arenberg, D. (1980). Enduring dispositions in adult males. *Journal of Personality and Social Psychology*, *38*, 793–800.

Costa, P. T., McCrae, R. R., Zonderman, A. B., Barbano, H. E., Lebowitz, B., & Larson, D. M. (1986). Cross-sectional studies of personality in a national sample: 2. Stability in neuroticism, extraversion, and openness. *Psychology and Aging*, *1*, 144–149.

Daniels, D., & Plomin, R. (1985). Origins of individual differences in infant shyness. *Developmental Psychology*, *21*, 118–121.

Darley, J., & Fazio, R. H. (1980). Expectancy confirmation processes arising in the social interaction sequence. *American Psychologist*, *35*, 867–881.

DeFries, J. C., Plomin, R., & LaBuda, M. C. (1987). Genetic stability of cognitive development from childhood to adulthood. *Developmental Psychology*, *23*, 4–12.

Diener, E., Larsen, R. J., & Emmons, R. A. (1984). Person × situation interactions: Choice of situations and congruence response models. *Journal of Personality and Social Psychology*, *47*, 580–592.

Digman, J. M. (1989). Five robust trait dimensions: Development, stability, and utility. *Journal of Personality*, *57*, 195–214.

Digman, J. M., & Inouye, J. (1986). Further specification of the five robust factors of personality. *Journal of Personality and Social Psychology*, *50*, 116–123.

Dodge, K. A. (1986). A social information processing model of social competence in children. In M. Perlmutter (Ed.), *Minnesota Symposium on Child Psychology* (Vol. 18, pp. 77–125). Hillsdale, NJ: Erlbaum.

Dusek, J. B., & Flaherty, J. F. (1981). The development of the self-concept during the adolescent years. *Monographs of the Society for Research in Child Development*, *46*, (4, Serial No. 191).

Dworkin, R. H., Burke, B. W., Maher, B. A., & Gottesman, I. I. (1976). A longitudinal study of the genetics of personality. *Journal of Personality and Social Psychology*, *34*, 510–518.

Dworkin, R. H., Burke, B. W., Maher, B. A., & Gottesman, I. I. (1977). Genetic influences on the organization and development of personality. *Developmental Psychology*, *13*, 164–165.

Elder, G. H., Jr. (1974). *Children of the Great Depression*. Chicago: University of Chicago Press.

Elder, G. H., Jr. (1979). Historical change in life patterns and personality. In P. B. Baltes & O. G. Brim, Jr. (Eds.), *Life-span development and behavior* (Vol. 2, pp. 117–159). New York: Academic Press.

Elder, G. H., Jr., & Caspi, A. (1988). Economic stress:

Developmental perspectives. *Journal of Social Issues*, *44*, 25–45.

Elder, G. H., Jr., Caspi, A., & Burton, L. M. (1988). Adolescent transitions in developmental perspective: Historical and sociological insights. In M. Gunnar & W. A. Collins (Eds.), *Minnesota Symposium on Child Psychology* (Vol. 21, pp. 151–179). Hillsdale, NJ: Erlbaum.

Emmerich, W. (1968). Personality development and the concepts of structure. *Child Development*, *39*, 671–690.

Emmons, R. A., Diener, E., & Larsen, R. J. (1986). Choice and avoidance of everyday situations and affect congruence: Two models of reciprocal interactionism. *Journal of Personality and Social Psychology*, *51*, 815–826.

Epstein, E., & Guttman, R. (1984). Mate selection in man: Evidence, theory, and outcome. *Social Biology*, *31*, 243–278.

Epstein, S. (1980). The self-concept: A review and the proposal of an integrated theory of personality. In E. Staub (Ed.), *Personality: Basic issues and current research.* (pp. 81–130). Englewood Cliffs, NJ: Prentice-Hall.

Epstein, S., & Erskine, N. (1983). The development of personal theories of reality from an interactional perspective. In D. Magnusson (Ed.), *Human development: An interactional perspective* (pp. 133–147). New York: Academic Press.

Erikson, E. (1950). *Childhood and society*. New York: Norton.

Eron, L. D., Huesmann, L. H., Dubow, E., Romanoff, R., & Yarmel, P. W. (1987). Aggression and its correlates over 22 years. In D. H. Crowell, I. Evans, & C. R. O'Donnel (Eds.), *Childhood aggression and violence* (pp. 249–262). New York: Plenum.

Feldman, K. A., & Newcomb, T. M. (1969). *The impact of college on students*. San Francisco: Jossey-Bass.

Feldman, S. S., & Aschenbrenner, B. G. (1983). Impact of parenthood on various aspects of masculinity and femininity: A short-term longitudinal study. *Developmental Psychology*, *19*, 278–289.

Finn, S. E. (1986). Stability of personality self-ratings over 30 years: Evidence for an age/cohort interaction. *Journal of Personality and Social Psychology*, *50*, 813–818.

Floderus-Myhred, B., Petersen, N., & Rasmuson, I. (1980). Assessment of heritability for personality based on a short form of the Eysenck Personality Inventory. *Behavior Genetics*, *10*, 153–161.

Freud, A. (1980). *Normality and pathology in childhood*. London: Hogarth Press and the Institute of Psycho-Analysis.

Funder, D., Block, J. H., & Block, J. (1983). Delay of gratification: Some longitudinal personality correlates. *Journal of Personality and Social Psychology*, *44*, 1198–1213.

Furstenberg, F. F., Jr., Brooks-Gunn, J., & Morgan, S. P. (1987). *Adolescent mothers in later life*. New York: Cambridge University Press.

Gardner, R. W., Holzman, P. S., Klein, G. S., Linton, H. B., & Spence, D. P. (1959). Cognitive control: A study of individual consistencies in cognitive behavior. *Psychological Issues*, *1*(Monograph No. 4).

Gelman, R., & Baillargeon, R. (1983). A review of some Piagetian concepts. In J. H. Flavell & E. M. Markman (Vol. Eds.), *Handbook of child psychology* (4th ed.):

Vol. 3. Cognitive development (pp. 167–230). New York: Wiley.

Gergen, K. J. (1982). *Toward transformation in social knowledge.* New York: Springer.

Giordano, P. C., Cernkovich, S. A., & Pugh, M. D. (1986). Friendship and delinquency. *American Journal of Sociology, 91,* 1170–1202.

Glenn, N. D. (1980). Values, attitudes, and beliefs. In O. G. Brim, Jr., & J. Kagan (Eds.), *Constancy and change in human development* (pp. 596–640). Cambridge, MA: Harvard University Press.

Goldsmith, H. H., Buss, A. H., Plomin, R., Rothbart, M. K., Thomas, A., Chess, S., Hinde, R. A., McCall, R. B. (1987). Roundtable: What is a temperament? Four approaches. *Child Development, 58,* 505–529.

Greenwald, A. G. (1980). The totalitarian ego: Fabrication and revision of personal history. *American Psychologist, 35,* 603–618.

Guttman, D. L. (1975). Parenthood: Key to the comparative psychology of the life cycle. In N. Data & L. Ginsberg (Eds.), *Life-span developmental psychology: Normative life crises* (pp. 167–184). New York: Academic Press.

Haan, N. (1981). Commmon dimensions of personality development. In D. Eichorn, J. A. Clausen, H. Haan, M. P. Honzik, & P. H. Mussen (Eds.), *Present and past in middle life* (pp. 117–151). New York: Academic Press.

Hanson, R. A. (1975). Consistency and stability of home environmental measures related to I.Q. *Child Development, 46,* 470–480.

Harkness, A. (1989). *Phenotypic dimensions of the personality disorders.* Unpublished doctoral dissertation, University of Minnesota.

Harter, S. (1983). Developmental perspectives on the self-system. In E. M. Hetherington (Vol. Ed.), *Handbook of child psychology* (4th ed.): *Vol. 4. Socialization, personality, and social development* (pp. 275–385). New York: Wiley.

Hartshorne, H., & May, A. (1928). *Studies in the nature of character: Vol. 1. Studies in deceit.* New York: Macmillan.

Helson, R., Mitchell, V., & Moane, G. (1984). Personality and patterns of adherence and nonadherence to the social clock. *Journal of Personality and Social Psychology, 46,* 1079–1096.

Helson, R., & Moane, G. (1987). Personality change in women from college to midlife. *Journal of Personality and Social Psychology, 53,* 176–186.

Higgins, E. T., & Eccles-Parsons, J. (1983). Social cognition and the social life of the child. In E. T. Higgins, D. W. Ruble, & W. W. Hartup (Eds.), *Social cognition and social development: A sociocultural perspective* (pp. 15–62). New York: Cambridge University Press.

Horn, J. L., & Donaldson, G. (1980). Cognitive development in adulthood. In O. G. Brim, Jr., & J. Kagan (Eds.), *Constancy and change in human development* (pp. 445–529). Cambridge, MA: Harvard University Press.

Huesmann, L. R., Eron, L. D., Lefkowitz, M. M., & Walder, L. O. (1984). Stability of aggression over time and generations. *Developmental Psychology, 20,* 1120–1134.

Huesmann, L. R., Eron, L. D., & Yarmel, P. W. (1987). Intellectual functioning and aggression. *Journal of Personality and Social Psychology, 52,* 232–240.

Ickes, W. (1982). A basic paradigm for the study of personality, roles and social behavior. In W. Ickes & E. Knowles (Eds.), *Personality, roles and social behavior.* (pp. 305–341) New York: Springer.

Jensen, A. R. (1973). Let's understand Skodak and Skeels, finally. *Educational Psychologist, 10,* 30–35.

Jensen, A. R. (1978). Genetic and behavioral effects of non-random mating. In C. E. Noble, R. T. Osborne, & N. Weyle (Eds.), *Human variation: Biogenetics of age, race, and sex* (pp. 51–105). New York: Academic Press.

Jones, M. C. (1981). Midlife drinking patterns: Correlates and antecedents. In D. Eichorn, J. A. Clausen, N. Haan, M. P. Honzik, & P. H. Mussen (Eds.), *Past and present in middle life* (pp. 223–242). New York: Academic Press.

Kagan, J. (1969). The three faces of continuity in human development. In D. A. Goslin (Ed.), *Handbook of socialization theory and research* (pp. 983–1002). Chicago: Rand McNally.

Kagan, J. (1980). Perspectives on continuity. In O. G. Brim, Jr., & J. Kagan (Eds.), *Constancy and change in human development* (pp. 26–74). Cambridge, MA: Harvard University Press.

Kagan, J. (1981). *The second year.* Cambridge, MA: Harvard University Press.

Kagan, J. (1984). *The nature of the child.* New York: Basic Books.

Kagan, J. (1989). *Unstable ideas: Temperament, cognition, and self.* Cambridge, MA: Harvard University Press.

Kagan, J., & Moss, H. A. (1962). *Birth to maturity.* New York: Wiley.

Kagan, J., Reznick, J. S., & Snidman, N. (1987). The physiology and psychology of behavioral inhibition in children. *Child Development, 58,* 1459–1473.

Kagan, J., Reznick, J. S., & Snidman, N. (1988). Biological bases of childhood shyness. *Science, 240,* 167–171.

Kandel, D. B. (1978). Similarity in real-life adolescent friendship pairs. *Journal of Personality and Social Psychology, 36,* 306–312.

Keil, F. C. (1989). *Concepts, kinds, and cognitive development.* Cambridge, MA: MIT/Bradford Press.

Kelly, E. L. (1955). Consistency of adult personality. *American Psychologist, 10,* 659–681.

Kohlberg, L. (1966). A cognitive-developmental analysis of children's sex-role concepts and attitudes. In E. E. Maccoby (Ed.), *The development of sex differences* (pp. 82–173). Stanford, CA: Stanford University Press.

Kohn, M. (1977). *Class and conformity.* Chicago: University of Chicago Press.

Kohn, M., & Schooler, C. (1978). The reciprocal effects of the substantive complexity of work and intellectual flexibility: A longitudinal assessment. *American Journal of Sociology, 84,* 24–52.

Kohn, M., & Schooler, C. (1983). *Work and personality: An inquiry into social stratification.* Norwood, NJ: Ablex.

Levinson, D. (1986). A conception of adult development. *American Psychologist, 41,* 3–13.

Lieberman, M. A., & Coplan, A. S. (1970). Distance from death as a variable in the study of aging. *Developmental Psychology, 2,* 71–84.

Livesley, W. J., & Bromley, D. (1973). *Person perception in childhood and adolescence.* New York: Wiley.

Livson, N., & Day, D. (1977). Adolescent personality antecedents of completed family size: A longitudinal study. *Journal of Youth and Adolescence, 6,* 311–324.

Livson, N., & Peskin, H. (1967). Prediction of adult psychological health in a longitudinal study. *Journal of Abnormal Psychology, 72,* 509–518.

Livson, N., & Peskin, H. (1980). Perspectives on adolescence from longitudinal research. In J. Adelson (Ed.), *Handbook of adolescent psychology* (pp. 47–98). New York: Wiley.

MacEvoy, B., Lambert, W. W., Karlberg, P., Karlberg, J., Klackenberg-Larsson, I., & Klackenberg, G. (1988). Early affective antecedents of adult Type A behavior. *Journal of Personality and Social Psychology, 54,* 108–116.

Magnusson, D. (1988). *Individual development from an interactional perspective.* Hillsdale, NJ: Erlbaum.

Markus, H. (1977). Self-schemata and processing information about the self. *Journal of Personality and Social Psychology, 35,* 63–78.

Mascie-Taylor, C. G. N., & Vandenberg, S. G. (1988). Assortative mating for IQ and personality due to propinquity and personal preference. *Behavior Genetics, 18,* 339–345.

Matas, L., Arend, R., & Sroufe, L. A. (1978). Continuity of adaptation in the second year: The relationship between quality of attachment and later competence. *Child Development, 49,* 547–556.

Matheny, A. P., Jr. (1980). Bayley's Infant Behavior Record: Behavioral components and twin analyses. *Child Development, 51,* 1157–1167.

Matheny, A. P., Jr. (1983). A longitudinal study of stability of components from Bayley's Infant Behavior Record. *Child Development, 54,* 356–360.

Matheny, A. P., Jr. (1989). Children's behavioral inhibition over age and across situations: Genetic similarity for a trait during change. *Journal of Personality, 57,* 215–235.

Matheny, A. P., Jr., & Dolan, A. B. (1975). Persons, situations, and time: A genetic view of behavioral change in children. *Journal of Personality and Social Psychology, 32,* 1106–1110.

Matza, D. (1964). *Delinquency and drift.* Berkeley: University of California Press.

McCall, R. B. (1977). Challenges to a science of developmental psychology. *Child Development, 48,* 333–344.

McCall, R. B. (1981). Nature–nurture and the two realms of development: A proposed integration with respect to mental development. *Child Development, 52,* 1–12.

McCall, R. B. (1983). A conceptual approach to early mental development. In M. Lewis (Ed.), *Origins of intelligence* (pp. 107–133). New York: Plenum.

McCall, R. B., Eichorn, D. H., & Hogarty, P. S. (1977). Developmental changes in mental performance. *Monographs of the Society for Research in Child Development, 38*(3, Serial No. 171).

McCrae, R. R., & Costa, P. T. (1985). Updating Norman's "adequate taxonomy": Intelligence and personality dimensions in natural language and in questionnaires. *Journal of Personality and Social Psychology, 49,* 710–721.

McCrae, R. R., & Costa, P. T. (1987). Validation of the five-factor model of personality across instruments and observers. *Journal of Personality and Social Psychology, 52,* 81–90.

McDevitt, S. C. (1986). Continuity and discontinuity of temperament in infancy and early childhood: A psychometric perspective. In R. Plomin & J. Dunn

(Eds.), *The study of temperament: Changes, continuities and challenges* (pp. 27–39). Hillsdale, NJ: Erlbaum.

McGuire, W. J., & McGuire, C. V. (1987). Significant others in self-space: Sex differences and developmental trends in the social self. In J. Suls (Ed.), *Psychological perspectives on the self* (pp. 71–96). Hillsdale, NJ: Erlbaum.

Mischel, W. (1968). *Personality and assessment.* New York: Wiley.

Mischel, W. (1977). The interaction of person and situation. In D. Magnusson & N. S. Endler (Eds.), *Personality at the crossroads: Current issues in interactional psychology* (pp. 333–352). Hillsdale, NJ: Erlbaum.

Mischel, W., Shoda, Y., & Peake, P. K. (1988). The nature of adolescent competencies predicted by preschool delay of gratification. *Journal of Personality and Social Psychology, 54,* 687–696.

Monson, T. C., Hesley, J. W., & Chernick, L. (1982). Specifying when personality traits can and cannot predict behavior: An alternative to abandoning the attempt to predict single-act criteria. *Journal of Personality and Social Psychology, 43,* 385–399.

Mortimore, J. T., Finch, M. D., & Kumka, K. (1982). Persistence and change in development: The multidimensional self concept. In P. B. Baltes & O. G. Brim, Jr. (Eds.), *Life-span development and behavior* (Vol. 4, pp. 264–310). New York: Academic Press.

Moskowitz, D. S. (1986). Comparison of self-reports, reports by knowledgeable informants, and behavioral observational data. *Journal of Personality, 54,* 294–317.

Moskowitz, D. S., & Schwartzman, A. E. (1989). Painting group portraits: Assessing life outcomes for aggressive and withdrawn children. *Journal of Personality, 57,* 723–746.

Moss, H. A., & Susman, E. J. (1980). Longitudinal study of personality development. In O. G. Brim & J. Kagan (Eds.), *Constancy and change in human development* (pp. 530–595). Cambridge, MA: Harvard University Press.

Myers, I. B. (1976). *Introduction to types.* Palo Alto, CA: Consulting Psychologists Press.

Nesselroade, J. R. (1977). Issues in studying developmental change in adults from a multivariate perspective. In J. E. Birren & K. W. Schaie (Eds.), *Handbook of the psychology of aging* (pp. 59–69). New York: Van Nostrand, Reinhold.

Nessleroade, J. R., & Baltes, P. B. (1974). Adolescent personality development and historical change: 1970–1972. *Monographs of the Society for Research in Child Development, 39,* (Serial No. 154).

Neugarten, B. L. (1977). Personality and aging. In J. E. Birren & K. W. Schaie (Eds.), *Handbook of the psychology of aging* (pp. 626–649). New York: Van Nostrand Reinhold.

Newcomb, T. M. (1943). *Personality and social change.* New York: Dryden Press.

Newcomb, T. M. (1961). *The acquaintance process.* New York: Wiley.

Newcomb, T. M., Koenig, K. E., Flacks, R., & Warwick, D. P. (1967). *Persistence and change: Bennington College and its students after twenty-five years.* New York: Wiley.

Norman, W. T. (1963). Toward an adequate taxonomy of personality attributes: Replicated factor structure in peer nomination personality ratings. *Journal of Abnormal and Social Psychology, 66,* 574–583.

Olweus, D. (1979). Stability of aggressive reaction patterns in males: A review. *Psychological Bulletin, 86*, 852–879.

Ozer, D. J., & Gjerde, P. F. (1989). Patterns of personality consistency and change from childhood through adolescence. *Journal of Personality, 57*, 483–507.

Patterson, G. R. (1982). *Coercive family process.* Eugene, OR: Castalia.

Patterson, G. R. (1988). Family process: Loops, levels, and linkages. In N. Bolger, A. Caspi, G. Downey, & M. Moorehouse (Eds.), *Persons in context: Developmental processes* (pp. 114–151). New York: Cambridge University Press.

Patterson, G. R., & Bank, L. (in press). Some amplifying mechanisms for pathologic processes in families. In M. Gunnar (Eds.), *Minnesota Symposium on Child Psychology* (Vol. 22). Hillsdale, NJ: Erlbaum.

Peabody, D., & Goldberg, L. R. (1989). Some determinants of factor structures from personality-trait descriptions. *Journal of Personality and Social Psychology,*

Pianta, R. C., Sroufe, L. A., & Egeland, B. (1989). Continuity and discontinuity in maternal sensitivity at 6, 24, and 42 months in a high risk sample. *Child Development, 60*, 481–487.

Plomin, R. (1986). *Development, genetics, and psychology.* Hillsdale, NJ: Erlbaum.

Plomin, R., & DeFries, J. C. (1985). *Origins of individual differences in infancy: The Colorado Adoption Project.* New York: Academic Press.

Plomin, R., DeFries, J. C., & Fulker, D. W. (1988). *Nature and nurture during infancy and early childhood.* New York: Cambridge University Press.

Plomin, R., DeFries, J. C., & Loehlin, J. C. (1977). Genotype–environment interaction and correlation in the analysis of human behavior. *Psychological Bulletin, 88*, 245–258.

Plomin, R., & Rowe, D. C. (1979). Genetic and environmental etiology of social behavior in infancy. *Developmental Psychology, 15*, 62–72.

Pulkkinen, L. (1982). Self-control and continuity from childhood to late adolescence. In P. B. Baltes & O. G. Brim, Jr. (Eds.), *Life-span development and behavior* (Vol. 4, pp. 63–105). New York: Academic Press.

Pulkkinen, L. (1986). The role of impulse control in the development of antisocial and prosocial behavior. In D. Olweus, J. Block, & M. Radke-Yarrow (Eds.), *Development of antisocial and prosocial behavior: Research, theories, and issues* (pp. 149–175). New York: Academic Press.

Pulkkinen, L. (1988). A two-dimensional model as a framework for interindividual differences in social behavior. In D. H. Saklofske & S. B. G. Eysenck (Eds.), *Individual differences in children and adolescents: International perspective* (pp. 27–37). London: Hodder & Stoughton.

Retherford, R. D., & Sewell, W. H. (1988). Intelligence and family size reconsidered. *Social Biology, 35*, 1–40.

Riegel, K. F. (1972). Time and change in the development of the individual and society. *Advances in child development and behavior, 7*, 81–113.

Roberts, G. C., Block, J. H., & Block, J. (1984). Continuity and change in parents' child rearing practices. *Child Development, 55*, 586–597.

Rodgers, W. L., & Thornton, A. (1985). Changing patterns of first marriage in the United States. *Demography, 22*, 265–279.

Rose, R. J., & Ditto, W. B. (1983). A developmental–genetic analysis of common fears from early adolescents to early adulthood. *Child Development, 54*, 361–368.

Rossi, A. (1980). Aging and parenthood in the middle years. In P. B. Baltes & O. G. Brim, Jr. (Eds.), *Life-span development and behavior* (Vol. 3, pp. 138–205). New York: Academic Press.

Rothbart, M. K., & Derryberry, D. (1981). Development of individual differences in temperament. In M. E. Lamb & A. L. Brown (Eds.), *Advances in developmental psychology* (Vol. 1, pp. 37–86). Hillsdale, NJ: Erlbaum.

Rothbart, M. K., & Goldsmith, H. H. (1985). Three approaches to the study of infant temperament. *Developmental Review, 5*, 237–260.

Rowe, D. C. (1987). Resolving the person–situation debate: Invitation to an interdisciplinary dialogue. *American Psychologist, 42*, 218–227.

Rutter, M. (1987). Psychosocial resilience and protective mechanisms, *American Journal of Orthopsychiatry, 57*, 316–331.

Ryder, R. G. (1967). Birth to maturity revisited: A canonical reanalysis. *Journal of Personality and Social Psychology, 7*, 168–172.

Ryff, C. D. (1984). Personality development from the inside: The subjective experience of change in adulthood and aging. In P. B. Baltes & O. G. Brim, Jr. (Eds.), *Life-span development and behavior* (Vol. 6, pp. 244–278). Orlando, FL: Academic Press.

Scarr, S., & McCartney, K. (1983). How people make their own environments: A theory of genotype–environment correlations. *Child Development, 54*, 424–435.

Scarr, S., & Weinberg, R. A. (1983). The Minnesota adoption studies: Malleability and genetic differences. *Child Development, 54*, 260–267.

Schaie, K. W. (1983). The Seattle Longitudinal Study: A twenty-one year exploration of psychometric intelligence in adulthood. In K. W. Schaie (Eds.), *Longitudinal studies of adult psychological development* (pp. 64–135). New York: Academic Press.

Schaie, K. W., & Parham, I. A. (1976). Stability of adult personality traits: Fact or fable? *Journal of Personality and Social Psychology, 34*, 156–158.

Secord, P. F., & Backman, C. W. (1965). Interpersonal approach to personality. In B. H. Maher (Ed.), *Progress in experimental personality research* (Vol. 2, pp. 91–125). New York: Academic Press.

Siegler, I. C., George, L. K., & Okun, M. A. (1979). A cross-sequential analysis of adult personality. *Developmental Psychology, 15*, 350–352.

Simonton, D. K. (1989). The swan-song phenomenon: Last-works effects for 172 classical composers. *Psychology and Aging, 4*, 42–47.

Snyder, M. (1984). When beliefs create reality. In L. Berkowitz (Ed.), *Advances in experimental social psychology* (Vol. 18, pp. 248–305). Orlando, FL: Academic Press.

Snyder, M., & Ickes, W. (1985). Personality and social behavior. In E. Aronson & G. Lindzey (Eds.), *Handbook of social psychology* (3rd ed., Vol. 2, pp. 883–947). New York: Random House.

Snyder, M., & Swann, W. B., Jr. (1978). Hypothesis testing processes in social interaction. *Journal of Personality and Social Psychology, 36*, 1202–1212.

Snyder, M., Tanke, E. D., & Berscheid, E. (1977). Social perception and interpersonal behavior: On the self-fulfilling nature of social stereotypes. *Journal of Personality and Social Psychology, 35,* 656–666.

Sroufe, L. A. (1979). The coherence of individual development. *American Psychologist, 34,* 834–841.

Sroufe, L. A. (in press). Pathways to adaptation and maladaptation: Psychopathology as developmental deviation. In D. Cicchetti (Ed.), *First Rochester Symposium on Developmental Psychopathology.* Hillsdale, NJ: Erlbaum.

Sroufe, L. A., Fox, N., & Pancake, V. (1983). Attachment and dependency in developmental perspective. *Child Development, 54,* 1615–1627.

Steinberg, L. (1985). Early temperamental antecedents of adult Type A behaviors. *Developmental Psychology, 22,* 1171–1180.

Steinberg, L. (1986). Stability (and instability) of Type A behavior from childhood to young adulthood. *Developmental Psychology, 22,* 393–402.

Swann, W. B., Jr. (1983). Self-verification: Bringing social reality into harmony with the self. In J. Suls & A. G. Greenwald (Eds.), *Psychological perspectives on the self* (Vol. 2). Hillsdale, NJ: Erlbaum.

Swann, W. B., Jr. (1985). The self as architect of social reality. In B. R. Schlenker (Ed.), *The self and social life.* New York: McGraw-Hill.

Swann, W. B., Jr. (1987). Identity negotiation: Where two roads meet. *Journal of Personality and Social Psychology, 53,* 1038–1051.

Thomas, W. I., & Thomas, D. (1928). *The child in America.* New York: Knopf.

Tomkins, S. S. (1979). Script theory: Differential magnification of affects. In H. E. Howe, Jr., & R. A. Dienstbier (Eds.), *Nebraska Symposium on Motivation* (Vol. 26, pp. 201–236). Lincoln: University of Nebraska Press.

Tomkins, S. S. (1986). Script theory. In J. Aronoff, A. I. Rabin, & R. A. Zucker (Eds.), *The emergence of personality* (pp. 147–216). New York: Springer.

Vandenberg, S. G. (1972). Assortative mating, or who marries whom? *Behavior Genetics, 2,* 127–157.

Wachtel, P. L. (1977). *Psychoanalysis and behavior therapy.* New York: Basic Books.

Waters, E. (1978). The reliability and stability of individual differences in infant–mother attachment. *Child Development, 49,* 483–494.

West, D. J. (1982). *Delinquency.* Cambridge, MA: Harvard University Press.

Willerman, L., Turner, R. G., & Peterson, M. (1976). A comparison of the predictive validity of typical and maximal personality measures. *Journal of Research in Personality, 10,* 482–492.

Wilson, R. S. (1983). The Louisville Twin Study: Developmental synchronies in behavior. *Child Development, 54,* 298–316.

Witkin, H. A., & Goodenough, D. R. (1981). Cognitive styles: Essence and origins. *Psychological Issues,* (Monograph No. 51).

Wohlwill, J. F. (1980). Cognitive development in childhood. In O. G. Brim, Jr., & J. Kagan (Eds.), *Constancy and change in human development* (pp. 359–444). Cambridge, MA: Harvard University Press.

Woodruff, D. S., & Birren, J. E. (1972). Age changes and cohort differences in personality. *Developmental Psychology, 6,* 252–259.

Word, C. O., Zanna, M. P., & Cooper, J. (1974). The nonverbal mediation of self-fulfilling prophecies in interracial interaction. *Journal of Experimental Social Psychology, 10,* 109–120.

Wright, J. C., & Mischel, W. (1987). A conditional approach to dispositional constructs: The local predictability of social behavior. *Journal of Personality and Social Psychology, 53,* 1159–1177.

Chapter 22

The Interpersonal Self

Hazel Markus and Susan Cross
University of Michigan

The self can be distinguished as one important aspect of the individual's personality. It is the insider's grasp of the personality; in Sullivan's (1940) terms, the self is what one "takes oneself to be." The self-system, consisting of various forms of self-relevant knowledge and the processes that construct, maintain, and defend this self-knowledge, develops as individuals organize and provide meaning to their own experiences (e.g., Combs & Syngg, 1949; Epstein, 1973; Kegan, 1982; Markus, 1977; Rogers, 1951; Rosenberg, 1979; Sarbin, 1962).

What one "takes oneself to be" is an interpersonal achievement, deriving almost entirely from the individual's relations with others. Achieving some organization of one's share of existence requires the participation of others, although the role of others in self-construction and self-management is variable. Sometimes other people are coproducers of self-feeling and self-understanding. At other times they serve as silent standard bearers, as active monitors, or as partners in ongoing interior dialogues. Even the appreciation of one's unique or unshared aspects of the self requires interaction with others.

Self-concept, identity, and personality researchers approach a consensus on the assumption that it is difficult—perhaps impossible—to escape the influence of others, or to extract a "pure" self from the interpersonal context. Why this is true is a matter of considerable speculation, however. Bowlby (1969) argues that individuals have a need for each other and they come preadapted to expect another who is tuned to their needs. Epstein (1988) claims that there is a need to maintain relatedness to others that is second in importance only to seeking pleasure and avoiding pain. Still others, like Sullivan (1940) and Fairbairn (1952), assert that the need to establish and maintain relations with others is *the* primary motivational force. More specifically, Harre (1980) suggests not only that we have a need for relatedness and for being noticed by others, but that we have an overriding need to be regarded favorably by these others. He argues that seeking the respect of others is the deepest human motive. Other theorists (Baldwin, 1911; Mead, 1934; Sullivan, 1940) focus not on others as need gratifiers, but instead on others as the arbiters of existence. The claim is that individuals are aware of themselves as objects in the world only because other people are aware of them, or have been aware of them. In other words, without others, selves would not exist at all.

576

The goal of this chapter is to systematically explore the variety of ways in which the self can be considered an interpersonal creation. A review of a number of theorists who first elaborated the idea of an interpersonal self is followed by a description of some more recent theories and empirical work. The focus here is on the ways in which the "other" can create and constrain the individual's experience and understanding of the self. We cover the following topics:

1. *The role of others in the social construction of the self.* In this view of the interpersonal self, the thoughts, feelings, and behaviors of others are internalized or incorporated into the self so that individuals claim them as their own. This process is exemplified by children taking on the preferences, values, and beliefs of their various sociocultural contexts.

2. *The role of others in the evaluation and maintenance of the self.* This perspective on the interpersonal self focuses on the thoughts, feelings, and behaviors of others that are distinguished from the individual's own but that are used in self-management. Representations of others are thus carried in the self and used in the evaluation, motivation, control, or defense of the self. The form of this influence is diverse and quite idiosyncratic—a mother's admonition, a mentor's example, a friend's advice, a child's opinion, the recognition that "another has outperformed me," or a generalized view of "what they think of me at work." This section of the chapter also focuses on the structures that may represent or "carry" the other within the self-concept, as well as on individual differences in the degree to which people allow others to influence their behavior.

3. *The role of others as interdependent parts of the self.* In this approach to the interpersonal self, representations of others, especially others who are past, current, or potential partners in ongoing relationships (e.g., friends, spouses, bosses, coworkers, therapists, parents, children), can be conceptualized as parts of the self. To the extent that maintaining certain relationships is critical to self-definition, representations of these others will be continually active, integral parts of the self. This view of the interpersonal self differs from the preceding one in that here it is the whole other (and one's relationship with the other) that is represented within the self, rather than just some specific attribute of another, or some self-relevant information that is communicated by another.

OVERVIEW AND DEFINITION

Most current views of the self characterize it as a complex, dynamic entity that reflects ongoing behavior and that also mediates and regulates this behavior (Greenwald & Pratkanis, 1984; Kihlstrom & Cantor, 1984; Markus & Wurf, 1987; Rosenberg, 1979). The self-concept is viewed as a multifaceted phenomenon—as a set of images, schemas, conceptions, prototypes, theories, goals, or tasks (Carver & Scheier, 1981; Epstein, 1980; Greenwald, 1982b; Markus, 1983; Schlenker, 1980). Sociologists have converged on a similar view of identity, and many now refer to the multiplicity of identity (Burke, 1980; Lester, 1984; Martindale, 1980; McCall & Simmons, 1966; Stryker, 1968; Weigert, 1983).

Whatever the name given to the structures of the self, there is a consensus that they are social products. Their content and form is typically assumed to reflect either the direct or the indirect contribution of others, although the role of others is seldom made explicit. Thus a child's view of his or her own competence in math, for example (e.g., Dweck, 1986; Eccles, 1989; Phillips, 1984) is assumed to be some unspecified amalgam of the parent's views of the child, of the teacher's view, of the peers' views, and of the child's own direct observations. Other self-conceptions, such as one's "ought" selves, reflect what significant others hope or fear for the individual (e.g., a mother's view of her child as a doctor). Such conceptions may or may not be integrated into the individual's own repertoire of possible selves (Markus & Nurius, 1986). In some cases the representations that comprise the self-concept contain images, memories, or fantasies of other people (Singer, 1987). As people regulate their actions, these representations of others, or "internalized objects," as they are termed in the object relations literature, are assigned a diversity of roles in the initiation, maintenance, and evaluation of one's actions.

At any one time only a subset of this universe of representations of the self (the "working self-concept") is active in the regulation of the individual's ongoing actions and reactions. This active, shifting array of self-conceptions is influenced by the individual's motivational state and by the prevailing social circumstances. According to Markus and Wurf (1987), the working self-concept is influential in the shaping and controlling of *intra*personal behavior (self-relevant information processing; affect regulation; and motivational processes) and *inter*personal processes, which include social perception, social comparison, and social interaction. The ways in which the self can be seen to create and govern individual behavior have been the focus of a number of recent extensive reviews (Greenwald & Pratkanis, 1984; Markus & Wurf, 1987; Rosenberg, 1981; Singer & Salovey, 1985), and we do not re-review this material here. Furthermore, a focus on the self in action overlaps almost entirely with characterizations of the functioning of personality—a topic that is the focus of much of the current volume. Our intent, then, is to emphasize the interpersonal nature of the self.

THEORETICAL CONCEPTIONS OF THE INTERPERSONAL SELF

Nearly all of the major theorists of the self have been struck by the fact that however intensely private and uniquely individual the self *seems* to be, it is really a social self. These theorists can be distinguished, however, according to whether they view others primarily as one source of knowledge about the self or whether they view others as essential to self-development. We limit this brief theoretical review to those theorists who have explicitly focused on the self as the object of their theorizing, and, furthermore, those who have viewed some type of interaction between the self and others as critical to the formation and functioning of the self. For example, Freud (1921/1955) did not believe that interpersonal relations are essential for the realization of individual personality, even though the concept of the "superego" as the site of internal parental representations and ego ideals informed many later approaches to the social self. Yet Greenberg and Mitchell (1983), in an excellent comprehensive review of object relations theories, note that Freud, despite his views on the individual and the contained nature of the personality, did not overlook the importance of others. They quote his (1921/1955) statement that "in the individual's mental life someone else is invariably involved, as a model, as an

object, as a helper, as an opponent; and so from the very first, individual psychology, in this extended but entirely justifiable sense of the word, is at the same time social psychology as well" (Greenberg & Mitchell, 1983, p. 21).

James

For James (1890), the social self is one aspect of the entire self. The others include the material self, the spiritual self, and "pure ego." He claimed that we have an "innate propensity" to get ourselves noticed by others and that "no more fiendish punishment could be devised, were such a thing physically possible, than that one should be turned loose in society and remain absolutely unnoticed by all the members thereof" (p. 293). To be unnoticed engenders a "kind of rage and impotent despair . . . from which the cruelest bodily tortures would be a relief" (p. 294). He believed that "a man has as many social selves as there are individuals who recognize him and carry an image of him in their mind" (p. 294).

Cooley

One has the sense from James that although it would be a decidedly painful project, one could conceivably construct a self without the significant involvement of others. Cooley (1902), however, claimed that there is no self without the direct consideration of other people. He described the "looking-glass self" in which one constructs the self from the standpoint of important others. The self-concept reflects "the imagination of our appearance to the other person and the imagination of his judgment of that appearance" (p. 152).

Baldwin

With Baldwin (1911) came a more complex view of the social nature of the individual. As he saw it, the self is not just a reflection of information that has been received from others and that individuals struggle to piece together with their own self-conceptions into some type of harmonious whole. Rather, *every* self-conception is a product of one's interdependence with others. Baldwin asserted,

[I]t is impossible for any one to begin life as an individualist in the sense of radically separating himself from his social fellows. The social bond is established and rooted in the very growth of self-consciousness . . .[The individual] grows in personality and individuality by growing also in sociality. He does not have two lives, two sets of interests, two selves: one personal and the other social. He has but one self, which is personal and social in one, by right of the essential and normal movement of this growth. (p. 27)

Such claims led Baldwin to the belief that "the social relation is in all cases intrinsic to the life, interests, and purposes of the individual; he feels and apprehends the vitality of social relations in all the situations of his life" (p. 29).

Mead

In many respects, Mead (1934) was very much like Cooley (1902) in his theory that an individual "becomes an object to himself only by taking the attitudes of other individuals towards himself within a social environment or context of experience and behavior in which both he and they are involved" (p. 138). Yet, like Baldwin, Mead realized that attending to and incorporating the views of others is an ongoing, moment-by-moment process that lies at the heart of thinking itself. This process is not jut an inference from the self-relevant information provided by others. Mead described this mutually interdependent process as a "conversation of gestures." Thus one individual (A) in an interaction makes a gesture (A1). This serves as a stimulus for the other individual (B), who adjusts or shifts his or her own anticipated gesture (B1) so that it is an appropriate response to A1. Gesture B1 now serves as stimulus for individual A, who creates a gesture (A2) that is appropriate to it, and so the process continues, progressing to more complex levels of intersubjectivity. The second action of participant A is thus inherently social because it has been shaped by a consideration of B's response to the first gesture. And, moments later, what was self-initiated and what was aroused or invoked by the other can no longer be meaningfully distinguished. One assumes from Mead's theorizing that individuals have representations of themselves in a variety of dynamic relationships, and also some representation of the self as viewed by the "generalized other"

(the attitude of the group toward the individual), although the ways in which these others may be represented within the self and continue to structure experience remains unclear.

Sullivan

Sullivan (1940) is one of the key figures in what has been called "interpersonal psychiatry" (Greenberg & Mitchell, 1983). Theorists in this approach share the belief that the larger social and cultural context must be a central aspect of any personality theory. The basic drives and conflicts are thought to be a product of the real or imagined relations between the self and others. Sullivan, for example, became convinced that schizophrenia is connected to a disturbance in the capacity to relate to others, which in turn creates problems in the organization of the self. In fact, he argued that "a personality can never be isolated from the complex of interpersonal relations in which the person lives and has his being . . . personality is made manifest in interpersonal situations, and not otherwise" (1940, p. 32).

Sullivan thought of the self as a set of beliefs constructed from the perceived reactions of significant others, and he drew heavily on Mead (see Greenberg & Mitchell, 1983) in his theorizing. He claimed that when experiences are consistent with the appraisals of others, they are incorporated into the self; otherwise, they remain within the self but are unacknowledged. Furthermore, infants make an early distinction in their experience between anxious states and nonanxious states. Those experiences that invoke the mother's approval and tenderness make the child less anxious and these become classified as the "good-me." Those that make the mother more anxious become identified as the "bad-me." Experiences creating intense anxiety are not integrated into the self-system at all and are designated "not-me." At first all events are experienced according to the nature of the affective response evoked in the mother; eventually, however, the mother's response is not necessary. At this point, even without the mediation of the mother, good-me experiences generate security and bad-me experiences generate anxiety (Sullivan, 1940). According to Sullivan, selves are completely determined by the patterning of interpersonal relations.

What produces anxiety for the individual depends on one's family. In some cases, for example, it is sex that generates anxiety, whereas in others it may be affection or tenderness. The way in which the individual's experiences are organized into good-me, bad-me, and not-me depends on the interpersonal dynamics of the family. In families where anxiety is minimal, the individuals will have large, well-integrated good-me structures; where anxiety is wide-ranging, individuals will have large bad-me or not-me structures in the self (see Greenberg & Mitchell, 1983). In Sullivan's (1940) view, people constantly try to organize their experience so as to ensure good relations with others.

Bowlby

Bowlby (1969) was another interpersonal theorist who sought to specify how the other is represented and carried within the self-system. He thought that caregivers and infants are characterized by a reciprocal responsiveness that creates a tight interdependence between the two. Out of these moment-to-moment transactions come what he called "internal working models of the self." If the mother has been responsive to the child, has communicated that he or she is loved and worthy, and has allowed for independent exploration, the child will develop a model (or a self-schema) of the self as loved, valued, and capable of independence. If the caretaker has given a message of not understanding the child or has rejected the child's demands for attention and comfort, the child will develop a model of the self as unworthy or unloved. Bowlby says that models of the self are dynamic and are used by the child both to understand the caregiver's behavior and to plan his or her own behavior in response. The nature of the initial attachment relationship thus determines the child's working model of the self. If the relationship continues to be open and positive, the model of the self will grow in complexity and integration.

A number of other theories with provocative notions about the interpersonal nature of the self can also be identified, but they are much less well known by self-concept and identity theorists. Fairbairn (see Guntrip, 1971), for example, viewed relations with others as the fundamental need and argued that the ego can only be understood by considering its relationship to others. Many of these highly promising theories (e.g., those of Guntrip, Winnicott, and Mahler; see Greenberg & Mitchell, 1983) are likely to be reclaimed as personality and self-concept theorists endeavor to characterize the connected, related, or social nature of the self. Theorizing about the interpersonal self is likely to entail a move away from its current singular emphasis on traits, attributes, or drives as the defining elements of the self and toward a concern with relations with others as critical elements of the self. As this brief review intends to suggest, the literature on the self and personality is replete with theories that richly deserve extension and supporting empirical work.

THE SOCIAL CONSTRUCTION OF THE SELF

Others influence and constrain not only one's overt behavior, but also one's very thoughts and feelings. Psychologists and sociologists alike concur that self-feeling, self-understanding, self-awareness, and self-knowledge must somehow be products of social interaction (Aronson, 1984; Biddle & Thomas, 1966; Jones & Gerard, 1967; Mead, 1934; Mortimer & Simmons, 1978; Rosenberg & Turner, 1981). Yet, despite a growing understanding of the processes and mechanisms of early childhood socialization (see Harter, 1983; Maccoby & Martin, 1983), the precise ways in which the thoughts, feelings, and behaviors of others are internalized and become significant elements of the self-concept have received little direct empirical attention; their exact role in self-development and in the maintenance of the self-system is only now being closely analyzed.

People do what the others around them, especially the significant others, are doing. They take on the beliefs, attitudes, theories, or roles that are available in a given social context and that help them make sense of their experiences. Psychologists are now asking these questions: What form does the social interaction preceding internalization take (e.g., verbal, nonverbal, cognitive, affective, motoric)? What self-relevant structures (e.g., good-me vs. bad-me structures, internal working models, interpersonal schemas, role–person mergers), if any, are involved in the mediation of this social interaction? What do the relevant others—teachers, peers, family members—offer or provide to the self, and what and how are these contributions of the other incorporated into the self?

A point of agreement among the diverse questions and approaches guiding this work seems to be the assumption that the individual is an active participant in the development of the self. This is not a claim that the individual, especially the neonate, is always involved in conscious reflection and inference. Instead, the assumption is that individuals are active and do not just hold still, passively recording what others tell them about themselves. The individual is continually organizing the stimulus flow from the environment and achieving some understanding of it. Kegan (1982) claims, in fact, that "human being is the composing of meaning" (p. 19), and recent research efforts strongly support earlier theoretical insights that constructing meaning is not a solitary process—that other people have an essential role.

Who Am I?

Other people tell individuals who they are and what this means. They provide the important categories that individuals use in defining themselves. For example, a child's parents as the initial purveyors of American culture tell him or her that independence matters, that it is important to be independent and autonomous, and what it means to be independent and autonomous. Parental influence apparently goes far beyond how children dress, what they eat, whom they vote for, and how they spend their spare time. Families typically provide the categories for organizing one's experience. The well-known musical *Fiddler on the Roof* vivifies the importance of the family in providing self-knowledge and meaning. Tradition, Tevye, the protagonist, sings, is important because it tells "every man exactly who he is and what God expects him to do."

Shweder (1982) proposes that cultures provide information about 10 "themes of social existence." The answers given to these questions are likely to form a core of self-knowledge. The questions are as follows:

1. The problem of personal boundaries: What is me versus what is not-me?
2. The problem of sex identity: What is male versus what is female?
3. The problem of maturity: What is grownup versus what is childlike?
4. The problem of cosubstantiality: Who is of my kind and thus shares food or blood or both with me, versus who is not of my kind?
5. The problem of ethnicity: What is our way versus what is not our way?
6. The problem of hierarchy: Why do people share unequally in the burdens and benefits of our life?
7. The problem of nature versus culture: What is human versus what is animal-like?
8. The problem of autonomy: Am I independent, dependent, or interdependent?
9. The problem of the state: What do I want to do versus what does the group want me to do?
10. The problem of personal protection: How can I avoid the war of all against all?

How the answers to these questions are transmitted from the family to the child is still quite unclear. How do individuals learn what is valued and what is good and appropriate? It is likely that these problems are not explicitly discussed and actively negotiated. Many of the solutions to the problems are transmitted in the course of everyday conversations between parents and children, and among children themselves. Such conversations tell individuals what to feel, what to care about, and how to relate to other people (Heath, 1983; Shweder & Bourne, 1984). For example, children hear, "Only babies cry," "You have to learn to stand up for yourself," "Play by the rules," "If you don't look after yourself, who will?," "What did you do in school today?," "What do you want to be when you grow up?," and so on. The solutions to many of these problems of existence are embodied in the values that parents pass on to their children. Because of the press to impose some order and coherence on one's experience, to answer the "Who am I?" question, and to have some notion of how to be a person, individuals look to the other people in their immediate surroundings; as Shweder (1990) says, they "seize" the meanings others communicate.

The Mutual Shaping of the Self

The fact that many of the answers to the "Who am I?" questions outlined above typically seem obvious and unchallengeable is a consequence of internalization—the process by which one takes on the attitudes, beliefs, and behaviors of another and makes them one's own. Through internalization an individual adopts the understandings of others so that they seem the natural and inevitable consequences of his or her own thoughts. Research on identification theory assumes that when individuals have strong emotional ties to others, they will emulate these others in the hope of maintaining these ties and gaining love and acceptance (e.g., Bandura, 1969; Kelman, 1961). Such identification with a parent, for example, should lead to internalization of the parent's attitudes, beliefs, and characteristic behaviors. The groundwork for the processes of identification that seem to underlie most socialization, and that are doubtless critical to the development of the self, are to be found in the finely tuned interdependency that characterizes the caregiver–child relationship from its beginning (Bowlby, 1969; Stern, 1985; Vygotsky, 1962).

The acquisition of self-knowledge is at first a function of the imitation of one's significant others. Baldwin (1911) believed that imitation is typically given short shrift in the consideration of important social processes. Imitation, he felt, is not just slavish copying of the responses of another, a way to act without thinking. It is not a consequence of mere repetition of another's actions; rather, it is effortful and inventive, "a means to further ends, a method of absorbing what is present in others and making it over in forms peculiar to one's own temper and valuable to one's own genuis" (p. 28).

Caretaker–Child Interaction

Recent work by developmental psychologists such as Stern (1985) and Trevarthen (1980) has returned to a focus on the process of creative imitation and to a fine-grained analysis of the subtle, but powerful, role of the other in the development of self. Studies of early infant development suggest that concepts of the self and concepts of the caregiver are developed simultaneously out of the moment-to-moment transactions that occur as the caregiver feeds the hungry baby, soothes the crying baby, cuddles the gurgling baby, and in general tunes his or her talking, smiling, and gurgling so that it matches or mimics the baby's responses (Bretherton, 1988; Stern, 1985; Thompson, 1987). In the first 9 months caregivers appear

to imitate their babies quite exactly. The baby and the mother, for example, seem to coordinate their activities so that their feelings and actions are responsive to each other.

Stern (1985) hypothesizes that infants represent some aspects of their early social interactions in terms of episodes that are "small, coherent chunks of lived experiences." These episodes are made up of "sensations, perceptions, actions, thoughts, affects, and goals which occur in some temporal, physical and casual relationship so that they constitute a coherent episode of experience" (p. 95). Recurrent episodes are organized and represented preverbally as "representations of interactions that have been generalized" (RIGS). These, Stern suggests, are the basis of the infant's continual sense of a core self. This core self includes a sense of one's self as an agent, as a physical whole, as experiencing affect, and as being continuous with one's own past. Presumably this core self becomes the foundation for the more explicit knowledge of the self that comes later.

After 9 months, Stern (1985) argues that caregivers, when relating to their infants, try to match the affect carried in the infants' responses. Through some combination of their own verbal and nonverbal responses, caregivers match the timing, the intensity, or the overall shape of the infants' responses. Stern calls this matching "affective attunement." In many respects, this type of reciprocal interdependence is similar to the "conversation of gestures" proposed by Mead, in which the response of the other shapes and tunes the response of the self. The consequence of this process appears to be some awareness of both the self and the other.

The exact workings of such interpersonal processes are understandably extremely difficult to delineate. Earlier theorists assumed that becoming aware of the self involved an ability to see one's self from another's perspective. For example, in a study of chimpanzees, Gallup (1977) compared chimps reared in social isolation with chimps given considerable social experience. His hypothesis was that a chimp reared in isolation would not have the opportunity to examine the self from another's point of view, and thus it should not recognize itself in a mirror. After 10 days of either social experience or isolation, Gallup anesthetized the chimps and painted one of their ears and eyebrows bright red. He found a striking difference in self-recognition: When the mirror was introduced, none of the chimps reared in isolation showed any signs of self-recognition, whereas the socially reared chimps showed numerous signs of self-recognition; that is, they often touched the red ear and eyebrow when in the presence of the mirror.

According to Gallup (1977) this study showed that chimps have a sense of self and that others are necessary for its development. The basic paradigm has since been used repeatedly with infants. Investigators place a red mark on children's faces without their knowledge and then show them a mirror. However, these studies and the ensuing controversies have focused on whether or not infants have self-concepts and, if so, at what precise age they develop (e.g., Lewis & Brooks-Gunn, 1979). The way in which others contribute to self-recognition has not been given equal attention.

The assumption is that Gallup's isolated chimps were unable to assume the role of the other and thus showed no signs of self-recognition. Most self-concept researchers take as a given Mead's view that "the self can exist for the individual only if he assumes the role of the other" (1934, p. 196). Assuming the role of the other, however, is a complex capacity, and one that seems to require a level of cognitive differentiation not usually accorded to most animals or to the child embedded in his or her own egocentric perspective (Piaget, 1930). Notably, Neisser (1988), like Stern, has recently argued that some aspects of self-knowledge are actually quite directly perceived and may not require the ability to take the perspective of the other on the self. Neisser claims, for example, that individuals have a perception of themselves in the physical environment that derives primarily from kinetic information, which is available as the individual moves.

There are doubtless many routes to self-knowledge and many kinds of self-knowledge, and it is likely that some important individual differences can be explained by systematic variation in the elaboration or importance attached to various types of self-knowledge (i.e., self-knowledge that is inferred vs. self-knowledge as directly perceived; knowledge of self as interrelated vs. knowledge of self as separate or individuated). Lewis (1986), for example, reports that children labeled as "insecurely attached" were those who were first to recognize themselves in the mirror self-recognition task.

Internal Working Models of the Self

In the early stages of self-development, it is evident that others are less valuable for their views, images, or impressions of the self than they are for the affective quality and the contingency or close alignment of their responses with the child's. Contingent responding becomes the impetus for continued response (Murray & Trevarthen, 1985). Bretherton (1988) provides a very thorough review of the development of communicaion between the infant and the caretaker, and the ways in which various patterns of communication foster the development of internal working models. These models, in turn, are thought to mediate the development of attachment. A sensitively mothered child is one whose mother is responsive to signals of distress and to the signals for feeding, contact, and play. A child who is not sensitively mothered fails to have his or her immediate needs met, and also receives the message, "Your responses are not meaningful or important" (Ainsworth, Bell, & Stayton, 1974; Bretherton, 1988; Emde, 1983; Stern, 1985). Bretherton notes that insensitive mothering can include ignoring a child's bids for attention, or it can be a consequence of insisting on contact with the child or interfering when the child is attending elsewhere.

After the first year, however, self–other interactions are based less on the reciprocal interdependency of responses described earlier and more on the child's internal working models of the self (Bowlby, 1969; Sroufe, 1988). It is these models that will increasingly govern the individual's experience of the world. The nature of these earliest internal working models of the self (also called "self-schemas") that derive from social interaction have yet to be the focus of intensive inquiry. The functioning of such cognitive structures in adults has been detailed in a number of recent reviews (Markus & Zajonc, 1985; Singer & Salovey, 1985; Wyer & Gordon, 1984). Such models or schemas of the self are organized representations of past experience that "work" through their selective influence on the entire continuum of information processing. These models influence attention, encoding, storage, retrieval, inference, and planning and anticipation. They are revised and updated on the basis of new information.

A number of studies indicate that the responsiveness of the mother influences the child's emotional expressiveness, which in turn should be related to the nature of the internal working model (Grossman & Grossman, 1984; Grossman, Grossman, & Schwan, 1986). In one clinical study, observers compared the responsiveness of well and clinically depressed mothers (Radke-Yarrow, Cummings, Kucynsky, & Chapman, 1985). Depressed mothers responded predictably; their responses were not contingent upon their children's behavior, and thus it may have been difficult for the children to receive messages that their responses were meaningful or important. Caretakers may not be necessary for a sense that one exists (being able to effect any type of change in the environment could provide this evidence); they are, however, essential for the sense that "I am loved or worthy" and probably for any significant sense that "I am competent." Cassidy (1988), for example, found that kindergartners judged to have a secure relationship with their mothers presented a positive view of themselves and their relationship to their mothers when they used a doll family to complete various story beginnings.

Once formed, internal working models of self and its relationships are assumed to influence subsequent relationships throughout one's life. Simply, one's earliest relationships determine one's beliefs about the self and others, and these understandings will govern behavior in all subsequent relationships. Hazan and Shaver (1987), in an indirect test of these ideas, found attachment styles among the relationships of adults that matched those identified for mother and child. Furthermore, they noted that people with these different attachment orientations held different ideas about the course of romantic love, the trustworthiness of partners, and their own worthiness to be loved. Finally, the adult attachment patterns matched respondents' reports of their attachment histories. For example, secure respondents remembered their mothers as responsive and caring.

Differentiation of Self-Schemas

With the acquisition of language comes a differentiation in the self. There are now some aspects of self-experience that are labeled and thus objectified (Stern, 1985). This new verbal channel allows for a very efficient sharing of experience, and the interdependency between self and other will now be increasingly verbal. Yet labels such as "good," "smart," or "funny" are likely to capture only a small part of the rich

experiential units that may have previously organized the child's experience. This leaves a core of private experience that others will not have access to (Singer & Kolligian, 1987)—a subjective self that is different and separate from an objective self. Language may thus hasten the development of a sense of self as special or unique, as well as the sense that others' views of "me" may not be identical to one's own view, or to each other's views (e.g., what Daddy means by "good girl" is somewhat different from what Mommy means).

The child now begins to elaborate a series of self-schemas that build on the earlier sensorimotor senses of self and that integrate the views of others with one's own view of the self. There is no question that children of 7 or 8 have clearly articulated, stable self-schemas (Keller, Ford, & Meacham, 1978; Peevers & Secord, 1973). Eder (1989), in fact, suggests that children as young as 3½ have consistent views of themselves. To examine these preschool self-schemas, she devised a procedure in which two puppets describe themselves and then the child is asked, "How about you?" For example, one puppet says, "I usually play with friends," while another says, "I usually play by myself." Children were apparently willing and able to choose the puppet that was similar to themselves—an indication of some degree of self-understanding.

Self-concept researchers have gained a considerable understanding about the nature of the self in middle childhood and into adolescence (for excellent reviews, see Damon & Hart, 1982, 1988; Harter, 1983, 1988; Rosenberg, 1979). Damon and Hart (1988), for example, claim that children move through a series of stages in the development of self-understanding. In early childhood, self-knowledge typically focuses on characterizations of moods, preferences, and aversion. In middle childhood, children make more use of direct social comparison with others and describe the self relative to some standards. By early adolescence, the focus of self-knowledge is on interpersonal characteristics, and by late adolescence on beliefs, philosophy, and morals. The various ways in which others facilitate or impair these transitions in understanding deserve further focus. It may be that children cannot make explicit comparisons with specific others until middle childhood (e.g., Ruble & Rholes, 1981; Suls & Sanders, 1982), but information from others and about others is surely being used in developing understandings and expectations for the self. What, for example, is involved in creating the so-called "generalized other"?

As described by Selman (1980) the development of the self seems to involve a process of increasing differentiation from the other, and a growing ability to take the perspective of the other. It would be useful also to have a model of how the developing self retains the others in the self-concept and remains in some respects integrated or related to them, even while increasingly appreciating their separate perspectives and intrapsychic lives. Rosenberg (1986) maintains that the self remains interpersonal throughout development but that the form of its interpersonal nature changes. Young children are interpersonal in that others (family members, playmates) are typically included in self-description. Adolescents, however, are interpersonal in that they frequently describe themselves in terms of interpersonal feelings (e.g., "easy to talk to," "nice," "friendly," etc.). Furthermore, Selman (1980) claims that mature adolescents increasingly describe themselves in terms of their interactions with others (e.g., "can get along with others," "make friends easily," "have difficulties with people").

In support of the importance of others for developing adaptive schemas of the self, Damon and Hart (1988) report that delinquents provide fewer responses reflecting interpersonal strivings, such as gaining the approval of others or connecting with the family. Oyserman and Markus (1990), in a study exploring the relationship between the nature of the social environment and the configuration of possible selves, found that delinquent adolescents who had "feared" possible selves that were not offset or balanced by positive, "expected" selves were the most likely to report that "no one or nothing" had influenced them.

The importance of others in developing self-structures is also implied by findings that show differences in self-representation, depending on the nature of the relationship. Individuals' descriptions of themselves alone are not the same as their descriptions of themselves with their mothers, fathers, friends, or romantic partners (Harter, 1988; Leahy, 1985). Charting the nature of the role of others in continued self-development—the nature of their evaluations and judgements and the conditions under which these others are internalized into the self-schema or working model—is becoming an

agenda of increasing importance for developmental and social psychologists (see Harter, 1983; Rosenberg, 1988).

Self and the Larger Society

The preceding section emphasized how others in one's immediate social surroundings—for the most part, caregivers—are involved in the construction of the self. The role of others, where the others are the larger "society" in its various forms, is also significant. The incorporation of the social world beyond the family has been the dominant concern of sociologists, who emphasize the "roles" and "identities" that individuals can take on and internalize (Biddle, 1986; Burke, 1980; Sarbin & Scheibe, 1983; Turner, 1978; Weigert, Teitge, & Teitge, 1986). Very few of the major theorists of the self have paid much attention to the role of political forces, class structure, or other socioeconomic factors in creating the self. These types of structural factors locate individuals in society and are significant for self-construction because they determine the availability of roles (Heiss, 1981). Furthermore, sociologists claim that many self-conceptions are best understood as "role identities," which are views of the self behaving in particular roles (Callero, 1985; McCall, 1987; Turner, 1978; Weigert et al., 1986). Stryker (1987) defines identifies as "internalized role designations, corresponding to the social locations of persons in their various networks of interaction" (p. 89). The significant question from the point of view of this chapter is this: How do roles and role identities operate to create and structure the social self?

Individuals conform to expectations held by others because they perceive that powerful others will sanction them for noncompliance, or because they internalize the expectations of others, accepting them as their own, and thus exhibit the expected patterns of behavior because it seems right to do so. How imitation of the behavior of others influences the self-system has not been closely analyzed because, as we have emphasized earlier, most models of the self (particularly most psychological models of the self) do not leave much explicit room for others. In an attempt to address this problem, Stryker (1987) defines the self as a structure of salient identities and a set of corresponding personal traits. Weigert et al. (1986) suggest that the self is a "process involving knowledge and emotion shaped by the individual's roles and social position" (p. 42). Turner (1978) refers to "role–person mergers," and claims that when a person is merged with a role, there will be significant consequences for personality. Person and role are merged when individuals refuse to abandon a role even when faced with advantageous alternatives, when they acquire role-appropriate behaviors, and when they fail to engage in proper role compartmentalization.

Turner (1968) offers three principles to use in determining when role–person mergers will occur. These mergers will occur when the roles are used by others to identify the person; when they allow the person to maximize autonomy and positive self-evaluation; and when the investment in the role has been especially great. In a similar vein, Wiley and Alexander (1987) conceive of roles as dispositional schemas. The trait dimensions associated with a particular role are what guide behavior. The emphasis is less on individuals learning particular patterns of behavior and more on their learning the identity or set of traits that an actor in a given role is supposed to display.

Stryker (1984) has called for attention to the processes that "underwrite the linkage between identity salience and role performance" (p. 8). That individuals want to live out particular roles, or believe them to be important, does not adequately explain role performance. Presumably, the affective, cognitive, or sensorimotor representations and processes that elaborate one's identity are what create the link between identity and performance. The more salient a particular identity is, the more events and situations will be perceived and structured according to this identity.

Building on Turner's notions of the conditions fostering role–person mergers, Wiley and Alexander (1987) have outlined those conditions in which in-role behavior will influence what they call the "core self" or the "continuous self":

1. Enacting highly valued roles will influence the core self. Highly valued roles reflect the most important dispositional values of a society, the ones that all significant others can be expected to share. For example, a scientist is conceptualized as independent, creative, and hard-working.
2. As long as one component of a role is extremely reinforcing, the actor will choose to embrace the whole role.

3. Performing multiple roles that embody the same dispositions will lead the individual to ascribe these traits to the core self.
4. If a role, such as the female role, pervades the whole (one cannot escape the role and is always responded to by others as if this role is central to self), many of the traits associated with that role will be thought of as core self.
5. Certain roles constrain the other roles that one can embrace and/or the people with whom one interacts and thus make it more likely that the attributes associated with the role will be attributed to the self.

Other researchers have suggested that social change or upheaval may influence whether role–person mergers occur. Zurcher (1977) claims that in times of rapid social change, individuals may move from conceiving of themselves in terms of social roles to a more transcendental or "reflective" perspective on the self. Using the Twenty Statements Test (Kuhn & McPartland, 1954), Zurcher and his colleagues found that the modal type of self-description of college students had changed from a social role orientation in 1957 to a more situation-free orientation in 1970. They attributed this change to the social and cultural changes experienced in the United States as a whole during that period. This perspective is consistent with the findings of Turner (1976), who noted the shift in American young people from a "self-as-institution" to a "self-as-impulse" orientation.

THE ROLE OF OTHERS IN EVALUATING AND MAINTAINING THE SELF

In the preceding section, the focus has been on others who are internalized or merged with the self through social roles or relationships, and who thereby create the self. In this section, we begin by reviewing perspectives on the self in which others are involved much more indirectly in the construction of the self. We focus on the role of others in providing the self-relevant information that is used in the evaluation and maintenance of the self. We briefly review research on reflected appraisal, self-fulfilling prophecies, direct feedback, social comparison, and self-verification. This section concludes with an examination of individual differences in the degree to which one allows others to influence the self.

Interpersonal Processes

We come to see ourselves as others see us. This is one underlying assumption of those researchers and theorists who have investigated the role of information provided by others in the construction of the self. Other people's attitudes or "appraisals" of an individual may result in the individual's perceiving himself or herself as gifted, attractive, or "special," or as troublesome, homely, and unwanted. These appraisals may be in the form of direct feedback, or may be perceived, inferred, or assumed by the recipient. In the latter case, symbolic interactionists have termed these attitudes "reflected appraisals" (Sullivan, 1940), and have investigated how individuals' perceptions of other's responses toward them influence self-conceptions.

Reflected Appraisals

As described above, Cooley (1902) wrote of the "looking-glass self," describing it as the consequence of the individual's *imagination* of or presumptions about another person's judgment of himself or herself. These presumptions, or reflected appraisals, were in turn thought to influence self-appraisals. This theory has generated a diversity of research addressing the social nature of self-appraisals, particularly by symbolic interactionists. In a review of articles in the symbolic-interactionist tradition, Shrauger and Schoeneman (1979) concluded that perceived reactions of others are related to one's self-conceptions, but that self-conceptions are only moderately related to others' true judgments of the person. In other words, "What I think you think about me is related to what I think about myself, but what I think about myself is only slightly related to what you *really* think about me." This conclusion was confirmed by Felson (1989), who found that although fourth to eighth grade children's reflected appraisals of their parents did influence the children's self-appraisals, these reflected appraisals were not very accurate, and did not completely mediate their parents' *actual* appraisals of them. In earlier research Felson (1985) found that reflected appraisals of these children's peers were related to self-appraisals in the area of physical attractiveness, but not in athletic ability or academic ability. He suggests that in domains where "objective" information is available (e.g., grades in an academic area), perceptions

of others' opinions will be less important. But for characteristics that are socially defined (such as attractiveness), the reflected appraisals of others will be more important in shaping the individual's self-conceptions.

An individual's ability to perceive others' opinions or likelihood of incorporating those opinions into his or her own self-concept may also vary with age. Leahy and Shirk (1985) review research demonstrating a developmental trend in this process. Drawing upon work by Selman (1980) and others, they suggest that the ability to understand that the self may be an object of evaluation by others begins with the child's development of *self-reflective* thought. The magnitude of the influence of others' opinions on the individual's self-conceptions may peak in young adolescence (Elkind, 1967; Harter, 1986), decreasing in later adolescence (see also Harter, 1983, for a review). This sensitivity to other's opinions, coupled with heightened self-absorption (Elkind, 1967), may result in greater volatility of what Rosenberg (1986) has called the "barometric self-concept" (p. 124). The barometric self-concept is the portion of the self that fluctuates from moment to moment, responding to the real or imagined evaluations of others in the environment.

Not only is the impact of the perceived opinions of others variable with age, but the others whose opinions are viewed as important may vary as well. Rosenberg (1979) and Harter (1990) have found that parents are the most important source of information about the self for young children, whereas peers become more important in adolescence. In addition, children and adolescents may be able to make others more or less significant to them. Rosenberg (1973) reports research demonstrating that children in 3rd through 12th grades were able to protect their own self-esteem by disvaluing or discrediting the judgments of parents, teachers, or classmates whom they perceived as thinking poorly of them. Rosenberg concludes that we are most likely to see ourselves "as we think others who are important to us and whose opinion we trust see us" (1973, p. 857).

These others whose opinions we care about may take the form of an internal reference group or audience (Schlenker, 1985). These internal referents may be significant others that one cares about, or a fictitious or hypothetical person or group. In a test of the consequences of a private audience, Baldwin and Holmes (1987) found that subjects' responses to a particular experience (either reading a sexually permissive piece of fiction or a failure experience) were significantly influenced by a private audience (e.g., friends or parents) previously primed by the experimenter. Although the subjects denied the influence of these primed reference groups, the researchers found significant differences in subjects' responses when friends versus parents were primed (when the stimulus was sexually permissive material), and when an accepting versus a contingently accepting other was primed (when the stimulus was a failure experience).

Yet Mead (1934) argued that we do not see ourselves as we think particular others see us, but in terms of a "generalized other." Felson (1989) found that children have a generalized sense of how others view them, but are not very accurate in predicting how they are viewed by specific persons. Such a conclusion has been supported in a review by DePaulo, Kenny, Hoover, Webb, and Oliver (1987), who found that research indicates that the process of reflected appraisal is best understood as the ability to judge how one is viewed by other people in general, rather than the ability to judge how one is viewed by specific individuals (see also Kenny & Albright, 1987). We return in a later section to the role of others in providing standards or an internalized reference for the self.

Expectancies and the Self-Fulfilling Prophecy

Researchers in the psychological tradition have examined this indirect effect of others' attitudes and opinions in research concentrating on expectancy effects (Taylor, Wood, & Lichtman, 1983) and the self-fulfilling prophecy (for general reviews, see Darley & Fazio, 1980; Jussim, 1986; Miller & Turnbull, 1986; Rosenthal & Rubin, 1978). In these processes, others' expectations and subsequent treatment of an individual may influence the individual's self-conceptions and self-evaluations. Most research, however, has focused on the effects of expectancies on particular behaviors. For example, Word, Zanna, and Cooper (1974) found that white subjects treated black applicants for a job differently from white applicants, eliciting a poorer performance from the black applicants. Similarly, Snyder, Tanke, and Berscheid (1977) demonstrated that males' stereotypical beliefs about the relationships between physical attractiveness and sociability in females caused them to behave in a friendlier manner in a telephone conversation with women they had been told were attractive, leading the females to act in a way that confirmed these beliefs.

Jussim (1986) reviews research examining the influence of teachers' expectations on students' self-conceptions. He suggests that teacher perceptions will have an impact on skill development, on perceptions of control, and on the value placed on achievement. A teacher's expectancies may also interact with a student's current self-concept in producing self-concept change. For example, a student who has a self-schema of being "smart" may resist a teacher's lower expectations of him or her, acting in a way so as to disconfirm the expectancy (Swann & Ely, 1984), and reducing the effects of the expectancy on his or her self-concept. An individual who is unsure of his or her abilities will be more likely to confirm another's expectancies (Swann & Ely, 1984).

Darley and Fazio (1980), in an analysis of the effects of other's expectancies on self-concept change, suggest that self-perception theory (Bem, 1967) may explain the internalization of behavior in response to an expectancy. Self-perception theory states that people observe their own behavior, and infer their attitudes or abilities from that behavior. Thus, if a person responds like an extravert as a consequence of being asked "extraverted" questions, then the person may infer that he or she truly *is* an extravert, and behave accordingly in future situations (Fazio, Effrein, & Falender, 1981; Synder & Swann, 1978). But such inferences are importantly determined by the person's attributions. As Fazio et al. (1981) and Darley and Fazio (1980) have explained, such attributions to the self are constrained by the availability of other potential attributions. For example, the person may attribute his or her behavior to the behavior of the other person, or to some aspect of the situation (Fazio et al. 1981). However, Swann and Hill (1982) found that when a person was given self-discrepant feedback and had no opportunity to react against that feedback, more self-concept change was indicated than when the person was able to disconfirm the feedback.

Direct Feedback

Other research has investigated the effects of direct feedback from others on the self (for a review, see Shrauger & Schoeneman, 1979). This feedback is more likely to be incorporated into the self (1) when the other is perceived as very competent (Webster & Sobieszek, 1974); and (2) when the feedback is validated by others (Backman, Secord, & Pierce, 1963). These characteristics of the other interact with aspects of the information and the recipient in determining the degree of influence of the other on the recipient's self-conceptions (see Markus & Wurf, 1987, for a review). Inconsistent information is more likely to be rejected than is consistent or self-affirming information, especially if the information is inconsistent with a cherished, certain, or important self-conception (Fiske & Taylor, 1984; Jussim, 1986; Markus, 1977; Swann & Ely, 1984).

Social Comparisons

Not only do we come to see ourselves as others see us, but we also come to see ourselves differently depending on the others who surround us. Others may provide indirect information to the self by the individual's use of social comparison (Festinger, 1954). By comparing the self to others, the individual can make estimates of ability, attractiveness, personal characteristics, and correctness of behavior or opinions. Festinger identified two functions of comparison with others: "normative" and "comparative." In normative comparison, the individual learns norms, values, and attitudes that may be internalized and made self-relevant or self-defining. The comparative function of social comparisons provides the person with information about his or her abilities, characteristics, or attributes. Many of the normative functions of social comparisons have been described in the section on the social construction of the self; we focus here on the role of others in comparative functions.

Festinger (1954) assumed that the primary motivation of social comparison is an accurate self-evaluation of attitudes and abilities. As a result, he suggested that individuals prefer to compare themselves with similar others. In subsequent writing, researchers have outlined other motivations for social comparison (Wood, 1989), and have shown that in some situations individuals may make comparisons with dissimilar others (Brickman & Bulman, 1977; Crocker, Thompson, McGraw, & Ingerman, 1987).

In a recent review of the research, Wood (1989) succinctly clarifies three purposes that comparisons with others serve: self-evaluation, self-improvement, and self-enhancement. In self-evaluation, individuals compare themselves with others in order to obtain diagnostic or differentiating information about their abilities (see Scheier & Carver, 1983a, and Trope, 1986, for reviews). The conclusion from most of the early research by Festinger and others was that people can obtain the most informative comparisons from similar others (Festinger, 1954; Radloff, 1966). Much of the subsequent research attempted to spell out the basis for similarity (Rosenberg, 1973; Schachter, 1959) and the conditions under which similar versus dissimilar others would be chosen for comparison (Brickman & Bulman, 1977; Hakmiller, 1966; Kruglanski & Mayseless, 1987; Mettee & Smith, 1977; Thornton & Arrowood, 1966; see also Suls & Miller, 1977).

This evaluative aspect of social comparison may be influential in the individual's unique construction of the self. Social comparisons may give the individual information not only about how good or correct he or she is, but also about how unique or different he or she is from others. McGuire and Padawer-Singer (1976) have demonstrated that one's distinctive characteristics within a group may become importantly self-defining. For example, a tall person in a room full of relatively short people will be more likely to define himself or herself in terms of height; a blonde person visiting Japan may be more likely to define himself or herself in terms of hair color. Although this work has focused on relatively short-term or "spontaneous" self-descriptions, such comparisons may also form the basis of longer-lasting self-conceptions. For example, Tesser and Campbell (1986; see also Tesser, 1988) have suggested that as a result of comparing the self against "close" others, the developing child will tend to select those domains for self-definition in which he or she performs better than the comparison to others.

Wood (1989) describes Festinger's "unidirectional drive upward" as a drive toward self-improvement. To fulfill this goal, people tend to make upward comparisons, looking toward those who perform better than themselves in a particular domain. Some comparisons provide information about how to complete a task or how to improve one's performance on tasks (Feldman & Ruble, 1977). At other times, by comparing with others whose performance represents excellence in a domain, an individual may be provided with inspiration (Brickman & Bulman, 1977), or a sense of what is possible in that domain.

Others also influence the self as the person pursues self-enhancement goals (Festinger, 1954). For example, Morse and Gergen (1970) found that people evaluated themselves differently, depending on whether they shared a room with a person who appeared either socially desirable or socially undersirable. When a particular comparison is potentially threatening to the self-concept, the person may avoid the comparison (Brickman & Bulman, 1977; Martin, 1986) or seek downward comparisons (see Wills, 1981, and Wood, 1989, for reviews). Yet when threatening comparisons are very likely, persons may alter their perception of either themselves (e.g., "that ability isn't really so important to me"; Tesser, 1986), the situation or relationship (Tesser, 1986), or the comparison person (Brickman & Bulman, 1977; Wood, Taylor, & Lichtman, 1985). Research on the false-consensus and false-uniqueness biases has demonstrated how people distort the extent to which their abilities are shared by others and the commonality of their opinions, resulting in the sense of both uniqueness and a sense of belonging or correctness (Marks, 1984; Mullen et al., 1985; Orive, 1988; Ross, Greene, & House, 1977).

The relative importance of each of these motivations for social comparison may vary with age. Research has shown that the frequency of social comparisons for the purpose of self-evaluation increases during the middle elementary grades (Frey & Ruble, 1985; Masters, 1971; Ruble, Boggiano, Feldman, & Loebl, 1980; Ruble, Feldman & Boggiano, 1976; Ruble & Flett, 1988; Ruble & Rholes, 1981; Suls & Sanders, 1982). Frey and Ruble (1985) suggest that other goals in comparison —understanding social norms, learning how to do the task, ensuring equity, or affiliation—may precede the development of comparisons for self-evaluation. But once children have developed a belief that ability is a stable factor in performance, they may decrease overt comparisons in order to protect their own or others' feelings (Brickman & Bulman, 1977; Frey & Ruble, 1985, 1987). Suls and Mullen (1982) review findings showing that social comparison processes continue to vary across adulthood, becoming relatively less frequent in old age.

Self-Presentation and Self-Verification

Others' responses to a person's self-presentations may also affect or shape his or her self-concept. Tedeschi (1981; Tedeschi & Norman, 1985) suggests that a person seeks to elicit confirmation of valued identities through strategic or tactical impression management behaviors. These strategies may in turn aid in the maintenance of self-esteem. For example, feedback from others that supports an individual's desire to be seen as intelligent, kind, or compassionate may reduce the individual's perception of a discrepancy between the real and ideal self (Higgins, Strauman, & Klein, 1986; James, 1890), resulting in increased self-esteem.

Swann (1983) has incorporated these notions of impression management into a broader theory of self-verification. In response to research on the self-fulfilling prophecy, Swann and Ely (1984) found that there are times when individuals seek to disconfirm others' expectations in the service of verifying what they perceive to be more accurate or important self-conceptions. A nice illustration of this effect is Swann and Hill's (1982) study, in which subjects were given either self-confirming or disconfirming feedback about their interpersonal dominance. When the information was self-confirming, subjects accepted the feedback, passively playing the suggested role. If the feedback was contrary to their own beliefs about their dominance in interpersonal relationships, subjects reacted strongly, resisting the feedback and behaving so as to convince the other that this was not the kind of person they were. Self-perceived dominants who were labeled as submissive acted especially dominant, whereas self-perceived submissives who were labeled as dominant acted especially submissive.

How can people elicit self-verifying information from others? Swann (1983) suggests that three strategies are available to individuals. First, individuals may display signs or symbols of who they are (or think they are). For example, a male graduate student may begin smoking a pipe, grow his hair, and wear horn-rimmed glasses in order to communicate to others that he is an intellectual. Second, persons may select friends, relationships, and social situations that confirm these self-perceptions. Backman and Secord (1962) found that sorority women interacted more often with others who they believed perceived them as they perceived themselves. Third, persons may pursue "interaction strategies" that ensure that others will confirm their self-conceptions. So a dominant person may employ verbal and nonverbal cues (such as less eye contact and frequent interruptions), bringing others to defer to him or her. In addition, individuals may ignore, forget, or distort others' feedback that fails to confirm important self-conceptions. In sum, through strategic self-presentation (Tedeschi & Norman, 1985), selection of interaction partners, and particular interaction strategies, an individual may elicit from others information that confirms important self-conceptions.

Societal Influences

Others are not only influential in shaping standards or self-conceptions toward which to strive; they also determine how personal characteristics or statuses are to be evaluated. Is the obese person to be viewed as weak (as in the West) or wealthy (as in many Pacific islands)? Is the person who expresses strong feelings of dependence on another expressing a socially approved (Japan) or disapproved emotion? Is polygamy an accepted cultural institution (as in parts of Africa) or a deviant behavior (as in the United States)? In each of these examples, a given society has determined what behaviors, attitudes, or characteristics are acceptable and those that are unacceptable or deviant. As Becker (1963) writes, "social groups create deviance by making the rules whose infraction constitutes deviance, and by applying these rules to particular people and labeling them as outsiders" (quoted in Schur, 1971, p. 7).

But how do society's labels become a part of the self? How are they "taken" by the person, becoming a part of the individual's self-concept? We have described above some perspectives that suggest mechanisms through which social roles become part of the self. But the evaluative labels assigned to those roles may not necessarily be appropriated by the individual. In a review of the effects of social stigma on self-esteem, Crocker and Major (1989), affirm many of the negative consequences of stereotyping, but find that research conducted over the span of 20 years has demonstrated that "prejudice against members of stigmatized groups generally does *not* result in lowered self-esteem for members of those

groups" (p. 611). They go on to suggest that the stigmatized or oppressed may use a variety of self-protective strategies, such as altering valued abilities or devaluing other abilities, attributing negative appraisals to their group membership, and making selective comparisons *within* their own group. In an earlier work, Schur (1971) found that some members of deviant groups attempt "deviance disavowal," which may include rationalizing or redefining one's behavior, or believing that what one does is helpful and prosocial rather than deviant (as in the case of prostitutes). Such persons may also reject the stigmatizing label (as in "Black is beautiful"), may pay no attention to the label or the stigmatizing condition, or may avoid others who do not share the condition. As a result, the person does not incorporate the label or evaluation into his or her self-concept (see Jones et al., 1984, for a review).

Individual Differences in the Interpersonal Self

We have attempted above to demonstrate how others indirectly influence the self through such processes as reflected appraisals and social comparisons, and through broad social labels for particular characteristics or groups. In a following section, we address how others actually may be carried in structures of the self—not merely providing information to the self, but actually occupying some portion of the self-space. As a bridge to that discussion, we review some research indicating that there are individual differences in the degree to which people allow others to influence their selves or their identities.

Field Dependence

Witkin and his colleagues (Witkin & Goodenough, 1977; Witkin, Goodenough, & Oltman, 1979; Witkin, Moore, Goodenough, & Cox, 1977) were among the first to systematically analyze individual differences in how separate or distinct from others individuals felt themselves to be. They developed a theory of psychological differentiation that focuses on the degree of segregation of the self from the nonself. When the self is clearly segregated from others, particular features are identified as belonging to oneself and are recognized as separate from that of others. Differences in how individuals segregate themselves from others lead to differences in the extent to which the self can easily be used as a referent for behavior. When the self is not sharply segregated from others, it likely that others who comprise the field outside will be used as the referent for behavior. The tendency to rely on the self as referent was labeled a "field-independent" cognitive style, and the tendency to rely on the field (or others) as a referent was called a "field-dependent" style.

Witkin and colleagues argued that for a person who is field-dependent, other people constitute the main source of referents for organizing the person's own experience and work. When an individual does not make sharp self–nonself discriminations and thus incorporates others into the self, the person is said to reveal a basic orientation of "turning toward people." This type of orientation encourages attention to others and their activities, involvement with others, and competence in social relations. Summarizing a diverse array of studies comparing field-dependent and field-independent people, Witkin et al. (1977) concluded that field-dependent people, as a consequence of not clearly separating themselves from others, "are attentive to the views of others, sensitive to social cues, have an interpersonal orientation, encompass a strong interest in people, show a preference for being physically close to others, emotional openness, and in some circumstances, facility in getting along with others" (p. 662). There have been challenges to the empirical pictures drawn by Witkin and his colleagues, but overall the studies lend support to the idea that for some individuals, other people are highly salient and implicated in many aspects of their behavior.

Self-Monitoring

A more recent but in some respects, similar construct has identified differences in the extent to which individuals allow others to shape or influence their behavior. "Self-monitoring" (Snyder, 1979) is the extent to which an individual "is . . . sensitive to the expression and self-presentation of relevant others in social situations and uses these cues as guidelines for monitoring his or her own verbal and nonverbal self-presentation" (p. 89). Persons high in self-monitoring are very sensitive to such social cues, and adjust their behavior accordingly.

Persons low in self-monitoring, by contrast, are not so concerned with or perceptive of social information about appropriate behavior; as a result, their behavior appears to be controlled to a greater degree by their own affective states and attitudes. Individuals high in self-monitoring have been found in laboratory studies to adapt their behavior in "public" rather than "private" situations (Snyder & Monson, 1975); to adapt their behavior in self-reports (Snyder & Monson, 1975); and to demonstrate relatively less correlation between attitudes and behaviors than individuals low in self-monitoring (Snyder & Swann, 1976). Self-monitoring has also been shown to be negatively related to age (Reifman, Klein, & Murphy, 1989), indicating that the behavior of older persons may be directed by internal standards and beliefs more than by the dictates of situations.

Although Snyder (1979) does not directly relate this construct to Witkin and Goodenough's (1977) field dependence–independence, he does indicate that the degree of self-monitoring an individual exhibits may be related to the content of the self. He relates that the self-conceptions of individuals high in self-monitoring reflect great concern for relationships and involvement with other people. In contrast, Snyder claims that persons low in self-monitoring are more likely to "construe their identities in terms of enduring attributes that reside within themselves" (Ickes et al., 1978, p. 101; see also Sampson, 1978).

Personal and Social Identity

Cheek and Hogan (1981, 1983; Hogan, Jones, & Cheek, 1985) claim that identity is comprised of both personal and social aspects, but that individuals differ in which aspects they regard as most "true" or self-defining (see also Gordon, 1968; Sampson, 1978). In contrast to self-monitoring theory, they claim that personal and social orientations are independent dimensions rather than bipolar opposites. Personal identity is linked with the individual's thoughts, and emotions, particularly his or her self-knowledge and self-evaluations. Social identity is based on the impressions the individual makes, what others think of the individual, and his or her attraction and popularity with others. Social identity correlates positively with measures of concern for social appropriateness and an altruistic orientation, whereas personal identity is correlated with achievement orientation and a need for uniqueness (Cheek & Busch, 1982; Cutler, Lennox, & Wolfe, 1984). Cheek and colleagues (Cheek, 1989) claim that those who are high in social identity and low in personal identity will strive to get along with others, while those high in personal identity and low in social identity will pursue a strategy of trying to get ahead.

Sociation Versus Individuation

Greenwald (1982b) has proposed a model of the person that includes the self-system and the social system. Furthermore, he claims that some people are on average more socially oriented ("S-types"), whereas others are more individually oriented ("I-types"), and that these types will differ in their dominant tasks, motives, and strategies. Thus S-types will prefer impression management tasks, will show a need for approval, and are likely to conform. I-types will favor dissonance reduction, will reveal some tendencies to prefer isolation, and will attempt to ensure their independence. S-types, as opposed to I-types, may also have a tendency to enter a state of "sociation," in which the social system rather than the self-system is the controlling system for behavior. Sociation, as opposed to individuation, occurs when the individual's behavior is regulated or controlled by others, and will be associated with uniformity in behavior. I-types, in contrast, will prefer or seek the state of individuation, where the self-system is responsible for regulating behavior.

Public and Private Self-Consciousness

A related perspective investigates individual differences in self-focus. Deriving from self-awareness theory (Duval & Wicklund, 1972; Wicklund, 1975), research on dispositional self-consciousness examines the degree to which a person chooses to focus on covert or personal aspects of the self (private self-consciousness) and the degree to which one focuses on the self as a social object (public self-consciousness) (Scheier & Carver, 1983b). People who are high in public self-consciousness may be thought of as very aware of how they are perceived by others, and this information may later be used for behavioral modification (as in self-monitoring strategies).

In one study, women who were high in public self-consciousness reacted much more strongly to rejection by a group than did those low in public self-consciousness (Fenigstein, 1979). Yet other research has shown that being high in either public self-consciousness (Shaffer & Tomarelli, 1989) or private self-consciousness (Franzoi & Davis, 1985; Franzoi, Davis, & Young, 1985) is related to willingness to make intimate self-disclosures to others. Shaffer and Tomarelli (1989) suggest that individuals who are high in public self-consciousness self-disclose in order to make a good impression on their partners, while those high in private self-consciousness self-disclose in adherence to social reciprocity norms. (Subjects high in both or low in both public and private self-consciousness were less likely to partake in reciprocal self-disclosure.) Individuals high in public self-consciousness may be particularly likely to implicate others in the self through strategic self-presentation and impression management techniques.

Collectivism Versus Individualism

A final dimension that captures differences in the interpersonal self is the degree to which people are individualistic or collectivistic in their orientations (Hui, 1988; Hui & Triandis, 1986; Triandis, 1989; Triandis, Bontempo, Villareal, Asai, & Lucca, 1988). Individualists define the self independently of groups, believing that they can stand or fall on their own. They emphasis personal goals over group goals, and evidence less concern or attachment to the group. In contrast, collectivists see themselves in terms of the groups to which they belong, and value interdependence. They are willing to subordinate personal goals to group goals, and evidence intense emotional attachment to the group (Triandis, Leung, Villareal, & Clack, 1985; Triandis et al., 1988). Cultures as well as individuals may be described along this dimension. For example, Asian countries are more collectivistic than the United States (Triandis et al., 1988). Hui (1984, 1988) has developed a scale that measures individualism—collectivism in several situations, and has validated it with both Asian and American samples. In tests of this scale, he has found that individualists and collectivists are differentially concerned with social approval and responsibility sharing—values most often associated with collectivist cultures. In another study (Triandis et al., 1988), collectivist subjects were more likely to score highly on measures of social support, and scored lower than their individualist American counterparts on measures of loneliness.

These personality constructs illustrate the interpersonal self. Although they take into account different aspects of the self, together they present a picture of the self as differentially responsive or sensitive to others. In the following section, we review some recent theorizing and research that suggests ways in which others may be incorporated into structures of the self.

Structures That "Carry" the Interpersonal Self

What are the self-relevant products of social interactions with others? What structures of the self-system may carry or contain the influence of others or the interdependency with others? Object relations theorists (see Greenberg & Mitchell, 1983) assume that important others are internalized in some way, so that they are carried around within the individual, influencing all aspects of behavior. They have only very recently begun to worry about exactly what it is from important others that is internalized, or how these internal representations influence one's thoughts and feelings and one's actual interactions with these others. Cognitively oriented research in personality and social psychology has identified several elements that could be thought to carry one or another aspect of others within the self-system. These have been called "images," "schemas," "prototypes," "theories," "goals," "tasks," or "projects" (Carver & Scheier, 1981; Epstein, 1980; Greenwald 1982a; Greenwald & Pratkanis, 1984; Kihlstrom & Cantor, 1984; Markus, 1983; Markus & Sentis, 1982; Rogers, 1981; Schlenker, 1980). We review several of these structural views of the interpersonal self.

One way in which individuals may construct "social selves" is through the elaboration of an image of one's self *in the situation*. These "situated identities" "summarize the relationship between actors and their environments at a given point in time" (Wiley & Alexander, 1987, p. 106). As a result, situated identities represent the dynamic interplay or "joint construction" of the individual and others in his or her environ-

ment (Schlenker, 1985). The person engaged in a particular situated identity expresses a unique set of dispositional dimentions. For example, one's "volunteer at the local hospital" identity may include being "kind," "warm," and "helpful." Wiley and Alexander (1987) conclude that the "dispositional" dimensions of the situated identity are what become part of the self. This concept is similar to Rosenberg's (1986) construct of "interpersonal sentiments," which are feelings about the self in relation to others ("I am kind," cr "I am outgoing") or other's feelings toward the individual ("I am well liked"). Rosenberg suggests that the tendency to describe oneself in terms of interpersonal sentiments increases in adolescence, with the improved ability to take the role of others.

These constructs of dispositional dimensions or interpersonal sentiments are similar to other recent perspectives on the self. Notions of the self as a set of self-representations or "schemas" (Markus, 1977; Markus & Kunda, 1986), a hierarchical category structure (Rogers, 1981), an associative network (Bower & Gilligan, 1979), or a multidimensional space (Breckler & Greenwald, 1982) have been frequently examined in the last decade (see Gecas, 1982; Greenwald & Pratkanis, 1984; Kihlstrom & Cantor, 1984; Markus & Wurf, 1987, for reviews). But how can these more cognitive self-structures contain or represent others?

In the associational or network models, the self and others can be conceptualized as nodes in a cognitive network, which are interconnected by pathways that represent the relationships between them (Anderson & Bower, 1973; Bower, 1967). For example, thinking of one's self as "honest" may prime semantic or propositional links that include others toward whom one has exhibited that characteristic (e.g., telling one's parents that one has wrecked their car).

Other theories view the self as an arrangement of schemas that represent one's past experiences and personal characteristics (Markus, 1977; Markus & Kunda, 1986; Markus & Smith, 1981). Insofar as one's past experiences include others, it is conceivable that these others may also be represented in the self-schema. An individual's view of the self as friendly, for example, may include representations of specific situations in which the individual was friendly and/or a generalized view that others think of him or her as friendly. In another example, a person's self-representation of himself or herself as a parent may bring to mind representations of his or her children. A person's self-schema for "boss" may also activate images of his or her particular employees. To change such self-schemas may require changing the "others" that form the referent for the schemas. For example, at one point in life an individual's representation of the self as "boss" may include being controlling and very directive of particularly lazy or passive employees. At another point, this self-representation may have as a referent a very different set of employees, who are independent, responsible, and take initiative. Therefore, the self-schema for this role may have changed to include "relaxed," "supportive," or "easygoing." The self-schema may both carry a representation of the person to whom it refers and reflect one's unique responses to that person.

Recent studies suggest that self-schemas contain both public and private representations. In a study examining the consequences of public and private self-consciousness (Buss, 1980; Fenigstein, Scheier, & Buss, 1975), Nasby (1989) has demonstrated that self-descriptive characteristics may be differentially associated with a private or a public self-schema. Subjects were shown an initial list of trait adjectives, and later were asked to indicate on a second list whether they had previously been shown the words. Subsequently, subjects were asked to rate whether the trait terms were characteristic of their private view of themselves ("Does the adjective describe how you typically feel and think about yourself?") or their public view of themselves ("Does the adjective describe how think others typically 'see' you?"). Nasby found that the rate of false alarms for private words was highest for subjects high in private self-consciousness. Similarly, the false-alarm effect for public words was related to public self-consciousness. Although the differences between a public and a private self-schema remain to be specified, this study indicates that some aspects of the self-system may be decidedly public or social, whereas others may be more private in nature.

These self-schemas may not only include present conceptions of social relationships; others may also be represented in one's "desired identity images" (Schlenker, 1985; Schlenker & Weigold, 1989), one's "ought" or "ideal" selves (Higgins, 1987; Higgins et al., 1986; James, 1890), one's "committed image"

(Rosenberg, 1979), or one's "possible selves" (Markus & Nurius, 1986). Common to each of these conceptualizations is the idea that others may influence the self through the development of hopes, plans, guides, or standards for behavior. Cantor and Zirkel (Chapter 6, this volume) concisely describe these conceptions of the self; we limit our discussion here to elaborating how these structures may incorporate others.

In each of these conceptions the individual holds an image, desire, goal, hope, or standard toward which he or she strives. Schlenker's (1985) concept of desired identity images is overtly social, in that he suggests that these desired images influence and direct one's self-presentation and self-disclosures to others. The fulfillment of these desired images may also be limited by others, who may circumscribe one's opportunities to enact the scripts dictated by the desired identity, or who may not respond as one hopes, failing to affirm the desired image.

In Higgins's theory of self-guides, the hopes or expectations of others may become a standard for the self, or a "self-guide" (Higgins, 1987; Higgins et al., 1986). One's "ideal" selves or "ought" selves may first be influenced by significant others in one's family, school, or reference groups. Individuals' beliefs about what is possible for them, as well as what is required or expected from them, are importantly influenced by messages they receive from others in their social environment. Second, the standpoint from which an individual views these ideal or ought selves may also include the perspectives of others. As described by Higgins in Chapter 12 of this volume, a discrepancy between one's actual behavior and one's acquired guides may predict affective reactions such as guilt, shame, or disappointment.

Possible selves (Markus & Nurius, 1986) are those conceptions of the self that one hopes, wants, or seeks to be, as well as those feared conceptions that one seeks to avoid or is afraid of becoming. Like standards or self-guides, possible selves may be significantly constructed from the messages or influence of others in one's social world (Markus, Cross, & Wurf, 1990). With the encouragement of others, an individual may vividly elaborate hoped-for images of himself or herself as "being a famous musician," "becoming a good psychologist," or "having a happy family." Likewise, the social norms or expectations with which the individual is raised may result in feared selves such as "not doing anything of importance with my life" or "being very lonely when older." One's possible selves may also represent the self in relationship to another, as in hoped-for selves of "being happily married" and "having three or four children" or feared selves such as "never being loved" or "being a bad parent" (Cross & Markus, in press). Markus and Nurius (1986) suggest that these selves serve both as incentives for behavior and as standards for evaluation of the current self.

Another perspective on the representation of others in the individual's standards is found in Greenwald's self-evaluation theory (Greenwald, 1982a; Greenwald & Breckler, 1985; Greenwald & Pratkanis, 1984). Terming this perspective "ego-task analysis," Greenwald and colleagues evaluate the audience for one's actions, or the source for the standard of evaluation of one's actions, as being either the self, other people, or one's reference groups. The individual is thought of as having a private self, for whom internal, personal standards are the basis of achievement; a public self, which seeks the approval of significant others; and a collective self, which seeks to fulfill the individual's role in a reference group. The public self seeks the approval and rewards from specific others, whereas the collective self internalizes the values, norms, or attitudes of others.

All of these concerns with particular situated identities, self-schemas, standards, public or interpersonal selves, and sources of self-evaluation are related to the particular goals, "personal projects" (Little, 1983), or "life tasks" a person believes himself or herself to be working toward. Cantor and her associates (Cantor & Kihlstrom, 1983; Cantor & Zirkel, Chapter 6, this volume) have investigated the role of life tasks in understanding the self. Life tasks are defined as unique, self-relevant goals that the individual perceives to be confronting him or her at the time. These may include such objectives as finishing college, finding a mate, or preparing for retirement. Life tasks may be very private ("getting in shape") or very interpersonal ("being a good spouse"). As the person effectively employs his or her unique knowledge of the skills and attributes needed to perform well in such a task, he or she may be said to be using "social intelligence."

Very recently, Read and Miller (1989) developed what they termed "interpersonalism,"

which is a goal-based theory of persons in relationships. Although they have not explicitly focused on the self, they argue that focusing on goal-based structures such as goals, plans, resources, and beliefs should make it possible to explain how individuals in relationships understand, and fail to understand, each other. Their theory is potentially relevant to the interpersonal self because they propose the notion of "relational resources." These resources can be cognitive resources, which include relational memories and transactional memories (Wegner, Giuliano, & Hertel, 1985); affective resources, such as love and understanding; and other psychological resources.

In all of these approaches, the self may be theoretically understood as having structures that include others. Yet most of this inclusion is relatively indirect: Others are part of situations that shape one's behavior (Alexander & Wiley, 1981); others may serve as a referent for a self-conception; others may provide sources of standards or possibilities (Higgins et al., 1986; Markus & Nurius, 1986); or others may be implicated in one's life tasks (Cantor & Kihlstrom, 1983). In the next section, we review research and writing suggesting ways and situations in which the other may be very directly a part of the self.

OTHERS AS PART OF THE SELF

In this third and final "take" on the interpersonal self, what is critical is not just the other's role as an internalized object that is carried inside the self-concept and that functions as a guide to action or as the partner in an internal dialogue. Instead, the other is a participant in a relationship that allows an individual to experience a desired state of connectedness or relatedness. The relationship with the other is not an instrumental means to the end of finding out about the self, or to the end of learning how to behave, or to the end of being esteemed and admired. Instead, the relationship is an end in and of itself. The relationship itself is self-defining; thus, both the relationship and the other are represented within the boundaries of the self-concept.

Gender and Self—Other Interdependence

One literature that is directly centered on the significance of the other in constituting the self is recent feminist theory concerned with empathy. The goal of much of this work has been to analyze the central role of relationships in women's lives (Belenky, Clinchy, Goldberger, & Tarule, 1986; Block, 1984; Chodorow, 1978; Gilligan, 1982; Markus & Oyserman, 1989; Miller, 1986; Stewart & Lykes, 1985). These theorists suggest that relationships have a power and significance in women's lives that have gone largely unrecognized. Miller (1986) (see Jordan & Surrey, 1986), for example, suggests that a critical feature of the psychology of women is "the ongoing intrinsic inner awareness and responsiveness to the continuous existence of other or others and the expectation of mutuality in this regard" (Jordan & Surrey, 1986). From this perspective, much of the individual's self-worth or esteem is based on the feeling that one is "a part of relationships and is taking care of relationships." (Jordan & Surrey, 1986, p. 597)

Theorists differ in their views of why relationships may be importantly self-defining for women. Chodorow (1978) proposed that mothers and daughters, unlike mothers and sons, experience a sense of similarity and continuity with each other. As a result, women learn to focus on and value relationships more than do men. She claims that as children begin to individuate themselves and ask "Who am I?," girls are afforded a readily accessible answer: "I am like my mother." This answer is typically encouraged by mothers. Sons, however, do not experience this same sense of similarity and continuity with their mothers. By contrast, a feature of their social environment is difference from their mothers. Chodorow believes that the mother experiences the son as more of an "other," as an "external object," and thus the mother encourages the son to view himself as separate and distinct from the mother. The answer given to the "Who am I?" question by the son is "I am not like my mother." Block (1984), in fact, argues that male children experience a major discontinuity and sense of separation at about 18 months of age, when mothers begin distancing themselves and attempting to foster appropriate gender-role definitions.

In a recent test of Chodorow's theory Tolman, Diekmann, and McCartney (1989) examined the consequences of maternal employment and maternal absence on adult social connectedness as measured by the Interpersonal Orientation Scale (Swap & Rubin,

1983). Daughters whose mothers had been absent since early childhood were less connected than daughters whose mothers had never been absent or became absent later in the daughters' lives. As predicted by Chodorow's theory, there were no effects of maternal absence on sons, presumably because of their relatively greater differentiation from the mother.

For Miller (1986) the reason why women are likely to incorporate others into the self is not an issue of continuity versus distinctness from their mothers. It is, instead, an issue of the societal power differential between men and women. Women must learn to relate to others and be carefully attuned to others if they are to survive in a male-dominated society. Miller reasons,

> [S]ubordinates, then, know much more about the dominants than vice versa. They have to. They become highly attuned to the dominants, able to predict their reactions of pleasure and displeasure. . . . If a large part of your fate depends on accommodating to and pleasing the dominants, you concentrate on them. (pp. 10–11)

Gilligan (1982) has argued that because men and women attach very different meanings to relationships with others, they are likely to have two very different approaches to morality. The masculine approach is one born of separation and individuality. The other, the feminine approach, is focused on attachment and caring. A morality based on a concern with relationships follows from an appreciation of one's fundamental relatedness and of the extent to which one's self is comprised of relations with others. The reluctance to judge others and a tendency to accept others' points of view results from a desire to preserve the connection to these others (Belenky et al., 1986). In an extension of Gilligan's work, Lyons (1983) asked subjects to describe themselves and then coded their responses for mentions of relations with others or concern for others. Those who mentioned having relationships and/or concern for others in characterizing themselves were more likely to consider the responses of the others in their moral judgments. Conversely, those who described relationships in instrumental terms or referred to their skills in interacting with others more frequently used a consideration of rights in their moral judgments.

Markus and Oyserman (1989) claim that because of their characteristically different patterns of social interaction and interpersonal experiences, women are likely to construct different types of self-systems. Drawing on theorizing by Chodorow (1978), Erikson (1968), Gilligan (1982), and Stewart and Lykes (1985), they suggest that women are more likely to have what can be called "collectivist" "sociocentric," "ensembled," "communal," or "connected" self-schemas. In connectedness self-schemas, relations with others are the basic elements. By contrast, men are relatively more likely to have what can be called "individualist," "egocentric," or "separate" self-schemas. In separateness self-schemas, other individuals are represented not as part of the self, but as separate from it. The basic elements of such separateness self-schemas are attributes such as traits, motives, and beliefs.

Those with a connectedness self-schema will be particularly sensitive and responsive to others, and they will have well-elaborated knowledge and understanding of others. Because the elements of connectedness self-schemas are relationships, others are represented with the self. When one thinks about the self, these others are present also. When one thinks about these significant others, some aspects of the self are present also. Object relations theorists would call these others "internalized objects." Singer (1987) has persuasively argued that these internalized objects do not have to be viewed as mysterious entities:

> [They] are really ongoing memories and fantasies about people. These good mothers or bad mothers are not stuck in some limbo of the mind—they recur regularly when, as we initiate some action, we hear a voice from the past saying "that's my good girl" or "you're doing it again" or we see in our fleeting imagery a smiling face or a wagging finger. (p. 28)

As connectedness self-schemas become active and begin to exert their selective and directive influence on thought, individuals will automatically attend to and encode a diverse array of information—information about the self and information about the selves to whom the self is connected. As one consequence of the operation of these complex, connected self-schemas, females may have a greater capacity for empathy. "Empathy" is typically defined as the vicarious affective or cognitive responding to another's state of mind. With a connectedness self-schema, important others are represented as part of the self, and thus perceivers may be as sensitive to stimuli relevant to these others as they will be to what appear as more purely self-relevant stimuli. In this sense, information about the others is self-relevant information, and thus empathic responding may be an almost unavoidable response.

Research supports such an expectation. Hoffman (1977) found that females were significantly more empathic than males. Eisenberg and Lennon (1983) found large sex differences in favor of females when measures of self-report were used, but fewer differences when physiological measures of one's reaction to another's state were used. Davis (1980) proposed that empathy is composed of perspective taking (seeing things from another's point of view), empathic concern (a tendency to experience feelings of sympathy and compassion), and personal distress (the tendency to experience personal feelings of distress in the presence of distressed others), and developed an index to test these three facets. Women respondents scored significantly higher on all three facets of empathy (see also Franzoi et al., 1985; Ickes, 1987). Davis and Oathout (1987) replicated these findings and further reported that the empathy scores of women were related to many more self-reported behaviors than was true for men. Finally, Hall (1978), in a review of 75 studies, found that females are significantly better than males in decoding or interpreting visual and auditory cues about another's affective state.

Culture and Self–Other Interdependence

In the last decade, psychologists and anthropologists alike have become increasingly intrigued by the differences between Western and Eastern or Asian views of the individual (Gergen, 1977; Heelas & Lock, 1980; Marsella, DeVos, & Hsu, 1985; Roland, 1989; Shweder & Levine, 1984; Triandis, 1989; Triandis et al., 1988; Westen, 1985; White & Kirkpatrick, 1985). One of the distinctive differences among cultures in the view of the self is the degree to which they see the self as separate from others or as connected to others. Many Eastern cultures insist on the fundamental connectedness of human beings to each other. From this perspective, individuals are only parts that when separated from the larger social whole cannot be fully understood (Phillips, 1976; Shweder & Levine, 1984). For example, Lebra (1976), in describing the Japanese, claims that the Japanese are "most fully human in the context of others" (p. 64).

Many Western cultures hold to theory of the individual that has been succinctly summarized by Geertz (1975). The individual is "a bounded, unique, more or less integrated motivational and cognitive universe, a dynamic center of awareness, emotion, judgment, and action organized into a distinctive whole and set contrastively against other such wholes and against a social and natural background" (p. 48). From this view, the self is basically a bundle of attributes, and it is this bundle that causes behavior. Furthermore, the self is basically separate from the social context and is invariant across these social roles and relationships. When psychology's underlying model of the self is made explicit in this way, it becomes easier to see why more progress has not been made in implicating others in the structure and functioning of the social or the interpersonal self. The Western model of the self, with its emphasis on separation, distinctness, and uniqueness, pushes others into the background and does not really accord them a significant role (for a lively debate on the pros and cons of individualism, see Hogan, 1975, and Waterman, 1981).

Despite the extensive theorizing (see earlier sections) that focuses on the role of others in the self, most models of personality and of the self (with some recent exceptions, described in the section on gender) are attribute-based (see Cantor & Zirkel, Chapter 6, this volume). Recently, however, several Japanese theorists have begun an attempt to characterize the nature of the Japanese self. Because of the emphasis on interdependence in Japan, many observers have been led to assume that there is no self as we know it among Eastern cultures, and that researchers should refrain from imposing a Western concept such as "self" on these cultures. Hamaguchi (1985) suggests instead that the concept of self is equally important in Asian cultures but that it is a different type of self. For the Japanese, Hamaguchi argues,

> [A] sense of identification with others (sometimes including conflict) pre-exists and selfness is confirmed only through interpersonal relationships. . . . [Selfness] is not a constant like the ego but denotes a fluid concept which changes through time and situations according to interpersonal relationships. (p. 302)

A normative task of many Eastern cultures is to maintain relatedness among individuals; this requires seeing oneself as part of a larger social whole and recognizing that one's behavior is contingent on, and to a large extent organized and made meaningful by, reference to the thoughts, feelings, and actions of others. The Japanese experience of the self, for example, seems to include a sense of interdependence and of one's status as a participant in a larger social unit. American culture, by contrast, does not value such an overt connectedness among individuals. It is based on a belief in the inherent separateness of individuals. A normative task of this culture is to become independent from others and to discover and express one's unique attributes. The individual's behavior should take others into account, but behavior is organized and made meaningful primarily by response to one's own internal repertoire of thoughts, feelings, and behavioral intentions.

Markus and Kitayama (1989) have focused explicitly on the different types of self-systems that may emerge in collectivist or individualist cultures. They contrast a Western or independent self with an interdependent self. In the independent view, the most significant self-representations are within or inside the individual. The others in the social context are important but they are important primarily as standards of social comparison, as sources of reflected appraisal, or as sources of direct feedback that can be used to verify or validate the self. In the interdependent view, the individuals are characteristically defined not by their unique attributes but by their social relationships. The significant self-representations are those of the self in relationship to specific others. Interdependent selves are also thought to include representations of personal attributes and abilities, but these representations are less important in controlling observable behavior, and are not assumed to be particularly diagnostic of the self.

Although the concerns of cross-cultural research have been rapidly expanding, relatively few cross-cultural studies have focused exclusively on the nature of the self. Recently, Kitayama, Markus, Tummula, Kurokawa, and Kato (1989) used a cognitive-reference-point task to expore the idea that individuals from an Eastern cultural background should have an extensive store of information not only about themselves, but also about the others to whom they are committed, obligated, or responsible. They built on a study by Holyoak and Gordon (1983), who found that when they asked subjects "How similar are you to your best friend?," most people reported, "Not very similar."

When they asked another group of subjects, "How similar is your best friend to you?," most people reported, "Very similar." They explained this finding using Tversky's (1977) distinctive-feature model of similarity judgments. Tversky has shown that if people are asked to compare two objects—one they have some knowledge about and another they know much less about—and determine how similar they are, there will be an asymmetry in the similarity ratings of the two objects.

Kitayama et al. (1989) gave the self–other similarity task to students from Eastern (India) and Western cultural backgrounds. With American students, they replicated the original Holyoak and Gordon (1983) results, finding that the other was perceived as much more similar to the self than vice versa. This was not the case for the Indian subjects. In fact, there was a nonsignificant reversal of this finding. These data are consistent with the idea that for individuals with an interpersonal view of the self, knowledge about others is highly accessible, and thus the asymmetry in similarity judgments originally observed is not evident.

In one of the very few other studies on cultural differences in self-conception, Cousins (1989) compared the self-descriptions of American students with the self-descriptions of Japanese students. He used two types of free-response formats, the Twenty Statements Test (TST) and a questionnaire requiring subjects to describe themselves in several situations (me at home, with friends, at school). The Japanese responses to the TST were concrete and role-specific ("I play tennis on the weekend"), while the American descriptions included more global psychological characterizations ("I am optimistic"). However, when a specific interpersonal context was provided, so that respondents knew the situation—and presumably who was there, and what was being done to whom or by whom—this pattern of results was reversed. When self-description was contextualized, the Japanese responded with more global psychological characterizations of themselves than did Americans. In contrast, when thinking about themselves in specific situations, Americans tended to qualify their self-descriptions, claiming, for example, "I am sometimes lazy at home." Cousins (1989) argued that for Japanese subjects the TST isolated the "I" from the all-important relational or situational context, and thus self-description became artificial or unnatural.

SUMMARY AND DISCUSSION

We have attempted to identify the role of the other in the constuction and makeup of the self. Early theorists, particularly Sullivan, Baldwin, and Mead, suggested that the self is a social creation, and that the public and private aspects of the self are inseparably intertwined. Recent research with primates and infants supports the idea that the self is a social product, and goes on to describe the intersubjectivity between caregiver and child that produces a socially connected, relational self.

We have also reviewed research that demonstrates how others may indirectly be involved in the maintenance and enhancement of the self. As a result of others' appraisals of the individual and social comparisons, as well as through processes such as self-affirmation or self-verification, others are used by the individual to evaluate, improve, or enhance the self, or to confirm or reaffirm important self-definitions. The structures that carry the other may include situated identities, schemas, standards, possible selves, or life tasks.

A great many concepts have been developed to examine the degree to which an individual is oriented toward others. Individual differences in field dependence, self-monitoring, public self-consciousness, and collectivism have been shown to reliably predict those people who show greater concern with others in relation to the self. Although the self–other relationship varies for each construct (e.g., differentiation of the self from others, concern for altering one's public behavior, etc.), together they point to the varieties of ways in which others may be represented in the self or responded to by the self.

Finally, we have reviewed research indicating that for some people others may constitute a critical portion of the self. Initial findings from studies focusing on gender differences in the self-concept and on cultural differences in the self-concept suggest that in some cases it may be the relationship that is the defining element of the self, rather than an attribute or trait.

Many questions remain to be answered about the extent to which the self can be considered "interpersonal" and about the processes and structures through which others influence or become part of the self. Most empirical research has yet to capture the sense of the self as a product of the mutual shaping and negotiation that is described in much of the early theorizing. The most pressing questions are those concerned with the variety of ways in which the others can be represented or reflected in the self and the different ways in which these others function within the self-system. Who are represented in the self—specific others or generalized others? Is the whole person represented, or only some important aspects? Is it the case that all self-representations are inherently social and actually require others for their evaluation, maintenance, or defense?

The most evident roadblock to greater specification of an interpersonal self is the lack of theories or models that meaningfully incorporate the role of the other. This difficulty is no doubt related to the fact that most researchers and theorists are tied to a Western model of the self. In this view of the self, the self is a bounded, separate entity comprised of attributes such as traits, motives, or goals. Beginning with James (1890), one can see a tendency in all areas of psychology to accord a higher level of maturity or morality to those with self-contained, independent selves. Even though developmental and social-psychological research continues to reveal the thoroughgoing social nature of the individual, and to highlight the behavioral interdependency among people, there is still an overwhelming commitment to the ideology of an indepent self (see Sampson, 1985). Why is this? Why aren't there more models that systematically implicate the other in the immediate, on-line working of the self-system?

The metaphors for the units of the self continue to be entity- or product-like rather than process- or relation-like. Different units are needed to reflect the open and flexible nature of the interpersonal self and to represent the self in continuing relations to significant others. For example, developmental researchers who are concerned about the nature of the attachment relationship often use the labels of "secure," "avoidant," and "ambivalent" as if these were qualities of individuals. The focus on the other, or the representation of this other, in creating and maintaining a particular type of secure, avoidant, or ambivalent relationship is thus virtually lost.

Increasingly, self-concept and identity researchers are grappling with this problem. Thorne (1989) has shown that certain tendencies of personality—extraversion, for example—

do not reside as substances within the individual, but depend for their expression on certain interpersonal configurations. Tomkins (1979) and Carlson (1981) have elaborated the idea of "scenes" and "scripts" as the organizing units of the personality, where these scenes reflect salient features of interpersonal experience. Cantor and Kihlstrom's (1987) emphasis on life tasks and Little's (1983) concern with personal projects also have the potential to meaningfully implicate the other, and ongoing interaction with this other, into the workings of the self-system. Currently, these researchers are elaborating what individuals are doing in their lives. And very often, what individuals are trying to do is to maintain relationships or to negotiate a sense of self across somewhat divergent relationships.

Even though most self-concept researchers would claim that thoughts about the self always involve beliefs and expectations about others, some researchers focused on the study of emotional disorder are arguing for an emphasis on interpersonal schemas or relationship schemas as the important elements of the self. Luborsky (1984), for example, describes a "core conflictual relationship theme," which is associated with a wish (e.g., "to assert myself"), a response from the other (e.g., "They dominate me") and a response from the self (e.g., "I withdraw"). Safran, Segal, Hill, and Whiffen (in press) propose an "interpersonal schema." Such a structure, like Bowlby's "internal working model," includes beliefs and expectations about other people, beliefs about the self, and beliefs about what is necessary to maintain relatedness. This knowledge is thought to be implicit in the strategies employed to maintain relatedness, and self–other interactions may be what are represented in memory. Similarly, Horowitz (1988) describes "role–relationship models," which are schemas of the characteristics of self and other, plus scripts for various interactions.

Other questions about the interpersonal self are equally compelling. Is the entire self to be considered interpersonal, or only some aspects of it? Do only some individuals have what might be called truly interpersonal selves? What are the range of consequences associated with holding an interpersonal self? And, finally, what is the connection between these interpersonal selves and interpersonal behavior? With a view of the self as constantly responding, adjusting, and incorporating the responses of others, we necessarily move toward a more dynamic view of the self and toward a view of behavior as reciprocally determined. We also move away from a view of self-structures as "causing" behavior.

A full understanding of the interpersonal self will involve an appreciation of how the attitudes, beliefs, and behaviors of others shape the individual—both early in life, as the individual constructs some core sense of self, and throughout life, as the actual, anticipated, or remembered evaluations and concerns of significant others are continually organized into the working self-concept.

REFERENCES

Ainsworth, M. D. S., Bell, S. M., & Stayton, D. (1974). Infant–mother attachment and social development. In M. P. Richards (Ed.), *The Introduction of the child into a social world* (pp. 95–135). Cambridge, England: Cambridge University Press.

Alexander, C. N., & Wiley, M. G. (1981). Situated activity and identity formation. In M. Rosenberg & R. Turner (Eds.), *Social psychology: Social perspectives* (pp. 269–289). New York: Basic Books.

Anderson, J. R., & Bower, G. H. (1973). *Human associative memory.* Washington, DC: V. H. Winston.

Aronson, E. (1984). *The social animal.* San Francisco: W. H. Freeman.

Backman, C., & Secord, P. (1962). Liking, selective interaction, and misperception in congruent interpersonal relations. *Sociometry, 25,* 321–335.

Backman, C., Secord, P., & Pierce, J. (1963). Resistance to change in the self-concept as a function of consensus among significant others. *Sociometry, 26,* 102–111.

Baldwin, J. M. (1911). *The individual and society.* Boston: Boston Press.

Baldwin, M. W., & Holmes, J. G. (1987). Salient private audiences and awareness of the self. *Journal of Personality and Social Psychology, 52,* 1087–1098.

Bandura, A. (1969). *Principles of behavior modification.* New York: Holt, Rinehart & Winston.

Becker, H. S. (1963). *Outsiders: Studies in the sociology of deviance.* New York: Free Press.

Belenky, M. F., Clinchy, B. M., Goldberger, N. R., & Tarule, J. M. (1986). *Women's ways of knowing: The development of self, voice, and mind.* New York: Basic Books.

Bem, D. J. (1967). Self-perception: An alternative interpretation of cognitive dissonance phenomena. *Psychological Review, 74,* 183–200.

Biddle, B. J. (1986). Recent developments in role theory. *Annual Review of Sociology, 12,* 67–92.

Biddle, B. J., & Thomas, E. J. (Eds.). (1966). *Role theory: Concepts and research.* New York: Wiley.

Block, J. H. (Ed.). (1984). *Sex role identity and ego development.* San Francisco: Jossey-Bass.

Bowlby, J. (1969). *Attachment and loss: Vol. 1. Attachment.* New York: Basic Books.

Bower, G. H. (1967). A multicomponent theory of the memory trace. In K. W. Spence & J. T. Spence (Eds.), *The psychology of learning and motivation* (Vol. 1, pp. 229–325). New York: Academic Press.

Bower, G. H., & Gilligan, S. G. (1979). Remembering information related to one's self. *Journal of Research in Personality, 13,* 420–432.

Breckler, S. J., & Greenwald, A. G. (1982). *Charting coordinates for the self-concept in multidimensional trait space.* Paper presented at the 90th annual meeting of the American Psychological Association, Washington, DC.

Bretherton, I. (1989). Open communication and internal working models: Their role in the development of attachment relationships. *Nebraska Symposium on Motivation, 36.*

Brickman, P., & Bulman, R. J. (1977). Pleasure and pain in social comparison. In J. M. Suls & R. L. Miller (Eds.), *Social comparison processes: Theoretical and empirical perspectives* (pp. 149–186). Washington, DC: Hemisphere.

Burke, P. (1980). The self: Measurement requirements from an interactionist perspective. *Social Psychology Quarterly, 43,* 18–29.

Buss, A. H. (1980). *Self-consciousness and social anxiety.* San Francisco: W. H. Freeman.

Callero, P. L. (1985). Role-identity salience. *Social Psychology Quarterly, 48,* 203–215.

Cantor, N., & Kihlstrom, J. F. (1983). *Social intelligence: The cognitive basis of personality* (Tech. Rep. No. 60). Ann Arbor: University of Michigan.

Cantor, N., & Kihlstrom, J. F. (1987). *Personality and social intelligence.* Englewood Cliffs, NJ: Prentice-Hall.

Carlson, R. (1981). Studies in script theory: Adult analogs of a childhood nuclear scene. *Journal of Personality and Social Psychology, 40,* 501–510.

Carver, C. S., & Scheier, M. F. (1981). *Attention and self-regulation: A control-theory approach to human behavior.* New York: Springer.

Cassidy, J. (1988). The self as related to child–mother attachment at six. *Child Development, 59,* 121–134.

Cheek, J. M. (1989.) Identity orientations and self-interpretation. In D. M. Buss & N. Cantor (Eds.), *Personality psychology: Recent trends and emerging directions* (pp. 275–285). New York: Springer-Verlag.

Cheek, J. M., & Busch, C. M. (1982). *Self-monitoring and the inner–outer metaphor: Principled versus pragmatic self?* Paper presented at the meeting of the Eastern Psychological Association, Baltimore.

Cheek, J. M., & Hogan, R. (1981). *The structure of identity: Personal and social aspects.* Paper presented at the meeting of the American Psychological Association, Los Angeles.

Cheek, J. M., & Hogan, R. (1983). Self-concepts, self-presentations, and moral judgments. In J. Suls & A. G. Greenwald (Eds.), *Psychological perspectives on the self* (Vol. 2, pp. 249–273). Hillsdale, NJ: Erlbaum.

Chodorow, N. (1978). *The reproduction of mothering: Psychoanalysis and the sociology of gender.* Berkeley: University of California Press.

Combs, A. W., & Snygg, D. (1949). *Individual behavior: A perceptual approach to behavior.* New York: Harper.

Cooley, C. H. (1902). *Human nature and the social order.* New York: Scribner's.

Cousins, S. (1989). Culture and selfhood in Japan and the

U.S. *Journal of Personality and Social Psychology, 56,* 124–131.

Crocker, J., & Major, B. (1989). Social stigma and self-esteem: The self-protective properties of stigma. *Psychological Review, 96,* 608–630.

Crocker, J., Thompson, L. L., McGraw, K. M., & Ingerman, C. (1987). Downward comparison, prejudice, and evaluations of others: Effects of self-esteem and threat. *Journal of Personality and Social Psychology, 52,* 907–916.

Cross, S., & Markus, H. (in press). Possible selves across the life span. *Human Development.*

Cutler, B. L., Lennox, R. D., & Wolfe, R. N. (1984). *Reliability and construct validity of the Aspects of Identity Questionnaire.* Paper presented at the meeting of the American Psychological Association, Toronto.

Damon, W., & Hart, W. (1982). The development of self-understanding from infancy through adolescence. *Child Development, 53,* 841–869.

Damon, W., & Hart, W. (1988). *Self-understanding in childhood and adolescence.* New York: Cambridge University Press.

Darley, J. M., & Fazio, R. H. (1980). Expectancy confirmation processes arising in the social interaction sequence. *American Psychologist, 35,* 867–881.

Davis, M. H. (1980). A multidimensional approach to individual differences in empathy. *JSAS: Catalog of Selected Documents in Psychology, 10*(4), 85.

Davis, M. H., & Oathout, H. A. (1987). Maintenance of satisfaction in romantic relationships: Empathy and relational competence. *Journal of Personality and Social Psychology, 53,* 397–410.

DePaulo, B. M., Kenny, D. A., Hoover, C. W., Webb, W., & Oliver, P. V. (1987). Accuracy of person perception: Do people know what kinds of impressions they convey? *Journal of Personality and Social Psychology, 52,* 303:315.

Duval, S., & Wicklund, R. A. (1972). *A theory of objective self-awareness.* New York: Academic Press.

Dweck, C. (1986). Motivation processes affecting learning. *American Psychologist, 41,* 1040–1048.

Eccles, J. S. (1989). Bringing young women to math and science. In M. Crawford & M. Gentry (Eds.), *Gender and thought: Psychological perspectives* (pp. 36–58). New York: Springer-Verlag.

Eder, R. A. (1989). *Uncovering young children's psychological selves: Individual and developmental differences.* Unpublished manuscript, Southern Methodist University.

Eisenberg, N., & Lennon, R. (1983). Sex differences in empathy and related capacities. *Psychological Bulletin, 94,* 100–131.

Elkind, D. (1967). Egocentrism in adolescence. *Child Development, 38,* 1025–1034.

Emde, R. N. (1983). The pre-representational self and its affective core. *Psychoanalytic Study of the Child, 38,* 165–192.

Epstein, S. (1973). The self-concept visited. *American Psychologist, 28,* 404–416.

Epstein, S. (1980). The self-concept: A review and the proposal of an integrated theory of personality. In E. Staub (Ed.), *Personality: Basic issues and current research.* Englewood Cliffs, NJ: Prentice-Hall.

Epstein, S. (in press). Cognitive-experiential self-theory: Implication for developmental psychology. *Minnesota symposium on child psychology.* Hillsdale, NJ: Erlbaum.

Erikson, E. H. (1968). *Identity, youth and crisis.* New York: Norton.

Fairbairn, W. R. D. (1952). *An object-relations theory of the personality.* New York: Basic Books.

Fazio, R. H., Effrein, E. A., & Falender, V. J. (1981). Self-perceptions following social interactions. *Journal of Personality and Social Psychology, 41,* 232–242.

Feldman, N. S., & Ruble, D. N. (1977). Awareness of social comparison interest and motivations: A developmental study. *Journal of Educational Psychology, 69,* 579–585.

Felson, R. B. (1985). Reflected appraisal and the development of self. *Social Psychology Quarterly, 48,* 71–78.

Felson, R. B. (1989). Parents and the reflected appraisal process: A longitudinal analysis. *Journal of Personality and Social Psychology, 56,* 965–971.

Fenigstein, A. (1979). Self-consciousness, self-attention, and social interaction. *Journal of Personality and Social Psychology, 37,* 75–86.

Fenigstein, A., Scheier, M. F., & Buss, A. H. (1975). Public and private self-consciousness: Assessment and theory. *Journal of Counseling and Clinical Psychology, 43,* 522–527.

Festinger, L. (1954). A theory of social comparison processes. *Human Relations, 7,* 117–140.

Fiske, S. T., & Taylor, S. E. (1984). *Social cognition.* Reading, MA: Addison-Wesley.

Franzoi, S. L., & Davis, M. H. (1985). Adolescent self-disclosure and loneliness: Private self-consciousness and parental influences. *Journal of Personality and Social Psychology, 48,* 764–776.

Franzoi, S. L., Davis, M. H., & Young, R. D. (1985). The effects of private self-consciousness and perspective taking on satisfaction in close relationships. *Journal of Personality and Social Psychology, 48,* 1584–1594.

Freud, S. (1955). Group psychology and the analysis of the ego. In J. Strachey (Ed. and Trans.), *The standard edition of the complete psychological works of Sigmund Freud* (Vol. 18, pp. 65–143). London: Hogarth Press. (Original work published 1921)

Frey, K. S., & Ruble, D. N. (1985). What children say when the teacher is not around: Conflicting goals in social comparison and performance assessment in the classroom. *Journal of Personality and Social Psychology, 48,* 18–30.

Frey, K. S., & Ruble, D. N. (1987). What children say about classroom performance: Sex and grade differences in perceived competence. *Child Development, 58,* 1066–1078.

Gallup, G. G. (1977). Self-recognition in primates: A comparative approach to the bidirectional properties of consciousness. *American Psychologist, 32,* 329–338.

Gecas, V. (1982). The self-concept. *Annual Review of Sociology, 8,* 1–33.

Geertz, C. (1975). On the nature of anthropological understanding. *American Scientist, 63,* 47–53.

Gergen, K. J. (1977). The social construction of self-knowledge. In T. Mischel (Ed.), *The self: Psychological and philosophical issues* (pp. 139–169). Totowa, NJ: Rowman & Littlefield.

Gilligan, C. (1982). *In a different voice: Psychological theory and women's development.* Cambridge, MA: Harvard University Press.

Goffman, E. (1959). *The presentation of self in everyday life.* Garden City, NY: Doubleday/Anchor.

Gordon, C. (1968). Self-conceptions: Configurations of

content. In C. Gordon & K. J. Gergen (Ed.), *The self in social interaction* (pp. 115–136). New York: Wiley.

Greenberg, J. R., & Mitchell, S. A. (1983). *Object relations in psychoanalytic theory.* Cambridge, MA: Harvard University Press.

Greenwald, A. G. (1982a). Ego task analysis: An integration of research on ego-involvement and self-awareness. In A. Hastorf & A. M. Isen (Eds.), *Cognitive social psychology.* New York: Elsevier/North-Holland.

Greenwald, A. G. (1982b). Social psychology from the perspective of the self. In J. Suls (Ed.), *Psychological perspectives on the self* (Vol. 1, pp. 151–181). Hillsdale, NJ: Erlbaum.

Greenwald, A. G., & Breckler, S. J. (1985). To whom is the self presented? In B. R. Schlenker (Ed.), *The self and social life* (pp. 126–145). New York: McGraw-Hill.

Greenwald, A. G., & Pratkanis, A. R. (1984). The self. In K. S. Wyer & T. Srull (Eds.), *Handbook of social cognition* (Vol. 3, pp. 129–178). Hillsdale, NJ: Erlbaum.

Grossman, K. E., & Grossman, K. (1984, September). *The development of conversational styles in the first year of life and its relationship to maternal sensitivity and attachment quality between mother and child.* Paper presented at the Congress of the German Society for Psychology, Vienna.

Grossman, K. E., Grossman, K., & Schwan, A. (1986). Capturing the wider view of attachment: A reanalysis of Ainsworth's Strange Situation. In C. E. Izard & P. B. Read (Eds.), *Measuring emotions in infants and children* (Vol. 2, pp. 124–171). New York: Cambridge University Press.

Guntrip, H. (1971). *Psychoanalytic theory, therapy and the self.* New York: Basic Books.

Hakmiller, K. (1966). Threat as a determinant of downward comparison. *Journal of Experimental Social Psychology,* (Suppl. 1), 2 32–39.

Hall, J. A. (1978). Gender effects in decoding nonverbal cues. *Psychological Bulletin, 85,* 845–858.

Hamaguchi, E. (1985). A contextual model of the Japanese: Toward a methodological innovation in Japan studies. *Journal of Japanese Studies, 11,* 289–321.

Harre, R. (1980). *Social being: A theory for social psychology.* Totowa, NJ: Littlefield, Adams.

Harter, S. (1983). The development of the self-system. In E. M. Hetherington (Vol. Ed.), *Handbook of child psychology* (4th ed.): *Vol. 4. Socialization, personality, and social development* (pp. 275–386). New York: Wiley.

Harter, S. (1986). Processes underlying the construction, maintenance, and enhancement of the self-concept in children. In J. Suls & A. G. Greenwald (Eds.), *Psychological perspectives on the self* (Vol. 3, pp. 137–181). Hillsdale, NJ: Erlbaum.

Harter, S. (in press). Developmental differences in the nature of self-representations: Implications for the understanding, assessment, and treatment of maladaptive behavior. *Cognitive Therapy and Research.*

Harter, S. (1990). Causes, correlates and the functional role of global self-worth: A life span perspective. In R. J. Sternberg & J. Kolligian, Jr. (Eds.), *Competence considered.* New Haven, CT: Yale University Press.

Hazan, C., & Shaver, P. (1987). Romantic love con-

ceptualized as an attachment process. *Journal of Personality and Social Psychology, 52,* 511–524.

Heath, S. B. (1983). *Ways with words.* Cambridge, MA: Harvard University Press.

Heelas, P., & Lock, A. (1980). *Indigenous psychologies: The anthropology of the self.* New York: Academic Press.

Heiss, J. (1981). Social roles. In M. Rosenberg & R. Turner (Eds.), *Social psychology: Sociological perspectives* (pp. 219–266). New York: Basic Books.

Higgins, E. T. (1987). Self-discrepancy: A theory relating self and affect. *Psychological Review, 94,* 319–340.

Higgins, E. T., Strauman, T., & Klein, R. (1986). Standards and the process of self-evaluation: Multiple affects from multiple stages. In R. M. Sorrentino & E. T. Higgins (Eds.), *Handbook of motivation and cognition: Foundations of social behavior.* (pp. 23–63). New York: Guilford Press.

Hoffman, M. L. (1977). Sex differences in empathy and related behaviors. *Psychological Bulletin, 54,* 712–722.

Hogan, R. (1975). Theoretical egocentrism and the problem of compliance. *American Psychologist, 30,* 533–540.

Hogan, R., Jones, W. H., & Cheek, J. M. (1985). Socioanalytic theory: An alternative to armadillo psychology. In B. R. Schlenker (Ed.), *The self and social life* (pp. 175–198). New York: McGraw-Hill.

Holyoak, K. J., & Gordon, P. C. (1983). Social reference points. *Journal of Personality and Social Psychology, 44,* 881–887.

Horowitz, M. J. (1988). *Introduction of psychodynamics.* New York: Basic Books.

Hui, C. H. (1984). *Individualism–collectivism: Theory, measurement, and its relationship to reward allocation.* Unpublished doctoral dissertation, University of Illinois.

Hui, C. H. (1988). Measurement of individualism–collectivism. *Journal of Research in Personality, 22,* 17–36.

Hui, C. H., & Triandis, H. C. (1986). Individualism–collectivism: A study of cross-cultural researchers. *Journal of Cross-Cultural Psychology, 17,* 225–248.

Ickes, W. (1987). Sex-role influences in dyadic interaction: A theoretical model. In M. R. Walsh (Ed.), *The psychology of women* (pp. 95–128). New Haven, CT: Yale University Press.

Ickes, W. J., Layden, M. A., & Barnes, R. D. (1978). Objective self-awareness and individuation: An empirical link. *Journal of Personality, 46,* 146–161.

James, W. (1890). *Principles of psychology.* New York: Holt.

Jones, E. E., Farina, A., Hastorf, A., Markus, H., Miller, D., & Scott, R. (1984). *Social stigma: The psychology of marked relationships.* San Francisco: W. H. Freeman.

Jones, E. E., & Gerard, H. G. (1967). *Foundations of social psychology.* New York: Wiley.

Jordan, J. V., & Surrey, J. L. (1986). The self-in-relation: Empathy and the mother-daughter relationship. In T. Bernay & D. W. Cantor (Eds.), *The psychology of today's women.* Cambridge, MA: Harvard University Press.

Jussim, L. (1986). Self-fulfilling prophecies: A theoretical and integrative review. *Psychological Review, 93,* 429–445.

Kegan, R. (1982). *The evolving self: Problem and process in human development.* Cambridge, MA: Harvard University Press.

Kelman, H. C. (1961). Processes of opinion change. *Public Opinion Quarterly, 25,* 57–78.

Keller, A., Ford, L. M., & Meacham, J. A. (1978). Dimensions of self-concept in preschool children. *Developmental Psychology, 14,* 483–489.

Kenny, D. A., & Albright, L. (1987). Accuracy in interpersonal perception: A social relations analysis. *Psychological Bulletin, 102,* 390–402.

Kihlstrom, J., & Cantor, N. (1984). Mental representations of the self. In L. Berkowitz (Ed.), *Advances in experimental social psychology* (Vol. 17, pp. 1–47). New York: Academic Press.

Kitayama, S., Markus, H., Tummula, P., Kurokawa, & Kato (1989). *Self-centric cognitive bias: Is it culturally bound?* Unpublished manuscript, University of Oregon.

Kruglanski, A. W., & Mayseless, O. (1987). Motivational effects in the social comparison of opinions. *Journal of Personality and Social Psychology, 53,* 834–842.

Kuhn, M. H., & McPartland, T. (1954). An empirical investigation of self-attitudes. *American Sociological Quarterly, 5,* 61–84.

Leahy, R. L. (Ed.). (1985). *The development of the self.* New York: Academic Press.

Leahy, R. L., & Shirk, S. R. (1985). Social cognition and the development of the self. In R. L. Leahy (Ed.), *The development of the self* (pp. 123–150). New York: Academic Press.

Lebra, T. S. (1976). *Japanese patterns of behavior.* Honolulu: University of Hawaii Press.

Lester, M. (1984). Self: Sociological portraits. In J. A. Kotarbu & A. Fontana (Eds.), *The existential self in society.* pp. 18–68. Chicago: University of Chicago Press.

Lewis, M. (1986). Origins of self-knowledge and individual differences in early self-recognition. In J. Suls & A. G. Greenwald (Eds.), *Psychological perspectives on the self* (Vol. 3, pp. 55–78). Hillsdale, NJ: Erlbaum.

Lewis, M., & Brooks-Gunn, J. (1979). *Social cognition and the acquisition of self.* New York: Plenum.

Little, B. R. (1983). Personal projects: A rationale and method for investigation. *Environment and Behavior, 15,* 273–309.

Luborsky, L. (1984). *Principles of psychoanalytic psychotherapy.* New York: Basic Books.

Lyons, N. (1983). Two perspectives on self, relationships and morality. *Harvard Educational Review, 53,* 125–145.

Maccoby, E. E., & Martin, J. A. (1983). Socialization in the context of the family: Parent-child interaction. In E. M. Hetherington (Vol. Ed.), *Handbook of child psychology* (4th ed.): Vol. 4. *Socialization, personality, and social development* (pp. 1–101). New York: Wiley.

Marks, G. (1984). Thinking one's abilities are unique and one's opinions are common. *Personality and Social Psychology Bulletin, 10,* 203–208.

Markus, H. (1977). Self-schemata and processing information about the self. *Journal of Personality and Social Psychology, 35,* 63–78.

Markus, H. (1983). Self-knowledge: An expanded view. *Journal of Personality, 51,* 543–565.

Markus, H., Cross, S., & Wurf, E. (1990). The role of the self-system in competence. In R. J. Sternberg & J. Kolligian, Jr. (Eds.), *Competence considered.* New Haven, CT: Yale University Press.

Markus, H., & Kitayama, S. (1989). *Culture and the self.* Unpublished manuscript, University of Michigan.

Markus, H., & Kunda, Z. (1986). Stability and malleability of the self-concept. *Journal of Personality and Social Psychology, 51,* 858–866.

Markus, H., & Nurius, P. (1986). Possible selves. *American Psychologist, 41,* 954–969.

Markus, H., & Oyserman, D. (1989). Gender and thought: The role of the self-concept. In M. Crawford & M. Hamilton (Eds.), *Gender and thought* (pp. 100–127). New York: Springer-Verlag.

Markus, H., & Sentis, J. (1982). The self in social information processing. In J. Suls (Ed.), *Psychological perspectives on the self* (Vol. 1, pp. 41–70). Hillsdale, NJ: Erlbaum.

Markus, H., & Smith, J. (1981). The influence of self-schemas on the perception of others. In N. Cantor & J. F. Kihlstrom (Eds.), *Personality, cognition, and social interaction* (pp. 233–261). Hillsdale, NJ: Erlbaum.

Markus, H., & Wurf, E. (1987). The dynamic self-concept: A social psychological perspective. *Annual Review of Psychology, 38,* 299–337.

Markus, H., & Zajonc, R. B. (1985). The cognitive perspective in social psychology. In G. Lindzey & E. Aronson (Eds.), *Handbook of social psychology* (3rd ed., Vol. 1, pp. 137–230). New York: Random House.

Marsella, A., DeVos, G., & Hsu, F. (1985). *Culture and self.* London: Tavistock.

Martin, J. (1986). The tolerance of injustice. In J. M. Olson, C. P. Herman, & M. P. Zanna (Eds.), *Relative deprivation and social comparison: The Ontario Symposium* (Vol. 4, pp. 217–242). Hillsdale, NJ: Erlbaum.

Martindale, C. (1980). Subselves: The internal representation of situational and personal dispositions. In L. Wheeler (Ed.), *Review of personality and social psychology* (Vol. 1, pp. 193–218). Beverly Hills, CA: Sage.

Masters, J. E. (1971). Social comparison by young children. *Young Children, 27,* 37–60.

McCall, G. J. (1987). The structure, content, and dynamics of self: Continuities in the study of role-identities. In K. Yardley & T. Honess (Eds.), *Self and identity: Psychosocial perspectives* (pp. 133–145). New York: Wiley.

McCall, G. J., & Simmons, J. L. (1966). *Identities and interaction.* New York: Free Press.

McGuire, W. J., & Padawer-Singer, A. (1976). Trait salience in the spontaneous self-concept. *Journal of Personality and Social Psychology, 33,* 743–754.

Mead, G. H. (1934). *Mind, self, and society.* Chicago: University of Chicago Press.

Mettee, D. R., & Smith, G. (1977). Social comparison and interpersonal attraction: The case for dissimilarity. In J. M. Suls & R. L. Miller (Eds.), *Social comparison processes: Theoretical and empirical perspectives* (pp. 69–101). Washington, DC: Hemisphere.

Miller, J. B. (1986). *Toward a new psychology of women* (2nd ed.). Boston: Beacon Press.

Miller, D. T., & Turnbull, W. (1986). Expectancies and interpersonal processes. *Annual Review of Psychology, 37,* 233–256.

Morse, S., & Gergen, K. J. (1970). Social comparison, self-consistency, and the concept of self. *Journal of Personality and Social Psychology, 16,* 148–156.

Mortimer, J. T., & Simmons, R. G. (1978). Adult socialization. *Annual Review of Sociology, 4,* 421–454.

Mullen, B., Atkins, J. L., Champion, D. S., Edwards, C., Hardy, D., Story, J. E., & Vanderklok, M. (1985). The false consensus effect: A meta-analysis of 115 hypothesis tests. *Journal of Experimental Social Psychology, 21,* 262–283.

Murray, L., & Trevarthen, C. (1985). Emotional regulation of interactions between two-month olds and their mothers. In T. M. Field & N. A. Fox (Eds.), *Social perception in infants,* (pp. 177–197). Norwood, NJ: Ablex.

Nasby, W. (1989). Private and public self-consciousness and articulation of the self-schema. *Journal of Personality and Social Psychology, 56,* 117–123.

Neisser, V. (1988). Five kinds of self-knowledge. *Philosophical Psychology, 1,* 35–59.

Orive, R. (1988). Social projection and social comparison of opinions. *Journal of Personality and Social Psychology, 54,* 953–964.

Oyserman, D., & Markus, H. (1990). Possible selves and delinquency. *Journal of Personality and Social Psychology.*

Peevers, B. H., & Secord, P. F. (1973). Developmental changes in attribution of descriptive concepts to persons. *Journal of Personality and Social Psychology, 26,* 120–128.

Phillips, D. C. (1976). *Holistic thought in social science.* Stanford, CA: Stanford University Press.

Phillips, D. C. (1984). The illusion of incompetence among academically competent children. *Child Development, 55,* 2000–2016.

Piaget, J. (1930). *The child's conception of physical causality.* London: Routledge & Kegan Paul.

Radke-Yarrow, M., Cummings, E. M., Kuczynsky, L., & Chapman, M. (1985). Patterns of attachment in two- and three-year-olds in normal families and families with parental depression. *Child Development, 56,* 884–893.

Radloff, R. (1966). Social comparison and ability evaluation. *Journal of Experimental Social Psychology,* (Suppl. 1), Vol. 2. *2,* 6–26.

Read, S. J., & Miller, L. C. (1989). Inter-personalism: towards a goal-based theory of persons in relationships. In L. Pervin (Ed.), *Goal concepts in personality and social psychology* (pp. 413–472). Hillsdale, NJ: Erlbaum.

Reifman, A., Klein, J. G., & Murphy, S. T. (1989). Self-monitoring and age. *Psychology and Aging, 4,* 245–246.

Rogers, C. (1951). *Client-centered therapy: Its current practice, implications, and theory.* Boston: Houghton Mifflin.

Rogers, T. B. (1981). A model of the self as an aspect of the human information-processing system. In N. Cantor & J. F. Kihlstrom (Eds.), *Personality, cognition, and social interaction* (pp. 193–214). Hillsdale, NJ: Erlbaum.

Roland, A. (1989). *In search of the self in India and Japan.* Princeton, NJ: Princeton University Press.

Rosenberg, M. (1973). Which significant others? *American Behavioral Science, 16,* 829–860.

Rosenberg, M. (1979). *Concerning the self.* New York: Basic Books.

Rosenberg, M. (1981). The self-concept: Social product and social force. In M. Rosenberg & R. H. Turner (Eds.), *Social psychology: Sociological perspectives* (pp. 593–624). New York: Basic Books.

Rosenberg, M. (1986). Self-concept from middle childhood through adolescence. In J. Suls & A. G. Greenwald (Eds.), *Psychological perspectives on the self* (Vol. 3, pp. 107–136). Hillsdale, NJ: Erlbaum.

Rosenberg, M., & Turner, R. H. (1981). *Social psychology: Sociological perspectives.* New York: Basic Books.

Rosenberg, S. (1988). Self and others: Studies in social personality and autobiography. In L. Berkowitz (Ed.), *Advances in experimental social psychology* (Vol. 21, pp. 57–95). New York: Academic Press.

Rosenthal, R., & Rubin, D. B. (1978). Interpersonal expectancy effects: The first 345 studies. *Behavioral and Brain Sciences, 3,* 377–415.

Ross, L., Greene, D., & House, P. (1977). The "false consensus effect": An egocentric bias in social perception and attribution processes. *Journal of Experimental Social Psychology, 13,* 279–301.

Ruble, D. N., Boggiano, A. K., Feldman, N. S., & Loebl, H. H. (1980). Developmental analysis of the role of social comparison in self-evaluation. *Developmental Psychology, 16,* 105–115.

Ruble, D. N., Feldman, N. S., & Boggiano, A. K. (1976). Social comparison between young children in achievement situations. *Developmental Psychology, 12,* 192–197.

Ruble, D. N., & Flett, G. L. (1988). Conflicting goals in self-evaluative information seeking: Developmental and ability level analyses. *Child Development, 59,* 97–106.

Ruble, D. N., & Rholes, W. (1981). The development of children's perceptions and attributions about their social world. In J. Harvey, W. Ickes, & R. Kidd (Eds.), *New directions in attribution research* (Vol. 3, pp. 3–36). Hillsdale, NJ: Erlbaum.

Safran, J. D., Segal, Z. V., Hill, C., & Whiffen, V. (in press). Refining strategies for research on self-representations in emotional disorders. *Cognitive Therapy and Research.*

Sampson, E. E. (1978). Personality and the location of identity. *Journal of Personality, 46,* 552–568.

Sampson, E. E. (1985). The decentralization of identity: Toward a revised concept of personal and social order. *American Psychologist, 40,* 1203–1211.

Sarbin, T. R. (1962). A preface to a psychological analysis of the self. *Psychological Review, 59,* 11–22.

Sarbin, T. R., & Scheibe, K. E. (1983). *Studies in social identity.* New York: Praeger.

Scheier, M., & Carver, C. (1983a). Self-directed attention and the comparison of self with standards. *Journal of Experimental Social psychology, 19,* 205–222.

Scheier, M., & Carver, C. (1983b). Two sides of the self: One for you and one for me. In J. Suls & A. G. Greenwald (Eds.), *Psychological perspectives on the self* (Vol. 2, pp. 123–157). Hillsdale, NJ: Erlbaum.

Schlenker, B. R. (1980). *Impression management: The self-concept, social identity, and interpersonal relations.* Monterey, CA: Brooks/Cole.

Schlenker, B. R. (1985). Identity and self-identification. In B. R. Schlenker (Ed.), *The self in social life* (pp. 65–99). New York; McGraw-Hill.

Schlenker, B. R., & Weigold, M. F. (1989). Goals and the self-identification process: Constructing desired identities. In L. A. Pervin (Ed.), *Goal concepts in personality and social psychology* (pp. 243–290). Hillsdale, NJ: Erlbaum.

Schur, E. M. (1971). *Labeling deviant behavior: Its sociological implications.* New York: Harper & Row.

Selman, R. L. (1980). *The growth of interpersonal understanding.* New York: Academic Press.

Shaffer, D. R., & Tomarelli, M. M. (1989). When public and private self-foci clash: Self-consciousness and self-disclosure reciprocity during the acquaintance process. *Journal of Personality and Social Psychology, 56*, 765–776.

Shrauger, J. S., & Schoeneman, T. J. (1979). Symbolic interactionist view of self-concept: Through the looking glass darkly. *Psychological Bulletin, 86*, 549–573.

Shweder, R. A. (1982). Beyond self-constructed knowledge: The study of culture and morality. *Merrill-Palmer Quarterly, 28*, 41–69.

Shweder, R. A. (1990). Cultural psychology: What is it? In J. Stigler, R. A. Shweder, & G. Herdt (Eds.), *Cultural psychology: The Chicago Symposia on Culture and Human Development*. Chicago: University of Chicago Press.

Shweder, R. A., & Bourne, F. (1984). Does the concept of the person vary cross-culturally? In R. A. Shweder & R. A. Levine (Eds.), *Culture theory: Essays on mind, self and emotion* (pp. 158–199). New York: Cambridge University Press.

Shweder, R. A., & Levine, R. A. (Eds.). (1984). *Culture Theory: Essays on mind, self and emotion*. New York: Cambridge University Press.

Singer, J. L. (1987, August). *Psychoanalytic theory in the context of contemporary psychology*. Paper presented at the American Psychological Association Convention, New York.

Singer, J. L., & Kolligian, J., Jr. (1987). Personality: Developments in the study of private experience. *Annual Review of Psychology, 38*, 533–574.

Singer, J. L., & Salovey, P. (1985). *Organized knowledge structures and personality: Schemas, self-schemas, prototypes, and scripts*. Paper presented at program on Conscious and Unconscious Mental Processes of the John O. and Katherine T. MacArthur Foundation, Center of Advanced Study of Behavioral Sciences, Stanford, CA.

Snyder, M. (1979). Self-monitoring process. In L. Berkowitz (Ed.), *Advances in experimental social psychology* (Vol. 12, pp. 85–128). New York: Academic Press.

Snyder, M., & Monson, T. C. (1975). Persons, situations and the control of social behavior. *Journal of Personality and Social Psychology, 32*, 637–644.

Snyder, M., & Swann, W. B., Jr. (1976). When actions reflect attitudes: The politics of impression management. *Journal of Personality and Social Psychology, 34*, 1034–1042.

Snyder, M., & Swann, W. B., Jr. (1978). Hypothesis-testing in social interaction. *Journal of Personality and Social Psychology, 36*, 1202–1212.

Snyder, M., Tanke, E. D., & Berscheid, E. (1977). Social perception and interpersonal behavior: On the self-fulfilling nature of social stereotypes. *Journal of Personality and Social Psychology, 35*, 656–666.

Sroufe, L. A. (1988). The role of infant–caregiver attachment in development. In J. Belsky & T. Nezworsky (Eds.), *Clinical implications of attachment* (pp. 18–38). Hillsdale, NJ: Erlbaum.

Stern, D. N. (1985). *The interpersonal world of the infant: A view from psychoanalysis and developmental psychology*. New York: Basic Books.

Stewart, A. J., & Lykes, M. B. (1985). Conceptualizing gender in personality theory and research. In A. J. Stewart & M. B. Lykes (Eds.), *Gender and personality: Current perspectives on theory and research* (pp. 2–13). Durham, NC: Duke University Press.

Stryker, S. (1968). Identity salience and role performance: The relevance of symbolic interaction theory for family research. *Journal of Marriage and the Family, 30*, 558–564.

Stryker, S. (1984). Identity theory: Developments and extensions. Paper presented at Symposium on Self and Social Structure, British Psychological Society, University College, Cardiff, Wales.

Stryker, S. (1987). Identity theory: Developments and extensions. In K. Yardley & T. Honess (Eds.), *Self and identity: Psychosocial perspectives* (pp. 89–103). New York: Wiley.

Sullivan, H. S. (1940). *Conceptions of modern psychiatry*. New York: Norton.

Suls, J. M., & Miller, R. L. (Eds.). (1977). *Social comparison processes: Theoretical and empirical perspectives*. Washington, DC: Hemisphere.

Suls, J. M., & Mullen, B. (1982). From the cradle to the grave: Comparison and self-evaluation across the life span. In J. M. Suls (Ed.), *Psychological perspectives on the self* (Vol. 1, pp. 97–125). Hillsdale, NJ: Erlbaum.

Suls J. M., & Sanders, G. (1982). Self-evaluation via social comparison: A developmental analysis. In I. Wheeler (Ed.), *Review of personality and social psychology* (Vol. 3, pp. 171–197). Beverly Hills, CA: Sage.

Swann, W. B., Jr. (1983). Self-verification: Bringing social reality into harmony with the self. In J. Suls & A. G. Greenwald (Eds.), *Psychological perspectives on the self* (Vol. 2, pp. 33–66). Hillsdale, NJ: Erlbaum.

Swann, W. B., Jr., & Ely, R. J. (1984). A battle of wills: Self-verification versus behavioral confirmation. *Journal of Personality and Social Psychology, 46*, 1287–1302.

Swann, W. B., Jr., & Hill, C. A. (1982). When our identities are mistaken: Reaffirming self-conceptions through social interaction. *Journal of Personality and Social Psychology, 43*, 59–66.

Swap, W. C., & Rubin, J. Z. (1983). A measurement of interpersonal orientation. *Journal of Personality and Social Psychology, 44*, 208–219.

Taylor, S. E., Wood, J. V., & Lichtman, R. R. (1983). It could be worse: Selective evaluation as a response to victimization. *Journal of Social Issues, 39*, 19–40.

Tedeschi, J. (1981). *Impression management theory and social psychological research*. New York: Academic Press.

Tedeschi, J., & Norman, N. (1985). Social power, self-presentation, and the self. In B. R. Schlenker (Ed.), *The self and social life* (pp. 293–322). New York: McGraw-Hill.

Tesser, A. (1986). Some effects of self-evaluation maintenance on cognition and action. In R. M. Sorrentino & E. T. Higgins (Eds.), *Handbook of motivation and cognition: Foundations of social behavior* (pp. 435–464). New York: Guilford Press.

Tesser, A. (1988). Toward a self-evaluation maintenance model of social behavior. In L. Berkowitz (Ed.), *Advances in experimental social psychology* (Vol. 21, pp. 181–227). New York: Academic Press.

Tesser, A., & Campbell, J. (1986). Self-evaluation maintenance and the perception of friends and strangers. *Journal of Personality, 50*, 261–279.

Thompson, R. A. (1987). Empathy and emotional understanding: The early development of empathy. In N. Eisenberg & J. Strayer (Eds.), *Empathy and its development* (pp. 119–145). Cambridge, England: Cambridge University Press.

Thorne, A. (1989). Conditional patterns, transference, and the coherence of personality across time. In D. M. Buss & N. Cantor (Eds.), *Personality psychology:*

Recent trends and emerging directions (pp. 149–159). New York: Springer.

Thornton, D. A., & Arrowood, A. J. (1966). Self-evaluation, self-enhancement, and the locus of social comparison. *Journal of Experimental Social Psychology*, (Suppl. 1), *2*, 40–48.

Tolman, A. E., Diekmann, K. A., & McCartney, K. (1989). Social connectedness and mothering: Effects of maternal employment and maternal absence. *Journal of Personality and Social Psychology*, *56*, 942–949.

Tomkins, S. S. (1979). Script theory: Different magnification of affects. In H. E. Howe, Jr., & R. A. Dienstbier (Eds.), *Nebraska Symposium on Motivation* (Vol. 26, pp. 201–236). Lincoln: University of Nebraska Press.

Trevarthen, C. (1980). The foundations of intersubjectivity: Development of interpersonal and cooperative understanding in infants. In D. R. Olson (Ed.), *The social foundation of language and thought: Essays in honor of Jerome Bruner* (pp. 316–342). New York: Norton.

Triandis, H. C. (1989). The self and social behavior in differing cultural contexts. *Psychological Review*, *96*, 506–520.

Triandis, H. C., Bontempo, R., Villareal, M. J., Asai, M., & Lucca, N. (1988). Individualism and collectivism: Cross-cultural perspectives on self–ingroup relationships. *Journal of Personality and Social Psychology*, *54*, 323–338.

Triandis, H. C., Leung, K., Villareal, M. J., & Clack, F. L. (1985). Allocentric versus idiocentric tendencies: Convergent and discriminant validation. *Journal of Research in Personality*, *19*, 395–415.

Trope, Y. (1986). Self-enhancement and self-assessment in achievement behavior. In R. M. Sorrentino & E. T. Higgins (Eds.), *Handbook of motivation and cognition: Foundations of social behavior* (pp. 350–378). New York: Guilford Press.

Turner, R. (1968). The self-conception in social interaction. In C. Gordon & K. Gergen (Eds.), *The self in social interaction* (pp. 93–106). New York: Wiley.

Turner, R. (1976). The real self: From institution to impulse. *American Journal of Sociology*, *81*, 989–1016.

Turner, R. (1978). The role and the person. *American Journal of Sociology*, *84*, 1–23.

Tversky, A. (1977). Features of similarity. *Psychological Review*, *84*, 327–352.

Vygotsky, L. S. (1962). *Thought and language* (E. Haufmann & G. Vakar, Eds. and Trans.). Cambridge, MA: MIT Press.

Waterman, A. S. (1981). Individualism and interdependence. *American Psychologist*, *36*, 762–773.

Wegner, D. M., Giuliano, T., & Hertel, P. T. (1985). Cognitive interdependence in close relationships. In W. Ickes (Ed.), *Compatible and incompatible relationships* (pp. 253–276). New York: Springer.

Weigert, A. J. (1983). Identity: Its emergence within sociological psychology. *Symbolic Interaction*, *6*, 183–206.

Weigert, A. J., Teitge, J. S., & Teitge, D. W. (1986). *Society and identity*. Cambridge, England: Cambridge University Press.

Webster, M., & Sobieszek, B. I. (1974). *Sources of self-evaluation: A formal theory of significant others and social influence*. New York: Wiley.

Westen, D. (1985) *Self and society*. Cambridge UK: Cambridge University Press

White, G. M., & Kirkpatrick, J. (Eds.). (1985). *Person, self, and experience: Exploring Pacific ethnopsychologies*. Berkeley: University of California Press.

Wicklund, R. A. (1975). Objective self-awareness. In L. Berkowitz (Ed.), *Advances in experimental social psychology* (Vol. 8, pp. 233–275). New York: Academic Press.

Wiley, M. G., & Alexander, C. N. (1987). From situated activity to self-attribution: The impact of social structural schemata. In K. Yardley & T. Honess (Eds.), *Self and identity: Psychosocial perspectives* (pp. 105–118). New York: Wiley.

Wills, T. A. (1981). Downward comparison principles in social psychology. *Psychological Bulletin*, *90*, 245–271.

Witkin, H. A., & Goodenough, D. R. (1977). Field dependence and interpersonal behavior. *Psychological Bulletin*, *84*, 661–689.

Witkin, H. A., & Goodenough, D. R., & Oltman, P. K. (1979). Psychological differentiation: Current status. *Journal of Personality and Social Psychology*, *37*, 1127–1145.

Witkin, H. A., Moore, C. A., Goodenough, D. R., & Cox, P. W. (1977). Field-dependent and field-independent cognitive styles and their education implications. *Review of Educational Research*, *47*, 1–64.

Wood, J. V. (1989). Theory and research concerning social comparisons of personal attributes. *Psychological Bulletin*, *106*, 231–248.

Wood, J. V., Taylor, S. E., & Lichtman, R. R. (1985). Social comparison in adjustment to breast cancer. *Journal of Personality and Social Psychology*, *49*, 1169–1183.

Word, C. O., Zanna, M. P., & Cooper, J. (1974). The nonverbal mediation of self-fulfilling prophecies in interracial interaction. *Journal of Experimental Social Psychology*, *10*, 109–120.

Wyer, R. S. & Gordon, S. E. (1984). The cognitive representation of social information. In R. S. Wyer & T. K. Srull (Eds.), *Handbook of social cognition* (Vol. 2, pp. 73–150). Hillsdale, NJ: Erlbaum.

Zurcher, L. A. (1977). *The mutable self: A self-concept for social change*. Beverly Hills, CA: Sage.

Chapter 23
Emotion and Adaptation

Craig A. Smith
Vanderbilt University
Richard S. Lazarus
University of California–Berkeley

Subjectively, there are few psychological phenomena that compare with emotion. Emotions punctuate almost all the significant events in our lives: We feel proud when we receive a promotion; we become angry when we learn that our homes have been burglarized, we are joyful at the births of our children; and we experience profound grief at the death of someone we love. Furthermore, the emotions we experience seem to strongly influence how we act in response to these events: The joy and pride encourage renewed commitment to advance and protect career and family; the anger motivates us to seek justice and retribution; and the sadness pushes us to seek aid and comfort while coming to terms with our loss.

The centrality of emotion in human existence is no secret in the arts. Good drama is directed toward evoking emotion in the audience (Scheff, 1979), and thus serves as a study of the affective power of various social circumstances. In a complementary fashion, authors use emotional reactions as important clues to their characters' true motivations and personalities, revealing a pervasive assumption that emotions and personality are inextricably intertwined. Many of the trait words people use to describe others' personalities (e.g., "hostile," "timid," "spiteful," "cheerful," "aggressive," "cautious," etc.) refer directly to the persons' tendencies to respond to diverse situations with characteristic emotions (see Plutchik, 1980).

Given the central position that we cede to emotions in our personal lives and the prominence of emotion in literary studies of the human condition, one might expect emotion to serve as a central, organizing construct in scientific psychology, and especially in a psychology of personality. If to this we add the widespread—and no doubt justified—belief among professionals and laypersons that emotions have a major impact on our subjective well-being, our physical health, our social functioning, and our problem-solving performance, then understanding the emotions ought to be a major agenda for the social and biological sciences. Historically, however, the study of emotion in psychology has been severely neglected. Emotion has been considered an irrelevant epiphenomenon (e.g., Skinner, 1953), or has been used as a convenient chapter heading for a loosely organized collection of material not easily covered elsewhere (see Bolles, 1974; Lazarus, 1966; Tomkins, 1962).

This neglect, however, is currently showing healthy signs of dissipating. Psychologists from all subfields profess interest in emotional processes, and research on emotion-related topics is burgeoning. A number of volumes (e.g., Izard, Kagan, & Zajonc, 1984; Plutchik & Kellerman, 1980; Scherer & Ekman, 1984; Shaver, 1984), and even new journals (e.g., *Cognition and Emotion*), devoted to the study of emotion have recently appeared. The same can be found in sociology, anthropology, and the neurosciences.

What we think has happened is this: First, there was a loosening of the restrictive epistemology of behaviorism, which allowed investigators once again to examine thoughts about one's plight as factors in adaptation and emotion. Second, the cognitive revolution allowed researchers to center attention on emotion in common-sense or folk psychology terms, to recognize the dependence of our emotional lives on motivation, and to focus attention on the individual differences in what is important to the person. Although heartened by these developments, we maintain an uneasy sense that, with a few exceptions (e.g., Thoits, 1984), much of this work still fails to appreciate emotion's rightful place as a central and organizing construct within psychology. Instead, there is a tendency to treat it as yet another interesting, isolated subtopic.

We begin by addressing the question of what an emotion is. Next, we describe our own recent work directed at illuminating what we see as one of the important issues in emotion theory—the role of cognitive appraisal. We embed this work in a general model of emotion, which identifies the key variables and processes within a systems framework emphasizing person–environment relationships and cognitive mediation. In presenting our model, we illustrate how emotion theory makes firm contact with a variety of topics currently being pursued across diverse psychological disciplines, especially personality and social psychology.

DEFINITIONAL ISSUES: THE NATURE OF EMOTION

Unfortunately, although there is considerable agreement that certain psychophysiological states (e.g., anger, fear, and sadness) should be regarded as emotions, and that certain others (e.g., hunger and thirst) should not, there are many other states (e.g., startle, interest, guilt) about which there is little consensus (cf. Ekman, 1984; Ekman, Friesen, & Simons, 1985; Izard, 1977; Ortony, 1987; Plutchik, 1980; Tomkins, 1980). The lack of consensus occurs because there is no absolute agreement on the criteria that should be used to distinguish emotion from nonemotion. The "defining" criteria have been based on specific behaviors believed to be produced by the emotions (e.g., Watson, 1919), linguistic properties of the English words used to denote various states (e.g., Ortony, 1987; Ortony, Clore, & Foss, 1987), and distinctive patterns of physiological activity, such as characteristic facial expressions (e.g., Ekman, 1984; Izard, 1977; Tomkins, 1980). An examination of previous definitional attempts might lead to this conclusion: "Everyone knows what an emotion is, until asked to give a definition. Then, it seems, no one knows" (Fehr & Russell, 1984, p. 464).

In any definition we need to distinguish between what can be said about emotion in general, and what can be said about specific emotions such as anger, fear, guilt, shame, pride, love, and so forth. The most common solution, historically, has been to base the definition on descriptive characteristics of the general reaction, which, Hillman (1960) has suggested, provides substantial agreement in the abstract. Hillman quotes the following from Drever's (1952, pp. 80–81) *Dictionary of Psychology*:

> *Emotion:* differently described and explained by different psychologists, but all agree that it is a complex state of the organism, involving bodily changes of a widespread character—in breathing, pulse, gland secretion, etc.—and, on the mental side, a state of excitement or perturbation, marked by strong feeling, and usually an impulse toward a definitive form of behavior. If the emotion is intense there is some disturbance of the intellectual functions, a measure of dissociation, and a tendency towards action. . . .

Although this definition expresses some consensus at the descriptive level, it does not go far toward settling disputes over distinctions between emotion and nonemotion, or the specific reaction states that should be considered true emotions. Is surprise an emotion? Excitement? Relief? Love? How should we treat the so-called "aesthetic" emotions? Nor does it reveal much about the properties of specific emotions, or help us specify the processes and variables involved in the generation of emotion.

In seeking to distinguish emotion from nonemotion, the seemingly irreconcilable differences among various definitions suggest to us, as they have to others (e.g., Fehr & Russell, 1984; Shaver, Schwartz, Kirson, & O'Connor, 1987), that emotion may not be readily amenable to classical definition. Instead, it may be better to think of a set of prototype definitions that explicitly acknowledges that "emotion" may be an inherently fuzzy set, and perhaps to replace traditionally strict necessary and sufficient conditions with defining features that tend to be shared by most emotions and absent from most nonemotions (Fehr & Russell, 1984; Leeper, 1965; Rosch, 1978; Shaver et al., 1987). The very notion of a "fuzzy" set indicates the possible existence of *borderline* phenomena that have some characteristics prototypical of an emotion and other characteristics prototypical of a nonemotion, making the full category of "emotion" very difficult to define and many borderline states difficult to classify with assurance.

Wisdom suggests that in this chapter we should not try to resolve the question of which states are borderline states or genuine emotions, since the arguments are complicated and would require much space, and we are not totally confident about our own solutions. Instead, we compare emotions to related psychophysiological phenomena in order to identify the most important distinguishing characteristics of emotion. We draw upon these characteristics to describe the specific variables and processes involved in emotion, since delineating these specifics and their interrelationships in each kind of emotion represents the most pressing agenda for emotion theory and research.

THE ADAPTATIONAL PROBLEM AND THE EVOLUTION OF EMOTION

As Plutchik (1980) has cogently argued, each species faces a number of fundamental adaptational problems that it must adequately address in order to survive. The survival issues faced by most animal species include, among others, adequate nourishment, reproduction, and protection from external and internal threats to well-being.[1] Through natural selection, successful species develop mechanisms that enable them to meet these problems, and different species achieve solutions determined by both the environmental pressures they face and their biological potential.

Like many contemporary and recent theorists (e.g., Arnold, 1960; Ekman, 1984; Ellsworth & Smith, 1988a; Epstein, 1984; Izard, 1977; Lazarus, 1968; Lazarus, Kanner, & Folkman, 1980; Lazarus & Smith, 1988; Leeper, 1948, 1965; Leventhal, 1980; Plutchik, 1980; Roseman, 1984; Scherer, 1984b; Tomkins, 1962, 1980), we believe that emotions represent one class of solutions to these adaptational problems. Each emotion expresses a person's appraisal of a person–environment relationship involving a particular kind of harm or benefit. The appraisal is based on antecedent motivational and belief variables that confront (interact with) a set of environmental demands, constraints, and resources, and it generates action tendencies relevant to the specific conditions of harm or benefit confronted—tendencies that are embodied and expressed in a particular physiological pattern. However, emotions are not the only entities that serve adaptive functions; both within and across species, similar functions are also served by reflexes (e.g., startle) and physiological drives (e.g., hunger and thirst). Reflexes, physiological drives, and emotions all stimulate (motivate) the organism to behave in ways that enhance its potential to survive and flourish. In other words, each is a different "adaptational subsystem."[2]

Although serving similar general functions (i.e., promoting survival), the three adaptational subsystems are, in principle, distinguishable in an evolutionary sense. It is a reasonable inference that emotions evolved from simpler and more rigid adaptational systems such as reflexes and physiological drives (see Ellsworth & Smith, 1988a, 1988b; Epstein, 1984; Leeper, 1948, 1965; Scherer, 1984b; Tomkins, 1962). Undoubtedly, the most important evolutionary change was the movement away from specific built-in responses elicited by specific environmental stimuli toward increasing variability and complexity that decoupled the behavioral response from the environmental input. Along with this increasing variability and loss of behavioral rigidity, there simultaneously evolved an increasing dependence on intelligence and learning. As more complicated species evolved, they became less dependent on hard-wired reflexes, and a gap developed between environmental demand and action. This gap was filled increasingly by thought and judgment, as is most evident in humans (Piaget, 1952; Werner, 1948). Instead of surviving and flourishing because of a built-in program of adaptive reactions for every specific environmental condition, more advanced species survived by learning how to deal with their environments and mobilizing accordingly. Increasingly, judgment took over from innate reflexes, and emotions— drawing upon both motives and thought—have become the key adaptational process intervening between environmental challenges and actions (Tomkins, 1962). In short, innate reflexes were once the simplest solutions to the adaptational problem of getting along in the world, but in more complex creatures these evolved into emotional patterns.

In considering the role of the emotions in adaptation, one must remember that the fundamental adaptational task is to mobilize the most efficacious behavior in the face of the biological and social requirements of living. Remember, too, that in order to effectively produce contingent behavior, the organism must meet two fundamental conditions: First, it needs to reliably detect when environmental circumstances are relevant to one or another of its survival needs; second, this detection must result in behavior that increases the likelihood of satisfying the need. In our view, reflexes, physiological drives, and emotions all represent mechanisms connecting the detection of survival-relevant conditions with the production of survival-enhancing behavior, but they achieve this connection in different ways.

Reflexes

The task of pairing adaptive behaviors with survival-relevant conditions is easiest when a need is reliably signaled by a very specific cue or set of cues, and can be met by performing a specific behavior. It is this very specific linkage that innate reflexes accomplish, and the hallmark of the reflex is its stimulus specificity and response rigidity (Ekman, 1984; Ekman et al., 1985). Very specific patterns of stimulation ("releasing stimuli") elicit very specific patterns of behavior ("fixed action patterns") that ensure the need signalled by the releasing stimulus is met. These characteristic properties of reflexes are summarized in the first column of Table 23.1.

Reflexes (at one time, the term "instincts" might have been used) constitute an effective adaptational system for organisms that can afford to interact with their environments in highly stereotyped ways. However, their simplicity—the rigid pairing of a specific stimulus with a specific response—has high costs, particularly as organisms and their environmental interactions become more complicated. For an organism dependent on reflex, each new mode of interaction with the environment requires the development of a new reflex, and at some relatively modest level of complexity this requirement becomes highly disadvantageous. As the survival issues themselves become more complex, they become increasingly difficult to address through the performance of rigid behavioral sequences, and more flexible, context-sensitive responses become necessary. Furthermore, it becomes increasingly unlikely that specific survival issues will be reliably signaled by single stimuli. Thus, with increasing complexity there is increasing selective pressure to surmount the behavioral rigidity inherent in reflexes and to decouple specific stimuli from specific responses (see Epstein, 1984; Leeper, 1965; Scherer, 1984b; Tomkins, 1962). There

TABLE 23.1. Comparison of Reflexes, Physiological Drives, and Emotions

Property	Reflex	Physiological drive	Emotion
Stimulus source	Internal or external event (real)	Internal tissue deficit (real)	Internal or external event (real or imagined)
Periodicity	Reactive	Cyclical	Reactive
Stimulus specificity	High	Moderate–high	Low
Response flexibility	Low	Moderate	High
Examples	Startle, eye blink	Hunger, thirst	Anger, sadness, guilt

is still a need for mechanisms that both alert the organism when it faces survival-relevant circumstances and compel it to respond adaptively to those circumstances. However, there is much to be gained if the organism is somehow able to equate distinct stimuli that signal functionally similar conditions, and/or to respond to those conditions with a degree of behavioral flexibility.

Physiological Drives

Physiological drives, such as hunger and thirst, evolved in the service of particular internal, homeostatic needs. For instance, hunger serves to ensure that the organism's nutritional needs are met, and thirst ensures that the organism maintains an adequate fluid balance. These drives have tended to remain stimulus-specific even in the most complicated species, presumably because the homeostatic needs they serve can be reliably anticipated on the basis of specific internal cues, resulting in little selective pressure to abandon the specificity. For example, in many animal species (including humans), an impending need for nourishment can be predicted quite reliably from specific internal cues, such as the level of sugar in the bloodstream, and these cues elicit hunger (e.g., Thompson & Campbell, 1977).

Physiological drives are distinguished from reflexes by a moderate degree of response flexibility. In most higher animals drives tend to motivate specific *classes* of behavior, but the specific behavioral sequences within these classes are not determined by the drive itself. For instance, hunger motivates the organism to *eat* something, but for many species (including humans), the hunger itself does not determine either the specific behaviors to be performed to obtain and prepare the food, or the identity of appropriate foodstuffs. This response flexibility provides considerable adaptational advantages, but also entails considerable cost.

The major advantage is that the behavioral flexibility enables the organism to adjust its behaviors sensitively to its specific environmental contingencies. Thus, in hunger, if one strategy for obtaining food fails, the organism is relatively free to try another; if a favorite food becomes scarce, the organism is able to seek an alternative; and so on. The major cost is that this flexibility makes the drive in some sense incomplete: It must be supplemented with something that guides the organism toward specific appropriate behaviors. Thus, with hunger, appropriate strategies for obtaining food must come from somewhere, and the organism must have some means of identifying suitable foods.

The apparent evolutionary solution to this tradeoff has been to make the degree of behavioral flexibility associated with drives dependent upon the species' capacity for learning. The ability to draw upon past experience to guide present behavior seems to be a prerequisite for response flexibility (cf. Bolles, 1974; Ellsworth & Smith, 1988a; Epstein, 1984; Scherer, 1984b). Across species, organisms that demonstrate the most highly developed learning capabilities tend to be the ones that have acquired the greatest behavioral latitude in responding to specific physiological drives. For instance, human food preferences are dependent on culture and the individual's life experience (Rozin & Fallon, 1987).

Drives display an additional characteristic, "periodicity," that further distinguishes them from reflexes (and emotions). Unless anticipated, the homeostatic needs, and hence the drives that serve them, arise with great regularity. For example, after an extended period without nourishment (or fluid) an organism *will* become hungry (or thirsty, etc.) in a very predictable manner. In contrast, many reflexes, and all emotions, are "reactive." They arise in response to appropriate signals whenever those signals occur, and if the signal never arises then the reflex or emotion may never be experienced. As summarized in the second column of Table 23.1, physiological drives display periodicity, stimulus specificity, and moderate response flexibility, and they serve homeostatic needs.

Physiological drives—which are innate in all animal species, including humans—are not the only motivational forces to which complicated species respond. In humans, for example, there appear to be strong needs to explore, achieve, and gain mastery over the environment, as well as to maintain contact and form social bonds with others. Whether one refers to these needs as learned or acquired drives, or "social motives," the development of adaptational systems to satisfy them has depended on a powerful and abstract intelligence. Advanced intelligence also made possible the complex patterns of social organization that dominate the behavior of advanced species, and that are as important to survival and prosperity as meeting physiological needs.

This is not the place to argue about the extent to which social motives are innate or acquired or developmentally dependent on conditioning in the presence of the subsidence of physiological drives such as hunger and thirst. Human functioning and adaptation are heavily dependent upon the fate of social motives, and in our view, emotions are part of an evolutionary solution for ensuring their satisfaction. An understanding of human emotions would be impossible without reference to a motivational principle that identifies what is regarded by the individual as important or unimportant to personal well-being. A cognitive–relational theory of emotions, such as the one we propose below, cannot depend on the fate of innate physiological needs alone, but rests on the premise of individual differences in motivational patterns—patterns that set the stage for defining harm and benefit for each individual.

Emotions

As we have said, emotions emerged in complicated species to meet the need for high degrees of response flexibility to the often complex and subtle conditions of life that could generate harms and benefits. They developed in ways that differentiate them from both reflexes and drives in flexibility, variability, richness, and dependence on intelligence. As indicated in the last column of Table 23.1, emotions not only expanded the response flexibility that distinguishes drives from reflexes, but also lost the stimulus specificity that characterizes both reflexes and drives.

Unlike physiological needs, which are internal and reliably signaled by specific stimulus conditions, adaptationally significant external events present themselves to complex species in a variety of guises. For instance, one class of events with which the organism must be prepared to cope in order to survive is that of *threats* to its well-being. All threats share the property of having the potential of resulting in harm if they are not avoided or neutralized.

However, these dangers can take a variety of forms, and each can be signaled by a wide array of conditions. The danger may be any one of several predators, whose presence may be signaled by diverse stimuli (an odor, a sound, the sudden movement of a shadow, etc.). The

recognition of threat is further complicated by the fact that a predator is often not dangerous unless aggravated or hungry. Thus, the significance of any given signal may vary considerably across divergent contexts. In modern human existence, the danger from others may consist of subtle and concealed disapproval, patronizing statements that barely reveal a true attitude and require considerable social experience and intelligence to interpret, or poor matches between performance demands (e.g., at work) and the abilities and knowledge possessed by a person for meeting those demands. As a further complication, threats represent only one of several classes of significant events, each of which can take a variety of forms and be signaled in a multitude of ways.

In place of the unwieldy adaptational solution of developing a different reflex in response to every signal of every potentially significant event in all contexts, more complicated species have to stake their security on the capacity to evaluate the significance of what is happening. They need to be responsive to a wide variety of cues signaling a particular kind of significant event, and they need to be sensitive to the context in which these cues are encountered. In humans it is easy to demonstrate that, under the appropriate circumstances, just about any stimulus event can produce just about any emotion, and no single stimulus will always elicit a given emotion under all conditions (Ekman, 1984; Frijda, 1986).

The suggestion that emotions lack stimulus specificity does not imply that they are random response states. On the contrary, we see each distinct emotion as a response to a particular kind of significant event—a particular kind of harm or benefit (see Lazarus, 1968, 1982; Lazarus & Smith, 1988)—that motivates coping activity. However, because there is no simple mapping between objective stimulus properties and adaptive significance, the task of detecting significant events becomes quite formidable, and to accomplish it the organism must be able to somehow classify what is being confronted into a relatively small number of categories, corresponding to the various kinds of harm or benefit it may face. Above all, the emotional response is not a reaction to a stimulus, but to an organism (person)–environment *relationship*. Given the properties of the stimulus context and the organism's pattern of motivation, what must be detected is that the convergence of these two sets of characteristics results in harm or benefit. This is what it means to speak of a "relational" approach to emotion. Moreover, with the adaptational responses having become less innate, more flexible, more variable, and more dependent upon the species' cognitive capabilities, emotions are not only reactions to ongoing relationships with the environment but are also cognitive.

However, the adaptive solution has not been merely to produce a purely cold cognitive process of detection and evaluation. Instead, it comprises a complex psychobiological reaction that fuses intelligence with motivational patterns, action impulses, and physiological changes that signify to both the actor and observer that something of significance for well-being is at stake in the encounter with the environment. We call this psychobiological reaction an "emotion." It is a very complex reaction that simultaneously encompasses motives and cognitive evaluations of the adaptational requirements of the encounter, and, if the encounter is evaluated as having important consequences for personal well-being, it results in organismic involvement. Therefore, in place of "emotion" we often use the expression "cognitive–motivational–emotive configuration."

The divorce of emotional response from specific stimuli and its replacement with a cognitive evaluation of the significance of the organism–environment relationship is the centerpiece of the emotion process in humans. By centering on the person's *interpretation* or *evaluation* of what an encounter signifies for its well-being, the effective stimulus for emotion has shifted from a concrete *event* to an abstract *meaning*. In becoming meaning-centered, emotions have achieved a flexibility and adaptational power that is simply not possible for stimulus-centered adaptational systems such as drives and reflexes.

From this point of view, *anything* that implies harm or benefit to the person can produce an emotion. Thus, pain, hunger, or even emotional reactions themselves (e.g., anger) can evoke fear, guilt, shame, or some other emotion—even a positive one such as happiness or love—if they are interpreted as somehow being a harm or threat, or a benefit. Just as significantly, the critical event—be it internal, external, or a combination of both—need not have actually occurred. *Anticipated* circumstances can be as emotionally arousing as the actual occurrence, if not more so (e.g., Folkins,

1970; Nomikos, Opton, Averill, & Lazarus, 1968). Even purely imaginary experiences, which the person in no way expects to take place, are quite effective at evoking low-level emotional reactions, as a long tradition of imagery-based research will attest (e.g., Carroll, Marzillier, & Merian, 1982; Lang, 1979; Schwartz, Fair, Salt, Mandel, & Klerman, 1976; Smith, 1989; Smith, McHugo, & Lanzetta, 1986).

That emotions are reactions to abstract meanings conveyed by just about any set of circumstances implies an emotion process that is extraordinarily complex, variable, and flexible. Whereas any given drive can only be satisfied by performing a particular class of behaviors (e.g., eating something in hunger, drinking something in thirst), this does not appear to be the case for emotions, perhaps because the diverse range of circumstances that can elicit a given emotion cannot be effectively addressed by any single class of behavior. For example, anxiety arises when we perceive ourselves to be in a potentially dangerous situation, and we become motivated to avoid or escape the threat. But a wide variety of behaviors that eliminate or reduce the threat can satisfy this motivation—fleeing the situation, remaining in the situation but increasing vigilance, or even mounting a pre-emptory attack to eliminate the source of threat. Thus, an emotion provides the motivation to react to the situation in an ill-defined way—in this case, to avoid the perceived threat—but it does not greatly constrain the specific behaviors produced.

Finally, the dependence on meaning lends emotion a dynamic fluidity that allows the response to sensitively track the changing adaptational significance of the person–environment relationship as an encounter unfolds. Thus, if the anxious person's attempts to avoid the threat prove successful, and the perceived danger is eliminated, the person's anxiety will be transformed into relief, and vigilance abates. If the threat materializes, and there is recognition of an irremedial harm, the anxiety will be transformed into sadness or despair, and the psychophysiological and behavioral pattern will look quite different.

The idea that the adaptational power and flexibility of emotion depend upon the organism's cognitive capabilities provides the basis for Plutchik's (1984) assertion that cognition evolved in the service of emotion, and has also been invoked to explain why human beings, the most cognitive of creatures, also appear to be the most emotional (e.g., Hebb, 1949; Scherer, 1984b). Given the analysis above, it is not surprising that recent efforts to understand emotion have focused on the role of cognition, and in particular cognitive *appraisal*, in eliciting emotion.

APPRAISAL THEORY

How a given individual reacts emotionally to an encounter depends on an evaluation of what the encounter implies for personal well-being, which is what "appraisal" means in our usage. A fundamental proposition is that the evaluation causes the emotional response in accordance with a set of psychobiological laws, which we spell out later. That is, if we know how a person evaluates the relationship with the environment, we can predict that person's emotional reaction. In order to develop this position into a full-scale theory, and to make clear its utility, it is important to specify the causally relevant aspects of the appraisal process for each emotion. A large portion of our own recent collaboration (e.g., Lazarus & Smith, 1988; Smith, Lazarus, & Novacek, 1990) has been directed at developing a system of thought that specifies what a person must want and think in order to experience each kind of emotional response.

In developing the theory we wanted to integrate recent theoretical and empirical work relating specific types of cognitive activity to specific emotions (e.g., Ellsworth & Smith, 1988a, 1988b; Frijda, 1986; Roseman, 1984; Scherer, 1984b; Smith & Ellsworth, 1985, 1987; Weiner, 1985) with the more general theory of appraisal, stress, and coping developed by Lazarus and colleagues (e.g., Lazarus, 1966, 1968; Lazarus, Averill, & Opton, 1970; Lazarus & Folkman, 1984). We also wanted to clarify and refine the construct of "appraisal" so that it would refer only to the cognitive activities *directly* related to emotion. Finally, we hoped that by specifying the appraisals that produce individual emotions, the resulting theory would clarify how emotions motivate the organism to cope effectively with the adaptational demands confronting it.

Appraisal and Knowledge

Although emotions are evoked as a result of cognitive activity, not all cognitive activity is relevant to emotion, and even relevant cognitive activities are not all *equally* relevant. The task of interpreting the adaptational significance of our circumstances draws upon a highly complicated and only partially reliable arrangement of cues to determine what, if anything, the relationship to the environment implies for personal well-being. There appear to be at least two distinct types of cognition involved in this process.

First, there must be a well-developed representation of one's circumstances. Much social-psychological and personality research has been devoted to describing a vast array of attributional and inferential strategies that people use to go beyond the often paltry data directly available and construct rich representations of what is happening (e.g., Bruner, 1957; Heider, 1958; Jones et al., 1971; Lewin, 1936; Nisbett & Ross, 1980; Ross, 1977, 1987; Shaver, 1977). These representations, which reflect *knowledge* or *beliefs* about what is happening, are relevant to emotion because they are the data that the person evaluates with respect to their adaptational significance. These knowledge-centered representations, or "situational construals," however, do not directly produce emotions.

Instead, it is how these representations are *appraised* with respect to their significance for personal well-being—the second type of cognition—that directly determines the emotional state (see Lazarus & Folkman, 1984; Lazarus & Smith, 1988). Appraisals are strongly influenced by personality variables. Two individuals can construe their situations quite similarly (agree on all the facts), and yet react with very different emotions, because they have appraised the adaptational significance of those facts differently. This derives from the relational nature of emotions, in which the confluence of both an environmental configuration and personality traits is required to have a particular bearing on subjective well-being in the eyes of each individual.

The distinction between knowledge and appraisal can be understood as the difference between *distal* cognitive variables that influence emotions only indirectly, and *proximal* ones that have direct causal influences (see

House, 1981; Jessor, 1981). The appraisal construct encompasses the most proximal cognitive variables (Lazarus, 1966; Lazarus & Folkman, 1984), and in formulating our specific appraisal model, we have been quite restrictive about what we include as appraisal. We have not included a number of cognitive variables previously found to be relevant to emotion, because upon close inspection they reflect either the more distal, knowledge-based cognitive activities discussed above (e.g., locus of causality/control; Roseman, 1984; Smith & Ellsorth, 1985; Weiner, 1985) or the subjective properties of the emotional response itself (e.g., subjective pleasantness; Scherer, 1984b; Smith & Ellsworth, 1985), rather than being evaluative appraisals (see Lazarus & Smith, 1988, for a fuller account of this distinction).

Weiner (1985, p. 564), the foremost advocate of an attributional analysis of emotion, has himself acknowledged that knowledge or beliefs about how things work are more or less indeterminate with respect to their emotional consequences: "A word of caution . . . is needed. . . . Given a causal ascription, the linked emotion does not necessarily follow . . . [Attributional] dimension–affect relations are not invariant, but are quite prevalent in our culture, and perhaps in many others as well." What is needed to make the analysis more determinate is to add appraisal of the personal significance of what is happening for well-being.

Core Relational Themes and Appraisal Components

The appraisal task for the person is to evaluate perceived circumstances in terms of a relatively small number of categories of adaptational significance, corresponding to different types of benefit or harm, each with different implications for coping. A key proposition of a cognitive–relational theory of emotion is that the appraisal process results in the identification of a molar person–environment relationship, or what we call a "core relational theme," and that each distinct theme results in a distinct emotion (Lazarus & Smith, 1988). As indicated earlier, we think of this as a psychobiological law.

For each different emotion, one should be able to identify the core relational theme that summarizes the person's relationship to the en-

vironment in terms of a particular type of harm or benefit. For example, an ambiguous danger or threat produces anxiety; loss and helplessness produce sadness; offense to oneself or those one identifies with produces anger—much as Aristotle suggested in his *Rhetoric*—and so on for each emotion (see Abramson, Seligman, & Teasdale, 1978; Plutchik, 1980).

This molar level of description provides an economical summary of the appraised meaning leading to each distinct emotion. However, by itself, it is incomplete because it does not reveal the specific evaluations leading to the core relational theme. For example, knowing that an appraisal of "ambiguous danger" produces anxiety indicates very little about the specific cognitive decisions made in evaluating the situation as dangerous.

Therefore, the molar level of analysis must be supplemented by a more *molecular* one, which attempts to describe the specific appraisal questions and answers that result in each core relational theme. Knowledge of the details of appraisal would make it possible to describe and understand the details of the linkage between the core relational themes and the emotions that flow from them, as well as the similarities and differences among the various themes and emotions (see Smith & Ellsworth, 1985). For example, knowing about the component evaluations that combine to define uncertain threat and irretrievable loss, respectively, might suggest why subjective experiences of anxiety and sadness seem in many respects quite similar, why anxiety and sadness often co-occur in the same situation, and yet why they are so different as well (Ellsworth & Smith, 1988a).

We have made an effort to identify the major dimensional *components* of appraisal—that is, the specific questions evaluated in appraisal. The answers to these questions are then combined to produce the molar personal meanings that directly result in specific emotions (see Lazarus & Smith, 1988). To do this, we have drawn on a number of recent proposals attempting to identify the specific cognitions associated with particular emotions (e.g., Frijda, 1986; Roseman, 1984; Scherer, 1984b; Smith & Ellsworth, 1985, 1987; Weiner, 1985).

It is useful, we think, to view each appraisal component as addressing one of the two global appraisal issues originally proposed by Lazarus and his colleagues as relevant to well-being (e.g., Lazarus, 1966; Lazarus et al., 1970; Lazarus & Folkman, 1984). "Primary appraisal" concerns whether and how the encounter is relevant to the person's well-being, and "secondary appraisal" concerns the person's resources and options for coping with the encounter.[3] Both of these issues can be further subdivided, and at present we have identified a total of six appraisal components—two for primary appraisal, and four for secondary appraisal.

Consistent with the doctrine that emotion depends on antecedent motivations that are part of personality, the two components of primary appraisal are motivational relevance (or importance) and motivational congruence or incongruence. "Motivational relevance" is an evaluation of the extent to which an encounter touches upon personal goals and concerns—in other words, the extent to which there are issues in the encounter about which the person cares or in which he or she has a stake. This appraisal component is also included in the theoretical systems of Frijda (1986), Scherer (1984b), and Smith and Ellsworth (1987). "Motivational congruence or incongruence" refers to the extent to which a transaction is consistent or inconsistent with what one wants—that is, the extent to which it either thwarts or facilitates personal goals. This corresponds closely to Roseman's (1984) concept of "motive consistency," Scherer's (1984b) "goal conduciveness," and Smith and Ellsworth's (1985) "perceived obstacle."

The four components of secondary appraisal are accountability, problem-focused coping potential, emotion-focused coping potential, and future expectancy. "Accountability" provides direction and focus to the emotional response and the coping efforts motivated by it. It determines who (oneself or someone else) is to receive the credit (if the encounter is motivationally congruent) or the blame (if it is motivationally incongruent) for the harm or benefit. It is also closely related to locus of causality (Ellsworth & Smith, 1988a; Weiner, Graham, & Chandler, 1982), which is an attributional or knowledge factor, but differs from it in ways that highlight the earlier stated difference between knowledge and appraisal.

Accountability is a more proximal construct than locus of causality, intentionality, legitimacy, and controllability, which are often combined in evaluating accountability—that is, who gets the credit or blame (McGraw, 1987; Shaver, 1985). For example, under conditions of harm, people who are considered the locus of causality will be held less accountable to the extent that their harmful actions are perceived as unintentional, just, and/or unavoidable (Pastore, 1952; Shaver, 1985; Weiner, Amirkhan, Folkes, & Verette, 1987). The attribution of causality is "cold," with no necessary motivational consequences, whereas a determination of blame or credit is "hot" because it not only implies personal involvement but also implies that one's subsequent emotion and coping efforts should be directed toward the target of that judgment.

Often what makes the difference between an attribution of mere locus of causality and an appraisal of accountability, and hence blame, is a judgment of imputed control by the other person. In other words, if the other person who has caused the harm could have done otherwise, as when he or she has acted maliciously or has treated us too lightly and hence demeaned us, there will be accountability, blame, and anger. If, however, the other person could not have controlled what was done, then there will be an attribution of causal locus without accountability or blame. In this case, anger will not occur, or it will be directed at other sources of blame on the basis of complex social judgments about the accountability, say, of the authorities, or the system, or the like. The different motivational dynamics of locus of causality and accountability can often be observed when in the course of their jobs people must inflict harm on others, and even while acknowledging being the locus of causality they try to deflect the accountability and blame to their social role in the hope that the other person's anger will be similarly deflected (e.g., "I'm sorry, I really hate to do this, but I have to—it's my job").

The remaining three components of secondary appraisal all have to do with evaluation of the potential for improving an undesirable situation or maintaining a desirable one. The two subvarieties of coping potential correspond to one's evaluations of the ability to engage in the two major types of coping identified by Folkman and Lazarus (1980, 1985; Folkman, Lazarus, Dunkel-Schetter, DeLongis, & Gruen, 1986; Lazarus & Folkman, 1984). "Problem-focused coping potential" reflects evaluations of one's ability to act directly upon the situation to manage the demands of the encounter and actualize the personal commitments that are brought to it. This evaluation is closely related to the concept of power as discussed by Roseman (1984), and control and power as discussed by Scherer (1984b). "Emotion-focused coping potential" refers to the perceived prospects of adjusting psychologically to the encounter—in other words, of regulating the emotional state that harmful or threatening consequences generate. This evaluation is closely related to Scherer's concept of "the potential for adjustment to the final outcome via internal restructuring" (Scherer, 1984a, p. 39). "Future expectancy" refers to the perceived possibilities, for *any* reason (i.e., independent of whether the individual plays a role), for changes in the psychological situation that could make the encounter more or less motivationally congruent.

Appraisals for Each Emotion

The six appraisal components noted above, which combine into core relational themes, provide the conceptual machinery needed to generate hypotheses about the specific appraisals responsible for every emotion. One task is to identify the core relational theme and its specific harm or benefit, which is necessary and sufficient to produce each emotion. A second task is to describe this theme in terms of a particular combination of the six appraisal components.

Primary appraisal is involved in every emotional encounter. The evaluation of motivational relevance is necessary for emotion, since it defines the most elemental aspect of a person's level of affective involvement by indicating whether there is any personal stake in the encounter. In the absence of motivational relevance, the person's state of mind is likely to be one of indifference or passive tranquility (cf. Ellsworth & Smith, 1988b). Motivational congruence or incongruence combines with relevance to define the encounter as beneficial or harmful, actually or potentially (Lazarus et al., 1980).

Motivational relevance and motivational congruence or incongruence are not sufficient to shape the kind of emotion that will be experienced. The components of secondary appraisal are also needed to determine whether one will experience happiness, relief, pride, gratitude, hope, or the like on the positive side, or anger, guilt, shame, anxiety, sadness, envy, or the like on the negative side.

Table 23.2 combines the appraisal components with core relational themes, and depicts the specific appraisals for illustrative emotions. These hypotheses are generally consistent with the findings of a number of studies that have examined the relationships between cognitive activities and emotions (e.g., Ellsworth & Smith, 1988a, 1988b; Frijda, 1987; Roseman, 1984; Scherer, Wallbott, &

TABLE 23.2. Functional Analysis of Some Illustrative Emotions

Emotion	Proposed adaptive function	Core relational theme	Important appraisal components
Anger	Remove source of harm from environment and undo harm	Other-blame	1. Motivationally relevant 2. Motivationally incongruent 3. Other-accountability
Guilt	Make reparation for harm to others/motivate socially responsible behavior	Self-blame	1. Motivationally relevant 2. Motivationally incongruent 3. Self-accountability
Anxiety	Avoid potential harm	Ambiguous danger/threat	1. Motivationally relevant 2. Motivationally incongruent 3. Low/uncertain (emotion-focused) coping potential
Sadness	Get help and support in the face of harm/disengage from a lost commitment	Irrevocable loss	1. Motivationally relevant 2. Motivationally incongruent 3. Low (problem-focused) coping potential 4. Low future expectancy
Hope	Sustain commitment and coping	Possibility of amelioration/success	1. Motivationally relevant 2. Motivationally incongruent 3. High future expectancy

Summerfield, 1986; Smith & Ellsworth, 1985, 1987; Weiner et al., 1982), even though these studies have not always examined the relevant appraisals directly (see Lazarus & Smith, 1988). The hypotheses have recently received further direct support in an initial study explicitly designed to test them (Smith, Lazarus, & Novacek, 1990).

For each emotion in the table, we have listed the adaptive function for that emotion. Then we have listed the core relational theme that corresponds to the particular relationship with the environment in which that function is likely to be appropriate. Finally, we have listed the major appraisal components that combine to define that core relational theme. For example, anger motivates the person to eliminate, neutralize, or undo a source of harm (Cannon, 1929; Ellsworth & Smith, 1988a; Izard, 1977; Plutchik, 1980; Tomkins, 1963). The core relational theme that defines the relevant circumstances for this function is "other-blame." In other words, anger arises when someone else is being blamed for a harmful situation, although if the "other person" being blamed is the self one could speak of anger at the self. Since anger motivates the person to do something to remove the source of harm, the assignment of accountability or blame provides a target for these coping efforts, which is crucial for its subjective and behavioral characteristics.

Guilt motivates the individual to make reparations for harm he or she has caused to others, and generally to engage in socially responsible behavior (Ellsworth & Smith, 1988a; Izard, 1977). Consistent with these functions, the core relational theme producing guilt is "self-blame," which means holding oneself accountable for an important, motivationally incongruent situation. Like anger, guilt motivates the person to do something to remove the source of harm, but because the focus is on oneself, it takes the form of a desire to make reparations for any harm the person has caused (e.g., Carlsmith & Gross, 1969; Freedman, Wallington, & Bless, 1967). In addition, guilt is painful and therefore self-punishing (Wallington, 1973), which reduces the probability that the person will continue to engage in the harmful behavior in the future.

We consider the blame in self-directed anger to be qualitatively distinct from the self-blame associated with guilt; accordingly, we hold that feeling guilty and feeling angry at oneself are different emotional states with distinct motivational consequences. The blame in self-directed anger is quite literally "other-blame directed at the self." That is, the person observes himself or herself behaving undesirably and holds the observed person (who happens to be the self) accountable. This blaming process does not necessarily implicate one's self-concept or feelings of self-worth. In contrast, the self-blame in guilt calls into question one's self-worth. The distinction is expressed in the internal dialogue that often accompanies these two forms of blame, the blame associated with self-directed anger expressed in the second person and that associated with guilt in the first person (e.g., "You idiot, what did you do that for?" vs. "What have I done?"). This example highlights how seemingly small cognitive differences can lead to large differences in the nature of the emotional reaction.

Whereas accountability or blame is of central importance in differentiating anger from guilt, other appraisal components are more important in differentiating anxiety from sadness. Both anxiety and sadness are associated with harmful situations in which the prospects for amelioration are uncertain or poor, and these similarities may explain why these emotions are often evoked in conjunction with each other. Nevertheless, there are distinct motivational functions for these emotions; their hypothesized core relational themes, as well as the appraisal components that define them, reflect these distinct functions.

Anxiety motivates the person to avoid potential harm (Cannon, 1929; Izard, 1977; Plutchik, 1980; Tomkins, 1963), the core relational theme being an appraisal of uncertain "danger" or "threat." The component of secondary appraisal is poor coping potential, which derives from the inevitable uncertainty in anxiety about what will happen and when. If it arises from symbolic and existential threats—which is one of the major conceptualizations of anxiety (see Lazarus & Averill, 1972)—the danger to self is obviously vague and ambiguous; this translates into a condition of poor coping potential, since one cannot know what to do about danger of this kind. Emotion-focused coping potential may be especially important in anxiety. The sense of danger, and hence anxiety, will be particularly acute when, beyond seeing potential or actual harm in the situation, one believes that this harm—say, a loss of self or meaningfulness—cannot be tolerated emotionally if it occurs (or has occurred).

On the other hand, sadness promotes disengagement from commitments that have been lost and motivates the person to get help (Izard, 1977; Klinger, 1975; Plutchik, 1980). The core relational theme producing this emotion is "irrevocable loss" or "helplessness" (Abramson et al., 1978). Accordingly, the components of secondary appraisal that distinguish this theme from anxiety are a combination of negative future expectancy and poor coping potential. In sadness, one is totally pessimistic about amelioration, whereas in anxiety there is mainly uncertainty. And whereas emotion-focused coping potential is salient for anxiety, problem-focused coping potential is particularly salient in sadness; in a condition of irrevocable loss, nothing that can be done seems capable of restoring the prior status.

Thus far, we have considered only "negative" emotions—those arising under conditions of harm or threat. However, an exclusive focus on harm-related emotions does a disservice to the role of emotion in adaptation, because there is also motivational incongruence when a person perceives the absence of potential benefits and gains. Avoiding or ameliorating harm is, of course, a factor in survival. However, striving for gain enables the person (and the species) to grow and flourish. Accordingly, human adaptational subsystems also include hope, which sustains positive striving toward mastery and gain (Ellsworth & Smith, 1988b; Lazarus et al., 1980). It seems wise here to again recognize the difficulty of deciding what are genuine emotions by begging the question of whether hope should be regarded as an emotion or a borderline state.

As depicted in Table 23.2, the core relational theme for hope combines an appraisal that existing conditions are not yet the way the person wants them to be (importance, motivational incongruence) with a future expectation that these conditions could become or be made motivationally more congruent. Hope can be maintained as long as there is some (however slight) potential for improvement in an otherwise bleak set of conditions, as when we "hope against all hope." Thus hope springs from the conviction, which may well be a characteristic of some personalities, that even under dire circumstances there is still a chance that things could get better (Lazarus et al., 1980).

The analyses above require several qualifications. First, the emotions examined do not include all the emotions in the human repertoire, but are illustrative of some of the most important. They help us demonstrate how a more complete cognitive–relational theory of emotion might look. The richness of our English vocabulary of emotions (see Averill, 1975; Ortony et al., 1987; Shaver et al., 1987) suggests that there are many more emotional states, each produced by distinctive appraisals, than the few we have considered. For example, we have not analyzed a number of positive emotions, including happiness, pride, relief, and gratitude, that arise under various conditions of appraised benefit (Ellsworth & Smith, 1988b; Lazarus et al., 1980). A full theoretical statement must address positive or benefit-related emotions as well as those flowing from conditions of harm, and decisions must be made about which states should be considered bona fide emotions, nonemotions, or marginal instances.

Second, in discussing the primary appraisal of motivational relevance that gives rise to emotion, we have not considered the potential role of particular goals or stakes in providing emotional differentiation beyond what we have depicted. Stake-specific differentiation can sometimes occur between broad emotional categories such as guilt and shame. For instance, in guilt the stake is a moral value, while in shame it is an ego ideal. Moreover, consideration of particular stakes is likely to be especially important when attempting to differentiate among affective states *within* the broad emotion categories we have outlined here. For instance, many forms of anger specifically involve some sort of insult to one's personal identity, while others, such as annoyance, may be less stake-specific. Similarly, feelings of abandonment appear to involve a particular type of loss involving one's relationships with others, while the broader category of sadness is not specific with regard to the particular stake that has been lost or irreparably harmed (cf. Ortony et al., 1987).

Third, although we have given a relatively static description of the *structural* relations between appraisal and emotion, we do not minimize the importance of thinking about and studying emotion as a dynamic *process* (see Folkman & Lazarus, 1988b; Lazarus, 1989b). The theory of appraisal indicates how at any given moment the person's specific appraisals will produce a particular emotional state. Knowing these structural relations is, we believe, a crucial first step to understanding the emotion process in cognitive–relational terms. However, as an encounter unfolds—as the person attempts to cope with the adaptive impications of the circumstances and the environment reacts to those coping efforts—the adaptive significance of the encounter is likely to shift, and as the appraisal shifts so will the emotional state.

Fourth and last, emotion is a much richer and broader construct than stress, and should supersede stress in the study of coping and adaptation (see Lazarus, 1968, in press; Lazarus & Folkman, 1984; Lazarus & Launier, 1978). The concept of stress is largely unidimensional, and expresses little beyond the idea that the person–environment relationship is adaptationally significant and motivationally incongruent. In contrast, emotion is a multidimensional construct that reveals a wealth of information about the adaptational encounter, the reaction to it, and the personality of the individual. Thus, the observation of anger in contrast with anxiety, guilt, shame, and so on tells us much more than merely knowing that a person is undergoing stress. Although the distinction among harm, threat, and challenge (Lazarus & Folkman, 1984), or between eustress and distress (Selye, 1974), modestly enlarges the scope of stress beyond its traditional unidimensional character, even this usage pales in richness and clinical significance compared with emotion.

PERSONALITY, SOCIETY, AND BIOLOGY IN EMOTION

A general theory of emotion must take into account the respective contributions of personality, culture, social structure, and biology to the emotional process. Most theories take one of two extreme positions, considering emotions to be either largely innate—that is, fundamentally fixed products of our biological heritage and subject to only modest cultural influences—or largely socioculturally defined.

Many proponents of the biological position speak of an innate "affect program" for each emotion, which organizes the emotion process (e.g., Ekman, 1984; Ekman & Friesen, 1975; Izard, 1977; Tomkins, 1962, 1963). When the appropriate eliciting conditions for a particular affect program are present the program fires reflexively and runs its course, which includes preprogrammed action tendencies, physiolog-

ical changes, and subjective experiences. In support of this view, proponents cite evidence for cross-culturally universal associations between particular facial expressions and autonomic nervous system and hormonal response patterns for each emotion (e.g., Ekman & Friesen, 1971; Ekman, Sorenson, & Friesen, 1969; Izard, 1971, Levenson, 1988).

Proponents of the cultural position regard emotions as socially defined phenomena following conventional rules, or scripts, that vary widely across cultures (e.g., Averill, 1968, 1980; Hochschild, 1979; Sarbin, 1985). Evidence for this position typically includes observations of considerable cross-cultural diversity in both the conditions giving rise to particular emotions and the expressive and instrumental coping behaviors accompanying emotions that have been evoked.

Our view of emotion occupies a middle ground between these extremes. By tracing its evolution to the sensorimotor reflex we have assumed a substantial biological influence on the emotion process. Yet by emphasizing the loosening of reflexive ties between stimulus and reaction, and the importance of both cognitive activity and sociocultural learning factors, we have left much room for the influence of personality in emotion, which in turn is partially a product of developmental experience with the sociocultural environment (see Ryff, 1987; Shweder & LeVine, 1984). Emotion theory must go beyond the banal assertion that there is merit to both perspectives by offering specific proposals about the respective contributions of biology and the society.

The Biological Core of Human Emotion

Figure 23.1 depicts our overall theoretical model. The emotional response is at the innate biological center of the cognitive–motivational–emotive system. We assume that human beings (and, we believe, animals too) are constructed biologically to be constantly engaged in appraisals of ongoing and changing relationships with the environment. These relationships are evaluated in terms of a relatively small set of specific, innately determined appraisal issues, which we have identified above. Appraisals promote the detection and evaluation of adaptationally relevant conditions requiring action. They determine the emotional state, which prepares and motivates one to cope with the adaptational implications of what is happening.

If a person appraises the conditions being confronted in a manner that corresponds to a particular core relational theme of harm or benefit, the preprogrammed emotion is automatically generated as a feature of our biological heritage. Although the appraisal is itself a continuing component of the emotional response, it is by no means the entire response. As indicated in Figure 23.1, additional components include a distinctive subjective feeling state, the urge to respond behaviorally to the situation in a particular manner (e.g., action tendency; see Frijda, 1986; Scherer, 1984b), and a patterned physiological response consisting of facial muscle, postural, and neurohumoral activity associated with the action tendency and coping process.

These response components are systematically organized around the adaptive implications evaluated in the appraisal, and appear to have evolved to serve the two general functions of social communication and coping (Lazarus, 1968; Scherer, 1984a; Smith, 1989). The motor–physiological changes are, in part, detectable by observation (e.g., changes in facial expression, posture, vocal tone, etc.; see Ekman, 1984; Riskind, 1984; Scherer, 1986), and they communicate important information to others in the social environment about appraisal and possible actions (Scherer, 1982, 1984a; Smith, 1989). The motor–physiological changes in posture, muscle tone, hormonal activity, and autonomic activity prepare the person physiologically to engage in and sustain the coping activities motivated by the action tendency, which itself directly reflects the

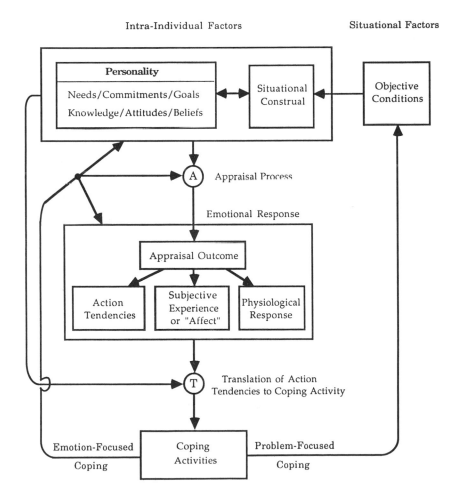

FIGURE 23.1. A model of the cognitive–motivational–emotive system.

624   RESEARCH TOPICS

adaptational demands implied by the continuing appraisal (Frijda, 1986; Lazarus, 1968; Smith, 1989). They also reflect changes in the organismic state resulting from a changed adaptational condition, as in relief or contentment after a threat has been removed.

The correlations between the appraisal and these response components appear to have two distinct levels of organization corresponding to the distinction we have drawn between core relational themes and appraisal components. The molar level of organization consists, as we have said, of core relational themes, and is parallel to the concept of affect programs. Particular action tendencies are probably emotion-specific and linked to specific relational themes. For example, "other-blame" generates anger and the impulse to attack the blameworthy agent, whereas an ambiguous threat generates anxiety and the impulse to avoid or escape the threat.

In addition, some of the innately determined motor–physiological consequences in emotion may be tied to molecular appraisal components. For example, Smith (1989) has provided evidence that activity of the corrugator supercilii muscles to pull the eyebrows together and down into a frown is associated with appraisals of motivational incongruence, and this association may extend over a broad range of emotions. It is possible that secondary appraisals having direct implications for subsequent coping (e.g., evaluations of coping potential) may have direct autonomic and postural effects consistent with the coping requirements.

The aspects of the emotional response described so far—the appraisals that define adaptationally significant core relational themes, and the subjective, physiological, and motivational consequences initiated by these evaluations—are, in our view, universal in our species. In considering this innate organization, which has yet to be detailed and demonstrated, it is important to consider what we have *not* included. The biologically fixed portion of the emotion system starts with the appraisal pattern and ends with the action tendency, leaving considerable flexibility and biological indeterminacy as to which stimulus configurations will result in which appraisals, and which actions (as opposed to action tendencies) will follow any given cognitive–motivational–emotive configuration. It is precisely at these two points—the process of appraisal and the translation of emotion into coping—

that personality and culture intersect with biology and play fundamental roles in the functioning of the cognitive–motivational–emotive system. These points of intersection give emotion the flexibility that differentiates it from reflexes and physiological drives and provides it with much of its adaptational power.

One way in which the sociocultural and biological points of intersection can be clarified is to make a statement with the following formal character: *If a person appraises his or her relationship to the environment in a particular way, then a specific emotion that is tied to the appraisal always results. Furthermore, if two individuals make the same appraisals they will experience the same emotion, regardless of the actual circumstances.*

Personality factors arising in the course of psychological development, as well as environmental variables (e.g., the immediate social structure), combine to influence the molecular appraisals—in effect, the specific meanings—that result in each core relational theme. These influences shape the "if" of the formal statement above. "If" means, in effect, that different individuals can appraise their relationships with the environment differently, or that the same individual can do so at different times or occasions. However, once a given appraisal pattern with its core relational theme has taken place, a particular emotion, with its subjective feeling state, action tendency, and motor–physiological response pattern, is generated as a *biological principle*. Each core relational theme has its own universal biological emotional outcome, which is invariant as long as the individual continues to appraise what is happening in a given way. The appraisal can, of course, change (1) as the person–environment relationship changes; (2) in consequence of self-protective coping activity (e.g., emotion-focused coping); (3) in consequence of changing social structures and culturally based values and meanings; or (4) when personality changes, as when goals or beliefs are abandoned as unserviceable.

Stated in a slightly different way, the "if" in the formula above provides for the flexibility and complexity made possible by intelligence and culture; the "then" provides the biological universal linking cognition to the emotional response. Change the "if" and the response configuration is also changed. Personality and environmental variables are the antecedents in this model, their emotional consequences being mediated by appraisals (influenced recursively by coping and its effects) whose biologically determined consequences constitute the emotional response.

Knowledge, Appraisal, Culture, and Personality

It will now be useful to examine more closely some of the intersections implied above between personality, culture, and biology. The upper portion of Figure 23.1 depicts some personality factors that contribute to the emotional response at two levels. First, they influence the cognitive representation, or knowledge about the person–environment relationship being appraised, which is identified as a situational construal in the figure; second, they make contributions to the appraisal process itself. The figure identifies two distinct types of personality factors. One consists of motivational characteristics, which include the values, goals, and commitments that a person brings into every encounter. These characteristics have parallels in other concepts, such as "current concerns" (Klinger, 1975), "personal projects" (Little, 1983; Palys & Little, 1983), and "personal strivings" (Emmons, 1986). The second factor consists of the person's knowledge base, which includes generalized beliefs, both concrete and abstract, about the way things are, how they work, the nature of the world, and the person's place in it. It also includes attitudes, expectations, and intuitive theories about the self (including self-concept) and the world (see Epstein, 1983; Lazarus & Smith, 1988; Lewis & Michalson, 1983; Ross, 1977). We suggest that the two personality factors have distinctive but interactive influences on both the way a person construes what is happening and the appraisal of that construal.

Personality Contributions to Knowledge about the Encounter

Cognitive representations of our relationships with the environment often go far beyond the perceptual data directly available. Certain aspects of the encounter are ignored; others are emphasized; missing information is filled in; and any number of inferences are made regarding the possible causes, intentions, and motiva-

tions underlying observed events (see Jones et al., 1971; Lewis, 1935, 1936; Nisbett & Ross, 1980; Ross, 1977, 1987; Shaver, 1977). Within the social-psychological and personality literatures, there is ample documentation that these constructive, inferential processes are systematically influenced by the motivations, knowledge, and expectations the person brings into an encounter.

Goals often have an important role in determining the aspects of the situation that are noticed, encoded, and emphasized; one is likely to look for and notice things that are motivationally relevant (cf. the "New Look" perception research movement of the 1940s and 1950s; e.g., Postman, Bruner, & McGinnies, 1948). For example, partisans on both sides of a rough football game will tend disproportionately to notice penalties committed by the opposing team, thereby strengthening their view of the other team as consisting of undeserving cheaters (Hastorf & Cantril, 1954). Similarly, pro-Arab and pro-Israeli viewers watching the very same news coverage of the 1982 Beirut massacre came away convinced that the other side received a greater number of favorable references and a smaller number of negative ones than their side did, in support of their view of the media as biased against them (Ross, 1987; Vallone, Ross, & Lepper, 1985).

Even when strong motivations are not involved, prior knowledge and expectations influence the interpretation and encoding of subsequent information. Thus, initial information about a person can produce a "halo effect" that influences how subsequent information about that person is interpreted (Asch, 1946), and facts and events consistent with one's "schema" or mental model of an episode are likely to be assumed to be present in the encounter, and to be incorrectly remembered subsequently as having been directly observed (e.g., Bower, Black, & Turner, 1979; Owens, Bower, & Black, 1979).

Although they have seldom outlined the specific beliefs and motivations underlying them, clinical and personality researchers have documented the existence of relatively stable individual differences in characteristic ways of construing certain types of encounters, often referred to as "attributional biases" (e.g., Dodge & Coie, 1987; Nasby, Hayden, & dePaulo, 1979) or "attributional" or "explanatory styles" (e.g., Peterson & Barrett, 1987; Peterson et al., 1982). These differences have been reliably associated with individual differences in coping and mood, presumably through the construal's influences on appraisal and emotional response. Recently it has been pointed out (Lazarus, 1989a) that emotion can be studied both as a personality trait (which is the dominant interest of clinical workers treating chronically dysfunctional emotional patterns), and as a state that is generated by particular encounters with the environment but that does not necessarily represent recurrent adaptational problems. A full approach to emotion requires both of these perspectives.

For example, chronically aggressive children, especially children whose aggression usually takes the form of angry reactions to perceived provocations, have been shown to have stronger tendencies than less aggressive children to attribute hostile intentions to the ambiguous actions of others (e.g., Dodge, 1980; Dodge & Coie, 1987; Dodge, Murphy, & Buchsbaum, 1984). Similarly, in adults the tendency to attribute negative events to internal, global, and stable causes, which is hypothesized to promote appraisals of helplessness and hence sadness and depression (Abramson et al., 1978), has been prospectively associated with enduring depression following poor performance on an exam (Metalsky, Halberstadt, & Abramson, 1987), relatively poor academic performance during the first year of college (Peterson & Barrett, 1987), and success and productivity of life insurance sales agents (Seligman & Schulman, 1986).

Personality Contributions to Appraisal

In addition to affecting emotion indirectly by systematically influencing the contents of knowledge a person draws upon in appraisal, personality contributes directly to the appraisal process itself. Primary appraisal makes sense only when one's relationship to the environment is considered in relation to needs, desires, or what one cares about—in effect, the goal hierarchy characteristic of a person as it intersects with the demands, constraints, and resources of the encounter. Without an analysis of what is (potentially) at stake in an encounter for that person, it is impossible to evaluate the appraisal components of motivational relevance and congruence or incongruence. If nothing the person cares about is at stake, then little or no emotion will result (see Lazarus,

1989b; Lazarus & Folkman, 1984; Lazarus & Smith, 1988).

The theoretical relationship between goal commitments and primary appraisal suggests that motivational measures—such as those developed by Little (1983) and Emmons (1986), as well as our own recent efforts—become necessary tools for predicting and understanding individual differences in emotional response, and make it possible to identify who will react to a particular situation with strong emotion and the specific encounters to which a particular individual is especially responsive emotionally (see Pervin, 1983).

A number of studies, both old and new, illustrate the promise of motivational measures in the prediction of emotional reactions. For example, Vogel, Raymond, and Lazarus (1959) showed that subjects having strong achievement goals and weak affiliation goals reacted to experimentally produced achievement-centered threats with more psychophysiological stress than to affiliation-centered threats; the reverse pattern was found for subjects with strong affiliation goals and weak achievement goals. Similarly, Bergman and Magnusson (1979) demonstrated that Swedish male high school overachievers, rated by their teachers as extremely ambitious, secreted more adrenaline in an achievement demanding encounter than other boys in the same class.

A study centered on health-related variables by Kasl, Evans, and Niederman (1979) showed that a combination of high academic achievement motivation and poor performance predicted risk of infectious mononucleosis among West Point cadets. Hammen, Marks, Mayol, and deMayo (1985) have also reported evidence that students for whom interpersonal issues were especially important were more likely to experience depression in relation to stressful events involving interpersonal relationships than they were to stressful events involving achievement concerns, while the reverse tended to be true for students with strong achievement concerns.

Finally, Gruen, Folkman, and Lazarus (1989) found that some day-to-day "hassles" and upsets were identified by respondents as being more important and central to their concerns than others. The contents of these "central hassles" varied considerably from individual to individual, presumably reflecting different patterns of commitment. Moreover, the central hassles were more strongly associated with symptoms of psychological dysfunction than the peripheral hassles.

In addition to motivation, which is most closely tied to primary appraisal, a second type of personality factor—beliefs and expectations—is crucial for emotional differentiation and acts as an antecedent of secondary appraisal. For example, beliefs about what is normatively appropriate, feasible, legitimate, or excusable in a given situation should strongly influence whether and to what extent an appraisal of accountability for a noxious event will be made and result in anger, say, instead of sadness.

Beliefs also affect expectations about the probable effectiveness of various courses of action and one's ability to perform those actions, which contribute to judgments of self-efficacy (Bandura, 1977, 1982; Maddux, Norton, & Stoltenberg, 1987), and therefore to evaluations of coping potential and future expectancy. Evaluations of efficacy partially determine whether an encounter will be appraised as a harm, threat, or potential gain, and in consequence contribute to anxiety, sadness, or hope (see also the research and analyses of Antonovsky, 1987, and Scheier & Carver, 1987). Expanding on his well-known studies of self-efficacy as a factor in performance, persistence, and the emotional reaction, Bandura (in press) has also recently provided a rich overview of the role of self-efficacy beliefs in the development of competence and incompetence.

Knowledge and beliefs can also contribute to primary appraisal by helping us define what is relevant to our goal commitments and what constitutes harm or benefit. For example, beliefs and expectations about a necessary but aversive encounter (e.g., how much pain it is normal to experience during a particular dental procedure and the gains that result from undergoing it) can significantly influence the degree to which an encounter is appraised as motivationally incongruent, and also influence appraisals of coping potential and future expectancy.

In our own recent work (Smith, Novacek, Lazarus, & Pope, 1990), we have been attempting to develop measures that reflect stable individual differences in "appraisal style." We have used the measurement strategy employed by Peterson et al. (1982) in the Attributional Style Questionnaire. Respondents are asked to report their probable reactions to an assortment of one-sentence descriptions of hypothetical situations. However, instead of asking about causal attributions in each situation, we ask about their appraisals along each of our six appraisal components, from which we hope to derive stable measures of an individual's characteristic appraisal style for each appraisal component. We conceive of these measures as reflecting the individual differences most proximal to the appraisal process, and they should enable predictions about the contextual appraisals that directly produce the emotional state. Research by others (e.g., Repetti, 1987; Solomon, Mikulincer, & Hobfoll, 1987) has demonstrated that proximal measures involving subjective appraisals are better predictors of emotional reactions than are (distal) objective measures.

Cultural Contributions to Appraisal

We have emphasized the contributions of personality to appraisal because emotions are responses of an individual person. Individuals, not cultures, perceive, construe, and appraise. Moreover, an individual's personal goals and beliefs should be important in shaping appraisals and their consequent emotions. Culture, however, significantly shapes an individual's beliefs and motivations over the course of personality development (see Ryff, 1987; Shweder & LeVine, 1984) by providing culturally shared meanings about what is socially important, what various circumstances imply for personal well-being, and therefore which emotions are appropriate under those circumstances (see, e.g., Hochschild, 1979).

It is common to contrast two broad forms of social influence: the living culture into which a person is born, and the social structure. "Culture" provides a set of meanings and symbols, many of which are internalized and carried with the person into transactions with the social and physical environment. The "social structure" produces a set of immediate demands, constraints, and resources that operate contemporaneously in adaptive transactions, though they can also be internalized and become part of an individual's personality. This contrast is well drawn by Schneider (1976, pp. 202–203):

Culture contrasts with norms in that norms are oriented to patterns of action, whereas culture constitutes a body of definitions, premises, statements, postulates, presumptions, propositions, and perceptions about the nature of the universe and man's place in it. Where norms tell the actor how to play the scene, culture tells the actor how the scene is set and what it all means. Where norms tell the actor how to behave in the presence of ghosts, gods, and human beings, culture tells the actor what ghosts, gods, and human beings are and what they are all about.

Coping and Emotion

Just as the top part of the model in Figure 23.1 depicts personality factors as influencing appraisal, the bottom portion depicts them as determinants of coping. The emotional response includes an action tendency—that is, an urge to respond to the encounter in a particular way: to attack in anger, cry in sadness, flee or avoid in anxiety, and so on. Nevertheless, at all but the most extreme levels of emotional arousal, people have the ability to suppress the action tendency and select from a wide array of coping options; this illustrates the flexibility of the emotion process.

For example, we are free to engage in any of a number of problem-focused coping activities that reflect active attempts to influence the person–environment relationship and to maintain or increase its degree of motivational congruence. We are also free to engage in any of a number of emotion-focused coping strategies that attempt to regulate the emotional response itself (cf. Folkman & Lazarus, 1980, 1985; Lazarus & Folkman, 1984). We are not constrained to a single coping strategy, and under stressful circumstances it appears that people most often engage in a combination of many problem-focused and emotion-focused strategies (Folkman & Lazarus, 1980; Lazarus & Folkman, 1984). Of the personality factors identified and discussed above, we suspect that beliefs are especially influential in affecting the actual coping activities to be engaged in, particularly beliefs about the coping options available and their probable effectiveness. Beliefs about the social appropriateness of the actions, which are often culturally defined—for example, the display rules about when and how it is appropriate to express an emotional state openly or to mask it behind some other expression (Ekman, 1984)—undoubtedly play a role too.

Explicit research on coping in the context of emotion theory is a neglected area of research, perhaps because the concept of coping has been used traditionally in stress theory and research and not in emotion (see Folkman & Lazarus, 1988b). Although specific action tendencies are almost universally assumed to flow from certain emotions such as anger and fear, biologically based action tendencies in coping and the consequences of beliefs for the coping process have received little research attention. Averill (1983) has even argued from his data on college students that attack is relatively uncommon in anger encounters, despite the usual expectation that it is a biologically generated action tendency. A basic unanswered question is this: What happens when the person copes in ways that run directly counter to the specific thrust of the action tendency itself? This would be the case when the impulse is to attack, but it is inhibited and perhaps even responded to by denial or suppression. Studies of the role of this pattern in stress-related disorders such as hypertension have been common but inconclusive.

The model portrayed in Figure 23.1 does not stop at coping, but is continuous (see Lazarus, 1968, 1989b), and depicts coping as influencing subsequent appraisal and emotion by at least two types of mechanisms: First, problem-focused coping consists of active attempts to alter the existing problematic relationship (Lazarus & Folkman, 1984). If the coping attempts are effective, and harm or threat is alleviated or removed, the change is likely to be reflected in subsequent appraisals, with consequent changes in emotion away from distress and toward positive states (see Folkman & Lazarus, 1989a). Ineffective attempts can influence subsequent appraisal as well, as when a nonresponsive environment alters the person's beliefs and expectations about both the nature or type of an encounter and the future sense of efficacy. Encounters originally appraised as subject to beneficial change can be reappraised as irremedial harms, producing corresponding emotional changes from hope to sadness or resignation.

Second, emotion-focused coping consists of managing distressing emotions that arise in any given encounter when the circumstances are refractory to change. Some forms of emotion-focused coping alter the emotional response directly without changing the meaning of what is happening (e.g., by affecting autonomic arousal through relaxation or exercise, or avoiding thinking about the appraisal, etc.). Other forms alter the appraised meaning of the encounter (e.g., by denial or distancing).

Even though cognitive dissonance encompasses a particular, limited type of motivational incongruence, many of the changes produced by emotion-focused coping overlap those identified in a long tradition of research into cognitive dissonance (e.g., Festinger, 1957; Wicklund & Brehm, 1976). For example, one can reconstrue the nature of the situation, such as by deciding that a perceived offense was really unintentional or unavoidable, or that an inferred event did not actually occur. Or one can alter personal beliefs about the meaning of the encounter, and hence its implications for well-being. In the face of a seemingly intractable unpleasant person–environment relationship, one can also give up cherished personal goals and values so that the encounter is no longer appraised as relevant to well-being, and it no longer has the power to evoke strong emotion (see Klinger, 1975).

Although emotion-focused coping alters the person instead of the environment, often by distorting reality, and although Western psychologists tend to assume (incorrectly, we think) that changing things by action is more adaptive than merely changing the way things are construed, emotion-focused coping is not inherently less adaptive than problem-focused coping (cf. Collins, Baum, & Singer, 1983; Lazarus, 1983; Strentz & Auerbach, 1988). On the contrary, both forms of coping have an important place in human adaptation. The two functions of coping (problem- and emotion-focused) are major strategies for achieving a better fit between persons and their environmental circumstances, and, in the long term, adaptive functioning requires maintaining a delicate balance between the two.

OTHER ISSUES

In this section we address briefly three topics of importance to emotion theory that have not yet been considered—namely, the characteristics of the appraisal process, the maladaptive aspects of emotion, and emotional development. Each of these also has relevance to personality and social psychology.

The Character of the Appraisal Process

In discussing appraisal and its role in emotion, we have focused primarily on the contents of appraisal, but have been relatively silent about the formal cognitive processes that underlie

this content. Unless we are clear about this, there is a danger that we will be interpreted as implying that appraisal is a conscious, volitional, verbally accessible process that requires deliberation and considerable time. On the contrary, we have been consistent in maintaining that appraisal can be automatic (even primitive) and instantaneous, and can occur outside of consciousness (see Lazarus, 1966, 1968, 1982, 1984; Lazarus & Smith, 1988).

In this connection, it is useful to maintain a distinction advanced by Leventhal (1980, 1984; Leventhal & Scherer, 1987) between "schematic" and "conceptual" processing, which has also been discussed by others, including Lazarus (1982, 1984), in discussions of cognition–emotion relationships. In combination these two qualitatively distinct forms of cognition give the emotion system the ability to react nearly instantaneously to adaptationally significant events, and yet to draw fully upon the power and flexibility of human cognitive capacities.

Through "schematic processing," the personal significance of an encounter is appraised automatically and nearly instantaneously on the basis of past experiences with similar encounters. That is, the appraisal can act much like the "social affordances" described by Baron (1988; Baron & Boudreau, 1987), with the adaptational implications of the environment leaping automatically and without deliberation into the person's mind, so to speak.

One way in which the operation of schematic processing can be understood is by using the concepts of activation and associative networks commonly invoked in the study of memory (e.g., Anderson & Bower, 1973), although we need not commit ourselves to this idea and use it only to illustrate the point about rapid processing of complicated material. When a person becomes involved in an encounter similar to some in the past, memories of these past encounters are likely to become quickly activated. Personal meanings strongly associated with those previous encounters are likely to be activated and available as contributors to the person's current emotional state. In this way, complicated and involved appraisals, drawing heavily on the person's knowledge and past experiences, can be arrived at quickly and automatically. In considering this type of mechanism, it is not necessary to think of the appraisal process as following a fixed or predefined sequence (as, e.g., Scherer, 1984b, does in his concept of "evaluation checks"), since the full appraised meaning associated with the past experience(s) can be activated in a single step.

Automatic or schematic processing, as we have described it, is quite passive, and it is important not to lose sight of the fact that humans are sentient, problem-solving beings who actively seek to understand the world and their reactions to it. Thus, schematic processing is accompanied by what Leventhal (1984) has termed "conceptual processing"—a set of more abstract, conscious, and deliberate cognitive processes—through which the person is able to evaluate the adaptational significance of the encounter more actively. Although conceptual processing of appraisal components could perhaps follow predefined sequences, as Scherer (1984b) has suggested, we are wary of a stage theory, since whatever issues and aspects of the encounter seem especially salient may well pre-empt attention at any given moment.

Conceptual processing is very important in much appraisal, as it permits the evaluation of the adaptational significance (hence the emotional response) and the availability of coping options to be finely tuned to the specific requirements of the encounter as it unfolds. It can also draw on highly complex, symbolic meanings, which we believe often underlie our garden-variety emotions. To the extent that they become associated with the encounter in memory, the results of conceptual processing become available for subsequent schematic processing and are an important aspect of emotional development. In any case, appraisal is a complex process that can occur on more than one level of cognitive processing.

Emotion and Dysfunction

Our focus has been on the functional, adaptive nature of emotion, the guiding thesis being that emotions evolved to ensure that the person responds effectively to the adaptational challenges that arise throughout the life course. However, emotions are often dysfunctional or maladaptive in individual cases. As such we can learn much about faulty appraisal and coping processes, and their personality determinants, from an examination of a person's emotional patterns.

For example, knowing that a person frequently reacts with high levels of anger and aggression reveals much about a troubled re-lationship with the environment, and suggests a number of specific points for possible intervention. Anger indicates that important personal goals are being threatened, and also that this person tends to blame someone else for this, perhaps because of a vulnerable self-esteem that leads to assumptions of malevolence or insulting attitudes on the part of others. The clinician will be prompted to explore the circumstances giving rise to the anger, as well as the client's motivational patterns and beliefs, in order to understand whether and why the client is misconstruing what is happening interpersonally. Why does the client react with anger as opposed to anxiety, guilt, or envy? And what is it about the client that leads to aggression rather than to a more productive coping process?

The answers to these questions may suggest the most appropriate points for intervention. For example, the client may be correctly appraising what is happening—there may indeed be malevolence in those toward whom anger is experienced—but the coping response to this may be counterproductive. The best intervention may be to try to inhibit or suppress the aggressive reactions, and instead to evolve more effective coping options. Alternatively, analysis of the problem may suggest that the appraisal of other-blame, and hence the anger, is inappropriate to the social conditions; perhaps this is the result of incorrect or "irrational" assumptions or beliefs that should be changed (see Ellis & Bernard, 1985). Many programs of cognitive therapy are predicated on this latter type of analysis of dysfunctional emotions.

Emotional Development

The theory of emotion we have been describing has been cast in terms of adult human experience. However, the analysis is also intended to apply to human infants and other complex mammalian species (see Lazarus, 1982, 1984). Yet by emphasizing intelligence, personality, and culture (as values and meanings) in the emotion process, we imply that emotion in the newborn infant will not be exactly the same as in the adult. After all, the appraisal dimensions we have proposed (e.g., future expectancy, accountability) require cognitive capacities, skills, social motives, and understandings that the newborn simply does not yet possess.

As we see it, the emotion system develops in

two distinct ways—one primarily reflecting a biologically determined maturational process, and the other reflecting socioculturally based learning, which must eventually influence the personality variables shaping appraisal and emotion in adaptational encounters.

In the largely biological maturational process the components of appraisal become increasingly differentiated as the infant acquires the formal cognitive capacities (*à la* Piaget) necessary to make the various evaluations of the significance of what is happening for personal well-being. Therefore, consistent with the observations of numerous developmentalists (e.g., Bridges, 1932; Emde, 1980; Izard, 1977; Lewis & Michalson, 1983; Piaget, 1981; Sroufe, 1979; Stein & Levine, 1987), we would expect the infant to demonstrate increasing emotional differentiation as it matures. The developing child should not experience a particular emotion until it is able, at least in rudimentary form, to make the appraisals that together comprise the core relational theme for that emotion (see Scherer, 1984b). The developmental research task is to delineate the unfolding of the appraisal process and the appreciation by the child of its environmental and motivational components in the case of each emotion as it emerges.

For example, the newborn may only be capable of rudimentary appraisals along the two components of primary appraisal, motivational relevance and motivational congruence or incongruence. This will restrict the newborn's emotional range to states of interested awareness, generalized pleasure, and generalized distress. Anger, as differentiated from generalized distress, should not appear until the infant is capable of some form of rudimentary accountability judgment, perhaps involving little more than the most primitive notion of causality. The differentiation between fear and sadness should not appear until the infant is capable of assessing coping potential/future expectancy, which would seem to require, at minimum, the ability to anticipate and form expectations about future events and perhaps even about one's own competence to influence outcomes. In all likelihood, the relatively fine-grained distinctions among emotion-focused coping potential, problem-focused coping potential, and future expectancy emerge even later, from a more general evaluation of coping potential. Emotions implicating the self, such as pride, shame, and guilt, would seem to require

the ability to maintain a rudimentary self-concept, and perhaps the ability to make a more sophisticated accountability judgment (involving notions of responsibility as well as causality) than might be required for, say, anger. Or perhaps a rudimentary self is a *sine qua non* of true emotions, as distinguished from undifferentiated contentment and distress.

Learning and culture interact with this biologically determined unfolding of cognitive abilities to give the cognitive–motivational–emotive system the full flexibility and power of which it is capable. Throughout the lifespan both the person's knowledge base and motivational hierarchy continue to change. Therefore, as the person's cognitive capacities and knowledge base increase, we should expect to see increasing sophistication and flexibility in both coping activities and the evidence used to make evaluations along the various appraisal dimensions.

In the newborn, appraisal of motivational congruence or incongruence may be based primarily (and almost reflexively) upon perceptual data, with pleasant sensations indicating motivational congruence, and unpleasant ones (e.g., physical discomfort, pain) indicating motivational incongruence (cf. Emde, 1980; Leventhal, 1980, 1984; Piaget, 1981; Sroufe, 1979). However, by adulthood, the evaluation of motivational congruence or incongruence is far more complex, involving subtle implications about the person's relationship with the environment with respect to personal needs and desires, and strategies of self-control. By adulthood, low to moderate sensations of physical discomfort should no longer be reliable indicators of motivational incongruence, and under the right circumstances may actively be sought, as when discomfort signals to the athlete that training is progressing as desired (see Lazarus & Smith, 1988). In a similar manner, the earliest appraisals of accountability may consist of little more than the primitive identification of a causal agent (e.g., identifying the direct source of undesired physical restraint), whereas by adulthood accountability is a highly complicated social judgment that combines causal information with beliefs about intentionality, justifiability, foreseeability, and so on.

Finally, we should see a similar development in the complexity and flexibility of the relationship between emotion and coping. Early on we would expect the emotionally produced action tendencies arising in an encounter to be acted on in a rather direct, impulsive, almost reflexive manner. Thus, in the infant, distress reliably produces crying, and in young children anger is very likely to produce overt aggression. However, as the child matures the capacity for behavioral control is much increased; in addition, through direct and vicarious experience, children acquire and can use complex knowledge of what is effective and normatively appropriate under various circumstances in choosing the coping activities that are acted on in an encounter. Although largely limited to Western culture, research on the development of children's knowledge of emotions provides an important step in the direction of studying the development of the emotion process (e.g., Gnepp, Klayman, & Trabasso, 1982; Harris, 1985; Stein & Levine, 1987).

CONCLUDING THOUGHTS

We have begun this chapter with an expression of regret that emotion has not served—as we think it should—as an integrating concept in psychology. In our discussion of emotion and dysfunction, we have intimated that emotions are instructive about persons because both emotions and the personality are organized around the problem of surviving, getting along, and flourishing over the life course. Our conclusion returns to this theme.

We have been saying that emotions are the product of *transactions* or *relationships* between the person and the environment (Lazarus & Folkman, 1987; Lazarus & Launier, 1978). This suggests one resolution to the person–situation debate (e.g., Bem & Funder, 1978; Endler & Magnusson, 1976; Epstein, 1979, 1983; Mischel, 1968; Mischel & Peake, 1982) and provides some statements about how personality and situational variables interact (see Figure 23.1).

Since the emotion process serves adaptation, theorists and researchers who would like to put the "person" back into personality research (e.g., Carlson, 1984)—that is, to move from the study of a disparate, seemingly random collection of "traits" to the study of an organized, coherent being who responds to the environment in ways that are intended to realize valued goals and to promote survival and personal growth in the face of potential harms, threats,

and challenges (see Pervin, 1983)—ought to concentrate on the emotional life. They are likely to find the personality variables most relevant to emotion to be a rich starting point for this synthetic (rather than analytic) perspective on persons. Of all the personality characteristics one could use to measure individual differences and to describe functioning persons, those that we have identified as being most relevant to emotion—the persons' goals and commitments, and knowledge and beliefs about self and the world relevant to avoiding harm and achieving those goals and commitments—are the very variables most likely to give rise to a coherent picture of personality. In other words, if one wants to understand whole persons and how they function in nature, what better place to begin than with a consideration of how the persons are equipped to handle the challenges, opportunities, and problems of living? This is, indeed, what emotions are all about.

NOTES

1. Although we find Plutchik's (1980) analysis to be important and thought-provoking, we disagree with one of his basic assumptions—namely, that there are eight survival issues universal to all animal species, and that the "basic" emotions for any species reflect that species' solutions to these specific issues. We see this assumption as simultaneously being too constraining and too broad. It is too constraining because, by imposing a constant set of survival issues across species, it overestimates the number of distinct issues facing very simple organisms and underestimates the number facing more complex species. As species and their interactions with the environment become more complex, they often face new, emergent problems, fundamental to *their* survival but irrelevant to simpler species (see Frijda, 1986, p. 86). For example, social beings, like humans, must find solutions to a number of fundamental issues surrounding the coordination of cooperative and competitive behavior among conspecifics—issues that need not be addressed by species whose members tend to lead their lives in isolation. At the same time, the assumption is too broad because it equates *emotion* with *any* solution a species has evolved to contend with a survival issue. By contrast, we view emotion as being one of

several types of solution (including physiological drives and reflexes) that species have evolved to foster adaptation.

2. We are referring to emotions, reflexes, and drives as "adaptational subsystems" rather than as "motivations" or "motives" in order to maintain a clear distinction between the *urges* (or tendencies) to behave in particular ways produced by emotions, drives, and reflexes, and the underlying *goals* or *needs* those urges serve. In the past, "motivation" has been used rather indiscriminately to refer to the underlying needs, the behavioral urges, and the processes that give rise to the urges in response to the needs. We believe that a clear understanding of emotions and their role in adaptation depends upon the ability to distinguish among these aspects of "motivation," and we have tried to select our language accordingly.

3. In referring to appraisal as "primary" or "secondary" we are *not* referring sequential properties and implying that primary appraisal necessarily precedes secondary appraisal in time. As we discuss in a later section of this chapter, whether and under what conditions appraisal may follow a sequential process are important and open issues for further research. Instead, we consider primary appraisal "primary" because it establishes the personal relevance of the encounter, and this relevance is hypothesized to be a prerequisite for strong emotion. That is, primary appraisal is responsible for the degree of emotional "heat" in a transaction. If the encounter is appraised as not relevant to well-being, then secondary appraisal is relatively unimportant because there will be little emotion of any kind. However, if primary appraisal indicates that the situation is relevant to well-being, then secondary appraisal plays a vital role in differentiating the emotional experience. Thus, secondary appraisal is "secondary" because its role in differentiating the emotional response is highly dependent on the outcome of primary appraisal (see Lazarus, 1968).

REFERENCES

Abramson, L. Y., Seligman, M. E. P., & Teasdale, J. D. (1978). Learned helplessness in humans: Critique and reformulation. *Journal of Abnormal Psychology, 87,* 49–74.

Anderson, J. R., & Bower, G. H. (1973). *Human associative memory.* Washington, DC: Hemisphere.

Antonovsky, A. (1987). *Unraveling the mystery of health.* San Francisco: Jossey-Bass.

Arnold, M. B. (1960). *Emotion and personality* (2 vols.). New York: Columbia University Press.

Asch, S. E. (1946). Forming impressions of personality. *Journal of Abnormal and Social Psychology, 41,* 258–290.

Averill, J. R. (1968). Grief: Its nature and significance. *Psychological Bulletin, 70,* 721–748.

Averill, J. R. (1975). A semantic atlas of emotional concepts. *JSAS: Catalogue of Selected Documents in Psychology, 5,* 330. (Ms. No. 421)

Averill, J. R. (1980). A constructivist view of emotion. In R. Plutchik & H. Kellerman (Eds.), *Emotion: Theory, research, and experience. Vol. 1. Theories of emotion* (pp. 305–339). New York: Academic Press.

Averill, J. R. (1983). Studies on anger and aggression: Implications for theories of emotion. *American Psychologist, 38,* 1145–1160.

Bandura, A. (1977). Self-efficacy: Toward a unifying theory of behavioral change. *Psychological Review, 84,* 191–215.

Bandura, A. (1982). Self-efficacy mechanism in human agency. *American Psychologist, 37,* 122–147.

Bandura, A. (in press). Reflections on nonability determinants of competence. In J. Kolligan, Jr., & R. J. Sternberg (Eds.), *Competence considered: Perceptions of competence and incompetence across the lifespan.* New Haven, CT: Yale University Press.

Baron, R. M. (1988). An ecological framework for establishing a dual-mode theory of social knowing. In D. Bar-Tal & A. W. Kruglanski (Eds.), *The social psychology of knowing* (pp. 48–82). New York: Cambridge University Press.

Baron, R. M., & Boudreau, L. A. (1987). An ecological perspective on integrating personality and social psychology. *Journal of Personality and Social Psychology, 53,* 1222–1228.

Bem, D. J., & Funder, D. C. (1978). Predicting more of the people more of the time: Assessing the personality of situations. *Psychological Review, 85,* 485–501.

Bergman, L. R., & Magnusson, D. (1979). Overachievement and catecholamine excretion in an achievement-demanding situation. *Psychosomatic Medicine, 41,* 181–188.

Bolles, R. C. (1974). Cognition and motivation: Some historical trends. In B. Weiner (Ed.), *Cognitive views of human motivation* (pp. 1–20). New York: Academic Press.

Bower, G. H., Black, J. B., & Turner, T. J. (1979). Scripts in text comprehension and memory. *Cognitive Psychology, 11,* 177–220.

Bridges, K. M. B. (1932). Emotional development in early infancy. *Child Development, 4,* 36–49.

Bruner, J. S. (1957). Going beyond the information given. In H. Gruber, K. R. Hammond, & R. Jesser (Eds.), *Contemporary approaches to cognition* (pp. 41–69). Cambridge, MA: Harvard University Press.

Cannon, W. B. (1929). *Bodily changes in pain, hunger, fear, and rage* (2nd ed.). New York: Appleton-Century.

Carlsmith, J. M., & Gross, A. E. (1969). Some effects of guilt on compliance. *Journal of Personality and Social Psychology, 11,* 232–239.

Carlson, R. (1984). What's social about social psychology? Where's the person in personality research? *Journal of Personality and Social Psychology, 47,* 1304–1309.

Carroll, D., Marzillier, J. S., & Merian, S. (1982). Psychophysiological changes accompanying different types of arousing and relaxing imagery. *Psychophysiology, 19,* 75–82.

Collins, D. L., Baum, A., & Singer, J. E. (1983). Coping with chronic stress at Three Mile Island: Psychological and biochemical evidence. *Health Psychology, 2,* 149–166.

Dodge, K. A. (1980). Social cognition and children's aggressive behavior. *Child Development, 51,* 162–170.

Dodge, K. A., & Coie, J. D. (1987). Social-information-processing factors in reactive and proactive aggression in children's peer groups. *Journal of Personality and Social Psychology, 53,* 1146–1158.

Dodge, K. A., Murphy, R. R., & Buchsbaum, K. (1984). The assessment of intention-cue detection skills in children: Implications for developmental psychopathology. *Child Development, 55,* 163–173.

Drever, J. (1952). *A dictionary of psychology.* Harmondsworth, England: Penguin.

Ekman, P. (1984). Expression and the nature of emotion. In K. R. Scherer & P. Ekman (Eds.), *Approaches to emotion* (pp. 329–343). Hillsdale, NJ: Erlbaum.

Ekman, P., & Friesen, W. V. (1971). Constants across cultures in the face and emotion. *Journal of Personality and Social Psychology, 17,* 124–129.

Ekman, P., & Friesen, W. V. (1975). *Unmasking the face: A guide to recognizing emotions from facial clues.* Englewood Cliffs, NJ: Prentice-Hall.

Ekman, P., Friesen, W. V., & Simons, R. C. (1985). Is the startle reaction an emotion? *Journal of Personality and Social Psychology, 49,* 1416–1426.

Ekman, P., Sorenson, E. R., & Friesen, W. V. (1969). Pan-cultural elements in facial displays of emotions. *Science, 164,* 86–88.

Ellis, A., & Bernard, M. E. (1985). What is rational–emotive therapy (RET)? In A. Ellis & M. E. Bernard (Eds.), *Clinical applications of rational–emotive therapy* (pp. 1–30). New York: Plenum.

Ellsworth, P. C., & Smith, C. A. (1988a). From appraisal to emotion: Differences among unpleasant feelings. *Motivation and Emotion, 12,* 271–302.

Ellsworth, P. C., & Smith, C. A. (1988b). Shades of joy: Patterns of appraisal differentiating pleasant emotions. *Cognition and Emotion, 2,* 301–331.

Emde, R. N. (1980). Levels of meaning for infant development. In W. A. Collins (Ed.), *Minnesota Symposium on Child Psychology* (Vol. 13, pp. 1–37). Hillsdale, NJ: Erlbaum.

Emmons, R. A. (1986). Personal strivings: An approach to personality and subjective well-being. *Journal of Personality and Social Psychology, 51,* 1058–1068.

Endler, N. S., & Magnusson, D. (Eds.). (1976). *Interactional psychology and personality.* New York: Wiley.

Epstein, S. (1979). The stability of behavior: I. On predicting most of the people much of the time. *Journal of Personality and Social Psychology, 37,* 1097–1126.

Epstein, S. (1983). A research paradigm for the study of personality and emotions. In M. M. Page (Ed.), *Nebraska Symposium on Motivation* (Vol. 30, pp. 91–154). Lincoln: University of Nebraska Press.

Epstein, S. (1984). Controversial issues in emotion theory. In P. Shaver (Ed.), *Review of personality and social psychology: Vol. 5. Emotions, relationships, and health* (pp. 64–88). Beverly Hills, CA: Sage.

Fehr, B., & Russell, J. A. (1984). Concept of emotion viewed from a prototype perspective. *Journal of Experimental Psychology: General, 113,* 464–486.

Festinger, L. (1957). *A theory of cognitive dissonance.* Stanford, CA: Stanford University Press.

Folkins, C. H. (1970). Temporal factors and the cognitive mediators of stress reaction. *Journal of Personality and Social Psychology, 14,* 173–184.

Folkman, S., & Lazarus, R. S. (1980). An analysis of coping in a middle-aged community sample. *Journal of Health and Social Behavior, 21,* 219–239.

Folkman, S., & Lazarus, R. S. (1985). If it changes it must be a process: Study of emotion and coping during three stages of a college examination. *Journal of Personality and Social Psychology, 48,* 150–170.

Folkman, S., & Lazarus, R. S. (1988a). Coping as a mediator of emotion. *Journal of Personality and Social Psychology, 54,* 466–475.

Folkman, S., & Lazarus, R. S. (1988b). The relationship between coping and emotion: Implications for theory and research. *Social Science in Medicine, 26,* 309–317.

Folkman, S., Lazarus, R. S., Dunkel-Schetter, C., DeLongis, A., & Gruen, R. J. (1986). The dynamics of a stressful encounter: Cognitive appraisal, coping, and encounter outcomes. *Journal of Personality and Social Psychology, 50,* 992–1003.

Freedman, J. L., Wallington, S. A., & Bless, E. (1967). Compliance without pressure: The effect of guilt. *Journal of Personality and Social Psychology, 7,* 117–124.

Frijda, N. H. (1986). *The emotions.* New York: Cambridge University Press.

Frijda, N. H. (1987). Emotion, cognitive structure, and action tendency. *Cognition and Emotion, 1,* 115–143.

Gnepp, J., Klayman, J., & Trabasso, T. (1982). A hierarchy of information sources for inferring emotional reactions. *Journal of Experimental Child Psychology, 33,* 111–123.

Gruen, R. J., Folkman, S., & Lazarus, R. S. (1989). Centrality and individual differences in the meaning of daily hassles. *Journal of Personality, 56,* 743–762.

Hammen, C. L., Marks, T., Mayol, A., & deMayo, A. R. (1985). Depressive self-schemas, life stress, and vulnerability to depression. *Journal of Abnormal Psychology, 94,* 308–319.

Harris, P. L. (1985). What children know about the situations that provoke emotions. In M. Lewis & C. Saarni (Eds.), *The socialization of affect* (pp. 161–186). New York: Plenum.

Hastorf, A. H., & Cantril, H. (1954). They saw a game: A case study. *Journal of Abnormal and Social Psychology, 49,* 129–134.

Hebb, D. O. (1949). *The organization of behavior.* New York: Wiley.

Heider, F. (1958). *The psychology of interpersonal relations.* New York: Wiley.

Hillman, J. (1960). *Emotion: A comprehensive phenomenology of theories and their meanings for therapy.* Evanston, IL: Northwestern University Press.

Hochschild, A. R. (1979). Emotion work, feeling rules, and social structure. *American Journal of Sociology, 85,* 551–575.

House, J. S. (1981). Social structure and personality. In M. Rosenberg & R. H. Turner (Eds.), *Social psychology: Sociological perspectives* (pp. 525–561). New York: Basic Books.

Izard, C. E. (1971). *The face of emotion.* New York: Appleton-Century-Crofts.

Izard, C. E. (1977). *Human emotions.* New York: Plenum.

Izard, C. E., Kagan, J., & Zajonc, R. B. (Eds.). (1984).

Emotions, cognition, and behavior. New York: Cambridge University Press.

Jessor, R. (1981). The perceived environment in psychological theory and research. In D. Magnusson (Ed.), *Toward a psychology of situations: An interactional perspective* (pp. 297–317). HIllsdale, NJ: Erlbaum.

Jones, E. E., Kanouse, D. E., Kelley, H. H., Nisbett, R. E., Valins, S., & Weiner, B. (Eds.). (1971). *Attribution: Perceiving the causes of behavior*. Morristown, NJ: General Learning Press.

Kasl, S. V., Evans, A. S., & Niederman, J. C. (1979). Psychosocial risk factors in the development of infectious mononucleosis. *Psychosomatic Medicine, 41*, 445–466.

Klinger, E. (1975). Consequences of commitment to and disengagement from incentives. *Psychological Review, 81*, 1–25.

Lang, P. J. (1979). A bio-informational theory of emotional imagery. *Psychophysiology, 16*, 495–512.

Lazarus, R. S. (1966). *Psychological stress and the coping process*. New York: McGraw-Hill.

Lazarus, R. S. (1968). Emotions and adaptation: Conceptual and empirical relations. In W. J. Arnold (Ed.), *Nebraska Symposium on Motivation* (Vol. 16, pp. 175–266). Lincoln: University of Nebraska Press.

Lazarus, R. S. (1982). Thoughts on the relations between emotion and cognition. *American Psychologist, 37*, 1019–1024.

Lazarus, R. S. (1983). The costs and benefits of denial. In S. Breznitz (Ed.), *The denial of stress* (pp. 1–30). New York: International Universities Press.

Lazarus, R. S. (1984). On the primacy of cognition. *American Psychologist, 39*, 124–129.

Lazarus, R. S. (1989a). Cognition and emotion from the RET viewpoint. In M. E. Bernard & R. DiGiuseppe (Eds.), *Inside rational–emotive therapy* (pp. 47–68). Orlando, FL: Academic Press.

Lazarus, R. S. (1989b). Constructs of the mind in mental health and psychotherapy. In A. Freeman, K. M. Simon, L. E. Beutler, & H. Arkowitz (Eds.), *Comprehensive handbook of cognitive therapy* (pp. 99–121). New York: Plenum.

Lazarus, R. S. (in press). Theory-based stress measurement. *Psychological Inquiry*.

Lazarus, R. S., & Averill, J. R. (1972). Emotion and cognition: With special reference to anxiety. In C. D. Spielberger (Ed.), *Anxiety and behavior* (2nd ed., pp. 242–283). New York: Academic Press.

Lazarus, R. S., Averill, J. R., & Opton, J. R., Jr. (1970). Toward a cognitive theory of emotion. In M. B. Arnold (Ed.), *Feelings and emotions: The Loyola Symposium* (pp. 207–232). New York: Academic Press.

Lazarus, R. S., & Folkman, S. (1984). *Stress, appraisal, and coping*. New York: Springer.

Lazarus, R. S., & Folkman, S. (1987). Transactional theory and research on emotions and coping. *European Journal of Personality, 1*, 141–169.

Lazarus, R. S., Kanner, A. D., & Folkman, S. (1980). Emotions: A cognitive–phenomenological analysis. In R. Plutchik & H. Kellerman (Eds.), *Emotion: Theory, research, and experience. Vol. 1. Theories of emotion* (pp. 189–217). New York: Academic Press.

Lazarus, R. S., & Launier, R. (1978). Stress-related transactions between person and environment. In L. A. Pervin (Ed.), *Perspectives in interactional psychology* (pp. 287–327). New York: Plenum.

Lazarus, R. S., & Smith, C. A. (1988). Knowledge and appraisal in the cognition–emotion relationship. *Cognition and Emotion, 2*, 281–300.

Leeper, R. W. (1948). A motivational theory of emotion to replace "emotion as disorganized response." *Psychological Review, 55*, 5–21.

Leeper, R. W. (1965). Some needed developments in the motivational theory of emotions. In D. Levine (Ed.), *Nebraska Symposium on Motivation* (Vol. 13, pp. 25–122). Lincoln: University of Nebraska Press.

Levenson, R. W. (1988). Emotion and the autonomic nervous system: a prospectus for research on autonomic specificity. In H. L. Wagner (Ed.), *Social psychophysiology and emotion: Theory and clinical applications* (pp. 17–42). New York: Wiley.

Leventhal, H. (1980). Toward a comprehensive theory of emotion. In L. Berkowitz (Ed.), *Advances in experimental social psychology* (Vol. 13, pp. 139–207). New York: Academic Press.

Leventhal, H. (1984). A perceptual motor theory of emotion. In K. R. Scherer & P. Ekman (Eds.), *Approaches to emotion* (pp. 271–291). Hillsdale, NJ: Erlbaum.

Leventhal, H., & Scherer, K. R. (1987). The relationship of emotion to cognition: A functional approach to a semantic controversy. *Cognition and Emotion, 1*, 3–28.

Lewin, K. (1935). *A dynamic theory of personality*. New York: McGraw-Hill.

Lewis, K. (1936). *Principles of topological psychology*. New York: McGraw-Hill.

Lewis, M., & Michalson, L. (1983). *Children's emotions and mood: Developmental theory and measurement*. New York: Plenum.

Little, B. R. (1983). Personal projects: A rationale and method for investigation. *Environment and Behavior, 15*, 273–309.

Maddux, J., Norton, L., & Stoltenberg, C. (1986). Self-efficacy expectancy, outcome expectancy, and outcome value: Relative effects on behavioral intentions. *Journal of Personality and Social Psychology, 51*, 783–789.

McGraw, K. M. (1987). Guilt following transgression: An attribution of responsibility approach. *Journal of Personality and Social Psychology, 53*, 247–263.

Metalsky, G. I., Halberstadt, L. J., & Abramson, L. Y. (1987). Vulnerability to depressive mood reactions: Toward a more powerful test of the diathesis–stress and causal mediation components of the reformulated theory of depression. *Journal of Personality and Social Psychology, 52*, 386–393.

Mischel, W. (1968). *Personality and assessment*. New York: Wiley.

Mischel, W., & Peake, P. K. (1982). Beyond deja vu in the search for cross-situational consistency. *Psychological Review, 89*, 730–755.

Nasby, W., Hayden, B., & dePaulo, B. M. (1979). Attributional bias among aggressive boys to interpret unambiguous social stimuli as displays of hostility. *Journal of Abnormal Psychology, 89*, 459–468.

Nisbett, R., & Ross, L. (1980). *Human inference: Strategies and shortcomings of social judgment*. Englewood Cliffs, NJ: Prentice-Hall.

Nomikos, M. S., Opton, E. M., Jr., Averill, J. R., & Lazarus, R. S. (1968). Surprise versus suspense in the production of stress reaction. *Journal of Personality and Social Psychology, 8*, 204–208.

Ortony, A. (1987). Is guilt an emotion? *Cognition and Emotion, 1*, 283–298.

Ortony, A., Clore, G. L., & Foss, M. A. (1987). The referential structure of the affective lexicon. *Cognitive Science, 11,* 341–364.

Owens, J., Bower, G. H., & Black, J. B. (1979). The "soap opera" effect in story recall. *Memory and Cognition, 7,* 185–191.

Palys, T. S., & Little, B. R. (1983). Perceived life satisfaction and the organization of personal project systems. *Journal of Personality and Social Psychology, 44,* 1221–1230.

Pastore, N. (1952). The role of arbitrariness in the frustration–aggression hypothesis. *Journal of Abnormal and Social Psychology, 47,* 728–731.

Pervin, L. A. (1983). The stasis and flow of behavior: Toward a theory of goals. In M. M. Page (Ed.), *Nebraska Symposium on Motivation* Vol. 30, pp. 1–53). Lincoln: University of Nebraska Press.

Peterson, C., & Barrett, L. C. (1987). Explanatory style and academic performance among university freshmen. *Journal of Personality and Social Psychology, 53,* 603–607.

Peterson, C., Semmel, A., von Baeyer, C., Abramson, L. Y., Metalsky, G. I., & Seligman, M. E. P. (1982). The Attributional Style Questionnaire. *Cognitive Therapy and Research, 6,* 287–300.

Piaget, J. (1952). *The origins of intelligence in children.* New York: International Universities Press.

Piaget, J. (1981). *Intelligence and affectivity.* Palo Alto, CA: Annual Reviews Monographs.

Plutchik, R. (1980). *Emotion: A psychoevolutionary synthesis.* New York: Harper & Row.

Plutchik, R. (1984). Emotions: A general psychoevolutionary theory. In K. R. Scherer & P. Ekman (Eds.), *Approaches to emotion* (pp. 197–219). Hillsdale, NJ: Erlbaum.

Plutchik, R., & Kellerman, H. (Eds.). (1980). *Emotion: Theory, research, and experience. Vol. 1. Theories of emotion.* New York: Academic Press.

Postman, L., Bruner, J. S., & McGinnies, E. (1948). Personal values as selective factors in perception. *Journal of Personality and Social Psychology, 43,* 142–154.

Repetti, R. L. (1987). Individual and common components of the social environment at work and psychological well-being. *Journal of Personality and Social Psychology, 52,* 710–720.

Riskind, J. H. (1984). They stoop to conquer: Guiding and self-regulatory functions of physical posture after success and failure. *Journal of Personality and Social Psychology, 47,* 479–493.

Rosch, E. (1978). Principles of categorization. In E. Rosch & B. B. Lloyd (Eds.), *Cognition and categorization* (pp. 27–71). Hillsdale, NJ: Erlbaum.

Roseman, I. J. (1984). Cognitive determinants of emotion: A structural theory. In P. Shaver (Ed.), *Review of personality and social psychology: Vol. 5. Emotions, relationships, and health* (pp. 11–36). Beverly Hills, CA: Sage.

Ross, L. (1977). The intuitive psychologist and his shortcomings: Distortions in the attribution process. In L. Berkowitz (Ed.), *Advances in experimental social psychology* (Vol. 10, pp. 173–220). New York: Academic Press.

Ross, L. (1987). The problem of construal in social inference and social psychology. In N. E. Grunberg, R. E. Nisbett, J. Rodin, & J. E. Singer (Eds.), *A distinctive approach to psychological research: The influence of Stanley Schachter* (pp. 118–150). Hillsdale, NJ: Erlbaum.

Rozin, P., & Fallon, A. E. (1987). A perspective on disgust. *Psychological Review, 94,* 23–41.

Ryff, C. D. (1987). The place of personality and social structure research in social psychology. *Journal of Personality and Social Psychology, 53,* 1192–1202.

Sarbin, T. H. (1985, June). *Emotions as situated actions.* Paper presented at the Conference on the Role of Emotions in Ideal Human Development, Heinz Werner Institute of Developmental Psychology, Clark University, Worcester, MA.

Scheff, T. J. (1979). *Catharsis in healing, ritual and drama.* Berkeley: University of California Press.

Scheier, M. F., & Carver, C. S. (1987). Dispositional optimism and physical well-being: The influenced of generalized outcome expectancies on health. *Journal of Personality, 55,* 169–210.

Scherer, K. R. (1982). Emotion as process: Function, origin and regulation. *Social Science Information, 21,* 555–570.

Scherer, K. R. (1984a). Emotion as a multicomponent process: A model with some cross-cultural data. In P. Shaver (Ed.), *Review of personality and social psychology: Vol. 5. Emotions, relationships, and health* (pp. 37–63). Beverly Hills, CA: Sage.

Scherer, K. R. (1984b). On the nature and function of emotion: A component process approach. In K. R. Scherer & P. Ekman (Eds.), *Approaches to emotion* (pp. 293–317). Hillsdale, NJ: Erlbaum.

Scherer, K. R. (1986). Vocal affect expression: A review and a model for future research. *Psychological Bulletin, 99,* 143–165.

Scherer, K. R., & Ekman, P. (Eds.). (1984). *Approaches to emotion.* Hillsdale, NJ: Erlbaum.

Scherer, K. R., Wallbott, H. G., & Summerfield, A. B. (Eds.). (1986). *Experiencing emotion: A cross-cultural study.* New York: Cambridge University Press.

Schneider, D. M. (1976). Notes toward a theory of culture. In K. Basso & H. Selby (Eds.), *Meaning in anthropology* (pp. 197–220). Albuquerque: University of New Mexico Press.

Schwartz, G. E., Fair, P. L., Salt, P., Mandel, M. R., & Klerman, G. L. (1976). Facial muscle patterning to affective imagery in depressed and nondepressed subjects. *Science, 192,* 489–491.

Seligman, M. E. P., & Schulman, P. (1986). Explanatory style as a predictor of productivity and quitting among life insurance sales agents. *Journal of Personality and Social Psychology, 50,* 832–838.

Selye, H. (1974). *Stress without distress.* Philadelphia: J. B. Lippincott.

Shaver, K. G. (1977). *Principles of social psychology.* Cambridge, MA: Winthrop.

Shaver, K. G. (1985). *The attribution of blame: Causality, responsibility, and blameworthiness.* New York: Springer.

Shaver, P. (Ed.). (1984). *Review of personality and social psychology: Vol. 5. Emotions, relationships, and health.* Beverly Hills, CA: Sage.

Shaver, P., Schwartz, J., Kirson, D., & O'Connor, C. (1987). Emotion knowledge: Further exploration of a prototype approach. *Journal of Personality and Social Psychology, 52,* 1061–1086.

Shweder, R. A., & LeVine, R. A. (Eds.). (1984). *Culture theory: Essays on mind, self, and emotion.* Cambridge, England: Cambridge University Press.

Skinner, B. F. (1953). *Science and human behavior.* New York: Appleton.

Smith, C. A. (1989). Dimensions of appraisal and physiological response in emotion. *Journal of Personality and Social Psychology, 56,* 339–353.

Smith, C. A., & Ellsworth, P. C. (1985). Patterns of cognitive appraisal in emotion. *Journal of Personality and Social Psychology, 48,* 813–838.

Smith, C. A., & Ellsworth, P. C. (1987). Patterns of appraisal and emotion related to taking an exam. *Journal of Personality and Social Psychology, 52,* 475–488.

Smith, C. A., Lazarus, R. S., & Novacek, J. (1990). *Appraisal components, relational themes, and emotion.* Manuscript submitted for publication, Vanderbilt University.

Smith, C. A., McHugo, G. J., & Lanzetta, J. T. (1986). The facial muscle patterning of posed and imagery-induced expressions of emotion by expressive and nonexpressive posers. *Motivation and Emotion, 10,* 133–157.

Smith, C. A., Novacek J., Lazarus, R. S., & Pope, L. K. (1990). *Antecedents of emotion: Situations, dispositions, attributions, and appraisals.* Manuscript in preparation, Vanderbilt University.

Solomon, Z., Mikulincer, M., & Hobfoll, S. E. (1987). Objective versus subjective measurement of stress and social support: Combat-related reactions. *Journal of Consulting and Clinical Psychology, 55,* 577–583.

Sroufe, A. L. (1979). Socioemotional development. In J. Osofsky (Ed.), *The handbook of infant development* (pp. 462–516) New York: Wiley.

Stein, N., & Levine, L. (1987). Thinking about feelings: The development and organization of emotional knowledge. In R. E. Snow & M. Farr (Eds.), *Aptitude, learning, and instruction: Vol. 3. Cognition, conation, and affect* (pp. 165–198). Hillsdale, NJ: Erlbaum.

Strentz, T., & Auerbach, S. M. (1988). Adjustment to the stress of simulated captivity: Effects of emotion-focused versus problem-focused preparation on hostages differing in locus of control. *Journal of Personality and Social Psychology, 55,* 652–660.

Thoits, P. A. (1984). Coping, social support, and psychological outcomes: The central role of emotion. In P. Shaver (Ed.), *Review of personality and social psychology: Vol. 5. Emotions, relationships, and health* (pp. 219–238). Beverly Hills, CA: Sage.

Thompson, D. A., & Campbell, R. G. (1977). Hunger in humans induced by 2-deoxy-D-glucose: Glucoprivic control of taste preference and food intake. *Science, 198,* 1065–1068.

Tomkins, S. S. (1962). *Affect, imagery, consciousness: Vol. 1. The positive affects.* New York: Springer.

Tomkins, S. S. (1963). *Affect, imagery, consciousness: Vol. 2. The negative affects.* New York: Springer.

Tomkins, S. S. (1980). Affect as amplification: Some modifications in theory. In R. Plutchik & H. Kellerman (Eds.), *Emotion: Theory, research, and experience. Vol. 1. Theories of emotion* (pp. 141–164). New York: Academic Press.

Vallone, R., Ross, L., & Lepper, M. R. (1985). The hostile media phenomenon: Biased perception and perceptions of media bias in coverage of the Beirut massacre. *Journal of Personality and Social Psychology, 49,* 577–585.

Vogel, W., Raymond, S., & Lazarus, R. S. (1959). Intrinsic motivation and psychological stress. *Journal of Abnormal and Social Psychology, 58,* 225–233.

Wallington, S. A. (1973). Consequences of transgression: Self-punishment and depression. *Journal of Personality and Social Psychology, 28,* 1–7.

Watson, J. B. (1919). *Psychology from the standpoint of a behaviorist.* Philadelphia: J. B. Lippincott.

Weiner, B. (1985). An attributional theory of achievement motivation and emotion. *Psychological Review, 92,* 548–573.

Weiner, B., Amirkhan, J., Folkes, V. S., & Verette, J. A. (1987). An attributional analysis of excuse giving: Studies of a naive theory of emotion. *Journal of Personality and Social Psychology, 52,* 316–324.

Weiner, B., Graham, S., & Chandler, C. (1982). Pity, anger, and guilt: An attributional analysis. *Personality and Social Psychology Bulletin, 8,* 226–232.

Werner, H. (1948). *Comparative psychology of mental development* (rev. ed.) Chicago: Follett.

Wicklund, R. A., & Brehm, J. W. (1976). *Perspectives on cognitive dissonance.* Hillsdale, NJ: Erlbaum.

Chapter 24

Personality and Health

Richard J. Contrada, Howard Leventhal, and Ann O'Leary
Rutgers University

Our chapter title sets at least three demanding tasks: specifying what we mean by personality, clarifying what we mean by health, and elaborating upon the interactions between the two domains. Hippocrates and Galen approached this problem at the psychological and physiologic levels by postulating four personality types, each of which was presumed to have an excess of a particular bodily fluid or humor: the depressive, "melancholic" temperament (black bile); the optimistic, "sanguine" temperament (blood); the irascible, "choleric" temperament (yellow bile); and the impassive, "phlegmatic" temperament (phlegm). These biopsychological dispositions were linked with propensities to fall ill with particular diseases.

HAS SCIENCE ADVANCED IN THE DOMAIN OF PERSONALITY AND HEALTH?

One reason for mentioning these early models of personality, temperament, and illness is that they continue to appear in relatively contemporary thinking about personality and health. For example, Eysenck (1967), following the lead of Immanuel Kant and Wilhelm Wundt, mapped two basic dimensions of personality, neuroticism and extraversion–introversion, and a more elaborate model of neurological excitation upon the Hippocratic matrix. And although the psychoanalytically oriented psychosomaticists (Alexander, 1950; Dunbar, 1947) presented a more complex set of person–disease linkages based upon both automatic physiological processes and symbolic bodily complaints, the correlational logic of their approach overlaps with the Hippocratic framework.

The main reason for mentioning this history, however, is that it creates the context for the two following questions: (1) Do we know more about the personality–health link now than did Hippocrates and Galen? and (2) Are the approaches now used to study these questions different in essential ways from those used in the past, and are they likely to generate "scientific" knowledge? We believe that the answer to both questions is a highly qualified "Yes." We say this fully aware of the numerous publications and the range of new tools being applied to the underlying question. Improved statistical procedures have generated a wide range of personality factors—for example, neuroticism (Eysenck, 1953), trait anxiety (Spielberger, Gorsuch, & Lushene, 1969), and hardiness (Kobasa, 1979)—and systematic interviewing methods have been used to define the Type A and Type C behavior patterns (Friedman & Rosenman, 1974; Price, 1982; Temoshok, 1987). These, among other personality factors, are presumed to relate to specific illness and/or health outcomes.

It is our thesis, however, that current approaches are deficient at three distinct points: (1) Personality is treated as a static variable rather than a set of processes; (2) the analysis of disease is too general and lacking in attention to physiologic processes; and (3) as a consequence of the first two points, current research fails to provide a persuasive picture as to how personality processes affect physiologic processes over the short and the long term so as to generate specific disease outcomes. We believe that these errors have survived in contemporary research because of a deceptively comfortable though faulty marriage between epidemiologic and personality research.

We set the stage for our analysis by examining the epidemiologic strategies that first bring personality–disease associations to light. We then discuss the steps that must be taken to determine whether these associations reflect a causal process. These steps include careful differentiation of the definition and assessment of disease, a process approach to personality, and the analysis of the physiologic paths linking the two. We then focus on two personality–disease relationships: Type A personality and cardiovascular disease, and Type C personality and cancer. In each of these sections, we describe the progress being made toward differentiating personality and disease concepts and toward providing a conceptual model and empirical evidence for their linkage.

EPIDEMIOLOGY AND PERSONALITY

Associations between personality and disease typically are initially uncovered in case–control studies, which are common in epidemiologic research. These are studies in which cases (persons with disease) are compared to controls (persons who are disease-free), with the two groups matched on factors such as age, gender, and education (Lilienfeld

& Lilienfeld, 1980). Less typically, the associations have been found in longitudinal designs, where assessments of personality are made at intake and disease rates are recorded over a period of years and correlated with the personality measure.

Although these methods are useful for generating hypotheses about factors responsible for differences in disease rates, they have a common difficulty: They are correlational, and therefore plagued with the problems of ruling out alternative explanations for observed associations (Feinstein, 1988). Like all correlational methods, they can never "prove" causation. By contrast, it is interesting to note that epidemiologists have achieved major successes in detecting environmental causes of disease. As is not the case for data from personality studies, there is a relatively high degree of distinctiveness in environmental pathogens and the vectors for their transmission (e.g., the famous case of the discovery of the Broad Street pump as the source of the water-borne pathogen in the London cholera epidemic of 1854; Lilienfeld & Lilienfeld, 1980; pp. 36–37). Distinctiveness was high because the agent was necessary for generating the disease and because it did not produce a large number of other diseases.

It has also been true that for many environmental pathogens, it has been possible to obtain follow-up data from natural experiments, quasi-experiments, and randomized trials. For example, natural variation of fluoride levels in drinking water allowed for the computation of a clear association between levels and dental caries. Because no sensible person could advance the hypothesis that persons with naturally healthy teeth settled in areas with high levels of fluoride in the drinking water and those with unhealthy teeth settled elsewhere, this natural experiment was consistent with the fluoride interpretation. The linkage between cigarette smoking and cancer is similarly distinctive, as the increments and declines of cancer incidence have followed, with an appropriate time lag, increments and declines in rates of smoking in different populations (e.g., physicians and women). No precise parallel exists for the personality–disease links. The pathways from personality to disease are complex and loosely defined; natural experiments are rare (twin studies may be an exception); and no simple experimental trial can be conducted to completely reverse the effect of a trait on a disease.

NECESSARY STEPS FOR LINKING PERSONALITY TO DISEASE

Identifying clear, "causal" links between personality and disease is further complicated by the nature of contemporary diseases. A hundred years of economic and environmental changes in the industrialized world have improved diet and hygiene, and have virtually eliminated infectious conditions such as gastroenteritis, influenza, pneumonia, and tuberculosis—conditions that had been the major causes of premature death and disability. With the exception of acquired immune deficiency syndrome (AIDS), chronic illnesses such as coronary disease, cancer, and diabetes have replaced infectious diseases as the major causes of death, disability, reduced quality of life, and medical expenditures (McKeown, 1976; McKinlay & McKinlay, 1986). These diseases have multiple causes and are linked to variations in lifestyle, such as diet, smoking, exercise, and traditional biomedical variables, as well as to emotional stress and personality (Krantz, Glass, Contrada, & Miller, 1981). These diseases have proven more elusive to diagnose, more difficult to link to particular antecedents, and far more difficult to control.

Epidemiological data are reasonable starting points for causal analysis of chronic disease, but they are reasonable only if the associations are repeatable and valid. Three frequent threats to validity are physical change (disease) preceding and causing observed personality characteristics; failure to use equally intensive diagnostic procedures in control and index groups, leading to underdetection of disease in the former (see Feinstein, 1988); and the presence of risk behaviors responsible for the disease outcome. Even when the association is repeatable and not subject to such obvious confounds, obtaining empirical data to demonstrate that the correlation reflects a causal connection requires conceptual and empirical elaboration of both ends of the correlation and of the process linking the two. Without such an elaboration, the research task is much like initiating the construction of a transcontinental railway beginning at both coasts without a map of the territory and adequate instruments to define the two building crews' locations; under these conditions, the two ends can never meet.

Defining Disease: An Essential Step for Causal Analysis

A valid analysis of associations between personality and disease depends upon an adequate model of the disease process. To laypersons, behavioral scientists included, terms such as "cancer" and "cardiovascular disease" are thought to refer to specific disease entities; this is not the case. "Cancer" refers to over 100 specific disorders that have some features in common but differ with respect to etiology, clinical manifestation, and course. Similarly, "cardiovascular disease" subsumes a number of conditions affecting the heart and blood vessels. Since the known biomedical risk factors often differ for specific disorders falling under such general rubrics, personality factors are likely to contribute in different ways to these different conditions.

Level of Diagnostic Precision

The disease endpoint is made yet more elusive when one realizes that diagnosis can be made at many different levels. All too often diseases are defined by their surface symptomatology and signs (e.g., a rash or tumor), though the definition may take into account the region or system of the body in which the symptom is located (e.g., a tumor of the lung). At a still more molecular level, the disease may be defined by its cellular makeup (e.g., a soft tissue tumor or an estrogen-sensitive tumor), and it may be diagnosed by its ultimate cause (e.g., an error in the genetic matrix, malnutrition, etc.) (Feinstein, 1973). It is possible that different personality variables will be related to different ways of defining a condition, and that each of these relationships will enhance our understanding of the way personality affects disease.

As an example, consider essential hypertension—a diagnosis based upon a sign, elevations of blood pressure, for which there is no specifiable cause. Esler et al. (1977) divided mildly hypertensive patients into two groups: one with elevated levels of renin (an enzyme whose secretion by the kidney is partially regulated by the sympathetic nervous system), and one with normal renin levels. Psychological testing showed that the high-renin group differed both from hypertensives with normal renin and from a normotensive control group on indices of suppressed hostility. Thus, by distinguishing two subgroups of hypertensive patients on the basis of a marker (renin), it was possible to provide evidence of an association between suppressed hostility and high blood pressure when the latter was diagnosed by a surface reading combined with a more molecular diagnosis (i.e., the presence of sympathetic nervous system activity). Defining the endpoint in terms of blood pressure only and ignoring the differentiation at an autonomic level would have blurred the relationship between personality and hypertension.

Symptoms and the Definition of Disease

Psychologists complain, with some justification, that symptom reports are too often used to define disease endpoints, instead of some presumably better "hard indicator" (Watson & Pennebaker, 1989). For two reasons, the complaint is particularly relevant to detecting relationships between personality and disease. First, there are data showing that measures of anxiety and neuroticism include many items measuring somatic symptoms. If so, many of the correlations between personality and symptom reports are relationships between two scales measuring the same thing. Second, people high in anxiety may also report more environmental stressors and also may exhibit a bias toward noticing symptoms and ascribing them to disease; both of these tendencies confound the interpretation of relationships between life stress and illness.

Notwithstanding these difficulties, symptoms may be more or less valid indicators of disease, depending upon the disorder under consideration. Acute, infectious conditions provoke activity in the body's immune or defense system, and the immune response is the source of most symptoms. By contrast, many chronic diseases such as the cancers and cardiovascular diseases are asymptomatic in their early stages, because they escape the body's defense systems. They become symptomatic only when the disease disrupts other bodily functions. Symptoms appear more useful, therefore, for defining acute, infectious conditions than for defining chronic conditions.

When, however, we examine the relation-

ship between symptoms and so-called "hard" (physiologic and anatomic) endpoints for either acute or chronic conditions, we may find it difficult to define disease by either set of factors alone. For example, it is not very surprising that during a flu epidemic, a high proportion of individuals may report symptoms and test negatively for a specific influenza antibody; they may have had a different "disease" than that detected by the test. It is somewhat more surprising to find a substantial percentage of individuals who test positively for the antibody and are asymptomatic. These individuals did not have, did not notice, or did not report symptoms or disruptions of everyday life (Drachman, Hochbaum, & Rosenstock, 1960). If we were testing the relationship between personality factors and influenza, would it make sense to call these latter persons "sick"? The presence of a positive antibody titer might be a better indicator of exposure, and within the exposed group, the presence of symptoms might be the better indicator of "sickness."

Symptoms and the Detection of Disease

Those who call for the use of "hard" endpoints often fail to recognize that many "hard" measures are difficult to secure, often of modest reliability, and often unethical to obtain in the absence of symptomatology. For example, would it be justified to perform an invasive procedure such as angiography to detect arterial occlusion in a functioning and asymptomatic individual? Symptoms may also play a critical role in detection of disease, as they are related to the use of health care and opportunities for diagnosis. And if symptoms are related to personality factors, it may be that disease detection, rather than the presence of a specific pathogen, produces the association between personality and "disease."

The Natural History of Disease

Because many diseases have complex and lengthy developmental histories, they may be labeled in different ways and identified with different indicators at different points in time; this further complicates their specification as endpoints. Moreover, different factors may be responsible for the development of a disease at different points along its path. For example, arterial disease may begin with minor arterial changes, such as deposition of fats forming streaks in artery walls, before progressing to stroke and/or coronary disease (Kuller, 1979). If the early stage is defined by its underlying cause, the diagnosis could be either excessive intake of unsaturated fats or the social environment and its ethnic diet (Feinstein, 1973); personality may have little to do with these early changes. On the other hand, the occurrence of a coronary event (i.e., a coronary embolism) later in life may be related to sudden high levels of catecholamine production that result from an interaction of an environmental stressor with a personality factor. It is important to note that the early phase does not necessarily lead to the later one. Different biochemical processes are involved at different stages, and environmental and personality factors may act in different ways at each of these points. Mortality may also change the disease composition in a population (e.g., coronary mortality in middle-aged males may remove one variety of the disease, such that different coronary conditions are the cause of mortality in individuals 70 years of age and over).

The lesson to be drawn from this discussion is that we are unlikely to draw reasonable conclusions about the relationship between personality and disease if we are ignorant of and ignore how a disease is initiated and promoted, and if we lack a model that identifies the possible barriers to initiation and promotion. With such a model we can formulate hypotheses about the relationship between personality factors and various disease endpoints. The task is to spell out those features of the disease process that involve potential points of contact between physiological processes and personality.

Defining Personality and Its Physiologic Linkages

The field of personality is often distinguished from other areas of psychological inquiry on the basis of its focus on consistencies in the behavior of individuals (Allport, 1961)—that is, regularities in behavior displayed by a person at different points in time and in different situations (Magnusson & Endler, 1977). Two classes of models have dominated the analyses of consistencies: "traits" and "processes." The type of model we choose will influence our conceptualization of the relationship of personality to physiologic processes and to disease.

Conversely, models of the relationship between personality and disease may stimulate basic changes in the way we conceptualize personality.

Personality as Traits

Trait models construe cross-situational consistencies as habits, and they view consistencies over multiple situations in a common domain (e.g., social behavior, work, etc.) as traits and attitudes (see Eysenck, 1953). Consistencies across domains such as extraversion, neuroticism, or openness to experience are said to be second-order factors reflecting basic underlying dimensions of personality (Eysenck, 1967). Trait measures have also been devised that are specific to the health domain—for example, illness behavior (Mechanic, 1962; Pilowsky, 1986) and body awareness (Miller, Murphy, & Buss, 1981). Although presumed to be domain-specific, these measures are often correlated with broader typological factors such as neuroticism.

Personality as Processes

It is our view that a process model of personality is essential for health research. A process perspective views behavior as the product of an interaction or transaction between personality dispositions and situational factors relevant to these dispositions (Atkinson, 1957; Bandura, 1978; Carver & Scheier, 1981; Lazarus & Folkman, 1984; Mischel, 1973; Rotter, 1954). From this perspective, instrumental and expressive behaviors are the outward manifestations of a set of cognitive and motivational/emotional structures that give meaning (cue) and value (incentive properties) to otherwise neutral stimuli (Lazarus, 1966; Leventhal, 1970), and that determine the selection of the coping response thought most likely to reach a desired outcome (outcome expectancies or benefits) at minimum cost. Subsequent to responding, an outcome evaluation is made that may lead to changes in expectations regarding the consequences of the response at issue, the ability to perform the responses, the reliability and validity of the cues defining pathways to the incentives, and the value of the incentives themselves (Abramson, Seligman, & Teasdale, 1978; Carver & Scheier, 1981; Leventhal, 1970).

More recent process views have emphasized

the self-regulative aspects of personality processes. Self-regulation models have added several facets to process models. First, they allow for innovation; that is, individuals invent new goals and new responses and do not simply repeat the past. Second, they suggest that individuals create and sustain situations where preferred goals are available and preferred coping reactions can be exercised (Bandura, 1978; Carver & Scheier, 1981; Kanfer, 1977; Lazarus, 1966; Leventhal, 1970). Third, they distinguish between coping with goals that are external (i.e., problem-focused coping) and coping with goals that are internal (i.e., emotion-focused coping), and propose that individuals may draw upon different coping repertoires regulating each of these two domains (Lazarus & Launier, 1978; Leventhal, 1970). It has also been suggested that different types of coping responses may occur simultaneously or in sequence, and that an individual may experience conflict in his or her efforts to deal with objective facets of a problem and associated emotional reactions (Lazarus & Folkman, 1984; Suls & Fletcher, 1985).

A fourth feature of many self-regulatory models is the postulate of a hierarchical structure of self-regulatory mechanisms, the levels differing in degree of abstraction (Carver & Scheier, 1981; Leventhal & Scherer, 1987). In these models, it is the setting as perceived, rather than the personality disposition, that is the direct determinant of behavior. Thus, the sensory and perceptual factors comprising a headache or an injury define a problem, and common-sense ideas about appropriate means of coping determine the selection of procedures used to resolve the problem (e.g., taking an aspirin for a headache) (Leventhal, Meyer, & Nerenz, 1980). Higher-order personality factors affect the way specific settings are represented or construed. Thus, personality dispositions such as maintaining a sense of optimism and self-worth, sustaining feelings of predictability or control over outcomes, and/or maintaining positive and minimizing unpleasant affects (anxiety, depression, pain/distress, etc.) help to determine the goal that is defined for that setting, the choice of actions for goal attainment, and the appraisal of outcomes of specific actions.

Finally, self-regulatory models of personality used in health research recognize both top-down and bottom-up communication between levels. Cognitive and subjective emotional processes affect somatic responses (these are top-down effects), and somatic responses influence cognitive and subjective emotional experiences (these are bottom-up effects) (Schwartz, 1979). For example, some individuals may be optimistic because they hold cognitions that lead them to represent the world as challenging and themselves as competent problem solvers (Kobasa, 1979). To persist, these cognitions need to be reinforced and sustained by high levels of problem-solving skill and high levels of energy, based, perhaps, upon a vigorous dopaminergic system. Bottom-up effects also can influence self-perception through a social route: The view that other people reflect to a person will be influenced by their observations of the person's temperament (i.e., his or her levels of skill and energy). Thus, temperament supports cognition (i.e., self-definition) through both internal and external feedback.

Physiologic Systems: Pathways to Health and Disease

Four physiologic systems define the pathways by which personality processes are assumed to initiate and promote disease. The systems are (1) the sympathetic–adrenomedullary (SAM) pathway or system; (2) the pituitary–adrenocortical (PAC) pathway or system; (3) the peptide communication system; and (4) the immune system, whose functions are surveillance, identification (as self or nonself), and destruction of foreign pathogens. (Borysenko, 1987, provides a readable review of the immune system.)

At one time the defensive activity of the immune system was thought to be stimulated only by bacterial or viral agents. Rapidly accumulating evidence has made it clear, however, that defensive actions by the immune system are influenced by activity in the SAM, PAC, and peptide systems, all three of which are linked to emotion, stress, and pain. Because the three communicate with one another and with the immune system, Pert (1986) has suggested that they constitute a single system. This conclusion requires that we alter our view of cognitive–emotional interactions and their correlated physiologic processes. The image of communication along a complex neural network is clearly insufficient, as these processes are not confined to networks. The old image must be amended by embedding the network in cellular and/or fluid media (i.e., by thinking of the body as a chemical factory). Rather than short-circuiting the network, these media both provide the nourishment that allows for communication in the network and are themselves media for communication. Thus, a variety of molecules, hormones, and peptides, produced at multiple sites, move through the body's fluid media, transit the cell walls of blood vessels, and communicate by contacting and attaching themselves to receptor sites on cells (immune cells, nerve cells, cells in various organs, etc.). This system forms a critical bridge between environmental stressors and personality on the one hand, and health and illness on the other.

It has long been known that both SAM and PAC activity are associated with stress and emotions (Asterita, 1985; Cannon & De La Paz, 1911; Frankenhauser, 1983; Henry & Stephens, 1977; Selye, 1956). The SAM system has been identified as the "effort" or the "fight-or-flight" system, and the PAC axis as the "distress" or "conservation–withdrawal" system (Frankenhauser, 1983; Henry & Stephens, 1977). SAM activity has been most strongly connected with emotions of acute onset, such as fear and anger. SAM activity is accompanied by the release or epinephrine, norepinephrine, and other catecholamines into the bloodstream. Social loss and disruption (Coe, Wiener, & Levine, 1983), clinical depression (Gibbons, 1964), chronic stress and anxiety, and feelings of being overwhelmed by threat and unable to cope are thought to activate the PAC system. The result of this activation is the release of adrenocorticotropic hormone (ACTH) and corticosteroids (cortisol in humans and other primates). Although the SAM and PAC systems are most frequently at center stage in discussion of physiologic linkages to affective events, most hormones, including growth hormone, prolactin, insulin, and sex hormones, are stress-responsive (see Asterita, 1985).

In recent years, a variety of peptides have been identified—such as the opioid peptides, cholecystokinin (CCK), substance P, vasoactive intestinal polypeptide (VIP), and others such as insulin and angiotensin—that were previously thought to act only within closed feedback systems. All of these peptides can be found in various forms in the periphery as well as in sites in the central nervous system (CNS). These peptides serve various functions, depending upon the place of action; for example,

in the CNS they have neuromodulating functions (Pert, 1986). Stress, especially when it is accompanied by pain, is known to stimulate the release of endogenous opioids, morphinelike peptides in brain and periphery (reviewed in Akil et al., 1984; Olson, Olson, & Kastin, 1987).

The complexity of the immune system precludes any but a cursory review of its key components. These include white blood cells or leukocytes, including B-cells, which secrete antibodies that combine with very specific nonself targets (or antigens); T-cells, which perform a variety of functions, including the amplification ("helper" T-cells) and suppression ("suppressor" T-cells) of other aspects of the immune response; and natural killer (NK) cells, thought to be an important defense against viruses and promotion of cancer. Because immune cells have receptor sites for most neurotransmitters, neuromodulators, and hormones, the SAM system (catecholamine release), the PAC system (cortisol release), and the other hormonal and peptide systems interacts with immunologic agents in the blood (SAM activity also has direct effects on lymphoid organs). Furthermore, immune system cells themselves secrete peptides (lymphokines), some of which are precursors of neurotransmitters (reviewed in Blalock, 1989). These serve communication functions within the immune system but also may affect CNS functions, as demonstrated by psychiatric effects of lymphokine treatment for cancer (Smedley, Katrak, Sikora, & Wheeler, 1983).

Multiple Routes From Personality to Disease

The four systems just reviewed are presumed to define the matrix for connecting personality to disease. What pathways might personality factors influence to generate health and/or illness?

Direct versus Indirect Effects

We have set the stage for the analysis of direct effects (i.e., cases in which the physiological correlates of personality processes initiate and/or promote disease). Two such paths have been spelled out in the literature: (1) Situations of threat that activate the SAM system are thought to elicit active emotions such as fear and anger and to increase the risk of coronary disease; and (2) situations of inescapable and/or uncontrollable threat that activate the PAC system are thought to elicit feelings of depression, of hopelessness, of being overwhelmed by threat, and of inability to cope, and are believed to increase the risk of cancer (Schneiderman & McCabe, 1985).

These cases contrast with indirect pathways, in which environment and personality and their interactions lead to disease via their effects on risk and health-promoting and illness behaviors. For example, cigarette smoking, which is more common among persons high on extraversion (Eysenck, 1967), is but one of several risk behaviors that can mediate between environment and personality and disease. Positive or health-promotive behaviors (eating three meals a day, getting 8 hours of sleep, engaging in moderate exercise), on the other hand, are related to enhanced health (e.g., an additional 7 years of longevity; Belloc & Breslau, 1972). It is no easy task to determine whether lifestyle behaviors mediate the relationship between a personality characteristic and health outcome, because health-promotive and health-damaging behaviors are weakly correlated (Langlie, 1979; Leventhal, Prohaska, & Hirschman, 1985); any given individual may engage in a mix of health-promotive and health-damaging behaviors; and there is no necessary linkage between any single personality factor and these behaviors. Finally, with the exception of cigarette smoking, heavy substance abuse, needle sharing, and high-risk sex, few of the health-damaging behaviors are powerful determinants of disease; also, most affect a broad spectrum of diseases, further reducing the specificity of their impact. Thus, when correlations between personality characteristics and health outcomes are mediated by health-damaging and health-promotive behaviors, we can expect the correlations to be relatively low (.10 to .30). We can also expect difficulties in ruling out indirect effects and detecting direct effects of personality on disease because of the many pathways and many possible interactions between them.

Direct Effects of Personality on Health

Unlike the trait view, in which multilevel factors integrate cognition, behavior, and phys-

iologic response to predict direct effects of personality on health, the interactionist view interposes situation–personality interactions and their resultant emotional states between the personality factor and illness. The SAM and/or PAC activity correlated with emotion is often presumed to be the key factor linking personality and disease. However, this change is not so great an improvement as it may seem, because it defines the state of emotional activation in overly simple terms. The hypotheses that fear or anger activate SAM activity and enhance coronary disease risk, and that inescapable and/or uncontrollable threat and loss of hope activate the PAC system and increase the probability of cancer, replace a trait with an emotional state; thus, disease and personality are still linked through a common, final endpoint. This is unsatisfactory for at least four reasons.

1. Cognition, affect, and action. Emotions such as fear, anger, and joy do not appear in isolation; they are embedded in meaning (cognition), and both cognition and affect are connected to complex action systems. Although modal syndromes such as depression link cognition, mood, and action components in characteristic ways, it is clear that different emotions can be linked to the same action tendency; for instance, both joy and anger are associated with approach (Leventhal, 1980), and sadness, calm, and euphoria are all associated with passivity. As the action tendency may have more potent effects on SAM and PAC activity than affect or mood may (Obrist, 1976), both need to be considered as determinants of disease.

2. Tonic versus phasic effects and the stages of illness. The simple state model focuses on phasic changes only, while both tonic and phasic physiologic responses may have an impact on disease processes and may do so at different stages in the disease history. For example, tonic moods and their associated SAM system activation may be responsible for the early changes initiating disease processes in hypertension, but may be irrelevant to the *initiation* of many cancers. Chronic SAM activity may be a barrier, however, to the *promotion* of cancer, as it appears to stimulate NK cell activity. The timing and overlap of these complex physiological processes with one another and with environmental assaults could be critical for initiation and promotion of different diseases (Leventhal & Tomarken, 1987).

3. *Self-regulation and environment selection.* Our process model also proposes that individuals act to avoid or generate environments, and that temperamental factors can influence cognition and support this activity. Thus, an individual's tonic level of activation may lead to the experience of under- or over-arousal and to action to reduce or increase levels of stimulation (e.g., the use of stimulants such as cigarettes and drugs in order to experience a change from baseline). The relation between phasic and tonic states may be important for predicting disease outcomes.

4. *Multiple determinants of physiologic activity.* The final complication introduced by our process model involves the interaction of multiple personality factors (e.g., of traits that moderate interpreting and coping with situations, and styles of monitoring and coping with feelings) as they affect physiologic activity and disease outcomes.

The issues above will not be resolved in the abstract, nor will they be resolved in the same way for different diseases. Steps toward their solution appear most advanced with respect to coronary heart disease and cancer; this is particularly important, because these are the two leading causes of mortality in the United States. It is to their analysis that we now turn.

TYPE A BEHAVIOR AND CORONARY DISEASE

The Nature and Biomedical Causes of Coronary Heart Disease

Despite a recent decline in cardiovascular mortality, diseases of the heart and blood vessels remain the nation's number one killer, accounting for over half of all deaths in the United States. Of the many varieties of cardiovascular disease, "coronary heart disease" (CHD) is by far the most prevalent. CHD typically represents the clinical manifestation of "coronary atherosclerosis," a slowly developing disorder that affects the coronary arteries, the blood vessels supplying heart tissue (Schneiderman, 1983). Atherosclerosis is initiated by injury to the endothelial cell layer that lines the inner walls of the coronary arteries. Endothelial injury sets in motion a number of processes that

promote the development of "atheromatous plaque"—an accumulation of lipids, lipoproteins, blood products, vascular tissue, and other substances, which narrows the arterial opening and reduces myocardial blood supply. It is believed that atherosclerosis may begin to develop in early childhood and may progress without symptom for decades.

Clinical CHD refers to a number of conditions that are precipitated by "myocardial ischemia" (i.e., insufficiency of oxygenated blood to the heart). A transient ischemic episode may produce a syndrome of severe chest pain referred to as "angina pectoris." However, reversible myocardial ischemia also may occur in the absence of pain, and a diagnosis of angina pectoris based on reports of severe chest pain may or may not reflect coronary atherosclerosis (or, indeed, any other medical condition). Prolonged and severe ischemia may produce a "myocardial infarction," or heart attack, in which a portion of the heart tissue dies. "Sudden cardiac death" refers to unexpected cardiac death occurring without symptoms or with symptoms of less than an hour's duration.

Epidemiologic research has identified three major risk factors for CHD—smoking, serum cholesterol, and high blood pressure—as well as others such as age, dietary intake of fat, sex (being male), obesity, sedentary lifestyle, and diabetes mellitus. Because this entire set of variables accounts for no more than about 50% of the new cases of CHD, investigators have examined other possible risk factors, including several psychosocial variables. Among the latter are occupational stress (Karasek, Theorell, Schwartz, Pieper, & Alfredsson, 1982), social support (Berkman, 1985), and personality. Of the entire array of proposed psychosocial risk factors, Type A behavior has been the target of the most intensive study.

Origins of the Type A Construct and Initial Linkage to CHD

The Type A construct has its roots in clinical observations that date back to the emergence of coronary disease as a common disorder (Jenkins, 1975). These descriptions were crystallized in the writing of two cardiologists, Meyer Friedman and Ray Rosenman (1974), who designated as "Type A" those individuals who characteristically display excessive achievement striving, competitiveness, impatience, hostility, and vigorous speech and motor mannerisms. Individuals who show a relative absence of these behaviors, and presumably who are less coronary-prone, were designated as "Type B."

Clinical observations and positive findings from cross-sectional research encouraged the large-scale study of Type A behavior. This work was spearheaded by Friedman and Rosenman, who developed a Structured Interview (SI) for assessing Type A behavior (Rosenman, 1978) and, along with their colleagues, initiated the critical study linking the behavior pattern to CHD, the Western Collaborative Group Study (WCGS; Rosenman et al., 1975). An 8½-year follow-up report of the WCGS sample of 3,500 initially healthy men showed that individuals characterized as Type A on the basis of the SI were about twice as likely as their Type B counterparts to develop angina, myocardial infarction, and sudden cardiac death. This relationship held when statistical adjustments were made to control for traditional coronary risk factors.

Measurement of Type A Behavior

The SI developed by Friedman and Rosenman consists of about 25 questions concerning Type A behavior (Rosenman, 1978). The questions are asked in a crisp, authoritative manner, with emphasis on key words and phrases. In addition, the interviewer will deliberately challenge the subject (e.g., by questioning or interrupting a response). The content of the subject's answers that is, whether or not the subject would be defined as Type A on the basis of self-report—carries very little weight in the SI assessment technique. What SI Type A ratings primarily reflect is the use of vigorous speech patterns, such as loud, rapid, and accelerated speech, explosive vocal intonations, and short response latencies. Also emphasized is the manifestation of hostility during the interview, including rather subtle attitudinal indicators such as boredom and condescension, as well as obvious irritation and outright surliness.

The Jenkins Activity Survey (JAS; Jenkins, Zyzanski, & Rosenman, 1979), a 50-item questionnaire, was constructed to circumvent the need to conduct and audit interviews. A statistical procedure identified a subset of 21 questions, responses to which best predicted Type A assessments based on the SI. Unfortunately,

although the relationship between JAS scores and SI assessments is statistically significant, the magnitude of this relationship is disappointingly low, the correlation between the two measures being about .30 (e.g., Matthews, Krantz, Dembroski, & MacDougall, 1982). This meager association reflects the weak relationship between self-reports of time urgency and a pressured drive to succeed, as reflected in JAS scores, and the subject's speech style and overt hostility, as evidenced during the structured interview (Matthews et al., 1982). These and other findings relating SI assessments to questionnaire scores have made it clear that Type A refers to a number of distinct behavioral tendencies rather than to a single entity (Matthews, 1982; Rosenman, Swan, & Carmelli, 1988).

Type A Components and Coronary Disease

Evidence that has accumulated since the WCGS supports the hypothesis that hostility may represent the "toxic" element of Type A behavior. Indirect support for this conclusion comes from a recent meta-analysis showing a significant, predictive association between Type A behavior and CHD when data were aggregated from studies employing the SI, but not from those using the JAS (Matthews, 1988). These findings point to the expressive attributes captured uniquely by the SI as the risk-enhancing elements of Type A behavior.

More direct evidence concerning the relative importance of hostility comes from a seminal investigation by Matthews, Glass, Rosenman, and Bortner (1977), who reanalyzed data from a subset of the WCGS sample. Individual ratings were made for approximately 40 variables derived from the SI, including vocal stylistic parameters, such as rapid, high-amplitude, and explosive speech; attitudinal characteristics, such as the subject's apparent "potential for hostility"; and self-report measures reflecting other Type A behaviors. Subjects who developed CHD could be distinguished from matched controls on the basis of seven individual SI variables—four involving anger-related behavior, (including potential for hostility), two reflecting vigorous speech patterns, and one concerning competitiveness.

The importance of hostility as the disease-promoting element of Type A behavior has been supported in several additional studies of the SI components. These include a further reanalysis of CHD incidence in the WCGS (Hecker, Chesney, Black, & Frautschi, 1988); a reassessment of the SI recordings from another prospective study originally reporting no relationship between global Type A and CHD (Dembroski, MacDougall, Costa, & Grandits, 1989); and three cross-sectional studies of the relationship between SI components and atherosclerosis as measured by diagnostic coronary angiography (for a review, see Dembroski & Costa, 1987). And though the JAS, designed explicitly to mimic the SI, has yielded unimpressive findings, the Cook–Medley Hostility Scale (Cook & Medley, 1954), derived from the Minnesota Multiphasic Personality Inventory (MMPI), has proven more successful in predicting cardiovascular morbidity and mortality, as well as a variety of other negative health outcomes (for reviews, see Matthews, 1988; Williams & Barefoot, 1988).

The status of Type A behavior as an epidemiological construct is currently undergoing transformation, with considerable attention being devoted to the determination of which facets of the behavior pattern are risk-enhancing and which are not, and to the specification of population characteristics that may moderate the relationship between Type A behavior and CHD (for a comprehensive review of these issues, see Matthews, 1988). Our working hypothesis is that certain Type A behaviors may enhance coronary risk, with those most likely to operate in this manner being hostile attributes measured by the SI and the Cook–Medley Hostility Scale (and, perhaps to a lesser extent, the vigorous speech and motor mannerisms captured uniquely by the SI). And, whereas Type A behaviors may lead to CHD indirectly, through health-damaging behaviors such as smoking and failure to seek medical care in a timely manner, our present examination of disease-promoting mechanisms focuses on more direct physiological pathways.

Mechanisms Linking Type A Behavior to CHD

Considerable attention has been devoted to the possibility that Type A behavior is associated with enhanced physiological responsiveness to psychological stressors and challenges, and that this hyperresponsiveness reflects processes involved in the development of CHD (Krantz & Manuck, 1984). Particular emphasis has been given to SAM activity, which is accompanied by a number of cardiovascular and metabolic adjustments that may be involved both in the initiation and progression of coronary atherosclerosis, and in the precipitation of clinical CHD (Schneiderman, 1983). One causal pathway involves the possible role of blood pressure and heart rate fluctuations in the induction of endothelial injury through mechanical stress. A second derives from evidence suggesting that circulating catecholamines may be a source of direct chemical injury to the endothelium. Either or both of these processes may provide a linkage between stress-induced sympathetic activity and the initiation of coronary atherosclerosis. The progression of arterial disease may be abetted through the metabolic effects of sympathetic activity, which include the release into the circulation of lipids that are major constituents of atheromatous plaque. Among several sympathetically mediated processes that may precipitate acute clinical CHD are the induction of arrhythmias, facilitation of thrombosis, and elevation of myocardial oxygen demand.

The PAC system may also play a role in coronary disease (Henry, 1983). For example, the glucocorticoids, such as cortisol, influence lipid metabolism, and the mineralocorticoids are involved in the regulation of electrolyte balance, which in turn plays a role in determining blood pressure and cardiac rhythm. Adding to the complexity is the possibility that male sex hormones may contribute to atherogenesis, and that female sex hormones may exert a protective effect. Notwithstanding these additional neuroendocrine influences, sympathetically mediated physiologic responses would seem to play a major role in mediating the relationship between Type A behavior and CHD.

Findings from nearly 75 psychophysiological studies conducted over the past decade are generally consistent with the foregoing line of reasoning (for reviews, see Harbin, 1989; Wright, Contrada, & Glass, 1985). There appears to be a modest but statistically reliable association between Type A assessments and physiologic responses to various psychological stressors and challenges. As with the epidemiologic data relating Type A to CHD, positive results have been obtained more frequently with the SI than with the JAS, and component analysis suggests that hostility and vigorous speech patterns may account for these effects (e.g., Dembroski, MacDougall, Shields, Petitto, & Lushene, 1978). Moreover, some of the studies involving the Cook–Medley Hostility Scale indicate positive associations between hostility and reactivity (e.g., Hardy & Smith, 1988). Other Cook–Medley studies have not produced significant findings (e.g., Smith & Houston, 1987), but this discrepancy may be due to the use of interpersonal stressors in the former set of studies and nonsocial performance challenges in the latter.

Several additional themes have emerged from psychophysiologic research on Type A behavior. First, data from studies involving female subjects have not yielded consistent evidence for greater reactivity among Type As than among type Bs (Harbin, 1989), an intriguing finding that cannot be accounted for entirely in terms of methodologic weaknesses (Contrada & Krantz, 1988). Second, the available literature provides only a limited basis for characterizing the situations that elicit enhanced physiologic activity among Type A individuals. Cognitive or psychomotor tasks have tended to yield positive results when task requirements and/or external incentives for good performance are moderate, rather than extremely low or excessively high (see Wright et al., 1985). Significant effects also have been obtained with some consistency in studies involving social threats (e.g., Dembroski, MacDougall, & Lushene, 1979; Glass et al., 1980; Hardy & Smith, 1988).

A third point worth mentioning here is that virtually all the available studies have been concerned with the relationship between Type A assessments and a single parameter of physiologic changes—namely, their *intensity.* Very few studies have attempted to determine the degree to which Type A behavior is associated with the *frequency* and *duration* of episodes of sympathetic activation (Contrada, Wright, & Glass, 1985). This gap in the empirical literature takes on significance when one considers that there is no *a priori* reason to suspect that intensity of sympathetic activation is more likely to reflect pathogenic processes than either the frequency or duration of such activations.

The role of physiologic reactivity in mediating the linkage between Type A and CHD gains plausibility from findings obtained in animal research (Schneiderman, 1983). Perhaps most relevant is a series of studies indicating that coronary atherosclerosis among cholesterol-fed cynomolgus monkeys was greatest in those exhibiting the largest heart rate response to a standardized laboratory challenge (e.g., Manuck, Kaplan, Adams, & Clarkson, 1989). It is most interesting, in view of the importance of hostility in the human literature, that heart rate reactivity and aggressive behavior are positively associated among male cynomolgus monkeys.

Trait-Interactional Models of Global Type A Behavior

Analysis of the *origins* of Type A behaviors has implicated a confluence of contributing factors, including genetically rooted temperamental tendencies, parent child interactions (Matthews & Woodall, 1988), and influences stemming from the larger sociocultural context (Price, 1982). Our focus in this chapter, however, is necessarily limited to attempts to specify processes underlying the *display* of Type A behavior in adults. First, we consider how four trait-interactional models might explain the intensity with which Type A behavior is exhibited on a particular occasion.

Three of these models treat within a single framework the full range of Type A behaviors reflected in both SI and JAS assessments: Glass's (1977) uncontrollability model; a self-evaluation perspective that may be constructed by integrating models proposed by Matthews (1982), Scherwitz, Berton, and Leventhal (1978), and Strube (1987); and Price's (1982) social learning analysis. The fourth is a somatopsychic feedback hypothesis (Krantz & Durel, 1983) that distinguishes between SI- and JAS-defined aspects of Type A behavior. The major components of each model are outlined in Table 24.1. Because all four approaches view the overt manifestation of Type A behavior as the outcome of a person–situation interaction, all imply three conceptual elements: an enduring *person factor* that accounts for temporal and cross-situational stability in Type A behavior; one or more *situational factors* that selectively engage individuals to the degree that they possess the person factor; and a *process* whereby situation and person factors interact and produce Type A behavior. To varying degrees, the four models also address the origins of negative affect and physiologic responsivity in Type As.

The person factor implied by Glass's (1977)

Table 24.1. Four Trait-Interactional Models of Type A Behavior

Model	Person factor	Situation factor	Psychological process	Behavioral responses	Affective responses	Physiological responses
Uncontrollability (Glass, 1977)	Motive to assert and maintain control over the environment	Stressors that threaten personal control	Threat appraisal; selection of effortful coping responses	Type A behaviors as a coping style aimed at maintaining control over the environment	Negative affect as a consequence of threatened loss of control and failed coping efforts	SAM activity as a correlate of effortful coping; PAC activity as a correlate of helplessness
Self-evaluation (Matthews, 1982; Scherwitz et al., 1978; Strube, 1987)	High and ambiguous standards for self-evaluation in Type A domains; dispositional self-consciousness	Factors that enhance self-awareness; ambiguous performance feedback	Negative self-evaluation; uncertainty about ability	Type A behavior as an effort to satisfy self-evaluative standards and generate self-diagnostic feedback	Negative affect as a consequence of negative self-evaluation and uncertainty about ability	SAM and PAC activity as a correlate of negative affect and behavioral efforts to satisfy standards and generate self-diagnostic feedback
Social learning (Price, 1982)	Three core beliefs: Self-esteem is contingent on external achievements; there are no universal moral laws; all resources are scarce	Opportunities and impediments relating to achievement and resources	Appraisal of threats to self-esteem; selection of behaviors on the basis of reinforcement expectations	Learned aspects of Type A as responses to threats relating to core beliefs	Negative affect as a consequence of threat appraisal	SAM and PAC activity as a correlate of negative affect and behavioral efforts at threat reduction
Somatopsychic feedback (Krantz & Durel, 1983)	Constitutionally based SAM responsiveness; Type A attitudes	Psychological and nonpsychological elicitors of SAM activity; cues congruent with Type A attitudes	Feedback from peripheral SAM activity interacts with situational cues and Type A attitudes	SAM feedback process gives rise to vigorous speech and hostile behavior	Negative affect is intensified by SAM feedback	SAM activity is determined by the interaction of constitutional predisposition and cognitive appraisal

model is a motive to assert and maintain control over environmental stressors. This motive is activated by stressors that signal the potential loss of control. The result is the overt display of Type A behaviors, which are conceptualized as an aggressive, problem-focused coping style. Glass has further hypothesized that the vigorous, *hyper*responsive behavior of Type A individuals should give way to behavioral *hypo*responsiveness, or helplessness, following prolonged exposure to an uncontrollable stressor. The notion that Type As are predisposed to respond to control-related threats is consistent with the behavioral responses of Type A and Type B subjects in the two-phase experimental procedure employed in learned helplessness research (Glass, 1977); with Type A individuals' greater sensitivity to manipulations that threaten personal freedom and arouse psychological reactance (Carver, 1980; Rhodewalte & Comer, 1982); and with Type A individuals' greater reluctance to give up control of a task to a more capable partner (Miller, Lack, & Asroff, 1985; Strube & Werner, 1985).

Unfortunately, all of the foregoing studies assessed Type A behavior using the JAS. Glass's uncontrollability hypothesis did receive partial support in a study in which SI-defined Type As responded to uncontrollable threat with behavioral and physiologic hyper-reactivity (Contrada et al., 1982). In addition, correlational studies have linked SI assessments to various control-related dispositions, such as dominance (Rosenman et al., 1988) and the desirability of control (Dembroski, MacDougall, & Musante, 1983), and the vigorous speech patterns emphasized in SI assessments have been associated with dominance and persuasiveness in research not explicitly concerned with the Type A concept (Dembroski et al., 1983).

According to one self-evaluation model (Scherwitz et al., 1978), Type A behavior is a reflection of high standards concerning achievement, competition, deadlines, and so forth. These standards become activated and direct behavior under conditions of heightened self-involvement. This notion is similar to that described by Carver and Scheier (1981), in which self-awareness is viewed as a consequence of individual differences in dispositional self-consciousness or of environmental conditions (e.g., the presence of others) that direct attention toward the self. When the Type A individual becomes aware of discrepancies between performance and goals, a self-regulatory process is activated that instigates behaviors aimed at reducing those discrepancies, and is manifested by the overt display of Type A behavior.

A related approach has been suggested by Matthews (1982), who hypothesizes that Type A behavior reflects a strong value for productivity and ambiguous standards for evaluating achievements. Strube (1987; Strube, Boland, Manfredo, & Al-Falaij, 1987) has proposed a self-evaluation model of Type A behavior that incorporates and extends the ambiguous-standards perspective. According to Strube, the overt display of Type A behavior reflects the desire for an accurate appraisal of important abilities. Thus, Type A behaviors may reflect both the desire to *satisfy* high standards for self-evaluation and an effort to *generate diagnostic information* concerning one's status as evaluated against such standards.

That many aspects of Type A behavior reflect high standards regarding achievement, competitiveness, and time seems self-evident, and in fact describes the content of several JAS items. There is evidence that these standards are translated into excessively high expectations regarding performance attainments in specific situations (Snow, 1978). Moreover, when faced with uncertainty about their abilities, Type As show greater efforts than Type Bs

to generate information they have reason to believe would allow a more definitive self-appraisal (Strube et al., 1987). Note, however, that there is very little evidence linking the self-evaluative models to SI-defined Type A behaviors (Matthews, 1982).

Price (1982) posits that Type A behavior reflects a cognitive system comprising three core beliefs, corollaries, and associated fears or threats:

1. The belief that one must constantly prove oneself reflects the assumption that self-worth is unstable and must be demonstrated repeatedly through tangible accomplishments; it is associated with the fear of insufficient self-worth and social disapproval and stimulates incessant achievement striving.
2. The belief that there is no universal moral principle implies that morally wrong behavior may be rewarded and morally correct behavior may not; it is associated with hostile behavior.
3. The belief that all resources are scarce fosters a view of life as a zero-sum game and instigates competitive behavior.

Research deriving from Price's (1982) model has been limited thus far to the development of a measure of the Type A belief system and demonstration of positive associations with Type A behavior and related constructs, including the SI and the Cook–Medley Hostility Scale (Watkins, Fisher, Southard, Ward, & Schechtman, 1989).

The person factor posited by the somatopsychic model is constitutional, rather than cognitive or motivational. Specifically, Krantz and Durel (1983) suggest that aspects of Type A behavior measured by the SI are caused by a physiologic responsivity to stress, reflecting a constitutionally based factor that is partially independent of conscious mediation. The notion is that among individuals predisposed in this manner to evince high levels of physiologic responses to stress, a feedback mechanism translates those responses into Type A behavior. This could entail a cognitive process such as that suggested by Schachter and Singer (1962), in which attitudinal aspects of Type A, in combination with situational cues, cause physiologic changes to be labeled as anger or another emotional state, which in turn stimulates such Type A behaviors as vigorous speech patterns and hostility.

Four sets of findings are consistent with the somatopsychic model of Krantz and Durel (1983). First, SI Type A assessments are predictive of blood pressure elevations in anesthetized subjects undergoing surgery—conditions that presumably minimize the operation of psychological processes requiring consciousness (for a review, see Contrada, Krantz, & Hill, 1988). Second, twin studies indicate significant heritability coefficients for SI-derived ratings of speech patterns and hostility ratings (Matthews, Rosenman, Dembroski, MacDougall, & Harris, 1984), and for physiological responses to psychological stressors (Rose, Grim, & Miller, 1984); both suggest a constitutional substrate for risk-enhancing features of Type A and their physiologic correlates. Third, individual differences in physiological responses to stressors are stable (Manuck, Kasprowicz, Monroe, Larkin, & Kaplan, 1989), and therefore may contribute to temporal and cross-situational consistency in Type A behavior. Fourth, antihypertensive medications that reduce cardiovascular responsiveness also appear to reduce the intensity of Type A behavior as measured by the SI, suggesting that sympathetic reactivity may be causally antecedent to Type A behavior (Krantz et al., 1988).

An interpretative analysis of the models depicted in Table 24.1 suggests the possibility of an integration. It may be argued that the first three models imply a system of cognitive structures that constitute an internal representation of the individual and his or her relationship to the world. These structures have two major components. The first is a set of self-evaluative standards and associated self-appraisals: One must remain in control of the environment (but will often lose control); be free of external constraints (but will often be constrained); aspire to high standards (but seldom actually satisfy them); be certain of how one is doing with respect to those standards (but can never know for sure). The second component is a generalized representation of the social and physical world that fosters the belief that people and environmental conditions constitute opportunities for and threats to the ability to be in control, be free of constraints, achieve high standards, and have an accurate self-appraisal.

Psychological processes implied by the first three models also take the same general form in that they involve the effects of representational structures upon threat appraisal and coping response selection. These processes, in turn, generate overt Type A behavior, negative affect, and physiologic reactivity. The models have different but not mutually exclusive emphases regarding the type of threat (e.g., "I am losing control" vs. "My abilities are in doubt"), the function of the selected coping response (e.g., restoration of control vs. assessment and reaffirmation of an ability), and the precise source of negative affect and physiological response (e.g., threat appraisal vs. effortful coping behavior).

The addition of a somatopsychic mechanism to the foregoing matrix of representational structures may be particularly relevant to the speech-stylistic and hostile aspects of Type A behavior. Although such behaviors might be construed as consequences of threatened loss of control (Glass, 1977), negative self-appraisals (Scherwitz et al., 1978), frustrated goals (Price, 1982), or thwarted efforts at self-evaluation (Strube et al., 1987), such accounts run into difficulty with the fact that most research generated by the first three models has involved the JAS, which, as noted earlier, shows considerable statistical independence from measures of hostility and vigorous motor mannerisms (e.g., Matthews et al., 1982; Rosenman et al., 1988). By contrast, the somatopsychic feedback notion is supported by findings based on the SI (see above), and is in accord with research indicating that the interaction of physiologic arousal and anger-related cues increases the intensity of self-reported anger and overt display of hostile aggression (for a review, see Contrada et al., 1988).

At the same time, peripheral physiologic reactivity appears to be neither necessary nor sufficient for the experience of emotion and display of emotional behavior (Leventhal, 1980). Somatopsychic feedback may therefore represent a process whereby emotional Type A behaviors are *supported* and/or *intensified*, rather than *generated*. The somatopsychic model may also require modification to account for the possibility that constitutionally based antecedents of Type A behavior operate independently of feedback from peripheral physiologic changes—for example, through CNS mechanisms responsible for integrated action–emotion responses (see Krantz et al., 1988).

The *initiating* mechanism responsible for precipitating hostility and related emotional responses in Type A individuals might be conceptualized in terms of cognitive structures, resembling those discussed earlier, that directly encourage threat appraisals likely to precipitate hostile affect. Such an approach is suggested both by Price's (1982) second and third Type A beliefs and by Krantz and Durel's (1983) discussion of attitudinal factors that direct the feedback-labeling process. This possibility is elaborated upon below after a consideration of previous attempts to conceptualize hostile aspects of Type A behavior.

Trait Models of Hostility

Conceptual analyses of hostility stand in contrast to those directed at global Type A behavior, in that the former have been correlational and descriptive rather than experimental and process-oriented. One effort to characterize the psychological attributes reflected in SI ratings of potential for hostility yielded the following descriptive labels: "anger experience," "anger expression," and "hostile attitude" (Musante, MacDougall, Dembroski, & Costa, 1989). Another produced a somewhat different set of terms—"frequency of anger experience," "intensity of anger experience," "antagonistic interview style," and "anger expression"—and attempted to define these attributes on the basis of their correlations with two more general personality traits, "neuroticism" and "disagreeableness" (Dembroski & Costa, 1987).

Table 24.2 summarizes the results of efforts to characterize the psychological attributes reflected in Cook–Medley scores. As with SI hostility ratings, trait approaches have spawned a plethora of terms designating distinct attributes presumably reflected in Cook–Medley scores. In an effort to determine which proposal best describes interrelationships among the Cook–Medley items, Contrada and Jussim (1989) utilized structural equation analysis to compare a single-factor model to multifactor models implied by Costa, Zonderman, McCrae, and Williams (1986), Houston, Smith, and Cates (1989), and Barefoot, Dodge, Peterson, Dahlstrom, and Williams (1989). Results in a sample of over 400 male and female undergraduates indicated that a single-factor model was extremely inadequate in accounting for interitem covariances. Whereas each of the more complex models achieved a modest degree of improvement, all showed a similar, very poor degree of overall fit with the data. These results draw into question both the adequacy of the full scale as a measure of a single trait and the cogency of conceptual analyses implying that the Cook–Medley captures multiple psychological attributes.

A Process Model of Hostility

We would argue that efforts to characterize the psychological attributes reflected by SI ratings of potential for hostility and Cook–Medley scores will most likely prove fruitful if conducted within the framework of a process model, rather as a search for an ever-increasing number of dispositional constructs. Such a model may be constructed by elaborating upon the four trait-interactional perspectives discussed earlier, in the light of the fuzzy set of attributes that have emerged from attempts to conceptualize hostile dispositions. Hostility may best be construed in terms of a system of interrelated cognitions that shape the individual's reactions to certain social situations. In this hostile world view, life is seen as a competitive struggle for survival and advancement, in which other people use unfair, deceptive, and manipulative means in the pursuit of selfish goals. Such a world view is implied by Price's (1982) second and third Type A beliefs (see Table 24.1), and would join the set of self-representational structures discussed earlier.

A hostile world sensitizes the person to hostile threats—that is, real or imagined efforts of specific individuals to manipulate, exploit, and/or deceive. This sensitization is reflected in the use of detection procedures, including vigilance and suspiciousness, that function to identify and characterize hostile threats. Threat detection instigates defensive responses, including avoidance, escape, and retaliatory aggression. Defensive maneuvers are accompanied by negative affective responses, which may include anger, fear, contempt, disgust, or distress, and concomitant physiologic activity.

A general trait-interactional model of Type A behavior is depicted in Figure 24.1. For the sake of simplicity, the diagram emphasizes a single direction of causal flow, though in fact feedback is likely at several points, as where behavioral, affective, and physiologic responses serve as inputs to threat appraisal. Interactions among the three outcome variables probably reflect the operation of higher-order mech-

TABLE 24.2. Conceptual Analyses of Attributes Measured by the Cook–Medley Scale

Study	Proposed construct(s)	Basis for proposed construct(s)
Smith & Frohm (1985)	One dimension: Cynical Hostility, a tendency to experience anger and resentment, to view others with distrust, and to be vigilant, calculating, and manipulative	Significant correlations with the following: seven Buss–Durkey subscales; low social desirability; trait anger, anxiety, and depression; Machiavellianism; external locus of control; Framingham Type A; low trust; cynicism; anger-in; anger-out; low hardiness; neuroticism; negative life events; frequency and severity of hassles; small number of and dissatisfaction with social supports
Costa et al. (1986)	Two dimensions: Cynicism, a tendency to hold a low opinion of human nature; and Paranoid Alienation, a tendency to experience feelings of persecution and emotional distance from others	Item-level principal-components analysis and correlations with other MMPI scales
Blumenthal et al. (1987)	Four dimensions: Anger and Hostility; Neuroticism; Ineffective Coping Style; and Social Maladjustment	Significant correlations with state and trait anger and anxiety; relevant subscales of the MMPI and Symptom Check List-90; and measures of perceived social support
Houston et al. (1989)	Two dimensions: Cynicism and a tendency to dislike or mistrust people privately, but to disavow negative feelings and inhibit aggression in order to avoid alienating others or appearing misanthropic	Clustering of subjects by item responses, and characterization of items that discriminated subject clusters and their pattern of relationships with measures of anger-in, social support, and physiological and affective responses to difficult tasks
Barefoot et al. (1989)	Five dimensions: Hostile Attribution, a tendency to interpret the behavior of others as reflecting harmful intent; Cynicism, a negative view of people in which they are seen as unworthy, deceitful, and selfish; Hostile Affect, a tendency to experience anger, impatience, and loathing in interpersonal interactions; Aggressive Responding, a tendency to express anger and engage in aggressive behavior; Social Avoidance, a tendency to refrain from social interaction	Conceptual grouping of items and pattern of correlations of item clusters with measures of neuroticism, extraversion, openness, conscientiousness, agreeableness, and hostility
Greenglass & Julkunen (1989)	One dimension: Cynical Distrust, an inability to trust others and a view of people as dishonest and unreliable	Item-level principal-components analysis and size of correlation with a measure of cynicism versus measures of other attributes

anisms that integrate the activity of parallel response generators, rather than direct cause–effect relationships. Note that differences between individuals in the occurrence of different sequences implied by the model (e.g., struggling to maintain control, defending against hostile threats) remain an empirical question rather than a matter specified *a priori* by postulating a single-factor model for the relationships among representational and constitutional person factors.

Frequency and Duration of Exposure: Transaction and Self-Regulation

As we have suggested in the introduction to this chapter, it may be fruitful to take a more

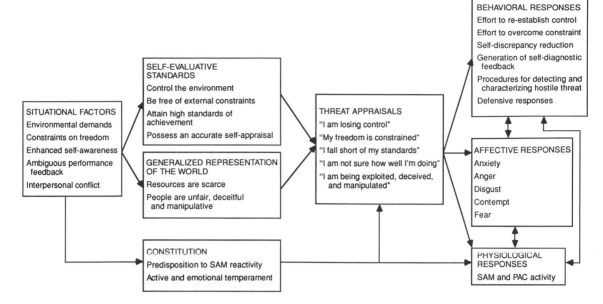

FIGURE 24.1. General trait-interactional model of Type A behavior.

transactional approach to the study of Type A behavior and health. Just such a step has been proposed by Smith (1989), who has expressed concern about the limitations of the mechanistic interaction model. As noted earlier, this model focuses on differences between Type A and Type B individuals with respect to behavioral and physiologic responses to predetermined experimental conditions, and ignores the possibility that Type A behavior may increase the frequency and duration of exposures to stressful situations. Smith (1989) reviews a number of studies, including several cited earlier, that support the transactional framework. For example, Type As may place objectively greater demands on themselves through their reluctance to delegate control to a partner with superior ability (e.g., Miller et al., 1985), and by engaging in behavioral strategies aimed at generating feedback they believe would be diagnostic of their abilities (Strube et al., 1987).

The transactional framework complements the trait-interactional view, rather than contradicting it, by identifying additional causal pathways whereby Type A behavior and associated pathogenic responses may be generated. There is, however, a need for elaboration of how components of a trait-interactional model for Type A behavior articulate with transactional processes. We would suggest that a

logical starting point for the analysis of this issue would be to consider the representational structures discussed earlier as a key element in the processes that increase the frequency and duration of exposures to disease-promoting person–situation transactions. In this view, both the occurrence of objectively real, risk-enhancing exposures, and the intensity of subsequent pathogenic responses to those exposures, may be construed as the product of self-regulatory processes guided by the individual's cognitive representation of self and world.

THE CANCER-PRONE PERSONALITY

Cancer is a complex collection of illnesses that can develop in any of a large number of sites in the body. They currently constitute the second most frequent cause of death in the United States, and despite many recent advances in their treatment, few physical afflictions provoke as much fear and awe. All cancers begin with the development of neoplastic (literally, "new-growth") cells whose reproduction becomes uncontrolled or autonomous, due to alterations in the cells' deoxyribonucleic acid (DNA) that are passed on to future cells as they reproduce. The majority of malignant tumors can be classified into two categories: "sarcomas," which arise from connective tissue, and "carcinomas," which arise from epithelial cells lining the outer or inner surfaces of the body. Efforts to identify psychosocial influences on cancer have used as models breast cancer (the most common cancer in women), lung cancer, cervical cancer, and malignant melanoma (a deadly skin cancer). Several of the studies, particularly "retroprospective" ones in which psychosocial data gathered in youth are used to predict the development of cancer in adulthood, have combined all types of cancer in analyses.

Numerous behavioral factors have been associated with the initiation of cancer (reviewed in Levy, 1985). Tobacco and alcohol use and dietary factors contribute the largest effects. Sexually promiscuous behavior resulting in the transmission of carcinogenic viruses, exposure to environmental pollutants, and geophysical factors such as radiation and ultraviolet light also contribute to risk of development of cancer. These factors exert their effects on initiation through several routes (reviewed in Levy, 1985, Ch. 2), including the alteration of cell DNA and perhaps, in some cases, effects on cancer-related immunologic processes.

Psychoimmunology and Cancer

The immune system plays an important role in defense against cancer, although the mechanisms are not yet well understood. One of the white blood cells involved in immune function, the natural killer or NK cell, seems to be particularly important in preventing carcinogenesis in a relatively nonspecific manner (i.e., it is effective against a wide variety of targets). It must be noted that this is somewhat controversial, since NK cell effects have been more difficult to demonstrate in humans than in murine (mouse) models (see Gorelik & Herberman, 1986, and Pross, 1986, for reviews and discussion). NK cells are able to destroy abnormal cells through "cytolysis," in which the NK cell secretes an acid that creates a hole in the membrane of the target cell. NK cell activity is thought to be a mechanism for control of initially altered cells and, after cancer has developed, of micrometastases that might result in recurrence following treatment.

Evidence has been accumulating for some years now that psychological processes exert

significant effects on immune function (reviewed in Jemmott & Locke, 1984; O'Leary, 1991). In fact, NK cell activity has been shown to be reduced by bereavement (Irwin, Daniels, Smith, Blood, & Weiner, 1987), marital separation (Kiecolt-Glaser et al., 1987), loneliness (Glaser, Kiecolt-Glaser, Speicher, & Holliday, 1985), and "stressed power motive" (Jemmott et al., in press), and to be enhanced by practice of relaxation techniques (Kiecolt-Glaser, Glaser, et al., 1985). It is important to note, however, that NK activity levels in these studies generally fall well within the "normal range," and these effects may be ephemeral; thus, their relevance to the development of cancer is unknown.

Personality and Cancer

Speculation that personality exerts an influence on the initiation and progression of cancer dates at least to the 2nd century A.D., with an assertion by Galen that "melancholy" women were more likely than "sanguinous" ones to develop breast cancer. The descriptions of the "cancer-prone personality" seem to be even more heterogeneous than those for Type A. A large number of studies implicate several quite different types of psychosocial variables as predictors of cancer outcome, though the evidence for most is variable, and the studies have been heavily criticized on methodological grounds (for an excellent critical review, see Fox, 1978). However, when the studies are viewed together, an impressionistic picture of a constellation of traits and coping styles that may constitute the "cancer-prone personality" begins to emerge. It has been labeled "Type C" (Morris & Greer, 1980; Temoshok, 1987) and is thought to represent a coping style that is the converse of that displayed by Type A individuals, with Type Bs falling in between the other two on a continuum (it must be noted, however, that no direct evidence for this assertion has yet been obtained). Personality factors such as nonexpressiveness and depression are associated with the development of cancer, more rapid progression, and worse prognosis. A variety of research designs have been used, and these vary with respect to the degree of confidence with which it can be concluded that psychosocial factors are causal. Retrospective studies are the least interpretable in that psychosocial factors may as easily be consequences as causes of cancer diagnosis. This criticism also applies to case–control studies, which contrast cancer patients with people who have some other disease or are disease-free. More convincing are "quasi-prospective" studies in which patients who will shortly have a biopsy to determine a malignant or benign condition are assessed and then compared in light of subsequent diagnosis, although these may suffer similar confounds in that cancer may produce psychological or psychobiological effects even in those not certain of their diagnosis. Longitudinal designs, which follow diagnosed subjects over time, are convincing to the extent that differences in cancer severity at the time of assessment can be controlled in data analysis. Among the best designs used in the studies described below are prospective and retro-prospective ones, in which psychosocial data are collected far in advance of cancer diagnosis. Probably the most readily interpretable studies use randomized psychosocial interventions; unfortunately, thus far only one has been reported.

An examination of the psychosocial variables found to be associated with worse outcome indicates that the majority can be placed into one of five categories: psychological depression, helplessness/hopelessness, low or lost social support, low negative emotionality, and emotional inexpressiveness. Following is a brief review of findings in each of these categories.

Depression

Depression is the psychological state most often described in early anecdotal reports of the cancer-prone personality, and several scientific investigations have examined this variable. Shekelle et al. (1981) found that elevated depression, reported while the subjects were medical students, was associated with increased risk of death from cancer 17 years later (odds ratio over 2.0). The relationship was maintained after controlling for a variety of behavioral risk factors. Studies showing cancer patients to be more depressed than others with no cancer (Jansen & Muenz, 1984), or than other cancer patients with less advanced disease (Pettingale, Burgess, & Greer, 1988), are less convincing, as the disease may have produced the depression.

Some investigations have yielded negative results—for example, for history of affective illness on later development of cancer (Niemi

& Jaaskelainen, 1978), and for depression assessed postdiagnosis on likelihood of recurrence (Greer, Morris, & Pettingale, 1979; Jamison, Burish, & Wallston, 1987). Higher self-reported depression has even been associated with *improved* outcome (Dattore, Shontz, & Coyne, 1980; Derogatis, Abeloff, & Melisaratos, 1979).

Thus, the findings regarding depression as a factor promoting cancer are mixed. It has been argued that self-report of distress is unreliable in cancer patients, who may be averse to admitting negative affect to themselves or others; however, this does not explain why reports of depression correlate with outcome in some studies but not in others.

Helplessness/Hopelessness

Two cognitive stances toward stressful situations, helplessness and hopelessness, which have themselves been linked to psychological depression (e.g., Seligman, 1975), have been shown to be more consistently related to cancer than depression. Helplessness/hopelessness was one of several interviewer-rated factors found to be associated with thicker melanoma tumors by Temoshok et al. (1985), and it has been found to predict outcome of cervical biopsy (Antoni & Goodkin, 1988; Schmale & Iker, 1969) and breast biopsy (Wirsching, Stierlin, Hoffman, Weber, & Wirsching, 1982), as well as recurrence of breast cancer (Greer et al., 1979; Jensen, 1987). Finally, hopeless reactions to life events have been reported to be predictive of the development of cancer in a large prospective study in Yugoslavia (Grossarth-Maticek, Kanazir, Schmidt, & Vetter, 1982).

We found only two studies reporting negative results for hopelessness—one a cervical biopsy study (Goodkin, Antoni, & Blaney, 1986), another a study of mixed cancers (Cassileth, Lusk, Miller, Brown, & Miller, 1985). The latter has been widely criticized on a number of grounds, perhaps the most important being the use of end-stage cancer patients.

Disrupted Social Support

Another set of factors speculated to contribute to carcinogenesis concerns the loss of significant others. Such losses, both early in life and recent, are associated with the development of depression (Brown & Harris, 1978); thus, these findings too are related to those regarding depression.

Included in this category are three sets of findings: early loss or lack of parental closeness as a predictor of cancer development (Shaffer, Duszynski, & Thomas, 1982); recent loss reported by newly diagnosed patients (Greene, 1954; Horne & Picard, 1979); and inadequacy of social support as a predictor or correlate of outcome. In this last category are indications that poorer support is associated with lower NK cell function in breast cancer (Levy, Herberman, Maluish, Schlein, & Lippman, 1985) and with greater likelihood of diagnosis of malignancy following cervical biopsy (Antoni & Goodkin, 1988). Finally, a recent randomized intervention study (Spiegel, Bloom, Kraemer, & Gottheil, 1989), which focused on enhancing social supportive bonds between members of treatment groups, was shown to increase survival time in women with metastatic breast cancer, from a mean of 19 months in untreated controls to 37 months in treated subjects.

A negative result for social ties and perceived adequacy of social support was obtained in the Cassileth et al. (1985) investigation, mentioned above.

The evidence for social disruption as a risk factor in cancer is reasonably compelling. It is of possible significance that all of the studies in the first two categories concerned male subjects, and indeed these represent the majority of studies involving men. It is possible that males have a more difficult time recovering from loss (whether early or recent) than females; in fact, women have been shown to suffer less morbidity than men following bereavement.

Negative Effects of Low Negative and High Positive Affect

Central to the proposed "Type C" construct is the nonexpression and/or nonexperience of negative emotion, particularly anger. Just as the Type A individual is angry, hostile, and explosive, the Type C person does not report anger and presents a pleasant, cheerful, or impassive face to the world.

Early evidence for low negative emotionality in cancer-prone individuals was provided by Kissen and colleagues (Kissen, Brown, & Kissen, 1969; Kissen & Eysenck, 1962), who found lower neuroticism and less "awareness of autonomic activity" to be predictive of lung cancer diagnosis. Low neuroticism and low anxiety also predicted diagnosis of breast malignancy (Morris, Greer, Pettingale, & Watson, 1981). Stavraky (1968) reported decreased hostility, measured through a projective technique, in shorter-surviving patients with mixed cancers. The short-surviving breast cancer patients studied by Derogatis et al. (1979) reported less psychological symptomatology in every subscale of a symptom checklist except phobic anxiety, and endorsed fewer negative and more positive mood adjectives. In the Greer et al. (1979) study mentioned earlier, recurrence-free survival from breast cancer was more frequent in those who had reacted to their diagnoses with "fighting spirit" or with denial (rather than "stoic acceptance" or helplessness). Wirsching et al. (1982) reported cancer patients to be "more distant," "not engaged," emotionally suppressed (but with "sudden outbursts"—see the following section on under- versus overexpression of emotion), more rational, and less emotional than those found to have benign conditions. The prospective study by Grossarth-Maticek et al. (1982) similarly found interviewer-rated "rational, antiemotional" behavior to be predictive of later development of cancer. The "nonverbal Type C" factor found to be associated with worse prognostic indicators by Temoshok et al. (1985) included several descriptors indicative of low emotionality: "bland" rather than "intense," "emotionally constricted" rather than "labile," and "appeasing" rather than "hostile." Jensen (1987) found "repressive coping" to predict breast cancer recurrence; this variable was operationalized as low reported anxiety combined with high social desirability.

Possibly related to these findings concerning low emotionality are indications that less favorable prognosis is predicted by "good adjustment" to illness. Rogentine et al. (1979), for example, found that the report of less need for adjustment to malignant melanoma was associated with later recurrence; similarly, those breast cancer patients studied by Levy et al. (1985) who were rated as being better adjusted to their illness had lower NK cell function.

For this variable, too, negative and contradictory results have been reported. For example, short-term breast cancer survivors received lower scores than longer survivors on one measure of anxiety, but higher ones on another (Jamison et al., 1987). Pettingale et al. (1988) also found reports of higher anxiety among lymphoma patients with more advanced disease. The Cassileth et al. (1985) study found no effect of need for adjustment to illness.

Interestingly, several studies have obtained associations between higher reported positive affect and worse outcome. Thus, the warm, hearty, "substable" person was identified by Hagnell (1966) as being at greater risk of cancer; cancer patients expressing more positive affect on questionnaire or checklist measures (Derogatis et al., 1979; Greer et al., 1979), more "positive attitude" (Derogatis et al., 1979), or more positive daydreaming (Jensen, 1987) suffered worse outcomes; more socially "harmonizing" women were more likely to be diagnosed with breast cancer (Wirsching et al., 1982). Contrary to this trend is a single finding: Levy and colleagues (1988) found greater joy to predict survival time in recurrent breast cancer. It is interesting to note that all of these findings involved women (in the Hagnell study the effect was obtained for women but not men). It has been argued that women in our society are socialized to "manage" their emotions to provide a soothing emotional environment, and that this is the function of many of the traditionally female occupations (Hochschild, 1983). Thus, at least some aspects of the cancer-prone personality may be the result of socialization processes (it is also interesting to note the resemblance between the Type A behavior pattern and expectations that our society holds for adult males).

Low Emotional Expressiveness

Several investigations have focused on the overt display of emotion demonstrated by subjects in their social environments. Results concerning emotional expression generally report less expression on the part of cancer patients relative to others, or to those with less favorable prognosis. Two studies obtained results indicating less frequent expression of anger in breast biopsy patients later found to have malignancies (Greer & Morris, 1975; Jansen & Muenz, 1984). In the latter study, which also used a quasi-prospective design, women later found to have breast cancer were more likely to have described themselves as "keeping anger inside." Breast cancer patients in the Jensen (1987) study who later suffered neoplastic spread and reported less expression of negative affect on a questionnaire measure. The survival-enhancing intervention developed by Spiegel et al. (1989) may have affected emotional responses of treated subjects, in that members were encouraged to discuss their feelings about their illness.

A negative result for emotional expressiveness was obtained by Greer et al. (1979), who obtained no effect of questionnaire-assessed anger expression on breast cancer recurrence.

On the other hand, there is some evidence that *increased* expression of emotion can be linked to unfavorable outcome. Greer and Morris (1975) found increased incidence both of under- and of overexpression in breast cancer patients (48% and 20%, respectively), compared with controls (15% and 10%). Shorter-surviving mixed cancer patients were shown by Stavraky (1968) to have less hostility, but also more loss of emotional control, than long-surviving patients; and although Wirsching et al. (1982) rated women later found to have breast cancer as being more emotionally suppressed, these women also showed "eruption of affect." It has been speculated that failure to attend to emotional states may produce disregulation, resulting in increased emotional lability (Jensen, 1987; Schwartz, 1983).

Summary of Personality Findings

The evidence that has been gathered for the impact of personality on cancer outcome, while far from robust, is at least quite suggestive, particularly in view of the inattention paid in most of these studies to the control of biological sources of variance (see Fox, 1978). An important question that remains unanswered, however, concerns the unity of the concept: Is there one, or are there many, cancer-prone "personalities"? If there are more than one, are particular types of cancer influenced differentially by different psychosocial factors? Conceptualizations have for the most part assumed a single underlying factor, sometimes referred to as "Type C." A fuller understanding of the nature of the "cancer-prone personality" and the mechanisms by which it exerts its effects can best be achieved by examining the psychosocial factors that comprise it in conjunction with physiological processes that may mediate its effects on cancer outcome. As described previously, immune function, particularly cytotoxic activity of NK cells, is thought to be one mediator of cancer initiation and recurrence, and NK cell function has in turn been related to psychosocial variables. Thus, it represents one possible mediator of psycho-oncologic relationships. Furthermore, it is possible to speculate about the physiologic processes mediating effects of personality factors on NK cell function.

Neuroendocrine Mediation of Psychoimmunological Relationships

Both catecholamines and cortisol have been demonstrated to affect NK cell numbers and function. Catecholamines seem to have enhancing effects. For example, injection of norepinephrine and epinephrine have been shown to increase NK activity (Hellstrand, Hermodsson, & Strannegård, 1985; Locke et al., 1984). A recent study of people with AIDS (O'Leary, Temoshok, Sweet, & Jenkins, 1989) demonstrated that greater sympathetic reactivity—reflected by greater peripheral autonomic responses to emotional reliving—was highly correlated both with NK activity and with duration of survival. It has also recently been demonstrated that persistently low NK cell activity in a healthy young adult population is associated with considerably lower levels of urinary norepinephrine and marginally significant reductions in urinary epinephrine, as well as with increased depression (Levy et al., 1989).

On the other hand, there is evidence for *suppressive* effects on NK activity of cortisol and pharmacologic corticosteroids *in vivo* (Onsrud & Thorsby, 1981) and *in vitro* (Gatti et al., 1987). Moreover, as described earlier, depression is associated with increased PAC activation.

A Two-Pathway Model for Emotion Influence on NK Function

Psychoimmunologic mediation of oncologic outcomes may occur, therefore, via at least two distinct pathways: SAM activity and PAC activity. Less strong or frequent sympathetic response, and stronger or more frequent cortisol release, are both predicted to have negative effects on NK cell activity and eventual cancer outcome. As illustrated in Figure 24.2, it is presumed here that either pathway could produce its results independently of the other; that is, that neither is necessary and either could be sufficient to result in a deleterious cancer outcome. Thus, the best outcome would be ex-

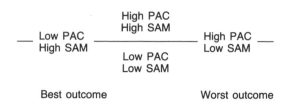

FIGURE 24.2. Range of possible cancer outcomes, depending on levels of PAC and SAM activation.

pected for individuals with low PAC and high SAM activation and the worst for those with high PAC and low SAM activation, with intermediate outcomes expected for those in the other two groups. Figure 24.3 illustrates this model. PAC activity is thought to be elevated in connection with depression, helplessness/hopelessness, and social disruption, whereas low SAM activity accompanies a set of variables collectively termed "emotional avoidance," including stoicism, low neuroticism and distress, good adjustment, and low emotional expression.

Pathway 1: Depression. Depression, and the associated factors of helplessness/hopelessness and disrupted social support, are hypothesized to constitute a single physiologic pathway for reduced NK function and worse cancer outcome. Psychological depression is associated with a number of cognitive and affective conditions that are presumed to be products of the person's environment and learning history, and that include (in addition to social loss, as discussed above) irrational thinking patterns associated with self-deprecatory cognitions (Abramson et al., 1978; Beck, 1983), learned helplessness (Seligman, 1975), and reduced reinforcement activity (Lewinsohn, 1974). There is also evidence for heritability of unipolar depression; thus, constitutional factors may be important in addition to environmental or learning history ones.

In addition to direct effects of PAC activity on biologic processes, it is suggested that this pathway may exert indirect behavioral effects on the development of cancer by promoting such risk-enhancing behaviors as the use of tobacco and alcohol and sexual promiscuity. These could exert carcinogenic effects through either alteration of DNA or immune suppression.

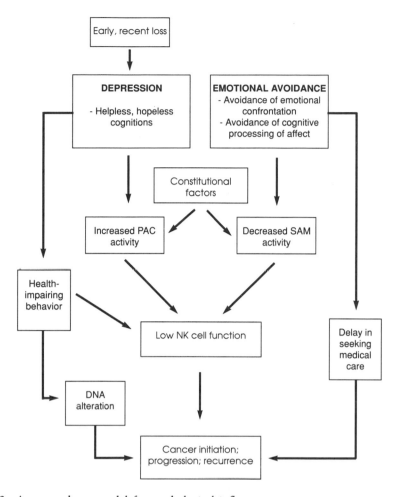

FIGURE 24.3. A two-pathway model for psychological influence on cancer.

Pathway 2: Emotional Avoidance. The second pathway is proposed to account for two sets of findings reported above: low negative/high positive emotionality, and low expression of emotion. We speculate that these effects may be consequences of an emotionally avoidant style, in which negative affect, particularly anger, is actively avoided. The possible effects of such a coping stance might include (1) the avoidance of situations likely to elicit negative affect; (2) unwillingness to express negative affect to others, due to the likelihood of consequent escalation of affect; (3) disinclination to dwell upon events associated with such affect, perhaps in connection with the active use of distraction following distressing events; and the resulting (4) reduced depth of processing of affective episodes, culminating in poor encoding in memory and thus poor retrieval, which

may combine with the other factors to reduce questionnaire reports of past distress. Over the course of time, such a person should experience less than the usual amount of negative emotion. This would mean less frequent, strong, and long-lasting SAM activation, which should be linked to poorer NK cell function.

In addition to its effects on SAM activity and NK cell function, emotional avoidance may be associated with a lower tendency to notice possible cancer symptoms or to seek medical diagnosis and treatment. Thus, like depression, emotional avoidance may exert harmful effects through behavioral processes as well as physiological ones.

Emotional avoidance as described here bears considerable resemblance to the concept of "repression" described originally by Freud, and early psychosocial oncology researchers used this concept to describe the cancer-prone individual (Bahnson & Bahnson, 1969). The two concepts, emotional avoidance and repression, may be regarded as equivalent, if it is assumed that the process itself need not occur out of the subject's conscious awareness (Erdelyi, 1985). However, this raises a potential contradiction to the proposition that repression of affect is associated with lower SAM activity. There is evidence that repressive or inexpressive persons evidence greater sympathetic response than do others during threatening laboratory procedures (e.g., Weinberger, Schwartz, & Davidson, 1979). In fact, it has been speculated that the overarousal associated with repression is responsible for repression's effects on cancer outcome (Morris & Greer, 1980; Temoshok, 1987). However, as we have mentioned at the outset, although the individuals we study may become highly aroused in laboratory situations, they may seldom expose themselves to threatening situations in their everyday lives. The small set of findings showing negative effects of overexpression of emotion may reflect the impossibility of avoiding negative affect altogether.

An important question concerns the independence of these two pathways, depression and emotional avoidance. A possible connection between them has been suggested by Temoshok (1987), who asserts that the cancer-prone style produces a fragile equilibrium for the person, both socially and intrapsychically. When stress becomes overwhelming—as it may at the time of a cancer diagnosis—the coping outcome may take one of three forms: a lapse into helplessness/hopelessness; continuation of Type C coping efforts; or the development of more adaptive coping methods. This process model provides an interesting link between the two psychophysiological pathways posited here. Temoshok's argument hinges on the assertion that the emotionally avoidant style is "masking" an underlying depression. Unfortunately, we know of no evidence that emotional avoidance or repression is predictive of depression. On the other hand, depression, when it is characterized by fatigue and psychomotor retardation, may be associated with reduced sympathetic activity, and would thus place the person in the highest risk category in Figure 24.2.

Here, as with depression, the possible contribution of temperamental factors and their heritable, perhaps immutable effects on these processes must be emphasized. Low sympathetic reactivity—activity may in some cases have nothing whatsoever to do with the avoidance of emotion, but rather with low constitutional emotionality.

Discussion

It must be stressed that the present model describes but one of many possible psycho-oncologic mediation processes, and is by no means presumed to be applicable to all cancers. Even within a particular cancer model, a variety of different processes may operate to link psychosocial to physiologic phenomena, and it is very likely that such processes differ for different types of cancer. NK activity is stimulated by the lymphokines interferon and Il-2, and lymphokine production by T-cells is known to be influenced by stress (Glaser, Rice, Speicher, Stout, & Kiecolt-Glaser, 1986). Opioid peptides are another possible pathway for effects of personality/emotional processes on tumor defense, immune function, and specifically NK cell activity. These have a variety of immunologic effects, which are complex and variable, depending upon which immune measures and which opioids are examined (reviewed in Morley, Kay, Solomon, & Plotnikoff, 1987; see also Mandler, Biddison, Mandler, & Serrate, 1986; Shavit et al., 1985).

Furthermore, pathways other than those affecting immune function may also operate. For example, the ability of cells to spontaneously repair damaged DNA has been shown to be reduced during periods of stress (Kiecolt-Glaser, Stephens, Lipetz, Speicher, & Glaser, 1985), and glucocorticoids can function as cofactors in the transformation of virally infected cancer cells (Pater, Hughes, Hyslop, Nakshatri, & Pater, 1988). Since sex hormones are stress-responsive, and these play an important role in some cancers, these too may account for some variance in psychosocial—oncologic relationships.

This model can be used to illustrate several implications for continuing research in the area. First, it points to the need for assessment of physiologic mechanisms that may mediate psycho-oncologic effects. Second, it is vital that behavioral risk factors be examined as well, so that the direct and indirect effects of emotional and other psychological processes can be separated. Finally, attention must be paid to temporal factors that may influence the nature of results obtained, as described earlier in this chapter. Of utmost importance is the need for tailoring hypotheses to the specific cancer model under consideration. Different types of cancers present unique physiologic and behavioral profiles; adequate assessment of relevant factors must take these into account.

This model also highlights several issues for psychosocial treatments designed to improve cancer outcome. First, an effective strategy for intervention would include comprehensive assessment of the psychological and biological factors contributing to the clinical picture of the individual. Effective interventions exist for depression; these include pharmacologic, cognitive, and behavioral approaches, and any of these may be helpful for a depressed patient. Social support may be enhanced through social skills training, marital counseling, or group interventions such as that used by Spiegel et al. (1989). Interventions addressing the emotional avoidance pathway present a different and perhaps greater challenge. As mentioned previously, the intervention study by Spiegel and colleagues may have influenced this factor, in that patients were encouraged to discuss their emotions during the sessions. The cancer model, with its objective outcomes, may be a useful one in which to test clinical processes that have been embraced by some (but by no means all) mental health care providers. Such phenomena as "getting in touch" with feelings, "working through" the emotional effects of traumatic events, and the analysis of defense may be relevant to the cancer-prone style and its physiological concomitants, and may be convincingly tested in the context of cancer and its outcomes.

GENERAL SUMMARY AND CONCLUSIONS

We have begun this chapter by questioning the extent and solidity of scientific knowledge regarding the linkage between personality and health. The findings of descriptive epidemiology, in both retrospective case–control and prospective longitudinal studies, define the problem for analysis but do not provide a causal model. To understand how personality factors affect disease, we must constantly clarify our conceptualizations of personality, disease, and the physiologic pathways linking them. Adequate differentiation of disease (i.e., the pro-

cesses involved in its initiation, promotion, and progression, and the indicators of these changes) and the adoption of a process model of personality make clear that developing a causal model will not be a simple task.

The complete process model of personality here proposed requires, first, an interactional perspective for the conceptualization and assessment of person and situation. Added to this is a transactional or self-regulative view that requires the analysis of strategies for controlling (i.e., generating, maintaining and avoiding) both specific types of situations and specific emotions. It also requires the analysis of the interactions among the biological substrate, temperament, self-concept, and the social environment. In addition, it demands careful analysis of both indirect (health-damaging and health-promotive lifestyle and illness behaviors) and direct connections between personality and disease. The direct effects involve extremely complex interactions among the neurologic, SAM, PAC, peptide, and immune systems. Understanding the ways in which these systems communicate with and influence one another requires major revision of the network image of nervous system and soma, as the network is literally afloat in fluid media filled with an abundance of varied (peptide) messengers ready to attach to specific receptor sites on a variety of cells.

The complexity of the metamodel has required that we focus here on the relationship of personality to a limited number of diseases; we have chosen Type A behavior and CHD, and Type C personality and cancer, because the extensive literature in each of these areas provides a view of what has been done and what remains to be done to complete an analysis of these complex relationships. Both literatures reveal the many steps needed between the uncovering of an initial epidemiologic relationship and a causal explanation. Problems of identification and measurement of the specific disposition are present in both areas: Are hostility or speech characteristics, depression and loss of hope or combative aggressiveness, the toxic and/or protective dispositions? The analysis of processes, both personality and physiologic, raises questions about interactions and transactions between environment and person: How common are specific types of environments? Do these individuals create their environments in efforts to present and protect specific images of self? And are these images and coping procedures reinforced by temperament both internally (energy supporting cognition) and externally (temperament creating an image of self in the social environment)?

Efforts to conceptualize and test the linkages between personality and disease raise many fascinating questions about our conceptualization of personality. For example, is it reasonable to consider smoking as separate from Type A behavior in predicting coronary disease? A self-regulative perspective suggests that smoking could be an integral component of Type A behavior as a strategy for regulating affect. Thus, while it can be measured separately, it should be conceptualized as a link on the path from Type A to disease rather than an independent predictor (i.e., as something that explains away the relationship of Type A to disease).

The key issue, however, is defining the pathways. Two stand out at this moment. The most familiar, SAM activity, may provoke cardiac risk and reduce cancer risk by stimulating NK immune function. It appears to be activated by emotional states such as fear and anger. The second, PAC activity, which seems to be activated by depression and hopelessness, appears to suppress immune function and to enhance cancer risk. The balance between the two and its fluctuation over time may be a critical determinant of disease outcome. The difficulty in developing a detailed and clear picture may be a result in part of focusing on chronic conditions. It is not inconceivable that attention to acute, infectious disease would simplify the explanatory task.

It would be unfortunate, however, if this provisional view of the pathways between personality and disease were the main theme derived by our readers. In our judgment, the more important message is that advances in understanding depend upon further conceptual differentiation in the three major domains we have covered (i.e., personality, physiology, and disease). As the number of peptides mounts and the component structures and functions are isolated for cognitive and emotional processing, expressions of euphoria for consensus on the "five factors of personality" seem naive and out of place. A synthesis of carefully studied components is essential and inevitable, and must be distinguished from a false synthesis that is merely descriptive. The analysis of the linkage of personality and disease will make a modest but valuable contribution to our understanding of the human condition, and a significant contribution to our conceptualization of personality and social behavior.

ACKNOWLEDGMENT

Preparation of this chapter was supported by Grant No. AG03501 from the National Institute on Aging. The authors are listed in alphabetical order.

REFERENCES

Abramson, L. Y., Seligman, M. E. P., & Teasdale, J. D. (1978). Learned helplessness in humans: Critique and reformulation. *Journal of Abnormal Psychology, 87*, 49–74.

Akil, H., Watson, S. J., Young, E., Lewis, M. E., Khachaturian, H., & Walker, J. M. (1984). Endogenous opioids: Biology and function. *Annual Review of Neuroscience, 7*, 223–255.

Alexander, F. (1950). *Psychosomatic medicine*. New York: Norton.

Allport, G. W. (1961). *Pattern and growth in personality*. New York: Holt, Rinehart & Winston.

Antoni, M. H., & Goodkin, K. (1988). Host moderator variables in the promotion of cervical neoplasia: I. Personality facets. *Journal of Psychosomatic Research, 32*, 327–338.

Asterita, M. F. (1985). *The physiology of stress*. New York: Human Sciences Press.

Atkinson, J. W. (1957). Motivational determinants of risk taking behavior. *Psychological Review, 64*, 359–372.

Bahnson, M. B., & Bahnson, C. B. (1969). Ego defenses in cancer patients. *Annals of the New York Academy of Sciences, 164*, 546–559.

Bandura, A. (1978). The self system in reciprocal determinism. *American Psychologist, 33*, 344–358.

Barefoot, J. C., Dodge, K. A., Peterson, B. L., Dahlstrom, W. G., & Williams, R. B. (1989). The Cook-Medley Hostility Scale: Item content and ability to predict survival. *Psychosomatic Medicine, 51*, 46–57.

Beck, A. T. (1983) Cognitive therapy of depression: New perspectives. In P. J. Clayton & J. E. Barrett (Eds.), *Treatment of depression: Old controversies and new approaches* (pp. 265–290). New York: Raven Press.

Belloc, N. B., & Breslow, L. (1972). Relationship of physical health status and health practices. *Preventive Medicine, 1*, 409–421.

Berkman, L. F. (1985). Measures of social networks and social support: Evidence and measurement. In A. M. Ostfeld & A. D. Eaker (Eds.), *Measuring psychosocial variables in epidemiologic studies of cardiovascular disease* (DHHS Publication No. PHS 85-2270, p. 51–79). Washington, DC: U.S. Government Printing Office.

Blalock, J. E. (1989). A molecular basis for bi-directional communication between the immune and neuroendocrine systems. *Physiological Reviews, 69*, 1–32.

Borysenko, M. (1987). The immune system: An overview. *Annals of Behavioral Medicine, 9,* 3–10.

Brown, G. W., & Harris, T. O. (1978). *Social origins of depression.* London: Tavistock.

Cannon, W. B., & De La Paz, D. (1911). Emotional stimulation of adrenal secretion. *American Journal of Physiology, 28,* 64–70.

Carver, C. S. (1980). Perceived coercion, resistance to persuasion, and the Type A behavior pattern. *Journal of Research in Personality, 19,* 467–481.

Carver, C. S., & Scheier, M. F. (1981). *Attention and self-regulation: A control-theory approach to human behavior.* New York: Springer.

Cassileth, B. R., Lusk, E. J., Miller, D. S., Brown, L. L., & Miller, C. (1985). Psychosocial correlates of survival in malignant disease. *New England Journal of Medicine, 312,* 1551–1555.

Coe, C. L., Wiener, S. G., & Levine, S. (1983). Psychoendocrine responses of mother and infant monkeys to disturbance and separation. In L. A. Rosenblum & H. Moltz (Eds.) *Symbiosis in parent–offspring interactions.* (pp. 189–214). New York: Plenum.

Contrada, R. J., Glass, D. C., Krakoff, L. R., Krantz, D. S., Kehoe, K., Isecke, W., Collins, C., & Elting, E. (1982). Effects of control over aversive stimulation and Type A behavior on cardiovascular and plasma catecholamine response. *Psychophysiology, 19,* 408–419.

Contrada, R. J., & Jussim, L. (1989). [Dimensionality of the Cook–Medley Hostility Scale]. Unpublished raw data.

Contrada, R. J., & Krantz, D. S. (1988). Stress, reactivity, and Type A behavior: Current status and future directions. *Annals of Behavioral Medicine, 10,* 64–70.

Contrada, R. J., Krantz, D. S., & Hill, D. R. (1988). Type A behavior, emotion, and psychophysiologic reactivity: Psychological and biological interactions. In B. K. Houston & C. R. Snyder (Eds.), *Type A behavior pattern: Research, theory, and intervention* (pp. 254–274). New York: Wiley.

Contrada, R. J., Wright, R. A., & Glass, D. C. (1985). Psychophysiologic correlates of Type A behavior: Comments on Houston (1983) and Holmes (1983). *Journal of Research in Personality, 19,* 12–30.

Cook, W. W., & Medley, D. M. (1954). Proposed hostility and pharisaic-virtue scales for the MMPI. *Journal of Applied Psychology, 38,* 414–418.

Costa, P. T., Zonderman, A. B., McCrae, R. R., & Williams, R. B. (1986). Cynicism, paranoid alienation in the Cook and Medley Ho scale. *Psychosomatic Medicine, 48,* 283–285.

Dattore, P. J., Shontz, F. C., & Coyne, L. (1980). Premorbid personality differentiation of cancer and noncancer groups: A test of the hypothesis of cancer proneness. *Journal of Counseling and Clinical Psychology, 48,* 388–394.

Dembroski, T. M., & Costa, P. T. (1987). Coronary-prone behavior: Components of the Type A pattern and hostility. *Journal of Personality, 55,* 211–235.

Dembroski, T. M., MacDougall, J. M., Costa, P. T., & Grandits, G. A. (1989). Components of hostility as predictors of sudden death and myocardial infarction in the Multiple Risk Factor Intervention Trial. *Psychosomatic Medicine, 51,* 514–522.

Dembroski, T. M., MacDougall, J. M., & Lushene, R. (1979). Interpersonal interaction and cardiovascular responses in Type A subjects and coronary patients. *Journal of Human Stress, 5,* 28–36.

Dembroski, T. M., MacDougall, J. M., & Musante, L. (1983). Desirability of control versus locus of control. *Health Psychology, 3,* 15–26.

Dembroski, T. M., MacDougall, J. M., Shields, J. L., Petitto, J., & Lushene, R. (1978). Components of the Type A coronary-prone behavior pattern and cardiovascular responses to psychomotor challenge. *Journal of Behavioral Medicine, 1,* 159–176.

Derogatis, L. R., Abeloff, M. D., & Melisaratos, N. (1979). Psychological coping mechanisms and survival time in metastatic breast cancer. *Journal of American Medical Association, 242,* 1504–1508.

Drachman, R. H., Hochbaum, G. M., & Rosenstock, I. M. (1960). A seroepidemiologic study in two cities. In I. M. Rosenstock, G. M. Hochbaum, H. Leventhal (Eds.), *The impact of Asian influenza on community life: A study in five cities.* (DHEW Publication No. PHS 766, pp. 27–51). Washington, DC: U.S. Government Printing Office.

Dunbar, H. F. (1947). *Mind and body: Psychosomatic medicine.* New York: Random House.

Erdelyi, M. H. (1985). *Psychoanalysis: Freud's cognitive psychology* (pp. 212–265). New York: Freeman.

Esler, M., Julius, S., Zweiflier, A., Randall, O., Harburg, E., Gardiner, H., & DeQuattro, V. (1977). Mild high-renin essential hypertension: Neurogenic human hypertension? *New England Journal of Medicine, 296,* 405–411.

Eysenck, H. J. (1953). *The structure of human personality.* London: Methuen.

Eysenck, H. J. (1967). *The biological basis of personality.* Springfield, IL: Charles C Thomas.

Feinstein, A. (1973). An analysis of diagnostic reasoning: 1. The domains and disorders of clinical macrobiology. *Yale Journal of Biology and Medicine, 46,* 212–232.

Feinstein, A. (1988). Scientific standards in epidemiologic studies of the menace of daily life. *Science, 242,* 1257–1263.

Fox, B. H. (1978). Premorbid psychological factors as related to cancer incidence. *Journal of Behavioral Medicine, 1,* 45–133.

Frankenhauser, M. (1983). The sympathetic–adrenal and pituitary–adrenal response to challenge: Comparison between the sexes. In T. M. Dembroski, T. H. Schmidt, & G. Blümchen (Eds.), *Biobehavioral bases of coronary heart disease* (pp. 91–105). Basel: Karger.

Friedman, M., & Rosenman, R. H. (1974). *Type A behavior and your heart.* New York: Knopf.

Gatti, G., Cavallo, R., Sartori, M. L., del Ponte, D., Masera, R., Salvadori, A., Carignola, R., & Angeli, A. (1987). Inhibition by cortisol of human natural killer (NK) cell activity. *Journal of Steroid Biochemistry, 26,* 49–58.

Gibbons, J. C. (1964). Cortisol secretion rate in depressive illness. *Archives of General Psychiatry, 10,* 572–575.

Glaser, R., Kiecolt-Glaser, J. K., Speicher, C. E., & Holliday, J. E. (1985). Stress, loneliness, and changes in herpes virus latency. *Journal of Behavioral Medicine, 8,* 249–260.

Glaser, R., Rice, J., Speicher, C. E., Stout, J. C., & Kiecolt-Glaser, J. K. (1986). Stress depresses interferon production concomitant with a decrease in natural killer cell activity. *Behavioral Neuroscience, 100,* 675–678.

Glass, D. C. (1977). *Behavior patterns, stress, and coronary disease.* Hillsdale, NJ: Erlbaum.

Glass, D. C., Krakoff, L. R., Contrada, R. J., Hilton, W. F., Kehoe, K., Mannucci, E. G., Collins, C., Snow, B., & Elting, E. (1980). Effects of harassment and competition upon cardiovascular and plasma catecholamine responses in Type A and Type B individuals. *Psychophysiology, 17,* 453–463.

Goodkin, K., Antoni, M. H., & Blaney, P. H. (1986). Stress and hopelessness in the promotion of cervical intraepithelial neoplasia to invasive squamous cell carcinoma of the cervix. *Journal of Psychosomatic Research, 30,* 67–76.

Gorelik, E., & Herberman, R. B. (1986). Role of natural killer (NK) cells in the control of tumor growth and metastatic spread. In R. B. Herberman (Ed.), *Cancer immunology: Innovative approaches to therapy.* (pp. 151–176). Boston: Martinus Nijhoff.

Greene, W. A. (1954). Psychological factors and reticuloendothelial disease. *Psychosomatic Medicine, 15,* 220–230.

Greenglass, E. R., & Julkunen, J. (1989). Construct validity and sex differences in Cook–Medley hostility. *Personality and Individual Differences, 10,* 209–218.

Greer, S., & Morris, T. (1975). Psychological attributes of women who develop breast cancer: A controlled study. *Journal of Psychosomatic Research, 19,* 147–153.

Greer, S., Morris, T., & Pettingale, K. W. (1979). Psychological response to breast cancer. Effect on outcome. *Lancet, ii* 785–787.

Grossarth-Maticek, R., Kanazir, D. T., Schmidt, P., & Vetter, H. (1982). Psychosomatic factors in the process of carcinogenesis. *Psychotherapy and Psychosomatics, 38,* 284–302.

Hagnell, O. (1966). The premorbid personality of persons who develop cancer in a total population investigated in 1947 and 1957. *Annals of the New York Academy of Sciences, 125,* 846–855.

Harbin, T. J. (1989). The relationship between the Type A behavior pattern and physiological responsivity: Quantitative review. *Psychophysiology, 26,* 110–119.

Hardy, J. D., & Smith, T. W. (1988). Cynical hostility and vulnerability to disease: Social support, life stress, and physiological response to conflict. *Health Psychology, 7,* 447–459.

Hecker, M. H. L., Chesney, M. A., Black, G. W., & Frautschi, N. (1988). Coronary-prone behaviors in the Western Collaborative Group study. *Psychosomatic Medicine, 50,* 153–164.

Hellstrand, K., Hermodsson, S., & Strannegård, Ö. (1985). Evidence for a β-adrenoreceptor-mediated regulation of human natural killer cells. *Journal of Immunology, 134,* 4095–4099.

Henry, J. P. (1983). Coronary heart disease and arousal of the adrenal cortical axis. In T. M. Dembroski, T. H. Schmidt, & G. Blümchen (Eds.), *Biobehavioral bases of coronary heart disease* (pp. 365–381). Basel: Karger.

Henry, J. P., & Stephens, P. M. (1977). *Stress, health, and the social environment.* New York: Springer.

Hochschild, A. R. (1983). *The managed heart: Commercialization of human feeling.* Berkeley: University of California Press.

Horne, R. L., & Picard, R. S. (1979). Psychosocial risk factors for lung cancer. *Psychosomatic Medicine, 41,* 503–514.

Houston, B. K., Smith, M. A., & Cates, D. S. (1989).

Hostility patterns and cardiovascular reactivity to stress. *Psychophysiology, 26,* 337–342.

Irwin, M., Daniels, M., Smith, T. L., Blood, E., & Weiner, H. (1987). Impaired natural killer cell activity during bereavement. *Brain, Behavior and Immunity, 1,* 98–104.

Jamison, R. N., Burish, T. G., & Wallston, K. A. (1987). Psychogenic factors in predicting survival of breast cancer patients. *Journal of Clinical Oncology, 5,* 768–772.

Jansen, M. A., & Muenz, L. R. (1984). A retrospective study of personality variables associated with fibrocystic disease and breast cancer. *Journal of Psychosomatic Research, 28,* 35–42.

Jemmott, J. B., III, Hellman, C., Locke, S. E., Kraus, L., Williams, R. M., & Valeri, C. R. (in press). Motivational syndromes associated with natural killer cell activity. *Journal of Behavioral Medicine.*

Jemmott, J. B., III, & Locke, S. E. (1984). Psychosocial factors, immunologic mediation, and human susceptibility to infectious disease: How much do we know? *Psychological Bulletin, 95,* 78–108.

Jenkins, C. D. (1975). The coronary-prone personality. In W. D. Gentry & R. B. Williams (Eds.), *Psychosocial aspects of myocardial infarction and coronary care* (pp. 5–23). St. Louis: C. V. Mosby.

Jenkins, C. D., Zyzanski, S. J., & Rosenman, R. H. (1979). *Manual for the Jenkins Activity Survey.* New York: Psychological Corporation.

Jensen, M. R. (1987). Psychobiological factors predicting the course of breast cancer. *Journal of Personality, 55,* 317–342.

Kanfer, F. H. (1977). The many faces of self-control, or behavior modification changes its focus. In R. B. Stuart (Ed.), *Behavioral self-management: Strategies, techniques, and outcomes* (pp. 1–48) New York: Brunner/Mazel.

Karasek, R. A., Theorell, T. G., Schwartz, J., Pieper, C., & Alfredsson, L. (1982). Job, psychosocial factors and coronary heart disease: Swedish prospective findings and U.S. prevalence findings using a new occupational inference method. *Advances in Cardiology, 29,* 62–67.

Kiecolt-Glaser, J. K., Fisher, L. D., Ogrocki, P., Stout, J. C., Speicher, C. E., & Glaser, R. (1987). Marital quality, marital disruption, and immune function. *Psychosomatic Medicine, 49,* 13–34.

Kiecolt-Glaser, J. K., Glaser, R., Williger, D., Stout, J. C., Messick, G., Sheppard, S., Ricker, D., Romisher, S. C., Briner, W., Bonnell, G., & Donnerberg, R. (1985). Psychosocial enhancement of immunocompetence in a geriatric population. *Health Psychology, 4,* 25–41.

Kiecolt-Glaser, J. K., Stephens, R. E., Lipetz, P. D., Speicher, C. E., & Glaser, R. (1985). Distress and DNA repair in human lymphocytes. *Journal of Behavioral Medicine, 8,* 311–320.

Kissen, D. M., Brown, R. I. F., & Kissen, M. (1969). A further report on personality and psychosocial factors in lung cancer. *Annals of the New York Academy of Sciences, 164,* 535–545.

Kissen, D. M., & Eysenck, H. J. (1962). Personality in male lung cancer patients. *Journal of Psychosomatic Research, 6,* 123–127.

Kobasa, S. C. (1979). Stressful life events, personality and health: An inquiry into hardiness. *Journal of Abnormal and Social Psychology, 37,* 1–11.

Krantz, D. S., Contrada, R. J., Durel, L. A., Hill, D. R., Friedler, E., & Lazar, J. D. (1988). Comparative effects of two beta-blockers on cardiovascular reactivity and Type A behavior in hypertensives. *Psychosomatic Medicine, 50*, 615–626.

Krantz, D. S., & Durel, L. A. (1983). Psychobiological substrates of the Type A behavior pattern. *Health Psychology, 2*, 393–411.

Krantz, D. S., Glass, D. C., Contrada, R. J., & Miller, N. E. (1981). Behavior and health. In National Science Foundation (Ed.), *Five year outlook on science and technology: 1981 source materials* (Vol. 2, pp. 561–588). Washington, DC: U.S. Government Printing Office.

Krantz, D. S., & Manuck, S. B. (1984). Acute psychophysiologic reactivity and risk of cardiovascular disease: A review and methodological critique. *Psychological Bulletin, 96*, 435–464.

Kuller, L. H. (1979). Natural history of coronary heart disease. In M. L. Pollock & D. H. Schmidt (Eds.), *Heart disease and rehabilitation* (pp. 32–56). Boston: Houghton Mifflin.

Langlie, J. (1979). Interrelationships among preventive health behaviors: A test of competing hypotheses. *Public Health Reports, 94*, 216–225.

Lazarus, R. S. (1966). *Psychological stress and the coping process*. New York: McGraw-Hill.

Lazarus, R. S., & Folkman, S. (1984). *Stress, appraisal, and coping*. New York: Springer.

Lazarus, R. S., & Launier, R. (1978). Stress related transactions between person and environment. In L. A. Pervin & M. Lewis (Eds.), *Perspectives in interactional psychology* (pp. 287–327). New York: Plenum.

Leventhal, H. (1970). Findings and theory in the study of fear communications. *Advances in Experimental Social Psychology, 5*, 119–186.

Leventhal, H. (1980). Toward a comprehensive theory of emotion. In L. Berkowitz (Ed.), *Advances in experimental social psychology* (Vol. 13, pp. 139–207). New York: Academic Press.

Leventhal, H., Meyer, D., & Nerenz, D. (1980). The common sense representation of illness danger. In S. Rachman (Ed.), *Medical psychology* (Vol. 2, pp. 7–30). New York: Pergamon Press.

Leventhal, H., Prohaska, T. R., & Hirschman, R. S. (1985). Preventive health behavior across the life span. In J. C. Rosen & L. J. Solomon (Eds.), *Prevention in health psychology* (Vol. 8, pp. 191–235). Hanover, NH: University Press of New England.

Leventhal, H., & Scherer, K. R. (1987). The relationship of emotion to cognition: A functional approach to semantic controversy. *Cognition and Emotion, 1*, 3–28.

Leventhal, H., & Tomarken, A. J. (1987). Stress and illness: Perspectives from health psychology. In V. Kasl & C. L. Cooper (Eds.), *Stress and health: Issues in research methodology* (pp. 27–55). Sussex, England: Wiley.

Levy, S. M. (1985). *Behavior and cancer*. San Francisco: Jossey-Bass.

Levy, S. M., Herberman, R. B., Maluish, A. M., Schlien, B., & Lippman, M. (1985). Prognostic risk assessment in primary breast cancer by behavioral and immunological parameters. *Health Psychology, 4*, 99–113.

Levy, S. M., Herberman, R. B., Simons, A., Whiteside, T., Lee, J., McDonald, R., & Beadle, M. (1989). Persistently low natural killer cell activity in normal adults: Immunological, hormonal and mood correlates. *Natural Immunity and Cell Growth Regulation, 8*, 173–186.

Levy, S. M., Lee, J., Bagley, C., & Lippman, M. (1988). Survival hazards analysis in first recurrent breast cancer patients: Seven-year follow-up. *Psychosomatic Medicine, 50*, 520–528.

Lewinsohn, P. H. (1974). A behavioral approach to depression. In R. J. Friedman & M. M. Katz (Eds.), *The psychology of depression: Contemporary theory and research* (pp. 157–185). Washington, DC: Winston–Wiley.

Lilienfeld, A. M. & Lilienfeld, D. E. (1980). *Foundations of epidemiology*. New York: Oxford University Press.

Locke, S., Kraus, L., Kutz, I., Edbril, S., Phillips, K., & Bonner, H. (1984). Altered natural killer cell activity during norepinephrine infusion in humans. In *Proceedings of the First International Workshop on Neuroimmunomodulation* (p. 297). Bethesda, MD.

Magnusson, D., & Endler, N. S. (1977). Interactional psychology: Present status and future prospects. In D. Magnusson & N. S. Endler (Eds.), *Personality at the crossroads: Current issues in interactional psychology* (pp. 3–31). Hillsdale, NJ: Erlbaum.

Mandler, R. N., Biddison, W. E., Mandler, R., & Serrate, S. A. (1986). Beta-endorphin augments the cytolytic activity and interferon production of natural killer cells. *Journal of Immunology, 136*, 934–939.

Manuck, S. B., Kaplan, J. R., Adams, M. R., & Clarkson, T. B. (1989). Behaviorally elicited heart rate reactivity and atherosclerosis in female cynomolgus monkeys (*Macaca fascicularis*). *Psychosomatic Medicine, 51*, 306–318.

Manuck, S. B., Kasprowicz, A. L., Monroe, S. M., Larkin, K. T., & Kaplan, J. R. (1989). Psychophysiologic reactivity as a dimension of individual differences. In N. Schneiderman, S. M. Weiss, & P. G. Kaufmann (Eds.), *Handbook of research methods in cardiovascular behavioral medicine* (pp. 365–382). New York: Plenum.

Matthews, K. A. (1982). Psychological perspectives on the Type A behavior pattern. *Psychological Bulletin, 91*, 293–323.

Matthews, K. A. (1988). CHD and Type A behavior: Update on and alternative to the Booth–Kewley and Friedman quantitative review. *Psychological Bulletin, 104*, 373–380.

Matthews, K. A., Glass, D. C., Rosenman, R. H., & Bortner, R. (1977). Competitive drive, pattern A, and coronary heart disease: A further analysis of some data from the Western Collaborative Group Study. *Journal of Chronic Diseases, 30*, 489–498.

Matthews, K. A., Krantz, D. S., Dembroski, T. M., & MacDougall, J. M. (1982). Unique and common variance in Structured Interview and Jenkins Activity Survey measures of the Type A behavior pattern. *Journal of Personality and Social Psychology, 42*, 303–313.

Matthews, K. A., Rosenman, R. H., Dembroski, T. M., McDougall, J. M., & Harris, E. (1984). Familial resemblance in components of the Type A behavior pattern: A reanalysis of the California Type A twin study. *Psychosomatic Medicine, 46*, 512–522.

Matthews, K. A., & Woodall, K. L. (1988). Childhood origins of overt Type A behaviors and cardiovascular reactivity to behavioral stressors. *Annals of Behavioral Medicine, 10*, 71–77.

McKeown, T. (1976). *The role of medicine: Dream, mirage, or nemesis?* London: Nuffield Provincial Hospitals Trust.

McKinlay, J. B., & McKinlay, S. M. (1986). Medical measures and the decline of morality. In P. Conrad & R. Kern (Eds.), *The sociology of health and illness: Critical perspectives* (pp. 7–23). New York: St. Martin's Press.

Mechanic, D. (1962). The concept of illness behavior. *Journal of Chronic Disease, 15,* 189–194.

Miller, S. M., Lack, E. R., & Asroff, S. (1985). Preference for control and the coronary-prone behavior pattern: "I'd rather do it myself." *Journal of Personality and Social Psychology, 49,* 492–499.

Miller, L., Murphy, R., & Buss, A. (1981). Consciousness of body: Private and public. *Journal of Personality and Social Psychology, 41,* 337–406.

Mischel, W. (1973). Toward a cognitive social learning reconceptualization of personality. *Psychological Review, 80,* 252–283.

Morley, J. E., Kay, N. E., Solomon, G. E., & Plotnikoff, N. P. (1987). Neuropeptides: Conductors of the immune orchestra. *Life Sciences, 41,* 527–544.

Morris, T., & Greer, S. (1980). A "Type C" for cancer? *Cancer Detection and Prevention, 3*(1), 102. (Abstract)

Morris, T., Greer, S., Pettingale, K. W., & Watson, M. (1981). Patterns of expressing anger and their psychological correlates in women with breast cancer. *Journal of Psychosomatic Research, 25,* 111–117.

Musante, L., MacDougall, J. M., Dembroski, T. M., & Costa, P. T. (1989). Potential for hostility and dimensions of anger. *Health Psychology, 8,* 343–354.

Niemi, T., & Jaaskelainen, J. (1978). Cancer morbidity in depressive persons. *Journal of Psychosomatic Research, 22,* 117–120.

Obrist, P. (1976). The cardiovascular–behavioral interaction—as it appears today. *Psychophysiology, 13,* 96–107.

O'Leary, A. (1991). Stress, emotion, and human immune function. *Psychological Bulletin,* in press.

O'Leary, A., Temoshok, L., Sweet, D. M., & Jenkins, S. R. (1989). Autonomic reactivity and immune function in men with AIDS. *Psychophysiology, 26,* 547.

Olson, G. A., Olson, R. D., & Kastin, A. J. (1987). Endogenous opiates: 1986. *Peptides, 8,* 1135–1164.

Onsrud, M., & Thorsby, E. (1981). Influence of *in vivo* hydrocortisone on some human blood lymphocyte populations. I. Effect on NK cell activity. *Scandinavian Journal of Immunology, 13,* 573–579.

Pater, M. M., Hughes, G. A., Hyslop, D. E., Nakshatri, H., & Pater, A. (1988). Glucocorticoid-dependent oncogenic transformation by Type 16 but not Type 11 human papilloma virus DNA. *Nature, 335,* 832–835.

Pert, C. B. (1986). The wisdom of the receptors: Neuropeptides, the emotions, and bodymind. *Advances, 3,* 8–16.

Pettingale, K. W., Burgess, C., & Greer, S. (1988). Psychological response to cancer diagnosis: I. Correlations with prognostic variables. *Journal of Psychosomatic Research, 32,* 255–261.

Pilowsky, I. (1986). Abnormal illness behavior: A review of the concept and its mechanics. In S. McHugh & T. M. Vallis (Eds.), *Illness behavior: A multi-disciplinary model* (pp. 391–395). New York: Plenum.

Price, V. A. (1982). *Type A behavior pattern: A model for research and practice.* New York: Academic Press.

Pross, H. F. (1986). The involvement of natural killer cells in human malignant disease. In E. Lotzova & R. B. Herberman (Eds.), *Immunobiology of natural killer cells* (Vol. 2, pp. 11–27). Boca Raton, FL: CRC Press.

Rhodewalte, F., & Comer, R. (1982). Coronary-prone behavior and reactance: The attractiveness of an eliminated choice. *Personality and Social Psychology Bulletin, 8,* 152–158.

Rogentine, G. N., Van Kammen, D. P., Fox, B. H., Docherty, J. P., Rosenblatt, J. E., Boyd, S. C., & Bunney, W. E. (1979). Psychological factors in the prognosis of malignant melanoma A prospective study. *Psychosomatic Medicine, 41,* 647–655.

Rose, R. J., Grim, C. J., & Miller, J. Z. (1984). Familial influences on cardiovascular stress reactivity: Studies of normotensive twins. *Behavioral Medicine Update, 6,* 21–24.

Rosenman, R. H. (1978). The interview method of assessment of the coronary-prone behavior pattern. In T. M. Dembroski, S. M. Weiss, J. L. Shields, S. G. Haynes, & M. Feinleib (Eds.) *Coronary-prone behavior* (pp. 55–69). New York: Springer.

Rosenman, R. H., Brand, R. J., Jenkins, C. D., Friedman, M., Straus, R., & Wurm, M. (1975). Coronary heart disease in the Western Collaborative Group Study: Final follow-up experience of 8½ years. *Journal of the American Medical Association, 233,* 872–877.

Rosenman, R. H., Swan, G. E., & Carmelli, D. (1988). Some recent findings relative to the relationship of Type A behavior to coronary heart disease. In S. Maes, C. D. Spielberger, P. B. Defares, & I. G. Sarason (Eds.), *Topics in health psychology* (pp. 21–29). New York: Wiley.

Rotter, J. B. (1954). *Social learning and clinical psychology.* Englewood Cliffs, NJ: Prentice-Hall.

Schachter, S., & Singer, J. E. (1962). Cognitive, social and physiological determinants of emotional state. *Psychological Review, 69,* 379–399.

Scheier, M. F., & Carver, C. S. (1985). Optimism, coping, and health: Assessment and implications of generalized outcome expectancies. *Health Psychology, 4,* 219–247.

Scherwitz, L., Berton, K., & Leventhal, H. (1978). Type A behavior, self-involvement, and cardiovascular response. *Psychosomatic Medicine, 40,* 593–609.

Schmale, A., & Iker, H. (1969). The psychological setting of uterine cervical cancer. *Annals of the New York Academy of Sciences, 164,* 807–813.

Schneiderman, N. (1983). Behavior, autonomic function and animal models of cardiovascular pathology. In T. M. Dembroski, T. H. Schmidt, & G. Blümchen (Eds.), *Biobehavioral bases of coronary heart disease* (pp. 304–364). Basel: Karger.

Schneiderman, N., & McCabe, P. M. (1985). Biobehavioral responses to stressors. In T. M. Filed, P. M. McCabe, & N. Schneiderman (Eds.), *Stress and coping* (pp. 13–61). Hillsdale, NJ: Erlbaum.

Schwartz, G. E. (1979). The brain as a health system. In G. C. Stone, F. Cihen, & N. E. Adler (Eds.), *Health psychology.* San Francisco: Jossey-Bass.

Schwartz, G. E. (1983). Disregulation theory and disease: Applications to the repression/cerebral disconnection/cardiovascular disorder hypothesis. *International Review of Applied Psychology, 32,* 95–118.

Seligman, M. E. P. (1975). *Helplessness: On depression, development, and death.* San Francisco: W. H. Freeman.

Selye, H. (1956). *The stress of life.* New York: McGraw-Hill.

Shaffer, J. W., Duszynski, K. R., & Thomas, C. B. (1982). Family attitudes in youth as a possible precursor of cancer among physicians: A search for explanatory mechanisms. *Journal of Behavioral Medicine, 5,* 143–163.

Shavit, Y., Terman, G. W., Martin, F. C., Lewis, J. W., Liebeskind, J. C., & Gale, R. P. (1985). Stress, opioid peptides, the immune system, and cancer. *Journal of Immunology, 135,* 834–837.

Shekelle, R. B., Raynor, W. J., Ostfield, A. M., Garron, D. C., Bieliauskas, L. A., Liu, S. C., Maliza, C., & Paul, O. (1981). Psychological depression and 17-year risk of death from cancer. *Psychosomatic Medicine, 43,* 117–125.

Smedley, H., Katrak, M., Sikora, K., & Wheeler, T. (1983). Neurological effects of recombinant human interferon. *British Medical Journal, 286,* 262–264.

Smith, T. W. (1989). Interactions, transactions, and the Type A pattern: Additional avenues in the search for coronary-prone behavior. In A. W. Siegman & T. M. Dembroski (Eds.), *In search of coronary-prone behavior* (pp. 91–116). Hillsdale, NJ: Erlbaum.

Smith, T. W., & Frohm, K. D. (1985). What's so unhealthy about hostility? Construct Validity and psychosocial correlates of the Cook and Medley Ho Scale. *Health Psychology, 4,* 503–520.

Smith, T. W., & Houston, B. K. (1987). Hostility, anger expression, cardiovascular responsivity, and social support. *Biological Psychology, 24,* 39–48.

Snow, B. (1978). Level of aspiration in coronary-prone and non-coronary-prone adults. *Personality and Social Psychology Bulletin, 4,* 416–419.

Spiegel, D., Bloom, J. R., Kraemer, H. C., & Gottheil, E. (1989). Effect of psychosocial treatment on survival of patients with metastatic breast cancer. *Lancet, ii,* 888–891.

Spielberger, C. D., Gorsuch, R. L., & Lushene, R. E. (1969). *The State–Trait Anxiety Inventory: Preliminary test manual for Form B.* Tallahassee: Florida State University.

Stavraky, K. M. (1968). Psychological factors in the outcome of human cancer. *Journal of Psychosomatic Research, 12,* 251–259.

Strube, M. J. (1987). A self-appraisal model of the Type A behavior pattern. In R. Hogan & W. H. Jones (Eds.), *Perspectives in personality: Theory, measurement and interpersonal dynamics* (pp. 201–250). Greenwich, CT: JAI Press.

Strube, M. J., Boland, S. M., Manfredo, P. A., & Al-Falaij, A. (1987). Type A behavior pattern and the self-evaluation of abilities: Empirical tests of the self-appraisal model. *Journal of Personality and Social Psychology, 52,* 956–974.

Strube, M. J., & Werner, C. (1985). Relinquishment of control and the Type A behavior pattern. *Journal of Personality and Social Psychology, 48,* 688–701.

Suls, J., & Fletcher, B. (1985). The relative efficacy of avoidant and non-avoidant coping strategies: A meta-analysis. *Health Psychology, 4,* 249–288.

Temoshok, L. (1987). Personality, coping style, emotion and cancer: Towards an integrative model. *Cancer Surveys, 6,* 545–567.

Temoshok, L., Heller, B. W., Sagebiel, R. W., Blois, M. S., Sweet, D. M., DiClemente, R. J., & Gold, M. L. (1985). The relationship of psychosocial factors to prognostic indicators in cutaneous malignant melanoma. *Journal of Psychosomatic Research, 29,* 139–154.

Watkins, P. L., Fisher, E. B., Southard, D. R., Ward, C. H., & Schechtman, K. B. (1989). Assessing the relationship of Type A beliefs to cardiovascular disease risk and psychosocial distress. *Journal of Psychopathology and Behavioral Assessment, 11,* 113–125.

Watson, D., & Pennebaker, J. W. (1989). Health complaints, stress, and distress: Exploring the central role of negative affectivity. *Psychological Review, 96,* 234–254.

Weinberger, D. A., Schwartz, G. E., & Davidson, R. J. (1979). Low-anxious, high-anxious, and repressive coping styles: Psychosomatic patterns and behavioral and physiologic responses to stress. *Journal of Abnormal Psychology, 88,* 369–380.

Williams, R. B., & Barefoot, J. C. (1988). Coronary-prone behavior: The emerging role of the hostility complex. In B. K. Houston & C. R. Snyder (Eds.), *Type A behavior pattern: Research, theory, and intervention* (pp. 189–211). New York: Wiley.

Wirsching, M., Stierlin, H., Hoffman, F., Weber, G., & Wirsching, B. (1982). Psychological identification of breast cancer patients before biopsy. *Journal of Psychosomatic Research, 26,* 1–10.

Wright, R. A., Contrada, R. J., & Glass, D. C. (1985). Psychophysiological correlates of Type A behavior. In E. S. Katkin & S. B. Manuck (Eds.), *Advances in behavioral medicine* (pp. 39–88). Greenwich, CT: JAI Press.

Chapter 25

Personality and Politics

Dean Keith Simonton
University of California–Davis

The fundamental tenet of personality psychology is that people vary: Considerable individual differences exist on an impressive array of traits, and this variation presumably translates into consistent patterns of behavior across diverse situations. Equally manifest to any observer of the political scene is the parallel axiom that people differ in their relevant attitudes and actions. This personal diversity is apparent in ideology, party affiliation, candidate preferences, policy choices, and political leadership, just to list the more obvious examples. For the personality psychologist fascinated with political phenomena, the central question is this: How do the personal traits that are so conspicuous in everyday life determine the more exceptional events that characterize the world of politics? Owing to the inherent complexity of politics, this issue breaks down into three subsidiary questions (cf. Elms, 1976; Greenstein, 1987). First, how does personality affect the political follower, whether the common citizen, voter, or passive participant in politics? Second, how is personality involved in the policy and performance of the political leader? Third, how does personality enter into the attitudes and behaviors of the political activist, the individual who often occupies the middle ground between follower and leader?

Now all three of these subsidiary issues are important, even if not equally so. Nevertheless, from a purely historical perspective, investigators have tended to favor the follower as the subject of inquiry. Such is the clear emphasis of the classic investigation in this area, that of *The Authoritarian Personality* (Adorno, Frenkel-Brunswik, Levinson, & Sanford, 1950). One cause for this focus may have been postwar bewilderment about how a whole nation could succumb to the Nazi ideology of Adolf Hitler. Because the personality syndrome that defines authoritarianism is unrestricted to a particular time or place, this question also enjoyed immediate relevance for comprehending political movements in contemporary democracies as well, where the dispositions of the masses can quickly be converted into national policies. Yet another reason why studies of the follower have been so prominent was simply that such inquiries are far more readily executed. Given a batch of personality tests in one hand, and a batch of attitude questionnaires in the other, it is a relatively easy matter to administer these measures to a sample of subjects, whether college students or survey respondents.

In contrast to studies of the followers, investigations of leaders and activists have tended to be more restricted, at least until recently. The most frequent approach to the examination of leaders has been the psychobiographical analysis of particular leaders (see Cocks, 1986; Glad, 1973; Tetlock, Crosby, & Crosby, 1981). Objects of such treatment include Hitler (Binion, 1976; Langer, 1972), Gandhi (Erikson, 1969), Woodrow Wilson (Freud & Bullitt, 1967; George & George, 1956), Richard M. Nixon (Brodie, 1983; Chesen, 1973; Mazlish, 1972), Lyndon B. Johnson (Kearns, 1976), and Jimmy Carter (Glad, 1980). Nonetheless, in recent years remarkable progress has been made in the quantitative and nomothetic analysis of political leaders (e.g., Hermann, 1977a) and, to a far lesser extent, activists (e.g., Costantini & Craik, 1972, 1980; Knutson, 1974). These advances may be said to have begun with David Winter and his colleagues, who all endeavored to show how the motives of public figures, U.S. presidents in particular, can be assessed at a distance and the impact of these motives on performance objectively measured (e.g., Donley & Winter, 1970; Wendt & Light, 1976; Winter, 1973, 1980, 1988). Other researchers have developed methods to gauge the cognitive styles of leaders; this work has been led by Peter Suedfeld, Philip Tetlock, and their associates (e.g., Suedfeld & Rank, 1976; Tetlock, 1981a). Still other investigators have tried to extend standard personality instruments and techniques, such as the Q-sort and adjective checklist, to biographical materials concerning otherwise inaccessible political leaders (e.g., Historical Figures Assessment Collaborative [HFAC], 1977; Milburn, 1977; Simonton, 1986c). Finally, several adventurous political scientists have applied personality concepts and methods in the study of political actors (e.g., Etheredge, 1978; Hermann, 1980, 1980b).

This current work has immensely enhanced our understanding of the part that personality plays in politics. After all, followers must ultimately have leaders to follow, and even the activists serve largely as go-betweens from leaders to followers. Without a full appreciation of the role of personality in political leadership, our knowledge can only be fragmented and incomplete. Because it is my belief that the psychometric examination of political leaders represents the leading edge of current personality research, the present chapter is primarily a review of this innovative work. I think it is fair to assert that the heyday of personality studies conducted on the typical citizen is past; the

personality traits germane to citizen ideology and candidate preferences have been inventoried many times (e.g., DiRenzo, 1974; Elms, 1976; Greenstein, 1987). In addition, although I am not deliberately neglecting the literature on political activists, this work still represents a minuscule fraction of the entire corpus of published investigations. Finally, even though the emphasis is on the connection between personality and political leadership, little space is granted to psychobiographical treatments. For the most part, such analyses have leaned heavily on both theoretical perspectives and methodological approaches that cannot be considered a central current in mainstream personality research (see Simonton, 1981a, 1983b). Indeed, political psychobiography, with only few exceptions, is an enterprise of political scientists, historians, and psychoanalysts who lack formal training in contemporary personality theory and research methodology.

All this is not to say that this chapter surveys nomothetic studies of political leadership to the exclusion of all other issues in the personality-and-politics domain, but only that these matters are treated mostly to the degree that they shed light on the central topic of concern (see also Hermann, 1977a, 1986). I begin by presenting the highlights of the diverse empirical findings. Then I turn to a discussion of some of the most critical substantive problems that must be confronted by researchers in this area.

SOME EMPIRICAL FINDINGS

The majority of studies have concentrated on more narrowly defined personality traits, with the goal of showing how individual variations on these select dispositions correspond with concrete contrasts in political attitudes and behaviors. Less common are those investigations that attempt to gauge a wider range of traits in order to discern a more complex pattern of personality profiles.

Specific Personality Traits

The attributes of character that leave the biggest impression on political affairs involve both cognitive inclinations, which govern how an individual perceives and thinks about the world, and motivational dispositions, which energize and channel individual actions in the

below, I examine examples from four
ct research programs—the first two large-
concerning cognition (or attitudes), and the
st two motivation (or affect).

Authoritarianism

As noted in the introduction, the classic investigation on the personality–politics connection is the work conducted by Adorno et al.
(1950) on authoritarianism. On the basis of
extensive interviews conducted at the University of California–Berkeley, these researchers
were able to devise a series of measures that
captured various components of personality
deemed most supportive of fascist policies and
practices. Hence, an anti-Semitism scale
gauged whether an individual possessed extremely prejudicial (and often contradictory)
stereotypes about Jews. Because anti-Semitic
people often exhibited negative attitudes about
other ethnic groups as well, a more comprehensive ethnocentrism scale was created to
assess any strong bias in favor of conventional,
majority-culture values. A political–economic
conservatism scale more directly measured a
person's ideological orientation in the world of
politics, and a conservative inclination was
shown to correlate positively with ethnocentric
and anti-Semitic beliefs.

But the jewel of all these novel assessment
devices is clearly the F Scale, which purports to
evaluate an individual's "potentiality for fas-
cism." Such a proclivity would necessarily subsume the more narrow attitudes addressed by
the preceding Berkeley scales, and in fact scores
on the F Scale were shown to correlate positively with all three. In addition, the F Scale
assessed a broad authoritarian syndrome that
was ultimately rooted in a psychodynamic
theory. In other words, those persons who hold
authoritarian beliefs are suffering from a kind of
personality disorder; their attitudes serve as
outward manifestations of deeper emotional
problems. In this way the researchers on the
authoritarian personality tried to integrate
cognitive and motivational sides of political
behavior. Whatever the success of this theoretical integration, the F Scale soon became one
of the most widely used instruments in personality and social psychology. Study after
study showed that high scores on this measure
indeed predicted a diverse array of real-life political attitudes and behaviors.

Even if this literature has quite successfully

proven that personality matters in politics, the
authoritarian research has provoked its share of
criticisms (see Christie & Jahoda, 1954). For
current purposes, the most potent complaint is
that the F Scale displays a pronounced political
bias: It assesses authoritarianism on only one
end of the political spectrum—the right-wing
or conservative pole. Yet reactionary extremists
may not have a monopoly on authoritarianism.
If this syndrome entails an unquestioning and
rigid submission to specific authority figures,
then leftists of the more extreme persuasions
can readily compete on that score, as the Red
Guards brandishing The Quotations of Chairman
Mao during the Cultural Revolution amply
illustrated. Several investigators have attempted to preserve the essential part of the
authoritarian personality while rendering it free
of particular ideological commitments. The
Dogmatism Scale of Rokeach (1960) is one
such attempt at a more or less content-free
instrument. In addition, Eysenck (1954) has
introduced a two-dimensional model—tough-
versus tender-minded and radical versus conservative—which tries to accommodate all major political positions. When this discussion
turns to the work on integrative complexity,
this issue reappears.

Notwithstanding any criticisms and refinements, the basic notion underlying authoritarianism remains sound. The denizens of
any country vary appreciably in authoritarianism, and this variation has crucial consequences for political events. At the same
time, we must recognize that authoritarianism
is not just a permanent trait, but an alterable
state besides. Even if we can assume that authoritarianism is normally distributed in the
population of any given nation, certain circumstances may serve to raise or lower the
mean level of authoritarianism. Some of these
external conditions have to do with child-
rearing practices, such as severity of discipline,
which make a permanent imprint on the magnitude of authoritarianism later observed. But
other exogenous inputs may be more transient,
yet no less critical as determinants of the political milieu. In particular, research suggests that
any individual tendencies toward authoritarianism may be aggravated when a person confronts severe threat (Sales, 1972).
In such stressful instances, authoritarianism
serves as a sort of defense mechanism or self-
protective coping behavior. Hence, whenever
a nation is faced with an extremely threatening

situation or crisis, the average level of authoritarianism in the population may shift upwards; this change in the personality emphasis of the populace then causes a corresponding increase in the kinds of political attitudes and actions that typify the authoritarian.

A series of archival investigations has demonstrated this very real causal linkage. In the first such inquiry, Sales (1972) looked at how economic ups and downs affected the rates of conversion to authoritarian versus nonauthoritarian churches in the United States. Whereas a nonauthoritarian church grants its members considerable latitude in both behavior and belief, an authoritarian church is one that enforces absolute obedience to doctrine and prescription. Just as hypothesized, economic prosperity inspired growth in the membership of nonauthoritarian churches, whereas economic hardship encouraged conversions to the authoritarian denominations. In a posthumously published follow-up study, Sales (1973) isolated cultural indices of the several components of the authoritarian syndrome, and showed that threatening conditions brought about the expected shifts in these indicators. Thus, during the Great Depression, comic strip characters exhibited more power and toughness; magazine articles became more cynical; books on superstitious topics (e.g., astrology) saw improved sales; interest in psychology and psychoanalysis declined (anti-intraception); and punishment for sex crimes became more harsh.

Subsequent work only reinforces Sales's conclusion that threatening environmental conditions nurture the expression of authoritarianism. For example, a troubled economy is associated with the preference of the American people for highly authoritarian television programs (Jorgenson, 1975). And threatening circumstances have even been shown to affect the appearance of parapsychological research in the professional journals, a presumed index of superstitious beliefs (McCann & Stewin, 1984). Nor is this nomothetic principle restricted to the United States: The popularity of astrology and mysticism, as gauged by book sales, was strongly tied to the state of the German economy between the two world wars (Padgett & Jorgenson, 1982). The significance of this fact is obvious, for it was in this historical interval that Hitler rose to power, ultimately leading to the very chain of events that originally motivated the Berkeley research on the authoritarian personality.

Integrative Complexity

Despite the attempt to ground authoritarianism in unconscious motives, the primary component of this trait from the standpoint of politics may remain the cognitive: Those who score high on the F Scale tend to think in extremely rigid, simplistic categories, to conceive of the world in terms of quite polarized stereotypes, and to display a conspicuous intolerance for ambiguity in their environment. This aspect of authoritarianism links directly with the more recent research on "integrative complexity," a construct that explicitly stresses the role of information-processing sophistication on political thought and conduct. The parallel between the two research traditions extends to the trait-versus-state issue as well. People vary significantly in their capacity for integratively complex thinking, which requires finely differentiated and yet fully integrated representations of the milieu. At the same time, external circumstances may serve to raise or lower the amount of integrative complexity shown, stressful events being particularly likely to provoke more simple-minded cognition. Yet one remarkable contrast between the two lines of research is that whereas authoritarianism measures have concentrated on the follower, the measures of integrative complexity have been applied to actual leaders, including revolutionaries, legislators, diplomats, and chief executives. This application was accomplished by adapting a regular psychometric instrument, the Paragraph Completion Test (Schroder, Driver, & Streufert, 1967), to documentary materials. Once this content-analytical coding method was devised, scores on integrative complexity could be obtained from letters, speeches, or interviews. Individual variations on this trait could then be correlated with assessments of leader performance and policy.

The first such inquiry was conducted by Suedfeld and Rank (1976), who wondered why some revolutionaries are more successful than are others. By "success" the investigators meant that once a regime has been overthrown, the central agents differ in whether they manage to stay in power as the new government consolidates. Presumably it takes a fanatical single-mindedness of purpose to pull off a revolution, but to participate in the actual governing of a nation requires a more complex mode of thought, and some revolutionaries may be quite incapable of making the necessary shift.

By examining the integrative complexity of 19 key figures in five revolutions, Suedfeld and Rank demonstrated a significant tendency for the failures to persist in their simple-minded habits of thought, whereas the successes managed to alter their pattern of thinking in order to formulate more realistic policies. The contrast between Lenin and Trotsky illustrates this marked discrepancy.

Subsequent investigations have shown that integrative complexity predicts successful outcomes in other domains as well. For example, low scores on this variable tend to be characteristic of decision makers engaged in "groupthink," which results in suboptimal, even foolish choices, such as the Bay of Pigs fiasco early in the Kennedy administration (Tetlock, 1979; cf. Janis, 1972). Other studies indicate that international crises are less likely to lead to war if the participants avoid conceptual simplicity when dealing with the key points of contention (Raphael, 1982; Suedfeld & Tetlock, 1977; Suedfeld, Tetlock, & Ramirez, 1977). Curiously, should a war break out, integrative complexity may even determine success on the battlefield. Robert E. Lee's odds of victory or defeat during the American Civil War were partly a function of whether his complexity score was superior to that of his opponent. The one Union general whose integrative complexity tended to surpass that of Lee was no less than Ulysses S. Grant (Suedfeld, Corteen, & McCormick, 1986).

Integrative complexity influences not just performance, but policy preferences besides. For instance, after an objective content analysis of the speeches by 35 senators in the 82nd Congress of the United States, Tetlock (1981a) showed that those who advocated isolationism had lower integrative complexity scores than those who defended America's continued active involvement in world affairs (see also Hermann, 1977b, 1980a). Significantly, the relevance of this characteristic extends beyond this specific policy matter, for integrative complexity scores correspond to a legislator's placement on the classic liberal-to-conservative political spectrum. To show this, Tetlock (1983) used 1975 and 1976 voting records to classify American senators into liberal, moderate, and conservative predispositions. The policy statements of the conservative senators were considerably lower on the integrative complexity dimension than was the case for their moderate and liberal colleagues. Because the left

wing appears to feature about the same integrative complexity as that found in the political center, one might conclude that this finding parallels the results of the research on authoritarianism. This apparent convergence, however, is complicated by two considerations.

First, because the conservative senators represented the minority viewpoint in the mid-1970s, they may have adopted a rhetorical strategy of public confrontation: The party out of power may concentrate less on convincing opponents in the Senate chamber and more on registering a simple, direct protest with the American people. In line with this interpretation is Tetlock's (1981b) demonstration that the speeches of U.S. presidential candidates are far lower in integrative complexity than are the pronouncements of the same politicians when they become presidents—a dramatic shift that is practically instantaneous. Nevertheless, when Tetlock compared two Congresses dominated by conservatives with three dominated by liberals and moderates, no complete reversal of roles was seen (Tetlock, Hannum, & Micheletti, 1984). The liberals and moderates declined in integrative complexity, to be sure, but the conservatives did not show a proportionate increase on the same dimension. Furthermore, the same connection between integrative complexity and political ideology holds for justices of the U.S. Supreme Court, regardless of the circumstances (Tetlock, Bernzweig, & Gallant, 1985).

Second, because the extreme left, unlike the extreme right, has never found a voice in the U.S. Senate (or a place on the bench of the Supreme Court), the discovery of low integrative complexity on the left may be simply impossible. Never has this country selected communists, or even socialists, to serve in either august body. Therefore, to test properly whether leftists can boast their share of dogmatic cognition, we must turn to legislatures where the full range of ideologies tends to earn representation. Hence, Tetlock (1984) content-analyzed confidential interviews with 89 members of the British House of Commons. In line with expectation, both extreme socialists and extreme conservatives exhibited a predilection for simple, undifferentiated, and unidimensional mental habits, and both poles were decidedly distinguishable from the more respectable integrative complexity manifested by the moderate conservatives and the moderate socialists. So idealogues of all persuasions tend to display a more rigid and narrow kind of information processing.

The clear linkage between cognitive style and political ideology notwithstanding, we must still acknowledge that integrative complexity is both a trait of individuals and a state susceptible to modification by extrinsic conditions, just as was found for authoritarianism. Thus, political crises and violence may motivate momentary drops in integrative complexity in both leaders and followers (Ballard, 1983; Porter & Suedfeld, 1981; Suedfeld, 1980; Suedfeld et al., 1986). In addition, the leaders of competing nations interact with each other in such a manner that the integrative complexity of one leader is sure to affect the complexity of the rival leader, yielding an intricate feedback process that unfolds over time (Tetlock, 1985). When all of these factors are added up, the precise way in which integrative complexity intervenes in politics as a personality trait—as opposed to a rhetorical strategy or transient coping mechanism—is not always easily deciphered. Even so, the research gathered to date does suggest that integrative complexity shapes both performance and policy (see also Hermann, 1980b).

Power, Achievement, and Affiliation Motives

Common sense suggests that cognition alone cannot account for all that happens in the political arena: Behind each event, each decision or goal, must dwell an impetus, a motivating force. People differ not only in information-processing capacity, but also in fundamental drives, and such differences may have political manifestations. The difficulty in demonstrating this seemingly straightforward proposition involves measurement. How do we go about assessing the ulterior or even unconscious motives of political actors? One conceivable solution is to take full advantage of cultural indicators, such as was done in establishing the association between economic threat and authoritarianism. In Winter's (1973) book *The Power Motive*, we witness this very application. After setting down a solid case that the Don Juan legend provides an archetype of the need for power, Winter showed how imperialistic military adventures are positively associated with the legend's popularity, as revealed by the emergence of new renditions in European literature (cf. McClelland, 1975).

Nevertheless, an alternative approach is feasible—one that has the advantage of being more directly applicable to political leaders. Just as the Paragraph Completion Test was converted to a scheme by which documents could be scored for integrative complexity, so can Murray's (1938) projective measure, the Thematic Apperception Test, be modified to score letters, speeches, and the like on the human drives most pertinent to politics. This extension was first accomplished by Donley and Winter (1970), who used inaugural addresses to gauge the power and achievement motives for 20th-century U.S. presidents. After a series of follow-up studies, almost all American chief executives have now been assessed on the three most politically relevant motives—power, achievement, and affiliation (Wendt & Light, 1976; Winter, 1973, 1987b; Winter & Stewart, 1977; cf. Winter, 1988). In these assessments, the need for power concerns the drive to control or influence others; the need for achievement involves the quest for excellence or unprecedented accomplishment; and the need for affiliation involves the desire for friendship, love, or companionship.

Scores on the three motives have then been related to a wide range of performance and policy variables. For example, such scores correspond to the two-dimensional typology advocated by Barber (1977) in his popular book *The Presidential Character*: Active rather than passive presidents are notable for their high needs for achievement and power but low need for affiliation; affectively positive rather than negative presidents are noticeably high in power needs but low in achievement needs (Winter & Stewart, 1977; cf. Winter, 1980). More detailed research findings are as follows:

1. The need for power emerges as the most influential motive behind presidential leadership. For one thing, those chief executives who score higher on power motivation may be more likely to enter the United States into a war (Winter, 1973, 1987b; Winter & Stewart, 1977; cf. McClelland, 1975, Ch. 9) and to expand U.S. territorial holdings (Winter, 1973). Curiously, a high power motive may also allow a president to prevent an international crisis from escalating into a full-fledged military conflict, perhaps by enabling the president to project a more imposing image of national strength (Winter, 1973). Power-prone presidents may be something of a liability, however, insofar as they are not positively

disposed toward completing arms limitation agreements with rival nations (Winter & Stewart, 1977; cf. Winter, 1987b). In domestic affairs, the power-oriented chief executive tends to enjoy better relations with the press (Wendt & Light, 1976), but also has a greater chance of attracting an assassination attempt (Wendt & Light, 1976; Winter, 1973; see also Simonton, 1986c). The power motive may bear some relation to political affiliation as well, for Democratic presidents tend to score higher than Republican chief executives (Wendt & Light, 1976). Finally, a conspicuous power drive may be responsible for a president's making more "great decisions" in office (Winter, 1987b), and for a president's going down in history as one of the more highly regarded chief executives (Winter, 1987b; Winter & Stewart, 1977). For the most part, the power motive seems to produce a vigorous and competent presidency, albeit one potentially dangerous to either the nation or the president himself.

2. By contrast, the achievement motive has fewer implications for the exercise of political leadership. The main problem in identifying a unique role for this trait is that in presidents, unlike in the general population, power and achievement motives tend to be highly positively correlated (Wendt & Light, 1976; Winter & Stewart, 1977). Whenever this correlation is controlled for, the need for achievement all too often has minimal relevance apart from its linkage with the need for power (Winter & Stewart, 1977). However, one consequence is that those presidents strong in the achievement motive may experience higher rates of Cabinet turnover, as continuity and conviviality are sacrificed for the sake of getting the job done (Wendt & Light, 1976; Winter & Stewart, 1977). The achievement motive is also linked with arms limitations, albeit at only a modest level (Winter & Stewart, 1977). Nevertheless, an exceptional achievement motive may still prove pertinent to our understanding of a leader's behavior. In an interesting deduction from nomothetic principles, Winter and Carlson (1988) showed that many of the paradoxes of Richard Nixon's political career can be explicated, once we consider that he was driven far more by a desire for achievement and affiliation than by power.

3. In general, an affiliation-oriented presidency tends to be more flexible in dealing with both foreign and domestic issues (Winter & Stewart, 1977). And at the specific level of foreign policy, an above-average need for affiliation is related to a greater probability of successful agreements to limit armaments (Winter, 1987b; cf. Hermann, 1980a). But at the domestic level, a president may be somewhat less effective. Whereas chief executives who score high in achievement and power motivation apparently select Cabinet secretaries according to competence and expertise, presidents who are driven primarily by a quest for friends and social approval are inclined to appoint Cabinet officials who make better cronies than experts (Winter & Stewart, 1977). An immediate repercussion is that affiliative presidents suffer higher chances of having a scandal break out in their administration (Winter & Stewart, 1977). By placing so much weight on surrounding themselves with chums who cannot easily be fired, and who tend to be trusted far more than their competence and integrity would justify, such presidents virtually invite moral infractions by those pals with the sleaziest ethical standards.

The relevance of the three motives has been demonstrated for other leaders besides U.S. presidents, so their influence may be ubiquitous (e.g., Hermann, 1980a, 1980b; Winter, 1980). Nevertheless, I should emphasize the fact that the foregoing results, though often provocative, are frequently tentative besides. Thus, sometimes different patterns of relationships emerged as the sample of presidents examined via this methodology was enlarged from the original 11 to the current 34 (Donley & Winter, 1970; Winter, 1987b). Moreover, as is often the case for projective measures, alternative quantifications of the three core motives do not always correlate highly, even when assessed by the same researcher (Simonton, 1988c). Also, critics have sometimes questioned the validity of inferring motives from public pronouncements, whether formal speeches or spontaneous responses (e.g., Rasler, Thompson, & Chester, 1980). Lastly, bivariate relationships often vanish when subjected to more sophisticated multivariate analyses that introduce appropriate statistical controls. As a case in point, the power motive is at best only an indirect antecedent of presidential greatness, a factor that operates only through such direct determinants as war and assassination (Simonton, 1986c, 1987b, 1988c).

Even so, taken as a whole, the research conducted by David Winter and his associates provides sufficient indications that the motives of politicians may indeed influence the effectiveness and direction of their leadership (see also Walker & Falkowski, 1984; Winter, 1980, 1987a). This conclusion is only bolstered by the next pair of motivational traits, which are closely bound to power and affiliation needs.

Dominance and Extraversion

Up to this point, it has been shown that the personality psychologist is by no means confined to standard psychometric "pencil-and-paper" measures when examining political phenomena. Cultural indicators can serve as proxy indices of cognitive and motivational dispositions among the masses, and content-analytical coding methods can be operationalized directly from more orthodox personality instruments. There remains yet a third methodological strategy—that of abstracting individual traits immediately from biographical data. Several psychologists initiated the development of this procedure for historical figures (Cox, 1926; HFAC, 1977; Thorndike, 1936, 1950); however, it was a political scientist, Lloyd Etheredge (1978), who first established the utility of this technique for unearthing the tie between personality and political leadership. Etheredge's specific goal was to test the "interpersonal generalization theory." Individuals all have preferred patterns of social relationships, and these interpersonal dispositions may slant a political leader's perspective on the optimal interactions among sovereign nations. Desirable international relations are those that are isomorphic with favored interpersonal relations (see also Hermann, 1980a, 1980b).

This hypothesis was tested on a collection of 36 presidents and presidential advisers who made American foreign policy from 1898 to 1968, the period when the United States emerged as a world power. To determine the impact of personality and policy, Etheredge had to accomplish two things. First, the policy makers had to be distinguished on pertinent personality variables on the basis of biographical information. The variables selected were dominance over subordinates and extraversion—how much an individual likes to lord it over others and how friendly and outgoing that individual tends to be with others. Etheredge was able to obtain measures of each characteristic that were both reliable (accord-

ing to interrater concurrence) and consistent with alternative measures (content-analytical indicators of the power and achievement motives).

Second, occasions had to be identified in which the policy makers disagreed over some issue in international relations. Because a president picks his own advisers, and because political precedents are so powerfully pervasive, such conflicts do not happen often; when they do, however, personality biases may be revealed. Etheredge found 62 instances of such disagreements: 49 of these had to do with the use of force or threat to settle international problems, and another 13 concerned inclusionary issues (i.e., whether to include or exclude the Soviet Union and members of the Soviet bloc). For each of the policy debates Etheredge recorded who took what side, and then determined the number of times that the side advocated fit with the policy maker's personality. In fully 75% of the cases the position advocated was in absolute concordance with interpersonal disposition. Dominant individuals preferred to employ force to achieve policy goals in international affairs, and extraverted individuals tended to recommend inclusionary gestures toward America's ideological rivals.

On the basis of these results, Etheredge conceived a two-dimensional typology describing how the personality makes itself felt in foreign affairs. Once we distinguish high- versus low-dominance types and extraverted versus introverted types, we obtain a fourfold classification. High-dominance introverts are "bloc-excluding leaders" who try to restrict potentially disruptive forces by setting up exclusive blocs, such as alliances. Low-dominance introverts are mere "maintainers," passively committed to preserving the status quo in international affairs. Low-dominance extraverts, by contrast, function as "conciliators"—leaders whose involvement in foreign relations is both conspicuous and ineffectual, as their interest is not backed up by vigor. Finally, the high-dominance extraverts set out to actively reform international affairs by bringing all powers into a more orderly system, becoming thereby "world-integrating leaders." To illustrate, Wilson was a bloc-excluding leader; Coolidge was a maintainer; Harding and Eisenhower were both conciliators; and the two Roosevelts, Kennedy, and Lyndon Johnson were all world-integrating leaders.

The important lesson to be gained from Etheredge's study is that the formulation of foreign policy is not a totally rational procedure. Except when extrinsic considerations dictate a consensus on recommendations, policy makers will project their own preferences in interpersonal relationships on the global scene (see also Hermann, 1977a, 1980a, 1980b).

General Personality Profiles

The collection of politically germane traits presented above makes an impressive list. If there were no space limitations on this chapter whatsoever, I could continue by enumerating more personality characteristics that have been associated with political activities in some fashion (e.g., Cell, 1974; Hermann, 1980a, 1980b; Hoffer, 1978; Leitner, 1983; Mahoney, Coogle, & Banks, 1984; Milburn, 1977; Miller & Stiles, 1986; Rokeach, Homant, & Penner, 1970; Stiles, Au, Martello, & Perlmutter, 1983; Zullow, Oettingen, Peterson, & Seligman, 1988). The drawback to compiling such trait inventories is obvious: As items proliferate we soon become inundated with so many variables that conceptual confusion soon replaces analytical clarity. This mess is only aggravated by the apparent but undefined overlap between the variables. Obviously authoritarianism and integrative complexity cover some of the same facets of cognitive style, just as the power motive and interpersonal dominance cover similar personal needs. Consequently, what is required is a research strategy by which a more exhaustive range of personality traits can be evaluated and their impact on political events determined. Such a procedure would give us the capacity to generate rich personality profiles for political actors—profiles that predict a corresponding array of attitudes and behaviors. To be complete, this framework should deal with both cognitive and motivational dispositions, and both personal and social orientations.

Below, I briefly describe two initial attempts at deriving a broader scheme for assessing personality in politicians. Both investigations were limited to assessments of American presidents, although the techniques are certainly generalizable to other varieties of political leadership (cf. Hermann, 1980a, 1980b; Simonton, 1983a, 1984b; Winter, 1980). Both studies also derive personality measures from biographical data rather than through content analysis of primary materials.

The Gough Adjective Check List Study

In the first study (Simonton, 1986c), personality descriptions were first abstracted from biographical data on all 39 presidents. A team of naive raters then converted these raw data to ratings on the 300 descriptors in the Gough Adjective Check List (ACL; Gough & Heilbrun, 1965). Due to floor and ceiling effects, the presidents could only be reliably differentiated on 110 of the adjectives. This subset of traits was then subjected to a factor analysis in order to obtain a smaller set of cohesive personality dimensions. The 14 factors that resulted were as follows (with characteristic ACL adjectives in parentheses): Moderation ("moderate" and "modest" vs. "temperamental" and "hasty"), Friendliness ("friendly" and "outgoing" vs. "unfriendly" and "cold"), Intellectual Brilliance ("wide" and "artistic" interests), Machiavellianism ("sly" and "deceitful" vs. "sincere" and "honest"), Poise and Polish ("poised" and "polished" vs. "simple" and "informal"), Achievement Drive ("industrious" and "persistent"), Forcefulness ("energetic" and "active"), Wit ("humorous" and "witty"), Physical Attractiveness ("handsome" and "good-looking"), Pettiness ("greedy" and "self-pitying"), Tidiness ("methodological" and "organized"), Conservatism ("conservative" and "conventional"), Inflexibility ("stubborn" and "persistent"), and Pacifism ("peaceable" vs. "courageous"). (For standardized scores, see Simonton, 1986c.)

The derived dimensions correlate in a predictable manner with alternative assessments of the presidents, including those originating in content analysis (for details, see Simonton, 1986c; 1987b, pp. 146–147). To offer a few examples: Winter and Stewart's (1977) indicator of power motivation correlates positively with Forcefulness but negatively with Pacifism and Moderation, whereas their measure of achievement motivation correlates positively with Achievement Drive; Forcefulness correlates positively with Etheredge's (1978) indicator of interpersonal dominance, and Friendliness with his gauge of extraversion; Machiavellianism is negatively associated with historians' ratings of presidential idealism (Maranell, 1970); and Intellectual Brilliance correlates with two alternative indicators of intelligence (Cox, 1926; Thorndike, 1950).

Admittedly, the 14 measures are not entirely orthogonal, but the correlations that exist among the dimensions make substantive sense. For instance, moderate presidents tend to be friendly, conservative, and pacifistic, but neither forceful nor inflexible. At any rate, given the 14 measures, we can then employ a cluster analysis to determine which presidents exhibit the most similar personality profiles. Figure 25.1 shows the dendrogram that results.

Besides using the scores to cluster those presidents with the more nearly comparable pro-

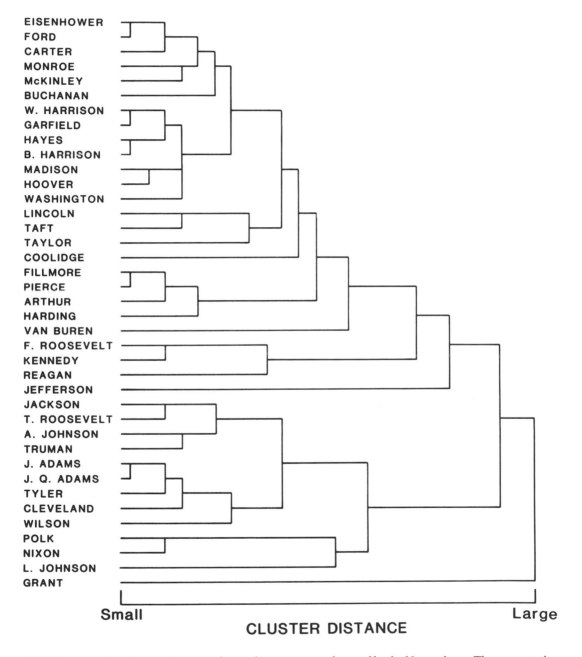

FIGURE 25.1. Dendrogram depicting the similarity in personality profiles for 39 presidents. The most similar presidents are grouped together on the left, the least similar on the right. From "Presidential Personality: Biographical Use of the Gough Adjective Check List" by D. K. Simonton, 1986, *Journal of Personality and Social Psychology, 51,* 149–160. Copyright 1986 by the American Psychological Association. Reprinted by permission.

files, we can also use them to link personality with biographical and performance variables (Simonton, 1986c, 1987b). As an example of a biographical antecedent, those chief executives who come from large families tend to be higher on Moderation and on Poise and Polish, but lower on Forcefulness and Inflexibility. From the perspective of political leadership, presidents who succeed best as legislators usually display the most Machiavellianism, Forcefulness, Moderation, and Poise and Polish, but the least Inflexibility (cf. Alker, 1981). Inflexible presidents do not get along well with Congress, at least in the sense that they are obliged to use the veto power more often and are more likely to have their appointees to the Supreme Court and the Cabinet rejected by the Senate. One of the more intriguing findings has to do with how controversial a chief executive becomes, as defined by how much historians later disagree on the merits of his presidency (Murray & Blessing, 1983). Controversiality is positively correlated with Achievement Drive, Forcefulness, Pettiness, and Inflexibility, and negatively correlated with Moderation, Friendliness, and Wit. More examples of valuable trait–performance correlations are given later, so it may suffice here to say that this historiometric inquiry clearly indicates the impact of personality on politics.

The Presidential Style Study

Despite the apparent utility of applying the Gough ACL to biographical descriptions, the effects of personality on political leadership may be a more complex affair. Instead of using highly generalized personality traits that are descriptive of any *Homo sapiens*, it may prove advantageous to develop richer constructs. One solution is the "presidential style Q-sort," which assesses presidents on 82 ways of differentiating the leadership style that an American politician carries into office (Simonton, 1988c; cf. HFAC, 1977; Milburn, 1977; Stogdill, Goode, & Day, 1977). With a few minor modifications, this instrument was applied to the biographical materials exploited in the preceding study, again using a team of naive judges. A factor analysis was performed on the 49 items on which the 39 chief executives from Washington to Reagan could be reliably differentiated; this analysis yielded five broad stylistic dimensions, which may be briefly described as follows:

1. *Interpersonality.* The interpersonal president emphasizes good relationships with his Cabinet members and top aides, stresses teamwork, is flexible and always willing to compromise, and is exceptionally courteous and considerate toward his staff.

2. *Charisma.* The charismatic president displays his charisma in the pleasure he takes in dealing with the press and with executing the ceremonial responsibilities of the office; viewing the presidency as a vehicle for self-expression, he has a flair for the dramatic, uses rhetoric effectively, and consciously refines his public image so as to convey a clear-cut, highly visible personality; and he is a dynamo of energy and determination who can maintain his popularity and who is characterized by others as a world figure.

3. *Deliberation.* The deliberative president commonly understands the implications of his decisions and is able to visualize alternatives and weigh long-term consequences; being cautious and conservative in action, he keeps himself thoroughly informed by reading briefings and background reports. Only infrequently does he indulge in emotional outbursts.

4. *Creativity.* The creative president frequently initiates new legislation and programs and is generally innovative in his role as an executive, but is far from a "middle-of-the-roader."

5. *Neuroticism.* The neurotic president most often suffers health problems that tend to parallel difficult and critical periods in office; places political success over effective policy; and adopts an indirect, complicated approach to the office.

The stylistic factors correlate in meaningful ways with alternative gauges of presidential personality. For instance, Charisma is more strongly associated with the power motive and Creativity with the achievement motive in Winter and Stewart's (1977) schema; and in Barber's (1977) classification, active presidents are charismatic and, especially, creative, whereas positive presidents are interpersonal in style. The five styles exhibit interesting correlations with the ACL descriptors. For instance, the interpersonal leader is good-natured, pleasant, and easy-going, but not distrustful; the charismatic leader is outgoing, natural, and witty, but neither shy nor withdrawn; the deliberative leader is organized, insightful, polished, methodical, intelligent, and sophisticated; the creative leader is inventive and artistic; and the neurotic leader is evasive. (For correlations between the five styles and the 14 personality dimensions, see Simonton, 1988c.) Furthermore, the five styles are linked with several performance indicators, and they can also be distinguished according to biographical experiences, both personal and professional (Simonton, 1988c). So leadership style has clear relevance in the political world.

CENTRAL SUBSTANTIVE ISSUES

Up to now, this discussion has proceeded as if the primary obstacle to the personality study of politics were a simple matter of measurement. Once the appropriate assessment techniques are devised—whether from cultural indicators, content analyses, or biographical data—the apparent assumption has been that the analysis of politicians and politics may proceed unencumbered. The truth of the matter is different, for a number of critical problems must be considered first—issues that immensely complicate the personality portraits of political leaders. These concerns are three: situational constraints, interaction effects, and curvilinear functions.

Situational Constraints

Avid observers of the political scene frequently draw inferences about a leader's character without taking into full consideration the situational factors that constrain the leader's choices. Social psychologists have devised a name for this very sort of slip—the "fundamental attribution error" (Ross, 1977). This inferential mistake occurs whenever an observer offers judgments about an actor's personality without paying sufficient attention to external determinants of the observed behaviors. Leo Tolstoy (1865–1869/1952) made a good case for the prevalence of this error in the Epilogue to his *War and Peace*. After scrutinizing the career of Napoleon, Tolstoy concluded that epoch-making leadership was not a matter of being the "right person" but rather of happening to be "at the right place at the right time." Tolstoy maintained that "A king is history's slave. . . . In historic events, the so-called great men are labels giving names to events, and like labels they have but the smallest con-

nection with the event itself" (pp. 343–344). This situational interpretation may be styled the "eponym" theory, in which historical personalities merely serve as convenient tags for epochs of history: The bigger and more eventful the period so labeled, the larger looms the corresponding name—regardless of what personality lurked behind this name. Empirical studies of monarchal eminence, presidential greatness, and the vice-presidential succession effect suggest that the fundamental attribution error indeed may be a confounding phenomenon.

Monarchal Eminence

After examining the reign and life spans of all kinds of political leaders, Sorokin (1925) noted that the most famous monarchs of history tend to be those who reigned the longest. Among the French, Louis XIV ("the Great") ruled many times longer than, say, the far less illustrious Francis II. When all other factors are held constant, the more years that a monarch governs, the more events that occur during the reign, and hence the more impressive is the ruler's eponymic value as a label. What makes this connection perplexing is that reign span in hereditary monarchies depends very little on personality traits; in the vast majority of cases length of tenure hinges solely on how old the ruler was upon succession and how long a ruler happened to live. The "Age of Louis XIV" accordingly offers a handy periodization simply because he assumed the throne at age 5 and lived to age 77. To be sure, personality variables may affect both the reign span and the quantity of events that infuse the historical interval, but we cannot assume so without the proper evidence.

Hence, the comparative inputs of individual and situation have been directly evaluated for 342 European monarchs who ruled over 14 European nations from the late Middle Ages to the Napoleonic era (Simonton, 1984b). Figure 25.2 summarizes the findings most critical to the question at hand. The arrows indicate the probable direction of causal influence, and the percentages assigned to each arrow depict the proportion of variance accounted for by that particular causal effect. Clearly the main determinant of leader eminence is historical activity, the last being a direct count of the number of notable events that can be tabulated under a given reign. The single best predictor of the

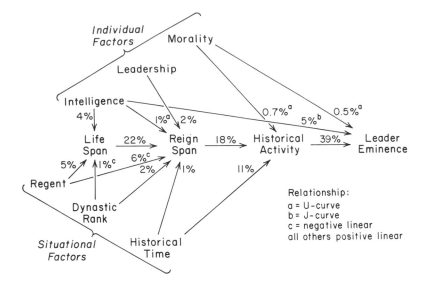

FIGURE 25.2. Summary of the main direct and indirect determinants of the differential eminence attained by 342 monarchs. Both the form of the function and the percentage of variance explained are shown. From "Leaders as Eponyms: Individual and Situational Determinants of Monarchal Eminence" by D. K. Simonton, 1984, *Journal of Personality, 52,* 1–21. Copyright 1984 by Duke University Press. Reprinted by permission.

historical activity count is reign span (with another situational factor, the date the ruler ascended the throne, close behind), and the most critical antecedent of reign span is indeed lifespan. The three links in this central spine of eponymic causality all entail effects that explain between one- and two-fifths of the variance.

This magnitude of effect contrasts sharply with the three personality variables examined—intelligence, leadership, and morality. Gauged from biographical data (Simonton, 1983a; Woods, 1906, 1913), these individual factors do indeed impinge on the causal network at diverse points: Intelligence influences lifespan, reign span, and eminence; leadership affects reign span; and morality determines both historical activity and eminence. Nonetheless, these effects, while important, are puny in comparison to the influx of situational factors. So Tolstoy's theory does not require serious qualification. As further support for this inference, we can note that a ruler's personal responsibility for the events that fill his or her reign is not a relevant consideration when predicting eventual historical distinction (Simonton, 1984b). For instance, battles in which the monarch personally led the armies make the same contribution to the overall eminence score as do those battles fought while the

monarch was lounging far away in the luxuries of the royal palace.

Presidential Greatness

Similar results obtain for U.S. chief executives. A huge data base of biographical, personality, and historical variables has been scanned systematically for sound predictors of the greatness ratings that are sporadically offered by the experts (e.g., Maranell, 1970; Murray & Blessing, 1983; Schlesinger, 1948). Out of the impressive supply of potential predictors, over four-fifths of the variance in the ratings can be anticipated using a mere six variables. Roughly in order of predictive utility (in terms of stability and incremental addition to variance), these are years in office, number of war years, assassination, scandals, status as war hero, and intellectual brilliance (Simonton, 1986a, 1986c, 1988c; cf. Simonton, 1981b, 1986b).

Now there can be no doubt that intellectual brilliance (as measured by the Intellectual Brilliance Factor in the ACL study) marks a personal trait of leaders, and this correlation fits what has been found for monarchs (Simonton, 1984b) and for leaders of all varieties (Simonton, 1985a). But the personological status of the remaining predictors is less obvious. The number of years that a president held office, the most consistent and powerful predictor, is identical to the reign span that proves so conspicuous in the creation of monarchal eminence. Indeed, longer-tenured presidents do make superior eponyms, for years in office correlates positively with a large number of historical activity tabulations, such as the quantity of legislation, major Supreme Court decisions, treaties, and military interventions (Simonton, 1981b, 1986b). To be sure, one might assert that this variable truly reflects quality of personal leadership, under the assumption that only effective chief executives are ever re-elected. Yet the data fail to support this conjecture. Re-election bears no relation with assessed greatness once tenure duration is statistically controlled, whereas the latter variable does persist as a predictor even after the effect of re-election is partialed out (i.e., taking presidents elected the same number of times, those who serve the longest still earn a higher greatness rating). In addition, the primary predictors of years in office, including re-election, are situational rather than individual in nature (Simonton, 1986b, 1987b).

The same situational dominance prevails in the other variables as well. Even if we can say that the power motive raises the probability of leading the United States into a war and of becoming an assassination target (Wendt & Light, 1976; Winter & Stewart, 1977), it is the number of war years and successful assassinations that are the predictors of greatness, and these latter two variables are governed so much by situational influences (not excluding plain chance) that the power motive and other personality attributes prove irrelevant as correlates (Simonton, 1986c, 1987b, 1988c). This is not to say that personality is utterly irrelevant, but only that it is not an easy matter to tease out individual from situational factors. To a respectable though unmeasurable extent, posthumous evaluations of a president's performance are permeated with the fundamental attribution error (cf. Ballard & Suedfeld, 1988).

The Vice-Presidential Succession Effect

To be fair, there is ample reason to suspect that this basic mistake is committed not just by naive academics, but by experienced political professionals. One of the most useful predictors of objective performance in the White House is whether the incumbent entered office via vice-presidential succession upon the death or resignation of his immediate predecessor. Such "accidental presidents" tend to get along horribly with members of Congress, especially the Senate. Specifically, accidental presidents are obliged to rely on the veto power more often in exerting their will over legislation, see a larger number of these same vetoes overturned notwithstanding their expressed desires, and suffer more frequent rejection of their nominees to the Supreme Court and the executive cabinet (Simonton, 1981b, 1985b, 1986b). To provide the most recent instance, Gerald Ford was often criticized for the abnormal rate at which he vetoed bills that landed on his desk—and for the inordinate frequency at which these bills became law without his signature.

One might simply dismiss the poor performance of these unexpected executives by blaming the criteria by which a politician is picked to occupy the secondary spot on the party presidential ticket. Yet vice-presidents do not appreciably differ from presidents on any pertinent item of biographical background, political experience and competence, personality characteristics, or leadership style (Simonton, 1985b, 1986b, 1988c). In addition, the disadvantages plaguing the accidental president only hold during the unelected term of office, when he is filling out the unexpired term of his predecessor (Simonton, 1985b). Such fill-ins are rarely nominated to run for reelection (Simonton, 1981b), but should they be lucky enough to be granted the opportunity, and then be fortunate enough to achieve election to a second term of their own, the performances of the new administrations are indistinguishable from the normal baseline. Obviously, because the same person has served both before and after the general election, we cannot ascribe this substantially improved performance to a sudden change in personality or expertise.

A more plausible interpretation may be that the peculiar context in which the president came to power, especially the heavy dependence on random "luck," compels those on Capitol Hill to ignore the genuine assets possessed by the unelected incumbent. Only when the new leader wins a term in a more "legitimate" manner will this attribution of leadership suddenly become more generous. The mandate urges members of the legislative branch to see leadership skills not seen before. It is worth recalling that the first person to enter the White House through the constitutional back door—namely, John Tyler—was derisively referred to, despite political and personal credentials far superior to those of William Harrison ("Tippecanoe"), as "His Accidency."

It is obvious, then, that personality psychologists must duly weigh situational factors before crediting any leader's actions to internal causes, whether intentions or dispositions.

Interaction Effects

Individual and situation may sway political leadership in more than a simple, additive fashion. Besides straightforward "main effects," success as a leader may require being "the right person at the right place at the right time"—some type of individual × situational interaction effect. Although there have been many attempts to document the existence of multiplicative functions in the world of political action (e.g., Hermann, 1980b; Simonton, 1980, 1986b), perhaps more pertinent illustrations are the matching hypothesis and the Johnson–Wilson effect.

The Matching Hypothesis

No matter what a politician's intrinsic merits, he or she is hardly going to move into a nation's highest office without fitting the "mood of the people" or the "spirit of the times." A synchronous match must appear between leader attributes and the modal expectations of the mass of followers. To be sure, in democracies this fit between political candidate and responsible citizen adopts an obvious form—namely, that a voter will cast a ballot according to the extent that agreement exists on the key issues of the day. But other forms of matching are less intellectual in nature, and entail the selection of a personality disposition deemed appropriate for the political Zeitgeist. Three examples may establish this point:

1. Lewis Stewart (1977) has proposed a provocative theory that establishes a correspondence between the political circumstances in which a politician seeks office and the birth order of the aspirant. The fundamental thesis is Adlerian: A child's ordinal position in the family hierarchy directly affects personality development, most notably the acquisition of social skills and orientations. Because these dispositions carry over into adulthood, and

because of their clear relevance for effective performance in specific political situations, birth order should correspond to the prevalent Zeitgeist. In particular, Stewart argued that the first-born is favored during times of international crisis and war, the only child during social disruption and upheaval (as in the Great Depression), the middle child during peaceful reconciliation and retrenchment (years of status quo maintenance), and the later-born when revolution erupts. Stewart tested his hypothesized scheme on data regarding both American presidents and British prime ministers, and found that the predicted co-occurrence of person and context far exceeded chance-level expectation. To offer a fascinating illustration, in the overwhelming majority of election years, the major contenders for the presidency had the same birth order!

Moreover, other researchers have confirmed various aspects of Stewart's (1977) thesis, albeit not deliberately and often only obliquely (Simonton, 1987b, Ch. 4): The middle-born child enjoys certain advantages during less turbulent times, when the emphasis is more on negotiation and compromise (Goertzel, Goertzel, & Goertzel, 1978), and revolutionaries are more likely to be later-born children from large families (Matossian & Schafer, 1977; Walberg, Rasher, & Parkerson, 1980; cf. Rejai & Phillips, 1979). Also, it has been discovered that first-born chief justices tended to preside when the American Supreme Court apparently expanded its power or pursued an innovative direction, whereas under a middle-born the Supreme Court tended to be more passively preoccupied with consolidating prior gains (Weber, 1984). Finally, a couple of studies of the American presidency indicate that birth order may determine the willingness of a politician to adopt a subsidiary role with respect to an incumbent, whether that role be the vice-presidency (Wendt & Muncy, 1979) or status as the hand-picked successor (Barry, 1979). Needless to say, none of these inquiries actually measured personality, but merely posited individual differences on some intervening variables, such as dominance or extraversion. Even so, the results lend support to the notion that personality and context enter into complex interaction effects.

2. Winter (1987b) gauged a significant individual × situational interaction far more directly. I have already mentioned the latest assessments of the power, achievement, and

affiliation motives for all elected presidents from Washington through Reagan. These scores were combined with comparable motive scores for American society, based on the content analysis of standard cultural documents (popular novels, children's readers, and hymns) that was independently developed by McClelland (1975, Ch. 9). The discrepancy between a president's motive scores and those of contemporary U.S. culture was then calculated by subtracting the standardized scores, yielding a measure of president–society motive congruence. Across approximately two dozen general elections, the magnitude of motive congruence was shown to correlate positively with (a) the percentage of the popular vote received, (b) the margin of victory over the second-place candidate (these both for election to the president's first term), and (c) the probability of re-election to a second term. Hence, presidential election success evidently requires a match between leader motive profile and the modal motive profile of the American people. The ironic feature of this motive congruence is that there is no reason to conclude that these well-matched chief executives serve as effective leaders. On the contrary, Winter (1987b) provided evidence that increases in president–society congruence go with *decreases* in (a) the capacity to avoid war in times of international crises, (b) the number of landmark decisions made, and (c) the president's final reputation with posterity (as represented by the consensus of historians). Consequently, a motivational kinship between leader and follower may produce a popular but inferior presidency, an all-too-common occurrence in American political history (Simonton, 1987b).

3. Along the same lines, McCann and Stewin (1987) built upon the research concerning the impact of external threat and authoritarianism reviewed earlier. Given this linkage, and considering that one component of authoritarianism is the tendency to identify with powerful figures, these investigators predicted that threat conditions should elicit in the American voter a preference for presidents displaying dominance, toughness, and authority. To test this hypothesis, the power motives for presidents from Coolidge through Reagan were adapted and extended from Winter's work, and several indicators of threat were defined, such as the unemployment rate, changes in car registration, fluctuations in the gross national product, and even subjective ratings by experts in

American history. The correlations between the power ratings of the presidents and the external threat measures were consistently positive. In addition, McCann and Stewin confirmed a corollary hypothesis, one directly comparable to that examined by Winter (1987b): The greater the discrepancy between the president's power needs and the magnitude of prevailing threat, the lower the proportion of the popular vote received in the concurrent election. These results extend what has been said earlier about authoritarians; the threatening circumstances that dominated the Weimar period in Germany would certainly nurture the rise of a power-obsessed leader like Hitler.

It is clear from all of these studies that individual × situational interaction effects may be rather common in electoral politics. The last example shows how such interactions may even affect the day-to-day operation of the government.

The Johnson–Wilson Effect

It must be apparent by now that one of the more influential personality variables in the realm of politics is some form of dogmatism. Whether we style this trait "authoritarianism" or "inflexibility," or call its inverse" "integrative complexity" or "flexibility," it underlies both how followers perceive leaders from the bottom and how leaders perform at the top. However, this attribute operates in interaction with situational variables, not just as a main effect. I have noted previously how presidential inflexibility, as gauged in the Gough ACL study, predicts veto behavior (Simonton, 1986c). In truth, the connection between these variables is more complex, for the trait interacts with two contextual factors. The first factor is the size of the electoral mandate. For highly flexible presidents, the scope of victory in the general election strongly determines their proclivity for exploiting the veto power. The larger the margin in the electoral college, the more bills are sent back to Congress for reconsideration. By contrast, highly inflexible presidents fail to weigh the magnitude of their electoral mandate when deciding to reject a piece of legislation. Here a personality trait moderates the correlation between situation and performance: An exceptional inflexibility simply swamps the otherwise important influence of electoral backing, rendering the situation impotent.

The second interaction effect incorporates a different and perhaps more critical situational factor—the extent to which the president's own party controls Congress. This party control × inflexibility interaction has powerful repercussions for the probability that a president's vetoes will be overturned by the House and Senate (Simonton, 1987a). For those chief executives who can boast unusual flexibility, the correlation between the degree of Congressional support and the number of overridden vetoes is negligible, for these presidents are able to bargain and negotiate deftly regardless of how many allies they can count in Congress. But for those presidents who are characterized as rather inflexible, this adaptation to political reality is foreclosed, and thus the correlation between party control and veto overrides becomes substantial. Therefore, the inflexible president is very much at the mercy of the powers that be on Capitol Hill. If the context is friendly, no one ever needs to suspect that the president possesses a potentially tragic flaw; should the setting turn adverse, however, this personality quirk comes out in full force, and undermines the best intentions of America's top politician.

This second interaction is christened the "Johnson–Wilson effect," after two of our most rigid chief executives, Andrew Johnson and Woodrow Wilson. Both men had a respectable supply of personal virtues, and both made effective leaders under the proper circumstances, yet both fell apart when they were obliged to face potent opposition. When the last-described situation arose, both reverted to extremely stubborn and self-defeating behaviors, including excessive and fruitless reliance on the executive veto. This reactive behavior at the level of the individual parallels the link between external threat and authoritarianism that emerges at the societal level.

Curvilinear Functions

In the search for a nexus between personality and some political criterion, the bias of many investigators seems to rest on the side of simplistic linear functions. Nevertheless, the real world beyond a psychologist's limited understanding may be overflowing with more complex mathematical functions. Interaction (or multiplicative) effects introduce additional sophistication to theoretical modeling, and tests for curvilinear relationships add another dimension of complexity still. Nonlinear functions are far less rare in the natural sciences, and are slowly edging their way into the behavioral sciences as well (Simonton, 1984a). In lifespan developmental psychology, for instance, it now has been well established that outstanding achievement, including effectiveness as a leader, is a curvilinear function of a person's age; the form is often described as an inverted backward-J curve (Simonton, 1988a). Such nonlinear curves may become more prominent in research on personality and politics.

Some theoretical models certainly suggest the existence of curvilinear functions. Take the connection between intelligence and leadership as a case in point. Even though intelligence is the one and only individual-difference construct that consistently correlates with leadership, the typical linear coefficient tends to be modest, on the order of .25 (Simonton, 1985a). The reason why the association may not be stronger is that an excessive intellectual gap between leader and follower undermines the latter's ability to comprehend the former. As Gibb (1969, p. 218) expressed it,

> One of the most interesting results emerging from studies of the relation between intelligence and leading is the suggestion that leaders may not exceed the nonleaders by too large a margin. Great discrepancies between the intelligence of one member and of others militate against his emergence into and retention of the leadership role. . . . The evidence suggests that every increment of intelligence means wiser government, but that the crowd prefers to be ill-governed by people it can understand.

The optimal intelligence for exercising effective leadership is therefore based on a tradeoff between intellectual superiority and comprehension.

For example, one formal model has shown that with a group of followers with a mean intellectual competence at the average level, the probability of a group member exerting influence over others is a curvilinear, concave downward function of that person's intelligence (Simonton, 1985a). A graph of the resulting function is shown in Figure 25.3. The prediction of a peak at about 1.2 standard deviations above the mean has been confirmed in a large number of studies (Simonton, 1985a). In-

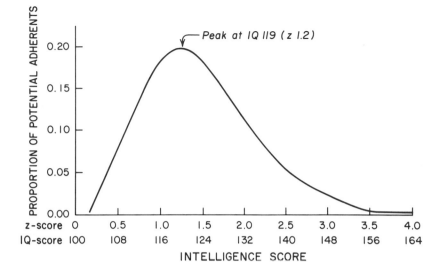

FIGURE 25.3 The predicted proportion of probable adherents as a function of the intelligence of a given group member (given both as IQ scores and as z scores). The average intelligence of the group is presumed to be at the average level. From "Intelligence and Personal Influence in Groups: Four Nonlinear Models" by D. K. Simonton, 1985, *Psychological Review*, 92, 532–547. Copyright 1985 by the American Psychological Association. Reprinted by permission.

terestingly, indirect evidence on behalf of this model may be found in the American experience: Notwithstanding the positive association between presidential greatness and intellectual brilliance, the latter attribute correlates negatively with the margin of victory in the Electoral College (Simonton, 1986c). Indeed, many of the nation's brightest candidates failed to receive a majority of the votes cast, becoming minority presidents. Woodrow Wilson, for instance, earned less than half the popular vote two elections in a row. Whether we accept this negative function as a consequence of the curve shown in Figure 25.3, the fact remains that we have here an instance of how a personality variable may relate in a nonmonotonic manner with a creditable measure of political performance.

But we need not resort to theoretical speculation, for immediate empirical examples can be given of curvilinear functions. Earlier in this chapter, I have already observed how the relationship between dogmatism (or integrative complexity) is probably a curvilinear U-shaped function of placement on the political spectrum: The highest scores are obtained by extremists on the right or left, whereas the lowest scores are enjoyed by moderates in the middle (e.g., Tetlock, 1984). Curiously, such dogma-

tism may itself be a curvilinear function of the level of formal education attained, with the highest scores displayed by those who have either little training or a great deal, including higher degrees; at least, such a U-shaped function holds for American presidents (Simonton, 1981b; 1987b, Ch. 5). Both cultural illiteracy and ivory-tower idealism are detrimental to cognitive flexibility.

Further illustrations concern how individual factors impinge on the eponymic causal chain that leads to monarchal eminence (Simonton, 1984b). To return to Figure 25.2, it is clear that some of these effects are nonlinear. For example, the relation between eminence and intelligence is described by a J-shaped curve; here, this signifies that once intellect descends below a certain minimal level, further decreases have little consequence, except that the extremely dull may gain a few points in notoriety. If we disregard the modest upturn in the lowest intellectual levels, this curve roughly replicates the positive correlation between intellectual brilliance and presidential greatness (Simonton, 1986c).

Yet the most thought-provoking curvilinear functions in Figure 25.2 may be those that concern morality. We would like to believe that goodness means success and evil brings failure, but in the world of *Realpolitik* the saint and the sinner may prove equally prominent as makers of history. For every honored leader who strives to impose high ideals on the rest of the world, whether through religious crusades or holy alliances, some other leader may opt for the low road to fame and fortune, perhaps taking instruction from Machiavelli's *The Prince*, and win a less admirable but no less permanent place in the annals of civilization. In the study of 342 European monarchs (Simonton, 1984b), morality produced two U-shaped curves. In the first, those kings, queens, and regents who presided over the most intensive historical activity were those either most or least moral. In contrast, those rulers who were neither principled nor unscrupulous left a less prominent mark. In the second function, the same U-shaped curve obtains between morality and leader eminence. Here the ambiguity of political distinction becomes more conspicuous, for the regard of posterity can actually be split into a pair of antithetical attributes, corresponding to fame and infamy. In the middle ground of the bifurcation comes pure nonentity.

Interestingly, a somewhat similar U-shaped curve has been isolated for the U.S. presidents. This set of leaders can be differentiated on a bipolar factor that has been labeled "dogmatism" (Simonton, 1981b; Wendt & Light, 1976), but that more specifically contains idealistic inflexibility at one pole and pragmatic flexibility at the other (cf. Maranell, 1970). Even if we cannot exactly call this a moral-versus-immoral dimension, it remains true that those presidents who score highest on this factor score lowest on Machiavellianism (Simonton, 1986c). More important, presidential greatness is a U-shaped function of dogmatism (Simonton, 1986b). Those chief executives who best make a name for themselves are either idealistic crusaders or pragmatic wheeler-dealers.

All in all, the very existence of some empirical examples, in conjunction with the theoretical anticipation of other instances, should warn researchers to be on the lookout for further cases of curvilinear functions.

CONCLUSION

Based on the survey just completed, personality psychologists evidently have much to say about how individual traits may intervene in political events. Especially crucial are such variables as authoritarianism; integrative complexity; flexibility; intelligence; dominance and the power motive; extraversion and the affiliation motive; and morality, idealism, and Machiavellianism—a fairly representative sample of cognitive and motivational attributes. These aspects of character have been assessed by a noteworthy diversity of methods, including aggregate cultural indicators, content analysis of speeches and interviews, and biographical data; the assessments often entail ingenious extensions of standard psychometric instruments to gauge leaders at a distance. Most significantly, the resulting personality traits have been tied to an impressive array of significant political criteria, including a politician's ideology, foreign policy, administrative competence, legislative success, and even historical reputation.

Despite the wealth of nomothetic findings that have so far accumulated, considerably more remains to be done. Political psychologists with a personality bent must become more sensitive to potential situational influences, individual × situational interaction effects, and nonlinear functions. And more work certainly must focus on political figures other than heads of state, such as diplomats, legislators, governors, and leaders of nationalist revolts (see, e.g., Hermann, 1977a, 1980a, 1980b; McConaughy, 1950; Stogdill et al., 1977; Swede & Tetlock, 1986; Walker & Falkowski, 1984; Winter, 1980). As part of this broadening, additional attention must also be paid to leaders outside the United States. American politicians, and especially U.S. presidents, have undergone detailed analysis far out of proportion to their psychological and political importance (cf. Simonton, 1987b). Perhaps this provincial emphasis is simply a matter that differential psychology has always been an American preoccupation—"*ganz Amerikanish,*" said Wundt long ago of James McKeen Cattell's first endeavor to examine individual differences. Even so, a wealth of data is available on leaders in other nations, even in distinct civilizations. We have discussed examples of subjecting diverse revolutionaries and monarchs to psychological scrutiny, and some beginning spadework has been done on Soviet Politburo members (Hermann, 1980a), southern African political leaders (Winter, 1980), Italian legislators (DiRenzo, 1977), Canadian prime ministers (Ballard, 1983; Ballard & Suedfeld, 1988), and other European-style politicians (Hermann,

1980b). Yet the body of information on Islamic, Japanese, and especially Chinese leaders is most remarkable, and awaits full exploitation (cf. Simonton, 1988b). By widening personality studies to include such a diversity of subject pools, we can ensure that any nomothetic results that do emerge are indeed cross-culturally and transhistorically invariant.

But beyond the manifest need to extend the scope of the politicians sampled, researchers can devise ever more techniques for assessing personality at a distance. Even if we already have at our disposal a respectable inventory of pertinent traits, one can easily conceive of other standard constructs that might become useful predictors of political thought and conduct in the real world. In addition, more effort needs to be directed at unearthing the character traits that presumably intervene between biographical antecedents on the one hand and political leadership consequences on the other. For example, birth order seems to affect a politician's probable behavior, presumably via some personality trait or profile that emerges in the family environment (Barry, 1979; Stewart, 1977). At present we possess only hypotheses.

These comments all converge on a single affirmation: If past research seems successful, future research should prove even more exciting. We all possess and perceive personalities, and each one of us lives inescapably in a political world. Few can resist speculations about the character of those singular individuals, our leaders, who are the most prominent agents of happenings that literally govern our lives. Therefore, to appreciate the interface between personality and politics is to enhance our understanding of events fundamental to our existence.

REFERENCES

Adorno, T. W., Frenkel-Brunswik, E., Levinson, D. J., & Sanford, R. N. (1950). *The authoritarian personality*. New York: Harper & Row.

Alker, H. A. (1981). Political creativity. In L. Wheeler (Ed.), *Review of personality and social psychology* (Vol. 2, pp. 167–188). Beverly Hills, CA: Sage.

Ballard, E. J. (1983). Canadian prime ministers: Complexity in political crises. *Canadian Psychology, 24*, 125–129.

Ballard, E. J., & Suedfeld, P. (1988). Performance ratings of Canadian prime ministers: Individual and situational factors. *Political Psychology, 9*, 291–302.

Barber, J. D. (1977). *The presidential character* (2nd ed.). Englewood Cliffs, NJ: Prentice-Hall.

Barry, H., III. (1979). Birth order and paternal namesake as predictors of affiliation with predecessor by presidents of the United States. *Political Psychology, 1*, 61–66.

Binion, R. (1976). *Hitler among the Germans*. New York: Elsevier.

Brodie, F. M. (1983). *Richard Nixon: The shaping of his character*. Cambridge, MA: Harvard University Press.

Cell, C. P. (1974). Charismatic heads of state: The social context. *Behavior Science Research, 9*, 255–305.

Chesen, E. S. (1973). *President Nixon's psychiatric profile*. New York: Weyden.

Christie, R., & Jahoda, M. (Eds.). (1954). *Studies in the scope and method of* The authoritarian personality. New York: Harper.

Cocks, G. (1986). Contributions of psychohistory to understanding politics. In M. G. Hermann (Ed.), *Political psychology* (pp. 139–166). San Francisco: Jossey-Bass.

Costantini, E., & Craik, K. H. (1972). Women as politicians: The social background, personality, and political careers of female party leaders. *Journal of Social Issues, 28*, 217–236.

Costantini, E., & Craik, K. H. (1980). Personality and politicians: California party leaders, 1960–1976. *Journal of Personality and Social Psychology, 38*, 641–661.

Cox, C. (1926). *The early mental traits of three hundred geniuses*. Stanford, CA: Stanford University Press.

DiRenzo, G. J. (Ed.). (1974). *Personality and politics*. Garden City, NY: Doubleday.

DiRenzo, G. J. (1977). Politicians and personality: A cross-cultural perspective. In M. G. Hermann (Ed.), *The psychological examination of political leaders* (pp. 149–173). New York: Free Press.

Donley, R. E., & Winter, D. G. (1970). Measuring the motives of public officials at a distance: An exploratory study of American presidents. *Behavioral Science, 15*, 227–236.

Elms, A. C. (1976). *Personality in politics*. New York: Harcourt Brace Jovanovich.

Erikson, E. H. (1969). *Gandhi's truth*. New York: Norton.

Etheredge, L. S. (1978). Personality effects on American foreign policy, 1898–1968: A test of interpersonal generalization theory. *American Political Science Review, 78*, 434–451.

Eysenck, H. J. (1954). *The psychology of politics*. London: Routledge & Kegan Paul.

Freud, S., & Bullitt, W. C. (1967). *Thomas Woodrow Wilson*. Boston: Houghton Mifflin.

George, A. L., & George, J. L. (1956). *Woodrow Wilson and Colonel House*. New York: Day.

Gibb, C. A. (1969). Leadership. In G. Lindzey & E. Aronson (Eds.), *Handbook of social psychology* (2nd ed., Vol. 4, pp. 205–282). Reading, MA: Addison-Wesley.

Glad, B. (1973). Contributions of psychobiography. In J. N. Knutson (Ed.), *Handbook of political psychology* (pp. 296–321). San Francisco: Jossey-Bass.

Glad, B. (1980). *Jimmy Carter: In search of the great White House*. New York: Norton.

Goertzel, M. G., Goertzel, V., & Goertzel, T. G. (1978). *Three hundred eminent personalities*. San Francisco: Jossey-Bass.

Gough, H. G., & Heilbrun, A. B., Jr. (1965). *The Adjec-*

tive Check List manual. Palo Alto, CA: Consulting Psychologists Press.

Greenstein, F. I. (1987). *Personality and politics.* Princeton, NJ: Princeton University Press.

Hermann, M. G. (Ed.). (1977a). *The psychological examination of political leaders.* New York: Free Press.

Hermann, M. G. (1977b). Some personal characteristics related to foreign aid voting of Congressmen. In M. G. Hermann (Ed.), *The psychological examination of political leaders* (pp. 313–334). New York: Free Press.

Hermann, M. G. (1980a). Assessing the personalities of members of the Soviet Politburo. *Personality and Social Psychology Bulletin, 6,* 332–352.

Hermann, M. G. (1980b). Explaining foreign policy behavior using the personal characteristics of political leaders. *International Studies Quarterly, 24,* 7–46.

Hermann, M. G. (Ed.). (1986). *Political psychology.* San Francisco: Jossey-Bass.

Historical Figures Assessment Collaborative (HFAC). (1977). Assessing historical figures: The use of observer-based personality descriptions. *Historical Methods Newsletter, 10,* 66–76.

Hoffer, P. C. (1978). Psychohistory and empirical group affiliation: Extraction of personality traits from historical manuscripts. *Journal of Interdisciplinary History, 9,* 131–145.

Janis, I. L. (1972). *Victims of groupthink.* Boston: Houghton Mifflin.

Jorgenson, D. O. (1975). Economic threat and authoritarianism in television programs: 1950–1974. *Psychological Reports, 37,* 1153–1154.

Kearns, D. (1976). *Lyndon Johnson and the American dream.* New York: Wilson.

Knutson, J. N. (1974). *Psychological variables in political recruitment: An analysis of party activists.* Berkeley, CA: Wright Institute.

Langer, W. C. (1972). *The mind of Adolf Hitler.* New York: Basic Books.

Leitner, L. M. (1983). Construct similarity, self-meaningfulness, and presidential preference. *Journal of Personality and Social Psychology, 45,* 890–894.

Mahoney, J., Coogle, C. L., & Banks, P. D. (1984). Values in presidential inaugural addresses: A test of Rokeach's two-factor theory of political ideology. *Psychological Reports, 55,* 683–686.

Maranell, G. M. (1970). The evaluation of presidents: An extension of the Schlesinger polls. *Journal of American History, 57,* 104–113.

Matossian, M. K., & Schafer, W. D. (1977). Family, fertility, and political violence, 1700–1900. *Journal of Social History, 11,* 137–178.

Mazlish, B. (1972). *In search of Nixon.* New York: Basic Books.

McCann, S. J., & Stewin, L. L. (1984). Environmental threat and parapsychological contributions to the psychological literature. *Journal of Social Psychology, 122,* 227–235.

McCann, S. J., & Stewin, L. L. (1987). Threat, authoritarianism, and the power of U.S. presidents. *Journal of Psychology, 121,* 149–157.

McClelland, D. C. (1975). *Power: The inner experience.* New York: Irvington.

McConaughy, J. B. (1950). Certain personality factors of state legislators in South Carolina. *American Political Science Review, 44,* 897–903.

Milburn, T. W. (1977). The Q-sort and the study of political personality. In M. G. Hermann (Ed.), *The*

psychological examination of political leaders (pp. 131–144). New York: Free Press.

Miller, N. L., & Stiles, W. B. (1986). Verbal familiarity in American presidential nomination acceptance speeches and inaugural addresses (1920–1981). *Social Psychology Quarterly, 49,* 72–81.

Murray, H. A. (1938). *Explorations in personality.* New York: Oxford University Press.

Murray, R. K., & Blessing, T. H. (1983). The presidential performance study: A progress report. *Journal of American History, 70,* 535–555.

Padgett, V., & Jorgenson, D. O. (1982). Superstition and economic threat: Germany 1918–1940. *Personality and Social Psychology Bulletin, 8,* 736–741.

Porter, C. A., & Suedfeld, P. (1981). Integrative complexity in the correspondence of literary figures: Effects of personal and societal stress. *Journal of Personality and Social Psychology, 40,* 321–330.

Raphael, T. D. (1982). Integrative complexity theory and forecasting international crises. *Journal of Conflict Resolution, 26,* 423–450.

Rasler, K. A., Thompson, W. R., & Chester, K. M. (1980). Foreign policy makers, personality attributes, and interviews: A note on reliability problems. *International Studies Quarterly, 24,* 47–66.

Rejai, M., & Phillips, K. (1979). *Leaders of revolution.* Beverly Hills, CA: Sage.

Rokeach, M. (1960). *The open and the closed mind.* New York: Basic Books.

Rokeach, M., Homant, R., & Penner, L. (1970). A value analysis of the disputed Federalist Papers. *Journal of Personality and Social Psychology, 16,* 245–250.

Ross, L. (1977). The intuitive psychologist and his shortcomings: Distortions in the attribution process. In L. Berkowitz (Ed.), *Advances in experimental social psychology* (Vol. 10, pp. 173–220). New York: Academic Press.

Sales, S. M. (1972). Economic threat as a determinant of conversion rates in authoritarian and non-authoritarian churches. *Journal of Personality and Social Psychology, 23,* 420–428.

Sales, S. M. (1973). Threat as a factor in authoritarianism: An analysis of archival data. *Journal of Personality and Social Psychology, 28,* 44–57.

Schlesinger, A. M. (1948, November 1). Historians rate the U.S. presidents. *Life,* pp. 65–66, 68, 73–74.

Schroder, H. M., Driver, M. J., & Streufert, S. (1967). *Human information processing.* New York: Holt, Rinehart, and Winston.

Simonton, D. K. (1980). Land battles, generals, and armies: Individual and situational determinants of victory and casualties. *Journal of Personality and Social Psychology, 38,* 110–119.

Simonton, D. K. (1981a). The library laboratory: Archival data in personality and social psychology. In L. Wheeler (Ed.), *Review of personality and social psychology* (Vol. 2, pp. 217–243). Beverly Hills, CA: Sage.

Simonton, D. K. (1981b). Presidential greatness and performance: Can we predict leadership in the White House? *Journal of Personality, 49,* 306–323.

Simonton, D. K. (1983a). Intergenerational transfer of individual differences in hereditary monarchs: Genes, role-modeling, cohort, or sociocultural effects? *Journal of Personality and Social Psychology, 44,* 354–364.

Simonton, D. K. (1983b). Psychohistory. In R. Harré & R. Lamb (Eds.), *The encyclopedic dictionary of psychology* (pp. 499–550). Oxford: Blackwell.

Simonton, D. K. (1984a). *Genius, creativity, and leadership.* Cambridge, MA: Harvard University Press.

Simonton, D. K. (1984b). Leaders as eponyms: Individual and situational determinants of monarchal eminence. *Journal of Personality, 52,* 1–21.

Simonton, D. K. (1985a). Intelligence and personal influence in groups: Four nonlinear models. *Psychological Review, 92,* 532–547.

Simonton, D. K. (1985b). The vice-presidential succession effect: Individual or situational determinants? *Political Behavior, 7,* 79–99.

Simonton, D. K. (1986a). Dispositional attributions of (presidential) leadership: An experimental simulation of historiometric results. *Journal of Experimental Social Psychology, 22,* 389–418.

Simonton, D. K. (1986b). Presidential greatness: The historical consensus and its psychological significance. *Political Psychology, 7,* 259–283.

Simonton, D. K. (1986c). Presidential personality: Biographical use of the Gough Adjective Check List. *Journal of Personality and Social Psychology, 51,* 149–160.

Simonton, D. K. (1987a). Presidential inflexibility and veto behavior: Two individual–situational interactions. *Journal of Personality, 55,* 1–18.

Simonton, D. K. (1987b). *Why presidents succeed.* New Haven, CT: Yale University Press.

Simonton, D. K. (1988a). Age and outstanding achievement: What do we know after a century of research? *Psychological Bulletin, 104,* 251–267.

Simonton, D. K. (1988b). Galtonian genius, Kroeberian configurations, and emulation: A generational time-series analysis of Chinese civilization. *Journal of Personality and Social Psychology, 55,* 238–247.

Simonton, D. K. (1988c). Presidential style: Biography, personality, and performance. *Journal of Personality and Social Psychology, 55,* 928–936.

Sorokin, P. A. (1925). Monarchs and rulers: A comparative statistical study. I. *Social Forces, 4,* 22–35.

Stewart, L. H. (1977). Birth order and political leadership. In M. G. Hermann (Ed.), *The psychological examination of political leaders* (pp. 206–236). New York: Free Press.

Stiles, W. B., Au, M. L., Martello, M. A., & Perlmutter, J. A. (1983). American campaign oratory: Verbal response mode use by candidates in the 1980 American presidential primaries. *Social Behavior and Personality, 11,* 39–43.

Stogdill, R. M., Goode, O. S., & Day, D. R. (1977). The leader behavior of United States senators: An example of the use of informants. In M. G. Hermann (Ed.), *The psychological examination of political leaders* (pp. 122–129). New York: Free Press.

Suedfeld, P. (1980). Indices of world tension in the *Bulletin of the Atomic Scientists. Political Psychology, 2,* 114–123.

Suedfeld, P., Corteen, R. S., & McCormick, C. (1986). The role of integrative complexity in military leadership: Robert E. Lee and his opponents. *Journal of Applied Social Psychology, 16,* 498–507.

Suedfeld, P., & Rank, A. D. (1976). Revolutionary leaders: Long-term success as a function of changes in conceptual complexity. *Journal of Personality and Social Psychology, 34,* 169–178.

Suedfeld, P., & Tetlock, P. (1977). Integrative complexity of communications in international crises. *Journal of Conflict Resolution, 21,* 169–184.

Suedfeld, P., Tetlock, P. E., & Ramirez, C. (1977). War,

peace, and integrative complexity. *Journal of Conflict Resolution, 21,* 427–442.

Swede, S. W., & Tetlock, P. E. (1986). Henry Kissinger's implicit theory of personality: A quantitative case study. *Journal of Personality, 54,* 617–646.

Tetlock, P. E. (1979). Identifying victims of groupthink from public statements of decision makers. *Journal of Personality and Social Psychology, 37,* 1314–1324.

Tetlock, P. E. (1981a). Personality and isolationism: Content analysis of senatorial speeches. *Journal of Personality and Social Psychology, 41,* 737–743.

Tetlock, P. E. (1981b). Pre- to post-election shifts in presidential rhetoric: Impression management or cognitive adjustment. *Journal of Personality and Social Psychology, 41,* 207–212.

Tetlock, P. E. (1983). Cognitive style and political ideology. *Journal of Personality and Social Psychology, 45,* 118–126.

Tetlock, P. E. (1984). Cognitive style and political belief systems in the British House of Commons. *Journal of Personality and Social Psychology, 46,* 365–375.

Tetlock, P. E. (1985). Integrative complexity of American and Soviet foreign policy rhetoric: A time-series analysis. *Journal of Personality and Social Psychology, 49,* 1565–1585.

Tetlock, P. E., Bernzweig, J., & Gallant, J. L. (1985). Supreme Court decision making: Cognitive style as a predictor of ideological consistency of voting. *Journal of Personality and Social Psychology, 48,* 1227–1239.

Tetlock, P. E., Crosby, F., & Crosby, T. L. (1981). Political psychobiography. *Micropolitics, 1,* 191–213.

Tetlock, P. E., Hannum, K. A., & Micheletti, P. M. (1984). Stability and change in the complexity of senatorial debate: Testing the cognitive versus rhetorical style hypothesis. *Journal of Personality and Social Psychology, 46,* 979–990.

Thorndike, E. L. (1936). The relation between intellect and morality in rulers. *American Journal of Sociology, 42,* 321–334.

Thorndike, E. L. (1950). Traits of personality and their intercorrelations as shown in biography. *Journal of Educational Psychology, 41,* 193–216.

Tolstoy, L. (1952). *War and peace* (L. Maude & A. Maude, Trans.). Chicago: Encyclopaedia Britannica. (Original work published 1865–1869)

Walberg, H. J., Rasher, S. P., & Parkerson, J. (1980). Childhood and eminence. *Journal of Creative Behavior, 13,* 225–231.

Walker, S. G., & Falkowski, L. S. (1984). The operational codes of U.S. presidents and secretaries of state: Motivational foundations and behavioral consequences. *Political Psychology, 5,* 237–266.

Weber, P. J. (1984). The birth order oddity in Supreme Court appointments. *Presidential Studies Quarterly, 14,* 561–568.

Wendt, H. W., & Light, P. C. (1976). Measuring "greatness" in American presidents: Model case for international research on political leadership? *European Journal of Social Psychology, 6,* 105–109.

Wendt, H. W., & Muncy, C. A. (1979). Studies of political character: Factor patterns of 24 U.S. vice-presidents. *Journal of Psychology, 102,* 125–131.

Winter, D. G. (1973). *The power motive.* New York: Free Press.

Winter, D. G. (1980). Measuring the motives of southern African political leaders at a distance. *Political Psychology, 2,* 75–85.

Winter, D. G. (1987a). Enhancement of an enemy's power motivation as a dynamic of conflict escalation. *Journal of Personality and Social Psychology, 52,* 41–46.

Winter, D. G. (1987b). Leader appeal, leader performance, and the motive profiles of leaders and followers: A study of American presidents and elections. *Journal of Personality and Social Psychology, 52,* 196–202.

Winter, D. G. (1988, July/August). What makes Jesse run? *Psychology Today,* pp. 20, 22, 24.

Winter, D. G., & Carlson, D. G. (1988). Using motive scores in the psychobiographical study of an individual: The case of Richard Nixon. *Journal of Personality, 56,* 75–103.

Winter, D. G., & Stewart, A. J. (1977). Content analysis as a technique for assessing political leaders. In M. G. Hermann (Ed.), *The psychological examination of political leaders* (pp. 28–61). New York: Free Press.

Woods, F. A. (1906). *Mental and moral heredity in royalty: A statistical study in history and psychology.* New York: Holt.

Woods, F. A. (1913). *The influence of monarchs.* New York: Macmillan.

Zullow, H. M., Oettingen, G., Peterson, C., & Seligman, M. E. P. (1988). Pessimistic explanatory style in the historical record: CAVing LBJ, presidential candidates, and East versus West Berlin. *American Psychologist, 43,* 673–682.

Chapter 26

Personality Assessment: A Conceptual Survey

Leonard G. Rorer
Miami University, Ohio

I know nothing stays the same
But if you're willing to play the game
It will be coming around again.
CARLY SIMON

The problem with personality assessment is that there is little agreement as to what one is assessing, much less how to assess it; from this it follows that there is little agreement concerning the domain that it covers. I could start by giving a dictionary definition of personality:

> An individual's enduring persistent response patterns across a variety of situations. It is comprised of relatively stable patterns of action often referred to as TRAITS, dispositional tendencies, motivations, attitudes and beliefs which are combined into a more or less integrated self-structure. (Harré & Lamb, 1983, p. 460)

But we should remember that all such definitions are ultimately circular. All words in the dictionary are defined in terms of other words in the dictionary. We cannot learn the meaning of a word by itself, but only in context. Even dictionaries define words by giving examples of their use. Concepts, including "personality" and "assessment," cannot be defined explicitly; they must be defined implicitly.

I am going to start by assuming that readers have a general understanding of the everyday meaning of these words. There is not much disagreement about that. The disagreement comes when we try to explicate this common-sense understanding and analyze just what we mean by "personality" and "assessment." I take the goal of personality assessment to be the description of people, but only that part of the description having to do with personality. It does not relate to physical appearance or physiological functioning, or behavior as such (a description of how someone ate his or her spinach would not be a personality description, although we might infer personality characteristics from that description); rather, it relates to a person's manner of behaving, his or her moods, and the situations and behaviors he or she chooses as opposed to the ones he or she avoids. This illustrates how our intuitive understanding guides us, and how it is impossible to be explicit about that understanding.

This chapter defines personality assessment, in part, by describing things it includes and things it excludes. As a start, personality assessment applies to such things as intellectual (but not athletic) abilities, aptitudes, attitudes,

693

interests, and behavioral or personality traits. This chapter also defines personality assessment by describing what personality assessors do, and the rationale that they provide for what they do. However, this is not a how-to-do-it chapter on personality assessment. Readers who want more applied or more detailed instructions could start with Wiggins (1973), an outstanding summary at the time it was published, or the more recent handbook by Goldstein and Hersen (1984). Rather, I try to describe what personality assessors do in the conceptual sense, and to make explicit the often implicit philosophical basis of what has been called personality assessment for the last 60 years or so. I do this historically, but I do not describe particular instruments or techniques. A number of excellent accounts of this kind already exist (e.g., Goldberg, 1971; McReynolds, 1986; McReynolds & Ludwig, 1987).

In order to develop my theme that all personality assessment assumes, and can only be understood in the context of, some model of both personality and assessment, I start with a brief review of some early antecedents. I then describe what I call the "traditional" assessment model. This description includes a fairly detailed look at various strategies of scale construction. Following this, I first review the philosophy of science in the context of which the traditional model was developed, and next summarize some of the modern challenges to that philosophy. Following that, I describe the behavioral and cognitive challenges to the traditional model, more recent developments within the traditional framework, and alternative models that have been developed in the context of the more modern philosophies of science.

EARLY HISTORY OF PERSONALITY ASSESSMENT

Ancient Times to the Early 20th Century

It seems likely that people must have been interested in describing other people from earliest times, and that those descriptions would have included personality as well as physical characteristics and physical (athletic) abilities. The writings of the Greeks from the 5th century B.C. contain personality descriptions based on their humoral theory, which posited four characteristics (sanguinity, irritability, melancholy, and placidity) in terms of which people could be described. These characteristics were thought to be related to the amounts of the four humors in the blood (McReynolds, 1986).

Given the interest that people have in describing one another, it is striking that the development of a systematic means of description is so recent. Early descriptions were tied to beliefs about personality determinants, and were couched in terms of external indicators (astrology), physical descriptions (e.g., a lion-like appearance indicated courage), and hypothesized physiological determinants (e.g., the four humors). The idea of behavioral indicators does not seem to have occurred until the very end of the 17th century, and then only in scattered references (McReynolds, 1986). It was not until the last half of the 19th century that Galton started collecting systematic measurements of behavioral as well as physical characteristics of people: "Galton largely created the bases for the quantitative assessment of individual differences. He pioneered the use of questionnaires, rating scales, word association techniques, test batteries, and other evaluation methods" (McReynolds, 1986, p. 52). He seems also to have been the first to try to find measures of intellectual capacity; he focused mostly on sensorimotor tasks such as reaction time, but also developed the digit span test, a form of which is included in leading intelligence measures to this day.

There were scattered instances of the development and use of checklists and rating scales early in this century. Checklists suggest that there is something that one can have or not have, such as a broken leg or a rash all over the body, or a headache or hallucinations. Rating scales suggest that things exist in some degree or quantity, such as height and weight, or the severity of the headache or the frequency of the hallucinations. Checklists can also apply to things that exist in various degrees, in which case they are really dichotomous rating scales with an arbitrarily selected cutting point. When we use physical descriptors such as "tall" or "short," or psychological descriptors such as "cheerful" or "sad," we are using ascription rules (Rorer & Widiger, 1983) to translate an implicit rating scale into a checklist. An ascription rule tells us how high or low the rating must be on a descriptor before we ascribe it to the person. When we make such an ascription, we say that we have described the person, although we should more accurately say that we have described that aspect of the person (i.e., that we have described the person's height or the person's cheerfulness).

Binet and Woodworth

The next important step forward was taken by Binet and Woodworth, who, although they may not have been the first to have assembled a set of items into a scale, are clearly the ones who popularized the idea. This seemingly simple step represented the start of psychological assessment as we know it today. In the case of the Binet intelligence test, the items were empirically ordered in terms of increasing difficulty to approximate what we would today call a Guttmann scale. The score was taken to represent, at the first level of inference, a child's level of achievement; in relation to the child's age it was taken to indicate the need for remedial education; and, given the additional assumption that children of a given age have had roughly the same educational background, it was inferred to be a measure of the child's intellectual ability or intelligence. If two children who have been exposed to the same educational experiences perform differently, then it is reasonable to assume that the difference in performance is due to differences in ability.

"Ability" is an ambiguous word; so is "ambiguous." A term can be ambiguous either because it is not clear, or because it has more than one meaning and it is not clear which meaning is intended. "Ability" is ambiguous in the second sense. We use it to refer to both a present level of performance ("He can [is able to] run a mile in 8 minutes") and to a potential level of performance ("With the correct training program, he could [has the ability to] run a mile in 6 minutes"). Sometimes the context makes clear which meaning is intended, but in many cases it does not. The picture is muddied further by the fact that ability in the second sense sometimes refers simply to the *fact* that one could learn to do something and sometimes to the *rate* at which one could learn to do it. The controversies having to do with ability testing in general and intelligence (intellectual ability) testing in particular have to do with ability in the second sense.

For our purposes, it is important to note only that the question as to whether a particular test is an achievement test (an ability test in the first sense) or an intelligence test (an ability test in the second sense) is misguided. The same test may be either one, depending on the level of the inference we make. We can say that the individual is able to speak French or to repeat five digits backwards now; that the individual could learn to speak French or to repeat five digits backwards with proper training; or that the person could learn to speak French or to repeat five digits backwards in some (long or short) period of time. The first statement refers to the performance on the test; the second and third are inferences that might be made on the basis of present test performance and other information.

The 116 items in Woodworth's Personal Data Sheet (PDS) constituted a scale of Psychoneurotic Tendencies, which was designed to be used to identify emotionally unstable soldiers in World War I. According to McReynolds (1986), this was the first instance in which a set of items was combined into a single quantitative scale to measure an aspect of personality. The item pool was developed rationally, but the initial set of 200 items was empirically reduced to 116 by eliminating items that were endorsed by more than 25% of normal and inductee samples. This last step was, again according to McReynolds (1986), the first instance in which empirical procedures were used to select items. The elaborate theories of personality inventory construction have all been developed in the little more than 70 years since the introduction of the PDS.

Two significant developments occurred during the 1920s: the development of (1) projective instruments and (2) empirical item selection strategies using an external criterion. As we consider in more detail later, projective instruments used vague stimuli and a free-response format to gather a sample of verbal behavior from which inferences concerning internal psychodynamic structure could be made. Empirically keyed scales were initially constructed on the basis of occupational groups, but starting in the 1930s interest shifted to psychiatrically diagnosed or otherwise identified maladjusted groups; this shift culminated in the publication of the Minnesota Multiphasic Personality Inventory (MMPI) in 1943.

THE TRADITIONAL PERSONALITY ASSESSMENT MODEL

From the present vantage point it seems that psychologists were in much greater agreement as to what they were about 30–50 years ago than they are today. Psychologists—clinical psychologists, at least—seemed to know what personality assessment was. It is still the case, in the clinical psychology training program of which I am a member, that when a student says that he or she wants to learn to "do assessments," the reference is to the traditional kind that were performed 30–50 years ago, without much thought as to whether there might be other kinds. I am going to describe this model of personality assessment in the context of the 1940s and 1950s, even though I realize that it is still widely held today. What I am referring to as the "traditional" assessment included an anamnesis, sometimes based on a standard form but often obtained by interviewing the client; at least one projective test, usually a Thematic Apperception Test (TAT) or a Rorschach; an objective test of psychopathology, usually the MMPI; some measure of intellectual functioning, probably the Wechsler Adult Intelligence Scale (WAIS) for an adult or the Wechsler Intelligence Scale for Children (WISC) or Stanford–Binet for a child; and an interview focused on the client's problems and presenting complaints. Other tests were often added, depending on the results of these first tests and the questions to be answered. The goal of this assessment was twofold: first, to arrive at a diagnosis; and second, to describe the person's personality structure or "psychodynamics." It was assumed that the diagnosis and the personality structure existed, and that they could be discovered (revealed, understood) by means of the assessment battery.

In the context of the times, the approach made sense. The one clear triumph in understanding mental disorders had been the discovery of syphilis as the cause of general paresis and tabes dorsalis early in this century, and it provided a model for further research focused on identifying disease entities for which treatments could then be sought. Kraepelin (1907/1981) is usually credited with being the first to attempt a comprehensive nosology of psychopathology, and Bleuler (1911/1950) provided an exemplary model in his attempt to describe the schizophrenias. That enterprise continues today with the continuing revisions of the *Diagnostic and Statistical Manual of Mental Disorders* (the latest of which is DSM-III-R; American Psychiatric Association, 1987). This model, which I refer to as the "diagnostic" model, had been successful in medicine for some 50 years. Under this model it was assumed

that if diagnostic categories could be established, then appropriate treatments, which would vary from category to category, could be identified.

Although psychodynamic interpretations might superficially seem different, it is important to remember that they were based on the same model. One could *be* a hysteric or an obsessive–compulsive (or, more accurately, one could be a person who had hysteria or obsessive–compulsive neurosis), in the same sense that one could be a consumptive or a person who had diabetes. Certain early life experiences were thought to determine certain personality structures and dispositions, which in turn were thought to determine one's life pattern. There was a limited number of these crucial experiences, and therefore a small number of diagnostic categories. Psychodynamic formulations and the diagnostic system were inextricably intertwined. Given a diagnosis, one could infer a developmental personality pattern, and vice versa. Given the assumption of psychological etiology, the purpose of the psychodynamic formulation was to identify the kinds of life experiences on which psychotherapeutic treatment should focus. In conjunction with the life history, the psychodynamic formulation might target the particular life experiences that were crucial for this client, or might indicate that the particular experiences remained to be discovered.

The traditional assessment procedures are all tied to the diagnostic model. Meehl and Golden (1982) have provided a clear exposition of the logic by which diagnostic categories are established and the methods by which individuals are assigned to such categories. The recent history of acquired immune deficiency syndrome (AIDS) provides a familiar example of how nosological categories are identified. It was first noticed that there had been an unexplained increase in the incidence of Kaposi sarcoma; next that these cases tended to be confined to a particular category of the population (gay males); and then that gay males seemed to be developing a rather vague disorder that might be described as general malaise (fatigue, fever, etc.), and that they also seemed to have a decreased resistance to other infections. When this was combined with reports of a similar disorder in Africa, it seemed that there was a sufficient reason to think that medicine was dealing with a genuine disease entity, and a search was launched for an etiological agent (in this case the presumption was high that it was a virus). Most believe that the virus has now been identified, but there are still some skeptics who believe that the disorder is caused by a pair of viruses (only the less lethal of which has been identified), and others who believe that it is not caused by a virus at all.

There are at least two tests to identify antibodies to the virus, but they are imperfect, and one may have the virus for some period of time (no one knows how long) before one develops antibodies. The diagnosis is based on the tests, the person's history, and the other symptoms that the person has, and is therefore probabilistic. It is known that the virus can be transmitted through the blood, and it is believed that it can be transmitted by sexual contact (though the mechanism of transmission is not known, and some individuals have had hundreds of sexual contacts with persons carrying the virus without themselves getting it). It is not known whether the virus can be transmitted in other ways. Thus, we are still learning about the disease; as we learn, the methods of diagnosis and treatment, as well as the definition and understanding of the disorder, change. It is an open concept.

Once an etiological agent has been identified, then a positive diagnosis can be made by associating the agent with the person. Prior to determining the cause of a disorder (and to some extent afterward, as well) we are operating on the basis of a hypothetical construct, an open concept, for which there is no explicit definition and no infallible (pathognomonic) indicator. In the absence of such an indicator, we are forced to make diagnoses on the basis of probabilistic signs and symptoms. It is not possible at this point to specify any combination (conjunction) of signs that must be present, or any set (disjunction) from which a certain number will suffice. (Certain sets or combinations may be arbitrarily specified for research or reporting purposes, as in the case of DSM-III-R). Rather, it is assumed that the more positive indicators one has, the greater the probability that one falls into the category. It may also be the case, or may be assumed to be the case, that the number of positive indicators is related to the severity of the disorder, if it is a disorder that can vary from mild to severe. These are not necessarily unrelated, because the more severe the disorder, the more signs and symptoms it would be expected to produce; the clearer the signs and symptoms would prob-

ably be; and therefore the higher the probability with which it could be identified.

The traditional assessment procedures followed from this model. Anamnesis responses, personality inventory items, and projective test scores were treated as diagnostic signs. The number of positive responses was summed, and this number was assumed to be related to the probability and the severity of the disorder to which the signs were presumed to be related. Within the context of the prevailing psychodynamic model, the psychodynamic formulation was intended to identify the specific etiological agents associated with the diagnosis in this individual's case.

Projective Tests

Projective tests were characterized primarily by the use of ambiguous stimuli and free-response formats. To the extent that they produced quantitative scores, the logic of their use was no different from that of personality inventories. The Rorschach, for example, could be scored for response categories such as Form, Color, and Human Movement. These scores were initially related to diagnostic categories on theoretical grounds, but the relations were not supported by subsequent empirical studies.

In addition, the free-response protocols could be interpreted in terms of the theory, which assumed that one's basic personality structure determines the nature of one's responses in all aspects of one's life. It followed that if a tester used vague or ambiguous stimuli to which a person could respond in a variety of ways, then the particular response that was selected must be a function of the person's dynamic structure. Stimuli that were suggestive of basic response categories but still vague enough to be interpreted in several different ways were thought to provide the best opportunity to trigger the crucial, revealing responses.

The validity of the process obviously depends crucially on the verisimilitude or utility (depending on one's epistemological position) of the theory. It also depends on the accuracy of the subjective scoring of the protocols for psychodynamic content—a process requiring that the response be interpreted in terms of the theory. This creates an infinite regress, because the responses are now, for the interpreter, a form of projective test, and there is no way of knowing whether the interpretation is a function of the psychodynamics of the respondent or the interpreter (see Meehl, 1982, for an analysis of this problem with respect to psychoanalytic interpretations in general). Evidence of high agreement among interpreters would help deal with this problem, though it would not solve it. In any event, the inter-interpreter reliabilities are not high, so the problem remains.

In my view, the huge literature on the psychodynamic interpretation of these instruments has shown their utility to be negative. Of more relevance to this chapter, I do not know of any developments in the assessment theory underlying the subjective interpretation of these instruments in the context of psychoanalytic theory in the last 50 years. Therefore, I have nothing more to say in this chapter about projective techniques as such, and move on to the discussion of personality inventories. I return to the problem of the interpretation of protocols in the sections on cognitive assessment and narrative analysis.

Personality Inventories

By "personality inventory" I mean a set of stimuli (usually verbal items) to which the respondent is instructed to respond by means of a limited number of structured response options. Various techniques are used to identify sets of items that form scales. Here, I describe the underlying logic of seven of these scale construction strategies.

The Rational Strategy

In general, if one wants information from someone, the easiest and best way to get it is to ask directly. As we have seen, the Woodworth PDS was constructed on this basis. Its goal was to identify inductees who might be unfit for military service, and it was therefore composed of items describing psychological conditions that might render someone unfit for military service. Such direct items are the most efficient means of obtaining information if the respondent (1) can understand the question, (2) knows the answer to the question, and (3) is willing to answer the question honestly. In the case of the PDS, it was obviously easy for a respondent to malinger, and there was an equally obvious motivation for many of them to do so.

The PDS took a step forward by assembling a set of such items into a scale. The implicit assumptions were that the items were all related to the same construct (psychological fitness for military service), and that the more such items one endorsed, the less likely it was that one was fit for service—in other words, that there was a monotonic relation between scores on the scale and fitness for military service.

The designation of this means of scale construction as "rational" may be something of a misnomer. In the modern sense of this word, "rational" refers to thoughts and actions that are reasonable in the light of well-established empirical knowledge. Its use here is in reference to the historical distinction between rationalist and empiricist philosophies. In that use it was meant to contrast rational with empirical approaches to scale construction. The contrast is one of disapprobation, and the emphasis is on the fact that rational scales were constructed without empirical checks on their validity. Thus, "rational" here refers to acting in the absence of, or with disregard for, empirical information.

The Rational–Theoretical Strategy

One may rationally select items for a scale, not because one is interested in the answer to the item itself, but because the response is thought to be related to a construct in which one is interested. If, for example, one is interested in measuring human needs (e.g., Murray, 1938), then one may include an item of the form "Whenever I have a new sheet of stamps, I always carefully remove the border from an outside stamp before using it"—not because one really cares whether the person uses stamps with the border on them, but because one thinks the response might be related to a construct called Need for Order.

There is obviously no clear line between rational and rational–theoretical scales. Each of the items in the PDS was thought to be significant in its own right, but they were also thought to be related to the construct of Psychoneurotic Tendencies. However, the latter construct was not of theoretical interest in the same sense as something like Need for Order, which is embedded in a theory. The distinction really refers to the investigator's orientation and purpose: Is one interested in the answer itself, or in the answer as an indicator of a construct from a particular theoretical orientation?

Rational and rational–theoretical means of scale construction fell out of favor from the 1930s through the 1960s. Beginning in the 1970s, however, the cycle that had reached the empiricist extreme during the 1940s and 1950s returned to the point at which rational–theoretical approaches were described as the preferred first step in personality inventory scale construction, within the context of a sophisticated construct validation model (Jackson, 1971).

The Internal-Consistency Strategy

In the absence of an external criterion that the scale is intended to predict, are there ways in which one might improve on the procedures described above? If one's theory is that the construct being measured is a unitary construct, then one may believe that all items in the scale should be positively correlated with one another. Internal-consistency coefficients (e.g., coefficient α) or correlations between each item and the total of the remaining items may be used to insure scale homogeneity. In this case, empirical information concerning the relations among responses is being used as one kind of check on the adequacy of the items to measure the intended construct. However, nothing in the procedure guarantees that the items are measuring the intended construct, as opposed to some other construct. Nor is there any guarantee that they are measuring a single construct; they may be measuring two or more constructs that happen to be positively correlated in the sample being studied. In fact, it is possible to get high α coefficients even for a scale measuring two constructs that are uncorrelated in the population (O. P. John, personal communication, August 9, 1989).

Investigators who adopt the internal-consistency approach believe that a scale should measure only one construct, and that this construct should be homogeneous. If the construct can be broken into constituent parts, then a scale should be constructed to measure each of those parts. The scales can then be combined either statistically or subjectively to provide a measure of the superordinate construct.

Although a great deal has been written about the desirability of scale homogeneity, the limits of this desirability are only rarely considered. If all items correlated perfectly, then obviously one would need only one item, not the whole scale. If the items correlated at the limits imposed by their individual reliabilities, then additional items might add reliability, but no new information. If one combines items in a scale, one is implicitly acknowledging that no individual item is designed to measure the construct as such, but rather only some aspect or instance of the construct. Items measuring different aspects or instances of a construct obviously should be less than perfectly correlated after one allows for less than perfect reliability. How much less remains an unanswered theoretical question, probably because, as a practical matter, test constructors have not been confronted with the problem of items that seemed too highly correlated.

The Empirical, Criterion-Group Strategy

None of the procedures described above uses empirical data to assess the relation between item responses and the construct of interest. Empirical, criterion-group keying is straightforward: Assemble a pool of items, administer them to the group one wishes to describe (the criterion group), and key them in terms of the predominant response of the group. Items can be differentially weighted to reflect their endorsement frequencies. Individuals who take the scale can then be described in terms of the extent to which their answers correspond to those of the group. Note that if one considers the prototypical member to be the one who has the most characteristics that identify the group, then the prototypical member may receive a score higher than the average for the group (i.e., he or she would or will be more like the group prototype than the average member of the group). Thus, as scores on the scale increase, they first indicate increasing similarity to a typical member, and then decreasing similarity. Scores are linearly related to group prototypicality, but not to group representativeness. (In some groups, such as that of people with schizophrenia, the prototypical member is not one who has every possible schizophrenic sign). Not many scales have been constructed this way.

The Empirical, Contrasted-Groups Strategy

The empirical, contrasted-groups method is the strategy that is most often meant when writers refer simply to "empirical scale construction." The shorthand designation causes few problems because most empirically keyed scales were developed by the contrasted-groups strategy. In this procedure, an item pool is administered both to a group of interest (the criterion group) and to a group from whom they are to be differentiated (the reference group). The latter is generally a group representative of people in general, but may be a narrower group representative of, say, psychiatric hospital patients, and may in principle be any other group. One retains those items that are answered signficantly differently by the members of the two groups. This procedure should be cross-validated (although it seldom is) to remove those items that may have initially been included because of Type I errors.

The items that are included by these two empirical procedures are obviously very different—a fact that is sometimes overlooked in interpreting responses to scales that have been developed by these empirical procedures. The first method retains items that are common to the two groups; the second does not. For example, in the physical realm the former procedure includes items relating to having two arms, two legs, and two eyes, whereas the latter does not. Depending on the item pool with which one begins, a criterion-group scale may be composed entirely of Barnum-type statements—that is, statements that are true of almost everyone. Thus, the scale may not be very descriptive of the criterion group in the sense that it contains no information to distinguish members of that group from any other group.

The contrasted-groups procedure, on the other hand, may retain items that are not representative of the criterion group, because, even though they are answered by only a minority of the criterion group, that minority is larger than the minority of the reference group who endorse the item. For example, an item such as "I sometimes see things that are not there" may be answered by only a minority of a group of psychiatric patients, but may be answered by almost none of the members of the reference group, and so will be included in the scale, even though it is not representative of the criterion group. The more nearly similar the criterion group is to the reference group, the more misleading the items will be as a description of the criterion group, because only those items relating to the small area of differ-

ence will be retained. The criterion group will be caricatured by items that describe only a fringe minority or relatively unimportant characteristics of the group.

Both rational and empirical scales have been developed on the basis of two distinctly different population models. One posits distinct groups, or "taxa" (e.g., Meehl & Golden, 1982). The other posits traits or characteristics that are assumed to be normally distributed in the population. In either case, there must be some independent way in which to identify criterion-group members so as to be able to construct the scale, although once the scale is constructed it may turn out to be a better indicator than the one that was used in the first place (Dawes & Meehl, 1966; Meehl & Golden, 1982).

The way in which the criterion group is constructed may pose a problem for subsequent interpretation. Consider the continuous case first. Here the usual procedure is to identify individuals falling at the extreme ends of the continuum and to select items that discriminate between these two groups. Unfortunately, those items that best discriminate individuals who fall at the extreme ends of the continuum may not discriminate among those who fall toward the center, and it is the latter for whom the scale is most needed, because those at the extremes can probably be identified without use of the scale. The same problem occurs in a slightly different form when distinct groups are assumed to exist. Here, in an effort to get a "clean" criterion group one selects only clear-cut cases of, say, schizophrenia. The resulting scale may well identify such clear-cut cases, but, again, one does not need the scale for that. Rather, one needs the scale for assistance in diagnosing borderline cases, and there is nothing in the procedure to guarantee that the scale will be very good at that.

In contrasts of the rational and the empirical approaches, the attention paid to item content has often been overemphasized. It is true that the rational approaches utilize item content exclusively, and that the ultimate basis of empirical scale construction strategies is endorsement frequency. But it is not true, in general, that content has been ignored in assembling item pools for empirical scale construction. Vocational inventories contain items relating to occupations and interests; personality (or should we call them psychopathology?) inventories, such as the MMPI, contain items relating to psychological problems; and so on. One of the reasons why the MMPI has endured as long as it has is probably because Hathaway had an unusual sensitivity to what his patients said. Other inventories with items that seem more clever or original have not fared as well.

The Empirical, Itemmetric Strategy

The fact that item content has typically been considered in assembling item pools for empirical scales is made clearer by considering those cases in which scales have been constructed on the basis of criteria other than item content. Examples include endorsement frequencies, social desirability scale values, and differential endorsement frequencies. In the first two cases the goal has been to develop scales that would measure acquiescent and social desirability response tendencies. Unfortunately, the interpretation of scales constructed in this fashion turns out to be problematic, because neither endorsement frequency nor social desirability is independent of item content, or of each other. In the third case the goal has been to test the radical empiricist theory of scale construction. I comment briefly on each of these in turn.

Response Styles. Unless one adopts the radical empiricist approach, one assumes that the responses to personality inventory items are responses to the content of those items. The "response style" hypothesis stated, first, that individuals might be responding, not to the item content, but rather on the basis of a preference for some response category, such as "true" or "false"; and, second, that such response preferences might be enduring tendencies reflective of a basic personality style. The hypothesis stimulated a great deal of research aimed at building measures of response styles, particularly acquiescence response style, so as to use these scales to remove the stylistic components from responses and get purer content measures.

The first part of the hypothesis seemed to be supported when scales constructed on the basis of endorsement frequencies were shown to account for sizable proportions of the response variance. Given the experimental assumption that such scales would be composed of diverse content, and would therefore not be subject to content interpretations, it was inferred that these scales must measure response styles. The

assumption turned out to be false. The methodologically superior approach of item reversal showed that such scales were more accurately interpreted in terms of their content, and that the stylistic contribution to variance in personality inventories was small. There was never any support for the hypothesis that stylistic tendencies represent enduring personality characteristics (see Rorer, 1965, for a detailed review).

Nonetheless, it has become part of the enduring wisdom that "standard practice" calls for the construction of balanced scales. "Balanced" sometimes seems to mean an equal number of true- and false-keyed items, and other times to mean an equal number of positively and negatively phrased items. It is my impression that there is not a clear appreciation of the fact that these are not the same. In the first case one could have a scale of positively phrased items, half of which were keyed true and half false, whereas in the second case one could have a true-keyed scale composed of an equal number of positively and negatively phrased items. Acquiescence response style, renamed "agreement acquiescence" by Bentler, Jackson, and Messick (1971), would be controlled by the former, but not the latter.

However, Paulhus (in press) notes that "The original proponents of the importance of acquiescence, Messick and Jackson, shifted their focus to acceptance acquiescence." The latter refers to the tendency to ascribe many characteristics (even seemingly contrary ones) to oneself, without respect to keying. The importance of acceptance acquiescence was challenged by Block (1971), and has received little attention. Paulhus (in press) was able to find only two personality instruments designed to measure or control for it, and both of these are measures of socially desirable responding. Thus, balanced keying has come to be part of the accepted wisdom, even though the original proponents "concluded that the effects of agreement acquiescence are insignificant" (Paulhus, in press).

Social Desirability. In contrast to "response styles," which relate to a tendency to prefer a certain response option independently of the item content, "response sets" refer to a tendency to respond to item content with the intent of presenting a certain picture of oneself. When it is used in the literature, "social desirability" usually seems to refer to a response set—a reference that is made clear by "social desirability response tendency" or some similar designation. However, it should be emphasized that "social desirability" is ambiguous in the sense of having two distinct meanings. One is the one that has just been suggested: a tendency to put oneself in a good light, to give the socially desirable response, even if it may not be the most accurate one. The tendency may be either conscious or unconscious. In either case, it is a form of dissimulation.

One would like to be able to partial these response tendencies out so as to get a better estimate of what a correct content response would be. Dissimulation scales have been constructed in two ways: (1) empirically, by contrasting the responses of people presumed to be making themselves look good or bad with people presumed to be answering honestly, or at least more honestly; and (2) rationally, by selecting items judged to be either desirable but unlikely to be true, or undesirable but likely to be true.

The early work which popularized the notion of social desirability was based on the Social Desirability (SD) scale, constructed from the MMPI item pool by selecting items judged to be either socially desirable or undesirable, without regard to their likely veridicality (e.g., Edwards, 1957). Edwards contrasted his scale with the MMPI Lie (L) scale, and noted that they loaded on different factors (I and III, respectively). He stated simply that the SD scale measured socially desirable responding (a potentially misleading designation) and that responses could be accounted for by the social-desirability scale values (SDSVs, determined by having subjects rate the social desirability of the items on a 9-point scale) of the items. In this second sense, social desirability is not a response set; it is simply a psychometric fact that is neutral with respect to the veridicality of the responses.

However, social desirability has not been construed in terms of this narrow psychometric definition. It has been claimed that the first factor of the MMPI measures social desirability, presumably in contrast to content, and that desirability scales should be used to partial social desirability out of other scales—a suggestion that makes sense in relation to social desirability in the first sense as a response tendency, but makes no sense in relation to social desirability in the second sense as a psychometric fact.

Some behaviors and characteristics are more desirable than others. We cannot measure behaviors and characteristics independently of their social desirability. Any form of psychopathology provides an example. One of the reasons why we are interested in measuring anxiety, depression, psychoticism, or any other form of psychological maladjustment is precisely because such maladjustment is not desirable. If we were to partial social desirability out of psychoticism, what we would presumably have left would be psychoticism that is not socially undesirable. What, pray tell, would that be? Certainly not what any clinician is interested in measuring. Attitudes, behaviors, beliefs, characteristics, dispositions, tendencies, and traits do differ in their social desirability, and a measure with that desirability partialled out is simply a measure of something other than the original construct. To remove that part of the meaning that is associated with social desirability is to change the meaning.

In the more than 30 years since Edwards popularized research into social desirability, investigators have first lumped all the dissimulation and desirability measures together under the general rubric of "social desirability," and then rediscovered that there are really two kinds of measures there (e.g., Paulhus, 1986). There is not much disagreement about the first kind, though it has been suggested that terms such as "lie" and "dissimulation" are overly pejorative and should be replaced. Paulhus (1986) has suggested "impression management."

There is continuing disagreement about the interpretation of the second kind of measure. However, no one has improved on Block (1965), who showed empirically that peer ratings indicated that item content describes respondents accurately. And no one has responded to Norman (1967), who pointed out that the method of scale construction precludes inferences concerning response tendencies on logical grounds (see the section on "Normative, Ipsative, and Idiothetic Strategies," below). Paulhus (1986, in press) concluded that the second kind of measure probably does measure self-deception, but only to the extent that such self-deception is part of normal healthy functioning; he noted that social desirability in this sense should not be partialled out of personality measures, because it is part of what the personality scales are designed to measure. Thus, whether or not one believes that the scales include a component of self-deception, the conclusion is the same: There is no justification for using these scales to partial out social desirability.

Radical Empiricism. The radical empiricist position, dubbed the "deviation hypothesis" by Berg (1967), stated that scales composed of items with no obvious content relation to the construct being measured, or scales composed of sets of geometric drawings with no content at all, could be constructed to perform as well as scales with relevant content. The proposed methodology was a straightforward, brute-force application of the empirical, contrasted-groups strategy. All that was necessary was to assemble a sufficiently large pool of potential items and a sufficiently large group of subjects and let the computers do the rest. If such scales could have been constructed, they would have solved one of the long-standing problems of personality assessment, because they would have been virtually immune to dissimulation. Unfortunately, after some apparent early successes had raised hopes, all such attempts ultimately failed (e.g., Goldberg & Slovic, 1967; Norman, 1963). The failure of this ultimate test of the empiricist approach during the 1960s undoubtedly played a role in the increasing emphasis on theoretical and conceptual coherence during the 1970s and 1980s.

The Factor-Analytic Strategy

The logical extension of the principle of scale homogeneity is exploratory factor analysis, especially if one is constructing a set of scales rather than a single scale. In contrast to the rational and empirical strategies, which assume that one knows what one wants to measure, the factor-analytic strategy assumes that one does not know what one wishes to measure. The goal of the procedure is first to determine that, and then to build measures of the constructs identified by the factor analysis. The model assumes that one is identifying dimensions along which people differ, and is therefore not appropriate for distinct groups (taxa).

Conceptually, there are two stages of the factor-analytic process: One first determines how many dimensions (factors) are needed to reproduce the responses to the items, and then how best to position the dimensions (axes) so as to provide the most meaningful or interpretable outcome. The second step requires a decision that is important both conceptually and mathematically, but may not make a lot of practical difference—namely, whether to require the dimensions to be orthogonal or to allow them to be correlated. Orthogonal solutions are mathematically simpler, and allow one to calculate the independent contribution of each factor to each variable. However, such a solution is not desirable if the most "natural" solution involves factors that are, in fact, correlated in the population one is studying. To use another example from the physical realm, if one had a set of variables related to the height and weight of people, and if one wanted a two-factor solution that would describe the relations among these variables with respect to the dimensions of height and weight, then one could not insist on an orthogonal solution, because height and weight are correlated in the general population. In an orthogonal solution, if the first factor represented height, then the second factor would represent that aspect of weight that is independent of height—namely, the tendency of people to be fat or thin for a given height.

Although there are algorithms that will perform both steps on the basis of designated criteria, thereby making the process both objective and empirical, sophisticated practitioners often run numerous analyses using a variety of algorithms to see which gives the "best" solution, or attempt to improve on the results by making subjective adjustments. The primary criteria seem to be the meaningfulness and comprehensibility of the result in terms of previous findings and the investigator's theoretical beliefs. Once the dimensions to be measured have been decided upon, the items that correlate most highly with each dimension can be empirically selected to construct scales to measure those dimensions (see Comrey, 1988, for a very readable description of his factor-analytic reasearch program).

The construct is now defined by the content of the items in the scale. The investigator may, on the basis of that content, argue that the construct corresponds to a construct in some theoretical framework, or he or she may argue that a new construct, requiring a new theoretical formulation, has been discovered. If the result were to be interpreted within the traditional framework that I have described, then one would have to assume that there are certain dimensions that one is trying to identify (discover). Few factor-analytic investigators would interpret their results that way these days; they would probably opt instead for a constructivist approach within which it would be acknowledged that a number of different descriptions might be possible, with the selection ultimately to be made on the basis of pragmatic criteria.

Test Interpretation

Even if a scale has been empirically constructed by either the criterion-group or the contrasted-groups method, we still do not know, except by looking at the content of the items, what characteristics of the group may be involved in making the distinction. Thus, the means of interpreting or understanding an empirically constructed scale is not a great deal different from that of a rationally or factor-analytically constructed scale. Furthermore, consulting the content of the items does not tell us what other characteristics, not represented in the item pool, may be related to those represented in the scale. Thus, no matter how a scale has been constructed, the only way in which to know what it indicates is to investigate its empirical correlates. The same reasoning applies to sets or patterns of scales.

Empiricist investigators therefore began studying groups of people who scored high or low on a given scale. The characteristics of such a group could turn out to be similar to those of the group on the basis of which the scale was constructed. Indeed, the scale might turn out to be a means of selecting a more homogeneous group (Meehl & Golden, 1982). But the characteristics might turn out to be very different.

In addition, it was observed that some patterns of MMPI scale scores occurred much more often than others. This raised the hope that such patterns might be the road to the discovery of true diagnostic groups; that is, that the groups identified by these patterns might provide a new and improved diagnostic system. The result was a proliferation of "cookbooks" describing a number of these groups in different populations (e.g., Gilberstadt & Duker, 1965; Hathaway & Meehl, 1951; Marks & Seeman, 1963). Although the hope of a new diagnostic system was not realized, the science of test interpretation was fundamentally altered. Related studies made it clear that logically reasoned interpretations were no match for empirically derived ones. And psychologists were forced to confront the problem of Bayesian inverse probabilities: The probability of being schizophrenic, given a high score on a schizophrenia scale, is not the same as the probability of having a high score on the schizophrenia scale, given that one is

schizophrenic (e.g., Dawes, 1962; Rorer, Hoffman, Laforge, & Hsieh, 1966).

If one has identified the criterion one wishes to predict, then the logical extension of the finding that the empirical interpretation of scales is superior to subjective interpretation is that the empirical selection of scales may be superior to subjective selection, and it turns out that it is. One should therefore have the computer determine empirically which scales should be included in the prediction set and how they should be weighted. Because the number of possible scale combinations is large, the number of possible empirical correlates endless, and the number of possible populations limited only by the investigator's imagination, modern computerized cookbooks rely on a combination of empirically derived and clinically inferred descriptors. Butcher (1987) provides an up-to-date survey.

It is a historical fact that such cookbooks have been constructed almost entirely on the basis of the MMPI, although there is no logical reason why that should be the case. Is there an empirical one? More generally, if one is building an empirical prediction system, does it matter whether the scales have been assembled rationally, empirically, or factor-analytically? In a pioneering study, Goldberg (1972) asked just that question. The surprising answer, confirmed in subsequent studies (Burisch, 1986), is that it does not. Scales assembled randomly or solely on the basis of itemmetric considerations (SDSVs or endorsement frequencies) have little validity, but the other systematic means of scale construction seem about equally effective, at least with cooperative subjects. The results in other settings may well be different. Thus, when the empirical scale construction strategy is carried to its logical conclusion, it has an ironic result: Empirical scale construction results in no predictive advantage; one can do as well assembling scales rationally, and one can do it a lot more cheaply. The same is not true of scale interpretation, where the evidence in favor of empirical interpretation is overwhelming.

LOGICAL EMPIRICISM AND ITS CRITICS

To understand the traditional assessment model, it is necessary to keep in mind some of the tenets of logical empiricism, in the context of which the traditional assessment model was developed. That position has not been accepted in philosophy for at least 25 years, and is finally beginning to lose support in psychology. In this and the following section, I indicate some of the problems with the empiricist position as I describe it, and briefly describe some more modern alternatives.

1. In order to be scientifically acceptable or meaningful, statements had to be "objective," by which it was generally understood that they had to refer to something "observable." The logical empiricists realized early on that such a criterion was much too strict, and readily accepted statements that were only indirectly confirmable. Physicists have never had any reluctance to talk about things that are in principle unobservable (e.g., atoms, quarks, black holes), but psychologists, thinking that they were being scientific, competed with one another to see who could be the most rigorous—that is, the most objective.

2. Given the goal of objectivity, the problem was to make that which is subjective, objective. There is, ultimately, no way to do that. Nevertheless, it was thought that unobservable entities could be dealt with by means of operational definitions. Unfortunately, it has never been possible to give an acceptable formulation of an "operational definition," and most philosophers of science now agree that it cannot be done (Suppe, 1977). Even if it were possible to formulate operational definitions, one has to have some way of determining the extent to which the operational definition corresponds to the subjective experience, and there is no objective way to do that. One solution is to pretend, as some behaviorists did, that one can ignore subjective experience, and that one should put an end to the traditional personality assessment enterprise (see below).

3. It was believed that it was possible to obtain theory-free data, and that assessment procedures could, and therefore should, be theory-free. It was only after the demise of empiricism in philosophy, and the behavioral and cognitive revolutions in psychology, that we were able to appreciate that all assessments and all assessment procedures are meaningful and understandable only in a theoretical context.

4. The goals of scientific research were thought to be prediction and control. Prediction and control required that one know the cause of an event. To establish the cause of an event, and therefore to be able to predict it, one had to show that it was a special case (instantiation) of a general covering law. The task of the scientist was to develop theories (laws) from which deductions could be made, and then to test those predictions experimentally. If the experimental result corresponded to the prediction, then the theory was said to be confirmed, the event was said to be explained, and the law was taken to state the cause of the event. Acceptable scientific research was narrowly limited to laboratory or controlled experimentation. Observational or correlational procedures were rejected, because it was thought that only controlled experiments could establish causal relations.

A realist position allows a far different view of causality. The goal is not to discover general laws, but to describe structures. Causal explanations are provided by a description or account in some theoretical context, and can be of many kinds. Controlled experimentation is not the only, or even the most desirable, means of providing causal explanations. The gene, our understanding of which has changed radically over the years, explains the phenomena of inheritance. The double helix provides an explanation at another level. Both are structures. Astronomical theories explain the movements of the stars and planets, which obviously cannot be studied experimentally in the laboratory. Thus, both the goals and methods of science have changed. (For a more detailed summary of the philosophy of science as it relates to psychology, see Rorer, in press.)

The empiricist view of science created a tension within the field of personality assessment. The instruments developed in the diagnostic context were objectively scorable and quantitative, and therefore scientifically respectable. The projective tests, developed within the psychodynamic framework, were not. Some who worked within the latter framework tried to make their research enterprise conform to the sicentific model; others rejected it, as they should have, but had no strong candidate to put in its place.

CHALLENGES TO THE TRADITIONAL MODEL

As it turned out, the entire assessment enterprise was to be attacked—first from the right by the behaviorists, who claimed that it was not sufficiently scientific, and then from the left by the cognitivists, who claimed that it was too constricted by an outmoded philosophy of science to be able to deal with the problem to which it was addressed. Here, I first consider the behaviorist attack, which was launched within the empiricist framework.

Behavioral Assessment

Although behavioral methods of treatment enjoyed some popularity during the 1920s as a result of the writings of Watson, behavior therapy or behavior modification did not become a recognized speciality until the 1960s, when it was embraced by academicians as a scientifically respectable alternative to psychoanalysis for the treatment of psychological (behavioral) problems. Hayes (1986) distinguishes among three kinds of behaviorists. "Traditional methodological behaviorists" accept the early logical empiricist notion that science can deal only with that which is publicly observable. "Contemporary methodological behaviorists," in parallel with the liberalization of the logical empiricists' meaning criterion, would include the study of "inferred events that are thought to exist at another level but that cannot be addressed directly by science" (Hayes, 1986, p. 39). "Radical behaviorists," following Skinner, reject public observability as a criterion of scientific meaningfulness, and focus instead on the contingencies surrounding an observation. In contrast to methodological behaviorists, radical behaviorists reject logical empiricism as a philosophical basis. It is a contextualist position, focusing on the subjectively determined act in context (Hayes, 1986).

In my reading of the literature, behavior therapists and behavior assessors seem to invoke methodological rather than radical behaviorism as the justification for their procedures, even though there may be references to Skinner. The general claim is that behavior therapy is objective, because it relies upon overt behavior, whereas psychoanalysis is not (Freud's claim to the contrary notwithstanding), because it focuses upon private events; behavior therapy is therefore claimed to be more scientifically respectable than psychoanalysis or any of the related psychodynamic theories (Kazdin, 1979). This belief was widely shared in academic circles in the 1960s

and 1970s, and it has survived, albeit less strongly, through the 1980s.

Behavioral theorists reject internal structures or dispositions as causes of behavior, and therefore reject both internal dynamics and disease processes as accounting for disordered behavior. Because they reject the disease concept, they reject the diagnostic model according to which people could be put in categories. Disordered behavior is not a sign of an internal dysfunction; it *is* the dysfunction. The task of the behavioral assessor, therefore, is not to obtain data on the basis of which inferences can be made to internal states, dispositions, or events, but rather to obtain samples of the behavior to be modified.

Note that this fundamental difference in theoretical approach does not necessarily imply any difference in the data that one may collect, but only a difference in the way the data are treated once they have been collected. Both approaches may use self-reports, behavioral rating scales, objective tests, and physiological reactions—in one case treating them as signs of the disorder to be corrected, and in the other as samples of the behavior to be modified. Nevertheless, the change in focus from covert to overt behavior and from signs to samples resulted in a different emphasis on the kinds of data to be obtained. The behaviorists were interested in observing *in situ*, or in constructing situations in which the problematic behavior would be exhibited, or in obtaining verbal reports of the behavior to be changed.

Thirty years of research on test development and theory had been based on the premise that one could not just take behavior, especially verbal reports, at face value. It was this research on which the claim of scientific respectability for clinical psychology had been based. With the behaviorists' emphasis on behavioral contingencies, this work was seemingly undone at a stroke, again in the name of scientific respectability.

Just how different are these positions? Not as different as it might seem (e.g., Meehl, 1986). First, it should be noted that, in general, behaviorists do not study behavior, but rather the results of behavior (lever presses, maze turns, quantity of food eaten, etc.). Second, behavior as such is not observable. Movement is, but it requires inferences to convert movement to behavior. Third, even though they might deny it, I think many behaviorists do consider their observations, such as heart rate, blushing, perspiring, and trembling, to be indicators of internal states—in this case a state of anxiety.

Cognitive Assessment

"Cognitive assessment" is another ambiguous designation. Until the mid-1970s, at least, it referred either to intellectual assessment, usually with reference to the administration of an IQ test, or to neuropsychological assessment, which was understood to mean the assessment of cognitive or intellectual dysfunction (brain damage) as a result of trauma, illness, or degeneration. That is, it referred to the assessment of either cognitive abilities or the impairment of cognitive abilities. In this sense it may be taken to refer to the assessment of cognitive processes—in particular, to the quality or efficiency of cognitive processes. In the present context, however, "cognitive assessment" has quite a different meaning. It refers to the assessment of beliefs—the contents, both conscious and unconscious, of the mind, including the contents of cognitive (reasoning) processes. It includes the assessment of meaning and understanding.

Ericsson and Simon (1981) have provided an excellent, concise summary of psychologists' views of cognition since the turn of the century. They begin by noting,

> The nature of data, and of admissible procedures for gathering and interpreting them, cannot be discussed very long in theory-free terms. The epistemological question (how the experimenter gains reliable information about the subject) is closely interwoven with the psychological question (how the subject gains and retains reliable information about the world). (p. 16)

> We have also long known, both from experiments and from everyday experience, how subjects' behaviors are affected by expectation, context, and measurement procedures. The notion that there can be "neutral" methods for gathering data has been refuted decisively. (p. 17)

The first method used by psychologists was what we would now call "naive introspection." Early psychologists such as William James considered it the major tool for psychological investigation. Binet defined psychology in terms of introspection. Titchner considered a phenomenological account, a description of con-

sciousness, to be the starting point of a psychological description, but his aim was then to go beyond this and use the contents of consciousness to uncover its structure. In order to do this he tried to train his subjects to report only their immediate perceptual or imaginal experience, before that experience had been interpreted at all. He thought that in this way he could find the basic sensory units or attributes out of which all other experiences were then constructed.

The procedure was attacked from both sides. The Gestaltists claimed that the phenomenal experience was primary and could not be decomposed by analytic introspection. For them the immediate reports of naive subjects' experiences constituted the basic source of data. They emphasized the importance of conceptual understanding for learning and retention. The behaviorists, led by Watson, objected to the use of anything other than observable data. For Watson, the verbal reports, and not the events to which they supposedly referred, constituted the data. He cited the variability in the reports produced by different laboratories as evidence that such reports were inevitably contaminated by the subjects' prior experiences. He and many subsequent behaviorists thought that by sticking to observational data, they could avoid this problem and collect theory-free data.

Note that everyone relied on verbal reports as their primary data. The Gestaltists made extensive use of think-aloud procedures, but Watson did it first (Ericsson & Simon, 1981)—unless we count Freud, who had been having patients free-associate for years. The behaviorists and traditional personality assessors rejected verbal reports as evidence of direct experience, but starting in the 1970s cognitive assessors were once again asking clients to think aloud, and were accepting such reports as descriptive of the clients' phenomenal experience.

Cognitive therapies were first introduced by Ellis (e.g., 1962) and Kelly (1955), although not under that name, but did not gain even minimal acceptance until the 1970s. Mischel's (1973) article "Toward a Cognitive Social Learning Reconceptualization of Personality" is commonly cited as the turning point in the acceptability of cognitive formulations of personality.

An excellent current summary of *cognitive* assessment techniques can be found in a volume entitled, *Behavioral Assessment: A*

Practical Handbook (Parks & Hollon, 1988). These authors begin by noting the problems. Much cognitive processing takes place—and at any given time most thoughts, beliefs, and memories are—outside of conscious awareness. In contrast to earlier assumptions, it is now recognized that memory retrieval is largely a constructive, or reconstructive, process: "While people can often describe the products of their information processing, the actual processes followed may need to be inferred on the basis of carefully structured assessment paradigms" (p. 161).

Parks and Hollon (1988) describe instruments that are designed to measure thoughts, attitudes, beliefs, attributional styles, expectations, irrational thinking processes, and self-schemas. These assessment procedures are categorized as "recording," "endorsement," "production," and "inferential" methods. Recording methods include listening to private speech (i.e., barely audible speech), especially of children, when they are unaware that their speech is being recorded; having people think aloud as they perform a task or solve a problem; asking people to free-associate; and asking people to respond to stimuli out loud. Endorsement methods involve presenting the subject with a set of items that have been either rationally constructed or empirically selected. Production methods include thought listing (listing one's thoughts in response to a stimulus), thought sampling (the same, except that thoughts are recorded in response to a beeper at random or fixed intervals), and event recording (recording one's thoughts during some designated event). Inferential methods are indirect in nature:

> The purpose of the assessment is not readily discernible from the procedure . . . Virtually all depend on inference; investigators do not ask subjects to report their operating self-schemata, personal constructs, etcetera. Rather, these cognitive structures are inferred from subjects' performance on a variety of cognitive and/or behavioral tasks, typically developed and validated in the basic cognitive psychology literature. (Parks & Hollon, 1988, p. 168)

"What's going on here?" readers may ask. How are these different from what personality assessors were doing 50 years ago, before they tried to get (pseudo)scientific? In one way or another people are being asked to state their thoughts, and those thoughts are either being accepted at face value or are being used to infer cognitive structures, beliefs, attitudes, and attributional styles. Sundberg (1981) has provided a fascinating history of cognitive assessment, showing that interest in thoughts and beliefs has been there all along. The inferences currently being made in cognitive assessment are more closely tied to the data than are the inferences of dynamic therapists. If someone suffers from a social phobia, the interest is in the thoughts that occur when the person is entering, or thinking about entering, the phobic situation. There may be some general theory concerning the kinds of thoughts that are most likely to lead to social anxiety (e.g., those having to do with evaluation by others), but the client's formulation of the belief is accepted, in contrast to inferring some repressed fear from early childhood as the real problem. Within the context of modern epistemologies it is no longer necessary to justify such procedures. It is sufficient to show that a persuasive argument can be made that the inferred relations make sense, or that the same kinds of thoughts occur in other people with similar problems.

Finally, before concluding this section I should note that there have been dramatic advances in cognitive assessment in its original sense. The computer has made possible the research program envisioned and attempted unsuccessfully by Galton, Cattell, and others just before and after the turn of the century. It now seems that it may be possible one day to measure intelligence in terms of neurological speed and efficiency (e.g., Glaser, 1981; Sternberg, 1981). With respect to both ability and content, cognitive assessment has completed the cycle to psychology's beginnings.

DEVELOPMENTS WITHIN THE TRADITIONAL MODEL

In this section, I describe three areas of research that represent developments within the traditional model, but which clearly reflect the influence of modern philosophies of science on that model. First, I describe some recent developments in the theory of personality inventory construction. Second, I make brief reference to a continuing effort to construct a comprehensive taxonomy of trait-descriptive adjectives. And, third, I briefly describe a very different approach to the construction of diagnostic indicators.

Personality Inventories

Multimethod Sequential Strategies

Jackson (1971) is usually credited with writing the manifesto for personality inventory construction in the 1970s and 1980s. He rejected the radical empiricist philosophy and called for an explicit concern with item content. Inventories were to be constructed within a theoretical framework; items written to measure constructs within that framework had to meet several criteria, including conceptual comprehensibility, to be included in scales. Jackson also argued that items should measure only one construct, should be free of social desirability, and should be keyed equally "true" and "false"—all criteria that I have already rejected.

Conceptually, the shift in thinking is indicated by the shift from criterion validation to construct validation (e.g., Embretson [Whitely], 1983; Messick, 1981). Whereas judgments or ratings would previously have been accepted as the criteria against which scales would be validated, it was now recognized that judgments and scales are both indicators of open rather than operationally defined constructs. Multitrait–multimethod matrices provide a systematic way of examining the relations among the indicators developed by different methods to measure a set of constructs. Divergent validity was seen to be as important as convergent validity, even if such data are not often provided in practice.

The shift in thinking is also reflected in the development and utilization of confirmatory factor analysis. Exploratory factor analysis had been used to discover the variables to be measured; now those variables can be derived on theoretical grounds, and confirmatory factor analysis can be used to determine the extent to which the instrument corresponds to the theory. Thus, empirical checks are still used, but in a very different way; for if the results do not fit the theory, it may well be the instrument rather than the theory that gets revised.

Finally, the concept of structural fidelity that Loevinger (1957) articulated long ago can comfortably be incorporated into the theory of inventory construction. The properties of the measurement model should mirror the properties of the construct of which it is an indicator. For example, a bipolar scale with "love" at one end and "hate" at the other is not appropriate for a theory including "ambivalence" (large amounts of love and hate existing simultaneously) as a construct. Such a theory requires separate, possibly orthogonal, scales for "love" and "hate."

Normative, Ipsative, and Idiothetic Strategies

Normative Strategies. Under the traditional model, most inventories have been constructed normatively. Scores on a scale indicate an individual's standing relative to a reference population on whatever the scale measures. All descriptors are relative to some (usually implicit) population or standard. With physical objects, the immediate measure, such as 6 feet, is relative to a standard; however, when we translate that measure into a descriptor via an ascription rule (Rorer & Widiger, 1982), the descriptor is relative to some population. Thus, 6 feet may indicate a tall woman relative to the general population of women, but a short man relative to other players in the National Basketball Association. When "very often" is used to describe the rate at which earthquakes occur, the rate is lower than when "sometimes" is used to describe the amount of shooting in a Western movie (Pepper, 1981). In psychology we do not have an objective standard such as a meter stick or a clock. Our measures are relative to start with, and are meaningful only when the reference population is specified.

The meaning of scores on normative personality scales is more basically relativistic than is always acknowledged. If we keep in mind that scales serve as indicators of constructs, and that the raw scores (which are meaningless) are translated into deviation scores relative to some population, the scores on two scales may indicate that an individual scores relatively higher on indicator A than on indicator B relative to this reference population; however, it does not necessarily follow that the individual has more of trait A than of trait B in any absolute sense, because that relation may change with a different reference population or with a different set of indicators for the same constructs.

Ipsative Strategies. Some personality inventories have been constructed ipsatively by the use of forced-choice items on which each of the possible responses is scored on a different scale. Each person has a fixed number of points, equal to the number of items, that can be divided up among the scales. Thus, everyone's average raw score is the same, and the scaled results indicate the salience of a scale relative to the other scales for that person, *relative* to the reference population used in norming the scales. In this case it is the person's deviation relative to that person's other scores that is then normed relative to the reference population. As before, the indicated relation between two constructs might change with a different reference population or with a different set of indicators for the same constructs, and in this case it might also change if the two scales were compared with a different set of scales.

Idiothetic Strategies. In an article that should be a citation classic, but is not, Norman (1967) showed that the correlation between respondents' ratings of the social desirability of an item and their responses to the item could not be used to infer a relation between the ratings and the responses for an individual, because the estimator of the relation included population variance components. He even noted that in some published studies the *SDSVs* and the responses had been collected on different samples of respondents, thereby precluding any possibility that the correlation could indicate a relation at the individual level. He further showed that if one were willing to assume that the relation was constant for everyone, then the correlation between the interaction components (the doubly centered residuals with the main effects removed) provided an appropriate estimate of the within-individual relationship. A similar point was made by Gollob (1968a, 1968b) with respect to factor-analytic techniques.

More recently, Lamiell (1981, 1987) has advocated an alternative approach that he calls "idiothetic." Lamiell begins by noting the distinction, made by others, between personality psychology and individual-differences research. The latter he acknowledges to be appropriate for selection or classification purposes. However, as Norman and Gollob noted, individual-differences methods are inappropriate for drawing inferences concerning personality theory, which is concerned with relations that hold at the individual level for each individual.

Lamiell (1987) argues persuasively that the problem is rooted in the nomothetic–idiographic debate. Psychologists believed, and still believe, that the goal of personality research is to establish nomothetic laws—that is, laws that hold for each individual in the pop-

ulation—and that the way to do this is by means of individual-differences research. The latter is seen as appropriately objective and scientific, in contrast to idiographic research, which is believed to be subjective and therefore not scientifically respectable under the empiricist model. The problem is that individual-differences research cannot establish nomothetic laws, if they exist, of the kind that are desired.

According to Lamiell, the basic error is what William James called the "psychologist's fallacy": "This fallacy occurs whenever the empirical properties of *data* are uncritically assumed to reflect psychological properties of the *persons*[,] observations on whom generated the analysis of those data" (Lamiell, 1987, p. 91). He begins with an example with which few psychologists will have much trouble. If a poll shows that a population is split 51% to 49% on an issue, it does not follow that individuals do not have strong opinions on the issue—that is, that each individual's opinion is about 51–49% on the issue. For example, the fact that the population is fairly evenly divided on abortion rights does not mean that individuals do not hold strong views on the issue. Similarly, 90% or even 100% of the individuals may only slightly favor the same alternative. Thus, one cannot reason from the percentage split in the population to the strength of conviction of any individual.

The following is my formulation of the point that I understand Lamiell to be making. The basic fallacy is what logicians call the "fallacy of division" (Copi, 1982). The fallacies of composition and division are the reverse of each other, and they both involve a confusion between the distributive and collective uses of general terms. The fallacy of composition occurs when one argues from "attributes of the individual elements or members of a collection to attributes of the collection or totality of those elements" (Copi, 1982, p. 125). The fallacy of division occurs "when one argues from the attributes of a collection of elements to the attributes of the elements themselves" (p. 126). The *distributive* use of a term refers to each of the members or the collection individually; the *collective* use refers to the members all together, as a whole. For example, it may be that college students (distributively) may register for no more than six courses each term, but that college students (collectively) register for hundreds of courses each term.

Consider the following arguments, which are

taken from Copi (1982). (1) Humans are mortal; Socrates is a human; therefore Socrates is mortal. (2) American Indians are disappearing; that man is an American Indian; therefore that man is disappearing. The first argument is valid, because "humans" is used distributively, that is, it applies to each member of the class. The second argument is invalid, because "American Indians" is used collectively, and therefore does not apply to each of the members of the class.

> The Fallacy of Division is committed when one argues that since a whole (or a class) has a specified attribute, therefore every part of that whole (or every member of that class) also has that attribute. Thus it would be an example of the Fallacy of Division to argue that since the United States is a wealthy nation, therefore United States citizen Jane Doe must be wealthy. It would also illustrate the Fallacy of Division to argue that because barbers have been cutting hair for hundreds of years, therefore the new barber at the corner barber shop must be very experienced. (Copi, 1982, p. 128)

Simply put, the correlations computed in individual-differences research are properties of the class, and applying them to individuals is an instance of the fallacy of division. There is no way to get from the relation between two traits or characteristics in the population to the relation between those traits within an individual. It follows, for example, that correlations between traits and behaviors in no way answer the question as to whether an individual with a particular trait is likely to exhibit a particular behavior. The latter is, in any event, a logical and not an empirical question (Rorer, 1989).

I now turn from Lamiell's critique of current research to his constructive suggestion for an alternative. Again, I am going to make the argument somewhat differently than he does, so there is the possibility that I am making a different argument. Personality researchers who have adopted the normative or nomothetic model have assumed that the meaning of terms such as trait descriptors is given by a person's standing relative to a reference population; for example, if we say that someone is average in friendliness it means that there are about as many people who are more friendly as there are people who are less friendly than that individual.

But there is another possibility. In making judgments about physical objects, people have explicit reference scales for characteristics such as height, weight, and temperature. There are also scales for hardness (of rocks) and intensity (of earthquakes). Perhaps what people do when they make judgments of other attributes is to use implicit scales of each of the attributes. Conceptually, these scales would range from none of the attribute to the maximum amount of it. As is the case with physical scales, the conceptual end points may not exist; for example, one may conceive of a scale from zero weight to infinite weight, even though there may be no objects with either zero or infinite weight, nor any way to measure them if there were. Lamiell calls this "idiothetic" measurement, and presents evidence that this, rather than normative measurement, may be what people have in mind when they make such judgments. Idiothetic measurement, if it can be implemented, will have the advantage of being relative to a standard rather than a population or other constructs.

Such a reconceptualization would also make sense out of several decades of rating scale research that psychometricians have found puzzling. The classic instance was the Navy's experience with scales labeled "poor," "fair," "average," "good," and "excellent." The scales were relabeled "average," "above average," "good," "very good," and "excellent" when it was found that the lowest rating ever given was "average." Similarly, at my university the teacher evaluation forms have a scale from 0 to 4, and the middle category, 2, is labeled "average." The average rating, however, is approximately 3.

It has been suggested that such results reflect leniency error, response bias, or some other form of rater irrationality. Another possibility—one closer to what students tell me about their thinking process in making the ratings—is that they have an implicit standard of, say, good teaching, and that they rate their professors relative to that scale. Relative to that scale, as opposed to relative to one another, their professors are viewed as above average (i.e., above the midpoint). The situation is obviously more complicated than that, because, as pointed out above in the discussion of ascription rules, people do make normative adjustments when making ratings. The debate about whether individuals make normative or idiothetic judgments when asked for personality ratings may be like the debate over whether persons add or average information in making judgments: The answer is that sometimes they do one, sometimes they do the other, and often they do both.

However, it is important to distinguish the empirical question about what people do from the logical question about the appropriateness of inferences from data. Whatever studies may eventually show about how the average individual goes about making such judgments, three points seem clear: (1) Inferences concerning personality structure cannot be made from individual-differences data; (2) investigators should take seriously the possibility that respondents are making idiothetic, rather than normative, judgments, when interpreting their data; and (3) more research on the implementation of idiothetic measurement is sorely needed.

Taxonomic Approaches

I have indicated that factor-analytic research starts with the assumption that the ways in which individuals may differ psychologically are unknown, and attempts to establish empirically what those dimensions are. In order for a dimension to emerge, it must exist and it must be represented in the item pool. How can one know that all possible dimensions are represented in the item pool? One approach is to assume that any important differences among people will come to be represented in the natural language. If so, one could then start with the natural language and try to systematize the information that is included there. There is a long-standing and continuing effort to develop just such a taxonomy of trait-descriptive terms, and a description of those efforts would logically be a part of this chapter. John (Chapter 3, this volume) provides an excellent summary.

Taxometric Methods

I am going to return to the diagnostic model to describe briefly an area that would also require an entire chapter to describe adequately. Suppose that one is interested, not in dimensions along which individuals might differ, but in categories or classes of people that in some sense really exist; that is, the classes are nonarbitrary. Meehl (e.g., Meehl & Golden, 1982) has termed such classes "taxa," and the means of identifying them "taxometric methods." If

one suspects that an entity (in our case specifically a diagnostic entity) exists, is there some way to determine which of the purported indicators of that entity are valid? The answer, surprising to those who have been schooled in traditional criterion-group research, is yes.

Let us start with the case where the criterion group is known to exist, but for some reason cannot be assembled—for example, people who will commit suicide or die of cancer. We want to know whether we can find an indicator that will identify these people in advance. Suppose we have two groups for which the suicide rate is known, even though we do not know which members of each group will commit suicide. If the suicide rates for the two groups are different, then it is possible to identify indicators (even perfect indicators) that will tell us which members of each group will commit suicide. Dawes and Meehl (1966) refer to this as "mixed-group validation."

Now consider an example such as schizophrenia, where it is not known whether any such disorder exists in the taxonomic sense, or if there may be more than one disorder. Given a sizable sample, one can determine the optimum cutting point on a potential indicator by noting the covariance between two other potential indicators for various regions of the first indicator. The optimum cut on the first indicator is in the region of that indicator for which the covariance between the other two indicators is a maximum. The optimum cutting point on the other two indicators can then be found in similar fashion. Given a set of indicators for which optimum cuts have been determined, Bayesian probabilities of taxon membership can be determined for each individual in the sample on the basis of that person's score on each indicator. Details are given in Meehl and Golden (1982).

Both of these procedures are examples of what have come to be known as "bootstrap procedures," by which it is meant that marginally valid indicators can be used to identify more valid (even perfectly valid) indicators. For example, clinical judgments might be used to form two groups that differ in suicide rate. Suppose that 50% of those whom a clinician identifies as suicide risks subsequently attempt suicide, whereas only 10% of those who are identified as nonrisks do so. These groups can now be used to identify more valid indicators of suicide risk (Dawes, 1967). This may seem paradoxical at first, but should not if one considers the history of medicine. Today's sophisticated diagnostic techniques have all been developed on the basis of the crude indicators that existed a couple of hundred years ago.

NONTRADITIONAL MODELS

Postempiricist Philosophies of Science

The demise of empiricism ended the search for a line of demarcation between science and metaphysics (nonscience); removed the requirement for justification of knowledge claims; and opened the way for the return of the study of cognition, consciousness, and meaning to psychology. Scientists are still expected to be able to defend their positions with good reasons and strong arguments, but modern philosophers are more humble, more aware and acknowledging of our limitations. It is accepted that we can never know anything for sure. All knowledge is filtered through our perceptual apparatus, and there is no way to know how that apparatus distorts the information we receive. Given that absolute knowledge is impossible, all we can ask is whether we have good reasons for believing what we do.

The early positivists limited meaningful statements to reports of sense data. The later empiricists accepted the meaningfulness of statements concerning physical objects that were independently verifiable, but the ontological question concerning the reality of physical objects was still considered to be metaphysical. Without the empiricists' requirement for justifiable knowledge, it is possible to embrace realism on the basis of reasonableness. Somewhat ironically, as the changing philosophy of science has made it easier for psychologists to hold a realist position, fewer of them have done so; instead, they have embraced a constructivist position that emphasizes the arbitrary nature of psychological entities (e.g., Gergen, 1985; Hampson, 1988). There is a middle ground. Although I acknowledge the logical problems, I believe that one can reasonably argue for an ontological realism while holding a pragmatic, constructivist epistemology. Given this view, constructs are admittedly constructed, but reality, which we cannot know directly, places limits on the extent to which different constructions will work. Those that work, we keep. With respect to psychological constructs, in particular, there are probably many that will work to varying degrees.

In a recent article Kukla (1989) outlined some of the nonempirical issues to be dealt with in psychology. Many of these would provide no problem for an empiricist. Theory construction, for example, was always considered to be in the context of discovery rather than the context of justification. The philosophers certainly considered their own analytical work to be appropriate. The development of theoretical systems by means of logical deduction was a highly esteemed activity, as was the analysis of empirical theories for conceptual coherence. In many cases theoretical analysis can result in new knowledge. Conceptual innovations allow us to understand existing knowledge in a different way. Copernicus's heliocentric theory is an example of a conceptual innovation that included no new empirical information, but facilitated the development of other theories explaining the movements of the heavenly bodies.

Some philosophers believe that there may be other fundamental issues involving a priori knowledge and basic presuppositions that are not empirically reconcilable. Behaviorists (discussed above) and phenomenologists (to be discussed below) do not disagree about the use of introspective reports; they disagree about what those reports mean. Resolving the differences between them is not an empirical matter. It involves examining the presuppositions of the two positions. Kukla (1989) suggests that psychology may not need more data as much as it needs conceptual innovations concerning the data we already have. This chapter suggests that a good case can be made that this is true of personality assessment.

With this background I now describe two overlapping approaches that fall clearly in the postempiricist era—and, as we shall see, in the pre-empiricist era as well.

Narrative Analysis: Hermeneutics

Cognitive assessment, in my view, differs fundamentally from behavioral assessment in its incorporation of meaning as an important aspect of human functioning. Cognitive models of personality and personality dysfunction focus on beliefs and on the logic of an individual's thinking. The behaviorists used simplified experimental situations (e.g., Skinner boxes) and nonhumans, and so eliminated much of the role that meaning plays in determining human behavior. In the simplified experimental situation, the stimulus was clear; in real life, it is not. An individual may perceive me as a man for census purposes, a man in the social classification sense, a man in the sexual sense, a professor, his or her professor, a father, his or her father, a lover, a psychologist, or a psychotherapist. What I am as a stimulus to another person is not an objective fact that can be known by observation.

Likewise, the fact that the response in the box is defined in terms of its effect rather than the behavioral topography does not make a lot of difference, because in that setting one can ignore the question of whether the animal intended to press the lever, whereas in ordinary human affairs the question of intent is crucial. If someone else's hand comes in contact with me, it makes a great deal of difference whether this person is giving me a friendly greeting, congratulating me, teasing me, hitting a mosquito, punching me, or just swinging his or her arm; and, again, this is not an objective fact that can be determined by observation. It is something that must be determined contextually, and even then the person may mislead me as to his or her intent.

The behaviorist focuses on the relation between a stimulus and a response and attempts to explain the latter in terms of the manipulation of the former. The cognitive theorist notes that the same objective stimulus may produce different response topographies in different people (e.g., a grade of B may cause some to leap in glee and others to weep), and attempts to explain those differing responses in terms of the intervening cognitions of the people. The behaviorist would argue that, in principle, the explanation can be found in the person's prior history without resorting to cognitions. For the cognitivist, the meaning of the stimulus to the perceiver and the intent (meaning) of the response to the responder are crucial. They use the methods I have described to try to determine those meanings; as we have seen, those methods are the methods of traditional personality assessment.

A growing number of theorists believe that these methods are insufficient and inappropriate for the study or understanding of meaning. The traditional methods of natural science were designed for the study of material things, and meaning is not a material thing; it is an emergent property. Just as water has emergent properties that cannot be predicted from the properties of oxygen and hydrogen, and life has emergent properties that cannot be predicted from a knowledge of the properties of the elements of which living organisms are constituted, meaning is a further property that has emerged as a consequence of, or along with, consciousness.

Meaning is not a thing or substance; it is an activity. Because each of us has direct access only to our own experience of meaning, the realm of meaning is difficult to investigate, cannot be investigated by natural science methods, and has therefore not been the object of much study in psychology. Meaning is expressed linguistically, and linguistic data can be understood only by means of hermeneutic reasoning or understanding.

"Hermeneutics" originally referred to the study and understanding of the Bible, but was then broadened to include the study and understanding of all texts. Now, some psychologists believe that human experience is constructed in the same way as, and therefore must be understood in the same way as, a text. Understanding cannot come in the form of general laws from which deductions are made, but only in terms of the life history—the narrative that represents the person's experience. Individual or personality psychology differs from differential or individual-differences psychology. It is represented by studies of lifespan development, such as case histories and biography, for which the appropriate methodology is hermeneutics.

Polkinghorne (1988), on whose exposition the following is based, uses the term "narrative" to refer broadly to the attempts that we make to understand our actions and those of others by creating narratives (accounts, stories, scenarios, etc.). If asked why I am typing at my computer, I would explain by describing my commitment to write this chapter and my desire to finish it quickly, given that I am already far past the deadline to which I originally agreed. Most people would accept this as an appropriate explanation of my actions, on the grounds that I have made my actions understandable by giving them meaning—something that can not be experimentally or objectively determined. There is a reason why I am typing rather than playing golf or watching television.

Experience is neither material nor static; it is constantly changing as we create narratives to make sense out of what we are perceiving and thinking. Our understanding of various actions and events may change as the result of additional experiences. To return to an earlier example, I may have been angry when I thought the other person was trying to hurt me when he or she hit me, but when I learn that the other person was killing a mosquito that was biting me my anger turns to appreciation, because I have rewritten the narrative. The construction of experience does not proceed logically; it proceeds sequentially, associationally, pictorially, and emotionally. Logical thought is (unfortunately) but a small part of the narrative construction and experience.

One of the empiricists' goals was to construct a language that would permit objective communication. It is now acknowledged that this cannot be done. We learn language contextually. As we learn new words, our understanding of old words changes. The meaning of a sentence changes, depending on the context in which it is used. And so with stories and the larger context in which they are embedded. Hermeneutics makes this contextualism explicit. Texts must be analyzed in relation to our knowledge of the author and the times when the author wrote, and in relation to our own intuitive understanding of human experience.

Psychoanalysts' use of the case study was an early attempt at a hermeneutic approach to individual psychology. Although Freud's theory evolved as he attempted to explain new cases, psychoanalysis was an attempt to find a representation that would work for all people for all time. A hermeneutic analysis would emphasize the turn-of-the-century European Jewish culture from which Freud and his colleagues came, the sexual repressiveness of Western society in general, the mechanistic theories of physics and the knowledge of anatomy and physiology at the time, Freud's own life history, and so forth. Such an analysis would facilitate our understanding of psychoanalysis, and would lead to the conclusion that psychoanalysis is but one way in which to understand human behavior. To the extent that psychoanalysis imposes a construction, a personologist working from a hermeneutic approach would probably not find it very useful, because that investigator would want to understand the constructions of the person being studied.

Murray's (1938) *Explorations in Personality* reports a later effort to understand individuals on the basis of detailed information about them. After that, academic interest in biographical study virtually disappeared from psychology

until the 1970s, when works such as *The Seasons of a Man's Life* (Levinson, 1978) began to appear, and there was increasing interest in the study of lifespan development. More recently there has been an increasing number of articles on qualitative research in general, and on narrative analysis and hermeneutics in particular. For representative examples, one might try recent papers by Mishler (e.g., 1979) or Rosenwald (e.g., 1988). Gergen, Hepburn, and Fisher (1986) applied hermeneutics to the process of personality assessment as it is currently practiced, with devastating results. They found that items on the Rotter Internal-External Scale "could plausibly be used as indicators of virtually any common trait term within the English language" (p. 1261). So much for the idea that an item can be thought to represent just one trait.

Phenomenological Perspectives

Some will think that this should have been the major section of this chapter; others will wonder why it is here at all. Such is the divided state of personality assessment.

We have seen that at the turn of the century there was great interest in finding true or justifiable knowledge. The interest is understandable. The church had for centuries claimed to be the arbiter of true knowledge, and the rationalist philosophers had attempted to provide a philosophical basis for that claim in pure reason. The empiricists launched a challenge that carried the day into the middle of this century. The arbiter of true knowledge was science, not the church. Justifiable knowledge came from experience, not from mere, meaningless, metaphysical speculation.

The empiricists had originally sought true knowledge by limiting their data to sense data, but there were problems with that position. From a philosophical point of view, it was open to the charge of being solipsistic, and so it was revised to require intersubjective testability. It was not until the second half of this century that it was realized that the structuralists' program of introspection at the turn of the century should have shown on psychological grounds that sense data were unacceptable as an epistemological criterion, because it was impossible to free them of the effects of prior learning (Rorer, in press).

At the turn of the century there was still

RESEARCH TOPICS

another claim that sense data were the correct road to true knowledge. Husserl's efforts provided the foundation of phenomenology (Jennings, 1986), which was swept aside by the rising tide of empiricism. Husserl did not reject the use of empirical methods to gain true knowledge of the material world, but he argued that this solved only half of the problem. The other half was to understand the process of knowing. Because consciousness is a process rather than a material thing, it cannot be studied by methods appropriate to studying things. Husserl sought to provide a means whereby one could obtain absolute knowledge of conscious phenomena, something he felt was essential if psychology was to understand how naive experiential reports are contaminated by preconceptions. Before a psychologist can study the relation between a stimulus and a perception, it is important to know what the perception is, and phenomenological methods were designed to provide that information. The basic idea was that one could learn to put aside one's preconceptions and experience the essence of an experience—that part of the experience that would be equally true at any other time and place (i.e., in any other context). Essences cannot be established by reason or induction, but must be immediately experienced. The means of achieving this experience was the reduction, the purpose of which is to move from psychological consciousness to pure consciousness—from a concern with empirical facts to a concern with essences. These are inseparable. The act of knowing and that which is known are not independent. For a more complete description, see Jennings (1986), on whose excellent exposition my account is based.

As with any school of knowledge, phenomenology has evolved and has developed different subschools (Henley, 1988; Valle, King, & Halling, 1989). The belief that one can acquire true or absolute knowledge has been abandoned by all except religious fanatics. Phenomenologists would now acknowledge that essences cannot be grasped independently of preconceptions. The aspects on which Snyder (1988) believes they would agree are the following:

1. the importance of experience in its own right, rather than as a reflection of an independently existing reality;
2. the emphasis on intentionality (i.e, the di-

rectedness of consciousness towards something, or alternatively, that consciousness is consciousness of something) as the fundamental structure around which the exploration of experience can occur, as opposed to the consideration of psyche in terms of mental contents that like physical entities do not have a referential aspect;
3. the importance of describing this experience in as clear and direct a manner as possible;
4. through emphasizing essence, the importance of understanding the fundamental nature of whatever is being investigated;
5. the route toward this understanding and subsequent description is directly given through intuition and is not fundamantally dependent on any other epistemological avenue (e.g., the application of inductive reason to experimental data). (p. 404)

Clearly, someone with this orientation is going to have a very different view of personality assessment than any of those whom we have considered so far. Many phenomenologists do not do assessments, because they believe that assessment necessarily treats the person as object, neglecting the person as subject. Fischer (1989) is an exception. She terms her approach a "human science" approach, in contrast to the prevailing "natural science" approach. The emphasis is on considering the person as a whole, and on the differentiations that can be made within that whole, in contrast to the normative framework of traditional assessment. The individual's experiences, not the underlying traits indexed by standard tests, are considered primary. Linear causal explanations are rejected in favor of descriptions of the whole.

Within human science, both research and applied work begin with different data than that which mainstream psychology has accumulated. Like behaviorists, we do begin with publicly observable events. . . . However, in contrast, we regard these events as implying the person's lived history, present world, and goals. . . . We do use test scores, traditional research, and other theories' constructs to help us expand and refine our understandings of those observed events. But we regard these resources as tools, ones derived from earlier life events. (Fischer, 1989, pp. 164–165)

The assessor recognizes that the client's experience of his or her situation must be taken into account. The assessor's own experience also is inevitably involved. . . . Disciplined, examinable descriptions, then, are achieved not by trying to exclude the assessor's subjectivity (individuality, perspective, involvement) but by explicitly taking it into account. (Fischer, 1989, p. 165)

SUMMARY AND CONCLUSIONS

Because all forms of personality assessment presuppose, and are embedded in, a philosophy of science, changes in the philosophical *Zeitgeist* have strongly influenced personality assessment. One cannot understand the historical development of personality assessment unless one puts it in the context of changes in the philosophy of science. In the late 19th century empiricism and phenomenalism, among others, competed with religion to be recognized as the path to true knowledge. The ascendance of empiricism in philosophy set the course of psychology for 50 years. The extremes of empiricism were replaced during the 1960s by an equally extreme rejection of empiricism. Now we see more moderate positions that acknowledge the impossibility of identifying true knowledge, or of distinguishing science from nonscience. There is increasing interest in the late-19th-century pragmatism that was among the casualties swept aside by empiricism.

Paralleling these developments in philosophy, first empirical and then behavioral assessment rose in favor, while cognitive, phenomenalistic, and rational approaches diminished. But then positions that had been temporarily eclipsed by the dominance of logical empiricism in psychology were again seen as viable alternatives, and positions that flourished during the heyday of empiricism have quietly faded away. Rational considerations have returned to personality inventory construction as brute-force empirical procedures have given way to a demand for conceptual coherence between measures and theories. As cognitive behaviorists have challenged methodological behaviorists to acknowledge that it is the construal or evaluation of an object or event, rather than the object or event itself, in terms of which behavior is best explained, cognitive assessments have supplanted or replaced behavioral assessments.

A growing number of researchers believe that the meaning an individual attaches to objects or events can be understood and explained only in the context of that person's life, and that the methodology appropriate for the study of lives is narrative analysis or hermeneutics. There has been a corresponding growth in the number of textbooks and classes devoted to or including qualitative as well as quantitative research methods. Introspectionism, the lessons from which should have precluded the rise of empiricism, has not returned as the means of studying cognitive structure, but there is growing interest in phenomenological reports as a means of understanding personality. Unlike the traditional case studies that attempted to fit every individual into a single psychodynamic framework, modern cognitive and phenomenological assessments focus on the individual's framework for understanding his or her life.

Personality assessment is not a unified enterprise; it is a divided camp. Many traditional personality assessment researchers find themselves uncomfortable with the current changes. If the rigid rules of objectivity and operationism do not hold, does that mean that "anything goes"? No. The current positions are a far cry from the world-views position, popular in the 1960s, which held that any representation of reality is as good as any other. Alternate views are possible (e.g., wave and particle theories of light, cognitive and behavioral explanations of behavior), but not any view (e.g., demonological theories of behavior). However, there is no firm line of demarcation between acceptable and unacceptable views. There may well be many different ways of representing the world, with no way to say that one is correct and the rest false; however, it is reasonable to believe that there is a world out there, and that some representations will therefore work better than others. To keep the ones that work and discard the ones that do not is to adopt a pragmatic position with which most scientists should find themselves comfortable. The judgment as to which ones work best, or have the best hope of working best, is not a judgment that can be made objectively, so reasonable people may reasonably disagree.

It is important to take seriously the distinction between research on individual differences and research on personality theory. The individual-differences structure of the population is not the same as the personality structure of the individual. Evidence concerning the dimensions on which individuals differ does not provide an explanation for the behavior of those individuals. Most of what is included in traditional personality assessment would better be described as individual-differences assessment.

The data and methods of analysis that are

appropriate for identifying individual differences are not the same as those that are appropriate for developing personality theory, and the differences may run deeper than has been realized. So far, the efforts that have been made have been to reconcile the two approaches—to adapt individual-differences methods to idiographic ones by means of idiothetic procedures. That approach is creative and deserves support. But it may be that the ultimate resolution of much of the tension in the field will come from realizing that traditional personality assessment procedures are appropriate for the study of individual differences, whereas behavioral, cognitive, hermeneutic, and phenomenological methods are appropriate for developing personality theory.

ACKNOWLEDGMENTS

Preparation of this chapter was supported in part by National Institute of Mental Health Grant No. MH-39077.

Bobbie G. Hopes provided advice and encouragement throughout the preparation of this chapter. William H. Henricks at Miami University, and Lewis R. Goldberg, Sarah E. Hampson, Oliver P. John, and Tina K. Rosolack at Oregon Research Institute responded with incredible speed to my urgent plea for assistance under great time pressure. The chapter benefited greatly from their comments and suggestions. My thanks to all.

REFERENCES

American Psychiatric Association. (1987). *Diagnostic and statistical manual of mental disorders* (3rd ed., rev.). Washington, DC: Author.

Bentler, P. M., Jackson, D. N., & Messick, S. (1971). Identification of content and style: A two-dimensional interpretation of acquiescence. *Psychological Bulletin, 76*, 186–204.

Berg, I. A. (1967). The deviation hypothesis: A broad statement of its assumptions and postulates. In I. A. Berg (Ed.), *Response set in personality assessment* (pp. 146–190). Chicago: Aldine.

Bleuler, E. (1950). *Dementia praecox or the group of schizophrenias* (J. Zinkin, Trans.). New York: International Universities Press. (Original work published 1911)

Block, J. (1965). *The challenge of response sets: Unconfounding meaning, acquiescence and social desirability in the MMPI.* New York: Appleton-Century-Crofts.

Block, J. (1971). On further conjectures regarding acquiescence. *Psychological Bulletin, 76*, 205–210.

Burisch, M. (1986). Methods of personality inventory development—comparative analysis. In A. Angleitner & J. S. Wiggins (Eds.), *Personality assessment via questionnaires: Current issues in theory and measurement* (pp. 109–120). New York: Springer.

Butcher, J. N. (Ed.). (1987). *Computerized psychological assessment: A practitioner's guide.* New York: Basic Books.

Comrey, A. L. (1988). Factor-analytic methods of scale development in personality and clinical psychology. *Journal of Consulting and Clinical Psychology, 56*, 754–761.

Copi, I. M. (1982). *Introduction to logic* (6th ed.). New York: Macmillan.

Dawes, R. M. (1962). A note on base rates and psychometric efficiency. *Journal of Consulting Psychology, 26*, 422–424.

Dawes, R. M. (1967). How clinical judgment may be used to validate diagnostic signs. *Journal of Clinical Psychology, 23*, 403–410.

Dawes, R. M., & Meehl, P. E. (1966). Mixed group validation: A method for determining the validity of diagnostic signs without using criterion groups. *Psychological Bulletin, 66*, 63–67.

Edwards, A. L. (1957). *The social desirability variable in personality assessment and research.* New York: Dryden Press.

Ellis, A. (1962). *Reason and emotion in psychotherapy.* New York: Lyle Stuart.

Embretson (Whitely), S. (1983). Construct validity: Construct representation versus nomothetic span. *Psychological Bulletin, 93*, 179–197.

Ericsson, K. A., & Simon, H. A. (1981). Sources of evidence on cognition: A historical overview. In T. V. Merluzzi, C. U. Glass, & M. Genest (Eds.), *Cognitive assessment* (pp. 16–51). New York: Guilford Press.

Fischer, C. T. (1989). Personality and assessment. In R. S. Valle & S. Halling (Eds.), *Existential–phenomenological perspectives in psychology* (pp. 157–178). New York: Plenum.

Gergen, K. J. (1985). The social constructionist movement in modern psychology. *American Psychologist, 40*, 266–275.

Gergen, K. J., Hepburn, A., & Fisher, D. C. (1986). Hermeneutics of personality description. *Journal of Personality and Social Psychology, 50*, 1261–1270.

Gilberstadt, H., & Duker, J. (1965). *A handbook for clinical and actuarial MMPI interpretation.* Philadelphia: W. B. Saunders.

Glaser, R. (1981). The future of testing: A research agenda for cognitive psychology and psychometrics. *American Psychologist, 36*, 923–936.

Goldberg, L. R. (1971). A historical survey of personality scales and inventories. In P. McReynolds (Ed.), *Advances in psychological assessment* (Vol. 2, pp. 293–336). Palo Alto, CA: Science and Behavior Books.

Goldberg, L. R. (1972). Parameters of personality inventory construction and utilization: A comparison of prediction strategies and tactics. *Multivariate Behavioral Research Monographs, 72*(2).

Goldberg, L. R., & Slovic, P. S. (1967). Importance of test item content: An analysis of a corollary of the deviation hypothesis. *Journal of Counseling Psychology, 14*, 462–472.

Goldstein, G., & Hersen, M. (Eds.). (1984). *Handbook of psychological assessment.* New York: Pergamon Press.

Gollob, H. F. (1968a). Confounding of sources of variation in factor-analytic techniques. *Psychological Bulletin, 70,* 330–344.

Gollob, H. F. (1968b). A statistical model which combines features of factor analytic and analysis of variance techniques. *Psychometrika, 33,* 73–115.

Hampson, S. E. (1988). *The construction of personality: An introduction* (2nd ed.). London: Routledge.

Harré, R., & Lamb, R. (1983). *The encyclopedic dictionary of psychology.* Cambridge, MA: MIT Press.

Hathaway, S. R., & Meehl, P. E. (1951). *An atlas for the clinical use of the MMPI.* Minneapolis: University of Minnesota Press.

Hayes, S. C. (1986). Behavior philosophy in the late 1980's. *Theoretical and Philosophical Psychology, 6,* 39–43.

Henley, T. B. (1988). Beyond Husserl. *American Psychologist, 43,* 402–403.

Jackson, D. N. (1971). The dynamics of structured personality tests: 1971. *Psychological Review, 78,* 229–248.

Jennings, J. L. (1986). Husserl revisited: The forgotten distinction between psychology and phenomenology. *American Psychologist, 41,* 1231–1240.

Kazdin, A. E. (1979). Fictions, factions, and functions of behavior therapy. *Behavior Therapy, 10,* 629–654.

Kelly, G. A. (1955). *The psychology of personal constructs* (2 vols.). New York: Norton.

Kraepelin, E. (1981). *Clinical psychiatry* (7th ed.) (A. R. Diefendorf, Trans.). Delmar, NY: Scholars' Facsimiles & Reprints. (Original work published 1907).

Kukla, A. (1989). Nonempirical issues in psychology. *American Psychologist, 44,* 785–794.

Lamiell, J. T. (1981). Toward an idiothetic psychology of personality. *American Psychologist, 36,* 276–289.

Lamiell, J. T. (1987). *The psychology of personality: An epistemological inquiry.* New York: Columbia University Press.

Levinson, D. J. (1978). *The seasons of a man's life.* New York: Ballantine Books.

Loevinger, J. (1957). Objective tests as instruments of psychological theory. *Psychological Reports, 3* (Monograph No. 9), 635–694.

Marks, P. A., & Seeman, W. (1963). *The actuarial description of personality: An atlas for use with the MMPI.* Baltimore: Williams & Wilkins.

McReynolds, P. (1986). History of assessment in clinical and educational settings. In R. O. Nelson & S. C. Hayes (Eds.), *Conceptual foundations of behavioral assessment* (pp. 42–80). New York: Guilford Press.

McReynolds, P., & Ludwig, K. (1987). On the history of rating scales. *Personality and Individual Differences, 8,* 281–283.

Meehl, P. E. (1982). Subjectivity in psychoanalytic inference: The nagging persistence of Wilhelm Fliess's Achensee question. In J. Earman & C. W. Savage (Eds.), *Minnesota studies in the philosophy of science: Vol. 10. Confirmation of theories* (pp. 349–411). Minneapolis: University of Minnesota Press.

Meehl, P. E. (1986). Trait language and behaviorese. In T. Thompson & M. D. Zeiler (Eds.), *Analysis and integration of behavioral units* (pp. 315–334). Hillsdale, NJ: Erlbaum.

Meehl, P. E., & Golden, R. (1982). Taxometric methods. In P. Kendall & J. Butcher (Eds.), *Handbook of research methods in clinical psychology* (pp. 127–181). New York: Wiley.

Messick, S. (1981). Constructs and their vicissitudes in educational and psychological measurement. *Psychological Review, 89,* 575–588.

Mischel, W. (1973). Toward a cognitive social learning reconceptualization of personality. *Psychological Review, 80,* 252–283.

Mishler, E. G. (1979). Meaning in context: Is there any other kind? *Harvard Educational Review, 49,* 1–19.

Murray, H. A. (1938). *Explorations in personality.* New York: Oxford University Press.

Norman, W. T. (1963). Relative importance of test item content. *Journal of Consulting Psychology, 27,* 166–174.

Norman, W. T. (1967). On estimating psychological relationships: Social desirability and self-report. *Psychological Bulletin, 67,* 273–293.

Parks, C. W., Jr., & Hollon, S. D. (1988). Cognitive assessment. In A. S. Bellack & M. Hersen (Eds.), *Behavioral assessment: A practical handbook* (3rd ed., pp. 161–212). New York: Pergamon Press.

Paulhus, D. L. (1986). Self-deception and impression management in test responses. In A. Angleitner & J. S. Wiggins (Eds.), *Personality assessment via questionnaires: Current issues in theory and measurement* (pp. 143–165). New York: Springer.

Paulhus, D. L. (in press). Measurement and control of response bias. In J. P. Robinson, P. R. Shaver, & L. Wrightsman (Eds.), *Measures of personality and social-psychological attitudes.* New York: Academic Press.

Pepper, S. (1981). Problems in the quantification of frequency expressions. In D. W. Fiske (Ed.), *Problems with language imprecision* (pp. 25–42). San Francisco: Jossey-Bass.

Polkinghorne, D. E. (1988). *Narrative knowing and the human sciences.* Albany: State University of New York Press.

Rorer, L. G. (1965). The great response style myth. *Psychological Bulletin, 63,* 129–156.

Rorer, L. G. (1989). *Misconceptions concerning states and traits.* Unpublished manuscript.

Rorer, L. G. (in press). Some myths of science in psychology. In D. Cicchetti & W. Grove (Eds.). *Thinking clearly about psychology: Essays in honor of Paul E. Meehl.* Minneapolis: University of Minnesota.

Rorer, L. G., Hoffman, P. J., Laforge, G. E., & Hsieh, K. C. (1966). Optimum scores to discriminate groups of unequal size and variance. *Journal of Applied Psychology, 50,* 153–164.

Rorer, L. G., & Widiger, T. A. (1982, May). *Ascription rules for trait descriptive adjectives.* Paper presented at the meeting of the Midwestern Psychological Association, Minneapolis.

Rorer, L. G., & Widiger, T. A. (1983). Personality structure and assessment. *Annual Review of Psychology, 34,* 431–463.

Rosenwald, G. C. (1988). A theory of multiple-case research. *Journal of Personality, 56,* 239–264.

Snyder, D. M. (1988). Comment on Jennings. *American Psychologist, 43,* 403–404.

Sternberg, R. J. (1981). Testing and cognitive psychology. *American Psychologist, 36,* 1181–1189.

Sundberg, N. S. (1981). Historical and traditional approaches to cognitive assessment. In T. V. Merluzzi, C. U. Glass, & M. Genest (Eds.), *Cognitive assessment* (pp. 52–76). New York: Guilford Press.

Suppe, F. (1977). *The structure of scientific theories* (2nd ed.). Urbana: University of Illinois Press.

Valle, R. S., King, M., & Halling, S. (1989). An introduction to existential–phenomenological thought in psychology. In R. S. Valle & S. Halling (Eds.), *Existential–phenomenological perspectives in psychology* (pp. 3–16). New York: Plenum.

Wiggins, J. S. (1973). *Personality and prediction: Principles of personality assessment.* Reading, MA: Addison-Wesley.

PART V
OVERVIEW

Chapter 27

Personality Theory and Research: Prospects for the Future

Lawrence A. Pervin
Rutgers University

As we survey the outstanding contributions to this volume, two overall impressions stand out: an emphasis on the complexity of personality, and diversity in the concepts and research methods utilized. Both indicate the liveliness of the field today and suggest that its prospects for the future are exciting.

COMPLEXITY OF PERSONALITY FUNCTIONING

> However much psychologists may disagree about the best way to conceptualize the structure of personality or to define its units, on one point—its complexity—there is unanimity.
> —MacKinnon, (1951, p. 118)

If this statement was true in 1951, it is all the more true today. Complexity is recognized and emphasized in a variety of ways. First, it is recognized that phenomena of interest and importance may only appear under very specific and limited conditions. Thus, it is emphasized that a phenomenon (e.g., motive) may only

appear under certain conditions of arousal, and that a person may show similar patterns of behavior across domains but only within specific parameters (e.g., high conflict or anxiety) within each domain. What is striking is that those who emphasize the psychodynamic, trait, and social-cognitive views would all emphasize this order of complexity, despite their otherwise fundamental theoretical differences. Furthermore, the sensitivity of these phenomena to variations in internal and external conditions in no way is seen as lessening their fundamental importance to an understanding of personality functioning. And this recognized sensitivity in no way makes a statement concerning the relative importance of internal and external factors. Indeed, it gives expression to the importance of both internal and external factors in virtually all important aspects of personality functioning.

Second, complexity is recognized in the multiple determination of most important aspects of human behavior: "It is likely that behaviors are complex and are influenced by multiple determinants. To expect any psychological variable to correlate with some behavioral criterion on the order of .5 or greater is to deny the complexity of human behavior" (Ahadi & Diener, 1989, p. 398). Not only may there be multiple determinants of a phenomenon, but the same phenomenon can be caused by different sets of determinants. Thus, in understanding phenomena we may discover many causes, all of which are potentially relevant but no one of which is necessary or sufficient (Holzman, 1986).

Third, and in part following from the first two points, complexity is recognized in the task of prediction and in the relation between understanding and prediction. Although prediction is a desirable goal, not only are there times when we can predict without understanding but there also are times when we may understand a great deal without being able to predict. As Meehl (in press) notes, our fascination with correlations and tests of statistical significance often leads us to assume progress in understanding a phenomenon when none is present; this is due in part to what he calls the "crud" factor. The history of fads in personality research, noted in the introductory chapter, is undoubtedly relevant here. Perhaps equally serious, though, is the potential for discarding interest in a phenomenon or theory because of difficulties in establishing significant correlations or high-level predictions.

As a clinician, I have often been impressed with how much I understood about a patient and how much trouble I had in making individual predictions. In part this was due to unforeseen, perhaps chance events (Bandura, 1982). However, in other cases it was due to missing some relevant ingredient or failing to appreciate the import of a particular detail. In predicting complex events, it is possible to understand a great deal and yet to fare poorly in prediction because an essential variable is missing. Economists understand a great deal about the forces governing economic systems, yet their record in prediction is poor, not only because of unforeseen events (e.g., changes in weather conditions, accidents, wars) but also because of the complexity of interacting forces governing the events of interest. Given the complexity of factors determining development over the lifespan and daily behavior in the natural environment, it may be that all we will ever be capable of is prediction at a general level, rather than in detail, and only within specific ranges of circumstances. Appreciation of the limits on prediction in complex systems, with associated implications for research, has been formulated in chaos theory:

> The existence of chaos affects the scientific method itself. The classic approach to verifying a theory is to make predictions and test them against experimental data. If the phenomena are chaotic, however, long-term predictions are intrinsically impossible. This has to be taken into account in judging the merits of the theory. The process of verifying a theory thus becomes a much more delicate operation, relying on statistical and geometric properties rather than on detailed predictions.
>
> Chaos brings a new challenge to the reductionist view that a system can be understood by breaking it down and studying each piece. This view has been prevalent in science in part because there are so many systems for which behavior of the whole is indeed the sum of its parts. Chaos demonstrates, however, that a system can have complicated behavior that emerges as a consequence of simple, nonlinear interaction of only a few components. (Crutchfield, Farmer, Packard, & Shaw, 1986, p. 56)

Recognition of the complexity of the phenomena of interest to us is increasingly given in terms such as "pattern," "organization," and "system." Of course, an emphasis on patterns, organizations, and systems is not new to the field; it goes back to many of the significant figures noted in the historial introduction (see Chapter 1)—Allport, Lewin, Murphy, and Murray. The fact that a systems view is not new should not, however, lead us to ignore its importance in the present context. Once more, what is striking is the diversity of theoretical perspectives emphasizing such concepts as hierarchical organization; patterns of relationships among variables; dynamic processes and open systems; equipotentiality and equifinality; integrated and conflicted relationships among the parts; nonlinear relationships; goals and self-regulative or self-corrective mechanisms; and adaptive functions or competencies. A systems view does not tell us what units to employ or which strategies to follow in research; that is, it is not a substitute for creative theory, methodological development, or technological innovation. However, a systems view can help us to keep in focus the complexity of the phenomena, can help us to focus our attention on system processes, and (we may hope) can assist us in avoiding some of the controversies that have bogged us down in the past.

DIVERSITY, PLURALISM, AND WIDENING HORIZONS

One of the very positive developments in the field of personality has been the expanded range of phenomena of interest and concepts employed. Personality psychologists have returned to an interest in phenomena as diverse as overt behavior, affect, daydreams, and fantasies; they appreciate, but are not intimidated by, the difficulty of exploring many of these phenomena. Concepts such as purpose, intention, and meaning have become acceptable, and research methods as diverse as laboratory investigation, questionnaires, clinical and biographical case studies, experience sampling, and field studies are utilized (Craik, 1986; Runyan, 1988; West, 1986). The strengths and limitations of these methods are different and the data obtained from various measures may not always be in agreement; once more, this points to the complexity of the task at hand (Kagan, 1988). At least for the present, however (and, we may hope, for the future), the time of dismissal of some phenomena as not legitimate for investigation and of hegemony of some research methods over others has passed.

Accompanying these developments has been some investigators' readiness to establish links between differing theoretical perspectives and among disciplines or subdisciplines. Here, in particular, I have in mind the links being established between psychoanalytic and social-cognitive theorists and clinicians. This is not to say that there are large areas of agreement, or even that the majority of representatives of each view are concerned with the concepts and data of the other. This may be asking too much and may not be necessary for the development of either approach or the field as a whole. What is occurring, however, and what I believe is important and healthy for the field, is that at least some individuals are prepared to take seriously the contributions of alternative approaches, including both the phenomena observed and the concepts utilized. Similarly, we see the beginning of efforts to understand the links between traits and motives, as well as between cognitive and motivational perspectives; these reflect more generally the effort to understand the interplay between structure and process or between stability and change in personality (Pervin, 1984, 1985; Pyszczynski & Greenberg, 1987).

Furthermore, personality psychologists are establishing important links with social and developmental psychologists, as well as with biopsychologists, sociologists, and anthropologists. The expanded range of phenomena of interest to personality psychologists, the greater appreciation of the complexity of these phenomena, and advances by members of these other disciplines have dictated that these links be formed. As emphasized by a number of the contributors to this handbook, most important human phenomena of interest to personality psychologists have biological, intrapsychic, interpersonal, and sociocultural components.

WHAT LIES AHEAD?

Having noted the difficulty of predicting complex events, even given a reasonable level of understanding, does one dare to predict what lies ahead? Reflecting back on the 1968 *Handbook of Personality: Theory and Research* (Borgatta & Lambert, 1968), could one have anticipated the developments and changes reflected in the current handbook? What does this suggest about the next 20 years? Will progress dictate another handbook prior to then, or will another at that point not even be necessary?

Some reflections on the present and potential developments for the future come to mind. As I noted a few years ago (Pervin, 1985), there is a sense of excitement and vitality in the field of personality—not only in this country, but in Europe as well. As noted, personality psychologists appear to be interested in more phenomena, as well as in exploring these phenomena in a greater variety of ways. In addition, there is the sense of an infusion of new blood into the field—a group of young personality psychologists prepared to tackle old problems in both traditional and new ways. Awareness of similar points in the past, described in the historical introduction (see Chapter 1), should caution us about excessive optimism. Yet there would appear to be more grounds for real progress at this time and less danger of the field being dominated by fads. For one thing, because the field has gone down that path there may be greater awareness of the risks associated with it. For another, research in the field today seems to be more programmatic in nature, less firmly tied to specific questionnaires or tests, and more closely related to developments in other parts of psychology. At the same time, it is clear that we do not have a shared paradigm and it is unclear whether we indeed are building a base of cumulative knowledge.

For the future, two developments in particular appear to me to be key. The first relates to developments in other disciplines and our relation to them. On the one hand, there is a danger that we will fail to keep in touch with developments in fields such as biopsychology, neuropsychology, computer science, sociology, and anthropology. At this point developments in biology, neuroscience, and artificial intelligence are so rapid and important that we run the risk of being out of touch with fundamental progress in allied areas. On the other hand, there is the danger that we will become disenchanted with our slow progress relative to these other fields and seek to reduce all personality phenomena to their terms. The challenge would appear to be, then, to keep in touch with developments in other fields, while keeping in mind what is central and distinctive about the field of personality.

The second development relates to technology. Often I have heard debate concerning whether the field needs better theory or better research. Of course, some of each is always welcome but my own sense is that the real stumbling block concerns methods of gathering data about basic phenomena of interest to us. At one point I thought that the field awaited its Einstein or Mendeleev. I still think that it does, but I also think that it awaits technological advances in our ability to observe and record such essential phenomena as cognitions and affects. The field of biotechnology is currently one of the most exciting areas of science. I listen with some envy to my friends describing their feeling that almost daily they expect a breakthrough to be made, either by them or by someone else. It is clear that theoretical developments have been important, but technological advances in genetic research have provided the basis for a great leap forward. Is it possible that technological advances of a similar order lie ahead for our own field?

Finally, I would like to note an area that goes back to the earliest days of the field and yet remains one of the least understood—the problem of will or volition (Kimble & Perlmutter, 1970; Libet, 1985). As I have emphasized (Pervin, 1989), James's (1892) description of the problem of getting out of a warm bed on a cold day ("Now how do we *ever* get up under such circumstances?") provides the basis for an entire psychology of volition that remains worthy of our consideration today. Parts of the field appear to be beginning to address the issue (Frese & Sabini, 1985; Kuhl & Beckmann, 1985; Lewis, in press; Uleman & Bargh, 1989), but the attention being given to the problem would in no way appear to be commensurate with its theoretical and applied importance. Almost everyone experiences some breakdown in volition—whether in the form of an inability to take desired action (e.g., inhibition or procrastination) or in the form of an inability to inhibit undesired action (e.g., compulsions or addictions); whether minor or major; whether involving cognitions, emotions, or overt behavior. Thus, the question of will or volition brings into focus many of the problems of concern to us as personality psychologists: how the person attempts to regulate and integrate various cognitive and affective processes in the pursuit of immediate and long-term goals.

What is distinctive about personality is the focus on the person as a system, thereby involving the interplay between consistency and diversity, stability and change, and integration and conflict, as well as the study of people in a variety of contexts and over a long enough time period for patterns to emerge, in their private world of thought and feeling as well as in their public behaviors. The contributors to this volume have reviewed the past and set the stage for the future. Let us hope that the next *Handbook of Personality* will trace its roots to these contributions.

REFERENCES

Ahadi, S., & Diener, E. (1989). Multiple determinants and effect size. *Journal of Personality and Social Psychology, 56,* 398–406.

Bandura, A. (1982). The psychology of chance encounters and life paths. *American Psychologist, 37,* 747–755.

Borgatta, E. F., & Lambert, W. W. (Eds.). (1968). *Handbook of personality: Theory and research.* Chicago: Rand McNally.

Craik, K. H. (1986). Personality research methods: An historical perspective. *Journal of Personality, 54,* 18–50.

Crutchfield, J. P., Farmer, J. D., Packard, N. H., & Shaw, R. S. (1986). Chaos. *Scientific American, 255,* 46–57.

Frese, M., & Sabini, J. (Eds.). (1985). *Goal directed behavior: The concept of action in psychology.* Hillsdale, NJ: Erlbaum.

Holzman, P. S. (1986). Similarity and collaboration within the sciences. In D. W. Fiske & R. A. Shweder (Eds.).

Metatheory in social science: Pluralisms and subjectivities (pp. 347–352). Chicago: University of Chicago Press.

James, W. (1892). *Psychology: A briefer course.* New York: Holt.

Kagan, J. (1988). The meanings of personality predicates. *American Psychologist, 43,* 614–620.

Kimble, G. A., & Perlmutter, L. C. (1970). The problem of volition. *Psychological Review, 82,* 1–25.

Kuhl, J., & Beckmann, J. (Eds.). (1985). *Action control: From cognition to behavior.* New York: Springer-Verlag.

Lewis, M. (in press). The development of intentionality and the role of consciousness. *Psychological Inquiry.*

Libet, B. (1985). Unconscious cerebral initiative and the role of conscious will in voluntary action. *Behavioral and Brain Sciences, 8,* 529–566.

MacKinnon, D. W. (1951). Personality. *Annual Review of Psychology, 2,* 113–136.

Meehl, P. E. (in press). Appraising and amending theories: The strategy of Lakatosian defense and two principles that warrant it. *Psychological Inquiry.*

Pervin, L. A. (1984). The stasis and flow of behavior: Toward a theory of goals. In M. M. Page (Ed.), *Personality: Current theory and research* (pp. 1–53). Lincoln: University of Nebraska Press.

Pervin, L. A. (1985). Personality. *Annual Review of Psychology, 36,* 83–114.

Pervin, L. A. (1989). Goal concepts in personality and social psychology: A historical perspective. In L. A. Pervin (Ed.), *Goal concepts in personality and social psychology* (pp. 1–18). Hillsdale, NJ: Erlbaum.

Pyszczynski, T., & Greenberg, J. (1987). Toward an integration of cognitive and motivational perspectives on social inference: A biased hypothesis-testing model. In L. Berkowitz (Ed.), *Advances in experimental social psychology* (Vol. 20, pp. 297–340). New York: Academic Press.

Runyan, W. M. (1988). Progress in psychobiography. In D. P. McAdams & R. L. Ochberg (Eds.), *Psychobiography and life narratives* (pp. 327–338). Durham, NC: Duke University Press.

Uleman, J. S., & Bargh, J. A. (Eds.). (1989). *Unintended thought.* New York: Guilford Press.

West, S. G. (1986). Methodological developments in personality research. An introduction. *Journal of Personality, 54,* 1–17.

Index